ΝΟΜΟΘΕΤΗΣ·

THE

INTERPRETER,

Containing the genuine Signification of ſuch obſcure

WORDS and TERMS

Uſed either in the

Common or Statute

LAWES

OF THIS

REALM.

Firſt Compiled by the Learned Dr. COWEL, and now Enlarged from the *Collections* of all others who have written in this kind.

WITH

An Addition of many Words omitted by all former Writers, and pertinent to this Matter, with their ETYMOLOGIES as often as they Occur:

AS ALSO

TENURES whether *Jocular*, or others *Statutes* and *Records*, wherein the Alterations are expreſſed, and their Agreement or Diſſonancy, with the Law *at preſent* Declared.

Whereto is ſubjoyned,

An APPENDIX, containing the ancient Names of Places here in *ENGLAND*, very neceſſary for the Uſe of all Young Students, who intend to Converſe with old *Records*, *Deeds* or *Charters*.

The Second Edition, wherein many Errors and Miſtakes in the former are carefully Corrected.

By *THO. MANLEY* of the *Middle-Temple*, Eſq;

THE LAWBOOK EXCHANGE, LTD.
Clark, New Jersey
2004

ISBN 1-58477-406-1

Second printing 2005

The quality of this reprint is equivalent to the quality of the original work.

Printed in the United States of America on acid-free paper

The Lawbook Exchange, Ltd.
33 Terminal Avenue
Clark, New Jersey 07066-1321

Please see our website for a selection of our other publications and fine facsimile reprints of classic works of legal history:
www.lawbookexchange.com

Library of Congress Cataloging-in-Publication Data

Cowell, John, 1554-1611.
Nomothetas, The interpreter: containing the genuine signification of such obscure words and terms used either in the common or statute lawes of this realm / first compiled by the learned Dr. Cowel, and now enlarged from the collections of all others who have written in this kind ... — 2nd ed. / wherein many errors and mistakes in the former are carefully corrected by Tho. Manley.
p. cm.
Originally published: 2nd ed. / wherein many errors and mistakes in the former are carefully corrected by Tho. Manley. London: Printed by the assigns of R. Atkins and E. Atkins for H. Twyford, Tho. Basset, J. Place, and H. Sawbridge, 1684.
ISBN 1-58477-406-1 (cloth: alk. paper)
1. Law—England—Dictionaries. 2. Names, Geographical—England—Dictionaries. I. Title: Interpreter. II. Manley, Thomas, 1628-1690. III. Title.

KD313.C682 2004
349.42'03—dc22 2003058940

ΝΟΜΟΘΕΤΗΣ·

THE

INTERPRETER,

Containing the genuine Signification of ſuch obſcure

WORDS and TERMS

Uſed either in the

Common or Statute

LAWES

OF THIS

REALM.

Firſt Compiled by the Learned Dr. COWEL, and now Enlarged from the *Collections* of all others who have written in this kind.

WITH

An Addition of many Words omitted by all former Writers, and pertinent to this Matter, with their ETYMOLOGIES as often as they Occur:

AS ALSO

TENURES whether *Jocular*, or others *Statutes* and *Records*, wherein the Alterations are expreſſed, and their Agreement or Diſſonancy, with the Law *at preſent* Declared.

Whereto is ſubjoyned,

An APPENDIX, containing the ancient Names of Places here in *ENGLAND*, very neceſſary for the Uſe of all Young Students, who intend to Converſe with old *Records*, *Deeds* or *Charters*.

The Second Edition, wherein many Errors and Miſtakes in the former are carefully Corrected.

By *THO. MANLEY* of the *Middle-Temple*, Eſq;

London, Printed by the Aſſigns of *Richard Atkins* Eſq; and Sir *Edward Atkins* Knight, for *H. Twyford*, *Tho. Baſſet*, *J. Place*, and *H. Sawbridge*, 1684.

The PREFACE.

I Shall not Apologize for this Work, as knowing it to be more convenient to leave it to the Judgment of learned Readers, whoſe Underſtanding knows how to ſet a Value upon Laborious Improvements : Yet in regard it hath been the Method by Others taken up, and is indeed ſomewhat in the Mode, I think it not amiſs to follow in a beaten Track, and to render You in ſhort the Reaſons inducing me to Undertake, what, I hope, I may without Boaſt ſay I have Endeavored to perform.

The Ground-Work upon which I Build, is Cowell's Interpreter, an Excellent Book both as to its Matter and Compoſure, and did not deſerve that ſevere Arraignment that it hath of late ſuffered : Thoſe intermixtures of His in the Civil Law being abſolutely neceſſary to be known, by him who would have the Repute of a learned and well read Common Lawyer; and his few Defects (for they are not many for ſo great an Undertaking) might, at leaſt, after ſo many Years have been paſſed over in ſilence. And let Others boaſt of themſelves what they pleaſe; I am not aſhamed to own Him, and to acknowledge, that I only follow and make more publickly uſeful that Path which his Induſtry firſt laid Open to us : Wherein to uſe his own words, That whoever ſhall obſerve moſt Faults therein, I, by gleaning after, will Collect as many omitted by him, as he ſhall ſhew committed by me.

'Tis true, I have drawn in whatever I could find conſiderable either in other Authors, or could attain from any Perſons Learned, not ſparing Pains to ſearch into the Cabinets of Antiquity; So that, I hope, in this Collection *will be found whatever is most desirable for attaining Knowledge in this kind.*

I have in the perusing Cowell, *omitted several Matters, as unfit for the time; contracted and abbreviated Others; In some places commenting upon, and dilucidating his Matter, and adding thereto what of the* Law *hath been either new made, or altered since his time; so that his Defects therein are supplied.*

I have also gleaned after the Book, intituled, The Law Dictionary, *wherein are many good things, which I have hinted, as every ingenious* Reader *will discern; but withall, have added some* Centuries *of words therein totally omitted.*

As for Etymologies, I have followed the course laid open before me, retaining such as were apt, amending some that were a little too wide, rejecting others that seemed impertinent, and in their places inserting what seems more agreeable to that sort of Learning; in all places avoiding, as much as possible, the impropriety of extracting terms from two different Languages.

I have reserved to it the former Name, and call it The Interpreter, *which is most proper, as opening those obscure terms which otherwise are with great difficulty understood, although the Students of the* Law *be no* Tyroes *in other Learning; or, at least, ought not to be, for a* Lawyer *should profess* Philosophy: *And this Book thus compleated, I hope will attain the end aimed at,* viz. *To be most useful and advantagious not only to the* Students *of the* Law, *but to all Gentlemen who are desirous to improve their Knowledge; which I dare assure them, if with diligence they peruse the same.*

I need not subjoyn the Characters of any other Language used therein, because I write to the Learned, nor anticipate them with Advertisements; but leave the whole to their more discerning Judgments, to find the same in their proper places.

T. M.

ΝΟΜΟΘΕΤΗΣ

OR THE

INTERPRETER.

A.

A Is the letter of the Alphabet with the *Hebrews*, *Greeks*, *Latines*, and other Nations, and called by the *Heb. Aleph*; the *Arab. Aliph*; *Chaldee* and *Syriac*, *Olaph*; *Armenians*, *Alp*; *Æthiopians*, *Alph*; and *Greeks Alpha*. *A.* prefixt to words in *English* stands equivolent with *un* in *French*, as a man, *un homme*. But *A.* prefixt according to the *Greek* acceptation becomes privative, and signifies as much as *without*; *v. g.* in *Greek* Ὄνομα, a name, by prefixing *A.* it becomes Ἀνωνυμὸς, *sine nomine*, without a Name, or that will not own his Name.

Abactors, (*Abactores*) Drivers away, or indeed stealers of Cattel or Beasts, not by one and one, but in great numbers at once; and therefore by *M. S.* thus distinguished from *fur*, *qui unam ovem surripuerit, ut fur coërcetur, qui gregem ut Abactor*.

Abate, May be derived from the French word *Abatre, destruere, prosternere*, to break down or destroy; in the vulgar sense, it signifies to diminish, or take away, as to *abate* the courage of a Man; It is in the Writers of the Common Law used both actively and passively, as to *abate* a Castle or Fortlet, *Old Nat. Brev. fol.* 45. Which in *Westm.* 1. *cap.* 17. is plainly interpreted to beat it down: and to *abate* a Writ, is by some exception to defeat, or overthrow it, *Britton*, *cap.* 48. And in this active voice, it hath two significations, one general, another special; general, as in the former examples; and again, in *Kitchin*, *fol.* 173. *Abater Meason* is to ruine, or cast down a House; special, as in the *Old Nat. Brev. fol.* 115. A stranger *abateth*, that is, entreth upon a House or Land, void by the death of him that last possessed it, before the Heir take his Possession, and so keepeth him out; wherefore as he that putteth him out of Possession, is said to disseise; so he that steppeth in between the former Possessor and his Heir, is said to *abate*. And in the Stat. *De conjunctim Feoffatis*, 34 Ed. 1. Stat. 2. The Writ of the Demandant shall be *abated*, that is, shall be disabled, frustrated, or overthrown. So in *Stamford's Pleas of the Crown*, fol. 148. the Appeal *abateth* by Cousinage, that is, the accusation is defeated by deceit, *Anno* 11 *H.* 6. *cap.* 2. The Justices shall cause to be abated the said Writ; and hence cometh a word of Art *Abatamentum*. Vide *Intrusion*: *Abatement*, derived from the Frenh *Abatement*, sometimes signifies the Act of the *Abater*, as in the abatement of the Heir into the Land before he hath agreed with the Lord, *Old Nat. Brev.* 91. Sometimes the affection or passing of the thing *abated*, as abatement of the Writ, *Kitch. fol.* 214. And in this signification, it is as much as *exceptio dilatoria* with the *Civilians*, *Brit. cap.* 51. or rather an effect oft it; for the exception alledged, and made good, works the abatement. And this exception may be taken either to the insufficiency of the matter, or to the incertainty of the allegation, by the misnaming of the Plaintiff, Defendant, or place; to the variance between the Writ and the Specialty, or Record; to the incertainty of the Writ, Count or Declaration; or to the death of the Plaintiff or Defendant, *New Terms of the Law*, verb. *Abatement of a Writ*, &c. To prevent *abatement* of Writs of Error. See the Stat. 16 *Car.* 2. *cap.* 2. *Co. Entries*, *fol.* 63. *c.* & 205. *d.* & 519. *c.* Abatement is called in Latine *Intrusio*, but it may rather be called *Interpositio*, or *intratio per interpositionem*, to distinguish it from intrusion after the death of Tenant for life: And in his *Com.* on *Lit. fol.* 277. he shews the difference between Abatement, Disseisin, Intrusion, Deforcement, Usurpation and Purpresture. He that will read more of this, may read the *New Book of Entries*, verb. *Brief*. See also *Writ*, *Misnosmer* and *Variance*, and the Book called *The Digest of Writs*.

Abator, Is he that abateth, that is, intrudeth into a House or Land, void by the death of the former Possessor, and not yet entred, or taken up by his Heir, *Old Nat. Brev. fol.* 115. *Perkins, fol.* 76.

Abbacy, In Latine *Abbatia*, or *Abbathia*, is the Government of a Religious House, with the Revenues and Persons subject to an Abbat, as a Bishoprick is to a Bishop. The word is used *Anno* 34 & 35 *H.* 8. *cap.* 17, 18. *Sciant, &c. quod ego Issabella Comitissa Pembrock pro salute animæ meæ, &c. Dedi Deo & Abbathiæ de* N. *totam wicham juxta prædictam Abbathiam, &c.*

Abbat or **Abbot**, *Abbas* in Latine, in French *Abbe*, a Spiritual Lord having the Rule of a Religious House, according to our Common Law: Skilful Linguists derive it from the Syriack *Abba Pater*; *Justinians Novel Constitut.* 115 *Sect* ὑπολειπον, terms him *Archimandrita*; others *Cænobiarcha*, or *Archimonachus*, Hotoman *in verb. Feuda*. Of these, some here in *England* were mitred, some not, *Stows Annals, pag.* 442. Such as were mitred, were exempted from the Jurisdiction of the *Diocesan*, having themselves Episcopal Authority within their Limits, and were also Lords of the Parliament. Of this kind, thus saith *Corasius, Aliqui* Abbates *habent jurisdictionem Episcopalem, ad quos cum Ecclesia pleno jure pertineat, in eorum Monasteriis Episcopus nihil exercet, cap. ea quæ*. And these were called *Abbots Soveraign*, 9 *R.* 2. *cap.* 4. And *Abbots Generals*, as Mr. *Ferne* noteth in his *Glory of Generosity*, pag. 126. The other sort were subject to the *Diocesan* in all Spiritual Government, *cap. Monasteria* 18. *quæst. cap. Abbas & ca. visitandi, cum quatuor sequentibus ibid. Omnes* 16. *quæst.* 7. *& ca. cum venerabilis, extra de religiosis domibus.* And as *Abbots*, so were there Lords Priors also, who both had exempt Jurisdiction, and were Lords of Parliament, as Sir *Edward Coke* makes out, *De jure Eccles. fol.* 28. a. Of which Lords *Abbots* and Priors that sat in Parliament, some reckon but Twenty Six, but Sir *Edward Coke* says, They were Twenty Seven *Abbots* and Two Priors, *Co. super Lit. fol.* 97. In the Parliament 20 *R.* 2. there were but Twenty Five *Abbots* and Two Priors: But *Anno* 4 *Ed.* 3. *In dorso Claus. ejusdem, An. membran.* 41. more are named. Such an *Abbot* with the Monks of the same House, being called *The Covent*, made a Corporation; but such *Abbot* was not chargeable by his Predecessors Act, but by their common Seal, or for such things as came to the use of his House; neither for the Debt of his Monk before his entry in Religion, though the Creditor had a Specialty. See for this the *Abridgment* under the same Title.

Abbathy, *Anno* 31 *H.* 8. *cap.* 13. See *Abbacy*.

Abbettor. See *Abet*.

Abbrochment, (*Abbrocamentum*) Is a forestalling of a Market or Fair, by buying up the Wares before they are exposed to Sale in the Market or Fair, and then vending them again by Retail.

Abbuttals, (From the French *Abutter*, that is, to limit or bound) are the *buttings* and boundings of Land either to the East, West, North or South, shewing how it lies in respect to the other places, *Cro. Rep.* 2. *par. fol.* 184. *Latera autem nunquam aiunt* abuttare, *sed terram proximam adjacere.* And *Camden* says, Limits were distinguisht by Hillocks raised on purpose, which were call'd *Botentines*; whence we may guess our *Butting* to Spring.

Abeyance, Hath by some been derived from the French *Abeyer*, that is, *allatrare*, to bark at, as Dogs do at a stranger; but I rather suppose it may come from the French word *Bayer*, to expect: So Children are said *Bayer a la mamme*, who seeing the Dugg, they strivingly expect it: So also *bayer a l' argent, qui spe atq; animo pecuniæ incumbunt*. This word in *Littleton*, cap. *Discontinuance*, we find thus used, The right of Feesimple lieth in abeyance, that is, according to his own interpretation, only in the remembrance, intendment and consideration of the Law; The Frank-tenement of the Glebe of a Parsonage is in no Man, so long as the Parsonage remains void, but is in *Abeyance*. And it is a maxim in Law, *That of every Land there is Feesimple in some Man, or else it lies in Abeyance*. Considering and comparing these places with the signification of the French word *Bayer*, it seems more than probable, that our ancient Law-Books would signifie hereby a kind of hope, or longing expectation, because things in *abeyance*, though at present in no Man, yet in hope and expectation they belong to him that is next to enjoy them. And also in French, a man that earnestly gazes at any thing, is termed *un Bayard*, a greedy Beholder. This *abeyance* cannot be better compared, than to that which the *Civilians* call *Hæreditatem jacentem*. For as *Bracton* saith, *lib.* 1. *cap.* 12. *num.* 10. *Hæreditas jacens nullius est hominis ante additionem, &c.* So that (as the *Civilians* say) Lands and Goods do *jacere*; So the Common Lawyers say, That things in like estate are in *Abeyance*, as the *Logicians* terme *in posse*, or in understanding; and as we say, *in nubibus*, in the Clouds, that is, in consideration of the Law. Read more of this in the *New Terms of the Law, fol.* 6. & *Plow. Rep. Walsingham's* Case. See also *lib.* 3. *cap.* 11. *fol.* 145. & *Perkins fol.* 12. *Co.* on *Lit. fol.* 342. *b.*

Abet (*Abettare*) May be said to proceed from the French *Bouter*, *impellere* or *excitare*: In our Common-Law it signifies as much as to encourage, or set on. *Abetment*, (*abettum*) the Substantive implies the same, *Stamf. Pl. Cor.* 105. And *Abettor* (Abettator) for him that encourageth, or setteth on, *Old Nat. Brev. fol.* 21. but both Verb and Noun are always taken in the worst sense. As *Abettors* of Murder, are such as command, procure, or counsel others to commit a Murder; and in some Cases such *Abettors* shall be taken as Principals, in other but as Accessories; and their presence or absence at the doing of the Fact, differences the Case. There are also *Abettors* in Treason, but they are as Principals; for there are no *Accessories* in *Treason*.

Abishersing, (As *Rastal* in his *Abridgment* expounds it,) Is to be quit of Amerciaments before whomsoever of transgression proved. It is called in the *New Terms of the Law Misbersing*; It signifies originally a Forfeiture, but much miswritten by the ignorance of Clerks; which Opinion *Spelman* in his *Glossary* seems to confirm.

Old

Old Authors have termed it a Freedom or Liberty, because whoever hath this word inserted in a Charter or Grant, hath not only the Forfeitures and Amerciaments of all others within his Fee for Transgressions, but also is himself free from the controul of any within that Compass.

Abjuration, (*Abjuratio*) Is a renouncing by Oath, and signifieth in our Law a sworn Banishment, or forswearing of the Realm, *Stamf. Pl. Cor. lib.* 2. *cap.* 40. saith out of *Polyd. Virgil* 1. So great was the devotion towards the Church in King *Edward the Confessors* Time, till the 22 of *H.* 8. that if a Man having committed Felony, could get into the Church or Church-yard before he were apprehended, he might not be taken thence to the usual Trial at Law, but confessing his Fault to the Justices at their coming, or to the Coroner, might be admitted to his Oath, to *abjure* or forsake the Realm, *Anno* 7 *H.* 7. *cap.* 7. The form and effect of this you have in the *Old Abridgment of Statutes*; an ancient Tract, *De Officio Coronatorum*, Cromptons *Office of Coroner*, fol. 260. b. *New Book of Entries*, verb. *Abjuration*. Hornes *Mirror of Justices*, lib. 1. cap. *Del Office del Coroner*. This part of our Law was in some sort practised by the *Saxons*, as appeareth by the Laws of King *Edward*, set out by Mr. *Lambard*, *num.* 10. but more directly by the *Normans*, evidenced by the *Grand Customary*, cap. 24. where the form of the Oath is likewise set down, with the rest of the proceedings therein, very agreeable with Ours. This Clemency something resembles that of the *Roman* Emperors towards such as fled to the Church, *Lib.* 1. *Co. tit.* 12. or to the Images themselves, *Eod. tit.* 25. And also that of the Cities of Refuge mentioned by *Moses*, *Exod.* 21. 13. *Numb.* 15. 6. 11, 12. *Deut.* 19. 2. *Josh.* 20. 2. Of all the Circumstances belonging to this *Abjuration*, read the *New Terms of the Law*, and *Stamf. ubi supra*. But this grew at last to be but a perpetual confining of the Offendor to some Sanctuary, wherein, upon *abjuration* of his Liberty and free Habitations, he would chuse to spend his life, as appears *Anno* 22 *H.* 8. *cap.* 14. And by 21 *Jac. cap.* 28. this benefit is wholly taken away, and consequently *Abjuration*, 2. *Inst. fol.* 629. See *Sanctuary*.

Abolition, (25 *H.* 8. *cap.* 21.) A destroying. The Licence given to a criminal Accuser, to desist from further prosecution.

Abbridge, (*Abbreviare*) Cometh of the French *Abreger*, to make shorter in words, yet still retains the sense and substance; but in the Common Law it seems more particularly used for making a Declaration or Count shorter, by substracting or severing some of the substance. As for example, a Man is said to *abridge* his Plaint in Assise, or a Woman her Demand in an Action of Dower, that hath put into the Plaint, or Demand, any Land not in the Tenure of the Tenant or Defendant, if the Tenant pleads Nontenure, Joynt-tenancy, or the like, in abatement of the Writ; the Demandant may *abridge* his Plaint, that is, he may leave out that part, and pray that the Tenant may answer to the rest, to which he hath not yet pleaded; and the reason is, because the certainty is not set down in such Writs: And though the Demandant hath *abridged* his Plaint in part, yet the Writ remains good still for the rest: So that here *abridger* is not *contrahere*, but rather *subtrahere*, *Bro. tit. Abridgment*, & Anno 21 *H.* 8. *cap.* 3. Of this the *Civilians* have no use, by reason of certain cautelous Clauses they ordinarily affix to the end of every Article in their Lebel or Declaration.

Abridgment, (*Abreviamentum*) See *Abridge*.

Abrogate, *Abrogare*, To disannul or repeal, as to *abrogate* a Law, that is, to lay aside or repeal it, *anno* 5 & 6 *E.* 6. *cap.* 3.

Absentees, or **Des Absentees**, A Parliament so called, held at *Dublin* 10. *May*, 28 *H.* 8. and mentioned in Letters Patents, dated 29 *H.* 8. See *Co. Inst. fol.* 358.

Abuttals. See *Abbuttals*.

Accedas ad Curiam, Is a Writ that lies for him who hath received false Judgment in a Court-Baron or Hundred-Court, being directed to the Sheriff, as appeareth by *Dyer*, *fol.* 169. *num.* 30. Like as the Writ *de falso Judicio* lies for him that hath received false Judgment in the County-Court: The form you may see in *F. N. B. fol.* 18. *d.* And in the *Register. fol.* 9. *b.* where it is said, This Writ lies as well for Justice delayed, as Judgment falsly given: It is a Species of the Writ *Recordare*, *Reg. Orig. fol.* 56. & *F. N. B. ubi supra*.

Accedas ad Vice-comitem, Is a Writ directed to the Coroner, commanding him to deliver a Writ to the Sheriff, who having a *Pone* delivered him, suppressed, *Reg. Orig.* 83.

Acceptance, Is a thing in good part, and as it were a kind of agreeing to some Act done before, which might have been undone and avoided if such acceptance had not been: For example, If a Bishop before the Stat 1 *Eliz.* lease part of the possessions of his Bishoprick for term of years, reserving Rent, and dies, and after another is made Bishop; who accepts, that is, takes or receives the Rent when it is due, and ought to be paid; by this acceptance the Lease is made good, which else the new Bishop might have avoided: The like is, if Baron and Feme seized of Land in right of the Feme, joyn and make a Lease or Feoffment by Deed, Reserving Rent; the Baron dies, the Feme receives or accepts the Rent: by this the Feoffment or Lease is confirmed, and shall bar her of bringing a *Cui in vita*, *Co. on Lit. fol.* 211. *b.*

Accessory or **Accessary**, (*Accessorius vel Accessorium:*) *Particeps criminis*, Is used in our Common-Law otherwise than among the *Civilians*; for whereas with them it is generally taken for any thing depending upon another, here, though it be so likewise, yet most commonly and notoriously it signifieth a Man guilty of a felonious Offence, not principally, but by participation, as by command, advice or concealment. And a Man may be *accessory* to the offence of another after two sorts, by the Common Law, or by Statute; and by the Common Law two ways also, *viz.* either before or after the Fact; Before the Fact, as where one commandeth or adviseth another to commit a Felony, and is not present at the execution thereof; for his presence maketh him also a Principal; wherefore there cannot be an *accessory* before the Fact in Manslaughter,

slaughter, because Man-slaughter is sudden, and premeditated, *Co. lib.* 4. *fol.* 44. 2. *Accessory* after the Fact, is, when one receiveth him whom he knoweth to have committed a Felony, 3. *Accessory* by Statute, is he that abetteth, counselleth or concealeth, committing, or having committed an Offence made Felony by Statute; for though the Statute make no mention of Abettors, yet they are by interpretation included. Of all these consult, *Stamf. Pl. Cor. lib.* 1. *cap.* 45, 46, 47, 48. There is also an *accessory* of an *accessory*, as he that wittingly receiveth an *accessory* to a Felony; But a Woman in such case shall not be an *accessory* for helping her Husband, *Lib. Ass.* 26. *Pl.* 51. *Coron. Fitz.* 197. *Stamf. Pl. Cor. lib.* 1. *cap.* 48. And the Law of *England* is, that so long as the Principal is not attainted, the *Accessory* may not be medled with, *Stamf. ubi supra, Co. lib.* 4. *fol.* 43. *b.* In the highest and lowest Offences, there are no *Accessories*, but all are Principals; as in Treason, *crimen læsæ Majestatis*, the highest; and in Riots, Forcible Entries, and other Trespasses, *Vi & Armis*, the lowest, *Co.* on *Lit. fol.* 71. Of this Subject, read more in *Cromp. Just. fol.* 37. *b.* 38, 39. If a Man counsel a Woman to murther the Child she hath in her Womb, and afterward the Child is born, and then murthered by the Woman, in the absence of him that so gave the counsel; yet he is *accessory* by his counselling before the Birth of the Infant, and not countermanding it, *Dyer, fol.* 186. *pl.* 2.

Accompt, (*Computus*,) Is in the Common Law taken for a Writ, or Action, which lies against a Man, that by means of Office or Business undertaken, is to render an account to another; as a Bayliff towards his Master or Guardian in Soccage towards his Ward, and the like; as you shall find particularized in *Fitz. Nat. Brev. fol.* 116. But if an Accomptant be not allowed reasonable Expence and Costs, or charged with more Receipts than he ought, his next Friend may sue a Writ of *Ex parte talis* out of the Chancery, directed to the Sheriff, to take four Mainpernors, to bring his Body before the Barons of the Exchequer at a certain day, and to warn the Lord to appear there the same day.

Accord, That is, Agreement between Two, or more, to satisfie a Trespass or Offence done by one to another, for which he hath agreed to make satisfaction, in recompence; which shall be a good bar in Law, if the other, after the Accord performed, should commence any new Action for the same Trespass, *Terme de la Ley, fol.* 14.

Accroche, From the French *Accrocher*, to fix: This word is used *Anno* 25 *E.* 3. *Stat.* 3. *cap.* 8. and signifies there as much as to Encroach, and the French used it for delay, as *Accrocher un processe*, to delay the proceedings in a Suit for some time. Vide *Encroachment*.

Achat, Cometh of the French, *Achat, emptio*, or *nundinatio*, and is taken to signifie a Contract or Bargain, *Brook, tit. Contract.* from whence haply *Purveyors* in the 36 *E.* 3. were ordained to be call'd *Achators*, because of their frequent Bargain making; hence also with seeming reason enough may be deriv'd the word *Acates*, signifying Provision brought in the Market for great Feasts.

Acquietancia de Shiris & Hundredis, To be free from Suit and Service in Shires and Hundreds, to which purpose it is said, *In Regist. Priorat. de Cokesford, Quod Prior non debet facere sectam ad Comitatum* Norwici *vel in Hundredo pro Manerio de* Rudham *cum pertin.*

Acquietandis Plegiis, This Writ we find in the *Register of Writs*, fol. 158. being in truth a *Justicies*, and lies for a Surety against a Creditor, that refuseth to acquit him after the Debt is paid.

Acquital, Is derived from the French *Acquitter*, as that from the Latine Compound *Acquietare*, and signifyeth in Law to discharge, or keep in quiet, and that the Tenant be safely kept from any Entries or Molestations for any manner of Service issuing out of the Land to any Lord, that is, above the Mesne; hereof we say, *Et quietus est*, that is, he is discharged, *Co.* on *Lit. lib.* 2. *sect.* 148. It signifies also ordinarily a deliverance, and setting free from the suspicion or guilt of an Offence, as he that is discharged of a Felony by Judgment, is said to be *acquietatus de felonia*, and if it be drawn in question again, he may plead *auter foits acquit.* This is two-fold, *Acquital in Law*, and *Aquital in Fact*; *Acquital in Law* is, when Two are indicted, the one as Principal, the other as Accessary; the Principal being discharged, the Accessary by consequence is also *acquitted*, and in this case as the Accessary is *acquitted* by Law, so is the Principal in Fact, *Stamf. Pl. Cor.* 168. *Aquital in Fact* is either by *Verdict*, or by *Battel*; By *Verdict*, when by a Jury he is found *Not Guilty* of the Offence whereof he is charged; By *Battel*, as when in an Appeal, the Plaintiff yieldeth himself *Creant*, or vanquisht in the Field; the Judgment shall be, that the Appeller shall go quit, and that he shall recover his Damages, *Co.* 2. *Inst.* 385.

Acquittance, *Acquietantia*, Cometh from the French *Quiter*, that is, *accepto ferre*, signifieth a Release or Discharge in Writing of a sum of Money, or other Duty which ought to be paid or done. Also the Verb (*acquit*) the Participle (*acquitted*) and the Noun (*acquittal*) signifie a discharge or clearing from an Offence objected, as acquitted by Proclamation, *Smith de Rep. Ang.* pag. 76. *Stamf. Pl Cor.* 168. *Brook*, tit. *Acquital.* This word differs from that which in the Civil Law is called *Acceptitatio*, because that may be by word withou tWriting, and is nothing but a fained Payment and Discharge, where no real Payment is had. Nor can it be said to be *Apocha*, which is a witnessing the payment or delivery of Money, which discharges not, unless the money be paid, *Termes de Ley*, verb. *Acquitance.*

Acre, From the German *Acker*, that is, *ager*, is a quantity of Land containing in length forty Perches, and four in breadth, or according to that proportion, be the length more or less; and if a Man erect any new Cottage, he must lay four *Acres* of Land to it after this Measure, *Anno* 31 *Eliz. cap.* With this Measure agrees *Crompton*, in his *Jurisdiction of Courts*, fol. 222. though he saith also, That according to the Customs of divers Countries the Perch differeth, being in some

ſome places, and moſt ordinarily but 16 foot and a half, but in *Staff.* 24 foot, as was ajudged in the Exch. in the Caſe between Sir *Ed. Aſton* & Sir *Job. B.* In the Statute made concerning ſowing Flax (24 *H.* 8. c.4. eight ſcore Perches make an Acre, which is forty multiplied by four.

Action, *Actio*, Is defined by *Bracton, lib.* 3. *cap.* 1. In the ſame manner as by *Juſtinian lib* 4. *Inſtit. titulo de Actionibus*, viz. *Actio nihil aliud eſt quam jus proſequendi in judicio quod alicui debetur*, & is divided into *perſonalem, realem, et mixtam*, Co. *Inſt* 2. *fol.* 40. A perſonal Action is that which one man may have againſt another, by reaſon of any Contract for Money or Goods, or for any Offence done by him, or ſome other, for whoſe Fact he is anſwerable, *Bract. lib.* 3. *cap.* 3 *.nu.* 2. A real Action is defined to be, whereby a Defendant claims Title to have a Freehold in any Lands or Tenements, Rents or Commons, in Fee-ſimple, Fee-tail, or for life, *Bract. ibid. nu* 3. And every Action real is either *Poſſeſſory*, that is, of his own Poſſeſſion & Seiſin, or *Aunceſtrel* of the Seiſin or Poſſeſſion of his Anceſtor, *Co. lib.* 6. *fol.* 3. *Writs of Right, Writs of Entry*, &c. And their ſeveral Appendixes, as *Grand-cape, Petit-cape, Receipt, View, Ayd-Prayer*, &c. being real Actions, took place, & ſwell'd the Titles of our Year-Books heretofore, but now grown much out of uſe.

Action mixt, Is that which lyeth as well againſt or for the thing which we ſeek, as againſt the perſon that hath it, and is called *Mixt*, as having a reſpect both to the thing and the perſon, *Bract. lib.* 3 *ca.* 3. *nu.* 5. For example, the diviſion of an Inheritance between Co-heirs, or Co-partners, called in the Civil-law (*Actio familiæ exciſcundæ*): Secondly, The diviſion of any particular thing being common to more, called alſo (*actio de communi dividundo*): which *Bracton, Cujacius, Weſenbachius*, allow to be mixt; of which *Britton* diſcourſeth at large in his 71. Chap. In *the Terms of the Law*, verb. *Action mixt*: It is ſaid to be a Suite by the Law, to recover the thing demanded, and damages for the wrong done; as in Aſſize of *No. Diſſ.* which Writ, if the Diſſeiſor make a Feoffment to another, the Diſſeiſſee ſhall have againſt the Diſſeiſor, and the Feoffee, or other Tenant, and thereby ſhall recover Seiſin of his Land, and Damages for the mean Profits, and the wrong done; and ſo is an Action of Waſt, and *Quare Imp.*

Action, Is alſo divided by the Civilians into *Civilem & Prætoriam*, whereof one ariſeth out of the Civil-Law in general, the other from ſome *Prætorian* Edict. And a diviſion not unlike this may be made in the Common-Law of *England*, one part growing from the ancient Cuſtoms, the other from the Statute, *Bro. tit. Action ſur le Stat.*

Actions, Alſo are divided into civil, penal and mixt, *Co. Vo.* 6. *fol.* 61. *a.* Action civil is that which tends only to the recovery of that which by reaſon of any Contract, or other like cauſe, is due to us: As if a man by Action ſeek to recover a ſum of Money formerly lent, &c.

An Action penal, Aims at ſome penalty or puniſhment in the party ſued, be it Corporal or Pecuniary: As in the Action *Legis Aquiliæ*, in the Civil-Law; and in the Common-Law, the next Friends of a man feloniouſly ſlain or wounded, ſhall purſue the Law againſt the Offendor, and bring him to condigne puniſhment, *Br. l.* 3. *c.* 4.

Action mixt, Seeks both the thing whereof we are deprived, and a penalty for the unjuſt detention. As in an Action for Tythes upon the Statute 2 & 3. *E.* 6. *cap.* 13. See *Co.* on *Lit. fol.* 262. *b.*

Action, Is alſo (according to the form of the Writ) divided into ſuch as are conceived to recover either the ſimple value of the thing challenged, or the double, treble or quadruple, *Bract. lib.* 3. *cap.* 3. *nu.* 6. So doth a *Decies tantum* lye againſt *Embraceors*, F. N. B. *fol.* 171. And againſt Jurors that take money for their Verdict of either or both Parties: And any other Action upon a Statute that puniſhes any Offence by reſtitution, or fine proportionable to the Tranſgreſſion.

Action, Alſo is *Prejudicial*, (otherwiſe called *Preparatory*) or *Principal*. *Prejudicial*, is that which grows from ſome doubt in the Principal: As if a man ſue his younger Brother for Land deſcended from his Father, and it is objected, that he is a Baſtard, *Bract. lib.* 3. *cap.* 4. *num.* 6. For this poynt of baſtardy muſt be tryed, before the cauſe can further proceed, and therefore termed *prejudicialis, quia prius judicanda.*

Action, Is either *Aunceſtrel* or *perſonal*, *Stam. Pl. Cor.* 59. *Aunceſtrel* ſeems to be that which we have by ſome right deſcending, from our Anceſtor: and that Perſonal, which has beginning in & from our ſelves. There is alſo *Action Anceſtrel Droiturel* & *Action Aunceſtrel Poſſeſſory*, which ſee in *Co.* 2. *In. f.* 291.

Action upon the Caſe, *Actio ſuper caſum*, Is a general Action given for redreſſe of wrongs done without force againſt any man, and by Law not eſpecially provided for; for when you have any occaſion of Suit, that neither hath a fit, nor certain form preſcribed; then the Clerks of the Chancery in ancient time conceived a fit form of Action for the Fact in queſtion, which the Civilians call *Actionem in factum*, and the Common Lawyers, *Actionem ſuper caſum.* And whereas in the Civil-Law, there are two ſorts of theſe Actions; one termed *Actio in factum præſcriptis verbis*; the other *Actio in factum prætoria*; the former grounded upon words paſſed in Contract; the other more generally upon any Fact touching either Contract, or Offence formerly not provided againſt: This Action upon the Caſe ſeemeth more to reſemble the *Actio Prætoria in factum*, then the other; becauſe in the peruſal of the Book of *Entries*, & *Bro.* Abridgment; I find that an Action upon the Caſe lieth as well againſt Offences, as breach of Contract. See more of this in *Treſpaſs.*

Action upon the Statute, *Actio ſuper Statutum*, Is brought upon the breach of a Statute, whereby an Action is given that lay not before; As where one commits Perjury, to the prejudice of another, he who is endammaged, ſhall have a Writ upon the Stat. that is, where the Stat. gives the Suit or *Action* to the party grieved, or otherwiſe to one perſon certain: And this *Action* ſeems to be like any Action in the *Law imperial*, either upon *Edictum Prætoris, Plebiſcitum*, or *Senatus-conſultum* for as the *Prætor*, ſo the common people *in Comitiis*, and the Senators or Nobility, in *Curia*, or *Senatu*, had power to make Laws, whereupon the Prætor, or other Judges permitted Action: So our High Court of Parliament maketh Stat. againſt ſuch Offences as are either newly grown, or more and more encreaſed, and the Judges are obliged

C to

to entertain their Pleas, that commence Actions against the Breakers of them.

Action, Is perpetual or temporal (*perpetua vel temporalis*) and that is called perpetual, whose force cannot be determined by time, Of which sort were all civil Actions among the *Romans viz*. Such as grew from Laws, Decrees of the Senate, or Constitutions of the Emperors, whereas Actions granted by the Prætor, fell within the year. So we have in *England* perpetual and temporary Actions: And indeed all Actions may be called *perpetual*, that are not expresly limited. As divers Statutes give action, so they be pursued within the time by them prescribed: As for example, the Statute of 1 *Ed*.6. *cap*. 1. gives Action for three years after the Offences commited, and no longer. And the Staute of 7 *H*. 8. *cap*. 3. doth the like for four years; and that of 31 *Eliz*. *cap*. 5. for one year and no more; and the Act for uniformity 14 *Car* 2. *cap*. 4. limits some things to two, some to three moneths, and some to more. But as by the Civil-Law, no actions were at last so perpetual, but that by time they might be prescribed against; So in our Common-Law though actions may be called perpetual, in comparison of those that be expresly limited by Statute, yet there is a means to prescribe against real actions within five years, by a Fine levied, or a Recovery suffered; as you may see Further in the words *Fine* and *Recovery*, and also *Limitation of Assize*.

* **Action popular**, Is given upon the breach of some penal Statute, which every man that will may sue for himself and the King, by Information, or otherwise: and because this action is not given to one especially, but generaly to any of the Kings people that will sue, it is called an *Action popular*; but in this case, when one hath begun to pursue an action, no other may sue it; and in this as it seems, it varies from an *Action popular* by the Civil-Law, *Termes de Ley*.

Action, Is farther divided *Actionem bonæ fidei & stricti juris*, which division hath good use in the Common-Law, though the termes are not to be found in any of their Writers; therefore we refer them to the Civilians, and particularly *Wesemb*. in his *Paratitles, De Oblig. & act*.

Action of a Writ, Is a phrase of speech used when one pleads some matter, by which he shews the Plaintiff had no cause to have the Writ he brought, yet it may be that he may have another Writ or Action for the same matter. Such a Plea is called *a Plea to the action of the Writ*; whereas, if by the Plea, it should appear that the Plaintiff hath no cause to have an action for the thing demanded, then it shall be called *a Plea to the action*, *Termes de Ley*.

Acts of Parliament, Are positive Laws, which consist of two parts, that is, the words of the Act, and the sense and meaning, which both joyned together make the Law.

Acton Burnel, A Statute so called, made 13 *E*. 1. *Anno* 1285. ordaining the *Statute Merchant*, and was so termed from a place named *Acton Burnel*, where it was made, being a Castle sometime belonging to the Family of *Burnel*, afterwards of *Lovel in Shropshire*.

Actuary, (*Actuarius*) Is the Clerk or Scribe, that Registers the Canons and Constitutions of the Convocation.

Addition, (*Additio*) Is both the English and French word made of the Latine, and signifieth in our Common-Law a Title given to a man besides his Christian and Sir-name, shewing his Estate, Degree, Mistery, Trade, place of Dwelling, &c. As for example, additions of Estate are *Yeoman*, *Gentelman*, *Esquire*, and such like; additions of degree, are names of Dignity, as *Knight*, *Earl*, *Marquess*, *Duke*: additions of Mistery, are *Scrivener*, *Painter*, *Mason*, *Carpenter*, and all other of like nature; for Mistery is the Craft or Occupation, whereby a man gets his Living: Addition of Towns, as *London*, *Kingston*, *Chester*, *&c*. and where a man hath Houshold in two places, he shall be said to dwell in both of them; so that his addition in either shall suffice. For the use of these additions in original Writs of actions personal, Appeals and Indictments: It is provided by the Statute, 1 *H*. 5. *cap*. 5. that in Suits or Actions, where process of *Utlary* lies, such additions should be to the name of the Defendant, to shew his Estate, Mistery, and place where he dwells; and that Writs, not having such *additions*, shall abate, if the Defendant take exception thereto, but not by the Office of the Court; and this was ordained by that Statute, that one man might not be vexed or troubled by the *Utlary* of another, but that by reason of the certain *addition*, every person may be known, and bear his own burden: For more particular additions of Town, see *Bro. tit. Addition*. See also *Crompton Just. of Peace, fol*. 95. 96. *Co*. 2. *part*, *Inst. fol*. 595. & 666. and Stat. 27. *El*. *cap*. 7.

Addoubors, See *Redoubers*.

Adeling, Or *Etheling*, from the Saxon *Ædelan*, or the Dutch *Edel*, signifying Excellent, and was a Title of Honour among the *Angles*, properly pertaining to the Kings Children, and Successors of the Crown; whereupon King *Edward*, the Confessor being himself without Issue, and intending to make *Edgar* (to whom he was great Unkle by the Mothers side) the Heir of his Kingdom, gave the honourable stile of *Adeling*. *Rog. Hovenden, parte poster. suor. Annal. fol*. 347, *a. Vide etiam Leges sancti Ed. Conf. M. S. a. Will. Conq. recept. cap. antepenult*. See more of this word in *Spelman's Glossary*.

Adjournment, (*Adjournamentum*) the same with the French *Adjournment*, and signifies *denunciatio*, or *diei dictio*,) that is, by our Common-Law an assignment of a day, or a putting off untill another day and place. So adjournment in *Eyre* (25 *E*. 3. Statute of *Purveyors*, *cap*. 18.) is an appoyntment, of a day, when the Justices in *Eyre* mean to sit again, and *Adjournment* hath the same signification in 2 *E*. 3. *cap*. 11. See *Bro. Abridg. tit. Adjournment*. The bastard Latin word (*ajournamentum*) is used among the *Burgundians*, as Mr. *Skene* notes in his Book *de verbo Signif. verbo Adjornatus*, out of *Cassanæus de consuet. Burg*. See *Prorogue*.

Adjudication, (*Adjudicatio*) A settlement by Judgment, Decree or Sentence, 16 & 17 *Car*. 2. *cap*. 10.

Ad inquirendum, Is a Writ *judicial*, commanding inquiry to be made of any thing touching a cause depending in the Kings Court for the better execution of Justice; as of *Bastardy*, *Bondmen*, and such like; whereof, see great diversity in the Table of the *Judicial Register*, *verbo ad inquirendum*.

Ad jura Regis, Is a writ that lies for the *Kings* Clerk against him that sought to eject him, to the Prejudice of the *Kings Title* in Right of his Crown, *Reg. of Writs fol.* 61. *a.*

Admeasurement, (*Admensuratio*) Is a Writ which lyeth for the bringing of those to a Mediocrity, that usurp more than their part: and it lieth in two cases, one is termed *Admeasurement of Dower*, *Admensuratio dotis*, where the Widow of the deceased holdeth from the Heir or his Gardian, more in the name of her Dower, than of right is belonging unto her, *Regist. Orig. fol.* 171. *a Fitzherb. Nat. Brev. fol.* 148. The other is *Admeasurement of Pasture*, *Admensuratio Pasturæ*, which lyeth between those that have Common of Pasture appendant to their Freeholds, or Common by Vicinage, in case any one or more of them do surscharge the Common with more Cattel than they ought, *Reg. Orig. fol.* 156. *b. F. N. B. fol.* 125. * This Writ lies not for the Lord, nor against the Lord, but the Lord may distrain the Beasts of the Tenant that are surplusage: But if the Lord overcharge the Common, the Commoner hath no remedy by the Common-Law, but an Assize of his Common, *Termes de la Ley* 24.

† **Adminicle,** (*Adminiculum*) Aid or support *Anno* 1 *Ed.* 4. *cap.* 1.

Administrator, (*Adminstrator* in Lat.) Is in the sense of our Common-Law taken for one that hath the goods of a man dying intestate, commited to his charge by the Ordinary, and is accountable for the same, when ever it shall please the Ordinary to call him thereto. In this peculiar sense, this word is not used in all the Civil or Canon-Law, but more generally for those that have the Goverment of any thing. However the signification came to be restrained among us, it much matters not. But there was a Statute made 31 *E.* 3. *cap.* 11. whereby power was given to the Ordinary, to appoint these Administrators, and to authorise them as fully as Executors, to gather up and dispose the Goods of the deceased, so as they should be accountable for the same as Executors. And before that by the Satute *Westm.* 2. 13 *E.* 1. *cap.* 19. It was Ordained, that the goods of persons dying intestate, should be commited to the Ordinaries disposition, who should be bound to answer his Debts as far as his Goods would extend. * Against such an *Administrator*, and for him an Action will lye as for an *Executor*, and he shall be charged to the value of the Goods, and no farther, unlesse by his own *false Plea* or *Wast*: If the *Administrator* die, his Executors are not Administrators; but it behoves the Ordinary to commit a new Administration. And if a stranger, that is not *Administrator* or Executor, take the Goods, and administer of his own wrong, he shall be charged and sued as an *Executor*; and not as *Administrator*; but if the Ordinary make a letter, *Ad colligendum bona defuncti*, he that hath such a letter, is not Administrator; but the Action lies against the Ordinary, as if he had the goods in his own hand *Termes de Ley tit. Administrator.*

* **Administrator durante minore ætate,** Cannot sell the Goods of the deceased, unless it be of necessity, for payment of Debts, or *bona peritura*, for he hath his Office *pro bono & commodo* of the Infant, and not for his prejudice, and his Adminstration ceaseth at the Infants age of Seventeen years, *Co.* 5. *Rep. Prince's* Case. Where one hath Goods only in an inferior Diocess, yet the Metropolitan of the same Province pretending that he had *bona notabilia* in divers Diocesses, commits *Administration*; this is not void, but voidable by sentence, because the Metropolitan hath power over his whole Province; but if the Ordinary of a Diocess commit *administration*, when the party hath *bona notabilia*, such administration is meerely void, because by no means he can have jurisdiction of the Case.

Administratrix, (Lat.) She that hath such power and goods committed to her.

Admiral, (*Admiralius*, *Admirallus*, *Admiralis Capitaneus*, or *Custos maris*,) and derived of the French *Amerel*, signifieth both there, and with us, a high Officer or Magistrate, that hath the Government of the Kins Navy, and the hearing of all Causes belonging to the Sea, *Cromp. Jur. fol.* 88. *An.* 13. *R.* 2. *Cap.* 15. 15 *R.* 2. *cap.* 3. 2 *H* 4. *cap.* 11. 2 *H.* 4. *cap.* 6. 23 *H.* 8. 15. This Officer is in all Kingdoms of *Europe* that border upon the Sea. This Magistrate among the *Romans* was called *Præfectus classis*, as appeareth by *Tully*, in *Verrem.* 7. Mr. *Gwin.* in his *Preface to his Reading*, believes this Office was first created in the time of *Edw.* 3. his reason is this, because *Britton* that wrote in *Edw.* the First time, in the beginning of his Book, taking upon him to name all the Courts of Justice, maketh no mention of this Court, or Magistrate; and *Richard* the Second, in the Tenth Year of his Reign, limited his Jurisdiction to the power he had in his Grand-father *Edw.* 3 his Days; but contrary to this, it appears by some ancient Records, that not only in the Days of *Edward* the first, but also of King *John*, all Causes of Merchants and Mariners, and things happening within the main Sea, were ever tryed before the Lord Admiral. To this purpose, he hath his Court call'd *The Admiralty*: He hath Cognisance of the Death or Mayhem of a man committed in any great Ship riding in great Rivers, beneath the Bridges of the same next the Sea; also to arrest Ships in great Streams, for the Voyages of the King and Realm, and hath Jurisdiction in such Streams during the said Voyages. And Mr. *Pryn* in his *Animadversions* on *Co. Inst.* 4. *pa.* 75. says, he had Jurisdiction, both within and without the Kings Dominions, and might judge them in a summary way, according to the Laws of *Oleron*, and other Sea-Laws.

Admission, Is when the Patron presents to a Church, being void, and the Bishop upon examination, admits the Clerk able, by saying *Admitto Te habilem*, *Co.* on *Lit. fol.* 344. *a.*

Admittendo clerico, Is a Writ granted to him that hath recovered his right of Presentation against the Bishop in the *Common Bench*, the form of which you may have in *F. N. B. Fol.* 38. And *Reg. Orig. fo.* 33. *a.*

Admittendo in Socium, Is a Writ for the Association of certain persons to Justices of Assize before appointed, *Reg. Orig. fol.* 206. *a.*

† **Adnichiled,** 28. *H.* 8. *cap.* 7. From the *Lat. Nihil*, or as it was written of old *Nichil*, signifies annulled, made void, or brought to nothing.

Ad quod Damnum, Is a writ that lies to

the Sheriff, to inquire what Damage it may be to others for the King to grant a *Fair* or *Market*; or other person to give any Lands holden in Fee-simple, in *Mortmain*, to any House of Religion, or other Body Politick; for in that case the Land is said to fall in *manum mortuam*, into a dead hand; that is, it is in such an estate and condition, that the chief Lords lose all hope of *Heriots*, *service*, of Courts and *Escheats* upon any trayterous or felonious offence commited by the Tenant; for a Body-politick dyeth not, neither can perform personal Service, or commit Treason or Felony, as a single person may. And therefore it seems convenient, that before any such Grant be made, it be known what prejudice, it is like to work either to the Grantor, or others, *Fitz. Nat. Brev. fol.* 221. *Termes de ley* 25. Vide *Mortmain*.

Ad terminum qui præteriit, Is a writ of Entry, that lies where a man having leased Lands or Tenments for term of life, or years, and after the term expired, is held from them by the Tenant, or other stranger, that occupieth the same, and deforceth the Lessor. In such case this writ lyeth for the Lessor and his Heirs, *Fitzh. Nat. Brev. fol.* 201.

Advent, Is a time comprising a Moneth, or thereabouts, and begins upon the Sunday, that falls either upon St. *Andrews*-day, being the 30*th* of *November*, or next after it, and continues till the Feast of the Nativity of our Lord, commonly called *Christmas*, though Sir *Edward Cook.* 2. *part, Inst. fol.* 265. mistakes, in saying it ends eight dayes after the *Epiphany*; herein our Ancestors reposed much Reverence and Devotion, in regard of the near approach of that Solemn Feast; insomuch that it is sad, *Inter Plac. de temp. Regis Johan. Ebor.* 126. that *In adventu Domini nulla assisa debet capi*; all Contentions in Law were then remitted. Whereupon there was a Statute made *Anno* 3 *E.* 1. being *Westm.* 1. *cap.* 48. that notwithstanding the said usual Solemnity, it might be lawful (in respect of Justice and Charity, which ought at all times to be regarded) to take Assises of *Novel Disseisin*, *Mortdancester*, and *Darrein-presentment* in the time of *Advent, Septuagesima and Lent*. This is also one of the times from the beginning whereof to the end of the Octaves of the *Epiphany*, the Solemnizing of Marriage was forbidden, by reason of certain Spiritual Joy that the Church ought to conceive in the remembrance of her Spouse, *Christ Jesus*, and was not without special licence to be entertained, according to the old Verses,

> *Conjugium* Adventus *prohibet*, Hilariq; *relaxat*,
> Septuagena *vetat*, *sed* Paschæ *octava reducit*,
> Rogatio *vetitat*, *concedit* Trina Potestas.

Vide *Rogation*-week and *Septuagessima*. This Solemn Feast had its name of *Advent*, because it did so immediately precede the appearing of our Lord, and therefore was *præparatio Sancta in Adventum Domini*.

Adultery, (*Anno* 1 *H.* 7. *cap.* 4. and in divers other both places and Authors termed Advowtry,) in Latine *Adulterium* (as it were *Ad alterius thorum ascendere*,) is properly the Sin of Incontinence between two married persons; yet if but one be married, it is Adultery, which is severely punisht by the Laws of God, and the antient Laws of the Land. King *Edmund* a Saxon *Leg. suar cap.* 4. *Adulterium affici jussit instar Homicidii*. *Canutus* the Dane, *Hominem adulterum in exilium relegari jussit, fœminam nasum & aures præcidi, Leg. par.* 2. *cap.* 6. and afterwards, *cap.* 50. *Qui uxoratus faciet Adulterium, habeat Rex vel Dominus superiorem, Episcopus inferiorem. Leg. Hen.* 1. *cap.* 12. See a notable Case concerning Adultery in *Co.* 2. *Inst.* concerning *Margaret*, the Wife of *John de Camois*, who with her Husbands consent lived in Adultery with Sir *William Panell*, yet lost her Dower. See *Dower*. *Rex. &c. Præcipimus tibi quod diligenter inquiri facias per legales homines de* Visn. Candeur *Si* Robertus Pincerna *habens suspectum* Will. Wake *qui cum uxore sua adulterium committeret, prohibuit ei ingressum domus suæ, & si idem* Will. *post prohibitionem illam, domus ipsius* Roberti *ingreßus adulterium prædictum commisit, inde præfatus* Robertus *mentula eum privavit, & si inquisitio dederit, quod ita sit tunc eidem* Roberto *& suis qui cum eo erant ad hoc faciend. terr. & catalla sua occasione illa in manum nostram seisita, in pace esse facias donec aliud inde tibi præcipimus, &c.* Claus. 14. Joh. m. 2.

Ad ventrem inspiciendum, Is a writ mentioned in the Statute of Essoines, 12 *E* 2. See more in the Title *Ventre inspiciendo*.

Advocatione decimarum, Is a Writ that lieth for the claim of the fourth part, or upward, of the Tythes that belong to any Church, *Reg. Orig. fol.* 29. *b.*

Advowtry. See *Adultery*.

Advow, *Alias* Avow, *advocare*, cometh of the French word *Advoüer*, alias *avoüer*, and signifieth as much as to justifie or maintain an Act formerly done: For Example, One takes a Distresse for Rent, or other thing, and he that is distrained sueth a Replevin; now he that took the Distress, or to whose use the Distress was taken by another, justifying or maintaining the act, is said to *avow*, *Termes de Ley* 73. Hence comes Advowant and Advowry, *Old. Nat. Brev. fol.* 43 *Bracton.* uses the Latine word in the same signification (as *Advocatio Disseisinæ*) *lib.* 4. *cap.* 26. and *Caßanæus, de consuet. Burg. pa.* 1210. Uses *advocare* in the same signification. And *pag.* 1213. the Substantive *desavohamentum*, for a disavowing, or refusal to avow, * This word *Advowee* or *Avowee* (in Latine *Advocatus*) is used for him that hath right to present to a Benefice, 25. *E.* 3. Stat. 5. where we find also *Advowee paramount*, for the highest Patron, *viz.* the King: *Advocatus est ad quem pertinet jus Advocationis alicujus Ecclesiæ, ut ad Ecclesiam, nomine proprio, non alieno poßit præsentare, Fleta, lib.* 5. *cap.* 14. *Fitz. Nat. Brev. fol.* 39. useth in the same sense.

Advowee Paramount. By the Statute of Provisors, 25. *E.* 3. is taken for the King, the highest Patron.

Advowzen, Or Advowson; *Advocatio* signifieth in our Common-Law a right to present to a Benefice, and is as much as *jus Patronatus* in the *Canon-Law*; The reason why it is so termed, proceedeth from this, because they that originally obtained the right of presenting to any Church, were Maintainers of, or great Benefactors to that Church, either by building, or increasing it; and are therefore sometimes termed *Patroni*, sometimes

Advo-

Advocati and sometimes *Defensores cap* 4. & 2. *de jure Patronatus in decretal.* And Advowson being an old bastard French word, is used for the right of presenting, as appeareth by the Statute of *Westm.* 2. *cap* 5 Now *Advowson* is of two sorts; first *Advowson in gross*, that is, sole or principal, not belonging to any Mannor, as parcel of its right; and secondly, *Advowson apendant*, which depends upon a Mannor, as appurtenant to it, termed therefore by *Kitchin* an *Incident*, that it may be separated from the subject. O. this Mr. *John Skene de verbo* Sig. hath these words, *Dicitur Advocatio Ecclesiæ, vel quia Patronus alicujus Ecclesiæ ratione sui juris advocat se ad eandem Ecclesiam, & asserit se in eadem habere jus Patronatus, eamq; esse sui quasi clientis loco vel potiùs cùm aliquis (nempe Patronus) advocat alium jure suo ad Ecclesiam vacantem eumque loco alterius (veluti defuncti) præsentat & quasi exhibet.*

Aelmefeoh, *Pecunia Eleemosynaria, scilicet, Denarii sancti Petri.* Vide *Almsfeoh.*

Ætate probanda, Is a Writ that the Kings Tenant holding in chief, by Chivalry, and being Ward, by reason of Nonage, obtaineth to the Escheator of the County where he was born, or where the Land lyeth, to inquire whether he be of full age, to receive his Lands into his own hands, *Reg. Orig. fol.* 294, 295. *F. N. B. fol.* 253. & 257. he saith, that this Writ is sometime directed to the Sheriff, to impanel a Jury against a day certain, before Commissioners authorized under the Great Seal to deal in such a case.

Aerie, Or *Ayry* of Goshawks (*Aëria accipitrum*,) Is the proper term for Hawkes, for that which of other Birds we call a Nest. Thus it is used, 9 *H.* 3. *cap.* 12. in the Charter of the Forrest, and divers other places. It cometh from the French word (*Aire*) signifying as much as (*par*) in Latine, or (*a payre*) in English; and therefore when the Frenchman saith, *un home de bone aire*, he means a man coming of a good Payre, that is, a good Father and Mother.

Aesnecy. Vide *Esnecy*.

Afeerers, (*Afferatores aliàs Affidati*,) May probably be derived from the French (*Affier*) that is, *affirmare, confirmare*; and signifieth in the Common-Law such as are appointed in Court-Leets, upon Oath, to set the Fines on such as have committed faults arbitrarily punishable, and have no express penalty appointed by the Statute. The form of their Oath, you may see in *Kitchin, fol.* 46. The reason of this denomination may seem to be, because they that be appointed to that Office, do affirm upon their Oaths, what penalty they think in conscience the Offender hath deserved: Another probable derivation may be from (*feere*,) an old English word signifying a Companion, as (*Gefera*) doth among the *Saxons*, by Mr. *Lambard*'s testimony (*verb. contubernalis*,) in his explication of *Saxon* words, and so it may be gathered that *Kitchin* taketh, *cap. Amercements, fol.* 78. in these words, *Mes tiel amerciament soit affire per pares*; where (*Pares*) is put for *Affeerers*, and the reason hereof may be, for that in this business they are made Companions, or Equals. We find this word used, 25 *E.* 3. *Stat.* 7. *viz.* The same Justices before their rising in every Sessions, shall cause to be affeered the Amercements; and also to the same effect, 26 *H.* 6. *cap.* 6. And *Kitchin* *fol.* 78. joyns these three words together, as *Synonima's*, viz. *Affidati, Amerciatores, Affirors*, *Affidare* in the Canon-Law, is used for *Fidem dare, ca. fina. de cognatio spirit. in Decretal.* & *ca. super eo de testibus.* *Bracton* hath *Affidare mulierem*, to be betrothed to a Woman, *lib.* 2. *cap.* 12. But in the Customary of *Normandie, cap.* 20. this word (*Affeurer*,) the Latine Interpreter expresseth by (*Taxare*,) that is, to set the value of a thing, and the same with *æstimare*, &c. which seems indeed the best Etymology. See *Co. li.* 8. *fol.* 40. *b.*

Affidatus, Signifies a Tenant by Fealty, witness this Charter, *Ego Rogerus*, &c. *dedi*, &c. Willielmo Wallensi *pro suo servitio unam acram*, &c. *pro hac donatione & concessione devenit prædictus Will.* Affidatus *meus*, &c. *Affidati non proprie Vassalli sunt, sed quasi vassalli, qui in alicujus fidem & clientelam sunt recepti*, &c. *Affidatio accipitur pro mutua fidelitatis connexione tam in sponsaliis quam inter Dominum & Vassallum. Proles de affidata & non maritata, non est hæres, M. S. penes Arth. Trevor. Ar.*

Affirme, *Affirmare*, Signifies to ratifie or confirm a former Law or Judgment: So is the Substantive (*affirmance*) used *anno* 8 *H.* 6. *cap.* 12. And so is the Verb it self by *West, part* 2. *Symbole, tit. Fines, sect.* 152. if the Judgment be affirmed, &c. and also by **Crompton** in his *Jurisd. fol.* 166. 19 *H.* 7. *cap.* 20.

Affiance, Is the plighting of Troth betwixt a Man and a Woman, upon agreement of Marriage to be had between them; the Latine word, (*affidare*) from whence this is derived, is as much as *fidem ad alium dare*, and this word *affiance* is used by **Littleton**, *cap. Dower, sect.* 39.

Affidavit, In Law signifies an Oath, as to *make Affidavit*, is to testifie a thing upon Oath.

Afforest, Is to turn a piece of Ground into Forest, *Charta de Foresta, cap.* 1. & 3c. *anno* 9 *H.* 3. what that is, see more at large in *Forest.*

Affray, Cometh of the French word (*Effrayer*) *terrere*, to affright, and therefore may be without word or blow given, and so is the word used in the Statute of *Northampton*, 2 *E.* 3. *cap.* 3. It is commonly taken for a Skirmish, or Fighting, between two or more; In our Books it is many times confounded with an *Assault*, as appears by *Lambert*, in his *Eirenarcha, lib.* 2. *cap.* 3. & *lib.* 1. *cap.* 17. yet as it is there said, they differ in this, that where an *Assault* is but a wrong to the Party, an *Affray* is a wrong to the Common-wealth, and therefore both inquirable and punishable in a Leet. It may be said likewise, that an *Assault* is but of one side, but an Affray is the fighting of many together; besides this signification already mentioned, it may be taken for a terror wrought in the Subject by an unlawful sight of Violence, &c. as if a man shew himself furnisht with Armor or Weapons not usually worn, it may strike a fear into others unarmed, 2 *E.* 3. *cap.* 3. 4 *H.* 6. 10 8 *E.* 4. 5.

Affri, *Vel Affra*, Bullocks or Beasts of the Plough, *Vicecomes liberet ei omnia catalla debitoris, exceptis bobus &* Affris *carucæ, West.* 2. *cap.* 18. And in *Northumberland* to this day, they call a dull or slow Horse a *false Aver*, or *Afer, Spelm.* Whence also with probability enough, may be drawn the word *Heyfer* for a young Cow.

Age, *Ætas*, French *aage*, and signifieth in the

the Language of the Vulgar a mans life, from his Birth to the day of his Death; but in the Common-Law it is particularly used for those special times, which enable men and women to do that, which before for want of age, and consequently of Judgment, they might not do: And these times in a man be two, at Fourteen years he is at the age of discretion, Twenty one years is his full age, *Littleton*, *lib.* 2. *cap.* 4. the Law takes notice of him at several other ages, as at twelve years, to take the Oath of Allegiance in a Leet; at fourteen to consent to Marriage, and in soccage to choose his Guardian, *Dyer*, *fol.* 162. at fifteen for the Lord to have aid *pur faire Fitz Chivalier*, F.N.B. *in brevi de rationabili auxilio.* In a Woman they be Six, *Bro. Gard.* 7. First at seven years of age, her Father being the Lord, might heretofore distrain his Tenants for aid *pur file marier*, for at those years she may consent to Matrimony, *Bract. lib. cap.* 36. *nu.* 3. Secondly, At nine years old she is Dowable, for then, or within half a year after, she is able *Promereri dotem & virum sustinere*, Fleta, *lib.* 5. *cap.* 22. *Lit. lib.* 1. *cap.* 5. which *Bracton loco citato* does notwithstanding limit to twelve years Thirdly, At twelve years she is able finally to ratifie and confirm her former consent given to Matrimony. Fourthly, At fourteen years she is enabled to receive her Lands into her own hands, and shall be out of Ward, if she be of that age at her Ancestors death. Fifthly, At sixteen years she shall be out of Ward, though at the death of her Ancestor, she was under fourteen; The reason is, because then she may take a Husband able to perform Knights-Service. Sixthly, At twenty one years she is able to Alienate her Lands and Tenements; besides, as to a man we may add, that at fifteen years he shall be sworn to keep the King's Peace, *Anno* 34 *E.* 1. *Stat.* 3. The age of twenty one did heretofore compel a Man to be a Knight that had twenty pound Lands *per annum* in Fee, and that by 1 *E.* 2. *Stat.* 1. which is since repealed by 17 *Car.* 1. *cap.* 20. That age also enables him to contract and deal by himself in the management of his Estate, which until that time he cannot do with security of those that deal with him. The age of twelve binds to appearance before the Sheriffs and Coroner for enquiry after Robberies, *Anno* 52 *H.* 3. *cap.* 24. The age of fourteen years enables to enter an Order of Religion, without consent of Parents, *Anno* 4 *H.* 4. *cap.* 17. See *Co.* on *Lit. fol.* 78. *b.*

Age prier, (*Ætatem precari*, or *ætatis precatio*) Is a petition or motion made in Court by one in his minority (having an Action brought against him for Lands coming to him by descent) that the action may cease till he arrive to his full age, which the Court in most cases ought to yield unto: This is otherwise in the Civil-Law, which enforceth Children in their minority to answer by their Tutors or Curators; *W. de minor.* 25. *an.*

Agenhine. See *Hogenhine.*

Agent and Patient, Is, when a man is the doer of a thing, and the party to whom it is done, as where a Woman endows her self of the fairest possession of her Husband; Also if a man be endebted to another, and after makes the party to whom he is so endebted his Executor, and dies, the Executor may retain so much of the Deceased's Goods in his hands as his own Debt amounts to, and by this retainer he is the Agent and Patient, that is, the party to whom the Debt is due, and the party that pays the same. *Sed quære de hoc*, for that it is resolved, *Co. lib.* 8. *fol.* 138. In *Bonham's* Case, that a Man shall not be judge in his own cause, *Quia iniquum est aliquem sui rei esse judicem.*

Agist, From the French (*Gist*) a Bed or resting place, or (*gister*) *jacere*, or *gister*, *stabulari*, a word proper to a Deer, *cum sub mensem Mayum e locis abditis in quibus delituit emigrans in loco delecto stabulari incipit: unde commoda & propinqua sit pabulatio*, *Budæus in Posterior. lib. Philologiæ.* It signifieth in our Common-Law to take in and feed the Cattel of Strangers in the Kings Forest, and to gather the Money due for the same to the Kings use, *Charta de Foresta*, *an.* 9 *H.* 3. *cap.* 9. The Officers that do this, are called *Agistors*, in English Guest-takers, *Cromp. jur. fol.* 146. These are made by the Kings Letters Patents under the Great Seal of *England*, of whom the King hath four in every Forest, where he taketh any Pawnage; *Manwood's* Forest Laws, *cap.* 11. *fol.* 80. In what their Office consists; see the same *Manwood*, *part* 1. *p.* 336. Their Function is termed *Agistment*, as *Agistment upon the Sea-banks*, *Anno* 6 *H.* 6. *cap.* 5. This word *Agist* is also used for the taking in of other Mens Cattel into any Ground at a certain rate *per week.* See 4 *part*, *Inst. fol.* 293.

Agreement, (*Agreamentum*, which is according to *Plowden*, *aggregatio mentium*) Is a joyning or putting together of two or more minds in any thing done, or to be done, and this is threefold: 1. An agreement executed already at the beginning, and of that mention is made, 25 E. 3. *cap.* 3. of Clothes, which saith, *That the Goods bought by Forestallers, being thereof attainted, shall be forfeit to the King, if the Buyer have made* Gree *with the Seller:* Where the word (*Gree*) which otherwise is called Agreement executed, that is, payment for the things, or satisfaction. 2. An agreement after an act done by another, and is executed also; this is where one does an Act, and another agrees to it afterwards. 3. An agreement executory, or to be done *in futuro*, for which see 26 *H.* 8. *cap.* 3. And this may be divided into two parts, one which is certain at the beginning, the other when the certainty doth not appear at first, and the Parties agree that the thing shall be performed, or paid, upon the certainty known.

* **Agraria Lex**, Was a Law made by the *Romans* for the distribution of Lands among the common people.

Ayde, *Auxilium*, Is all one in signification with the French (*Aide*) and differs only in pronunciation; But in our Law it is applied to divers significations, as sometimes it signifies *a Subsidy*, as 14 *E.* 3. *Stat.* 2. *cap.* 1. sometimes *a Prestation due from Tenants to their Lords*, as towards the relief due to the Lord Paramont, *Glanvile*, *lib.* 9. *cap.* 8. This the King, or other Lord, might of old lay on their Tenants for knighting his eldest Son at the age of fifteen years, or marrying his Daughter at seven, *Reg. Orig. fol.* 87. *a.* and that at what rate themselves listed; But the Statute of *Westm.* 1. *anno* 3 *E.* 1. ordained a re-

straint

ſtraint for ſo unlimited a demand; And 25 E. 3. *Stat.* 5. *cap.* 11. provides, That the rate ſet down by the former Statute ſhould hold in the King as well as other Lords; of which, mention is made 27 *H.* 8. *cap* 10. This Impoſition ſeems to have deſcended to us from *Normandy*, (or rather from a more ancient Original, *The Feodal Laws*) for in the *Grand Cuſtumary*, *cap.* 35. you have a Tractate, intituled, *Des aydes Chevelz i. auxiliis capitalibus*, whereof the firſt is, *a fayre Peyne fitz de ſon Seigneur Chevalier*, to make his eldeſt Son Knight; The ſecond *pur eine file marier*; to marry the eldeſt Daughter, both theſe, and all charges incident thereunto, are taken away and diſcharged by the *Stat.* 12 *Car.* 2. *cap.* 24. This word is alſo particularly uſed in matter of Pleading, for a Petition made in Court for the calling in of help from another that hath an intereſt in the cauſe in queſtion, and is likely both to give ſtrength to the Party that prayeth in ayd of him, and alſo to avoid a prejudice growing toward his own right, except it be prevented; as when *Tenant* for term of *life*, by *curteſie*, *Tenant in tail after poſſibility of iſſue extinct*, *for term of years*, *at will*, by *Elegit*, or by *Statute Merchant*, being impleaded touching his Eſtate, may *petere auxilium*, that is, pray in ayde of him in the Reverſion, that is, deſire the Court that he may be called in by Writ, to alledge what he thinketh good for the maintenance both of his Right, and his Own; *Termes de la Ley:* But this courſe hath been much diſuſed: *Fitzherbert* mentions both *Prier in Ayde*, and *Prier Ayde de Patron*, *&c. auxilium petere a Patrono*, *Nat. Brev. fol.* 50. *d.* And the New Book of *Entries*, *verbo Ayde de parcener*, *fol.* 411. *col.* 4. This word is alſo found in 13 *R.* 2. *cap.* 17. This *Ayde prier* is ſometimes alſo uſed in the King's behoof, that there may be no proceeding againſt him, until the Kings Council be called and heard, to ſay what they think fit for avoiding the Kings prejudice or loſs; as if the King's Tenant holding in chief, be demanded a Rent of a common perſon, he may pray in Ayd of the King; Alſo a City or Burrough that hath a Fee-Farm of the King, any thing being demanded againſt them which belongeth thereunto, may pray in Ayd of the King, &c. *Termes de Ley*, 35, 36. Of this you may read the Statute *De Bigamis*, *Anno* 4 *E.* 1. *cap.* 1. 2, 3. & *an.* 14 *E.* 3. *Stat.* 1. *cap.* 14. The Civil-Law in Suits begun between two, allow a third to come in (*pro intereſſe*) and he that cometh in for his Intereſt, cometh either *aſſiſtendo* or *opponendo*, *&c.* See 19 *Car.* 2. *cap.* 8. Vide *Receit.*

Ayel, (*Avus*) Cometh of the French word (*Aieul*) and ſignifies a Writ, which lies where the Grand-Father and great Grand-Father, (called by our common Lawyers (*Beſayel*) but in true French (*Beſayeul*) was ſeiſed in his Demeſne, as of Fee of any Lands and Tenements in Fee-ſimple the day that he died, and a ſtranger abateth or entreth the ſame day, and diſpoſſeſſeth the Heir, *F.N.B. fol.* 222. *Plow. Com. fol.* 449. *b.*

Airy of Hawkes. See *Aery*.

Alba firma. *Cenſus annualis qui Centenario ſive Domino Hundredi penditur. Ideo* Alba *dicta quod non ex more priſci ſaeculi in annonâ qua tunc* Black mail *nuncupata fuit* (*hoc eſt cenſus vel firma nigra, ſed argento, quaſi cenſu albo reddebatur.* Spelman. *Duplex eſt tenura in Com. Weſtmerland, ſcil, una per* Albam firmam, & *alia per Cornagium*, *&c.* 2 Part Inſt. fol. 10.

Alderman, Sax. Ealdorman, Lat. *Aldermanus* ſignifies as much as *Senator* or *Senior*, and was among the *Saxons* as *Earl* among the *Danes*, *Camb. Brit. fol.* 107. *Lamb.* in his explication of Saxon words, *verbo Senator. Rog. Hoveden. part. poſterior ſuor. annal. fol.* 346. *b.* At this day we call them Aldermen, who are Aſſociates to the chief Civil Magiſtrate of a Town-Corporate or City, 24 *H.* 8. *cap.* 13. See *Spelman's Gloſſary* at large on this word, where you ſhall find that here we had anciently a Title of *Aldermannus totius Angliæ*, witneſs this Inſcription upon a Tomb in *Ramſey-Abby*, *Hic requieſcit D. Alwinus inclyti Regis Eadgari cognatus, totius Angliæ Aldermannus, & hujus ſacri Cœnobii miraculoſus Fundator.*

Alepiman, (*Alepimannus*) *Omnis* Alepiman *de tota Soca de* Hecham *debet ſingulis annis unum denarium de Chevagio*; & *operabitur per tres Dies in autumpno, exceptis illis qui ab hac ſervitute liberi ſunt.* Conſuetudinar. de Hecham Prior Lew. M. S. pag. 21. *Videtur* Alepimannos *iſtos mancipia fuiſſe*; *Chevagii enim ſolutio ſervitutis judicium eſt.* Spelman.

Aler ſans jour, Is French, and ſignifies properly in Engliſh to go without day; the meaning whereof is to be finally diſmiſſed the Court, becauſe there is no further day aſſigned for appearance, *Kitchin*, *fol.* 146.

Ale-ſilver, A Rent or Tribute yearly paid to the Lord Mayor of *London*, by thoſe that ſell Ale within the City, *Antiq. Purveyance*, *fol.* 183.

Ale-taſter, Is an Officer appointed in every Court-Leet, and ſworn to look to the Aſſize of Bread and *Ale*, or Beer, within the Precincts of that Lordſhip, *Kitchin*, *fol.* 46. where you may ſee the form of his Oath.

Alias. Vide *Capias alias.*

Alien, (*Alienare*) Cometh of the French word (*aliener*) and ſignifieth as much as to tranſfer the property of any thing to another. To *Aliene in mortmain*, is to make over Lands or Tenements to a Religious Houſe, or other Body Politick, *Stamf. Prær. Reg. fol.* 48. See *Mortmain.* To *aliene* in Fee, is to ſell the Fee-ſimple of any Land or Tenement, or of any Incorporeal right, *Weſtm.* 2. *cap.* 25. *an.* 13 E. 1.

Alien, *Alius*, *Alienus*, *Alienigena*, ſignifies one born in a ſtrange Country: It is uſually taken for the contrary to a *Denizen*, or natural Subject, that is, one born in a ſtrange Country, and never here infranchiſed, *Bro. Denizen* 4. Yet a man born out of the Land, ſo it be within the Limits of the King's Obedience, beyond the Seas, or of Engliſh Parents out of the King's Obedience; ſo the Parents at the time of the Birth be of ſuch obedience, is no *Alien* in account, but a Subject, *Stat.* 2. 25 E. 3. commonly called the Statute *De natis ultra mare.* Alſo, if one born out of the King's allegiance, come and dwell in *England*, his Children begotten here, are not *Aliens*, but *Denizens*, *Co. Rep. lib.* 7. *Calvin's* Caſe. See *Denizen.*

Alienation, Is to make a thing another mans, or to alter and put the Poſſeſſion of Lands or Tenements, or other things, from one man to another. And in ſome caſes a man hath power so to do without the assent or licence of another, and in some not; as if Tenant *in Capite* alien his Estate without the King's licence, then by the Stat. of 1 *E.* 3. *cap.* 12. a reasonable Fine shall be taken, whereas at the Common-Law, before that Statute, they were held forfeit, &c. *Co. lib.* 6. *fol.* 28. But if a man will *alien* Lands in Fee-simple to a Religious House, or Body-Corporate, it behoves him to have the King's licence to make this *Alienation*, otherwise the Lands shall be forfeit, by the Statute of 15 R. 2. *cap.* 5.

Alimony, *Alimonia*, Maintenance: But in a legal sense, signifies that allowance which a married Woman sues for, upon any occasional separation from her Husband; wherein she is not charged with *Elopement* or *Adultery*. This *Alimony* was heretofore called *rationabile estoverium*, as we may see by this Writ. *Rex, &c. Præcipimus tibi quod de Maritagio Emmæ de Pinckeney uxoris Laurentii Penir, qui excommunicatus est, eo quod prædictam Emmam affectione maritali non tractat, eidem Emmæ* rationabile estoverium *suum invenias, donec idem Laurentius vir suus eam tanquam uxorem suam tractaverit, ne iteratus clamor ad nos inde perveniat*, T. 29. Aug. Anno Regni nostri 7. Rot. Claus. 7. Hen. p. 1. m. 3.

Allay, French, In Latine *Allaya*, Is used for the temper or mixture of other Metals with Silver and Gold, *Anno* 9 *H.* 5. *Stat.* 2. *cap.* 4. and *Stat.* 1. *cap.* 11. The reason of which *Allay* is, with a baser metal to augment the weight of the Silver or Gold, so much as may countervail the Princes charge in Coynage, *Anton. Faber. de Nummariorum debitorum solutionibus, cap.* 1.

Allocation, (*Allocatio*) Properly a placing or adding to; but in the sense of Law it is an allowance made upon an account in the Exchequer.

Allocatione facienda, Is a Writ directed to the Lord Treasurer and Barons of the Exchequer, upon complaint of some Accountant, commanding them to allow him such sums as he hath by vertue of his Office lawfully and reasonably expended, *Regist. Orig. fol.* 206. *b.*

Allodium, See *Fee.* *Allodian* Lands are free Lands, which pay no Fines or Services.

Alluminor, Is derived from the French word *Allumer*, *i. accendere*, and denotes one that by his Trade coloureth or painteth upon Paper or Parchment: And the reason is, because he gives light and ornament by his colours to the Letters, or other Figures coloured. The word is used *Anno* 1 R. 3. *cap.* 9. At this day we call such a one a *Limner*.

Almaine rivets, Is a light kind of *Armor* for a man, with Sleeves of Maile, or Plates of Iron, for the defence of his Arms; this may seem to have been the Pattern of the Rocket, not long since in use among us, having loose Sleeves, which the livery Clokes of Noblemens Coachmen may also seem to imitate.

Almner or **Almoner**, (*Eleemosynarius*) Is an Officer of a Kings or Princes House, whose Office is diligently to collect all Fragments of Victuals, and distribute them daily to the Poor; charitably to visit all Sick, Leprous, Prisoners, poor Widows, and other necessitous and vagrant People, that have no constant abode: likewise to receive, and faithfully distribute all cast Horses, Robes, Money, and other things given in Alms. He ought also by frequent Admonitions, to move the King to bestow his Alms, and especially upon *Saints*, or *Holy-days*, and to advise him not to give his rich Robes to Players, Sycophants, Flatterers, Whisperers, or Minstrels, but that he command them to be bestowed as an increase of his *Alms*, *Fleta. lib.* 2. *cap.* 22. He hath the forfeiture of all *Deodands*, and the Goods of Felons *de se*, which he is to dispose in Alms to the Poor, *Termes de Ley*, 39.

Almoine. See *Aumone*, and *Frank Almoyne.*

Almesfeoh or **Aelmesfeoh**, Saxon, that is, Alms-Money; it was taken for *Peter-pence*, anciently paid in *England* on the First of *August*, and first given by *Ina* King of the *West-Saxons*: It was called also *Romefeoh*, *Romescot*, and *Heorthpening*. Seldens *Hist. Tythes, pag.* 217.

Almond, *Amygdalum*, Is well known to every mans sight, being the Kernel of a Nut, of whose nature and diversities, read *Gerards Herball*, *lib.* 3. *cap.* 87. This is noted among Merchandise, that are to be garbled, *Anno* 1 *Jac. cap.* 19.

Alnage, French *Aulnage*; the measuring with an Ell, 17 E. 4. *cap.* 5. See *Alnager.*

Alnager, **Alnageor**, **Aulnager**, **Alneger.** In Latine *Ulniger* or *Ulnator*; that, is, a Measurer by the Ell; it may be derived from the French word *Aulne*, an Ell, and signifieth a publick sworn Officer of the Kings, who by himself, or his Deputy, looks to the *Assize of Woollen Cloth* made through the Land, and to the Seals for that purpose ordained, 25 E. 3. *Stat.* 4. *cap.* 1. and 3 R. 2. *cap.* 2. who is accountable to the King, for every Cloth so sealed in a Fee or Custom thereunto belonging, *Anno* 17 R. 2. *cap.* 2. Read of this more, 27 E 3, 4. 1 *H.* 4. 13. 7 *H* 4. 10. 11 *H.* 4. 6. 12 *H.* 4. 4. 11 *H* 6. 9. 31 *H.* 6. 5. 4 E. 4. 1. 8 E. 4. 1. & 1 *H* 3. 8. There are now three Officers belonging to the Regulation of Clothing, all which were anciently comprised in one Person. These bear the distinct Names of *Searcher*, *Measurer*, and *Alneger*; which last, though in a several Language, it be the same with *Measurer*; yet long Usage and Custom have brought them to distinct Offices, and that which was anciently called *Alnager*, is now become Collector of the Subsidy granted to the King, by the fore-mentioned Statutes, still holding the same Name, because the Collection of that Subsidy was by *Edw.* the Third committed to the *Alneger*, and he nevertheless not abridged of measuring, till by his own neglect separated: Insomuch as there is now a peculiar *Measurer* to every particular Cloth made in *England* and *Wales*: And to prevent Abuses, an *Office of Searching* is establisht by an Act of Parliament, who ought by peculiar Seal to denote the Defects which each Cloth contains. All these were anciently under the Cognisance of the *Alneger*, as you may read at large in a Treatise, entitled, *The Golden Fleece*, See 4. *Inst. fol.* 31.

Alnetum est ubi alni arbores crescunt, A place where Alder-Trees grow, *Doomesday*-Book.

Alodium, Signifies a Mannor, and *Alsidarii*,

darii, or *Alodarii*, the Lords of the ſame Mannor. The old Tranſlation of the Saxon Laws uſeth this word for *Bockland*. And *Aloacii*, or rather, as I believe, *Alodacii*, for them that hold *Bockland* or *Charterlands*.

Altarage, *Altaragium*, This word includes not only the offerings made upon the Altar, but alſo all the profit that ariſes to the Prieſt by reaſon of the Altar, *Obventio Altaris*, as appears by an Order made in the Term of St. *Michael* 21, *viz.* in the Exchequer, between *Turner* Vicar of *Weſthaddon* in *Com. Northampton* and *Andrews*, whereby is declared, that by *Altaragium* is meant Tithes of Wooll, Lamb, Colt, Calf, Pigs, Goſlings, Chickens, Butter, Cheeſe, Hemp, Flax, Honey, Fruits, Herbs, and other ſuch ſmall Tithes, with offerings that ſhall be due in the Pariſh of *Weſthaddon*. See the Order at large, *Inter ordines in cuſtodia Rememerator. Reg. ibid.* And the like Caſe was for *Norton* in *Northamptonſhire*, of a latter date, *Oblationes ſive nummorum ſive panum tali vel tali Altari, vel ex devotione vel ex conſuetudine, aut à Parochianis, aut ab extraneis facta* Altaragii *nomine cenſebantur*, Gloſſ. in Mat. Paris.

Alto & Baſſo, or in Alto & in Baſſo. By this is meant the abſolute ſubmiſſion of all Differences, ſmall and great, high and low, *Pateat Univerſis, &c. quod* W. T. *de* Y. & T. G. *de* A. *poſuerunt ſe in* alto & baſſo *in arbitrio quatuor hominum, &c. de quadam querela, &c. Dat. apud* A. *die Mercurii prox. poſt Feſt concept. B. Mar. Virg. anno* 2 H. 5. And the like ſignification it hath in *Plac. coram Rege Hill.* 18 E. 1. *Ipſe Prior venit & Bogo ſimiliter & ponunt ſe in gratiam, miſericordiam & voluntatem Regis de* Alto & Baſſo, *ad quod mandantur Turri London, &c.*

Amabyr. See *Chevage*.

Ambidexter, Properly denotes a man that can equally uſe both his Hands; But in a legal ſence, it ſignifies, That Juror or Embraceor that taketh Money on both Parties for the giving of his Verdict, for which he forfeits *Decies tantum*, ten times ſo much as he taketh, 38 E. 3. 12. *Cromp. Juſt. of Peace, fol.* 156. *b.*

Ame. Vide *Aume*.

Amenable, From the French word *Amener*, *Adducere*, to lead unto; or as ſome *Amaynable*, deducting it from (*Maine*) a hand; it ſignifies *Tractable*, that may be lead or governed. It is applied in our Law Books to a Woman, that is governable by her Husband.

Amendment, *Emendatio*, Signifieth in our Common-Law, a correction of an Error committed in a Proceſs, and eſpied before Judgment, *Termes de la Ley, Bro. tit. Amendment, per tot.* but if the fault be found after Judgment given, then the party that will redreſs it, is driven to his Writ of Error, *Bro. tit. Error.*

Amerciament, *Amerciamentum*, Signifieth the pecuniary puniſhment of an offendor againſt the King, or other Lord in his Court, that is found to be in *miſericordia*, that is, to have offended, and to ſtand at the Mercy of the King or Lord. There ſeems to be a difference between *Amerciaments* and Fines, *Kitchin, fol.* 214. for Fines, as they are taken for puniſhments, be certain, and grow expreſly from ſome Statute, but *Amerciaments* are ſuch as be arbitrarily impoſed by *Affeerors*, which *Kitchin, fol.* 78. in ſome manner confirms in theſe words, *L'amerciament eſt aſſire per pares.*) *Manwood* in his *Foreſt Laws, part* 1. *fol.* 166. ſaith, An *Amerciament* is more eaſie, or more merciful penalty, and a *Fine* more ſharp or grievous. His words are theſe, *If the Pledges for ſuch a Treſpaſs do appear by common Summons, but not the Defendant himſelf, then the Pledges ſhall be impriſoned for that default of the Defendant. But otherwiſe it is, if the Defendant himſelf do appear, and be ready in Court before the Lord Juſtice in* Eyre, *to receive his Judgment, and pay his Fine; But if ſuch Pledges do make default, in that caſe the Pledges ſhall be* Amerced, *but not* Fined. The Author of the *New Terms of Law* ſaith, That *Amerciament* is properly a penalty aſſeſſed by the Peers or Equals of the Party amerced, for an Offence done; for the which he putteth himſelf upon the mercy of the Lord: Who alſo maketh mention of an *Amerciament Royal*, and defines it to be a pecuniary puniſhment laid upon a Sheriff, Coroner, or ſuch like Officer of the King, by Juſtices for ſome Offence. *Ratcliff* Baron of the Exchequer, 2 *H.* 7. *fol.* 7. See *Miſericordia*.

Amortization, *Amortizatio*, French *Amortiſſement*, *eſt prædiorum translatio in* manum mortuam *quod tamen ſine venia Principis non fiat. Jus amortizationis eſt privilegium ſeu licentia capiendi in* manum mortuam. In the Statute *De libertatibus perquirendis*, 27 E. 1. This word *Amortiſement* is uſed. See *Mortmayne*.

Amortiſe, (From the French word *amortir*) is to aliene Lands or Tenements to any Corporation, Guild or Fraternity, and their Succeſſors, which cannot be done without licence of the King and the Lord of the Mannor, 15 R. 2. *cap.* 5. See *Mortmayn*, and the Statute for *Amortizing Lands* made *tempore*, Ed. 1.

Amoveas manum. See *Ouſter le mayn*.

Amy, *Amicus*, As in Law *Prochein amie* is the next to be intruſted for an Orphant, or Infant.

Ampliation, *Ampliatio*, properly an enlargement, but in ſence of Law, denotes a deferring of Judgment, till the Cauſe be further examined.

Amneſtia, *Oblivio*, as an *Amneſtia*, or Act of Oblivion, ſuch as was granted by his moſt Gracious Majeſty at his Reſtoration.

An, jour & Waſte, (*Annus, dies & Vaſtum*) Look *Year*, *Day*, and *Waſte*.

Anealing of Tile, 17 E. 4. *cap.* 4.

Ancorage, (*Ancoragium*) A duty taken of Ships for the *Pool* of the *Haven*, where they caſt Anchor, *M. S. Arth. Trevor. Ar.* For no man can let any Anchor fall on the Kings Ground in any Port, without paying for it to the Kings Officers appointed by Patent.

Anceſtor, *Anteceſſor*, The ſignification is well known; and the Law makes this difference between that and Predeceſſor, that *Anceſtor* is applied to a natural perſon, as J. S. and his Anceſtors; the other to a Body-Politick or Corporate, as a Biſhop and his Predeceſſors, *Co.* on *Lit. lib.* 2. *cap.* 4. *ſect.* 103.

Anceſtrel, As *Homage Anceſtrel*, that is, Homage that hath been done or performed by ones *Anceſtors*. See *Homage*.

Ancient, In the *Middle-Temple*, such as are past their Reading, and never Read, are *Ancients*. In *Gray's-Inn* the Society consists of *Benchers*, *Ancients*, *Barristers*, and *Students* under the Bar, and here the *Ancients* are of the more *Ancient Barristers*. The *Inns* of *Chancery* consist of *Ancients* and *Students*, or *Clerks*, and among the *Ancients*, one is yearly the *Principal*, or *Treasurer*.

Ancient demeasne or **demayn**, (*Vetus Patrimonium Domini*) Is a certain *Tenure*, whereby all the Mannors belonging to the Crown in the days of *Saint Edward*, or *William the Conqueror*, were held. The numbers and names of which Mannors, as of all others belonging to common persons, after a Survey made of them, he caused to be written in a Book, now remaining in the Exchequer, and called *Doomsday*. And those, which by that Book appear, to have at that time belonged to the Crown, and are contained under the Title, *Terra Regis*, are called *Ancient Demesne*, *Kitchin*, *fol.* 98. Of these Tenants were two sorts; one that held their Land frankly by Charter, the other by Copy of Court-Roll, or by the Verge at the Will of the Lord, according to the Custom of the Mannor, *Britton*, *cap.* 66. *num.* 8. The benefit of this *Tenure* consists in these Points. 1. The Tenants holding by Charter, cannot be impleaded out of their Mannor, or, if they be, they may abate the Writ, by pleading their Tenure. 2. They are free of Toll for all things concerning their Livelihood and Husbandry. 3. They may not be empannelled upon any Enquest, *F. N. B. fol.* 14. *d.* & *fo.* 228, *&c.* By whom it appears, these Tenants held originally by ploughing the King's Lands, plashing his Hedges, or such like, towards the maintenance of his Houshold; for which cause they had such Liberties granted. No Lands ought to be esteemed *Ancient Demesn*, but such as are held in *Soccage*. See *Monstraverunt* and *Demayn*.

Anciently, (French *Anciennete*, that is, *Antiquitas*) It is used *in statuto Hiberniæ*, 14 *H.* 3. for Seniority. As, *The eldest Sister can demand no more than her other Sisters, by reason of her* Ancienty.

Andena, A swath in Mowing. See *Dole*.

Annats, *Annates*, Are all one with First-Fruits, *Anno* 25 *H.* 8. *cap.* 20. See *First-Fruits*. The reason of the name is, because the rate of *First-Fruits* paid of Spiritual Livings, is after the value of *one years* profit. *Annates more suo appellant primos fructus unius anni sacerdotii vacantis aut dimidiam eorum partem*, Pol. Virgil. de Invent. rer. lib. 8. cap. 2. Here observe, That First-Fruits, *Primitiæ* & *Annates*, are all one, *Co.* 12. *Rep. fol.* 45.

Annienteo, Cometh of the French word *Anneantir*, that is, *Abjicere*; it signifieth in Law as much as frustrated, or brought to nought, *Lit. lib.* 3. *cap. Warranty*, and *sect.* 741.

Anniversary days, (*Dies Anniversarii*) Were in former times, solemn Days appointed in Commemoration of the Deaths or Martyrdoms of Saints, and once every year celebrated: Also Days whereon, at the return of every year, Men were wont to pray for the Souls of their deceased Friends, mentioned in the Statute, 1 *Ed.* 6. *cap* 14. and 12 *Car.* 2. *cap.* 13. This was in use among our Ancestors the *Saxons*, as may be seen, *Lib. Rames*, *Sect.* 134.

Annua Pensione, Is a Writ whereby the King having due unto him an Annual Pension from an Abbot or Prior, for any of his Chaplains (whom he should think fit to nominate, being as yet unprovided of sufficient Living) doth demand the same of the said Abbot or Prior; and also willeth him for his Chaplains better assurance, to give him his Letters Patent for the same, *Reg. Orig. fol.* 165. & 307. & *F. N. B. fol.* 231. Where you may see the Names of all the Abbies and Priories bound to this, in respect of their Foundation or Creation; as also the form of the Letters Patent usually granted upon this Writ.

Anno Domini, Is that reckoning of Time from the Birth of our Saviour, which is generally used in all publick Writings, with an Addition of the year of the King's Reign. The *Romans* began their *Æra* from the building of their City; The *Greeks* reckon'd by *Olympiads*: And the Christians from the Birth of *Jesus Christ*. *The day of the Month, Year of our Lord, and year of the Kings Reign, are the usual dates of Deeds*, Co. 2. *Inst. fol.* 675.

Annuity, *Annuus redditus*, Signifies a yearly Rent to be paid for term of Life, or Years, or in Fee; and is also used for the Writ that lieth against a man for the recovery of such a Rent, if it be not satisfied every year according to the Grant, *Reg. Orig. fol.* 158. *F. N. B. fol.* 152. The Author of the *New Terms of Law* defineth *Annuity* to be a certain sum of Money granted to another in Fee-simple, Fee-tail, for term of Life or Years, to receive of the Grantor or his Heirs, so that no Free-hold be charged therewith, whereof a man shall never have Assize, or other Action, but a Writ of *Annuity*. Saint *Germain* in his Book stiled *Doctor and Student*, *Dial.* 1. *cap.* 3. Sheweth divers differences between a Rent and an *Annuity*, *viz.* That every Rent, be it Rent-Charge, Rent-Service, or Rent-Seck, is going out of Lands; but an *Annuity* goeth not out of any Land, but chargeth only the person; that is to say, the Grantor, or his Heirs, that have *Assets by descent*; Or the House, if it be granted by a House of Religion, *Lit. sect.* 220. 2. A second difference is, That for the recovery of an *Annuity*, no Action lieth, but only a Writ of *Annuity* against the Grantor, his Heirs or Successors, *Fitz. Nat. Brev.* 152. But of a Rent, the same Actions lye as do of Land, as the Case requireth. 3. The third Difference is, That an *Annuity* is never taken for *Assets*, because it is no Free-hold in Law, neither shall be put in execution upon a *Statute-Merchant*, *Staple*, or *Elegit*, as a Rent may, *Doct.* & *Stu. cap.* 30. See also, *Dyer*, *fol.* 345. *pl.* 2. Also an *Annuity* cannot be severed, *Co. lib.* 8. *fol.* 52. *b.* See more *Leighs Comment. verbo Annuity*.

Annis-seed, *Semen Anysi*, a Medicinal Seed not unknown, *Gerard's Herbal. lib.* 2. *cap.* 397. It is noted among the Garbleable Drugs and Spices, 1 *Jac. cap.* 19.

Anoysance, Alias *Noysance*, alias *Nusance*, in Latine *Nocumentum*, in French *Nuisance*, hath a double signification, being used as well for any hurt done to a publick place, as a High-way, Bridge, or common River; or to a private, by laying any thing that may breed Infection, by incroaching, or otherwise; As also, for the Writ that is brought upon such transgression; whereof see more in *Nusance:* This word *Anoysance*, you may find, *Anno* 22 *H.* 8. *cap.* 5.

Ansel weight. See *Aunsel.*

Apostata capiendo, Is a Writ that lieth against one, that having entred and profess'd some Order of Religion, breaks out again, and wanders up and down the Country, contrary to the Rules of his Order; for the Abbot or Prior of the House, certifying this into the Chancery, under their Common Seal, and praying this Writ directed to the Sheriff, for the Apprehension of such Offender, and delivery of him again to his Abbot or Prior, or their lawful Attorney, were wont to obtain the same. The form whereof, with other circumstances, you may find, *Reg. Orig. fol.* 71. & 267. and *Fitz. Nat. Brev. fol.* 233. *C.* This is now out of use.

Apparitor, 21 *H.* 8. *cap.* 5. Signifies a Messenger that cites Offenders to appear in the Spiritual Court, and serves the Process thereof.

Apparlement, Cometh of the French *Pareilment*, that is, *Similiter, Perinde, Ibidem*, in English, *likewise*; it signifies a resemblance or likelihood, as *Apparlement* of War, 2 R. 2. *Stat.* 1. *cap.* 6.

Appeal, *Apellum*, Cometh of the French word *Appeller*, that is, *Accire:* It signifies in our Common-Law as much as *Accusatio* with the Civilians; for as in the Civil-Law, Cognisance of Criminal Causes is taken either upon *Inquisition, Denunciation* or *Accusation;* so in Ours, upon *Inditement* or *Appeal*; *Inditement* comprehending both *Inquisition* and *Denunciation*: And *Accusation* or *Appeal*, is a lawful Declaration of another mans Crime (which by *Bracton* must be Felony at the least) before a Competent Judge, by one that setteth his Name to the Declaration, and undertaketh to prove it upon the penalty that may ensue of the contrary. To declare the whole course of an *Appeal*, is not proper for this place, I refer you to *Bracton, lib.* 3. *tract.* 2. *cap.* 18. *cum sequent.* Britton, *cap.* 22, 23, 24, 25. Smith, *lib.* 3. *de repub. Ang. ca.* 3. And Stamf. *pl. Cor. lib.* 2. *ca.* 6, 7, &c. *usque* 17. An *Appeal* is commenced two ways, either by *Writ*, or by *Bill, Stamf. ubi supra*, and it may be gather'd by him, *fol.* 148. that an *Appeal by Writ* is, when a Writ is purchased out of the Chancery by one to another, to this end, that he Appeal a third of some Felony committed by him, finding Pledges that he shall do it, and deliver the Writ to the Sheriff to be recorded. *Appeal by Bill* is, when a man of himself giveth up his Accusation in Writing to the Sheriff or Coroner, offering to undergo the burthen of Appealing another therein named. This point of our Law, among others, is taken from the *Normans*, as appears plainly by the *Grand Custumary*, cap. 68. where there is a solemn Discourse both of the effects of this *Appeal, viz.* The Order of *Combat*, and of the Tryal by *Inquest*; of either of which it is in the Defendant's power to make choice. See *New Book of Entries*, verbo *Appell, Lib. Ass. fol.* 78. and 3. *part. Inst. fol.* 131.

Appeal of Mayhem, *Appellum Mahemii*, Is an accusing of one that hath *maimed* another. But that being no Felony, the *Appeal* is but a kind of Action of *Trespass*, because there is nothing recover'd but Damages. *Bracton* calls this *Appellum de plagis & Mahemio*, and writes a whole Chapter about it, *lib.* 3. *tract.* 2. *ca.* 24. See *Coke, vol.* 4. *fol.* 43. *a.* In King *Johns* Time, there is an *Appeal* recorded against a Jew, *Qui fecit ementulari quendam nepotem suum.*

Appeal of wrong Imprisonment, (*Appellum de pace & imprisonamento*) Is used by *Bracton* for an Action of *Wrong Imprisonment*, whereof he writeth, *lib.* 3. *tract.* 2. *ca.* 25.

Appeal, (*Appellatio*) Many times used in the Common, as it is in the Civil-Law, which is the removing a Cause from an Inferior Judge to a Superior, *as Appeal to Rome*, 24 *H.* 8. *ca.* 12. and 1 *Eliz. ca.* 1. So Saint *Paul* Appealed from *Festus* to *Cæsar*. But more commonly for a private Accusation of a Murderer, by a person who had interest in the party murthered, or of any Felon, by one of his Complices with him. And those that are so appealed, are call'd *Appellees*, 28 *E.* 1. See *Approver*

Appendant, *Appendens*, Is a thing belonging to another that is more worthy, as *Accessorium Principali* with the Civilians, or *Adjunctum Subjecto* with the Logicians. An Hospital may be *Appendant* to a Mannor, *Fitzh. Nat. Brev. fol.* 142. Common of Fishing *appendant* to a Free-hold, *Westm.* 2. *ca.* 25. 13 *Ed.* 1. *Appendants* are ever by Prescription. See *Co.* on *Lit. fo.* 121. *b.*

Appennage or **Apennage**, French, *A Childs part*, properly the Portion of the Kings younger Children in *France*, where they have a Law which they call, *The Law of Apenages*, whereby the Kings younger Sons have Dutchies, Counties, or Baronies granted to them, and their Heirs, or Heirsmales of their Bodies, the Reversion reserved to the Crown, and all Matters of Regality; as Coynage, Levying Taxes, and the like: It is derived *ab appendendo*, or from the German word *Avanage*, which signifies a *Portion*. See *Gerard de Heylan & Spelman's Glossary, in verbo* Appennagium.

Appertinances, (*Pertinentiæ*) Is derived of the French word *Appertiner, i. Pertinere*, to belong to. It signifies in the Common-Law things both Corporeal, belonging to another thing, as the more Principal; as Hamlets to a chief Mannor, Common of Pasture, Turbary, Piscary, and such like; and incorporeal, as Liberties and Services of Tenants, *Brit. ca.* 39. Where we may observe, That he accounts Common of Pasture, Turbary and Piscary, to be things corporeal. *Vide Corporal.*

Apportionment, *Apportionamentum*, Is a dividing of a Rent into parts, according as the Land, whence the whole Rent issueth, is divided among two, or more. As if a man have a Rent-service issuing out of Land, and he purchases parcel of the Land, the Rent shall be apportioned according to the value of the Land. So if a man hold his Land of another by Homage, Fealty, Escuage and Rent, if the Lord of whom the Land is holden, purchase parcel of the Land, the Rent shall be *apportioned*. And if a man let Lands for years, reserving Rent, and after a Stranger recovers part of the Land, then the Rent shall be be *apportioned*, and the Lessee shall pay, having respect to that which is recovered, and to that which remains in his Hands according to the value. But a Rent-charge cannot be *apportioned*, nor things that are entire: As if one hold Land by Service, to pay his Lord yearly at such a Feast, a Horse, a Hawk, a Rose, or a Cherry, or the like; then, if the Lord purchase part of the Land, this Service is gone, because a Horse, a Hawk, a Rose, a Cherry, &c. cannot be divided or *apportioned*, without damage to the entirety. In some Cases Rent-charge shall be *apportioned*, as if a man hath a Rent-charge issuing out of Land, and his Father purchases parcel of the Lands charged in Fee, and dies, and this parcel descends to his Son, who hath the Rent-charge; there this Charge shall be *apportioned*, according to the value of the Land; because such portion of the Land purchased by the Father, comes not to the Son by his own act, but by descent, and course of Law. Common Appendant is of common right, and severable; and though the Commoner purchase parcel of the Land, whereto the Common is appendant, yet the Common shall be *apportioned*. But in this case, Common Appurtenant, and not Appendant by such Purchase is extinct, *Co. lib.* 8. *fol.* 79. *Termes de Ley* 48, 49.

Apposer. See *Forreign Apposer.*

Apprendre, (French) As a Fee or Profit *Apprendre*, 2 & 3 *E.* 6. *cap.* 8. A Fee or Profit to be taken or received.

Apprentice, *Apprenticius*, (French *Apprenti*, and that from *Apprendre* to learn, whence their *apprentisage*, and our *apprentiship*) signifieth with us one that is bound in Word, or Writing, to serve another man of Trade for certain years, upon condition, That the Artificer, or Master, shall in that mean time indeavour to instruct him in his Art or Mystery, *Smith, de Rep. Angl. lib.* 3. *cap.* 8. saith, They are a kind of Bondmen, differing only, that they be Servants by Covenant, and for a time. Barristers at Law were heretofore called *Apprentices of the Law*; So saith Mr. *Selden* in his Notes upon *Fortescue*, *p.* 3. And so the Learned Mr. *Plowden* stiled himself. Sir *Henry Finch* in his *Nomotechnia*, gives himself the same Title. And Sir *Edward Coke*, 2. Part, *Inst. fol.* 564. holds, That *Apprenticii Legis* are called *Homines consiliarii & in Lege Periti*. And in another place --- *Apprentices, and other Counsellors of Law.*

Appropriation, *Appropriatio*, Proceedeth from the French *Approprier, id est, Aptare, accommodare*, and properly signifieth in the Law of *England*, a severing of a Benefice Ecclesiastical, which originally, and in nature is, *Juris divini & in Patrimonio nullius*, to the proper and perpetual use of some Religious House, or Dean, &c. and Chapter, Bishoprick or Colledge: And the reason of the Name may be this, because, that whereas Parsons ordinarily be not accounted *Domini*, but *Usu-fructuarii*, having no right of Fee-simple, *Lit. tit. Discontinuance.* These, by reason of their perpetuity, are accounted Owners of the Fee-simple, and therefore are called *Proprietarii*. And before the time of *Richard* the Second, it was lawful (as it seems) to *appropriate* the whole Fruits of a Benefice to an Abby or Priory, they finding one to serve the Cure. But that King redressed that Evil by a good Law, whereby he Ordained, That in every Licence of *Appropriation* made in *Chancery*, it should be expresly contained, That the Diocesan of the place should provide a convenient sum of Money yearly to be paid out of the Fruits, towards the sustenance of the Poor of that Parish, and that the Vicar should be well and sufficiently endowed, 15 *R.* 2. *ca.* 6. Touching the first Institution, and other things worth the learning about *Appropriations*, Read *Plowd* in *Grendon's* Case, *fol.* 496. *b.* & *seq.* As also, *Termes de Ley verbo* Appropriation. To an *Appropriation*, after the Licence obtained of the King in Chancery, the consent of the Diocesan, and the Patron and Incumbent are necessary, if the Church be full; but if it be void, the Diocesan, and Patron may conclude it, *Plowd. ubi supra.* To dissolve an *Appropriation*, it is enough to present a Clerk to the Bishop, and he to institute and induct him; For that once done, the Benefice returns to the former nature, *Fitz. Nat. Brev. fol.* 35. and *Co. lib.* 7. *fol.* 13.

Approvement, Mentioned 43 *Eliz. ca.* 11. Is, where a man hath Common in the Lords wast Ground, and the Lord encloses part of the wast for himself, having nevertheless sufficient Common with egress and regress for the Commoners. This inclosing is called *Approvement*. See *Reg. Jud. fol.* 8, 9.

Approver, *Approbator*, Cometh of the French *Approver, Approbare*; It signifies one that confessing Felony of himself, appealeth or accuseth another, one or more to be guilty of the same; and he is called so, because he must *prove* that which he hath alledged in his Appeal, *Stamf. Pl. Cor. fol.* 142. And that Proof is by Battle, or by the Country, at his election that is appealed. The form of this Accusation you may in part gather by *Crom. Just. of Peace*, *fol.* 250, & 251. That it is done before the Coroner, either assigned unto the Felon, by the Court, to take and record what he saith, or else called by the Felon himself, and required for the good of the Prince and Common-wealth to record that which he saith, &c. The Oath of the *Approver*, when he beginneth the Combat, see also in *Cromp. pag. ult.* As also the Proclamation by the Herald. Of the Antiquity of this Law, you may see something in *Horne's Mirror of Just. lib.* 1. *in fine*, *cap. del Office del Coroner*; and more at large, *Bracton lib.* 3. *tract.* 2. *ca.* 21. & 34. *Stamf. Pl. cor. lib.* 2. *ca.* 52. *cum seq.* 3. *Part, Inst. fol.* 129.

Approvers of the King, *Approbatores Regis*, Be such as have the letting of the Kings Demeans in small Mannors, to his best advantage. 51 *H.* 3. *Stat.* 5. And in 1 *E.* 3. *ca.* 8. The Sheriffs call themselves the *Kings Approvers*.

Approve, *Approbare*, Signifies in the Common-Law, to augment, or rather, to examine to the uttermost. As for Example, *To approve Lands* is to make the best benefit thereof by approving the Rent, or increasing it. And in *Crom. Jurisd. fol.* 152. the Substantive *Approvement* is used for the Profits themselves. So is it likewise in the Statute of *Merton*, *ca.* 4. *anno* 2 *H.* 3. Land newly *approved*, *Old Nat. Brev. fol.* 79. and 9 *H.* 6. *ca.* 10. Bayliffs of Lords in their Franchises, be called their *Approvers*; But by 2 *E.* 3. *ca.* 12. *Approvers* be certain men especially sent into several

Coun-

Counties of the Realm, to increaſe the Farms of Hundreds and Wapentakes, which formerly were ſet at a certain rate to the Sheriffs, who likewiſe demiſed them to others, the County Court excepted. And *Approvers* in the Marches of *Wales* were ſuch as had licence, *de vendre & achater beaſts, &c.* as appears by a Charter thereof from one *Richard de Lingeyne* to *Janin de Brompton*, dated the 11th day of *July*, in the 4th year of *Henry* the Fourth, and 2. *Part, Inſt. fol.* 474. *Quod nullus libere tenens infra Baroniam illam ſe appruira poſſit de vaſto ſuo, &c.*

Aquage, (*Aquagium, quaſi aquæ agium*) *Non liceat facere dammas, &c. in aliquibus watergangeis, &c.* Ordinatio Mariſci de Romeney facta tempore, *H.* 3. *& Ed.* 1. *pag.* 72. See *Watergage.*

Arbitrator, May be taken to proceed either from the Latine (*arbitrator*) or the French (*arbitre*) and ſignifieth an extraordinary Judge in one or more Cauſes between party and party, choſen by their mutual conſents, *Weſt. Sym. Part* 2. *tit. Compromiſe, ſect.* 21. who likewiſe divideth *Arbitrement* into general, that is, including all Actions, Quarrels, Executions and Demands, and eſpecial which is of one or more Matters, Facts, or Things ſpecified, *ibid. ſect.* 2, 3, 4. The *Civilians* make a difference between *arbitrum* and *arbitratorem, lib.* 76. *π pro ſocio*; for though they both ground their power upon the compromiſe of the Parties, yet their liberty is divers; For *Arbiter* is tied to proceed and judge according to Law, with equity mingled. *Arbitrator* is permitted wholly to his own diſcretion, without ſolemnity of Proceſs, or courſe of Judgment, to hear and determine the Controverſie committed unto him. So it be *juxta arbitrium boni viri.* See *Alto & Baſſo.*

Arbitrement, Is an Award, or Determination, made by one or two, at the requeſt of two Parties at leaſt. To every *Arbitrement* five things are incident, *ſcil.* 1. Matter of Controverſie. 2. Submiſſion. 3 Parties to the ſubmiſſion. 4. Arbitrators. And 5. Giving up of the *Arbitrement, Dyer* 217, *Pl.* 60. How an *Arbitrement* may be avoided. See 7 *H.* 6. *ca.* 40. And *Termes de Ley*, [illegible]54. Alſo no party ſhall be bound by any *Arbitrement*, unleſs the Award be delivered unto him. As it is, *Co. lib.* 5. *fol.* 103. And *lib.* 8 *fol.* 98.

Arches Court, (*Curia de arcubus*) Is the chief and moſt ancient Conſiſtory that belongeth to the Archbiſhop of *Canterbury*, for the debating of Spiritual Cauſes; and is ſo called from the Church in *London*, dedicated to the Bleſſed Virgin, commonly called the Church of St. *Mary le Bow*, where it is held; and the Church is named *Bow Church*, from the faſhion of the Steeple, whoſe top raiſed of Stone Pillars, is builded *Archwiſe*, like ſo many bent Bows. The Judge of this Court, is termed *The Dean of the Arches*, or *The Official of the Arches Court. Dean of the Arches*, becauſe with this Officialty is commonly joyned a peculiar Juriſdiction of Thirteen Pariſhes in *London*, termed a *Deanry*, being exempt from the Authority of the Biſhop of *London*, and belonging to the Archbiſhop of *Canterbury*; of which the Pariſh of *Bow* is one, and the principal, becauſe the Court is there kept. Others conceit that he was firſt called *Dean of the Arches*, becauſe the *Official* to the Archbiſhop being many times employed abroad in Ambaſſages for the King and Realm; the *Dean of the Arches* was his Subſtitute in this Court, and by that means the Names became confounded. The Juriſdiction of this Judge is ordinary, and extendeth it ſelf through the whole Province of *Canterbury.* So that upon any Appeal made, he forthwith, and without any farther examination of the Cauſe, ſends out his Citation to the Appellee, and his Inhibition to the Judge from whom the Appeal was made Of this you may read more in *Hiſt. de Antiquitate Eccleſ. Brittan.* And 4 *Part, Inſt. fol.* 337.

Archives, *Archiva*, A derivative from *Arca*, a Cheſt. The *Rolls*, or any place where Ancient Records, Charters, and Evidences are kept; alſo the *Chancery*, or *Exchequer-Office.* Alſo the private Repoſitory in *Libraries.*

Arma moluta, Seem to be ſharp Weapons that do cut, and not blunt, which do only break or bruiſe, *Bract. lib.* 3. *tract.* 2. *ca.* 23. & *Stamf. Pl. Cor.* 78, 79. *Bractons* words be theſe, *Arma moluta plagam faciunt, ſicut gladius & hujuſmodi; Ligna vero & lapides, bruſuras, orbes & ictus, qui judicari non poſſunt ad plagam, ad hoc ut inde venire poſſit ad duellum.*

Armor, *Arma*, In underſtanding of Law, is extended to any thing that a man in his wrath or fury taketh into his hand, or wears for a defence, wherewith to caſt at, or ſtrike another, *Cromp. Juſt. of Peace, fol.* 65. *a.* So *Armorum appellatio non utique ſcuta & gladios ſignificat, ſed & fuſtus & lapides.*

Argentum Dei, Gods Money, That is, Money given in earneſt upon the making of any Bargain.

Arabant, *Ad Curiam Domini*, Was intended of thoſe who held by the Tenure of ploughing and tilling the Lands of the Lord, *infra Curiam*, i. e. *manerium ſuum, Spel.Gloſſ. verb. Arabant.*

Arpens or **Arpen**, Engliſh *Arpent*, ſignifies an Acre, and according to the old French account, mentioned in *Doomſ-day* Book, one hundred Perches make an *Arpent*, 18 Foot a Perch, 12 Inches a Foot, *Columel. lib.* 5. *ca.* 1. *Demyarpent* they take for *Jugum*, or *Jugerum.*

Array, (*Arraya*, alias *Arraiamentum*) Cometh of the *Obſolete* French word *Array*, that is, *Ordo*, or it may probably be derived from *raye, linea*; It ſignifies in a legal acceptation, the ranking or ſetting forth of a Jury or Enqueſt of men empannelled upon a Cauſe, 18 *H.* 6. *ca.* 14. Thence we ſay to *Array* a Pannel, *Old N. B. fol.* 157. The *Array* ſhall be quaſht, *ibid.* By the Statute, every *Array* in an Aſſize ought to be made four Days before, *Bro.tit.Panel.nu.*10. To challenge the *Array*, *Kitchin, fol.* 92. See *Challenge.* To lead and conduct perſons armed and *arrayed*, 14 *Car.* 2. *ca.* 3.

Arrayers, Is uſed 12 *R.* 2. *ca.* 6. for ſuch Officers as had care of the Soldiers Armor, and to ſee them duly accoutred in their kinds. Such were the Commiſſioners of *Array*, appointed by King *Charles* the Firſt, 1642. And *Edward* the Third, in the firſt year of his Reign, appointed ſuch Commiſſioners to *array* men againſt the *Scots.*

Arraigne or **Arraine**, From the French *Arranger*, that is, to ſet a thing in order in his place, and the ſame ſignification it hath in Law: For example, He is ſaid to *Arraine* a Writ of

Novel Disseisin in a County, that sitteth it for Tryal before the Justices of the Circuit, *Old Nat. Brev. fol.* 109. *Lit. pag.* 78. useth the word in the same sence, *The Lease arraineth an Assize of Novel Disseisin.* To *arraign the Assize*, is to cause the Tenant to be called, to make the Plaint, and set the Cause in such order, as the Tenant may be enforced to answer thereto, *Co.* on *Lit. fol.* 262. *b.* Also a Prisoner is said to be *arraigned*, when he is indicted and brought forth to his Tryal. *Arrained* within the Verge for Murther, *Stamf. Pl. Cor. fol.* 150. The method of this *Arraignment* you may read in Sir *Thomas Smith, de Rep. Ang. lib.* 2. *ca.* 23. The famous *Spelman* thinks it should be *Arrame*, and that derived from *Arramare*, an obsolete Latine word, proceeding from the old French *arramir*, *jurare*, *solenniter profiteri*; but we rather stick to the old and common Writing.

Arrerages, *Arreragia*, Deduced from the French *Arrierages*, as that from *arriere*, *a retro*, behind. It signifies the remainder of an Account, or sum of Money in the hands of an Accountant. It is used sometimes more generally for any Money unpaid at a due time, as *Arrearages* of Rent. That this word is borrowed from *France*, appears by *Tiraquel de utroque retractu, tom.* 3. *p.* 32. *num.* 10.

Arrentation, From the *Spanish Arrendare*, which is as much as *ad certum reditum dimittere*, it is mentioned *Ordin. Foresta*, 34 *E.* 1. *ca.* 6. Signifies the licencing an Owner of Lands in the Forest to enclose them (*bassa haya & parvo Fossato*, with a low Hedge, and little Ditch) under a yearly Rent: *Saving of the Arrentations*, is saving power to give such Licences for a yearly Rent.

Arrest, *Arrestum*, Cometh of the French *Arrester*, to stop or stay, and is metaphorically used for a Decree, or Determination of a Cause debated, or disputed to and fro: As *Arrest du Senat.* is *Placitum Curiæ*: In our Common-Law it is taken most of all for a stay or stop, as a man apprehended for Debt, &c. is said to be *arrested*. To move or plead in *arrest* of Judgment, is to shew cause why Judgment should be staid, though there be a Verdict in the Case: To plead in *arrest* of taking the Enquest upon the former Issue, is to shew cause why an Enquest should not be taken, *Bro. tit. Repleader. Bud.* (saith Mr. *Lambert, Eirenar. lib.* 2. *c.* 2. *p.* 94.) in his Greek Commentaries, thinks that the French word *Arrest*, which with them (as we said) signifies the Decree, or Judgment of the Court, took beginning from the Greek ἀρεστόν, *i. Placitum*, as we may say the pleasure of the Court; yet, I believe, rather that we receive the same from the *Normans* Law, because we use it in the same sence with them; for commonly with us an *Arrest* is taken for the Execution of the Commandment of some Court, or of some Officer of Justice; but howsoever the name began, an *Arrest* is a certain restraint of a mans person, depriving him of his own will, and binding him to become obedient to the will of the Law: Precepts, and Writs of the higher Courts of Law, do use to express it by two several words, as (*Capias*) and (*Attachies*) to take, or catch hold of: And, it seems, this word is spread farther then *France*, for *Gale* a *German* Writer sheweth by his Tractate, *De Arrestis Imperii*, that it is used in the Imperial Territories in the same signification, *c.* 1. *n.* 1. For preventing *Arrests of Judgment*, see 16 & 17 *Car.* 2. *ca.* 8.

Arrestandis bonis ne dissipentur, Is a Writ which lies for him whose Cattel or Goods are taken by another, who, during the Controversie, doth, or is like to make them away, and will hardly be able to make satisfaction for them afterward, *Reg. Orig. fol.* 126. *b.*

Arrestando ipsum qui pecuniam recepit ad proficiscendum in obsequium Regis, &c. Is a Writ that lieth for the Apprehension of him that hath taken Prest-money towards the Kings Wars, and hides himself when he should go, *Reg. Orig.* 24. *b.*

Arresto facto super bonis mercatorum alienigenorum, Is a Writ that lies for a *Denizon* against the Goods of Strangers of another Country found within the Kingdom, in recompence of Goods taken from him in that Foreign Country, after denial of Restitution, *Reg. Orig. fol.* 129. *a.* This among the Civilians is called *Clarigatio*, but now barbarously *Reprisalia*.

Arretted, *Arrectatus*, Is he that is convented before a Judge, and charged with a Crime, *Stamf. Pl. Cor. lib.* 2. 45. *Arrectatus* may seem a Compound, *quasi ad rectum vocatus*; It is sometimes used for imputed, or laid unto; as, no folly may be *arretted* to him being under age, *Lit.cap. Remitter*; the Latine Substantive *Rettum* is used in the *Reg. Orig.* And *Chaucer* useth the Verb *Arretteth*, that is, lays blame, as it hath been interpreted: It may with some reason seem, that that word is the same with the *Rectum*, because *Bracton* saith, *Rectum habere Malefactorem*, that is, to have the Malefactor forth-coming, so as he may be charged, and put to his Tryal, *lib.* 3. *tract.* 2. *ca.* 10. And in the same *chap. nu.* 3. *Rectatus de morte hominis*, that is, charged with the death of a man.

Arsura, The trial of Money by Fire after it was coyned.

Articles of the Clergy, *Articuli Cleri*, Statutes made touching Persons and Causes Ecclesiastical, 9 *E.* 2. and 14 *E.* 3. *Stat.* 3.

Arundinetum, A place where R[illegible]s grow, we find it mentioned in the Book of *Doomsday*.

Arthel, *Anno* 26 *H.* 8. *ca.* 6. Is a Brittish word, and more truly written *Arddelw*, which the *South-Wales* Men Write *Arddel*, and signifies (according to Doctor *Davies* Dictionary) *Astipulari*, *asserere*, in English to *Avouch*. *O dele'r dyn a'i Ledrad yn ei law, rhaid iddo geisio Arddelw, &c.* that is, If a man be taken with stolen Goods in his hands, he must be allowed a lawful *Arddelw* (Vouchee) to clear him of the Felony, which is part of the Law of *Howel Dda*; but probably so abused in *Henry* the Eigth his Time, by the delay, or exemption of Felons, and other *Criminals* from Justice, that provision by the forementioned *Statute* was made against it.

Assay of Measures and Weights, Derived from the French *Essay*, *i.* a Proof or Trial, is the Examination used by the *Clerk of the Market*, Reg. Orig. fol. 279. *Ac assisam & assayam panis, vini & cervisiæ*, Paten. 37 H. 8. *Tho. Marrow.*

Assayer of the King, (*Assayator Regis*) French *Assayeur*, Is an Officer of the Mint, for the

the due tryal of Silver, indifferently appointed between the *Master of the Mint*, and the Merchants that bring Silver thither for Exchange, 2 *H. 6. ca.* 12. Vessels of Gold shall be *assayed*, 28 *E.* 1. *ca.* 20. and 18 *Car.* 2. *ca.* 5. *Mandatum est, &c. quod convocatis in præsentia sua omnibus monetariis, Assayatoribus, &c. de cambiis Regis* London, *&c. provideat tot & tales, &c. qui, &c. ne Rex, &c. damnum incurrat*, Clauf. 17 H. 3. m. 8.

Assault, *Insultus* or *assultus*, Cometh of the French verb *Assayler*, i. *Adoriri, Invadere*, and that French word may be derived from the Latine *Assilire*, that is, *vim Afferre, Oppugnare*. It signifies in Law a violent kind of injury offered to a mans person, of a higher nature then Battery; for it may be committed by offering of a Blow, or by a threatning Speech, *Lambar. Eiren. lib.* 1. *ca.* 3. As to threaten a Collector with harsh words, so that he dare not, for fear execute his Office, hath been reckon'd *an Assault*. To strike at a man, though he be neither hurt nor hit, hath been adjudged the like, 22 *Lib. Ass. Pl.* 60. That *Assault* doth not always imply a blow, or striking, appears, in that in Trespass for *Assault and Battery*, a man may be found guilty of the *Assault*, and excused of the *Battery*, 25 *E.* 3. *ca.* 24. The *Feudists* call this *Assultum*, and define it thus, *Assultus est impetus in personam aut locum, sive hoc pedibus fiat, vel equo aut machinis aut quacunq; alia re assiliatur*, Zasius de Feud. pa. 10. nu. 38. And *assilire est vim Adferre*, Lib. Feud. 1. tit. 5. *sect.* 1.

Assach, Seemeth to be a Welsh word, and to signifie so much as a kind of excuse, or strange purgation, by the Oaths of 300 men. This of old was used in *Wales*; for so I find it explained in an old Manuscript, *Assach est un Jur.* 300 *homes in Gales*, but now it is utterly out of use, 1 *Hen.* 5. *ca.* 6.

Assart, *Assartum*, In the Opinion of *Manwood, part* 2. *ca.* 9. *nu.* 5. Of the *Forest Laws*, comes from the French *Assartir*, signifying to make plain, *Assartum est quod redactum est ad culturam*, Fleta, lib. 4. cap. 21. *Item respondere*: It is saith the same *Manwood, ca.* 9. *nu.* 1. An offence committed in the Forest, by pulling up by the roots the Woods, that are thickets and covert for the Deer, and by making them plain as arable Land: This is reputed the greatest offence or trespass, that can be done in the Forest to *Vert or Venison*, containing in it *Wast*, or more; for whereas *Wast of the Forest*, is but the felling and cutting down of the Coverts, which may grow up in time again; *an Assart* is a plucking them up by the Roots, and utterly destroying them, that they can never grow again. And this is confirmed out of the *Red Book in the Exchequer*, in these words, *Assarta vero, occasiones nominantur, quando, &c. Forestæ nemora vel dumeta, pascuis & latibulis ferarum opportuna succiduntur; quibus succisis & radicibus avulsis terra subvertitur & excolitur*. And again, out of the *Reg. Orig. fol.* 257. *a b.* in the Writ, *ad quod damnum*, sent out in case where a man sueth for licence to Assart his Grounds in the Forest, and to make it several for Tillage; So that it is no offence, if done with licence. To this may *Bracton* also be added, *lib.* 4. *ca.* 38. *nu.* 11. where he saith, That the words *Boscus efficitur assartum*, signifie as much as *redactus in culturam*. Of this, you may read more in *Cromp. Jur. fol.* 203. And *in Charta de Foresta*, 9 *H.* 3. *ca.* 4. where the English word is not written *Assart*, but *Assert*. And in *Manwood*, part 1. p. 171. The word is used, 4 *E.* 1. *Stat.* 1. in the same signification. That which we call *Assartum*, is elsewhere termed *disboscatio*: *Decis*, Genu. 78. *Quietus de Essartis*, we find in a Charter of *Henry* the First to the *Abbot* of *Rames*, *Sect.* 198. & *in Pat.* 18 E. 3. p. 1. m. 19. & *quibusdam Sartis quæ, &c. Assart* was also anciently used for a parcel of Land *assarted*, as appears by a Charter of *Roger* Earl of *Mortimer*, without date; which is in the custody of Mr. *Thomas Bridgwater*.

Assembly unlawful, Coming from the French *Assembler*, id est, *Aggregare*, to flock together, whence also is the Substantive *Assembly, Congregatio*; in a legal sence, signifying the meeting of Three, or more persons, to do an unlawful act, although they do it not, *Lamb. Eiren. lib.* 1. *ca.* 19. See *unlawful Assembly*.

Asset, From the French *Assez*, i. *Satis*, *Bract. lib.* 5. *tract.* 3. *ca.* 8. *nu.* 2. And although this word wear the vizard of a Substantive, yet is it in truth but an Adverb, and signifies Goods enough to discharge that burthen, which is cast upon the Executor or Heir, in satisfying the Testators or Ancestors Debts and Legacies. See *Bro. tit. Assets per discent*, that whosoever insists upon *Assets*, intends thereby that the party charged hath enough descended, or come to his hands, to discharge the thing in demand. The Author of the *New Terms of Law* maketh two sorts of *Assets*. *Assets per descent*, and *Assets enter maynes*: *Assets per descent* is, where a man is bound in an Obligation, and dies seised of Land in Fee-simple, which descend to his Heir, then his Land shall be called *Assets*, that is enough or sufficient to pay the same Debt, and by that means the Heir shall be charged as far as the Lands so to him descended will extend. But if he have alienated before the Obligation be put in suit, he is discharged. Also when a man seised of Lands in tail, or in the right of his Wife, aliens the same with Warranty, and hath in value as much Lands in Fee-simple, which descends to his Heir, who is also Heir in tail, or Heir to the Woman; now if the Heir, after the decease of his Ancestor, being a *Writ of Formedon*, or *sur cui in vita*, for the Land so alienated; then he shall be barred, by reason of the warranty, and the Land so descended, which is as much in value as that which was sold, and so thereby he hath received no prejudice; therefore this Land is called *Assets per descent*. 2. *Assets enter maynes* is, when a man indebted, makes Executors, and leaves them sufficient to pay, or some commodity or profit is come to them in right of their Testator; this is called *Assets in their hands*.

Assigne, *Assignare*, It hath two significations, one general, as to appoint a Deputy, or set over a right unto another; in which sence *Britton* saith (*fol.* 122.) This word was first brought into use for the favour of Bastards, because they cannot pass under the name of Heirs, and therefore were and are comprised under the name of *Assignees*. The other signification is special as to *point at*, or *set forth*, so we may say to *assign Errors*, *Old N.B. fol.* 19. that is, to shew where the Error is committed. *To assign false Judgment*, Id. fol. 17. that is, to declare how

how and where the Judgment is unjust. To *assign a false Verdict*, Id. fol. 112. And *to assign Perjury*, Anno 9 R. 2. cap. 3. *To assign the Cessor*, Old Nat. Brev. *fol.* 1341. To shew how the Plaintiff had cessed, or given over. *To assign Waste*, is to shew wherein especially the Waste is committed, *Reg. Orig. fol.* 72. *Assign* in the general signification is used, 20 *E.* 1. And 11 *H.* 6. *ca.* 2. in these words, *Justices assigned to take assises*. And the Substantive *assignment* hath the same signification, *West. Symbol.* par. 1. lib. 2. sect. 496. as the *assignment of a Lease* is the setting over the interest to another. In which manner is used also the word *Assignee*, *assignatus* for one that is appointed or deputed by another, to do any Act, or perform any Business, or enjoy any Commodity. And such an *Assignee* may be either by Deed, or in Law: *Assignee by Deed* is he that is appointed by a person, as when a Lessee of a term assigns the same to another, he is his *Assignee by Deed*; *an Assignee in Law*, is he whom the Law so makes, without any appointment of the person, *Dyer*, *fol.* 6. *nu.* 5. So an Executor is *Assignee in Law* to the Testator. *Perkins* (tit. *Grants*) saith, That *an Assignee* is he that occupieth a thing in his own Right, and *Deputy* is he that doth it in the right of another.

Assize, Cometh of the French *Assise*, which in the *Grand Custumary of Normandy*, ca. 24. is thus defined. *Assize* is an Assembly of Knights, and other substantial men, with the Bayliff, or Justice, in a certain place, and at a certain time appointed: And again, *ca.* 55. *Assize* is a Court, in the which, whatsoever is done, ought to have perpetual strength. This word is properly derived from the Latin Verb *assideo* to sit together. *Littleton* in his Chapter *Of Rents* saith, That it is *Æquivocum*, setting down three several significations of it; one, as it is taken for a *Writ*; another, as it is used for a *Jury*; the third, as for an *Ordinance*. *Assize* then is taken for a Writ directed to the Sheriff, for the recovery of possession of things immovable, whereof any one, and his Ancestors, have been disseized. And this is as well of things corporeal, as right incorporeal, being of four sorts, as here follow in Order.

Assize of Novel Disseisin, *Assisa Novæ Disseisinæ*, lies where a Tenant in Fee-simple, Fee-tail, or for term of Life, is lately disseised of his Lands or Tenements, or else of a Rent-service, Rent-seck, or Rent-charge, of Common of Pasture, of an Office, of a Toll, Tronage, Passage, Pawnage, or for a Nusance levied, and divers other such like; for confirmation whereof, you may read *Glanvile*, lib. 10. cap. 2. *Bract. lib.* 4. *tract.* 1. *per totum*, Britton, ca. 70. & *seq.* *Reg. Orig.* fol. 197. F. N. B. *fol.* 117. 178, 179. *New Book of Entries*, fol. 74. col. 3. *West.* 2. *c.* 25. *anno* 13 *E.* 1. And to this may aptly be added the bill of *Fresh force*, which is directed to the Officers, or Magistrates of Cities, or Towns-Corporate, being a kind of *Assise*, for Recovery of Possession in such places, within forty Days after the *Force*, as the ordinary *Assise* is in the County, F. N. B. *fol.* 7. This the *Civilians* call, *Judicium Possessorium recuperandi*.

Assise of Mort d'Ancestor, *Assisa mortis antecessoris*, Lyeth where my Father, Mother, Brother, Sister, Uncle, Aunt, &c. died seised of Lands, Tenements, Rents, &c. that he had in Fee-simple, and after his death a stranger abateth: And it is good as well against the Abator, as any other in Possession. How this may be extended, see *Bract. lib.* 4. *tract.* 3. *per totum*, *Brit. cap.* 70. *Fitz. Nat. Brev. fol.* 114. *Reg. Orig. fol.* 223. This the *Civilians* call *Judicium Possessionum adipiscendi*.

Assise of Darrein Presentement, *Assisa ultimæ presentationis*, Lies where I and my Ancester have presented a Clerk to a Church, and after the Church being void by his Death, or otherwise, a stranger presents his Clerk to the same Church in disturbance of me: And how otherwise this Writ is used. See *Bract. lib.* 4. *tract.* 2. *Reg. Orig. fol.* 30. *F. N. B. fol.* 195.

Assise de utrum, Lyeth for a Parson against a Lay-man, or a Lay-man against a Parson, for Land or Tenement doubtful, whether it be Lay-fee, or free-alms. And of this, see *Bract. lib.* 4. *tract.* 5. *cap.* 1. *Brit. cap.* 95. The reason why these Writs be called *Assises*, may be divers. First, because they settle the Possession, and so an outward right in him that obtaineth by them. Secondly, They were originally executed at a certain time and place formerly appointed. For by the *Norman Law*, the time and place must be known forty days before the *Justice* sat upon them: And by our Law likewise fifteen days of preparation, except they be tried in those standing Courts of the King at *Westminster*, as appeareth by F. N. B. *fol.* 177. Lastly, They may be called *Assises*, because they are tried most commonly by special Courts, set and appointed for that purpose, as may well be proved not only out of the *Custumary of Normandy*, but our Books also; which shew, that in ancient times, Justices were appointed by special Commission to dispatch Controversies of Possession, one or more, in this or that only County, as occasions fell out, or Disseisins were offered, and that as well in Term-time as out of Term: Whereas, of later days, we see that all these *Commissions of Assises*, *of Eyre*, *of Oyer and Terminer*, *of Gaol-delivery*, *and of Nisi prius*, are dispatcht all at one time, by two several Circuits in the year, out of Term, and by such as have the greatest sway of Justice, being all of them either the Kings *ordinary Justices* of his Benches, *Barons* of the Exchequer, *Sergeants* of the Law, and such like; concerning which, hear the learned Lord *Verulam* in his Use of the Law, *fol.* 13. *ad* 21.

All the Counties of this Realm (says he) *are divided into six Circuits, and two men learned in the Law are assigned by the Kings Commission in every Circuit, who ride twice a year through those Shires allotted to that Circuit; these we call Justices or Judges of Assise, who have five several Commissions by which they sit.* The first is a *Commission of Oyer and Terminer* directed to them, and many others of the best account in their Circuits: But in this Commission the Judges of Assise are of the *Quorum*, so as without them, there can be no proceedings. This Commission gives them power to deal with Treasons, Murders, and all manner of Felonies and Misdemeanors, and this is their largest Commission. The second is of *Gaol-delivery*, and that only to the Judges themselves, and the Clerk of the *Assize associate*; by this Commission they are to to deal with every Prisoner in *Gaol*, for what offence soever he be there: The third Commission is directed to themselves only, and the *Clerk of the Assise* to take *Assises*, by which they are called *Justices of Assise*; and the Office of these Justices, is to do right upon Writs called *Assize*, brought before them by such as are wrongfully thrust out of their Lands. The fourth Commission is to take *Nisi prius*, directed to none but the Judges themselves and their *Clerks of Assises*, by which they are called Justices of *Nisi prius*. The fifth is a *Commission of Peace* in every County of their Circuit: And all the Justices of Peace, having no lawful impediment, are bound to be present at the *Assises*, to attend the Judges, as occasion shall fall out; if any make default, the Judges may set a Fine upon him at their pleasure and discretions: The Sheriff of every Shire, is also to attend in person, or by a sufficient Deputy, allowed by the Judges, who may fine him, if he fail, &c.

Assise, In the second signification, according to *Littleton*, is used for a *Jury*; For (to use his own Example) it is set down in the beginning of the Record of an *Assise of Novel Disseisin*; as *Assisa venit recognitura*, which is as much to say, as *Juratores veniunt recognituri*: And the reason why the Jury is called an Assise, he giveth to be this, because by a *Writ of Assise*, the Sheriff is commanded, *Quod faciat duodecem liberos & legales homines de vicineto, &c. Videre tenementum illud & nomina eorum imbreviari, & quod summoneat eos per bonas summonitiones, quod sunt coram Justiciariis, &c. parati inde facere recognitionem, &c.* This is (to speak shorter) *Metonymia effecti*, for they are called the *Assises*, because they are summoned by vertue of the Writ so called. And yet the Jury summoned upon a *Writ of Right*, is likewise called *the Assise*, though it be not an Assise, but is so termed καταχρηστικῶς, or abusively. *Assise* in this signification is divided into *magnam & parvam*, *Glanv. lib. 2. cap. 6, 7, &c.* and *Brit. cap. 12.* where it appeareth, wherein the *Great Assize* differeth from the *Petit Assize*. The former four kinds of *Assises* used in Actions only *Possessory* be called *Petit Assises*, in respect of the *Grand Assise*; for the *Law of Fees* is grounded upon two Rights, one of Possession, the other of Property. And as the *Grand Assise* serveth for the right of Property, so the *Petit Assise* serveth for the right of Possession. *Horn's Mirror of Just.* lib. 2. cap. *de Novel Disseisin*. *Assise* in the third signification, according to the same *Littleton*, is an Ordinance or Statute, as the *Statute of Bread and Ale* made 51 *H.* 3. is termed the *Assise of Bread and Ale*, *Assisa panis & cervisiæ*, Reg. Orig. fol. 279. *The Assise of Clarendon*, *Assisa de Clarendon*, whereby those that be accused of any heinous Crime, and not able to purge themselves by Fire and Water (perhaps *Ordeale*, *Ordalium*) but must abjure the Realm, had liberty of forty days to stay, and try what Succour they could get of their Friends towards their sustenance in Exile, *Stamf. Pl. Cor. fol.* 118. which he seemeth to have taken out of *Bract. lib. 3. tract. 2. cap. 16. num. 2.* See also *Roger Hoveden, parte posterior. suor. annal.* fol. 313. *in Henrico Secundo.*

Assise of the Forest, *Assisa de Foresta*, Is a Statute or Condition, touching Orders to be observed in the Kings Forest. *Manwood's Forest Laws*, part 1. p 35. *Cromp.* in the Court of Justices of the Forest, *per totum*, *fol.* 146. And the *Assise of the King*, Anno 18 *Ed.* 1. *Stat.* 1. called *The Statute for view of Frank-pledge*. And these be called *Assises*, because they set down and appoint a certain Measure, Rate or Order in the things they concern. Of *Assise*, in this signification *Glanvile* speaks, *Lib. 9. cap. 10. in fine*. *Generaliter verum est quod de quolibet placito quod in comitatu deducitur & terminatur, misericordia quæ inde provenit, vicecomiti debetur: Qua quanta sit, per nullam assisam generalem determinandum est:* And thus much touching *Littleton's* Division. But if we mark well the Writers of the Law, we shall find this word *Assise* more diversly used, than he (*Littleton*) hath noted. For it is sometime used for the measure or quantity it self, (and that *per Metonymiam effecti*) because it is the very scantling described or commanded by the Ordinance; as we say, when Wheat, &c. is of such a price, then the Bread, &c. shall be of such *assise*. This word is further taken, for the whole *Process in Court* upon the *Writ of Assise*, or for some part thereof, as the Issue or Verdict of the Jury; For Example, *Assizes of Novel Disseisin, &c.* shall not be taken, but in their Shires, and after this manner, &c. *Mag. Chart.* c. 12. and so it seems to signifie, *West.* 2. *cap.* 25. 13 *Ed.* 1. In these words, *Let the Disseisor alledge no false Exceptions, whereby the taking of the Assises may be deferred, &c.* And 34 *E.* 1. *Stat.* 2. If it be found by *Assise*; the *Assise is arrained*, to *aver by the Assise*, the *Asise by their default* shall pass against them. And also, 1 *H.* 6. c. 2. *Assises* awarded by default of the Tenants, &c. Lastly, by *Merton*, cap. 4. an. 20 H. 3. *certified by the Assize, quit by the Assise, &c.* And in this signification *Glanvile* calleth it, *Magnam Assisam Domini Regis, quæ ex duodecem ad minus legalium hominum Sacramentis consistit*, lib. 2. cap. 7. *Bract.* useth it in like sort, as *Assisa cadit in transgressionum*, lib. 4. cap. 30. & *assisa cadit in perambulationum*, Id. c. 31. num. 2. *Fleta* defineth an Assise in this signification, thus, *Assisa in jure possessorio, est quædam recognitio duodecem hominum juratorum, per quam Justiciarii certiorantur de articulis in brevi contentis.* And Assise also thus signifying, is said sometime to pass (*per modum Assisæ*) and sometime *in modum juratæ*, in manner of an *Assise*, when only the *Disseisin* is in question, is put to the trial of the twelve, in manner of a *Jury*, when any exception is objected, to disable the interest of the *Disseisin*, and is put to be tried by the twelve, before *the Assise* can pass: As for example, *Quæstio status, causa successionis, causa donationis, pactum sive conditio vel conventio, voluntas & dissimulatio, transactio vel quieta clamatio, vel remissio, confirmatio sive consensus, propria usurpatio rei propriæ, difficultas judicii, justum Judicium, finis, Chirographum, intrusio in rem alienam vel disseisina, si incontinenti rejiciatur, negligentia quæ per transitum temporis excludit actionem*, Fleta, *lib.* cap. 10. *sect.* 1. Whom read also to this point, c. 11. sect. *si autem a Domino*, and at large, *cap.* 16. *ejusd. lib.* & *lib.* 5. *cap.* 6. *sect. Item vertitur assisa*. And note, That *Assise* in this signification is taken four ways, *Old Fitz. Nat. Brev. fol.* 105. The first is *Assise at large*, which is taken as well upon other Points, as upon the Disseisin, *v. g.* where an Infant bringeth an Assise, and the Deed of his Ancestor is pleaded, whereby he claimeth his Right, or or founded his Title, then the *Assise* shall be taken at large; that is, the Jury shall enquire not only whether the Plaintiff were disseised or not by the Tenant, but also of these two Points, *viz.* Whether his Ancestor were of full Age, of good Memory, and out of Prison, when he made the Deed pleaded. Another Example out of *Kitchin, fol. 66.* The Tenant pleadeth a Foreign Release, in bar to an *Assise*, whereupon the Cause was adjourned; At the day the Tenant maketh default, therefore the *Assise* was taken at large, that is, not only whether the Plaintiff were disseised, but also whether there be any Foreign Release. A third Example you may read in *Littleton*, cap. *Estates upon Condition.* The second manner of Assise in point of Assise (*Assisa in modum Assise*) which is, when the Tenant, as it were, setting Foot to Foot with the Demandant, without farther circumstance, pleadeth directly to the Writ, *no Wrong, no Disseisin.* The third manner is, Assise out of the point of Assise (*Assisa extra Assisam, vel in modum juratæ*) *viz* when the Tenant alledgeth some by exception, that must be tried by a Jury, before the Principal Cause can proceed; as if he plead a Foreign Release, or Foreign Matter triable in another County. For in this case, the Justices refer the Record to the Court of Common-Pleas, for the trial of the Foreign Pleas, before the Disseisin can come to be discussed. Of this sort, read divers Examples in *Bract. lib.* 4. *part* 1. *cap.* 34. and *Britton, cap.* 52. The fourth and last manner is, *Assise of Right of Damages*; and that is, when the Tenant confesseth an *Ouster*, and referring it to a Demurrer in Law, whether it were rightly done or not, is adjudged to have done wrong; for then shall the Demandant have a Writ to recover Damages, which is called *Assise to recover Damages*, as also the whole Process. *Assise* is further taken for the Court, place or time, when and where the Writs and Processes of the *Assise* be handled or taken. And in this signification *Assise* is general; as when the Justices go their several Circuits, every couple with their Commission, to take all *Assises* twice in the year, which is called the *General Assises*; for he that speaketh of any thing done at that time, and in that place, will commonly say it was done at the *General Assises*. It may likewise be special in this signification, as if a special Commission should be granted to certain (as in ancient times they often were, *Bract. lib.* 3. *cap.* 11. *in fine*) for taking an *Assise* upon one Desseisin or two; any thing done in the Court before them, a man will say was done at such a *Special Assise*. And in this signification *Glanvile* useth it, *Lib.* 9. *cap.* 12. in these words, *Si contra Dominum suum & non infra Assisam tunc distingitur ipse occupator, &c.* And *lib.* 13. *cap.* 32. M. Skene *de verbor.* Sig. *tit. Assise*, saith, That in *Scotland* this word hath five significations, touching the Fifth, he hath these words, An *Assise* is called a certain number of Men lawfully summoned, received, sworn and admitted, to judge and discern in divers civil Causes, &c. whereof there be two kinds; one ordinarily in use, which may be called *a little Assise*, of the number of thirteen or fifteen persons; the other, *a great Assise*, consisting of twenty five persons, &c.

Assisa continuanda, Is a Writ directed to the Justices assigned to take an Assise, for the continuance of a Cause, where certain Records alledged, cannot in time be procured by the Party that would use it, *Reg. Orig. fol.* 217.

Assisa proroganda, Is a Writ directed to the Justices of *Assize*, for the stay of proceedings, by reason of the Kings business, wherein the party is employed, *Reg. Orig. fol.* 208. & 221.

Assisors, *Assisores, sunt qui assisas condunt aut taxationes imponunt*, saith *Spelman.* In *Scotland*, according to *Skene*, they are the same with our Jurors, and their Oath is this.

We shall leil, suith say,
And na suith conceale, far na thing we may,
Sa far as we are charg'd upon this Assise,
Be God himself, and be our part in Paradise,
And as we will answer to God, upon
The dreadful day of Dome.

Association, *Associatio*, Is a Patent sent by the King, either of his own motion, or at the suit of the Plaintiff, to Justices appointed to take Assises of *Novel Disseisin*, or of *Oyer* and *Termin.*, *&c* to take others unto them as Fellows and Collegues in that business. As if the King makes three Justices of Assise, and afterwards one of them dies, there the King may grant a Patent of *Association* to another, to *associate* him to the two, in place of him that is dead, and a Writ which shall be close, directed to the two Justices that are alive to admit him, *F. N. B.* 185. & 111. The Examples, and sundry Uses hereof, may be found in several places, but particularly in the *Register Origin. fol.* 201, 202, 205, 206, 207, 223, 224.

Assoyle, (*Absolvere*) Signifies to deliver, or set free from an Excommunication, *Stamf. Pl. Cor. lib.* 2. *cap.* 18. *fol.* 71. *b.* whose words are to this effect, otherwise the Defendant should remain in Prison, till the Plaintiff were *assoyled*, that is, delivered from his Excommunication. So in 1 *H.* 4. *cap.* 10. mention being made of King *Edward* the Third, it is added, *Whom God assoyle.*

Assumpsit, Is a voluntary Promise made by word, whereby a man assumeth, or taketh upon him, to perform or pay any thing unto another. This word includeth any verbal Promise made upon consideration, which the *Civilians* express by divers words, according to the nature of the Promise, calling it sometimes *Pactum*, sometime *Sponsionem*, sometime *Promissionem*, *Pollicitationem*, or *Constitutum.* The word is derived from the Latine Verb *Assumpsit*, and bears the sence of, he hath assumed upon him, or undertaken.

Astrihilthet, or **Atrahilthet**, Is a Saxon word, and denotes, say LL. divi Edwardi, cap. 30. *Hi qui pacem Regis habent, vel manu vel brevi, &c. Qui si nimis confidens in pace quam habet, per superbiam alicui forisfecerit, damnum restauret & iterum tantundem, quod Angli vocant* Atrihilthet. See *Hoveden, pag.* 606.

Atia. See *Odio & Atia.*

At large, *Ad largum.* See *Verdict at large, Lit. fol.* 98. To vouch *at large*, *Old Nat. Brev. fol.* 108. To make Title *at large*, *Kitchin, fol.* 68. See *Bar.*

Attache, *Attachiare*, Cometh from the French *Attacher*, that is, *figere, nectere, alligare*;

In the Common-Law, it signifies to take or apprehend by Commandment or a Writ or Precept, *Lamb.* in his *Eirenarch. lib.* 1. *cap.* 16. maketh this difference between an *Arrest*, and an *Attachment*, that an *Arrest* proceedeth out of lower Courts, by Precept; and an *Attachment* out of higher Courts, by Precept or Writ; and that a Precept to Arrest hath these formal words, (*Duci facias*) and a Writ of *Attachment* these words, (*Præcipimus tibi quod* Attachies *talem & habeas eum coram nobis,&c.*) Whereby it appeareth, that he which arresteth, carrieth (or ought to carry) the Party arrested to a person of higher power to be disposed of forthwith; he that attacheth, keepeth the Party attached, and presents him in Court at the day assigned. Yet we may take notice, that an *Attachment* issueth out of a Court-Baron, which is an Inferior Court, *Kitchin Attachment in Court-Baron, fol.* 79. Another difference there is, that an Arrest only lies upon the Body of a Man, but an *Attachment* chiefly upon his Goods: And this also makes it differ from a *Capias*, which lays hold only of the Body, whereas a man may be *attached* by an hundred Sheep. Other Differences between a *Capias*, an *Attachment*, and a *Distress*, may be these. First, an *Attachment* differs from a *Capias*; that in a Court-Baron, a man may be *attached* by his Goods, but a *Capias* shall not go out thence. Secondly, A *Capias* (be it the *Grand Cape*, or the *Petit Cape*) taketh hold of immovable things, as Lands or Tenements, and properly belong to Actions real, as may be gather'd from their Forms, *F. N. B.* whereas *Attachment* hath place rather in personal Actions, *Bract. lib.* 4. *tract.* 4. *cap.* 5. *num.* 5. See *Skene* de verbo *Sign.* tit. *Attachiamentum.* In the next place, an *Attachment* differs from a *Distress*, *Kitch. fol.* 78. holds, That the Process in a Court-Baron, is *Summons*, *Attachment* and *Distress*, *Old Nat. Brev. fol.* 27. That the Process in a *Quare impedit*, is *Summons*, *Attachment*, and one *Distress*. And *fol.* 28. speaking of the Writ, *Ne admittas*, saith, The Process is one Prohibition, and upon that *Attachment* and *Distress*. And *fol.* 32. in a Writ of *Indicavit*, after the *Attachment* returned, the *Distress* shall go out of the Rolls of the Justices. *Bracton* on the other side, *Lib.* 5. *tract.* 3. *cap.* 4. *num.* 2. thinks, that *Attachiamentum & magnum Cape, sunt districtiones*; wherewith agrees *Fleta*, lib. 5. cap. 24. but with this distinction, that *Attachiamentum est districtio personalis, & Cape magnum districtio realis.* So that upon the whole matter, there are but two Differences between an *Attathment* and a *Distress*, *viz.* That an *Attachment* reacheth not to Lands, as a *Distress* doth; and a *Distress* toucheth not the Body (being properly taken) as an *Attachment* doth. Yet are they divers times confounded, as appears by the fore-mentioned places, and *Glanv.* lib. 10. cap. 3. and *Fleta*, lib. 2. cap. 66. But to conclude, in common acceptation of Law, an *Attachment* is an apprehension of a man by his Body, to bring him to answer the Action of the Plaintiff. A *Distress* is the taking Goods for some real Cause, as Rent, &c. whereby to force him to *Replevy*, and so become Plaintiff in an Action of Trespass against him that distrained him. There is also an *Attachment* out of Chancery, and may be had of course upon Affidavit made of the Service of the *Sub-pœna*, and the Defendants not appearing, or else Issues upon not performing some Order or Decree: And they are of two sorts, one simple, which is that beforementioned, originally sent out for apprehension of the Party: The other, after Return made by the Sheriff, *Quod Defendens non est inventus in balliva sua*, with Proclamation made through the whole County, that the party appear by a day assigned, and that he be *attached* nevertheless, if he may be found. This second kind hath an affinity with the *Canonists* (*viis & modis*) at which, if the party appear not, he is Excommunicate; and with the *Civilians*, *Viis & modis una cum intimatione*; for if in the Chancery he come not in upon this *Attachment* with Proclamation, a *Writ of Rebellion* issues forthwith, *West.* 2. *part*, *Symboleog.* tit. *Proceedings in Chancery.*

Attachment of Priviledge, Is by vertue of a Mans Priviledge, to call another into that Court whereto himself belongeth; and in respect whereof he is Priviledged, *New Book of Entries*, verbo *Priviledge, fol.* 431.

There is also a *Forein Attachment*, which is of a Foreigners Goods found in some Liberty or City, to satisfie some Creditor of his within such Liberty or City. And by the Custom of *London*, a man may *attach* Money or Goods in the hand of a Stranger, while he is within their Liberty. As if A. owes B. ten pounds, B. may *attach* this ten pounds in the hands of C. *Calthorps Rep. pag.* 66.

There is also an *Attachment of the Forest*, which is one of the three Courts there held, *Manwood, p.* 90, *&c.* 99. The lower Court is called the *Attachment*; the middle one, the *Swainmote*; the highest, the *Justice in Eyres seat.* The *Court of Attachment* seemeth to be so called, because the *Verderors* of the Forest have therein no other Authority, but to receive the *Attachments* of Offendors against Vert and Venison, taken by the rest of the Officers, and to enroll them, that they may be presented and punisht at the next *Justice Seat*, *Manwood, par.* 1. *p.* 93. and this *attaching* is by three means, 1. By Goods and Chattels. 2. By the Body, Pledges and Mainprise. 3. By the Body only. This Court is kept every forty days. See *Crompton* in his *Court of the Forest.* For the diversity of *Attachments*, see *Reg. Orig.* verbo *Attachiamentum, in Indice.*

Attaint, *Attincta*, Is used for a Writ that lieth after Judgment, against a Jury, that hath given a false Verdict in any Court of Record, be the Action Real or Personal, if the Debt or Damages amount to above the sum of Forty Shillings. For the Form and Use of it, see *F. N. B. fol.* 105. and the *New Book of Entries, fol.* 84. *col.* 1. The reason why it is so called, seemeth to be, because the party that sueth it out, endeavoureth thereby to stain the Jury with Perjury, by whose Verdict he is grieved, whose punishment by the Common-Law consisted in these particulars; 1. *Quod amittat liberam Legem in perpetuum*, he shall never be received as a Witness, or admited a Juror, &c. 2. *Quod forisfaciat omnia bona sua & catalla.* 3. *Quod terræ & tenementa in manus Domini Regis capiantur.* 4. *Quod uxores & liberi extra domus suas ejicerentur.* 5. *Quod domus suæ prosternentur.* 6. *Quod arbores suæ prosternentur.* 7. *Quod prata sua arentur.* 8. *Quod corpora sua carceri mancipentur*, Co. on Lit. lib. 3. cap. 8. sect. 514. See also *Glanvile, lib.* 2. *cap.* 19. *Fitz. Nat. Brev. fol.* 109. 110. *Termes de* *de Ley*, verb, *Attaint.* Fortescue, *cap.* 26. Smith, *de Rep. Anglor. lib.* 3. *cap.* 2. And 11 *H.* 7. *cap.* 21. & 23 *H.* 8. *cap.* 3. It is a Substantive made of the French (*Atteindre*) i. *assequi vel attingere*, because he is catcht and overtaken; or rather of the French (*teindre*) in Latine (*tingere*) to stain, die, or colour, or give a tincture, *unde Gallice Teint*, *Latinè Tinctus*, as we in English say attainted or tainted of Treason, that is stained *Minsh.*

Attainted, *Attinctus*, Is used in our Common-Law, particularly for such as are found guilty of some Crime or Offence, especially Felony or Treason: Howbeit a man is said to be *attainted* of Disseisin, *Westm.* 1. *cap.* 24. & 36. *anno* 3 *Ed.* 1. and so the French use it, as *Estre attaint & vayncu en ascun case*, that is, to be cast away in any case. A man is *attainted* by two means, By Appearance, or by Process, *Stamf. Pl. Cor. fol.* 44. *Attainder* by Appearance, is by Confession, by Battel, or by Verdict, *Id. fol.* 122. *Confession*, whereof *Attaint* groweth, is double, one at the Bar before the Judges, when the Prisoner, upon his Inditement read, being asked whether *Guilty* or not *Guilty*, answers *Guilty*, never putting himself upon his Country; the other is, before the Coroner in Sanctuary, where he was in former times upon his Confession constrained to abjure the Realm, and therefore this kind of Attaint was called Attainder by *Abjuration*, Id fol. 182. *Attainder by Battel* is, when the party appealed by another, and chusing to try the truth by Combat, rather than by Jury, is vanquisht, *Id. fol.* 44. *Attainder by Verdict* is, when the Prisoner at the Bar, answering to the Indictment, *Not Guilty*, hath an Enquest of Life and Death passing upon him, and is by their Verdict found Guilty, *Id. fol.* 108. & 192. *Attainder by Process* otherwise called *Attainder by Default* or *Utlawry*, is, where a party flieth, and is not found, until he have been five times publickly called in the County, and at the last Outlawed upon his Default, *Id. fol.* 44. The same Author, *fol.* 108. makes a difference between *Attainder* and *Conviction*. And with this agreeth the Statute 34 & 35 *H.* 6. *cap.* 14. and 1 *E.* 6. *cap.* 12. Add hereto 2 & 3. *E.* 6. *cap.* 33. And *Stamf. fol.* 66. saith, A man by our ancient Laws, was said to be convicted presently upon the Verdict (*Guilty*) but not to be *attainted*, till it appeared he was no Clerk, or being a Clerk, and demanded of his Ordinary, could not purge himself; whereby it appeareth, that *Attainder* is larger than *Conviction*, *Conviction* being only by the Jury: And *Attainder* is not before Judgment, *Perkins, Grants, num.* 27. 29. This ancient Law touching the Purgation and Conviction of Clerks, is altered by 23 *Eliz. cap.* 2. as you may read further in *Clergy*.

Attainder, *Attincta* and *Attinctura*, Is when a man hath committed Felony or Treason, and Judgment is passed upon him. The Children of a person *attainted* of Treason, cannot be Heirs to him, or any other Ancestor; and if he were Noble and Gentile before, thereby his Posterity are Degraded and made Base; and this corruption of Blood cannot be salved, but by Act of Parliament. See *Attaint*, *Attainted* and *Felony*.

How far the tenure of *Gavel-kind* salves in such case, we will not dispute, only set down what Tenants in that kind have among themselves as a Maxim, *viz.*

The Father to the Bough,
The Son to the Plough.

But many of those Tenures are within the last Century, altered by Statute; the Reasons whereof are not to our purpose here.

Attendant, *Attendens*, Signifies one that oweth a Duty or Service to another, or after a sort dependeth of another. For Example, There is a *Lord*, *Mesne*, and *Tenant*, the *Tenant* holdeth of the *Mesne* by a penny, the *Mesne* holdeth over by two pence: The *Mesne* releaseth to the *Tenant* all the right he hath in the Land, and the Tenant dieth; his Wife shall be endowed of the Land, and she shall be *Attendant* to the Heir of the third part of the penny, not of the third part of the two pence; For she shall be endowed of the best Possession of her Husband. And *Kitchin fol.* 109. saith, That where the Wife is endowed by the Guardian, she shall be *Attendant* to the Heir at his full age: With whom agrees *Perkins* in *Dower*, 424.

Atturney, *Atturnatus*, Cometh of the French word (*Tourner*) *vertere.* Thence cometh the Participle (*tourne*) *Versus*, *Conversus*, and the Substantive (*tour*) *vices*, as *Chacun a son tour, quilibet sua vice.* It signifies in a legal acceptation, one appointed by another Man to do any thing in his stead, and is as much as *Procurator* or *Syndicus* in the Civil-Law: *West. Symb. part.* 1. *lib.* 2. *sect.* 559. defines them thus, Atturneys be such persons, as by the Consent, Commandment, or Request of another, do take heed, see to, and take upon them the Charge of other mens Business in their absence. And it seemeth that in ancient time, those of Authority in Courts, had it in their power, whether they would suffer men to appear, or sue by any other then themselves; as it is evident by *F. N. B. fol.* 25. In the Writ *Dedimus Potestatem de atturnato faciendo*, where it appears, that men were forced to procure the Kings Writs, or Letters Patent, to appoint *Atturneys* for them; but since that, it is provided by several Statutes, that it should be lawful so to do without any such matter, as 20 *H.* 3. *cap.* 10. 6 *E.* 1. *cap.* 8. 27 *E.* 1. *Stat.* 2. 12 *E.* 2. 1. 15 *E.* 2. *cap. unico*, 7 *R.* 2. *cap.* 14. 7 *H.* 4. 13. 3 *H.* 5. 2. 15 *H.* 6. 7. and 17 *H.* 7. 2. And you may see great diversity of Writs in the Table of the *Register Origin.* wherein the King, by his Writ, commandeth the Judges to admit of *Atturneys*; whereby there grew at last so many unskilful *Atturneys*, and so many Mischiefs by them, that provision for restraining them was requisite. Wherefore *anno* 4 *H.* 4. *cap.* 18. It was Ordained, That the Justices should examine them, and displace the unskilful. And again, 33 *H.* 6. *cap.* 7. that there should be but a certain number of them in *Norfolk* and *Suffolk*. In what Cases at this day a man may have an *Atturney*, and in what not, see *Fitzh. ubi supra.*

Atturney is either general or special. *Atturney General* is he, that by general Authority is appointed to manage all our Affairs or Suits; As the *Atturney General of the King*, which is as much as *Procurator Cæsaris* was in the *Roman* Empire. *Atturney General* of the Duke, *Cromp. Jurisd. fol.* 105.

105. *Atturney Special* or *Particular*, is he that is imployed in one or more Causes particularly specified: *Atturneys General* be made after two sorts, either by the Kings Letters Patents, or by appointment before Justices in *Eyre* in open Court, *Glanvile, lib.* 11. *cap.* 1. *Britton, cap.* 126. There be also in respect of the divers Courts, *Atturneys at large*, and *Atturneys special*, belonging to this, or that Court only. The Name is borrowed of the *Normans*, as appears by the *Custumary, cap.* 65. And the word *Attornati*, or as some read it *Turnati*, is found in the same signification in the Title, *De statu regularium ca. unico, sect. porro in sexto*, where the *Gloss* saith, That *Atturnati dicuntur Procuratores, apud acta constituti*: Our old Latine word for it seems to be *Responsalis, Bract. lib.* 4. 31. & *lib.* 5. *part* 2. *cap.* 8. And so it is in *Scotland* at this day, but especially for the Defendants Attorney. *Skene de* verb. *signif. Responsalis*, as *Sigonius* witnesseth in his first Book, *pag.* 11. *De Regno Italiæ*, was in ancient time the Title of the Popes Embassador.

Atturney of the Court of Wards and Liveries, Atturnatus Regis in Curia Wardorum & Liberaturarum, Is the third Officer in that Court; at his admission into the Office, he taketh an Oath before the Master of the said Court, well and truly to serve the King, &c. But *the Court of Wards and Liveries* being it self taken away by the Statute, 12 *Car.* 2. *cap.* 24. This Office is gone, and therefore we will say no more of it.

Atturney of the Court of the Dutchy of Lancaster, *Atturnatus Curiæ Ducatus* Lancastriæ, Is the second Officer in that Court, and seemeth for his skill in Law, to be then placed as *Assessor* to the Chancellor of that Court, being for the most part some Honourable Person, and chosen rather for some special trust reposed in him, to deal between the King and his Tenents, than for any great Learning; as was usual with the Emperors of *Rome*, in the choice of their Magistrates.

Attournment, *Attornamentum*, Signifies the Tenants acknowledgment of a new Lord; for otherwise, he that buyeth any Lands or Tenements which are in the Occupation of a third, cannot get the Possession. Yet see 27 *H.* 8. *cap.* 16. the words used in *Attournment*, are set down by *Littleton*, lib. 3. cap. *Attornment* 10. *viz. I agree to the Grant made to you, &c.* or, more usually, *Sir, I attourn to you by force of the same Grant;* or, *I become your Tenant*, or else deliver unto the Grantee a penny by way of *Attournment*; you may in the same place see divers other Cases, whereto *Attournment* appertaineth, and that it is the transposing those Duties the Tenant ought to his former Lord, unto another, and is either by word, or by act, &c. *Attournment* also is voluntary or compulsory, by the Writ termed, *Per quæ servitia, Old Nat. Brev. fol.* 155. Or sometime by Distress, *F. N. B. fol.* 147. Lastly, *Attournment* may be made to the Lord himself, or to his Steward in Court, *Kitchin, fol.* 70. There is also *Attournment in Deed*, and *Attournment in Law*, Co. vol. 6. fo. 113. a. *Attournment in Law* is an Act, which though it be no express *Attournment*, yet in intendment of Law is all one.

Attornato faciendo vel recipiendo, Is a Writ which a Man owing suit to a County, Hundred, Wapentake, or other Court, and desiring to make an *Atturney* to appear for him, whom he doubteth, whether the Sheriff or Bayliff will admit, or not, purchaseth to command him to receive and admit him. The form thereof, see *F. N. B. fol.* 156.

Avage or **Avisage**, Is a Rent or Payment which every Tenant of the Mannor of *Writtel* in *Essex*, upon St. *Leonards* day, the Sixth of *November*, pays to the Lord, *viz.* for every Pig not a year old, a half-penny; for every yearling Pig, one peny; for every Hog above a year old, two pence; for the priviledge of *Pawnage* in the Lords Woods.

Audiendo & terminando, Is a Writ, but more properly a Commission, directed to certain persons, when any riotous Assembly, Insurrection, or heinous Misdemeanor or Trespass, is committed in any place for the appeasing and punishment thereof, which you may read at large in *F. N. B. fol.* 110. See *Oyer* and *Terminer*.

Audience Court, *Curia Audientiæ Cantuariensis*, Is a Court belonging to the Archbishop of *Canterbury*, of equal Authority with the *Arches Court*, though inferior both in Dignity and Antiquity: The Original of this Court was, because the Archbishop of *Canterbury* heard many Causes extrajudicially at Home in his own Palace, in which, before he would finally determine any thing, he did usually commit them to be discust by certain men learned in the Civil and Canon Laws, whom thereupon he termed *his Auditors*; and so in time it grew to one special Man, who at this day is called (*Causarum negotiorumq; audientiæ Cantuariensis auditor seu officialis.*) And with this Office was joyned heretofore the Chancery of the Archbishop, which medleth not with any point of contentious Jurisdiction, that is, deciding of Causes between Party and Party, (except such as are ventilated *pro forma* only, as the Confirmation of Bishops Elections, or such like) but only of Office, and especially such as are *voluntariæ jurisdictionis*, as the granting the Custody of *Spiritualities*, during the vacation of Bishopricks; Institutions to Benefices, dispensing with Banes of Matrimony, &c. But this is now distinguished from the *Audience*. Of this *Audience Court*, you may read more in the Book, *De Antiquit. Eccles. Brittan. Historia*, and 4. *Inst. fol.* 337.

Audita querela, Is a Writ that lieth against him, who, having taken a Statute-Merchant, or Recognisance in the nature of a Statute-Staple, or a Judgment or Recognisance of another, and craving, or having obtained execution of the same from the Mayor and Bayliffs, before whom it was entred, at the complaint of the Party, who entred the same, upon suggestion of some just cause, why Execution should not be granted, as a Release, or other Exception. This Writ is granted by the Lord Chancellor of *England*, upon view of the Exception suggested, to the Justices of either Bench, willing them to grant Summons to the County, where the Creditor is, for his appearance at a certain day before them. See more in *Old Nat. Brev. fol.* 66. and *Fitz. Nat. Brev. fol.* 102.

Auditor, (*Auditor*) According to our Law, is an Officer of the King, or some other great personage, which yearly, by examining the Accounts of all under-Officers accountable, makes up a general Book; which shews the difference between their Receits and Charge, and their Allowances commonly termed *Allocationes*: As namely, the *Auditors* of the *Exchequer* take the Accounts of those Receivers, who collect the Revenues of the Augmentation, as also of the Sheriffs, Escheators, Collectors and Customers, and set them down, and perfect them; concerning which, see the Stat. 33 *H.* 8, *cap.* 33. and 4. *Inst. fol.* 106.

Auditors of the Prests or **Imprests**, Are also Officers in the *Exchequer*, who take and make up the great Accounts of *Ireland*, *Berwick*, the Mint, and of any Money imprested to any man for the Kings Service. See *Practice of the Exchequer*, p. 83.

Auditor of the Receits, Is also an Officer of the *Exchequer*, that files the Tellers Bills, and makes an Entry of them, and gives the Lord Treasurer a Certificate of the Money received the week before. He maketh also *Debenturs* to every Teller, before they pay any Money, and taketh their Accounts: He keepeth *the black Book of the Receits*, and the *Treasurers Key of the Treasury*, and seeth every Tellers Money lockt up in the New Treasury.

Aventure, (But more properly *Adventure*) Is a Mischance, causing the death of a Man, without Felony; as when he is suddenly drowned or burnt, falling into the Water or Fire, or kill'd by any Disease or Mischance, *Britton*, *cap.* 7. where you may see how it differs from *Misadventure*. See *Misadventure*.

Avenage, (From the Latine *Avena*, Oats) Signifies a certain quantity of Oats paid to a Landlord in lieu of some other Duties, or, as a Rent from the Tenant.

Avenor, Is an Officer belonging to the Kings Stables, and provides Oats for his Horses; he is mentioned 13 *Car.* 2. *Cap.* 8.

Avera, Is found in *Doomsday* Book, and signifies a Days-work of a Plough-man, that is, eight pence, 4 *Inst. fol.* 269.

Average, (*Averagium*) By *M. Skenes* Opinion, is derived from the word *Averia*, Cattel, and consequently signifieth Service which the Tenant owes to the Lord by Horse, or carriage of Horse. It seemeth with us to have two significations; First, *Rastall*, tit. *Exposition of words*, maketh mention of the King's *Averages*, which I take to be the King's Carriages by Horse or Cart. Then, *Anno* 32 *H.* 8. *cap.* 14. and 1 *Jac. cap.* 32. it is used for a certain contribution that Merchants, and others, do make proportionably towards their Losses, who have their Goods cast into the Sea, for the safeguard of the Ship, or of the other Goods and Lives of them in the Ship, in the time of a Tempest. And this Contribution seemeth to be so called, because it is proportioned after the rate of every mans *Average*, or Goods carried. In this last sence it is also used in the Stat. 14 *Car.* 2. *cap.* 27. *Average*, Is also a little duty, which those Merchants, who send Goods in another mans Ship, do pay the Master of it, for his care over and besides the Freight: For in the Bills of Lading, they usually say, ---*Paying so much Freight for the said Goods with Primage and* Average *accustomed*.

Averiis captis in Withernam, Is a Writ, for the taking of Cattel to his use, that hath his Cattel unlawfully taken by another, and driven out of the County where they were taken, that they cannot be *replevyed*, *Reg. Orig. fol.* 82. When one Beast is spoken of, we say, *Quidam equus vel bos*; but when more, it is not said in the plural number, *Equi* or *boves*, but *tot averia*.

Averment, *Verificatio*, Cometh from the French *Averrer*, i. *testari*, signifies commonly an offer of the Defendant, to make good or justifie an Exception pleaded in abatement or bar of the Plaintiffs Action; and there is reason, why it should rather signifie the act, then the offer of justifying the Exception. For, *Anno*, 34 *Ed.* 1. *Stat.* 2. And the Demandant will offer to *aver* by the Assise or Jury, where to offer to *averre*, and to *averre* must needs differ; And again in the same Statute, And the Demandant will offer to *aver* by the Country, &c. Thirdly, In the English *Nat. Brev. fol.* 57. *These Errors shall be tried by* Averment, *&c.* This *Averment* is twofold, *general* and *particular*; a *general Averment*, which concludes every Plea, &c. or in Bar of Replication and other pleadings, containing matters Affirmative, ought to be *averred* with these words, *Et hoc paratus est verificare*, *&c. Particular Averment*, is when the life of Tenant for Life, or Tenant in Tail is *averred*, *&c.* And an *Averment* contains as well the Matter as the Form thereof, *Co.* on *Lit. fol.* 362. *b.*

Averpeny, (*Quasi Average-peny*) Is Money contributed towards the King's *Averages*, or to be freed thereof, *Rastall Exposit. verb.* Aver-peny *est quietum esse de diversis denariis pro averagiis Dom. Regis.* See *Average*.

Augmentation, *Augmentatio*, Was the Name of a Court, erected 27 *H.* 8. as appeareth by the 27th Chapter of that years Parliament; and the end thereof was, that the King might be justly dealt with, touching the profit of such Religious Houses, and their Lands, as were given to him by Act of Parliament the same year, not printed: For the dissolving of which Court, Authority was given to Queen *Mary*, by the Parliament held the First year of her Reign, *Sess.* 2. *cap.* 10. which she afterward put in execution by her Letters Patent. The Name of the Court sprung from hence, That the Revenues of the Crown were *augmented* so much by the suppression of the said Houses, as the King reserved unto the Crown, and neither gave nor sold away to others. But the Office of *Augmentation* remains to this day, wherein there are many Records of great Use and Importance.

Avisage. See *Avage*.

Aulneger. See *Alneger*.

Aumone, (French *Aumosne*, that is, Alms) Tenure in *Aumone*, is a Tenure *per liberam Eleemosynam*, *Britton*, *fol.* 164. As where Lands are given to some Church, or Religious House, upon condition, That some Service or Prayers shall be offered at certain times, for the good of the Donors Soul. See *Frank Almoine*.

Aumonier. French *Ausmonier*. Vide *Almoner*.

Ave, Is the Name of a Writ, for which, see *Ayle*.

Auncel-weight, Is as if we should say, *Hand-sale-weight*, being a kind of weight with Scales hanging, or Hooks fastned to each end of a Staff, which a Man lifting up upon his fore-finger or *hand*, discerneth the quality or difference between the *weight*, and the thing *weighed*. In which, because there was wont to be great deceit, it was forbidden by several Statutes, as 25 *E.* 3. *Stat.* 5. *cap.* 9. and 34 *E.* 3. *cap.* 5. and 8 *H.* 6. *cap.* 4. and the even Ballance Commanded; yet nevertheless this *weight* continued in use in divers parts of *England*, notwithstanding the Constitution of *Henry Chichely*, Archbishop of *Canterbury*, 1430. *Pro abolitione ponderis vocati*, Le Auncel-weight, &c. *qui utitur Excommunicandus*, but now it is utterly abolished by a late Statute made 22 *Car.* 2. *cap. ult.*

Auncient Demeasne. See *Antient Demesne*.

Avoydance, Hath a double signification; the one, when a Benefice becomes *void* of an Incumbent; the other, when we say in Pleadings in *Chancery*, confessed or *avoided*, traversed or denied is true, &c. See *Voidance*.

Avowee, *Advocatus*. See *Advowee*, Britton, *cap.* 29. saith, That *Avowee* is he to whom the Right of *Advowson* of any Church appertaineth, so that he may present in his own Name: And is called *Avowee*, for a difference from those that sometimes present in another Mans name; as a Guardian, that presenteth in the name of his Ward; and for a difference also from those, which have the Lands, whereto an *Advowson* appertaineth, but only for term of their Lives, or of Years, or by Intrusion, or by Disseisin.

Avowry, Is where one takes a Distress for Rent, or other thing, and the other sues *Replevin*, then the taker shall justifie his Plea for what cause he took it; and if in his own Right, he ought to shew it, and *avow* the taking. But if he took it in the right of another, then when he has shewed the Cause, he shall make Cognisance of the taking, as Bayliff or Servant to him in whose right he did it, *Termes de Ley*, 73 & 21 *H.* 8. *cap.* 19. For the more speedy and effectual proceeding upon Distresses and *Avowryes*. See 17 *Car.* 2. *cap.* 7.

Avoir du pois, It is in true French *Avoir due poix*, that is, *Habere pondus*, or *justi esse ponderis*. In Law it signifies two things: First, a kind of weight diverse from that which is called *Troy-weight*, containing twelve Ounces to the Pound, whereas this containeth Sixteen. And in this respect it may probably be conjectured, That it is so called, because it contains a greater weight than the other. Secondly, It signifieth such Merchandise as are weighed by this weight, and not by *Troy-weight*, as in the Statute of *York*, 9 *E.* 3. in *Proœmio*, 27 E. 3. *Stat.* 2. *cap.* 10. 2 R. 2. *cap.* 1. See *Weights*.

Aurum Reginæ, The Queens Gold, *Rot. Pat.* 52 *H.* 3. *m.* 6. Vide *Queen-Gold*.

Austurcus, A Goshawk; In some Deeds there is reserved as a Rent to the Lord, *unum Austurcum*.

Awayte, 13 *R.* 2. *cap.* 1. Seems to be that which we now call *Way-laying*, or lying in *wait* to do a Mischief.

Award, May be derived from the French *Agarder*, and is properly the Judgment of one that is neither assigned by Law, nor appointed by the Judges, for the ending a matter in Controversy, but is chosen by the parties themselves that are at Variance. And may seem to be called an *Award*, because it is imposed on both Parties, *ad custodiendum seu observandum*. Spelm.

Awme, Mentioned, 1 *Jac. cap.* 33. and 12 *Car.* 2. *cap.* 4. Is a Measure of Rhenish-wine, containing forty Gallons; yet you may read in an old printed Book these words, ---*The Rood of Rhenish-wine of Dordreyght is ten* Awames, *and every* Awame *is fifty Gallons*. Item, *the Rood of* Antwerpe *is fourteen* Awames, *and every* Awame *is thirty five Gallons*.

Auxilium ad filium militem faciendum & filiam maritandam, Is a Writ formerly directed to every County, where the King, or other Lord, hath Tenants, to levy of them reasonable *Aide* towards the Knighting of his Son, and Marriage of his Daughter. See *Aide*, and *F. N. B. fol.* 82. But this is utterly taken away by a Statute made, 12 *Car.* 2. *cap.* 24.

Ayde, Is where a particular Proprietor is impleaded, and not being able to defend the thing for which he is impleaded, he prayeth *Ayde* of some better able; which is performed two ways: First, In a Plea real, *Tenens petit auxilium de* A. S. *sine quo respondere non potest*. 2. In a Plea personal, and then the Defendant *petit auxilium ad manutenendum exitum*.

B.

Bachelor, *Bacchalaureus*, Cometh of the French word *Bachalier*, that is, *Tyro*, a Learner; and thereupon I gather, those that be called *Bachelors* of the Companies of *London*, be such of each Company, as are springing towards the estate of those that are imployed in Council, but as yet are Inferiors. For every of the Twelve Companies hath a Master, two Wardens, the Livery, and the *Bachelors*. I have read in an old Monument, this word *Bachelor* attributed to the Lord Admiral of *England*, if he be under a Baron. This word is used, 13 *Rich.* 2. *Stat.* 2. *cap.* 1. and signifieth the same with *Knight-Bachelor*, 3 E. 4. cap. 5. that is, a *Simple Knight*, and not a *Knight Baneret*. Touching the farther Etymology of this word, *Baccalaurei*, (*teste Renano*) *a bacillo nominati sunt, quia primi studii autoritatem quæ per exhibitionem baculi concedebatur jam consecuti fuissent, &c.*

Backberinde, Is a Saxon word, and almost good English at this day, signifying so much as *bearing* upon the *back*, or about a Man. *Bracton* uses it for a sign or circumstance of theft apparent, which the *Civilians* call *Furtum manifestum*, for dividing *furtum* into *manifestum & non manifestum*, he defineth *Furtum manifestum* in this sort, *Furtum vero manifestum est, ubi latro deprehensus est seisitus de aliquo latrocinio*, scil. Handhabend & Backberinde & *insequutus fuerit per aliquem cujus res illa fuerit*, lib. 3. tract. 2. cap. 32. *Manwood* in his *Forest Law*, part 2. Noteth it for one of the four Circumstances or Cases, wherein a Forrester may arrest the

Body of an Offendor against Vert or Venison in the Forest. For by the Assise of the Forest of *Lancaster* (saith he) *taken with the manner*, is, when one is found in the Kings Forest in any of these four degrees, *viz. Stable-stand, Dog-draw, Backbear* and *Bloody-hand*; in which place you may find all these interpreted.

Badger, Cometh from the French *Bagage*, that is, *Sarcinia* a bundle or fardle; and thence is derived *Bagagier*, a Carrier of bundles: It is used with us for one that is licenced to buy Corn, or other Victuals in one place, and carry them to another to sell; and such a one is exempted in the Statute made in the 5 & 6 of *Ed. 6. cap.* 14. from the punishment of an Ingrosser within that Statute. See *Crompton's Just. of Peace, fol.* 69, 70.

Bay or Penn, Is a Pond-head made up of a great heighth, to keep in store of Water, so that the wheel of the Furnace or Hammer belonging to an Iron-Mill, may stand under them, and be driven by the Water coming out of them by a Passage or Floodgate, call'd the *Penstock*, and falling upon the said Wheels. This word is mentioned in the Statute 27 *Eliz.* cap. 19.

Baile, (*Ballium, plevina, manucaptio*) Cometh of the French (*bailler, tradere.*) It is used in our Common-Law properly for the freeing or setting at liberty of one arrested or imprisoned upon Action, either Civil or Criminal, under Surety taken for his appearance at a day and place certainly assigned, Bract. *lib.* 3. *tract.* 2. *cap.* 8. *num.* 8. & 9. The reason why it is called *Bayle*, is, because by this means the party restrained is delivered into the hands of those that bind themselves for his forth-coming: There is both *common* and *special Bail*; *Common Bail* is in Actions of small Concernment, and is called *common*, because any Sureties in that case are taken; whereas, upon Causes of greater weight, or apparent specialty, *special Bail* or Surety must be taken, as Subsidy-men at the least, and that to the value. *Manwood* in his *Forest Laws*, part 1. pag. 167. makes a great difference between *Bail* and *Mainprise*, saying, He that is *mainprised*, is always said to be at large, and to go at his own Liberty out of War, after that he is let to *Mainprise*, until the day of his appearance, by reason of the said common Summons, or otherwise: But it is not so, where a Man is let to *Bail* by four or two Men, by the Lord Chief Justice in *Eyre* of the Forest, until a certain day, for there he is always accounted by the Law, to be in their Ward and Custody for the time: And they may, if they will, keep him in Prison or Ward during that time. So that he which is so *bailed*, shall not be said by the Law to be at large, or at his own Liberty. See *Lam. Eiren. lib.* 3. *cap.* 2. *pag.* 330. *Bail* is also a certain limit within the Forest, according as the Forest is divided into the particular Charges of several Foresters, *Crompton* in the Oath of *Bowbearer, fol.* 201. See *Mainprise*, and 4 *Inst. fol.* 178.

Bailment, Is a delivery of things, whether Writings, Goods, &c. to another, sometimes to be delivered back to the *Baylor*, that is, to him that so delivered it; sometimes to the use of the *Bailee*, that is, of him to whom it is delivered, and sometimes also it is delivered to a third person: This delivery is called a *Bailment*.

Bayliff, (*Ballivus*) Cometh of the French word *Bayliff*, that is, *Præfectus provinciæ*, and as the Name, so the Office it self in ancient time was answerable to that of *France* and *Normandy*; For as in *France* there be several Parliaments, which be high Courts, from which lies no Appeal; and within the Precincts of the several Parts of that Kingdom, that belong to each Parliament, there be several Provinces, unto which, within themselves, Justice is Ministred by certain Officers called *Bayliffs*. So in *England* we see many several Counties or Shires, within the which Justice hath been Ministred to the Inhabitants of each County, by the Officer whom we now call *Sheriff* or *Viscount*; the one of which Names descends from the *Saxons*, the other from the *Normans*. And I cannot expresly prove, That this *Sheriff* was ever called a *Bayliff*; yet it is probable, that might have been one of his Names, because the County is many times called *Balliva*, a Bayliwick. As in the Return of a Writ, where the Person is not arrested, he saith, *Infra-nominatus* A. B. *non est inventus in balliva mea*, Kitchin Ret. Brev. fol. 287. And again, in *Bracton, lib.* 3. *tract.* 2. *cap.* 33. *num.* 3. and 5 *Eliz.* 23. and 14 *E.* 3. *Stat.* 1. *cap.* 6. And, I think, the word *Bayliff* used, *cap.* 28. of *Magna Charta*, compriseth as well *Sheriffs*, as *Bayliffs* of Hundreds So 14 *E.* 3. *Stat.* 1. *cap.* 9. But as the Realm is divided into Counties, so every County is again divided into Hundreds; within which it is manifest, that formerly the Kings Subjects had Justice ministred to them by the several Officers of every Hundred, which were called *Bayliffs*. See *Lupanus de Magistrat. Francor.* lib. 2. cap. *Balivi.* And the *Grand Customary* of *Normandy*, cap. 1. And the truth hereof *Bracton* attests, *lib.* 3. *tract.* 2. *cap.* 34. *num.* 5. Where it appeareth, That *Bayliffs* of Hundreds might hold Plea of Appeal and Approvers. But since that time, these Hundred-Courts (certain Franchises excepted) are by the Statute 14 *E.* 3. *Stat.* 1. *cap.* 9. dissolved into the County Courts, as you may read in County and Hundred. And the *Bayliffs* Name and Office is grown into such contempt, that now they are only Officers to serve Writs, and do such base Offices within their Liberties, *Cromp. Just. of Peace, fol.* 49. *a.* Yet is the Name still in good esteem otherwise, for the chief Magistrates in divers Towns be called *Bayliffs*; as in *Ipswich, Yarmouth, Colchester*, and other places: And there be other to whom the King gives the Custody of his Castles, which are called *Bayliffs*, as the *Bayliff* of *Dover*-Castle.

These ordinary *Bayliffs* are of two sorts, *Bayliffs Errants*, and *Bayliffs of Franchises*; *Bayliffs Errant, Ballivi Itinerantes*, be those which the Sheriff maketh and appointeth to go hither and thither in the County to serve Writs, to Summon the County, Sessions, Assizes, and such like. *Bayliffs of Franchises, Ballivi Franchesiarum aut Libertatum*, be those that be appointed by every Lord within his Liberty, to do such Offices within his Precincts, as the *Bayliff Errant* doth at large in the County. Of these, read Sir *Thomas Smith, De Rep. Ang. lib.* 2. *cap.* 16. There be also *Bayliffs of the Forest, Manwood, part.* 1. *pag.* 113. There be likewise *Bayliffs of Husbandry*, belonging to private men of great Substance, who seem

to

to be so called, because they dispose of the under-servants, every man to his Labour and Task, check them for misdoing their business, gather the Profits to their Lord and Master, and deliver an Account for the same at the years end, or otherwise, as it shall be called for. The Office or Duty of a Bayliff of a Mannor, or Houshold, (which in ancient time seemeth to have been all one) *Fleta* well describeth, *Lib.* 2. *Cap.* 72. 73. This word is also used in the Canon-Law, *cap. dilecto de sentent. excom. in sexto* & c. 1. *de pœnis in clement.* Where the Glossographer saith, It is a French word, signifying as much as *Præpositus*, and *Baliva* and *Balivatus* is used among our Interpreters of the Civil and Canon Law for *Provincia*, as *Balliva* here with us in *England* is taken for a County or Shire.

Bailiff of the Moot. See *Moot*.

Bale, a Pack, or quantity of Goods or Merchandise, as a *Bale* of Silk, Cloth, &c. the word is used in 16 *R.* 2. *Cap.* 1. and still in use.

Balenger, By the Statute 28 *H.* 6. *Cap.* 5. seems to be a kind of Barge, Boat, or Water-Vessel.

Baliva, In the Statute of *Marlbridge*, 52 *H.* 3. *Cap.* 2. It is said,----*ubi* Balivam *habeat vel jurisdictionem*. Here *Baliva* is well expounded by the Statute it self; for in this place it signifies *Jurisdiction*, *Co. Inst. Fol.* 105.

Balivo amovendo, Is a Writ to remove a Bayliff out of his Office, for want of sufficient living in his Bayliwick, *Reg. Orig. fol.* 78.

Balkers or **Balkors**. See *Conders*.

Ban or **Bans**, *Bannum* signifyeth a publick Notice given of any thing: The Word is ordinary among the *Feudists*, and grown from thence to other uses, as to that which we here in *England* call a *Proclamation*, whereby any thing is publickly commanded or forbidden, *Vincent. de Franchis. descis* 521. & 360. *Hottoman verbo* Bannus, *in verbis Feudalibus*, saith, That there is both *bannus* and *bannum*, and that they signifie two divers things. But in *England* we use this word *Bans*, especially in publishing of Matrimonial Contracts in the Church, before Marriage, That if any Man can say ought against the intention of the Parties, either in respect of Kindred, precontract, or otherwise, they may take their Exception in time. And in the Canon-Law, *Bannæ sunt Proclamationes sponsi & sponsæ in Ecclesiis fieri solitæ*, Cap. 27. *extra desponsal*, &c. Yet our word (*Banning*) seems to come thence, being an exclamation against, or Cursing of an other. *Bracton* in one place mentions *Bannus Regis* for a Proclamation, or Silence made in Court by the Cryer, before the meeting of Champions to a Combat, *Lib.* 3. *Tract.* 2. *Cap.* 21. *In terra ditionis suæ* Bannum, *id est*, *Interdictum misit*, *quod est Prohibitio*, &c. Histo. Norm. Edit. 1619. *Fol.* 85. *b*.

Bane, (Proceeds from the Saxon *Bana*, a Murderer,) and signifies the destruction or overthrow of any thing, *Bract. Lib.* 3. *Tract.* 2. *Cap.* 1. *Nu.* 1. He which is the Cause of another Mans Death is said to be *Labane*, a Malefactor. So when a Man receives a Mortal Prejudice by any thing, we commonly say, such a thing was his *Bane*.

Baneret, *Bannerettus*, *Miles vexillarius*, in Mr. *Skenes* Opinion, seemeth to be compounded of *baner* and *rent*. But *Cambden* in his *Brittania*, *pag.* 109. derives it from the German *Bannerheyres*. Sir *Tho. Smith*, *Lib. de Rep Ang. Cap.* 18. saith, That a *Baneret* is a Knight made in the Field, with the Ceremony of cutting off the point of his Standard, and making it, as it were, a *Banner*: And accounted so honourable, that they are allowed to display their Arms in the Field in the King's Army, as Barons do. These are *Cambden's* Words, *loco supra citato*, *Baneretti*, *cum Vassalorum nomen jam desierat*, *a Baronibus secundi erant*; *quibus inditum nomen a vexillo*, *Concessum illis erat Militaris virtutis ergo quadrato vexillo*, (*perinde ac Barones*) *uti*, *unde* & Equites Vexillarii *à nonnullis vocantur*, &c. Of creating a Knight *Baneret*, read M. *Segar-Norroy* his Book, *Lib.* 2. *Cap.* 10. That they be next to Barons in Dignity, appears by the Statute, 14 *R.* 2 11. and by 5 *R.* 2. *Stat.* 2. *Cap.* 4. It may be conjectured, That they were antiently called by Summons to the Court of Parliament. And 13 *R.* 2. *Stat.* 2. *Cap.* 1. we find, That a *Baneret* for praying a Pardon for a Murtherer, is subject to all one Punishment with a Baron. *Henry* the Seventh made divers *Banerets* upon the *Cornish* Commotion, *Anno* 1495. See further *Seldens* Titles *of Honour*, *fol.* 799. and *Co. Inst.* 4. *fol.* 6.

Bank, *Bancus* cometh of the French *Banque*, i. *Mensa*. In our Common-Law, it is most usually taken for a Seat or Bench of Judgment; as *Bank le Roy*, the Kings Bench, *Bank de Common Plees*, the Bench of Common-Pleas, *Kitchin. fol.* 102. called also in Latine *Bancus Regis*, & *Bancus communium Placitorum*, Cromp. Just. *fol.* 67. & 91. *Cambden* also in his *Brit.* calls them, *Bancum Regium* & *Bancum Communem*; there is another sort of *Bank*, which signifies a place where a great Sum of Money is let out to use, returned by Exchange, or otherwise disposed to Profit. *Jus Banci* was of old allowed to the Judges of the Superior Courts, for Inferiour Courts were not allowed that Priviledge. See *Free-bank* and *Free-bench*.

Bankrupt, *Quasi bankus ruptus*, or *Bankrupt*, because when the *Bank* or *Stock* is *broken* or exhausted, the Owner is said to be a *Bankrupt*. The composition of the French Word, I take to be this, *Banque*, that is, *Mensa*; and *Route*, that is, *Vestigium*, Metaphorically taken for the sign left in the Earth, of a Table once fastened into it, and now taken away. So that the Original seemeth to be drawn from those *Romane Mensarii*, which, as appeareth by many ancient Writers, had their *Tabernas* & *Mensas* in certain publick places, where they sied, and deceived Men that had put them in trust with their Money, they left but the Signs or Carkasses behind them. But *Bankrupt* with us signifieth his or her act, that having gotten other Mens Goods into his Hands, hideth himself in places unknown, or in his own private House, not minding to restore to his Creditors what is due to them. In the Statute made 34 *H.* 8. *Cap.* 4. The French Word *Banque Route faire*, is literally translated to make *Bankrupt*. And by 1 *Jac. Cap.* 15. a *Bankrupt* is thus described. *All and very such persons using, or that shall use the Trade of Merchandise, by way of Bargaining, Exchange, Bartery, Chevisance, or otherwise in Gross, or by seeking* *his, her, or their Trade of Living by Buying and Selling, and being a Subject born within this Realm, or any the Kings Dominions, or Denizen, who at any time since the first day of this present Parliament, or at any time hereafter shall depart the Realm, or begin to keep his, her, or their House or Houses, or otherwise, to absent him or her self, or take Sanctuary, or suffer him or her self willingly to be arrested for any debt or other thing not grown or due, for Money delivered, Wares sold, or any other just or lawful cause, or good consideration or purpose, or hath or will suffer him or her self to be outlawed, or yield him or her self to Prison, or willingly, or fraudulently hath, or shall procure him or her self to be arrested, or his or her Goods, Money, or Chattels to be attached or sequestred, or depart from his or her Dwelling-house, or make, or cause to be made any fraudulent Grant, or Conveyance of his, her, or their Lands, Tenements, Goods or Chattels, to the intent, or whereby his, her, or their Creditors, being Subjects born, as aforesaid, shall, or may be defeated, or delayed for the recovery of their just and due Debts; or being arrested for Debt, shall after his or her arrest, lye in Prison Six Months, or more, upon that Arrest, or any other Arrest or Detention in Prison for Debt, and lye in Prison six Months upon such Arrest or Detention, shall be accounted and adjudged a* Bankrupt *to all intents and purposes.* But a later Act, made 14 *Car.* 2. *Cap.* 23. hath provided, That no person whatsoever, who shall adventure in the *East-India* or *Guiney*-Company, or in the *Royal Fishing* Trade, shall be esteemed a Merchant or Trader within any Statute of *Bankrupt*, or lyable to the same.

Bannum vel Bauleuga, The utmost bounds of Mannor or Town, so used, 47 *H.* 3. *Rot.* 44 *Carta, &c. Notum facio, me eleemosynam nostram Christo concessisse & omnibus Sanctis suis, &c.* viz. *primo Terram illam à Twiwella usq; Thorney, ubi* Bannum *nostrum cessat.*

Banishment, *Exilium, abjuratio,* Cometh of the French word *Banissement*, and hath a signification known to every Man: But there be two kinds of *Banishment* in *England;* one voluntary, and upon Oath, whereof you may read *Abjuration*; the other upon Compulsion, for some Offence or Crime. As if a Lay-man succour him that having taken Sanctuary for an Offence, obstinately refuseth to abjure the Realm, he shall lose his Life and Member. If a Clerk do so, he shall be *banished, Stamf. Pl. Cor. fol.* 117. This punishment is also of our modern *Civilians* called *Bannimentum*, which was antiently termed (*deportatio*) if it were perpetual, or (*religatio in insulam*) i for a time, *Vincent. de Iranchis, Pet. de Belluga in suo speculo, fol.* 125. *nu.* 4.

Barator. See *Barretor.*

Barberies, (*Oxycantha*) A Thorny Shrub, known to most men to bear a Berry or Fruit red, and of a sharp Tast. These Berries, as also the Leaves of the said Tree, are medicinable, as *Gerard* sheweth in his *Herbal, Lib.* 3. *Cap.* 21. you find them mentioned among Drugs to be garbled, *Anno* 1 *Jac. Cap.* 9.

Barbican, (*Barbicanum*) A Watch-Tower or Bulwark, *Mandatum est, &c. Custodi Castri Regis & Honoris de* P. *quoddam* Barbicanum *ante portam, &c. & in eodem* Barbicano *quandam portam cum ponte Versatili, &c. de novo facere, &c. T. Rege* 10. *Aug.* Claus. 17. E. 2. m. 39.

Barcaria or **Barquarium,** Cometh of *Berr* a Tan-house; but in a legal sense more usually denotes a Sheep-coat, and derived from the French word *Bergery.*

Barcarii, or rather **Berquarii,** May be taken for Shephards; for we usually say, *Bercarium* a Shephard, and both seem to come from the French Word *Beragier.*

Bard, alias **Beard,** See *Clack.*

Bargain and Sale, As it seemeth by *West. Symb. Par.* 1. *Lib.* 2. *Sect.* 436. Is properly a Contract made of Mannors, Lands, Tenements, Hereditaments, and other things, transferring the property thereof from the *Bargainor* to the *Bargainee*; whereto the Author of the *New Terms of Law* addeth, That it ought to be for Money, saying withal, that it is a good Contract for Land, *&c.* and that Fee-simple passeth thereby, though it be not said in the Deed, *To Have and to Hold the Land to him and his Heirs*: And though there be no Livery and Seisin made by the Vendor, so it be by Deed indented, sealed and enrolled, either in the County where the Land lies, or within one of the Kings Courts of Record at *Westminster* within six Months after the date of the Deed, according to 27 *H.* 8. *cap.* 16.

Barkary, *Barcaria,* Is a Heath-house, *New Book of Entries,* tit. *Assise. corp. polit.* 2. Some call it a Tan-house.

Baron, (*Baro*) Is a French Word, and hath divers significations here in *England.* First, It is taken for a Degree of Nobility next unto a Viscount, *Bract. Lib.* 1. *Cap.* 8. *Num.* 4. saith, They are called *Barones, quasi, robur belli.* And in this signification it is borrowed from other Nations, with whom *Baroniæ* be as much as *Provinciæ, Petr. Belluga in specul. Princip. fol.* 119. So then *Barons* seem to be such, as have the Government of Provinces, as their Fee holden of the King; some having greater, some lesser Authority within their Territories: Yet it may probably be thought, that of old times here in *England*, they were called *Barons* that had such Signiories, as we now call *Court-Barons*, as they be at this day in *France* called *Seigneurs*, that have any such Mannor or Lordship. And the Learned in Antiquities have affirmed, That soon after the Conquest, all such came to the Parliament, and sate as Peers in the Upper-House. But when by experience it appeared, that the Parliament was too much pestered by such multitudes, it grew to a custome, that none should come, but such as the King for their extraordinary Wisdom and Quality, thought good to call by Writ; which Writ also then ran (*hâc vice tantum.*) But then Men seeing this estate of Nobility to be but casual, and to depend meerly upon the Princes Pleasure, they sought a more certain Hold, and obtained of the King Letters Patent, to settle such Honour upon them, and their Heirs-Male, and these were intituled *Barons by Patent*, or Creation, whose Posterity be now by Inheritance, and true descent of Nobility, those *Barons* that be called *Lords of the Parliament*, of whom the King may create at his pleasure. Yet nevertheless, there are *Barons by Writ*, as well as *by Letters Patent*, and they may be discerned by their Titles, because the *Barons by Writ* are those that to the Title of Lord, have their own Sirnames annexed, whereas *Barons by Letters Patents*

are

are named by their *Baronies*. These *Barons* which were first made *by Writ*, may now justly be called *Barons by Prescription*, for that they have continued *Barons* by themselves and their Ancestors beyond the Memory of Man. The Original of *Barons* by Writ, *Cambden* in his *Brit. Pa.* 109. referreth to *Henry* the Third. *Barons by Letters Patent*, or Creation (say our Antiquaries) commenced in the time of *Richard* the Second; the manner of whose Creation, read in *Stows Annals, p.* 1121 *Seldens* Titles *of Honour, fol.* 687. *Fernes Glory of Generosity, pag.* 125, 126. *Skene de verb.* Sign. *tit.* Baro. And Sir *Tho. Smith, Lib.* 1. *de Rep. Ang cap.* 17. saith, That none in *England* is created a *Baron*, unless he can dispend 1000 *li. per Annum*, or at least 1000 Marks. To these *Segar* (by Office *Norroy*) *lib.* 4. *cap.* 13. *Of Honour, Civil and Military*, addeth a third kind of *Baron*, calling them *Barons by Tenures*, and those be the Bishops of the Land, all which, by vertue of *Baronies* annexed to their Bishopricks, have always had place in the Upper-House of Parliament, and are termed *Lords-Spiritual*.

Baron in the next signification, is an Officer, as *Barons of the Exchequer* be to the King, of which the Principal is called *Lord Chief Baron* (*Capitalis Baro*) and the three other (for so many there be) are his Assistants in Causes of Justice, between the King and his Subjects, touching Causes appertaining to the *Exchequer*. The *Lord Chief Baron* is at this day the Chief Judge of the Court, and in matter of Law, Information, and Plea, answereth the Bar, and giveth Order for Judgment thereupon. He alone in the Term-time doth sit upon *Nisi prius* that come out of the King's Remembrancers Office, or out of the Office of the Clerk of the Pleas, which cannot be dispatcht in the Mornings for want of time. He taketh Recognizances for the King's Debts, for appearances and observing of Orders. He taketh the Presentation of all Officers in Court under himself, and o the Mayor of *London*, and sees the King's Remembrancer to give them their Oaths: He taketh the Declaration of certain Receivers, Accounts of the Lands of the late Augmentation made before him by the Auditors of the Shires; and giveth two *Parcel-makers* places by vertue of his Office. The *second Baron*, in the absence of the Lord chief Baron, answers the Bar in matters aforesaid. He also taketh Recognizances for the Kings Debts, appearences, and observing of Orders: He giveth yearly the Oath to the late Mayor and Escheator of *London*, for the true Account of the Profits of his Office: He taketh a Declaration of certain Receivers Accounts. He also examineth the Letters and Sums of such Sheriffs foreign Accounts, as also the Accounts of Escheators and Collectors of Subsidies and Fifteenths as are brought unto him by the Auditors of the Court. The *third Baron*, in the Absence of the other two, answereth the Bar in matters aforesaid, and taketh Recognizances as the former. He giveth yearly the Oath of the late Mayor and Gawger of *London* for his true accounting. He also taketh a Declaration of certain Receivers Accounts, and examineth the Letters and Sums of such of the former Accountants as are brought unto him The *fourth Baron* is always a Cursitor of the Court, and hath been chosen of some one of the Clerks of the Remembrancers Offices, or of the Clerk of the Pipes Offices; He at the days of prefixion, taketh Oath of all High-Sheriffs, and their Under-Sheriffs, and of all Escheators, Bayliffs, and other Accountants, for their true accounting. He taketh the Oath of all Collectors, Controulers, Surveyors and Searchers of the Custome-Houses, that they have made true Entrances in their Books. He opposeth all Sheriffs upon their Summons in open Court: He informeth the rest of the *Barons* of the Course of the Court in any matters concerning the Kings Prerogative: He likewise, as the other *Barons*, taketh the Declaration of certain Receivers Accounts, and examineth the Letters and Sums of such of the former Accountants as are brought unto him.

These *Barons of the Exchequer* are ancient Officers, for I find them Named, *Westm.* 2. *cap.* 11. *Anno* 13. *E.* 1. and they be called *Barons*, because *Barons* of the Realm were wont to be employed in that Office, *Fleta, Lib.* 2. *Cap.* 24. Sir *Tho. Smith* saith of them, That their Office is to look to the Accounts of the Prince, and to that end they have Auditors under them, as also to decide all Causes appertaining to the King's Profits, coming into the Exchequer by any means. This is proved in part by the Statutes of 20 *E.* 3. *cap.* 2. 27 *E.* 3. *Stat.* 2. *Cap.* 18. 5 *R.* 2. *Stat* 1. *Cap.* 9. and 12 and 14 *R.* 2. 11. And hereupon they have of late been Men learned in the Common Laws of the Realm, whereas in ancient time they were other, *viz. Majores & discretiores in Regno, sive de Clero essent, sive de Curia. Ockham* in his *Lucubrations, De fisci regii ratione. Hornes Mirror of Just.* saith, That the *Barons* were wont to be two, and they Knights, *Cap. de la place del Escheker.*

There are also *Barons* of the Cinque-Ports; 31 *E.* 3. 2. and 33 *H.* 8. *Cap.* 10. which are two of every the seven Towns of *Hastings, Winchelsea, Rye, Rumney, Hithe, Dover*, and *Sandwich*, that have places in the lower House of Parliament, *Cromp. Jur. fol.* 28.

Baron in the third Signification, is used for the Husband in relation to his Wife, which is so ordinary in all Law-Books written in French, that it would be vain to mention any one.

The Chief Magistrates of *London* were also called *Barons*, before they had a Lord Mayor, as will appear by several ancient Charters, particularly one of *H.* 3. in these words, *Henricus Rex. Sciatis nos concessisse et hac præsenti charta nostra confirmasse* Baronibus *nostris de Civitate* London, *quod eligant sibi* Mayer *de seipsis singulis annis, &c.* See *Spelm. Gloss.* at large upon this word.

Baronet, *Baronettus*, Is a Dignity or degree of Honour, and hath precedency before Banerets, *Knights of the* Bath, and *Knights* Bachelors, excepting only such Banerets as are made *sub Vexillis Regiis in aperto bello, & ipso Rege personaliter præsente*. This Order was erected by King *James*, 1611, as may appear in *Rot. Pat.* 10 *Jac. part.* 10. *m.* 8. & 14 *Jac. par.* 2. *m.* 24. with an *Habendum sibi & Heredibus masculis.* Therefore we may believe, that where the word *Baronets* is mentioned in our old Statutes, and ancient Authors, it is mistaken for *Banerets*, 2. *Inst. fol.* 667. And *Seldens Titles of Honor, fol.* 736.

Barony, (*Baronia*, *Baronagium*,) Is that

Honour

Honour that gives title to a *Baron*, under which Notion are contained not only the Fees and Lands of Temporal *Barons*, but of Bishops, who have two Estates, one as they are Spiritual Men, without Possession, as was the Tribe of *Levi* among the *Israelites*, being sustained only by the First-Fruits and Tenths of the other Tribes, *Josh. ca.* 13. *ver.* 14. The other respect they have, groweth from the bounty of our English Kings, whereby they have *Baronies* at the least, and by that are Lords of Parliament. This *Barony* (according to *Bracton, lib.* 2. *cap.* 34.) is a right indivisible, and therefore if an Inheritance be to be divided among Coparceners, though some capital Messuages may be divided, yet, *Si capitale Messuagium sit caput Comitatus, vel caput* Baroniæ: he saith, They may not be parcel'd. The reason is, *Ne sic caput per plures particulas dividatur, & plura Jura Comitatuum &* Baroniarum *deveniant ad nihilum, per quod deficiat regnum, quod ex Comitatibus &* Baroniis *dicitur esse constitutum.* There are other *Barons* which bear that Title to this day, but are no *Barons* of Parliament. Such were those constituted by *Hugh Lupus* Earl of *Chester*, in the County Palatine there; as the *Baron* of *Malpas*, the *Baron* of *Kinderton* &c.

Barre, *Barra* Cometh of the French (*Barre*) or *Barriere*, that is *Repagulum*, *Obex*, *Vectis*. In the legal sense, denotes a peremptory exception against a Demand or Plaint, and is by the Author of the *Terms of the Law* said to be such a Plea, as is sufficient to destroy the Action of the Plaintiff for ever: And is divided into *a Barre to common Intendment*, and *a Barre special*. A *Barre to common Intendment*, is an ordinary or general *Barre*, that ordinarily disableth the Declaration or Plea of the Plaintiff. A *Barre special*, is that which is more than ordinary, and falleth out in the case in hand, upon some special circumstance of the Fact, *Plow. Com. Colthirsts* Case, *fol.* 26. *a. b.* As for Example, An Executor being sued for his Testators Debt, Pleadeth, That he had no Goods left in his hands at the day when the Writ was taken out against him; This is a good *Barre to common Intendment*, or (*prima facie.*) But yet the case may so fall out, that more Goods might fall to his hands since that time; which if the Plaintiff can shew by way of Replication, then except he have a more especial Plea or *Barre* to be alledged, he is to be condemned in the Action. See also *Plow. de casu supra citato, fol.* 28. and *Bro. tit.* Barre, *num.* 101. and *Kitchin, fol.* 215.

Barre also in the same signification, is divided into *barre material*, and *barre at large*, *Kitchin, fol.* 68. A *barre material*, as it seemeth, may be otherwise called a *barre special*; As when one in the stop of the Plaintiffs Action, pleadeth some particular matter, as a descent from him that was the undoubted Owner, a Feoffment made by the Ancestor of the Plaintiff, or such like. A *barre at large* is, when the Tenant or Defendant, by way of exception, doth not Traverse the Plaintiffs Title, by Pleading Not Guilty, nor confess or avoid it, but only maketh to himself a Title in his *barre*. As if in an Assise of *Novel Disseisin*, the Tenant Plead a Feoffment of a Stranger unto him, and gives but a colour only to the Plaintiff; of this, there may be an example found, 5 *H.* 7. *fol.* 29. *Barre* is also in regard of the effect, divided into *barre perpetual*, and *barre pro tempore*: *Perpetual* is that, which overthroweth the Action for ever. *Barre pro tempore* is that, which is good for the present, and may fail hereafter. See *Brook, tit.* Barre, *nu.* 23. Where he saith, That to plead *Plene administravit* is good, until it may appear, that more Goods come to the Executors hands afterward; which also holdeth for an Heir, that in an Action of his Ancestors Debt, Pleadeth *Riens per descent*. This word is also used for a *material Barre*, as the place where Serjeants or Counsellors stand to Plead Causes in Court, or Prisoners to answer to their Indictment; from which our Common Lawyers are termed *Barristers*, *Anno* 24 *H.* 8. *cap.* 24.

Barrator or **Barretor**, *Barectator*, (French *Barateur*,) a Deceiver; Signifies a common Wrangler, that setteth men at ods, and is himself never quiet, but at Brawle with one or other. To this effect, you may read, *Lamb. Eiren. P.* 342. who saith also, That *Barattor* may seem to be derived from the Latine *Barator* or *Balatro*, that is, a vile Knave, or Unthrift; and by a Metaphor a spot in a Common-wealth. See the Statute of *Champetry*, 33 *Edw.* 1. *Stat.* 2. *cap. unico*, and *West.* 1. *cap.* 32. *Anno* 3 *E.* 1. Mr. *Skene de Verb. signif. tit.* Barratry, saith, That *Barrators* be Symonists, so call'd of the Italian word *Barrataria*, signifying Corruption or Bribery in a Judge, giving a false Sentence for Money; whom you may read more at large, as also *Hortensius Cavalcanus* in his *Tract de Brachio regio, par.* 5. *nu.* 66. See also *Egidius Bossius in practica criminali titulo de officialibus corrupt. &c.* num. 2. & 6. & Co. lib. 8. fol. 36., 37.

Barraster or **Barrister**, *Barrasterius*. See *Utter-Barrister*.

Barre-Fee, is a Fee of Twenty Pence, that every Prisoner acquitted of Felony payeth to the Gaoler, *Crompt. Just. of Peace, fol.* 158. *b.* See 21 *H.* 7. 16. *b.*

Barrel, Is a Measure of Wine, Oyl, *&c.* containing the eighth part of a Tun, the fourth of a Pipe, and the second of a Hogshead, that is, thirty one Gallons and an half, 1 R. 3. *cap.* 13. But this Vessel seemeth not to contain any certain quantity, but differeth according to the Liquor; For a *Barrel* of Beer containeth Thirty six Gallons, and a Barrel of Ale but Thirty two, *Anno* 23 *H.* 8. *cap.* 4. and by 12 *Car.* 2. *cap.* 23. The said Assise of Thirty two Gallons of Wine-Measure, which is about Twenty eight Gallons of Old-Standard, well packed, and containing in every *Barrel* usually a thousand full Herrings at least, is, and shall be taken for good, true, and lawful Assise of *Herring-barrels*, *An.* 13. *Eliz. c.* 11.

Barriers, Cometh of the French Word (*Barres*) and signifieth with us that which the Frenchmen call (*leu de* Barres, *i. Palæstram*) a Martial Sport or Exercise of Men Armed, and fighting together with short Swords, within certain *Barres* or Lists, whereby they are separated from the Spectators: It is now grown out of use here in *England*.

Barter, May probably be derived from the French *Barater*, that is, *Circumvenire*. It signifies in our Books Exchange of Wares for Wares, *Anno* 1 R. 3. *Cap.* 9. And so the Substantive (*Bartry*) 13 *Eliz. cap.* 7. The reason may be, because

because they that Chop and Change in this manner do endeavour, for the most part, one to over-reach and circumvent the other.

Barton, Is a term used in *Devonshire*, and other parts, for the Demesne Lands of a Mannor; some times for the Mannor-House it self; and in some places for Out-Houses and Fold-Yards. In the Stat. 2 & 3 *E.* 6. *cap.* 12. *Barton* Lands and *Demesne* Lands are used as *Synonyma's*. See *Barton*.

Base Court, Is any Inferiour Court, that is not of Record, as the *Court Baron*, &c. Of this read *Kitchin*, *fol.* 95. 96. &c.

Base Fee, Vide *Base Estate*.

Base Estate, Is in true French *Bas Estat*. It signifies that Estate which *Base Tenants* have in their Land. Now *Base Tenants* be they (according to *Lambard*, in his Explication of Saxon Words, *verb. Paganus*,) which perform to their Lords Services in Villenage, The Author of the *Termes of Laws*, saith, That to hold in *Fee Base*, is to hold at the Will of the Lord. *Ketchin*, *fol.* 41. makes *Base-tenure* and *Frank-tenure*, to be contraries, and puts Copiholders in the number of *Base Tenants*; whence it may probably be conjectured, That every *Base Tenant* holdeth at the Will of the Lord, but yet that there is a difference between a Base Estate and Villenage; which *Fitzh.* in his *Nat. Brev. fol.* 12. seemeth to intermingle. For to hold in *Villenage*, is to do all that the Lord will command. So that if a Copyholder have but a *Base Estate*, not holding by doing every Commandment of his Lord, he cannot be said to hold in *Villenage*. And I will not undertake to determine, whether Copy-holders by custome, and continuance of time, have shaken off that extreme Servitude, wherein they were at first, although *Fitz. loco citato* saith, Tenure by Copy hath grown but of late years.

Basels, *Baselli*, A sort of Coyn, abolished by *Henry* the Second, *Anno* 1158. *Holinsheds Chron. pag.* 67.

Baselard, *Bastardus*, By the Stat. 12 *R.* 2. *cap.* 6. Is made to signifie a Weapon, which Mr. *Speight* in his Exposition upon *Chaucer*, called *Pugionem*, *vel Sicam*.

Bastard, *Bastardus*, From the Brittish *Bastard*, that is, *Nothus* or *Spurius*, Is one that is born of any Woman not married; so that his Father is not known by order of Law, and therefore is called *filius Populi*, the Child of the People. Such cannot Inherit Land, as Heir to his Father, nor can any but the Heir of his Body take Land as his Heir, *Lit. Sect.* 401. If a Child be begotten by him that marries the Mother, after the Childs birth, yet it is in the judgment of Law a *Bastard*, Stat. 20 *H.* 3. 9. and 1 *H.* 6. 3. *Co.* on *Lit.* 244. If a man take a Wife who is great with Child by another, who was not her Husband, yet the Child, though born but one day after the Marriage, shall be Heir to the Husband. So if one marry a Woman, and never Bed her, but dye before Night, and she have a Child after, yet it seems it shall be accounted his Child. See the *English Lawyer*, 117. If a Man or Woman Marry a second Wife or Husband, the first living, and by that second have Issue, such Issue is a *Bastard*, 39 *E.* 3. 14. 7 *H.* 4. 49. 18 *E.* 4. 26. If a Woman elope with a stranger, and hath a Child by him, yet if the husband be *infra quatuor Maria*, he is legitimate, and shall inherit, 44 *E.* 3. 10. 7 *H.* 4. 10.

Bastardy, (*Bastardia*) Cometh of the French word *Bastard*, and signifies a defect of Birth, objected to one begotten out of Wedlock, *Bract. lib.* 5. *cap.* 19. How *Bastardy* is to be proved, or enquired into, if it be pleaded; See *Rastals Entries*, *tit. Bastardy*, 104. and *Kitchin*, *fol.* 64. who mentions *Bastardy special* and *Bastardy general*: *Bastardy general* is a Certificate from the Bishop of the Diocess to the Kings Justices, after just Enquiry made, that the Party enquired of is a *Bastard*, or not a *Bastard*, upon some question of Inheritance. *Bastardy special* is a Suit commenced in the Kings Court, against him that calleth another *Bastard*; so termed, because *Bastardy* is the principal and special Case in Tryal, and no Inheritance contended for. And by this it appeareth, that in both these significations *Bastardy* is rather taken for Examination or Tryal, whether a mans birth be Legitimate or not, than for *Bastardy* it self. See *Bro.* titul. *Bastardy*, *n.* 29. and Doctor *Ridlyes* Book, *pag.* 203. 204.

Baston, Is a French word signifying a Staff or Club, and by the Statutes of our Realm, denotes one of the Warden of the *Fleets* Servants or Officers, that attendeth the Kings Court with a painted Staff, for the taking into Custody such as are committed by the Court, and so it is used, 1 *R.* 2. 12. 5 *Eliz. cap.* 23. See *Trayle Baston*.

Batable Ground, Was the Land lying between *England* and *Scotland*, heretofore, when the Kingdoms were distinct, in question to whom they belonged, 23 *H.* 8. 6. and 32 *H.* 8. 6. The word seems as if we should say, *Debatable Ground*, or Land about which there is Debate, according to the Opinion of *Skene*. See Lamb. *Brit.* tit. *Cumberland*.

Battayle, *Duellum*, Signifies in our Common-Law a Trial by Combat: The manner whereof, because it is long, full of Ceremonies, and now totally disused, the better to understand, I refer you to *Glanvile*, *lib.* 2. *cap.* 3. 4. 5. *Bract. lib.* 3. *tract.* 2. *cap.* 21. *fol.* 140. Britton, *cap.* 22. And Sir *Tho. Smith de Rep. Ang. lib.* 2. *cap.* 7. & *lib.* 3. *cap.* 3. See *Combat*.

Battery, (From the French *Batre*, to strike, or the Saxon Batte, a Club,) Is a violent striking or beating any Man; for which, in regard it tends to the breach of the Peace, the Party injured may either indict the other at the Sessions, or have his Action of Trespass of Assault and *Battery* against him, and recover what the Jury will give him; which Action will lie as well before as after the Indictment. In some Case a Man may justifie the moderate beating of another, as the Parent his Child, the Master his Servant or Apprentice, &c. This *Battery* the *Civilians* call *Injuriam personalem, quia personæ infertur per verbera*, &c. *Wesemb. parat.* π. *de injur.* & *fam. libell.*

Batus, A Boat, and *Batellus*, a little Boat. *Concessit etiam idem Hugo Wake, &c. quod prædict. Abbas, &c. de Croyland habeant tres Batellos in Harnolt, &c.* Chart. E. 1. 20 Jul. 18 Regni. See *Libera Batella*. Hence we have an old word *Batswaynes*, for such as now we call *Boat-swaynes*, vulgarly *Boson of a Ship*.

K Baubels,

Baubels, (*Baubella*) Is an old Word signifying *Jewels*, *Ro. Hoveden. part. poster. suor. annal. fol.* 449. *b.*

Beacon, A kind of Saxon Word betokening a *Signal*: It is well known, 8 *Eliz. Cap* 13. *Beaconage* (*Beconagium*) Money paid towards the Maintenance of a *Beacon*; and we still use the Word *Beckon*, to give notice unto. See the Stat. 5 *H.* 4. and *Dorf. Pat.* 28 *H.* 6. *part* 2. *m.* 21. *Pro signis Anglice* Beacons & *Vigiliis.*

Bead, (Saxon Bead, a Prayer;) So that to say over ones *Bead*, is to say over ones Prayers: They are used to that purpose in many parts of the World, and are mentioned in 27 *H.* 8. *cap.* 26. and 3 *Jac. cap.* 5.

Bearding alias **Barding** of Wool. See *Clacke.*

Bearers, Signifies such as bear down or oppress others, and is all one with Maintainers, 4 *Ed.* 3. *cap.* 11.

Beasts of the Forest, Are those that are otherwise called *Beasts of Venery*, and are five; the Hart, the Hind, the Hare, the Bore, and the Wolf: *Antiquitas Britaniæ*, Written before the Conquest, *fol.* 43. *Holinsh.* Description of *England*, *pag.* 206. *b.* 30. Book of St. *Albans*, *fol.* 30. *Budæus*, *lib.* 2. *de Philologia*, and divers others.

Beasts of Chase, Also are Five, *viz.* The Buck, the Doe, the Fox, the Martern, and Roe, *Manwoods Forrest Law*, *Part* 2. *Cap.* 4. *Num.* 2.

Beasts and Fowl of Warren, Are only these, The Hare, the Coney, the Pheasant, and the Partridge, as appears by the *Register of Writs*, fol. 95. *in brevi de transgressione*, F. N. B *fol.* 86. 87. *Co.* on *Lit.* 233.

Beastials. See *Bestials.*

Beaupleader, (*Pulchrè Placitando*,) Is made of two French Words, *Beau*, *Formosus*, *Pulcher*, and *Pleader*, *Disputare*, *Causam agere*, and signifies in Common-Law, a Writ upon the Statute of *Marlbridge*, 52 *H.* 3. *cap.* 11. Whereby it is provided, That neither in the Circuit of Justices, nor in Counties, Hundreds, or Court-Barons, any Fines shall be taken of any Man for *Fair-Pleading*, that is, for not Pleading fairly or aptly to the purpose; upon which Statute this Writ was ordained, against those that violate the Law herein. See *F. N. B. fol.* 270. whose definition is to this effect: The Writ upon the Statute of *Marlbridge*, for not *Fair Pleading*, lyeth, where the Sheriff, or other Bayliff, in his Court, will take Fine of the Party, Plaintiff or Defendant, for that he Pleadeth not fairly. And it was as well in respect of the vitious Pleadings, as of the Fair Pleadings, by way of amendment, 2. *par. Inst. fol.* 122.

Bedel, *Bedellus*, Is derived from the French Word *Bedeau*, which signifies a Messenger or Apparator of a Court, that cites men to appear, and answer. It is also an inferior Officer of a Parish or Liberty, well known in *London* and the Suburbs. *Manwood* in his *Forest-Laws*, *cap.* 21. saith, That a *Beadle* is an Officer or Servant of the Forest, that doth make all manner of Garnishments of the Courts of the Forest; and also all manner of Proclamations, as well within the Courts of the Forest as without; and also to execute all the Process of the Forest: He is like unto a Bayliff Errant of a Sheriff in his County. *Edgarus*, &c. viz. *Vicecomitibus*, *Bedellis*, &c. *Ne introeant*, &c. Ingulphus Hist. Croyl.

Bedelary, *Bedelaria*, is the same to a *Bedel*, as *Baliva* a *Baylíwick* is to a *Bayliff*, *Lit. lib.* 3. *cap.* 5.

Bederepe, A Saxon Word, signifying a Service which some Tenants were antiently bound to perform, , as to Reap their Landlords Corn in Harvest; in imitation of which, some are yet tyed to give one, two, or more days Work, when commanded. *Debent venire in Autumno ad precariam quæ vocatur* a le Bederepe, *Pla. in Craft. Pur.* 10 H 3. Rot. 8.

Benefice, *Beneficium*, Is generally taken for all Ecclesiastical Livings, be they Dignities, or other. And *Anno* 13 R. 2. *Stat.* 2. *Cap.* 2. *Benefices* are divided into Elective, and of Gift. In the same sence it is used also in the Canon-Law, *Duarenius de Beneficiis*, *lib.* 2. *cap.* 3.

Beneficio primo Ecclesiastico habendo, Is a Writ directed from the King to the Chancellor or Lord Keeper, to bestow the Benefice that first shall fall in the Kings Guift, above or under such a value, upon this or that Man, *Reg. Orig. fol.* 307. *b.*

Benevolence, *Benevolentia*, Is used both in the Chronicles and Statutes of this Realm, for a voluntary gratuity given by the Subjects to the King, *Stowes Annals*, *Page* 701. By the Statute, *Anno* 1 R. 3. It is called a *New Imposition* and in that respect by him found fault with. But *Stow*, *Page* 791. saith, The Invention grew first from *Edward* the Fourth's days: You may find it also *Anno* 11 H. 7. *cap.* 10. to have been yielded to that worthy Prince, in regard of his great expences in Wars and otherwise: It is also mentioned and excepted out of the Pardon, 1 E. 6. *cap.* 15 Other Nations call it *Subsidium Charitativum*, given sometimes to Lords of the Fee by their Tenants, sometimes to Bishops by their Clergy. *Mattheus de afflictis descis.* 136. *Cassan. de consuet. Burg. pag.* 134. 136. *Baldus consitio*, 120. *vel.* 6. *pag.* 230. Of this *Menochius* makes mention, *Lib.* 2. *cent.* 2. *cap.* 178. & 179. Also by Act of Parliament, 13 *Car.* 2. *cap.* 4. it was given to our present Soveraign, King *Charles* the second.

Berghmayster, From the Dutch *Berg*, a Hill, Is a chief Officer among the *Derbishire Miners*, who also performs the Duty of a Coroner, *Juratores dicunt, quod in principio quando Mineratores veniunt in campum minera quærentes, inventa minera veniunt ad Balivum qui dicitur* Berghmayster, & *petent ab eo duas Metas*, &c. Esc. de Anno 16 E. 1. num. 34. In Turri London. See *Berghmoth.*

Berghmoth or **Berghmote**, May be deduced from the Saxon *Bergh*, a *Hill*, and *Gemote*, an Assembly; which is as much as to say, An Assembly, or Court upon a Hill. *Juratores etiam dicunt quod Placita del* Berghmoth *debent teneri de tribus septimanis in tres septimanas super mineram de Pecco.* Esc. 16 E. 1. *ut supra.* Hear what Mr. *Manlove* in his ingenious Treatise of the Customs of *Miners*, saith,

(Court,
3 E 6. ---*And suit for* Ore *must be in* Berghmote
Art. 9. *Thither for Justice*, Miners *must resort*, &c.
16E1 c.2.*And 2 great Courts of* Berghmote *ought to*
3E.6A.10.*In every year upon the Minery*, &c. (*be*
To swear Berghmaysters *that they faithfully*
Perform their Duties on the Minery, &c.

Bernet, *Incendium*, Comes from the Saxon *Bynnan*, to burn: It is one of those Crimes, which by the *Laws* of *H.* 1. *cap.* 13. *Emendari non possunt.* See *Opentheff.*

Bery or **Bury**, Signifies a *Habitation*, which is still made out in the names of Places, as St. *Edmonds-Bury*, &c. So we usually say, That in a Warren there are *Coney Buries*, or *Cony-berries.* Anciently it was taken also for a Sanctuary.

Berton, Is that part of a great Country-Farm, where the Barns, Stables, and other inferiour Offices stand, and wherein their Cattel are fodder'd, and other Country-business managed. See *Claus.* 32 E. 1. *m.* 17.

Berwica, A Word often found in the Book of *Doomsday*, signifying a Village, and is the termination of many Words, signifying somewhat appurtenant to a Mannor: As there is a Village near *Kingston* upon *Thames*, called at this day the *Wicke* or *Weeke*; and we commonly say, *Bayliwick*, &c. *Spelman* thinks it may be *Manerium minus ad majus pertinens*, &c.

Besaile, *Proavus*, is borrowed of the French *Bysayeul*, (i. *pere de mon pere grand*,) the Father of my Grand-father. In the Common-Law it signifies a Writ, that lyeth where the Great Grand-father was seised in his Demesne, as of Fee of any Lands or Tenements in Fee-simple, the day that he dyed; and after his Death, a stranger abateth or entreth the same day upon him, and keepeth out his Heir, &c. The form and use of this Writ is more at large to be read in *F. N. B. fol* 221.

Besca, A Spade or Shovel, derived from the French *Bescher*, *fodere*, to Dig. Hence perhaps *Una* bescata *terræ inclusa*, *Mon. Ang. p.* 2. *fol.* 642. May signifie a piece of Land usually turned up with a Shovel or Spade, as Gardiners use to fit their Grounds to sow and plant in.

Bestials, Cometh of the French *Bestials*, which is *pecus*, Beasts of any sort, *Anno* 4 E. 3. *cap.* 3. It is written *Bestayle*, and taken to denote all kind of Cattel, purvey'd for the Kings Provision. It is also mentioned, to signifie all kind of Cattel, 1 *Jac.* 33. and 12 *Car.* 2. *cap.* 4.

Bidale, or **Bid-all**, Is the invitation of Friends to drink at some poor Mans House, who thereby hopes to receive some assistant benevolence from the Guests for his Relief; still in use in the West of *England*, and falsly written by some *Bildale*, and mentioned 26 *H.* 8. *cap.* 6. The same is used also in the County-Palatine of *Chester* by persons of quality, toward the relief of their own or Neighbours poor Tenants.

Bidding of the Beads, Was a charge or warning that the Parish Priest gave to his Parishoners at certain special times, to say some particular Prayers, or do other acts of Devotion in behalf of some deceased Friends Soul; in imitation of which, the Ministers of the Church of *England* are commanded by the Canons on the Sunday precedent, to give notice of the Festivals in the following week, that the Parishioners may the better observe them; this is mentioned 27 *H.* 8. *cap.* 26. we may easily find *bidding* in the Saxon word bidden, to pray or desire; and *Bead*, a Prayer.

Bidripe, *Bidripa.* See *Bederepe.*

Biga, Properly a Cart with two Wheels, and not as some have offered, a Chariot drawn with coupled Horses; these Words prove it sufficiently, *Et quod eant cum* Bigis & *carris*, &c. *super Tenementum suum*, &c. Mon. Ang. fol. 256. b.

Bigamus, Is any person that hath at several times married two or more Wives successively after each others death, or a Widow, as appears by the Statutes, 18 *E.* 3. *cap.* 2. 1 *E.* 6. *cap.* 12. 2. *part Co. Inst. fol.* 273.

Bigamy, *Bigamia*, Signifies a double Marriage, being a Compound Greek Word; it is used in Common-Law, for an Impediment that hindreth a Man to be a Clerk, by reason he hath been twice Marryed, 4 E. 1. 5. which seems to be grounded upon the Words of St. *Paul* to *Timothy*, *Epist.* 1. *cap.* 5. *vers.* 2. *Oportet ergo Episcopum irreprehensibilem esse & unius uxoris virum.* The Canonists have founded their Doctrine upon this, That he that hath been twice marryed may not be a Clerk: And him that hath marryed a Widow, they reckon to have been twice marryed. Both which they do not only exclude from Holy Orders, but also deny them all priviledge that belongs to Clerks. But the Author of the *New Termes of the Law* saith, This Law is abolisht by 1 *E.* 6. 12. and to that may be added, 18 *Eliz. cap.* 7. which alloweth to all men that can read as Clerks, though not within Orders, the Benefit of Clergy, even in case of Felony, not especially excepted by some other Statute. So is *Brook tit.* Clergy, *plac.* 20. to the same purpose.

Bilanciis deferendis, Is a Writ directed to a Corporation, for the carrying of Weights to such a Haven, there to Weigh the Wools that such a Man is licensed to transport, *Reg. Orig. fol.* 270. *a.*

Bilawes or rather **By-laws**, That is, Laws made *Obiter*, or by the *By*, such as are made in Court-Leets or Court-Barons, for the peculiar good of those that make them, farther than the Common or Statute-Law doth bind. The like are generally allowed by Letters Patents of Incorporation to any Guild or Fraternity, for the better regulation of Trade among themselves, or with others, *Co. vol.* 6. *fol.* 63. *a. Kitchin*, *fol.* 45. 79. These in *Scotland* are called *Burlaw* or *Birlaw. Skene de verb signif. verb. Burlaw*, which saith he, are Laws made and determined by consent of Neighbours, elected and chosen by common approbation in the Courts called *Birlaw-Courts*, where they take Cognisance of Complaints between Neighbour and Neighbour, which men so chosen, are Judges and Arbitrators to the effect aforesaid, and are called *Birlaw-men*; for *Bawr* or *Bawrsman* in Dutch is *Rusticus*, and so *Birlaw* is is no other but *Leges Rusticorum.* By 14 *Car.* 2. *cap.* 5. The Wardens and Assistants for making and regulating *Norwich*-Stuffs, are impowred to make *By-Laws.* See 20 *Car.* 2. *cap.* 6.

Bilinguis, In general is a man of a double tongue, but in a legal sense, is used for a Jury that passeth between an English-man and an Alien, whereof part ought to be English-men and part strangers, 28 E. 3. *cap.* 13. This we call vulgarly a *Party-Jury*, but in proper Language, it is a Jury *de medietate linguæ.* See *Medietas Linguæ*

Bill, *Billa,* Hath several significations in Law. First, According to *West. Symb. Pag.* 1. *lib.* 2. *sect.* 146. It is all one with an Obligation, saving that it is commonly called *a Bill,* when in English; and an Obligation, when in Latine But now by a *Bill* we ordinarily understand a single Bond, without a Condition; by an Obligation a Bond with a Penalty and Condition, *West. part* 2. *Symbol. tit. Supplications, sect.* 52. Secondly, A *Bill* is a Declaration in Writing, that expresseth either the wrong the Complainant hath suffered by the Defendant, or else some fault that the Party complained of hath committed against some Law or Statute of the Commonwealth. Such *Bill* is sometimes exhibited to Justices *Iitnerant,* at the General Assises, by way of Indictment or Information; but more especially to the Lord Chancellor or Lord Keeper for unconscionable wrongs done: Sometimes it is preferred to others having Jurisdiction, accordingly as the Law, whereupon they are grounded, doth direct. It containeth the Fact complained of, the Damages thereby suffered, and petition of Process against the Defendant for redress.

Billa vera, Is a term of Art in the Common-Law, for the Grand Inquest impannelled and sworn before the Justices in *Eyre, &c.* indorsing a *Bill,* whereby any Crime punishable in that Court is presented unto them with these two words which do signifie thereby, That the Presentor hath furnished his Presentment with probable evidence, and worthy of farther consideration: And thereupon the Party presented, is said to stand Indicted of the Crime, and so bound to make Answer unto it, either by confessing or traversing the Indictment: and if the Crime touch the life of the Person Indicted, it is yet referred to another Inquest, called *The Jury of Life and Death,* who, if they find him guilty, then he stands convicted of the Crime, and is by the Judge to be condemned to death. See *Ignoramus.* See also *Indictment.*

Bill of Store, Is a kind of Licence granted at the Custome-House to Merchants, to carry such Stores and Provisions as are necessary for their Voyage, Custome-free.

Bill of Sufferance, Is a Licence granted at the Custome-house to a Merchant, to suffer him to Trade from one English Port to another, without paying Custome, *Anno* 14 *Car.* 2. *cap.* 11.

Billets of Gold, Are Wedges or Ingots of Gold; the word is derived from the French *Billot,* that is, *Massa Auri,* 27 E. 3. *Stat.* 2. *cap.* 14.

Binny Pepper, *Anno* 1 *Jac. cap.* 19.

Bissextile, *Bissextilis,* Vulgarly called *Leap-year,* because the sixth day before the Calends of *March* is twice reckoned, *viz.* on the twenty fourth and twenty fifth of *February*; so that the *Bissextile-year* hath one day more than other years, and happens every fourth year; This Intercalation of a day was first invented by *Julius Cæsar*, to make the year agree with the course of the Sun. And to prevent all ambiguity that might grow thereupon, it is ordained by the Statute *de Anno Bissextili,* 21 *H.* 3 That the day increasing in the *Leap-year,* and the day next before shall be accounted but one day, *Britton, fol.* 209. and *Dyer,* 17 *Eliz.* 345.

Birlaw, See *Bilaw* and *Byrlaw.*

Black maile, Is half English, half French, for in French *Mail* signifyeth a small piece of Money. It denotes in the Counties of *Cumberland, Northumberland, Westmerland,* and the Bishoprick of *Durham,* a certain rate of Money, Corn, Cattel, or other consideration, paid unto some inhabiting near the Borders, being men of Name and Power, allyed with certain known to be great Robbers and Spoile-takers within the said Counties; to the end, to be by them Protected and kept in safety from the danger of such as do usually rob and steal in those parts, *Anno* 43 *Eliz. cap.* 13. See *Mayle.* These Robbers are of late years called *Moss-Troopers,* and several Statutes made against them.

Black Rod, Is the Usher belonging to the Garter, so called of the *Black Rod* that he carrieth in his hand: He is Gentleman-Usher to the King, and also Usher of the Parliament. He is called in the *Black Book, fol.* 255. *Lator virgæ nigræ,* and *Hostiarius*; and elsewhere *Virgi-bajulus:* His duty is *Ad portandum Virgam coram Domino Rege, ad Festum Sancti Georgii infra Castrum de Windsore.* He also keeps the Chapter-House-Door, when a Chapter of the Order is sitting: His habit is the same with the Register of the Order, and *Garter,* principal King at Arms, which he wears only at the solemn times of that Festival of St. *George.* He carries, as we said, a *Black Rod,* on whose top is a Lyon, Gold. His Fee is 30 *li per Annum,* and hath antiently been made by Letters Patent under the Great Seal, and hath a great Power; for to his Custody all Noblemen, called in question for any Crime, are first committed.

Blade, *Bladum, Spelman* says, *De segete tantum intelligitur*; But in the Saxon it signifies more generally, Fruit, Corn, Hemp, Flax, Herbs, *&c.* Hence *Bladier* is taken for an Ingrosser of Corn or Grain: This may appear by a Release of *Will. de Mohun* to his Brother, of all the Mannor of *T. Salvo instauro suo & Blado,* excepting his Stock and Corn on the Ground.

Blancks, French *Blanc,* that is *candidus,* white; It signifies a kind of Money Coyned in the parts of *France* by King *Hen.* 5. that were subject to *England,* the value whereof was Eight Pence, *Stowes Annal pag* 586. these were forbidden to be currant within this Realm, 2 *H.* 6. *cap.* 9. The reaosn why they vvere called *Blanks,* may be, because at the time these were Coyned in *France,* there was also a Piece of Gold Coyned, which was called a *Salus,* of the value of 22 Shillings, from which this Silver was distinguished by the colour.

Blench,

Blench, Is the title of a kind of tenure of Land, as to hold Land in *Blench*, is by Payment of a Sugar loaf, a Bever-Hat, a couple of Capons, and such like; if it be demanded in the name of *Blench*, *id est*, *nomine albæ firmæ*. See *Alba firma*.

Blockwood. See *Logwood*.

Blomary, Is one of the Forges belonging to an Iron-Mill, through which the Iron passeth before it comes to the Finary. Of this you may read at large, 27 *Eliz. cap.* 19.

Bloated Fish or Herring, Are such as are not throughly dryed; they are spoken of, 18 *Car.* 2. *cap.* 2.

Bloudy hand, See *Backberend*. It signifies the Apprehension of a Trespasser in the Forest against Venison, with his *hands*, or other part *bloody*, though he be not found chasing or hunting. Of which, see *Manwood*, *cap.* 18. *num.* 9.

Bloudwit, Is a compound, from the Saxon Blod, *Sanguis* and *Wyte*, an old English Word signifying *Misericordia*. It is often used in ancient Charters, and intends an Amerciament for Blood shed. *Skene de verbor. Signif.* writes in *Bluidveit*, which, says he, is in English as much as *Injuria* or *Misericordia*. It being as the Scottishmen call it, an *Unlaw* for Wrong or Injury, as is the effusion of *Blood*. For he that hath *Bloodwit* granted him, hath free liberty to take all Amerciaments of Courts for shedding of *Blood*. *Fleta* saith, *Quod significat quietantiam misericordiæ pro effusione sanguinis*, lib. 1. cap. 47. *Si aliqui pugnantes, &c. extraxerint sanguinem* Prior *habebit* Bloudwit, 1. *amerciamentum inde in curia sua.* Ex Reg. Priorat de Cockesford.

Blubber, A kind of Whale-Oyl, so called, before it is thorowly boyled, spoken of 12 *Car.* 2. *cap.* 18.

Boc hord, Is, as it were, *Bookboard*, or a hoard for Books, that is, a place where Books, Writings, or Evidences are kept; we may term it in Latine *Librorum horreum*.

Bocland, Sax. *quasi* Bookeland, a Possessi on or Inheritance held by Instruments in writing. Bocland *vero ea possidendi transferendiq; lege coercebatur, ut nec dari licuit nec vendi, sed hæredibus relinquenda erat, in scriptis aliter permitteretur*; Terra *inde* Hæreditaria *nuncupata inter leges* Aluredi, *cap.* 36. See *Charter-land*, *Copyhold* and *Freehold*, and *Land boc*. See also *Glossarium in decem scriptores*.

Bodies Politick. See *Corporation*.

Boilary or **Bullary of Salt**, A Salt-house or Salt-Pit, where Salt is Boiled, *Co.* on *Lit. fol.* 4. *b*.

Bolting, Is a term of art used in *Greys-Inn*, whereby they intend private arguing of Cases; the manner of it is this, An *Antient* and two *Barristers* sit as Judges; three Students bring each a Case, out of which the Judges choose one to be argued, which done, the *Students* first begin and argue, and after them the *Baristers*. *Bolting* hath also a more common acception, which Country Housewives say is the Sifting of their Meal or Flour through a Bag, to make it finer; which Bag they call a *Bolter*; and why may not the Law-term be drawn hence, because the *bolting* of Cases is the through sifting and debating of them.

Bonis arrestandis, Is a Writ, for which see *Arrestandis bonis*.

Bona fide, We say, that is done *Bonâ fide*, that is done really, with a good Faith, without Fraud or Deceit. It is mentioned 12 *Car.* 2. *cap* 18 and 15 *Car.* 2. *cap.* 5.

Bonaght or **Bonaghty**, An Exaction in *Ireland*, imposed at the Will of the Lord, *Antiq. Hib pag.* 60. *Cambden* in his *Brit.* tit *Desmond.* says, That *James* Earl of *Desmond* imposed upon the people those most grievous Tributes of *Coyn*, *Livery*, *Cocherings*, *Bonaghty*, *&c.*

Bona notabilia, Are such Goods as a Party dying hath in another Diocess than that wherein he dies, amounting to 5 *li* at least, which, whoso hath, his Will must be proved before the Archbishop of the Province; unless by Composition or Custome other Diocesses are authorised to do it, where *Bona notabilia* are rated at a greater sum. Book of Canons, 1 *Jac. can.* 92. 93. *Perkins*, *sect.* 489. See *Probate of Testaments*.

Bona Patria, An Assise of Country-men, or good Neighbours: Sometimes called *Assisa bonæ Patriæ*, when Twelve, or more, are chosen out of the Country to pass upon an Assise; and they are called *Juratores*, because they swear judicially in presence of the Party, *Skene verb. Bona Patria.* Vide *Assisors*.

Bond, **Bondage** and **Bondmen**, The Book of *Doomsday* calls *Bondmen*, *Servi*, and differences them from *Villani*, *Villeynes*. *Et de toto tenemento quod de ipso tenet in* Bondagio, *&c. Mon. Ang.* 2 *par. fol.* 609. *a*.

Bonis non amovendis, Is a Writ to the Sheriffs of *London*, &c. to charge them, that one condemned by Judgment in a Nation, and prosecuting a Writ of Error, be not suffered to remove his Goods, until the Error be tryed, *Reg. Orig. fol.* 131. *b*.

Booting or **Boting Corn**, Certain Rent-Corn anciently so called: The Tenants of the Mannor of *H.* in *Com.* B. heretofore paid *Booting Corn* to the Prior of *Rochester*, *Antiquit. of Purveyances*, *fol.* 418. See *Bote*.

Bordarii, B: Tenants that occupy part of the Demesnes, which are called *Bordlands*.

Bordagium, The Tenure of *Bordlands*, which see. *Item ordinatum est, quod omnes qui terras & tenementa tenent per* Bordagium, *habeant super singulis* Bordagiis, *quæ per prædictum servitium tenentur, capitalem quandam mensionem in loco ad hoc consueto, &c.* Ordin. Just c. Itin. in Insula de Jersey.

Bordarii seu Bordmanni, We often meet with these words in *Doomsday*; some think they are Peasants, Husbandmen, or Cottagers, *Dicuntur* Bordarii *vel quod in Tugurio* (*quæ cotagia vocant*) *habitabant*, *&c.* Spelman. See *Bordlands*.

Bord-halfpeny, Is a Duty paid in Fairs and Markets, for setting up Tables, *Bords* and Stalls, for the selling of Wares. In many old Charters, divers are freed from this Payment: Some have corrupted it to *Borthalpeny* and *Brod-halpeny*.

Bordlands, Signifie the Demesnes, which Lords keep in their hands for the Maintenance of of their *Bord* or Table. Bordlands *sunt Dominicum ad mensam*, *Bract. lib.* 4. *tract.* 3. *cap.* 9. *num.* 5. which was antiently termed *Bordagium* or *Bordage*. Saxon *Diction. verbo Bord*. See also *Antiquity of Purveyances*, *fol.* 49.

Borow or **Borough**, In Latine *Burgus*, *Burgum*; May be derived either from the French *Burg*, i. *pagus*; or from the Saxon *Borhoe*, *pignus*, It signifies with us a Corporate-Town, that is not a City, 2 E. 3. *cap.* 3. namely such as send Burgesses to the Parliament, whose number you may see in *Cromp. Jurisd. fol.* 24. It may probably be conjectured, That anciently it was taken for those Companies consisting of ten Families, which were to be Pledges for one another. See *Bract. lib.* 3. *tract.* 2. *cap.* 10. See *Head-borow* and *Borow-head*, and *Lamb. Duty of Consta. pag.* 8. *Linwood* upon the *Provincial* (*ut singula de sensibus*) speaks to this effect, *Aliqui interpretantur Burgum esse castrum, vel locum ubi sunt crebra castra, vel dicitur Burgus, ubi sunt per limites habitacula plura constituta*: But afterwards defines it thus, Burgus *dici potest villa quæcunq; alia a civitate, in qua est Universitas approbata*. Some derive it from the Greek Word πυργὸς, that is, *Turris*. See *Skene de verb*. Signif. *Verstegan* in his *Restitution of decayed Intelligences*, saith, That Burg or Burgh, whereof we take our *Borough*, metaphorically signifies a Town having a Wall, or some kind of closure about it. All places that in old time had amongst our Ancestors the name of *Borough*, were one way or other fenced or fortified, *Lit. sect.* 164.

Borow-head alias **Head-borough**, *Capitalis Plegius*, made up of *Borhoe*, a Pledge, and Head, *Lamb. Duty of Constables*, where in the Explication of this and other Saxon Words of that nature, he rehearseth some ancient Customs of *England*, during the Reign of the Saxons. This *Borow-head* was the chief man of the *Decury*, elected by the rest to speak and do in their behalfs those things that concerned them. See *Borowholders*.

Borow-hold alias **Borsholders**, Be *quasi Borhoe-ealders*, and signifieth the same Officers that be called *Borow-heads*, *Lamb. Duty of Consta. Bracton* calleth them *Borghy-Aldere*, *lib.* 3. *tract.* 2. *cap.* 10,

Borow English, Is a customary descent of Lands or Tenements, whereby, in all places where this Custom holds, Lands and Tenements descend to the youngest Son; or if the Owner of the Land have no Issue, then to the younger Brother; as in *Edmunton*, some part of *Richmond*, and other places, *Kitchin*, *fol.* 102. And the reason of this Custom (says *Littleton*) is, for that the youngest is presumed in Law to be least able to shift for himself.

Borow Goods Devisable, I find these words in the Statute of *Acton Burnel*, 11 E. 1. *cap. unico*: And suppose that as before the Statute of 32 & 34 *H.* 8. no Lands were Divisable at the Common-Law, but in ancient Baronies, so perhaps at the making the Statute of *Acton Burnel*, it was doubtful, whether Goods were devisable but in ancient *Borows*: For it seemeth by the Writ *De rationabili parte bonorum*, that anciently the Goods of a Man were partible between his Wife and Children.

Borthalpeny. See *Bord-halpeny*.

Boscage, *Boscagium*, Is such Sustenance as Wood and Trees yield to Cattel, *viz.* Mast; it may be derived from the Greek Word βόσκειν, *Pascere*.

Boscaria, May be either Wood-houses, from *Boscus*; or Ox-houses, from *Bos*. *Ut ipsi possint domus* & Boscaria *satis competentia ædificare*, Mon. Ang. 2. *pa. fol.* 302.

Boscus, Is an ancient Word used in the Law of *England* for all manner of Wood: The *Italian* uses *Bosco* in the same sense, and the French *Boys*. *Boscus* is divided into Wood or Timber, *Haut-bois*; and Coppice or Under-Wood, *Subbois*: The High-Wood is properly called *Saltus*, and in *Fleta Maeremium*.

Bosinnus. A certain Rustical Pipe: By Inquisition after the Death of *Lawrence Hastings*, Earl of *Pembroke*, 22 E. 3. The Mannor of *Aston Cantlow in Com. War.* is returned to be held *in Capite* of the King, by these Words, *Quod quidem Manerium per se tenetur de Domino Rege in Capite per servitium inveniendi unum hominem Peditem cum quadam Arcu sine Corda, cum uno* Bosinno *sine tappa*, &c. Ex Record. Tur Lond.

Bote, Signifieth Compensation, *Lamb. Explicat*. Saxon Words: Thence cometh *Manbote* alias *Monbote*, that is compensation or amends for a Man slain, which was bound to another. In King *Ina*'s Laws, set out by Mr. *Lambert*, *cap.* 96. is declared what Rate was ordained for the expiation of this Offence. Hence also comes our common Phrase, *To give to boote*, that is, *compensationis gratia*. See *Skene de verb. signif. tit.* Bote. See also *Hedge-bote*, *Plowbote*, *House-bote*, *Theft-bote*, &c. in their proper places.

Boteless, *Sine remedio. Inter. Plac. Trin.* 12 E. 2. *Ebor.* 48. We retain the Word still in common speech, as it is *bootless* to attempt such a thing that is, it is vain to attempt.

Botha, A Booth or Tent to stand in, in Fairs or Markets.------*Et duas Mensuras liberas ad* Bothas *suas Faciendas*, Mon. Ang. 2 par. Fol. 132.

Bothna, **Buthna**, **Buthena**, Seems to be a Park where Cattel are enclosed and fed, *Hector Boetius*, *lib.* 7. *cap.* 123. *num.* 35. And *Aulus Gellius*, *lib.* 11. *cap.* 1. *Bothena* also signifies a Barony, Lordship, or Sheriffwick. And *Domini Bothenæ* are Lords of the Barony, Mannor, &c. *Skene de verb. Signif.*

Botiler Of the King, *Pincerna Regis*, *Anno* 43 E. 3. *cap.* 3. Is an Officer that provideth the Kings Wines; who (as *Fleta*, *lib.* 2. *cap.* 21. saith) may by vertue of his Office out of every Ship laden with Sale-Wines, *unum dolium eligere in prora navis ad opus Regis*, & *aliud in puppi*, & *pro qualibet Pecia reddere tantum* 20 *solid. Mercatori. Si autem plura habere voluerit, bene licebit, dum tamen Pretium fide dignorum judicio pro Rege apponatur.*

Bottomry or **Botomary**, *Anno* 16 *Car.* 2. *cap.* 6. Is, when the Master of a Ship borrows Money upon the Keel or Bottom of his Ship, and binds the Ship it self, That if the Money be not paid at the day limited, the Creditor shall have the Ship. *Ceo est* Bottomage *quand argent est borow sur le Keil del neif et le neif oblige al payment de ceo*, &c. Latches Rep. fol. 252. *Scarboroughs* Case. Though

Others.

Others say, when *A. B.* lends a Merchant Money, and is to be paid a greater Sum at the return of the Ship, standing to the hazard of the Voyage, though he receive greater Interest than six *per cent.* it is not Usury, but *Bottomry.*

Bovata terræ, An Oxgate of Land is as much as an Ox can till. *Octo bovata terræ faciunt unam carucatam, octo carucatæ faciunt unum feodum militis: 18 acræ terræ faciunt* Bovatum *terræ,* M. S. cum notis in Stat. Vide *Oxgange.*

Bouche of Court, Or according to the Vulgar *Budge of Court,* is a certain quantity of provision allowed there to a servant. For so is the French *Avoir Bouche a Court,* to have an allowance at Court. This antiently extended as well to Noblemens Houses, who were Subjects, as to the Kings Court; as may appear by this Deed, of which we will repeat only what is material to our purpose.

C*Est Endenture fait parentre luy Nobles hommes Monsieur* Tho. Beauchamp, *Counte de Warwike, d'une part, & Monsieur* Johan Russel *de Strengesham Chivalier de autre part, tesmoigne que le dit* Johan *est, &c. Et avera pur la pees, &c.* Bouche au Court *pur luy mesme, &c. Done a nostre Chastell de Warwike le 29 jour del moys de March l'an du reigne le Roy* Richard *le* Second, *pur le Conquest, sisme.*

Boveria, An Ox-house or Ox-stall, *Loca ubi stabulantur* Boves; according to *Gloss. in 10 Scriptores.* And *Mon. Ang. 2 par. fol.* 210. hath these Words---*Ad faciendum ibi* Boverias *suas & alias domos usibus suis necessariis.*

Bound or **Boundary,** *Bunda,* For the derivation, see *Co.* 4. *Inst. fol.* 318. how it is used, we may see 8 E. 3. Itin. Pick. fol. 6. *Secundum metas, maras, bundas & Marchias Forestæ.*

Bow-bearer, According to *Cromp. Jur. fol.* 201. Is an under Officer of the Forest, sworn to the true performance of his Office, in these words, *I will true Man be to the Master Forester of this Forest, and to his Lieutenant; and in the absence of them I shall truly oversee, and true Inquisition make as well of sworn Men as unsworn in every Bailiwick, both in the North Bail and South Bail of this Forest; and of all manner of Trespasses done either to Vert or Venison, I shall truly endeavour my self to attach, or cause them to be attached in the next Court of attachment, there to be presented, without any concealment had to my knowledge.* So help me God.

Bozones. See *Busones.*

Bracton, Was a famous Lawyer of this Land, renowned for his Knowledge both in the Common and Civil Laws, as appeareth by his Books every where extant. He lived in the days of *Henry* the Third, *Stamf. prær. fol* 5. *b.* And, as some say, was Lord chief Justice of *England.*

Brandy, A kind of Strong-water, made chiefly in *France* of the Lees of Wine; mentioned in the Act 20 *Car.* 2. *cap.* 1. Upon an Argument in the Exchequer, *Anno* 1668. It was Resolved, That *Brandy* was a Spirit. But 25. *Novemb.* 1669. by a Grand Committee of the whole House of Commons, it was voted to be a Strong-Water, and not a Spirit.

Brasium, Seems to signifie Malt, because in the ancient Statutes *Brasiator* is taken for a Brewer, and still for a Maltster, 18 E. 2. It was resolved, That *Venditio* Brasii *non est venditio victualium, nec debet puniri sicut venditio panis, vini & cervisiæ & hujusmodi contra formam statuti.*

Breach Carnium, By *Breach carnium, Thomas Crew,* Master of the Hospital of St. *John Baptist,* without the North-Gate at *Chester,* claims, *Quod omnes Tenentes sui infra eorum libertates residentes sint quieti de venditione carnium.* Pla. in Itin. apud Cest. 14 H. 7.

Bread of Treat or Trite, *Panis Tritici,* Is one of those sorts of Bread mentioned in the Stat. of *Assise of Bread and Ale,* 51 *H.* 3. *Stat.* 1. where we may read of *Wastel Bread, Cocket Bread,* and *Bread of Treat,* which may answer to three sorts now in use with us, called *White, Wheaten,* and Houshold *Bread.* See *Cocket.*

Brede, Signifieth Broad; *Bracton* useth this Word, *lib.* 3. *tract.* 2. *cap.* 15. *nu.* 7. proverbially thus, *Too large and too brede*; that is, too long and too broad.

Brehon, The Irishry call their Judges *Brehones,* and consequently the Irish Law is termed *Brehon Law.* See 4 *Inst. fol.* 358.

Bretoyse or **Bretois,** *Henricus de Penebrugge dedit omnibus liberis, &c. omnes libertates & liberas consuetudines secundum Legem de* Bretoyse, *&c.* where *secundum Legem de* Bretois, must needs signifie the Law of the Marches, then in practise among the *Britains*; because *Penebrugge* or *Pembridge* is in *Herefordshire,* a Town bordering on *Wales.*

Breve, Which haply may be so called from the *brevity* of it, is any Writ directed either to the Chancellor, Judges, Sheriffs, or other Officers, whose variety and forms you may see in the *Register per totum.* The Word is used in the Civil Law according to several senses. See *Skene de verbor. Signif. verb.* Breve. And *Bracton, lib.* 5. *tract.* 5. *cap.* 17. *num.* 2. Breve *quia* Breviter *& paucis verbis intentionem proferentis exponit, &c.*

Brevibus & Rotulis liberandis, Is a Writ or Mandat to a Sheriff, to deliver unto the new Sheriff, chosen in his room, the County, with the appurtenances, *una cum Rotulis,* brevibus, and all other things belonging to that Office, *Reg. Orig. fol.* 295. *a.*

Bribery, Is a high Offence, *viz.* when any Man in judicial place, or any great Officer, takes any Fee, Pension, Gift, or Reward, for doing his Office, of any person, save the King only, *Fortescue, cap.* 51. and 3 *Inst. fol.* 145.

Bribors, Cometh of the French *Bribeur, id est Mendicus:* It seemeth in a legal signification one that pilfereth other mens Goods, *Anno* 28 E. 2. *Stat.* 1. *cap. unico.*

Briga, French *Brigue,* that is, strife or contention. *Et posuit terram illam in* Brigam, *&c.* he made strife about the Land, *Ebor. Hill.* 18 E. 3. *Rot.* 28.

Brigandine, *Lorica,* Is a Coat of Mail; this Word is used 4 & 5 *P. & M. cap.* 2. Some confound it with *Habergeon,* and others with *Brigantine,* which is a far different thing, being a swift sayling Vessel used at Sea, being long, but low built.

Brigbote,

Brigbote or **Brugbote**, *Est quietum esse de auxilio dando ad reficiendum Pontes. Fleta, lib.* 1. *cap.* 47. It is compounded of *Brig*, a Bridge; and *Bote*, a compensation or yielding of amends. See *Bote* and *Bruckbote*. *Seldens Titles of Honor, fol.* 622.

Britton, Was a famous Lawyer, that lived in the days of King *Edward* the First, at whose Command, and by whose Authority, he writ a learned Book of the Law of this Realm; The tenor whereof runeth in the Kings Name, as if it had been Penned by himself, answerably to the Institutions which *Justinian* assumeth to himself, though composed by others, *Stamf. prær. fol.* 6. & 21. Sir *Edward Coke* Saith, That this *Britton* writ his Book in the Fiftieth year of *Edward* the First, *Lib.* 4. *fol.* 126. *a.* & *lib.* 6. *fol* 67. *a.* Mr. *Guin* in the *Preface to his Reading*, mentioneth, That this *John Britton* was Bishop of *Hereford*.

Brocage, Is commonly taken for the wages or Hire of a Broker. In 12 *R.* 2 *cap.* 2. it is taken for the means used by a spokesman. *Anno* 1 *Jac. cap.* 21. It is written *Brokerage*. See also 11 *H.* 4. *num.* 28. not printed.

Brochia, A great Can or Pitcher, *Bracton, lib.* 2. *tract.* 1. *cap.* 6 hath these Words, *Si quis teneat per servitium inveniendi domino Regi, certis locis & temporibus, unum hominem & unum equum & saccum cum* Brochia, &c. By which it seems that he intends *Saccus* to carry dry, and *Brochia* liquid things. See *Saccus*.

Brodehalpeny, In some Copies *Broadhalfpeny*, and in others *Bordhalpeny*. It signifies to be quit of a certain Custome exacted for setting up of Tables or Boards in Fairs or Markets: and those that were freed by the Kings Charter of this Custome, had this Word put in their Letters Patents; by reason whereof at this day, the freedom it self, for brevity of speech, is called *Broadhalpeny*. It seems to be derived of three Saxon Words, *Bret* or *Bred*, that is, a Board: and *Halve*, that is in the behalf of, as we say in Latine (*cujus rei gratia,*) and *Penning*, a Toll, which in all makes a Toll in behalf of or for a *Board*.

Broggers. See *Brokers*.

Broke, Commonly called Sir *Robert Broke*, was a great Lawyer, and Lord Chief Justice in Queen *Maries* time, *Cromp. Just. of Peace, fol.* 22. *b.* He made an Abridgment of the whole Law, from him Intituled *Brokes Abridgment*.

Broker, *Brocarius*, Seemeth to come of the French Word *Broieur*, that is, *Tritor*, a Grinder or Breaker into small pieces; because he that is of that Trade, to deal in matters of Money and Merchandise between Englishmen and Strangers, draws the Bargain into particulars, not forgetting to grind out something to his own Profit. These Men be called *Broggers*, 10 *R.* 2. *cap.* 10. In *Scotland* they be called *Broccarii*, that is, according to *Skene de Signif. verbor. Mediators* or *Intercessors* in any Transaction, Paction or Contract, as in Buying, Selling, or Contracts of Marriage. *Broggers of Corn* are used in a Proclamation of Queen *Eliz.* for *Badgers*, *Bakers Chron.* in her Reign. He that will know what these *Brokers* were wont and ought to be, let him read the Statute 1 *Jac. cap.* 21. These, in the Civil-Law, are termed *Proxineti*, as also of some *Licitatores* & *mediatores*, tit. *de Proxinet. in Digestis*. There is another sort of *Brokers*, commonly called *Pawn-brokers*, who commonly have a shop, and let out Money to Necessitous People upon Pawns, not without Extortion: These we may call more properly *Friperers*, and are neither of that Antiquity or Credit as the other; nor does the Statute allow them to be *Brokers*, though they are vulgarly so called.

Broderers, This may take his derivation from the French *Brodeur*, and that of *Bordur*, *fimbria*, the Edge or Hemme of a Garment, which we yet call *Border*, and that because it is usually distinguisht from the rest by some conceited or costly Work: He that worketh it, is known among us by the name of an *Embroiderer*.

Brothel-houses, King *Hen.* 8. by Proclamation 30 *March*, 37 year of his Reign, suppressed all the Stews or *Brothel-houses* which long had continued on the *Bankeside* in *Southwark*, 3 *Inst. fol.* 205. and *Rot. Parl.* 14 *R.* 2. *nu.* 32.

Bruckbote, Is compounded of two German Words, (*Kruck*, *Pons* a Bridge,) and *bote*, *compensatio*, Reward; It signifieth with us a Tribute or Duty, toward the mending or re-edifying of Bridges, whereof many are freed by the Kings Charter; and thereupon the Word is used for the very liberty or exemption from this Tribute. See *Pontage* and *Brig-bote*.

Bruere, We call that which the Latines name *Erica*, and signifies *Heath*: Bruaria 2. *leucarum longitudine & latitudine*, Doomsday. *Hac autem appellatione forenses vocant steriles campos licet Ericam non edant*, Spelm.

Buckstall, By 19 *H.* 7. *cap.* 11. seems to be a Deer-hay, Toyle, or large Net to catch Deer, which by that Statute none may keep, but he that hath a Park of his own, under the Penalty of 40 *li.* What it is to be quit of *Buckstalls*, see 4 *Inst. fol.* 306.

Buckwheat, Is mentioned 15 *Car.* 2. *cap.* 5. and in truth the same with French Wheat, and well known in many Countries among us of late years.

Budge of Court. See *Bouch de Court*.

Buggery, According to *Co. Rep.* 12. *pag.* 36. Comes from the Italian *Buggerare*. It hath been defined to be *Carnalis copula contra naturam & hac vel per confusionem specierum, sc.* a Man or Woman with a brute Beast, *vel Sexuum*, a Man with a Man, or a Woman with a Woman, see *Levit.* 18. 22, 23. This Offence committed either with Man or Beast is Felony without Benefit of Clergy, being a Sin against God, Nature, and the Law, 25 *H.* 8. revived, and 3 *Eliz.* 17. It was brought into *England* by the *Lombards*, as appears *Rot. Parl.* 50 *E.* 3. *num.* 58. See F. N. B. 269. and *Dalton*. In ancient times such Offendors were to be burned by the Common-Law. This most detestable Sin was most justly excepted out of the Act of *General Pardon*, 12 *Car.* 2. *cap.* 8. made after his Majesties Happy Restoration.

Bull, Seemeth to be derived from the Greek βουλὴ, *consilium*, as *Polidore Virgil* saith, *De invent. rer. lib.* 8. *cap.* 2. It is an Instrument so called, granted by the Bishop of *Rome*, and sealed with a Seal of Lead, containing in it his Decrees, Commandments, or other Acts, according to the nature

nature of the thing for which it is granted: And these Instruments have been heretofore used, and of force in this land; but by the Statute of 28 *H.* 8. *cap.* 16. It was Enacted, That all *Bulls*, Briefs, Faculties and Dispensations, of whatsoever name or nature, had or obtained from the Bishop of *Rome*, should be altogether void, see *Rast.* 328. The word is often used in other Statutes, as 1 & 2 *P.* & *M. cap.* 8. 13 *Eliz. cap.* 2. *Mat. Paris*, *Anno* 1237. describes its Seal thus, *In* Bulla *Domini Papæ stat imago* Pauli *a dextris crucis in medio* Bullæ *figurata* & *Petri a sinistris.* But now, as we said, they are disused among us, and therefore need no further Description.

Bullenger, The Commons Petition, that certain Commissions issued to Cities, for the preparing Boats and *Bullengers* may be repealed, the Parliament not having consented thereto, *Rot. Parl.* 2 *H.* 4. *num.* 22.

Bullion, Cometh of the French *Billen*, the Ore or Metal whereof Gold is made: It signifies with us Gold or Silver in Mass or Billet, 9 E. 3. *Stat.* 2. *cap.* 2. And sometime the Kings Exchange, or place, whither such Gold in the lump is brought to be tried or exchanged, *Anno* 27 E. 3. *Stat.* 2. *cap.* 14. 4 *H.* 4. 10. See *Skene de verbor.* Signif. *verbo.* Bullion. *Gervase* of *Tilbury* says, (writing of the Salt-springs in *Worcestershire*) That of old they called a certain quantity of Salt *Bullion*.

Bultell, Is the branny remainder of Meal that hath been dressed. And the Bag wherein it is dressed, is called a *Bulter*, or rather a *Boulter*; the word is mentioned in the Statute, entituled, *Assisa panis* & *cervisia*, 51 H. 3. Hence *bulted* or *boulted* Bread.

Bunda. See *Bounds.*

Burcheta, A kind of Gun, mentioned in the *Forest Records.*

Burgbete, Compounded of *Burg*, *castellum*, and *Bote*, *compensatio*, signifies a Tribute or Contribution toward the building or repairing of Castles or Walls of Defence, or toward the edifying a Burrough or City; from this divers had exemption by the ancient Charters of the Saxon Kings, whereupon it is usually taken for the exemption or liberty it self, *Rast.* Exposition of words. *Fleta* says, *Significat quietantiam reparationis murorum Civitatis vel* Burgi, *lib.* 1. *cap.* 47.

Burg-English. See *Borow-English.*

Burgage, *Burgagium*, Is a Tenure proper to Cities, *Borows* and Towns, whereby the *Burgers*, Citizens or Townsmen, hold their Lands or Tenements of the King, or other Lord, for a certain yearly Rent. *Old Tenures.* It is a kind of Socage, *Swinburne*, *part* 3. *sect.* 3. *num.* 6. *Habetur inter ignobiles tenuras qui ad militiam non pertinet*, 37 *H.* 8. 20. Anciently some called a Dwelling-house in a Borow-Town, a *Burgage.*

Burghbrech or **Borghbrech**, *Angli omnes decemvirali olim fide-jussione pacem regiam stipulati sunt, quod autem in hanc commissum est*, Burghbrech *dicitur*, &c. *Vide* Leg. Canuti, cap 55. Burghbrich *est Læsio libertatis aut septi*, Polychron, lib. 1. cap 50.

Burgheristhe, I suppose it should be *Burgheriche*, that is, *Violatio pacis in villa.* The word is used in *Doomsday*, and so expounded by Mr. *Agar* of the *Exchequer.*

Burghmote, A Court of a Borow or City, *Et habeatur in anno ter* Burges motus, &c. & *intersit Episcopus* & *Aldermanus*, & *doceant ibi Dei rectum* & *sæculi*, Leg. Canut. M. S. cap. 44. Hence in the City of *London* they still have their *Wardmote*, &c.

Burgesses, *Burgenses*, Are properly the Inhabitants of a Borow or Town driving a Trade there; yet we usually apply it to the Magistrates: And particularly we call those *Burgesses* who serve in Parliament for any such Borow or Corporation. See *Glanvile*, *lib.* 7. *cap.* 9. In *Germany* and other Countries they confound *Burgesse* and Citizen, but we distinguish them, as appears by the Stat. 5. *R.* 2. *cap.* 4. where the several Degrees are thus enumerated, *Count*, *Baron*, *Baneret*, *Chivalier de Countee*, *Citizen de Citee*, *Burgesse de Burgh.* See the Statute of *Merton*, *cap.* 7. and *Co.* on *Lit. fol.* 80.

Burglary, *Burglaria*, Is compounded of two French words, *Bourg*, *pagus*, & *Larecin*, *furtum*, or *Laron*, *fur*, Co. lib. 4. fol. 39. It is in the legal sence defined to be, a felonious entring into another Mans dwelling wherein some person is, or into a Church in the night-time, to the end, to commit some Felony, as to kill some Man, or to steal somewhat thence, or do some other felonious Act, albeit he execute not the same, *Westm. Symb. part.* 2. *tit.* Indictments, *sect.* 56. *Burglary* in the natural signification, is nothing but the robbing of a House; but as it is *vox artis*, the Lawyers restrain it to robbing a House by night, or breaking in with an intent to rob or do some other Felony. The like Offence committed by day, they call *House robbing*, by a peculiar name. How many ways *Burglary* may be committed, see *Cromp. Just. of Peace*, *fol.* 28, 29, 30. and 3. *par. Inst. fol.* 363. The Offenders shall not have benefit of Clergy, 18 *Eliz.* 7.

Burghware, A Citizen or Burgess, *Quasi vir* Burgi, it is used in the Charter of *William the Conquerer* to the *Londoners*, *Willielmus Rex salutat Willielmum Episcopum* & *Goffredum Portgeresium* & *omnem* Burghware *infra* London, &c.

Burlimen. See *Sucking.*

Bursa, A Purse,--*Reddendo inde ad* Bursam *Abbatis*, &c. Ex lib. Cart. Priorat. Leom.

Burse, A word used in *Doomsday*, of which Mr. *Agar* thus; It may be this word is written for *Bury*, which sometimes I read in this Book, and *Bure* is that which the Dutchmen call a *Bore*, *Colonus*, a Peasant.

Busca or **Buscus**, Underwood or Brushwood. See *Boscus.*

Busones Comitatus, *Justiciarii vocatis ad se quatuor vel sex vel pluribus de Majoribus comitatus, qui dicuntur* Busones *comitatus* & *ad quorum nutum dependent vota aliorum*, Bract. lib. 3. tract. 2. cap. 1. num. 1. *sed quære.*

Butt, As a *Butt* of *Malmsey*, containing at least 126 Gallons, *Anno* 1 R. 3. *cap.* 13. It signifies also the place where *Archers* are wont with their Bows and Arrows to shoot at a Mark, which we at this day call *Shooting at the Butts.*

Butlerage of Wines, Signifies that Imposition of sale *Wine* brought into the Land, which

which the Kings Butler, by vertue of his Office, may take every Ship, 1 *H.* 8. *cap.* 5. For which, see more in *Botyler of the King*, the Statute 12 *Car.* 2. *cap.* 24. for taking away Purveyances extends not to this ancient Duty. See *Calthorps Rep. Of special Cases, pag.* 23. and 4. *Inst. fol.* 30.

Butsecarle, Buthscarle, Butesecarle, or **Botescarle,** The same with *Boatswaine* or *Mariner*, Seld. Mar. Clauf. 184.

Buzones Judiciorum. See *Busones comitatus.*

Bydalle, 26 *H.* 8. *cap.* 6. See *Bidale.*

Byzlaw or **Burlaw.** See *Bylaw*, *Skene de Signif. verb. pag.* 33.------**Bye,** *An Habitation, Doomsday*

C.

L*itera* C. *apud veteres nota fuit condemnationis, unde proverbium inter Græcos* τὸ χῖ<?>

Literally: *unde proverbium inter Græcos* τὸ χδὲν ἡδίκεσε ὑδὲ τὸ K.

Cablish, Cablicia, Among the Writers of the *Forest Laws*, signifieth *Brushwood*, *Cromp. Jurisd. fol.* 165. *Manwoods Forest Laws, cap.* 25. *num.* 3. *pag.* 541. calls it *Browsewood.* See *Itiner. Lanc.* 10 E. 3. fol. 172. *Itiner. Pick.* But Sir *Henry Spelman* thinks it more properly signifies *Windfaln-wood*, because of old written *Cadibulum*, from *Cadere*.

Caballa, Belonging to a Horse, from the Latine word *Caballus* : *Doomsday*, Mr. *Agar*.

Cabo de bona Esperanza. See *cape de bona Esperanza.*

Cade, Of Herrings is 500; of Sprats 1000. Book of Rates, *fol.* 45.

Calamus, Is a Cane, Reed, or Quill, the divers kinds whereof you have in *Gerards Herbal, lib.* 1. *cap.* 24. This is comprised among Merchandise, and Drugs to be garbled, by 1 *Jac. cap.* 19.

Calendring of Worsteds, Spoken of 5 *H.* 8. *cap.* 4. and 35 *H.* 8. *cap.* 5. It signifies to Smooth, Trim, and give them a Gloss; and is a Trade used both in *London* and *Norwich*.

Calangium, Challenge, Claim, or Dispute : *Sciant, &c. quod ego* Godefridus, &c. *dedi, &c. sine aliqua reclamatione seu* calangio, *&c. Boscum qui fuit in* calangio *inter ipsum &* Walterum, Mon. Ang. 2. par. fol. 252. b.

Calcetum & Calceata, A Cawsey or Cawseway; perhaps so called *quia pedibus calcatur.*

Calends, *Calendæ*, Was among the *Romans* the first day of every Month, to which if we add *Pridie*, it is the last day of every Month, as *Pridie Calend Septem.* is the last of *August*; if any number be set before it, as *Decimo, Nono, Octavo,&c. calend. Sept.* is the 22, 23, 24. of *Aug.* In *March, May, July* and *October*, the *Calends* begin at the Sixteenth day, in other Months at the Fourteenth; and they must ever bear the name of the Month following, and be numbred backwards from the first day of the said following Months. See more in *Hoptons Concordance, pag.* 69. See also *Ides* and *Nones*. *Dictum de Kenelworth* is dated the day before the *Calends* of *November*, 1256. In the Dates of Deeds, the day of the Month by *Nones, Ides* and *Calends*, is sufficient, 2. *Inst. fol.* 675.

Campe-fight. See *Champion*, and 3. *Inst. fol.* 221.

Candlemass-day, The Feast of the Purification of the Blessed Virgin *Mary*, *February* the Second, and instituted in the Memory and Honour of the Purification of the said Virgin, being the fortieth day after her happy Child-birth, according to the Law of *Moses*, *Levit.* 12. 6. It is nominated *Candlemas*, because, before Mass, that day is said to be consecrated, and set apart for sacred use, *Candles* for the whole year, and made a Procession with some of the said hallowed *Candles*, in Memory of the Divine Light, wherewith Christ inlightned the Church, at his presentation in the Temple, when by old *Simion* entitled, *A Light to lighten the Gentiles*, as it is in the Gospel of St. *Luke*, *cap.* 2. *vers.* 32. This is no day in Court, for the Judges sit not, and is the Grand Day in that Term of all the Inns of Court.

Cantel, Seems to signifie the same with that we now call *Lumpe*, as to buy by Measure, or by the *Lumpe*. See *Polton, temps, H.* 3. *E.* 1. or *E.* 2. *cap.* 4. & 9. It signifies also a piece of any thing, as a *Cantel* of Bread, Cheese, and the like.

Cantred, Is as much in *Wales* as an Hundred in *England*; for *Cantre* in the Brittish-tongue signifieth *centum*, the word is used, 28 *H.* 8. 3.

Capacity, *Capacitas*, An ability or fitness to receive : In Law it signifies, when a Man, or Body Politick, is able to give or take Lands, or other things, or to sue Actions. As an Alien born, hath a sufficient *capacity* to sue in any personal Action, but in a real Action it is a good Plea to say, *He is an Alien born*; and pray, *If he shall be answered*, Dyer, fol. 3. pla. 8. If a Man enfeoff an Alien and another Man, to the use of themselves, or, &c. it seems that the King shall have the moiety of the Land for ever, by reason of the *incapacity* of the Alien, *Dyer, fol.* 283. *pla.* 31. By the Common-Law, no Man hath *capacity* to take Tythes, but Spiritual Persons, and the King, who is a Person mixt; our Law allowing him two *capacities*, a Natural and a Politick. But a Layman, who is not *capable* of taking Tithes, was yet *capable* to discharge Tithes in the Common-Law in his own Land, as well as a Spiritual Person. See *Co. lib.* 2. *fol.* 44.

Cape de bona Speranza, Or the *Cape of Good Hope*, a Promontory that lies in *Africa*, within the Tropick of *Capricorne*, on the edge of *Ethiopia* inferior, and first discover'd by the *Portuguese*, under the Command of *Bartholomew Dyas*. See *Speeds* Map of *Asia*, in his *Theatr. Brit.* It is mentioned in the Statute, 12 *Car.* 2. *cap.* 18.

Cape, Is a Writ Judicial, touching plea of Land or Tenements, so termed (as most Writs be) of that word in it self, which beareth the chiefest end and intention thereof. And this is divided into *Cape Magnum & cape parvum*, both which (as is before said in *Attachment*) take hold of things immovable, and seem to differ between

them-

themselves in these Points; First, Because *Cape magnum*, or the *Grand Cape*, lieth before appearance, and *Cape parvum* afterwards. Secondly, The *Cape magnum* summoneth the Tenant to answer to the Default, and over to the Demandant. *Cape parvum* summoneth the Tenant to answer to the Default only, and therefore is called *Cape parvum*, or in the *French English*, *Petit Cape*, Old Nat. Brev. fol. 161. 162. Yet *Ingham* saith, That it is called *Petit Cape*, not because it is of small force, but that it consisteth of few words; *Cape magnum* in the *Old Nat. Brev.* is thus defined, This is a Judicial Writ, and lieth where a man hath brought a *Præcipe quod reddat* of a thing that toucheth Plea of Land, and the Tenant make default at the day to him given in the Writ original, then this Writ shall go for the King, to take the Land into the Kings hands, and if he come not at the day given him by the *Grand Cape*, he hath lost his Land, &c. A President and Form of this Writ, you may see in the *Register Judicial*, *fol.* 2. *b.* It seemeth after a sort to contain in it the effect (*missionis in possessionem & primo & secundo decreto*) among the *Civilians*: For as the first Decree seiseth the thing, and the second giveth it from him that the second time defaulteth in his appearance. So this *Cape* both seiseth the Land, and also assigneth to the Party a farther day of appearance, at which, if he come not in, the Land is forfeited; yet is there difference between these two Courses of the Civil and Canon-Law. First, For that *missio in possessionem* toucheth both movable and immovable Goods, whereas the *Cape* is extended only to immovable. Secondly, That the Party being satisfied of his Demand, the *remanet* is restored to him that defaulted; but by the *Cape*, all is seised without Restitution. Thirdly, *Missio in possess.* is to the use of the Party agent, the *Cape* is to the use of the King: Of this Writ, and the explication of the true force and effect thereof, Read *Bracton*, *lib.* 5. *tract.* 3. *ca.* 1. *num.* 4, 5, 6. See *Cape ad valentiam*.

Cape parvum, In the *Old Nat. Brev. fol.* 162. is thus defined, This Writ lieth in case where the Tenant is summoned in Plea of Land, and cometh at the Summons, and his appearance is of Record; and after he maketh default at the day that is given to him, then shall go this Writ for the King, &c. Of this likewise you may see the Form in the *Register Judicial*, *fol.* 2. Of both these Writs, Read *Fleta*, *lib.* 6. *ca.* 44. *Sect. Magnum & seq.*

Cape ad valentiam, Is a Species of *Cape magnum*, so called of the end whereunto it tendeth. In the *Old Nat. Brev. fol.* 161. 162. it is thus described, This Writ lieth, where any impleaded of certain Lands, and I vouch to warrant another, against whom the Summons *ad Warrantizandum* hath been awarded, and the Sheriff cometh not at the day given, then if the Demandant recover against me, I shall have this Writ against the Vouchee, and shall recover so much in value of the Land of the Vouchee, if he have so much; and if he have not so much, then I shall have execution of such Lands and Tenements as descend unto him in Fee-simple; or if he purchase afterward, I shall have against him a resummons; and if he can say nothing, I shall recover the value. Here note, That this Writ lieth before Appearance.

Capias, Is a Writ of two sorts, one before Judgment, called *Capias ad respondendum*, in an Action personal, where the Sheriff upon the first Writ of Distress returns, *Nihil habet in balliva nostra*, and the other is a Writ of Execution after Judgment, being of divers kinds, *viz. Capias ad satisfaciendum*, *Capias pro fine*, *Capias utlagatum*, *Capias utlagatum & inquiras de bonis & catallis*, *&c.*

Capias ad satisfaciendum, Is a Writ of Execution after Judgment, lying where a man recovers in an Action personal, as Debt or Damages, or *detinue* in the Kings Court; and he against whom the Debt is recovered, and hath no Lands nor Tenements, nor sufficient Goods, whereof the Debt may be levied. For in this Case, he that recovereth, shall have this Writ to the Sheriff, commanding him, that he take the Body of him, against whom the Debt is recovered, and he shall be put in Prison, until satisfaction made.

Capias pro fine, Is, where one being by Judgment fined unto the King, upon some Offence committed against a Statute, doth not discharge it according to the Judgment; for by this is his Body taken and committed to Prison, until he content the King for his Fine, *Coke*, *lib.* 3. *fol.* 12. *a.*

Capias utlagatum, Is a Writ of Execution, which lieth against him that is Outlawed upon any Suit, by which the Sheriff, upon the Receipt thereof, apprehendeth the Party Outlawed, for not appearing upon the *Exigent*, and keepeth him in safe Custody till the return of the Writ, and then bringeth him into Court, there farther to be ordered for his Contempt.

Capias utlagatum & inquiras de bonis & catallis, Is a Writ all one with the former, but it gives a farther power to the Sheriff, besides the apprehension of his Body, to enquire of his Goods and Chattels. The form of all these Writs, see the *Old Nat. Brev. fol.* 154. and see *Termes de la Ley*, *verbo Processe*. Lastly, You may find great variety of this kind in the *Register Judicial*, *verbo Capias*.

Capias in Withernam de averiis, Is a Writ lying for Cattel in *Withernam*, *Reg. Orig. fol.* 82. 83. See *Withernam*.

Capias in Withernamium de homine, Is a Writ that lieth for a Servant in *Withernam*, *Regist. Orig. fol.* 79. 80. See *Withernam*.

Capias conductos ad proficiscendum, Is a Writ that lieth for the taking up such as having received Prest-Money to serve the King, slink away, and come not in at the time: This is an Original Writ directed to the *Sergeant at Arms*, to Arrest and bring them in, having included a Clause of assistance, *Reg. Orig. fol.* 191. 4. *Inst. fol.* 121.

Capite, From *Caput*, the Head; and so *Tenure in Capite*, is to hold of the King, the Head of the Common-Wealth. It is a Tenure that holds immediately of the King, as of his Crown, be it by Knight-service or Soccage, and not of any Honor, Castle or Mannor; and for this it is called a *Tenure*, which holds meerly of the King; For as the Crown is a Corporation, a Seignory in in groſs; ſo the King, who poſſeſſes the Crown, is in the Eye of the Law, perpetually King, never in his Minority, F. N. *B. fol.* 5. Yet a man may hold of the King, and not in *Capite*, that is, not immediately of the Crown in groſs, but by means of ſome Honor, Caſtle, or Manner belonging to the Crown: Of this *Kitchin*, *fol.* 129. ſaith well, That a Man may hold of the King by Knight-ſervice, and not in *Capite*, becauſe it may be he holds of ſome Honor by Knights-ſervice, that is in the Kings hands, by deſcent from his Anceſtors, and not immediately of the King, as of his Crown. And this *Tenure in Capite* is otherwiſe called, Tenure holding of the perſon of the King, *Dyer*, *fol.* 44. *Broke*, *tit.* Tenure, *num.* 65. 99. But this *Tenure* is now aboliſhed, and by 12 *Car.* 2. *ca.* 24. all turned into free and common Soccage.

Captain, alias **Capitayne**, *Capitaneus*, Is one that leadeth, or hath Command of a Company of Soldiers; and is either General, as he that hath the Governance of the whole Hoſt; or eſpecial, as he that leads but one Band. There is another ſort of *Captains*, *Qui urbium præfecti ſunt, quibus plebs ab aliquo ſuperiorum gubernanda committitur.* So we have *Captains* of Caſtles here in *England*, as of *Dover*, the Iſles of *Jerſey*, *Guernſey*, *Wight*, &c.

Caption, *Captio*, When a Commiſſion is executed, and the Commiſſioners names ſubſcribed and returned, that is called the *Caption*.

Capture, *Captura*, A taking, an Arreſt, a Seizure, 14 *Car.* 2. *ca.* 14.

Caput Baroniæ, Is the chief Manſion-Houſe of a Nobleman, which (if there be no Son) muſt deſcend to the eldeſt Daughter, and not be divided.

Careta & Carectata, A Cart or Cartload, *Quinq; Carectatas clauſturæ ad prædictæ terræ clauſturam ſuſtinendam*, Mon. Ang. 2. *par. fol.* 340. *a.*

Caretarius, A Carter. See *Carecta* and *Carreta*.

Carke, Seems to be a quantity of Wooll, whereof thirty make a *Sarpler*, 27 H. 6. cap. 2. See *Sarpler*.

Carno, Is an immunity, as appears in *Cromp. Juriſd. fol.* 191. where it is ſaid, That the Prior of *Malton* made Claim for him and his men to be quit of all Amerciaments within the Foreſt, and alſo to be quit of Eſcapes, and all manner of Gelds, as Foot-gelds, Buckſtalls, Trites, *Carno*, and Summage, &c.

Carpemeales, A courſe ſort of Cloth made in the North of *England*, mentioned 7 *Jac.* 16.

Carreta, alias **Carecta**, Was anciently taken for a Carriage, Cart, or Waine-load; as *Carreta fœni* is uſed in an old Charter, for a load of Hay.

Carracke, alias **Carricke**, Is a Ship of Burthen, and ſo is call'd of the Italian word *Carico* or *Carco*, which ſignifies a Burthen: This word is mentioned in the Star. 2 R. 2. *ca.* 4. and 1 *Jac. ca* 33.

Carroway-ſeeds, alias **Carruway-ſeeds**, Is a Seed ſpringing of the Herb ſo called, of whoſe operation you may read in *Gerards Herbal, lib.* 2. *ca.* 396. It is reckoned among the Merchandiſe, that ought to be garbled, by 1 *Jac. ca.* 19.

Cartell. See *Chartell.*

Carucage, *Carucagium*, As Hidage was a Taxation by Hides of Land, ſo *Carucage* was by *Carucas* of Land, *Mon. Ang.* 1. *par. fol.* 294.

Caruca, A Plough, Mr. *Agar* out of *Doomeſday*.

Carucata, A Plough-land, *Doomeſday*, Mr. *Agar*. It is a certain quantity of Land, by which the Subjects have been ſometimes taxed; whereupon the Tribute levied upon a *Carue* of Land, was called *Caruagium*, *Bracton*, *lib.* 2. *ca.* 26. *num.* 8. & *ca.* 17. It may contain Houſes, Mills, Paſture, Meadow, Wood, &c. *Co.* on *Lit. ſect.* 119. It is ſometime uſed for a Cartload, as *Una carrucata Ligni in Foreſta noſtra*, Mon. Ang. 2. *par. fol.* 311. *Littleton*, *cap. Tenure in Socage*, ſaith, That *ſoca*, *idem eſt quod* Caruca: Yet *Stow* in his *Annals*, *pag.* 271. makes me doubt, where he ſaith, The ſame King *Henry* took *Caruage*, that is to ſay, two Marks of Silver of every Knights Fee towards the Marriage of his Siſter *Iſabella* to the Emperor, where *Caruage* cannot be taken for a Plough-land, except there were ſome other further diviſion, whereby to raiſe of every Plough-land ſo much, and ſo conſequently of every Knights Fee, that is, of every 680 Acres, two Marks of Silver. *Raſtal*, in his *Expoſition of words*, ſaith, That *Carvage* is to be quit, if the King ſhall Tax all the Land by *Carues*, that is, a Priviledge, whereby a man is exempted from *Carvage*. *Skene de verbor.* Signif. *verb.* Carucata *terræ*, deriveth it from the French *Charrow* (more truly *Charrue*) a Plough, and ſaith, That it contains ſo great a portion of Land as may be tilled and laboured in a year and a day with one Plough; which alſo is called *Hilda*, or *Hida terræ*, a word frequently uſed in the *Britain Laws*. *Lambert* among his Precedents, towards the end of his *Eirenarcha*, tranſlates *Carucatam terræ*, a Plough-land. The word *Carve* is mentioned in the Statute *Of Wards and Reliefs*, made 28 *E.* 1. And in *Magna Charta*, cap. 5. See *Co.* on *Lit. fol.* 69. *a.*

Carvage, *Carvagium.* See *Carucata.*

Caſſatum & Caſſata, By the Saxons called *Hide*; by *Bede*, *familia*, is a Houſe with Land ſufficient to maintain one Family.

Caſſia fiſtula, Is a Tree that beareth black, round, and long Cods, wherein is contained a pulpe, ſoft and pleaſantly ſweet, ſerving for many uſes in Phyſick. This Tree, with the Vertues, you may find deſcribed in *Gerards Herbal*, lib. 3. cap. 77. The Fruit is mentioned in the Statute 1 *Jac. cap.* 19. among the Drugs and Spices to be garbled.

Caſſia lignea, Is a ſweet Wood, not unlike to *Cynamon*, whereof you may read in *Gerards Herbal*, lib. 1. cap. 19. and compriſed among Merchandiſe to be garbled.

Caſtell, *Caſtellum*, Is well known. In the time of *Henry* the Second, there were in *England* 1115 *Caſtles*, every *Caſtle* contains a Mannor; ſo that the Conſtable of a *Caſtle*, is the Conſtable of a Mannor, 2. *par. Inſt. fol.* 31.

Caſtellaine, *Caſtellanus*, Is a Keeper or Captain,

Captain, sometimes called a *Constable of a Castle*, *Bract. lib.5. tract.2. cap.16. & lib. 2. cap.32 num.2.* In like manner it is used, 3 *E.1. cap 7.* In the Books *De Feudis* you shall find *Guastaldus* to be almost of the same signification, but something more large, because it is also extended to those that have the Custody of the Kings Mansion-houses, called of the *Lombards, Curtes, in* English *Courts*, though they be not places of Defence or Strength. *Manwood* in his *Forest Laws* saith, That there is an Officer of the Forest called *Castellanus*.

Castleward, *Castelgardum, vel wardum Castri*, Is an Imposition laid upon such of the Kings Subjects as dwell within a certain compass of any Castle, towards the maintenance of such as do Watch and Ward the *Castle*, Mag. Chart. *cap.* 20. and 32 *H.* 8. *cap.* 48. It is used sometime for the very Circuit it self, which is inhabited by such as are subject to this Service, as in *Stowes Annals, pag.* 632. And there to take *Castleward*, viz. *De qualibet districtione infra feodum ipsius ducis ad* Castellum *de* Halton, *ducti & ibidem una de causa, si per solam noctem pernoctaverit, quatuor denarios*, Pl. apud Cestr. 31 E. 3.

Casu consimili, Is a Writ of Entry granted where the Tenant by Curtesie, or Tenant for terme of Life, or for the Life of another, doth alien in Fee, or in Tayle, or for terme of anothers Life. And it hath the Name of this for that the Clerks of the *Chancery* did, by their Common consent, frame it to the likeness of the Writ called *In casu proviso*, according to their authority given them by the Stat. *West.* 2. *cap* 24. which, as often as there chanceth any new Case in *Chancery*, something like to a former Case, and yet not especially fitted by any Writ, licenceth them to lay their Heads together, to frame a new form answerable to the new Case, and as like some former Case, as they may. And this Writ is granted to him in the Reversion against the Party to whom the said Tenant so alienateth to his prejudice, and in the life-time of the said Tenant. The form and effect whereof read more at large in *F. N. B, fol.* 206.

Casu proviso, Is a Writ of Entry given by the Statute of *Gloucester, cap* 7. In Case where a Tenant in Dower alieneth in Fee, or for term of Life, or in Tayl, and lieth for him in Reversion against the Alienee, whereof read *F. N. B. fol.* 205

Catalls alias **Chattells**, *Catalla*, Cometh from the *Normans*, for in the Eighty Seventh Chapter of the *Grand Custumary*, you shall find that all moveable Goods with them are called *Chattells*; the contrary whereof is *Fief.ibid.* which we call *Fee*. But as it is used in our Common-Law, it comprehends all Goods moveable and immoveable, but such as are in the nature of Freehold, or parcel thereof, as may be gather'd out of *Stamf. Prærog. cap.* 16. And *Anno* 1 *Eliz. cap.* 2. Howbeit *Kitch.* in his Chapter *Catalla fo.* 32. saith, That ready Money is not accounted any Goods or *Chattells*, nor Hawks nor Hounds; the reason for Hawks and Hounds he gives, is, because they are *Feræ naturæ*; but why Money is not, though he set not down the cause, yet it may be gathered to be, for that Money of it self is not of worth, but as by consent of men for their easier traffick, or permutation of things necessary for life. It is reckoned a thing rather consisting in imagination, than in Deed. And here note, That *Chattells* be either *personal* or *real*: *Personal* may be so called in two respects, one, because they belong immediately to the person of a man; as a Bow, a Horse, &c. the other, for that being any way with-held injuriously from us, we have no means to recover them but by personal Action: *Chattells real* be such, as either do not appertain to the person, but to some other thing by way of dependency, as a Box with Charters of Land; the Body of a Ward, Apples upon a Tree, or a Tree it self growing on the Ground, *Cromp. Justice of Peace, fol.* 33. *b.* or else such as are necessary, issuing out of some immoveable thing to a person, as a Lease or Rent for term of years. And also to hold at will is a *Chattell real, Termes de la Ley, verbo* Chattel. The *Civilians* Comprehend these things, as also Lands of what kind or holds soever, under *bona*; *bona autem dividuntur in mobilia & immobilia, mobilia verò in ea quæ se movent vel ab aliis moventur*, V. legem. 49. & l. 208. *de verb.* Signif. *& interpretes ibidem. Bracton* also *cap* 3. *lib.* 5. *num.* 3. *&* 4. seemeth to be of the same Judgment.

Catallis captis, nomine districtionis, Is a Writ that lyeth within a Borough, or within a House, for Rent going out of the same, and warranteth a Man to take the Doors, Windows or Gates for Rent, *Old Nat. Brev. fol.* 66.

Catallis reddendis, Is Writ which lyeth where Goods being delivered to any man to keep until a certain day, and be not upon demand delivered at a day. And it may be otherwise called a *Writ of Detinue*. See more of it *Reg. Orig. fol.* 139. and *Old Nat. Brev. fol.* 63. This is answerable to *actio depositi* in the Civil-Law.

Catchpole, Though it now be used as a word of contempt, yet in ancient times it seemeth to have been used without Reproach; for such as we now call *Sergeants of the Mace*, or any other that use to arrest Men upon any cause, 25 *E.* 3. *Stat.* 4. *cap.* 2. *Hospitalarii tenent in* Hereford *unum Messuagium quod* Philippus *filius Odonis tenuit per Serjeantiam*, Chachepollii, *quod eis legavit in puram Eleemosynam*, Rot. *de Serjeantiis in* Heref. *temp.* H. 3. *in custod* Camerar. Scaccar.

Cathedral, See *Church*.

Cathedraticke, *Cathedraticum*, Is a sum of two Shillings paid to the Bishop by the Inferior Clergy, *In argumentum subjectionis & ob honorem* Cathedræ. See Hist. of *Procurations* and *Synodalls*, *pag.* 82.

Caulceis, 6 *H.* 6. *cap.* 5. *Causyes*, 1 E. 4. 1. Perhaps it should be written *Causewayes*, from the old French word *Cauz*, now *Caillon*, a Flint or other Stone; in Latine *Calceta*,--- *pro ponte & calceto reparand. Pat.* 18 *H.* 6. *p.* 2. *m.* 22. Sometimes it may be written *Calceya*, *Casea*, and *Calsetum*, in old Records.

Causam nobis significes, Is a Writ which lyeth to a Mayor of a Town or City, &c. that formerly by the Kings Writ being commanded to give Seisin unto the Kings Grantee of any Lands or Tenements, doth delay so to do, willing him to shew cause why he so delayeth the performance of his Charge, *Co. lib.* 4. *casu* Communalty *de* Sadlers. *fol.* 55. *b.*

Causa Matrimonii prælocuti, Is a Writ which

which lies in case where a Woman giveth Lands to a Man in Fee-simple, to the intent he shall marry her, and refuseth so to do in reasonable time, being required thereunto by the Woman; the form and other use thereof, see *Reg. Orig. fol.* 233. and *F. N. B.* 205.

Cautione admittenda, Is a Writ that lyeth against the Bishop, holding an Excommunicate person in prison for his Contempt, notwithstanding that he offereth sufficient Caution or Pledges to obey the Commandments and Orders of Holy Church from henceforth. The form and effect whereof you may find in *Reg. Orig. pag.* 66. and *F. N. B fol.* 63.

Caya, A Key or Waterlock, from the Saxon Cæg. See *Kay*.

Ceapgilde, A word derived from the Saxon *Ceap*, signifying *pecus*, Cattel and *Gild*, *solutio*, that is, *solutio pecudis*, from this Saxon word *Gild*, haply we may have our common English word *yield*, as *yield* or *pay*.

Cellerarius, alias **Cellarius**, Was the *Butler* in a Monastery: In the Universities of *England* they are sometimes called *Manciple*, sometimes *Caterer* and *Steward*.

Censarii, Such as might be taxed, *Doomesday*.

Century. See *Hundred*.

Cepi corpus, Is a Return made by the Sheriff, that upon a *Capias*, *Exigend*, or other Process, hath taken the Body of the Party, *F. N. B. fol.* 26.

Cerage, *Ceragium*. See *Waxshot*.

Cert Money, *Quasi certa Moneta*, The Head peny, or common Fine, yearly given by the Resiants and Tenants of several Mannors to the ancient Records, is called *Certum Leta*. See *Common Fine*.

Certiorari, Is a Writ out of the *Chancery* to an Inferior Court, to call up the Records of a Cause therein depending, that conscionable Justice may be therein administred upon Complaint made by Bill, that the Party which seeketh the said Writ, hath received hard dealing in the said Court, *Termes de Ley*. See the divers Forms and Uses of this, *F N. B. fol.* 242. as also the *Register* both *Original* and *Judicial* in the Tables *verbo* Certiorari, *Crompton* in his *Justice of Peace*, *fol.* 117. saith, That this Writ is either returnable in the *Kings Bench*, and then hath these words, *Nobis mittatis*, or in the *Chancery*, and then hath in *Cancellaria Nostra*, or in the *Common Bench*, and then hath *coram Justiciariis nostris de Banco*. The word *Certiorari* is used divers times in the digest of the Civil-Law; but our later Criticks think it so barbarous, that they suspect it to be rather foysted in by *Tribonian*, than to be originally used by those men of whose works the said *Digest* is compiled: *Prateus in suo Lexico*.

Certificat, *Certificatorium*, Is used for a writing made in any Court, to give notice to another Court of any thing done therein. As for example, A *Certificate* of the Cause of Attaint, is a transcript made briefly, and in few words, by the *Clerk of the Crown*, *Clerk of the Peace*, or *Clerk of Assize*, to the Court of the *Kings Bench*, containing the tenor and effect of every Indictment, Outlawry, or Conviction, and Clerk attainted, made or pronounced in any other Court, 34 *H.* 8. 14. Or this, see more in *Certificat d'Evesq*; *Bro. f.* 119.

Certification of Assise of Novel Disseisin, &c. *Certificatio Assisæ Novæ Disseisinæ*, &c. Is a Writ granted for the reexamining or review of a matter passed by *Assise* before any Justices, and is called *Certificatio Novæ Disseisinæ*, *Old Nat. Brev. fol.* 181. Of this, see also *Reg. Orig. fol.* 200. and the *New Book of Entries* verb. *Certificate of Assise*. This word hath use, where a man appearing by his Bayliff to an Assise brought by another, hath lost the day, and having something more to plead for himself, as a Deed of Release, &c. which the Bayliff did not, or might not plead for him, desireth a farther examination of the Cause, either before the same Justices or others, and obtaineth Letters Patents to them to that effect. The form of these Letters Patents, you may see *F. N. B. fol.* 181. and that done, bringeth a Writ to the Sheriff, to call both the Party for whom the *Assise* passed, and the Jury that was empannelled upon the same, before the said Justices at a certain day and place: And it is called a *Cerificate*, because in it there is mention made to the Sheriff, that upon the Parties Complaint of the defective examination, or doubts, yet remaining upon the *Assise* passed, the King hath directed his Letters Patents to the Justices for the better certifying of themselves, whether all points of the said *Assise* were duly examined. See farther, *Old Nat. Brev.* and F. N. *b. ubi supra.* Of this you may also read *Bract. lib.* 4. *cap.* 19. *num.* 4. *in fine* & 5. 6. where he discusseth the reason of this Point very learnedly. And lastly, *Horne* in his *Mirror of Just. lib.* 3. *cap. final. sect. en ayde des memoyres*, &c.

Certificando de recognitione stapulæ, Is a Writ directed to the Mayor of the *Staple*, &c. commanding him to certifie the Chancellor of a Statute of the *Staple*, taken before him between such and such, in case where the party himself detaineth it, and refuseth to bring it in, *Reg. Orig. fol* 152. *b.* In like manner may be said of *Certificando de statuto mercatorio*, Eod. fol 148. And *de certificando in cancellarium de inquisitione de idemptitate nominis*, fol. 195. And *certificando quando recognitio*, &c. And *certificando quid actum est de brevi super statutum mercatorium*, fol. 151. And *certificando in loquela Warrantiæ*. fol. 12.

Cervisarii, The Saxons had a Duty called *Drinckleum*, that is, *retributio potus*, Canutus *Laws*, *cap.* 8. 28. 38. whereupon such Tenants may be called *Carvisarii*, *Doomesday*, Mr. *Agar*.

Cessor, Is he that ceaseth or neglecteth so long to perform a Duty belonging unto him, as that by his *cesse* or *cessing*, he incurreth the danger of Law, and hath or may have the Writ *Cessavit* brought against him, *Old Nat. Brev. fol.* 136. And note, that where it is said in divers places, *The Tenant cesseth*, without any more words, that is to be understood, the Tenant *cesseth* to do that which he ought, or is bound to do by his Land or Tenement.

Cessavit, Is a Writ that lyes in divers Cases, as appeareth by *F. N. B. fol.* 280. upon this general ground, that he against whom it is brought hath for two years neglected to perform such Service, or to pay such Rent as he is tyed to by by his Tenure, and hath not upon his Land or Tenement sufficient Goods or Chattels to be distrained. Consult more at large *F. N. B.* 280. *Fleta, lib.* 5. *cap.* 34. *sect. visa sunt. Termes de Ley.* See *Cessavit de Cantaria*, Reg. Orig. 238. *Cessavit de feodi firma*, Reg, Orig. 237. *Cessavit per biennium, ibid.* See the *New Book of* Entries, *verbo* Cessavit.

Cesses, By 22 *H.* 8. *cap.* 3. Seems to signifie Assessment or Taxes: *Cesse* or *Ceasse* in *Ireland* is an exaction of Victuals at a certain rate for the Deputies Family, and the Souldiers in Garrison. See the Earl of *Straffords* Tryal.

Cession, Is when an Ecclesiastical person is created Bishop, or when a Parson of a Parsonage takes another Benefice without Dispensation, or otherwise not qualified, &c. In both cases their first Benefices are become void, and are said to become void by *Cession*: And to those that he had who was created Bishop, the King shall present for that time, whoever is Patron of them; and in the other case the Patron may present.

Cessure or **Cesser**, Is likewise taken to signifie a giving over, or giving of place, *Westm.* 2. *cap.* 41.

Cestui qui vie, Is in true French *Cestuy a vie de qui*, that is, he for whose life any Land or Tenement is granted, *Perkins Grants*, 97.

Cestui que use, *Ille cujus usui vel ad cujus usum*, is broken French, and this may be better modelled (*Cestui al use de qui*) It is an ordinary speech among Lawyers, signifying him to whose *use* any other man is enfeoffed in any Lands or Tenements. See the *New Book of Entries*, *verbo* Uses, and in *Replevin*, *fol.* 508. *col.* 3. *verbo* Trespass, *fol.* 606. & 123. *col.* 3. *num.* 7. And see 1 *R.* 3. *cap.* 1. and *Co. lib.* 1. *fol.* 133. *Anno* 12 *Car.* 2. *cap.* 30.

Cestui qui trust, Is he who hath a *trust* in Lands or Tenements committed to him, for the benefit of another, 12 *Car.* 2. *cap.* 30.

Chafewax, Is an Officer in Chancery, that fitteth the *Wax* for the sealing of the Writs, and such other Instruments as are there made to be sent out. This Officer is borrowed from the French, for there *calefactores ceræ sunt qui Regiis literis in cancellaria ceram imprimunt:* Corasius.

Chaffers, Seem to signifie Wares or Merchandise, 3 *E.* 4. 4. and we yet use *chaffering* for buying and selling.

Chaldron, or **Chaldern of Coals**, Contains thirty six Bushels of Coals, heaped up, and according to the sealed Bushel kept at *Guild-hall, London*, for that purpose, 16, 17 *Car.* 2, *cap.* 2. It is written *Chawdren*, 9 *H.* 5. 10.

Challenge, *Calumnia*, Cometh of the French word *Chalenger*, that is, *sibi asserere*, and in a legal sence signifies an exception taken either against persons or things; Persons, as in Assise to the Jurors, or any one or more of them; or in a case of Felony by a Prisoner at the Bar, *Smith de Rep. Ang. lib.* 2. *cap.* 12. *Britton*, *cap.* 52. *Bracton*, *lib.* 2. *tract.* 2. *cap.* 22. Against things, as a Declaration, *Old Nat. Brev. fol.* 76. *Challenge* made to the Jurors, is either made to the *Array*, or to the *Polles*: *Challenge* to the *Array*, is when the whole number is excepted against as partially empannelled; *Challenge* to or by the *Polle*, when some one or more are excepted against as not indifferent, *Termes de la Ley.* *Challenge* to the Jurors is also divided into *Challenge principal*, and *Challenge per cause*, that is, upon Cause or Reason. *Challenge principal* (otherwise by *Stamf. pl. cor. fol.* 157, 158. called *Peremptory*,) is that which the Law alloweth without cause alledged, or farther examination, *Lamb Eiren. lib* 4. *cap.* 14. as a Prisoner at the Barr, arraigned upon Felony, may peremptorily *challenge* to the number of twenty, one after another, of the Jury empannelled upon him, alledging no cause, but his own dislike, and they shall be still put off, and new taken in their Places. But in case of High-Treason, no *Challenge peremptory* is allowed, 33 *H.* 8. 23. *Fortescue* saith, That a Prisoner in this case may *challenge* thirty five men, *cap.* 27. but that Law was abridged by 25 *H.* 8. *cap.* 3. And here observe, That there is some difference, *Challenge principal* and *Challenge peremptory*; *peremptory* being used only in matters Criminal, and alledged without other cause than barely the Prisoners fancy, *Stamf. pl. cor. fol.* 124. But *principal* in civil Actions for the most part, and with naming some such cause of exception, as being found true, the Law alloweth, without farther scanning: For example, If either Party say, that one of the Jurors is the Son, Brother, Cousin, or Tenant to the other, or espoused his Daughter; this exception is good and strong enough, if it be true, without farther examination of the Parties Credit; and how far this *Challenge* upon Children reacheth, you have a notable example in *Plowden*, in the Case of *Vernon* against *Mannors*, *fol.* 425. Also in the plea of the death of a Man, and in every Action real, as also every Action personal, where the Debt or Damages amount to forty Marks, it is a good *challenge* to any man, that he cannot dispend forty shillings by the year of Free-hold, 11 *H.* 7. *cap.* 21. The ground of this *challenge* you may see farther in *Fleta*, *lib.* 4. *cap* 8. *Challenge* upon reason or cause, is when the Party doth alledge some such exception against one or more of the Jurors, as is not forthwith sufficient upon acknowledgment of the truth thereof, but rather arbitrable and considerable by the rest of the Jurors: As for example, If the Son of the Juror have marryed or espoused the Daughter of the adverse party, *Termes de la Ley*, *verbo* Challenge. This *Challenge per cause*, seems by *Kitchin*, *fol.* 92. to be termed *Challenge for favor*, or rather *Challenge for favour* is said there to be one species of *Challenge per cause*, where you may read what *Challenges* be commonly accounted *principal*, and what not. See the *New Book of Entries*, *verbo* Challenge, and the *Old Nat. Brev. fol.* 158. 159. That this word *Challenge* is turned into Latine by the word *Calumnia*, appeareth by *Bracton*, *lib.* 3. *tract.* 2. *cap.* 18. & *lib.* 4. *tract.* 3. *cap.* 6. & *lib.* 5. *cap.* 6. See farther *Fleta*, *lib.* 1. *cap.* 32. *Co.* on *Lit.* 156. 157, &c. and *calangium.*

Chamberdekins or **Chaumberdakins**, Were *Irish* Beggars, which by the Statute of 1 *H.* 5. *cap.* 8. were by a certain time, within the said Statute limited to avoid this Land, *Termes de la Ley*, *fol.* 114.

Chamberer, Is used for a *Chamber-Maid*, 33 *H.* 8. *cap.* 21.

Chamberlain, *Camerarius*, Cometh of the

the French *Chambellan*, that is, *cubicularius vel præfectus cubiculi*: It is diverſly uſed in our Chronicles, Laws and Statutes, as *Lord Great Chamberlain of England*, *Lord Chamberlain of the Kings Houſe*, *the Kings Chamberlain*, 13 E. 1. cap. 41. and 17 R. 2. cap. 16. To whoſe Office it eſpecially appertaineth to look to the Kings *Chambers* and Wardrobe, and to govern the under-ſervants belonging to the ſame, *Fleta, lib. 2. cap. 6. 7. Chamberlain* of any of the Kings Courts, 7. E. 6. 1. *Chamberlain* of the Exchequer, 51 *H.* 3. *Stat.* 5. 10. *E.* 3. 11. 14 *E.* 3. 14. 26 *H.* 8. 2. *Chamberlain* of *North-Wales*, *Stow pag.* 641. *Chamberlain* of *Cheſter*, Cromp. Jur. *fol.* 7. and *Chamberlain* of *London*. This Officer is commonly the Receiver of all Rents and Revenues belonging to that City whereto he is *Chamberlain*. *Vide Fleta, lib. 2. cap.* 70. To the *Chamberlain* of *Cheſter*, when there is no Prince of *Wales* and Earl of *Cheſter*, belongs the receiving and returning of all Writs coming thither out of any the Kings Courts. The Latine word ſeemeth to expreſs the Function of this Officer, for *Camerarius dicitur a camera*, i. *Teſtudine ſive fornice, quia cuſtodit pecunias quæ in cameris præcipue reſervantur*, *Onuphrius de interpret. voc. Eccleſ.* It ſeemeth to be borrowed from the *Feudiſts*, who define the word *Camera* thus, *Camera eſt locus in quem theſaurus colligitur, vel conclave in quo pecunia reſervatur.* Zaſius de Feudis, par. 4. num. 7. And *Peregrinus de jure Fiſci*, lib. 6. tit. 3. ſaith, That *Camerarius vel* Chamberlingus (*quem Quæſtorem antiqui appellarunt*) *in rebus fiſci primum locum tenet, quia Theſaurarius & cuſtos eſt publicæ pecuniæ*. There be two Officers of this Name in the Kings Exchequer, who were wont to keep a Controulment of the *Pelle of Receipt* and *Exitus*, and kept certain Keys of the Treaſury and Records: They kept alſo the Keys of that Treaſury, where the Leagues of the Kings Predeceſſors, and divers ancient Books, as *Doomſday*, and the *Black Book* of the *Exchequer* ramain. There is mention of this Officer in the Stat. 34 & 35 *H.* 8. *cap.* 16. There be alſo *Under-Chamberlains* of the Exchequer, which ſee in *Under-Chamberlain*.

Champarty, (*Cambi partia*) alias *Champerty*, Seemeth to come from the French *Champert*, *Vectigal*, and ſignifieth in our Common Law a Maintenance of any Man in his Suit depending, upon condition to have part of the things (be it Lands or Goods) when it is recovered, *F. N. B. fol.* 171. This ſeems to have been an ancient grievance in our Realm, for notwithſtanding the Statutes of 3 *E.* 1. 25. 13 *E.* 1. 49. 28 *E.* 1. 11. 33 *E.* 1. *Stat.* 2. & 3. and 1 R. 2. *cap.* 4. and a form of a Writ framed unto them; Yet *Anno* 4. *E.* 3. 11. it was again Enacted, That whereas the former Statute provided redreſs for this in the Kings Bench only, (which at that time followed the Court) from thenceforth it ſhould be lawful for Juſtices of the Common-Pleas likewiſe, and Juſtices of Aſſiſes, in their Circuits, to inquire, hear and determin this and ſuch like Caſes, as well at the Suit of the King, as of the Party. How far this Writ extendeth, and the divers forms thereof applyed to ſeveral Caſes, ſee in *F. N. B fol.* 171. *Reg Orig fol.* 183. and the *New Book of Entries, verbo* Champerty, every *Champerty* implieth Maintenance, *Cromp. Jur. fol.* 39. See alſo *Cromp. Juſt. of Peace. fol.* 155. 2. *par. Inſt. fol.* 208. But every Maintenance is not *Champerty*, for *Champerty* is but a *Species* of Maintenance, which is the *Genus*. The word *Champerty* ſeems very ſignificantly to derive it ſelf from *campus* a Field, and *partitio* a dividing; becauſe the Parties in *Champerty* agree to divide the thing in diſpute.

Champertors, *Vel campi participes ſunt qui per ſe, vel per alios placita movent, vel movere faciunt & ea ſuis ſumptibus proſequuntur ad campi partem, vel pro parte lucri habenda*, 33 E. 1. Stat. 2. Artic. ſuper Chart. cap. 11. Alſo it was Ordained by the Stat. 33 *H.* 8. confirmed by 37 *H.* 8. 7. That Juſtices of Peace, at their Quarter-Seſſions, ſhould have authority as well by the Oaths of twelve Men, as by the Information of any other perſon to inquire of the Offendors and Offences againſt the Laws and Statutes made and provided touching *Champerty*, *Maintenance*, &c. *Termes de la Ley, fol.* 114, 115.

Champion, (*Campio*) Is thus defined by *Hottoman*, *In verbis feudalibus: Campio eſt certator pro alio datus in duello, a campo dictus, qui circus erat decertantibus definitus*; and therefore called *Campefight*. In the Common-Law, it is taken no leſs for him that tryeth the Combat in his own caſe, than for him that fighteth in the Quarrel or Place of another, *Bract. lib.* 3. *tract.* 2. *cap.* 21. *num.* 24. ſeems to uſe this word for ſuch as hold by *Sergeanty*, or ſome Service of another, as *Campiones faciunt Homagium Domino ſuo*, lib. 2. cap. 35. Of this, read more in *Battel* and *Combate*. Alſo in *fol.* 36. of Sir *Edward Biſhes* notes upon *Upton*, you will find, That *Henricus de Ferneberg* for thirty Marks Fee, did by a Charter, under his Seal, covenant to be *Champion* for *Roger Abbot* of *Glaſtonbury*, *Anno* 42 *H.* 3. See 3. *Inſtit. fol.* 221.

Champion of the King, His Office is at the Coronation of our Kings, when the King is at Dinner, to ride armed into *Weſtminſter-hall*, and by a Herald make a Challenge, That if any Perſon ſhall deny the Kings Title to the Crown, he is there ready to defend it; which done, the King drinks to him, and ſends him a gilt Cup with a cover full of Wine, which he hath for his Fee. This Office ever ſince the Coronation of *Richard* the *Second*, when *Baldwin Frevile* laid claim to it, was from him adjudged to his Competitor Sir *Jo. Dymocke*, (both claiming from *Marmion*) and hath ever ſince continued in the Family of the *Dymockes*, who hold the Mannor of *Scrivelsby in Com. Lincoln.* hereditarily from the *Marmions* by *Grand Sergeanty*, Cambd. *in part. fin. Mich.* 1. *H.* 6. and accordingly Sir *Edward Dymocke* performed this Office at his preſent Majeſties Coronation, *April* the 23d. 1661.

Chancellor, *Cancellarius*, Cometh of the French (*Chancelier*) *Vincent Lupanus de magiſtratibus Francorum*, ſaith, That *Cancellarius* is no Latine word, though he citeth Latine Writers that uſe it; with him agrees *Petrus Pithæus, lib. 2. adverſariorum*, cap. 12. And whereas *Lupanus* would derive it from the *verb Cancello*, *Pithæus* thinks he hath ſome (though not ſufficient) colour for his Opinion, and therefore rather deriveth it from *Cancellis*, an incloſed or ſeparated place, a Chancell; or place incompaſſed with bars, to defend the Judges and other Officers from the preſs of the People. *Cancellarius* at firſt, as *Lupanus* thinks

thinks, signified the *Registers* in Court; *Graphari-os, sc. qui conscribendis & excipiendis judicum actis dant operam.* But this Name in our days is highly advanced, and not only in other, but in our Kingdom also, is given to him that is the chief Man for matter of Justice (in private Causes especially) next unto the Prince; for whereas all other Justices are tyed to the Law, and may not swerve from it in Judgment: The *Chancellor* hath in this the Kings absolute Power to moderate and temper the written Law, subjecting himself only to the Law of Nature and Conscience, ordering all things *juxta æquum & bonum.* And therefore *Stamford* in his *Prerogative*, cap. 20. *fol.* 65. saith, That the *Chancellor* hath two Powers, one *absolute*, the other *ordinary*; meaning, that though by his *ordinary* Power, in some Cases, he must observe the form of proceeding as other ordinary Judges; yet that in his *absolute* Power he is not limited by the written Law, but by Conscience and Equity, according to the circumstances of the Matter in question. But how long he hath had this Power, some would doubt; For *Polydore Virgil*, lib. 9. Hist. Ang. hath these Words of *William the Conqueror*, *Instituit item scribarum collegium qui Diplomata scriberent, & ejus collegii Magistrum vocabat* Cancellarium, *qui paulatim supremus factus est Magistratus, qualis hodie habetur.* And see *Fleta*, lib. 2. cap. 13. This high Officer seems to be brought from *France* to us, as many other Officers and Usages be. But Mr. *Dugdale* in his *Origines Judiciales* makes this an Error, giving us a Catalogue of *Chancellors* before that time: He that with us beareth this Magistracy, is called the *Lord Chancellor of England*, *Anno* 7 R. 2. cap. 14. and by the Stat. 5 *Eliz.* cap. 18. the Lord *Chancellor* and *Keeper* have all one Power. He is made by the King, by delivery of the Great Seal to him, and taking an Oath. See *Lord Keeper*. See *Fleta*, lib. 2. cap. 12. 13. And *Co. Inst.* 4. *fol.* 78. 79. There are divers other inferior Officers that be called *Chancellors*, as *Chancellor* of the Exchequer, 25 *H.* 8. 16. whose Office hath been thought by many, to have been created for the qualifying of Extremities in the Exchequer. He sitteth in the Court and the Exchequer-Chamber, and with the rest of the Court ordereth things to the Kings best benefit: He is always in Commission with the Lord Treasurer, for the letting of the Lands that came to the Crown, by the dissolution of Abbeys, and hath by Privy-Seal from the King Power, with others, to compound for Forfeitures of Bonds upon Penal Statutes: He hath also much to do in the Revenue come by the dissolution and First-Fruits, as appears by the Acts of uniting them to the Crown.

Chancellor of the Dutchy of Lancaster, 3 *E.* 6. 1. and 5 *E.* 6. 26. Whose Office is principally in that Court to judge and determine all Controversies between the King and his Tenants of the *Dutchy* Land, and otherwise to direct all the Kings Affairs belonging to that Court.

Chancellor of the Order of the Garter, *Stowes Annals*, 706. *Chancellor* of the University, 9 *H.* 5. 8. 2 *H.* 6. 8. *Chancellor* of the Court of *Augmentations*, 27 *H.* 8. 27. & 32 *H.* 8. 20. & 33 *H.* 8. 39. *Chancellor* of the First-fruits, 32 *H.* 8. 45. *Chancellor* of Courts, 32 *H.* 8. 28 Chancellor of the Diocess, 32 *H.* 8. 15.

Chance-medley, Signifies the casual killing of a Man, not altogether without the Killers Fault, though without an Evil Intent, *Stamf. pl. cor. lib.* 1. *cap.* 8. calls it, *Homicide by Misadventure*, *West. Symb. par.* 2. *Tit.* Indictments, *sect.* 5. calls it, *Homicide mixt.* It is also called *Manslaughter by misadventure*, for which the Offendor shall have his Pardon of Course, as appears by the Statute of 6 E. 1. 9. but here is to be considered whether he that commits this Manslaughter by *Chance-medley* was doing a lawful thing; for if the act were unlawful, it is Felony. As if two are Fighting together, and a third man comes to part them, and is kill'd by one of the two, without any malice fore-thought, or evil intent in him that killed the Man; yet this is Murther in him, and not Manslaughter by *Chance-medley* or Misadventure, because they two that fought together were doing an unlawful act: And if they were met with prepensed Malice, the one intending to kill the other, then it is Murther in them both. See *Skene de verbor signif. verb.* Melletum, where he says this in *Scotland* is called *Chaudmelle.*

Chancery, *Cancellaria*, Is a Court of Equity and Conscience, moderating the rigour of other Courts, that are not strictly tyed to the Letter of the Law, whereof the Lord *Chancellor of England* is the chief Judge, *Cromp. Jur. fol.* 41. Or else the *Lord Keeper of the Great Seal*, 4 Eliz. cap. 18. The Officers belonging to this Court, are, The Chancellor or Keeper of the Broad Seal, twelve Masters of the *Chancery*, whereof some always sit by turns on the Bench, as Assistants; the six Clerks, who have each of them about twenty Clerks under them, in nature of Atturneys in the Court; two chief Examiners, who have each of them several Clerks: One chief Register, who hath usually four or five Deputies: The Clerk of the Crown, the Warden of the Fleet, the Usher, Sergeant at Arms, and Cryer of the Court; the Cursitors and their Clerks, the Clerks of the Petty-Bag, the Clerk of the Hanaper, the Controller of the Hanaper, the Clerk of Appeals, the Clerk of the Faculties, the Sealer, the Chafe-Wax; the Clerk of the Patents, Clerk of Presentations, Clerk of Dismissions, Clerk of Licences to alienate, Clerks of the Enrolments, Clerk of the Protections, Clerk of the *Subpœnas*, Clerk of the *Affidavits*, &c. which see described in their several places, *Co.* 4. *Inst. fol.* 82.

Changer, Is an Officer belonging to the Kings Mint, mentioned in the Statute of 2 *H.* 6. *cap.* 12. where also Written after the old Way *Changour*, whose business was chiefly to exchange Coyn for Bullion brought in by Merchants or others.

Chantry, See *Chauntry*.

Chapel, *Capella*, Cometh of the French *Chapelle*, that is, *ædicula*, and is of two sorts, either adjoyning to a Church as a Parcel, of the same, which Men of Worth do Build, *ut ibidem familiaria Sepulchra sibi constituant*, or else separate from the Mother-Church, where the Parish is Wide, and commonly called a *Chappel of ease*, because it is built for the ease of one or more Parishioners that dwell too far from the Church, and

O served

served by some inferior Curate, provided at the charge of the Rector, or of them that have benefit by it, as the composition or custome is: Whence the word is derived, the *Canonists* differ in Opinion, neither will we trouble our selves about it, since it makes not much to our purpose. There is a free *Chappel*, which seemeth to be such as hath maintenance perpetual towards the upholding thereof, and Wages of the Curate, by some Lands charitably bestowed on it, without the Charge of the Rector or Parish, 37 *H.* 8. *ca.*4 *Anno* 1 *E.* 6. *ca.* 14.

Chapellaine or **Chaplaine**, *Capellanus*, Is he that performeth Divine-Service in a *Chappel*; and therefore in the Common-Law it is used most ordinarily for him that is depending upon the King, or other Man of worth, for the Instructing him and his Family, to Pray and Preach in his private House, where commonly they have a *Chappel* for that purpose, as 21 *H.* 8. 13. where it is set down what persons may priviledge one or more *Chaplains*, to discontinue from their Benefices for their peculiar Service.

Chapelry, (*Capellania*) Is the same thing to a *Chappel*, as a Parish is to a Church. See the Statute of 14 *Car.* 2. *cap.* 9.

Chaperon, A Hood or Bonnet mentioned in the Stat. 1 R. 2. 17. and in Heraldry is that Title *Escutcheon*, which is fixt on the Fore-head of the Horses that Draw a Herse to a Funeral.

Chapiters, *Capitula*, Cometh of the French *Capitre*, i. *caput libri*, It signifies in our Common-Law a Summary, or Content of such matters as are to be enquired of, or presented before Justices in *Eyre*, Justices of *Assise*, or of *Peace* in their Sessions: So it is used *Anno* 3 *E.* 1. *cap.* 27. in these Words, And that no Clerk of any Justice, Escheator or Commissioner in *Eyre*, shall take any thing for delivering *Chapiters*, but only Clerks of Justices in their Circuits. And again, *Anno* 13 *E.* 1. *cap.* 10. in these Words, And when the time cometh, the Sheriff shall certifie the *Chapiters* before the Justices in *Eyre*, how many Writs he hath, and what, &c. *Britton* also useth the word in the same Sense, *chap.* 3. *Chapiters* or *Capitula* be now called *Articles* most ordinarily, and are delivered as well by the Mouth of the Justice in his Charge, as by the Clerks in writing to the Inquest; whereas in ancient times, as appeareth by *Bracton* and *Britton*, they were after an Exhortation given by the Justices for the good observation of the Laws and King's Peace, first read distinctly and openly in the whole Court, and then delivered in Writing to the Grand Inquest. And the same order doth *Lambert* wish to be kept in these days, *Eirenarc. lib.* 4. *cap.* 4. *pag.* 393. *Horne* in his *Mirrour of Justice*, calleth them *Articles*, and expresseth what they were wont to contain, *lib.* 3. *cap. de Articles in Eyre.* An example of these *Chapiters* or *Articles*, you have in the Book of *Assises*, *fol.* 138. *num.* 44. As also in *Roger Hoveden*, *parte poster. suor. annal in Richardo primo*, *fol.* 423.

Chapter, *Capitulum*, Signifieth in our Common-Law (as in the Canon-Law) whence it was borrowed, *Congregationem clericorum in Ecclesia Cathedrali, conventuali, regulari vel collegiata*, & in another sense, *Locum in quo fiunt communes tractatus collegiatorum.* It hath other significations, though not worth the repeating in this place, which you may read in *Linwoods Provincialis Gloss. in ca. Quia incontinentiæ, de constitutionibus verb.* Capitulis. Such a Collegiate company is metaphorically termed *Capitulum*, that is, a little Head, for such a Corporation is a kind of Head, not only to Rule and Govern the Diocess in the Vacation of a Bishoprick, but also in many things to advise the Bishop when the See is full, *Panormitan.* in cap. *Capitulum extra de rescriptis.*

Charre of Lead, A *Charre of Lead* consists of Thirty Pigs, each Pig containing six Stone wanting two Pound, and every stone being twelve pound, *Assisa de ponderibus*, Rob. 3. R. Scot. cap. 22. sect 2.

Charte, *Charta*, Paper, Parchment, or any thing to write on; also a Card which Mariners use at Sea, mentioned 14 *Car.* 2. *cap.* 33. See *Charter.*

Chartel, A Letter of Defiance or Challenge to a Duel, in use heretofore, when Combats were in Practice, to decide difficult, and not otherwise to be determined, Controversies in Law.

Charta Pardonationis se Defendendo, Is the Form of a Pardon, for Slaying another Man in his own Defence, *Reg. Orig. fol.* 287.

Charta Pardonationis utlagariæ, Is the Form of a Pardon for a Man that is Outlawed, *Reg. Orig. fol.* 288, 388.

Charter, *Charta*, French *Charters*, that is, *Instrumenta*: It is taken in our Law for Written Evidence of things done between Man and Man; whereof *Bracton*, *lib.* 2 *cap.* 16. *num.* 1. saith thus, *Fiunt aliquando donationes in scriptis, sicut in* Chartis, *ad perpetuam rei memoriam propter brevem hominum vitam*, &c. and a little after, *num.* 12. *Et sciendum quod* Chartarum *alia Regia, alia privatorum, & regiarum alia privata, alia communis, & alia universalis. Item privatorum alia de Feoffamento puro & simplici, alia de Feoffamento conditionali, & secundum omnia genera Feoffamentorum fieri potest. Item privatorum alia de recognitione pura vel conditionali: Item alia de quiete-clamantia; Item alia de confirmatione*, &c. and so through the whole Chapter. *Britton* likewise in his Thirty Ninth Chapter, divideth *Charters* into the *Charters* of the King, and *Charters* of private persons: *Charters* of the King are those, whereby the King passeth any Grant to any person or more, or to any Body-Politick, as a *Charter* of Exception, that a Man shall not be empannelled upon any Jury, *Kitchin*, *fol.* 114. & *fol.* 177.

Charter of Pardon, Whereby a Man is forgiven a Felony, or other Offence committed against the King's Crown and Dignity, *Bro. tit. Charter of Pardon. Charter of the Forest*, wherein the Laws of the *Forest* are comprised, *Anno* 9 *H.* 3. Cromp. Jur. *fol.* 147. *Pupilla oculi*, par. 5. cap. 22. *Manwood*, par. 1. of his *Forest Laws*, fol. 1. where he setteth down the *Charter* of *Canutus*, and *fol.* 11. where he sets down that which was made, 9 *H.* 3. with the *Charter* of the Forest which we use. *Skene* saith, That the Laws of the Forest in *Scotland* do agree, *De verbo* Signif. *verbo* Venison. *Charter of Land*, *Brooke*, *eodem titulo.* That which we call a *Charter*, the *Lombards in libris Feudalibus*, call

call *Præceptum*, *Præceptionem*, *Hottoman*, *Verbo Præceptum in verbis feudalibus.* Of these *Charters* you have also a long discourse in *Fleta*, *lib.* 3. *cap.* 14. who expoundeth every substantial part of a Deed of Gift particularly in Order. See *Magna Charta.*

Charter-Land, (*Terra per Chartam*) Is such as a Man holdeth by *Charter*, that is, by Evidence in Writing, otherwise called *Freehold*, *Anno* 19 *H.* 7. *cap.* 13. and *Kitchin*, *fol.* 86. And these in the Saxons time were called *Bockland*, which *Lamb.* in his Explication of Saxon Words, *verbo*, Terra *ex scripto* saith, Was held with more commodious and easie Conditions than *Folkland* was, that is, Land held without Writing; and the reason is, because that was *Hæraditaria, libera atq; immunis*, whereas *fundus sine scripto censum pensitabat annuum atq; Officiorum quadam servitute est obligatus; Priorem viri plerunq; nobiles atq; ingenui, posteriorem rustici fere & pagani possidebant.----Illam nos vulgo* Free-hold, & *per* Chartam *hanc ad voluntatem Domini appellamus.* Thus far Mr. *Lambard.*

Charter party, *Charta partita*, A Deed or Writing divided, is only a Paper of Indentures among Merchants and Seafaring-men, containing the Covenants and Agreements made between them touching their Merchandise and Maritime-Affairs, 32 *H.* 8. 14. 12 *Car.* 2. *cap.* 18. *Latches Rep. fol.* 225. *Ballo's* Case, and 2. *Inst. fol.* 637.

Chartis reddendis, Is a Writ which lies against him that hath *Charters of Feoffment* delivered him to be kept, and refuseth to deliver them, *Old Nat. Brev. fol.* 66. *Orig. fol.* 159.

Chase, *Chacea*, Cometh of the French Word *Chasser*, that is, *Sectari Belluas*: It signifies in the Common-Law two things, First, As much as *Actus* in the Civil-Law, that is, a driving of Cattel to or from any place, as to *chase* a Distress to a Fortlet, *Old Nat. Brev. fol.* 45. Secondly, It is used for a Receit for Deer, and Wild Beasts of a middle nature, between a Forest and a Park, being commonly less than a Forest, and not having so many Liberties as the Court of *Attachment*, *Swainemote*, and *Justice-seat*; and yet of a larger compass, and stored with greater diversity both of Keepers and Wild Beasts or Game than a Park. And *Crompton* in his *Jurisdictions*, *fol.* 148 saith, That a Forest cannot be in the hands of a Subject, but it forthwith loseth the Name, and becometh a *Chase*; Yet *fol.* 197. he saith, That a Subject may be Lord and Owner of a Forest, which, though it seem a contrariety, yet are both his sayings in some sort true; for a King may give or alienate a Forest to a Subject, yet so, as when it is once in a Subject, it loseth the true property of a Forest, because that the Courts called a *Justice-seat*, the *Swain mote*, and *Attachment* forthwith do vanish; none being able to make a Lord chief Justice In *Eyre* of the Forest but the King, as *Manwood* well sheweth in his *Forest-Laws*, *cap.* 3. & 4. and yet it may be granted in so large a manner, that there may be *Attachment* and *Swain-mote*, and a Court equivalent to a *Justice-seat*, as appeareth by him in the same Chapter, *num.* 3. So that a *Chase* differeth from a Forest in this, because it may be in the hands of a Subject, which a Forest in his proper and true nature cannot; and from a Park, in that it is not inclosed, and hath not only a larger compass, and more store of Game, but of Keepers also and Officers. See *Forest.*

Chatell, See *Catals.*

Chauncemedley. See *Chance-medley.*

Chaunter *Cantator*, A Singer in the Quire, 13 *Eliz. cap.* 10. At St. *Davids* in *Pembrokeshire*, the *Chaunter* is next the Bishop, for there is no Dean, *Cambd. Britan.*

Chauntry, *Cantaria* Is a Church, or Chappel, endowed with Lands, or other yearly Revenue, for the Maintenance of one or more Priests daily to sing Mass for the Souls of the Donors, and such others as they do appoint, 37 *H.* 8. 4. 1 *E.* 6. 14. and 15 *Car. cap.* 9. Of these *Chantryes* there were Forty seven belonging to St. *Paul's* Church in *London*, for which, see *Dugdales* History of that Church.

Chawdren of Sea-Coals, 9 *H.* 5. 10. See *Chaldron.*

Checkroll, Is a *Roll* or Book containing the Names of such as are Attendants in Pay to great Personages, as their Houshold-Servants, 19 *Car.* 2. *cap.* 1. It is otherwise called *The Checquer-Roll*, *Anno* 24 *H.* 8. 13. 3 *H.* 7. 13. And seems to take its Etymology from the *Exchequer*, which see.

Clerk of the Checke. See *Clerk.*

Chemin. See *Chimin.*

Chensers, Mentioned 27 *H.* 8. *cap.* 7. *Quære* if they be not such as pay Tribute or *Cense*, Chief-rent or Quit-rent, for so the French *Censier* signifies.

Cherset. See *Churchesset.*

Chevage, *Chevagium*, Cometh of the French Word *Cheif*, id est, *caput*: It signifieth with us a Sum of Money paid by Villians to their Lords, in acknowledgment of their Villenage, Whereof *Bracton*, *Lib.* 1. *cap.* 10. saith thus, Chevagium *dicitur recognitio in signum subjectionis & Dominii de capite suo.* It seems also to be used for a Sum of Money yearly given to one by another of Might and Power, for his Avowment, Maintenance and Perfection, as to their Head and Leader, *Lamb. Eirenarch. lib.* 2. *cap.* 5. writeth it *Chivage*, or rather *Cheifage*. *Est apud Wallos* Chevagii *genus quod* Amabr. *vocant*, *Principi walliæ pro maritandis filiabus olim ab omnibus (ut asserunt) hodie a quibusdam etiam liberis persolutum*, says the learned *Spelman* on the Word *Chevagium*, see *Co.* on *Lit. fol.* 140.

Chevisance, Cometh of the French Word *Chevir*, that is, *Venir a cheife de quelque chose*, to come to the head or end of a Business. This Word is used 37 *H.* 8. *cap.* 9. 13 *Eliz. cap.* 5. & 8. 10 *R.* 2. *cap.* 1. & 3 *H.* 7. 5. for a Bargain or Contract. It signifies also an unlawful Contract in point of Usury, spoken of 21 *Jac.* 17. 12 *Car.* 2. *cap.* 13.

Chevitiæ & Chevisæ, Heads of Ploughed-Lands, *Novem Acras Terræ cum* Chevisis *ad ipsas pertinentibus*, Mon. Ang. 2 Par. Fol. 116.

Cheife. See *Capite.*

Cheifage. See *Chevage.*

Chief pledge, (*Plegius, vel vas capitalis,*) 20 H 6.cap 8. For the better understanding of this Word, see *Borow-head.*

Childwit, Is Compounded of two Saxon Words, *Child* and *Wit*; the meaning of the former every one understands; for the latter, see *Bloodwit.* It signifies a power to take a Fine of your Bond-Woman gotten with Child without your consent; Within the Mannor of *Writtle* in *Com. Essex*, every reputed Father of a Bastard gotten there, pays to the Lord for a Fine, three shillings four pence, and the custom is there also called *Childwit.*

Chimin, French *Chemin*, Signifies in Lavv phrase a Way: It is divided into two sorts, The Kings High-Way, and a private Way, *Kitchin, fol.* 35. The Kings High-Way, *Chiminus Regius*, is that by which the Kings Subjects, and all under his Protection, have free Liberty to pass, though the property of the soyl of each side, where the Way lyeth, may perhaps belong to some private man. A Way private is that, by which one man or more have liberty to pass, either by Prescription or by Charter, through another Mans Ground. And this is divided into *Chimin in gross*, and *Chimin appendant*, Kitchin, fol. 117. *Chimin in gross* is that Way which a Man holdeth principally and solely in it self: *Chimin appendant* is that which a Man hath adjoyned to some other thing as appurtenant thereto. For Example, If a Man hire a Close or Pasture, and Covenant for Ingress and Egress to and from the said Close, through some other Ground, by which otherwise he cannot pass: Or *Chimin in gross* may be that, which the *Civilians* call *personal*; as when one Covenanteth for a Way through another Mans Ground for himself and his Heirs: *Chimin appendant* on the other side, may be that which they call *real*; as when a Man purchaseth a Way through another Mans ground, for such as do or shall dwell in this or that House for ever, or be Ovvners of such a Mannor. See *Co.* on *Lit. fol.* 56.

Chiminage, *Chiminagium*, Signifieth a Toll for Wayfarage through the Forest, *Cromp. Jur. fol.* 189. and *Manwoods Forest Law*, p. 86. The *Feudists* call it *Pedagium.* See *Chimin.*

Chimney-Money, Otherwise called *Hearth-money*, by 14 *Car.* 2. *cap.* 12. Every *Fire-Hearth* and *Stove, &c.* (except such as pay not to Church and Poor) shall be chargeable with *Two Shillings per Annum* at *Michaelmas* and *Lady-day* to the King, &c. See *Smoke-money, Hearth-money*, and *Fuage.*

Chirgemote, Circgemot or **Chirchgemot**, A Saxon Word signifying *Forum Ecclesiasticum*; *Quousq;* Chirgemot *discordantes inveniet vel amore congreget, &c.* Leg. H. 1. cap. 8. and 4 *Inst. fol.* 321.

Chirographer of Fines, *Chirographus Finium & Concordiarum*, Cometh of the Greek χειρόγραφον, (a Compound of χείρ, *Manus*, a hand, and γράφω, *Scribo*, to Write,) so that in plain English, it is a Writing of the Hand: It signifies in the Common-Law, that Officer of the Common Pleas who ingrosseth *Fines* in the Court, acknowledged into a perpetual Record, after they be acknowledged and fully passed by those Officers by whom they are formerly examined, and that Writeth and Delivereth the Indentures of them unto the Party, 2 *H.* 3. *cap.* 8. and *West. Symbol. par.* 2. *tit.* Fines, *Sect.* 114. & 129. *F. N. B. fol.* 147. This Officer also maketh two Indentures, one for the Buyer, another for the Seller, and makes one other Indented Piece, containing also the effect of the *Fine*, which he delivereth over to the *Custos Brevium*, that is called *The foot of the Fine.* The *Chirographer* also, or his Deputy, doth Proclaim all the *Fines* in the Court every Term, according to the Statute; and then reparing to the Office of the *Custos Brevium*, there indorseth the Proclamations upon the backside of the Foot thereof; and alway keepeth the Writ of Covenant, as also the Note of the *Fine.*

Chivage. See *Chevage.*

Chivalry, (*Servitium militare*) Cometh of the French *Chevalier*, and signifieth in our Common-Law a Tenure of Land by Knights Service: For the better understanding whereof, it is to be known, That there is no Land, but is holden mediately or immediately of the Crown by some Service, and therefore all our Free-Holds that are to us and our Heirs are called *Feuda* or *Feoda*, Fees; as proceeding from the Benefit of the King, for some small yearly Rent, and the performance of such Services as originally were laid upon the Land at the Donation thereof; for as the King gave to the great Nobles, his immediate Tenants, large Possessions for ever, to hold of him for this or that Service or Rent; and they again in time parcelled out to such others as they liked the same Lands, for Rents and Services, as they thought good. And these Services are by *Littleton* divided into two sorts, *Chivalry* and *Socage*, the former is martial and military, the other clownish and rustical; *Chivalry* therefore is a tenure of Service, whereby the Tenant is bound to perform some noble or military Office unto his Lord; and is of two sorts, either Regal, that is, such as may hold only of the King, or such as may hold of a common person: That which may hold only of the King is properly called *Servitium* or *Sergeantia*, and is again divided into *grand* or *petit*, great or small; Great, commonly called *Grand Serjeanty*, is that where one holdeth Lands of the King by Service, which he ought to do in his own person; as to bear the Kings Banner or his Spear, or to lead his Hoste, or to find a Man at Arms to Fight within the four Seas, &c. *Litl. Tit.* Sergeanty. *Petit Sergeanty*, is where a Man holdeth Land of the King, to yield him annually some small thing towards his Wars, as a Sword, Dagger, Bow, *&c. Littl. tit.* Petit Sergeanty. *Chivalry* that may hold of a common person, is called *Scutagium, Escuage*, that is, Service of the Shield, and this is either uncertain or certain. *Escuage* uncertain is likewise two-fold, First, Where the Tenant is bound to follow his Lord, going in Person, to the Kings Wars against his Enemies, either himself, or to send a sufficient Man in his place, there to be maintained at his Cost so many days, as were agreed upon between the Lord and his first Tenant at the granting of the Fee. And the days of such Service seem to have been rated by the quantity of the Land so holden; as if it extend to a whole Knights Fee, then the Tenant was bound to follow his Lord Forty Days, and a Knights Fee was so much Land,

Land, as in those days was accounted a sufficient living for a Knight, and that was 680 Acres as some hold, or as others 800, or 15 Pounds *per Annum, Cambd. Brit. pag.* 110. Sir *Thomas Smith* saith, *Census equestres* is forty pounds Revenue in Free Lands. But if it extend to half a Knights Fee, then the Tenant is bound to follow his Lord but twenty days; If to a fourth part, then ten days, *F. N. B. fol* 83, 84. The other kind of this *Escuage uncertain* is called *Castleward*, where the Tenant by his Land is bound either by himself or some other, to defend a Castle as often as it shall come to his course. *Escuage certain*, is where the Tenant is set at a certain sum of Money to be paid in lieu of such uncertain Service; as that a man shall pay yearly for every Knights Fee twenty shillings, *Stow Annal. pag.* 238. for half a Knights Fee ten, or some like rate: And this Service, because it is drawn to a certain Rent, groweth to be of a mixt nature; not meerly Socage, for that it smelleth not of the Plough, and yet Socage in effect, being now neither personal service nor uncertain, *Lit. tit.* Socage. This Tenure called *Chivalry*, hath other Conditions annext to it, as *Homage, Fealty, Wardship, Relief*, and *Marriage*, Bract. *lib.* 2. *cap.* 35. which what they signifie look in their places: *Chivalry* is either *general* or *special*, *Dyer, fol.* 161. *num.* 47. *General* seemeth to be, where it is only said in the Feoffment, That the Tenant holdeth *per servitium militare*, without any specification of *Sergeanty, Escuage, &c. Special*, That which is declared particularly, what kind of Knights-Service he holdeth by. But there is a great alteration made in these things by the Statute, made 12 *Car.* 2. *cap.* 24. which saith, All Tenures by Knights-Service of the King, or of any other person, Knights-service *in capite* or *Socage*; *in capite* of the King, and the Fruits and Consequences thereof hapned, or which shall or may happen or arise thereupon, or thereby, are taken away and discharged: And all Tenures of Houses, Mannors, Lands, &c. shall be construed and adjudged to be turned into Free and common Socage, *&c.*

Choral, *Choralis*, Is such a person of whom Mr. *Dugdale* in his Hist. of St. *Pauls* Church, *pag.* 172. says, There were Six, whom he calls *Vicars Chorals*, belonging to that Church, and signifies one that by vertue of any of the Orders of Clergy, was in ancient time admitted to sit and serve God in the Quire, which in Latine is termed *Chorus*.

Chose, *Res*, In French a thing: It is in the Common-Law used with divers *Epithetes* worthy the interpretation; as *Chose local* is such a thing as is annexed to a place: For Example, a Mill is *Chose local, Kitchin, fol.* 18. *Chose transitory*, seemeth to be that thing which is moveable, and may be taken away, or caried from place to place. *Chose in Action*, is a thing incorporeal, and only a Right, as an Annuity, an Obligation of Debt, a Covenant, or Voucher by Warranty, *Bro. tit. Chose in Action*: And it seemeth, that *Chose in Action* may be also called *Chose in suspence*, because it hath no real existence or being, neither can be properly said to be in possession, *Bro. ibid.*

Chop church, *Ecclesiarum permutatio*, Is a word used, 9 *H* 6. 65. As for example, If two Parsons of several Churches change their Benefices, and resign them into the hands of the Ordinary to that intent, and the Patrons make Presentations accordingly, and one of them is admitted, instituted and inducted accordingly, and the other is admitted and instituted, but dyeth before Induction; the other Parson shall not retain the Benefice in which he was inducted, for the change is not perfected, being not executed. By the fore-mentioned Book, it seems, in those days a kind of Trade; yet *Brooke* in his *Abridgement* says, It was only permissible by Law; without peradventure it was a Nickname, for such as used to change Benefices; for we to this present usually say, *To chop and change*. See *Spelm. de conc. vol.* 2. *fol.* 642.

Church-reve, Is the same with *Church-warden*; *Reeve* in the Saxon being as much as Guardian in the French, and signifies the Guardian or Overseer of the Church; as *Shire-Reeve* is the Guardian of the Shire or County, and *Port-Reeve* of the Port or Haven, though afterwards it became a name of Office. The word is now out of use, but used by *Chaucer*, speaking of the Jurisdiction of Archdeacons. See Church-wardens.

Church-wardens, *Ecclesiarum Gardiani* be Officers yearly chosen, by the consent of the Minister and Parishioners, according to the custom of every several place, to look to the *Church, Church-yard*, and such things as belong to both, and to observe the behaviors of their Parishioners for such faults as appertain to the Jurisdiction or Censure of the Court-Ecclesiastical. These be a kind of Corporation, enabled by Law to sue for any thing belonging to their Church, or Poor of their Parish. See *Lamb. Duty of Church-wardens*.

Churchesset, *Ciricsceat*, *Chirset* or *Curcscet*, A Saxon word mentioned in *Doomsday*, and interpreted by Mr. *Agar*, *Quasi Semen Ecclesiæ*, Corn paid to the *Church*. *Fleta* calls it *Circsed, lib.* 1. *cap.* 47. and thereof writes thus, It signifies a certain Measure of Wheat, which in times past every Man on St. *Martins* day gave to the Holy Church as well in times of the *Britains* as of the *English*; yet many great persons after the coming of the *Romans* gave that Contribution, according to the ancient Law of *Moses*, in the name of First-fruits; as in the Writ of King *Canutus* sent to the Pope is contained, in which they call that Contribution, *Chirch-sed*, as one would say *Church-seed*, Seld. *Hist. Tythes, pag.* 216.

Cinnamon, *Cinnamomum*, Is a Tree whereof the Bark is known to be pleasant, and a comfortable and medicinal Spice, which you have described in *Gerards Herbal, lib.* 3. *cap.* 142. This is reckoned among garbleable Spices, *Anno* 1 *Ja. cap.* 19.

Cinque Ports, *Quinq; Portus*, Be those special Havens that lie toward *France*, and therefore have been thought fit by our Kings from time to time to be such as ought most vigilantly be guarded against Invasion: In which respect the places where they be, have an especial Governor or Keeper called, by his Office, *Lord Warden of the Cinque Ports*, and divers Priviledges granted unto them, as a particular Jurisdiction, their *Warden* having the Authority of an Admiral among them, and sending out Writs in his own

Name. *Crompton* in his *Jurisdictions, fol.* 28. nameth *Hastings, Rumney, Rye, Dover, Sandwich, Winchelsea* and *Hythe*, whereof some, because the number exceedeth five, must either be added to the first Institution by some later Grant, or be accounted as Appendants to some of the rest. See *Gardeine of the Cinque Ports*, and the Stat. 32 *H.* 8. *cap.* 48 See *Quinq; Portus*, and 4. *Inst. fol.* 222.

Cippus. A pair of Stocks to put Offendors in,----*Habeant, necnon* Cippos & *conclusoria in singulis villis, ad correctionem delinquentium*, Mon. Ang. 2 par. fol. 349. a.

Circuity of Action, (*Circuitus Actionis*) Is when an Action is rightfully brought for a Duty, but yet about the Bush, as it were, for that it might have been as well otherwise answered and determined, and the Suit saved; and because the same Action is more than needful, it is called *Circuity of Action*; as if a Man grant a Rent-charge of ten Pounds out of his Mannor of *Dale*, and after the Grantee disseises the Grantor of the same Mannor, and he brings an Assise, and recovers the Land, and twenty Pounds damages, which twenty Pounds being paid, the Grantee of the Rent Sues his Action for ten Pound of the Rent due during the time of his Disseisin, which if no Disseisin had been, he must have had. This is called *Circuity of Action*, because it might have been more shortly answered; for whereas the Grantor shall receive 20 *li.* Damages, and pay 10 *li.* Rent, he might have received but the 10 *li.* only for the Damages, and the Grantee might have cut off, and kept back the other ten pounds in his hands, by way of detainer for his Rent, and so thereby might have saved his Action.

Circumspecte Agatis, Is the Title of a Statute made 13 *E.* 1. *Anno Domini*, 1285. prescribing some Cases to the Judges, wherein the Kings Prohibition lies not, *Co. lib.* 7. *fol.* 44. *lib.* 5. *fol.* 67. and 2 *par. Inst. fol.* 487.

Circumstantibus, In English *By-standers*, Is a word of Art, signifying the supply or making up of the number of Jurors (if any impannell'd do not appear, or appearing, be challenged by either party) by adding to them so many other of those that are present or standing by, as will serve the turn 35 *H.* 8. *cap.* 6. 5. *Eliz. ca.* 25.

Ciricseat. See *Churchesset*.

City, *Civitas*, Is such a Town-Corporate as hath a Bishop and a Cathedral-Church, of which it is said thus, The same place is in Latine called *Urbs,--Civitas*, and *Oppidum*: It is named *Civitas*, in regard it is governed in Justice, and order of Magistracy. *Oppidum*, for that it contains a great number of Inhabitants; and *Urbs*, because it is in due form begirt about with Walls. Yet *Crompton* in his *Jurisdictions*, where he reckoneth up the *Cities*, leaveth out *Ely*, although it have a Bishop and Cathedral-Church, and putteth in *Westminster*, though it hath at present no Bishop. And *Anno* 35 *Eliz cap.* 6. *Westminster* is called a *City* And 27 *Eliz. cap.* 5. of the Statutes not Printed, it is alternatively termed a City or Borow. It appeareth by the Statute 35 *H.* 8. 10. that then there was a Bishop of *Westminster*, though now but a Deanry, and entituled *The Dean and Chapter of the Collegiate Church of St.* Peter *in* Westminster *Civitas* according to *Aristotle, li. Politicor. cap.* 1 is defined to be a certain or uniform Government of the Inhabitants, *Et Cæsar, Civitatem vocat, populum eodem jure utentem*, Cambd. Brit. pag. 310. But this is the general definition of a Commonwealth, and not of a *City* at the least, as we now a dayes take it. *Cassanæus* in *Consuetud. Burg. pag.* 15. saith, That *France* hath within the Territories of it one hundred and four *Cities*, and giveth reason of this his saying, because there be so many Seats of Archbishops and Bishops. Sir *Edward Coke* makes *Cambridge* a *City, Mich.* 7 *R.* 1. *Rot.* 1. yet there is no mention that it ever was an Episcopal See. *Co. on Lit. fol.* 109. and by the Stat. 11 *H.* 7. *cap.* 4. It is called only *The Town of Cambridge*.

Clacke, As to *Clacke, force* and *Bard*, alias Beard Wools, *Anno* 8 *H.* 6. *cap.* 22. whereof the first, *viz.* to *Clacke* Wool, is to cut off the Sheeps Mark, which maketh it to weigh less, and so yield the less Custome to the King: To *force* Wool, is to clip off the upper and more Hairy part of it. To *bard* or *beard* it, is to cut off the Head and Neck from the rest of the Fleece.

Clayme, *Clameum*, Is a Challenge of Interest in any thing that is in the possession of another, or at the least out of his own, as *claims by charter, claime by descent*, Old Nat. Brev. fol. 11. *Si dominus infra annum clameum qualitercunq; apposuerit, Bract. lib.* 1. *cap.* 10. See the definition, and divers sorts of *claimes* in *Plowden, fol.* 359. *Stower*'s Case.

Clamea admittenda in Itinere per Atturnatum. Is a Writ whereby the King Commands the Justices in *Eyre* to admit of ones *claime* by *Atturney*, that is employed in the Kings Service, and cannot come in his own person, *Reg. Orig. fol.* 19.

Clapboard, 35 *Eliz. cap.* 11. Is *board* cut in order to make Cask or Vessels.

Clarentius. See *Herald*.

Claves Insulæ, Is a term of Art used in the *Isle of Man*, for those twelve to whom all ambiguous and weighty Cases are referred.

Clausum fregit, Signifies as much as an *Action of Trespass*, and so call'd, because in the Writ such a one is summoned to answer *quare clausum fregit*, that is, why he did such a Trespass.

Clausum Paschæ, Stat. *Westm.* 1. *In crastino clausi Paschæ*, or *in crastino octabis Paschæ*, which is the same, that is the Morrow of the *Utas* of *Easter*, 2 *par. Inst. fol.* 157. It is called *Clausum Paschæ*, because *Pascha claudat*.

Clausura Heye, *Johannes Stanley* Ar. *clamat quod ipse & hæredes sui sint quieti de clausura* Heye *de* Maulesfield. *scil. clausura unius rodæ terræ circeter* hayam *prædict.* Rot. plac. *in Itinere apud Cestriam, Anno* 14 H. 7.

Clergy, (*Clerus, Clericatus*) Is diversly taken, sometimes for the whole number of those that are *de clero Domini*, of the Lords Lot or Share, as the Tribe of *Levi* was in *Judæa*, sometime for a Plea to an Indictment or an Appeal, and is by *Stamf. pl. cor. lib.* 2. *cap.* 41. thus defined. *Clergy* is an ancient liberty of the Church, which hath been confirmed by divers Parliaments, and is, when a Priest, or one within Orders, is arraigned of Felony before a Secular Judge, he may pray his *Clergy*, which is as much as if he prayed to be delivered

delivered to his Ordinary, to purge himself of the Offence objected: And this might be done in *Co. lib.* 4 *fol.* 46 *a.* This liberty is mentioned in *Articulis cleri*, 9 *E.* 2. *cap.* 15. and what persons might have their Clergy, and what not, see *Stamf. pl. cor. lib.* 2. *cap.* 42. 43. Howbeit there be many Statutes made since he writ; whereby the benefit of Clergy is abridged: As *Anno* 8 *Eliz. cap.* 4. *Anno* 14 *Eliz.* 5. 18 *Eliz.* 4. 6, 7. 23 *Eliz.* 2. 29 *Eliz.* 2. 31 *Eliz.* 12. 39 *Eliz.* 9. 15. and divers other since. Of this, see *Cromptons Justice of Peace*, *fol.* 102, 103, 104, 105. and *Lamberts Eiren. lib.* 4. *cap.* 14. *pag.* 543. And here note, That the ancient course of the Law in this point of Clergy is much altered; for by the Statute, 18 *Eli. ca.* 7. Clerks be no more delivered to their Ordinaries to be purged, but now every man, though not within Orders, is put to read at the Bar, being found Guilty, and convicted of such Felony as this Benefit is granted for, and so burnt in the Hand, and set free for the first time, if the Ordinaries Commissioner, or Deputy, standing by, do say, *Legit ut clericus*, or otherwise suffereth death for his Transgression.

Clerico capto per Statutum Mercatorum, &c. Is a Writ directed to the Bishop, for the delivery of a Clerk out of Prison that is in custody upon the breach of a *Statute-Merchant*, *Reg. Orig. fol.* 147.

Clerico admittendo, Is a Writ directed to the Bishop, for the admitting of a Clerk to a Benefice upon a *Ne admittas*, tryed and found for the Party that procureth the Writ, *Reg. Orig. fol.* 31.

Clerico convicto commisso Gaolæ in defectu ordinarii deliberando, &c. Is a Writ for the delivery of a Clerk to his Ordinary, that formerly was convicted of Felony, by reason his Ordinary did not challenge him according to the Priviledges of Clerks, *Reg. Orig. fol.* 69. *a.*

Clerico infra sacros Ordines constituto non Eligendo in Officium, Is a Writ directed to the Bayliffs, &c. That have thrust a Bayliwick or Beadleship upon one in Holy Orders, charging them to release him again, *Reg. Orig. fol.* 143. *a.*

Clerk, *Clericus*, hath two significations, one as it is in the Title of him that belongeth to the holy Ministry of the Church, that is (as we reckon) either Minister or Deacon, or what other Degree or dignity soever; though according to former times not only *Sacerdotes & Diaconi*, but also *Subdiaconi, Lectores, Acolythi, Exorcistæ, & Ostiarii* were within this account, as they be at this day, where the Canon-Law hath full power. And in this signification a Clerk is either Religious (otherwise called regular) or Secular, *Anno* 4. *H.* 4. *ca.* 12. The other signification of this word noteth those that by their Function, or course of Life, practise their Pen in any Court, or otherwise; as namely, the Clerk of the Rolls of Parliament, Clerks of the Chancery, and such like, whose peculiar Offices shall be set in order.

Clerk of the Acts, Is an Officer of the Navy, who receives and enters the Commissions and Warrants of the Lord Admiral, and Registers the Acts and Orders of the Commissioners of the Navy, and is mentioned in the Statute, 16 *Car.* 9. 5.

Clerk of the Parliament Rolls, *Clericus Rotulorum Parliamenti*, Is he that recordeth all things done in the High Court of Parliament, and engrosseth them fairly into Parchment Rolls, for their better keeping to Posterity. Of these there be two, one of the Higher, the other of the Lower, or House of Commons, *Cromp. Jurisd. fol* 4. & 8. *Smith de Rep. Ang. pag.* 38. See also *Vowels* Book, touching *The Order of Parliament*.

Clerk of the Crown in Chancery, *Clericus Coronæ in Cancellaria*, Is an Officer there, that by himself, or his Deputy, is continually to attend the Lord Chancellor, or Lord Keeper, for special Matters of State, by Commission, or the like, either immediately from His Majesty, or by Order of his Council, as well ordinary as extraordinary, *viz.* Commissions of Lieutenancy, of Justices-Errant, of Assise, of *Oyer* and *Terminer*, of Gaol-delivery, of the Peace, and such like, with their Writs of Association, and *Dedimus potestatem*, for taking of Oaths. Also all general Pardons upon Grants of them at the Kings Coronation, or at a Parliament; the Writs of Parliament, with the Names of Knights and Burgesses, are returned into his Office. He hath also the making of all special Pardons, and Writs of Execution upon Bonds of *Statute-Staple* forfeited, which was annexed to his Office in the Reign of Queen *Mary*, in consideration of his continual and chargeable Attendance; both these being before common for every Cursitor or Clerk of Court to make.

Clerk of the Crown, *Clericus Coronæ*, Is a Clerk or Officer in the Kings Bench, whose business is to read, frame and record all Inditements against Traitors, Felons, and other Offendors there arraigned upon any publick Crime. He is otherwise termed *Clerk of the Crown-Office.* And *Anno* 2 *H.* 4. *cap.* 10. he is called *Clerk of the Crown* in the Kings Bench.

Clerk of the Estreats, *Clericus Extractorum*, Is a Clerk belonging to the Exchequer, who every Term receiveth the *Estreats* out of the Lord Treasurers Remembrancers Office, and writeth them out to be Levyed for the King: He also maketh Schedules of such Sums *estreated* as are to be discharged.

Clerk of Assise, *Clericus Assisæ*, Is he that writeth all things judicially done by the Justices of *Assise* in their Circuits, *Crompt. Jurisd. fol.* 227.

Clerk of the Pell, *Clericus Pellis*, Is a Clerk belonging to the Exchequer, whose Office is to enter every Tellers Bill into a Parchment-Roll called *Pellis receptorum*, and also to make another Roll of Payments, which is called *Pellis exituum*, wherein he setteth down by what Warrant the Money was paid.

Clerk of the Warrants, *Clericus Warrantorum*, Is an Officer belonging to the Court of Common-Pleas, which entreth all *Warrants* of Atturney for Plaintiff and Defendant, and inrolleth all Deeds of Indentures of Bargain and Sale, which are acknowledged in Court or before any Judges out of the Court. And he doth estreat into the Exchequer all Issues, Fines and

and Amerciaments, which grow due to the King any way in that Court, and hath a standing Fee of ten pounds of the King, for making the same Estreats. See *Fitzh. Nat. Brev. fol.* 76.

Clerk of the Petty Bag, *Clericus Parvæ Bagiæ*, Is an Officer of the Chancery, of which sort there be three, and the Master of the Rolls their cheif. Their Office is to Record the Return of all Inquisitions out of every Shire, all Liveries granted in the Court of Wards, all *Ouster le maynes*, to make all Patents of Customers, Gaugers, Controulers and Aulnegers, all *conge de esliers* for Bishops, all *Liberates* upon extents of *Statute-Staple*, the recovery of Recognisances forfeited, and all *Elegits* upon them; the Summons of the Nobility, Clergy and Burgesses to the Parliament: Commissions directed to Knights and other of every Shire, for Sessing the Subsidies; Writs for the nomination of Collectors for the Fifteenths, and all Traverses upon any Office, Bill, or otherwise, and to receive the Money due to the King for the same. This Officer is mentioned 33 *H.* 8. *cap.* 22.

Clerk of the Kings Great Wardrobe, *Clericus magnæ* Gardrobæ *Regis*, Is an Officer of the Kings House, that keepeth an account, or Inventory, in Writing of all things belonging to the *Kings Wardrobe*. This Officer is mentioned 1 *E.* 4. *cap.* 1.

Clerk of the Market, *Clericus Mercati*, Is an Officer of the Kings House, *Anno* 1 E. 4. *cap.* 1. and 13 *R.* 2. *cap.* 4. whose duty is to take charge of the Kings Measures, and to keep the Standards of them, that is, the Examples of all the Measures that ought to be through the Land; as of all Ells, Yards, Lagens, Quarts, Pottles, Gallons, *&c.* Of Weights, Bushels, and such like; and to see that all Measures in every place be answerable unto the said Standard, *Fleta, lib.*2. *cap.* 8, 9, 10, 11, 12. Of which Office, as also of our diversity of *Weights and Measures*, you may there find a Treatise worth the reading. *Britton* also in his Thirtieth Chapter, saith in the Kings Person to this effect, *We will that none have Measures in the Realm, but we our selves, but that every man take his Measures and Weights from our Standards*; and so goeth on with a Tractate of this Matter, that well shews the ancient Law and Practice in this point: Touching this Officers Duty, you have also a good Statute, *Anno* 13. *R.* 2. *cap.* 4.

Clerk of the Kings Silver, *Clericus Argenti Regis*, Is an Officer belonging to the Court of Common-Pleas, to whom every Fine is brought, after it hath been with the *Custos Brevium*, and by whom the effect of the Writ of Covenant is entred into a Paper-Book, and according to that Note, all the Fines of that Term are also Recorded in the Rolls of the Court, and his Entry is in this Form. He putteth the Shire over the Margin, and then saith, A. B. *Dat Domino Regi dimidium Marcæ*, (or more, according to the value) *pro licentia Concordandi* C. *cum* C. D. *pro talibus terris in tali villa & habet Chirographum per pacem admissum*, *&c.*

Clerk of the Peace, *Clericus Pacis*, Is an Officer belonging to the Sessions of the *Peace*: His Duty is in the Sessions, to read Indictments, to enroll the Acts, and draw the Processe; to Record the Proclamations of Rates for Servants Wages, to enrol the Discharge of Apprentices, to keep the Counterpart of the Indenture of Armour, to keep the Register-Book of Licences given to Badgers and Laders of Corn, and of those that are licensed to shoot in Guns, and to certifie into the Kings Bench Transcripts of Indictments, Outlawries, Attainders and Convictions had before the Justices of the *Peace* within the time limited by Statute, *Lamb. Eirenar. lib.* 4. *cap.* 3. *fol.* 379.

Clerk of the Signet, *Clericus Signeti*, Is an Officer continually attendant upon his Majesties Principal Secretary, who always hath the Custody of the *Privy Signet*, as well for Sealing His Majesties private Letters, as also such Grants as pass his Majesties Hand by Bill *signed*. Of these there be four that attend in their course, and have their Dyet at the Secretaries Table; more largely you may read of their Office in the Statute made *Anno* 27 *H.* 8. *cap.* 11.

Clerk of the Privy-Seal, *Clericus Privati Sigilli*, Is an Officer (whereof there be four) that attendeth the Lord Keeper of the *Privy-Seal*; or if there be none such, upon the Principal Secretary, Writing and making out all things that be sent by Warrant from the Signet to the *Privy-Seal*; and are to be passed to the *Great Seal*: As also to make out (as they are termed) *Privy-Seals* upon any special occasion of His Majesties Affairs; as for loan of Money, and such like. Of this Officer and Function, you may read 27 *H.* 8. 11. He that now is called *The Lord Keeper of the Privy-Seal*, seemeth in ancient time to have been called *The Clerk of the Privy-Seal*, and to have been reckoned in the number of the great Officers in the Realm. Read the Statute, 12 *R.* 2. *cap.* 11.

Clerk of the Juries, or Jurata Writs. *Clericus Juratorum*, Is an Officer belonging to the Court of Common-Pleas, which maketh out the Writs called *Habeas Corpora, & Distringas*, for appearance of the Jury either in Court, or at Assises, after that the Jury or Panel is returned upon the *Venire facias*. He entreth also into the Rolls the awarding of these Writs, and maketh all the Continuances from the going out of the *Habeas Corpora* to the Verdict.

Clerk of the Pipe, *Clericus Pipæ*, Belongs to the Exchequer, who having all Accounts and Debts due to the King delivered and drawn out of the Remembrancers Office, chargeth them down into the great Roll; who also Writeth Summons to the Sheriff to Levy the said Debts upon the Goods and Chattels of the Debtors. And if they have no Goods, then doth he draw them down to the Lord Treasurers Remembrancer, to write Estreats against their Lands. The ancient Revenue of the Crown remaineth in charge before him, and he seeth the same answered by the Farmers and Sheriffs to the King. He maketh a Charge to all Sheriffs, of their Summons of the *Pipe* and *Green-wax*, and seeth it answered upon their accounts. He hath the drawing and ingrossing of all Leases of the Kings Land.

Clerk of the Hamper or Hanaper. *Clericus Hanaperii*, Is an Officer in the Chancery, *Anno* 2 *E.* 4. *Cap.* 1. otherwise called *Warden*

Warden of the Hamper in the ſame Statute, whoſe buſineſs is to receive all Money due to the Kings Majeſty, for the Seals of Charters, Patents, Commiſſions and Writs; as alſo Fees due to the Officers for enrolling and examining the ſame. He is tyed to attendance on the Lord Chancellor, or Lord Keeper, daily in the Term-time, and at all times of Sealing, having with him Leather Bags, in which are put all Charters, &c. after they be Sealed by the Lord Chancellor, and thoſe Bags being Sealed up with the Lord Chancellors Private Seal, are to be delivered to the *Controuler of the Hamper*, who, upon receipt of them, doth, as you may read in his Office. This *Hamper* repreſented a Shadow of that which the *Romans* termed *Fiſcum*, that contained the Emperors Treaſure.

Clerk of the Pleas, *Clericus Placitorum*, Is an Officer in the Exchequer, in whoſe Office the Officers of the Court, upon ſpecial priviledge belonging to them, ought to ſue, or be ſued, upon any Action.

Clerk of the Treaſury, *Clericus Theſaurariæ*, Belongs to the Common-Pleas, and hath the Charge of keeping the Records of the Court, and maketh out all the Records of *Niſi prius*, hath the Fees due for all Searches, and hath the certifying of all Records into the Kings Bench, when a Writ of Error is brought, and maketh out all Writs of *Superſedeas de non moleſtando*, which are granted for the Defendants, while the Writ of Error hangeth. Alſo he maketh all Exemplifications of Records being in the *Treaſury*. He is taken to be the Servant to the chief Juſtice, and removeable at his pleaſure, whereas all other Officers are for terme of Life. There is alſo a Secondary, or Under-Clerk, of the Treaſury for aſſiſtance, which hath ſome allowances. There is likewiſe an Under-Keeper, who always keepeth one Key of the *Treaſury* Door, and the chief Clerk of the Secondary another, ſo that one cannot go in without the other.

Clerk of the Eſſoyns, *Clericus Eſſoniorum*, Is an Officer belonging to the Court of Common-Pleas, who only keepeth the *Eſſoyne-Roll*, and hath for Entring every *Eſſoine* ſix pence, and for every Exception to bar the *Eſſoine*, in caſe where the Party hath omitted his time, ſix pence. He hath alſo the providing of Parchment, and cutting it out into Rolls, and marking the numbers upon them, and the delivery out of all the Rolls to every Officer, and the Receiving of them again when they be written, and the binding and making up of the whole bundles of every Term; and this he doth as Servant to the chief Juſtice, for the chief Juſtice is at charge for all the Parchment of all the Rolls.

Clerk of the Outlawries, *Clericus Utlagariarum*, Is an Officer belonging to the Court of Common-Pleas, being only the Servant, or Deputy, to the King's Atturney-General, for making out the Writs of *Capias Utlagatum* after *Outlawry*; and the Kings Atturneys name is to every one of thoſe Writs. And whereas Seven pence is paid for the Seal of every other Writ betwixt Party and Party, there is but a Peny paid for the Seal of this, becauſe it goeth out at the King's Suit.

Clerk of the Sewers, *Clericus Sewarum*, Is an Officer belonging to the Commiſſioners of the *Sewers*, writing all things that they do by vertue of their Commiſſion; for which, ſee *Sewers*. And ſee the Stat of 13 *Eliz. cap.* 9.

Clerk Controllar of the Kings Houſe, Whereof there be two, is an Officer in Court, that hath Place and Seat in the *Counting-Houſe*, and authority to allow or diſallow the Charges and Demands of Purſuivants and Meſſengers of the *Green-Cloth*, Purveyors, or the like. He hath alſo the Over-ſight and *Controlling* of all Defaults, Defects, and Miſcarriages of any the Inferior Officers, and as before-mentioned, to ſit in the *Counting-Houſe* with the ſuperior Officers, *viz.* the Lord Steward, Treaſurer, *Controller* and Cofferer, either for correcting or bettering things out of Order, with ſeveral other Matters. This Officer you have mentioned, 33 *Hen.* 8. *cap.* 12.

Clerk of the Nichils or **Nihils**, *Clericus Nihilorum;* Is an Officer in the Exchequer, that maketh a Roll of all ſuch Sums as are *Nihiled* by the Sheriffs upon their Eſtreats of Green-Wax, and delivereth the ſame into the Lord Treaſurers Remembrancers-Office, to have execution done upon it for the King.

Clerk of the Check, Is an Officer in Court ſo called, becauſe he hath the *Check* and Controlment of the Yeomen of the Guard, and all other ordinary Yeomen or Uſhers belonging either to the King, Queen or Prince, either giving leave, and allowing their abſenſes or defects in attendance, or diminiſhing their Wages for the ſame. He alſo rightly by himſelf, or Deputy, taketh the view of thoſe that are to Watch in the Court, and hath the ſetting of the Watch. This Officer is mentioned *Anno* 33 *H.* 8. *cap.* 12. There is an Officer of the ſame name in the Kings Navy, ſpoken of 19 *Car.* 2. *cap.* 1.

Clerk-Marſhal of the Kings Houſe, ſeems to be an Officer that attends the Marſhal in his Court, and Recordeth all his proceedings, 33 *H.* 8. 12.

Cloſh, Is an unlawful Game forbidden by the Statute, made in the ſeventeenth year of *E.* 4. *cap.* 3. and is inhibited alſo by the Statute of 33 *H.* 8. *cap.* 9. but there it is more properly called *Claſh;* for it is the throwing of a Bowl at Nine-Pins of Wood, or nine Shank-bones of an Ox or Horſe; and it is now ordinarily called *Kailes* or *Nine-Pins*, *Termes de la Ley.*

Cloth of Ray, *Anno* 27 *E.* 3. *Stat.* 1. *cap.* 4.

Clove, Is the two and thirtieth part of a Weigh of Cheeſe, that is Eight Pound, 9 *H.* 6. *cap.* 8.

Cloves, *Caryophylli*, are a Spice known by ſight to every Man; they are Flowers of a Tree gathered and hardned by the Sun: Of their nature, you may read in *Gerards Herbal*, *lib.* 3. *cap.* 144. This is compriſed among ſuch Spices as are to be garbled, 1 *Jac.* 19.

Clough, A Valley, *Doomſday-Book.*

Cocherings, An Exaction or Tribute in *Ireland.* See *Bonaght.*

Cocket or **Coket**, *Cockettum*, Is a Seal apper-

taining

taining to the Kings Custom-house, *Reg. Orig. fol.* 192. and also a Scroll of Parchment Sealed and delivered by the Officers of the Custom-house to Merchants, as a warrant that their Merchandise be Customed, 11 *H.* 6. 16. which Parchment is otherwise called *Litera de* Coketto, or *Literæ testimoniales de* Coketto, *Reg. Orig. fol* 179. So is the word used, 5 & 6 *E.* 6. *cap.* 14. and 14 *E.* 3. *Stat.* 1. *cap.* 21. This word is also used for distinction of Bread, in the Statutes of *Bread* and *Ale*, made 51 *H.* 3. where you have mention made of *Bread-Cocket*, *Wastel-Bread*, *Bread* of *Treete*, and *Bread* of *Common-Wheat*.

Codicil, *Codicillus*, Is a Schedule or Supplement to a Will, or other Writing; it is used as an addition to a Testament, when any thing is omitted, which the Testator would add, explain, alter or retract, and is of the same nature with a Testament, but that it is without an Executor, *Swinburne, pag.* 1. *sect* 5. And *Touchstone of Wills, pag.* 21. 22.

Coffee, Mentioned 15 *Car.* 2. *cap.* 11. A kind of Drink, originally used among the *Turks* and *Persians*, and from them brought to us: It is thick, blackish and bitter, made from Berries of that Nature and Name, and now greeably in use as a wholsom Liquor.

Cofferer of the Kings Houshold, Is a principal Officer of His Majesties Court, next under the Controller, that in the Counting-House, and elsewhere at other times hath a special Charge and Over-sight of other Officers of the House for their good Demeanor and Carriage in their Offices, to all which he pays their Wages. He is made mention of 39 *Eliz. cap.* 7.

Cofez, *Cottages.* See *Doomsday* Book, thus interpreted by Mr. *Agar.*

Cogs, *Cogones*, A kind of Boats or Vessels used in the River *Ouse* and *Humber*, they are mentioned 23 *H* 8. *cap.* 18. See *Mat. Westm. Anno* 1066.

Cognatione. See *Cosinage.*

Cognisor or **Conusor**, Is he that passeth or acknowledgeth a Fine of Lands or Tenements to another. *Cognisee* or *Conusee* is he to whom the Fine is acknowledged, *West. Symb. part.* 2. *tit.* Fines, *sect.* 2. 32 *H* 8. 5.

Cognisance, Id est, *Intelligentia*, *Cognitio*, with us is used diversly, sometimes signifying a Badge on a Serving-mans Sleeve, whereby he is discerned to belong to this or that Master. Sometime an acknowledgement of a Fine or Confession of a thing done, as *Cognoscens latro*, *Bracton, lib.* 3. *tract.* 2. *cap.* 3. 20. 32. *Cognoscere se ad Villanum*, Id. lib. 4. tract. 3. cap. 16. As also to make *Cognisance* of taking a Distress, sometime as an Audience or hearing of a Matter judicially, as to take *Cognisance.* Sometime a Power or Jurisdiction, as Cognisance of Pleas, is an ability to call a Cause or Plea out of another Court, which no Man can do but the King, except he can shew Charters for it, *Manwood*, *cap.* 3. *num* 2. See the *Terms of the Law*, and *New Book of Entries*, verbo *Conusance.*

Cognitionibus mittendis, Is a Writ to a Justice or other that hath Power to take a Fine, who having taken acknowledgment thereof, deferreth to certifie it into the Court of Common-Pleas, commanding him to certifie it, *Reg. Orig.* 68. *b.*

Cogware, Seems to be a sort of course Clothes made in the North of *England*, mentioned in the Stat. 13 *R.* 2. *cap.* 10. where there is mention also of *Cogmen*, that is, Buyers of, Makers or Dealers in such *Cogware.*

Coyfe, A Title given to *Sergeants at Law*, who are called *Sergeants of the Coyfe*; from the Lawn Coyfe they wear on their Heads under their Cap when they are created, and always after. See *Sergeant.*

Coyne, *Cuneus vel cuna*, Seemeth to come from the French (*Coigne*) *Angulus* a Corner, which probably verifieth the Opinion of such as hold the ancientest sort of *Coyne* to be cornered, and not round, of this Lawyers Substantive *Cuna*, comes their Verb *Cunare* to *coyne*, *Cromp. Just of Peace, fol.* 220.

Coynage, Besides the general signification, it hath relating to Money, is used for the weighing and stamping of Tinne after it is cast and wrought, *Cambden*, *Brit. fol.* 186. and 11 *H.* 7. *cap* 4. Some Authors write it *Cunage.*

Coket. See *Cocket.*

Coleberti, *Coleberti*, Are Tenants in Free-Socage, *Doomsday-Book*, or such as being Villains were manumitted.

Coliander-seed, or rather **Coriander-seed**, *Semen Coriandri*, Is the Seed of an Herb so called, medicinable and wholsome for divers good purposes, which see in *Gerards Herball*, *lib.* 2. *cap.* 379. It is numbred among the Drugs that are to be garbled, *Anno* 1 *Jac. cap.* 19.

Collateral, *Collateralis*, Cometh of the Latine *Laterale*, that which hangeth by the side: And in the legal Sense it differs not from the same acceptation; for *Collateral* Assurance is that which is made over and beside the Deed it self. For example, If a Man Covenant with another, and enter Bond for the performance of his Covenant, the Bond is termed *Collateral assurance*, because it is external, and without the nature and essence of the Covenant. And *Cromp. Jur. fol.* 185. saith, That to be subject to the feeding of the Kings Deer, is *collateral* to the soyl within the Forest. In like manner we say, That the liberty to pitch Booths or Standings for a Fair in another Mans Ground, is *collateral* to the Ground. The private Woods of a common person within a Forest, may not be cut without the Kings Licence; for it is a Prerogative *collateral* to the soyl, *Manwood Forest Laws*, *cap.* 8. *num.* 2.

Collateral Warranty. See *Warranty.*

Collation of Benefice, *Collatio Beneficii*, Signifies properly the bestowing of a Benefice by the Bishop that hath it in his own Gift or Patronage, and differeth from Institution in this, that Institution into a Benefice is performed by the Bishop, at the motion or presentation of another who is the Patron of the same, or hath the Patrons right for the time; yet is *collation* used for Presentation, 25 *E.* 3. *Stat.* 6. And there is a Writ in the *Register*, 31. *b.* called *De* Collatione *facta uni post mortem alterius*, &c. directed to the Justices of the Common-Pleas, commanding them to direct their Writ to the Bishop, for the admitting

ting of a Clerk in the place of another, presented by the King, who dyed during the Suit between the King and the Bishops Clerk, for Judgment once passed for the Kings Clerk, and he dying before he be admitted, the King may give his Presentation to another.

Collatione Heremitagii, Is a Writ whereby the King conferreth the Keeping of an *Hermitage* upon a Clerk, *Reg. Origin. Fol.* 303 308.

Collusion, *Collusio*, Is in our Common-Law a deceitful Agreement or Compact between two or more, for the one Party to bring an Action against the other to some evil purpose, as to defraud a third of his Right, &c. See the *Terms of the Law*, *fol.* 142. and *Bro. tit.* Collusion. See also the Case of *Collusion*, *Reg. Orig. fol.* 179. *a. West.* 2. *cap.* 32. and 8 *H.* 6. *cap.* 26. which gives the *Quale Jus*, and inquiry in such Cases; Gifts made by *Collusion*, see 50 *E.* 3. *cap.* 6.

Colour, *Color*, Signifies in a legal acceptation a probable Plea, but in truth false, and hath this end, to draw the Tryal of the Cause from the Jury to the Judges. As for example, *A.* brings an Assise of Land against *B.* and *B.* saith, He himself did Let the same Land to one *C.* for term of Life, and afterwards did grant the Reversion to *A.* the Demandant; and afterward *C.* the Tenant for term of Life died, after whose decease *A.* the Demandant claiming the Reversion by force of the Grant (whereto *C.* the Tenant did never Attorn) entred, upon whom *B.* entred, against whom *A.* for that entry brings this Assise, &c. This is a good *Colour*, because the common People think the Land will pass by the Grant without Attornment, where indeed it will not pass, &c. Also in an Action of Trespass, *color* must be given, of which there are an infinite number, take this one for a Patern of the rest In an Action of Trespass, for taking away the Plaintiffs Beasts, the Defendant saith, That before the Plaintiff had any thing in them, he himself was possessed of them as of his proper Goods, and delivered them to *A.* to deliver to him again, when, &c and *A.* gave them to the Plaintiff, and the Plaintiff supposing the property to be in *A.* at the time of the Gift, took them, and the Defendant took them from the Plaintiff, whereupon the Plaintiff brings an Action, that is, a good *Color* and a good Plea. See more hereof *Doctor and Student*, *lib.* 2. *cap.* 13. and *Broke*, *tit. Color in Assise*, *Trespass*, *&c. fol.* 104

Color of Office, *Color Officii*, Is always taken in the worst part, and signifies an Act evilly done by the countenance of an Office, and it bears a dissembling Face of the Right of an *Office*, whereas the *Office* is but a Vail to the Falsehood; and the thing is grounded upon Vice, and the Office is as a shadow to it, it is but *colore Officii*, when as *virtute Officii*, by vertue of the *Office*, is taken always in the best part; and where the *Office* is the just cause of the thing, and the thing is pursuing the *Office*, *Plowd.* in *Dive* and *Manningham*'s Case, *fol.* 64. *a.*

Combat, *Duellum*, Is a French Word signifying the same with *certamen*, *prælium*, *pugna*, and in our ancient Law was a formal Tryal of a doubtful Cause or Quarrel, by the Sword or Bastons of two Champions: Of this you may read at large both in divers *Civilians*, as *Paris de Puteo de re militari & duello*, *Alciat. de duello*; *Hotoman disputatio feudalium*, *cap.* 42. and others, and Common Lawyers, namely *Glanvile*, *lib.* 14. *cap.* 1. *Bract. lib.* 3. *tract.* 2. *cap.* 3. *Britton*, *cap.* 22. *Hornes Mirrour of Justices*, *lib.* 3. *cap. des exceptions in fine proxim. & cap. juramentum duelli*, Dyer, *fol.* 301. *num.* 41, 42. *Camden* in his *Brit. fol.* 519. mentions a *Combat* between *Alan de la Zouch*, and *John* Earl of *Warren*, in the year 1269. The last Tryal by Combat in *England*, was in the sixth year of King *Charles* the First, between *Donald* Lord *Rey* Appellant, and *David Ramsey* Esq; Defendant, both *Scotch-men*; but after many Formalities, the matter was referred to the Kings Will and Pleasure, *Bakers Chron. fol.* 500. See *Co.* on *Lit. fol.* 294. *b. Origines Juridiciales*, *fol.* 65. and *Spelmans Gloss.* at large, *verbo* Campus.

Comin Seed, *Semen Cumini*, Is a Seed brought forth by an Herb so called, which you see described in *Gerards Herbal*, *lib.* 2, *cap.* 416. This is placed among the garbleable Drugs, 1 *Jac.* 19.

Comitatu Commisso, Is a Writ or *Commission*, whereby the Sheriff is authorised to take upon him the command of the County, *Reg. Orig. fol.* 295. *Co. Rep. lib.* 3. *fol.* 72.

Comitatu & Castro Commisso, Is a Writ whereby the Charge of a County, together with the keeping of a Castle, is committed to the Sheriff, *Reg. Orig. fol.* 295. *a.*

Commandry, (*Præceptoria*) Was a Mannor or Chief Messuage, with Lands and Tenements appertaining thereto, belonging to the Priory of St. *John of Jerusalem* in *England*, and he which had the Government of any such Mannor or House, was called a *Commander*; who could not dispose of it, but to the use of the Priory, only taking thence his own sustenance, according to his Degree, who was usually a Brother of the same Priory, *Termes de la Ley*, *verbo Commandry*, By some other Books it appears, That the chief Prior of St. *Johns* was a Commander of a Nunnery, and constituted the Prioress of the said Nunnery, who was under his Obedience, and removeable at his Will, notwithstanding she had Covent and Common Seal, and had her Possessions several, and was wont to Lease the Land for term of years, *Fullbecks Parallels*, *fol.* 2. *a.* Of these *Commandrys*, also you may read *Petrus Gregorius*, *lib. de Beneficiis*, *cap.* 11. *num.* 11. These in many places of *England* are termed by the name of Temples, because they sometimes belonged to the *Templers*, of whom you may read 26 *H.* 8. *cap.* 2. and 32 *H.* 8. *cap.* 24. Thus *New-Eagle*, in the County of *Lincoln*, is still called *The Commandry of Eagle*, as belonging of old to the said Priory. Such also were *Slebach* in *Pembrokeshire*, and *Shenghay* in *Cambridgeshire*. See *Preceptores*.

Comitatus, Of dead Farmes, and Debts desperate, whereof there is no hope, one Roll shall be made and entituled, *Comitatus*, and read every year upon the account of Sheriffs, 10 *E.* 1. *cap. unico*.

Combe, In *Doomsday-Book* signifies a *Valley*, as Mr. *Agar* Reports.

Commandement, *Preceptum*, Is used diversly in the Common Law: Sometimes for the

the *Commandment* of the King, when, upon his meer Motion, and from his own Mouth, he sendeth any Man to Prison, *Stamf. pl. cor. fol.* 72. or of the Justices. And this *Commandment* of the Justices is either *absolute* or *ordinary*. *Absolute*, as when upon their own Authority, in their Wisdom and Discretion, they commit a Man to Prison for a Punishment. *Ordinary* is, when they commit one rather for safe Custody than Punishment: And a Man committed upon an *ordinary Commandment* is bayleable, *Stamf. pl. cor.* 73. Again, *Commandment* is used for the Offence of him that willeth another Man to transgress the Law, or to do any thing contrary to the Law, as Theft, Murder, or such like, *Bract. lib.* 3. *tract.* 2. *cap.* 19. *Les Civilians appell cest* Commandment, *Angelus de maleficiis*, Termes de Ley, 145.

Commendam, Is a Benefice, that being void, is Commended to the Care of some Sufficient Clerk to be supplyed, till it may be conveniently provided of a Pastor; and that this was the true original of this practice, may be read at large in *Durandus de sacris Ecclesiæ Ministeriis & Beneficiis, lib.* 5. *cap.* 7. He to whom the Church is *commended* hath the Fruits and Profits thereof only for a certain time, and the nature of the Church is not changed thereby, but is as a thing deposited in the Hands of him to whom it is commended, who hath nothing but the custody thereof, which may be revoked. When a Parson is made a Bishop, there is a Cession of his Benefice by the Promotion; but if the King gives him power to retain his Benefice, he shall continue Parson, and is said to hold it in *Commendam, Hub. Rep. fol.* 144. *Latches Rep.* 236. 237. See *Ecclesia Commendata in Gloss.* 10. *scriptor.*

Comminalty, or rather **Communalty** or **Commonalty**, Signifies the middle sort of the Kings Subjects, 2 *Inst. fol.* 539. *Tout le Commune d'Engle-terre*, are such of the *Commons* as raised beyond the ordinary Peasants, come to have the managing of Offices, and by that means are one degree under Burgesses, which are Superior to them both in Order and Authority, as in Companies incorporated, they are said to consist of Master, Wardens, and *Commonalty*; the first two being the chief, the middle sort such as are usually called *of the Livery*.

Comen, But I suppose rather *Comon* or *Common*, In Latine *Communia, quod ad omnes pertinet*, Signifieth in our Common-Law, That Soyl or Water, whereof the use is common to this or that Town or Lordship, as Common of Pasture, *Communia Pasturæ, Bract. lib.* 4. *cap.* 19. & 40. Common of Fishing, *Communia Piscariæ*, Id. lib. 2. cap. 34. Common of Turbary, *Communia Turbariæ*, that is, liberty of digging Turf, *Id. lib.* 4. *cap.* 41. Common of *Estovers, Communia Estoveriorum, Kitchin, fol.* 94. Common is divided into *Common in gross, Common appendant, Common appurtenant*, and *Common pur caus. de Vicinage*, that is, by reason of Neighborhood. *Common in gross*, is a liberty to have Common alone, that is, without any Land or Tenement in another mans Land to himself for Life, or to him and his Heirs, and it is commonly passed by deed of Grant, or specialty, *Old Nat. Brev. fol.* 31 & 37. *Common appendant* and *Common appurtenant* be in a manner confounded, as appeareth by *F. N. B. fol.* 180. and are defined to be a liberty of *Common*, appertaining to, or depending on such or such a Freehold. Onely *Kitchin, fol.* 94. seemeth to make this difference, That he which hath Common *appendant*, hath it without limitation of this or that kind of Beasts, but that is controlled by *Dyer, fol.* 70. *b. num.* 19. He that hath Common *appendant*, hath it but for Beasts Commonable, as Horses, Oxen, Kine, and Sheep, being accounted fittest for the Ploughman, and not of Goats, Geese and Hogs. Hereto may be added another Difference, *viz.* That Common *appurtenant* may be severed from the Land whereto it is *appurtenant*, but not Common *appendant*, of whose Original you may read *Coke, lib.* 4. *fol* 37. in these words, Common *appendant* by the ancient Law had beginning in this manner, When a Lord infeoffed another in Arable Lands, to hold of him in Socage, as all Tenure in the beginning, according to *Littleton*, was, The Feoffee, to maintain the Service of his Plough, had Common in the Wasts of his Lord, for his necessary Beasts to manure and compost his Land, and that for two causes; one, for that as then it was taken, it was (*tacite*) implyed in the Feoffment, by reason the Feoffee could not manage the Land without Cattel, and Cattel could not be sustained without Pasture; and so by consequent the Feoffee had, as a thing necessary and incident, Common in the Wasts and Land of his Lord. And this appeareth by ancient Books, *temp. E.* 1. *tit.* Common 24. & 17 *E.* 2. *tit.* Common 23. & 20 *E.* 3. *tit.* Admeasurement 8 & 18 *E.* 3. and by the rehersal of the Statute of *Merton, cap.* 4. The second reason was, For maintenance and advancement of Tillage, which is much regarded and favoured in the Law; thus far *Coke*. *Common pur cause de vicinage*, is a liberty that the Tenants of one Lord in one Town, have to Common with the Tenants of another Lord in another Town, which kind of Common, they that Challenge, may not put their Cattel into the Common of the other Town, for then they be distrainable; but turning them into their own Fields, if they stray into their Neighbours Common, they must be suffered, *Termes de la Ley*. Common of Pasture, the Civilians call *jus compascendi, cum sc. plures ex municipibus, qui diversa prædia possidebant, Saltum communem ut jus compascendi haberent mercarentur*: It is called *jus compascuum*.

Commissary, *Commissarius*, Is a Title of Ecclesiastical Jurisdiction, appertaining to such a one as exerciseth Spiritual Jurisdiction (at the least so far as his Commission permitteth) in places of the Diocess so far distant from the chief City, as the Chancellor cannot call the Subjects to the Bishops principal Consistory, without their too great molestation. This Commissary is of the Canonists termed *Commissarius* or *Officialis foraneus*. *Lynwoods Provin. cap.* 1. *de accusat.* &c. And he is ordained to this especial end, That he supply the Bishops Jurisdiction and Office in the Out-places of the Diocess, or else in such Parishes as be peculiar to the Bishop, and exempted from the Jurisdiction of the Arch-deacon; for where either by Prescription or Composition, there be Arch-deacons that have Jurisdiction within their Arch-deaconries, as in most places they there have, this *Commissary* is superfluous, and most commonly doth rather vex and disturb the Country for

for his Lucre, than of Conscience seek to redress the Lives of Offendors. And therefore the Bishop taking Prestation-Money of his Arch-deacons yearly *pro exteriori Jurisdictione*, as it is ordinarily called, doth by superonerating their Circuit with a *Commissary*, not only wrong the Arch-deacons, but the poorer sort of Subjects much more, as common practice too frequently teacheth.

Commission, *Commissio*, Is for the most part in the understanding of the Law as much as *Delegatio* with the *Civilians*. See *Broke*, *tit.* Commission, and is taken for the Warrant, or Letters Patent, that all Men exercising Jurisdiction either ordinary or extraordinary, have for their power to hear or determine any Cause or Action. Of these, see divers in the Table of the *Register Original*, *verbo* Commissio; yet this word sometimes is extended further than to matters of Judgment, as the *Commission* of Purveyors, 11 *H.* 4. *cap.* 28. But with this Epithite (*High*) is used for the Honourable *Commission-Court* instituted and founded upon the Statute 1 *Eliz. cap.* 1. but for divers reasons utterly abolished and taken away by the Statute made 16, 17 *Car.* 1. *cap.* 10.

Commission of Association, Mentioned 18 *Eliz. cap.* 9. Is a *Commission* under the Great Seal, to *associate* two or more learned persons, with the several Justices in the several Circuits and Counties in *Wales*.

Commission of Anticipation, Was a *Commission* under the Great Seal, to Collect a Subsidy before the day, *Anno* 5 *H.* 8. *Co.* 12 *Rep. fol.* 120.

Commission of Rebellion, *Commissio Rebellionis*, Is otherwise called *a Writ of Rebellion*, *breve rebellionis*, and is sent forth, when a man, after Proclamation made by the Sheriff, upon an Order of the *Chancery*, under great penalty to present himself to the Court by a certain day. And this *Commission* is directed by the way of Command to certain persons, to the end, that they, three, two, or one of them do apprehend, or cause to be apprehended the Party as a Rebel and Contemner of the Kings Laws, wheresoever they find him within the Kingdom, and bring him, or cause him to be brought to the Court upon a day therein assigned. The true Copy of this *Commission* or *Writ* you have in *Cromp. Jurisd. Court de Star-Chamber* as also in *West.* touching *Proceedings in Chancery*, *sect.* 24.

Commissioner, *Commissionarius*, Is he that hath *Commission*, as Letters Patent, or other lawful Warrant, to execute any publick Office, as *Commssioners* of the Office of *Fines* and *Licences*, *West. par.* 2. *Symbol. tit.* Fines, *sect.* 106. *Commissioners* in *Eyre*, *Anno* 3 *E.* 1. *cap.* 26. *Commissioners* of Sewers, 23 *H.* 8. 5. 12 *Car.* 2. *cap.* 6. with infinite other such like.

Committee, Is he or they to whom the consideration, or ordering of any matter is referred, either by some Court, or consent of Parties to whom it belongeth. As in Parliament, a Bill being read, is either consented unto, and passed, or denyed, or neither of both, but referred to the consideration of some discreet Men appointed by the House farther to examine it, who thereupon are called *Committees*: *Committee* of the King, *West. par.* 2. *Symb. tit.* Chancery, *sect.* 144. This word seemeth to be something strangely used in *Kitchin*, *fol* 160. where the Widow of the Kings Tenant being dead, is called *The Committee of the King*, that is, one committed by the ancient Law of the Land to the Kings Care and Protection.

Common Bench, *Bancus Communis*, Is sometimes used for the Court of Common Pleas, *Anno* 2 *E.* 3. *cap.* 11. so called, as Mr. *Cambden* saith in his *Brittania*, *pag.* 113. *Quia communia placita inter subditos ex jure nostro*, *quod commune vocant*, *in hoc disceptantur*, that is, the Pleas or Controversies tryed between common persons. See more in *Common Pleas*.

Common Fine, *Finis Communis*, Of this *Fleta*, *lib.* 1. *cap.* 48. *sect. quibus*, hath these words, *Quibus expeditis* (speaking of the business finished by Justices in *Eyre*) *consueverunt Justiciarii imponere villatis*, *juratoribus hundredis & toti comitatui concelamentum & omnes separatim americare*, *quod videtur voluntarium*, *cum de perjurio & concelamento non fuerint convicti*; *sed potius dispensandum esset cum eis quod animas in statera posuerint pro pacis conservatione.* And a little following he saith, *Quod communes misericordiæ vel fines comitatuum amerciatorum in finibus itinerum Justiciariorum*, &c. which words of his have relation to the Statute, *Westm.* 1. *cap.* 18. which read, It is called in some places *Head-silver*, in others *Certum Letæ*, and was, as it seems, first granted to the Lord, towards the charge of his Purchase of the Leet, whereby the Resiants had now an ease to do their Suit Royal within the Mannor, and not be compelled to go to the Sheriffs Tourn to do it. And for this *Common Fine* the Lord must prescribe, and cannot distrain for it without a Prescription, as appears in *Godfryes* Case, in 11 *Rep. fol.* 44. *b.* The Clerk of the Market shall take no *Common Fine*, 13 *R.* 2. *cap.* 4.

Commoigne, A Brother Monk, residing in the same Covent, 3. *par. Inst. fol.* 15.

Common Pleas, *Communia Placita*, Is the Kings Court now held in *Westminster-hall*, but in ancient time moveable, as appears by *Mag. Charta*, *cap.* 11. and also 2 *E.* 3. *cap.* 11. & *Pupilla oculi*, part 5. cap. 22. But Mr. *Gwin* in the *Preface to his Reading* saith, That until the time that *Henry* the Third granted the great Charter, there were but two Courts in all, called *The Kings Courts*, whereof one was the *Exchequer*, the other the *Kings Bench*, which was then called *Curia Domini Regis*, and *Aula Regia*, because it followed the King and Court; and that upon the Grant of that Charter, the Court of *Common Pleas* was erected and setled in one certain place, *viz. Westminster*. And because this Court was settled at *Westminster*, therefore after that, all Writs ran, *Quod sit coram Justiciariis nostris apud Westmonasterium*; whereas before it was *Coram me vel Justiciariis meis*, simply without addition of place, as he well observeth out of *Glanvile* and *Bracton*: The one writing in *Henry* the Seconds time, before the Court was erected; the other in the later time of *Henry* the third, who erected this Court. All civil Causes, both real and personal, are or were in former times tryed in this Court according to the strict Law of the Realm. And by *Fortescue*. *cap.* 50. it seemeth to have been the only Court for real Causes; The chief Judge of that Court is called

The Lord Chief Justice of the Common Pleas, assisted with three or four Associates, which are created by Letters Patents from the King, and, as it were enstalled or placed upon the Bench by the Lord Chancellor and Lord Chief Justice of the Court, as appeareth by *Fortescue*, *cap.* 51. who expresses all the Circumstances of this admission. The rest of the Officers belonging to this Court, are, The *Custos brevium*, three Protonotories, Chirographer, fourteen Filacers, four Exigenters, Clerk of the Warrants, Clerk of the Juries, or *Jurata* Writs, Clerk of the Kings Silver, Clerk of the Treasury, Clerk of the Essoines, Clerk of the Outlawries; whose distinct Functions, look in their proper places. See *Common Bench*.

Common day in Plea of Land, *Anno* 13 R. 2. *Stat.* 1. *cap.* 17. signifieth an ordinary day in Court, as *Octabis Michaelis*, *Quindena Paschæ*, *&c.* as you may see in the Statute made *Anno* 51 *Hen.* 3. concerning general days in the Bench.

Common Intendment, Is common meaning; so *bar to Common Intendment* is an ordinary or general bar, which commonly disables the Plaintiffs Declaration. Of *common Intendment*, a Will shall not be supposed to be made by Collusion, *Co.* on *Lit. fol.* 78. *b.* See *Intendment*.

Commons House of Parliament, Is the *Lower-House* so called, because the *Commons* of the Realm, that is, the Knights of Shires, Citizens and Burgesses, sit there, *Cromp. Jur.* 9.

Common Law, *Lex Communis*, Hath three significations; First, for the Laws of this Land simply, without any other Law, as Customary, Civil, Spiritual, or whatsoever other Law joyned to it; as when it is disputed in our Laws of *England*, what ought of right to be determined by the *Common Law*, and what by the Spiritual Law, or Admirals Court, or otherwise. Secondly, It is taken for the Kings Courts, as the *Kings Bench* or *Common Pleas*, only to shew a difference between them and base Courts, as Customary-Courts, Courts-Baron, County-Courts, Pipowders, and such like; as when a Plea of Land is removed out of ancient Demesne, because the Land is Frank-fee, and pleadable at the *Common-Law*, that is to say, in the Kings Court, and not in ancient Demesne, or in any other base Court. Thirdly, and most usually, By *Common-Law* is understood such *Laws* as were generally taken and holden for *Law* before any Statute was made to alter the same. As for example, Tenant for Life or for Years were not punishable for Wast at the *Common-Law*, till the Statute of *Gloucester*, *cap.* 5. which gives an Action of Wast against them. But Tenant by the Curtesie, and Tenant in Dower, were punishable for Wast at the *Common-Law*, that is, by the usual and common received Laws of the Realm before the said Statute was made.

Commorth. See *Comorth*.

Commotes, Signifies in *Wales* a part of a Shire, as a Cantred or Hundred, 28 *H.* 8. *cap.* 3. See Stat. *Walliæ*, 12 *E.* 1. and 21 *H.* 8. *cap.* 26. It denotes a great Lordship, and may include one or divers Mannors, *Co.* on *Lit. fol.* 5.

Commune, See *Comminalty*.

Communi Custodia, Was a Writ that lay for that Lord whose Tenant holding by Knights-service, dies, and leaves his eldest Son under age, against a Stranger that entreth the Land, and obtaineth the Ward of the Body. See *Old Nat. Brev. fol.* 89. and *Reg. Orig. fol.* 161. *a.* But this is now become of no use since the Stat. 12 *Car.* 2. *cap.* 24. hath taken Wardships with the Dependances.

Communia Placita non tenenda in Scaccario, Is a Writ directed to the Treasurer and Barons of the *Exchequer*, forbidding them to hold Plea between two common persons in that Court where neither of them belong to it, *Reg. Orig. fol.* 187. *b.*

Communication, *Communicatio*, A talking or conferring with, where there is only a Discourse between two or more, without any perfect Agreement; this may be called a *Communication*, being such as no Action can be grounded upon. See *Nudum Pactum*.

Comorth, *Comortha*, It signifies a Contribution, 4 *H.* 4. *cap.* 27. and 26 *H.* 8. *cap.* 6. prohibits the levying any such in *Wales*, or the Marches, *&c.* It seems this was a collection made at Marriages, and when young Priests said or sung their first Masses, and sometimes for Redemption of Murders or Felonies.

Companion of the Garter, Is one of the Knights of that most honorable Order, 24 *H.* 8. *cap.* 13. See *Garter*.

Compositio mensurarum, Is the Title of an ancient Ordinance for *Measures*, not Printed, and mentioned in the Statute of 23 *Hen.* 8. *cap.* 4.

Compromise, *Compromissum*, We usually say *Comprimise*, is a mutual *Promise* of two or more Parties at Difference, to refer the ending of their Controversies to the Arbitriment and Equity of one or more Abitrators, *West. part.* 2. *Symbol. tit.* Compromise, *sect.* 1. defines it thus, A *Compromise* or submission is the faculty or power of pronouncing Sentence between Parties at Controversie, given to Arbitrators by the Parties mutual private consent, without publick authority.

Computation, Is used in the Common-Law for the true and indifferent construction of time, so that neither the one party nor the other shall do wrong, nor the determination of times referred at large, be taken one way or other, but computed according to the just censure of the Law. As if Indentures of Demise are ingrossed, bearing Date the eleventh day of *May*, 1669. *To Have and to Hold* the Land in *S.* for three years from henceforth, and the Indentures are delivered the fourth day of *June*, in the year aforesaid. In this case, *from henceforth* shall be accounted from the day of the delivery of the Indentures, and not by any *Computation* from the Date: And if the said Indenture be delivered at four of the Clock in the Afternoon of the said fourth Day, this Lease shall end the third day of *June* in the third year; for the Law in this *Computation* rejects all Fractions or Divisions of the day, for the incertainty, which always is the Mother of Contention; so where the Statute of Inrolments made

made *Anno* 27 *Hen.* 8. *cap* 16. is, That the Writings shall be Inrolled within six Months after the Date of the same Writings indented; if such Writing have Date, the six Months shall be accounted from the Date, and not from the Delivery; but if it want Date, then shall it be accounted from the Delivery, *Co. lib.* 5. *fol.* 1. If any Deed be shewed to a Court at *Westminster*, the Deed, by Judgment of the Law, shall remain in Court all the Term in which it is shewed, for all the Term in Law is but as one day, *Co. lib.* 5. *fol.* 74. If a Church be void, and the true Patron doth not present within six months, then the Bishop of the Diocess may collate his Chaplain; but these six months shall not be *computed* according to the 28 days to the month, but according to the *Calendar*; and there is great diversity in our common Speech in the singular number, as a *Twelve-month*, which includes all the year, according to the *Calendar*; and *twelve months* which shall be *computed* according to 28 days to every month, *Co. lib.* 6. *fol.* 61. *b.*

Computo, Is a Writ so called of the effect, because it compelleth a Bayliff, Receiver or Chamberlain, to yield his Account, *Old Nat. Brev. fol.* 58. It is founded upon the Statute of *West.* 2. *cap.* 2. *Anno* 13 *E.* 1. which, for your better understanding, you may read. And it lieth also for Executors of Executors, 15 *E.* 3. *Statut. de provis. Victual. cap.* 5. Thirdly, Against the Guardian in Socage, for Wast made in the Minority of the Heir, *Marlb. cap.* 17. And see farther, where, how, and for what it lies, *Reg. Orig. fol.* 135. *Old Nat. Brev. ubi supra*, & *F. N. B. fol.* 116.

Comprint, Properly signifies to *Print* together; but as it is used in common Speech among Dealers in Books, it intends a surreptitious *Printing* of anothers Copy, to make a gain thereby to himself. This is contrary to the Statutes made 14 *Car.* 2. *cap.* 33. 16 *Car.* 2. *cap.* 6. 16 & 17 *Car.* 2. *cap.* 7. and 17 *Car.* 2. *cap.* 4. *apud Oxon.*

Conabel, (French *Convenable*, that is, convenient;) the Word is of little use in these days, but you may read it in *Artic. decani & capit. S.* Pauli *Priorat. S.* Helenæ, *Dat.* 21 *June* 1439. We Ordain, That there be made a Hache of *Conabel* heythe, &c. that no strange *Peopille* may enter, &c. as you and them think honest and *Conabel*.

Concealers, Be such as find out *concealed* Lands, that is, such Lands as are privily kept from the King by common person, having nothing to shew for them, *Anno* 39 *Eliz. cap.* 22. They be so called, *a concelando*, as *mons a movendo* by an Antiphrasis. They are called a *troublesom or disturbant sort of men*, turbulent persons, 3 *par. Inst. fol.* 188.

Concessi, A word of frequent use in Conveyances, creating a Covenant in Law, as *Dedi* makes a Warranty, *Co.* on *Lit. fol.* 384.

Conclusion, *Conclusio*, Is when a Man by his own act upon Record, hath charged himself with a Duty, or other thing. As if a Freeman confess himself to be the Villain of *A.* upon Record, and afterward *A.* takes his Goods, he shall be *concluded* to say in any Action or Plea afterwards, that he is free, by reason of his own confession. So if the Sheriff upon a *Capias* to him directed, returns that he hath taken the Body, and yet hath not the Body in Court at the day of the Return; he shall be amerced, and if it were upon a *Capias ad sat.* the Plaintiff may have his Action against the Sheriff for the Escape; for by such Returns the Sheriff hath *concluded* himself. And this Word *Conclusion* is taken in another sense, as for the end or later part of any Declaration, Bar, Replication, &c. As where to the Bar there ought to be a Replication, the *Conclusion* of his Plea shall be, *Et hoc paratus est verificare.* If in Dower, the Tenant pleads, That he was never seised to render Dower, the *Conclusion* shall be, *Et de hoc ponit se super Patriam.* And in what manner the *Conclusion* shall be, according to the nature of several Actions. See *Kitchin, fol.* 219, 220.

Concord, *Concordia*, Is in the Common-Law, by a peculiar signification, defined to be the very Agreement between parties, that intend the levying of a Fine of Lands one to the other, how and in what manner the Land shall pass: In the form whereof, many things are to be considered, *West. part.* 2. *Symb. tit.* Fines *and* Concords, *sect.* 30. whom read at large. *Concord*, Is also an Agreement made upon any Trespass committed between two or more, and is divided into a *Concord executory*, and a *Concord executed.* See *Plowd. fol.* 5. & 6. *Reniger* and *Fogassa's* Case, where it appeareth by some Opinion, That the one bindeth not, as being imperfect; the other absolute, and tyes the parties; And yet by some other Opinion in the same Case, it is affirmed, That Agreements executory be perfect, and do no less bind than Agreements executed, *fol.* 8. *b.*

Concubinage, *Concubinatus*, In common acception signifies the keeping of a Whore, or Concubine, but in a legal, is an Exception against her that sueth for her Dower; whereby it is alledged, that she was not a Wife lawfully marryed to the Party in whose Lands she seeketh to be endowed, but his Concubine, *Britton, cap.* 107. *Bract. lib.* 4. *tract.* 6. *cap.* 8.

Conders, May seem to proceed from the French *Conduire*, i. *Gubernare*, they be such as stand upon high places near the Sea-coast at the time of Herring-fishing, to make signs with Boughs, &c. in their hands unto the Fishers, which way the shole of Herrings passeth; for that does appear better to such as stand upon some high Cliff on the Shore, by a kind of blue colour that the said Fish causeth in the Water, than to those that be in the Ships. These be otherwise called *Hewers* (probably from the French *Huyer*, *exclamare*) and *Balkers*, *Directors* and *Guiders*, as appeareth by the Statute made *Anno* 1 *Jacobi, cap.* 23.

Condition, *Conditio*, Is a restraint or bridle annexed to a thing, so that by the not performance, the party to it shall receive prejudice and loss, and by the performance, commodity and advantage, *West. part.* 1. *Symb. lib.* 2. *sect.* 156. and *Co. lib.* 3. *Pennant's* Case, *fol.* 64. Of these *Conditions* there are divers kinds, *Condition collateral*, *Condition in fact*, *Condition in Law*, *Condition exprest*, and *Condition implyed*, &c. *Condition collateral*, is that which is annexed to any collateral act, as that the Lessee shall not go to *Canterbury*, *Co. lib.* 3. *fol.* 65. *Condition in Fact*, is that which is exprest in plain words in any Feoffment, Lease

or

or Grant: *Condition in Law* is implyed, though not at all exprest in the Grant. Also *Conditions* are either precedent, and going before the Estate, and are executed, or else subsequent and executory. *Condition precedent*, doth get and gain the thing or Estate made upon *Condition*, by the performance of it. *Condition subsequent*, keeps and continues the thing or Estate made upon *condition*, by the performance of it. *Condition precedent* is, when a Lease is made for Life to one upon *condition*, That if the Lessee will pay to the Lessor 20 *li.* at such a day, then he shall have Fee-simple: Here the *Condition* precedes the Estate in Fee-simple, and upon performance of the *condition*, gains the Fee-simple. *Condition subsequent* is, when one grants to *J. S.* his Manor of *Dale* in Fee-simple, upon *condition*, that the Grantee shall pay to him at such a day 20 *l.* or else that his Estate shall cease; here the *Condition* is *subsequent*, and following the Estate in Fee, and upon the performance thereof continues the Estate. See more of this in *Co. lib.* 3. *fol.* 64. and in *Lit. lib.* 3. *cap* 5. and *Perkins* in the last Title *Of Conditions*.

Cone and Key, *Bract. lib.* 2. *cap.* 37. *num.* 3. A Woman at the Age of fourteen or fifteen years may take the charge of her House, and receive *Cone and Key*, that is, *computum & clavem. Cone* or *Colne* in the Saxon signifying *computus*, and *Key*, *clavis*, wherewith there is something agreeable, *Glanvile, lib.* 7. *cap.* 9.

Confederacy, Is when two or more *confederate* themselves to do any hurt or damage to another, or to do any unlawful thing. And though a Writ of Conspiracy doth not lye, if the party be not Indicted, and in lawful manner acquitted, for so are the words of the Writ; yet false *confederacy* between divers persons shall be punished, though nothing be put in *ure*, and this appears by the Book of 27 *Assise, placit.* 44. where there is a Note, That two were Indicted of *Confederacy*, each of them to maintain other, whether their matter were true or false; and though nothing was supposed to be put in *ure*, the Parties were put to answer, because this thing is forbidden by the Law. So in the next Article in the same Book, Enquiry shall be made of Conspirators and *Confederators* which bind themselves together, &c. falsly to indite or acquit, &c. the manner of their binding, and between whom; which proves also, That *Confederacy* to indite or acquit, though nothing be done, is punishable by the Law. And it is to be observed, That this *Confederacy* punishable by Law, before it is executed, ought to have four Incidents. First, To be declared by some manner of prosecution, as by making of Bonds or Promises the one to the other. Secondly, To be Malicious, as for unjust Revenge. Thirdly, To be false against an Innocent. And lastly, To be out of Court, and voluntary, *Termes of the Law, fol.* 162, 163.

Confession of Offence, Is, when a Prisoner is Appealed or Indicted of Treason or Felony, and brought to the Bar to be Arraigned, and his Indictment is read unto him; And the Court demands what he can say thereto, then either he confesses the Offence, and the Indictment to be true, or estranging him from the Offence, pleads Not Guilty, or else gives an indirect Answer, and so in effect stands mute. *Confession* may be made in two sorts, and to two several ends: The one is, He may confess the Offence whereof he is indicted openly in the Court before the Judge, and submit himself to the Censure and Judgment of the Law, which *Confession* is the most certain Answer, and best satisfaction that may be given to the Judge to condemn the Offendor, so that it proceeds freely of his own accord, without any threats, force, or extremity used: For if the *Confession* arise from any of these Causes, it ought not to be Recorded. As if a Woman was indicted for the Felonious taking of Bread, to the value of two shillings, and being thereof arraigned, she confest the Felony, and said, That she did it by the Commandment of her Husband, and the Judges, in pity, would not record her *Confession*, but caused her to plead Not Guilty to the Felony; whereupon the Jury found, That she stole the Bread by compulsion of her Husband, against her will, for which cause she was discharged, 27 *Ass. pl.* 50. The other kind of *Confession* is, when the Prisoner *confesses* the Indictment to be true, and that he hath committed the Offence whereof he is Indicted, and then becomes an Approver, that is, an Accuser of others who have committed the same Offence whereof he is Indicted, or other Offences with him, and then prays the Judge to have a Coroner assigned him, to whom he may make relation of those Offences, and the full circumstances thereof. There is also a third kind of *Confession* made by an Offendor in Felony, which is not in Court before the Judge, as the other two are; but before a Coroner in a Church, or other priviledged place, upon which the Offendor, by the ancient Law of the Realm, was to abjure.

Confirmation, *Confirmatio*, Cometh of the Verb *Confirmare*, *quod est firmum facere*, and therefore it is said, That *Confirmatio omnes supplet defectus, licet id quod actum est, ab initio non valuit, Co.* on *Lit. lib.* 3. *cap.* 9. *sect.* 515. It is a Conveyance of an Estate or Right *in esse*, whereby a voidable Estate is made sure and unavoidable, or whereby a particular Estate is increased. Nay, it is a strengthening of an Estate formerly, and yet voidable, though not presently void. For example, A Bishop granteth his Chancellorship by Patent, for the term of the Patentees life; this is no void Grant, but voidable by the Bishops death, except it be strengthened by the *Confirmation* of the Dean and Chapter. *Qualibet* confirmatio *aut est perficiens, crescens aut diminuens.* 1. *Perficiens*, As if Feoffee upon a condition make a Feoffment, and the Feoffor *confirm* the Estate of the second Feoffee: So if Disseisee *confirm* the Estate of the Disseisor, or his Feoffee. 2. *Crescens*, Doth always enlarge the Estate of a Tenant; as Tenant at Will, to hold for years; or Tenant for years to hold for life. 3. *Diminuens*, As when the Lord of whom the Land is holden, *confirms* the Estate of his Tenant to hold by a less Rent. See more of this, *West. Symb. part.* 1. *lib.* 2. *sect.* 500. *F. N. B. fol.* 169, 226, 271. and *Lit. lib.* 3. *cap.* 9. *Co.* 9. *Rep. Beaumont's* Case.

Confiscate, *Confiscatus*, May be derived either from the Latine *Confiscare*, or the French *Confisquer*, that is, *in publicum addicere*; all these words are drawn from *Fiscus*, which (as *Minshew* saith)

saith) originally signifieth a *Hamper* or *Basket*, but *Metonymically* the Emperors Treasure, because it was anciently kept in such Hampers. And though our King doth not put his Treasure in such things, yet as the *Romans* have said, That such Goods as were forfeited to the Emperour, were *bona confiscata*, in like manner do we say of such Goods as are forfeited to the Kings Exchequer. And the Title to have these Goods is given to the King by such Law, when they are not claimed by some other. As if a man be indicted, That he feloniously stole the Goods of another man, when, in truth, they are the proper Goods of him indicted; and they are brought in Court against him as the manner is, and he then asked, what he says to the said Goods, to which he disclaims; by this Disclaimer he shall lose the Goods, although that afterwards he be acquitted of the Felony, and the King shall have them as *confiscated*: But otherwise it is, if he do not disclaim them. The same Law is, where Goods are found in the Felons Possession, which he disavows; and afterwards is attainted of other Goods, and not of them, there the Goods which he disavows are *Confiscate* to the King; but had he been attainted of the same Goods, they should have been said to be forfeited, and not *confiscate*, notwithstanding his disavowment. So if an Appeal of Robbery be brought, and the Plaintiff leaves out some of his Goods, he shall not be received to enlarge his Appeal: And for as much as there is none to have the Goods so left out, the King shall have them as *confiscate*, according to the old Rule, *Quod non capit Christus, capit fiscus.* And as in the case aforesaid, the Law punishes the Owner for his negligence and connivency; so also the Law abhors malice in seeking the life of any without just cause. And therefore if *A.* hath the Goods of *B.* by delivery or finding, and *B.* brings an Appeal against *A.* for taking them feloniously, and it is found, That they were the Plaintiffs Goods, and that the Defendant came lawfully by them: In this case the Goods are not *confiscate* to the King, because of the false and malicious Appeal. See more in *Stamf. pl. cor. lib. 3. cap. 24. 3. Inst. fol. 227.*

Confraryre, *Confraternitas*, A Fraternity or Brotherhood, as the *Confrairie de St.* George, or *les Chivaleers de la blue Gartier*, the honourable Society of the Knights of the Garter.

Confreres, *Confratres*, Brethren in a Religious House, Fellows of one Society, 32 *H.* 8. *cap.* 24.

Congeable, Cometh of the French *Conge*, that is, *Venia*, and signifies in our Common-Law as much as lawful, or lawfully done, or done with leave, as the Entry of the Disseisee is *congeable*, and so *Littleton* uses it in his 410 *Section*, and *Cro. 2. par. fol.* 31.

Conge d' Accorder, Signifies leave to Accord or Agree, it is mentioned in the Statute of *Fines*, 18 *E.* 3. in these words, *When the Original Writ is delivered in presence of the Parties before the Justices, a Pleader shall say this,* Sir Justice Conge d' Accorder; *And the Justice shall say to him*, What saith Sir R. *and shall name one of the Parties, &c.*

Conge d' Eslire, *Venia Eligendi*; Is very French, and signifieth in our Common-Law the Kings permission Royal to a Dean and Chapter in time of Vacation, to chuse a Bishop; or to an Abby or Priory of his own foundation, to chuse the Abbot or Prior, *F. N. B. fol.* 169, 170. Touching this matter, *Gwin* in his *Preface to his Readings* saith, That the King of *England* as Soveraign Patron of all Arch-bishopricks, Bishopricks, and other Ecclesiastical Benefices, had of ancient time free appointment of all Ecclesiastical Dignities, whensoever they chanced to be void in vesting them first, *per baculum & annulum*, and afterwards by his Letters Patents, and that in process of time he made the Election over to others under certain Forms and Conditions, as, that they should at every Vacation, before they chuse, demand of the King *Conge d' Eslire*, that is, licence to proceed to Election, and then after the Election, to crave his Royal assent, &c. And further, he affirmeth by good proof out of Common-Law-Books, That King *John* was the first that granted this, and that it was afterwards confirmed by *Westm.* 1. *cap.* 1. which Statute was made *Anno* 3 *E.* 1. And again, by the Statute *Articuli Cleri, cap.* 2. which was ordained, 25 *E.* 3. *Stat.* 3.

Congius, An ancient Measure, containing about nine pints, *Et reddat quinq; congios celiæ & unum Ydromelli, &c. Charta Edmundi Regis de anno* 946.

Conisance. See *Cognizance.*

Conjuration, *Conjuratio*, Is a Compound of *con* and *juro*, and so it signifieth a plot or compact made by Men, combining themselves together by Oath or Promise, to do any publick harm: But in our Common-Law it is specially used for such as have personal conference with the Devil, or Evil Spirits, to know any Secret, or to effect any purpose, *Anno* 5 *Eliz. cap.* 16. And the difference between *Conjuration* and Witchcraft seemeth to be this, That the one by Prayers and Invocations of Gods powerful Names, compels the Devil to say or do what he commandeth him; the other dealeth rather by a friendly and voluntary Conference and Agreement between him or her and the Devil, or Familiar, to have her or his desires or turns served, in lieu of Bloud, or other Gift offered unto him, especially of his or her Soul. And both these differ from Enchantments or Sorceries, because they are personal Conferences with the Devil, as is already said; but these are but Medicines, and ceremonial forms of words, called commonly *Charms*, without Apparition.

Consanguineo, Is a Writ, for the which see *Avo, & Reg. Orig. de Avo, proavo & consanguineo, fol.* 226. *a.*

Conservator of the Truce and safe Conducts, *Conservator Induciarum & salvorum Regis conductuum*, Was an Officer appointed in every part of the Sea by the Kings Letters Patent, and had forty pounds for his yearly stipend at the least. His charge was to enquire of all Offences done against the Kings *Truce and safe Conducts* upon the main Sea, out of the Liberties of the Cinque-Ports, as the Admirals customably were wont to do, and such other things as are declared, 2 *H.* 5. *cap.* 6. Touching this matter, read also the Statute of 4 *H.* 5. *cap.* 7.

Conservator of the Peace, *Conservator vel Custos Pacis*, Is he that hath an especial charge, by vertue of his Office, to see the Kings *Peace* kept, which *Peace Lambard* in effect defineth to be a with-holding or abstinence from that injurious force and violence, which boysterous and unruly persons are in their natures prone to use towards others, were they not restrained by Laws, and fear of punishment. Of these *Conservators* he farther saith thus, That before the time of King *Edward* the Third, who first erected Justices of *Peace*, there were sundry persons, that by the Common-Law had interest in keeping the Peace, Of those, some had that charge, as incident to their Offices which they did bear, and so included within the same, that they were nevertheless called by the name of their Office only: Some others had it simply, as of it self, and were thereof named *Custodes pacis*, Wardens, or *Conservators of the Peace*. The former and later sort he again subdivideth, which read in his *Eirenarcha*, *lib.* 1. *cap.* 3. The Corporation of the great Level of the *Fens* does consist of a Governor, six Bayliffs, twenty *Conservators* and Commonalty, as by Act of Parliament, 15 *Car.* 2. *Cap.* 17. appears. The Chamberlain of *Chester* is a *Conservator of the Peace* in that County, by verue of his Office, 4. *Inst. fol.* 212. And Pety-Constables are by the Common-Law *Conservators of the Peace*, &c. *Conservator* of the Priviledges of the Hospitalers and Templers, &c. *West.* 2. *cap.* 43. 4 *Inst. fol.* 341.

Consideration, *Consideratio*, Is that with us which the Greeks called συνάλλαγμα, that is the material cause of a Contract, without which it would not be effectual or binding. This *Consideration* is either expressed, as if a man bargain to give twenty shillings for a Horse; or else implyed, as when the Law it self enforceth a *Consideration*, as if a man come into a common Inn, and there staying some time, taking both Meat and Lodging for himself and his Horse, the Law presumeth that he intends to pay for both, though nothing be farther covenanted between him and his Host. And therefore if he discharge not the House, the Host may stay his Horse, *Fulbeckes Parall. tract. Contracts, fol.* 6. Also there is a *consideration* of Nature and Bloud, and valuable *consideration*: And therefore if a Man be indebted to divers others, and yet in *consideration* of natural affection, gives all his Goods to his Son or Cousin, this shall be construed a fraudulent Gift within the Act of 13 *Eliz. cap.* 5. because this Act intends a valuable *consideration*.

Consistory, *Consistorium*, Is a word borrowed of the *Italians*, or rather *Lombards*, and signifies as much as Tribunal. It is *Vocabulum utriusq; juris*, and is used for the place of Justice in the Court-Christian or Spiritual. Every Archbishop, and Bishop hath a *Consistory* Court, held before his Chancellor or Commissary in his Cathedral Church, or other convenient place of his Diocess, for Ecclesiastical Causes, 4. *Inst. fol.* 338. See further concerning this, *Seldens* Hist. of *Tythes*, *pag.* 413, 414.

Consolidation, *Consolidatio*, It is used for uniting two Benefices in one, *Broke*, *tit. union*, and *Anno* 37 *H.* 8. *Cap.* 21. This is taken from the Civil-Law, where it signifies properly an uniting of the possession or profit with the property. For example, if a man have by Legacy *usum-fructum fundi*, and afterwards buy the Property or Feesimple of the Heir, *Hoc casu consolidatio fieri dicitur*. See *Union and Unity of Possession*.

Conspirators. See their full Description, 33 *E.* 1. *Stat.* 2.—2. *par. Inst. fol.* 384. & 562. See *Conspiracy*.

Conspiracy, *Conspiratio*, Though both in Latine and French it is used for an Agreement of Men, to do any thing either good or bad; yet in Common-Law it is alway taken in *pejorem partem*. It is defined *Anno* 33 *E.* 1. *Stat.* 2. to be an Agreement of such as do confeder, and bind themselves by Oath, Covenant, or other Alliance, That every of them shall bear and aid the other, falsly and malitiously to Indite, or falsly to move or maintain Pleas, and also such as cause Children within age, to appeal Men of Felony, whereby they are imprisoned, and so grieved; and such as retain Men in the Countries with Liveries or Fees, to maintain their malicious Enterprises. And this extendeth as well to the Takers, as to the Givers. And Stewards and Bayliffs of great Lords, which by their Seigniory, Office or Power, undertake to bear or maintain Quarrels, Pleas or Debates, that concern other Parties, than such as touch the Estate of their Lords, or themselves. See 4 *E.* 3. *cap.* 11. 3 *H.* 7. *cap.* 13. and also 1 *H.* 5. *cap.* 3. and 18 *H.* 6. *cap.* 12. and the *New Book of Entries*, *verb. Conspiracy*. In the places before-mention'd, *Conspiracy* is taken more generally, and is confounded with Maintenance and Champerty: But in a more special signification, it is taken for a *confederacy* of two at the least, falsly to indict one, or to procure one to be indicted of Felony. And the punishment of *conspiracy*, upon an Indictment of Felony, at the Kings Suit, is, that the Party attainted, lose his *Frank-Law*, to the intent that he be not empannelled upon Juries or Assises, or such like Employments, for the testifying of truth. And if he have to do with the Kings Court, that he make his Attorney, and that his Lands, Goods and Chattels be seised into the Kings hands, his Lands estreated, his Trees rased, and his Body committed to Prison. 27 *Ass.* 59. *Cromp. Just. of Peace*, *fol.* 156. *b.* This is called *Villanous Judgment*. See *Villanous Judgment* But if the Party grieved sue upon the Writ of *Conspiracy*, then see *F. N. B. fol.* 114, 115. *Conspiracy* may be also in cases of less weight, *Idem fol.* 116, &c. As *Conspiracies* made by Victuallers, touching selling of Victuals, shall be grievously punished. See 37 *H.* 8. 23. and 3. *part. Inst. fol.* 143. See *Frank-Law*.

Conspiratione, Is a Writ that lies against *Conspirators*, *F. N. B. fol.* 114. *d. Cromp. de Jurisd. fol.* 209. See also the *Register fol.* 134.

Constable, *Constabularius*, Is a Saxon word compounded of *Koning*, and *Staple*, which do signifie the stay or hold of the King, *Lam. Duties of* Constables, *num* 4. But I have heard it made heretofore of these two words, *Comes stabuli*, which seemeth to me the more probable, because we have the Officer from *France*, as most others, and not from the Saxons. And *Tilius* in his *Commentaries de rebus Gallicis*, lib. 2. cap. *de Conestabili*, hath the same Etymology, giving the reason thereof, *qui praeest stabulo*; which Office is ancient here in *England*, and mentioned by *Bracton*, seeming to answer him that was called *Tribunus celerum* under the first Kings of *Rome*, and *Magister equitum* afterward. This word is

diversly

diversly used in our Common-Law: First, For the *Constable* of *England*, who is also called *Marshal*, *Stamf. pl. cor. fol.* 65. of whose great Dignity and Authority, a man may find many arguments and signs both in the Statutes and Chronicles of this Realm. His Office consisteth in the care of the common Peace of the Land, in deeds of Arms, and matters of War, *Lamb. ubi supra*, with whom agreeth the Statute of *Anno* 13 *R.* 2. *cap.* 2. *Stat.* 1. and *Smith, de Rep. Anglor. lib.* 2. *cap.* 25. Of this Officer or Magistrate, Mr. *Guin* in the *Preface to his Reading*, saith to this effect, The Court of the *Constable* and *Marshal* determineth Contracts touching deeds of Arms out of the Realm, and handleth things concerning War within the Realm, as *Combates*, *Blasons of Armory*, &c. But he may not deal with Battel in Appeals, nor generally with any other thing that may be tryed by the Laws of the Land, and read *Fortescue*, *cap.* 32. This Office was belonging heretofore to the Lords of certain Mannors, *Jure feodi*, and why it is discontinued, see *Dyer*, *fol.* 285. *pl.* 39. Out of this high Magistracy (saith Mr. *Lambert*) were drawn these lower *Constables*, which we call *Constables of Hundreds* and *Franchises*, and first ordained by the Statute of *Winchester*, 13 *E.* 1. which appointeth for the Conservation of the Peace, and view of Armor, two *Constables* in every Hundred and Franchise, which were called in Latine *Constabularii capitales*. And these be now *High Constables*, because continuance of time, and increase both of People and Offences, hath again, under these, made others in every Town called *Petit Constables*, in Latine *subconstabularii*, which are of like nature, but of inferior Authority to the other. Of these also read *Smith*, *lib.* 2. *cap.* 22. Besides these, there be Officers, of particular places called by this Name, as *Constable* of the Tower, *Stamf. pl. cor. fol.* 152. & *anno* 1 *H.* 4. *cap* 13. *Stows Annals*, *pag.* 812. *Constable* of the *Exchequer*, 51 *H.* 3. *Stat.* 5. *Constable* of *Dover-Castle*, *Camb. Brit.* 239. *F. N. B. fol.* 240. otherwise called *Castellane Westm.* 1. *cap.* 7. *Anno* 3 *E.* 1. But these be *Castellani* properly, as *Lambert* takes notice, though conjoyned in name with the others. See the Statute 32 *H.* 8. *cap.* 38. *Manwood*, *cap.* 13. maketh mention of a *Constable* of the Forest.

Constat, Is a sort of Certificate made by the Clerk of the Pipe, and Auditors of the Exchequer, at the request of any person who intends to plead in that Court for the discharge of any thing, 3 & 4 *E.* 6. 4. 13 *Eliz.* 6. A *Constat* is held to be superior to a Certificate, because this may err or fail in its contents, that cannot, as certifying nothing but what is upon Record. Also the exemplification of the inrollment of Letters Patents is termed a *Constat*, *Co. super Lit. fol.* 225. The difference between a *Constat*, *Inspeximus* & *Vidimus*, you may read at large in *Cokes* 5. *Rep. Pages* Case.

Customs and Services, *Consuetudinibus & servitiis*, Is a Writ of right close, which lyeth against the Tenant, that deforceth his Lord of the Rent or Service due to him. Of this, see more at large in the *Old Nat. Brev. fol.* 77. *F. N B. fol.* 151. and *Reg. Orig. fol.* 159.

Consultation, *Consultatio*, Is a Writ whereby a Cause being formerly removed by Prohibition from the Ecclesiastical-Court, or Court-Christian, to the Kings Court, is returned thither again; for the Judges of the Kings Court, if, upon comparing the Libel with the Suggestion of the Party, they do find the Suggestion false, or not proved, and therefore the Cause to be wrongfully called from Court-Christian, then upon this *Consultation* or Deliberation, they Decree it to be returned again; whereupon the Writ in this Case obtained, is called a *Consultation*. Of this you may read the *Reg. Orig.* 44, 45. *usq; ad* 58. *Old Nat. Brev. fol* 32. & *Fitz. Nat. Brev. fol.* 50.

Contenement, *Contenementum*, Seemeth to be the Freehold-Land which lyeth to a mans Tenement or Dwelling-House that is in his own Occupation: For in *Magna Charta*, *cap.* 14. you have these words, A Free-man shall not be amerced for a small Fault, but after the quantity of the Fault, and for a great Fault after the manner thereof, saving to him his *Contenement* or Free-hold. And a Merchant likewise shall be amerced, saving to him his Merchandises, and a Villain, saving to him his Waynage. And *Bracton*, *lib.* 3. *tract.* 2. *cap.* 1. *num.* 3. hath these words, *Et sciendum quod miles, & liber homo non amerciabitur nisi secundum modum delicti, secundum quod delictum fuit magnum vel parvum & salvo* contenemento *suo, mercator vero non nisi salva Merchandisa sua & villanus nisi salvo Wainagio suo*, which mercy seemeth to have been learned from the Civil-Law, where *executio non potest fieri in boves, aratra, aliave instrumenta rusticorum.* And Sir *Henry Spelman* says, Contenementum *est æstimatio & conditionis forma, qua quis in repub. subsistit.*

Contingent use, Is such a *use* as by the limimitation may, or may not happen to vest. Of which you may read to further satisfaction in *Chudleigh's* Case, *Co. Rep.* 1.

Continuance, Seems to be used in the Common-Law as *Prorogatio* in the Civil. For example, *Continuance* until the next Assises, *F. N. B. fol.* 154 & 244. In both places it is said, That if a Record in the Treasury be alledged by the one Party, and denyed by the other; a *Certiorari* shall be sued to the Treasurer and the Chamberlain of the *Exchequer*, who, if they certifie not into the Chancery, that such a Record is there, or that it is likely to be in the Tower, the King shall send to the Justices, repeating the Certificate, and will them to continue the Assise. In this signification it is likewise used by *Kitchin*, *fol.* 199. & 202. and 11 *H.* 6. *cap.* 4.

Continual Claim, Is a *Claim* made from time to time within every year and day to Land, or other thing, which, in some respect, we cannot attain without danger. As if I be disseised of Land, into which, though I have Right unto it, I dare not enter, for fear of Death or Beating. It behoveth me to hold on my Right of Entry to the best opportunity of me and mine Heir, by approaching as near it as I can once every year as long as I live, and so I save the Right of Entry to my Heir. *Termes de la Ley.* Again, if I have a Slave or Villain broken from me, and remaining any where within the ancient Demesne of the King, being in the hands of the King, I cannot maintain the Writ *De Nativo Habendo* as long as he contineueth there; but if I *Claim* him within the year

and

and day, and so continue my *Claim* until I can find him within that compass, I may lawfully lay hold of him as mine own. *F. N B. fol.* 79. See more in *Lit. verb. Continual Claim.* And the *New Book of Entries*, tit. *Eodem*, and *Fleta*, *lib.* 6. *cap.* 53. See also *Lit. lib.* 3. *cap.* 7. and the Stat. 32 *Hen.* 8. *cap.* 33.

Continuando, Is a word used when the Plaintiff would recover Damages for several Trespasses in the same Action: For in one Action of Trespass, you may recover Damages for divers Trespasses, laying the first with a *Continuando* to the whole time, and is in this form, *Continuando transgressionem prædictam*, *&c. a prædicto die*, *&c. usq; talem diem*, so including the last Trespass.

Contours. See *Countors.*

Contrabanded Goods, Are such as are prohibited by Act of Parliament or Proclamation, to be imported into, or exported out of this into other Nations.

Contract, Is a Covenant or Agreement, with a lawful consideration or cause, *West. Symb. part* 1. *lib.* 1. *sect* 10. or else one thing must be given for another, which is called *Quid pro Quo*; as if I sell my Horse for Money, or Covenant to make you a Lease of my Mannor of *Dale*, in consideration of twenty pound; these are good *Contracts*, because one thing is given for another. But if a man make Promise to me, That I shall have twenty shillings, and that he will be Debtor to me thereof, and after I ask the twenty shillings, and he will not deliver it; yet I shall never have Action to recover, because the Promise was no *Contract*, but a bare Promise, and *ex nudo Pacto non oritur Actio.* But if any thing were given for the twenty shillings, though it were but to the value of a peny, then had it been a good *Contract.*

Contra formam Collationis, Is a Writ that lies, where a man hath given Lands in perpetual Alms to any late Houses of Religion, as to an Abbot and Covent, or to the Warden or Master of any Hospital and his Covent, to find certain poor Men, and do other Divine-Service; if they alien the Lands, then the Donor or his Heirs shall have the said Writ to recover the Lands. But this Writ shall be always brought against the Abbot, or his Successor, and not against the Alienee, although he be Tenant; but in all other Actions, where a man demands Free-hold, the Writ shall be brought against the Tenant of the Land. This is founded upon the Statute of *Westm.* 2. *cap.* 1. And of this see *Reg. Orig. fol.* 238. and *F. N. B. fol.* 210.

Contra formam Feoffamenti, Is a Writ that lies for the Heir of a Tenant, infeoffed of certain Lands or Tenements, by Charter of *Feoffment* of a Lord, to make certain Services and Suits to his Court, and is afterwards distrained for more than is contained in the said Charter, *Reg. Orig. fol.* 176. *Old Nat. Brev.* 162. This Writ lies not for the Plaintiff, Who Claims by Purchase from the first Feoffee, but for the Heir to the first Feoffee.

Contributione facienda, Is a Writ that lyeth where more are bound to one thing, and yet one is put to the whole burden, *Fitz. Nat. Brev. fol.* 162. bringeth these examples, If Joynt-Tenants, or Tenants in Common, hold a Mill *pro indiviso*, and equally take the Profits thereof; the Mill falling to decay, and one or more of them refusing to contribute towards the reparation, the rest shall have this Writ to compel them. And if there be three Coparceners of Lands that owe suit to the Lords Court, and the eldest perform the whole, then may she have this Writ to compell the other two to a contribution of the charge, or to one of them, if one only refuse. The *Old Nat. Brev.* frameth this Writ to a Case, where one only Suit is required for Land, and that Land being sold to divers, Suit is required of them all, or some of them by Distress, as intirely, as if all were still in one, *fol.* 103 See *Reg. Orig. fol.* 176.

Controller, *Contrarotulator*, Cometh of the French *Contrerouleur, antigraphus*, which in *Rome* was used for him, *Cui id muneris injunctum erat, ut observet pecuniam, quam in usum Principis vel civitatis collegerunt exactores*, Budæus in annot. prio. in pand. tit. *De quæstoris officio.* In *England* we have divers officers of this Name, as *Controller of the Kings House*, Stamf. pl. cor. fol. 52. & 6 H. 4. 3. *Controller of the Navy*, 35 Eliz. cap. 4. *Controller of the Customs*, Cromp. Jurisd. fol. 105. *Controller of Callis*, 21 R. 2. cap. 18. *Controller of the Mint*, 2 H. 6. 12. *Controller of the Hamper*, who is an Officer in the Chancery, daily attending in Term-time on the Lord Chancellor, or Lord Keeper, to take all things sealed from the Clerk of the Hamper, to note the just number and effect of all things so received, and to enter the same into a special Book, with all the Duties appertaining to his Majesty, and other Officers for the same, and so chargeth the Clerk of the Hamper thereof. *Controller* of the Pipe, *Contrarotulator Pipæ*, is an Officer of the Exchequer, that writeth out Summons twice every year to the Sheriffs, to levy the Farms and Debts of the Pipe, and also keepeth a *Contra-rollment* of the Pipe. *Controller* of the Pell is another Officer of the Exchequer, of which sort there be two, *viz.* the two Chamberlains Clerks, that do, or should, keep a *Controlment* of the Pell of Receipts and goings out. See *Fleta*, *lib.* 1. *cap.* 18. and 12 *E.* 3. *cap.* 3. who say, This Officer was originally one that took Notes of any other Officers Accounts or Receits, to the intent, to discover him, if he dealt amiss; and was ordained for the Princes better security, howsoever the same sithence may be in some things otherwise applyed.

Controvor, French *Controuveur*, He that of his own head devises or invents false Bruits, or fained News. 2. *Inst. fol.* 227.

Convenable, Convenient or fitting, 27 *E.* 3. *Stat.* 2. *cap.* 21. and 2 *Hen.* 6. *cap.* 2. See *Covenable.*

Conventicle, *Conventiculum*, A private Assembly of a few Folks, under pretence of exercise of Religion; first given to the Meetings of *Wickliff*, in this Nation, above 200 years past, but now applyed to the illegal Meetings of the prisent Non-conformists. It is mentioned 1 *H.* 6. *cap.* 3. and declared against in Parliament, 16. *Car.* 2 *cap.* 4. and 17 *Car.* 2. *cap.* 1. *apud Oxon.*

Conventio, Is a word frequently used both in ancient and modern Law-pleadings, for

a *Covenant*

a *Covenant* or Agreement, as *A. B. queritur, &c. de C. D. &c. pro eo quod non teneat* Conventionem, &c.

Convention, Is a Writ that lyeth for any *Covenant* in writing not performed, *Reg. Orig. fol.* 185. *Old Nat. Brev. fol.* 101. *Fitzherbert* calls it *a Writ of Covenant, Nat. Brev. fol.* 145. where he divideth *Covenants* into personal and real, making a large Discourse of them both; as also how this Writ lyeth for both.

Conventuals, Are Religious Persons united together in a *Covent*, or House of Religion. See *Fryer Observant.*

Conventual Church, See *Parish.*

Convict, *Convictus*, Is he that is found Guilty of an Offence by Verdict of the Jury, *Stamf. pl. cor. fol.* 186. Yet *Crompton* out of *Dyer, fol.* 275. saith, That *Conviction* is, either when a Man is Outlawed, or appeareth and confesseth, or else is found Guilty by the Inquest, *Cromp. Just. of Peace, fol.* 9. *a. Conviction* and Attainder are often confounded. See *Attaint and attainted.*

A Convict Recusant, Is one that hath been legally presented, indicted, and *convict* for refusing to come to Church to hear the Common-Prayer, according to the several Statutes of 1 *Eliz.* 2. 23 *Eliz.* 1. and 3 *Jac.* 4. This term is usually given to Papists, though any other refusing to come to Church in like manner, are as properly *Recusants.* See *Jury.*

Convocation, Is commonly taken for the General Assembly of the Clergy, to consult of Ecclesiastical matters in time of Parliament; and as there are two Houses of Parliament, so there are two places called *Convocation-Houses*; the one called, *The Higher*, where the Archbishops and Bishops sit severally by themselves; the other, *The lower Convocation-House*, where all the rest of the Clergy sit, 25 *H.* 8. *cap.* 19. Vide *Prolocutor.*

Conusance. See *Cognisance.*

Conusant, Knowing or understanding, as if the Son be *Conusant*, and agrees to the Feoffment, &c. *Co.* on *Lit. fol.* 159. *b.*

Conusor. See *Cognizor.*

Coopertura, A thicket or covert of Wood, *Chart. de Forest. cap.* 12.

Coparceners, *Participes*, Be otherwise called *Parcerners*, and in Common-Law are such as have equal Portion in the Inheritance of their Ancestor; and as *Littleton* in the beginning of his third Book saith, *Parceners* be either *by Law*, or *by Custom: Parceners by Law*, are the Issue Female, which (no Heir-male being) come in equality to the Lands of their Ancestors, *Bro. lib.* 2. *cap.* 30. *Parceners by Custom*, are those that by custom of the Country challenge equal part in such Lands; as in *Kent*, by the Custom called *Gavelkind.* This among the *Feudists* is called *Adaequatio, Hot. in verbis* Feud. *verbo* Adæquatio. Of these you may see in *Littleton* at large, in his first and second Chapters of his Third Book. And *Britton, cap.* 27. intituled, *De Heritage divisable.* The Crown of *England* is not subject to *Coparcenary*, 25 *H.* 8. *cap.* 22.

Cope, By *Doomsday-Book*, as Mr. *Agar* hath interpreted it, signifies a Hill. It denotes also, according to Mr. *Manlove*, in his Treatise *Of the Liberties and Customs of Mints, &c.* printed 1653. A Custom or Tribute due to the Lord of the Soyl, or else to the King, out of the Lead-Mines in some part of *Derbyshire*, his words are these,—

Egress and regress to the Kings-High-way,
The Miners have, and Lot *and* Cope *they pay, &c.*

And a little after

Six pence a Load for Cope *the Lord demands, &c.*

Copie, *Copia*, Is according to the French *Le double de quelque escripture*, and signifies in a legal sense the example or transcript of an original writing; as the *Copy* of a Charter, the *Copy* of a Court-Roll, *&c.*

Copia libelli deliberanda, Is a Writ that lyeth, in case where a Man cannot get the *Copy* of a *Libel* at the hands of the Judge Ecclesiastical, *Register Orig. fol.* 51.

Copy-hold, *Tenura per* copiam *rotuli curiæ*, Is a Tenure for which the Tenant hath nothing to shew but the *Copy* of the Rolls made by the Steward of his Lords Court, for the Steward, as he inrolleth and maketh Remembrances of all other things done in the Lords Court; so he doth also of such Tenants, as be admitted in the Court, to any parcel of Land or Tenement belonging to the Mannor; and the Transcript of this is called *The Copy of the Court-Roll*, which is all the Tenant taketh from him, and keeps as his only Evidence, *Co. lib.* 4. *fol.* 25. *b.* This Tenure is called *a base Tenure*, because it holdeth at the Will of the Lord, *Kitchin, fol.* 80. *cap. Copy-holds, F. N. B. fol.* 12. where 'tis said, That it is wont to be called *Tenure in Villenage*, and that of *Copy-hold* is but a new Name; yet it is not simply at the Will of the Lord, but according to the custom of the Mannor: So that if a *Copy-holder* break not the custom of the Mannor, and thereby forfeit his Tenure, he seemeth not so much to stand at the Lords courtesie for his Right, that he may be displaced hand-over-head at his pleasure. These Customs of Mannors be infinite, varying in one point or other almost in every several Mannor: First, Some *Copy-holds* are *fineable* at will, and some *certain*; that which is *fineable* at will, the Lord rateth at his pleasure; but if it exceed two years Revenue, the *Chancery, Kings Bench, Common Pleas*, or *Exchequer*, may reduce them to reason. That which is *certain*, is a kind of Inheritance, and called in many places *Customary*, because the Tenant dying, and the *Hold* being void, the next of Blood, paying the Customary Fine, as two shillings for an Acre, or such like, may not be denyed his Admission. Secondly, Some *Copy-holders* have by Custom, the wood growing upon their own Land, which by Law they could not have, *Kitchin, ubi supra.* Thirdly, *Copy-holders*, some be such as hold by the *Virge* in ancient Demesne; and although they hold by *Copy*, yet are in account a kind of *Freeholder*; for if such a one commit Felony, the King hath *annum, diem & Vastum*, as in case of *Freehold.* Some other hold by Common-Tenure, called *Meere-Copy-hold*, and they committing Felony, their Land escheateth to the Lord of the Mannor, *Kitchen fol.* 81. *chap. Tenent per virge in ancient Demesne*; what *ancient Demesne* is, see in the proper place. See *Tenant by Copy of Court-Roll.* This is the Land that in the Saxons times was called *Folk-land, Lamb.* Explication of Saxon Words, *verbo Terra ex scripto, West Symbol. part.* 1. *lib.* 2. *sect.* 646. defines a *Copy-holder* thus, *Tenant by Copy of Court-Roll*, is he which is admitted Tenant of any Lands or Tenements within a Mannor, that, time out of mind, by Use and Custom of the Mannor, have been demisable and demised to such as will take the same in Fee, or Fee-tail for Life, Years, or at Will, according to the Custom of the Mannor, by *Copy of Court-Roll* of the said Mannor, where you may read more of these things.

Coram non judice, Is, when a Cause is brought in a Court, whereof the Judges have not any Jurisdiction; there it is said to be *Coram non judice*, *Croke 2 par. fol.* 351. *Powel*'s Case.

Coraage, Is an Imposition extraordinary, growing upon some unusual occasion, and seems to be of certain Measures of Corn, *Bract. lib.* 2. *cap.* 16. *num.* 6. uses *Corus tritici* for a Measure of Corn; and in the same Chapter, *num.* 8 hath these words, *Sunt enim quædam communes*, &c. In English thus, There are certain common *Prestations*, which are not called *Services*, neither do they arise from Customs, unless some necessary occasion happen, or that the King comes. Such are Hidage, *Coraage* and Carvage, and many others, which are performed in cases of necessity, by the common consent of the whole Kingdom, and which appertain not to the Lord of the Fee; nor is he bound to acquit his Tenant thereof, unless he hath especially tyed himself thereto by his own Deed.

Cord of Wood, ought to be eight foot long, four foot broad, and four foot high by Statute.

Cordage, Is generally applyed to all Stuff for the making of Ropes, and also to all kind of Ropes belonging to the rigging of Ship, mentioned 15 *Car.* 2. *cap.* 13. *Seamans Dictionary.*

Cordiner, Cometh of the French *Cordovannier*, id est, *sutor calcearius*, A Shoomaker, (we call him vulgarly a *Cordwainer*) and is so used in divers Statutes, as *Anno* 3 *H.* 8. *cap.* 10. & *Anno* 5 *H.* 8. *cap.* 7. and others.

Cornage, *Cornagium*, From the Latine *Cornu*, and in our Common-Law signifieth a kind of *Grand Sergeanty*; the Service of which Tenure is to blow a Horn, when any Invasion of the Northern Enemy is perceived. And by this many men hold their Land Northward, about the Wall, commonly called, *The Picts-Wall*, *Cambd. Brit. pag.* 609. and *Littleton*, *fol.* 65. But by Stat. 12 *Car.* 2. *cap.* 24. All Tenures are turned into free and common Socage. *Co.* on *Lit. fol.* 107. saith, That in old Books, it was called, *Horne-geld, sed quære.* See *Horne-gold*, 2 *Inst. fol.* 9.

Corner-Tile. See *Gutter-Tile.*

Corody, *Corodium* signifies in the Common-Law a sum of Money, or allowance of Meat, Drink and Clothing, due to the King, from an Abbey, or other House of Religion, whereof he is the Founder, towards the reasonable Sustenance of such a one of his Servants, being put to his Pension, as he thinketh good to bestow it on. And the difference between a *Corody* and a Pension seemeth to be, that a *Corody* is allowed towards the Maintenance of any the Kings Servants that liveth in the Abbey; a Pension is given to one of the Kings Chaplains, for his better maintenance in the Kings Service, until he may be better provided of a Benefice. Of both these, read *F.N.B. fol.* 230, 231, 233. who there setteth down all the *Corodies* and Pensions certain, that any Abbey, when they stood, was bound to perform unto the King. There is mention also of a *Corody*, in *Stamf. Prarog.* 44. And this appears an ancient Law, for in *Westm.* 2. *cap.* 25. It was Ordained, That an Assise shall lie for a *Corody*: It is also apparent by the Statute 34 & 35 *H.* 8. *cap.* 16. That *Corodies* belonged sometimes to Bishops from Monasteries. And by the *New Terms of Law*, That a *Corody* may be due to a common person, by Grant from one to another, or of common right, to him that is a Founder of a Religious House, not holden in *Frank-almoine*, for that Tenure was discharged of all *Corodies* in it self: By which Book it appeareth also, That a *Corody* is either certain or uncertain, and that it may be for Life, for Years, in Tail, or in Fee. See *Termes de la Ley.*

Corodio habendo, Is a Writ, whereby to exact a *Corody* of an Abbey, or Religious House. See *Corody*, see also *Reg. Orig. fol.* 264.

Coronatore eligendo, Is a Writ which, after the death or discharge of any *Coroner*, is directed to the Sheriff out of the Chancery, to call together the Free-holders of the County, for the choice of a new Coroner, and to certifie into the Chancery, both the Election, and name of the Party elected, and to give him his Oath. See *Westm.* 2. *cap.* 10. and *F. N. B. fol.* 163. and *Reg. Orig. fol.* 177.

Coroner, *Coronator*, Is an ancient Officer of this Land so called, because he dealeth wholly for the King and Crown. There be four of them commonly in every County, and they are chosen by the Free-holders of the same upon Writ, and not made by Patent, *Cromp. Jur. fol.* 126. This Officer, though now he be some inferior Gentleman, that hath some smattering in the Law; yet if we look to the Statute of *Westm.* 1. *cap.* 10. we shall find, That he was wont and ought to be a sufficient Man; that is, the most wise and discreet Knight that best will and may attend upon such an Office; yea, there is a Writ in the *Register*, *Nisi sit miles*, *fol.* 177.*b.* whereby it appeareth, That it was cause sufficient to remove a *Coroner* chosen, if he were not a Knight, and had not a 100 *li.* Rent of Free-hold: And the Lord Chief Justice of the *Kings Bench* is the Soveraign *Coroner* of the whole Realm, that is, where-ever he remaineth, *Lib. Ass. fol.* 49. *Coke lib.* 4. *Casu de* Wardens, &c. His Office especially concerneth Pleas of the Crown; but if you will see what anciently belonged to him. Read *Bract. lib.* 3. *tract.* 2. *cap*, 5. *De Officio* Coronatorum *circa homicidium*, & *cap.* 6, 7, 8. and *Britton*, *cap.* 1. *Fleta* also *lib.* 1. *cap.* 18. and *Hornes Mirror of Justices*, *lib.* 1. *cap. del office del* Coroners. But more aptly for the present times, *Stamf. pl. cor. lib.* 1. *cap.* 51. Note, there be certain special *Coroners* within divers Liberties, as well as those ordinary Officers in every County, as the *Coroner* of the Verge, which is a certain compass about the Kings Court, whom *Cromp.* in his *Jurisd. fol.* 102.

calleth

calleth, *The Coroner of the Kings House*, of whose Authority, see *Co. Rep. lib. 4. fol. 46*. And there are certain Charters belonging to Colledges, and other Corporations, whereby they are licenced to appoint their *Coroner* within their own Precincts. See farther of this, *F.N.B. fol. 76. Smith, lib. 2. cap. 21. de Rep. Anglor. Lamb. Eiren. lib. 4. cap. 3. pag. 380.* Also of the Office of *Coroner* in *Scotland*, see *Skene de verbor.* Sig *verbo. Iter.*

Corporal Oath. See *Oath*.

Corporation, *Corporatio*, Is that which the *Civilians* call *Universitatem*, or *Collegium*, and is a Body-Politick, authorised by the Kings Charter, being of capacity to take and grant, having a common Seal, &c. These are constituted either by Prescription, by Letters Patent, or by Act of Parliament, and are either *Spiritual* or *Temporal*; Of *Spiritual*, some are Corporations of dead persons in Law, and some otherwise; some by Authority of the King only, some by mixt Authority. Those that are *Temporal*, some are by the Authority of the King, and also some by the Common-Law of the Realm.

Corporation Spiritual, and of dead persons in the Law, Is, where the *Corporation* consists of an Abbot and Covent, which had beginning of the King and the Pope, when he had to do here, *Corporation Spiritual, and of able Persons in Law.* Is, where it consists of a Dean and Chapter, a Master of a Colledge or Hospital, and this had beginning from the King only.

Corporation Temporal by the King, Is, where there is a Mayor and Commonalty. *Corporation Temporal* by Authority of the Common-Law, is, the Parliament consisting of the *King*, the Head; the Lords *Spiritual* and *Temporal*, and *Commons*, the Body.

If Land be given to a Mayor and Commonalty for their Lives, they have an Estate by Intendment, not determinable: So it is, if a Feoffment be made of Land to a Dean and Chapter, without mention of Successors. Release of a Mayor for any sum of Money due to the *Corporation* in his own name, is not good in Law, in case of a sole *Corporation*, as Bishop, Parson, Vicar, Master of Hospital, &c. no Chattel either in Action or Possession, shall go in succession; but the Executors or Administrators of the Bishop, Parson, &c. shall have them; but otherwise it is in case of a *Corporation* aggregate, as a Dean and Chapter, Mayor and Commonalty, and such like; for they, in Judgment of the Law, never dye. Yet the case of the *Chamberlain* of *London* differs from all these, for his Successor may, in his own name, have Execution of a Recognisance acknowledged to his Predecessor, for Ophanage-Money, and the reason is, because in this case the *Corporation* of the *Chamberlain* is by Custom, which hath enabled the Successor to take such Recognisances, Obligations, &c. that are made to his Predecessor. And this Custom is founded upon great reason, for the Executors or Administrators of the *Chamberlain* ought not to intermeddle with such Recognisances, &c. which by the said Custom are taken in the *Corporate* capacity of the *Chamberlain*, and not in his private.

Corpus cum Causa, Is a Writ issuing out of the Chancery, to remove both the Body and the Record, touching the cause of any man lying in Execution upon a Judgment for Debt, into the Kings Bench, &c. there to lye until he have satisfied the Judgment, *Fitz. Nat. Brev. fol.* 251. *e.*

Corpus Christi day, The next *Thursday* after *Trinity-Sunday*, is a Feast instituted in honor of the Blessed Sacrament. It is mentioned 32 *H.* 8. 21. by which Statute also *Trinity Term* is always to begin the *Friday* next after this Feast.

Corrector of the Staple, Is a Clerk belonging to the *Staple*, that writeth and recordeth the Bargains of Merchants there made, 27 *E.* 3. *Stat.* 2. *cap.* 22, & 23. The *Romans* called them *Mensarios.*

Corruption of Blood, Is an Infection growing to the state of a Man attainted of Felony or Treason; for he loseth all to the Prince, or other Lord of the Fee, as his case is, so his Issue cannot be Heirs to him, or to any other Ancestor, of whom they might have claimed by him. And further, if he were noble or a Gentleman before, he and his Children are made unnoble and ungentile. But if the King will pardon the Offendor, it will cleanse the *Corruption of the Blood* of those Children which are born after the Pardon, and they may inherit the Land of their Ancestor purchased at the time of the Pardon, or afterwards, but so cannot they who were born before the Pardon. But there are divers Limitations even in Treason, made by Statutes which save *Corruption of Blood*, though a Man be attainted, 27 *E.* 3. *cap.* 77. 13 *H.* 7. *cap.* 17. 5 *Eliz. cap.* 1. 11. 18 *El. cap.* 1. 6. 14. 31 *Eliz. cap.* 4. 1 *Mar. cap.* 12. 1 *Jac. cap.* 12.

Corse present, Are words borrowed from the French *Corps presentè*, signifying a *Mortuary*, which may be thus termed; for that where a *Mortuary* was wont to be due, the Body of the best Beast was according to the Law or Custom offered or presented to the Priest. See 21 *H.* 8. *cap.* 6.

Corselet, Is a French word, signifying a little Body, in Latine *Corpusculum*; we generally use it for an Armor to cover the whole Body, 4 & 5 *P. & M. cap.* 2. wherewith Pike-men, commonly set in the Front and Flanks of the Battel, are armed, for the better resistance of the Enemies Assaults, and the surer Guard of the Gunners placed behind, who were more slightly armed, for their speedier advancing, and retreating to Fire. See *Barret's Discourse of War, lib.* 3. *Dialog.* 2.

Cosenage, *Cognatione*, Is a Writ that lies, where the *Tresayle*, (that is, *Tritavus*, the Father of the *Besayle*, or of the great Grand-father) is seised in his Demesne, as of Fee, at the day of his death, of certain Lands or Tenements, and dyeth, and then a stranger entreth, and abateth; for then shall his Heir have this Writ of *Cosenage*, the form whereof see in *F.N.B. fol.* 221. of this, read also *Britton* at large, *cap.* 89.

Cosening, Is an Offence unnamed, whereby any thing is done guilfully, in or out of Contracts, which cannot be fitly termed by any special Name, *West Symbol. part.* 2. *tit.* Indictments, *sect.* 68. It is called in the Civil-Law, *Stellionatus*, of *Stellio*, a Beast, which is *Lacertæ genus versutissimum*, as *Cujacius* in his *Particles* calleth it: And *Pliny*,

Pliny, lib. 3. *cap.* 10. says, *Nullum animal invidet homini fraudulentius.*

Cot, In the old Saxon signifying *Cottage*, and so still in many places of *England*, as *Verstegan* testifies in his *Restitution*, of decayed Intelligences in Antiquities. It is also a kind of refuse wooll, clung or clotted together, that it cannot be pulled asunder, *Anno* 13 R. 2. *Stat.* 1. *cap.* 9.

Cotage, *Cotagium*, Is a small House, without Land belonging to it, 4 *E.* 1. *Stat.* 1. and the Inhabitant of such a House is called a *Cotager*, but by a later Statute no man may build a *Cotage*, but he must lay four Acres of Land to it.

Cotarii, *Cotagers, Doomsday.*

Coterelli, Used in the same Book for *Cotageri* also.

Cotuchani, *Bores*, or Husbandmen. *Vide* the Book of *Doomsday.*

Coucher, Signifies a *Factor*, residing in some Foreign Country for Traffick, as formerly in *Gascoigne*, for buying Wines, 3 & 4 *E.* 6. *cap.* 10. It is used for the general Book, wherein a Corporation, &c. Register their particular Acts.

Covenable, *Rationabilis*, Is a French word denoting fit or convenient. So 4 *H.* 8. *cap.* 12. *covenably* endowed, that is, endowed as is fitting. It was also written *convenable*, 27 *E.* 3. *Stat.* 2. *cap.* 17. *Plowd. fol.* 472. *a.*

Covenant, *Conventio*, Is the consent of two, or more, to one thing, to do or give somewhat, *West. Symbol. part* 2. *lib.* 1. *sect.* 4. It seemeth to be as much as *Pactum Conventum* with the *Civilians*, which you read oftentimes in *Tully*, *Pactum conventum quod & vulgo vestitum vocant, opponitur nudo pacto, vel ut ab omni juris solemnitate destituto, Hujus exempla, &c. Oldendorpius.* And *Covenant* in this signification is either a *Covenant in Law*, or a *Covenant in Fact*, *Coke, lib.* 4. *Noke's* Case, *fol.* 80. or *Covenant express*, and *Covenant in law*, Co. lib. 6. fol. 17. a. *Covenant in Law* is, that which the Law intendeth to be made, though in words it be not exprest, as if the Lessor do demise and grant, &c. to the Lessee for a certain term, the Law intendeth a *Covenant* on the Lessors part, That the Lessee shall quietly enjoy his Lease for his term against all Incumbrances. *Covenant in fact* is, that which is expresly agreed between the Parties. There is also a *Covenant* meerly *personal*, and a *Covenant real*, *F. N. B. fol.* 145. And he seemeth to say, That a *Covenant real* is, whereby a Man tyeth himself to pass a thing *real*, as Lands or Tenements; as a *Covenant* to levy a Fine of Land, &c. A *Covenant meerly personal* of the other side is, where a Man *covenanteth* with another by Deed to build him a House, or any other thing, or to serve him, or to infeoff him, &c.

Covenant, Is also the Name of a Writ, for which see *Conventione*; Instruments of *Covenant* you may see good store in *West Symbol. part* 1. *lib.* 2. *sect.* 100. See also the *New Book of Entries verbo* Covenant. This word hath also an evil interpretation, as the late *Solemn League and Covenant* was a seditious Conspiracy, Voted illegal and irreligious by Parliament, 1661. and Provision made against it by Stat. 14 *Car.* 2. *cap.* 4.

Covent, *Conventus*, Signifies the Society of an Abby or Priory, as *Societas* signifies the number of Fellows in a Colledge, *Bract. lib.* 2. *cap.* 35.

Coverture, Is a French word, signifying any thing that *covers*, as Apparel, a *Coverlet*, &c. and deduced from the *couvir*, that is, *tegere*; In Law, it is particularly applyed to the Estate and Condition of a marryed Woman, who by the Laws of our Realm is *sub potestate viri*, and therefore disabled to make Bargain with any, to the prejudice of her self, or her Husband, without his Assent and Privity, or at the least without his Allowance and Confirmation, *Bro. hoc tit. per tot.* And *Bracton, lib.* 2. *cap.* 15. saith, That *Omnia quæ sunt uxoris, sunt ipsius viri, nec habet uxor potestatem sui, sed vir.* And again, *lib.* 4. *cap.* 24. *Vir est caput mulieris.* And also *Lib.* 5. *tract.* 2. *cap.* 3. That in any Law matters, *sine viro respondere non potest.* And in the same Book, *Tract.* 5. *cap.* 23. *Vir & uxor sunt quasi unica persona, quia caro una & sanguis unus; Res licet sit propria uxoris, vir tamen ejus custos, cum sit caput mulieris*, and *Lib.* 1. *cap.* 10. *nu.* 2. *uxores sunt sub virga viri.* And if the Husband alien the Wives Lands, during the Marriage, she cannot gain-say it during his life. See *cui ante divortium*, and *cui in vita.*

Covine, *Covina*, Is a deceitful Assent or Agreement between two, or more, to the prejudice of another. As if a Tenant for term of life, or Tenant in tail, will secretly conspire with another, that the other shall recover against the Tenant for life, the Land which he holds, &c. in prejudice of him in the Reversion. It cometh from the French Verb *Covenancer*, that is, *depacisci*, or rather *convenir*, id est, *convenire.*

Count, Signifieth as much as the original Declaration in a Process, though more used in real than personal Actions; as Declaration is more applyed to personal than real, *F. N. B. a.* 60. *d.* 71. *a.* 191 *e.* 217. *a. Libel* with the *Civilians* comprehends both. And yet *Count* and Declaration be sometimes confounded, as *Count* in Debt. *Kitchin, fol.* 281. *Count* or Declaration in Appeal. *Pl. cor.* 78. *Count* in Trespass, *Briton, cap.* 26. *Count* in an Action upon the Case for a Slander, *Kitch.* 252. The word seemeth to come from *France* and *Normandy*, for in the *Grand Customary, cap* 64. *Contours* are taken for such as a man retains to speak for him in any Court as Advocates, and *cap.* 63. *Pledeurs*, he makes an other sort of Spokesmen in the nature of Atturneys, for one that is himself present, but suffereth another to speak in his behalf. But *Contours* by *Horn's Mir.* of *Just. lib.* 2. *cap. des loyers*, are such Sergeants, skilful in the Law, which serve the common people to defend their Actions in Judicature for their Fee, whose Duty, if it be as is there described, and were observed, Men might have much more comfort of the Law than they have.

Countee, French *Comté*, which may well be derived from the Latine *Comes*, because they accompany the King, it was the most eminent Dignity of a Subject, before the Conquest, next to a Duke; and in ancient time were men of great Estate and Dignity, for which cause the Law gives them large Priviledges, as their persons may not be arrested for Debt, Trespass, &c. they may not be put upon Juries, &c. And of old the *Countee* was *Præpositus*, or *Præfectus Comitatus*, and had the Charge and Custody of the County, in which

Authority

authority the Sheriff hath now succeeded, *Co.lib.* 9. *fol.* 46. and is therefore called *Vice comes.* See *Earl.*

Countenance, Seemeth to be used for *Credit* or *Estimation*, *Old. Nat. Brev. fol.* 111. in these words, Also the Attaint shall be granted to poor Men that will swear, they have nothing whereof they may make Fine, saving their *Countenance*; So is it used 1 *E.* 3. *Stat.* 2. *cap.* 4 in these words, Sheriffs shall Charge the Kings Debtors with as much as they may levy with their Oaths without abating the Debtors *Countenance*. See *Contentment.*

Counter, *Computatorium*, May be derived from the Latine Verb *Computare*, to account. But we use it for the Names of the two City Prisons, commonly called the *Counters*, whereinto, he that once slippeth, is like to account ere he get out.

Countermand, Is, where a thing formerly executed, is afterward by some Act or Ceremony made void by the Party that hath first done it. As if a Man hath made his last VVill, whereby he devises his Land to *J. S.* and then he enfeoffs another of the same Land; there this Feoffment is a *Countermand* to the Will, and the Will, as to the disposition of the Land, is void. If a Woman, seised of Land in Fee, makes a Will in writing, and devises, that if *A.* of *B.* survives her, then she devises and bequeaths to him and his Heirs her Land, and afterward she intermarries with the said *A.* of *B*; there by taking him to Husband and Coverture at the time of her death, the Will is *countermanded.*

Counterplea, Is compounded of two French words, *Conter*, i. *Contra*, *adversus*; and *pleder*, *causam agere*, it signifieth properly in our Common-Law a Replication to *Ayde Prior*; for when the Tenant by Curtesie, or in Dower, prayeth in Ayde of the King, or him in the Reversion for his better Defence; or else if a Stranger to the action begun, desire to be received, to say what he can for the safeguard of his Estate; that which the Demandant alledgeth against this Request, why it should not be admitted, is called a *Counterplea.* And in this signification it is used 25 *E.* 3. *Stat.* 3. *cap.* 7. See also the *Terms of the Law, fol.* 172. and the Statute 3 *E.* 1. *cap.* 39.

Counter Rolls, *Anno* 3 *E.* 1. *cap.* 10. Sheriffs shall have *Counter-Rolls* with the Coroners, as well of Appeals, as of Enquests, &c.

Counters, French *Contours*, Have been taken for such Sergeants at Law as a man retains to defend his Cause for his Fee, *Hornes Mirrour of Justices, lib.* 2. *cap. des Loyer*, mentioned by *Chaucer* in these words,

> *A Sheriff had he been, and a* Contour,
> *Was no where such a worthy* Vavasour.

They were anciently called *Sergeant-Countors*, *Co.* on *Lit. fol.* 17. *a.*

County, *Comitatus*, Signifieth as much as Shire; the one descending from the French, the other from the Saxon, both containing a Circuit or Portion of the Realm, into which the whole Land is divided, for the better Government thereof, and the more easie administration of Justice; so that there is no part of the Kingdom that lyeth not within some County, and every County is governed by a yearly Officer, whom we call a *Sheriff*, which among other Duties, belonging to his Office, putteth in execution all the Commandements and Judgments of the Kings Courts, *Fortescue, cap.* 24. Of these *Counties*, there be four of especial mark, which therefore are termed *Counties Palatine*, as the *County Palatine of Lancaster*, *Chester*, *Durham* and *Ely*, *Anno* 5 *Eliz. cap.* 23. the Statute 33 *H.* 8. *cap.* 10. mentions the *County Palatine* of *Hexam*: Heretofore the Jurisdiction of a *County-Palatine* was of so high a nature, that whereas all Pleas, touching the Life or Mayhem of a Man, called *Pleas of the Crown*, be ordinarily held an sped in the Kings Name, and cannot pass in the Name of any other: The chief Governors of these, by especial Charter from the King, did send out all Writs in their own Name, and did all things touching Justice as absolutely as the Prince himself in other *Counties*, onely acknowledging him their Superiour and Soveraign. But by 27 *H.* 8. *cap.* 25. This Power is much abridged, to which I refer the Reader: As also to *Cromp. Juris. fol.* 137. Besides these *Countries* of both sorts, there be likewise *Counties* Corporate, as appeareth by the Stat. 3 *Ed.* 4. 5. And these be certain Cities, or ancient Boroughs of the Land, upon which the Princes of our Nation have thought good to bestow such extraordinary Liberties. Of these the Famous City of *London* is one and the principal, *York* another, 32 *H.* 8. *cap.* 13. the City of *Chester* a third, 42 *Eliz.* 15. *Canterbury* a fourth, *Lamb. Eiren. lib.* 1. *cap.* 9. *Norwich*, *VVorcester*, and many more, especially the *County* of the Town of *Kingstone* upon *Hull*, 32 *H.* 8. 13. The *County* of the Town of *Haverford West*, 35 *H.* 8. 16. and the *County* of *Litchfield*, *Cromp. Justice of Peace, fol.* 59. *a County* in another signification, is used for the *County-Court* which the Sheriff keepeth every Month within his Charge, either by himself or his Deputy, *Anno* 2 *E.* 6. *cap.* 25. *Cromp. Juris. fol.* 221. *Bract. lib.* 3. *cap.* 7. & *lib.* 3. *tract.* 2. *cap.* 12. Of these *Counties*, there are reckoned in *England* forty, besides twelve in *Wales*, making in all fifty two. The word *Comitatus*, is also used for a Jurisdiction or Territory among the *Feudists.*

County-Court, *Curia Comitatus*, By *Lambert* is otherwise called *Conventus*, in his Explication of Saxon words, and divided into two sorts; one retaining the general Name, as the *County Court*, held every moneth by the Sheriff, or his Deputy the Under Sheriff, whereof you may read in *Cromp. Juris. fol.* 231. The other called *The Turn*, held twice every year, of which see more in his proper place. And *Cromp. Juris. ibid.* This *County-Court* had in ancient times the Cognizance of great Matters, as may appear by *Glanvile, lib.* 1. *cap.* 2, 3, 4. by *Bracton* and *Britton* in divers places, and by *Fleta, lib.* 2. *cap.* 62. but was abridged by the Statute of *Magna Charta, cap.* 17. and much more by 1 *E.* 4. *cap.* 1. It had also, and hath the determination of certain Trespasses and Debts under forty shillings, *Britton, cap.* 27. 28. What manner of proceeding was of old used in this Court. Se *Fleta ubi supra.*

Counting-House of the Kings Household, *Domus Computus Hospitii Regis*, Is commonly called *The Green-cloth*, because the Table stands

stands always cover'd with a *Green-cloth*: Here sit the Lord Steward, Treasurer of the Kings-House, Controller, Master of the *Houshold*, Cofferer, two Clerks of the *Green-cloth*, and two Clerks Controllers, for daily taking the Accounts of all Expenses of the *Houshold*, making Provisions, and ordering Payment for the same; for the good Government of the Kings Servants, and paying the Wages of those below Stairs. *Vide* 39 *Eliz. cap.* 7. and 4. *Inst. fol.* 131.

Courratier, A French word signifying a *Horse-Courser*. 2. *Inst. fol.* 719.

Coursitour. See *Cursitour*.

Court, *Curia*, Cometh of the French *Court*, which signifies the Kings Palace or Mansion, but derived of the Latin word *Curia*, which, among the *Romans*, had divers significations; and with us also hath diversity of senses; as the House where the King remaineth with his ordinary Retinue, and also the place where Justice is judicially administred, of which you find thirty two several sorts in *Crompton*'s Book of *Jurisdictions* well described, and of them most are *Courts* of Record; some be not, and therefore are accounted *base Courts* in comparison of the rest. Besides these, there are also *Courts-Christian*, *Smith de Rep. Angl. lib.* 3. *cap.* 6. which are so called, because they handle matters especially appertaining to Christianity, and such as, without good knowledge in Divinity, cannot be well judged of, being held heretofore by Archbishops and Bishops, as from the Pope, because he challenged the superiority in all Causes Spiritual, but since his rejection they hold them by the Kings Authority, *virtute Magistratus sui*, as the Admiral of *England* holds his; whereupon it proceedeth, that they send out their Precepts in their own Names, and not in the Kings, as the Justices of the Kings *Courts* do. And therefore as the Appeal from these *Courts* did lie to *Rome*, now by the Statute, 25 *H.* 8. *cap.* 19. it lyeth to the King in his Chancery.

Court-Baron, *Curia Baronis*, Is a *Court* that every Lord of a Mannor (which in ancient times were called *Barons*) hath within his own Precincts. *Barons* in other Nations have great Territories and Jurisdictions from their Soveraign: But here in *England*, what they be, and have been heretofore, see in *Baron*. Of this *Court* and of a *Court-Leet*, you may read at large in *Kitchin*, who hath writ a whole Book of them. *Co.* 4. *Rep.* among his Copy-hold Cases, *fol.* 26. *b.* saith, That this *Court* is two-fold, as if a Man having a Mannor in a Town, to grant the Inheritance of the Copy-holders thereunto belonging to another; This Grantee may keep a *Court* for the Customary Tenants, and accept Surrenders to the use of others, and make both Admittances and Grants. The other *Court* is of Freeholders, which is properly called *The Court Baron*, wherein the Suitors, that is, the Free-holders, be Judges, whereas of the other the Lord, or his Steward, is Judge.

Court of Pye-Powders. See *Piepouders*.

Court of Requests, *Curia Requisitionum*, Is a *Court* of Equity, of the same nature with the Chancery, but inferior to it, being principally instituted for the help of such Petitioners, as in conscionable cases deal by Supplication with his Majesty. This *Court*, as Mr. *Gwin* saith in the *Preface to his Readings*, Had beginning from a Commission first granted by *Henry* the Eighth to the Masters of the Requests, whereas before that time, in his Opinion, they had no warrant of ordinary Jurisdiction, but travelled between the King and the Petitioner, by direction from the Kings mouth. But Sir *Julius Cæsar* in a Tractate of his on that Subject, plainly sheweth, That this Court was 9 *H.* 7. though then following the King, and not setled in any certain place, neither swayed particularly by the Masters of Requests, as you may see more in the same Book in several places, especially *pag.* 148. Also *à pag. prima usq; ad pag.* 46. This *Court* had assumed so great power to it self, that it grew burdensome and grievous, and therefore was taken away with some others, by a Statute made 16 & 17 *Car.* 1. *cap.* 10. and therefore being out of use, we need say no more of it here.

Court of the Legate, Was a *Court* obtained by Cardinal *Wolsey* of Pope *Leo* the Tenth, 9 *H.* 8. wherein he had power to prove Wills, and dispence with Offences against the Spiritual Laws, &c. but it was of short cotinuance, and fell utterly with him.

Court-Christian, *Curia Christianitatis*, Concerning which, *Linwood* thus, *In curia Christianitatis*, 1. *Ecclesiæ in qua servantur Leges* Christi, *cum tamen in foro Regio serventur Leges Mundi*. As in the Kings *Courts* humane Laws are maintained, so in the *Court-Christian* the Laws of *Christ* should be the Rule; and therefore the Judges are Divines, as Archbishops, Bishops, Archdeacons, and the like, 2. *par. Inst. fol.* 488. See also before in *Court*.

Court of Delegates. See *Delegates*.

Court of Chivalry, *curia Militaris*, Known also by the name of the *Marshal-Court*, the Judges are the Lord *High-Constable* of *England*, and the *Earl-Marshal* of *England*. This *Court* is the Fountain of Martial-Law, and the *Earl-Marshal* is not only one of the Judges, but also to see Execution done. See *Constable*, 4. *par. Inst. fol.* 123.

Courtilage. See *Curtilage*.

Courtesie of England. See *Curtesie of England*.

Coutheutlaughe, Is he that willingly receiveth a Man Out-lawed, and cherisheth or hideth him; in which case he was in ancient time subject to the same Punishment that the Out-law himself was, *Bracton, lib.* 3. *tract.* 2. *cap.* 13. *num.* 2. It is compounded of *Couthe*, that is, known, and *utlaughe*, an Out-law, as we now call him.

Cranage, *Cranagium*, Is a liberty to use a *Crane*, for the drawing up of Wares from the Vessels at any Creek of the Sea or Wharf, unto the Land, and to make profit of it: It signifieth also the Money taken, and paid for the same. *New Book of Entries, fol.* 3. *col.* 3.

Crastino sancti Vincentii, The Morrow after the Feast of St. *Vincent* the Martyr, being the 22 of *January*, is the Date of the Statutes made at *Merton*, *Anno* 20 *H.* 3.

Cravent or **Craven**, Was a word of

Oblo-

Obloquy, where in a Tryal by Battel upon a Writ of Right, the Victory should be proclaimed, and the vanquished acknowledge his Fault, or pronounce the word *Cravant, &c.* and thereupon Judgment was given forthwith, and then the *Recreant* should become infamous, 2. *par. Inst.* 247. 248. We retain the word still for a Coward: If the Appellant joyn Battel, and cry *Cravant, amittet liberam legem*; but if the Appellee cry *Cravant*, he shall be hanged, 3. *Inst. fol.* 221.

Crayer, A kind of small Vessel or Ship, mentioned in the Statute, 14 *Car.* 2. *cap.* 27.

Creansor, *Creditor*, Cometh of the French word *Croyance, persuasio*, and signifieth him that trusteth another with any Debt, be it in Money or Wares. This word is used in the *Old Nat. Brev.* in the Writ of *Audita Querela. fol.* 66. *a.*

Creast-tile. Vide *Roof-tile.*

Creeke, *Creca, Crecca, Creccum*, Seemeth to be a part of a Haven, where any thing is landed or disburthened out of the Sea; so that when you are out of the main Sea, within the Haven, look how many landing places you have, so many *Creeks* may be said to belong to that Haven. See *Cromp. Jurisdictions, fol.* 110. *a.* This word is mentioned 5 *Eliz.* 5. and 4 *H.* 4. 10, *&c.* and 14 *Car.* 2. *cap.* 28. and in *Plowd.* in the Case of *Reniger* and *Fogassa.*

Crocards, A sort of old Money. See *Pollards.*

Croft, *Croftum & Crofta*, is a little Close or Pightle adjoyning to a House, either for Pasture or Arable, as the Owner pleases: It seemeth to come of the old English word *Creaft*, signifying *Handy-craft*, because such Grounds are for the most part manured, and extraordinarily dressed, by the labour and skill of the Owner.

Croyses, *Cruce signati*, Is used by *Britton*, *cap.* 122. for *Pilgrims*: the reason may be, for that they wear the Sign of the *Cross* on their Garments. Of these, and their Priviledges, read *Bract. lib.* 5. *part.* 2. *cap.* 2. and *part.* 5. *cap.* 29. and the *Grand Customary* of *Normandy, cap.* 45. Under this word are also signified the Knights of the Order of St. *John* of *Jerusalem*, created for the Defence of *Pilgrims.* Such also were those Worthies of the Nobility and Gentry in the Reigns of King *Henry* the Second, *Richard* the First, *Hen.* 3. and *Ed.* 1. who *Cruce signati* were said to take upon them, the *Croisado*, for recovery of the Holy Land, *Gregor. Syntagm, lib.* 15. *cap.* 13. *&.* 14.

Cucking-stool, *Tumbrella*, Is an Engine invented for the punishment of Scolds, and unquiet Women, in ancient time called a *Tumbrell*, *Lamb. Eirenarch. lib.* 1. *cap.* 12. *Bracton* writes this word *Tymborella*, *Kitchin, cap. charge in Court-Leet, fol.* 13. *a.* saith Every one having view of *Frank-pledge*, ought to have a Pillory and a *Tumbrell*, where he seemeth by a *Tumbrell* to mean the same thing. This was a Punishment anciently inflicted upon Brewers and Bakers transgressing the Laws, who were thereupon in such a *stool* immerged over Head and Ears in *stercore*, some stinking Water.

Cuth, *Cognitus* known.

Cudutlaugh. See *Coutheutlaughe.*

Cui ante divortium, Is a Writ, that a Woman *divorced* from her Husband hath to recover Lands or Tenements from him, to whom her Husband did alienate them during the Marriage, because then she could not gainsay it, *Reg. Orig. fol.* 233. *F. N. B. fol.* 204.

Cui in vita, Is a Writ of Entry, that a Widow hath against him, to whom her Husband aliened her Lands or Tenements in his life-time, which must contain in it, that during his life-time she could not withstand it, *Reg. Orig. fol.* 232. *F. N. B. fol.* 193. See the *New Book of Entries, verbo* Cui in vita.

Cuinage. See *Cuynage.*

Culagium, Is when a Ship is laid up in the Dock to be repaired, *M. S. Ar. Trevor. Arm. de plac. Ed.*

Culvertage, *Culvertagium*, May be interpreted *Cowardise*, as *Omnes cum equis & armis jussit sub nomine* Culvertagii *convenire*, Mat. Paris, fol. 233.

Cuneus, A Mint or Place to coyn Money, *Mandatum est, &c. sciatis quod concessimus venerabili Patri nostro* Cicestr. *Episcopo quod habeat* Cuneum *suum in Civitate* Cicestriæ, &c. *T.* 29. *Apr. Claus.* 6. *Joh. m.* 3.

Cuntey, Cuntey, Is a kind of Tryal, as appeareth by *Bracton*, in these words, *Negotium in hoc casu terminabitur per* Cuntey Cuntey, *sicut inter cohæredes*, Bract. lib. 4. tract. 3. cap. 18. And again in the same place, *In brevi de recto negotium terminabitur per* Cuntey Cuntey. And thirdly, Lib. 4. tract. 4. cap. 2. *Terminabitur negotium per breve de recto, ubi nec duellum nec magna Assisa, sed per* Cuntey Cuntey *omninò*, which in mine Opinion is as much as by the Ordinary Jury.

Curfew, Cometh of two French words *Couvir*, that is *tegere*, and *Feu ignis*, Fire; We use it for the ringing of a Bell, by which the Conquerer willed every man to take warning for the raking up, or covering of his Fire, and the putting out of his Light. So that in many places at this day, where a Bell customably is rung towards Bed time, it is said to ring *Curfue*, *Stow's Annals in vita* Gul. Conquestor.

Curia. See *Court.*

Curia advisare vult, Is a Deliberation that the Court intends to take upon any point or points of a Cause before Judgment be resolved on; for this, see the *New Book of Entries, verbo* Curia advisare vult.

Curia claudenda, Is a Writ that lyeth against him who should fence and close up his Ground, if he refuse, or defer to do it, *Reg. Orig. fol.* 155. *F. N. B. fol.* 127. See also the *New Book of Entries, verbo* Curia claudenda.

Curia Penticiarum, Is a Court held by the Sheriff of *Chester*, in the place there commonly called *The Pendice*, *Pl. in Itin. apud Cestr.* 14 *H.* 7. probably so called at first, because it might be held under a *Penthouse*, or open Shed covered with Boards.

Curnocke Is four Bushels, or half a quarter of Corn, *Fleta, lib.* 2. *cap.* 12.

Cursitor, *Clericus de cursu*, Is an Officer or Clerk belonging to the Chancery, that maketh out original Writs, 14 & 15 *H.* 8. *cap.* 8. They be called *Clerks of the Course*, in the Oath of the Clerks of the Chancery appointed, 18 *E.* 3. *Stat.* 5. *cap. Unico.* They be of these twenty four in number, which have allotted to each of them several Shires, in which they make out such original Writs as are by the Subject required, and are a Corporation of themselves.

Curtesie of England, With us hath a proper signification, being used for a Tenure; for if a man marry an Inheritrix, that is, a VVoman seised of Lands in Fee-simple or Fee-tail general, or seised as Heir of the Tail special, and getteth a Child of her that cometh alive into the World, though both it and his wife dye forthwith; yet if she were in possession, he shall keep the Land during his life, and is called *Tenant per Legem Angliæ* or *Tenant by the Curtesie of England*, because this Priviledge is not allowed in any other Country except *Scotland*, *Glanvile*, *lib.* 7. *cap.* 18. *Bract. lib.* 5. *tract.* 5. *cap* 30. *num.* 7, 8, 9. *Britton cap.* 51. *fol.* 132. *Fleta*, *lib.* 6. *cap.* 56. *F. N. B. fol.* 149. *Littleton*, *lib.* 1. It is called *The Law of England*, *Westm.* 2. *cap.* 3. This in *Scotland* is called *Curialitas Scotiæ*. *Skene de verb.* Signif. *verbo* Curialitas, who there maketh a large Discourse of this Custome. See more *Termes de la Ley*.

Currier, Is one that dresses or liquors Leather, and is so called of the French word *Cuir*, id est, *Corium*, *Leather*; The word is used in all the Statutes made for the good making of *Leather*, as 1 *Jac. cap.* 22.

Curteyne, *Curtana*, Was the name of King *Edward the Confessors* Sword, which is the first Sword carryed before the King of this Land at his Coronation, *Mat. Paris in vita Henrici tertii.* And they say, The point of it is broken, which may seem therefore to be an Emblem of Mercy.

Curtilage, *Curtilagium*, signifieth a Garden, Yard or Field, or other piece of Ground lying near, or belonging to a Messuage, *West. Symbol. part* 2. *tit* Fines, *sect.* 26. And so it is used *Anno* 4 *E.* 1. *cap. Unico*, 35 *H.* 8, *cap.* 4. 39 *Eliz. cap.* 10. and *Coke*, *vol.* 6. *fol.* 64. *a.* and *Linwood*, *tit.* de Decimis, *cap.* sancta, *sect.* omnibus, *verbo* Curtelegiorum. So that in effect it is a Yard or a Garden belonging to a House. *Mihi dici videtur* Curtilagium (sayes the learned *Spelman*) *a* Curtellum & *ago scilicet locus ubi* curtis, *vel* curtilli *negotium agitur*.

Custode admittendo & Custode amovendo, Are Writs for the admitting or removing of Guardians, *Reg. Orig. in indice.*

Custodes libertatis Angliæ authoritate Parliamenti, Was the stile wherein VVrits, and other judicial Proceedings, did run during the late times of trouble, *viz.* From the Murther of King *Charles* the First, till the Usurpation of *Cromwel*, mentioned and declared tray-terous by the Stat. 12 *Car.* 2. *cap.* 3.

Custome, *Consuetudo*, Is all one in signification with our Common Lawyers and Civilians, being by both accounted a part of the Law; *Consuetudo quandocunq; pro lege servatur*, saith *Bracton*, *in partibus ubi fuerit more utentium approbata*; *Longævi enim temporis usus & consuetudinis non est vilis authoritas*, lib. 1. *cap.* 3. It may not unaptly be thus defined, *Custome* is a Law or Right not written, which being established by long use, and the consent of our Ancestors, hath been, and is daily practised. Our Ancestors, that is, *Majores*; and those of our Kindred that are *ultra tritavum*: So that allowing the Father to be so much elder than the Son, as *pubertas*, or the years of Generation do require, the Grand father, so much elder than him, and so *usq; ad tritavum*; We cannot say, That this or that is a *Custome*, unless we can justifie it hath continued so at least one hundred years. For *Tritavus* must be so much elder than the Party that pleadeth it, yet because that is hard to prove, it is enough for the proof of a *Custome*, if two or more Witnesses can depose, that they heard their Fathers say, That it was a *Custome* all their time, and that their Fathers heard their Fathers also say, That it was likewise a *Custome* in their time. It is to be proved by Record, the continuance of a hundred years will serve, *Davie's Rep. fol.* 32. *Custome* is either *general* or *particular*. *General*, I call that which is allowed through all *England*, whereof you may read divers in *Doct. & Stud. lib.* 1. *cap.* 7. very worthy to be known. *Particular*, is that which belongeth to this or that County as *Gavelkind* to *Kent*, or to this or that Lordship, City or Town. *Custome* differeth from *Prescription* for that *Custome* is common to more, and *Prescription* is particular to this or that man. Again, *Prescription* asketh not that length of time to set it up as *Custome* doth, but is pleadable in a far shorter time, *viz.* five years, one year, or less; example of five years *prescription* you have in the levying of a Fine; for if a Fine duly levyed of Lands and Tenements, be not impugned within five years, it excludeth all Claim for ever. And if a man omit his continual Claim for a year and a day, then the Tenant in possession prescribeth an immunity against the Entry of the Demandant and his Heir, *F. N. B. fol.* 79. *Termes de la Ley*, *verbo* Continual Claim; out of the Statutes you have greater diversity, which see collected in *Cowells Institutes*, tit. *Dusucap. & long. temp. præscript.* So that *Brissenius* in his 14. *lib. de verbo* Sig. saith, truly, That *Prescription* is an Exception founded upon so long time past, as the Law limiteth for the pursuit of any Action. An example may be taken from those Statutes 1 *H.* 8. *cap.* 4. which enacteth, That in all Actions popular, information shall be made within three years after the Offence committed, or else be of no force. Of like nature is the Statute 7 *H.* 8. *cap.* 13. which in some cases makes one years *Prescription* sufficient against Informations. *Custome* is also used for the Tribute or Toll, that Merchants pay to the King for the carrying in and out of Merchandise, 14 *E.* 3. *Stat.* 1. *cap.* 21. in which signification it hath the Latine name *Custuma*, *Reg. Orig. fol.* 138. *a.* 129. *a.* 4. *Inst. fol.* 29. And lastly, For such Services as Tenants of a Mannor owe unto their Lord, *New Book of Entries*, *verbo* Custome.

Custome House, Is a *House* in several Cities and Port-Towns, as *London*, &c. where the Kings *Customes* are received, and all business relating thereunto transacted. See 12 *Car.* 2. *cap.* 4.

Customary Tenants, *Tenants per consuetudinem*, Are such *Tenants* as hold by the *Custome* of the Mannor, as their special Evidence. See *coppy-holds*.

Custos brevium, Is the principal Clerk belonging to the Court of *Common-Pleas*, whose Office is to receive and keep all the Writs, and put them on Files, every Return by it self; and at the end of every Term to receive of the *Protonotaries* all the Records of *Nisi prius*, called *The postea*; for they are first brought in by the Clerk of the Assise of every Circuit to the *Protonotary* that entred the Issue in that matter, for the entring of the Judgment. And then do the *Protonotaries* get of the Court peremptory-day, for every party to speak what he hath to alledge in Arrest of Judgment, which day being past, he entreth the Verdict and Judgement thereupon into the Roll of the Court; and that done, he doth at the end of the Term deliver over to the *Custos brevium* all the Records of *Nisi prius*, which came to his hand that Term, which received, he bindeth into a bundle, and bestoweth them in apt place. The *Custos brevium* also maketh Entry of the Writs of Covenant, and the Concord upon every Fine, and maketh forth Exemplifications and Copies of all Writs and Records in his Office, & of all Fines levyed. The Fines after they be ingrossed, the parts thereof be divided between the *Custos brevium* and the *Chirographer*; whereof the *Chirographer* keepeth always the Writ of Covenant and the Note, the *Custos brevium* keepeth the Concord and Foot of the Fine, upon which Foot the *Chirographer* doth cause the Proclamations to be endorsed, when they be all proclaimed: This Office is in the Kings Gift. There is also a *Custos brevium & rotulorum* in the Kings Bench, who fileth such Writs as are there used to be filed, and all Warrants of Attorney, and transcribeth or maketh out the Records of *Nisi prius*, &c.

Custos placitorum coronæ, *Bract. lib.* 2. *cap.* 5. This seems to be all one with him whom we now call *Custos Rotulorum.* Of this Officer mention is made in the Writ *Odio, & Atia, Reg. Orig. fol.* 133.

Custos Rotulorum, Is he that hath the custody of the Rolls or Records of the Sessions of Peace, and, as some believe, of the Commission of the Peace it self, *Lamb, Eiren. lib.* 4. *cap.* 3. *pag.* 373. He is always a Justice of Peace and *Quorum* in the County where he hath his Office, and by his Office is rather termed an Officer or Minister then a Judge, because the Commission of the Peace layeth by express words this special Charge upon him, *Quod ad dies & loca prædicta, brevia, præcepta, processus & indictamenta prædicta coram te & aliis sociis tuis venire fac*, Lamb. ibid. Where yo may find a large Tract concerning this Office, who shall appoint the *Custos Rotulorum* in every County. See 37. *H.* 8. *cap.* 1. and 3. & 4. *E.* 6. *cap.* 1. & 2. *Inst. fol.* 674.

Custos of the Spiritualities, *custos Spiritualitatis vel Spiritualium*, Is he that exerciseth *Spiritual* or Ecclesiastical Jurisdiction of any Diocess in during the vacancy of the See. The appointment of whom, by the Canon Law, appertains to the Dean and Chapter, but at present with us in *England* to the Archbishop of the Province by Prescription; howbeit divers Deans and Chapters, if *Gwin* say truly in the *Preface to his Readings*, Do challenge this by antient Charters from the Kings of this Land.

Cutter of the Talleys, Is an Officer in the Exchequer, that provideth Wood for the *Talleys*, and *cuts* the summ paid upon them, and then casteth the same into the Court to be written upon.

Cuynage, Is a word us'd in the Statute of 11. *H.* 7. *cap.* 4. for the making up of Tin into that fashion as it is used to be framed, for the better carriage of it into other places.

Cyrickseat, Is a Saxon word, signifying a Tribute due to the Church, *Spelm. de Concil. vol.* 1. *fol.* 125. See *Churchesset*.

D.

Dakir, By the Stat. *de compositione ponderum & mensurarum*, 51 H. 3. A last of Hides consists of twenty *Dakirs*, and every *Dakir* of ten Hides: But by 1. *Jac. cap.* 33. a last of Hides is twelve dozen. See *Dicker of Leather*, *postea*.

Damage, *Damnum*, Generally signifieth any hurt or hinderance that a man taketh in his Estate, but in the Common Law it is a part of that the Jurors be to enquire of, passing for the Plaintiff or Defendant in a civil Action, be it personal or real. For after Verdict given of the principal cause, they are likewise ask'd their Consciences touching Costs (which be the Charges of Suit, called of the *Civilians Expensæ litis*) and *Damages*, which contain the hinderance that the Plaintiff or Demandant hath suffered, by means of the wrong done to him by the Defendant or Tenant, *Co.* on *Lit. fol.* 257. By the Statute 48. *E.* 3. 22. a means for the recovery of Damages was given to the Defendant in an Appeal, when he was acquitted of the Felony. And the Statute of *Westm.* 2. *Anno.* 13. *E.* 1. *cap.* 12. gave a more expeditious Redress than a Writ of Conspiracy against the Procurers and Abetters. This word *Damage* is taken in the Law in two several significations, the one *properly* and *generally*, the other *strictly* and *relatively*. *Properly*, as it is in cases where *Damages* are founded upon the Statute of 2. *H.* 4. *cap.* 1. and 8 *H.* 6. *cap.* 9. where Costs are included within this word *Damages*; for *Damage* in its proper and general signification is said *a demendo*, when a thing by diminution is made worse; and in this sense Costs of Suit are *Damages* to the Plaintiff, for by it his substance is diminished. But when the Plaintiff declares the wrong done to him, to the *damage* of such a summ, this is to be taken *relatively*, for the wrong which is passed before the Writ brought, and are assessed by reason of the Trespass aforesaid, and cannot extend to Costs of Suit, which are future, and of aanother nature. See *Co. lib.* 10. *fol.* 116. 117.

Damage cleere, *Damna clericorum*, Is now assessed by the tenth part in the *Common-Pleas*, and the twentieth part in the *Kings-Bench* and *Exchequer* of all *Damages* (exceeding five Marks) recovered either by Verdict, Confession, or Judgment of the Court, in all Actions upon the Case, Covenant, Trespass, Battery, false Imprisonment, Dower, and all others, wherein the *Damages* are incertain, which the Plaintiff must pay to the *Prothonotary*, or chief

Officer of that Court, wherein they are recovered, before he shall have Execution for them. This was no other originally than a gratuity given to the *Prothonotaries* and their Clerks, for drawing special Writs and Pleadings, which afterwards grew to a certainty, and was as some have fancied of old, a tenth part of the *Damages* recovered; For it appears by ancient Records, that it hath been incertain, sometimes a sixth, and at other times a third part. This is taken away by 17 *Car.* 2. *cap.* 6. from and after the 29. of *September*, 1672. and till that time to be paid out of such Moneys only as shall be actually levyed, or otherwise paid by the Defendants, and only for the proportion of the Money which shall be so levyed or paid, and no more or otherwise.

Damage Feasant, That is, doing hurt or *damage*, & is, when a strangers Beasts are in another mans Ground, without licence of the Tenant of the Ground, and there do feed, tread, and otherwise spoil the Corn, Grass, Woods, and such like; In which case the Tenant, whom they *damage*, may therefore take, distrain, and impound them as well in the Night as in the Day. But in other cases, as for Rent and Services, and such like, none may distrain in the Night, Stat. *de districtione scaccar. Anno* 51. Hen. 3.

Dane gelt, Dane-geld, or **Dane-gilt**, *Danegildum*, Is compounded of the word *Dane* and *Gelt*, that is, Money, and was a Tribute laid upon our Ancestors the Saxons, of twelve pence upon every Hide of Land through the Realm, by the *Danes*, who in those Dayes lorded it here, *Camd. Brit.* 83. with whom agree the Laws of St. *Edward*, set out by *Lambert* in his *Archaionomia*, *cap.* 11. *Stow* in his *Annols*, *pag.* 118. saith, This Tribute came to 40000 pounds *per annum*, and that it was released by *Edward the Confessor*. The Author of the *New Terms of the Law* saith, That this Tribute began in the Reign of King *Ethelred*, who being sore distressed by the continual Invasions of the *Danes*, to procure his Peace, was compelled to charge his People with insupportable Payments; for first, he paid them at five several times, 113000 pounds, and afterwards granted them 48000 pounds yearly. See *Rog. Hoveden, parte poster. suor. annal.* in H. 2. *fol.* 344. *a.* and *Ingulphus*, *fol.* 510. *a. Spelm. Gloss.* and *Seldens mare clausum*, *fol.* 190.

Danelage. See *Merchenlage*.

Darreine, Is a corruption from the French *Dernier*, id est, *ultimus*, and we use it in the same sense, as

Darreyne Continuance. See *Continuance*.

Darreyne Presentment, *Ultima praesentatio*. See *Assise of Darryene Presentment*.

Dates, Is the fruit of the Tree in Latine called *Palma*, in English the *Date Tree*, of which, who will understand the nature or diversities, may read *Gerrard's Herbal*, *lib.* 3. *cap.* 131. They be numbred among Spices and Drugs to be garbled, 1. *Jac.* 19.

Day, *Dies*, Is sometimes used in the Law for the *Day* of Appearance in Court, either originally, or upon Assignation, and sometimes for the Returns of Writs. For example, *Dayes in Bank*, be dayes set down by Statute, or Order of the Court, when Writs shall be returned, or when the Party shall appear upon the Writ served; and of this you may read the Statutes 51. *H.* 3. *cap.* 1. 2. *Marlb. cap.* 12. 52. *H.* 3. and 32. *H.* 8. *cap.* 21. To be dismissed without *day*, is to be finally discharged the Court, *Kitchin. fol.* 193. He had a *day* by the Roll, *Id. fol.* 197. that is, he had a *Day* of Appearance assigned him. *Day*, Year and Wast. See *Dies and Year*.

Deadly feud, *Feuda*, Is a Profession of an unquenchable hatred, until we be revenged even by the death of our Enemy. It is derived from the German word *Feed*, which as *Hottoman* saith, *In verbis* Feudalibus, *modò bellum, modò capitales inimicitias significat.* This word is used 43. *Eliz. cap.* 13.

Dead pledge, *Mortuum vadium*. See *Mortgage*.

Deafforested, That is, discharged from being *Forest*, or exempt from the *Forest-Laws*, 17. *Car.* 1. *cap.* 16.

Dean, *Decanus*, Is an Ecclesiastical Magistrate, so called of the Greek, *Δέκα*, *decem*, because he hath power over ten Canons at the least: Howbeit in *England* we use to call him a *Dean* that is next under the Bishop, and chief of the Chapter ordinarily in a Cathedral Church; the rest of the Society we call *Capitulum*, the Chapter; how diversly this word is used, read *Linwood, tit. de judic. ca. pri. verbo* Rural Dean. Where *Deans Rural* are said to be some that have Jurisdiction Ecclesiastical over other Ministers and Parishes near adjoyning, assigned unto them by the Bishop and *Archdeacon* being placed and displaced by them. As there be two Foundations of Cathedral Churches, the *old* and the *new* (the *new* be those which *Henry* the Eighth upon suppression of Abbot or Prior and Covent turned to *Dean* and Chapter); So there be two means of creating these *Deans*, for those of the *old Foundation* are brought to their Dignity much like Bishops, the King first sending out his *Conge de' eslire*, to the Chapter, the Chapter there chusing, the King yielding his Royal assent, and the Bishop confirming him, and giving his *Mandat* to install him. Those of the *new Foundation* are by a shorter course installed, by vertue of the Kings Letters Patents, without either Election or Confirmation. This word is also applyed to divers that are the chief of some peculiar Churches or Chappels, as *Dean* of the *Kings Chappel*, *Dean* of St. *Pauls*, *Dean* of the *Arches*, *Dean* of St. *Georges* Chappel in *Windsor*, *Dean* of *Bocking* in *Essex*, *&c.*

De bene esse, Are common Latine words, but their meaning something more dark; as thus, To take or do a thing *de bene esse* is to allow or accept for the present, till it comes to be more fully examined, and then to stand or fall, according to the merit, of the thing in its own nature so that *valeat quantum valere potest.* So in *Chancery*, upon motion for one of the less principal Defendants to be examined, the Court sometimes will order it *de bene esse*, that is, he may be examined, but so, that upon hearing, and fully examining the Case, his Deposition may be allowed or suppressed, as the Court shall think fit. See *Langham's* Case, *Cro.* 3. *par. fol.* 68. So also at Common Law, the Judges frequently take Bayl *de bene esse*, that is, to be allowed or disallowed upon the exception

exception or approbation of the Plaintiffs Atturney, however in the *interim* they have a well-being or conditional allowance.

Debentur, Was a kind of writing, given in the late Times of Usurpation, to the Souldier, to secure the payment of his Arrears. but that is now out of doors. The word is mentioned in the Act *Of Oblivion*, 12. *Car.* 2. *cap.* 8. They use *Debenturs* also in the Exchequer. See *Auditor of Receits.* In the Kings House also, *Debenturs* are given usually to the Kings Servants, for the payment of their Wages, Board wages, and the like.

Debet & solet, Are words frequently used by the writers of the Common-Law. For example, it is said in the *Old. Nat. Brev. fol.* 98. This VVrit *De secta Molendini* being in the *debet & solet*, is a VVrit of Right, &c. And again, *fol.* 69. a Writ of *Quod permittat* may be pleaded in the County before the Sheriff, and it may be in the *Debet* and in the *Solet*, or the *debet* without the *solet*, according as the Demandant claimeth; wherefore note, that those Writs that be in this sort brought have these words in them as formal words not to be omitted: And according to the diversity of the Case, both *debet* and *solet*, or *debet* alone; that is, if a Man sue to recover any Right by a Writ, whereof his Ancestor was disseised by the Tenant, or his Ancestor, then he useth only the word *debet* in his Writ, because *solet* is not fit, by reason his Ancestor was disseised, and the Custom discontinued; but if he sue for any thing that is now first of all denyed, then he useth both these words, *debet & solet*, because his Ancestors before him, and he himself usually enjoyed the thing sued for, as suit to a Mill, or Common of Pasture, until the present refusal of the Tenant. The like may be said of *Debet & Detinet*, as appeareth by the *Reg. Orig.* in the writ *de debito*, *fol.* 140 *a.*

Debito, Is a writ which lyeth, where a Man oweth to another a certain sum of Money upon an Obligation, or other Bargain, for any thing sold unto him, *F. N. B. fol.* 119. This writ is sometimes made in the *detinet*, and not in the *debet*, which properly falleth out, where a Man oweth an Annuity, or a quantity of Wheat, Barley, or such like which he refuseth to pay, *Old Nat. Brev. fol.* 75. See before *Debet & solet.*

Decem tales. See *Tales.*

Decies tantum, Is a writ that lyeth against a Juror, which hath taken Money for the giving of his Verdict; called so of the effect, because it is to recover ten times so much as he took: It lyeth also against Embracers, that procure such Enquest, 38. *E.* 3. *cap* 13. *Reg. Orig. fol.* 188. *F. N. B. fol.* 171 *New Book of Entries, verbo* Decies tantum.

Deceit, *Deceptio, fraus, dolus,* Is a subtle, wily shift or device, having no other name: Hereto may be drawn all manner of craft, subtilty, guile, fraud, wilinefs, slight, cunning, covin, collusion, practice and offence used to deceive another man by any means, which hath none other proper or particular name but offence, *West. Symbol. part.* 2. *tit.* Indictments, *sect.* 68. See *Cosening.*

Decenna and **Decenniers.** See *Deciners.*

Decennary, *Decennaria,* The limits or compass of ten *Friburgs.* See *Deciners.*

Deceptione, Is a writ that lyeth properly against him, that deceitfully doth any thing in the Name of another, for one that receiveth damage or hurt thereby, *F. N. B. fol.* 95. This writ is either *original* or *judicial*, as appeareth by the *Old Nat. Brev. fol.* 50. where you may read the use of both; for some satisfaction, take the words of that Book: This writ of *Deceit*, when it is *original*, lyeth in case where *deceit* is used by one Man to another, by which *deceit* he may be disherited, or otherwise evil intreated, as it appeareth by the *Register, &c.* And when it is *judicial*, then it lyeth out of the Rolls of Record; as in case where *Scire facias* is sent to the Sheriff, that he warn a man to be before the Justices at a certain day, and the Sheriff return the writ served, whereas the said man was not warned, by which the Party that sued out the *Scire facias* recovereth; then the Party which ought to have been warned shall have the said writ against the Sheriff. In the *Termes of the Law, verbo* Deceit, it is said, That the *original* writ of *deceit* lyeth, where any *deceit* is done by a man to another, so that he hath not sufficiently performed his Bargain or Promise: In the writ *judicial*, he concurreth with the former Book. See *Reg. Orig. fol.* 112. and the *Regist. Judicial,* in the *Table, verbo* Deceptione.

Decimation, *Decimatio,* The punishing every tenth Souldier by lot, was termed *Decimatio Legionis*: It may be stretched to signifie Tything, or paying the tenth part. There was another sort of *Decimation* in the late Times of Usurpation, which too many of his Majesties Loyal Subjects have so much sad cause to remember that I need not renew the Memory of it.

Decimis solvendis pro possessionibus alienigenarum, Is a Writ, or Letters Patents, yet extant in the *Register*, which lay against those that had farmed the Priors *Aliens* Lands of the Kings, for the Rector of the Parish, to recover his Tythe of them, *Reg. Orig. fol.* 179.

Deciners, alias **Decenniers**, alias **Dosiners,** *Decennarii*, Cometh of the French *Dizeine*, i. *Decas*, ten: It signifieth in the ancient Monuments of our Law, such as were wont to have the oversight and check of ten *Friburghs*, for the maintenance of the Kings Peace; and the Limits or Compass of their Jurisdiction was called *Decenna*, *Bract. lib.* 3. *tract.* 2. *cap.* 15. Of whom you may also read, *Fleta, lib.* 1. *cap.* 27. and *Reg. Orig. fol.* 98. *b.* These seemed to have large Authority in the Saxons time, taking cognisance of Causes within their Circuit, and redressing Wrongs by way of Judgment, as you may read in the Laws of King *Edward*, set out by *Lamb. num.* 32. In latter times mention is made of these, as in *Britton, cap.* 12. who saith in the Kings Person (as he writeth his whole Book in that manner) We will that all those that be fourteen years old, shall make Oath, That they will be sufficient and loyal to Us, and that they will neither be Felons, or assenting to Felons; and we will that all be *en dozeine & plevis per dozeners*, that is, profess themselves of this or that *dozeine*, and make or offer Surety of their Behaviour by these or those *Dozeniers*, except Religious Persons, Clerks, Knights, and their eldest Sons, and VVo-

VVomen: Yet the same Author in his 29. *chap.* toward the end, doth say, That all of twelve years old, and upward, are punishable for not coming to the Turn of the Sheriff, except Earls, Prelates, Barons, Religious Persons, and Women, *Stamf. pl. cor. fol.* 37. Out of *Fitzherbert* hath these words, The same Law is, where the *Dozeniers* make presentment, that a Felon is taken for Felony, and delivered to the Sheriff, &c. And *Kitchin* out of the *Register*, and *Bretton* saith thus, Religious Persons, Clerks, Knights, or Women shall not be *Deciniers, fol.* 33. from all which premises may be gathered, that of later times, this word signifieth nothing but such a one as by Oath of Loyalty to his Prince, is settled in the Combination or Society of a *Dozein*. And a *Dozein* seemeth to extend so far as every Leet extendeth, because in Leets onely this Oath is ministred by the Steward, and taken by such as are twelve years old, and upwards, dwelling within the compass of the Leet, where they are sworn, *F. N. B. fol.* 161. *a.* The particular of this Oath you may read in *Bracton, lib.* 3. *tract.* 2. *cap.* 1. *num.* 1. where he setteth down fifteen years for the age of those that are sworn to the Kings Peace, but *Lib.* 3. *tract.* 2. *cap.* 11. *num.* 5. he nameth twelve years, see *Inlaughe*: From hence we may note the diversities between the ancient and present times, in this point of Law and Government, as well for the age of those that are to be sworn, as also that *Decennier* is not now used for the chief man of a *Dozen*, but for him that is sworn to the Kings Peace. And lastly, That now there are no other *Dozens*, but Leets, and that no man ordinarily giveth other Security for the keeping of the Kings Peace, but his own Oath. And that therefore none answereth for anothers Transgression, but every man for himself. See *Frank Pledge*, and 2. *par. Inst. fol.* 37.

Declaration, *Declaratio*, Is a shewing in Writing the grief and complaint of the Demandant or Plaintiff, against the Defendant or Tenant, wherein he is supposed to have received wrong. And this ought to be plain and certain, both because it impeaches the Defendant, and also compels him to answer thereto. Such a *Declaration* in an Action real is termed a *Count*; Note, that the *Count* or *Declaration* ought to contain *Demonstration*, *Declaration* and *Conclusion*: In *Demonstration* are contained three things. *Quis queritur, contra quem, & pro qua causa.* In the *Declaration* there ought to be comprised, *Quomodo inter partes actio accrevit, quando & qua die, anno & loco & cui dabitur.* And in the *Conclusion*, he ought to aver, and profer to prove his Suit, and shew the Damages he hath sustained by the wrong done him. See *Count*.

Decretalls, *Decretales*, Are a Volume of the Canon-Law, containing the *Decrees* of sundry Popes, or else a digest of the Canons, of all the Councels that pertained to one matter, under one Head

Dedi, Is a Warranty in Law to the Feoffee and his Heirs, as if it be said in a Feoffment *A. B. hath given and granted, &c.* It is a Warranty, *Co.* on *Lit.* 384. *a.*

Dedimus potestatem, Is a Writ whereby Commission is given to a private man, for the speeding of some Act appertaining to a Judge. The *Civilians* call it *Delegationem*; And it is granted most commonly upon Suggestion, that the Party which is to do something before a Judge, or in Court, is so feeble, that he cannot travel: It is used in divers Cases, as to make a personal Answer to a Bill in *Chancery*, to make an Atturney for the following of a Suit in the County, Hundred, Wapentake, &c. *Old. Nat. Brev. fol.* 20. To levy a Fine, *West. Symbol. part* 2. *tit.* Fines, *sect.* 112. and divers other effects, as you shall see by *F. N. B.* in divers places. In what diversity of Cases this Writ or Commission is used. See in the Table of the *Register Orig. verbo* Dedimus Potestatem.

Deeds, *Facta*, Signifie in our Common-Law, Writings that contain the effect of a Contract made between man and man, which the *Civilians* call *literarum Obligationem*: They may be written in Parchment or Paper, but chiefly in Parchment, and to consist of three things, writing, sealing, and delivery: Of these *Deeds* there be two sorts, *Deeds* indented, and *Deeds* Poll, which division, *West* in his *Symbol. part.* 1 *lib.* 1. *sect.* 46. saith. Grows from the form or fashion of them, the one being cut in the fashion of dents in the top or side, and therefore called *Indentures*, the other being plain. And the definition of a *Deed* indented he expresseth thus, *Sect.* 47. A *Deed* indented, is a *Deed* consisting of two parts, or more, wherein it is expressed, That the Parties to the same *Deed* have to every part thereof interchangeably, or severally set their several Seals. See the rest there, where at last he shews the cause of the Name, *viz.* for that consisting of more parts, each part is indented, or cut one of them into the other, that by the cut it may appear they belong to one Business or Contract. A *Deed-Poll* or polled, he describeth thus, *Sect.* 46. A polled *Deed* is a *Deed* testifying that onely one of the Parties to the Bargain hath put his Seal thereto, after the manner there by him described. See also *Termes de la Ley, verbo* Fair.

Deemsters or **Demsters**, Are a kind of Judges in the *Isle of Man*, who, without Process, VVritings, or any Charge, decide all Controversies there; and they are chosen from among themselves, *Camb. Brit. tit.* Brittish Isles.

Deer-hays, *Anno* 19 *H.* 7. *cap.* 11. makes them to be Nets or Engins made of Cords to catch *Deer*.

De essendo quietum de Tolonio, Is a writ which lyeth for them, which are by Priviledge freed from the payment of *Toll*, of which read at large *F. N. B. fol.* 226.

De expensis Militum, Is a writ commanding the Sheriff to levy so much a day for the *expences* of a Knight of the Shire, and a like writ to levy two shilllings a day for every Citizen and Burgess called *De expensis Civium & Burgensium*, 4. Inst. fol. 46.

De facto, A thing actually done, done in very Deed.

Default, *Defalta*, Cometh from the French *Default*, and is an Offence in omitting that which we ought to do, *West. Symbol. part.* 2. *tit.* Inditement, *sect.* 2. Of this *Bracton* hath a large Discourse, *lib.* 5. *tract.* 3. By whom it appeareth, That a *Default* is most notoriously taken for nonappearance in Court at a day assigned. Of this you may read *Fleta, lib.* 6. *cap.* 14.

Defamation, *Defamatio*, Is, when a man speaks slanderous word of another man, of a Court of Justice, Magistracy, or Title of Land; for which the Party shall be punished according to the nature and quality of the Offence. Sometimes by Action upon the Case for Slander; at other times in the Ecclesiastical Courts; as if a man contrive any false lies against Prelates, Dukes, Earls, &c. then an *Actio de Scandalis Magnatum* will lie by the Stat. 2. *R.* 2. *cap.* 5. But for *Defamations* in the Spiritual Court to be determined, they ought to have three incidences. First, To concern matter meerly spiritual, and there tryable, as to call a man Heretick, Schismatick, Adulterer, &c. Secondly That it concern matter meerly spiritual. Thirdly, That is onely for punishment of the Fault, for the Souls health of him that offends. For the Slander or *Defamation* of a Title of Lands, see *Co. lib.* 4. *fol.* 18.

Defeizance, Cometh of the French *Deffayre* or *Deffayr*, that is, *infectum reddere quod factum est*, and signifieth a Condition relating to a Deed, as an Obligation, Recognisance or Statute, which being performed by the Obligor or Recognisor, the Act is disabled and annulled, as if it had never been done. And the difference between a Proviso or Condition in a Deed and a *Defeasance*, is this, that a Proviso or Condition is annexed or inserted in the Deed or Grant, whereas a *Difeasance* is usually a Deed by it self. For the form and manner of *Defeasances*, according to the diversity of the case, see *West Symbol. part* 1. *lib.* 2. *sect.* 156. & 230, 231.

Defend, *Defendere*, Signifies in our ancient Laws and Statutes as much as to forbid and prohibit, *Leg. Ed. Conf. cap.* 37. & 5. *R.* 2. *cap.* 7. In the same sence *Chaucer* uses it in these words,

Where can you say, in any manner Age,
That ever God defended *Marriage.*

And in 7 *E.* 1. we have a Statute intituled, *Statutum de* defensione *portandi arma, &c.* It is *defended*, that is, forbidden to distrain upon the Highway, *Co.* on *Lit. fol.* 161. nay, in common speech Men frequently say, *God defend*, instead of *God forbid*; and the *fence moneth* is more properly the *defence moneth*, that is, the forbidden moneth, or *tempus vetitum*, *Manwood's Forest Law*, *cap.* 13. *num.* 1. See *fence moneth*.

Defence, Is that which the Defendant ought to make immediately after the Count or Declaration made, that is, that he *defends* all the wrong force and damage, &c. and then to proceed either in his Plea, or to imparle. See more, *Termes de lay Ley*, *verbo* Defence.

Defendant, *Defendens*, Is he that is sued in an Action personal; as Tenant, is he which is sued in an Action real, *Termes de lay Ley*.

Defendemus, Is an ordinary word in a Feoffment or Donation, and hath this force, that it bindeth the Donor and his Heirs to *defend* the Donee, if any man go about to lay any servitude upon the thing given, other than is contained in the Donation, *Bracton*, *lib.* 2. *cap.* 16. *num.* 10. See also *Warrantizabimus & Acquietabimus*.

Defender of the Faith, *Defensor Fidei*, Is a peculiar Title given to the King of *England* by the Pope, as *Catholicus* to the King of *Spain*, and *Christianissimus* to the French King. It was first given by *Leo* the Tenth to King *Henry* the Eighth, for writing against *Martin Luther* in behalf of the Church of *Rome*, then accounted *Domicilium fidei Catholicæ*, *Stow's Annals*, *pag.* 863. The Bull for it bears Date *Quinto Idus*, *Octob.* 1521. and may be read at large in the Lord *Herberts* History of *Henry* the Eighth, *fol.* 105.

Deforcement, *Deforciamentum*, A withholding Lands or Tenements by *force* from the right Owner. See *Mat. Paris*, *fol.* 422. and *Co.* on *Lit. fol.* 331. *b.* See *Deforceor*.

Deforciant, The same with *Deforceor*, *Anno* 23 *Eliz. cap.* 3.

Deforceor, *Deforciator*, Cometh of the French *Forceur*, *expugnator*: In the sense of the Law it signifies one that overcometh, and casteth out by *force*; and differeth from Disseisor first in this, because a man may disseise another without *force*, which Acts is called *Simple disseisin*, *Britton*, *cap.* 53. next, because a man may deforce another that never was in possession. As for example, If more have right to Lands as common Heirs, and one entring, keepeth out the rest, the Law saith That he *deforceth* them, though he do not disseise them. *Old Nat. Brev. fol.* 118. And *Littleton* in his Chapter *Discontinuance*, *fol.* 117. saith, That he which is infeoffed by the Tenant in tail, and put in possession, by keeping out the Heir of him in the Reversion, being dead, doth *deforce* him, though he did not disseise him, because he entred when the Tenant in tail was living, and the Heir had no present Right. And a *Deforceor* differeth from an Intruder, because a man is made an Intruder by a wrongful Entry only into Lands or Tenements void of a Possessor, and a *Deforceor* also is, by holding out the right Heir, as abovesaid, *Bracton*, *lib.* 4. *cap.* 1. See more of this in *Polton de pace Regis*, *fol.* 34, 35.

Se Defendendo, In *defending* himself, as if one Man assail another, and he which is assailed fly till he come to a River side, or Wall, that hinders him to fly any further, and there he resists the Violence offered to him, and kill the other; this is said to be done *Se defendendo*, and the Law putteth him to sue out his Pardon of course, and Punisheth him by forfeiture of Goods, *Bacon's Collections of the Law*.

Degrading. See *Disgrading*.

Delegates, The Stat. 26 *H*, 8. *cap.* 19. sayes, Are Commissioners *delegated* or appointed by the Kings Commission, to sit upon an Appeal to him in the Court of *Chancery*, and is granted in three Cases. First, When a Sentence is given in any Ecclesiastical Cause by the Archbishop, or his Official. Secondly, When any Sentence is given in any Ecclesiastical Cause in places exempt. Thirdly, When Sentence is given in the Admiralty in Suits Civil and Marine, by order of the Civil-Law. 4 *par. Inst. fol.* 339. *Anno* 8 *Eliz. cap.* 5.

Deliverance. See *Replegiare*.

Delfe, From the Saxon *delpan* to dig; we still retain the word *Delve*, for dig; is a Quarry or Mine where Stone or Coal is digged, *Anno* 31 *Eliz.* 2. *cap.* 7. And *Camden* mentions a Charter of *Edward* the Fourth, wherein mention is made of a Mine or *Delfe* of Copper.

Demaine or **Demesne**, *Dominicum*, Is a French word otherwise written *Domaine*, and signifieth *Patrimonium Domini*, as Hotoman saith, *In verbis feudalibus*, *verbo* Dominicum, where by divers Authorities he proveth those Lands to be *Dominicum*, which a man holdeth originally of himself, and those to be *feodum* which he holdeth of a superior Lord. And by the word *Domanium* as *Demanium*, are properly signified the Kings Lands in *France*, appertaining to him in property. In like manner do we use it in *England*, although we have no Land (that of the Crown onely excepted) which holdeth not of a superior, for all dependeth either mediately or immediately of the Crown, wherefore no common person hath any *Demaynes* simply understood; For when a man in pleading, would signifie his Land to be his own, he saith, That he is or was seized thereof in his *Demayne*, as of Fee, *Lit. lib.* 1 *c.* 1. whereby he meaneth, that although his Land be to him and his Heirs for ever, yet it is not true *Demayne*, but depending upon a superior Lord, and holding by Service, or Rent in lieu of Service, and by both Service and Rent; yet these words have been used in the Kings Right, 37. *H.* 8. *cap.* 16. and 39 *El.* 22. But the application of this speech to the King and Crown-Land is crept in by error and ignorance of the word *Fee. Britton, cap.* 78. sheweth, That this word *Demayne* is diversly taken; sometimes more largely, as of Lands and Tenements held for life, &c. and sometimes more strictly, as for such onely as are generally held in Fee. This word sometime is used for a distinction between those Lands, that the Lord of the Mannor hath in his own hands, or in the hands of his Lessee, demised upon a Rent, for term of Years or Life, and such other Land appertaining to the said Mannor, which belongeth to Fee or Copy-holders. Howbeit, the Copy-hold belonging to any Mannor, is also in the Opinion of many good Lawyers accounted *Demaynes, Bracton, lib.* 4. *tract.* 3. *cap.* 9. *num.* 5. saith, *Est autem Dominicum, quod quis habet ad mensam suam & proprie, sicut sunt* Bordlands *Anglice. Item dicitur Dominicum Villenagium, quod traditur villanis quod quis tempestive & intempestive sumere possit pro voluntate sua & revocare.* Of this *Fleta* also writeth much after the same manner, *Lib.* 5. *cap.* 5. *sect. Dominicum autem.* And the reason why Copy-hold is accounted *Demaynes*, is because they that be Tenants to it, are judged in Law to have no other Right, but at the will of the Lord; so that it is reputed still after a sort to be in the Lords hands. And yet in common speech, that it is ordinarily called *Demeans*, that is, neither Free nor Copy. And here note, That *Demayne* is sometime used in a more special signification, and is opposite to *Frank-Fee*. For example, Those Lands which were in the possession of *Edward the Confessor*, are called *ancient Demaine*, and others be called *Frank Fee*, *Kitchin, fol.* 98. And the Tenants which hold any of those Lands be called *Tenants in ancient* Demaine, the others *Tenants in Frank-Fee, Kitchin, ubi supra.* And also Tenants of the Common-Law, *West. Symbol. part.* 2. *tit.* Fines. *sect.* 25. The reason is, because *Tenants in antient* Demain cannot be sued out of the Lords Court, *Termes de lay Ley, verbo* Ancient Demaine. And such Tenants, though they hold all by the *Verge*, and have none other Evidence, but Copy of Court-Roll, yet are they said to have *Free-hold, Kitchin* 81. See *Antient Demesne.* See more on this Subject in the learned *Spelman, verbo* Dominicum.

Demaine cart of an Abbot, Seems to be that *Cast* which the *Abbot* useth upon his own *Demaine, Anno* 6. *H.* 3. *cap.* 21.

Demand, *Postulatio*, signifies a calling upon a Man for any thing due. It hath also a more proper meaning distinguished from *Plaint*; for all civil Actions are pursued either by *Demands* or *Plaints*, and the Pursuer is called *Demandant* or *Plaintiff*, *viz. Demandant* in Actions *real*, and *Plaintiff* in *personal*. If a man release to another all *demands*, this is the best Release can be given, and shall enure most to his advantage that hath it, *Lit. fol.* 117. *a.* There are two manner of *Demands*, one in *Deed*, another in *Law*; In *Deed*, as in every *Præcipe* there is express *Demand*: In *Law*, as every Entry in Land, Distress for Rent, and such like acts are *demands* in Law. See more concerning Release of all *Demands, Co. lib.* 8. *fol.* 153. 154.

Demandant, *Petens*, Is the *Plaintiff* in a real Action so called, because he *demandeth* Lands, &c. *Co.* on *Lit. fol.* 127.

Demphaque. See *Haque* and *Haquebuz.*

Demise, *Dimissio*, Is applyed to an Estate either in Fee-simple, Fee-tail, or for term of Life, and so it is commonly taken in many Writs, 2. *par. Inst. fol.* 483. The Kings death is in Law termed *The demise of the Kings.*

Demsters. See *Deemsters.*

Demurrer, In Latine *Demorare*, Cometh of the French word *Demurer*, that is, *manere in aliquo loco.* It signifies in our Common-Law a kind of pause upon a point of difficulty in any Action, and used substantively; for in every Action the Controversie consisteth either in the Fact, or in the Law; if in the Fact, that is tryed by the Jury; if in the Law, then is the Case plain to the Judge, or so hard and rare, that it breedeth just doubt: I call that plain to the Judge, wherein he is assured of the Law, though perhaps the Party and his Councel yield not to it, and in such case the Judge, with his Associates, proceedeth to Judgment without farther work; but when it is doubtful to him and his Associates, there is then a stay made, and time taken, either for the Court to consider further of it, and to agree if they can; or else for all the Justices to meet together in the *Exchequer Chamber*, and upon hearing of that, the Councel shall stay on both parts to advise, and set down what is Law; and whatsoever they conclude, standeth firm without farther remedy, *Smith de Repub. Angl. lib.* 2. *cap.* 13. In *Chancery* the Defendant *demurrs* to the Plaintiffs Bills averring it to be defective in such or such a point, and demands the Judgment of the Court thereupon, whether he shall be compelled to make any further or other answer thereunto, *&c.* See *Moratur in Lege.*

Demy sanke ou Sangue, Of the half Blood, is, when the Man marries a Wife, and hath Issue by her a Son or a Daughter, and the Wife dies, and then he takes another Woman, and hath by her also a Son or Daughter; now these two Sons or Daughters are after a sort Brothers

thers or Sister, as we usually term them *half Brothers*, &c, or *Brothers of the half Blood*, because they had both one Father; but are not Brothers by the Mothers side, as having several Mothers, & therefore cannot be Heirs one to another, for he that shall Claim as Heir to one by Descent, must be of the whole Blood to him from whom he claims.

Denariata terræ. See *Farding-deal* of *Land.*

Denariatus, *Precium rei quæ* Denario *constat.* I have read *octo* Denariatus *annui redditus.*

Dena terræ, A hollow place between two Hills; you may find it in the beginning of *Doomsday Book.*

Dene, *Dena*, In the same Book signifies a *Dale.*

Denne, In the same Book stands for a *Town.*

Denelage, *Denelagia*, Is the Law that the Danes made here in *England*, out of which, and *Merchenlage* and *West Saxon-lage*, the Conqueror compounded certain Ordinances for his Subjects, *Camd. Brit. pag.* 94. & 183.

Denizen, From the French *Donaison*, i. *Donatio*, signifies in Law an Alien that is enfranchised by the Kings Charter, and inabled in all respects almost to do as the Kings native Subjects do, *viz.* to purchase and to possess Lands, and to be capable of any Office or Dignity; yet it is short of Naturalization, because a stranger naturalized, may inherit Lands by Descent, which a Man made onely a *Denizen* cannot. And in the Charter, whereby a Man is made *Denizen*, there is commonly contained some one Clause or other, that abridgeth him of that full benefit which natural Subjects do enjoy. And when a Man is thus infranchised, he is said to be under the Kings Protection, or *esse ad fidem Regis Angliæ*, before which time he can enjoy nothing in *England*, *Bract. lib.* 5. *tract.* 5. *cap.* 25. *num.* 3. Nay he and his Goods might be seised to the Kings Use, *Horne* in his *Mirrour of Justices*, *lib.* 1. *cap. de la Venue de francpledge*, and 2. *par. Inst. fol.* 741. See also the Statute 27 *H.* 8. *cap.* 24. and *Co. lib.* 7. *Calvin's* Case. It seems that *Donaiso* is the right Name so called, because his Legitimation proceeds *ex donatione Regis*, from the Kings Gift.

De non Residentia Clerici Regis, Is an antient VVrit, whereof see the form in 2 *par. Inst. fol.* 624.

Deodand, *Deodandum*, Is a thing given, or rather forfeited, as it were, to God, for the pacification of his Wrath, in case of Misadventure, whereby any Christian man cometh to a violent end, without the fault of any reasonable Creature. For example, If a Horse should strike his Keeper, and so kill him: If a man in driving a Cart, and seeking to redress any thing about it, should so fall as the Cart-wheel running over him, should kill him: If one should be felling of a Tree, and giving warning to company by, when the Tree were near falling, to look to themselves, and any of them should be slain nevertheless by the fall of the Tree. In the first of these cases, the Horse; in the second, the Cart-wheel, Cart and Horses; and in the third, the Tree, is to be a *Deodand*, that is, given to God; that is, to be sold and distributed to the Poor, for an Expiation of that dreadful Event, though effected by unreasonable, yea senseless and inanimate Creatures, *Stamf. pl. cor. lib.* 1. *cap.* 2. *Bract. lib.* 3. *tract.* 2. *cap.* 5. *Britton*, *cap.* 7. and *West. Symbol. tit.* Indictments, *sect.* 49. *Fleta*, *lib.* 1. *cap.* 25 *verbo* de Submersis, saith, That this is sold, and the price distributed to the Poor, for the Soul of the King, his Ancestors, and all faithful People departed this Life; which Law is in imitation of that in *Exodus*, *chap.* 21. See *Coke. lib.* 5. *fol.* 110. and *Plowdens Com. fol.* 260. *b.*

Omnia quæ movent ad mortem sunt Deodanda
What moves to death, we understand
Is forfeit as a Deodand.

This word is mentioned in the Statute *de Officio Coronatoris.* 4 *E.* 1. See 3. *par. Inst. fol.* 57.

De onerando pro rata portionis, Is a Writ that lyeth, where one is distrained for a Rent that ought to be paid by others *proportionably* with him. For example, A man holds ten Oxgangs of Land by Fealty, and ten shillings Rent of the King, and alienateth one Ox-gange to one, another to another in Fee; afterward the Sheriff, or other Officer cometh and distraineth onely one of them for the Rent; he that is distrained may have this Writ for his help, *F. N. B. fol.* 234.

Departer or **Departure**, From a Plea, or Matter, is where a man pleads a Plea in bar of an Action, and being replyed thereunto, doth in his Rejoynder shew another matter contrary to his first Plea, that is called a *Departure from his bar*, *Plowd. Com. fol.* 7. 8. *Reniger* and *Fogassa's* Case. It may also be applyed to a Plaintiff, who in his Replication shews new matter from his Declaration, *Co.* 2. *par. fol.* 147. *Bagshawes* Case. So if a Man plead a general Agreement in Bar, and in his Rejoynder alledge a special one; this shall be adjudged a *Departure* in pleading. So in in Trespass, if the Defendant will plead a Discent, and the Plaintiff that after this the Defendant enfeoffed him; and the Defendant saith, this Feoffment was upon condition, for the breach whereof he entred: This is a *Departure*, for it is new matter. Of this, see divers Examples in *Broke*, *tit. Departer de son plea.*

Departure in despight of the Court, Is, when a Tenant or Defendant appears to an Action and hath a day over in the same Term, or is called after, though he had no day given him, so that it be in the same Term; if he do not appear, but make Default, it is a *Departure in despight of the Court*, and therefore he shall be condemned. And here observe, That *Departure in despight of the Court*, is alwayes on the part of the Tenant or Defendant, and the Entry thereof is, *Quod prædictus A. licet solenniter exactus non revenit sed in contemptum curiæ recessit & defaltam fecit*: And this is when in Judgment of the Law he is present in Court, and being demanded, *departs in Despight of the Court.* This amounts to a Bar in respect of the *despight* and contempt *of the Court.* See *Co. lib.* 8. *fol.* 62.

Departers of Gold and Silver. See *Finers.*

Depopulation, *Depopulatio*, Is the laying waſt, deſtroying and unpeopling of a place *Co.* 12. *Rep. fol.* 30.

Depopulatores agrorum, Were great Offendors by the Common-Law, as appears by the Statute 4. *H.* 4. 2. and were called *Depopulatores agrorum*, becauſe by proſtrating and ruining of Houſes they ſeemed to *depopulate* Towns, that is, leave them without Inhabitants, 3. *par. Inſt. fol.* 204. See alſo 13 *El.* 10. and 14 *El.* 11.

Depoſition, *Depoſitio*, Is the teſtimony of a Witneſs ſet down in writing by way of anſwer to interrogatories exhibited in *Chancery*, where ſuch Witneſs is called a *Deponent*. *Depoſition* is alſo ſometimes uſed for death, as in *Provin. Ang. lib.* 2. *tit.* de Feriis; Where it is ſaid, *Ordinamus, quod feſtum* Depoſitionis *ſancti* Johannis *de* Beverlaco *celebretur, &c.* 7. *die Maij.*

Deprivation, *Deprivatio*, Is a bereaving or taking away, as when a Biſhop, Parſon, Vicar or Prebend, is *deprived* or depoſed from his Preferment for any matter in Fact or in Law; as if a Schiſmatick, or meer Lay man, be preſented, admitted, inſtituted and inducted; this is good cauſe of *Deprivation*. See other Cauſes of *Deprivation*, 13 *Eliz. cap.* 12. 21 *H.* 8. *cap.* 13. See alſo 2 & 3 *E.* 6. *cap.* 20. *Deprivation* of Biſhops and Deans, 39 *Eliz. cap.* 8. See alſo *Co. lib.* 4. *fol.* 76. and *lib.* 7. 43. *b.*

Deputy, Is he that exerciſes in another mans Right, either Office or other things; and his Forfeiture or Miſdemeanor ſhall cauſe the Officer, or him whoſe *Deputy* he is to loſe his Office: But a man cannot make his *Deputy* in all Caſes, except the Grant ſo be, as if it be with theſe, or ſuch like words, *To exerciſe and uſe by himſelf, or his ſufficient* Deputy; Or if the words go farther, *To himſelf, or his* Deputy, *or the* Deputy *of his* Deputy. Then he may make his *Deputy*, and his *Deputy* alſo may make a *Deputy*, or elſe not. As if the Office of a Parkerſhip be granted to one, he cannot grant this over to another, becauſe it is an Office of Truſt and Confidence, and ſhall not be forfeited. And there is great difference between a *Deputy* and Aſſignee of an Office, for an Aſſignee hath an intereſt in the Office it ſelf, and doth all things in his own Name; for whom his Grantor ſhall not anſwer, unleſs in ſpecial caſes. But a *Deputy* hath not any intereſt in the Office, but is onely the ſhadow of the Officer, in whoſe Name he doth all things. And where an Officer hath power to make Aſſignes, he may implicitly make *Deputies*, for *cui licet quod majus eſt, non debet quod minus eſt non licere*. And a Sheriff may make a *Deputy*, or Under-Sheriff, although he have not ſuch expreſs words in his Patent.

De quibus ſur diſſeiſin, Is a writ of Entry. See *Fitzh. Nat. Brev. fol.* 191.

Deraigne or **Dereyne**, *Diſrationare vel dirationare*, May ſeem to come of the French *Diſarroyer*, id eſt, *confundere*, to confound or diſorder, or *deſranger*, to put in diſorder; or of the *Norman* word *Deſrene*, which ſignifies nothing but a proof of the denial of a mans own Fact. In our Common-Law it is uſed diverſly. Firſt generally, To prove, as *Dirationabit jus ſuum hæres propinquior*, Glanvile, lib. 2. cap. 6. And *habeo probos homines, qui hoc viderunt & audierunt & parati ſunt hoc dirationare*, Id. lib. 4. cap. 6. And *dirationavit terram illam in curia mea*, Id. lib. 2. cap. 20. he proved, that Land to be his own, &c. And *pertinentiam eam dirationavit in vita ſua vel alio modo juſte perquiſivit*, Id. lib. 6. cap. 12. And *Bracton* uſeth it after the ſame ſort, in theſe words, *Habeo ſufficientem diſratiocinationem & probationem*, Lib. 4. tract. 6. cap 16. And ſo he uſeth *Dirationare, Lib.* 4. *cap.* 22. And ſo in *Weſtm.* 2. 13 *E.* 1. *cap.* 32. And to *derayne* the Warranty, *Old Nat. Brev. fol.* 146. And to *derayne* the Warranty Paramount, 31 *H.* 8. *cap.* 1. And *dereigner le Warranty* in *Plowden, Baſſet's* Caſe, *in fine* 2. *partis. fol.* 6. 7. 8. hath the ſame ſignification. So it is uſed, *Weſtm.* 2. *cap.* 5. 13 *E.* 1. in theſe words, And when the Parſon of any Church is diſturbed, to demand Tythes in the next Pariſh by a Writ of *Indicavit*; the Patron of the Parſon ſo diſturbed, ſhall have a Writ to demand the Advowſon of the Tythes, being in demand; and when it is *deraigned*, then ſhall the Plea paſs in the *Court-Chriſtian* as far as the ſame is *derayned* in the Kings Court. *Bract.* alſo *Lib.* 3. *tract.* 2. *cap.* 3. *num.* 1. ſpeaking of him that appealeth another for any Treaſon or Felony, hath theſe words, *Proponat accuſans appellum ſuum in hunc modum, ſc. debet dicere ſe interfuiſſe & vidiſſe certo loco, certo die, certa hora, & ſciviſſe ipſum accuſatum prælocutum fuiſſe mortem Regis vel ſeditionem ſuam, vel exercitus ſui, vel conſenſiſſe, vel auxilium & conſilium impendiſſe, vel ad hoc autoritatem præſtitiſſe, & hoc ego juxta conſiderationem curiæ* diſrationare *paratus ſum.* He uſeth it likewiſe as the *Normans* uſe *Diſraiſniam*, for him that offereth to juſtifie his denyal, as *Lib.* 3. *tract.* 2. *cap.* 28. *num.* 1. in theſe words, *Rex conſilio Epiſcoporum & bonorum miſit propter comitem, ut ſtatuto die veniret ad curiam, ad* diſrationandum *vel defendendum ſe ſi poſſit.* Laſtly, in ſome places the Subſtantive *Deraiment* is found uſed in the very literal ſignification of the French *Derayer* or *Diſranger*, that is, turning out of Courſe, as *dereinment* or departure out of Religion, 31 *H.* 8. *c.* 6. and *dereignment* or diſcharge of their Profeſſion, 33 *H.* 8. 29. which is ſpoken of thoſe religious men which forſook their Orders, or Profeſſion, as alſo 5 & 6 *E.* 6. *cap.* 13. So doth *Kitchin* uſe the word, *fol.* 152. ſaying, The Leſſee entreth into Religion, and afterward is *dereigned*. And *Britton* hath theſe words, *Semounſe diſrenable*, for a Summons that may be challenged as defective, or not lawfully made, *cap.* 21. Of this you may read more in *Skene de verb.* Signif. *verbo* Diſrationare, where he confoundeth it with our waging and making of Law.

Detinue, *Detinendo*, Is a Writ that lyeth againſt him, who having Goods or Chattels deliver'd him to keep, refuſeth to deliver them again. See of this *F. N. B. fol.* 138. To this is anſwerable in ſome ſort, *Actio depoſiti* in the Civil Law. And he taketh his Action of *Detinue*, that intendeth to recover the thing delivered, and not the Damages ſuſtained by the *Detinue*, *Kitchin. fol.* 176. See the *New Book of Entries, verbo* Detinue.

Deſcent. See *Diſcent*.

Detinet. See *Debito & debet*.

De ſon Tort demeſne, Seem to be certain words of form in an Action of Treſpaſs, uſed by way of Reply to the Plea of the Defendant: For example *A.* ſueth *B.* in an Action of Treſpaſs, *B.* anſwers for himſelf, That he did that which *A.* calleth *a Trespass*, by the Commandment of *C.* his Master. *A.* saith again, That *B.* did it *De son tort de demesne sans ceo que* C. *luy command, modo & forma, &c.*

Debt or **Det**, Is a Writ that lies, where any sum of Money is due to a man by reason of Account, Bargain, Contract, Obligation, or other Specialty, to be paid at a certain day, which is not paid, then he shall have this Writ; but Action of *Debt* will not lie for Money due to a Lord by his Tenant for any Rent-service, but he must distrain for it. So for Rent-charge or Rent seck, which any man hath for Life, in Tail, or in Fee; he shall not have any Action of *Debt* as long as the Rent continues, but his Executors may have an Action of *Debt* for the Arrearages due in the life of their Testator, by the Stat. 32 *H.*8. *cap.* 37. See more *Co. lib.* 8. 147.

Devastaverunt bona testatoris, Is a Writ lying against Executors, for paying Legacies and Debts without Specialty, to the prejudice of the Creditors that have Specialties, before the Debts upon the said Specialties be due: For in this case the Executors are as lyable to Action, as if they had wasted the Goods of the *Testator* riotously, or without cause, for such irregular and illegal Payments are accounted in Law a *wasting* of the Goods of the *Testator*, as much as if they had given them away without cause, or sold them, and converted them to their own use. See *Dyer, fol.* 232. *pla.* 5. And also the *Office of Executors, cap.* 12.

Devenerunt, Is a Writ directed to the Escheator, when any of the Kings Tenants holding *in Capite* dies, and when his Son and Heir within age, and in the King's Custody, dies, then shall this Writ go forth, commanding the Escheator, that by the Oaths of twelve good and lawful men he inquire what Lands or Tenements, by the death of the Tenant, come to the King. See *Dyer, fol.* 360. *pla.* 4. But see the Stat. 12. *Car.*2. *cap.* 24. and 14 *Car.* 2. *cap.* 11.

Devest, (*Devestir*) Is contrary to *Invest*; for as *Investire* signifies *possessionem tradere*, so *Devestire* is *possessionem auferre*, Feud. lib. 1. cap. 7.

Devise, or **Divise**, Cometh of the French *Divisir, separare*, or *Deviser*, to confer with. This word is properly attributed in the Common Law, to him that bequeaths his Lands or Goods by his last Will and Testament in writing, and he is called the *Devisor*. And here we are to observe, That the Laws of the Realm, and the Judges thereof, favour Wills and Testaments, and *Devises*, in yielding to them such a reasonable Construction as they think might best agree with the mind of the Deceased, and are more favourably interpreted in Wills then in Deeds: We will set down some few examples, as if one *devise* to *J.S.* by his Will all his Lands and Tenements, here not onely all those Lands that he hath in possession, but all those that he hath in Reversion, by vertue of the word *Tenements* pass. Again, if Lands be *devised* to a man, to have to him for ever, or to have to him and his Assigns; in these two cases the *Devisee* shall have a Fee simple: But if it be given by Feoffment in such manner, he hath but an Estate for term of Life.---If one *devise* to an Infant *in ventre matris suæ*, it is a good *devise*; but otherwise by Feoffment, Grant or Gift: for in those cases there ought to be one of ability to take presently, or otherwise it is void. See 14 *Eliz. Dyer* 304. and *Co.* on *Lit. fol.* 111. And this favourable allowance to Wills even the Heathens observed, as appears by these Verses.

Sed legum servanda fides; suprema voluntas
Quod mandat, fieriq; jubet, parere necesse est.

Laws must be reverenc'd; and what ere is laid
Upon us by a Will *must be obey'd.*

Devoyres of Caleys, Is as much to say as a Duty. It is used in the Statute of 2 *R.* 2. *Stat.* 1. *cap.* 3. and 5 *R.* 2. *Stat.* 2. *cap.* 2. where it signifies the Customs brought to, or carryed out from *Caleys*, while our Staple remained there. See 34 *E.* 3. *cap.* 18. paying their Customes and *Devoyres* to the King.

Devorce alias **Divorce**, *Divortium*, Is with our Common Lawyers accounted that separation between two, *de facto* marryed together, which is *a Vinculo matrimonii, non solum a mensa sed & a Thoro*, and therefore the Woman so *divorced* received all again that she brought with her. This is not but only upon a Nullity of the Marriage, upon some essential Impediment, as Consanguinity or Affinity within the Degrees forbidden, Pre-contract, Impotency, or such like, of which Divines reckon Fourteen, according to these Verses.

Error, Conditio, Votum, Cognatio, Crimen,
Cultus, Disparitas, Vis, Ordo, Ligamen, Honestas,
Si sis affinis; si forte, coire nequibis;
Si Parochi & duplicis desit præsentia testis,
Raptave sit mulier, &c.-----

For all these, see *Co. lib.* 6. *fol.* 66. *Co. lib.* 5. *fol.* 98. 19. *Lib. Ass. Pl.* 2. *Co. lib.* 7. *Kenne's* Case, And *Co.* on *Lit. fol.* 235. In the old Law, the Woman *divorced*, was to have of her Husband a writing, which was called *a Bill of Divorce.*

Dicker of Leather, Is a quantity consisting of ten Hides: The name may seem to come from the Greek δέκας, which something resembles the Latine word *Decem.*

Dictum de Kenelworth, Was an Edict between *Henry* the Third and his Barons, so called, because it was made at *Kenelworth* Castle in *Warwickeshire*, 51 *H.* 3. containing a Composition of those who had forfeited their Estates in that Rebellion.

Diem clausit extremum, Is a Writ that lyeth for the Heir of him that holdeth Land of the King, either by Knights-service or Socage, and dyeth, be he under or at full age, directed to the Escheator of the County, to inquire of what Estate the Party dyed seised, and who is next Heir to him, and of what value the Land is. The form whereof, and other circumstances, you may read in *F. N. B. fol.* 251.

Dyer, Was a learned Lawyer, and Lord chief Justice of the *Common-Pleas* in Queen *Elizabeths* time, who writ a Book of great account, called his *Commentaries* or *Reports.*

Dies, There are four sorts of *Dayes*, A *day natural*, and so the Scripture saith, *The Evening and the Morning made the first day.* 2. A day *artificial*, and

and that is *a crepusculo matutino usq; ad crepusculum vespertinum*. 3. *Dies astrologicus*, an Astrological day from Sun to Sun. 4. A *legal day*, and that is of two sorts, 1. *Dies Juridicus*. And 2. *Dies non Juridicus*. *Dies Juridici* are all dayes in Bank, Continuance, Essoin-dayes, and other dayes given in Term to the Parties in Court. *Dies non Juridici* are all Sundayes in the year, besides, in the several Terms particular dayes; as in *Easter* Term, *festum ascentionis Domini*; in *Trinity* Term, *festum sancti* Johannis Baptistæ; in *Michaelmas* Term, *festum omnium Sanctorum, & festum omnium Animarum*; and in *Hillary* Term, *festum Purificationis beatæ* Mariæ *Virginis*. And this was the ancient Law of *England*, and yet in use, 2. *par. Inst.* 264.

Dies datus, Is a *Respite* given to the Tenant or Defendant by the Court, *Broke, tit. Continuance*.

Dieta rationabilis, Is used in *Bracton* for a reasonable Dayes-Journey, *Lib.* 3. *part.* 2. *cap.* 16. It hath in the Civil-Law divers other significations not needful here to be set down, *v. vocab. Utriusq; juris*.

Dignitaryes, *Dignitarii*, Are such as are advanced to any Ecclesiastical Promotion, as Dean, Archdeacon, Prebendary, &c. 3. *par. Inst. fol.* 155.

Dignity Ecclesiastical, *Dignitas Ecclesiastica*, Is mentioned in the Statute 26 *H.* 8. *cap.* 3. and by the *Canonists* defined to be *administratio cum jurisdictione & potestate aliqua conjuncta*, Glos. in cap. 1. *de consuet. in sexto*, whereof you may read divers Examples in *Duarenus de sacris Eccl. minister. & Benefic.* lib. 2. cap. 6.

Dilapidation, *Dilapidatio*, A wastful destroying, or letting of Building run to ruine and decay, for want of Reparation, 13 *Eliz. cap.* 10. and the Money recovered for *Dilapidations* shall be employed in the repair of the same Houses, 14 *El.* 11.

Dioces, *Diocesis*, A Greek word compounded of διὰ and οἴκησις, and signifieth with us the Circuit of every Bishops Jurisdiction; for this Realm hath two sorts of Division, one into Shires or Counties, in respect of Temporal Policy; the other into *Dioceses*, in respect of Jurisdiction Ecclesiastical, of which last we reckon in *England* two and twenty, besides four in *Wales*.

Dieu son act, These are words oftentimes used in our Law; and it is a Maxime, that the *Act* of God shall prejudice no Man: And therefore if a House be beaten down by Tempest, or other *Act* of God, the Lessee for Life or Years shall not only be quit in an Action of Wast brought against him, but hath by the Law a special interest to take Timber to build the House again, if he will for his Habitation, *Co. lib.* 4. 63. & *lib.* 11. 82. *a.* So, when the Condition of an Obligation consists in two parts in the Disjunctive, and both are possible at the time of the Obligation made, and afterwards one of them becomes impossible by the *Act* of God; the Obligor is not bound to perform the other part, for the Condition shall be taken beneficially for him, *Co. lib.* 5. 22.

Dimihaque. See *Haque*.

Dimidietas, The moyety or one half of a thing.

Disability, *Disabilitas*, Is, when a Man is *disabled* of, or made incapable to inherit or take a Benefice, which otherwise he might have done, which may happen four wayes, By the act of the Ancestor, by the act of the Party, by act of Law, and by the act of God. 1. *Disability* by the act of the Ancestor, as if a man be attainted of Treason or Felony; by this Attainder his Blood is corrupt, and thereby himself and his Children *disabled* to inherit. 2. *Disability* by the act of the Party himself; as if one man make a Feoffment to another that then is sole, upon condition, that he shall enfeoff a third before *M*, and before *M.* or the Feoffment made, the Feoffee takes a Wife; he hath by that *disabled* himself to perform the Condition according to the Trust in him reposed, and therefore the Feoffor may enter, and outhim, *Lit. sect.* 357. So if I bind my self, that upon surrender of a Lease, I will grant a new Estate to the Lessee, and afterwards I grant over my Reversion: In this case, though I afterwards purchase the Reversion, yet I have forfeited my Obligation, because I was once disabled to perform it; *Co. lib.* 5. *fol.* 21. Also if a man be excommunicated, he cannot during that time sue any Action, but shall be thereby *disabled*, *Co. lib.* 8. *fol.* 69. and so in other cases. 3. *Disability* by act of Law, is properly when a man by the sole act of the Law is *disabled*, and so is an Alien born. And therefore if a man born out of the Kings Ligeance, will sue and Action, the Tenant or Defendant may say, That he was born in such a Country, out of the Kings Ligeance, and demand Judgment if he shall be answered; for the Law is our Birth-right, to which an Alien is an stranges, and therefore *disabled* to take any benefit thereby. 4. *Disability* by the act of God, as to be *Non compos mentis*, or *non sanæ memoriæ*, which so *disables* him, that in all cases where he gives or passes any thing or estate out of him, after his death it may be disannulled & avoided. And here observe, That it is a Maxime in our Law, That *a man of full age shall never be received to* disable *his own Person*, and this in capacity to *disable* himself, as to some is personal, extending onely to the Party himself; but as to others it is not personal, yet shall bind them as *Privyes*. Now there are four manner of *Privities*, viz. *Privity in Blood*, as Heir. *Privy in Representation*, as Executors or Administrators. *Privyes in Estate*, as Donee in Tail, the Reversion or Remainder in Fee, &c. And *Privyes in Tenure*, as Lord and Tenant. Two of these may *disable* the person of the dead, which was *Non sanæ memoriæ*, or, &c. and shall avoid his Grants or Feoffments, *viz. Privyes in Blood* may shew the *disability* of the Ancestor, and *Privyes* in *Representation* the infirmity of their Testator or Intestate, *Co. lib.* 4. *fol.* 123. 124. See *Lit. sect.* 405. and *Co. lib.* 8. *fol.* 43.

Disalt, Signifieth as much as to *disable*, *Littleton* in his Chapter of *Discontinuance*.

Discarcatio, An unloading.

Disboscatio, A conversion of wood Grounds into Arable or Pasture; and assarting. See *Assart*.

Disceyte. *Deceit and Deceptione*. See also the *New Book of Entries*, *verbo* Disceite.

Discent, *Discensus*, In the French *Descent*, signifieth

signifieth in the Common-Law, an order or means whereby Lands or Tenements are derived unto any man from his Anceſtors, as to make his *diſcent* from his Anceſtors, *Old Nat. Brev. fol.* 101. Is to ſhew how, and by what degrees the Land in queſtion came to him from his Anceſtors; as firſt from his great Grand-father to his Grand-father, from his Grand-father to his Father, and ſo to him, or in ſuch other like ſort. This *diſcent* is either *lineal*, or *collateral*; *Lineal diſcent* is conveyed downwards, in a right line from the Grand-father to the Father, and from the Father to the Son, and from the Son to the Nephew, &c. *Collateral diſcent* is ſpringing out of the ſide of the whole Blood, as Grand-fathers Father, Fathers Brother, &c. See *Termes de la Ley.* and *Lit. lib.* 3. *cap.* 6. *Stat.* 32 *H.* 8. *cap.* 33. *Co.* on *Lit. fol.* 237.

Diſclaymer, *Diſclamium*, Is a Plea containing an expreſs denyal or refuſal; as if the Tenant ſue a Replevin upon a Diſtreſs, taken by the Lord, and the Lord avow the taking of the Diſtreſs, ſaying, That he holdeth of him as of his Lord, and that he diſtrained for Rent not paid, or Service not performed; then the Tenant denying himſelf to hold of ſuch Lord, is ſaid to *diſclaime*, and the Lord proving the Tenant to hold of him, he loſeth his Land, *Termes de la Ley* 274. Alſo if a man deny himſelf to be of the Blood or Kindred of another in his Plea, he is ſaid to *diſclaime* his Blood, *F. N. B. fol.* 197. See alſo *Bro. tit. Diſclaymer*: If a man arraigned of Felony, do *diſclaime* Goods, being cleared, he loſeth them, *Stamf. pl. cor. fol.* 186. See alſo *Co. lib.* 8. *fol.* 62. *Lit. ſect.* 146. *Co. lib.* 3. *fol.* 26. *New Book of Entries, verbo* Diſclamer. *Skene de verbor. Sign. verb.* Diſclamation.

Diſcontinuance, *Diſcontinuatio*, Cometh of the French *Diſcontinuer*, that is, *ceſſare*, and ſignifieth in the Common-Law nothing elſe but an interruption, or breaking off, and is two-fold, *Diſcontinuance of Poſſeſſion*, and *Diſcontinuance of Proceſs*: The effect of *Diſcontinuance of Poſſeſſion* is this, that a man may not enter upon his own Lands or Tenements alienated, whatſoever his Right be unto it, of his own ſelf, or by his own authority; but muſt bring his Writ, and ſeek to recover *poſſeſſion* by Law. See the *Termes of the Law, verbo* Diſcontinuance. *Inſtitutes of the Common-Law*, cap. 43. *Co. Rep. lib.* 3. Caſe *Of Fines, fol.* 85. The effect of *Diſcontinuance of Plea or Proceſs*, when the inſtant is loſt, and may not be regained, but by a new Writ to begin the Suit a freſh: For to be *diſcontinued*, and to be put *ſine die*, is all one, and nothing elſe but to be diſmiſſed finally the Court, *Weſt. Symbol. part* 2. *tit.* Fines, *ſect.* 115. So *Cromptom* in his *Juriſdictions*, *fol.* 131. uſeth it in theſe words, If a Juſtice Seat be *diſcontinued* by the not coming of the Juſtices, the King may renew the ſame by his Writ, &c. In this ſignification *Fitzherbert* in his *Nat. Brev.* uſeth the word divers times, as *Diſcontinuance* of Corrody, *fol.* 193. To *diſcontinue* the Right of his Wife, 191. & 193. *Diſcontinuance* of an Aſſiſe 182 & 187. *Anno* 31 *Eliz. cap.* 1. 12 *Car.* 2. *cap.* 4. 14 *Car.* 2. *cap.* 10. *Co.* on *Lit.* 325.

Diſfranchiſe, To take away from any one his Priviledge or Freedom, 14 *Car.* 2 *cap.* 31. It is contrary to *Enfranchiſe*, which ſee.

Diſgrading or **Degrading**, *Degradatio*, Is the puniſhment of a Clerk, that being delivered to his Ordinary, cannot purge himſelf of the Offence whereof he was convicted by the Jury, and is the privation of him from thoſe Holy Orders which he had, as Prieſt-hood Deaconſhip, &c. *Stamf. pl. cor.* 130. & 138. There is likewiſe the *diſgrading* of a Knight, Lord, &c. So Sir *Andrew Harkley* Earl of *Carliſle* was convicted, *degraded*, and attainted of Treaſon, 18 *E.* 2. *Coram Rege Rot.* 34, 35. And it is not to be omitted, that by the Common-Law there be two ſorts of *diſgrading*, one *ſummary*, by word onely, and another *ſolemne*, by deveſting the Party *degraded* of thoſe Ornaments and Rites, which be the Enſigns of his Order or Degree. See *Selden*'s *Titles of Honour, fol* 787. So by the Statute of 13 *Car.* 2. *cap.* 15. *William* Lord *Mounſon*, Sir *Henry Mildmay*, and others therein named, were *degraded*, &c. See the Act at large.

Diſheriſon, Is an old word ſignifying as much as *diſinheriting*. It is uſed in the Statute of *Vouchers* made, 20 *E.* 1. and in 8. *R.* 2 *cap.* 4.

Diſheritor, One that *diſinheriteth*, or puts another out of his *Inheritance*, 3. *E.* 1. *cap.* 39.

Diſmes, *Decimæ*, Are Tythes, and ſignifieth the Tenth part of all the Fruits of the Earth, or Beaſts, or our Labour due unto God; and ſo conſequently to him that is of the Lords Lot, that is, our Paſtor. It ſignifieth alſo the Tenths of Spiritual Livings, yearly given to the Prince, called a *perpetual Diſme*, 2 & 3 *E.* 6. *cap.* 35. which in ancient time were paid to the Pope, till Pope *Urbane* gave them to *Richard* the Second, to Aid him againſt the French King *Charles*, and thoſe other that upheld *Clement* the Seventh againſt him, *Polydor. Virgil. Ang. Hiſt. lib.* 20. Laſtly, It ſignifieth a Tribute levyed of the Temporalty, *Holinſhed* in *H.* 2. *fol.* 111, Tythes are of three ſorts, *Predial*, *Perſonal*, *Mixt*: *Predial* Tythes are of things that come of the ground onely, as Corn, &c. *Perſonal* Tythes are paid of ſuch things as come of the labour and induſtry of Mans perſon, as Buying and Selling, &c. *Mixt* Tythes are of Calves, Lambs, Pigs, and ſuch like.

Diſparagement, *Diſparagatio*, Is in a legal ſenſe uſed eſpecially for matching an Heir in Marriage under his or her Degree, or againſt decency. See *Cowells Inſtitutes*, *tit.* de Nuptiis, *ſect.* 6. *Co*, on *Lit. fol.* 107. *Lit. lib.* 2. *cap.* 4.

Diſſeiſin, *Diſſeiſina*, Signifieth an unlawful diſpoſſeſſing a man of his Land, Tenement, or other immoveable or incorporeal Right, *Inſtitutes of the Common-Law*, *cap.* 15. And how far this extendeth, ſee *Bract. lib.* 4. *cap.* 3. And therefore the Aſſiſes be called *Writs of Diſſeiſin*, that lie againſt *Diſſeiſors* in any caſe, whereof ſome be termed *little Writs of Diſſeiſin*, being *Vicontiel*, that is, ſueable before the Sheriff, in the County-Court. *Old Nat. Brev. fol.* 109. becauſe they are determined by the Sheriff without Aſſiſe, *Reg. Orig. fol.* 198. *b.* as for Nuſances of no great prejudice: *Diſſeiſin* is of two ſorts, either *ſimple*, committed by day without Force and Arms, *Bract. lib.* 4. *cap.* 4. *Brit. cap.* 42, 43, 44. where you ſhall find in what eſpecially it is lawful, and in what not. *Brit. cap.* 53. And *diſſeiſin* by *force*, for which ſee *Deforceor*, ſee *Freſh-diſſeiſin*, *Rediſſeiſin*, and *Poſt-diſſeiſin*. See alſo *Skene de verbor.* Signif. *verbo* Diſſeiſina. How

 man

many wayes it is committed, see *Fleta, lib.* 4. *cap.* 1. *sect. fit autem, &c.* and when it is lawful, *cap.* 2. wrongful *Disseisin* is no descent in Law, 32 *H.* 8. *cap.* 33.

Disseisor, Is he that putteth another out of his Land, and *Disseisee* is the person so put out, 4 *H.* 4. *cap.* 7.

Disseisoresse, Is a Woman that *disseiseth* another, *Co.* on *Lit. fol.* 357. *b.*

Disseisin upon Disseisin, Is where a *Disseisor* is *disseised* by another.

Distress, Signifies a Compulsion in certain real Actions, whereby to bring a man to appear in Court, or to pay Debt of Duty denyed: The effect whereof most commonly is to drive the Party distrained to replevy the *Distress*, and so to take his Action of Trespass against the Distrainer, or else to compound Neighborly with him for the Debt or Duty for which the *distress* was made. In what cases a *distress* is lawful, see *New Termes of the Law.* The *Civilians* call it *Pignorum captionem*: There are divers things not distrainable, for a *distress* must be of a thing whereof a valuable property is in some Body, and therefore Dogs, Bucks, Coneys, and the like, that the *feræ naturæ*, cannot be distrained. 2. Although it be of a valuable property, as a Horse, (yet when a Man or Woman is riding of him) or an Axe (in a Mans hand cutting of wood, and the like, they are for that time priviledged, and cannot be distrained. 3. Valuable things shall not be distrained for Rent, for benefit and maintenance of Trades, which by consequence are for the Common-wealth, and are by authority of the Law there; as a Horse in a Smiths Shop shall not be distrained for the Rent issuing out of the Shop, nor the Materials in a Weavers Shop for making Cloth, not Cloth or Garments in a Taylors Shop, nor sacks of Corn or Meal in a Mill, nor in a Market, nor any thing distrained for *Damage-feasant*, for it is in *Custodia Legis.* 4. Nothing shall be distrained for Rent that cannot be rendred again in as good plight, as it was at the time of the *Distress* taken, as sheaves or shocks of Corn cannot be distrained for Rent, but for *Damage-feasant* they may. 5. Beasts belonging to the Plough *averia carucæ* shall not be distrained, but Goods or *animalia otiosa* may be distrained. 6. Furnaces, Cauldrons, or the like, fixed to the Freehold; or the Doors or Windows of a House, or the like cannot be distrained. When one takes a *Distress* that hath life, he must bring it to the common Pound, or keep it in an open place, where the Owner my give it food. See the Stat. *de districtione Scaccarii*, 51 H. 3. *Britton, cap.* 71. divides *Distress* into *real* and *personal*; *Distress real* is made upon immoveable Goods, as the *Grand-Cape* and *Petit Cape.* And thus it is interpreted by *Hotoman de verb.* Feudal, *verbo* Districtus. This differeth from an Attachment, in this point among others, that it cannot be taken by any common person, without the compass of his own Fee, *F.N.B.* 904. except it be presently after the Cattel, or other thing is driven or born off the Ground by him that perceiveth it to be in danger to be distrained. See *Attach* and the Stat. 17 *Car.* 2. *cap.* 7. *Distress personal* is made, by taking a mans moveable Goods, and detaining them for security of his appearance to the Suit. *Distress* is also divided into *finite* and *infinite*; *Finite* is that which is limited by Law, how often it shall be made to bring the Party to Tryal of the Action, *Old Nat. Brev. fol.* 43. *Distress infinite* is without limitation, until the Party come, as against a Jury that refuseth to appear *super certificatione Assisæ*, where the Process is a *Venire facias, habeas corpora*, and *Distress infinite, Old Nat. Brev.* 113. Then it is again divided into a *Grand Distress*, 52 *H.* 3. *cap.* 7. which *Fitzherbert* calleth in Latine *Magnam districtionem, Nat. Brev. fol.* 126. and an *ordinary Distress*: A *Grand Distress* is that which is made of all the Goods and Chattels the Party hath within the County, *Britton, cap.* 26. *fol* 52. But see whether it be not sometimes all one with a *Distress infinite, Id. fol.* 80. with whom also the Statute of *Marlbridge* agrees, 52. *H.* 3. *cap.* 7. 9, 12. See *Grand Distress* and *Attachment*, also *Old Nat. Brev. fol.* 71.

Districtus, Is sometimes used for the Circuit within which a man may be compelled to appearance, *Britton, cap.* 120. And whereas we say *Hors de son fee*, others use *extra districtum suum.* So likewise *Reg. Orig. fol.* 6.

Distringas, Is a Writ directed to the Sheriff, or any other Officer, commanding him to distrain one for Debt to the King, &c. or for his appearance at a day; as a *Distringas Jurat. &c.* There is great variety of this Writ in the Table of the *Register Judicial, verbo* Distringas.

Divise. See *Devise.*

Divided in the Exchequer, Seems to be one part of an Indenture, *Anno* 10 *E.* 1. *cap.* 11 and 28. *E.* 1. *Stat.* 3. *cap.* 2.

Dividend in the University, Is that share or part which every one of the Fellows does justly and equally divide among themselves of their Annual Stipend.

Divorce. See *Devorce.*

Docket, Is a Brief in writing, *An.* 2. & 3. P. & M. *cap.* 6. *West* writeth it *Dogget*, by whom it seemeth to be some small piece of Paper or Parchment, containing the effect of a larger writing, *Symbol. part.* 2. *tit.* Fines, *sect.* 106.

To do Law, *Facere Legem*, Is the same with to make Law, 23. *H.* 6. *cap.* 14. See *Make.*

Doctor and Student, Is a Book containing certain Dialogues between a *Doctor* of Divinity, and a *Student* at the Common-Law, wherein are contained Questions and Cases, as well of the Equity and Conscience used in the Common-Law, as also a Comparison of the Civil, Canon, and Common Law together, very worthy the reading. The Author is said to be one Saint *German*, and the Book was written in the time of *Henry* the Eighth.

Dog-draw, Is an apparent deprehension of an Offender against Venison in the Forest. There be four of these mentioned by *Manwood* in his *Forest Law, cap.* 18. *num.* 9. *viz. Stable-stand, Dog-draw, Back-bear*, and *Bloody-hand*; where he saith, That *Dog-draw* is where any man hath stricken or wounded a wild Beast, by shooting at him either with Cross-Bow, Long-Bow, or otherwise, and is found with a Hound, or other *Dog* drawing after him to recover the same.

Dogger, A kind of little Ship, 31 *E.* 3 *Stat.* 3. *cap. primo.*

Doggerfish, 31 *E.3.Stat.* 3. *cap.* 2. Seemeth to be *Fish* brought in those Ships to *Blackney-haven*, *&c.*

Dogger-men, *Anno* 2 *H.* 8. *cap.* 4.

Dogget, See *Docket*.

Doitkin, A base Coin prohibited by 3 *H.* 5. *cap.* 1. Hence probably we retain that phrase when we would undervalue a man, to say, *He is not worth a Doit or Doitkin.*

Dole, *Dola*, A Saxon word, signifying as much as *Pars* or *Portio* in Latine: It hath of old been attributed to a Meadow, and still so called, as *Dole-medow*, 4 *Jac. cap.* 11. because divers persons had shares in it; we still retain the word to signifie a share, as to deal a *Dole*; he dealt his *dole* among so many poor People, that is, he gave every one a share or part.

Dolefish, Seems to be that *Fish*, which the Fishermen yearly imploy'd in the North-Seas, do of custom receive for their allowance. See the Stat. 35 *H.* 8. *cap.* 7.

Dolg-bote, A recompence made for a Scar or Wound, *Sax. Diction. Inter Reg. Aluredi Regis, cap.* 23. *legitur* Dolgbot.

Dom-boc, A Saxon word signifying *Liber judicialis*, as appears by the Laws of King *Edward* the elder, *cap.* 8. This was probably a Book of Statutes proper to the English Saxons, wherein perhaps the Laws of former Saxon Kings were contained: That Chapter seeming to refer to the Laws of King *Ina, cap.* 29.

Domesday or Domesdei, *Liber Judiciarius* and *Censualis Angliæ*, Is a Book now remaining in the *Exchequer*. The Author of the *Old Nat. Brev. fol.* 15. saith, It was written in the time of St. *Edward the Confessor*, containing in it not only all the Lands through *England*, but also the Names of those in whose hands they were at that time: But *Lambert* proves it was made in the *Conquerours* time, with whom agrees *Camden* in his *Brit.* proving it out of *Ingulphus* that flourisht the same time, whose very words are these, *Totam terram descripsit, nec erat Hyda in tota Anglia, quin Valorem ejus & possessorem scivit, nec Lacus nec Locus aliquis quin in Regis rotulo extitit descriptus, ac ejus redditus & proventus, ipsa possessio & ejus possessor Regiæ notitiæ manifestatus, juxta Taxatorum fidem, qui electi de qualibet patria, territorium proprium describebant: Iste Rotulus vocat. est* Rotulus Wintoniæ, *& ab Anglis pro sua generalitate, quod omnia Tenementa totius terræ continuit,* Doomsday *cognominatur.* So it is called in the Statute 1 *R.* 2. *cap.* 6. This Book was also called *Liber Judicatorius*, or *Judiciarius, quia in eo Regni descriptio diligens continetur & tam de tempore Regis* Edwardi *quam de tempore Regis* Gulielmi, *sub quo factus est, singulorum fundorum valentia exprimitur*, as *Ockham* in his *Lucubrations, de fisci Regis ration*, testifies: *Gervas Tilburiensis* saith, It was called *Doomsday, Quod à predicto Judicio non liceat ulla ratione discedere.* It was finisht (saith *Stow*) in the Fourteenth year of *William the Conqueror*: *Camden* calls it *Censualem Gulielmi*, King *Williams Taxebook*. See more in *Spelm. Gloss.* and 4 *Inst.* 269.

Domicellus, Sir *Edw. Co.* 4. *Inst. fol.* 37 would seem to derive it from *Domoicel*, a French word, as he sayes, though mistaken, for it is an old Latine word, and anciently given as an addition to the Kings natural Sons in *France*, see *Spelm. Gloss. verbo* Domicellus. This word is also used in a Charter of Legitimation of several Children of *John* of *Gaunt*, 20 R. 2. confirmed by Parliament at *Westm.* 9. *die Febr.*

Dominica in Ramis Palmarum, Is *Palm Sunday* so called, because on that day they used to distribute branches of *Palm* & other green Boughs in commemoration of our Lords riding into *Jerusalem*, and the People cut *Palm* Boughs &c. to strow in the way, crying *Hosanna.*

Domo Reparanda, is a Writ for one against his Neighbour, by the fall of whose house he feareth hurt to his own, *Reg. Orig. fol* 153. In this case the *Civilians* have the Action *de damno infacto.*

Donative, Is a Benefice meerly given and collated by the Patron to a man, without either Presentation to the Ordinary or Institution by his Ordinary or Induction by his commandment *F. N. B. fol.* 35. Of this *Petr. Gregor. de benefic. cap.* 11. *num.* 10. hath these words, *Si tamen capellæ fundatæ per Laicos non fuerint a Diocesano approbatæ & (ut loquuntur) Spiritualizatæ, non censentur Beneficia, nec ab Episcopo conferri possunt, sed sunt sub pia dispositione fundatoris.* And Mr. *Gwin* in the *Preface of his Reading*, saith, That as the King might of ancient times found a free Chappel, and exempt it from the Jurisdiction of the *Diocesan* So he might also by his Letters Patents licence a common person to found such a Chappel, and to Ordain, That it shall be *donative*, and not presentable, and that the Chaplain shall be deprivable by the Founder and his Heirs, and not by the Bishop, And this is most likely to be the Original of these *Donatives* in *England*. *Fitzherbert* saith, That there be some *Chantryes* which a Man may give by his Letters Patents, *Nat. Brev.* 33. 42. All Bishopricks were in antient time *Donative* by the King, *Co. lib.* 3. *fol.* 75.

Donor and Donee, *Donor*, Is he who gives Lands or Tenements to another, and he to whom the same is given is the *Donee.*

Doome, (From the Saxon *Dom*) signifieth a Judgment or Sentence; a word much used in References to Arbitrators: We have several words that ends in *dom*, as Kingdom, Earldom, &c. so that it may seem to signifie the Jurisdiction of a Lord, or a King. See also *Mon. Ang.* 1. *Par. fol* 284. *a. Habeat Grithbrich. & Forstal, & Dom, & Som. & Wreche in Mari.*

Dorture, *Dormitorium*, *Anno* 25 *H.* 8. cap. 11. Is the common Room, Place or Chamber, where all the Fryers of one Covent slept and lay all Night.

Dote assignanda, Is a Writ that lies for a Widow, where it is found by Office, that the Kings Tenant was seized of Tenements in Fee or Fee-tail at the day of his death, &c. and that he holdeth of the King in chief, &c. For in this case the Widow cometh into the *Chancery*, and there maketh Oath, That she will not marry without the Kings leave, *Anno* 15 *E.* 3. *cap.* 4. and hereupon she shall have this Writ to the Escheator; for which see *Reg. Orig. fol.* 297. and *F. N. B. fol.* 263. And this sort of Widows is called *The Kings Widow.* See *Widow.*

Dote unde nihil habet, Is a Writ of Dower, that lyeth for the Widow against the

Tenant, which bought Land of her Husband in his life-time, whereof he was seised solely in Fee-simple or Fee-tail, in such sort as the issue of them both might have inherited it, *F. N. B. fol.* 147. *Regist. fol.* 170.

Dotis admensuratione. See *Admeasurement*, and the *Reg. Orig. fol.* 171.

Doubles, *Anno* 14 *H.* 6. *cap.* 6. signifie as much as Letters Patent, being a French word made of the Latin *Diploma*.

Double Plea, *Duplex placitum*, Is that wherein the Defendant alledgeth for himself two several matters, in bar of the Action, whereof either is sufficient to effect his desire in debarring the Plaintiff. And this is not to be admitted in the Common-Law; wherefore it is well to be observed, when a *Plea* is *double*, and when not; for if a man alledge several matters, the one nothing depending of the other, the *Plea* is accounted *double* If they be mutually depending one of the other, then is it accounted but single, *Kitchin, fol.* 223. and see *Brooke, tit.* Double Plea. And Sir *Tho. Smith* gives this reason, why our Law admitteth not a *double Plea*, because the Tryal is by twelve ignorant men, whose heads are not to be troubled with over many things at once, *Lib.* 2. *de Rep. Angl. cap.* 13.

Domus Conversorum, See *Rolls*.

Domus Dei, The Hospital of St. *Julian* in *Southampton* so called, *Mon. Ang.* 2. *par. fol.* 440. *b.*

Double Quarrel, *Duplex Querela*, Is a Complaint made by any Clerk, or other, to the Archbishop of the Province against an inferior Ordinary, for delaying of Justice in some Cause Ecclesiastical, as to give Sentence, to institute a Clerk presented, or the like: The effect whereof is, that the said Archbishop taking knowledge of some delay, directeth his Letters under his authentical Seal, to all and singular Clerks of his Province, thereby commanding and authorising them, and every of them to admonish the said Ordinary, within a certain number of dayes; namely nine dayes, to do the Justice required, or otherwise to cite him to appear before him or his Official at a day, in the said Letters prefixed, and there to alledge the cause of his delay. And lastly, To intimate to the Ordinary, that if he neither perform the thing enjoyned, nor appear at the day assigned, he himself will without further delay proceed to perform the Justice required. And this seemeth to be termed *a double Quarrel*, because it is most commonly made against both the Judge, and him at whose Petition Justice is delayed.

Dowager, *Dotata*, A Widow endowed. But chiefly an addition applyed in General to the Widows of Princes, Dukes, Earls, and Persons of Honour.

Dower, *Dos*, Signifieth in our Common-Law two things: First, That which the Wife bringeth to her Husband, otherwise called *Maritagium*, Marriage Goods; next and more commonly, that which she hath of her Husband after the Marriage determined, if she out-live him, *Glanvile, lib.* 7. *cap.* 1. *Bract. lib.* 2. *cap.* 38. *Britton, cap.* 101. And in *Scotland* it signifieth the same, *Skene de verb. Signif. verbo* Dos; the former is in French called *Dot*, the other *Dovayre*: And accordingly some Authors would distinguish the first by the name of *Dowry*. The second, Of *Dower*, but they are often confounded. Of the former our Law Books say very little; This onely may be noted, That whereas by the Civil-Law, Instruments are made before Marriage, which contain the quantity of the Wives *Dowry*, or Substance brought to her Husband, that he having the use of it during Marriage, may, after certain deductions, restore it again to his Wives Heirs or Friends after the Marriage dissolved. The Common-Law of *England*, whatsoever Chattels moveable or immoveable, or ready Money she bringeth, doth make them forthwith her Husbands own, to be disposed of as he will, leaving her at his curtesie to bestow any thing or nothing upon her at his death. Onely if she be an Inheritrix, the Husband holdeth the Land but during her life, except he have Issue by her; but then he holdeth it by the curtesie of *England* during his own life, see *Curtesie*. And again, if he have any Land in fee, whereof he was possessed during the Marriage, she is to have a third part thereof during her life, though she bring nothing to him, except she do by Fine release her Right during the Marriage. Therefore upon speech of Marriage between two, the Parents on both sides are commonly more careful in providing each for his Child than the Parties themselves; and by their means divers Bargains be made sometimes for the conveyance of Lands, &c. to them and by their Issue: And this said *To be given in Frank-Marriage.* Sometime to her during her life, and that before or at the Marriage: If before the Marriage, then it is called *a Joynture*; for a Joynture is a Covenant, whereby the Husband is tyed *ratione juncturæ*, in consideration of the Marriage, that the Wife surviving him shall have during her life, this or that Tenement or Lands, of thus much Rent yearly payable out of such Land, &c. with clause of Distress, and this may be more or less, as they do accord, *Britton, cap.* 102, 103, 104, 110. for *conventio vincit legem*, *Bract. lib.* 5. *tract.* 4. *cap.* 9. The diversities of these Joyntures you may read in *West Symbol. part* 1. *lib.* 2. *sect.* 128, 129, 130, 131, 132. 133. But if none of those Agreements be made before Marriage, then must the Wife stick to her *Dower*; and that is sometimes given *ad ostium Ecclesiæ*, at the Church-door, and may be what the Husband will, so it exceed not a third part of his Lands, *Glanvile, lib.* 6. *cap.* 1. or the half, as some say, *F. N. B. fol.* 150. And this *Dower* is either certainly set down and named, or not named, but onely in generality, as the Law requireth: If it be not named, then it is by Law the third part, and called *Dos Legitima*, *Bract. lib.* 4. *tract.* 6. *cap.* 6. *num.* 6. & 10. *Mag. Charta, cap.* 7. or the half, by the Custom of some Countries, as in *Gavelkind*, *F. N. B. fol.* 150. And though it be named, it seems that it cannot be above half the Lands of the Husband, *ibid.* And the Woman that will challenge this *Dower*, must make three things appear, *viz.* 1. That she was marryed to her Husband. 2. That he was in his life-time seised of the Land whereof she demandeth *Dower*. And 3. That he is dead, *Co.* 2. *Rep. fol.* 93. *Bingham's* Case. Of these things see *Glanvile, lib.* 6. *cap.* 1, 2, 3. *Bract. lib.* 2. *cap.* 38, 39. & *lib.* 14. *tract.* 6. *cap.* 1. & 6. and *Britton, cap.* 101, 102, 103, 104. and *F. N. B. fol,* 147, 148, 149, 150. And this

Custo

Customary *Dower* seemeth to be observed in other Nations as well as in ours. See also *Co.* on *Lit. fol.* 33. *b.* If the Wife be past the age of nine years at the death of her Husband, she shall be endowed: If a Woman elope, or go away from her Husband with an Adulterer, and will not be reconcil'd, she loseth her Dower by the Statute of *Westm.* 2 *cap.* 34. 2. *par. Inst. fol.* 433. *Camden* in his *Brit. tit.* Sussex, relates out of the Parliament Records, 30 *E.* 1. A memorable Case of *Margaret* the Wife of Sir *John Camoys*, cited also in 2. *Inst. fol.* 435. which for brevity sake I omit, and desire you there to read at large.

Dozein, *Decenna*, In the Statute for view of *Frank-pledge*, made 18 *E.* 2. one of the Articles for Stewards in their Leets to inquire of, is, If all the *Dozeins* be in the Assise of our Lord the King, and which not, and who received them, *Art.* 3. See *Dociners*. There is also a sort of *Devonshire* Kerseys called *Dozens*, 5 & 6 *E.* 6. *cap.* 6.

Drage, *Anno.* 6 *H.* 6. *cap.* 5. Seem to be Wood or Timber so joyned together, that swimming or floating upon the Water, they may bear a burden, or load of other Wares down a River.

Drawlatches, *Anno* 5 *E.* 3. *cap.* 14. and *Anno* 7 *R.* 2. *cap.* 5. *Lambert* in his *Eirenarcha*, *lib. cap.* 6. calleth them *Miching Thieves*, as Wasters and *Roberds* Men, *Mighty Thieves*, saying, That the words be grown out of use.

Dreit-Dreit. Signifies a double Right, that is, *Jus Possessionis & jus Dominii*, Bract. *lib.* 4. *cap.* 27. & *lib.* 4. *tract.* 4. *cap.* 4. & *lib.* 5. *tract.* 5. *cap.* 5. *Co.* on *Lit. fol.* 266.

Drenches or **Drenges**, *Drengi*, Were Tenants *in Capite*, sayes an ancient *M. S. Doomsday, tit. Lestr. Reg. Pictaviens Neuton.* They were, sayes *Spelman*, *E genere vassallorum non ignobilium, cum singuli qui in* Doomsday *nominantur, singula possiderent Maneria.* Such as at the Conquest being put out of their Estates, were afterward restored; for that they being before Owners thereof, were against him neither by their Persons or Counsels, *Co.* on *Lit. fol.* 5. sayes, *Dreuches* misprinted there for *Drenches*, are free Tenants of a Mannor. See also *Mon. Ang.* 2. *par. fol.* 598. *a.*

Drengage, *Drengagium*, The Tenure by which the *Drenches* held their Lands, of which see Trin. 21. *E.* 3. *Ebor. & Northumb. Rot.* 191. And we may observe, sayes the learned *Spelman*, *Qui e* Drengorum *classe erant, vel per* Drengagium *tenuere sua incoluisse Patrimonia ante adventum Normannorum.*

Drye Exchange, 3 *H.* 7. *cap.* 5. *Cambium siccum*, Seemeth to be a subtle term, invented to disguise a foul Usury, in which something is pretended to pass on both sides, whereas, in truth nothing passes but on the one side, in which respect it may be well called *Dry*: Of this *Lud, Lopes tractat. de Contract. & negotiat.* lib. 2. cap. 1. sect. *Deinde postquam*, writes thus, *Cambium est reale vel siccum, Cambium reale dicitur, quod consistentiam veri Cambii realem habet, & Cambium per trans & Cambium minutum*

Cambium autem siccum est cambium non habens existentiam Cambii sed apparentium ad instar arboris exsiccatæ, quæ humore vitali jam carens apparentiam arboris habet, non existentiam. See also *Sum. Syl. verbo* Usura. *Quæst.* 6.

Dry Rent, Rent-seck. See *Rent.*

Drift of the Forest, *Agitatio animalium in Foresta*, Is an exact view or examination what Cattel are in the *Forest*, that it may be known whether it be overcharged or not, and whose the Beasts be. This *Drift*, when, how often in the year, by whom, and in what manner it is to be made. See *Manwood's Forest Laws*, cap. 15. and 32 *H.* 8. *cap.* 35. and 4. *Inst.* 309.

Drinkham, Is a Contribution of Tenants towards a *Potatio*, or Ale, provided to entertain the Lord or his Steward; perhaps the same with a Scot-Ale.

Drofden, Among our Ancestors, the Saxons signified a Grove, or woody-place, where Cattel were kept, and the Keeper of them was called *Drofman.*

Droftland or **Dryftland**, Another Saxon word denoting anciently a yearly payment made by some to their Landlords, for driving their Cattel through the Mannor to Fairs and Markets. Mr. *Philips* mistaken Recompence, *fol.* 39.

Droit Right, The Law makes six kinds of it; 1. *Jus recuperandi.* 2. *Jus intrandi.* 3. *Jus habendi.* 4. *Jus retinendi.* 5. *Jus percipiendi.* 6. *Jus possidendi.* All these several sorts following the relation of their Objects, are the effects of the Civil-Law, *Co.* on *Lit. fol.* 266. & 345. *Co.* 8. *Rep. fol.* 151. 153. Of meer *Droit*, and very *Right.* See 27 *H.* 8. *cap.* 26.

Droit d' Advowson. See *Recto de advocatione Ecclesiæ.*

Droit Close. See *Recto clausum.*

Droit de Dower. See *Recto dotis.*

Droit sur Disclaymer. See *Recto sur Disclaymer.*

Droit Patens. See *Recto Patens*, and *Calthorp's* Rep. *fol.* 132.

Droffen, Druff, Dru, Druften, All according to the Book of *Doomsday*, signifie a Thicket of Wood in a Valley.

Duces tecum, Is a Writ commanding one to appear at a day in the *Chancery*, and to bring with him some Evidence, or other thing, that the Court would view. See the *New Book of Entries, verbo* Duces tecum. There is also another kind of *Duces tecum* directed to a Sheriff, upon return that he cannot bring his Prisoner without danger of Death, he being *adeo Languidus*, then the Court grants a *Habeas corpus* in the nature of a *Duces tecum licet languidus.*

Duell, *Duellum*, By *Fleta*, is a Fight between two Persons, for the Tryal of the Truth, the proof of which seemed to be on the Conquerours side, Stat. *de finibus levatis*, 27 *E.* 1. This sort of *Combat* is still disused, though the Law be still in force. See 3. *par. Inst. fol.* 221. and see *Combat.*

Duke, *Dux*, In ancient times among the *Romans* signified *Ductorem exercitus*, such as lead their Armies, who if by their Prowess they obtained any famous Victory, they were by their Souldiers saluted *Imperatores*, as *Hotoman de verb.* Feudal. *verb.* Dux, proveth out of *Livy, Tully*, and others: Since that they were called *Duces*, to whom the King committed the Government of any Province, *Id.* In some Nations to this day the Soveraigns of the Country are called by this Name, as *Florence*, or the great *Duke* of *Tuscany*, *Duke* of *Millayne*. In *England*, *Duke* is the next Secular Dignity to the of Prince *Wales*. After the coming in of the *Conquerour*, there were none bore this Title till *Edward* the Thirds dayes, who made *Edward* his Son Duke of *Cornwall*. Since that, there have been several made, whose Titles have descended by Inheritance to their Posterity; they were created with Solemnity *per cincturam gladii, cappæq; & circuli aurei in capite impositionem*. See *Camd. Brit. pag.* 166. *Zazium de feudis*, pag. 4. num. 7. *Cassan. de consuet. Burgund.* pag. 6. 10. And *Ferne's Glory of Generosity*, 139. At this day we have many of these created *Dukes* in *England*, whose Titles are very well known to every Body.

Dum fuit infra ætatem, Is a Writ which lies for him that before he came to his full Age, made a Feoffment of his Land in Fee, or for term of Life, or in Tail, to recover them again from him, to whom he conveyed them, *F. N. B. fol.* 192.

Dum non fuit compos mentis, Is a Writ that lyeth against the Alience or Lessee, for him that not being of sound Memory, did alien any Lands or Tenements in Fee-simple, Fee-tail, for term of Life, or for Years, *F. N. B. fol.* 202.

Dunum and Duna, A *Downe*, In which termination (a little, in some varied into *Don*) many Names of our Towns end, as *Ashdown*, *Cleydon &c.* Doomsd.

Duplicat, Is used by *Crompton* for second Letters Patents granted by the Lord *Chancellor* in a Case wherein he had formerly done the same, and was therefore thought void, *Cromp. Jur. fol.* 215. Also any Copy or Transcript of a writing is called a *Duplicat*; the word is used 14 *Car.* 2. *cap.* 10.

Durden, A thicket of Wood in a Valley.

Duresse, *Duritia*, Is in our Common-Law, a Plea used by way of Exception, by him that being cast in Prison at a mans Suit, or otherwise by Beating, or Threats hardly used, sealeth unto him a Bond during his Restraint; for the Law holdeth such specialty void, but rather supposeth it to be by Constraint, and *Duresse* pleaded shall avoid the Action. *Bro.* in his *Abridgment*, joyneth *Duresse*, and *Manass* together, that is, *duritiam & minas*. See the *New Book of Entries*, *verbo* Duress.

Dutchy-Court, Is a *Court* wherein all Matters appertaining to the *Dutchy* of *Lancaster*, are decided by the Decree of the Chancellor of that *Court*. And the original of it was in the Reign of *Henry* the Fourth, who after the deposing of *Richard* the Second, coming to the Crown, and having the *Dutchy* of *Lancaster* by Descent, in the Right of his Mother, he was seised thereof as King, and not as Duke; so that all the Liberties, Franchises, and Jurisdictions of the said *Dutchy* past from the King by the Great Seal, and not by Livery or Attornment; as the Possession of *Euerwick*, and the Earldom of *March*, and such others did, which had descended to the King by other Ancestors than the Kings: But at last *Henry* the Fourth passed a Charter by Authority of Parliament, whereby the Possessions, Liberties, &c. of the said *Dutchy* were severed from the Crown; yet *Henry* the Seventh reduced it to his former Nature, as it was in *Henry* the Fifth dayes, *Cromp. Jur. fol.* 136. The Officers belonging to this *Court*, are, The Chancellor, Atturney, Receiver-General, Clerk of the *Court*, the Messenger: Besides these, there be certain Assistants of this *Court*, as one Atturney in the *Exchequer*, one Atturney of the *Dutchy* in the *Chancery*, four learned men in the Law, retained of Councel with the King in the said *Court*. Of this *Court Gwin* in the *Preface to his Readings*, saith thus, The *Court* of the *Dutchy*, or *County Palatine* of *Lancaster*, grew out of the Grant of King *Edward* the Third, who gave the *Dutchy* to his Son *John of Gaunt*, and endowed it with such Royal Right as the *County-Palatine* of *Chester* had. And for as much as it was afterwards extinct in the Person of *Henry* the Fourth, by reason of the Union of it with the Crown; he separated the *Dutchy* from the Crown, and setled it in the natural Person of himself and his Heirs. In which estate it continued during the Reigns of *H.* 5. and *H.* 6. that descended of him: But when *Edward* the Fourth, by recovery of the Crown, recontinued the Right of the House of *York*, he appropriated that *Dutchy* to the Crown again; and yet so, that he suffered the *Court* and Officers to remain as he found them: And in this manner it came together with the Crown to *Henry* the Seventh, who again separated it, and so left it to his Posterity, who still injoy it.

Dyke-reeve, An Officer that hath the over-sight of the *Dykes* and Drains in *Deeping-Fens*, *&c.* mentioned 17 & 18 *Car.* 2. *cap.* 11.

E.

E. *Non solum est litera sed præpositio etiam & per se & in compositione significans Anglice* (out) as *è foro* out of Court; *Ejicio* to cast out, and the like.

Ealderman or Ealdorman, *Aldermanus*, Among the Saxons was as much as *Earl* among the Danes, *Camd. Brit. pag.* 107. It is as much as an *Elder* or *Statesman*, call'd by the *Romans* Senator, who were rather Counsellors at large, than bestowed upon any particular Office, as *Comites* were, see *County*. And that signification we retain at this day almost in all our Cities and Boroughs, calling those *Aldermen* that are Associates to the chief Officer in the Common-Council of the Town, 24 *H.* 8. *cap.* 13. Or sometime the chief Officer himself, as in *Stamford*.

Earl, Comes, According to *Lambert* in his Explication of Saxon words, *verbo Paganus*, is Saxon, and he interpreteth it *Satrapam*. *Verstegan* in his *Restitution of decayed Intelligence*, deriveth it from two Dutch words (*Ear*, that is, *Honor*,) and *Ethel*, that is, *Noble*: But whencesoever it is derived This Title in ancient time was given to those that were Associates to the King in his Counsels and Martial Actions; as *Comes* was to those that followed the Magistrates in *Rome*, and executed their Offices for them as their Deputies, and dyed alwayes

alwayes with the man. And the ancient manner of their Creation, was onely *per cincturam gladii comitatus*, without any formal Method of Creation. But the Conqueror, as saith *Camden*, gave this Dignity in Fee to his Nobles, annexing it to this or that County, and allotted them for their Maintenance a certain proportion of Money rising from the Princes Profits, for the Pleadings and Forfeitures of the Province. For example, He bringeth an ancient Record in these words, *Henricus* 2. *Rex Angliæ his verbis Comitem creavit. Sciatis nos fecisse* Hugonem Bigot *Comitem de* Norfolk, sc. *de tertio denario de* Norwic. *&* Norfolk, *sicut aliquis comes Angliæ liberius comitatum suum tenet*, which words (saith the same Author) an old Book of *Battel Abby* thus expoundeth, *Consuetudinaliter per totam Angliam mos antiquitus inoleverat. Comites provinciarum tertium denarium sibi obtinere, inde Comites dicti. Ferne, pag.* 12. sayes, One Duke or *Earl* had divers Shires under his Government, and had Lieutenants under him in every particular Shire called a *Sheriff*; and this appears by divers of our ancient Statutes, as namely by the Sentence of Excommunication pronounced by the Bishops against the Infringers of *Mag. Charta*, and *Charta de Foresta*, *Anno* 38 *H.* 3. *Roger Bigot* is named *Earl* both of *Norfolk* and *Suffolk*, and 1 E. 3. *Thomas Earl* of *Lancaster* and *Leicester*, *Humphry Bohun Earl* of *Hereford* and *Essex*, *Dyer*, *fol.* 285. *num.* 39. At this day, as long since, the Kings of *England* make *Earls* by their Charters, but give them no Authority over the County, nor any part of the profit rising of it, but onely some Annual Stipend out of the Exchequer, rather for Honors-sake, than any great Commodity; the Solemnity of their Creation is set down at large in *Stowes Annals*, *pag.* 1121. Their place is next after a Marquess, and before a Viscount. See more on this Subject in *Spelman's Glossary*, *verbo* Comites, and in *Seldens Titles of Honor*, fol. 676. and see Countee.

Easement, *Aisiamentum*, Is a Service which one Neighbour hath of another by Charter or Prescription, without profit, as a way through his Ground, a Sink, or such like, *Kitchin. fol.* 105. which, in the Civil-Law, is called *Servitus prædii*, *Glanvil*, *lib.* 12. *cap.* 14.

Ebere-murder, *Apertum murdrum*, Was one of those Crimes, which by *Henry* the First's Laws, *cap.* 13. *Emendari non possunt, hoc ex scelerum genere fuit nullo pretio expiabilium, &c.* Spelm.

Ecclesia, A Church or Place set apart, and consecrated to the Service of God. But *Fitzherbert*, will have it onely to intend a Parsonage, *Nat. Brev.* 32. When the question was, whether it was *Ecclesia sive capella, &c?* The Issue was, whether it had *Baptisterium & Sepulturam*; For if it had right to administer the Sacraments, and for *Sepulture*, it was in Law adjudged a Church, *Trin.* 20 *E.* 1. *in Banco Rot.* 117. 2. *Inst. fol.* 363.

Ecclesiastical persons, Are either *regular* or *secular*; *Regular* are such as lead a Monastick life, of this sort are Abbots, Priors, Monks, Fryers, &c. *Secular* are those whose ordinary Conversation is among those of the World, and profess to take upon them the Cure of Souls, and live not under any Rule of Religious Orders: Such are Bishops, Parish-Priests, &c.

Ele-fares, alias **Ele-vare**, 25 *H.* 8. Be the fry or brood of *Eles*.

Effractores, Is a Latine word, properly signifying *Breakers*; the Law termes them *Burglars*, that break open Houses to steal.

Egyptians, *Egyptiani*. We commonly call them *Gypsies*, and by our Statutes and the Laws of *England*, are a counterfeit kind of Rogues, that being English or Welsh People, accompany themselves together, disguising themselves in strange Habits, blacking their Faces and Bodies, and framing to themselves an unknown Language, wander up and down, and under pretence of telling Fortunes, curing Diseases, and such like, abuse the ignorant common People, by stealing all that is not too hot or too heavy for their carriage, *Anno* 1 *&* 2 *Phil. & Mar. cap.* 4. and 5. *Eliz. cap.* 20. These are very like those whom the *Italians* call *Cingari*, spoken of by *Franciscus Leo in suo thesauro fori Ecclesiastici*, part. *prim.* cap. 13.

Ejectione custodiæ, *Ejectment de gard*, Is a Writ which lyeth properly against him that casteth out the Guardian from any Land during the minority of the Heir, *Reg. Orig. fol.* 162. *F. N. B. fol.* 139. *Termes de la Ley*, *verbo* Gard. There be two other Writs not unlike this, the one is termed *Droit de gard*, or *Right of Ward*; the other *Ravishment de gard*, which see in their places.

Ejectione firmæ, Is a Writ which lyeth for the Lessee for term of years, that is cast out before his term expired, either by the Lessor or a Stranger, *Reg. Orig. fol.* 227. *F. N. B. fol.* 220. See *Quare ejecit infra terminum*, and the *New Book of Entries*, *verbo* Ejectione firmæ.

Eigne French, *Aisne*, *Maximus natu*, The first born as Bastard *Eigne*, and *Mulier puisne*, Lit. *sect.* 399. See *Mulier*.

Einecia, Is borrowed of the French *Aisne*, *Primogenitus*, And signifies in the Common-Law *Eldership*, Stat. of *Ireland*, 14 *H.* 3. *Skene de verbor.* Significatione, *verbo Eneya*, sayes, That in the Statute of *Marlbridge*, *cap.* 9. made in the time of *H.* 3. It is called *Enitia pars hæreditatis*: And likewise in another place of the same King, *Jus esniciæ*, that is, in proper Latine, *Jus primogenituræ*. See *Enitia pars*, and *Esnecy*.

Eyre alias **Eire**, From the old French word *Eire* that is, *Iter*, a Journey, as *à grand Eire*, that is, *Magnis itineribus*. It signifies in *Britton*, *cap.* 2. the Court of Justices *Itinerant*. And Justices in *Eyre* are those onely which *Bracton* in many places calleth *Justiciarios itinerantes*, of the *Eyre*, and *Lib.* 3. *tract.* 2. *cap.* 1. 2. saith, The *Eyre* also of the Forest is nothing but the *Justice-seat* otherwise called, which is or should by ancient Custome be held every three year by the Justices of the Forest, journeying up and down to that purpose, *Cromp. Jur. fol.* 156. *Manwood's Forest Laws*, *cap.* 24. Read also *Skene de verb.* Signif. *verbo* Iter, whereby as by many other places, you may see great Affinity between these two Kingdoms in the administration of Justice and Government. See *Justice in Eyre*.

Election, Is, when a man is left to his own free Will to take or do one thing or another, which he pleases; As if *A.* covenants to pay *B.* a pound of Pepper or Saffron before *Whitsontide*; it is at the *election* of *A.* at all times before *Whitsontide*, which of them he will pay; but if he payes it not before the said Feast, then afterwards it is at the *election* of *B.* to have Action for which he pleases, *Dyer, fol.* 18. *pl.* 104. 21 *H.* 7. 19. *Co. lib.* 5. *fol.* 59. and *lib.* 11. *fol.* 51.

Election de Clerk, *Electione Clerici*, Is a Writ that lyeth for the choice of a *Clerk* assigned to take and make Bonds called *Statute-Merchant*, and is granted out of the Chancery, upon suggestion made, that the *Clerk* formerly assigned is gone to dwell in another place, or hath hindrance to let him from following that business, or hath not land sufficient to answer his Transgression, if he should deal amiss, &c. *F. N. B. fol.* 164.

Elegit, (So called from the words in it, *Elegit sibi liberari*) Is a Writ Judicial, and lyeth for him that hath recovered Debt or Damages in the Kings Court against one not able in his Goods to satisfie, and directed to the Sheriff, commanding him that he make delivery of half the Parties Lands or Tenements, and all his Goods, Oxen and Beasts for the Plough excepted, *Old. Nat. Brev. fol.* 152. *Reg. Orig.* 299. & 301. And the Table of the *Register Judicial*, which expresseth divers uses of this Writ: In the *New Termes of the Law* it is said, That this Writ shall be sued within the year. The Creditor shall hold the moyety of the said Land so delivered unto him, till his whole Debt and Damages are satisfied, and during that term he is Tenant by *Elegit, Westm.* 2. *cap.* 18. See *Co.* on *Lit. fol.* 289. *b.*

Elke, A kind of *Ewe* to make Bows of 32 *H.* 8. *cap.* 9.

Eloyne, In French *Esloigner*, To remove or send away. So the word is used 13 E. 1. *cap.* 15. If such as be within age be *eloined*, so that they cannot sue personally, their next Friends shall be admitted to sue for them.

Elopement, Is when a marryed Woman departs from her Husband, and dwells with an Adulterer, for which, without voluntary reconcilement to the Husband, she shall lose her *Dower* by the Statute of *Westm.* 2. *cap.* 34. according to these old Verses.

Sponte virum Mulier fugiens & Adultera facta
Dote sua careat, nisi sponso sponte retracta.

Nor shall the Husband in such case be compelled to allow her any *Alimony*.

Emblements, Be the profits of Land which have been sowed; but the word is sometimes taken more largely for any Profits that arise and grow naturally from the Ground, as Grass, Fruit, Hemp, Flax, &c. If Tenant for life sow the Land, & afterwards dye, the Executor of the Tenant for life shall have the *Emblements*, and not he in Reversion: But if Tenant for years sow the Lands, and before he hath reaped, his term expires, there the Lessor, or he in Reversion, shall have the *Emblements*. See *Co. lib.* 11. *fol.* 51. and although it is commonly held, that if a man leases Lands at will, and after the Lessee sows the Land, and then the will is determined, that the Lessee shall have the *Emblements*; yet if the Lessee himself determines the Will before the severance of the Corn, he shall not have the *Emblements*. See *Co. lib.* 5. *fol.* 116.

Embraceor or Embrasour, 19 *H.* 7. 13. Is he that when a matter is in Tryal between Party and Party comes to the Bar with one of the Parties (having received some Reward so to do) and speaks in the Case, or privily labors the Jury, or stands there to surveigh or over-look them, thereby to put them in fear and doubt of the matter; the Penalty whereof is 20 *li.* and imprisonment at the Justices discretion by the afore-cited Statute. But persons learned in the Law may speak in the Case for their Clients.

Embracery, Is the offence of an *Embraceour*, to pre-instruct the Jury, &c. is *Embracery*, Noy's *Rep. fol.* 102.

Embre or embring dayes, 2 & 3 E. 6. *cap.* 19. Are those by the ancient Fathers called *Quatuor Tempora*, and of great Antiquity in the Church, being observed on the *Wednesday, Friday,* and *Saturday* next after *Quadragesima Sunday*, *Whitsunday, Holy rood day* in *September*, and *St. Lucyes day* in *December*. They are mentioned by *Britton, cap.* 53. and others. *Co.* in his *Inst. part* 3. *fol.* 200. saith, These *embring days* are the week next before *Quadragesima*; which must needs be a great mistake in the Printer, for it is not possible that learned man could be ignorant in a thing so well known.

Emendals, *Emenda*, Is an old word still used in the Accounts of the *Inner-Temple*, where so much in *Emendals* at the Foot of an Account, signifies so much in bank in the stock of the House for the supply of all emergent Occasions: *Spelman* sayes it is that, *Quod tribuitur in restaurationem damni.*

Empanel, *Impanellare vel Ponere in Assisis & Juratis*, Cometh of the French *Panne*, i. *Pellis*, or of *Paneau*, which denotes as much as a *Pane* with us, as a *pane* of Glass, or of a Window: In Law it signifieth the writing and entring the Names of a Jury into a Parchment Schedule, or Roll of Paper, by the Sheriff, which he hath summoned to appear for the performance of such publick Service as Juries are imployed in. See *Panel.*

Emparlaunce, *Licentia interloquendi*, Cometh of the French *Parler*, to talk, and in the Common-Law signifieth a Desire or Petition in Court, of a day to pause what is best to do: The *Civilians* call it *Petitionem induciarum.* And *Kitch. fol.* 200. interpreteth it in these words, If he *impart*, or pray continuance; when praying continuance is spoken *interpretative*. And *fol.* 201. he mentions *emparlance general*, and *emparlance special*; *Emparlance general* seemeth to be that which is made onely in one word, and in general termes. *Emparlance special*, where the Party requires a day to deliberat, eadding also these words, *Salvis omnibus advantagiis tam ad jurisdictionem Curiæ quam ad breve & narrationem*——or such like. *Britton, cap.* 53. useth it for the Conference of a Jury upon the cause committed to them. And an *Emparlance* or Continuance is thus entred, *Et modo ad hunc diem, scilicet diem veneris, &c. isto eodem Termino usq; ad quem diem prædictus A. habuit licentiam interloquendi, &c.* See *Imparlance.*

Emprovement. See *Improvement.*

Encheson, Is a French word much used in our Law Books, as in that Statute 50 *E.* 3. *cap.* 3. and it signifies as much as the Occasion, Cause or Reason for which any thing is done. So it is used by *Stamf. lib.* 1. *cap.* 12. in his Description of a *Deodand*. *Skene de verbor.* Signif. *verbo* Encheson

son, sayes, That *Edward*, the first King of *England*, *Westm.* 1. *cap.* 6. *Statutis & Ordainis*, That no man shall be an Merchande, with an reasonable *Encheson*.

Encroachment or Accroachment, Cometh from the French word *Accrocher*, to pull or draw to, and it signifies an unlawful gaining upon the Rights or Possessions of another: For example, If two mens Grounds lying together, the one presseth too far upon the other; or if a Tenant owe two shillings Rent-service to the Lord, and the Lord taketh three. See *Co.* 9. *Rep. fol.* 33. *Bucknal*'s Case. So it is said, That *Hugh Spencer* the Father, and *Hugh Spencer* the Son *encroached* unto them Royal Power and Authority, *Anno* 1 *E.* 3. *in proœm.*

Enditement or Indictment, *Indictamentum*, Cometh of the French *Enditer*, *indicare*; or according to Mr. *Lambert*, from the Greek ἐνδείκνυμι, Eirenar. *lib.* 4. *cap.* 5. *pag.* 468. It signifies in our Common-Law as much as *Accusatio* in the Civil-Law, though in some points it differ, *West. part.* 2. *Symb. tit.* Inditements, defineth it thus, An *Inditement* is a Bill or Declaration made in form of Law (for the benefit of the Common-wealth) exhibited as an Accusation of one for some Offence, either criminal or penal unto Jurors, and by their Verdict found and presented to be true, before an Officer having power to punish the same Offence. It seems to be an Accusation, because the Jury that enquireth of the Offence, doth not receive it, until the Party that offereth the Bill appearing, subscribe his Name, and proffer his Oath for the truth of it. It is alwayes at the Suit of the King, and differs from an Accusation in this, that the *Preferrer* is no way tyed to the Proof thereof upon any Penalty, if it be not proved, except there appear Conspiracy. See *Smith de Rep. Angl. lib.* 2. *cap.* 19. *Stamf. pl. cor. lib.* 2. *cap.* 23, 24. *& sic usq; ad* 34. *Enditements* of Treason ought to be very exactly and certainly penned, *Co.* 7. *Rep. Calvin*'s Case; and they must contain the day, year and place. See 37 *H.* 8. *cap.* 8. and 3. *par. Inst. fol.* 134.

Endowment, *Dotatio*, Signifieth the giving or assuming of Dower to a Woman; for which see more in *Dower*: But it is sometimes by a Metaphor used for the setting or severing of a sufficient portion for a Vicar towards his perpetual Maintenance, when the Benefice is appropriated, and so it is used in the Statutes, 15 *R.* 2. *cap.* 6. and 4 *H.* 4. *cap.* 12. See *Appropriation.*

Endowment de la pluis belle part, Is where a man dying seised of some Lands holden in Knights-service, and other some in Socage, the Widow is sped of her Dower rather in the Socage-Lands, than those holden in Knights-service, as being *le pluis belle part*, the fairer part, of which read *Littleton* at large, *Lib.* 1. *cap.* 5.

Enfranchise, Is to make Free, to incorporate a man into a Society or Body-Politick, or to make one a free *Denizen*.

Enfranchisement, Cometh of the French word *Franchise*, *libertas*, and signifies the incorporating of a man into any Society, or Body-Politick: For example, He that by Charter is made Denizen of *England*, is said to be *enfranchised*; and so is he that is made a Citizen of *London*, or other City, or Burgess of any Town Corporate, because he is made partaker of those Liberties that appertain to the Corporation, where into he is *enfranchised*: So a Villain is *enfranchised*, when he is made free by his Lord, and made capable of the benefits belonging to free men. And when a man is thus *enfranchised* into a City or Borough, he hath a Free-hold in his Freedom for his Life; wherefore, whatever shall be the cause of his *disfranchisement*, ought to be a Fact, and not onely an endeavoring or enterprising; what shall be sufficient cause to *disfranchise* a Free-man, and what not. See in *Co.* 11. *Rep. fol.* 98. *Bagg*'s Case.

Englecery, Englechery, Engleschire or Englesherp, In Latine *Englecería*, Is an old word, signifying nothing more than to be an *English* man. For example, If a man were privily slain or murder'd, he was in old time accounted *Francigena*, which word comprehended every Alien, until *Englecery* were proved, that is, until it was made manifest that he was an *English-man*, *Bract. lib.* 3. *tract.* 2. *cap.* 15. *fol.* 134. The original whereof was this, *Canutus* the Dane being King of *England*, having setled his Estate in Peace, at the Request of his Lords, discharged the Land of his Armies, upon condition, That whoever should kill an Alien, should be liable to Justice; and if the Manslayer escaped, the Town where the Man was slain should forfeit 66 Marks to the King, and if the Town was not able, then the Hundred should pay: And further, that every Man murthered should be accounted *Francigena*, except *Englecery* were proved; the manner of which see *Bract. ibid. cap.* 15. *num.* 7. See also *Hornes Mirrour of Just.* lib. 1. cap. *Of the Office of Coroners*, and *Fleta. lib.* 1. *cap.* 30. This *Englecery*, for the Abuses and Troubles that were afterwards perceived to grow by it, was utterly taken away by 14 Ed. 3. *cap.* 4. See *Co. lib.* 7. *fol.* 16. *Calvin*'s Case.

Enheritance. See *Inheritance.*

Enitia pars. See *Finecia.*

Enquest, Latine *Inquisitio*, Is the same with the French word, and all one in signification: Howbeit it is especially taken for an Inquisition by Jurors, or a Jury, which is the most usual tryal of all Causes both Civil and Criminal within this Realm; for in Causes civil, after proof is made on either side, of so much as each Party thinketh good for himself; if the doubt be in the Fact, it is referred to the discretion of twelve indifferent Men, empannelled by the Sheriff for that purpose, and as they bring in their Verdict, so Judgment passeth; For the Judge saith, The Jury findeth the Fact thus, and the Law is thus; For the *Enquest* in Criminal Causes, see *Jury*, and *Smith de Rep. Angl. lib.* 2. *cap.* 19. An *Enquest* is either *ex Officio*, of Office, or at the mise of the Party, *Stamf. pl. cor. lib.* 3. *cap.* 12. This word is used in the Statutes of 25 E. 3. *cap.* 3, 28 *E.* 3. 13. and almost in all Statutes that speak of Tryals by Jurors.

Entayle, *Feodum talliatum*, Cometh of the French *Entail*, i. *inscisus*, and in the Common-Law is used as a Substantive abstract, signifying *Fee-tail*, or *Fee-intailed*: *Littleton* in the second Chapter of his Book draweth *Fee-tail* from the Verb *Talliare*, (an *obsolete* and *superannuated* word, I am sure, if any,) whereas in truth it must come

 from

from the French *Taille*, *Jectura*, or *teiller*, *Jcindere*; and the reason is manifest, because *Fee-tail* in the Law is nothing but Fee abridged, scanted or curtail'd, or limited or tyed to certain Conditions. *Taille* in *France* is metaphorically taken for a Tribute or Subsidy, *Lupanus de Magistratibus Francorum*, lib. 3. cap. *Talea*. See Fee, see *Tail*.

Entendment, Cometh of the French word *Entendement*, *intellectus*, *ingenium*. In a legal sense it signifies as much as the true meaning or signification of a word or sentence. See of this *Kitchin*, *fol.* 244. When a thing is in doubt, then sometimes by *entendment* it shall be made out: As if an Inquisition be found before a Coroner, that a man was murthered at *A*, which is a Liberty, and it is not said in the Inquisition at *A*, within the Liberty of *A*, yet it shall be good by *entendment*; for peradventure the Liberty may extend beyond the Town, *Co. lib.* 5. *fol.* 121.

Enterpleder, *Interplacitare*, Is compounded of two French words, *Entre*, that is *Inter*, and *Pleder*, that is *Disputare*; and signifies in the Common Law as much as *Cognitio præjudicialis* in the Civil, that is, the discussing of a point incidently falling out before the principal Cause can take end: For example, Two several persons being found Heirs to Land, by two several Offices in one County, the King is brought in doubt to which of them, Livery ought to be made, and therefore first they must *interplede*, that is, formally try between themselves who is the right Heir, *Stamf. Prærog. cap.* 12. & 19. *Bro. tit.* Enterpleder, and *Co. lib.* 7. *fol.* 45.

Entierty or Intierty, A kind of French word signifying *Entireness*; it is *contra*-distinguished in our Books from moyety, and denoting the whole.

Entire Tenancy, Is contrary to *several Tenancy*, signifying a sole Possession in one man, whereas the other signifieth Joynt or Common in more. See *Bro. several Tenancy*, and the *New Book of Entries*, *verbo* Entire Tenancy.

Entry, *Ingressus*, Cometh of the French *Entree*, and properly the taking possession of Lands or Tenements. See *Plowd. Assise of fresh Force in* London, *fol.* 93. *b.* It is also used for a Writ of Possession, for which see *Ingressus*, and also read *West Symbol. part* 2. *tit.* Recoveries, *sect.* 2, 3. who there shews for what thing it lies, and for what not. Of this *Britton* in his 114 Chap. writeth to this effect, the Writs of *Entry* favour much of the right of Property: As for example, Some be to recover Customes and Services in the which are contained these two words, *Solet & Debet*, as the Writs *Quo Jure*; *Rationabilibus divisis*; *Rationabili estoverio*, and the like. And in this Plea of *Entry* there be three degrees; The first is, where a man demandeth Lands or Tenements of his own Seisin, after the term is expired. The second is where one demandeth Lands or Tenements, let by another after the term expired. The third, where one demandeth Lands or Tenements of that Tenant that had *Entry* by one, to whom some Ancestor of the Plaintiff did let it for a term now expired, according to which degrees, the Writs for more fit remedy are varied. And there is yet a fourth form, which is without degrees, and in case of a more remote Seisin, whereunto the other three degrees do not extend. The Writ in the second degree is called *a Writ of* Entry *in le Per*, and a Writ in the third degrees is called *a Writ of* Entry *in the Per & Cui*, and the fourth form without these degrees is called *a Writ of* Entry *in le Post*, that is to say after the Disseisin which such a one made to such a one; and if any Writ of *Entry* be conceived out of the right case, so that one form be brought for another, it is abateable. And in those four degrees be comprehended all manner of Writs of *Entry*, which are without number or certainty. Thus far *Britton*, by whom you may perceive that those words *Solet & Debet*, and also those other words *in le Per*, *in le Per & Cui*; and *in le Post*, which we meet with many times in the Books shortly and obscurely mentioned, do signifie nothing else but divers forms of this Writ, applyed to the case whereupon it is brought, and each form taking his name from the words contained in the Writ, and of this read *Fitzh. Nat. Brev. fol.* 193, 194. This Writ of *Entry* differeth from an Assise, because it lyeth for the most part against him who entred lawfully, but holdeth against Law, whereas an Assise lyeth against him that unlawfully disseised; yet sometimes a Writ of *Entry* lyeth upon an intrusion, *Reg. Orig. fol.* 233. *b.* See the *New Book of Entries*, *verbo* Entre brevis, *fol.* 254 *col.* 3. I have read also of a Writ of *Entry* in the nature of an Assise. Of this Writ in all his degrees, read *Fleta*, *lib.* 5. *cap.* 34. & *sequent.* Also there are five things which put the Writ of *Entry* out of the degrees, *viz. Intrusion*, *Succession*, *Disseisin* upon *Disseisin*, *Judgment* and *Escheat*. 1. *Intrusion*, Is where the Disseisor dies seised, and a stranger abates. 2. *Succession*, Is when the Disseisor is a man of Religion, and dies, or is deposed, and his Successor *enters*. 3. *Disseisin* upon *Disseisin*, Is when the Disseisor is disseised by another. 4. *Judgment*, Is when one recovers against the Disseisor. 5. *Escheat*, Is when the Disseisor dies without Heir, or doth Felony, whereby he is attaint, by which the Lord *enters* as in his Escheat. In all these Cases the Disseisee or his Heir shall not have a Writ of *Entry* within the degrees of the *Per*, but in the *Post*; because in those cases they are not in by Descent, nor by Purchase.

Entry ad Communem Legem, Is a Writ which lies where Tenant for term of Life, Tenant for term of anothers Life, Tenant by the Curtesie, or Tenant in Dower, aliens and dies, he in the Reversion shall have this Writ against whomsoever is in.

Entry in casu Proviso, Lies if Tenant in Dower alien in Fee, or for term of Life, or for anothers Life, living the Tenant in Dower, he in the Reversion shall have this Writ, which is provided by the Statute of *Glouc. cap.* 7.

Entry in casu consimili, Is a Writ that lies where Tenant for life, or Tenant by the curtesie aliens in Fee, he in the Reversion shall have this Writ by *Westm.* 2. *cap.* 24.

Entry ad terminum qui præteriit, Lies where a man leases Land to another for term of years, and the Tenant holds over his term; the Lessor shall have this Writ.

Entry sine assensu Capituli, Lies where an Abbot, Prior, or such as have Covent or Common-Seal, aliens Lands or Tenements of the right of his Church, without the assent of the

the Covent or Chapter, and dies, then the Successor shall have this Writ.

Entry causa Matrimonii prælocuti, Lies where Lands or Tenements are given to a man, upon condition, that he shall take the Donor to his Wife within a certain time, and he does not espouse her within the limited time, or espouses another; or otherwise disables himself, that he cannot take her according to the said condition, then the Donor and her Heirs shall have the said Writ against him, or against whoever else is in the said Land.

Entrusion, *Intrusio*, Signifieth a Violent or unlawful entrance into Lands or Tenements, being utterly void of a Possessor, by him that hath no Right, nor spark of Right unto him, *Bract. lib.* 4. *cap.* 2. For example, If a man step into any Lands, the Owner whereof lately died, and the right Heir neither by himself, or others, as yet hath taken Possession of them: The difference between an *Intruder* and an *Abator* is this, that an *Abator* entreth into Lands void by the death of a Tenant in Fee; and an *Intruder* enters into Lands void by the death of a Tenant for life or years, *F. N. B. fol.* 203. and *Co.* on *Lit. fol.* 277. yet the *Book of Entries* expresseth Abatement by the Latine word *Intrusionem*, *fol.* 63. *C.* which the *New Termes of Law* calls *Interpositionem aut introitionem per interpositionem.* See *Abatement*, see *Disseisin*, see *Britton, cap* 65. *Intrusio* is used also for the Writ brought against an *Entruder*, which see in *Fitzh. Nat. Brev.* 203. and Statute of *Marl. cap. ult.*

Entrusion de gard, Is a Writ that lies where the Infant within age entred into his Lands, and held his Lord out: for in this case the Lord shall not have the Writ *de communi Custodia*, but this. *Old Nat. Brev. fol.* 90.

Envoyce. See *Invoyce.*

Enure, Signifieth to take place or effect, to be available. As, a Release shall *enure* by way of extinguishment, *Littleton*, cap. *Release.* And a Release made to a Tenant for term of life, shall *enure* to him in the Reversion.

Eques Auratus, Is taken to signifie a Knight, and termed *Auratus*, because anciently none but Knights might beautifie and gild their Armor, or other Habiliments of War, *Fernes Glory of Generosity*, pag. 102. Yet in Law we never use *Eques Auratus*, but *Miles*, and sometimes *Chivalier*, *Co.* 4. *Inst. fol.* 5.

Equity, *Equitas*, Is of two sorts, and those of contrary effects; for the one doth abridge, and take from the letter of the Law, the other doth inlarge, and add thereto. The first is thus defined, *Æquitas est correctio legis generatim latæ, qua parte deficit.* *Equity* is the Correction of the Law generally made in that part wherein it fails, which Correction is much used in our Law: As for example, when an Act of Parliament is made, that whosoever doth such a thing shall be a Felon, and suffer death; yet if a Mad-man, or an Infant that hath no discretion, do the same, that shall not be Felons, nor suffer death therefore. The other *Equity* is defined to be an extension of the words of the Law to Cases unexpressed, yet having the same reason; so that when one thing is enacted, all other things are enacted that are of the like degree: As the Statute which ordains, that in an Action of Debt against Executors, he that doth appear by Distress shall answer, doth extend by *equity* to Administrators; for such of them as shall appear first by Distress, shall answer by *equity* of the said Act, *quia sunt in æquali genere.*

Erius alias **Iris,** Is the flower *de Lys* whose divers kinds you may read in *Gerards Herb. lib.* 1. *cap.* 34. The root of this is mentioned among Merchandise, or Drugs to be garbled, *Anno* 1 *Jac. cap.* 19.

Ermins, Seemeth to come of the French word *Ermine.* It signifieth a Furre of great price.

Erminstreet. See *Watlingstreet.*

Errant, *Itinerans*, May be derived from the old word *Erre*, i. *Iter*: It is attributed to Justices that go the Circuit, Stam. *pl. cor. fol.* 15. and to Bayliffs at large. See *Justices in Eyre* and *Bayliff.* See also *Eyre.*

Error, Cometh of the French *Erreur*, and signifieth especially an *Error* in Pleading, or in the Process, *Bro. tit.* Error. And thereupon the Writ which is brought for remedy of this oversight, is called *a Writ of Error*, in Latine *Breve de Errore corrigendo*, thus defined by *Fitzh.* in his *Nat. Brev. fol.* 20. A Writ of *Error* is that properly which lyeth to redress false Judgment given in any Court of Record, as in the *Common-Bench London*, or other City having power by the Kings Charter or Prescription, to hold Plea of Debt above twenty shillings, or Trespass. See the *New Book of, Entries, verbo* Error. This is borrowed from the French Practice, which they called *Proposition de erreur*, whereof you may read in *Gregorius de appellatione*, pag. 36. In what diversity of cases this VVrit lyeth see the *Register Original* in the Table, *verb. Errore corrigendo*, and *Reg. Jud. fol.* 34. There is likewise a Writ of *Error*, to reverse a Fine, *West. Symbol. part* 2. *tit.* Fines, 151. For preventing abatements by Writs of *Error* upon Judgments in the Exchequer. See 16 *Car.* 2. *cap.* 2. and 20 *Car.* 2. *cap.* 4. And for redressing and prevention of *Error* in Fines and Recoveries, see the Stat. 23 *Eliz. cap.* 3. for inrolling them.

Errore Corrigendo. See *Error.*

Escambio, Is a Licence granted to one, for the making over a Bill of Exchange to another over Sea, *Reg. Orig. fol.* 194. For by the Statute of 5 *R.* 2. *cap.* 2. No Merchant ought to exchange or return Money beyond Sea, without the Kings Licence.

Escape, *Escapium*, Cometh of the French *Eschapper*, that is, *effugere*, to fly from, and signifies in the Law a violent or privy evasion out of some lawful restraint. For example, If the Sheriff, upon a *Capias* directed to him, take one, and indeavour to carry him to the Goal, and he, in the way, either by violence, or by flight break from him, this is called *an Escape*, Stam. *pl. cor. fol.* 70. The same *Stamford* in his *Pleas of the Crown*, lib. 1. cap. 26. 27. nameth two kinds of *Escape*, the one *voluntary*, the other *negligent*: *Voluntary* is, when one arresteth another for Felony, or any other Crime, and afterward letteth him go whither he listeth. *Negligent escape* is, when one is arrested, and afterwards *escapeth* against his will

 that

that arrested him, and is not pursued by fresh Suit, and taken again before the Party pursuing hath lost the sight of him, *Id. cap.* 27. Of the course of Punishment by the Civil-Law in this point, read in *Practica criminali Claudii de* B. *attaindier*, reg. 143. Read also *Cromp. Just. fol.* 35. 36. 37. and *Termes de la Ley*. There is likewise an *escape* of Beasts, and therefore he that by Charter is *Quietus de escapio* in the Forest; is delivered of that punishment which, by order of the Forest, lyeth upon those whose Beasts be found within the Land forbidden, *Cromp. Jurisd. fol.* 196. See also *Co.* 3. *Reports, Ridgewayes* Case, and *ibid. Boytons* Case, *Plowd. Com. Platos* Case.

Eschange or Exchange, *Escambium* or *Excambium, Hanc terram cambiavit* Hugo Briccuino *quod modo tenet comes Moriton & ipsum Scambium valet Duplum*, Doomsday, *vide* Exchange.

Eschequer, *Scaccarium*, May be derived from the French word *Eschequier*, i. *abacus, tabula Lusoria*, and signifieth the Place or Court of all Receits belonging to the Crown, *Polyd. Virg. lib.* 9. *Hist. Ang.* saith, That the true word in Latine is *Statarium*; but it may with more probability be taken from the German word *Schatz*, denoting as much as *Thesaurus* or *Fiscus*. *Camden* in his *Brittannia, pag.* 113. saith, That this Court or Office took the Name from *tabula ad quam assidebant*, proving it out of *Gervasius Tilburiensis*, the Cloth which cover'd it being parti-colored or checquered. By the *Grand Custumair*, it is brought from the Normans, *cap.* 56. where you may find it thus described, The *Eschequer* is called *an Assembly of High Justicers*, to whom it appertaineth to amend that which the Bayliffs and other meaner Justiciers have evil done, and unadvisedly judged, and to do Right to all men without delay, as from the Princes mouth. *Skene de verbor.* Signif. *Scaccarium*, hath out of *Paulus Æmilius* these words, *Scaccarium dicitur quasi statarium, quod homines ibi in jure sistantur, vel quod sit stataria & perennis curia cum cæteræ curiæ essent indictivæ nec loco nec tempore statæ*. Also he addeth further, that it might be called *Scaccarium à similitudine Ludi scacchorum*, from the resemblance it has to the Game at *Chesse*, many persons meeting and pleading their Causes there, as if they were fighting in an arrayed Battel. And *Smith* deduces it from an old Saxon word *Scata*, signifying Treasure, whereof Account is made in the *Chequer*. This Court consisteth, as it were, of two parts, whereof one dealeth especially in the judicial hearing and deciding of all Causes appertaining to the Princes Coffers, anciently called *Scaccarium computorum*, as *Ockham* testifies in his *Lucubrations*. The other is called *The Receit of the Exchequer*, which is properly imployed in the receiving and paying of Money, *Cromp. Jur. fol.* 105. sayes, It is a Court of Record, wherein all Causes touching the Revenues of the Crown are handled: The Officers belonging to both these, you may read in *Cambdens Brit.* cap *Tribunalia Angliæ*, to whom I refer you. The Kings *Exchequer* now setled at *Westm.* was in divers Counties of *Wales*, 27 *H.* 8, *cap.* 5. but especially 26. and 4. *par. Inst. fol.* 103.

Eschete, *Eschaeta*, Cometh of the French *Escheoir, cadere, excidere*, and signifieth in a legal sense any Lands, or other Profits, that fall to a Lord within his Mannor by way of Forfeiture or, the death of his Tenant, dying without Heir general or special, or leaving his Heir within age, and unmarried, *Mag. Charta. cap.* 31. *F. N. B. fol.* 143, &c. *Escheat* is also used sometimes for the Place or Circuit within which the King, or other Lord hath *Escheats* of his Tenants, *Bract. lib.* 3. *tract.* 2. *cap.* 2. & *Pupillo oculi, part* 2. *cap.* 22. Thirdly, *Escheat* is used for a Writ which lyeth, where the Tenant having Estate in Fee-simple in any Lands or Tenements holden of a superior Lord, dyeth seised without Heir general or special; for in this case the Lord bringeth this Writ against him that possesseth the Lands after the death of his Tenant, and shall thereby recover the same in lieu of his Services, *F. N. B. fol.* 144. Those that we call *Escheats*, are in the Kingdom of *Naples* called *Excadentia*, or *bona excadentialia*, as *Baro locat excadentias eo modo quo locatæ fuerunt ab antiquo, ita quod in nullo debita servitia minuantur & non remittit gallinam debitam*, Jacob *de* Franchiis *in præludiis ad feudorum usum*, tit. 1. num. 23. & 29. And in the same signification, that we say the Fee is *escheated*; the *Feudists* say, *Feudum aperitur*. See *Co.* on *Lit. fol.* 92. *b.*

Escheator, *Escaetor*, Derived from *Escheat*, is an Officer that taketh notice of the *Escheats* of the King in the County, whereof he is *Escheator*, and certifieth them into the Exchequer. This Officer is appointed by the Lord Treasurer, and continueth in his Office but a year; neither can any be an *Escheator* above once in three years, *Anno* 1 *H.* 8. *cap.* 8. and 3 *H.* 8. *cap.* 2. See more of this Officer and his Authority in *Cromptons Justice of Peace*, see 29 E. 1. The form of his Oath, see in *Reg. Orig. fol.* 301. *b. Fitzherbert* calls him an Officer on Record, *Nat. Brev. fol* 100. because that which he certifieth by vertue of his Office, hath the credit of a Record. *Officium Escaetriæ*, is the Escheatorship, *Reg. Orig. fol.* 259. This Office having its chief dependance on the *Court of Wards*, is now in a manner out of date. See 4. *Inst. fol.* 225.

Escuage, *Scutagium*, Cometh of the French *Escu, clypeus*, a Shield. In Law it signifieth a kind of Knights-service, called *Service of the Shield*, whereby the Tenant is bound to follow his Lord into the *Scotch* or *Welsh* Wars at his own charge; for which see *Chivalry*. But note, that *Escuage* is either *uncertain* or *certain*: *Escuage uncertain* is properly *Escuage* and Knights-service being subject to Homage, Fealty, and (formerly) Ward and Marriage; and so called, because it is *uncertain* how often a man shall be called to follow his Lord into those Wars, and what his charge will be in each Journey. *Escuage certain* is, when a certain Rent is paid yearly in lieu of all Services, being no further bound then to pay his Rent, call'd *a Knights Fee*, or *the fourth part of a Knights Fee*, according to his Land; and this loseth the nature of Knights-service, though it hold the name of *Escuage*, being in effect but Socage, *F. N. B. fol.* 8. But see the Stat. 12 *Car.* 2. *cap.* 24. for taking away the *Court of Wards and Liveries*, and turning all Tenures into Free an Common Socage. See *Littleton. lib.* 2. *cap.* 3. and see *Capite*.

Esnecy, *Æsnecia*, Is a Prerogative given to the eldest Coparcener, to chuse first after the

Inheritance is divided, *Fleta, lib.* 5. *cap.* 10. *Sect. in divisionem. Salvo capitali Messuagio primogenito filio pro dignitate Æsneciæ suæ*, Glanvil, lib. 7. cap. 3. *jus* Æsnetiæ, *jus Primogenituræ. Skene de verb.* Sig. *Stat. Marlb. cap.* 9. calls it *Enitia pars hæreditatis.* See *Co.* on *Lit. fol.* 166. *b.*

Eskippeson, An *obsolete* word, signifying Shipping, as appears by an Indenture dated the Second of *Jan.* 50 E. 3. between *Thomas Beauchamp* Earl of *Warwick* of the one part, and *John Russell* Esq; on the other part, wherein, among other things, it is said, *Et que le dit* John *avera* Eskyppeson *son covenable pour son passage & repassage outre mere*, &c.

Esplees, *Expletia*, perhaps from *Expleo*, Seem to be the full profits that the Ground or Land yieldeth; as the Hay of the Meadows, the Feed of the Pasture, the Corn of the Arable; the Rents, Service, and such like Issues. The Profits comprised under this word the *Romans* call properly *Accessiones; nam accessionem ea generaliter omnia, quæ ex re de qua agitur orta sunt, veluti fructus, partus & omnis causa rei & quæcunq; ex re procedunt.* And note, that in a writ of right of Land, Advowson, or such like, the Demandant ought to alledge in his Count, that he or Ancestors took the *Esplees* of the thing in demand, otherwise the pleading is not good, *Termes de la Ley.*

Esperbarius et Sparberius, French *Esperver*, A Hawk, *Charta Forest, cap.* 13. *Reddit. folut.* W. Talboys *Arm ad manerium suum de Keyme pro omnibus serviciis secularibus unum* Esparverium, &c. *Comput.* David Gefferon *collect. Reddit. de Wragby*, Anno 35 Hen 6.

Esquier, *Armiger*, In French *Escuier*, i. *Scutiger*, was originally such a one attending a Knight in time of War, did carry his Shield; but this addition hath not of long time had any relation to that Office, but signifieth with us a Gentleman, or one that beareth Arms as a Testimony of his Nobility or Gentry, and is a meer Title of Dignity next to and below a Knight. They who by right claim this Title now, are all the younger Sons of Noble-men, the four *Esquires* of the Kings Body, the eldest Sons of all Baronets, Knights of the *Bath*, and Knights Batchelors; Those that serve the King in any Worshipful Calling, such as are created *Esquires* by the King, with a Collar of SS of Silver; the chief of some ancient Families are likewise *Esquires* by Prescription, those that bear any superior Office in the Common-wealth, a Justice of Peace while he is in Commission, and Utter-Barristers. In *Walsingham*'s History of *Richard* the Second, we read of one *John Blake*, who being *Juris Apprenticius*, has the addition of *Scutifer* given him. *Camden* in his *Brit. fol.* 111. having spoken of Knights, hath these words of them, *Hiis proximi fuere Armigeri qui & Scutiferi hominesq ad arma dicti, qui vel a clypeis gentilitiis quæ in nobilitatis insignia gestant; vel qui principibus & majoribus illis nobilibus ab armis erant, nomen traxerunt, &c.* The learned *Spelman* in his *Glossary* sayes, *A principe fiunt Armigeri, vel scripto, vel symbolo, vel munere: Scripto, cum Rex sic quempiam constituerit. Symbolo, quum collum ergo alicujus argenteo sigmatico, (hoc est torque ex SS. confecto) adornaverit, eumve argentatis calcaribus donaverit. Tales in occidentali Angliæ plaga* White spurs *dicti sunt. Munere, cum ad munus quempiam evocaverit, vel in Aula, vel in Repub.* &c. *Hotoman* in the Sixth Chapter of his *Disputations upon the Feods* saith, That those which the French call *Escuires*, were a military kind of Vassal, having *Jus scuti*, that is, they bear a Shield, and in it the Ensignes of their Family, in token of their Gentility or Dignity.

Essendi quietum de Tolonio, Is a Writ that lyeth for Citizens and Burgesses of any City or Town, that hath a Charter or Prescription to exempt them from Toll through the whole Realm, if it happen the same to be any where exacted of them, *F. N. B.* 226. *Reg. Orig. fol.* 258.

Essoine, *Essonium*, Cometh of the French *Essoine* or *Exonnie*, i. *causarius miles*, he that hath his presence forborn, or excused upon any just Case, as Sickness, or other Impediment. It signifieth in the Common-Law, the allegation of an excuse for him that is summoned, or sought for to appear, and answer to an Action real, or to perform Suit to a Court-Baron upon just cause of absence: It is as much as *excusatio* with the *Civilians.* The Causes that serve to *essoine* any man summoned are divers, yet drawn chiefly to five heads; whereof the first is, *Ultra Mare*, whereby the Defendant shall have forty dayes. The second, *De terra Sancta*, where the Defendant shall have a year and a day, and these must be laid in the beginning of the Plea. The third, *De malo Veniendi*, which is also called *The common assoine.* The fourth is, *De malo lecti.* And the fifth, *De servitio Regis.* For further knowledge of these, I refer you to *Glanvile*, in his whole First Book, and *Bracton, lib.* 5. *tract.* 2. *per totum*, and *Britton. cap.* 122, 123, 124, 125. and *Hornes Mirrour of Justices, lib.* 1. *cap.* de Essoines, who maketh mention of some more *Essoines* touching the Service of the King Celestial, and of some other points not unworthy to be known. Of these *Essoines* you may read further in *Fleta, lib.* 6. *cap.* 8. *& seq.* And that these came to us from the *Normans*, is well shewed by the *Grand Custumary*, where you may in a manner find all said that our Lawyers have spoken of this matter, *Cap.* 39, 40, 41, 42, 43, 44, 45.

Essoines and Proffers *Anno* 32 *H.* 8. *cap.* 21. See *Proffer.*

Essonio de malo lecti, Is a Writ directed to the Sheriff, for the sending of four lawful Knights to view one that hath *essoined* himself *de malo lecti, Reg. Orig. fol.* 8. *b.*

Establishment of Dower, Seemeth to be the assurance of *Dower* made to the Wife by the Husband, or his Friends, before or at Marriage; and Assigment is the setting it out by the Heir afterwards, according to the establishment, *Britton, cap.* 102. & 103.

Estandard or Standard, Cometh of the French *Estandart*, i. *signum, vexillum.* It signifies an Ensigne in War as well with us as with them. But it is also used for the standing Measure of the King to the scantling, whereof all the Measures in the Land, are, or ought to be framed by the Clerk of the Market, Alneger, or other Officer, according to their Functions; for it was established by the Statute of *Magna Charta, Anno* 9 *H.* 3. *cap.* 9. That there should be put one scantling of Weights and Measures through the whole

whole Realm, which is since confirmed by 14 E. 3. *cap.* 12. and many other Statutes; (one especially made 17 *Car.* 1. *cap.* 29. which sayes, From henceforth there shall be one Weight, one Measure and one Yard, according to the *Standard* of the Exchequer throughout all the Realm): It is not without great reason called a *Standard*, because it standeth constant and immoveable, and hath all Measures coming towards it for their Conformity: Even as Souldiers in the Field have their *Standard* or Colors, for their direction in their March or Skirmish to repair to. Of these *Standards* and Measures, read *Britton, cap.* 30.

Estate, May be deduced from the French word *Estat*, i. *Conditio*, and signifieth that Title or Interest which a man hath in Lands or Tenements; as *Estate simple*, otherwise called *Fee simple*; and *Estate conditional*, or upon Condition, which is as *Littleton* saith, *Lib.* 3. *cap.* 5. Either upon *condition in Deed*, or upon *condition in Law*: *Estate upon condition in Deed* is, where a man by Deed indented infeoffeth another in Fee, reserving to him and to his Heirs yearly a certain Rent payable at one Feast, or at divers, upon condition, that if the Rent be behind, &c. that it shall be lawful to the Feoffor, and to his Heirs, to enter into the Lands or Tenements, &c. *Estate upon condition in Law*, is such as hath a consideration in Law annexed to it, though not specified in writing: For example, If a Man grant to another by his Deed the Office of a Parkership for term of his life, this *Estate* is upon condition in the Law, or implyed by Law, *viz.* if the Parker shall so long well and truly keep his Park. I read also of an *Estate particular*, which is an *Estate* for Life, or for term of Years, *Perkins Surrenders* 581.

Esterling. See *Sterling*.

Estoppel, From the French *Estouper*, *oppilare, obstipare*, Denotes as much as an Impediment, or bar of an Action, growing from his own Fact that hath, or otherwise might have had his Action. For example, a Tenant maketh a Feoffment by Collusion to one, the Lord accepteth the Services of the Feoffee; by this he debarreth himself of the Wardship of his Tenants Heir, *F. N. B. fol.* 142. Divers other Examples might be shewed out of him, and *Broke hoc titulo*, *Co. lib.* 2. *fol.* 4. *Goddards* Case, defineth an *Estoppel* to be a Bar or Hinderance unto one to plead the truth, and restraineth it not to the Impediment given to a man by his own Act onely, but by anothers also, *Lib.* 3. the Case *Of Fines*, *fol.* 88. There are three kinds of *Estoppel*, *viz.* By matter of *Record*, by matter in *Writing*, and by matter in *Pais*; of which see *Co.* on *Lit. fol.* 352.

Estovers, *Estoverium*, Cometh of the French word *Estouver*, i. *fovere*, and in the sense of the Law signifieth Nourishment or Maintenance. For example, *Bracton*, *lib.* 3. *tract.* 2. *cap.* 18. *num.* 2. useth it for that sustenance which a man taken for Felony, is to have out of his Lands or Goods for himself and his Family, during his Imprisonment. And the Statute made 6 E. 1. *cap.* 3. useth it for an allowance in Meat or Cloth. It is also used for certain allowances of wood, to be taken out of another mans Woods. So it is used *Westm.* 2. *cap.* 25. *Anno* 13 E. 1. *West. Symb. part* 2. *tit.* Fines, *sect.* 26. saith, That the Name of *Estovers* containeth *House-bote*, *Hey-bote*, and *Plough bote*; as if he have in his Grant these general words, *De rationabili Estoverio in boscis*, &c. he may thereby claim these three. In some Mannors the Tenants have Common of *Estovers* out of the Lords Woods, and pay a certain small Annual Rent for the same, *Rationabile Estoverium*, vide *antea Alimony*.

Estrangers, Are sometimes taken for those that are not Privies or Parties to the levying of a Fine, or making of a Deed. Sometimes for those that are born beyond Sea.

Estray, *Extrahura*, From the old French *Estrayeur*, *pererrare*, signifies any Beast not wild, found within any Lordship, and not owned by any man; for in this case, it being cryed, according to Law, in the Market-Towns adjoyning, if it be not claimed by the Owner in a year and a day, it is the Lords of the Soyl. See *Britton, cap.* 17. *Vide etiam* Estrayes *in the Forest*, 27 H. 8. cap. 7. and *New Book of Entries*, *verbo* Trespass concernant Estray. The ancient Law of King *Ina* was, *Diximus de ignotis pecoribus, ut nemo habeat sine testimonio Hundredi, sive hominum Decennæ*, that is, the Suiters at a Court-Leet, *Spelm.*

Estreat, *Extractum*, Is used for the true Copy, or Duplicate, of an original Writing. For example, Of Amerciaments or Penalties set down in the Rolls of a Court, to be levyed by the Bayliff, or other Officer, of every man for his offence. See *F. N. B fol.* 57. & 76. and so also it is used *Westm.* 2. *cap.* 8.

Clerk of the Estreats, *Clericus extractorum*. See in *Clerk*.

Estrepe, French *Estropier*, i, *Mutilare*: To make Spoil by a Tenant for Life in Lands or VVoods, to the prejudice of him in the Reversion.

Estrepement or **Estrepament,** *Estrepamentum*, from the French word *Estropier*, *mutilare*: It signifies the spoil made by Tenant for life upon any Lands or VVoods, to the prejudice of the Reversioner, as namely in the Statute made *Anno* 6 E. 1. *cap.* 13. and it may seem by the derivation, that *Estrepement* is properly the unmeasurable soaking or drawing out of the heart of the Land by plowing or sowing it continually, without manuring, or other such usage as is requisite in good Husbandry; and yet *estropier* signifying *mutilare*, may not improperly be applyed to those that cut down Trees, or lop them, farther than the Law will bear. This signifies also a writ, which lyeth in two manners; the one is, when a man having an Action depending, (as a *Formedon*, or *Dum fuit infra ætatem*, or *Writ of Right*, or any other) wherein the Demandant is not to recover Damages, sueth to inhibit the Tenant for making wast during the Suit. The other sort is for the Demandant, that is adjudged to recover Seisin of the Land in question, and before Execution sued by the writ *Habere facias seisinam*, for fear of wast to be made, before he can get possession, sueth out this writ. See more in *F. N. B. fol.* 60, 61. *Reg. Orig. fol.* 76. and *Reg. Jud. fol.* 33. In ancient Records we often find *Vastum & extrepamentum facere*; and *Spelman* thinks Estrepamentum *vasti genus designare*.

Etate probanda, or rather *Ætate* **probanda,** Is a Writ of Office, and lyes for the

the Heir of the Tenant that held of the King in chief, to prove that he is of full age, directed to the Sheriff to enquire of his Age, and then he shall become Tenant to the King by the same Services that his Ancestors made to the King. But see the Statute 12 *Car.* 2. *cap.* 2. for abolishing the *Court of Wards and Liveries*, which hath in a manner utterly taken away this Writ.

Etheling or **Atheling**, Is a Saxon word signifying *Noble*, and among the English-Saxon was as the Title of Prince among us, or as the Kings eldest Son; such was *Edgar Atheling* the designed Successor of *Edward the Confessor*.

Everwickshire, *Yorkshire*, Heretofore so called, haply derived from the Latine *Eboracum*, from which *Eborac*, and *Evoric* or *Everwick* corruptly is no so strange variation; and the Saxon *Scyre*, which signifies *shire* or *share*.

Evesdroppers, Are such as stand under Walls or Windows by Night or by Day, to hear News, and to carry them to others, to make strife and debate among Neighbours: These are evil Members in the Common wealth, and therefore by the Stat. *Westm.* 1. *cap.* 33. are to be punished. And this Misdemeanor is presentable and punishable in the Court-Leet, *Kitchin*, *fol.* 11.

Evidence, *Evidentia* Signifies generally any Proof, be it Testimony of Men, Records or Writings. Sir *Tho. Smith* useth in both sorts *Lib.* 2. *cap.* 17. in these words, *Evidence* is authentical writings of Contracts after the manner of *England*; that is to say, written, sealed and delivered: And *Lib.* 2. *cap.* 23. speaking of the Prisoner that standeth at the Bar to plead for his Life, and of those that charge him with Felony, He saith thus, Then he telleth what he can say; after him, likewise all those who were at the Prisoners Apprehensions, or who can make any proof, which we in our Language call *Evidence* against the Malefactor. It is called *Evidence* because it makes the Issue *evident* to the Jury; for *Probationes debent esse* evidentes *& perspicuæ*, *Co.* on *Lit. fol.* 283.

Exactores Regis, The Kings *Exactor*, sometimes taken for the Sheriff. And in this sense the *Black-Book* in the Exchequer, *Part.* 1. *cap.* ult. *Tabulas, quibus Vicomes censum Regium colligit Rotulum* Exactorium *vocat*, but generally *Quicunq; publicas pecunias, tributa, vectigalia & res fisco debitas exigit, proprie nominantur* Exactor Regis.

Exaction, Is a wrong done by an Officer, or one pretending to have Authority, in taking a Reward or Fee for that which the Law allows not. The difference between *Exaction* and Extortion is this, Extortion is, where an Officer extorts more then his due. *Exaction* is, where he wrests a Fee or Reward, where none is due. See *Extortion*.

Examiners in Chancery, *Examinatores*, Are two Officers that *examine* upon Oath, Witnesses produced on either side, upon such Interrogatories as the Parties to any Suit do exhibit, to that purpose; and sometimes the Parties themselves are by particular order *examined* also by them. Heretofore there was such an *Examiner* in the *Star-Chamber*, but the Court being abolished, the Office and Officer is extinct.

Excambiator, Was anciently used for an Exchanger of Land, [such I suppose as we now call *Brokers*, that deal upon the *Exchange* between Merchants.] *In libro cartarum Priorat. Leominst. de anno* 2 Ed. 2. It is said, *Ita quod unusquisq; eorum qui damna sustinuit aliquo casu contingente, quod* Excambiator *refundat damna*, &c.

Exception, *Exceptio*, Is a stop or stay to an Action, being used in the Civil and Common-Law, both alike, and in both divided into *dilatory* and *peremptory*: Of these see *Bracton*, *lib.* 5. *tract.* 5. *per totum*, and *Britton*, *cap.* 91, 92.

Exchange, *Excambium vel Cambium*, Hath a peculiar signification in our Common Law, and is used for that Compensation which the Warrantor must make to the Warrantee, value for value, if the Land warranted be recovered from the Warrantee, *Bract. lib.* 2. *cap.* 16. *& lib.* 1. *cap.* 19. It signifieth also generally as much as *Permutatio* with the *Civilians*, as the Kings *Exchange*, 1 H 6. *cap.* 1. *&* 4. and 9 E. 3. *Stat.* 2. *cap.* 7. which is nothing else but the place appointed by the King for the *exchange* of Bullion, Gold, Silver or Plate, &c. with the Kings Coin. These places have been divers heretofore, as appeareth by the said Statutes: But now is there onely one, *viz.* The Tower of *London* conjoyned with the Mint, which in time past might not be, as appeareth by 1 *H.* 6. *cap.* 4.

Exchangeors, Are those that use to return Money beyond Sea, by Bills of *Exchange*, which by the Stat. 5. *R.* 2. *cap.* 2. ought not to be done without the Kings Licence. See *Escambio*.

Exchequer. See *Eschequer*.

Excheator. See *Escheator*.

Excise, Is a Charge or Imposition laid upon Beer, Ale, Syder and other Liquors, within the Kingdom of *England*, *Wales*, and *Berwick*, by Act of Parliament made 12 *Car.* 2. *cap.* 13. during the Kings life, and according to the Rates in the said Act mentioned. See 13 *C.* 2. *cap.* 13. and 15 *Car.* 2. *cap.* 3 and 17 *Car.* 2. *cap.* 4.

Excommengement, 23 *H.* 8. *cap.* 3. Is in Law-French, the same with *Excommunication* in English.

Excommunication, *Excommunicatio*, Is thus defined by *Panormitan*, Excommunicatio *est nihil aliud quam censura a Canone vel judice Ecclesiastico prolata et inflicta privans legitima communione Sacramentorum & quandoq; hominum.* And it is divided in *Majorem & Minorem*; *Minor est, per quam quis a Sacramentorum participatione conscientia vel sententia arcetur: Major est quæ non solum a Sacramentorum, verum etiam fidelium communione excludit, et ab omni actu legitimo seperat & dividit. Venatorius de senten. excom.* The form of an *Excommunication* was of old thus, *Auctoritate Dei Patris Omnipotentis & Filii & Spiritus Sancti & Beatæ Dei Genetricis* Mariæ, *omniumq; Sanctorum*, Excommunicamus, *Anathematizamus & à limitibus Sanctæ Matris Ecclesiæ sequestramus illos Malefactores* N. *consentaneos quoq; & participes & nisi resipuerint & ad satisfactionem venerint, sic extinguatur lucerna eorum ante viventem in sæcula sæculorum*, Fiat, Fiat, Fiat, Amen. *Ex emendat. Legum* Will. Conquestor *in lib. vocat, Textus Roffensis.*

Excommunicato capiendo, Is a Writ directed to the Sheriff for the apprehension of him who standeth obstinately *excommunicated* forty dayes, for such a one not seeking Absolution, hath, or may have his Contempt certified into the *Chancery*, whence issueth this Writ, for the laying of him up without Bail or Mainprise, until he conform himself, *F. N. B. fol.* 62. 5. *Eliz. cap.* 23. *Reg. Orig. fol.* 65, 67, 70.

Excommunicato deliberando, Is a Writ to the Under-Sheriff, for the delivery of an *excommunicate* person out of Prison, upon Certificate of the Ordinary of his Conformity to the Jurisdiction Ecclesiastical, *F. N. B. fol.* 63. and *Reg. Orig. fol.* 65. & 67.

Excommunicato recipiendo, Is a writ whereby persons *excommunicate*, being, for their obstinacy, committed to Prison, and unlawfully delivered thence, before they have given Caution to obey the Authority of the Church, are commanded to be sought for, and laid up again, *Reg. Orig. fol.* 67.

Executione facienda, Is a Writ commanding *execution* of a Judgment; The divers uses whereof, see in the Table of the *Register Judicial, verbo* Executione facienda.

Executione facienda in withernamium, Is a Writ that lies for the taking of his Cattel, that formerly hath conveyed out of the County the Cattel of another, so that the Bayliff having authority from the Sheriff to Replevy the Cattel so convey'd away, could not *execute* his Charge, *Reg. Orig. fol.* 82.

Execution, *Executio*, In the Common-Law signifies the last performance of an act, as of a *Fine* or a *Judgment*. And the *execution* of a *Fine*, is the obtaining possession actually of the things contained in the same by vertue thereof, which is either by Entry into the Lands, or by Writ; whereof see at large *West, part.* 2. *Symbol. tit.* Fines, *sect.* 136, 137, 138. Executing of Judgments and Statutes, and such like, see F. N. B. *in Indice* 2. *verbo* Execution. *Co.* in his 6. *Rep. Blomfields* Case, *fol.* 87. maketh two sorts of *Executions*, one *final*, another with a *quousq*; tending to an end: An *Execution final*, is that which maketh Money of the Defendants Goods, or extendeth his Lands, and delivereth them to the Plaintiff; for this the Party accepteth in satisfaction, and this is the end of the Suit, and all that the Kings Writ commandeth to be done. The other sort with a *quousq*; is tending to an end, and not final; as in the Case of a *Capias ad satisfaciendum*, &c. This is not final, but the Body of the Party is to be taken, to the intent and purpose to satisfie the Demandant, and his Imprisonment is not absolute, but until the Defendant do satisfie, *Idem. ibid.*

Executor, *Executor*, Is he that is appointed by any man in his last Will and Testament, to have the disposing of all his Substance, according to the Contents of the said Will. This *Executor* is either *particular* or *universal*; *Particular*, as if this or that thing onely be committed to his Charge: *Universal*, if all. And this is in the place of him whom the *Civilians* call *Hæredem designatum*, or *Testamentarium*; and the Law accounteth him one person with the Party whose *Executor* he is, as having all advantage of Action against all men that he had, so likewise being subject to every mans Action as himself was. This *Executor* had his beginning in the Civil-Law, by the Constitutions of the Emperors, who first permitted those that thought good by their Wills, to bestow anything upon godly and charitable Uses, to appoint whom they pleased to see the same performed; and if they appointed none, then they ordained, That the Bishop of the place should have Authority of course to effect it, *Lib.* 28. *cap. de Episcopis et Clericis.* And hence probably grew the use of *Universal Executors*, and also brought the Administration of their Goods, that die intestate, unto the Bishop.

Executor de son tort, Or *Executor* of his own wrong, Is he that takes upon him the Office of an *Executor* by intrusion, not being so constituted by the Testator; nor for want thereof, appointed by the Ordinary to Administer. How far he shall be liable to Creditors, see 43 Eliz. *cap.* 8. *Dyer* 166. and *vide etiam libellum vocat. The Duty of* Executors, *cap.* 14.

Exemplification of Letters Patents, *Anno* 13 Eliz. *cap.* 6. Is a Copy or Duplicate of *Letters Patent* made from the Inrolment thereof, and sealed with the Great Seal of *England*, which *Exemplifications* are as effectual to be shewed or pleaded as the Originals themselves. *Nota*, nothing but matter of Record ought to be *exemplified*, 3. *Inst. fol.* 173. See *Co.* 5. *Rep. Pages* Case.

Exemplificatione, Is a writ granted for the *exemplification* of an Original. See *Reg. Orig. fol.* 290.

Exemption, Is a Priviledge to be free from Service or Appearance, and therefore a Baron and Baroness *dignitatis causa*, are *exempted* to be sworn upon any Enquest, *Co. lib.* 6. *fol.* 53. Also Knights, Clerks, and Women are *exempted* to appear at the Sheriffs Turn, by the Statute of *Marlb. cap.* 10. And a man may be *exempted* from being put upon Enquests and Juries by the Kings Letters Patent, as the Colledge of *Physitians, London*, were by Letters Patent of *Hen.* 8. *Co. lib.* 8. *fol.* 108.

Ex gravi Querela, Is a Writ that lyeth for him to whom any Lands or Tenements in Fee within a City, Town or Borough, being devisable, are devised by Will, and the Heir of the Devisor entreth into them, and detaineth them from him, *Reg. Orig. fol.* 244. *Old. Nat. Brev. fol.* 87. See *F. N. B. fol.* 198.

Exhibit, *Exhibitum*, When a Deed, Acquittance, or other writing is in a Chancery Suit *exhibited* to be proved by Witness, and the Examiner writes on the back that it was shewed to such a one at the time of his Examination; this is there called *an Exhibit*. The word is mentioned 14 *Car.* 2. *cap.* 14.

Exigendary of the Common Bench, *Exigendarius de Banco Communi*, Is otherwise called *Exigenter*, 10 *H.* 6. *cap.* 4. and is an Officer belonging to that Court, for which see *Exigenter*.

Exigent, *Exigenda*, Is a Writ that lyeth where the Defendant in an Action personal cannot be found, nor any thing within the County whereby he may be attached or distrained; and is directed to the Sheriff, to proclaim and call five County-dayes one after another, charging him to appear under the pain of Outlawry, *Termes* *de la Ley*. This writ lyeth also in an Indictment of Felony, where the Party indicted cannot be found. *Smith de Rep. Ang. lib.* 2. *cap.* 19. It seemeth to be called an *Exigent*, because it exacteth the Party, that is, requireth his Appearance to answer the Law; for if he come not at the last dayes Proclamation, he is said to be *Quinquies exactus*, and then is Outlawed, *Crom. Jurisd. fol.* 188. And this *Manwood* also setteth down for the Law of the *Forest, cap.* 18. See the *New Book of Entries, verbo Exigent*.

Exigenter, *Exigendarius*, 18 *H.* 6. *cap.* 9. Is an Officer of the Court of *Common-Pleas*, of whom there be four in number: They make all *Exigents* and Proclamations in all Actions, where Process of Outlawry doth lie, and Writs of *Supersedeas*, as well as the *Protonotaries*, upon such *Exigents* as were made in their Offices. But the making Writs of *Supersedeas* is since taken from them by an Officer in the same Court, erected by King *James* by Letters Patent, towards the later end of his Reign.

Ex mero motu, Are words formally used in any Charter of the Prince, whereby he signifieth, that he doth that which is contained in the Charter of his own will and motion, without Petition or Suggestion made by any other; and the effect of these words are to bar all Exceptions that might be taken unto the Instrument, wherein they be contained, by alledging, that the Prince in passing that Charter was abused by any false Suggestion, *Kitchin, fol.* 152. *Co. lib.* 1. *fol.* 45.

Ex Officio, By a Branch of a Stat. made 1 *Eliz. cap.* 1. the Queen by her Letters Patent might authorize any persons, &c. to administer an Oath *Ex Officio*, whereby the supposed Offendor was forced to confess, accuse, or clear himself of any criminal Matter, &c. But this branch relating to the said Oath is repealed by the late Stat. 17 *Car.* 1. *cap.* 11.

Exoneratione sectæ, Is a Writ that lyeth for the Kings Ward, to be disburthened of all Suit, &c. to the County, Hundred, Leet, or Court-Baron, during the time of his Wardship, *F. N. B. fol.* 158.

Ex parte, Of the one part; In the Chancery it hath this signification, as a Commission *ex parte*, is that which is taken out and executed by one side onely; whereas a Joynt-Commission is by consent, and joyning of both.

Ex parte talis, Is a Writ that lyeth for a Bayliff, or Receiver, that having Auditors assigned to hear his Account, cannot obtain of them reasonable allowance, but is cast into Prison by them, *F. N. B. fol.* 129. The manner in this case is to take this Writ out of the Chancery, directed to the Sheriff, to take the four Mainpernors, to bring his Body before the Barons of the Exchequer at a day certain, and to warn the Lord to appear at the same time, *Termes de la Ley, verb.* Account.

Expectant, Is used in the Common-Law with this word *Fee*, and thus it is opposite to Fee-simple. For example, Lands are given to a man and his wife in *Frank marriage*, to *Have and to Hold* to them and their Heirs. In this case, they have Fee-simple: But if it be given to them, and the Heirs of their Body, &c. they have Tail and Fee *expectant*, *Kitchin, fol.* 153, *Mathæus de afflictis* useth the Adjective *Expectativa* substantively in the same signification, *Decis* 292, *num.* 2. *pag.* 412.

Explees. See *Esplees*.

Expeditate, *Expeditare*, Is a word usual in the Forest, to cut out the Balls of the great Dogs feet, for the preservation of the Kings Game: Every one that keepeth any great Dogs not *expeditated*, forfeiteth to the King three shillings four pence, *Cromp. Jurisd. fol.* 152. *Manwood* useth the same word in his *Forest Laws*, cap. 16. num. 6. 8. setting down the manner of *expeditating* Dogs heretofore, saying, That the three Claws of the fore-foot on the right side, shall be cut off by the skin; whereunto he also adds out of the Ordinance called the *Assise of the Forest*, that the same manner of *expeditating* Dogs shall be still used and kept, and no other. *Quære*, how it happens that *Crompton* and he differ. The one saying, the ball of the foot must be cut out; the other, that the three fore-claws are to be cut off by the skin, 4. *par. Inst. fol.* 308.

Expenditors, *Anno* 37 *H.* 8. *cap.* 11. Seems to signifie those that pay, disburse, or *expend* the Tax in the Statute mentioned, by *Anno* 7 *Jac. cap.* 2. *Paymaster*.

Expensis militum levandis, Is directed to the Sheriff, for levying the allowance for Knights of the Parliament, *Reg. Orig. fol.* 191.

Expensis militum non levandis ab hominibus de antiquo Dominico, nec a Nativis, Is a Writ to prohibit the Sheriff from levying any allowance for the Knights of the Shire, upon those that hold in ancient Demesne, &c. *Reg. Orig. fol.* 261.

Explorator, A Scout, *In memoriam* Henrici Croft *equitis aurati*, Exploratoris *in Hibernia Generalis, qui obiit*, *Anno* 1609. where *Explorator Generalis* signifies Scout-Master-General. Sometimes also it is used for a Hunts-man, as *Idem Abbas habens* exploratores *suos* (his Hunts-men) *ponere fecit retia, &c.* In *Itin. Pickering*, 8 Ed. 3. Rot. 4.

Extend, *Extendere*, In a legal sense denotes to value the Lands or Tenements of one bound by Statute, &c. that hath forfeited his Bond to such at an indifferent rate, as by the yearly Rent the Obligor may in time be paid his Debt. The course and circumstances hereof, see in *F. N. B. fol.* 131. *Brief de execution sur Statute-Merchant*.

Extendi facias, Is a Writ ordinarily call'd *a Writ of Extent*, whereby the value of Land, &c. is commanded to be made and levyed in divers cases, which see in the Table of the *Register Original*.

Extent, *Extenta*, Hath two significations, sometimes signifying a Writ or Commission to the Sheriff, for the valuing of Lands or Tenements, *Reg. Judic. in tabula*. Sometime the act of the Sheriff, or other Commission upon this Writ, *Bro. tit.* Extent, *fol.* 313. 16 & 17 *Car.* 2. *cap.* 5.

Extinguishment, In our Law signifies an effect of Consolidation: For example, If a man have due to him a yearly Rent out of any Lands, and afterwards purchase the same Lands, now both the Property and Rent are consolidated or or united in one Possessor; and therefore the Rent is said to be *extinguished*. In like manner it is, where a man hath a Lease for years, and afterwards buyeth the Property; this is a Consolidation of the Property and the Fruits, and is an *extinguishment* of the Lease, see *Termes de la Ley*. So if a man have a High-Way appendant, and after purchase the Land wherein the High-way is; then the way is *extinct*, and so it is of Common-Appendant. But if a man have an Estate in Land but for Life or Years, and hath Fee-simple in the Rent; then the Rent is not *extinguisht*, but in *suspence* for the time; and after the term, the Rent shall be revived.

Extirpatione, Is a Writ Judicial, that lyeth against him, who after a Verdict found against him for Land, &c. doth maliciously overthrow any House upon it, &c. and it is two-fold, one *ante Judicium*, the other *post Judicium*, *Reg. Jud. fol.* 13. 56. 58.

Extortion, *Extortio*, Is an unlawful or violent wringing of Money or Money-worth from any man: For Example, If any Officer, by terrifying any the Kings Subjects in his Office, take more than his ordinary Duties or Fees, he committeth this offence, and is inditable for it. To this (saith Mr. *West*) may be referred the Exaction of unlawful Usury, winning by unlawful Games; and in one word, all taking of more than is due, by colour or pretence of Right, as excessive Toll in Millers, excessive prices of Ale, Bread, Victuals, Wares, &c. *West Symbol part* 2. *tit.* Indictments, *sect.* 65. *Manwood* saith, That *Extortion* is *colore Officii*, and not *virtute Officii*. *Crompton* in his *Justice of Peace*, *fol.* 8. hath these words, Wrong done by any man is properly a Trespass, but excessive wrong by any man is called *Extortion*; and this is most properly in Officers, as Sheriffs, Mayors, Bayliffs, Escheators, and the like, that by colour of their Office do great Oppression, and excessive Wrong unto the People, in taking excessive Rewards or Fees, for the execution of their Office: Great diversity of Cases touching *Extortion*, you may read in *Cromp. Justice of Peace*, fol. 48, 49, 50. See the difference between *colore Officii & virtute vel ratione Officii*, Plow. *fol.* 64. *Dives* Case. This word is used in the same signification in other Countries; for *Cavalcanus de brachio Regio*, part 5. num. 21. thus describeth it, *Et* extortio *dicitur fieri, quando Index cogit aliquid sibi dari quod non est debitum vel quod est ultra debitum, vel ante tempus petit id, quod post administratam justitiam debetur.*

Extracts or **Extreats**. See *Estreats*.

Eyre. See *Eire*.

Ey, *Insula*, An Island, *Doomsday*.

Eyet, *Insuletta*, A small Island or Islet: It is corruptly called by the Moderns vulgarly *an Eyght*.

F

F. Who ever maliciously shall strike any person with a Weapon in the Church or Church-yard, or draw any weapon there with intent to strike, shall have one of his Ears cut off; and if he have no Ears, shall be marked on the Cheek with a hot Iron, with the letter F. that he may be known for a Fighter, or maker of Frays, 5 & 6 *E.* 6. *cap.* 4.

Fabrick-Lands, Are *Lands* given to the rebuilding, repair, or maintenance of Cathedrals, or other Churches, and mentioned in the Act *of Oblivion*, 12. *Car.* 2. *cap.* 8. In ancient time every one almost gave by his Will, more or less to the *Fabrick* of the Cathedral or Parish-Church where he lived. And these were called *Fabrick-Lands*, because given *ad* Fabricam *Ecclesiæ reparandum. In Dei nomine Amen*, &c. *Die veneris ante festum Nativitatis sancti* Johannis Baptistæ, *Anno Domini*, 1423. *Ego* Richardus Smith *de*, &c. *Item lego* Fabricæ *Ecclesiæ Cathedralis* Hereford xii d. *Item lego* Fabricæ *Capellæ beatæ* Mariæ *de* Bromyard xl. d. These *Fabrick Lands* by the Saxons were called *Timber-Lands*.

Faculty, *Facultas*, As it is restrained from the original and active signification, to a particular understanding in Law, is used for a Priviledge, or special Power granted unto a man by favour, Indulgence and Dispensation, to do that which by the Common-Law he cannot do; as to eat Flesh upon days prohibited, to Marry without Banes first asked, to hold two or more Ecclesiastical Livings; the Son to succeed the Father in a Benefice, and such like. And for the granting of these, there is an especial Court under the Archbishop of *Canterbury* called *The Court of the Faculties*, and the chief Officer thereof the Master of the *Faculties*, *Magister ad Facultates*, whose power to grant as aforesaid, was given by 25 *H.* 8. *cap.* 21. See 28 *H.* 8. *cap.* 16. and 4. *par. Inst. fol.* 337.——Engl. *Anno* 4 *E.* 4. *cap.* 1.

Faynt alias Feynt Action, Is as much as *fayned Action*, viz. such an *Action* as though the words of the writ be true, yet for certain Causes he hath no Title to recover thereby, whereas in a false *Action* the words of the writ are false; yet in *Co.* upon *Lit. fol.* 144. & 361. they seem to be confounded as *Synonyma*.

Faynt pleader, *Falsa placitatio*, Cometh of the French *Feynt*, a Participle of the Verb *feindre*, *simulare*, *fingere* and *pledoir*, *placitare*. It signifies a false, covenous, or collusory manner of *pleading*, to the deceit of a third Party, *Anno* 34 & 35 *H.* 8. *cap.* 24.

Faire alias **Feyre**, (*Feria*) Cometh of the French *Feire*, and signifies as much as *Nundinæ* with the *Civilians*, that is, a solemn or greater sort of Market granted to any Town by Priviledge, for the more speedy and commodious provision of such things as the Subject needeth, or the utterance of such things as we abound in above our own uses and occasions; both our English and the French word seemeth to come of *Feriæ*, because it is always incident to a *Fair* by priviledge, that a man may not be molested or arrested in it for any other Debt, than what was first contracted in the same, or at least was promised to be paid there, 17 *E.* 4. *cap.* 2. and 1 *R.* 3. *cap.* 6.

Fayre pleading, See *Beau-pleader*.

Fayling of Record, *Fayler de Record*, Is, when an action is brought against one, who pleads any matter of Record, and avers to prove it by *Record*: And the Plaintiff saith, *Nul tiel Record*, whereupon the Defendant hath a day given him

him to brings it in, at which day he *fails*, or brings in such a one as is no bar to this Action; this is said to be a *failer of Record*, &c. *Termes de la Ley* 346.

Fait, In Latine *Factum*, A Deed, which is a writing sealed and delivered, to prove and testifie the Agreement of the Parties, whose Deed it is, and consists of three principal Points, *Writing Sealing* and *Delivery*. By *writing* is shewed the Parties name to the Deed, their dwelling-places, degrees, thing granted, upon what Consideration, the Estate limited, the time when granted, and whether simply, or upon condition, &c. 2. *Sealing* is a farther testimony of their consents, as appears by these words, *In witness whereof, &c. In cujus rei testimonium, &c.* without which the Deed is insufficient. In the time of the Saxons our Ancestors they onely subscribed their Names, commonly adding the sign of the Cross, and in the end set down a great number of Witnesses, not using any kind of Seal, which fashion continued until the Norman Conquest; whose Custom by little and little prevailing, brought in the use of Seals. The first sealed Charter in *England*, is supposed to be that of *Edward the Confessor* to the Abbey of *Westminster*, which he being educated in *Normandy* brought thence: This change is mentioned by *Ingulphus*, who came in with the *Conqueror*, in these words, *Normanni Chirographorum confectionem (cum crucibus aureis & aliis signaculis sacris in Anglia firmari solitam) in ceram impressam mutant, modumq; scribendi Anglicum rejiciunt*; but this Custom was at first used only by the Nobility, as appears in the History of *Battell Abbey*, where *Richard Lucy* chief Justice of *England*, in the time of *Henry* the Second, is reported to have blamed a mean person for using a Seal, which (he said) pertained only to the Nobility; yet in *Edward* the Thirds time Seals became very common, according to every mans fancy. 3. *Delivery*, though it be set last, is not the least; for after a Deed is written and sealed, if it be not delivered, it is to no purpose: And therefore in all Deeds, care must be taken that the Delivery be well proved.

Faitours, Seemeth to be a French word antiquated, or something traduced; for the modern French word is *Faiseur*, that is, *factor*: It is used in the old repealed Statute, 7 *R.* 2. *cap.* 5. and in the evil part signifying a bad Doer. It may not improperly be interpreted an idle Liver, taken from *Faytardise*, which signifies a kind of numbe or sleepy Disease, proceeding of too much sluggishness, which the Latines call *Veturnus*; for in the said Statute it seemeth to be a *Synonymon* with Vagabond.

Falda, A Sheep-fold, *Et quod oves sit levantes & cubantes in propria* falda, &c. *Rot. Cart.* 16 Hen. 3. m. 6.

Faldage, *Faldagium*, Is a priviledge which anciently several Lords reserved to themselves, of setting up Folds for Sheep in any Fields within their Mannors, the better to manure them; and this not onely with their own, but their Tenants Sheep, which they called *Secta faldæ*. This *Faldage* in some places they call *a Fold-course* or *Free-fold*, and in some old Charters *Faldsoca*, that is, *Libertas faldæ* or *faldagii*.

Falesia or **Falazia**, A bank or hill by the Sea-side, *Co.* on *Lit. fol.* 5. *b.* See *Doomsday* Book.

Falke-land alias **Folke-land**. See *Copy hold, and free-hold.*

False Imprisonment, *Falsum imprisonamentum.* Is a Trespass committed against a man by *imprisoning* him without lawful cause: It is also used for the Writ which is brought upon this Trespass, *F. N. B. fol.* 86. 88. *Vide Booke*, and the *New Book of Entries, verbo* False Imprisonment.

False Judicio, Is a Writ that lyeth for *false Judgment* given in the County, Hundred, Court-Baron, or other Courts, being no Courts of Record, be the Plea real or personal, *Reg. Orig. fol.* 15. *F. N. B. fol.* 17. And the *New Book of Entries, verbo* False Judgement.

False Prophecies. See *Prophecies.*

Falso returno brevium, Is a Writ lying against the Sheriff, for false returning of Writs, *Reg. Judic. fol.* 43. *b.*

False Claim, Is, where a man *claimes* more than his due: As the Prior of *Lancaster*, by reason of a Charter, had the tenth of all the Venison, *viz. In carne tantum sed non in corio.* And because he made a *false Claim*, and said, That he ought to have the tenth of all Venison within the Forest of *Lancaster*, as well in *Carne* as in *Corio*; therefore he was *in misericordia de decima venationis suæ in Corio non percipiendo*, Manwoods Forest Laws, *cap.* 25. *num.* 3.

Falsify, Seemeth to signifie to prove a thing to be *false*, *Perkins*, *Dower* 383, 384, 485.

Familia, Is sometimes taken by our Writers for a *Hide*, sometimes called *a Manse*, sometimes *Carucata*, or a *Plough land*, containing as much as one Plough and Oxen can till in one year. *Bede* in his *Ecclesiastical History, lib.* 4. *cap.* 3. hath these words, *Donavit terram quinquaginta* Familiarum *ad construendum Monasterium*: And *Cressy* in his *Church-History, fol.* 723. *Ubi Beda* Familiam, *Saxonicus ejus interpres coætaneus passim Hide reddere t. Anglo-Normanni Carucata terræ*, Gloss. in Script.

Fanaticks, *Anno* 13 *Ca.* 2. *cap.* 6. Is used as a general Name for *Quakers*, *Anabaptists*, and all other Sectaries and Factious Dissenters from the Church of *England*.

Faonatio or **Feonatio**, From the French *Faonner* signifieth a bringing forth of Young, which in *Does* we properly call *Fawning*, *Carta Forestæ, cap.* 8.

Farding or **Farthing of Gold**, Seemeth to be a Coyn used in ancient times, containing in value the Fourth part of a Noble, *viz.* twenty pence in Silver, and in weight the sixth part of an ounce of Gold; that is, of five shillings in Silver, This word is used 9 *H.* 5. *Stat.* 2 *cap.* 7. thus, *Item*, That the King do to be ordained good and just weight of the Noble, half Noble, and *farthing of Gold*, with the Rates necessary to the same for every City, &c. By which place it plainly appeareth to have been a Coyn, as well as the Noble and half Noble.

Farandman, According to the interpretation of *Skene de verbor. Signif.* is a Merchant-Stranger, to whom, by the Laws of *Scotland*, Justice

Justice ought to be done with all expedition, that his Business or Journey be not hindred.

Fardel of Land, Is according to some Authors, the fourth part of a *Yard-Land*; yet *Noy* in his *Compleat Lawyer pag.* 57. will have two *fardels of Land* make a Nook, and four Nooks make a Yard Land.

Farding-deal, alias **Farundel of Land**, *Quadrantata terræ*, Signifieth the fourth part of an Acre, *Cromp. Jur. fol.* 220. *Quadrantata terræ* is read in the *Reg. Orig. fol.* 1 *b.* where you have *Denariata & Obolata, Solidata & Librata terræ*, which probably must arise in proportion of quantity, as an half-peny, peny, shilling, pound, rise in value or estimation; then must *Obolata* be half an Acre, *Denariata* an Acre, *Solidata* twelve Acres, and *Librata* twelve score Acres: And yet I find *Viginti libratas terræ vel reditus, Reg. Orig. fol.* 94. and *fol.* 248. whereby it seemeth, that *Librata terræ* is so much as yieldeth twenty shillings *per annum*, and *centum solidatas terrarum, tenementorum & redditum*, fol. 249. And in *F. N. B. fol.* 87. are these words, *Viginti libratas terræ vel reditus*, which argueth it to be so much Lands as twenty shillings *per annum*, see *Furlong*. Others hold *Obolata terræ* to be but half a Perch, and *Denariata* a Perch. See *Spelm. Gloss. verbo* Obolata terræ. *Sciatis, &c. me R. de J. dedisse Medietatem unius Feorwendel terræ, de meo Dominio, &c.* Mon. Ang. 2. *par. fol.* 913. *b.*

Fare, Signifies a Voyage or Passage, or according as we now use it, Money paid for passing by Water, 2 & 3 *P. & M. cap.* 16.

Farley or **Farleu**, In the Mannor of *West-slapton* in *Com. Devon*, if any Tenant die possessed of a Cottage, by custome he must pay six pence to the Lord for a *farley*, which probably may be in lieu of a Heriot; for in some Mannors Westward, they difference *Farleu* as the best good, from Heriot the best Beast.

Farme or **Ferme**, *Firma*, Derived from the Saxon word *Feormian*, which signifies to feed, or yield Victual; for in ancient time the reservation was as well in Victuals as Money. It is usually the chief Messuage in a Village or Town, whereto belongs great demeans of all sorts, and hath been used to be let for term of Life, Years, at Will. The Rent reserved upon such a Lease, is called *Farm*, and the Tenant or Lessee *Farmor*. See *Ferme*, and *Spelm. Gloss. verbo* Firma.

Farthing of Land, Seems to be a great quantity, and differs much from *Farding-deal*; for in a Book *Of Survey of the Mannor of* West-slapton *in* Com. Devon, there is an Entry thus made, *A. B.* holds six *Farthings of Lands* at 126 *li. per annum.* See *Fardel* and *Farding-deal*.

Fate, Fat or **Vate**, Is a great wooden Vessel, which among Brewers and Malsters is ordinarily used at this day to measure Malt by for expedition, containing eight Bushels, or a Quarter, mentioned 1 H. 5. *cap.* 10. 11 *H.* 6. *cap.* 8. It is also a leaden Pan or Vessel for the making of Salt at *Droitwhich* in the County of *Worcester*, whereof the several Owners or Propietors do claim Estates of Inheritance and Burges-ship. Also a great Brewing-Vessel used by all Brewers to run their Wort into.

Fautors, 16 *R.* 2. *cap.* 5. Are Favorers, Supporters or Abettors.

Fealty, *Fidelitas*, Cometh of the French *Feaulte*, that is *Fides*, and signifieth in our Common-Law an Oath, taken at the admittance of every Tenant to be true to the Lord, of whom he holdeth his Land: And he that holdeth Land by this onely Oath, holdeth in the freest manner that any man in *England* under the King may hold: Because all with us that have Fee-hold *per fidem & fiduciam*, that is, by *fealty* at the least, *Smith de Repub. Ang. lib.* 3. *cap.* 8. For *fidelitas* is *de substantia feudi*, as *Duarenus* saith, *de Feud.* cap. 2. num. 4. And *Mattheus de afflictis descis*, 320. num. 4. pag. 465. saith, That *fidelitas est substantiale feudi non servitium*: The particulars of his Oath, as it is used among the *Feudists*, you may read well exprest by *Zasius* in his *Tractate de feudis, part.* 7. *num.* 15, 16. which is worth the comparing with the usual Oath taken here in *England*. This *fealty* is also used in other Nations, as the *Lombards* and *Burgundians*, *Cassanæus de consuet. Burgund.* pag. 419, 420. And indeed the very creation of this Tenure, as it grew from the Love of the Lord towards his Followers, so did it bind the Tenant to Fidelity, as appeareth by the whole course of the *Feods*; and the breach thereof, is the loss of the Fee, *Duarenus in Commentariis feudorum*, cap. 14. num. 11. *Et Wesenbechius in tract. de feudorum*, cap. 15. num. 4. *Et sequen. Antonius Contius in methodo feudorum*, cap. *quibus modis feudum amittitur. Hotoman* in his *Commentaries de verbis feudalibus*, sheweth a double *fealty*; one general, to be performed by every Subject to his Prince; the other special, required onely of such as in respect of their Fee are tyed by this Oath to their Landlords: We may read of both in the *Grand Customary* of *Normandy*, being of course performed to the Duke by all resiant within the Dutchy. This *fealty* special is among us performed either by Freemen or Villains. The form of both see in *Anno* 14 *E.* 1. *Stat.* 2. in these words, When a Freeman shall do *fealty* to his Lord, he shall hold his right Hand upon a Book, and say thus, *Hear you my Lord* R, *that I* A. B. *shall be to you faithful and true, and shall owe my* Fealty *to you, for the Land that I hold of you, and truly shall do you the Customs and Services that I ought to do to you at the termes assigned: So help me God, and all his Saints.* And shall kiss the Book, but he shall not kneel. When a Villain shall do *Fealty* to his Lord, he shall hold his right Hand over the Book, and say thus, *Hear you my Lord* R, *that I* R. F. *from this day forth unto you shall be true and faithful and shall owe you* Fealty *for the Land which I hold of you in Villenage, and shall be justified by you both in Body and Goods: So help me God, and all his Saints.* See *Reg. Orig. fol.* 302. *a Fidelitas* (saith *Spelman*) *est fidei, obsequii & servitii ligamen, quo generaliter subditus Regi*, particularly, *Vassallus domino astringitur.*

Fee, *Feudum vel feodum*, Cometh of the French word *Fief*, i. *predium beneficiarium vel res clientelaris*, and is used in our Common Law, to signifie divers things: As first, all those Lands which we hold by perpetual Right, as *Hotoman* well noteth *verbo Feodum, de verbis feudalibus*. Our ancient Lawyers have not exprest what they fully meant by it, onely say, that by this Name go all Land and Tenements that are held by any acknowlegment of superiority to a higher Lord. They that write of this Subject, divide all Lands & Tenements where a man hath a perpetual Estate to him and his Heirs,&c. into *Allodium, & feudum.* 1. *Allodium,* They define to be every mans own Land, &c.which he possesseth meerly in his own Right,without acknowledgment of any Service, or payment of any Rent to another; and this is a property in the highest degree. 2 *Feudum,* Is that which we hold by the benefit of another, and in the Name whereof we owe Service,or pay Rent, or both, to a superior Lord: And all our Land here in *England*(the Crown-Lands being in the Kings own Hands,in the Right of his Crown excepted) is in the Nature of *feudum* or *fee*; for though many have Land by descent from their Ancestors,& others have dearly purchased Land with their Money; yet is the Land of such a nature,that it cannot come to any either by descent or purchase, but with the burthen that was laid upon him, who had *Novel Fee*, or first of all received it as a benefit from his Lord to him and to all such to whom it might descend,or any way be conveyed from him. So that in truth no man hath *directum Dominium,*the very property or demain in any Land, but onely the Prince in the Right of his Crown,*Camb.Brit.pag.* 93.For though he that hath *fee*, hath *jus perpetuum & utile Dominium*;yet he oweth a duty for it,& therefore is it not simply his own; which thing,I take those words, that we use for the expressing of our deepest rights in any Lands or Tenements to import; For he that can say most of his Estate, sayes thus, *I am seised of this or that Land or Tenement in my Demain as of* Fee, *Seisitus inde in Dominico meo ut de feudo,* and that is as much as if he said, It is my Demain or proper Land after a sort, because it is to me and my Heirs for ever; yet not simply mine,because I hold it in the nature of a benefit from another. Yet the Statute of 37 *H.* 8 16. useth these words of Lands invested in the Crown; but it proceedeth from the not knowing the nature of this word *Fee*, for *fee* cannot be without Fealty sworn to a Superior, as you may read partly in the word *Fealty*,but more at large in those,that write *de feudis*, and in particular *Hotoman* both in his *Commentaries* and *Disputations*. And note, that Land, &c. with us is termed *Fee* in two respects, one as it belongeth to us and our Heirs for ever, the other as it holdeth of another.*Britton, cap.*32. defineth it thus; *Fee* is a Right consisting in the person of the true Heir,or of some other that by just Title hath purchased it. *Fleta* saith, *Feudum est quod quis tenet ex quacunq; causa sibi & heredibus suis, sive sit tenementum sive reditus qui non proveniunt ex Camera & alio modo dicitur feudum, sicut ejus qui feoffant & quod quis tenet ab alio sicut dicitur, talis tenet de tali tot feuda per servitium militare,* Lib. 5. cap. 5. sect.*feudum autem.* And all that write *de feudis*, hold, that *feudatarius* hath not an intire property in his *Fee*. The divisions of *fee* in divers respects are many, and worthy to be known;but we divide them onely into *Fee absolute*,otherwise termed *Fee simple*; and *Fee conditional*, otherwise called *Fee-tayl*. *Fee-simple, feodum simplex* is that of which we are seized in these general words, To Us and Our Heirs for ever.*Fee-tayl, feodum talicatum* is that whereof we are seised to Us and our Heirs, with limitation, that is, the Heirs of our Body, &c. And this *Fee-tail* is either *general* or *special: General* is, where Land is given to a man and the Heirs of his Body; the reason whereof is given by *Littleton, lib.* 1. *cap.* 2. because a man seised of Land by such a Gift, if he marry one or more Wives, and have no Issue by them, and at length marry another by whom he hath Issue; this Issue shall inherit the Land. *Fee-tail special* is that, where a man and his wife be seised of Lands to them and the Heirs of their two Bodies. The reason is given likewise by *Littleton* in the same place, because in this case the wife dying without Issue,and he marrying another,by whom he hath Issue; this Issue cannot inherit the Land, being specially given to such Heirs, &c. This *Fee tail* hath the Original from the Statute of *Westm.* 2. *cap.* 1. made 13 E. 1. Yet see *Bracton, lib.* 2. *cap.* 5. *num.* 3. *in his verbis, Item quædam absoluta & larga, & quædam stricta & coarctata sicut certis hæredibus.* To whom add *Plowden, fol.* 235. *Willions* Case, for before that Statute, all Land given to a man and his Heirs, either *general* or *special*, was accounted in the nature of a *Fee*; and therefore held to be so firmly in him to whom it was given,that any limitation notwithstanding he might alien, and sell it at his pleasure, much like that which the *Civilians* call *Nudum præceptum*, binding rather by counsel and advice, than compulsion or restraint. But this seeming unreasonable to the wisdom of our Realm, that a man meaning well to this or that Posterity of himself, or his Friends,might be forthwith deceived of his Intention; the said Statute was made for redress of that inconvenience, whereby it is ordained, That if a man give Lands in *fee*, limiting the Heir,to whom it shall descend,with a Reversion to himself, or his Heirs, for default, &c.that the form and true meaning of his Gift shall be observed: He then that hath *fee*,holdeth of another by some duty or other,which is called *Service*; and of this Service, and the diversity thereof, see *Chivalry* and *Service*.Secondly,This word *Fee* is sometimes used with us for the compass or circuit of a Mannor or Lordship, *Bracton, lib* 2. *cap.* 5. *In eadem villa & de eodem feodo.* Thirdly, It is used for a perpetual Right incorporeal,as to have the Keeping of Prisons in *fee*, *Old Nat. Brev. fol.* 41. *Foster* in *fee*, *Eod fol.* 6. Rent granted in *fee*, *Eod. fol.* 8. Sheriff in *fee*, 28 *E.* 1 *Stat.* 3. *cap.* 8. Lastly, It is taken for a Reward or Wages given to one for the execution of his Office, as the *fee*,of a Forester, of a Keeper of a Park, or of a Sheriff for serving an Execution, limited by 20 *Eliz.cap.* 4. And also for that consideration given a Serjeant at Law or Counsellor, or a Physitian, for their Counsel and Advice in their Profession, which,as it is well observed by Sir *John Davis*, in his *Preface to his Reports*, is not properly *Merces*, but *Honorarium*; yet in the Law Language it is called a *Fee*.

Fee expectant, Is by the *Feudists* termed *feudum expectativum*, or *expectativa* substantively used, *Matthæus de afflictis descis* 292. *num.* 2. *pag.* 417. See *Expectant*.

Fee-farme, *Feudi firma*, Is a compound of *Fee*, and *ferme*, *prædium*, and signifieth in a legal sense Land held of another in *fee*, that is in perpetuity to himself and his Heir, for so much yearly Rent as it is reasonably worth, more or less, so it be the fourth part of the worth, *Old Tenures.* See *Exposition of the Statute of Gloucester, Anno* 6 *E.* 1. without Homage, Fealty or other Services,other than be specially comprised in the

 Feoff-

Feoffment; But by *Fitzh.* in his *Nat. Brev. fol.* 210. it seemeth, that the third part of the value may be appointed for the Rent, or the finding of a Chaplain to sing Divine-Service, &c. And the nature of it is thus, that if the Rent be behind and unpaid for the space of two years, then the Feoffor, or his Heirs, have Action to recover the Lands as their Demesnes, *Britton, cap. 66. num.* 4. But observe, that *West* in his *Symbol, part.* 1. *lib.* 2. *sect.* 463. that the Feoffment may contain Services and suit of Court, as well as Rent. And in *Termes de la Ley*, that Fee-farme, oweth Fealty, though not expressed in the Feoffment, for that Fealty belongeth to all kind of Tenures; this is near the nature of that which, among the *Civilians*, is called *Ager Vectigalis, qui in perpetuum licetur, i. hac lege, ut quamdiu pro eo Vectigal pendatur, tam diu neq; ipsis qui conduxerunt, neq; iis qui in locum eorum successerunt auferri eum liceat.*

Feed alias **Feud**, *Feida* alias *fayda*, Signifieth in the German Tongue, *Guerram*, that is, *Capitales inimicitias. Hottoman* Disput. *De feudis, cap.* 2. *Lambert* in his Exposition of Saxon words, writs it *Feeth*, and saith likewise, That it denotes *Capitales inimicitias*: And also that *Feud* now used in *Scotland*, and the North-parts of *England*, is the same, that is, a Combination of Kinred, to revenge the death of any of their Blood against the Killer, and all his Race. See *Skene de verbor.* Signif. *verbo* Affidatio.

Felo de se, Is he that commits *Felony* by murthering of himself, *Cromptons Just. of Peace, fol.* 28. and *Lamb. Eirenarc. lib.* 2. *cap.* 7. *pag.* 243.

Felony, *Felonia*, Seemeth to come of the French *Felonie*, (i.) *impetuositas. Felonia*, saith *Hotoman, de verbis feudalibus, non contumaciam vassalli in Dominum, hujusve in Vassallum perfidiam significat verum quodvis capitale facinus.* And again, Felonia, *Gothis & Longobardis dicitur quod Germanis hodie* Schelmarey, *Latinis* Scelus. Sir *Edward Coke* sayes, *Ideo dicta est* felonia, *quia fieri debet* felleo *animo*, lib. 4. fol. 124. *Hostiensis in sua summa, tit.* de Feudis. And others write of it thus, *Est culpa vel injuria propter quam Vassallus amittit feudum, &c.* But we account any Offence *Felony*, that is in degree next Petit Treason, and compriseth divers particulars, as Murther, Theft, killing of a mans Self, Sodomy, Rape, wilful burning of Houses, and such like; which are to be collected out of the Statutes, which have made many Offences *Felony* that before were not. *Felony* is differenced from lighter Offences in this, that the punishment thereof is death, yet not in all cases: For *Petit Larceny*, which is the stealing of any thing under the value of twelve pence, is *felony*, as appeareth by *Broke, tit.* Coron. *num.* 2. his reason is, because the Indictment against such a one must have these words, *Felonice Cepit*; and yet this is not punished by Death, though it be loss of Goods. Any other Exception I know not, but that a man may call that *Felony*, which is under *Petit Treason*, and punished by death. And of this may be reckoned two sorts, one lighter, that for the first time may have the benefit of the Clergy, another that may not. And these you must learn to know from the Statutes, for Clergy is allowed, where it is not expresly taken away. Of this read *Stam. pl. cor. lib.* 1. from the end of the second Chapter to the 39, and the Statutes. See also *Lamberts Justice of Peace. lib.* 2. *cap.* 7. in a Table drawn for that purpose. And also *Lib.* 4. *cap.* 4. *pag.* 404. And *Cromp. Justice of Peace, fol.* 32, *&c. Felony* is also punisht by loss of Lands not entailed, and Goods and Chattels as well real as personal; and yet by the 37H. 8. *cap.* 6. a difference is made in some cases touching Land. This Offence ordinarily worketh corruption of Blood, unless expresly provided against by Statute, as 39 *Eliz. cap.* 17. How many wayes *felony* may be committed. see *Termes de la Ley, pag.* 357, 358. and *Spelm. Glossary.*

Feme Covert, Is a marryed Woman, who is also said to be under *Covert-Baron*, 27 Eliz. 3.

Fence-moneth, *Mensis vetitus*, Is a moneth wherein it is unlawful to hunt in the Forest, because in that time the Female Deer do fawn. It begins alwayes fifteen dayes before *Midsummer*, according the Charter of the Forest, *viz. In initio quindecem dierum ante festum Sancti* Johannis Baptistæ, *quando Agistatores nostri conveniunt pro feonatione bestiarum nastrarum*; and it doth end fifteen dayes after *Midsummer*, which is upon St. *Cyrils-day*: And here observe, That every common *moneth* is but 28 dayes, but the *Fence-moneth* is 31 dayes, *Assisa Forestæ de Pickering, fol.* 20. Searjeant *Fleetwood* in his *Collection of the Forest Laws, fol.* 5. saith, That the *Fence-moneth* hath alwayes been kept with Watch and Ward in every Bayliwick through the whole Forest since the time of *Canutus. Manwood's* Forest Laws, *cap.* 13. and 20 *Car.* 2. *cap.* 3. Some ancient Foresters do call this *moneth, The Defence-moneth*, because then the Deer are to be defended from scare or fear. There are also certain *Defence-moneths*, or seasons for Fish, as appears by *Westm.*2. *cap.* 47. 13 *E.* 1. in these words, All Waters where *Salmons* be taken shall be in *defence* for taking of *Salmons* from the Nativity of our Lady unto St. *Martins-day*, and likewise that young *Salmons* shall not be taken nor destroyed by Nets, &c. from the midst of *April*, to the Nativity of St. *John Baptist.* See also 13 *R.* 2. *Stat.* 1. *cap.* 19.

Fengeld, A Tax or Imposition exacted for the repelling of Enemies, *M. S. Antiq.*

Feodal, *Feodalis vel feudalis*, Of or belonging to the Fee, Fee farme, or Fee simple, *Anno* 12 *Car.* 2. *cap.* 24.

Feodary, **Feudary** or **Feudatary**, *Feudatarius*, Was an Officer in the *Court of Wards*, appointed by the Master of that Court, by vertue of the Statute. 32 *H.* 8. *cap.* 46. to be present with the Escheator in every County at the finding of Offices, and to give in Evidence for the King as well for the value as the tenure: His Office also was to survey the Lands of the Ward after the Office found, and to return the true value thereof into Court; to assign Dower unto the Kings Widows, to receive all the Rents of the Wards Lands within his Circuit, and to answer them to the Receiver of the Court. This Officer is mentioned 32 *H.* 8. *cap.* 46. and is wholly taken away by 12 *Car.* 2. *cap.* 24. And in some antient Writings it appears, that Noblemen had their particular *Feodaries.*

Feoffment, *Feoffamentum*, By the Opinion of Sir *Tho. Smith de Repub. Anglor. lib.* 3. *cap.* 8. And *West. part.* 1. *Symb. lib.* 2. *sect.* 280. is descended

ded from the *Gothish* word *Feudum*, which we interpret *Fee*, and signifieth *donationem feudi*: But (as the same *West* addeth) it signifieth in our Common-Law any Gift or Grant of any Honors, Castles, Mannors, Messuages, Lands or other corporeal and immoveable things of like nature unto another in Fee-simple, that is, to him and his Heirs for ever, by the delivery of Seisin and the possession of the thing given, whether the Gift be made by Deed or Writing: And when it is in writing, it is called *a Deed of Feoffment*, and in every *Feoffement* the Giver is called *the Feoffor*, *Feoffator*, and he that receiveth by vertue of the same *Feoffe*, *Feoffatus*. And *Littleton* saith, That the proper difference between a Feoffor and a Donor is, that the Feoffor giveth in Fee-simple, the Donor in Fee-tail, *Lib.* 1. *cap.* 6. It is the ancient and most necessary Conveyance, because solemn and publick; and also because it cleareth all Disseisins, Abatements, Intrusions, and other defeasible Estates, where the Entry of the Feoffor is lawful, which neither Fine, Recovery, nor Bargain and Sale by Deed indented and inrolled doth, *Ephron* enfeoffed *Abraham*, *Gen.* 23. See *Co.* on *Lit. lib.* 1. *cap.* 1. *sect.* 1.

Feoffor and **Feoffee**, *Feoffor* is he that infeoffs, or makes a Feoffment to another of Lands or Tenements in Fee-simple. And *Feoffee*, is he that is infeoffed, or to whom the Feoffment is so made.

Ferdella terræ, Is ten Acrees. See *Virgata* and *Fardel*.

Ferdindel. See *Farding-deal*.

Ferdfare, *Significat quietantiam eundi in exercitum*. *Fleta lib.* 1. *cap.* 47. that is, to be quit from going to War.

Ferdwit, *Significat quietantiam murdri in exercitu*, Fleta, *lib.* 1. *cap.* 47. that is, to be quit of Murder committed in the Army, *Et sint quieti de Fictwite, Flictwite, & Ferdwite, & Hengwite, & Leirwite, &c.* Charta, 11 H. 3. m. 33.

Ferial-dayes, *Dies feriales*, *feriæ*, According to the proper Latine signification, signifies *Holy dayes*, or dayes vacant from Labor and Pleading; but in the Statute 27 *H.* 6. *cap.* 5. *Ferial-dayes* are taken for *Working-days*.

Ferling, *Ferlingus*, The fourth part of a peny, *Quadrans*, *Quando quarterium frumenti venditur pro* 12 *denar. tunc panis Wastelli de* Ferlingis *ponderabit* 5. *lib. &* 16. *sol. Assis. panis & cervis.* 51 H. 3. *Camden* in his *Brit. tit. Huntington*, sayes, There were in this Borough four *Ferlings*, that is, quarters of Wards.

Ferlingata terræ, The fourth part of a Yard-Land, *Decem acræ faciunt unam* Firlingatam, 4. Firlingatæ *virgatam*, 4. *Virgatæ bidam*, & 5. *Hidæ feodum militare*, Esc. 12 Ed. 2. n. 18. Ebor. In ancient Records is used both *Ferlingus & Ferdlingus terræ*. See *Mon. Ang.* 2. *par. fol.* 8.

Ferme or **Farme**, *Firma*, Cometh of the French *Ferme*, *prædium*, and signifieth with us House or Land, or both, taken either by Indenture of Lease, or Lease-parol. This in the North-parts is called *a Tacke*, in *Lancashire* a *Fermholt*, in *Essex a Wike*. We may Conjecture, that both the French and English word came from the Latine *firmus*; for I find *locare ad firmum*, to signifie with others as much as to set or let to *Farme* with us, the reason whereof, may be in respect of the sure hold they have beyond Tenants at Will. *Vide Vocabul. utriusq; juris, verbo* Afflictus. In the *Termes of the Law* it is derived from the Saxon *Feormian*, which signifieth to feed or yield Victual. For in ancient time the Reservations were as well in Victuals as Money: How many wayes *Farme* is taken, see *Plowden*, *fol.* 195. *Wriothesly's* Case.

Fermisona, The Winter-Season of Deer, as *Tempus pinguedinis* is the Summer-Season. See *Tempus pinguedinis*; *Rex dilecto* R. C. &c. *Cum mittamus dilectum valetium nostrum* Johannem *de* F. *ad instantem* Fermisonam *in parcis nostris ibidem, &c.* Claus. 30 Ed. 1. m. 18.

Ferrure, The shooing of Horses.

Festingmen, *Ut illud Monasterium sit liberatum ab illis incommodis quæ nos Saxonica lingua* Festingmen *dicimus*, Mon. Ang. 1. par. fol. 123. a. The Saxon Festenmon, signifies *Fidejussor*, a *Pledge*; so that to be free of *Festingmen*, in probability is to be free of *Frank-Pledge*, and not to be bound for any mans forth-coming, who should transgress the Law.

Feud. See *Feed*.

Feudal. See *Feodal*.

Feudary. See *Feodary*.

Feud-bote, Is a recompence for engaging in a *feud* or faction, and the contingent Damages. It having been the custome of ancient times, for all the Kindred to engage in the Kinsmans Quarrel; according to that of *Tacitus*, *De moribus Germanorum, suscipere tam inimicitias seu patris, seu propinqui, quam amicitias necesse est.*

Fictale, **Fildale** and **Filkale**, *Bracton*, *lib.* 3. *fol.* 117. A compotation or entertainment made for gain by Bayliffs to those of their Hundreds, or rather according to *Co.* 4, *Inst. fol.* 307. An extortion, *colore compotationis*, See *Scotale*.

Fieri facias, Is a Writ Judicial, that lyeth at all times within the year and day, for him that hath recovered in an Action of Debt or Damages, to the Sheriff, to Command him to levy the Debt or the Damages of his Goods against whom the Recovery was had, beginning from *Westm.* 2. *cap.* 18. *Anno* 13 *E.* 1. See *Old Nat. Brev. fol.* 152. See also great diversity thereof in the Table of the *Register Judicial*, *verbo* Fieri facias. See also *Scire facias*, and Title *Execution*.

Fifteenth, *Decima quinta*, Is a Tribute or Imposition of Money laid upon a City, Burrough, or other Town, through the Realm; not by the Pole, or upon this or that man, but in general upon the whole City or Town, and so called, because it amounteth to a *fifteenth* part of that which the City or Town hath been valued at of old; or to a *fifteenth* part of every Mans Goods and personal Estate, according to a reasonable valuation. This is now imposed by Parliament, and every Town through the Realm knoweth what a *fifteenth* for themselves doth amount to, because it is perpetually the same. Whereas the Subsidy, which is raised of every particular Mans Lands or Goods, must needs be uncertain, because the estate of every several man is uncertain. And in that regard, a *fifteenth* seems to be a Rate antiently laid upon every Town, according to the Land or Circuit belonging to it:

Whereof *Camden* in his *Brit.* makes frequent mention, particularly *pag.* 168. of Wells in *Somersetshire* thus, *Quo tempore ut testatur censualis Angliæ liber, Episcopus ipsum oppidum tenuit, quod pro quinquaginta hidis geldavit.* And *pag.* 172. Of Bath, *Geldabat pro viginti hidis, quando schira geldabat.* Thirdly, *pag.* 181. *Old Sarum* or *Salisbury, pro quinquaginta hidis geldabat.* And these Rates were taken out of *Doomsday* Book in the *Exchequer.* So that in old time this seemed to be a yearly Tribute in certainty; whereas now, though the Rate be certain, yet it is not levyed but by Parliament. See *Tax* and *Quinzime.*

Fightwite, A Saxon word, signifying a *Mulct* of 120 shillings, for making a Quarrel to the disturbance of the Peace. So that *Fightwite* is truly *forisfactura pugnæ*, M. S. *codex.*

Filacer, *Filazarius*, Possibly derived from the Latine *filum*, a Thred, Is an Officer in the *Common-Pleas* (so called) because he *files* those Writs whereon he makes Process: There are fourteen of them in their several Divisions and Counties, they make out all original Process, as well real as personal and mixt; and in Actions meerly personal, where the Defendants be returned or summoned, there goeth out the Distress infinite until Appearance; if he be returned *Nihil*, there Process of *Capias* infinite, if the Plaintiff will or after the third *Capias*, the Plaintiff may go to the *Exigenter* of the Shire, where his Original is grounded, and have an Exigent or Proclamation made. Also the *Filacer* maketh all sorts of Writs of view, in Causes where the view is payed; and upon all Replevins or Recordare's, Writs of *returno habendo.* Second Deliverance, and *Withernam*, They enter all Appearances and special Bayls, upon any Processe made by them. They make the first *Scire facias* upon special Bayls; Writs of *Habeas Corpus, Distringas Nuper-vice-comitem vel Ballivum & Duces tecum*, and all *Supersedeas* upon special Bail, or otherwise. Writs of *Habeas corpus cum causa* upon the Sheriffs Return, that the Defendant is detained with other Actions, Writs of adjornment of a Term, in case of Pestilence, War, or publick Disturbance, and (until an Order of that Court made 14 *Jac.* which limited the *Filacers* to all Matters and Proceedings before appearance, and the *Protonotaries* to all after) did enter Declarations, Imparlances, Judgments and Pleas; whereunto a Serjeants hand was not requisite, and made out writs of Execution, and divers other Judicial writs after Appearance. And in the *Kings Bench* of later times, there have been *Filacers* who make Process upon Original writs returnable in that Court, upon Actions *contra pacem.* The *Filacers* of the *Common-Pleas* having been Officers of that Court before the Statute of 10 *H.* 6. *cap.* 4. wherein they mentioned

Filiolus, A little Son properly, sometimes taken for a God-son, sometimes for a Nephew.

Filkale. See *Sothale* and *Fictale.*

File, *Filacium*, Is a Thread or Wyre, whereon writs and other exhibits in Courts and Offices are *filed*, for the more safe keeping of them.

Finders, 18 *E.* 3. *Stat.* 1. and 14 *R.* 2. *cap.* 10. Seem to be all one with those which now we call *Searchers.* See 17 *R.* 2. *cap.* 5. 1. *H.* 4. 13. and 31 *Hen.* 6. *cap.* 5. They are imployed for the discovery of Goods imported or exported, without paying Custome.

Fine, *Finis*, Hath divers Applications in the Common-Law, sometimes being used for a formal or ceremonious Conveyance of Lands or Tenements: Or as *West* saith, *tit.* Fines, *sect.* 25. of any thing inheritable, being *in esse tempore finis*, to the end to cut off all Controversies. The same *West* in his 2. *par. Symbol. sect.* 1. thus defines it, To be a Covenant made before Justices, and entred of Record. But *Glanvile* more nobly thus, *Lib.* 8. *cap.* 1. Finis *est amicabilis compositio &* finalis *concordia ex consensu & licentia Domini Regis vel ejus Justiciariorum.* And *Lib.* 9. *cap.* 3. *Talis concordia* finalis *dicitur, eo quod* finem *imponit negotio, adeo ut neutra pars litigantium ab eo de cætero poterit recedere.* And *Bracton, lib.* 5. *cap.* 28. *num.* 7. thus, Finis *ideo dicitur* finalis *concordia quia imponit* finem *litibus & est exceptio peremptoria.* The Author of the *New Termes of the Law* defineth it to be a *final* Agreement, had between persons concerning any Lands or Rent, or other thing whereof any Suit or Writ is between them, hanging in any Court. See the *New Book of Entries, verbo* Fines, and 27 *E.* 1. *Stat.* 1. *cap.* 1. This *Fine* is of so high a Nature, that *Bracton, lib.* 3. *cap.* 7. *num.* 3. saith of it thus, *Item immediate pertinet ad Regem querela* finis *facti in curia Domini Regis & non observati, & est ratio, quia nemo potest* finem *interpretare nisi ipse Rex, in cujus curia* fines fiunt. The *Civilians* would call this Solemn Contract, *Transactionem judicialem de re immobili*, because it hath all the Properties of a Transaction, if it be considered in the original use, *Wesemb. parat. tit. de Transact.* For it appeareth by the Writers of the Common-Law before recited, that it is nothing but a Composition or Concord acknowledged, and recorded before a competent Judge, touching some Hereditament, or thing immoveable, that before was in Controversie between the Parties to the same Concord: And that for the better credit of the Transaction, being, by imputation, made in the presence of the King, because it is levyed in his Court; and therefore doth it bind Women covert being parties, and others, whom ordinarily the Law disableth to transact, onely for this reason, that all presumption of deceit or evil meaning is excluded, where the King is privy to the act. [Originally the use of this *final* Concord was instituted and allowed, in regard that by the Law, and ancient Proceedings, no Plaintiff (giving real Security *de clamore suo prosequendo*,) could agree without Licence of the Court: So as *Fines* have been anciently levyed in personal Actions.] But subtilty of wit and reason hath in time wrought other uses of this Concord, which in the beginning was but one, *viz.* to secure the Title that any man hath in his possession against all men; to cut off Entails, and with more certainty to pass the Interest or Title of any Land or Tenement, though not controverted, to whom we think good, either for years or in fee: Insomuch, that the passing of a *fine*, in some cases, now is but *mera fictio Juris*, alluding to the use for which it was invented, and supposing a doubt or controversie, where in truth none is; and so not onely to work a present Prescription against the Parties to the Concord or *Fine*, and their Heirs, but within five years against all others, not expresly excepted (if it be levyed upon good consideration, and without covin) as Women-covert, persons under one and twenty years of age,

age, Prisoners, or such as be out of the Realm at the time when it was acknowledged. Touching this matter, see the Statutes, 1 *R*. 3. *cap*. 7. 4 *H*. 7. *cap*. 24. 32 *H*. 8. 36. and 31 *Eliz*. 2. This *Fine* hath in it five essential parts; 1. The Original Writ taken out against the Cognisor. 2. The Kings Licence, giving the Parties liberty to accord, for the which he hath a *Fine* called *The Kings Silver*, being accounted a part of the Revenue of the Crown. 3. The Concord it self which thus beginneth, *Et est concordia talis, &c.* 4. The note of the *Fine*, which is an abstract of the Original Concord, and beginneth in this manner, *sc. Inter* R. *Querentem & S. & E. uxorem ejus deforciantes, &c.* 5. The foot of the *fine*, which beginneth thus, *Hæc est* finalis *concordia facta in curia Domini Regis apud* Westm. *a die Paschæ in quindecem dies, anno, &c.* So as the foot of the *fine* includeth all, containing the day, year and place, and before what Justice made, *Co. vol.* 6. *fol.* 38, 39. *Teyes* Case, This *fine* is either *single* or *double*, A *single fine* is, that by which nothing is granted or rendred back again by the Conusees to the Conusors, or any of them. A *double fine* containeth a grant and render back again, either of some Rent, Common, or other thing out of the Land, or of the Land it self to all, or some of the Cognisors for some Estate, limiting thereby many times remainders to strangers, which be not named in the Writ of Covenant, *West. ubi supra, sect.* 21. Again a *Fine* is of the effect divided into a *fine executed*, and a *fine executory*. A *fine executed*, is such a *fine*, as of his own force giveth a present possession (at the least in Law) unto the Cognisee, so that he needeth no Writ of *Habere facias seisinam* for the execution of the same, but may enter; of which sort is a Fine, *Sur cognizance de droit come ceo que il ad de son* done, that is, upon acknowledgment that the thing mentioned in the Concord be *Jus ipsius Cognizati ut illa quæ idem habet de dono Cognitoris*, West. sect. 51. And the reason of this seemeth to be, because this *fine* passeth by way of Release of that thing, which the Cognisee hath already (at least by supposition) by vertue of a former Gift of the Cognisor, *Co. Rep. lib.* 3. *fol.* 89. Case *of Fines*, which is in very deed the surest *fine* of all *Fines executory* be such as of their own force do not execute the possession in the Cognisees, as *fines sur Conusance de droit tantum*, fines *sur dones*, Grant, Release, Confirmation or Render; for if such *fines* be not levyed, or such Render made unto them that be in possession at the time of the *fines* levyed, the Conusees must needs sue Writs of *Habere facias seisinam*, according to their several Cases, for the obtaining of their Possessions except at the levying such executory *fines*, the Parties unto whom the Estate is by them limited, be in possession of the Lands passed thereby: For in this case such *fines* do enure by way of extinguishment of right, not altering the estate of Possession of the Cognisee, but perchance bettering it, *West, ubi supra, sect.* 20. Touching the form of these *fines*, we must consider, upon what Writ or Action the Concord is to be made, and that is most commonly upon a Writ of Covenant; and then first there must pass a pair of Indentures between the Conusor and Conusee, whereby the Conusor covenanteth with the Conusee, to pass a *fine* unto him of such or such things, by a day set down: And these Indentures, as they are first in this proceeding, so are they said to lead the *fine*; Upon this Covenant, the Writ of Covenant is brought by the Conusee against the Conusor, who hereupon yieldeth to pass the *fine* before a Judge; and so the acknowledgment being recorded, the Cognisor and his Heirs are presently concluded, and all Strangers not excepted, after five years once passed. If the writ whereupon the *fine* is grounded be not a writ of Covenant, but of *Warrantia Chartæ*, or writ of Right, or a Writ of Mesne, or a Writ of Customs and Services (for all these *fines* may also be founded, *West* (*ubi supra sect.* 23.) then this form is observed, the Writ is served upon the Party that is to acknowledge the *fine*, and then he appearing, doth accordingly, see *Dyer*, *fol.* 179. *num.* 46. [*Fines* are now onely levyed in the Court of *Common-Pleas* at *Westminster*, in regard of the Solemnity thereof, ordained by the Stat. 18 *E.* 1. that before were levyed in other places.] This word *fine*, sometimes also signifieth a sum of Money paid for an Income to Lands or Tenements let by Lease, anciently called *Gersuma*; sometimes an amends, pecuniary punishment or recompence upon an Offence committed against the King and his Laws or against the Lord of a Mannor: In which case a man is said *Finem facere de transgressione cum Rege, &c.* Reg. Jud. fol. 25. a. And of the diversity of these *Fines*, with other matter worth the learning, see *Cromptons Justice of Peace*, *fol.* 141. 143. 144. and *Lambards Eiren. lib.* 4. *cap.* 16. *pag.* 555. But in all these diversities of Uses, it hath but one signification, and that is a *finall* Conclusion, or end of Differences between Parties. And in this last sense, wherein it is used for the ending and remission of an Offence, *Bracton* hath it, *Lib.* 2. *cap.* 15. *num.* 8. speaking of a common *fine*, that the County payeth to the King for false Judgments, or other Trespasses to be assessed by the Justices in *Eire* before their departure, by the Oath of Knights, and other good men, upon such as ought to pay it, with whom agreeth the Statute 3 *E.* 1. *cap.* 18. There is also a *common fine* in Leets, see *Kitchin*, *fol.* 13. Vide *Common Fine*. See *Fleta. lib.* 1. *cap.* 48. and *Co.* on *Lit. fol.* 126.

Fines for Alienation, Are reasonable *Fines* paid to the King by his Tenants in chief, for licence to *alien* their Lands according to the Stat. 1 *E.* 3. *cap.* 112. But see the Statute lately made, 12 *Car.* 2. *cap.* 24.

Fines pro licentia concordandi. See 21. *H.* 8. *cap.* 1. See *Fine*.

Fine force, Cometh of the French Adjective *Fin*, signifying sometimes crafty, sometimes artificial or exact, and the Substantive *force* in Latine *Vis*; so that it signifies an absolute necessity or constraint not avoidable; as when a man is constrained to do that which he can no way avoid, we say, He doth it *de fine force*, and in this sense it is used, *Old Nat. Brev. fol.* 78. and in the Statute 35 *H.* 8. *cap.* 12. and in *Perkins Dower* 321. In *Mantell* and *Woodlands* Case, *Plow. fol.* 94. And in *Eytons* Case, cited in *Foxleys* Case, *Co.* 6. *Rep. fol.* 111.

Fine adnullando levato de Tenemento quod fuit de antiquo dominico, Is a Writ to the Justices, for the *disanulling* of a *Fine* levyed of Lands holden in ancient Demesne

to

to the prejudice of the Lord, *Regist. Orig. fol.* 15.

Fine capiendo pro terris, &c. Is a Writ lying for one that, upon Conviction by a Jury, having his Lands and Goods taken into the Kings Hands, and his Body committed to Prison, obtaineth favour for a sum of Money, &c. to be remitted his Imprisonment, and his Lands and Goods to be redelivered unto him, *Reg. Orig. fol.* 142.

Fine levando de Tenementis tentis de Rege in Capite, &c. Is a Writ directed to the Justices of the *Common-Pleas*, whereby to licence them to admit of a *Fine* for sale of Lands holden *in Capite*, *Reg. Orig. fol.* 167.

Fine non capiendo pro pulchre placitando, Is a Writ to inhibit Officers of Courts, to take *Fines* for fair pleading, *Reg. Orig. fol.* 179. See *Pleder*.

Fine pro redisseisina capienda, &c. Is a Writ that lyeth for the release of one laid in Prison for a *Redisseisin*, upon a reasonable *Fine*, *Reg. Orig. fol.* 222.

Finary See *Blomary*.

Finors of Gold and Silver, Be those that purifie and separate those Mettals from other courser, by Fire and Water, *Anno* 4 *H.* 7. *cap.* 2. They be also in the same place called *Parters*, sometimes *Departers*.

Filicetum, A bracky Ground, *Ubi filices crescunt. Co.* 1. *Inst.* 4. *b.* See *Doomsday*.

Firdstole. See *Fridstole*.

Firebare, That without delay, they raise and repair the Signs and *Firebares* upon the highest Hills in every Hundred, that the whole Country by those Signs, as often as necessity shall require, may be fore-warned, &c. *Ordinatio pro Vigil. observand. a Linne usq; ad* Yarmouth *temp. E.* 2. Peradventure derived from the Saxon Fyrtop, a Beacon, or high Tower, near the Sea-side; wherein were Lights, either to direct Saylors in the Night, or to give warning of the Enemy.

Firebote, For the Composition of the word, see *Hay-bote*. It signifieth an allowance of Wood or Estovers, to maintain competent *fireing* for the use of the Tenant.

Firma, *Ad firmam noctis*, Was a Custom or Tribute paid towards the entertaining of the King for one Night, according to *Doomsday, Comes Meriton* T. R. E. *reddebat* firmam *unius noctis*; that is, entertainment for one Night, or the value of it. *Firma Regis*, anciently *pro villa Regis*, By a Charter of King *Edgar* to *Ely*, it is limited to a penalty, to pay one Nights *Ferme*, if the priviledges be broken by any man. See *Doomsday*.

First-fruits, *Primitiæ*, Are the Profits of every Spiritual Living for one year, given in ancient time to the Pope through all Christendome. But by the Stat. 26 *H.* 8. *cap.* 3. translated to the King here in *England*; for the ordering whereof, there was a Court erected 32 H. 8 *cap.* 45. but again dissolved *Anno primo Mariæ*, *Sess.* 2. *cap.* 10. And since that time, though those Profits be reduced again to the Crown by the Statute 1 *Eliz. cap.* 4. yet was the Court never restored, but all matters therein wont to be handled, were transferred to the *Exchequer*, See *Annates*.

Fish-garth, 23 *H.* 8. *cap.* 18. A Dam or Weare in a River, made for the taking of *Fish*, especially in the Rivers of *Owse* and *Humber*. See *Garth*.

Fitch. See *Furre*.

Fithwite, But more rightly *Fithewite*, From the Saxon Feohτ and pite, *mulcta*; so that it is a Fine laid upon one for fighting and breaking the Peace: *Si pugnaverint & percusserint se quamvis sanguinem non extraxerint, Prior habebit inde* Fithwite, that is, *amerciamenta*, *Ex Registro Priorat. de* Cokesford.

Fitzherbert, Was a famous Lawyer in the Dayes of King *Henry* the Eighth, and was chief Justice of the *Common-Pleas*; He wrote two Books of great Reputation, one *An Abridgement of the Common Laws*, another intituled, *De Natura Brevium*.

Fledwit, Cometh of the Saxon word *Fled*, that is, a *fugitive* and *wite*, which some make but a termination, signifying nothing of it self; howbeit others say, it signifies a Reprehension, Censure or Correction. It signifies in our Law, a discharge or freedome from Amerciaments, where one having been an outlawed Fugitive, cometh to the Peace of our Lord the King of his own accord. *Rastals* Exposition of words, and *Termes de la Ley*. See *Bloodwit* and *Childwit*. See *Fletwit*.

Fleet, A famous Prison in *London*, so called, as it seemeth, of the River upon whose side it standeth, *Camd. Brit. pag.* 317. Unto this none are usually committed, but for contempt to the King and his Laws, or upon absolute Command of the King, or some of his Courts. Or lastly, Upon Debt, when men are unable, or unwilling to satisfie their Creditors.

Flem and **Fleth,** Saxon *Flema*, an Outlaw, and *Flet*, a House, In a Plea of *Quo Warranto, Abbas de Burgo dicit quod clamat annum & vastum & medium tempus per hæc verba* Flem *&* Fleth, *Trin.* 7 *Ed.* 3.

Flemenes-firinth, But more truly *Flymena frymthe*. Vide *Leg. Inæ, cap.* 29. *&* 47. *Leg. etiam H.* 1. *cap.* 10. 12. It signifies the relieving of a Fugitive, *Cum Sacha & Socha, Tol & Team, Infangtheof &* Flemenes fyrythe *et Gridbrech, Forstal, Hamsocne, Blodwite, Ordel & Oreste*. Carta Edw. Conf. Mon. de Waltham. This word is variously written in old Charters, as *Flemeneferd, Flemenefrit, Flemenefremith, Flemanisflit, Flemeneward, Fremenefenda*, and *Flemenesfricthe*, but without question intending the same thing.

Flemenesfreme and **Flemenesfrenthe,** Are said to be the Chattels of Fugitives, *Mich.* 10 *H.* 4. *Hertf.* 59. *Coram Rege, Rot.* 59. See *Flemenesfyrinthe*.

Flemeswite, Signifies the liberty to challenge the Cattel or Amerciaments of your Man a Fugitive, *Rastals* Exposit. of words. *Fleta* writes it two different wayes, *viz. Flemenesfrevie* and *Flemenes freicthe*, and interprets it, *Habere catalla Fugitivorum, Lib.* 1. *cap.* 47. See *Flem* and *Flemenesferinthe*.

Fleta, A feigned Name of a learned Lawyer, that writing a Book of the Common Law of *England*, and other Antiquities in the *Fleet*, termed it thereof *Fleta*. He lived in the times of

Edw. the Second and *Edward* the Third. See his First Book, *cap.* 20. *sect. Qui ceperint*, and *lib.* 2. *cap.* 66. *sect. Item quod nullus.*

Fletwite alias **Fredwite**, *Skene de verb.* Signif. *verb.* Melletum, saith, That *Flichwit* is liberty to hold Courts, and take up the Amerciaments *pro melletis*, and the reason he gives is, because *Flicht* is called *Flitting*, in French *Melle*, which sometime is conjoyned with Hand-stroke, and in some Books *Placitum de melletis*, is the Plea of beating or striking. See *Fledwit.*

Flidethrift, But indeed more truly *Slidethrift*, otherwise called *Shovegroat*, Is the Game now known by the name of *Shovel-board*, mentioned 32 *H.* 8. *cap.* 9.

Flichtwite alias **Flitwite**, *Spelman* says, It signifies *Mulctam ob contentiones, rixas & jurgia impositam, & cui hæc a Principe conceduntur ; potest in curiâ suâ cognoscere, de hujusmodi trangressionibus & mulctas inde provenientes, &c. a delinquentibus exigere & sibimet retinere.*

Flight. See *Finer.*

Florences, A kind of Cloth so called, *Anno* 1 *R.* 3. *cap.* 8.

Flotages, That is, a swimming at the top, which we properly call *floating*, are such things as swim on the top of the Sea, or other great Rivers ; the word is used sometimes in the Commissions of *Water-Bayliffs.*

Flotson alias **Flotzam**, Is a word proper to the Seas, signifying any Goods that by Shipwrack be lost, and lye floating or swimming upon the top of the water, which with *Ietson*, and *Lagon*, and *Shares*, are given to the Lord Admiral by his Letters Patent. *Ietson* is a thing cast out of the Ship, being in danger of wreck, and beaten to the shore by the Waters, or cast on the shore by the Mariners, *Co. vol.* 6. *fol.* 106. *Lagon* alias *Lagan* or *Ligan*, is that which lyeth in the bottom of the Sea, *Co. ibid. Shares*, are Goods due to more by proportion. See *Coo. lib.* 5. Sir *Henry Constables* Case.

Foder, *Fodrum*, Signifies in plain English any kind of Meat for Horses, and other Cattel. But among the *Feudists* it is used for a Prerogative that the Prince hath to be provided of Corn, and other Meat for his Horses, by his Subjects, towards his Wars, or other Expeditions. *Arnoldus Clapmarius de arcanis Imperii*, lib. 1. cap. 11. and *Hotoman de verbis feudalibus*, *litera* F.

Fogage, *Fogagium*, Rank Grass not eaten in Summer, *Leg. Forestar. Scot. cap.* 15.

Folclands, *Copy-hold Lands*, so called in the time of the Saxons, as *Charter-Lands* were called *Boc-lands*, Kitchin 174. *Fundus sine scripto possessus* (sayes Master *Somner*) *censum pensitans annuum & officiorum servituti obnoxius, Terra Popularis.*

Folcmote or **Folkemote**, Saxon *Folkgemot*, that is, *Conventus populi*, compounded of *Folke populus*, and *Gemettan convenire*, signifies (as *Lambert* saith in his *Exposition of Saxon words*, verbo *Conventus*,) two kinds of Courts ; one now called *The County-Court*. The other, *The Sheriffs Turn.* This word is still in use in the City of *London*, and denotes *Celebrem ex tota civitate conventum*, Stowes *Survey of London.* But *Manwood* sayes in his *Forest Laws*, *Folke* is the Court holden in *London*, wherein all the *Folk* and People of the City did Complain of the Mayor and Aldermen, for misgovernment within the City. Mr. *Somner* in his *Saxon Dictionary* sayes. It is a general Assembly of the People, to consider and order Matters of the Common-wealth. *Omnes proceres Regni & milites & liberi homines universi totius Regni Brittanniæ facere debent in pleno* Folcmote *fidelitatem Domino Regi, &c.* In *Leg. Edw. Conf. cap.* 35.

Fold-course, *Cro.* 2. *par. fol.* 432. Vide *Faldage.*

Folgheres, or rather **Folgers**, Be *Followers*, if we interpret the word according to the true signification : *Bracton* saith it signifies, *Eos qui aliis deserviunt*, lib. 3. tract. 2. cap. 10.

Footgelde, Is an Amerciament for not cutting out the Balls of great Dogs feet in the Forest, for which see *Expeditate.* And to be quit of *Footgelde*, is a priviledge to keep Dogs within the Forest unlawed, without puishment or Control, *Cromp. Jur. fol.* 197. *Manwoods Forest Law, cap.* 25. *num.* 3. See *Foutgeld.*

Foot of the fine. See *Chirographer.*

Forage, *Fodder* for Cattel, *Cestes sont Covenants faits le vendredy prochein devant la feste de seint Jaques l' apostle, &c.* 30 E. 1. *Et le dit.* J. *trovera audit* N. *herbe & feyne &* forage *pour un Hakeney, &c.*

Forathe, *Liberalis autem home* (i.) Pegen *modo crimen suum non sit inter majora, habeat fidelem hominem qui possit pro eo jurare juramentum,* (i.) Forathe *si autem non habet, ipsemet juret, nec pardonetur ei aliquod juramentum*, Constit. Canuti Regis de Forest, cap. 12. cited by *Manwood* in his *Forest Law, pag.* 3.

Forbarre or **Forebar**, Is for ever to deprive, 9 *R.* 2. *cap.* 2. and 6. *H.* 6. *cap.* 4.

Forbusher of Armor, *Forbator*, *Si quis* forbator *arma alicujus resceperit adpurgandum, &c.* Leg. Aluredi, M. S. *cap.* 22.

Force, *Vis*, In our Common-Law it is most usually applyed *in pejorem partem*, signifying unlawful Violence. *West* thus defines it, *Symb. part.* 2. *tit.* Indictments, *sect.* 65. *Force* is an offence by which Violence is used to persons or things ; where also he divideth it thus, *Force* is either *simple* or *compound*, *Simple force* is that which is so committed, that it hath no other Crime adjoyned to it ; As if one by *force* do enter into another mans Possession, without doing any other unlawful act. *Mixt* or *compound force*, is that Violence which is committed with such a fact, as of it self onely is criminal: As if any by *force* enter into another mans Possession, and kill a man, or ravish a woman there, &c. He farther divideth it into true *force*, and *force* after a sort, and so proceedeth to divers other Branches worth the reading, as *forcible* Entry, *forcible* Detaining, unlawful Assembly, Routs, Riots, Rebellions, &c.

Forcible detaining or **holding of Possession**, Is a violent act of Resistance by strong Hand of Men weaponed with Harnesse, or other action of fear in the same place, or elsewhere, whereby the lawful Entry of Justices, or others, is barred or hindred, *West Symbol. part* 2 *tit*

tit. Indictments, *sect.* 65. Of this see *Cromp. Just. of Peace, fol.* 58. *usq*; *ad* 63.

Forcible Entry, *Ingressus manu forti factus*, Is a violent actual *Entry* into a House or Land, &c. or taking a Distress of any person weaponed, whether he offer violence or fear of hurt to any there, or furiously drive any out of the Possession thereof, *West Symbol. part* 2. *tit.* Indictments, *sect.* 65. *Cromp. Just. of Peace, fol* 58, 59. *usq*; *ad* 63. It is also used for a Writ grounded upon the Statute 8 *H.* 6. 9. whereof read *F. N.B. fol.* 248. See the *New Book of Entries, verbo* Forcible Entry. See *Lamb. Definition* in certain cases, *Eiren. lib.* 2. *cap.* 4. *pag.* 145.

Foreigne, *Fr: Forain Lat. Forinsecus*, is in Law used Adjectively, being joyned with divers Substantives in several senses, not unworthy the Exposition; as *Foreigne* Matter, that is, Matter triable in another County, *Pl. cor.* 154. Or Matter done in another County, *Kitchin, fol.* 126. *Forein Plea, Forinsecum placitum*, is a refusal of the Judge as incompetent, because the Matter in hand was not within his Precinct, *Kitchin, fol.* 75. & *an.* 4 *H.* 8. *cap.* 2. & 22 *H.* 8. *cap.* 2. & 14. *Forein Answer, Forinseca Responsio*, that is, such an Answer as is not triable in the County where it is made, 15 *H.* 6. *cap.* 5. *Foreign Service, Forinsecum servitium*, that is, such Service whereby a mean Lord holdeth over of another, without the compass of his own fee, *Bro. tit. Tenures, fol.* 251. *num.* 12. & 28. & *Kitchin, fol.* 209. Or else that which a Tenant performeth either to his own Lord, or to the Lord Paramount out of his Fee. Of these Services *Bracton* speaketh thus, *Item sunt quædam servitia quæ dicuntur* forinseca *quamvis sunt in Charta et de Feoffamento expressa et nominata, et quæ ideo dici possunt* forinseca, *quia pertinent ad dominum Regem et non ad Dominum capitalem, nisi cum in propria persona profectus fuerit in servitio, vel nisi cum pro servitio suo satisfecerit Domino Regi qu ocunq; modo et fiunt incertis temporibus cum casus et necessitas evenerit et varia habent nomina et diversa: Quandoq; enim nominantur* forinseca; *large sumpto vocabulo, quoad servitium Domini Regis; quandoq; scutagium; quandoq; servitium Domini Regis et ideo* forinsecum *dici potest, quia sit et capitur foris, sive extra servitium quod fit Domino Capitali. Vide* Bro. Tenures 28. 95. *Foreigne Service*, seemeth to be Knights-service, or Escuage uncertain, *Perkins Reservation* 650. *Foreigne Attachment, Attachiamentum forinsecum*, Is an Attachment of *Foreiners* Goods found within a Liberty or City, in the Hands of a third person, for the satisfaction of some Citizen, to whom the said *Foreiner* oweth Money. At *Lempster* (anciently *Leominstre*) there is the Burrough and the *Foreigne*, which last is within the Jurisdiction of the Mannor, but not within the Liberty of the Bayliff of the Burrough. *Foreigne Apposer* or *Opposer*, Is an Officer in the *Exchequer*, to whom all Sheriffs and Bayliffs do repair to be apposed by him of their Green Wax, after they are apposed of their Sums out of the Pipe-Office; and from thence draws down a Charge upon them to the Clerk of the Pipe: His business is to examine the Sheriffs Estreats with the Record, and to ask the Sheriff, what he sayes to every particular Sum therein. *Vide, The Practice of the Exchequer, fol.* 87. and 4. *Inst. fol.* 107.

Forera. *Terra transversalis seu Capitalis*. A Headland, or (as they vulgarly call it *Hadeland*, —*Uno capite abuttante super* Foreram *Rogeri Attecastel, Carta de anno* 47 E. 3.

Forest, *Foresta*, Sgnifies a great or vast Wood, in French *Lieu Forestier & Sauvage*, is *Locus sylvestris & saltuosus*. Such as have written upon the Common-Law, define it thus, *Foresta est locus ubi feræ inhabitant vel includuntur*, with whom agree several others. Some do say it is called *Foresta quasi ferarum statio vel tuta Mansio ferarum. Manwood* in his *Forest Laws*, cap. 1. num. 1. thus defineth it, A *Forest* is a certain Territory of woody Grounds, and fruitful Pastures, priviledged for wild Beasts, and Fowls of *Forest*, Chase, and Warren, to rest and abide in the safe Protection of the King, for his Princely delight and pleasure; which Territory of Ground so priviledged, is meered & bounded with unremoveable Marks, Meers and Boundaries, either known by matter of Record, or else by Prescription, and also replenisht with wild Beasts of Venery or Chase, and with great Coverts of Vert, for the succor of the said wild Beasts to have their abode in; for the preservation and continuance of which said place, together with the Vert & Venison, there are certain particular Laws, Priviledges and Officers belonging only to the same. The manner of making *Forests*, as the same Author well setteth down, *cap.* 2. *num.* 2. is this. The King sends out his Commission under the Great Seal of *England*, directed to certain discreet persons, for the view, perambulation, meering and bounding of the place he mindeth to a *Forest*; which bing returned into the *Chancery*, Proclamation is made throughout all the Shire where the Ground lyeth, That none shall hunt or chase any manner of wild Beasts in that Precinct, without the Kings special Licence; after which, He appointeth Ordinances, Laws, and Officers fit for the preservation of the Vert and Venison; and so it becometh a *Forest* by matter of Record. The Properties of a *Forest* are these in especial; First, A *Forest*, as it is truly and strictly taken, cannot be in the Hands of any but the King; the reason is given by *Manwood*, because none hath Power to grant Commission to be a Justice in *Eyre* for the *Forest* but the King, *cap.* 24. *num.* 1. The second property, be the Courts, as the *Justice-seat* every three years; the *Swainmote* thrice every year; and the *Attachment* once every forty dayes, *Idem. cap.* 21. *num.* 1. The third property, are the Officers belonging to it, for the preservation of the Vert and Venison: As first, the Justices of the *Forest*, the Warden or Keeper, Verderers, *Foresters*, Agistors, Regarders, Bayliffs, Beadels, and such like, which you may see, and their Duties, in *Manwood, cap.* 21. *num* 1, 2, 3, 4. But the chief property of a *Forest* both by *Manwood, cap.* 23. and *Crompt. pag.* 146. is the *Swainmote*, which, as they both agree, is no less incident to it, than a Court of Pye-powders to a Fair. Other Courts and Offices are not so requisite in those *Forests* that are in the Hands of Subjects, because they be not truly *Forests*. But if this fail, there remains nothing of a *Forest*, but it is turned into the nature of a Chace, see *Chace*. The *Forests* that I have read of in *England* are these, The *Forest* of *Windsor* in *Berkshire*, Cam. Brit, *pag.* 213. Of *Pickering*,

Cromp.

Cromp. 190. Of *Shirwood*, Id. *fol.* 202. Of *Englewood* in *Cumberland*, *Anno* 4 *H.* 7. *cap.* 6. And *Cromp.fol.* 42. Of *Lancaster*, Idem. fol. 196. Of *Wolmore*, *Stowes Annals*, pag. 462. Of *Gillingham*, Idem. pag. 113. Of *Knaresborough*, 21 H. 8. 17. Of *Waltham Caral*, Brit. 328. Of *Breden*, Idem. pag. 176. Of *White hart*, Id. 150. Of *Wiersdale*, Id. pag. 589. Of *Lownesall*, ibid. Of *Dean*, Id. pag. 266. 8 H. 6. 27. 19 H. 7. cap. 8. Of St. *Leonards* in *Sussex*, *Manwood*, pag. 1. 144. Of *Waybridge* and *Sapler*, Id. pag. 63. Of *Whitney*, Ibid 81. Of *Fekenham*, *Cambd.* pag. 441. Of *Rockingham*, Id. 396. *Forest de la mer*, Id. 467. Of *Huckestow*, Id. 456. Of *Ashdowne* in the County of *Sussex*, 37 H. 8. 16. Of *Whittlewood*, and *Swasy* in the County of *Northampton*, 32 H. 8. cap. 38. Of *Fronselwood* in the County of *Somerset*, Co. lib. 2. *Cromwells* Case, *fol.* 71. *Waterdown-Forest*, *Amdelworth* and *Dallington*, all in *Sussex*, besides several others. See 17 *Car.* 1. *cap.* 16.

Forestagium, Seems to signify some Duty or Tribute payable to the Kings *Foresters*, as *Chiminage*, or such like; *Et sint quieti de Theolonio & Passagio, & de* Forestagio, *&c.* Carta 18. E. 1. m. 10. n. 30.

Forestal. See *Forstal.*

Fore-closed, 33 *H.* 8. 39. Barred, and utterly excluded for ever, 2 *par. Inst. fol.* 298.

Forester, *Forestarius*, Is a sworn Officer of the *Forest*, appointed by the Kings Letters Patents, to walk the *Forest* both early and late, watching both the Vert and the Venison, attaching and presenting all Trespassers against them within their own Bayliwick or Walk, whose Oath you read in *Crompt. fol.* 201. And though these Letters Patent be ordinarily granted but *quamdiu se bene gesserint*; yet some have it to them and their Heirs, and thereby are called *Foresters in Fee*, Id. fol. 157. 159. By the same *Crompton* in Latine, *fol.* 175. *Forestarium feudi.*

Forejudger, *Forisjudicatio*, Signifies a Judgment, whereby a Man is deprived, or put by the thing in question: It seemeth to be compounded of *Fors*, i. *præter* and *judger judicare.* *Bracton, lib.* 4. *tract.* 3. *cap.* 5. hath these words, *Et non permittas quod A. capitalis Dominus feudi illius habeat custodiam hæredis, &c. quia in curia nostra* foris judicatur *de custodia*, &c. So doth *Kitchin* use it, *fol.* 29. and *Old Nat. Brev. fol.* 44. & 81. and the Stat. 5 *E.* 3. *cap.* 9. and 21. *R.* 2. *cap.* 12. *Forjudicatus*, with Authors of other Nations, signifieth as much as Banished, or as *Deportatus* in the ancient Roman Law, as appeareth by *Vincentius de Franchis*, *descis* 102. *Mathæus de afflictis*, Lib. 3. Feud. Rub. 31. pag. 625.

Forejudged the Court, Is, when an Officer of any *Court* is expell'd the same for some Offence, or for not appearing to an Action by Bill filed against him, and in the later he is not to be readmitted, till he shall appear, 2 *H.* 4. 8. He shall lose his Office, and be *forejudged the Court.* *Spelman* sayes, *Forjudicare interdum est male judicare.*

Foregoers, Be purveyors going before the King and Queen in Progresse, to provide for them, *Anno* 36 *E.* 3. *cap.* 5.

Forfeiture, *Ferisfactura*, Cometh of the French word *Forfaict*, id est, *scelus*; but in our Language signifieth rather the effect of transgressing a penal Law, then the Transgression it self; as *forfeiture* of Escheats, 25 *E.* 3. *cap.* 2. *Stat. de Proditionibus*: How Goods *forfeited*, and Goods confiscate differ, see *Stam.pl.cor.fol.* 186. where those seem to be *forfeited* that have a known Owner, having committed any thing whereby he hath lost his Goods; & those confiscate, that are disavowed by an Offendor, as not his own, nor claimed by any other; but we may rather say, that *Forfeiture* is more general, and Confiscation more particular, to such as forfeit onely to the Kings Exchequer. Read the whole Chapter, *Lib.* 3. *cap.* 24. Full *forfeiture*, *Plena forisfactura*, otherwise called *Plena vita*, is *forfeiture* of Life and Member, and all else that a man hath, *Manwood*, *cap.* 9. The *Canonists* use also this word *Forisfacturæ sunt pecuniariæ pœnæ delinquentium.*

Forfeiture of Marriage, *Forisfactura Maritagii*, Is a Writ lying against him, who, holding by Knights-service, and being under age, and *unmarried*, refuses her whom the Lord offers him without his disparagment, and *marryeth* another, *F. N. B. fol.* 141. *Reg. Orig. fol.* 163.

Forfang, *Antecaptio*, What we use to call *Pre-emption*, is the taking of Provision from any one in Fairs or Markets, before the Kings Purveyors are served with Necessaries for his Majesty. *Et sint quieti de* Wardwite, *et de utlewe et* Forvenge *et* Withfang, &c. *Carta* Hen. 1. *Hosp. sancti Barth.* London. *Anno* 1133.

Forseng, *Quietantiam prioris prisæ designat in hoc enim delinquunt Burgenses* Londonenses, *cum prisas suas ante prisas Regis faciunt*, Fleta, lib. 1. cap. 47. See *Forfange.*

Forgery, See the word next following, *viz. Forger of false Deeds.*

Forger of false Deeds, Cometh of the French *Forger*, i. *accudere*, to beat on an Anvil like a Smith, or else to fashion or bring into shape; and signifieth in our Common-Law either him that fraudulently maketh and publisheth *false Writings*, to the prejudice of any Mans Right, or else the Writ that lyeth against him that committeth this Offence, *F. N. B. fol.* 96. calleth it a *Writ of Deceit.* See *Termes of the Law*, *verbo* Forger of false Deeds, and *West. Symb. part.* 2. *tit.* Indictments, *sect.* 66. See the *New Book of Entries*, *verbo* Forger de Faits. This is a branch of that which the *Civilians* call *Crimen falsi*, *Nam falsarius est, qui decipiendi causa scripta publica falsificat. Speculator de crimine falsi, falsi crimen propriæ dicitur quod utilitatis privatæ causa factum est.* Connanus, lib. 5. cap. 7. num. 4. *Ad esse falsitatis tria requiruntur, mutatio veritatis, dolus et quod alteri sit nocivum*, &c. The penalty for this Offence is declared in the Statute of 5 *Eliz.* 14.

Forister. See *Forester.*

Foristel, *Forestal*, Properly signifies the stopping up of wayes; but now is vulgarly used for such as intercept and buy things before they come to the Market, *Doomsday.* See *Forestal.*

Formedon, *Breve de forma Donationis*, Is a Writ that lies for him that hath right to any Lands or Tenements, by vertue of any Entail growing from the Statute of *Westm.* 2. *cap.* 1. It lyeth in three sorts, and accordingly is termed *Forma donationis*, or *Formedon in the Descender*, Formedon in *the Reverter*, or Formedon *in the Remainder*: Formedon

medon *in the Descendor*, lyeth for the recovery of Lands, &c. given to one and the Heirs of his Body, or to a man and his Wife, and the Heirs of their two Bodies, or to man and his wife being Cosin to the Donor in *Frank marriage*, and afterwards alienated by the Donee; for after his decease, his Heirs shall have this Writ against the Tenant or Alienee, *F. N. B. fol.* 211. He maketh three sorts of this *Formedon in Descender*: The first is in the manner now exprest. The second is for the Heir of a Coparcener that aliens and dies, *fol.* 214. The third he calls (*In simul tenuit*) *fol.* 216. which lyeth for a Coparcener or Heir in *Gavelkind* before partition, against him to whom the other Coparcener or Heir hath alienated, and is dead. *Formedon in the Reverter* lyeth for the Donor or his Heirs, where Land entailed to certain and their Issue, with condition, for want of such Issue, to revert to the Donor and his Heirs, against him to whom the Donee alienateth, after the Issue extinct to which it was entailed, *F. N. B. fol.* 219. *Formedon in the Remainder* lyeth, where a man giveth Lands in tail, the remainder to another in tail; and afterwards the former Tenant in tail dyeth without Issue of his Body, and a Stranger abateth, then he in the Remainder shall have this Writ, *Fitzh. Nat. Brev. fol.* 217. see *Reg. Orig. fol.* 238, 242, 243. Of this also see the *New Book of Entries*, *verbo* Formedon, and *Coo.* on *Lit. fol.* 326.

Fornagium, Signifies the fee taken by a Lord of his Tenants bound to bake in his common Oven, as is usual in the Northern-parts of *England*, or for permission to use their own; also *Chimney* or *Hearth-Money*, see *Furnage*. *Et Dominus Rex proinde amittit per an. de exitibus* fornagii *sui* 10. *libras*, *Pl. coram Rege & ejus concil. in Parl.* 18 E. 1. *in Turri London.*

Fornication, *Fornicatio*, 1 H. 7. 4. Whoredome, the Act of Incontinency between single-persons; for if either Party be marryed, it is Adultery: The first Offence herein was punisht with three Moneths Imprisonment, the second was made Felony in the late Times of Usurpation, by a pretended Act made 1650. *cap.* 10. *Scobells Collection.*

Foreprise, *Foreprisum*, May be derived from the French words *For*, that is, *extra* and *prise*, *captio*, in which sense it is used in the Statute of *Exon*, 14 *E.* 1. but there written *Forsprise*; we still use it in Conveyances, wherein excepted and *foreprised* is a usual expression.

Forein, Many times used for a *Foreiner*, 34 & 35 *H.* 8. *cap.* 18. See *Foreine.*

Foreschoke, Seems to signifie originally as much as *Forsaken* in our Modern Language, or *Derelictum* with the Romans: It is especially used in one of our Statutes for Lands or Tenements seised by the Lord, for want of Services due from the Tenant, and so quietly held and possessed beyond the year and day. As if we should say, that the Tenant, which seeing his Land or Tenements taken into the Lords hand, and possessed so long, taketh not the course appointed by Law to recover them, doth in due presumption of Law disavow or *forsake* whatsoever right he hath unto them; and then such Lands shall be called *Forschoke* sayes the Stat. 10 *E.* 1. *cap. unico.*

Forses, *Catadupæ*, Watersals, *Cam. Brit. tit.* Westmerland.

Forstal, Is to be quit of Amerciaments, and Cattel arrested within your Land, and the Amerciaments thereof coming sayes, *Termes de la Ley*. But *Spelman* sayes, 'Tis *viæ obstructio vel itineris interceptio*, with whom agrees *Co.* on *Lit. fol.* 161. In *Doomsday* 'tis written *Foristel*, which see before. *Dediq; eis* forstallum, &c. *& terram quæ jacet ex utraq; part. ejusdem* forstalli, &c. Mon. Ang. 2. par. fol. 112. 60.

Forestalling, *Forestallatio*, Or according to *Spelman*, *viarum obstructio*, signifies the Buying or Bargaining for any Victuals or Wares coming to be sold towards any Fair or Market, or from beyond the Seas towards any City, Port, Haven, Creek, or Road of this Realm, and before the same be there, to the intent to sell the same again at a higher and dearer price, 51 *H.* 3. *Stat.* 6. *West Symbol. part.* 2. *tit.* Indictments, *sect.* 64.

Forestaller, In *Cromptons Jurisdiction*, *fol.* 153. Is used for stopping of Deer broke out of the *Forest*, from returning home again, or laying between him and the *Forest* in the way that he is to return. See *Regrators* and *Engrossers*, *Cromp. Just. of Peace*, *fol.* 69. In the *Termes of the Law*, 'tis thus defined, *Forstalling*, *Forstallamentum*, is the buying of Corn, Cattel, or other Merchandise, by the way, as it cometh towards the Market or Fair to be sold. *Fleta* sayes, *Significat obtrusionem viæ vel impedimentum transitus & fugæ averiorum*, lib. 1. cap. 47, who shall be adjudged a *forestal*. See in 5 & 6. E. 6. *cap.* 14. Forstal *est*, *si aliquis portaverit halec vel hujusmodi res ad forum*, *& statim alius venerit ei emerit ab ipso illas res*, *ut carius vendat*, *Prior habebit emendas ab ipso*. *Ex Reg. Priorat. de* Cokesford. See 3. *par. Inst. fol.* 195.

Fortescue, Was a learned Lawyer, and Lord Chancellor in the dayes of *Hen.* 6. who writ a Book in the Commendation of our Common-Law, intituled, *De Laudibus Legum Angliæ.*

Fortility, *Fortalitium vel forteletum*, Signifies a *fortified* place, or Bulwark or Castle; so 'tis said 11 *H.* 7. *cap.* 18. within the Towns and *Fortilities* of *Berwick* and *Carlisle.*

Fortlet, (*Fr:*) signifies a place of some Strength, *Old. Nat. Brev. fol.* 45.

Fortgingles, Otherwise *Farthingdel*, is the fourth part of an Acre or Peny, &c. See *Farthingdeal*, see the Book of *Doomsday.*

Fossa & furca. See *Furca.*

Fossatum, A Ditch, or rather a place fenced with a Ditch, *Ex dono* Henrici *Regis avi nostri unum* fossatum *tam largum quod naves possint ire et redire a flumine de* Withoma *usq; ad Tupholme Carta*, 20 H. 3. m. 9. where it seems to signifie the Trench of a cut River.

Fosseway, From *Fossus*, digged was anciently one of the four principal High-wayes of *England*, so called; because supposed to be digged and made passable by the *Romans*, and having a Ditch upon one side. See *Watling-street.*

Foster-land, Is *Land* given, assigned or set forth, for the finding of Food or Victuals for any person or persons; as in Monasteries, for the Monks, &c.

Fother or **Fodder**, Is a weight of about a Tun, or twenty hundred, which is a Wain or

Cart-

Cart-load. *Speight* in his *Annotations* upon *Chaucer*, in the Book of *Rates*, there is mention made of a *fodder* of Lead, which, according to *Skene*, is about one hundred twenty and eight ſtone.

Fourch, *Afforciare*, Seemeth to come of the Fr. *Fourchir*, i. *titubare Lingua*, and ſignifies a delay, putting off, or prolonging of an Action, & it ſeems no unpleaſant Metaphor, for as by ſtammering we draw out our Speech, not delivering that we have to ſay in ordinary time; ſo by *fourching* we prolong a Suit, that might be ended in a ſhorter ſpace. To *fourch* by Eſſoin, *Weſtm.* 1. *cap.* 24. *Anno* 3 *E.* 1. where you have words to this effect; Coparceners, Joynt-tenants, and Tenants in common, may not *fourch* by Eſſoine, to Eſſoine ſeverally, but have onely one Eſſoine, as one ſole Tenant may have. And *Anno* 6 *E.* 1. *cap.* 10. it is uſed in like ſort. The Defendants ſhall be put to anſwer without *fourching*, &c. See 23 *H.* 6. *cap.* 2. and 2. *par. Inſt. fol.* 250.

Foutgeld or **Footgeld**, Is a compound of two German words, *viz. Fous, pes*, and *Gyldan ſolvere*; and ſignifieth an Amerciament, for not cutting out the balls of the feet of great Dogs within the Foreſt, ſee *Expeditate*. And to be quit of *Footgeld*, is a priviledge to keep Dogs within the Foreſt, unlawed, without puniſhment or control, *Manwoods Foreſt Law, cap.* 25. *num.* 3.

Foundation, The *founding* of a Colledge or Hoſpital, is called *Foundatio quaſi fundidatio*, or *fundamenti locatio*, Co. lib. 10.

Founder, Is he that melteth Mettal, and maketh any thing of it, by caſting it into a mould, *Anno* 17 *R.* 2 *cap.* 1 derived from the Verb *Fundere*, to pour out. we alſo ſay, That whoever builds and endows a Colledge or Hoſpital is the *Founder*.

Fowles of Warren. See *warren*,

Frampole fences, Are ſuch as any Tenant of the Manner of *Writtle* in *Eſſex* hath againſt the Lords Demeſnes, whereby he hath the wood growing on the *Fence* and as many Trees or Poles as he can reach from the top of the Ditch with the Helve of his Axe, towards the repair of his *Fence*; but the reaſon of the name Etymologically we are yet to learn, and not willing to obtrude any idle fancy.

Franchiſe, *Franchesia, Libertas*, Is taken with us for a Priviledge or Exemption from ordinary Juriſdiction, and ſometimes an immunity from Tribute: It is either perſonal or real, *Cromp. Juriſd. fol.* 141. that is, belonging to a perſon immediately, or elſe by means of this or that Place, or Court of Immunity, whereof he is either chief or a Member. In what particular thing a *Franchiſe* commonly conſiſts, ſee *Britton, cap.* 19 *Franchiſe Royal*, 15 *R.* 2. *cap.* 4. and 2 *H.* 5. *cap.* 7. *in fine*, ſeemeth to be that where the Kings Writ runs, not as *Cheſter, Durham, &c.* which are called *Seigniories Royal, Anno* 28 H. 6. *cap.* 4. The Author of the *New Termes of the Law* ſaith, That *Franchiſe Royal* is, where the King granteth to one and his Heirs, that they ſhall be quit of Toll, or ſuch like. See *Franchiſe* in the *New Book of Entries, Bracton, lib.* 2. *cap.* 5. See *Sac.* See alſo *Old Nat. Brev. fol.* 4.

Francigena. See *Englecery*.

Francling, A Freeholder, *Qui liberè tenet*, See *Forteſcue de Laud. Leg. Ang. cap.* 29.

Frank-almoin, *Libera Eleemoſyna*, In French *Frank-auſmone*, Signifies a Tenure or Title of Lands or Tenements beſtowed upon God, that is, given to ſuch People as beſtow themſelves in the Service of God, for pure and perpetual Alms; whence the Feoffers or Givers cannot demand any terreſtrial Service, ſo long as the Lands, &c. remain in the hands of the Feoffees. With this agreeth the *Grand-Cuſtumary* of *Normandy, cap.* 32. Of this you may read at large, *Bracton, lib.* 2. *cap.* 5. *&* 10. See *F. N. B. fol.* 211. and the *New Book of Entries, verbo* Frank-almoine. *Britton*, in the forcited, makes another kind of this Land, given in Almes, but not in free Alms. As if an Abbot, &c. hold Lands of his Lord for certain Divine-Service to be done, as to ſing every *Friday* a Maſſe, or do ſome other thing, and if ſuch Divine-Service be not done, the Lord may diſtrain; in ſuch caſe the Abbot ought to do Fealty to the Lord; and therefore it ſhall not be ſaid a Tenure in *Frank-almoine*, but a Tenure by Divine-Service; for it cannot be *Frank-almoine*, if any certain Service be expreſſed.

Frank-banke. See *Free-bench*.

Frank-Chaſe, *Libera Chacea*, a Is Liberty of free *Chaſe*, whereby all Men having Ground within that compaſs, are prohibited to cut down wood, &c. without the view of the Foreſter, though it be in his own Demeſnes, *Cromp. Jur. fol.* 187.

Frank-fee, *Liberum feudum*, Is by *Broke, tit.* Demeſne, *num.* 32. thus expreſſed, That which is in the hands of the King or Lord of any Manor being ancient Demeſne of the Crown, (*viz.* the Demeſnes) is called *Frank-fee*, and that which is in the hands of the Tenant is ancient Demeſne only. See *Reg. Orig. fol.* 12. whereby that ſeemeth to be *Frank fee* which a man holds at the Common-Law to himſelf and his Heirs, and not by ſuch Service as is required in ancient Demeſne, according to the cuſtom of the Mannor. And again, in the ſame Book, *fol.* 14. there is a Note to this effect, That the Lands which were in the hands of King *Edward the Confeſſor* at the making of *Doomſday-Book*, is ancient Demeſne, and that all the reſt of the Realm is called *Frank-fee*, wherewith *Fitzherbert* agrees in his *Nat. Brev. fol.* 161. So that by this rule all the Land in the Realm is either ancinet Demeſne or *Frank fee*. The Author of the *Termes of Law* defines *Frank fee* to be a Tenure in Fee-ſimple of Lands pleadable at the Common-Law, and not in ancient Demeſne. *Fachineus, lib.* 7. *cap.* 39. makes *Feudum* francum *eſſe pro quo nullum ſervitium præſtatur Domino*, with whom agrees *Zaſius de feudis*, part. 12. ſaying That therefore it is *Feudum improprium, quia ab omni ſervitio liberum*.

Frank-ferme, *Firma Libera*, Is Land or Tenement, wherein the nature of *fee* is changed by Feoffment out of Knights-ſervice, for ſeveral yearly Services; and whence neither Homage, Wardſhip, Marriage, nor Relief may be demanded, nor any other Service not contained in the Feoffment, *Britton*, *cap.* 66. *num.* 3. See *Fee-ferme*.

Frank-fold, Is, where the Lord hath benefit of *folding* his Tenants Sheep within his

Mannor for the manuring of his Land, *Kel. Rep. fol.* 198. It is a compound irregular out of the French *Franc*, that is, *free*; and the Saxon *fald*, that is, a *fold*. See *Faldage*.

Frank-law *Libera Lex*, See *Cromp. Just. fol.* 156. where you shall find what it is by the contrary; for he that for an Offence, as Conspiracy, &c. loseth his *Frank law*, is said to fall into these Mischiefs; First, That he may never be impanelled upon any Jury or Assise, or otherwise used in testifying any truth. Next, If he have any thing to do in the Kings Court, he must not approach thither in person, but appoint his Attorney. Thirdly His Lands, Goods and Chattels must be seised into the Kings hands; and his Lands must be estreaped, his Trees rooted up, and his Body committed to Prison; for this the said Author citeth, *Lib. Assis. fol.* 59. *Conspiracy*, 24 *E.* 3. *fol.* 34. See *Conspiracy*.

Frank-marriage, *Liberum maritagium*, Is a Tenure in tail special, growing from these words in the Gift comprised, *Sciant &c. me* M. H. *de* W. *dedisse & concessisse & præsenti Charta mea confirmasse* J. A. *fil io meo &* Margeriæ *uxori ejus, filiæ veræ* T. N. *in liberum maritagium unum Messuagium, &c.* West Symbol. part 1. lib. 2. sect. 303. The effect of which words is, That they shall have the Land to them and the Heirs of their Bodies, and shall do fealty to the Donor till the fourth degree. See *Termes de la Ley*, *Glanvile*, *lib.* 7. *cap.* 18. and *Bract. lib.* 2. *cap.* 7. *num.* 4. divideth *Maritagium in liberum & servitio obligatum*, see *Marriage*. *Fleta* gives this reason why the Heirs do no Service until the fourth Descent, *Ne donatores vel eorum hæredes, per homagii receptionem a reversione repellantur.* And why in the fourth Descent, and downward, they shall do Service to the Donor, *Quia in quarto gradu vehementer præsumitur, quod terra non est pro defectu hæredum Donatoriorum reversura*, lib. 3. cap. 11.

Frank-pledge, *Franci-plegium*, From the French *Frank*, *liber*, and *pledge*, i. *fidejussor*, signifies a *Pledge* or Surety for Free men: For the ancient Custome of Free-men of *England*, for the preservation of the Publick Peace, was, That every free-born Man at fourteen years of age, after *Bracton* (Religious person, Clerks, Knights, and their eldest Sons excepted) should find Surety for his Truth towards the King and his Subjects, or else be kept in Prison; whereupon a certain number of Neighbours became customably bound one for another, to see each man of their *Pledge* forth-coming at all times, or to answer the Transgression committed, by any broken away: So that whosoever offended, it was forth-with inquired in what *Pledge* he was, and then they of that *Pledge* either brought him forth within 31 dayes to his Answer, or satisfied for his Offence. This was called *Frank-pledge*, and the Circuit thereof *Decenna*, because it commonly consisted of ten Housholds, and every particular person thus mutually bound for himself and his Neighbours, was called *Decennier*, because he was of one *Decenna* or another. This Custome was so kept, that the Sheriffs at every County-Court did, from time to time, take the Oaths of young Ones, as they attained the age of fourteen years, and see that they comprised in some *Dozen*; whereupon this Branch of the Sheriffs Authority was stiled *Viscus Franci Plegii*, *View of Frank-pledge*. See the Statute for *View of Frank-pledge*, made 18 *E.* 2. See also *Decennier*, *Leet*, *View of Frank-pledge*, and *Friborgh*. That we borrowed this Custome of the *Lombards*, manifestly appears in the Second Book of *Feuds*, *cap.* 53. upon which read *Hotoman*, *&c.* what Articles were wont to be enquired of in this Court. See in *Hornes Mirrour of Justices*, lib. 1. cap. *de la venue des* francs pledges; And what these Articles were in former times, see in *Fleta lib.* 2. *cap.* 52. and 4. *par. Inst. fol.* 73. In an ancient Charge of the Quest of *Wardmote*, in every Ward in *London*, It is said, *And if there be any person within the Ward that is not under* Frank-pledge, that is to say, *under Love and Law*, *&c.*

Free-bench, **Frank-bank**, *Francus bancus*, that is, sedes *libera*, signifies that Estate in Copy hold Lands, that the Wife being espoused a Virgin hath, after the decease of her Husband, for her Dower, *Kitchin*, *fol.* 102. *Bracton*, *lib.* 4. *tract.* 6. *cap.* 12. *num.* 3. hath these words, *Consuetudo est in partibus illis, quod uxores maritorum defunctorum habeant* francum bancum *suum de terris sockmannorum & tenent nomine dotis.* *Fitzherbert* calls it a *Custome*, whereby in certain Cities, the Wife shall have her Husbands whole Lands, &c. for her Dower, *Nat. Brev. fol.* 150. See *Plowden*, *fol.* 411. In the Case of *Newis*. Of this *Free bench*, several Mannors have several Customes, as at *East* and *West Enborne* in the County of *Berks*, If a customary Tenant die, the Widow, shall have her *Free bench* in all his Copy-hold Lands, *dum sola et casta fuerit*; but if she commit Incontinency, she forfeits her Estate: Yet if she will come into the Court riding backward on a black Ram, with his tayl in her hand, and say the words following, the Steward is bound by the Custome to readmit her to her *Free-bench*.

Here I am
Riding upon a black Ram,
Like a Whore as I am;
And for my Crincum Crancum,
Have lost my Binkum Bancum;
And for my Tayles game,
Have done this worldly shame,
Therefore I pray you, Mr. Steward let me have
my Land again.

The like Custome there is in the Mannor of *Torre* in *Devonshire*, and other Parts of the West.

Fredwit. See *Fletwit*.

Free-bord, *Francbordus*, In some places they claim as a *Free bord*, more or less ground beyond or without the Fence. In *Mon. Ang.* 2. *par. fol.* 241. It is said to contain two foot and a half, viz. *Et totum boscum vocat. Brendwood cum frankborda, Et duorum pedum & dimid. per circuitum illius bosci*, *&c.*

Free-Chappel, *Libera Capella*, In the Opinion of some is a *Chappel* founded within a Parish, for the Service of God, by the devotion and liberality of some good Man, over and above the Mother-Church, to which it was *free* for the Parishioner to come, or not to come, and endowed with Maintenance by the Founder and thereupon called *Free*. Others with more probability say, That those onely are *Free Chappels* that are of the Kings foundation, and by him exempted from the Jurisdiction of the Ordinary; but the King may Licence a Subject to found such a *Chappel*, and by his Charter exempt it from the *Diocesans* Jurisdiction. See *Reg. Orig.fol.*40, 41. These *Chappels* were all given to the King, with Chanteries, 1 *E.* 6. 14. *Free Chappel* of St. *Martin le Grand*, 3 *E.* 4. *cap.* 4. and 4 *E.* 4. *cap.*7.

Freedstll. See *Fridstoll.*

Freehold, Frank-tenement, *Liberum tenementum*, Is that Land or *Tenement* which a Man holdeth in Fee, Fee-tail, or at the least for term of Life, *Bract. lib.* 2. *cap.* 9. In the *Termes of the Law* 'tis said, That *Free-hold* is of two sorts, *Free-hold in Deed*, and *Free hold in Law*: *Free hold in Deed*, is the real possession of Land or *Tenements* in Fee, Fee-tail, or for Life. *Free-hold in Law*, is the Right that a Man hath to such Land or *Tenements* before his Entry or Seisure. It hath likewise been extended to those Offices which a man holdeth either in Fee, or for term of Life. *Britton* defines it to this effect, *Frank-tenement* is a possession of the Soyl, or Services issuing out of the Soyl, which a Free-man holdeth in fee to him and his Heirs, or at the least for term of his life, though the Soyl be charged with free Services or other *cap*, 32. *Free hold* is sometime taken in opposition to Villenage, *Bract. lib.* 4. 37, 38. *Lambert* in his Explication of Saxon words, verb. *Terra & scripto* saith, That Land in the Saxons time was called either *Bock-land*, that is, holden by Book or Writing; or *Folcland*, that, is holden without Writing. The former he reports was held with far better condition; and by the better sort of Tenants, as Noblemen and Gentlemen, being such as now we call *Free-hold.* The later was commonly in the possession of Clowns, being that we now call *Ad voluntatem Domini, At the will of the Lord.* The *Register Judicial, fol.* 68. and in divers other places saith, That he which holds Lands upon an Execution of a *Statute-Merchant*, until he be satisfied the Debt, *Tenet ut liberum* tenementum *sibi et assignatis suis.* And *fol.* 73, the same may be read of a Tenant by *Elegit*, where the meaning is not, that they be *Free-holders*, but as *Free-holders* for their time, that is, until they have gathered Profits to the value of their Debt. *Free holders* in the ancient Law of *Scotland* were called *Milites*, *Skene de verbor.* Signif. *verb.* Milites. *Doctor* and *Student*, that the possession of Land after the Law of *England*, is called *Frank-tenement* or *Free-hold*, *fol.*97. *a.*

Fraxinetum, A Wood of Ashen-Trees, *Doomsday.*

Frenchman, *Francigena*, Was heretofore wont to be used for every Outlandish-man, *Bract. lib.* 3. *tract.* 2. *cap.*See 15 *Englecerey.*

Frendless-man, Was the Saxon word for him that we call an *Outlaw*, and the reason might be, because upon his exclusion from the Kings Peace and Protection, he was denied all help of *friends* after certain dayes; *Nam forisfecit amicos*, Bract. *lib.* 3. *tract.* 2. *cap.* 12. *num.* 1. whose words are these, *Talem vocant Angli (utlough) & alio nomine antiquitus solet nominari, sc.* Frendless man, *& sic videtur quod forisfecit amicos, & unde si quis talem post Utlagariam & expulsionem scienter paverit, receptaverit vel scienter communicaverit aliquo modo, vel receptaverit, vel occultaverit, eadem pœna puniri debet, qua puniretur utlagatus, ita quod careat omnibus bonis suis & vita, nisi Rex ei parcat de sua gratia.*

Frendwite vel Infeng, *Significat quietantiam prioris prisæ ratione convivii*, Fleta, lib. 1. cap. 47.

Fresh Disseisin, *Frisca disseisina*, Cometh of the French *Fraiz*, i. *recens* and *disseisir*, *a possessione ejicere*; It signifies such a *Disseisin* as a man may seek to defeat of himself, and by his own power, without the help of the King or Judges, *Britton*, *cap.* 5. and that such *disseisin* as is not above fifteen dayes old, *Bracton*, *lib.* 4. *cap.* 5. whom you may read at large in this matter, concluding that it is arbitrary, and so doth *Britton*, *cap.* 65. But *cap.*43. he seemeth to say, That in one case it is a year. See him also, *cap.* 44.

Fresh fine, Is that which was levyed within a year past, *Westm.* 2. *cap.* 45. *Anno* 13 *E.* 1.

Fresh force, *Frisca fortia*, Is a *force* done within forty dayes, as seems by *F. N.B. fol.* 7. For if a man be disseised of any Lands or Tenements within any City or Borough, or *deforced* from them after the death of his Ancestor, to whom he is Heir, or after the death of his Tenant for life, or in tail; he may within forty dayes after his Title accrued, have a Bill out of the Chancery, to the Mayor, &c.See the rest there, and *Old Nat. Brev. fol.* 4.

Fresh suit, *Recens insecutio*, Is such a present and earnest following of an Offendor, as never ceaseth from the time of the Offence committed or discovered, until he be apprehended. And the effect of this in the *pursuit* of a Felon is, that the party *pursuing* shall have his Goods again, whereas otherwise they are the Kings. Of this see *Stamf. pl. cor. lib.* 3. *cap.* 10. *&* 12. where you shall find handled at large what *suit* is to be accounted *fresh*, and what not. And the same Author in his First Book, *cap.* 27. saith, That *fresh suit* may continue for seven years. See *Cokes Rep. lib.* 3. *Ridgewayes* Case. *Fresh suit* seemeth to be either within the View or without; For *Manwood* saith, That upon *fresh suit* within the View, Trespassers in the Forest may be attached by the Officers pursuing them, though without the limits and bounds of the Forest, *cap.* 19. *per totum.*

Friborgh, alias **Fridburgh**, alias **Frithburg**, *Frideburgum*, Cometh of two Saxon words, *viz.* *Freo*, i. *liber*, and *borgh fidejussor*, or of *frid Pax*, and *Borghe Sponsor*; this is called after the French *Frank-pledge*, the one being in use in the Saxons time, the other since the Conquest: Wherefore, for the understanding of this, read *Frank-pledge*. That it is all one thing, appears by *Lambert* in his Explication of Saxon words, verbo *Centuria*. And again, in the Law of King *Edw.* set out by him in these words, *Præterea est quædam summa & maxima securitas, per quam omnes statu firmissimo sustinentur*, viz. *ut unusquisq; stabiliat se sub fidejussionis securitate quam Angli vocant* Freoborghes. *Soli tamen Eboracenses dicunt eandem Tienmannatale quod sonat Latine decem hominum numerum. Hæc securitas hoc modo fiebat, quod de omnibus villis totius Regni sub decennali fidejussione debebant esse universi; ita quod si unus ex decem, forisfecerit, novem ad rectum eum haberent, quod si aufugeret daretur lege terminus ei* 31. *dierum, ut* *ut quæsitus interim & inventus ad justitiam Regis adduceretur, &c.* As in the Book *Bracton* maketh mention of *Fridburgum, lib.* 3. *tract.* 2. *cap.* 10. in these words, *Archiepiscopi, Episcopi, Cmites et Barones, et omnes qui habent Soc et Sak, Tol et Team, et hujusmodi libertates milites suos & proprios servientes, &c. sub suo* Fridburgo *habere debent Item et isti suos Armigeros & alios sibi servientes: Quod si cui forisfecerint, ipsi Domini sui habeant eos ad rectum etsi non habuerint, solvant pro eis forisfacturam, et sic observandum erit de omnibus aliis qui de alicujus manupastu.* Out of which words may be gathered the reason why great men were not combined in any ordinary *Dozein, viz.* because they were a sufficient Assurance for themselves and their Servants, no less than the ten were one for another in ordinary *Dozeins.* See *Frank-pledge*, and *Skene de verbor.* Signif. *verb.* Frieborge. *Fleta* writes this word *Frithborgh*, and useth it for the principal man, or at least for a man of every *Dozein. Frithborgh* (saith he) *est laudabilis homo testimonii liber vel servus, &c.* lib. 1. cap. 47. sect. *Frithborgh.* See *Hoveden, part. poster. annal. suor. in* Henrico 2. *fol.* 345.

Fridstoll & Frithstow, From the Saxon *Fird*, signifying *Peace*, and *Stoll* a *seat* or *stool*; so that it is a Seat, or place of Peace. In the Charter of Immunities granted to the Church of Saint *Peter* in *York*, confirmed *Anno* 5 *H.* 7. *Firdstoll* is expounded *Cathedra pacis et quietudinis.* There were many of these in *England*, but the most famous was at *Beverly*, bearing this Inscription, *Hæc sedes lapidea* Freedstoll *dicitur*, id est, *Pacis Cathedra, ad quam reus fugiendo perveniens omnimodam habet securitatem*, Camd.

Frier, *Frater*, In French *Frere*, is an Order of Religious persons, of which these are the four principal Branches, *viz.* 1. *Minors, Grey friers* or *Franciscans.* 2. *Augustines.* 3. *Dominicans* or *Black-fryers.* And 4. *White-fryers* or *Carmelites*, of which the rest descend. See in *Zachius de Rep. Eccl. pag.* 380. Vide *Linwood titulo de Relig. domibus, cap.* 1. *verb.* Sancti Augustin.

Frier observant, *Frater observans*, Is an Order of *Franciscans*, which are *Minors*, as well the *Observants* as the *Conventuals* and *Capuchines, Zach. de Rep. Eccles. tract. de Regular, cap.* 12. These we find mentioned *An.* 25 *H.* 8. *cap.* 12. They be called *Observants* because they are not combined together in any Cloyster, Convent or Corporation, as the *Conventuals* are; but only tye themselves to observe the Rites of their Order more strictly than the *Conventuals* do; and upon a singularity of Zeal, separate themselves from them, living in certain places, and Companies of their own chusing: And of these you may read *Hospinian, de Orig. & Progress. Monachatus*, fol. 878. cap. 38.

Friperie, Is deduced from the French *Fripier, interpolator*, one that scoureth up and cleanseth old Apparel to sell again: It is used for a kind of Broker, *Anno* 1 *Jac. cap.* 21.

Frithborgh. See *Freeborgh.*

Frithbrech, *Pacis violatio*, The breaking of the Peace, *Leg. Ethelredi*, cap. 6. See *Frythe.*

Frithmote per Frithmote, *J. Stanley Arm. clamat capere annuatim de villa de* Otton *quæ est infra feodum et Manerium de* Aldford *infra forestaria de la mer* 10. *sol. quos Comites cestriæ ante confectionem curiæ prædictæ solebant capere.* Pl. in Itin. apud Cestr. 14 H. 7.

Frithsoken, Frithsocne & Frithsoke, Signifies surety of Defence, *Tuendæ pacis Jurisdictio.* It seemeth to be drawn from these two words, *Frith* or *frid, pax*, and *socne libertas. Fleta* saith, It is *Libertas habendi Franci plegii*, or *locus immunitatis.*

Froborg or **Froburgh.** See *Friburgh* and *Frank-pledge.*

Froomortell, But more truly *Freomortell*, Is an Immunity or Freedom granted for Murder or Man-slaughter.

Frumgyld, Is an old Saxon word, which signifies the first payment made to the Kindred of a slain person, in Recompence of his Murder, *Leg. Edmundi, cap.* ultimo.

Frumstol, *Sedes primaria*, The chief Seat or Mansion-House, *Leg. Inæ Reg.* cap. 38.

Frussura, A demolishing, or pulling down, ---*Dedi eis nonam garbam tam in* Frussuris, *quæ de novo fiunt, in, &c.* Mon. Ang. 2. par. fol. 394.

Frustrum terræ, Or, according to *Spelman Frustum*, A small piece of Land, *Residuum quiddam præter acras numeratas vel campum mensuratum. Cum in* Doomsday Frustrum terræ *accipiatur pro ampla portione seorsum a campo villa, Manerio jacenti. Doomsday, tit.* Hantisc. Rex Abedestone; *In insula habet Rex unum* Frustrum terræ *unde exemit* 61 *Vomeres.*

Fryth, *Co.* on *Lit. fol.* 5. Expounds it a Plain between two Woods, and so is it used in *Doomsday*; *Chaucher* uses it for a Wood. *Camden* in his *Brit.* for an Arm of the Sea, or great River, and so we frequently use it at this day. *Smith* (in his *Englands Improvement*) makes it signifie all Hedgewood, except Thorns. It is a task to reconcile this, when they all disagree with the Saxon, with whom we know *frid* or *frith* signifies Peace.

Fuage or **Focage**, Derived *a foco*: In the Reign of *Edward* the Third, the black Prince of *Wales* having Acquitayne granted him, laid an Imposition of *Fuage* or *Focage* upon the Subjects of that Dukedome, *viz.* twelve pence for every Fire, call'd *Herth-Money, Rot. Parl.* 25 *E.* 3. 'Tis probable our *Herth-Money* took its original from hence.

Fuer, *Fuga*, From the French *Fuir, fugere*; Though it be a Verb, yet it is used substantively, and is two-fold; *Fuer in fait (in facto)* when a man doth apparently and corporally fly, and *fuer in ley (in lege)* when being called in the County he appeareth not, until he be Outlawed; for this is flight in interpretation of Law, *Stamf. pl. cor. lib.* 3. *cap.* 22.

Fugacia, Signifies a Chase, and is all one with *Chasea*: *Charta Matildis Imperatricis Miloni de* Glouc.

Fugitives Goods, *Bona fugitivorum*, Are the proper *Goods* of him that flyeth upon Felony, which after the flight lawfully found, do belong to the King, or Lord of the Mannor, *Co. vol.* 6. *fol.* 109. See *Waif.*

Fumage, *Fumagium*, Dung, or manuring with Dung, *Et sint quieti de* fumagio *& Maremio cariando, &c. carta* R. 2. *Priorat. de Hertland*, Pat. 5 E. 4. part 3. m. 13.

Fumathoes or **Fumadoes**, 14 *Car.* 2. *cap* 31, Our Pilchards garbaged, salted, hanged in in the Smoke, and pressed, are so called in *Italy* and *Spain*, whither they are carryed in great numbers.

Furca, (*Et fossa*) The Gallows and the Pit; In ancient priviledges it signified a Jurisdiction of punishing Felons, that is, Men by hanging, Women by drowning. *Skene de verbor.* Signif. *verb.* Fossa, hath these words concerning this matter, *Erectio* furcarum *est meri imperii & altæ Justitiæ, & significat. Dominium aeris, quia suspensi pendent in aere: Et merum Imperium consistit in quatuor, sicut sunt quatuor elementa: In aere ut hi qui suspendantur, In igne quando quis comburitur propter maleficium. In aqua quando quis ponitur in culeo & in mare projicitur ut parricida, vel in amnem immergitur ut Fœminæ* furti *damnatæ. In terra cum quis decapitatur & in terram prosternitur.*

Frussetum, A Wood, or Wood-ground, *Doomsday.*

Furlong, *Ferlingum terræ*, Is a quantity of Ground containing in most places forty Poles, every Pole sixteen foot and a half in length; eight of which *furlongs* make a Mile, *Anno* 35 *E.* 1. *cap.* 6. It is otherwise the eight part of an Acre; yet an old Book printed in *Henry* the Eighths time makes 600 foot, by fivescore to the hundred, a *furlong*, see *Acree.* In the former signification, the *Romans* call it *Stadium*, in the later *Jugerum*: A Pole is in some places called a *Perch*, and differs in length according to the Custom of the Country. See *Perch.*

Furnage, *Furnagium*, *Est tributum quod Domino* furni *a sectatoribus penditur ob usum* furni. For in many places the Tenants are bound to bake their Bread in the Lords Oven. *Est etiam lucrum seu emolumentum quod Pistori conceditur in Pistionis sumptus et mercedem et tunc potest Pistor de quolibet quarterio frumenti lucrare* 4. *Den. & furfur & duos panes ad* furnagium *Assisa panis & cervisiæ*, 51 H. 3. See *Fornagium.*

Furre, *Furrura*, Cometh from the French *Fourrer*, i. *pelliculare*, to line with Skins. The Statute 24 *H.* 8. *cap.* 13. mentions divers, as Sable, which is a rich *Furre*, of colour between black and brown, being the Skin of a Beast called a *Sable*, of bigness between a *Pole cat*; and an ordinary *Cat*, and shaped like a *Pole-cat*; bred in *Russia*, but the most and best in *Tartary.* *Lucernes* is the Skin of a Beast so called, being near the bigness of a Woolf, of colour between red and brown, something mailed like a Cat, and mingled with black spots; bred in *Muscovia* and *Russia*, and is a very rich *Furre.* *Genet* is the Skin of a Beast so called, of bigness between a Cat & a Weezle, mailed like a Cat, and of the nature of a Cat; bred in *Spain*, whereof there be two kinds, black and gray, & the black the more pretious *Furre*, having black spots upon it hardly to be seen. *Foynes* is of fashion like the Sable, bred in *France* for the most part; the top of the *Furre* is black, and the Ground whitish. *Marterne* is a Beast very like the Sable, the Skin something courser, it liveth in all Countries that be not too cold, as *England*, *Ireland*, &c. the best be in *Ireland.* *Minius* is nothing but the Bellies of Squirrels as some say; as others, it is a little Vermine, like unto a Weezle, Milk-white, and brought from *Muscovy.* *Fitch* is that which we otherwise call the *Pole cat* here in *England.* *Shankes* be the Skin of the Shankes or Leg of a kind of Kid, which beareth the *Furre* that we call *Budge.* *Calaber* is a little Beast, about the bigness of a Squirrel, of colour gray, and bred especially in *High Germany.*

Fustic, A kind of wood used by Dyers, and brought from *Barbadoes*, *Jamaica*, &c. spoken of in the Stat. 12 *Car.* 2. *cap.* 18.

G.

Gabel, *Gabella*, *Gabellum*, In French *Gabelle*, that is, *Vectigal*, hath the same signification among our old Writers that *Gabelle* hath in *France*: For Mr. *Camden* in his *Brit. pag.* 213. speaking of *Wallingford*, hath these words, *Continebat* 276 *Hagas*, i. *domos reddentes novem libras de* Gablo. And *pag.* 228. of *Oxford* these, *Hæc urbas reddebat pro felonio &* gablo *& aliis consuetudin ibus, per annum Regi quidem viginti libras et sex sextarios mellis, comiti vero Algaro decem libras.* Gabella, as *Cassaneus* defines it, *De cons. Burgund.* pag. 119. *Est* vectigal *quod solvitur pro bonis mobilibus*, id est, *pro iis quæ vehuntur*, distinguishing it from *tributum, quia tributum est propriè quod fisco vel Principi solvatur pro rebus immobilibus.* The Lord *Coke*, in his *Comment upon Littleton*, saith thus, *lib.* 2. *cap.* 12. *fol.* 213. Here note, for the better understanding of ancient Records, Statutes, Charters, &c. That *Gabel* or *Gavel*, *Gablum*, *Gabellum*, *Gabellettum*, *Galbellettum* and *Gavillettum*, do signifie a Rent, Custome, Duty or Service, yielded or done to the King, or any other Lord. But that *Gablum* did as well extend to Money as to other things in kind, is very plain by that Record in *Doomsday-Book* in *Windsore* in *Berk-shire*, where 'tis said, *Rex* Willielmus *tenet* Windsores, *in Dominio Rex* Edw. *tenuit ibi* xx. *hide, &c Et adhuc sunt in villa* C. *Hage* V. *minus*; *ex bis sunt* xxvi. *quiete de* Gablo *& de aliis exeunt* xxx. *solid.* And lastly, In the same Book in *Somerset-shire*, it is thus expressed under the Title of *Terra Regis* (which observe) *Rex tenet cedre* (I suppose it is that *Chedder*, so famous for its Cheese) *Rex* Edw. *tenuit, nunquam* Geldavit, *nec scitur quot Hidæ sunt ibi, &c. in Dominio, &c.* xx. *Bord cum* xvii. *Car. &* vii. Gablatores *redd.* xvii? These seven *Gablatores* did pay seventeen shillings, and from their paying of Rent were termed *Gablatores*: To me it seems probable, That this *Gablum* is to be distinguisht from a Rent or Payment made upon Contract or Bargain, and have relation to such a one as was imposed by the Power and Will of the Lord. And these different sorts of Payments are passed in *Doomsday-Book* under several expressions, according to the nature of them; where sometimes it is written, That one *Reddit* to such a one so much, without any other addition; and this, I believe, was Rent upon Agreement and Contract: Another *Reddit de consuetudine* so much, and a third *Reddit de* Gablo so much.

Gafold-gyld, Is a Saxon word, signifying the payment or rendring of Tribute or Custome. also it sometimes denotes Usury.

Gafol-land alias **Gaful-land**, *Terra censualis*, *Land* liable to Tribute or Tax. The *Saxon Dictionary* calls it *rented Land.* See *Gavel-*

Gage, *Vadium*, Signifies a Pawn or Pledge, and is derived from the French *Gager*, that is, *pignori dare. Glanvile, lib.* 10. *cap.* 6. saith *Quandoq; rei mobiles ponuntur in vadium, quandoq; res immobiles*; and a little after that thus, *Invadiatur res quandoq; ad terminum, quandoq; sine termino; Item quandoq; invadiatur res aliqua in mortuo vadio, quandoq; non.* And from that Chapter to the end of the twelfth in the same Book, he handleth this one thing; though the word *Gage* be retained as it is a Substantive, yet as it is a Verb the use hath turned the *G.* into a *W.* so as it is oftner written *Wage*, as to *wage deliverance*, that is, to give security that a thing shall be deliver'd: For if he that distrained, being sued, have not delivered the Cattel that were distrained, then he shall not only avow the Distress, but *gager* deliverance, that is, put in Sureties that he will deliver the Cattel distrained, *F.N.B. fol.* 74. & 67. yet in some cases he shall not be tyed to his Security, as if the Cattel dyed in the Pound, *Kitchin, fol* 145. Or if he claim a propriety in the Cattel sued for, *Termes de la Ley.* To wage Law, see *Law*; and also see *Mortgage*.

Gager deliverance. See *Gage*.

Gayle. See *Gaol*.

Gager del Ley, See *Wage, and wager of Law*.

Gagers, See *Gawgers*. This word is mentioned in 12 *Car.* 2. *cap.* 4.

Gaynage, *Wainagium Plaustri apparatus*, Is near the French *Gaignage, lucrum*, and signifieth in our Law the profit most properly that comes by the Tillage of Land, held by the baser kind of Soke-men or Villains. *Bracton, lib.* 1. *cap.* 9. speaking of such, hath these words, *Et in hoc legem habet contra Dominos* &c. *ut si eos destruant, quod salvum non possit eis esse* Wainagium *suum.* And again, lib. 3. tract. 2. cap. 1. *Miles & liber homo non amerciabitur nisi secundum modum delicti, secundum quod delictum fuit magnum vel parvum et salvo contenemento suo: Mercator non nisi salva Mercandisa sua, et Villanus non nisi salvo* wainagio *suo.* This in *Westm.* 1. *cap.* 6. *Anno* 3 *E.* 1. is called *Gaynure*, and again, *cap.* 17. And in Magna Charta, cap. 14. it is called *Gainage*. In the *Old. Nat. Brev. fol.* 117. 'tis termed *Gainor*, in these words, The writ of Aiel was *præcipe*, &c. *quod reddat unam bovatam terræ et unam bovatam marisci.* And the Writ was abated, for that the Oxgange is alwayes of a thing that lyeth in *Gainor*. This word was used onely concerning Arable Land, because they that had it in Occupation, had nothing of it, but the Profit and Fruit raised by their owns pain towards their Sustenance, nor any other Title, but at the Lords Will. *Gainor*, again in the same Book *fol.* 12. Is used for a Soke-man, that hath such Land in his Occupation. In the 32. Chapter of the *Grand Custumary* of *Normandy*, Geigneurs be *Agricolæ, qui terras eleemosinatas possident.* And *Britton* useth *Gainer* for to Plow or Till, *fol.* 42. & 65. *West. Symbol. part.* 2. *tit.* Recoveries, *sect.* 3. hath these words, *A Præcipe quod reddat* lyeth not in *Bovata Marisci*, 13 *E.* 3. *fol.* 3. nor *de selione terræ*, because of the incertainty; for a *selion*, is a piece of Land sometime containing an Acre, sometimes half an Acre, sometimes more, sometimes less: It lyeth not of a Garden, Cottage or Croft, 14 *Ass.* 13 8 *H.* 6. 3. 22 *Ed.* 4. 13. *de Virgata terræ*, &c. For they be not in Demesne, but in *Gain*, &c. Lastly, In the Statute of Distresses in the Exchequer, *Anno* 51 *H.* 3. are these words, No man of Religion, or other, shall be distrained by his Beasts that *gain* the Land. See *Wainage*.

Gainery, **Tillage** or **Agriculture**, Or the Profit accrewing thereby, or of the Beasts used therein.

Gainure, *Westm.* 1. *cap.* 6. & 17. Signifies the same with *gainery*.

Galege, *Galicæ*, Seemeth to come of the French *Galloches*, which signifieth a kind of Shooe worn by the *Gauls* in dirty weather; and at present the signification differs not much among us. The word is used *Anno* 4 *E.* 4. *cap.* 7. And 14 & 15 *H.* 8. *cap.* 9. where it is written plainly *Galoches*.

Galingal, Is a Medicinal Herb, the nature and diversity whereof is expressed in *Gerards Herbal*, lib. cap. 22. The root of this is mentioned for a Drugge to be garbled, 1 *Jac.* 19.

Gallehalpens, Were a kind of Coyn which with *Suskins* and *Dotkins* were forbidden by the Statute of 3 *H.* 5. 1.

Galloches. See *Galege*.

Galls, Be a kind of hard and round Fruit like a Nut, growing upon the Tree, in Latine called *Galla*: The divers kinds and uses whereof *Gerard* expresseth in his *Herbal.* lib. 3. cap. 34. This is a Drug to be garbled, 1 *Jac.* 19.

Gang-week. See *Rogation-week*.

Gaol, *Gaola*, Cometh of the French *Geol*, i. *Caveola*, A Cage for Birds, but is metaphorically used for a Prison; thence cometh the Master of a Prison to be called *Gaoler* or *Gayler*.

Garbe, Cometh of the French word *Garbe* alias *Gerbe*, i. *fascis*: It signifies with us a bundle or sheaf of Corn, *Charta de Foresta*, cap. 7. And *Garba sagittarum* is a sheaf of Arrows, containing twenty four, otherwayes called *Shaffa sagittarum. Skene de verbor.* Signif. *verb.* Garba.

Garbles, *Anno* 21 *Jac. cap.* 19. Signifies the Dust, Soyl, or Uncleanness that is severed from Spice, Drugs, &c.

Garbling of Bowstaves, *Anno* 1 R. 3. *cap.* 11. Is the sorting or culling out the good from the bad. As *garbling* of Spice is nothing but to purifie it from the dross and dust that is mixed with it. It may seem to proceed from the *Italian* Garbo, that is, fineness, neatness; thence probably we say, when we see a man in neat habit, *He is in a handsome* Garbe.

Garbler of Spices, 21 *Jac. cap.* 9. Is an Officer of great Antiquity in the City of *London*, who may enter into any Shop, Ware-house, &c. to view and search Drugs, *Spices*, &c. and to *garble* the same, and make them clean.

Garderobe. See *Wardrobe*, and 2. *Inst. fol.* 255.

Gard, *Custodia*, Signifieth a custody or care of Defence, but hath divers significations, sometimes applyed to those that attend upon the safety of the Prince, called the *Life-guard*, or *Yeomen of the guard*; sometimes to such as have the Education of Children under Age, or of an Ideot, sometimes to a Writ touching Wardship: Which Writs are of three sorts, one called *a Writ of Gard* or *Ward*, in French *Droit de gard, F. N. B fol.* 139.

The

The second is *Ejectment de garde*, Idem. fol. eod. The third is *Ravishment de gard*, Idem. fol. 140. See *Gardeyne*. See *Ward*.

Gardeyne or **Gardian**, *Custos*, Cometh of the French *Gardien*, and yet the German word *Warden* is nearer to it. It signifies generally him that hath the charge or custody of any person or thing; but more notoriously him that hath the Education or Protection of such People, as are not of sufficient Discretion to guide themselves and their own Affairs, as Children and Ideots, being indeed as largly extended as *Tutor* and *Curator* among the *Civilians*; for whereas *Tutor* is he that hath the government of a Youth, until he come to fourteen years of Age, And *Curator* he that hath the disposition and ordering of his Estate afterwards, until he attain to the Age of five and twenty years; or that hath the charge of a frantick person during his Lunacy, we use onely *Gardian* for both these: And for the better understanding of the Law in this point, we are to observe, That a *Tutor* is either *Testamentarius*, or a *Prætore datus ex lege Atilia*; or lastly, *Legitimus*. So we have three sorts of *Gardians* in *England*, one ordained by the Father in his last Will, another appointed by the Judge, the third cast upon the Minor by the Law and Custome of the Land: Touching the first, A man having Goods or Chattels, may appoint a *Gardian* to the Body or Person of his Child, by his last Will and Testament, until he come to the Age of fourteen years, and so the disposing and ordering his Estate so long as he thinks meet, which is commonly to one and twenty years of Age. The same he may do of Lands not holden *in Capite*, or by Knights-service: But the ancient Law in this case is very much altered by the Statute of 12 *Car*. 2. *cap*. 24. which, in all cases, gives the Father power to appoint a *Gardian* for his Child; But if the Father order no *Gardian* to his Child, the Ordinary may appoint one to manage his Goods and Chattels, till the Age of fourteen years, at which time he may choose him another *Gardian*, accordingly as by the Civil-Law he may his *Curator*; for we all hold one Rule with the *Civilians* in this case, and that is *Invito Curator non datur*. And for his Lands the next of Kin on that side, by which the Land cometh not, shall be *Gardian*, and was heretofore called *Gardian in Socage*. See more of the old Law in this case, 28 *E*. 1. *Stat*. 1. And *Fortescue de laudibus legum*, Ang. cap. 44. Stamf. Prærog. cap. 1. *Old Nat. Brev. fol.* 94. And *Skene de verbor.* Signif. *verbo* Varda, from whom you may learn great affinity, and yet some difference between the Law of *Scotland* and Ours in this point.

Guardia, Is a word used among the *Feudists* for the Latine *Custodia*, & Guardianus *seu* guardio, *dicitur ille, cui custodia commissa est*, Lib. Feudor. 1. tit. 2. & 11.

Gardeyne or **Guardian of the Spiritualties**, *Custos Spiritualium vel Spiritualitatis*, Is he to whom the *Spiritual* Jurisdiction of any Diocess is committed, during the vacancy of the See 25 *H*. 8. 21. And the *Guardian* of the *Spiritualties* may either be *Guardian* in Law, or *Jure Magristratus*, as the Archbishop is of any Diocess within his Province; or *Guardian* by delegation, as he to whom the Archbishop or Vicar-General doth for the time depute, 13 *Eliz. cap*. 12.

Gardeyne or **Gardian of the Peace**, *Custos pacis*. See *Conservator of the Peace*.

Gardeyne or **Gardian**, or rather **Warden of the Cinque Ports**, *Gardianus quinq; portuum*, Is a principal Magistrate that hath the Jurisdiction of those Havens in the East-part of *England*, which are commonly called *The Cinque Ports*, that is, the five *Ports* or Havens, who there hath all that Jurisdiction that the Lord High Admiral of *England* hath in places not exempt. And the reason why one Magistrate was assigned to so few Havens, was, because they, in respect of their situation anciently, required a more vigilant care than other Havens, being nearer, and more obvious to Enemies, by the narrowness of the Sea in those parts. *Cambden* in his *Brit. pag.* 238. saith, That the *Romans*, after they had setled themselves and their Empire here in *England*, appointed a Magistrate or Governor over those Eastern parts, whom they called *Comitem literis Saxonici per Brittanniam*, having another that did bear the same Title on the opposite part of the Sea, whose Office was to fortifie and furnish the Sea-Coasts with Munition against the Incursions and Robberies of the *Barbarians*; and farther signifieth his Opinion, That our *Warden of the Cinque-Ports* was first erected among us, in imitation of that *Roman* Policy. See *Cinque-Ports*.

Gardeyne de L' estemary, *Anno* 17 *Car*. 1. *cap*. 15. Warden of the *Stanneries*.

Gardeyne del Esglish, In English *Church-wardens*, Who are Officers chosen in every Parish, to have the care and custody of the Church Goods; and they may have an Action for the Goods of the Church, and divers other things they may do for the benefit of the Church. And by 43 *Eliz. cap*. 2. They are to joyn with the Overseers for the making of Rates, and other Provision for the Poor of the Parish.

Gare, *Anno* 31 *E*. 3. *cap*. 8. Is a course Wooll ful of Hairs, such as groweth about the Pezzle or shanks of Sheep.

Gariofilli, But more truly *Garyophylli*, Is that sort of Spice we call *Cloves*. There is a reservation in a Charter of *Hugh de Wygeton*, of the Priory of *Leominster*, *Anno* 1283. in these words, *Salva hæredibus meis post decessum meum uno clavo* Gariofil. *in præd. festo sancti* Mich. *pro omni servitio sæculari*.

Garnish, As to *garnish* the Heir, that is, to warn the Heir, 27 *Eliz. cap*. 3.

Garnishee, Is taken for the Party in whose hands Money is attached, within the Liberties of the City of *London*, so used in the Sheriff of *Londons* Court, because he has had *garnishment* or warning not to pay the Money, but to appear and answer to the Plaintiff-Creditors Suit.

Garnishment, Cometh of the French *Garnir*, i. *instruere*, and in a legal sense intends a warning given to one for his Appearance, for the better furnishing of the Cause and Court. For example, One is sued for the Detinue of certain Evidences and Charters, and saith, That the Evidences were delivered to him not onely by the Plaintiff, but another also, and therefore prayeth,

 that

that that other may be warned to plead with the Plaintiff, whether the said Conditions be performed, yea or no; And in this Petition he is said to pray *Garnishment*, *New Book of Entries*, *fol.* 211. *col.* 3. and *Termes de la Ley*, *Cromp. Jur. fol.* 211. Which may be interpreted either warning of that other, or else furnishing of the Court with Parties sufficient throughly to determine the Cause, because until he appear and joyn, the Defendant is, as it were, out of the Court, *F. N. B. fol.* 106. and the Court is not provided of all Parties to the Action. With this agrees *Britton*, *cap.* 28. where he saith, That Contracts, some be naked and *sans garnment*, and some furnisht, or (to use the liberal signification of the word) apparelled; but a naked Contract, *Nudum Pactum*, giveth no Action. And therefore it is necessary or needful, that every Obligation be apparell'd, which ought to be with these five sorts of *Garnements*, &c. Howbeit it is generally used for a warning in many places, particularly in *Kitchin*, *fol.* 6. *Garnisher le Court*, is to warn the Court; and reasonable *garnishment* in the same place intends reasonable warning, and again, *fol.* 283. and many other Authors. And in the Stat. 27. *Eliz. cap.* 3. upon a *Garnishment*, or two *Nichills* returned, &c. But this may well be thought a *Metonymy* of the effect, because by the warning of Parties, the Court is furnished and adorned.

Garranty. See *Warranty*.

Garsumme, A Fine or Amerciament. See *Doomsday*; 'Tis written in *Spelman Gloss. Gersuma*.

Garter, *Garterium*, In French *Jariter*, i. *Periscelis*; signifies with us both in divers Statutes and otherwise, one especial *Garter*, being the honourable, Ensign of a great and noble Society of Knights, called *Knights of the Garter*, and this is κατ' ἐξοχὴν, as being of all others the most excellent. This high Order, as appeareth by Mr. *Camden* 211. and many others, was first instituted by that famous King *Edward* the Third, upon good success in a Skirmish, wherein the Kings *Garter* (as it is said) was used for a Token: 'Tis true, *Polydore Virg.* gives it a more slight Original, but his grounds, by his own confession, grew from the Vulgar Opinion, however take it as it is. *Edward* the Third, King of *England* (sayes he) after he had obtained many great Victories, the Kings of *France* and *Scotland* being both Prisoners in the Tower of *London* at one time: King *Henry* of *Castile*, the Bastard expulsed, and *Don Pedro* restored by the Prince of *Wales*, did, upon no weighty occasion, first erect this Order, *Anno* 1350. *viz.* He dancing with the Queen, and other Ladies of the Court, took up a *Garter* that happened to fall from one of them, whereat some of the Lords smiling, the King said, That ere it were long he would make that *Garter* to be of high Reputation, and shortly after instituted this Order of the *Blue Garter*, which every Companion of the Order is bound daily to wear, being richly deckt with Gold and precious stones, and having these words fixt on it, HONI SOIT QUI MAL Y PENSE, which is commonly thus interpreted, *Evil to him* that *evil thinketh*, or rather thus, *To him be it that evil thinketh*, *Ferne* in his *Glory of Generosity*, fol. 120. agrees with *Camden*, and more particularly sets down the Victories by which this Order was occasioned. We will not (it being none of our Work) insist upon the cause of its beginning, [but leave you for the search thereof to an Ingenious and most Laborious piece of Work concerning this matter, given to the World by *Elias Ashmole* Esquire,] but how or whatever the beginning was, the Order is inferior to none in the World, consisting of 26 Martial and Heroical Nobles, whereof the King of *England* is the Soveraign, and the rest be either Nobles of the Realm, or Princes of other Countries, Friends and Allies of this Kingdome: The Honors being such, as Emperors and Kings of other Nations have desired, and thankfully accepted. He that will read more, let him converse with Mr. *Camden*, *Polidore*, *Ferne*, and the foresaid Mr. *Ashmoles* Books. The Ceremonies of the Chapter proceeding to Election, of the Investiture and Robes, Installation, and now with all other Observations. See Mr. *Segars Honor*, *Military and Civil*, lib. 2. cap. 9. fol. 65. and the same Mr. *Ashmole*. *Garter* also signifieth the Principal King of Arms among our English Heralds, created by King *Henry* the Fifth, *Stow*, *pag.* 584. and mentioned 14 *Car.* 2. *cap.* 33. See *Herald*.

Garth, Signifies a little Backside or Close in the North of *England*, Also a Dam or Wear in a River, for the catching of Fish, vulgarly call'd a *Fishgarth*. It seems to be an ancient British word, for *Gardd* in that Language signifies *Garden*.

Garthman, 13 *R.* 2. *Stat.* 1. *cap.* 19. & 17. *R.* 2. *cap.* 9. It is Ordained, That no Fisher or *Garthman* shall use any Nets or Engines to destroy the Fry of Fish, &c. whereby it seems to intend one that owns an open Wear where Fish are caught: We may haply derive it from the scotch word *Gart*, that signifies compelled or enforced, because the Fish are forced by the Wear to pass in at a Loop, where they are caught.

Gavel, Signifies Tribute, Toll, Custome, yearly Rent, Payment or Revenue; Of which we had of old several kinds, *Gavel-Corn*, *Gavel Malt*, *Oat-gavel*, *Gavel-Fodder*, as you may read in Mr. *Fab. Phillips* Book, stiled *The Mistaken Recompence*, fol. 39, 40. And *Taylors History of* Gavelkind, *pag.* 26, 27. & 102.

Gavelet, Is a special and ancient kind of *Cessavit* used in *Kent*, where the Custome of *Gavelkind* continueth, whereby the Tenant shall forfeit his Lands and Tenements to the Lord, of whom he holdeth, if he with-draw from him his due Rent and Services, which is done after this manner. If any Tenant in *Gavel-kind* with-hold his Rents and Services, let the Lord, seek by the Award of his Court from three weeks to three weeks, to find some Distress upon the Tenement until the fourth Court, alwayes with Witnesses and if within that time he can find no Distress on that Tenement, whereby he may have Justice of his Tenant, then at the fourth Court let it be awarded, that he take that Tenement into his Hand in name of a Distress, as if it were an Oxe or a Cow, and let him keep it a year and a day in his Hand without manuring: In which time, if the Tenant come and pay his Arrearages, and make him reasonable amends, let him re-enjoy it; but if he come not in that time, then let the Lord go to the next County-Court, with his Witnesses of

his

his own Court, and pronounce there his Process; and by the Award of his Court (after the County-Court holden) he shall enter, and manure those Lands and Tenements as his own; and if the Tenant come afterwards, and will re-have his Tenements, and hold them as he did before, let him make Agreement with the Lord according as it is anciently said.

Nighesith yeld, and Nighesith geld
Let him nine times pay, and nine times repay.

Hath he not since any thing given? nor hath he not any thing since paid? let him pay v. *lib.* for his Error, before he become Tenant or Holder again. See hereof 10 *H.* 3. *Fitz. cessavit* 60. and the Statute of *Gavelet*, where it appeareth to be a Writ used in the *Hustings* at *London*. And *Fleta* sayes, It is used in other Liberties, *lib. cap.* 55. In the *Collection of Statutes, London* 2. Is matter much tending to this purpose, That by this word *Gavelet*, the Lord shall have the Land for the ceasing of the Tenant. Mr. S. in his 31. page, *of the History of Gavel kind*, hath these words, *Et postea per quandam consuetudinem quæ vocatur* Gavelate, *usitatam in comitatu isto* (viz. Kanc.) *de terris & tenementis de* Gavel kind, *pro redditibus et servitiis quæ a retro fuerint de eisdem, per plures annos, devenerunt eædem terræ in manus cujusdam Abbatis, &c.* Now this *Consuetudo de Gavelate* (as he further adds) was not a Rent or Service, but betokeneth a Rent or Service with-held, denyed or detained, causing the forfeiture of the Tenement to the Lord, with which agree the Lord *Coke*, where he sayes, *Gaveletum*, is as much as to say, to cease, or to let to pay the Rent; *Breve de* gaveleto *in* London, *est, breve de Cessavit in Biennium, &c. Pro redditu ibidem quia tenementa fuerunt indistringibilia.* So that this Writ lay in *London* as well as *Kent.*

Gavel-kind, Is by Mr. *Lambert* in his *Exposition of Saxon words*, verbo *Terra & scripto*, compounded of three Saxon words, *Gyfe, Eal, Cyn*; *Omnibus cognatione proximis data.* But *Verstegan* in his *Restitution of decayed Intelligence*, cap. 3. Calls it *Gavel kind, quasi*, give all kind, that is, give to each Child his part. But *Taylor* in his *History of Gavel-kind*, would derive it from the Brittish *Gafael*, a Hold or Tenure, and *Cenned* or *Cennedh*, *Generatio aut familia*, and so *Gavel cenedh* might signifie *Tenura generationis, pag.* 92. *&* 132. But whatever is the true Etymology, it signifies in Law a Custome, whereby the Land of the Father is equally divided at his death among all his Sons, or the Land of the Brother equally divided at his death among all his Brethren, if he have no Issue of his own *Kitchin, fol.* 102.

Teutonicis priscis patrios succedit in agros,
Mascula stirps omnis ne foret ulla potens.

This Custome is still in force in divers places of *England*, but especially in *Kent*; *Urchenfield*, in *Herefordshire*, and elsewhere, though with some difference; but by the Statute of 35 *H.* 8. *cap.* 26. All *Gavel-kind* Land in *Wales* are made descendible to the Heirs, according to the course of the Common Law. *Cambden* in his *Brittannia, pag.* 239. saith in express words, *Cantiani eâ lege* Gulielmo Normanno *se dediderunt, ut patrias consuetudines illæsas retinerent, illamque imprimis quam* Gavelkind *nominant. Hæ terræ quæ eo nomine censentur liberis masculis ex æquis portionibus dividuntur vel fœminis si masculi non fuerint*, adding withall worth the noting, *viz. Hanc hæreditatem cum quintundecimum annum attigerint, adeunt, & sine Domini consensu, cuilibet vel dando vel vendendo, alienare licet. Hâc filii parentibus furti damnatis in id genus fundi, &c.* It appears by 18 *H.* 6. *cap.* 3. that in those dayes there were not above thirty or forty persons in *Kent* that held by any other Tenure, but it was altered afterwards in much Land in that County, upon the Petition of several Gentlemen there, by a Statute made 31 *H.* 8. *cap.* 3. See *Lamberts Perambulation* of *Kent*, *Sumners* Discourse on this Subject, [*Taylors* History of *Gavel-kind.*] *Vide etiam Termes de Ley*, and *Gavelet.* In *Mon. Ang.* 2. *par. fol.* 640. you may read thus, ---*Dedi totam terram, quam vendidit mihi* Michael *de Turnham sicut suum liberum* Gavilikind *& Stoikikind ad fundandum ibi Domum Religionis, &c.* ---In *Gavel-kind*, though the Father be hanged, the Son shall inherit; for their Custome is, The Father to the Bough, the Son to the Plough, *Doctor* and *Student, cap.* 10. *Coo.* on *Lit. lib.* 2. *cap.* 10. *sect.* 165. and *Co.* 9. *Rep. Shelleys* Case.

Gavelsester, *Sextarius Vectigalis*, Is a certain Measure of Rent-Ale; Among the Articles to be charged on the Stewards and Bayliffs of the Church of *Canterburies* Mannors, this of old was one, *De* Gavelsester *cujuslibet bracini braciati infra libertatem Maneriorum,* viz. *unam Lagenam & dimidiam Cervisiæ.* We may find it else-where under the name, of *Tolcester* thus, *De Tolcester cervisiæ, hoc est de quolibet bracino per unum annum lagenam de cervisia*, and is without dispute the same. In lieu of which the Abbot of *Abbinton*, of Custome, received that Peny, mentioned by *Selden* in his *Dissertation* annexed to *Fleta, cap.* 8. *num.* 3. and there (I believe) misprinted *Colcester-peny* for *Tolcester-peny*.

Gawgeor or **Gager**, *Gaugeator*, Comes of the French *Gawchir*, i. *in gyrum torquere*; and signifies with us an Officer of the Kings, appointed to examine all Tuns, Pipes, Hogsheads, Barrels, and Tertia's of Wine, Beer, Ale, Oyl, Honey, Butter, and give them a Mark of Allowance, before they be sold in any place. And because this Mark is a Circle, made with an Iron Instrument for that purpose: It seems that from thence he taketh his Name. Of this Office you may find many Statutes, the first whereof is 27 *E.* 3. commonly called the Statute of *Provision* or *Purveyors, cap.* 8. The others are 4 *R.* 2. *cap.* 1. 18 *H.* 6. 17. 23 *H.* 6. 16 1 *R.* 3. 13. 28 *H.* 8. 14. And lastly, 12 *Car.* 2. *cap.* 4.

Gawge-peny, May be thought to be the *Gawgers* Fee, by *Anno* 23 *H.* 6. *cap.* 16.

Geld, *Geldum*, Among the Saxons signified *pecunia vel tributum*, also the compensation for a Crime: Hence, in our ancient Laws *Wergild* was used for the value of a Man slain, and *Orfgeld* of a Beast. *Et sint quieti de* Geldis, *& Danegeldis, & Horngeldis, & Forgeldis, & de Blodwita, & Fitwita, & Flitwita, & Leirwita & Heinwita, et Fremenefuda, et Werd-peny, et Aver-peny, et Toling peny,* Charta Rich. 2. Priorat. *de* Hertlande *in* Devon, *Pat.* 5 *E.* 4. *part* 3. *m.* 13. See *Gilde.*

Geldable. See *Gildable.*

Gemote, Is a Saxon word signifying *Conventus*, an Assembly: 'Tis used in the Laws of *Edward* the *Confessor, cap.* 35. for a Court, *viz. Omnis homo pacem habeat eundo ad* gemotum *& rediens de* gemoto, *nisi probatus fur fuerit.* See *Mote.*

General Issue. See *Issue.*

¶ **Geneath,** *Villanus*, as *Regis Geneath* is the Kings Villain, *Leg. Inæ.* M. S. *cap.* 19.

Generosa, Seems of late to be a good Addition; for if a Gentlewoman be named *Spinster* in any Original Writ, Appeal or Indictment, she may abate, and quash the same, 2. *Inst. fol.* 668.

Genets alias **Jenets.** See *Furre.*

Gentleman, *Generosus*, Is an irregular compound of two Languages, the one from the French *Gentil*, that is, *Honestus, vel honesto loco natus*; the other from the Saxon *Mon*, as if you would say, a man well born. The *Italian* followeth the very word, calling those *Gentil huomini*, whom we call *Gentlemen.* The *Spaniard* keepeth the meaning, calling him *Hidalgo* or *Hijo d'algo*, that is, the Son of some Man, or of a Man of Reckoning: The *French* also call him *Gentil homme.* So that *Gentlemen* be those, whom their Blood and Race doth make noble and known: In Greek they are Εὐγενεῖς, in Latine *Nobiles, Smith de Rep. Ang. lib.* 1. *cap.* 20. Under this Name are comprised all above Yeomen, so that Noblemen be truly called *Gentlemen*; but by the Course and Custome of *England*, Nobility is either Major or Minor; the greater contains all the degrees from Knights upward, the lesser, all from Barons downward, *Smith ubi supra, cap.* 21. The reason of the Name may grow from this, that they observe *gentilitatem suam*, that is, the Race and Propagation of their Blood, by giving of Arms, which the common sort neither doth, nor may do; for by the Coat that a *Gentleman* giveth, he is known to be, or not to be descended from those of his Name, that lived many hundred years since, *Gentiles homines.* See in *Tiraquel de Nobilitate*, cap. 2. pag. 53, *Cicero* in his *Topicks* of this matter, speaks thus, *Gentiles sunt qui inter se eodem sunt nomine ab ingenuis oriundi, quorum majorum nemo se servitutem servivit, qui capite non sunt diminuti.* And in the First Book of his *Tusc. Quest.* be calleth *Tullus Hostilius*, one of the Kings of *Rome, Gentilem suum.* These words, *gentilis homo*, for a *Gentleman*, was adjudged a good addition, *Hill.* 27 *E.* 3. The addition of Knight is ancient, but of Esquire or *Gentleman* rare before the First of *Hen.* 5. *cap.* 5. See 2. *par. Inst. fol.* 595. & 667.

Gersuma, *Sumptus*, In ancient Charters it is used for a Fine or In-come; as *dare in Gersumam.* And *Gersumam capere, de nativa nostra impregnata sine licentia nostra quod dicitur Childwit. Mat. Paris* writes it *Gersoma*, and in *Scotland* they say *Gressume*, and in *Doomsday* we find it *Garsumme. Vide antea* Garsumme, and *Spelm. Gloss.*

Gestu & fama, Is a Writ, but grown out of use, *Lamb. Eiren.* lib. 4. cap. 14 pag. 531.

Gethbrech. But more truly *Grithbrech*, *Si pacem quis fregerit ante mediocres Forestæ, quod dicunt* Gethbrech, *emendet Regi decem solidis, Constitut. Canuti de Foresta*, cap. 18. See *Grithbrech.*

Giggemils, Were for the fulling of woollen Cloth, and forbidden, 5 *E.* 6. *cap.* 22. They were a kind of Fulling-Mills.

Gild alias **Geld,** 18 *Car.* 2. *cap.* 1. It is used as a Verb, and as a Substantive also; and as it is a Sustantive; it is latined *gilda*, and signifies a Tribute, or sometimes an Amerciament, or thirdly, a Fraternity or Company combined together, with Orders and Laws made among themselves, by the Princes Licence. *Camden* citeth many Antiquities, by which it appears to signifie a Tribute or Tax, as *pag.* 135. 139. 159. 168. 178. *Crompton* in his *Jurisdictions, fol.* 191. sheweth it to be an Amerciament, as *Footgeld*, And *fol.* 197. he interpreteth it to be a Prestation within the Forest, in these words, To be quit of all manner of *gelds*, is to be discharged of all manner of Prestations, to be made for gathering of sheaves of Corn, of Lamb and of Wooll, to the use of the Foresters. *Camden*, pag. 349. dividing *Suffolk* into three parts, calleth the first *Geldable*, because Tribute is thence gathered; the second *Libertatem S. Ethelredi*, and the Statute of 27 *E.* 3. *Stat.* 2. *cap.* 13. and 11 *H.* 7. *cap.* 9. use *gildable* in the same sense, and so doth the Stat. 27 *H.* 8. *cap.* 26. From hence *Lamberd* is perswaded (*ubi supra*) that the common word *Gild* or *Gild-hall* doth proceed: And in *Reg. Orig. fol.* 219. we may read *gildam mercatoriam*, that is the *Merchant-gild*, which was liberty or priviledge granted to Merchants, whereby they are enabled to hold certain Pleas of Land within their own Precincts. This word *Gildes* or *Guilds* is so used, 37 *E.* 3. 51. and 15 *R.* 2. *cap.* 5. And *Gildhalda Teutonicorum* is used for the Fraternity of *Easterling* Merchants in *London*, called the *Stilyard*, 22 H. 8. 8. See *Co. lib.* 8. *fol.* 125. This word is also mentioned 15 H. 6. 6. and 15. *Car.* 2. *cap.* 7.

Gildale, A Compotation, where every one paid his share. See *Sothale.*

Gildable or **Geldable,** That is, lyable to pay Tax or Tribute; and therefore *Camden* calls one part of *Suffolk Geldable.* It is mentioned 27 *Hen.* 8. *cap.* 26. It is also expounded in an Old *M. S.* to be that Land or Lordship which is *sub districtione curiæ Vicecom.* 2. par. Inst. fol. 701. *Jur dicunt, quod Prior de* Sempringham, *tenet tres Carucatas terræ in S, et non sunt* geldabiles, Ex Rot. Hundr. *in* Turr. Lond. *de* Anno 3 E. 1. *Linc.* See *Gild.*

Gild-hall, The chief *Hall* of the City of *London, Gildarum nomine continentur non solum minores Fraternitates et sodalitia sed ipsæ etiam Civitatum communitates*, sayes the learned *Spelman.* See *Gild.*

Gildhalda Teutonicorum, The *Stilyard.* See before *Gild.*

Gild-merchant, *Gilda Mercatoria*, See *Gilde.*

Gildwite. See *Gyltwite.*

Ginger, *Zinziber*, Is a Spice well known, being the Root of a Plant, that groweth in hot Countries, as *Spain, Barbary, &c.* The true form whereof you have expressed in *Gerards Herbal*, lib. 1. cap. 38. This is a Spice whose Root is to be garbled, 1 *Jac.* 19.

Gynny Pepper, *Piper de Guinnea*, Is otherwise called *Indian Pepper*, of the place whence it cometh; the Nature, and farther Description whereof

whereof you have in *Gerards Herbal*, lib. 2. cap. 66. This is mentioned among Drugs and Spices to be garbled, by 1 *Jac.* 19.

Gisarmes, but more truly **Guisarmes**, 13 *E.* 1. *Stat.* 3. *cap.* 6. Is according to *Skene de verb.* Signif. *verbo* Gysarum, a kind of Hand-Axe, *Fleta*, lib. 1. cap. 24. sect. *Item quod quilibet*, writes it *Sisarmes. Spelman* sayes, *Est armorum genus longo manubrio & porrecto cuspide.*

Glawnce ore. See *Plowden*, *fol.* 320. The Case of *Mines*.

Glanvil, Was a learned Lawyer, and chief Justice in *Henry* the Seconds dayes, who writ a Book *Of the Common Laws of England*, which is the ancientest of any extant, touching that Subject, *Stamf. præ. cap.* 1. *fol.* 5. He was then called in Latine *Ranulphus de Glanvilla.* He died in *Richard* the Firsts dayes, at the Siege of *Acres*, in the Coast of *Palestine*, being with him in his Voyage to the Holy Land, *Plowden*, *fol.* 368. *Stowels* Case.

Glyn, Signifies a Valley. See *Doomsday-Book*.

Gleabland, **Gleba**, **Church-land**, *Dos ad Ecclesiam pertinens*, Chart. *Elredi* Regis Magnæ Brit. Monast. *de* Croiland, *apud* Ingulphum. *Imprimis totam insulam Croilandiæ pro gleba Ecclesiæ --Dono. Linwood* sayes, *Gleba est terra in qua consistit Dos ecclesiæ*, mentioned in the Stat. 14 *Car.* 2. *cap.* 25. we most commonly take it for Land belonging to a Parish-Church, beside the Tythe. *Skene* sayes, *The four aickers of Land quhilk is granted to the Ministers of the* Evangel *within this Land, is called* ane Gleebe, *the quhilke fuld be free fra payment of ony Teinds*, De verbor. *Sig.* verb. *Mansus.*

Go, Is used sometime in a special Signification, as to *go* to God, is to be dismissed the Court; so also is to *go* without day, *Broke*, *tit.* Fayler de Records, *num.* 1. See *Smith de Rep. Angl. lib.* 2. *cap.* 13. and *Kitchin*, *fol.* 193.

Goaling of Vagabonds, That is, sending them to the *Gaol*, 35 *Eliz. cap.* 7.

Godbote, Was a Fine or Amerciament for Crimes and Offences against *God*, an Ecclesiastical or Church Fine.

Good behaviour. See *Good abearing.*

Goats, No man may Common with *Goats* within the Forest without especial Warrant. *Nota*, That *Capriolus non est bestia, venationis Forestæ*, Manwoods *Forest-Law*, cap. 25. num 3.

Good abearing, *Bonus gestus*, Is by a special signification, an exact carriage or behaviour of a Subject to the King and his Liege People, whereunto Men upon their evil course of Life, or loose Demeanor, are sometimes bound: For as *Lambard* in his *Eirenarcha*, *lib.* 2. *cap.* 2. saith, He that is bound to this, is more strictly bound, than to the Peace; for the Peace is not broken without an Affray, but this Surety *de bono gestu* may be forfeited by the number of a Mans Company or by his or their Weapons or Harness. Whereof see more in that learned Writer in the same Chapter, as also in *Cromp. Just. of Peace*, *fol.* 119, 120, 121, 122, 123, 124, 125, 126, 127.

Good Country, *Bono Patria*, Is an Assise or Jury of *Countrymen* or *good* Neighbors. *Skene de verbor.* Signif. *verb.* Bona patria.

Goole, From the French *Goulet*, or the Latine *gula*, In *Anno* 16 & 17 *Car.* 2. *cap.* 11. is a breach in a Bank, or Sea-wall, or a passage worn by the flux and reflux of the Sea.

Gorce, May be fetcht from the French *Gort*, that denotes a Wear, [it is a Pool or Pit of Water to keep Fish in; by the Grant whereof the Soyl it self passes, and a *Præcipe quod reddat* lyes of it, as you may see in 4 *E.* 3 29. *b.* and 8 *E.* 3. 13. *a.* and *F. N. B. fol.* 191.] It is also a stop in a River; It is accorded, that all such *Gorces*, Mills, Wears, Stankes, Stakes and Kiddles, which be levyed, and set up in the time of King *Edward*, the Kings Grand-father, and after, whereby the Kings Ships and Boats be disturbed, that they cannot pass in such River as they were wont, shall be out, and utterly pulled down, without being renewed, 25 *E.* 3. *cap.* 4. *Co.* on *Lit. fol.* 5. would derive it from *Gurges*, but with what reason, I will not inquire.

Gote, 23 *H.* 8. 5. A Ditch, Sluce or Gutter, I suppose with more ease drawn from the Latine word *Guttur*, than the Saxon *Geotan*, that signifies, as one saith, *Fundere.*

Graduates, *Graduati*, Are Schollars as have taken degrees in an University, 1 *H.* 6. 3.

Graffer, *Graffarius*, Signifies a Notary or Scrivener, and is used in the Statute 5 *H.* 8. *cap.* 1. Why may it not be derived from the Greek Verb γράφω, *Scribo*: I am sure it is apt enough.

Gralle, **Gradale** seu **Graduale**, A *Gradual*, or Book containing some of the Offices of the *Roman* Church. *Gradale*, sayes *Linwood*, *sic dictum a* gradalibus *in tali libro contentis*, *Provincial Ang. lib.* 3. The word is mentioned in *Plowden*, *fol.* 542. and 37 *H.* 6. 32. It is sometimes taken for a *Masse-Book*, or part of it instituted by Pope *Celestine*, *Anno* 432. according to *Cotgrave.*

Grand Assise. See *Assise*, and *Magna Assisa.*

Grand Cape. See *Cape* and *Attachment.*

Grand dayes, Are those in every Term solemnly kept in the Inns of Court and Chancery, *viz.* In *Easter* Term *Ascension-day*, in *Trinity* Term St. *John Baptists-day*, in *Michaelmas* Term *All-Saints-day*, (and of late *All-Souls-day*) and in *Hillary* Term the Feast of the Purification of our *Lady*, commonly call'd *Candlemas-day.* And these are *Dies non Juridici*, no *Dayes* in Court.

Grand Distresse, *Magna Districtio*, Is so called for quality and extent thereof, for thereby the Sheriff is commanded. *Quod distringat tenentem, ita quod ipse nec aliquis per ipsum ad ea manum apponat, donec habuerit aliud præceptum, & quod de exitibus eorundem nobis respondeat, & quod habeat corpus eis, &c.* This Writ lies in two Cases, either when the Tenant or Defendant is attached, and so returned, and appears not, but makes default; then a *grand Distress* is to be awarded: Or else when the Tenant or Defendant hath once appeared, and after makes default, then this Writ lies by the Common-Law in lieu of a *Petit Cape*, 2. *par. Inst. fol.* 254. 51 *H.* 3. *cap.* 9. *Westm.* 1. *cap.* 44. and *Fleta lib.* 2. *cap.* 69. *sect. penult.* See *Distresse.*

Grand Sergeanty. See *Chivalry* and *Seargeanty*.

Grange, *Grangia*, Is a House or Farm, not onely where Corn is laid up, as Barnes be, and *Granaries, &c.* but allso Stables for Horses, Stalls for Oxen, Styes for Hogs, and other things necessary for Husbandry: And by the grant of a *Grange* such places will pass, *Provinc. Angl. lib. 2. tit.* de Judiciis, *cap.* Item Omnis.

Grant, *Concessio*, Signifies a Gift in writing of such a thing as cannot aptly be passed or conveyed by word onely, as Rents, Reversions, Services, Advowsons in gross, Common in gross, Tythes, &c. Or made by such persons as cannot give but by Deed, as the King, and all Bodies Politick, which differences be often in speechneglected, and then it is taken generally for every gift whatsoever, made of any thing by any person; and he that *granteth* is named the *Grantor*, and he to whom it is made the *Grantee*, *West Symbol. part.* 1. *lib.* 2. *sect.* 334. A thing is said to lie in *grant*, which cannot be assigned without Deed, *Coke, lib.* 3. *fol.* 63. *Lincoln* Colledge Case.

Graynes, *Grana Paradisi*, alias *Cardamomum*, Is a Spice Medicinable and wholesome, whereof you may see divers kinds in *Gerards Herbal.* lib 3. cap. 148. These are comprised among Merchandise to be garbled by 1 *Jac.* 19.

Great men, Are sometimes understood of the Temporal Lords in the higher House of Parliament, as 43 *E.* 3. *cap.* 2. and 8 *R.* 2. *in Proœm.* and sometimes of the Members of the House of Commons, as 2 *R. Stat.* 2. *in principio.*

Grava, A little Wood, *Doomsday.*

Greath-breach or **Greach-breach**, Is intended for a breaking of the Peace by *Saxton*, in his *Description of England*, and *Rastal*, tit. *Exposition of words*, but mistaken for *Grithbrech* See *Grithbrech.*

Gree, Cometh of the French word *Gre* that is good-liking, and in Law signifies Contentment or Satisfaction, as in 1 *R.* 2. *cap.* 15. To make *gree* to the Parties, is to give them contentment or satisfaction for an Offence done unto them. So in 25 E. 3. *cap.* 19. That Judgment shall be put in dispence, till *gree* be made to the King of his Debt. See *Agreement.*

Green-Cloth. See *Counting-House.*

Greenhew, Is all one with Vert, *Manwoods Forest Law*, cap. 6. num. 5. See *Vert.*

Green-Silver, *Argentum Viride*, By Custome in the Mannor of *Writtle* in *Essex*, every Tenant having his Fore-door opening to *Greenbury*, pays a half-peny yearly to the Lord of the Mannor, by the Name of *Green-silver.*

Green-wax, Is a word used in 42 E. 3. 9. and 7 *H.* 4. 3. and signifies the Estreats of Fines, Issues and Amerciaments in the Exchequer, under the Seal of that Court made in *Green-wax*, to be levyed in the County. See *Foreigne Apposer.*

Gressume, See *Gersuma*,

Greve, *Præpositus*, Is a word of Power and Authority, signifying as much as *Comes*, or *Vicecomes. Lamb.* in his *Exposition of Saxon words*, verbo *Præfectus*, makes it all one with *Reve*. The Saxon word is *Geresa*, of which we have divers words compounded, as *Shyreve*, *Portreve*, *&c.* which, by the Saxons, were written *Scyregeresa*, *Portgeresa*. See *Shireeve* and *Portgreve*. *Hovedon part. poster. annal.* fol. 346. saith, *Greve dicitur, ideo quod jure debeat Grith*, i. *pacem ex illis facere qui patria inferunt væ*, i. *miseriam vel malum.*

Grithbrech Is a *breach* of the Peace, *In causis Regiis* Grithbrech 100 *sol.—emendabit*, *Leg.* H. 1. cap. 36. *& Charta* Willelmi Conq. *Eccles. sancti Pauli in Hist. ejusd.* fol. 90.

Grills, A kind of little Fish, 22 E. 4. 2.

Grithstole, *Sedis pacis*, A Sanctuary, See *Frodmortell.*

Grocers, By 37 E. 3. 5. Were Merchants that engrossed all Merchandise vendible; but now it is a particular and well-known Trade, incorporated into a Company which is one of the Twelve, and have a very Handsome Hall, from them stiled *Grocers hall.*

Groome, *Vallettus*, 33 H. 8. *cap.* 10. Is the Name of a Servant in some inferior place. *Verstegan* in his *Restitution of decayed Intelligence*, saith, That he findeth it to have been in times past a Name for Youths, who albeit they served, yet were they inferior to Men-servants, and were sometimes sent on foot of Errants, serving in such manner as Lackeys do now.

Grosse bois, Is great Wood, and properly signifies such wood as is either by the Common-Law or Custome of the County Timber, 2. *par. Inst. fol.* 642.

Grossome, Signifies a Fine, and is corrupted from *Gersum.* For *Plow. fol.* 271. saith thus, *Et le dit* J. K. *grant per mesme le indenture a payer en la fine de le dit terme de* 10. *Ans al dit* W. N. *deze Mille de tiles ou le value de eux en argent en nosme de* Grossome; And in *fol.* 285. it is written *Gressame.*

Growme, By 43 E. 3, *cap.* 10. Seems to be an Engine to stretch woollen Cloth with after it is woven.

Growth-half-peny, A Rate paid in some places for Tythe of every fat Beast, Oxe, other unfruitful Cattel, *Claytons Rep. pag.* 92.

Gruarii, Derived from the French *Gruyer* signifies generally the principal Officers of the Forest of whom you may read in the Forest Records.

Guest-Takers or **Gist-Takers.** See *Agistors.*

Guydage, *Guydagium*, Is that which is given for safe Conduct through a strange Territory, or unknown wayes. *Cassaneus de consuetud. Burgun.* pag. 119. whose words be these, *Est* guidagium *quod datur alicui, ut tutò conducatur per loca alterius*, Co. 2. Inst. fol. 526. calls it an old legal word.

Guild. See *Gild.*

Guildhalda Teutonicorum. See *Gild.*

Gule of August, *Gula Augusti*, *Westm.* 2. *cap.* 30. 27 E. 3. Stat. 3. cap. *unico* F. N. B. *fol.* 62. alias *Goule de August.* And *Plowden*, *fol.* 316. Case of *Mines* is the very day of St. *Peter ad vincula*, which was wont, and is still celebrated upon the first of *August.* And in probability called *The Gule of August*, from *gula*, a Throat. The reason we have in *Durands Rationale Divinorum*, lib. 7. cap. *de festo sancti Petri ad vincula*, where he saith,

That

That one *Quirinus* a *Tribune* having a Daughter that had a Disease in her Throat, went to *Alexander*, then Pope of *Rome*, the sixth from St. *Peter*, and desired of him to borrow, or see the Chain that St. *Peter* was chained with under *Nero*, which Request obtained; his said Daughter kissing the said Chain, was cured of her Disease, and *Quirinus* with his Family baptized. *Tunc dictus* Alexander *Papa*, saith *Durand*, *hoc festum in Calendis* Augusti *celebrandum instituit & in honorem beati* Petri *Ecclesiam in urbe Fabricavit, ubi ipsa vincula reposuit & ad vincula nominavit & Calendis* Augusti *dedicavit. In qua festivitate populus ille ipsa vincula hodie osculatur.* So that this day that before was only called *The Calends of August*, was upon this occasion termed indifferently either of the Instrument that wrought the Miracle, St. *Peter's day ad vincula*; or of that part of the Maid whereon the Miracle was wrought, the *Gule of August*. See *Hospinian de origine festorum*, fol. 85. *Averagium æstivale fieri debet inter* Hock-day *et* gulam Augusti: *Rentale Manerii Regalis de* Wy.

Gultwit, Is an amends for Trespass, according to *Saxton*, in his *Description of England*, cap. 11. But we may suppose it mistaken for *Gyltwit*, because no such word is found either in *Spelmans Glossary*, the *Saxon Dictonary*, or ancient Record.

Guest, *Hospes*, Is used by *Bracton* for a Stranger or *Guest*, that lodges with us the second night, *Lib.* 3. *tract.* 2. *cap.* 10. In St. *Edw.* Laws, publisht by *Lamb. num.* 27. it is written *Gest*. Of this see more in *uncouth*.

Gumme, Is a clammy or tough Liquor issuing out of Trees, and hardned by the Sun. Of these there be divers sorts brought from beyond See, that are Drugs to be garbled, as appeareth by the Statute 1 *Jac.* 19.

Gutter-tile alias **Corner-tile**, Is a *Tile* made three-corner-wise, especially to be laid in *Gutters*, and at the *corners* of *tyled* Houses and Dove-houses, 17 *E.* 4. 4.

Gwabr-merched, Is a Brittish word, signifying a Fine made to some Lord of Mannors upon the Marriage of their Tenants Daughters, or otherwise upon their committing Incontinency. See *Marchet* and *Lairwite*.

Gwalstow, A place of Execution, *Omnia* Gualstown, id est, *occidendorum loca totaliter Regis sunt in soca sua*.

Gyltwyte, *Habeatq; ipse Episcopus* (sc. *Oswaldus Ep. Weorgeceastre*) *&c. debita trangressionum & pœnam delictorum quæ nos dicimus* Ofersegenesse *&* Gyltwit, *& omnia quæcunq; Rex in suis hundredis habet. Ex ipso Autographo* Eadgari *Regis dat. anno* 964. *Penes Regem*; It signifies a Compensation for Trespass or Fraud.

H.

Habeas Corpus, Is a Writ which a man indicted of a Trespass before Justices of Peace, or in a Court of any Franchise; and being apprehended and imprisoned for the same, may have out of the Kings Bench to remove himself thither at his own Costs, and to answer the Cause there, *F. N. B. fol.* 250. And the order in this case is, first to procure a *Certiorari* out of the *Chancery*, directed to the said Justices, for the removing of the Indictment into the Kings Bench, and upon that to procure this Writ to the Sheriff, for the causing of his Body to be brought at a day, *Reg. Jud. fol.* 81. where you may find divers Cases, wherein this Writ is to be used.

Habeas corpora, Is a Writ that lies for the bringing in of a Jury, or so many of them as refuse to come upon the *Venire facias*, for the Tryal of a Cause brought to Issue, *Old Nat. Brev. fol.* 157. See great diversity of this Writ in the Table of the *Register Judicial*, *verbo* Habeas corpora, and the *New Book of Entries*, *verbo* Eodem.

Habendum, Is a word of form in a Deed or Conveyance, every of which must have two parts, *viz.* the *Premisses* and the *Habendum*: The Office of the *premises* is, to express the Names of the Grantor, Grantee, and the thing granted. The Office of the *habendum* is, to limit the Estate, so that the general implication of the Estate, which, by construction of Law passeth in the *premisses*, is by the *habendum* controlled and qualified. As in a Lease to two persons, *habendum* to the one for life, the Remainder to the other for life, altereth the general implication of the Joynt-tenancy in the Free-hold, which should pass by the premisses, if the *habendum* were not, *Co. vol*, 2. *fol.* 55. *Bucklers* Case. See *use*.

Habere facias seisinam, Is a Writ Judicial, which lyeth where a man hath recovered Lands in the Kings Court, directed to the Sheriff, and commanding him to give *seisin* of the Land recovered, *Old Nat. Brev. fol* 154. See great diversity thereof in the Table of the *Register Judicial*, verbo *Habere facias seisinam*. This Writ is sometimes issuing out of the Records of a Fine executory, directed to the Sheriff of the County where the Land lyeth, and commanding him to give to the Cognisee, or his Heirs, *seisin* of the Land, whereof the Fine is levyed, which Writ lyeth within the year after the Fine, or Judgment, upon a *Scire facias*, and may be made in divers forms, *West Symbol.* 2. *tit.* Fines, *sect.* 136. There is also a Writ called *Habere facias seisinam ubi Rex habuit annum, diem & vastum*, which is for the delivery of Lands to the Lord of the Fee, after the King hath taken his due of Lands of him that was convicted of Felony, *Orig. fol.* 165.

Habere facias visum, Is a Writ that lyes in divers Cases, where view is to be taken of the Lands or Tenements in question, *F. N. B. in Indice*, verbo *View*. *Bracton*, *lib.* 5. *tract.* 3. *cap.* 8. & *lib.* 5. *part.* 2. *cap.* 11. See *View*, Reg. Jud. *fol.* 1. 26, 28, 45, 49, 52.

Haberjects or **Haubergets**, *Haubergettæ*, A kind of Cloth, *una sit latitudo pannorum tinctorum, russatorum &* Haubergettarum, *scil. duæ ulnæ infra listas*, Mag. Chart. cap. 25. 26. *Et pupilla occuli*, part 5. cap. 22.

Habiliments of War, 31 *Eliz. cap.* 4. Are Armor, Harness, and Provision of *War* of all sorts, without which no *War* can be maintained, 3. *par. Inst. fol.* 79.

Hables, Is the plural of the French *Hable*, signifying a Port or Haven of the Sea; whence Ships set forth into other Countries, and where they

they do arrive when they return from their Voyage: This word is used 27 *H.* 6. 3.

Hadbote, Was a Recompence made for the violation of Holy Orders, or violence offer'd to persons in Holy-Orders, *Saxon-Dictionary.*

Hade of Land, *Hada terræ; Sursum reddidit in manus Domini duas acras terræ continens decem seliones & duas* Hadas, *Anglice*, Ten Ridges, and two *Hades, jacent inter. terr. &c. Maner de Orleton, Anno* 16 Jac.

Hærede deliberando alii qui habet custodiam terræ, Is a Writ directed to the Sheriff, willing to Command one, having the Body of him that is Ward to another, to deliver him to him, whose Ward he was by reason of his Land, *Reg. Orig. fol.* 161. This is now out of use by 12 *Car.* 2 *Cap.* 24.

Hærede abducto, Is a Writ that lyeth for a Lord, who having the Wardship of his Tenant under age, by right cannot come by his Body, for that he is conveyed away by another, *Old Nat. Brev. fol.* 93. See *Ravishment de Gard*, and Hærede *rapto in Reg. Orig. fol.* 163. but now of no use.

Hæretico comburendo, Is a Writ that lies against him that is a Heretick, *viz.* that having once been convicted of *Heresie* by his Bishop, and having abjured it, afterwards falleth into it again, or into some other, and is thereupon committed to the secular Power, *F.N.B. fol.* 269. This Writ lies not at this day, according to the Opinion of Sir *Edw. Coke* in his Twelfth Rep. *fol.* 93

Haga, is used as a kind of Latine word for a House in a City or Burrough: In *Doomsday* Book in *Sussex, Terra Rogerii*, num. 11. Radulfus *tenet unam* Hagam *de* xii. *denar.* Will. *quinq;* hagas *de* 5 *fol. &c.* In an old Book, sometimes belonging to the Abbey of *St. Austins* in *Canterbury*, we find that King *Stephen* sent his Writ to the Sheriff and Justices of *Kent* in this manner, *Stephanus Rex Anglorum, Vice-comiti & Justiciariis de* Kent, *salutem, Præcipio quod faciatis habere Ecclesiæ Sancti* Augustini *& Monachis* hagam *suam quam Gosceold eis dedit, &c.*

Hafne Courts, *Hafne*, Is a Danish word signifying a Haven or Sea-port, in Letters Patent of *Richard* Duke of *Gloucester*, Admiral of *England*, 14. *Aug.* 5 E. 4. are these words, *Ulterius dicunt quod dicti Abbas & conventus & predecessores sui habent & habere consueverunt per idem tempus in prædictis villis* (Bancaster & Ringsted) *cum hulmo, quasdam curias portus vocatas* Hafne Courts *tenendas ibidem, &c.* Haven Courts, 4 *Inst. fol.* 147.

Hagbut, See *Haque* and *Haquebut.*

Haja, A Hedge, and sometimes taken for a Park or Enclosure, *Vallatum fuit, &c. Fossata* Haja *& Palatio*, Bract. lib. 2. cap. 40. num. 3. Hence *Hajement* for a Hedge-fence, *Rot. Inq.* 36 E. 3. *in Scac. de Foresta.*

Haiebote, Is an irregular compound of the French *Haye*, i. *Sepes*, and the Saxon *Bote*, *compensatio* & used for a permission to take Thorns or Freeth to make or repair Hedges. See *Hedgebote.*

Half-haque, See *Haque.*

Halsfang. See *Pillory* and *Healfang.*

Half-merk. *Dimidia Merkæ*, Is a Noble *F.N.B. fol.* 5. where he saith, That in case a Writ of Right be brought, and the seisin of a Demandant, or his Ancestor, alledged, the seisin is not traversable by the Defendant, but he may tender or proffer the *Half-mark* for the enquiry of this seisin; which is in plain terms, that the Defendant shall not be admitted to deny, that the Demandant or his Ancestor, was seised of the Land in question, and to prove his denyal; and that he shall be admitted to tender *half a Mark* in Money, to have an Enquiry made, whether the Demandant, *&c.* were so seised or not. And in this signification we find the same words in the *Old Eng. Nat. Brev. fol.* 26. Know, that in a Writ of Right of an Advowson brought by the King, the Defendant shall not proffer the *half mark, &c.* whereof *Fitzherbert*, *ubi supra*, giveth this reason, because in the Kings Case, the Defendant shall be permitted to traverse the Seisin, by Licence obtained of the Kings Sergeant. To which effect seee *F. N. B. fol.* 31.

Half-Seal, Is used in the Chancery for the *sealing* to *Delegates*, appointed upon any Appeal, either in Ecclesiastical or Marine Causes, 8 *Eliz.* 5.

Half-Tongue, See *Medietas Linguæ.*

Halymote alias **Healgemote**, Is a Court-Baron, *Manwoods Forest Laws*, *cap.* 23. And the Etymology is the meeting of the Tenants of one *Hall* or Mannor. See *Gwins Preface to his Reading, Omnis causa terminetur, vel Hundredo, vel Comitatu, vel* Halymote, *locum habentium*, Leg. Hen. 1. cap. 10. The Name is still kept in several places in *Herefordshire.* It is sometimes taken for a Convention of Citizens in their publick Hall; as in *London* every Company hath a Hall, wherein they keep their Courts, 4 *Inst. fol.* 249. It may also signify a Holy or Ecclesiastical Court.

Hall, *Halla*, The Saxon word is *Healle*, and antiently denoted a chief Mansion-house or Habitation; which word we retain in many Counties of *England* to this day, especially in the County-Palatine of *Chester*, where every Gentleman of Qualities Seat is termed a *Hall.*

Hallage, Is a Fee due for Cloaths brought for Sale to *Blackwel-Hall* in *London, Co. vol.* 6. *fol.* 62. *b.* Also the Toll due to the Lord of a Fair or Market, for such Commodities as are vended in the Common *Hall* of the place.

Hallamshire, Is a part of *York-shire*, in which the Towns of *Sheffield* stands, 21 *Jac. cap.* 23.

Ham, A House, also a Village or little Town: This is a termination of many Towns in *England*, as *Nottingham, Buckingham, Walsingham*, &c.

Hambles, See *Hables.*

Hambling, or **Hameling of Dogs**, Is the same with expeditating; *Manwoods Forest Law, cap.* 16. *num.* 5. says, This is the ancient term that Foresters used for that matter, and *num.* 12. he adds, *Canutus* in his 31 Canon, doth call *The lawing of Dogs*, *Genu-scissio*, which was a kind of cutting or laming of *Dogs* in the *hams*, which the old Foresters called *Hamling.* See *Expeditate.*

Hamlet, as also **Hamel** and **Hampsel**, Are diminutives of *Ham*, which signifies Habitation,

bitation. *Cambd. Brit. pag.* 149. & 354. *Kitchin* hath *Hamel* in the same sense, who also useth *Hampsel* for an old House or Cottage decayed, *fol.* 103. *Hamlet*, as *Stow* useth it in *Edw.* 3. seemeth to be the Seat of a Free-holder; for there he saith, The King bestowed two Mannors and nine *Hamlets* of Land upon the Monastery of *Westminster*, for the keeping of yearly Obits for his Wife, Queen *Elianor* deceased. *Spelman* making a difference betwixt *Villam integram, villam dimidiam* & Hamlettam, hath these words, *Hamlettam vero qua medietatem friborgi non obtinuit, hoc est ubi quinq; Capitales Plegii non sint deprehensi*. The Statute of *Exton*, 14. *E.* 1. mentions it thus, *Lez nosmes de toutes les villes* & Hamlets *que sont en son Wapentake*, &c.

Hamfare, An Assault made upon a House. See *Gloss. in scriptores*.

Hamsoken, See *Homesoken*, *Skene de verbor. Signif.* writeth it *Haimsuken*; and deriveth it from *Haim* a German word, signifying a House, and *Suchen*, that is, to seek, search, or pursue: It is used in *Scotland* for the Crime of him that violently, and contrary to the Kings Peace, assaulteth a Man in his own House, which, (as he saith) is punishable equally with Ravishing a Woman. *Significat etiam quietantiam misericordiæ intrationis in alienam domum vi & injuste. Fleta lib.* 1 *cap.* 47. Our antient Records express Burglary under this word *Hamsocne*. In a Charter of Donation from King *Edmund* to the Church of *St. Mary Glaston*, we have these words, *Concedo libertatem & potestatem, jura, consuetudines & omnes forisfacturas omnium terrarum suarum*, i. *Burgberith & Hundred-setena, Athas & Ordelas & Infangtheofas*, Hamsocne & *Fridebrice & Forestel & Toll & Team in omni Regno meo*, &c.

Hand-borow, A Surety, a manual Pledge, that is, an inferior Undertaker; for *Head-borow* is a superior or chief Instrument, *Spelm.*

Hand in and hand out, 17 *E.* 4. *cap.* 2. Is the name of an unlawful Game.

Handful, Is four Inches by the Standard, *Anno* 33 H. 8. 5. &c.

Hand-gun, Is an Engine prohibited to be used, and carried about by the Statute, 33 H. 8. 6. And though a Dag was invented of late time, and after the making of the said Act, and is not known by the name of a *Hand-gun*, but by its own special name; yet the carrying a Dag is within the said Act. See *Co. lib.* 5. *fol.* 71, 72.

Handy-warp, A kind of Cloth made at *Cocksal, Bocking*, and *Braintree* in *Essex*, and mentioned in the Statute 4 & 5 *Phil. & Mar.* 5.

Hanfare. See *Hinefare*.

Hangwite alias **Hangwit**, or **Heng-wit**, Cometh of the Saxon words *Hangian, pendere* and *wite, mulcta. Rastal* saith, It is a liberty granted to a man, whereby he is quit of a Felon or Thief hanged without Judgment, or escaped out of Custody. By some it hath been interpreted, *Mulcta pro homine injuste suspenso*, and elsewhere *Mulcta pro latrone præter juris exigentiam suspenso vel elapso*. It may also signify a Liberty, whereby a Lord challengeth the Forfeiture due for him, who hangs himself within his Fee, *sed quære*. See *Bloodwit*.

Hanper, *Hanaperium*, The *Hanaper* of the Chancery, *Anno* 10. R. 2. *cap.* 1. seems to signify the same, that *Fiscus* doth originally in the Latine. See *Clerk of the Hanaper*.

Hanse, According to *Ortelius* in the Index to his *Additament* to his *Theatre*, ver. *Ansiatici*, Is an old Gothish word: It signifieth a certain Society of Merchants combined together, for the good usage and safe passage of Merchandise from Kingdom to Kingdom. This Society was, and in part yet is, endowed with many large priviledges of Princes respectively within their Territories. It had four principal Seats or Staples, where the Almain or German Merchants being the Erectors of this Society had an especial House, one of which was here in *London*, call'd *Gildhalda Teutonicorum*, or among us vulgarly the *Steel-yard.---Et quod habeant Gildam mercatoriam cum* Hansa, *&c.* Charta Hen. 7. *Ballivis & Burgens. Montgomer.*

Happe, Cometh of the French *Happer*, i. *Rapere*, to snatch or catch: And signifies the same with us, as to *happe* the possession of a Deed-poll, *Littleton, fol.* 8. To *happe* the Rent, as if partition be made by two Parcenors, and more Land be allowed to one than the other; and she that has most of the Land charges it to the other, and she *happeth* a Rent, she shall remain an Assise without specialty.

Haque, Is a Hand-gun about three quarters of a yard long, 33 *H.* 8. *cap.* 6. and 2 & 3 *E.* 6, *cap.* 14. There is also the *Half-haque* or *Demy-haque*. See *Haquebut*.

Haquebut, Is a sort of *Gun*, which we otherwise call a *Harquebuss*, being both French words, 2 & 3 *E.* 6. 14. 4 & 5 *Phil. & Mar. cap.* 2.

Haratium, or **Haracium** (from the *French Haras*) signifies a race of Horses and Mares, kept for breed. *Spel Gloss. verb. Haracium. Et decimas de dominio suo, de pratis, de bladis parcis*, Haratiis, *molendinis & de Vivariis*, Mon. Ang. part 1. fol. 339.

Hariot alias **Heriot**, *Heriotum*, Is in the Saxon Tongue *Heregate*, which is derived from *Here, exercitus*; and *Geat* is a Beast, and in the Saxons time signified a Tribute given to the Lord for his better preparation towards War. *Lambert* in his *Explication of Saxon words, verbo* Hereorum, The name is still retained, but the use is altered; for whereas by *Lamberts* Opinion, it did signify so much as Relief doth now with us: Now it is taken for the best Cattle that a Tenant hath at the hour of his death, due to the Lord by Custome, *Kitchin, fol.* 133, 134. makes *Heriot* Service and *Heriot* Custom; for interpretation whereof, you shall find these words in *Broke, tit.* Hariot, *num.* 5. *Hariot* after the death of the Tenant for life is *Hariot-Custom. Hariot-Service* is after the death of Tenant in Fee-simple. In the Book called *Les Termes de la Ley*, 'tis said, That *Hariot-Service* is often expressed in the Grant of a Man, that he holds by such Service to pay *Hariot* at the time of his death, that holdeth in Fee-simple. *Hariot-Custome* is, when *Hariots* have been paid time out of mind by Custom, and this may be after the death of Tenant for life. And for this the Lord may distrain or seise. See *Plowd. fol.* 95, 96. *Bracton, lib.* 2. *cap.* 36. *Doct.* and *Stud. cap.* 9. But of right neither the Lord nor Officer should take *Hariot*, before it be presented at the

next

next Court holden after the Tenant is dead, that ſuch a Beaſt is due for a *hariot*. If the Lord purchaſe part of the Tenancy, *Hariot-ſervice* is extinguiſht, but it is not ſo in *Hariot-cuſtome*, *Co*.8. *Rep. Talbots* Caſe. If the Lord ought to have a *hariot* when his Tenant dieth, and the Tenant deviſeth away all the Goods; yet the Lord ſhall have his *hariot*, for the Law preferreth the Cuſtom before the Deviſe, *Co.* on *Lit. lib.* 3. *cap.* 3. *pag.* 185. See *Dyer*, *fol.* 199. *num.* 58. This in *Scotland* is called *Herrezelda*, compounded of *Here* in *Dutch*, in Latine *Herus*, that is, a Lord or Maſter; and *Zeild* a Gift, Tribute or Taxation. *Skene de verb.* Signif *verbo* Herrezelda.

Hart, Is a Stagg of five years old compleat, *Manwoods Foreſt Laws, cap.* 4. *num.* 5. which he hath out of *Budæus de Philolog. lib.* 10. And if the King or Queen do hunt him, and he eſcape away alive, then afterward he is called a *Hart-Royal*; And if the Beaſt by the King or Queens hunting be chaſed out of the Foreſt, and ſo eſcape, Proclamation is commonly made there-about, that in regard of the Paſtime, that the Beaſt hath ſhewed to the King or Queen, None ſhall hurt him, or hinder him from returning to the Foreſt; and then he is a *Hart-royal* proclaimed.

Harth-Peny, and **Harth-Silver**, and **Harth-Money**. See *Chimney-Money* and *Peter-Pence*.

Haubergets. See *Haberjects*.

Haw, A ſmall quantity of Land ſo called, as a *Hemp-haw*, a *Bean-haw*, lying near the houſe; But ſome Manuſcripts ſay, That *Hawes vocantur manſiones*. And *Co.* on *Lit. fol.* 5. ſays, That in an old Plea, relating to *Feverſham* in *Kent*, *Hawes* are interpreted to ſignifie the ſame.

Haward, See *Hayward*.

Hawberke, Cometh of the French *Haubert*, *Lorica*, whereupon he that holdeth Land in *France*, by finding a Coat or Shirt of Mayle, and to be ready with it when he ſhall be called, is ſaid to have *Hauberticum feudum*; whereof *Hotoman* writeth thus, *Hauberticum feudum Gallicâ Linguâ vulgo dicitur pro Loricatum*, i. *datum vaſſallo ea conditione, ut ad edictum Loricatus ſive Cataphractus ſit praeſto. Nam ut Lorica Latinis proprie, tegmen de loro factum quo majores in bello utebantur*, &c. *frequentiſſime autem pro aenea armatura integre uſurpatur*; *ſic apud Gallos* Haubert *proprie Loricam annulis contextam ſignificat, quam vulgus Cote de Maille appellat*, Hotom. *in verb.* Feudal. *verbo* Hauberticum Feudum. *Hauberke*, with our Anceſtors, ſeemeth to ſignifie as in *France* a Shirt or Coat of Male, and ſo it ſeemeth to be uſed, 13 *E.* 1. *Stat.* 3. *cap.* 6. Though in theſe days the word is otherwiſe written, as *Halbert*, and ſignifies a Weapon well enough known.

Hawes, In *Doomſday* Book ſignifies Manſions or Dwelling-houſes.

Hawkers, Be a ſort of deceitful Fellows that go from place to place, buying and ſelling Braſs, Pewter, and other Merchandiſe, that ought to be uttered in open Market: The appellation ſeemeth to grow from their uncertainty, like thoſe that with *Hawks* ſeek their Game where they can find it; you may read the word 25 *H.* 8. 6. and 33. H. 8. 4. We now call thoſe *Hawkers* that go up and down the Streets crying *News-Books*, and ſelling by Retail; and thoſe who ſell them by Whole-ſale from the Preſs are called *Mercury's*.

Haye, A Hedge, alſo a piece of Ground incloſed with a Hedge. See *Haia*.

Hayward alias **Haward**, Is a compound of two French words, *viz.* Hay i. *Sepes*, and *Gard*, i. *Cuſtodia*, and ſignifies one that keepth the common Herd of the Town; and the reaſon may be, becauſe one part of his Office is to look that they neither break nor crop the Hedges of incloſed Grounds: He is an Officer ſworn in the Lords Court, and the form of his Oath you may ſee in *Kitchin*, *fol.* 46.

Hazarders, Are ſuch as play at *Hazard*, a Game at Dice ſo called; *Hazardor communis ludens ad falſos talos adjudicatur quod per ſex dies in diverſis locis ponatur ſuper Colliſtrigium*, Inter place Trin. 2 H. 4. Suſſex 10.

Headborow, Derived from the Saxon *Head*, id eſt, *caput*, & *Borge*, i. *Pignus*; ſignifies him that is chief of the *Frank-Pledge*, and him that had the principal Government of them within his own Pledge And as he was called *Headborow*, ſo was he alſo called *Burrow-head*, *Burſholder*, *Third-borow*, *Tything-man*, *Chief-pledge* or *Burrow-elder*, according to the diverſity of Speech in ſeveral places. Of this ſee *Lambert* in his *Explication of Saxon words*, *verbo* Centuria, and in his *Treatiſe of Conſtables*, and *Smith de Rep. Angl.* lib. 2. cap. 22. This Officer is at preſent call'd a *Conſtable*. See *Conſtable*.

Head-pence, Was an Exaction of 40 *li.* or more, heretofore collected by the Sheriff of *Northumberland*, of the Inhabitants of that County twice in ſeven years, that is, every third and every fourth year, without any Account made to the King, which was therefore by the Statute of 23. H. 6. *cap.* 7. clearly put out for ever. See *Common Fine*.

Head-Silver, See *Head pence*.

Healfang, Is compounded of two Saxon words, *viz. Hals*, i. *Collum*, and *Fang*, *capere*: It is that puniſhment *qua alicui collum ſtringatur*. See *Pillory*.

Hearth-Money, See *Chimney-Money*.

Heck, Is the name of an Engine, to take Fiſh in the River of *Owſe* by *York*, *Anno* 33 Hen. 8. 18.

Heda, A Haven or Port, *Doomſday*.

Heyre, *Haeres*, Though the word be borrowed of the Latine, yet it hath not altogether the ſame ſignification with us that it hath with the *Civilians*; for whereas they call *Haeredem, qui ex teſtamento ſuccedit in univerſum jus Teſtatoris*; The Common-Law calls him *Heir*, that ſucceeds by right of Blood in any mans Lands or Tenements in Fee; for by the Common-Law nothing paſſeth *Jure haereditatis*, but only Fee; Moveables, or Chattels immoveable, are given by Teſtament to whom the Teſtator liſteth, or elſe are at the diſpoſition of the Ordinary, to be diſtributed as he in conſcience thinketh meet. *Caſſanaeus in conſuetud. Burg.* pag. 909. hath a diſtinction of *haeres*, which, in ſome ſort, accordeth well with our Law; for he ſaith, There is *Haeres ſanguinis et haereditatis*. And a man may be *Haeres ſanguinis* with us, that is, *Heir* apparent to his Father or Anceſtor; and yet may, upon diſpleaſure, be defeated of his Inheritance, or at leaſt the greateſt part of it. Every heir having Lands by descent, is bound by the binding acts of his Ancestors, if he be named, *Qui sentit commodum, sentire debet & onus*, Co. on Lit. fol. 7, 8.

Last-heir. See *Last*.

Heir-loome, Seemeth to be compounded of *Heir* and *Loome*, that is, a Frame to weave in; the word by Time hath a more general signification than at first it did bear, comprehending all Implements of Houshold, as Tables, Presses, Cupboards, Bedsteds, Wainscot, and such like; which, by the Custome of some Countries, having belonged to a house certain descents, are never inventoried after the decease of the Owner as Chattels, but accrue to the *Heir* with the house it self by custome. *Spelman* says of it, *Omne utensile robustius quod ab ædibus non facilè revellitur, ideoq; ex more quorundam locorum ad hæredem transit, tanquam membrum hæreditatis.* And *Co.* on *Lit. fol.* 18. sayes, *Consuetudo Hundredi de* Stretford *in* Com. Oxon. *est quod hæredes tenementorum infra Hundredum prædictum existen. post mortem antecessorum suorum habebunt*, &c. *Principalium, Anglicè an* Heyre loome, *viz. de quodam genere catallorum, utensilium*, &c. *optimum plaustrum, optimam carucam, optimum ciphum*, &c.

Heinfare alias **Hinefare,** *Discessio famuli á Domino*, The word is compounded of *Hine*, a Servant, and *Fare*, an old English word signifying a Passage.

Hebberman, One that fishes below *London* Bridge for Whitings, Smelts, &c. commonly at *Ebbing-water*, and therefore so called, mentioned in the Articles for the *Thames Jury*, printed 1632.

Hebbing-Wears, They are mentioned in the Stat. 23 *H.* 8 *cap*, 5.

Heisa, *Servitium, Inter placita de temp.* Jo. *Regis* Northampton 50.

Henchman or **Heinsman,** A German word, signifying *Domesticum, aut unum de familia*; It is used with us for one that runneth on foot, attending upon a man of honor, 3 *E.*4, 5 24 H. 8. 13. It is written *Henxman*, 6 H. 8. 1.

Henfare, An Amerciament for flight for Murder: *Doomsday*.

Henghen, A Prison, or House of Correction, *Si quis amicis destitutus, vel alienigena, ad tantum laborem veniat, in prima accusatione ponatur in* Henghen, &c. *Leg. Hen.* 1. *cap.* 65.

Hengwite, *Significat quetantiam misericordiæ de Latrone suspenso absq; consideratione*, Fleta, lib. 1. cap. 47. See *Hankwit*.

Heneward, A Duty to the King in *Cambridge-shire: Doomsday*.

Herald, Heralt or **Harold,** Italian *Heraldo*, French *Herault*, *quasi* herus *altus*. *Verstegan* thinks it may be derived from two Dutch words, *viz. Here, exercitus*, and *Healt, pugil magnanimus*: As if he should be called *The Champion of the Army.* With us it signifieth an Officer at Arms, whose business is to denounce War, to proclaim Peace, or otherwise be employed by the King in Martial Messages, or other business: The *Romans* called them *Plurally Feciales. Polydore, lib.* 19. describes them thus, *Habent insuper Apparitores ministros, quos* Heraldos *dicunt, quorum præfectus Armorum Rex vocitatur, hii belli et pacis nuntii ducibus, Comitibusq; a Rege factis insignia aptant ac eorum funera curant.* Nay more, They are the Judges and Examiners of Gentlemens Arms, marshal all the Solemnities at the Coronations of Princes, manage Combates, and such like: There is one and the same use of them with us and the French, whence we have their Name; and what their Office is with them, see *Lupanus*, lib. 1. *de Magist. Francor, cap.* Heraldi. There be divers of them with us, whereof three being the chief, are called *Kings at Arms.* And of them *Garter* is the principal, instituted and created by *Henry* the Fifth, *Stowes Annals*, pag. 584. whose Office is to attend Knights of the Garter at their Solemnities, and to marshal the Funerals of all the greater Nobility; as Princes, Dukes, Marquesses, Earls, Viscounts and Barons. And in *Plowden*, in *Reniger* and *Fogassa*'s Case, we read that *Edward* the Fourth granted the Office of King of *Heralds* to one *Garter*, *Cum feudis et proficuis ab antiquo*, &c. *fol.* 12. The next is *Clarentius*, Ordained by *Edward* the Fourth, for he attaining the Dukedom of *Clarence*, by the death of his Brother *George*, whom he beheaded for aspiring to the Crown, made the *Herald*, which properly belonged to the Duke of *Clarence*, a King at Arms, and called him *Clarentius*: His proper Office is to marshal and dispose the Funerals of all the lesser Nobility, as Knights and Esquires through the Realm, on the South-side of *Trent*. The third is *Norroy* or *North-roy*, whose Office is the same on the North-side of *Trent* that *Clarentius* hath on this side, as may well appear by his Name, signifying the Northern King, or King of the North parts. Besides these, there be six other properly called *Heralds*, according to their Original, as they were created to attend Dukes, &c. in Martial Expeditions, *viz. York, Lancaster, Somerset, Richmond, Chester* and *Windsore*. Lastly, There be four other called *Marshals*, or *Pursuyvants at Arms*, reckon'd after a sort in the number of *Herlads*, and do commonly succeed in the place of the *Heralds*, when they die, or be preferred; And those be *Blue-mantle, Rouge-cross, Rouge-dragon* & *Portcullis*. The *Feciales* among the *Romans* were Priests, *Nam Numa Pompilius divini cultus institutionem in octo partes divisit, & ita etiam sacerdotum octo ordines constituit*, &c. *Septimam partem sacræ constitutionis collegio eorum adjecit, qui Feciales vocantur: Erant autem ex optimis domibus, viri electi*, &c. *quorum partes in eo versabantur, ut fidei publicæ inter populos præessent, neq; justum aliquod bellum fore censebatur, nisi id per Feciales esset indictum*, Corasius Miscel. *juris civilis*, lib. 1, cap. 10. num. 12. Kings at Arms are mentioned in Stat. 14 *Car.* 2. 33. Of these, see more in *Spelmans Glossary*.

Herbage, *Herbagium*, Signifies the Fruit of the Earth, produced by Nature for the bite or mouth of the Cattel. But is most commonly used for a liberty that a man hath to feed his Cattel in another mans Ground, as in the Forest, &c. *Cromp. Jur. fol.* 197. *Occurrit frequens pro jure depascendi alienum solum ut in Forestis*, says the learned *Spelman*.

Herbenger, From the French *Herberger*, that is, *Hospitio accipere*, signifieth an Officer in the Kings house, that allotteth the Noblemen, and those of the Houshold their Lodgings, *Kitchin, fol.* 176. uses it for an Inn-Keeper.

Herciebant, From the French *Hercer*, to Harrow, *Arabant et* Herciebent *ad curiam Domini*, that

that is, they did plough and harrow at the Mannor of the Lord, 4. *Inst. fol.* 270.

Hereditaments, *Hæreditamenta*, Signifie all such things immoveable, be they corporeal or incorporeal, as a man may have to himself, and his heirs, by way of Inheritance. See 32 *H* 8. *cap.* 2. or not being otherwise bequeathed, do naturally, and of course descend to him which is next heir of Blood, and fall not within the compass of an Executor or Administrator as Chattels do. It is a word of large extent, and much used in Conveyances; for by the grant of *Hereditaments*, Isles, Seigniories, Mannors, Houses and Lands of all sorts, Charters, Rents, Services, Advowsons, Commons, and whatever may be inherited, will pass, *Co.* on *Lit fol.* 6. *Hæreditamentum est omne quod jure hæreditario ad hæredem transeat.*

Herefare, Is a going in a Military expedition, a going to a *Warfare*. See *Subsidy*.

Heregeat, See *Hariot*.

Heregeld, Is a Tribute or Tax levyed for the Maintenance of an Army. See *Subsidy*.

Heriot, See *Hariot*.

Heresliita or **Heresllia**, Denotes a hired Souldier, that departs without Licence, derived from the Saxon *Here*, *exercitus*, and *Sliten*, to depart, according to *Co.* 4. *Inst. fol* 128. Whom I rather incline to follow, than him who would in stead of *sliten*, to depart; put in *slitan*, *scindere*.

Heretico comburendo, Is a Writ that lies against a *Heretick*, who having been once convicted by the Bishop of *Heresie*, and having abjured it, after Relapses into the same, or some other, and is thereupon committed to the Secular Power. *Britton*, *lib.* 1. *cap.* 17. saith, That by the Common-Law, such as feloniously burn the Corn or houses of others, Sorcerers and Sorceresses, Sodomitical persons and *Hereticks* should be burnt.

Hebdomas, A Week, derived from ἑπτὰ, seven; as *septimana* from *septem*. *Julius Cæsar* divided the year into Twelve Months, each Moneth into four Weeks, and each Week into seven Days, according to the number of the seven Planets. See more of this matter at large, *Skene de verbor. Signif. verbo* Hebdomas.

Hermitage, *Heremitagium*, A solitary place, the recess or cell of a *Hermit*. See *Mon. Ang.* 2. *par. fol.* 339.

Hermitorium, Some Authors have confounded it with *Heremitagium*, but more rightly it may denote the Chappel, or place of Prayer belonging to a *Hermitage*; for so it is said in an old Charter, *Capellam sive Hermitorium*.

Herysfar, A Place of Immunity.

Hesta or **Hestha**, May be understood for a Capon, derived from the French *Hestoudeau*, a Caponet: *Spelm.* see *Rusca*.

Hestcorne, King *Athelstane* in his return out of the North, after a Victory, went to *Beverley*, where he gave to God, &c. *Quasdam avenas, vulgariter dictas* Hestcorne *percipiendas de Dominiis & Ecclesiis in illis partibus quas*, &c. Mon. Ang. 2. par. fol. 367.

Hexam, Was anciently a County of it self, and a Franchise, where the Kings Writ went not; But by the Stat. 14 *Eliz.* 13. *Hexam* and *Hexamshire* shall be within the County of *Northumberland*. See 4. *Inst. fol.* 222. It was also of old a Bishoprick, and in Latine stiled *Episcopatus Hugustaldensis*. See *Monast. Ang.* 2. *par. fol.* 91.

Hide of Land, *Hida terræ*, *Saxonice*, *Hydeland* is a certain quantity of Land, such as might be plowed with one Plough in a year, *Termes da Ley*. By others it is an hundred and twenty Acres: By *Beda*, who calls it *Familiam*; it is as much as will maintain a Family: Others hold it to be four yard *Land*. *Cromp.* in his *Jur. fol.* 220. says, It contains a hundred Acres, every Acre in length forty Perches, and in breadth four, every Perch sixteen foot and a half. And again, *fol.* 222. a *hide of Land* contains a hundred Acres, and eight *hides*, or eight hundred Acres makes a Knights Fee. But *Co.* on *Lit. fol.* 69. says, That a Knights Fee, a *hide*, or Plough-land, a Yard-land, or Oxgang of Land, contain no certain number of Acres. The distribution of *England* by *hides of Land* is very ancient, mention being made thereof in the Laws of King *Ina*, *cap.* 14. And *Henry* the First, to marry his Daughter to the Emperor, took of every *hide of land* three shillings, *Spelman*. And see *Camb. Brit. fol.* 158

Hide Lands, *Sunt terræ ad* hidam *seu tectum pertinentes*.

Hide and Gayne, *Old Nat. Brev. fol.* 71. *Co. lib.* 4. *Tirringhams* Case; signifies arable Land. See *Co.* on *Lit. fol.* 85. Of old to *gaine* the Land, was as much as to till or manure it. See *Gainage*.

Hidage, *Hidagium*, Is an extraordinary Tax to be paid for every *hide of land*. Bracton, *lib.* 2. *cap.* 6. writes thus of it, *Sunt etiam quædam communes præstationes, quæ servitia non dicuntur, nec de consuetudine veniunt, nisi cum necessitas intervenerit, vel cum Rex venerit, sicut sunt* hidalgia, *coragia & caruagia & alir plura de necessitate, & ex consensu communi totius Regni introducta & quæ ad Dominum feudi non pertinent*, &c. This was a frequent kind of taxing as well for provision of Armor, as payments of Money; but especially in the Reign of King *Ethelred*, who when the *Danes* landed at *Sandwich*, taxed all his Land by *hides*, so that every 310 *hides* of Land found one Ship armed, and every eight *hides* found one Jack and one Saddle for the defence of the Realm. And afterwards *William the Conqueror* took of every *hide* throughout *England* six shillings. In the *Terms of the Law*, *Hidage* is taken to be quit of that Tax, which was also called *Hyde-gyld*.

Hidell, 1 H. 7, *cap.* 5. Seemeth to signifie a place of Protectiom, as a Sanctuary.

Hierloome, See *Heyreloome*.

Hiis testibus, These words were anciently added in Deeds after the *In cuius rei testimonium*, and written with the same hand as the Deed, which Witnesses were called, the Deed read, and then their Names entred: And this Clause of *hiis testibus* in Subjects Deeds continued till the Reign of *Hen.* 8. but now is quite left off, *Co.* on *Lit. fol.* 6.

Hine, A Servant, or one of the Family, but more properly a Servant at Husbandry; and the Master *hine* is he that Oversees the rest, 12 *R.* 2. 4.

Hinefare, See *Hinefare*, *Si quis occidit hominem Regis et facit* heinfarum, *dat Regi* xx s &c. *Doomsday*, tit. *Arcanfeld*.

Hine-geld, *Significat quietantiam transgressionis illatæ in servum transgredientem*.

Hir ciscunda, The division of an Inheritance among the *heirs*, *Goldm. dict.* *Actio* Hirciscundæ. See *Action* mixt.

Hird, *Domestica familia*, *Inter pla.* Trin. 12. E. 2. Ebor. 48. M. S.

Hith, See *Hyth*.

Hirst or **Hurst**, A little Wood. See *Doomsday*.

Hoblers, *Hobellarii*, These were Souldiers lightly armed, and ordinarly horsed, but ready for any quick motion; so that we may not improperly call them *light horse-men*: But afterwards they were Men that, by their Tenure, were tyed to maintain a little light Nag, for the certifying of any Invasion made by Enemies, or such like peril towards the Sea-side; as *Portsmouth*, of whom you may read 18 *E.* 3. *Stat.* 2. *cap.* 7. and 25. *E.* 3. *Stat.* 5. *cap.* 8. and *Camd. Brit. fol.* 272, &c.

Hock-tuesday-money, Was a Duty given to the Land-lord, that his Tenants and Bondmen might solemnise that *day* on which the English master'd the *Danes*, being the second *Tuesday* after *Easter* week. See Mr. *Phillips Mistaken Recompence*, fol. 39.

Hocketto or **Hocqueteur**, Is an old French word for a Knight of the Post, a decayed man, 3. *par. Inst. fol.* 175. *Que nul enquerelant neu respoignant soit surpris neu cheson per* Hockettours, *parent que la veritie ne soit ensue*, Stat. *Ragman*.

Hogenhine, (But more rightly *Third-night awn hine*,) Is he that comes Guestwise to an Inn or house, and lies there the third Night, after which he is accounted of his Family in whose house he lyeth; and if he offend the Kings Peace, his Host must be answerable for him, *Bracton, lib.* 3 *tract.* 2. *cap.* 10. In the Laws of King *Edward*, set forth by *Lambert*, he is call'd *Agenhine*, where you may read more of this matter, Vide *Third-night-awne-hine*.

Hogs-head, Is a measure of Wine or Oyl, containing the fourth part of a Tun or 63 Gallons, *Anno* 1 R. 3. *cap.* 13.

Holstings, See *Hustings*.

Hockeday, Otherwise called *Hock-tuesday*, or *Hock-tide*, was the second *Tuesday* after *Easter* week. In *Monast. Ang. part.* 2. *fol.* 550. It is said, *Inter alia---senescallus Cur. de la Hele habebit de celerario quinq; albos panes, &c. Et ad le* Hokeday *totidem*. See *Hock-tuesday-money*.

Holme, *Hulmus*, An Isle or Fenny-ground, according to *Beda* and *Doomsday*, sometimes found in ancient Deeds and Records, *Co.* on *Lit. fol.* 5. and, as it seems, in a different signification, in *Mon. Ang.* 2. *par. fol.* 292. *Cum duobus* holmis *in campis de Wedone*.

Homage, *Homagium*, Probably derived from *homo*, because when the Tenant does this Service to his Lord, he says, *I become your man*; It is also called *Manhood*, *Co.* on *Lit. fol* 64. The French word imports as much as *Fides clientelaris*; for in the original Grants of Lands and Tenements by way of Fee, the Lord did not only tye his Tenants to certain Services, but also took a Submission, with Promise and Oath, to be true and loyal to him as their Lord and Benefactor. This submission was and is called *Homage*, the form whereof you have in the second Statute 17 E. 2. in these words, "When a Free-man shall "do *Homage* to his Lord, of whom he holdeth "in chief, he shall hold his hands together be-"tween the hands of his Lord, and shall say thus, *I become your Man from this day forth for life, for member, and for worldly honor, and shall owe you my Faith for the Land I held of you, saving the Faith that I owe unto our Soveraign Lord the King, and to mine other Lords.* And in this manner the Lord of the Fee, for which *homage* is due, taketh *homage* of every Tenant as he cometh to the Land or Fee, *Glanvil, lib.* 9. *cap.* 1. except they be Women, who perform not *homage*, but by their husbands: yet *Fitzherbert* in his *Nat. Brev. fol.* 157. saith the contrary. Read *Glanvil* more at large of this in the said First, and also the second, third and fourth. The reason of this, *Skene* giveth *de verb.* Signif. *verbo* Homagium, because *Homage* specially concerneth Service in War. He saith also, That consecrated Bishops do no *homage*, but only Fealty; and yet we find the Archbishop of *Canterbury* do *homage* on his Knees to our Kings at their Coronation; and it hath been held, that the Bishop of *Soder*, in the *Isle of Man*, is *Homager* to the Earl of *Derby*. And in the *Reg. Orig. fol.* 296. that a Woman taking Livery of Lands holden by Knights-service, must do *homage*, &c. Concerning the *homage* of consecrated Bishops, read *Fulbecke, fol.* 20. in these words. By our Law a Religious man may do *homage*, but may not say to his Lord *Ego devenio homo vester*, because he hath professed himself to be only Gods man; But he may say, *I do unto you* homage, *and to you shall be faithful and loyal.* See of this *Britton, cap.* 68. *Homage* is either new with the Fee, or Auncestrel, that is, where a man and his Ancestors, time out of mind, have held their Lands by *homage* to their Lord, whereby the Lord is tyed to warrant the Land unto his Tenant. This *homage* is used in other Countries as well as Ours, and was wont to be called *Hominium*. See Hotoman *de verbis feudalibus. verbo* Homo. *Skene* divided it into *Ligeum & non ligeum, de verbor.* Signif. *verbo* Homage; for the which see *Leige* and *Hotoman, disputatione de feudis tertia. Homage* is sometimes used for the Jury in a Court-Baron, *Smith de Rep. Ang. lib.* 2. *cap.* 27. The reason is because it consisteth most commonly of such as owe *homage* unto the Lord of the Fee; And these, by the *Feudists*, are called *Pares Curiæ*. Of this *homage* you may read in the 29. Chapter of the *Grand Custumary* of *Normandy*, and others not used by us. See further in *Hotoman Disputat. de feudis*, pag. 861. Of *homage* in *Scotland* read *Skene de verb.* Signif. *tit.* Homagium, to whom you may also add a large Discourse in *speculo Durandi*, commonly called *Speculator* among the *Civilians*, tit. *De feudis*. The Steward of the Lord may take Fealty, but not *Homage*. See the Stat. 12 *Car.* 2. *cap.* 24.

Homage Auncestrel, Is, where a man and his *Ancestors*, time out of mind, held their Land of their Lord and his *Ancestors* by *homage*. And if such Lord have received *homage*, he is bound to acquit the Tenant against all other Lords above him of every manner of Service,

and

and if the Tenant hath done *homage* to his Lord, and is impleaded, and vouches the Lord to warranty, the Lord is bound to warrant him; and if the Tenant lose, he shall recover in value against the Lord so much of the Lands as he had at that time of the Voucher, or any time after. To this effect *Littleton;* upon which *Coke* says, In this example here put, There must be a double Prescription both in the Blood of the Lord and the Tenant; and therefore, I think, there is little or no Land at all at this day holden by *homage Ancestrel.* Yet (as one avers) in the Mannor of *Whitney* in *Herefordshire,* whose Lord is of the same Name, and the Family has continued there many Ages, is one *West* a Tenant, who can prescribe to hold his Land of *Thomas Whitney* Esq; the present Lord, by *homage Ancestrel.*

Homager, One that does, or is bound to do *homage*: As the Bishop of *Sodor,* in the *Isle of Man* is said to be *Homager* to the Earl of *Derby.* See *Homage.*

Homagio respectuando, Is a Writ directed to the Escheator, commanding him to deliver Seisin of Lands to the heir that is of full age, notwithstanding his *homage* not done, which ought to be performed before the heir have Livery, or his Lands, except there fall out some reasonable cause to hinder it, *F. N. B. fol* 269.

Home-soken, But more truly *Ham-soken* and *Ham-soca,* (for the derivation, see *Hamsoken*) Is by *Bract. lib.* 3. *tract.* 2. *cap.* 23. thus defined, *Homesoken dicitur invasio domus contra pacem Domini Regis.* It appeareth by *Rastal* in the Title, *Expositions of words,* That in ancient times some men had immunity to do this; for he defineth *Homesoken* to be an Immunity from Amerciament, for entring into Houses violently, and without Licence; which seemeth to be altogether unreasonable, I rather believe it should be a Power granted by the King to some person, for the punishment of such a Transgression. *Si quis* Hamsocam *violaverit, jure Anglorum Regi emendet,* 5. Libr. Leg. Canuti, *cap.* 39. See *Hamsoken.*

Homicide, *Homicidium,* Is the killing of a Man, and it is divided into *voluntary* and *casual*: *Homicide voluntary* is that which is deliberate, and committed of a set-mind, and purpose to kill; and this is either with precedent Malice, or without: The former is Murther, and is a felonious killing through malice prepensed of any person living in this Realm, under the Kings Protection, *West. part* 2. *Symbol. tit.* Indictments, *sect.* 37. &c. *usq;* 51. Where you may see divers subdivisions of this matter. See also *Glanvile, lib.* 14. *cap.* 3. *Bract. lib.* 3. *tract.* 2. *cap* 4. 15. & 17. *Britton, cap.* 5. 6. 7. See *Murder, Manslaughter* and *Chance-medley.*

Homine eligendo ad custodiendam peciam sigilli pro mercatoribus aedici, Is a Writ directed to a Corporation, for the choice of a new Man to keep the one part of the Seal, appointed for *Statutes-Merchant,* when the other is dead, according to the Statute of *Acton Burnel,* Reg. Orig. fol. 178.

Homine replegiando, Is a Writ to bail a Man out of Prison; In what Cases it lies, see *F. N. B. fol.* 6. *Reg. Orig. fol.* 77. and the *New Book of Entries, verbo* Homine replegiando.

Homine capto in Withernamium, Is a Writ to take him, that hath taken any Bondman or woman, and led him or her out of the Country, so that he or she cannot be *replevied* according to Law, *Reg. Orig. fol.* 79. See also *Withernam.*

Hominatio, *Doomsday. Idem quod Homagium,* Spel Glofs. verb. Hominatio

Hondhabend, A derivative from the Saxon *Hond,* that is, a hand, and *habens, having;* and signifies a circumstance of manifest theft, when one is deprehended with the things stollen in his *hand, Bract. lib.* 3. *tract* 2. *cap.* 31. & 54. who also uses *Handberend* for the same, *ibid. cap.* 8.

Hond-peny, *Sint quieti de cheuagio,* Hondpeny, &c. *Priveleg. de Semplingham.* But there is no Declaration made, what is intended by it, *Ideo Quare.*

Honor, *Honor,* Is, beside the general signification, used more especially for the nobler sort of Seigniories, whereupon other inferior Lordships and Mannors do depend, by performance of Customs and Services to those that are Lords over them: And it seems that none were *Honors* originally, but such as belonged to the King, though afterwards given in Fee to Noblemen. The manner of creating these *Honors,* may in part be collected out of the Statutes 34 H. 8. 5. where *Hampton Court* is made an *Honor.* And 33 H. 8. *cap.* 37, 38. whereby *Ampthil* and *Grafton* be also made *Honors.* And 37 H. 8. *cap.* 18. whereby the King hath Power given by his Letters Patent, to erect four several *Honors,* of *Westminster,* of *Kingston* upon *Hull,* St. *Osithes* in *Essex,* and *Dodington* in *Berk-shire*: This word is used in the same signification in other Nations. In reading, I have observed divers other *honors* in *England,* of *Aquila, Camd. Brit.* 231. Of *Clare Idem.* 351. Of *Lancaster,* Idem. 581. Of *Tick-hill,* ibid. Of *Wallingford, Nottingham, Boloine, Magna Charta, cap.* 31. Of *West-Greenwich, Camd.* pag. 239. Of *Bedford, Pupilla oculi,* part 5. cap. 22. Of *Barkhamsted,* Bro. *tit. Tenure,* num. 16. *Wittam, Camd* pag. 333. Of *Plimpton,* Cromp. Jur. *fol.* 115. Of *Crevecure* and *Haganet fobert,* 32. H. 8. 48. Of *East-Greenwich* in *Kent, Windsor,* in *Berk-shire,* and *Beaulieu* in *Essex,* 37. H. 8, 88. Of *Peverel* in the County of *Lincoln,* Reg. Orig. fol. 1. besides many other, which we think not fit to name. See *Bakers Chronicle,* fol. 117. *Inquis.* 10 Ed. 2. *Co.* 4. *Inst. fol.* 224. &c.

Honour Courts, Are *Courts* held within the *Honors* aforesaid, mentioned 33. H. 8. 37. and 37 H. 8. 18.

Honorary Services, Are such as are incident to *Grand Sergeanty,* and annexed commonly to some *Honor.* See 12 *Car.* 2. *cap.* 29.

Hontfangenethef, This should rather have been written *Hondfangenethef,* and signifies a *Thief* taken with *Hond-habend,* that is, having the thing stollen in his Hand.

Hornebeame Pollengers, Are *Trees* so called, that have been usually lopped, and are above twenty years growth, and therefore not tythable, *Plowden, fol.* 470. *Soby's* Case.

Hornegeld, Is a Compound from the Saxon word *Horn, cornu,* and *geld, solutio,* signifying a Tax within a Forest, to be paid for *horned* Beasts,

Cromp

Cromp. Jurisd. 197. And to be free thereof, is a priviledge granted by the King unto such as he thinketh good, *Idem ibid.* & *Rastall* in his *Exposition of words*, *Quietum esse de omni collectione in Foresta de bestiis cornutis assess.* 4. Inst. fol. 369. Et *sint quieti de omnibus Geldis*, & *Dane-geldis*, & *Volgeldis*, & *Sene-geldis*, & Horn-geldis, &c. *Diploma*, H. 3. *Canonicis* & *Monialibus de Semplingham.* See *Subsidy.*

Hors de son fee, Is an Exception to avoid an Action brought for Rent, issuing out of certain Land by him that pretendeth to be the Lord, or for some Customs and Services; for if he can justifie that the Land is without the compass of his *fee*, the Action falls. *Vide broke*, *hoc titulo.* See *District.*

Hospitallers, *Hospitalarii*, were the Knights of a Religious Order, so called, because they built an *Hospital* at *Jerusalem*, wherein Pilgrims were received. To these Pope *Clement* the Fifth transferred the Templers, which Order, by a Councel held at *Vienna* in *France*, he suppressed for their many and great Offences. The institution of their Order was first allowed by Pope *Gelasius* the Second, *Anno* 1118. and confirmed here by Parliament, and had many priviledges granted them, as Immunities from payment of Tythes, &c. you shall find their Priviledges reserved to them by *Mag. Charta, cap.* 37. and you shall see the Right of the Kings Subjects vindicated from the Usurpation of their Jurisdiction, by the Statute of *Westm.* 2. *cap.* 43. Their chief abode is now in *Malta*, an Island given them by the Emperour *Charles* the Fifth, after they were driven from *Rhodes* by *Solyman* the Magnificent Emperour of the *Turks*; and for that they are now called *Knights of Malta.* They are mentioned 13 *E.* 1. *cap.* 43. and 9 H. 3. *cap.* 37. *Tho. Walsingham* in Hist. *Ed.* 2. and *Stows Annals*, *ibid.* All the Lands and Goods of these Knights here in *England* were given to the King, by 32 H. 8. *cap.* 34. See *Mon. Ang.* 2. *par. fol.* 489.

Hosteler, *Hostellarius*, Cometh of the French *Hosteler*, i. *Hospes*, and signifieth with us those that otherwise are called *Innkeepers*, 9 *E.* 3. *Stat.* 2. *cap.* 11. We now usually term those that in the Stable look to the Guests Horses in an Inn *Hostlers.*

Hotchpot, *In partem positio*, Is a word brought from the French *Hutspot*, among the Dutch it signifies flesh cut into pieces, and sodden with Herbs or Roots, not unlike that which the *Romans* call'd *Farraginem.---Festus.* But *Littleton* saith, That literally it signifies a pudding mixed of divers ingredients, but by a Metaphor, signifyeth a Commixture, or putting together of Lands of several Tenures, for the equal division of them, *fol.* 55. For example. A man seised of thirty Acres of Land in Fee, hath issue two Daughters, and gives with one of his Daughters, to a Man that marries her, ten Acres of the same Land in *Frank-marriage*, and dies seized of the other twenty Acres. Now if she that is thus married will have any part of the twenty Acres whereof her Father died seized, she must put her Lands, given in *Frank-marriage*, in *Hotchpot*, that is, she must refuse to take the sole Profits of the Lands given in *Frank-marriage*, and suffer the Land to be commixt, and mingled together with the other Land whereof her Father died seised; so that an equal division may be made of the whole between her and her Sister, and thus for her ten Acres she shall have fifteen, else her Sister will have the whole twenty of which her Father died seised. See *Co.* on *Lit. lib.* 3. *cap.* 12. and *Britton*, *fol.* 119. There is also in the Civil Law *Collatio bonorum* answerable to this, whereby if a Child advanced by the Father, do after his Fathers decease challenge a Childs part with the rest, he must cast in all that formerly he had received, and then take out an equal share with the others.

Housebote, A compound of *house* and *bote*, i. *compensatio*, signifies *Estovers*, or an allowance of necessary Timber out of the Lords Wood, for the repair and support of a *House* or Tenement. [And this belongs of common right to any Lessee for years or for life: But if he take more than is needful, he may be punisht by an Action of Wast.] *Housebote* sayes *Co.* on *Lit. fol.* 41. Is two-fold, *viz. Estoverium ædificandi* & *ardendi.*

House-robbing or **House-breaking**, Is the robbing of a man in some part of his *House*, or his Booth or Tent, in any Fair or Market, and the Owner, or his Wife, Children or Servants being within the same; for this is Felony by 23 H. 8. *cap.* 1. and 3 *E.* 6. *cap.* 9. And since it is made Felony, though none be within the *House*, Booth, or Stall, by 39 *Eliz.* 15. See *Burglary*, and *West*, *part* 2. *Symb. tit.* Indictments, *sect.* 67.

Hudegeld, *Significat quietantiam transgressionis illatæ in servum transgredientem*, Fleta, *lib.* 1. *cap.* 47. It may be thought in that place of *Fleta* to be misprinted for *Hine-geld*, which see, & *quære.*

Hopcomb, Signifies a Valley in *Doomsday* Book, so also do *Hope*, *Hawgh* and *Howgh.*

Hosthas, A Service to the King in *Closhaw*, says *Doomsday*; but I think rather it should be written *Hasta*, because it is supposed a Military Service.

House, *Domus*, In a *House* four things are necessary, 1. *Habitatio hominis.* 2. *Delectatio inhabitantis.* 3. *Necessitas luminis.* 4 *Salubritas aeris.* For any hurt or hindrance to the first, third, and fourth of these an Action lyeth: For *Probibetur ne quis faciat in suo, quod nocere possit alieno.* The *house* of every man is to him as his Castle and Fortress, as well for his defence against injury and violence, as for his repose; according to the Maxim, *Domus sua cuiq; est tutissimum refugium.* See *Co.* 5. *Rep. Semaines* Case. The priviledge that the Law gives to *houses* for the habitation of men is great; for first, it ought to have the precedency in a *Præcipe quod reddat* before Lands, Meadows, Pastures and Woods. Secondly, The *house* of a man hath priviledge to protect him against an Arrest, by force of a Process of the Law, at the Suit of the Subject, *Co Rep.* 11. *Bowles* Case. Thirdly, Those that dig for *Salt-peter*, shall not dig in the *Mansion-house* of any Subject without his assent; for then He, nor his Wife, nor Children, cannot be in safety, nor his Goods preserved from Thieves. 4. He that kills a man which will rob and spoil him in the *house*, shall forfeit nothing.

Hue and Cry, *Hutesium* & *clamor*, Is derived of two French words *Huer* and *Crier*, both signifying to shout or *cry* aloud. *Manwood* in his *Forest Law. cap.* 19. *num.* 11. saith, That *Heu* is Latine, [Est *vox dolentis*, as signifying the Complaint of the Party,] and *Cry* is the pursuit of the Felon upon the High-way upon that Complaint; for if the party robbed, or any in the Company of one robbed or murdered, come to the Constable of the next Town, and will him to raise the *Hue and Cry* [that is, make the Complaint known, and follow the Pursuit,] after the Offendor, describing the Party, and shewing as near as he can which way he went; the Constable ought forthwith to call upon the Parish for Ayd in seeking the Felon, and if he be not found there, then to give the next Constable notice, and the next, until the Offendor be apprehended, or at least until he be thus pursued unto the Sea-side. Of this read *Bracton*, *lib.* 3. *tract.* 2. *cap.* 5. *Smith de Rep. Anglor. lib.* 2. *cap.* 20. and the Stat. 13 *E.* 1. of *Winchester*, *cap.* 3. & 28 *E.* 3. 11. & 27 *El.* 13. The *Normans* had such a pursuit with a *Cry* after Offendors, which they call'd *Haro*, whereof you may read the *Grand Custumary*, *cap.* 54. and it may probably be derived from *Harier*, *flagitare*. *Hue* is used alone, 4 *E.* 1. *Stat.* 2. This the *Scots* call *Hutesium*, and *Skene de verb.* Signif. *verb. Hutesium*, saith, It is deduced from the French *Oyer*, i. *Audite*, (or rather *Oyes*) being a *Cry* used before a Proclamation; The manner of their *Hue and Cry* he thus describeth, If a Robbery be done, a Horn is blown, and an Out-cry made, after which, if the Party fly away, and not yield himself to the Kings Bayliff, he may be lawfully slain, and hanged upon the next Gallows. Of this *Hue and Cry*, see *Cromp. Just. of Peace. fol.* 160. and in Rot. *Claus.* 30 H. 3. m. 5. We find a Command to the Kings Treasurer, to take the City of *London* into the Kings Hand, because the Citizens did not *secundum Legem & consuetudinem Regni* raise the *Hue and Cry* for the death of *Guido de Aretio*, and others who were slain.

Huers. See *Conders*.

Huissier. See *Usher*.

Hulme. See *Holme*.

Hundred, *Hundredum Centuria*, Is a part of a Shire properly so called, because it contained ten Tythings, called in Latine *Decennas*, either because at first there were a *hundred* Families in each *Hundred*, or else found the King a *hundred* able Men for his Wars. These were first Ordained by King *Alfred* the 29*th* King of the *West Saxons*, *Stows Annal*, *Pag.* 105. Of these *Lambert* in his *Explication of Saxon words*, *verbo* Centuria, saith, *Aluredus Rex, ubi cum Guthruno Daco fædus inierat prudentissimum illud Olim a Jethrone Mosi datum consilium, Angliam primum in Satrapias Centurias & Decurias partitus est. Satrapiam, shire a schyran (quod partiri significat) nominavit; Centuriam* Hundred & *Decuriam*, Tything *sive Tienmantale*, i. *Decemvirale collegium appellavit atq; iisdem nominibus vel hodie vocantur*, &c. And again afterward, *Decrevit cum porro Aluredus, liberæ ut conditionis quisq; in centuriam ascriberetur aliquam atq; in Decemvirale aliquod conjiceretur collegium*, &c. This form of dividing Counties into *Hundreds*, for better Government, King *Alfred* had from *Germany*, where *Centa* or *Centena* is a Jurisdiction over a *hundred* Towns, and contains the punishment of Capital Crimes. Hence may be learnt the original and old use of *Hundreds*, which still keep the Name and remain in some sort the same, for their several Services in divers respects, but their Jurisdiction is transferred to the County Court, some few excepted, which have been by Priviledge annexed to the Crown, or granted to some great Subject, and so remain still in the nature of a Franchise. And this has been ever since the Stat. 14 *E.* 3. *Stat* 1. *cap.* 9. whereby these *Hundred* Courts formerly farmed out by the Sheriff to other men, were reduced all, or the most part, to the County-Court, and so remain at present, so that where you read now of any *hundred* Courts, you must know, that they be several Franchises, wherein the Sheriff hath not to deal by his ordinary Authority, unless they of the *Hundred* refuse to do their duty. See *West Symbol. part.* 1. *lib.* 2. *sect.* 288. See *Turne* in the *Terms of the Law*. This word *Hundredum* is said to be quit of money or Customs due to the *Hundredors*.

Hundreders, *Hunredarii*, Are Men empannelled, or fit to be empannelled of a Jury upon a Controversie, dwelling in the *Hundred* where the Land in question lies, *Cromp. Jur. fol.* 217. and 35 H. 8. 6. It signifies also him that hath the Jurisdiction of a *Hundred*, and holdeth the *hundred* Court, 13 *E.* 1. *cap.* 38. 9 *E.* 2. *Stat.* 2. & 2 *E.* 3. *cap.* 4. and sometimes it is used for the Bayliff of an *Hundred*. Hornes *Miror of Justices*, lib. 1. cap. *del Office del Coroner*.

Hundred-Lagh, Signifies the *hundred* Court, from which all the Officers of the Kings Forest were by the Charter of King *Canutus cap.* 9. See *Manwood, vide etiam Warscot*.

Hundred-peny, *Est autem pecunia quam subsidii causa vicecomes olim exigebat ex singulis Decuriis sui Comitatus, quas Tethingas Saxones appellabant. Sic ex* Hundredis Hundred-peny, *Spelm. Pence of the hundred*, Cam. Brit. *fol.* 223.

Hundred setena, *Et habeant Sakam & Socam*, on *Strond & on streame*, on *Wode & on feld*, *Grithbrice*, Hundred-setena, *Adas & Ordelas*, &c. *Carta Edgari Regis*, *Man. Glaston. Anno* 12 *Regni*, *Mon. Ang.* 1 *par. fol.* 16. This word *Setena* in Composition signifies Inhabitants.

Hurst, A little wood, *Doomsday*. See *Hirst*.

Huscarle, Is as much to say as *Housecarle*, that is, a Domestick or Menial Servant; the word is often found in *Doomsday*, where we find the Town of *Dorchester* paid to the use of *Housecarles* one Mark of Silver. See *Karles*.

Hus & Hant, *Quidem* H. P. *captus per queremoniam mercatorum Flandriæ & imprisonatus effert Domino Regi* Hus & Hant *in plegio ad standum recto & ad respondendum*, &c. *in curia Regis apud* Shepway, *Pla. cur. Regis*, 27 H. 3. Rot. 9. *Quare annon sit commune plegium sicut* Johannes Doe & Richardus Roe. See 4. *Instit. fol.* 72.

Huseaus, Of the French *Houseau*, i. *ocrea*, a kind of Boot, or somewhat made of course Cloth, and worn over the Stocking; a *Buskin*, or as the vulgar call it a *Spatterdash*.

Husfastne, Is he that holdeth House and Land, *Bracton*, *lib.* 3. *tract* 2. *cap.* 10. hath these words, *Et in Franco plegio esse debet omnis qui terram tenet & domum qui dicuntur* Husfastne, & *etiam alii, qui illis deserviunt et dicuntur Folgheres*, &c. Some have corruptly written it *Hurderefest* & *Hurdefest*, but

but more truly *Heordfeste*; which see in *Glosse in decem scriptor.*

Husseling people, The Parishioners of *Leominster*, in a Petition to King *Edward* the Sixth, set forth that in their Town there were to the number of 2000 *Husseling people*, &c. that is 2000 Communicants, for *Hussel* in the Saxon Tongue signifies the Holy Sacrament.

Hustings, *Hustingum*, Derived from *Hus Domus*, and *Thing*, *Causa*, is as much as *Domus causarum*, *antiquissima & celeberima* Londoniarum *Civitatis curia suprema*, 11 H. 7. 21. *F. N. B. fol.* 23. 9 *E.* 1. *cap. unico* 10. Of this Antiquity, we find this mention in the Laws of King *Edward the Confessor*, *Debet etiam in* London *quæ est caput Regni & Legum, semper curia Domini Regis singulis septimanis die Lunæ* Hustingis *sedere & teneri. Fundata enim erat olim & ædificata ad instar & ad modum & in memoriam veteris magnæ Trojæ, et usq; in hodiernum diem, Leges & jura et dignitates, libertates, regiasq; consuetudines antiquæ magnæ Trojæ in se continet——et consuetudines suas una semper inviolabilitate conservat.* See *Taylors Hist. Gavelkind, pag.* 55. This Court is held before the Lord Mayor and Aldermen of *London*; an Error or Attaint lies there of a Judgment, or false Verdict in the Sheriffs Court, as appears by *F. N. B. fol.* 23. Other Cities and Towns also have had a Court of the same Name, as *Winchester*, *Lincoln*, *York* and *Shepey*, and others, where the Barons or Citizens have a Record of such things as are determinable before them, *Fleta, lib.* 2. *cap.* 55. *Stat.* 10. *E.* 2. *cap. unico* 4. *Inst. fol.* 247. and *Gloss. in decem scriptores* on this word.

Hyde of Land. See *Hide*.

Hydegyld, A Ransome paid to save ones Skin, *viz.* that it be not beaten. Also the same with *Hidage*.

Hyth, A Port or little Haven to lade or unlade Wares at, as *Queen-hyth, Lamb-hyth, &c. New Book of Entries, fol.* 3. & *Mon. Ang.* 2. *par. fol.* 142. *sayes,—De tota Medietate* Hythæ *sua in, &c. cum libero introitu et exitu.*

I.

I. *Hæc litera est etiam verbum seu rectius pronomen, scilicet ego unde derivatur possessivum (meus) ut ab altero pronomine, (viz. tu, tuus)* in English *Mine and Thine*; or as we use *Meum* and *Tuum*, the proper guides of Right; and whose being misunderstood, hath been the ground of all Quarrels.

Jacke, *Olim Wambasium*, A kind of defensive Coat worn by Horsemen in War, not made of solid Iron, but many Plates fastned together, which some by Tenure were bound to find upon an Invasion. See *Hidage*.

Jactivus & Jectivus, A Latine word signifying him that loseth by default, *Placitum suum neglexerit &* Jactivus *exinde remansit, formul. solen.* 159.

Jamaica, Is an *American* Iland, lying on the South of *Cuba*; in length from East to West fifty Leagues, and in breadth twenty, the middle under the eighteenth degree of Northern Latitude: It was in part taken from the *Spaniard* by the *English* in the year 1655. and is mentioned in the Stat. 15 *Car.* 2. *cap.* 5.

Jamaica-wood, Mentioned 15 *Car.* 2. *cap.* 5. Is a kind of speckled *wood*, of which are made Cabinets, called there *Granadillo*. The Tree (as they say) is low and small, seldom bigger than a mans Leg.

Jampnum, Furz or Gorse; also a gorsie Ground, *Cro.* 1. *part. fol.* 179. a word much used in Fines, and the name seems to derive it self from the French *Jaulne*, i. yellow, because the Blossoms of it are of that colour, *Co.* on *Lit. pag.* 5. says *Jampna*, signifies a waterish place. *Manwood* in his *Forest Law, cap.* 25. *num.* 3. sayes, No man may cut down Furze or Whins, within the Forest without good Licence.

Jarre, Any great Earthen Pot, we commonly call a Vessel of Oyl, containing twenty gallons a *Jarr*.

Jarrocke, 1 *R.* 3. *cap.* 8. Is a kind of *Cork* so called, by this Statute prohibited to be used in the dying of Cloth.

Identitate nominis, Is a Writ that lies for him, who upon a *Capias* or *Exigent* is taken and committed to Prison for another man of the name, whereof see the form, and farther use in *F. N. B. fol.* 267. See *Reg. Orig. fol.* 194.

Ides, *Idus*, Are eight days in every month so called, in *March*, *May*, *July* and *October*, they begin at the eighth day of the month, and continue to the fifteenth; in the rest they begin at the sixth and end at the thirteenth. But here observe, that only the last day is called the *Ides*, the first being termed the eighth *Ides*, the second the seventh, that is, the eighth or seventh before the *Ides*, and so of the rest, and therefore when we speak of the *Ides* of such a month, we must understand it of the fifteenth or thirteenth day of that month. See *Calends*.

Ideot, Is a word in Greek properly signifying a private man, who has no publick Office. Among the Latines it is taken for *illiteratus, imperitus* and in our Law for *non compos mentis*, or a natural Fool. The words of the Statute, 17 *E.* 2. *cap.* 9. are *Rex habebit custodiam terrarum fatuorum naturalium*, whereby it appears he must be a natural Fool, that is, a Fool *à nativitate*: For if he were once wise, or became a Fool by chance or misfortune, the King shall not have the custody of him, *Stamf. Prerog. cap.* 9. *F. N. B. fol.* 232. If one have understanding to measure a yard of Cloth, number twenty, rightly name the days of the week, &c. he shall not be counted an *Ideot*, or natural Fool, by the Laws of the Realm. See 4 *Rep. Beverlyes* Case.

Ideota inquirenda vel examinanda, Is a Writ to the Escheator or Sheriff of any County, where the King hath notice that there is an *Ideot* naturally born, so weak of understanding, that he cannot govern or manage his Inheritance, to call before him the Party suspected of *Ideocy*, and examine him. And also to inquire by the Oaths of twelve men whether he be sufficiently witted to dispose of his own Lands with discretion or not, and to certifie accordingly into the Chancery; for the King hath the Protection

of

of his Subjects, and by his Prerogative the Government of their Lands and Substance that are naturally defective in their own discretion, *Stat. de Prærog. Regis, edit.* 17 E. 2. cap. 8. whereof read *Stamf. Prærog. cap.* 9. and of this Writ read *F.N.B. fol.* 232. and Reg. *Orig. fol.* 267.

Jeman, Sometimes used for Yeoman, as by this following, *Sciant*, &c. *Quod ego* J. S. *de* B. *in com.* H. Jeman *dedi, &c.* Dat. 10. Jan. 9 H. 6.

Jeofayle, , Is a compound of three French words *j'ay faille*, i. *ego lapsus sum*, and in a legal sense denotes an over-sight in pleading, touching which you have a Statute 32 H. 8. 30. whereby it is Enacted, That if the Jury have once past upon the Issue, though afterward there be found a *Jeofayle* in the pleading, yet Judgment shall likewise be given according to the Verdict of the Jury. See *Bro. tit. Repleader.* The Author of the *New Terms of Law* saith, That a *Jeofayle* is, when the Parties to any Suit have in pleading proceeded so far, that they have joyned Issue, which shall be tryed, or is tryed by a Jury, and this Pleading or Issue is badly pleaded or joyned, that it will be Error if they proceed: Then some of the said Parties may, by their Councel, shew it to the Court as well after Verdict given, and before Judgment, as before the Jury be charged; the shewing of which Defects, before the Jury charged, was often, when the Jury came into Court to try the Issue, then the Councel which will shew it, shall say, *This Inquest you ought not to take*; and if it be after Verdict, then he may say, *To judgment you ought not to go*; and because of this many delays grew in Suits, for the redress of which divers Statutes were made, *viz.* 32 H. 8. 30. beforementioned, and others in Queen *Elizabeth* and King *James* his Days, *viz.* 18 *Eliz.* 14. 21 *Jac.* 13. yet the fault little amended.

Jetsen, Jetzon and **Jotson**, From the French *Jetter, ejicere*, is any thing thrown out of a Ship, being in the danger of wreck, and by the Waves driven to the shore. See *Flotson, Co. lib.* 5. *fol.* 106.

Jews, *Judæi.* See *Judaism*, anciently we had a Court of the Justices assigned for the Government of the *Jews.* See 4. *Inst. fol.* 254 *Rex—Vic. Wigor. salutem. Præcipimus tibi quod clamari et observari facias per totam Ballivam tuam, quod omnes Judæi deferant in superiori indumento suo ubicunq; ambulaverint vel equitaverint infra villam vel extra quasi duas tabulas albas in pectore factas de lineo panno vel de pergameno, ita quod per hujusmodi signum manifestè possint* Judæi, *a Christianis discerni* T. *comite apud* Oxon 30. *Martii claus.* 2 H. 3. p. 1. 10. *in Dorso.*

Ignitegium, See *Curfew.*

Ignoramus, Is a word properly used by the Grand Inquest, impannelled in the Inquisition of Causes criminal and publick, and written upon the Bill, when they mislike their Evidence as defective, or too weak, to make good the Presentment; the effect of which word so written is, that all farther enquiry upon that Party for that fault is thereby stopped, and he delivered without further answer. It hath a resemblance of that ancient Custom of the *Romans*, where the Judges, when they absolved a person accused, did write *A.* upon a little Table provided for that purpose, *i. Absolvimus*; if they judged him guilty, they writ *C. id est, condemnamus*; if they found the cause difficult and doubtful, they writ *N. L.* that is, *Non liquet. Asconius Redianus in oratione pro Milone, Alexander ab Alexandro, Genial. dierum*, Lib. 3. cap. 14.

Ikenild-street, Is one of the four famous ways that the *Romans* made in *England*, called *Stratum Icenorum*, because it took beginning *ab Icenis*, which were the People that inhabited *Norfolk, Suffolk*, and *Cambridgshire, Camd. Brit. fol.* 343. *Leg. Edw. Conf. cap.* 12. See *Watling-street.*

Illeviable, That may or cannot be levyed, and therefore *Nihil* is a word set upon a Debt *Illeviable.*

Imbargo, A stop or stay, most commonly upon Ships by publick Authority, 18 *Car.* 2. *cap.* 5.

Imbezle or **Imbesil**, To wast, scatter and consume; as if a person intrusted with Goods wast and diminish them, we say, He hath *imbesil'd* the Goods, 14 Car. 2. *cap.* 31.

Imbracery. See *Embracery.*

Imparlance, *Interlocutio vel interloquela*, Is a motion made in Court upon the count of the Demandant by the Tenant, or Declaration of the Plaintiff by the Defendant, whereby he craveth Respite, or any other day to put in his Answer. See *Bro. tit. Continuance.* See also *Dies datus.* This *Imparlance* is either *general* or *special*; *Special* is with this Clause, *Salvis omnibus advantagiis tam ad jurisdictionem curiæ quam breve & narrationem*, Kitchin, fol. 200. *General*, is made at large, without inserting that or any other like Clause. See *Emparlance.*

Imparsonee, As Parson *imparsonee*, *Persona imparsonata*, is he that is inducted, and in possession of a Benefice, *Dyer, fol.* 40. *num.* 72. says a Dean and Chapter, are Parsons *imparsonees* of a Benefice appropriate unto them.

Impeachment of Wast, *Impetitio vasti*, Cometh of the French *Empeschment*, i. *impedimentum*, and signifies a Restraint from committing of *Wast* upon Lands and Tenements. See *wast.* And therefore he that hath a Lease without *impeachment of Wast*, hath by that a property or interest given him in the houses and Trees, and may make *wast* in them without being *impeached* for it, that is, without being questioned, or demanded any recompence for the *wast* done. See *Co. lib.* 11. *Bowles* Case, *fol.* 82.

Impediens, *Hæc est finalis concordia facta in curia Domini Regis apud* Westm. *in Octabis sancti* Hillarii, *Anno Regni Regis* Henrici *filii Regis* Johannis *septimo coram*, &c *inter* Willielmum *de* Mohun *querentem &* Willielmum Bruere *impedientem*, &c. Where *impedientem* is used for *Defendentem* or *Deforciantem.*

Impetration, *Impetratio*, An obtaining by Request or Prayer: It is used in our Statutes for the pre-obtaining of Benefices, and Church-Offices in *England* from the Court of *Rome*, which did belong to the disposition of the King, and other Lay-Patrons of this Realm; the penalty whereof was the same with Provisors, 25 E. 3. See 38 E. 3. *Stat.* 2. *cap.* 1.

Impierment, 23 *H.* 8. 9. Signifies as much as impairing or prejudicing; For the words of the Statute are, *To the great* impediment *and diminution of their good names.*

Imple-

Implements, Cometh either of the French word *Employer*, to employ; or the Latine *Impleo*, to fill up, and is used for all things necessary for a Trade, or furniture of a Houshold: And in that sense you shall often find the word used in Wills, and Conveyances of moveables.

Implead, From the French *Playder*, to sue, arrest, or prosecute by course of Law.

Impost, Is a French word signifying Tribute, and derived of the Verb *Imposer*, i. *injungere*, and signifieth the Tax received by the Prince, for such Merchandise as are brought into any Haven within his Dominions from foreign Nations, 31 *Eliz.* 5. It may in some sort be distinguished from Custom, because Custom is rather that profit the Prince maketh of Wares shipped out; yet are they frequently confounded.

Imprimerie, A Print, Impression; also the Art of Printing, and likewise a Printing-house, *Anno* 4. *Car.* 2. *cap.* 33.

Impropriation, Of which there are in *England* 3845. See *Appropriation*

Improvement. See *Approve.*

Imprisonment, *Imprisonamentum*, Is the restraint of a mans Liberty, whether it be in the open Field, or in the Stocks, or Cage in the Streets, or in a mans own House, as well as in the Common Gaol. And in all these places the Party so restrained, is said to be a Prisoner, so long as he hath not his Liberty freely to go at all times, to all places whither he will, without Bail or Mainprise.

In alto & imo, The same with *Alto* and *Basso*, which see.

Inborh and **Outborh**, Saxon. *Vide Camdens Britan.* in *Ottadinis*, Where he says, speaking of *Edelingham*, the Barony of *Patricke* Earl of *Dunbarre*, which also was *Inborow* and *Outborow* between *England* and *Scotland*, as we read in the Book of *Inquisitions*, that is, (as he believes) he was to allow and observe in this part the ingress and egress of those that travelled to and fro between both Realms; for English men in ancient time called in their Language an *Entry* and *Forecourt* or *Gate-house*, Inborow.

In casu consimili, Is a Writ, See *Casu consimili.*

In casu proviso, Is a Writ. See *Casu Proviso.*

Inchanter, *Incantator*, Is he that by Charms or Verses Conjures the Devil. The Ancients called them *Carmina*, because in those days their Charms were in Verse, 3. *part* Inst *fol.* 44.

Inchantress, *Incantatrix*, Is a Woman that uses Charms and Incantations. See *Inchanter.*

Incident, *Incidens*, Signifies a thing necessarily depending upon another as more principal. For example, A Court Baron is so *incident* to a Mannor, and a Court of Pypowders to a Fair, that they cannot be severed by Grant; for if a Mannor or Fair be granted, these Courts cannot be severed, *Kitchin*, *fol.* 36. See *Co.* on *Lit. fol.* 151.

Incroch, *Incrociare.* See *Encrochments.* Admirals and their Deputies do *incroch* to themselves Jurisdictions, &c. 15 *R.* 2. *cap.* 4.

Incumbent, Is a derivative from the Latine Verb *Incumbo*, to mind diligently, and is a Clerk resident on his Benefice with Cure, *Co.* on *Lit. fol.* 119. and called *Incumbent* of that Church, because he doth or ought to bend his whole study to discharge his Cure, 10 *H.* 6. 7. and 1 & 2 *P.* & *M. cap.* 17.

Indecimable, *Indecimabilis*, That is not tytheable, or ought not to pay Tythe, 2. *par.* Inst. *fol.* 490.

Indenture, *Indentura*, Is a Writing comprising some Contract between two, and being *indented* in the top answerable to another, that likewise containeth the same Contracts: This the Greeks call'd συγγραφον or συγγραφὴν which the *Civilians* have defined to be *Scriptura inter creditorem & debitorem* indentata *in cujus scissura literis capitalibus hæc dictio* Συγγραφή, or plurally τὰ σύγγραφα, *scribitur*; and it differs from χειρόγραφον *quia hoc manu unius tantum puta debitoris scribitur & penes debitorem relinquitur. Pruinc. constitut. de Offic. archidicano*, cap. *prim.* verbo *in scriptis.* It differs from a Deed-Poll, which is a single Deed *unindented*, *Co.* on *Lit. fol.* 229.

Indefeisible, That cannot be defeated or made void, as a good and *indefeisible* Estate.

Indefensus, One that is impleaded, and refuseth to answer, *M. S. de temp.* E. 3.

Indicavit, Is a Writ or Prohibition that lyeth for a Patron of a Church whose Clerk is Defendant in Court-Christian, in an Action of Tythes commenced by another Clerk, and extending to the fourth part of the Church, or of the Tythes belonging to it; for in this case the Suit belongeth to the Kings Court by the Stat. *Westm.* 2. *cap.* 5. Wherefore the Patron of the Defendant being like to be prejudiced in his Church and Advowson, if the Plaintiff obtain in the Court-Christian, hath this means to remove it to the Kings Court, *Reg. Orig. fol.* 35. See *Old Nat. Brev. fol* 31. and *Britton*, *cap.* 109.

Inditor, Is he that inditeth another for any Offence, 1 E 3. *cap.* 11. And *Inditee* is he that is *indited*, 21 *Jac. cap.* 8.

Indictment, *Indictamentum*, See *Enditement.*

Indivisum, Is used for that which Two hold in Common, without Partition, *Kitchin*, *fol.* 241. in these words, He holds *pro indiviso*, &c.

Indorsement, *Indorsamentum*, Is any thing written on the back of a Deed, as a Condition written on the back of an Obligation is commonly called *An Indorsement*, *West Symbol. part* 2. *sect.* 157.

Induction, *Inductio*, A leading into: It is most commonly taken for the giving possession to an Incumbent of his Church, by leading him into it, and delivering him the Keys, by the Commissary, or Bishops Deputy, and by his ringing one of the Bells, *Croke*, *Rep.* 3. *part fol.* 258.

In esse, 21 *Jac.* 2. *In being*: The learned make this difference between things *in esse*, and things *in posse*, as a thing that is not, but may be, they say, Is *in Posse*, or *Potentia*; but a thing apparent and visible, they say, Is *in esse*, that is, has a real being, *eo instanti*, whereas the other is casual, and but a possibility.

Infang alias **Infeng**, *Significat quietantiam prioris prisæ ratione convivii*, Fleta, lib. 1. cap. 47.

Infangthefe, **Hinfangthefe** or **Infangtheof**, Is compounded of three Saxon words; the Preposition *In*, *fang* or *fong*, to take or catch, and *thefe* a Robber: It signifieth a Priviledge or Liberty granted unto Lords of certain Mannors to judge any *Thief* taken within their Fee. *Bracton*, *lib.* 3. *tract.* 2. *cap.* 35. saith, *Dicitur* Infangthef *latro captus in terra alicujus de hominibus suis propriis*, *seisitus Latrocinio*. Utfangthefe *vero dicitur latro extraneus*, *veniens aliunde de terra aliena & qui captus fuit in terra ipsius*, *qui tales habet libertates*, *&c.* In the Laws of King *Edward the Conf.* set out by Mr. *Lambert*, cap. 26. you have it thus described, *Infangthefe*, *justitia cognoscentis latronis sua est*, *de homine suo*, *si captus fuerit super terram suam*: *Illi verò qui non habent has consuetudines coram justitia Regia rectum faciant in Hundredis*, *&c.* The definition hereof see also in *Britton*, *fol.* 90. and *Rog. Hovenden*, *part. poster suor. annal. fol.* 345. And *Skene de verb.* Signif. who writeth of it at large, reciting diversity of Opinions. Touching this, and *Outfangthefe*, *Fleta*, *lib.* 1. *cap.* 47. says, *Infangthefe* (for so he writes it) *dicitur latro captus in terra alicujus*, *seisitus aliquo latrocinio de suis propriis hominibus*, Anno 1 & 2 P. & M. cap. 15.

In forma pauperis, When any man that hath a just cause of Suit either in the Chancery, or any other the Courts of Common-Law, will come either before the Lord Keeper, Master of the Rolls, either of the chief Justices, or chief Baron, and make Oath, that he is not worth five pounds, his Debts paid, either of the said Judges will in his own proper Court admit him to sue in *forma Pauperis*, and he shall have Council, Clerk or Attorney assigned to do his business, without paying any Fees.

Information. See *Enditement*. *Information* for the King, *Informatio pro Rege*, is the same that for a common person we call a Declaration, and is not always done directly by the King, or his Attorney, but sometimes by another, *qui sequitur tam pro Domino Rege quam pro seipso*, upon the breach of some penal Law or Statute, wherein a penalty is given to the Party that will sue for the same.

Informatus non sum, or more truly **Non sum Informatus**, Is a formal Answer made of course by an Attorney, that is commanded by the Court to say what he thinketh good in defence of his Clyent, who being not instructed to say any thing material; says, He is not *informed*, by which he is deemed to leave his Clyent undefended, and so Judgment passeth for the adverse Party. See the *New Book of Entries*, *tit. Non sum informatus*, and Judgment 12.

Informer, *Informator*, Is any one who *informs* or prosecutes in any the Kings Courts of Common-Law, *viz.* Exchequer, Kings Bench, Common-Pleas, Assises or Sessions, those that offend against any Law, or penal Statute: These, in some cases, are called *Promoters*; the *Civilians* term them *Delatores*.

Ingressu, Is a Writ of Entry, whereby a man seeketh Entry into Lands or Tenements: It lies in many cases, and hath many several forms. See *Entry*. This Writ is also call'd in particular, *Præcipe quod reddat*, because those be formal words in Writs of Entry. The Writs, as they lie in divers Cases, are these, set down in the *Old Nat. Brev.* viz. *Ingressu ad Terminum qui præteriit*, *fol.* 121. *Reg. Orig. fol.* 227. which lyeth where the Lands or Tenements are let to a man for term of years, and the Tenant holdeth over his term *Ingressu dum non fuit compos mentis*, *Reg. Orig.* 218. which lies when a man selleth Land or Tenement, being out of his wits, &c. *Ingressu dum fuit infra ætatem*, Old N. B. fol. 123. Reg. Orig. fol. 228. lies where one under age sells his Lands, &c. *Ingressu super disseisina in le quibus*, *Old N.B.* 125. *Reg. Orig.* 229. lies where a man is disseised, and dyeth, for his Heir against the Disseisor. *Ingressu in le Per*, *Old Nat. Brev.* 126. *Reg. Orig. fol.* 229. *Ingressu sur cui in vita*, Vet. N. B. 128. Reg. Orig. 230. both which see in *Entry*. *Ingressu causa matrimonii prælocuti*, Vet. N. B. fol. 130. Reg. Orig. 233. which see in *causa Matrimonii prælocuti*. *Ingressu in casu proviso*, Vet. N. B. 132. Reg. Orig. 235. which see in *casu proviso*. *Ingressu cui ante divortium*, Vet. N. B. fol. 130. Reg. Orig. 233. For which see *Cui ante divortium*. *Ingressu in casu consimili*, for which see *Casu consimili*. *Ingressu sine assensu capituli*, Reg. Orig. fol. 230. Is a Writ given by the Common-Law to the Successor of him that alienated *sine assensu capituli*, &c. and is so called from those words contained in the Writ, *Co.* on *Lit. fol.* 325. And *Ingressu ad communem Legem*, Vet. N. B. 132. Reg. Orig. 234. which lieth where the Tenant for term of Life, or of anothers Life, Tenant by Courtesie, or Tenant in Dower, maketh a Feoffment in Fee, and dieth: He in the Reversion shall have the aforesaid Writ against whomsoever that is in the Land, after such Foffment made.

Ingrossator magni Rotuli. See *Clerk of the Pipe*.

In grosse, Is that which belongs to the person of the Lord, and not to any Mannor, Lands, &c. As Villain in *gross*, Advowson in *gross*, *&c. Co.* on *Lit. fol.* 120.

Ingrossing of a Fine, Is making the Indentures by the *Chirographer*, and the delivery of them to the Party unto whom the Cognisance is made, *Fitz. Nat. Brev. fol.* 147.

Ingrosser, *Ingrossator*, From the French *Grosier*, that is, *Solidarius venditor*, Is one that buys Corn growing, or dead Victuals to sell again, except Barley for Malt, Oats for Oatmeal, or Victuals to Retail; Badging by Licence, and buying of Oyls, Spices and Victuals, other than Fish or Salt, *Anno* 5 *E.* 6. *cap.* 14. 5 *Eliz.* 14. 13 *Eliz.* 25. but *West. Symbol.* part 2. *tit.* Inditements *sect.* 64. says, This definition rather doth belong to unlawful *ingrossing*, than to the word in general. See *Forestaller*, and 3. *par.* Inst. *fol.* 195. *Ingrosser* is also a Clerk that writes Records or Instruments of Law in skins of Parchment: As in *Henry* the Sixth's time, he who is now called *The Clerk of the Pipe*, was call'd *Ingrossator Magni Rotuli*; and the *Controuler of the Pipe* was called *Duplex ingrossator*, Spelm.

Inheritance,

Inheritance, *Hæreditas*, Is a perpetuity in Lands or Tenements to a man and his Heirs: For *Littleton, lib.* 1. *cap.* 1. hath these words, This word *Inheritance* is not only understood where a man hath *inheritance* of Lands and Tenements by descent of Heritage, but also every Fee-simple or Fee-tail that a man hath by his Purchase, may be said by *Inheritance*, for that his Heirs may *inherit* after him. *Several inheritance* is that which two or more hold severally, as if two men have land given them to them and their Heirs of their two Bodies; these have joint Estates during their Lives, but their Heirs have several *Inheritance, Kitchin, fol.* 155. See *Terms de la Ley, verbo* Enheritance.

Inewardus, One attending the King in *Hereford* and *Cambridge shires, Doomsday*.

Inhibition, *Inhibitio*, Is a Writ to *inhibit* or forbid a Judge from farther proceeding in the Cause depending before him. See *F. N. B. fol.* 39. where he putteth *prohibition* and *inhibition* together. *Inhibition* is most commonly a Writ issuing out of a higher Court-Christian to a lower and inferior, upon an Appeal, *Anno* 24 *H.* 8. *cap.* 12. And *Prohibition* out of the Kings Court to a Court-Christian, or to an inferior Temporal Court.

Injunction, *Injunctio*, Is a writ grounded upon an Interloquutory Order in Chancery; sometimes to give possession to the Plaintiff, for want of the Defendants Appearance; sometimes to the Kings ordinary Court, and sometimes to the Court-Christian, to stay proceedings in a cause upon Suggestion made, that the rigour of the Law, if it take place, is against equity, and conscience in that case. See *West. Symb. part* 2. *tit. Proceeding in Chancery*, sect. 25.

Inlagh or **Inlaugh**, *Inlagatus vel homo sub lege*, signifies him that is some *Frank-Pledge*, and not Outlawed, of whom take *Bractons* words, *Lib.* 3. *Tract.* 2. *cap.* 11. *Minor vero et qui infra ætatem duodecem annorum fuerit, utlagari non potest nec extra legem poni; quia ante talem ætatem non est sub lege aliqua nec in decenna, non magis quam fæmina, quæ utlagari non potest, quia ipsa non est sub lege*, i. Inlaugh *Anglice*, sc. *in franco plegio sive decenna sicut masculus duodecem annorum et ulterius*, &c. Inlaughe *significat hominem subjectum legi*, Fleta, lib. 1. cap. 47.

Inlagary, *Inlagatio*, Is a restitution of one Outlawed, to the Kings Protection, and to the benefit or estate of a Subject, *Bracton, lib.* 3. *tract.* 2. *cap.* 14. *num.* 6. 7, 8. *Britton, cap.* 13.

Inland, *Inlandum, Terra Dominicalis, Pars Manerii Dominica, terra interior*; For that which was let out to Tenants, was called *Utland*. In the *Testament* of *Brithericus* in *Itinerar. Cantii*, 'tis said thus according to *Lamberts* Interpretation, *To Wulfee* (*I give*) *the* Inland *or Demeans, and to Elfeyth* Outland *or Tenancy*.----This word is often found in *Doomsday*.

Inleased, From the French *Enlass*, intangled or insnared; the word we may read in the Champions Oath, *Co.* Inst. 2. *par. fol.* 247.

Inmates, Be those that are admitted to dwell for their Money joyntly with another man, though in several Rooms of his Mansion-house, passing in and out by one Door, and not being able to maintain themselves; which are inquirable in a Leet, *Kitchin, fol.* 45. where you may read who are properly *Inmates*, and who not.

Innes of Court, *Hospitii Curiæ*, Are so called, because the Students therein do study the Laws, to enable them to Practise in the *Courts* of *Westminster*, or elsewhere; and also because they use all other gentile Exercises, as may make them more serviceable to the King in his *Court*, *Fortescue*, *cap.* 49. Of these there are four well known, *viz.* the *Middle-temple*, *Inner-Temple*, *Lincolns-Inn* and *Grayes-Inn*, which with the two *Sergeants-Inns*, and eight *Inns* of *Chancery* (as Sir *Edward Coke* says) make the most famous University for the Profession of Law only, or of any one humane Science in the World; concerning which, see *Dugdales Origines Judiciales*.

Inn, **Hospitium**, Common *Inns* are instituted for Passengers; for the proper Latine word is *Diversorium*, because he that lodgeth there is *quasi divertens se a via*; and therefore if a Neighbour which is not a Traveller, as a Friend at the request of the Inn-Keeper lodge there, and his Goods are stollen, he shall not have an Action, for the Writ is *Hospitandos homines per partes, ubi hujusmodi* hospitia *existunt transeuntes & in eisdem* hospitantes, Co. 8. Rep. *Calyes* Case: Neither shall the Inn-Keeper answer for any thing that is out of his *Inn*, but only for such things as are *infra hospitium*, the words are *eorum bona & catalla infra hospitia illa existentia*. Any person found tipling in any *Inn* or Ale-house, shall be adjudged within the Statutes against Drunkenness, 21 *Jac.* and 1 *Car.* 1. *cap.* 4.

Infant, *Infans*, Before the Age of one and twenty years, a Man or Woman is called an *Infant* in the Law, *Co.* on *Lit. lib.* 1. *cap.* 21. & *lib.* 2. *cap.* 28. An *Infant* of eight years of Age, or above, may commit *Homicide*, and be hanged for it, *viz.* if it may appear by hiding the person, by excusing, or by any other act that he had knowledge of Good and Evil, and of the danger of the Offence, for here *Malitia supplebit ætatem*; yet *Co.* upon *Lit. sect* 405. saith, That an *Infant* shall not be punisht till the age of fourteen, which, says he, is the age of discretion.

Innotescimus, Letters Patents so called, which are always of a Charter of Feoffment, or some other Instrument not of Record, and so stiled in the words of the conclusion, *Innotescimus per præsentes*. An *Innotescimus* and *Vidimus* are one and the same. See *Co. Rep.* 5. *Pages* Case.

Innuendo, From *Innuo*, to beck or nod with the Head, is a word frequently used in Writs, Declarations and Pleadings, and the Office of it is only to declare and ascertain the person or thing which was named or left doubtful before; as to say, He (*innuendo*, the Plaintiff) is a Thief, where there was mention before of another person; but this *innuendo* must neither inlarge the sense of the words, nor make a supply, or alter the Case where the words are defective. See *Huttons Rep. fol.* 44.

Inpeny and **Outpeny**, Concerning which, you may read in the *Register* of the *Monastery* of *Cokesford*, pag. 25. thus, *De* Inpeny & Out-

Outpeny *consuetudo talis est in Villa de East-Rudham de omnibus terris quæ infra Burgagium tenentur, viz. quod ipse qui vendiderit vel dederit dictam tenuram alicui, dabit pro exitu suo de eadem tenura unum denarium & similiter proingressu suo, &c.* These words and Custom are also mentioned in the Rolls of a Court there held, about the Feast of the *Epiphany*, *Anno* 12. R. 2. *Spelm.*

Inquirendo, Is an Authority given to a person or persons, to enquire into something for the Kings advantage, which, in what cases it lyeth, see *Reg. Orig. fol.* 72 85, 124, 265, 266, 267.

Inquisition, *Inquisitio*, Is a manner of proceeding in matters Criminal, by the Office of the Judge, or by the great *Inquest* before Justices in *Eyre*. See *Eyre*, and the places in *Bracton* and *Britton* there quoted. *Hostensis* defines it thus, *Inquisitio nihil aliud est quam alicujus criminis manifesti ex bono et æquo judicis competentis canonice facta investig. tio. ca. qualiter de accusat.* in the *Decretals*. *Inquisition* is also with us used for the King in Temporal Causes and Profits, in which kind it is confounded with Office. *Stamf. Prærog. fol.* 51. See *Office*.

Inquisitors, *Inquisitores*, Are Sheriffs, Coroners, *super visum corporis*, or the like, who have power to inquire into certain Cases. Statute of *Marlbridge, cap.* 18. *Britton, fol.* 4. and *Westm.* 1, *Enquirors* or *Inquisitors* are included under the Name of *Ministri*, 2 *par.* Inst. *fol.* 211.

Inrollment, *Irrotulatio*, Is the Rigistring, Recording, or Entring of any lawful Act in the Rolls of the *Chancery*, as a Recognisance acknowledged, or a Statute, or a Fine, levied, or in the Rolls of the Exchequer, Kings Bench, or Common-Pleas, or in the *Hustings* of *London*, or by the Clerk of the Peace in any County. See *West. Symbol.* part 2. tit. *Fines*, *sect.* 133. and 27 H. 8. 16.

Insidiatores viarum, Waylayers, or such as lie in wait, are words which by 4 *H.* 4. *cap.* 2. are not to be put in Inditements, Arraignments, Appeals, &c.

Insimul tenuit, Is one Species of the Writ called a *Formedon*. See *Formedon*.

Insinuation, *Insinuatio*, 21 *H.* 8. 5. Is a covert, and cunning creeping into a mans favour. *Insinuation* of a Will is, among the *Civilians*, the first production of it, or the leaving it *Penes Registrarium*, in order to its Probate.

Inspeximus, Letters Patent so called, because they begin after the Kings Title with this word *Inspeximus*, and is the same with Exemplification. See *Co.* 5. *Rep. Pages* Case.

Installment, A settlement, or sure placing in, 20. *Car.* 2. *cap.* 2. Sometimes it is confounded with Abatement.

Instant, In Latine *Instans*, and defined by the *Logicians* to be *Unum indivisible in Tempore, quod non est Tempus, nec pars temporis, ad quod tamen partes temporis copulantur*, and is much considered in Law; and though it cannot be actually divided, yet in conceit it may, and applyed to several Purposes, as if they were several times. Whereof see in *Plowdens Commentaries*, *Fulmerston* and *Stuards* Case, where the Statute of 31 *H.* 8. is expounded concerning an Abbots letting of Lands, &c. and there it is debated, that when the Termor takes the second Lease, he surrenders his former Term; and so at the same *instant* of taking the second Lease, the former is expired. And in the Case between *Petit* and *Hales*, he who kills himself, commits not Felony till he be dead, and when dead, he is not in being, so as to be termed a Felon; but he is so adjudged in Law *eo instante*, at the very *instant* of this Fact doing; and there are many other Cases in Law, where the *instant* time, that is not dividable in nature; in the consideration of the mind is divided.

Institution, *Institutio*, Is, when the Bishop says to a Clerk who is presented to a Benefice, *Instituo te Rectorem talis Ecclesiæ cum cura animarum & accipe curam tuam & meam.* Every Rectory consists of a *Spiritualty* and *Temporalty*. As to the *spiritualty*, viz. *Cura animarum*, he is a compleat Parson by *institution*. But as to the *Temporalties*, as Gleab-land, &c. he has no *Franktenement* therein till Induction, *Co.* 4 *Rep. Digbyes* Case. The first beginning of *Institutions* to Benefices was in a National Synod held at *Westminster* by *John de Crema*, the Popes Legate, *Anno* 1124. Which see in *Seldens History of Tythes*, pag. 375.

Insuper, Is a word used by *Auditors* in their Accounts in the Exchequer, when they say, so much remains *insuper* to such an Accountant, that is, so much remains due upon such an Account, *Anno* 21 *Jac. cap.* 2.

Intakers, Were a sort of Thieves in *Riddesdale*, in the farthest Northern parts of *England*, mentioned 9 *H.* 5. *cap.* 8. and so called, because they dwelling within the Liberty, did *take* in and receive such Booties of Cattel, and other things, as their Confederates the Outparters brought in to them. See *Outparters*.

Intendment of Law, *Intellectus Legis*, The understanding, intention, and true meaning of Law, *Co.* on *Lit. fol.* 78. says, The Judges ought to judge according to the common *intendment of Law*.

Intension, Is a Writ that lies against him that enters after the death of Tenant in Dower, or other Tenant for Life, and holds out him in the Reversion or Remainder; For which see *F. N. B. fol.* 203. And every Entry upon the Possession of the King is called an *Intension*; as where the Heir of the Kings Tenant enters after Office, and before Livery, this is called an *Intension upon the King*, as appears in *Stamf. Prærog. fol.* 40, &c.

Inter Canem & Lupum, *M. filia* N. *de* Okele *Appellat.* J. C. *pro raptu & pace Regis fracta die Martis prox. &c.* Inter Canem & Lupum, i. *in, crepusculo, scilicet Anglice Twilight*, i. *inter diem et noctem, &c.* Inter *placita de* Trin. 7 E. 1. Rot. 12. Glouc.——*In placit. de domo combusta maliciose, hora vespertina, sc.* Inter Canem & Lupum *venerunt malefactores, &c. Plac. Cor. Reg. apud Novum Castrum*, 24 E. 1. Rot. 6.

Inter-commoning, Is where the Commons of two Mannors lie together, and the Inhabitants of both have time out of mind depastured their Cattel promiscuously in each.

Interdiction, *Interdictio*, Is used in the Common-Law in the same signification that it hath in the Canon-Law, where it is thus defined, *Interdictio est censura Ecclesiastica prohibens administrationem*

strationem divinorum, and thus it is used, 24 *H.* 8. *cap.* 12.

Interdicted of Water and Fire, Were, in old time, those who for some Crime were banisht, which Judgment, though not by express Sentence pronounced, yet by giving Order, That no man should receive them into his House, but deny *Fire and Water*: They were condemned, as it were, to a civil death; and this was called *Legitimum exilium*. Livy.

Interest, *Interesse*, Is usually taken for a Term, or Chattel real, and more particularly for a future Term; in which case, it is said in pleading, That he is possessed *de interesse termini*: But *ex vi Termini* in a legal sense, extends to *Estates*, Right and Titles that a man hath of, in, or to, or out of Lands; for he is truly said to have an *interest* in them, *Co.* on *Lit. fol.* 345.

Interlocutory Order, *Ordo interlocutorius*, Is that which decides not the Cause, but only settles some interveneing matter relating to the cause; As where an Order is made, by motion in *Chancery*, for the Plaintiff to have an Injunction to quiet his Possession, till the hearing of the Cause. This, or any such Order, not being final, is *interlocutory*.

Interpleder. See *Enterpleder*.

Intestates, *Intestati*; There are two kinds of *Intestates*, one that makes no Will at all; another that makes a Will, and nominates Executors, but they refuse; in which he dies as an *Intestate*, and the Ordinary commits Administration, 2. *par.* Inst. *fol.* 397. See the Stat. 22 & 23 *Car.* 2. *cap.*

Intierty. See *Entierty*.

Intrusion, *Intrusio*, Is, when the Ancestor dies seised of any Estate of Inheritance, expectant upon an Estate for life; and then Tenant for life dies, between whose death, and the Entry of the Heir, a Stranger doth interpose and *intrude*, *Co.* on *Lit. fol.* 277. *lib.* 3. *cap.* 8. *sect.* 475. *Bracton*, *lib.* 4. *cap.* 2. To the same purpose defines it thus, *Intrusio est ubi quis, cui nullum jus competit in re nec scintilla juris, possessionem vacuam ingreditur, quæ nec animo nec corpore possidetur*, &c. with whom agreeth *Fleta*, *lib.* 4. *cap.* 30. *sect.* 1. & 2. *Britton. cap.* 65. The *New Book of Entries*, *verbo* Entrusion. See *Entrusion*. See *Disseisin*. See also *Abatement*, and the Stat. 21 *Jac. cap.* 14.

Intrusione, Is a Writ that lies against the *Intruder*, *Regist. fol.* 233.

Invadiationes, Mortgages or Pledges, *Confirmamus eis omnes alias donationes, venditiones* & invadiationes *rationabiliter factas*, Mon. Ang. 1. par. fol. 478.

Inventory, *Inventorium*, Is a Description or Repertory, orderly made of all dead Mens Goods and Chattels, prized by four or more credible men, which every Executor or Administrator is bound to exhibite to the Ordinary at such times as he shall appoint, *West. Symbol. part* 1. *lib.* 2. *sect.* 696. where likewise you may see the form. This *Inventory* proceeds from the Civil Law, for whereas by the ancient law of the *Romans*, the Heir was obliged to answer all the Testators Debts, by which means Heritages were more prejudicial to many than profitable. *Justinian*, to encourage men the better to take upon them this charitable Office, Ordained, That if the Heir would make and Exhibit a true *Inventory* of all the Testators Goods coming to his hands, he should be no further charged than to the value of the *Inventory*, *lib ult. Cod. de jure deliberando*, &c.

In ventre sa mere, French, in the Mothers Belly: Is a Writ mention'd in the *Register*, And *Anno* 12 *Car.* 2. *cap.* 24.

Invest, *Investire*, Is derived of the French word *Invester*, and signifies to give possession. *Hotoman de verbis feudalibus, verbo* Investitura: *Investitura barbarum nomen, barbaricam quoq; rationem habet, Nam ut ait feudista*, lib. 2. tit. 2. *Investitura proprie dicitur quando hasta vel aliquod corporeum traditur a domino.* We use likewise to *invest* the Tenant, by delivering them a Verge or Rod in their hands, and ministring them an Oath, which is called *Investing*. Others define it thus, *Investitura est in suum jus alicujus introductio*, a giving Livery of Seisin or Possession.

Invoyce, 12 *Car.* 2. *cap.* 34. Is a particular of the value, custom and charges of any Goods sent by a Merchant in another mans Ship, and consigned to a Factor or Correspondent in another Country.

Inure, signifies to take effect, as the Pardon inureth, *Stamf. prær. fol* 40. See *Enure*.

Jocalia, Jewels, *Edward* the first employ'd one *Andevar ad* Jocalia *sua impignoranda*, Claus. 29 E. 1.

Jocarius, A Jester, In a Deed of *Richard* Abbot of *Bernay* to *Henry Lovet*, without date; among the Witnesses to it, was *Willielm. tunc* Jocario *Domino Abbatis*.

Joclet, A Saxon word signifying *Prædiolum*, a little Farm; in some parts of *Kent* yet called *Yoclet*, as requiring but a small yoke of Oxen to till it, Saxon *Diction*.

Jotson. See *Jetsen* & *Flotzon*.

Joynder, Is the coupling or joyning of two in a Suit or Action against another, *F. N. B. fol.* 118, 201, 221. and in many other places, as appeareth in the *Index*, *verbo* Joynder.

Joint-tenants, *Simul tenentes*, or *qui conjunctim tenent*, Lib. intrationum, tit. *Formedon in view*, 3. be those that come to, and hold Lands or Tenements by one Title *pro indivisio*, or without partition, *Co.* on *Lit. lib.* 3. *cap.* 3. *sect.* 277. These are distinguished from sole or several *Tenants*, from *Parceners*, and from *Tenants* in Common; and anciently they were called *Participes*, and not *Hæredes*: And these must *joyntly* implead, and *joyntly* be impleaded by others, which properly is common between them and Coparceners; but *Joynt-tenants* have a sole quality of survivorship, which Coparceners have not; for if there be two or three *Joynt-tenants*, and one hath Issue and dies, then he or those *Joynt-tenants* that survive, shall have the whole by Survivorship. See *Co.* on *Lit. ibid. sect.* 180. See more of this *Termes de la Ley*, *verbo* Joynt-tenants.

Joyning of Issue, *Junctio Exitus*. See *Issue*.

Joynture, *Junctura*, Is a Covenant whereby the Husband, or some other Friend in his behalf, assureth unto his Wife, in respect of marriage, Lands or Tenements for term of Life, or other-

otherwise, *West Symbol. part* 2. *lib.* 2. *tit.* Covenants, *sect.* 128. 27 *H.* 8. *cap.* 10. It is so called either because granted *ratione junctura in matrimonio*, or because the Land in *Frank-marriage* is given joyntly to the Husband and Wife, and after to the Heirs of their Bodies, whereby the Husband and Wife be made Joynt-tenants during the Coverture, *Co. lib.* 3. *Butler* and *Bakers* Case, *fol.* 27. See *Frank-marriage. Joynture* is also used as the abstract of Joynt-tenants, *Co. lib.* 3. *fol.* 3 Marquess of *Winchesters* Case. *Junctura* is also by *Bracton* and *Fleta* used for joyning of one Bargain to another, *Fleta lib.* 2. *cap.* 60. And therefore *Joynture* in the first signification may be so called, in respect that it is a Bargain of Livelihood for the Wife, adjoyned to the Contract of Marriage. See also the *Terms of the Law*, *eodem verbo*.

Journeys accounts, *Dieta computata*, Is a term in the Law to be thus understood, if a Writ be abated without the default of the Plaintiff or Demandant, he may purchase a new Writ, which if it be purchased by *Journeys accounts* (that is, within as little time as he possibly can after the abatement of the first Writ,) then this second Writ shall be as a continuance of the first, and so shall oust the Tenant or Defendant of his Voucher, Plea of Non-tenure, Joynt-tenancy fully administred, &c. or any other Plea which arises upon matter happening after the date of the first Writ; and fifteen days have been held a convenient time for the Purchase of the new Writ. See for this Writ by *Journeys accounts*, *Co. lib.* 6. *fol.* 9. *Spencers* Case.

Journal; A Diary or Day-Book, *Journals* of Parliaments are not Records, but only Remembrances; and are neither of necessity, nor have been of long continuance. See *Hub. Rep. fol.* 109.

Journey choppers, 8 *H.* 6. 5. were Regrators of Yarn; whence the first part of the word is derived, is somewhat obscure; but *Choppers* are to this time known to be *Changers*: As to *chop* and change is a familiar phrase. See *Chop-Chirch*.

Journey-man, Cometh of the French word *Journee*, that is, a day or days-work, so that properly it is one that wrought with another by the day, though now by the Statute made *Anno quinto Eliz. cap.* 4. it be extended to those likewise, that covenant to work with another in his Trade or Occupation by the year.

Ire ad largum, To go at large, is a term frequent in the Law.

Irregularity, *Irregularitas*, Disorder: In the Canon Law it is taken for an Impediment, which hinders a man from taking holy Orders; as if he be base born, notoriously defamed of any notable Crime, maimed, or much deformed, or has consented to procure anothers death, and the like.

Irrepleviable or **Irreplevisable**, That neither may nor ought to be *replevyed* or set at large upon upon Sureties; as the Distress shall be *irreplevisable*, 13 E. 1. *cap.* 2.

Isinglass, *Gluten Piscium*, A kind of Fish-glue or Fish-gum, brought from *Iseland*, and those parts, and used in Medicines, and by some in the adulterating of Wines, but for that prohibited by Statute made 12 *Car.* 2. *cap.* 25.

Issue, *Exitus*, Cometh of the French *Issuer*, i. *emanare*: It hath divers Applications in the Common-Law, sometime being used for the children begotten between a man and his Wife, sometimes for Profits growing from Amerciaments or Fines, and sometimes for profits of Lands or Tenements, *Westm.* 2. 13 *E.* 1. *cap.* 39. Sometimes for that point of matter depending in Suit, whereupon the Parties joyn, and put their Cause to the Tryal of the Jury: And yet in all these it hath but one signification, which is an effect of a Cause proceeding, as the children be the effect of the Marriage between the Parents; the profits growing to the King or Lord, from the punishment of any mans Offence, is the effect of his Transgression; the point referred to the tryal of twelve men, is the effect of Pleading or Process. *Issue* in this last signification is either *general* or *special*; *General issue* seemeth to be that whereby it is referred to the *Jury*, to bring in their Verdict, whether the Defendant have done any such thing, as the Plaintiff layeth to his charge. For example, If it be an Offence against any Statute, and the Defendant plead *Not Guilty*; this being put to the Jury, is called *The general issue*. And if a man complain of a private wrong, which the Defendant denyeth, and pleads no wrong nor Disseisin; and this be referred to the Jury, it is likewise the *general issue*, *Kitchin*, *fol.* 225. See *Doct.* and *Stud. fol.* 158. The *special issue* then must be that, when special matter being alledged by the Defendant for his defence, both Parties joyn thereupon, and so grow rather to a Demurrer; if it be *quæstio juris*, or to tryal by the Jury, if it be *quæstio facti*, 4 *H.* 8. 3. 18 *Eliz. cap.* 12. and the *New Book of Entries*, *verbo* Issue.

Itinerant, *Itinerans*, Travelling, or taking a Journey. Those were anciently called Justices *itinerant*, who were sent with Commission into divers Counties to hear such Causes especially as were termed Pleas of the Crown. See *Justices in Eyre*.

Judaisme, *Judaismus*, The Custome, Religion, or Rites of the *Jews*: This word was often used by way of exception in old Deeds. The Statute *de Judaismo* was made 18 E. 1. At which Parliament the King had a Fifteenth granted him *pro Expulsione* Judæorum. *Judaismus* was also used for a Mortgage —--*Pro hac autem donatione dederunt mihi dicti Abbas & Canonici sex Marcas sterl. ad acquietandam terram prædictam de* Judaismo *in quo fuit impignorata per* Rob. *fratrem meum, &c.* Ex magno Rot. Pipæ de Anno 9. E. 2.

Judge and **Judges**, *Judex & judices*, All their Commissions are bounded with this express limitation, *Facturi quod ad justitiam pertinet secundum legem & consuetudinem Angliæ*. The *Judg* at his Creation takes an Oath, That he shall indifferently minister Justice to all them that shall have any Suit or Plea before him, and this he shall not forbear to do, though the King by his Letters, or by express word of mouth should command the contrary, &c. It is a Maxim in the Law, *Aliquis non debet esse* Judex *in propria causa*. King *Henry* the Fourth, when his eldest Son the Prince was by the Lord chief Justice, for some great misdemeanors, committed to Prison, he thanked God that he had a Son of that Obedience, and a *Judge* so impartial, and of such undaunted Courage; the story

story is well known, and may be read at large both in *Stow* and *Daniel*, *in vita*, Hen. 5. *Fortescue* in his Book *de Laudibus legum Angliæ* 53. speaketh of a *Judge*, complaining of a Judgment given against a Gentlewoman of *Salisbury*, who being accused by her own Man, without any other proof, for murdering her Husband, was thereupon condemned and burnt: The Man, who accused her, being within a year after convicted for the same Offence, confest, That his Mistress was altogether innocent of that cruel Fact. But this *Judge* (as the same Author Adds) *sæpius mihi fassus est, quod nunquam in vita sua animum ejus de hoc facto purgaret.* In *septimo Hen.* 4. the King demanded of *Gascoigne* Justice, If he saw one in his presence kill *J. S.* and another (which was not culpable) should be indicted of this before him, what he would do in this Case? To which he answer'd, That he ought to respite the Judgment against him, and to relate the matter fully to the King to procure him a Pardon; for there he cannot acquit him, and give Judgment according to his private knowledge. But where they have a judicial knowledge, there they may and ought to give Judgment according to that. See the like Case determined by King *James*, in his Disputations at *Oxford*, *Rex Plat. p.* 109. 113, 114, 115. *Plow. fol.* 83. *Partridge* against *Strange*.

Judgment, *Judicium*, *quasi juris dictum*, Is the Censure of the Judges so called, and is the very Voyce and final Doom of the Law; and therefore is always taken for unquestionable truth. The ancient words of *Judgment* are very significant, viz. *Consideratum per curiam*, &c. because *Judgment* is or ought to be given by the Court, upon consideration of the Record before them; and in every *Judgment* there ought to be three persons, *viz. Actor, reus & Judex*: Of *Judgments* some be final, and some not final. See *Co.* on *Lit. fol.* 39. and *Co.* 9. *Rep. Downams* Case.

Judicium Dei, The Judgment of God, so our Ancestors call'd those now prohibited Tryals of Ordeal, and its several kinds, *Si super defendere non posset* Judicio Dei, *scilicet Aqua vel ferro, fieret de eo justicia*, Leges Ed. Conf. cap. 16. See *Spelmans Gloss.* on this word.

Judgment or Tryal by the holy Cross, Long since disused. See *Cressyes Church History*, *fol.* 960.

Jug, A watery place, according to *Doomsday*.

Jugum, Half an Arpent, 50 Perches, so mentioned in *Doomsday*, as the same Book interprets, *Jugum terræ*, to contain half a Plowland.

Juncaria or Joncaria, (From *junctus*, the Latine word for a Rush;) is a soyl or place where Rushes grow, *Co.* on *Lit. fol.* 5. *Cum Piscariis, Turbariis*, Juncariis, *& communibus pasturis ad messuagium prædictum pertin.* Pat. 6 E. 3. pag. 1. m. 25.

Juncture. See *Joynture*.

Jura Regalia. See *Regalia*.

Jure Patronatus. See the *New Book of Entries*, *verbo* Jure Patronatus *in Quare impedit*, *fol.* 465. *col.* 3.

Jurats, *Jurati*, 2 & 3 *E.* 6. *cap.* 30. As the Mayor and *Jurats* of *Maydstone*, *Rye*, *Winchelsey*, *Tenderton*, &c. are in the nature of Aldermen, for Government of their several Corporations So *Jersey* hath a Bayliff and twelve *Jurats*, or sworn Assistants to Govern the Island, *Camd. Brit. Romeny Marsh* is also incorporate of one Bayliff, twenty four *Jurats*, and the Commonalty thereof by Charter dated 23 *Feb.* 1 *E.* 4.

Jury, *Jurata*, May be derived from the Latine *Jurare*, to swear, and signifies either twenty four or twelve Men sworn to inquire of the matter of Fact, and declare the truth upon such Evidence as shall be delivered them, touching the matter in question. Of which *Jury*, who may, and who may not be impannelled, see *F. N. B. fol.* 165. And here observe, That in *England* there be three sorts of Tryals, *viz.* one by Parliament, another by battel, and the third by Assise or *Jury*, *Smith de Rep. Angl. lib.* 2. *cap.* 5, 6, 7. Of the two former read him, and see *Battel*, *Combat*, and *Parliament*. The tryal by Assise, (be the Action civil or criminal, publick or private, personal or real,) is referred for the Fact to a *Jury*, and as they find it, so passeth the Judgment; and the great Favor that by this the King shews to his Subjects, more than the Princes of other Nations, you may read in *Glanvil*, *lib.* 2. *cap.* 7. where he call it, *Regale beneficium clementiæ principis de consilio Procerum populis indultum, quo vitæ hominum & status integritati tam salubriter consulitur, ut in jure, quod quis in libero soli tenemento possidet, retinendo, duelli casum declinare possint homines ambiguum*, &c. This *Jury* is not only used in Circuits of Justices Errant, but also in other Courts and Matters of Office; as if the *Escheator* make Inquisition in any thing touching his Office, he doth it by *Jury* or Inquest. If the Coroner inquire how a Subject found dead, came to his end, he useth an Enquest. The Justices of Peace in their Quarter-Sessions, The Sheriff in his County and Turn, The Bayliff of a hundred, The Steward of a Court-Leet or Court-Baron, if they inquire of any Offence, or decide any Cause between Party and Party, they do it in the same manner: So that where it is said, All things be tryable by Parliament, Battel or Assise, Assise in this place is taken for a *Jury* or Enquest, empannelled upon any Cause in a Court where this kind of Tryal is used; and though it be commonly supposed that this Custom of ending and deciding Causes proceeded from the *Saxons* and *Britains*, and was of favour permitted to us by the Conquerour; Yet I find by the *Grand Custumary* of *Normandy*, *cap.* 24. that this course was likewise used in that Country, for Assise is in that Chapter defined to be an Assembly of wise men, with the Bayliff, in a place certain, at a time assigned forty days before, whereby Justice may be done in Causes heard in the Court: Of this Custom also, and those Knights of *Normandy*, *Johannes Faber* maketh mention in the *Rubrick* of the Title *de militari testamento*, *in Institut.* This *Jury* though it appertains to most Courts of the Common-Law, yet is it most notorious in the half year Courts of the Justices Errants, commonly called the *Great Assises*; and in the Quarter-Sessions, and in them it is most ordinarily called a *Jury*: And that in civil Causes, whereas in other Courts it is termed oftener an *Enquest*; and in the Court-Baron, a *Jury* of the Homage: In the General Assise, there are usually many *Juries*, because there be store of Causes both civil

civil and criminal, commonly to be tryed, whereof one is called *The Grand Jury*, and the rest *Petit Juries*, whereof it seemeth there should be one for every Hundred, *Lamb. Eirenarch. lib.* 4. *cap* 3. *pag.* 384. The Grand *Jury* consists ordinarily of twenty four grave and substantial Gentlemen, or some of the better sort of Yeomen, chosen indifferently by the Sheriff out of the whole Shire, to consider of all Bills of Inditement preferred to the Court, which they do either approve by writing upon them *Billa vera*, or disallow by indorsing *Ignoramus*: Such as they do approve, if they touch Life and Death, are farther referred to another *Jury* to be considered of, because the Case is of such Importance; but others of lighter moment, are upon their allowance, without more work, fined by the Bench, except the Party traverse the Inditement, or challenge it for insufficiency, or remove the Cause to a higher Court by *Certiorari*, in which two former Cases it is referred to another *Jury*, and in the later transmitted to a higher, *Lamb. Eir. lib.* 4. *cap.* 7. and presently upon the allowance of this Bill by the Grand Inquest, a man is said to be indited; such as they dissallow, are delivered to the Bench, by whom they are forthwith cancelled or torn. The *Petit Jury* consists of twelve men at the least, and are empanell'd as well upon criminal as upon civil Causes: Those that pass upon Offences of Life and Death, do bring in their Verdict either Guilty, or not Guilty, whereupon the Prisoner, if he be found guilty, is said to be convicted, and so afterward receiveth his Judgment and Condemnation, or otherwise is acquitted, and set free: of this read *Fortescue, cap.* 47. Those that pass upon civil Causes real, are all, or so many as can conveniently be had of the same Hundred, where the Land or Tenement in question doth lye, being four at the least, and they upon due examination bring in their Verdict either for the Demandant or Tenant. Of this also see *Fortescue, cap.* 25, 26 According to which, Judgment passeth afterward in the Court, where the Cause began: And the reason hereof is, because these Justices of Assise are in this case, for the ease of the Country, only to take the Verdict of the *Jury* by vertue of the Writ called *Nisi prius*, and so return it to the Court where the Cause is depending. See *Nisi prius*, and *Lambert* in his *Explication of Saxon words, verbo* Centuria, His words are these, *In singulis centuriis Comitia sunto atq; liberæ conditionis viri duodeni ætate superiores, una cum Præposito sacra tenentes, juranto, se adeo virum aliquem innocentem haud condemnaturos, sontemve absoluturos.* See also the *Custumary* of Normandy. cap, 69. *Vide etiam Enquest.* See *Twelve men*, and *Lamberts Eiren.* lib. 4 cap. 3. pag. 384.

Juridical days, *Dies Juridici*, *Days* on which the Law is administred, *days* in Court. See *Dies.*

Jurisdiction, *Jurisdictio*, Is a dignity which a Man hath conferred on him to do Justice in Cases of Complaint made before him: Of this there are two kinds, one which a man hath by reason of his Fee, doing Right in all Plaints relating to his Fee; by vertue thereof, the other is collated by a Prince to a Bayliff, which division we find in the *Grand Custumary* of *Normandy*, *cap.* 2. which is not unfit for the constitution of our Government: For under the name of Bayliff there, we may comprehend all that have Commission from the Prince to give Judgment in any Case, See *Co.* 4. *Inst.* in the *Proæmium.* The *Civilians* divide *Jurisdictionem* into *Imperium* & Jurisdictionem, & *imperium in merum & mixtum*; Of which you may read several Tractates.

Juris utrum. Is a Writ that lyeth for the Incumbent, whose Predecessor hath alienated his Lands or Tenements; the divers uses of which Writ see in *F. N. B. fol.* 48.

Jus Coronæ, The Right of the Crown is part of the Law of *England*, and differs in many things from the general Law, relating to the Subject. See *Co.* on *Lit. fol.* 15. *b.*

Jus Curialitatis Angliæ, See *Curtesie of England.*

Jus hæreditatis, The right of Inheritance. See *Heir.*

Jus Patronatus, Is the right of presenting a Clerk to a Benefice. See the *New Book of Entries*, *verbo* Jure Patronatus *in Quare impedit*, *fol.* 465. *col.* 3.

Justes, Cometh of the French *Joustes*, i. *decursus*, and signifieth with us contentions between Martial Men and Persons of Honor, with Spears on Horseback, 24 *H.* 8. *cap.* 13.

Juror, *Jurator*, Is one of those twenty four or twelve Men, which are sworn to deliver a Truth upon such Evidence as shall be given them touching the matter in question, of which see *F. N. B. fol.* 165. and the Statute 16 & 17 *Car.* 2. returning able and sufficient *Jurors.*

Justice, *Justiciarius*, Signifies him that is deputed by the King to do Right by way of Judgment; the reason why he is called *Justice* and not *Judex*, is, because in ancient time the Latine word for him was *Justitia*, and not *Justiciarius*, as appeareth by *Glanvile*, *lib.* 2. *cap.* 6. and *Rog. Hovenden, part. poster. suor. annal. fol.* 413. Another reason why they are called *Justiciarii*, and not *Judices*, is, because they have their Authority by Deputation, as *Delegates* to the King, and not *jure Magistratus*, and therefore cannot depute others in their stead, the *Justice* of the Forest only excepted, who hath that liberty especially given him by 32 *H.* 8. 35. for the Chancellor, Marshal, Admiral, and such like, are not called *Justiciarii*, but *Judices*: Of these *Justices* there are divers sorts in *England*, of the manner of whose creation with other appurtenances, read *Fortescue*, *cap.* 51. These in *Magna Charta*, *cap.* 12. and other Statutes, are called *Justicers.*

Justice or chief Justice of the Kings Bench, *Capitalis justitia vel justiciarius de Banco Regis*, Is a Lord by his Office while he enjoys it, and the *chief* of the rest; His Office especially is to hear and determine all Pleas of the Crown, *viz.* such as concern Offences committed against the Crown, Dignity, and Peace of the King; as Treasons, Felonies, Mayhems, and such like; which you may read in *Bracton*, *lib.* 3. *tract.* 2. *per totum*, and in *Stamf. Pl. Cor.* from the first to the 51. *chap.* of the first Book. He also, with his Assistants, heareth all personal Actions and real also, if they be incident to his Jurisdiction. See *Cromp. Jur. fol.* 67. Of this Court *Bracton*, *lib.* 3. *cap.* 7. *num.* 2. saith thus, *Placita* *vero civilia in rem & personam in Curia Domini Regis terminanda, coram diversis* justiciariis *terminantur; & illarum curiarum habet unam propriam, sicut aulam Regiam; &* justiciarios capitales *qui proprias causas Regis terminant & aliorum omnium per querelam vel privilegium sive libertatem; ut si sit aliquis qui implacitari non debeat, nisi coram Rege.* This *Justice* hath no Patent under the Great Seal, but is made by Writ in this short form.

> *Rex, &c.* M. H. *salutem, sciatis quod constituimus vos* justiciarium *nostrum capitalem ad placita coram nobis tenenda, durante beneplacito nostro. Teste, &c.*

Of the ancient Dignity of this *chief Justice*, we find that in the time of King *John*, and others our ancient Kings, it often occurs in Charters of Priviledges, *Quod non ponatur respondere nisi coram nobis vel capitali* justitia *nostra.* The Court was first called *The Kings Bench*, because the King sometime sat in it in his own Person, and was moveable with the Court, 9 *H.* 3. 11. The Oath of the *Justices* see in the Stat. 18 *E.* 3. *Stat.* 4. and in *Origines Juridiciales* a Catalogue of all the Lords *chief Justices* in *England.* See Oath, and see *Kings Bench.*

Justice, or chief Justice of the Common Pleas, *Dominus Justiciarius Communium Placitorum.* He is also a Lord by his Office, and, with his Assistants, originally did hear and determine all Causes at the Common-Law, that is, all civil Causes between common Persons, as well personal as real, for which cause it is called *The Court of Common Pleas*, as differencing it from the *Pleas* of the Crown, or the Kings *Pleas*, which are special, and appertaining to him only. Of this, and the jurisdiction thereof, see *Cromp.* Jur. *fol.* 91. and 4. *Inst. fol.* 99. This Court was always setled in a place, as appears by the Stat. 9 *H.* 3. 11. The Oath of him and his Associates, see 18 *E.* 3 *Stat.* 4. See *Oath.*

Justice of the Forest, *Justiciarius Forestæ*, Is also a Lord by his Office, and hears and determines all offences within the *Forest*, committed against Vert or Venison: Of these there be two, whereof one hath Jurisdiction over all *Forests* on this side *Trent*, the other of all beyond. The chiefest point of their Jurisdiction consisteth upon the Articles of the Kings Charter, called *Charta de Foresta*, made *Anno* 9 *H.* 3. concerning which, see *Camden, Brit. pag.* 214. See *Protoforestarius.* The Court where this *Justice* sits and determines, is called *The Justice Seat of the Forest*, held once every three years, as you may read in *Manwoods Forest Laws, cap.* 24. He is also called *Justice in Eyre of the Forest*; and is the only *Justice* that may appoint a Deputy, by the Statute of 32 *H.* 8. 35.

Justices of Assise, *Justiciarii ad capiendas Assisas*, are such as were wont by special Commission to be sent (as occasion was offered) into this or that County, to take *Assises* for the ease of the Subjects; for whereas these Actions pass always by Jury, so many men might not, without great damage and charge, be brought up to *London*, and therefore *Justices* for this purpose, by Commission particularly authorised, were sent down to them. For it seems, that the *Justices* of the *Common Pleas* had no power to take *Assises* till the Stat. of 8 *R.* 2. *cap.* 2. for by that they were enabled to it, and to deliver Gaols. And the *Justices* of the *Kings Bench* have by that Statute such Power affirmed unto them, as they had one hundred years before. These *Commissions ad capiendas Assisas*, have of late years been setled and executed only in *Lent*, and the *long Vacation*, when the *Justices*, and other learned Lawyers, may be at leisure to attend those Controversies; whereupon it also falls out, that the Matters that were wont to be heard by more general Commissions of *Justices in Eyre*, are heard all at one time with these *Assises*, which was not so of old, as appears by *Bracton, lib.* 3. *cap.* 7. *num.* 2. *Habet etiam* justiciarios *itinerantes de Comitatu in Comitatum, quandoq; ad omnia placita; quandoq; ad quædam specialia, sicut* Assisas, &c. *& ad Gaolas deliberandas, quandoq; ad unam vel duas & non plures.* And by this means the *Justices* of both Benches being worthily accounted the fittest of all others, and their Assistants, were imployed in these Affairs. But no *Justices* of either Bench, nor any other, may be *Justices of Assise* in his own County, *Anno* 8. *R.* 2. 2. and 33 *H.* 8. 24. And those who now are called *Justices of Assise*, and twice every year go the Circuit, by two and two through all *England*, dispatch their several business by several Commissions, *Cromp.* Jur. *fol.* 210. For they have one Commission to take *Assises*, another to deliver Gaols, another of *Oyer* and *Terminer*, *&c.* That *Justices of Assise*, and *Justices in Eyre* did anciently differ, appeareth by 27 *E.* 3. *cap.* 5. And that *Justices of Assise* and *Justices of Gaol-delivery* were divers, is evident by 4 *E.* 3. 3. The Oath taken by *Justices of Assise* is all one with that taken by the *Justices* of the *Kings Bench*, *Old Abridgment of Statutes*, tit. *Sacramentum justiciariorum.* See *Oath.*

Justices of Oyer and Terminer, *Justiciarii ad audiendum et terminandum*, Were *Justices* deputed upon some special or extraordinary Occasion, to hear and determine some peculiar Causes. *Fitzherbert* in his *Nat. Brev.* saith, That the Commission *d' Oyer and Terminer* is directed to certain Persons upon any great Assembly, Insurrections, heinous misdemeanors, or Trespasses committed. And because the occasion of granting this Commission should be maturely weighed, It is provided by the Staute made 2 *E.* 3. *cap.* 2. That no such Commission ought to be granted, but that they shall be dispatched before the *Justices* of the one Bench or other, or *Justices Errant*, except for horrible Trespasses, and that by the special favour of the King. The form of this Commission, see *F. N. fol.* 110.

Justices in Eyre, *Justiciarii itinerantes*, Are so termed of the old French word, *Erre, Iter*, as (*a grand Erre*, i. *magnis itineribus*,) proverbially spoken. These in ancient time, were sent with Commission into divers Counties to hear such Causes especially, as were termed *Pleas of the Crown.* And this was done for the Ease of the People, who must else have been hurried to the Kings Bench, if the Cause were too high for the County-Court: They differed from the *Justices of Oyer and Terminer*, because they (as we said before) were sent upon one or few special Causes, and to one place, whereas the *Justices in Eyre* were sent through the Provinces and Counties of the Land, with more indefinite and general Commission, as appeareth by *Bracton*, *lib.* 3. *cap.* 11. 12, 13. and *Britton*, *cap.* 2. And again, because the *Justices of Oyer and Terminer* were sent uncertainly upon any uproar, or other occasion in the Countrey; but these in *Eyre* (as Mr. *Gwin* sets down in the *Preface to his Reading*,) were sent but every seven years once, with whom agrees *Horne* in his *Mirror of Justices*, lib. 2. cap. *queux poient estre actours*, &c. *Et* lib. 2. cap. *des peches criminals*, &c. *al suite del Roy*, &c. And lib. 3. cap. *de Justices in Eyre*: Where he also declares what belongs to their Office. [But there is a Book entituled, *Orig. juridiciales*, which says, They went oftener.] These were instituted by King *Henry* the Second, as *Camden* in his *Britannia* witnesseth, *pag.* 104. and *Hovenden par. post. suor. annal. fol.* 313. hath of them these words, *Justiciarii itinerantes, constituti per* Henricum *Secundum*, *qui divisit Regnum suum in sex partes, per quarum singulas tres* justiciarios *itinerantes constituit*, &c. In some respect they resembled our Justices *of Assise* at present, though their authority and manner of proceeding much differ, *Co.* on *Lit. fol* 293.

Justices of Gaol-delivery, *Justiciarii ad Gaolas deliberandas*, Are such as are sent with Commission to hear and determine all Causes appertaining to such as for any Offence are cast into the *Gaol*; part of his Authority is to punish such as let to Mainprise those Prisoners that be not bailable by Law, nor by the Statute *de finibus*, *cap.* 3. *F. N. B. fol.* 151. These seem in ancient time to have been sent into the Country upon this several occasion; but aftewards *Justices of Assise* were likewise authorised to this, *Anno* 4 *E.* 3. *cap.* 3. Their Oath is all one with other of the Kings *Justices* of either Bench, *Old Abridgment of Statutes*, tit. *Sacramentum justiciariorum*. See *Oath*.

Justice of the Hundred, *Justiciarius Hundredi, erat ipse Hundredi Dominus*, *qui & Centurio & Centenarius appellatur*, *Hundrediq; Aldermannus*, saith *Spelman*.

Justicements, From *Justicia*, All things belonging to *Justice*, *Co.* on *Westm.* 1. *fol.* 225.

Justices of Laborers, Were *Justices* heretofore appointed to redress the frowardness of *laboring-men*, that would either be idle, or have unreasonable Wagee. See 21 *E.* 3. *cap.* 1. 25 *E.* 3. *cap.* 8. and 31 *E.* 3. *cap.* 6.

Justices of Nisi Prius, Are all one at this time with *Justices of Assise*, for it is a common Adjournment of a Cause in the *Common-Pleas*, to put it off to such a day, *Nisi prius justiciarii venerint ad eas partes ad capiendas Assisas*; and upon this Clause of Adjournment they are called *Justices of Nisi prius* as well as *Justices of Assise*, by reason of the Writ or Action that they have to deal in. Their Commission you may see in *Cromp. Jur. fol.* 204. yet with this difference between them, that *Justices of Assise* have Power to give Judgment in a Cause, but *Justices of Nisi prius* only to take the Verdict. But in the nature of both their Functions, this seems to be the greatest difference, that *Justices of Nisi prius* have to deal in Causes personal as well as real; whereas *Justices of Assise*, in strict acception, meddle only with the possessory Writs called *Assise*.

Justices of traile baston, Were a kind of *Justices* appointed by King *Edward* the First, upon occasion of great Disorders grown in the Realm, during his absence in the *Scotch* and *French* Wars. In the *Old N. B. fol.* 52. they are stiled *Justices of Tryal baston*: But by *Holinshed* and *Stow*, *Traile-baston*, so called (say they) of *trailing*, or drawing the staff of *Justice*: Or according to *Co.* 12. *Rep. fol.* 25. for their summary proceedings, who says also, They were, in a manner, *Justices in Eyre*, and their Authority founded on the Statute of *Ragman*. Their Office was to make Inquisition through the Realm, by the Verdict of substantial Juries, upon all Officers, as Mayors, Sheriffs, Bayliffs, Escheators, and others touching Extortion, Bribery, and other such Grievances; as intrusions into other mens Lands, Barretors, and Breakers of the Peace, with divers other Offendors; by means of which Inquisitions, many were punisht by Death, many by Ransome, and the rest flying the Realm; the Land was quieted, and the King gained great Riches towards the support of his Wars. See *Mat. Westm.* in *Anno* 1305. As to the name *Traile-baston*, there are divers Opinions, some think that *Baston* signifies the Beam of a pair of Scales, and so is metaphorically applyed to the just poysing of recompence for Offences committed. Others think it may be deriv'd from the French (*Treilles*, i. *Cancelli*) Bars or Lattices, a Grate with cross-bars: Others from the word *Treille*, i. *Pargula*, a Frame or Rayl, such as Vines use to run upon; and *Baston*, a Staff or Pole, inferring, that the *Justices* imployed in this Commission, had Authority to proceed without any solemn Judgment-Seat, but might without more work proceed where-ever they could apprehend the Malefactors they sought for. If I may be admitted to give my thoughts, I suppose, it may be deriv'd from the French word *Trayl*, i. to draw; and *Baston*, a Staff; and the reason of this my supposition, is, that the Kings of *England* having in those times many occasions in *France*, by reason of their frequent Wars there, and observing that the Marshals of *France* had a large Power, with which they were invested by the delivery of a *Baston*, (or as we call it a *Battoon*) the Ensign of their Office and Authority. When they returned and found strange disorders grown here, in imitation of that, erected these *Justices*, who (as they say) had a *Baston* delivered them as the Badge of their Office, so that whoever was brought before them was *Traille al Baston*, *traditus ad Baculum*; whereupon with submission, may their Name easily be deduced, and they called *Justices de trail Baston*, or *Justiciarii ad trahendum offendentes ad baculum vel* baston. We find a Commission of *Trail-baston*, *coram Rogero de Grey & Sociis suis* Justic. *apud* S. *Albanum*, *Anno Regni Regis* E. 3. *post conquestum* 5. See *Spelmans Gloss. verbo Trail-baston*.

Justices of the Pavilion, *Justiciarii Pavilionis*, Are certain Judges of a *Pye-powder Court*, of a most transcendent Jurisdiction, anciently authorised by the Bishop of *Winchester*, at a Fair held on St. *Giles's* Hills near that City, by vertue of Letters Patent granted by King *Edward* the Fourth. See the Patent at large in *Prynnes Animadv.* on 4. *Inst. fol.* 191.

Justices of the Peace, *Justiciarii ad pacem*,

pacem, Are they that are appointed by the Kings Commission to attend the *Peace* of the County where they dwell; of whom some, upon special respect, are made of the *Quorum*, because some business of importance may not be dispatcht without the presence or assent of them, or one of them. See *Quorum*. The Office and Power of these is so various, being grounded upon several Statutes, that we cannot here recite them, concerning which, both *Fitzherbert*, *Lambert* and *Crompton* have written Books to their own great Commendation, and the general benefit of the whole Realm. See also *Smith de Repub. Anglor. lib.* 2. *cap.* 19. They were called *Guardians of the Peace* till the thirty sixth year of *Edward* the Third, *cap.* 12. where they are called *Justices*, *Lamb. Eiren. lib.* 4. *cap.* 19. *pag.* 578. Their Oath see also in *Lamb. lib.* 1. *cap.* 10.

Justices of Peace, &c. within Liberties, *Justiciarii ad pacem infra libertates*, Are such in Cities and other Corporate Towns, as those others be of any County, and their Authority or Power is all one within their several Precincts, 27 *H.* 8. *cap.* 25.

Justice-Seat, Is the highest Court that is held in a Forest, and is always held before the Lord chief *Justice in Eyre of the Forest*, upon warning forty days before; and there the Judgments are always given, and the Fines set for Offences, that were presented at the Courts of Attachments, and the Offendors indited at the *Swainmotes*, concerning which, see *Manwoods Forest-Law*, *cap.* 24.

Justiciar, French *Justicier*, A Justice or *Justicer*, The Lord *Bermingham. Justiciar* of *Ireland*, *Baker*, *fol*, 118.

Justicies, Is a Writ directed to the Sheriff, for the dispatch of *Justice* in some special Cause of which he cannot by his ordinary Power hold Plea in his County-Court. Hereupon the Writ *de excommunicato deliberando*, is called a *Justicies* in the *Old Nat. Brev. fol.* 35. Also the Writ *de homine replegiando*, Ibid. *fol.* 41. And the Writ *de secunda superoneratione pasturæ*, Ibid. *fol.* 73. There are many Presidents of this in *F. N. B. fol.* 117. in Account, and *fol.* 152. in Annuity, and *fol.* 119. in Debt. *Kitchin*, *fol.* 74. says, That by this Writ of *Justicies*, the Sheriff may hold Plea of a great sum, whereas, of his ordinary Authority, he can hold no Pleas, but of sums under forty shillings, with whom agrees *Crompton*, *fol.* 231. It is called a *Justicies*, because it is a Commission to the Sheriff *ad justiciandum aliquem* to do a man justice, and requires no return, or any Certificate of what he hath done, *Bract. lib.* 4. *tract.* 6. *cap.* 13. *num.* 2 mentions a *Justicies* to the Sheriff of *London*, in a Case of *Dower*. See the *New Book of Entries*, *verbo*, Justicies.

Justification, *Justificatio*, Is an affirming or shewing good reason in Court, why he did such a thing as he is call'd to answer, as to *justifie* in a Cause of Replevin, *Broke*, tit. *Replevin*.

Justificators, *Justificatores*, Seem to signifie Compurgators, or such as by Oath *justifie* the innocency, Report or Oath of another, as in the case of waging Law; also Jury-men, because they *justifie* that Party, for whom they deliver their Verdict. See *Spelmans Gloss*.

K.

Kalender month, Mentioned 16 *Car.* 2. *cap.* 7. consists of 30 or 31 days, (excepting *February*, which never hath more than 28, unless in *Leap-year*, and then but 29,) twelve of which *months* being those mentioned in the *Kalender* make a year, which we call vulgarly in the singular number, *A twelve-month*. But if in the plural number, we say *Twelve-months*, then shall it be accounted a *month* of weeks, which is but 28 days. See *Co. lib.* 6. *fol.* 81. *Catesbyes* Case.

Kantref, According to the description of Mr. *Humfry Lloyd*, out of the Laws and Ordinances of *Howel-dda*, a *Kantref* had its denomination from one hundred Towns, and signifies as much, under which were contained so many Commots, which the *Welsh* call *Cwmmwd*, and signifies *Provincia* or *Regio*, and consisted of twelve Mannors or Circuits, and two Townships. We find the word mentioned in *Mong. Ang.* 1. *part fol.* 319. thus,—*Le primier Conquereur de trois* Kantref *de la terre de* Brecknoch, *estoit* Bernard *de* Nesmarch Norman. See *Cantred*.

Karle, A Saxon word, properly denoting a Man, but with any addition a Servant or *Clown*. Hence they called a Sea-man, a *Buscarle*, and a Menial Servant, a *Huscarle*. See *Huscarle*. We may read this word frequently in *Seldens Mare Clausum*, *Doomsday*, and other ancient Records: And probably from hence by corruption comes the modern word *Churle*.

Karrata fæni, A Cartload of Hay, *Mon. Ang. part* 1. *fol.* 548. See *Caretta*.

Kay, *Kaya & Caya*, Is a convenient place fitted on the shore, for the loading and unloading of Vessels; we commonly call it a *Wharf*. The Verb *Cajare* in old time (says one) signifies (as *Scaliger* Reports) to keep in or restrain, and the Ground where *Kays* are made is forced and kept in with strong Planks and Posts.

Kayage, *Kayagium*, The Money or Toll paid for Wharfage, for loading or unloading of Goods or Wares, *Rot. pat.* 1 *E.* 3. *m.* 10. and 20 *E.* 3. *m.* 1.

Kedel, 12 *E.* 4. *cap.* 7. See *Kiddle*.

Keeper of the Great Seal, *Custos magni sigilli*, Is a Lord by his Office, and stiled *Lord Keeper of the Great Seal of England*: He is one of the Kings Privy-Council; through whose hands pass all Charters, Commissions, and Grants of the King under the *Great Seal*; without which *Seal* all such Instruments by Law are of no force. For the King is in the interpretation of Law a Corporation, and passeth nothing firmly but under the said *Seal*, which is as the publick Faith of the Kingdom in the high esteem and reputation, justly attributed thereto. This *Lord Keeper* by the Statute 5 *Eliz.* 18. hath the same Place, Authority, Preheminence, Jurisdiction, Execution of Laws, and all other Customs, Commodities, and Advantages as hath the *Lord Chancellor of England* for the time being. He is constituted, by the delivery of the *Great Seal* to him, and taking his Oath, *Co.* 4. *Inst. fol.* 87.

Keeper of the Privy-Seal, *Custos privati sigilli*, Is a Lord by his Office, through whose hands pass all Charters signed by the King before they come to the *Great Seal*, and some things which do not pass the *Great Seal* at all: He is of the Kings Privy-Council, and was anciently called *Clerk of the Privy-Seal*, 12 R. 2. *cap.* 11. *Gardien del Privy-Seal*, in Rot. Parl. 11 H. 4. num. 28. And Lord *Privy-Seal*, and one of the great Officers of the Kingdom, by 34 *H.* 8. 4.

Keeper of the Touch, 12 *Henr.* 6. 14. Seems to be that Officer in the Kings Mint, at this day called *The Master of the Assay*. See *Mint*.

Keeper of the Forest, *Custos Forestæ*, Is also called *Chief Warden of the Forest*, *Manwood Forest Laws*, *part* 1. *pag.* 156. and hath the principal Government of all things, and the check of all Officers belonging to the same; and when it pleaseth the Lord chief Justice in *Eyre of the Forest* to keep his Justice-Seat, he sends out his Warrant, or general Summons, to him forty days before, for the warning of all under-Officers to appear before him at a day assigned in the Summons, which see in *Manwood*, *ubi supra*.

Kennets, A sort of course Welsh Cloth, mentioned 33 H. 8. 3.

Kernes, Idle Persons, Vagabonds, *Necknon de illis qui dicuntur homines otiosi, & malefactoribus, qui etiam* kernys *dicuntur*, Ordin. Hibern. 31 E. 3. m. 11. 12.

Kernellatus, Fortified, or according to the old fashion embattell'd; according to which the Duke of *Lancaster* claimed to him and his Heirs *Castrum suum de* Halton, *Kernellatum*, 31 E. 3. *Pl. de quo Warrant. apud Cestriam.*

Keyles or **Keeles**, *Ciuli*, A kind of long Boats, of great Antiquity, mentioned 23 H. 8. 18. *Longæ naves quibus Britanniam primo ingressi sunt Saxones*, Spelm.

Kidder, *Anno* 5 *Eliz. cap.* 12. says, *Every person being a common Badger*, Kidder, *Lader or Carryer*. Whereby it signifies one that Badges, or carries Corn, dead Victual, or other Merchandise up and down to sell, called also *Kyddiers*, 13 *Eliz. cap.* 25.

Kiddle, Kidel or **Kedel**, *Kiddellus*, A Dam or Wear in a River to catch Fish. The word is ancient, For in *Magna Charta*, *cap.* 24. it is said, *Omnes* kidelli *deponantur de cætero penitus per Thamesiam & Medeweyam & per totam Angliam nisi per Costeram maris*. And in a Charter granted by King *John*, Power was granted to the City of *London*, *De* kiddellis *amovendis per Thamesiam*, *& Medeweyam*, Anno 1 H. 4. cap. 12. It was among other things accorded, That a Survey should be made of the Wears, Mills, Stanks, Stakes and *Kidels* in the great Rivers of *England*. In an Inquisition taken at *Derby* the 15. of *Novemb.* 4 *Eliz.* after the death of *Thomas Fenderne*, *&c.* 'Tis said, *Et fuit seisitus de uno* kidello, *vocat.* a Wear *ac de libera piscaria in Potlok. esc. Bundello* 3.

Kilketh, An ancient servile kind of Payment, for in an old Manuscript 'tis thus written, *Kilketh pro qualibet Hundredeca* 2. *denar.*

King, *Rex*, Is thought by *Camben* in his *Brit. pag.* 105. to be contracted from the Saxon word *Cyning* or *Coning*, signifying him that hath the higest Power, and absolute Rule over the whole Land; and therefore the *King* is in intendment of Law cleared of those defects which common persons are subject to; for he is always supposed to be of full age, although never so young, *Cromp. Jur. fol.* 134. *Kitchin*, *fol.* 1. He is taken as not subject to death, but is a Corporation in himself, *Cromp. ibid.* He is *supra Legem* by his absolute Power, *Bract. lib.* 1. *cap.* 8. *Kitch. fol.* 1. And though for the better and more equal course in making Laws, He do admit the three Estates, that is, Lords Spiritual, Lords Temporal, and the Commons unto Council; yet this derogates not from his Power; for whatever they Act, He by his negative Voyce may quash. See concerning this, *Smith de Rep Anglor. lib.* 1. *cap.* 3. and *Bracton*, *lib.* 2. *cap.* 16. *num.* 3. and *Britton*, *cap.* 39. He pardoneth Life and Limb to Offenders against his Crown and Dignity, except such as he bindeth himself by Oath not to forgive, *Stamf. pl. cor. lib.* 2. *cap.* 35. And *Habet omnia jura in manu sua*, Bracton, lib. 2. cap. 24. num. 1. He may alter or suspend any particular Law that seems hurtful to the Publick, *Blackwood in Apologia Regum*, cap. 11. For the *Kings* Oath, see *Bracton*, *lib.* 3. *cap.* 9. *num.* 2.

Again, The *Kings* only Testimony of any thing done in his presence, is of as high nature and credit as any Record; Whence it comes, That in all Writs or Precepts sent out for the dispatch of Justice, He useth no other Witness than himself, always using these words at the end, *Teste Meipso*. Lastly, He hath in the right of his Crown many Prerogatives above any common person, be he never so potent and honourable; whereof you may read at large in *Stamfords Tractate* upon the Statute thereof made 17 *E.* 2. Also in *Bracton*, *lib.* 2. *cap.* 24. *num.* 1 & 2.

King of Heralds, *Rex Heraldorum*, Is a principal Officer at Arms, that hath the Preeminence of the Society. See *Herald* and *Garter*. Among the *Romans* he was called *Pater Patratus*.

King of the Minstrels, His power and Priviledge appears by the following Charter.

JOhan per le grace de Dieu, Roy de Castile & de Leon, Duke de Lancastre, a touts ceux, que cestu nos letres verront ou orront. Saluz Sachez nous avoir ordonez constitut et assignez nostre bien ame le Roy des Minstraulx *deins nostre Honeur de Tuttebury quare est, ou qui pur le temps serra pur prendre et arrester touts le* Minstraulx *deins meisme nostre Honeur & Franchise, queux refusount de fair lour services &* Minstralcy *as eux appurtenants, a faire de ancient temps a Tuttebury suis dit annuelment les jours del assumption de nostre Dame. Donants & grantants au dit* Roy des Minstraulx *pur le temps esteant plein poyer & mandement de les faire resonablement, justifier et constrener de faire lour services & Minstralcyes en maner come appeint, & come illonques ad este use & de ancient temps accustome. En Testimoignance de quel chose nous avons fait faire cestes nos Letres Patents, don souz nostre Privy-Seal a nostre castel de Tuttebury le* xxii. *jour de* August *le an de Regne nostre tresdulces le Roy* Richard *Second*, *quart.* Confirmed by Hen. 6. 22. Feb. 21. year of his Reign.

Kings

Kings Bench, *Bancus Regius*, Is the Court or Judgment Seat, where the *King* of *England* was sometimes wont to sit in his own Person; and therefore it was moveable with the Court or *Kings* Houshold, and called *Curia Domini Regis*, and *Aula Regia*, as *Gwin* Reports in the *Preface to his Reading*; and that therein, and in the Court of Exchequer, which were the only Courts o the *King* till *Henry* the Thirds days, were handled all matters of Justice, as well Civil, as Criminal. This Court of the *Kings Bench* was wont in ancient Times to be specially exercised in all Criminal Matters, and Pleas of the Crown, leaving the handling of private Contracts and Civil Actions to the Common-Pleas, and other Courts, *Glanvile lib.* 1. *cap.* 2, 3, 4. and *lib.* 10. *cap.* 18. *Smith de Rep. Angl. lib.* 2. *cap.* 11. *Co.* 4. *Inst. fol.* 70. and hath president of it, the Lord Chief Justice of *England*, with three or four Justices Assistants; or according to *Fortescue. cap.* 51. four or five, and Officers thereto belonging, the Clerk of the Crown, a Protonotary, and other inferior Ministers and Atturneys. See *Justice of the Kings Bench.*

Kings Silver, Is properly that Mony due to the *King* in the Court of Common Pleas *pro licentia concordandi*, in respect of a Licence then granted to any man for passing a Fine, *Co. vol.* 6. *fol.* 39. & 43.

Kings Swan-herd, *Magister deductus Cygnorum*, Pat. 16. R. 2. Pars 1. m. 38. *Radulphum Scot Custodem Cygnorum nostrorum*, &c. No Fowl can be a Stray but a *Swan*, *Co.* 4. *Inst. fol.* 280.

Kintal, Is a certain Weight of Merchandise, most commonly of one hundred pounds, or something under or over, according to the several uses of divers Nations. *Plowden fol.* 3. mentions 2000 *Kintals* of Woad in the Case of *Reniger* and *Fogassa*.

Kirbyes Quest, Is an ancient Record remaining with the Remembrancer of the Exchequer, the meaning and Etymology whereof will appear by what follows. *Memorandum, quod anno Domini* 1277. *Anno Regni Regis* Edwardi *filii Regis* Henrici *quinto, misit idem Rex per totam Angliam Ballivos inquirere, sub juramento & in secreto de universis terris Angliæ per* Johannem de Kirby *Thesaurarium suum, quisquis teneret & cujus feodi & quantum & cujus Regis tempore feoffati essent.* Ex Regist. Glaston. Cænobii penes Rad. Sheldon Ar. fol. 71.

Knave, An old Saxon word for a Man-Servant, and so is used, 14 *E.* 3. *Stat.* 1. *cap.* 3. And *Verstegan* in his *Restitution of decayed Intelligence*, c. 10. believes it is borrowed of the Dutch *Cnapa*, which signifies the same thing. And that is some kind of Officer or Servant, as *Scild-knapa* was he that bore the Weapon or Shield of his Superior, whom the Latines call *Armigerum*; and the French *Escuyer*.

Knight, *Miles*, Is almost one with the Saxon *Cnite*; with us it signifies a person that beareth Arms, who for his virtue, and specially Martial Prowess, is by the King, or one having the Kings Authority, singled from the ordinary sort of Gentlemen, and raised to a higher step of Dignity. This among all Nations, takes his Name from the *Horse*, because in ancient times they served in the War on Horse-back. The *Romans* called them *Equites*: The *Italians* term them *Cavallieri*: The French *Chevaliers*: The Germans *Reyters*: The Spaniard *Gavallaros*, &c. It appears by the Stat. *Anno* 1 *E.* 2. *cap.* 1. That in ancient times a Gentleman having a full *Knights* Fee, and holding his Land by *Knights*-service, might be urged by distress to procure himself to be made *Knight* when he came to full age. But by the Statute 17 *Car.* 1. *cap.* 20. It is Ordained, That no man shall be compelled to take the Order of *Knight-hood*, &c. The manner of making *Knights*, *Camd.* in his *Brit. pag.* 111. shortly expresseth in these words, *Nostris vero temporibus qui equestrem dignitatem suscipit, flexis genubus educto gladio leviter in humero percutitur. Princeps his verbis Gallice effatur, sois Chevalier au nom de Dieu*, that is, *sis eques nomine Dei.* The solemnity of making *Knights* among the *Saxons*, *Stow* mentions in his *Annals, pag.* 159. See the Priviledges belonging to a *Knight* in *Fernes Glory of Generosity*, pag. 116. Of these there be two sorts, *Knights Spiritual* and *Knights Temporal*, *Cassanæus in gloria Mundi*, part. 9. considerat. 2. Discourses at large of them. The *temporal* or second sort of *Knights*, *Ferne* in his *Glory of Generosity*, pag. 103. makes here among us three-fold, *Knights* of the *Sword*, *Knights* of the *Bath*, and *Knights* of the *Garter*, *Skene de verbor.* Significat. *verbo* Milites, saith, That in the ancient Laws of *Scotland*, Free-holders were called *Milites*, which may seem to have been a Custom with us. Also by divers places in *Bracton*, who saith, That *Knights* must be in Juries, which turn Free-holders do now serve. See *Seldens Titles of Honor, fol.* 770.

Knights of the Garter, *Equites Garterii*, or *Periscelidis*, are an Order of *Knights* first created by King *Edward* the Third, after he had obtained many notable Victories, who, for furnishing of this Honorable Order, made a choice out of his own Realm, and all Christendom, of the best and most excellently Renowned Knights in Virtue and Honor, bestowing this Dignity upon them, and giving them a blue *Garter*, decked with Gold, Pearl, and Precious Stones, and a Buckle of Gold, to wear daily on the left Leg only, a Kirtle, Crown, Cloak, Chaperon, a Collar, and other stately and magnificent Apparel, both of stuff and fashion; exquisit and heroical to wear at high Feasts, as to so high and Princely an Order was meet. Of which he and his Successors, Kings of *England*, were ordained Soveraigns, and the rest Fellows and Brethren, to the number of twenty six, *Smith de Rep. Anglor. lib.* 1. *cap.* 20. This Honorable Society is a Colledge or Corporation, having a common Seal belonging to it, and consisting of a Soveraign Guardian, which is the King of *England*, that always Governs this Order by himself, or his Deputy; Of twenty five Companions called *Knights of the Garter*, of fourteen secular Chanons that be Priests, or must be within one Year after their admission; thirteen Vicars, also Priests, and twenty six poor Knights, that have no other Sustenance, or means of Living, but the allowance of this House, which is given them in respect to their daily Prayer to the honor of God and St. *George*. There be also certain Officers belonging to this Order, *viz.* The Prelate of the

Garter, which Office is inherent to the Bishop of *Winchester* for the time being; the Chancellor of the *Garter*; the Register, who is always Dean of *Windsor*; The Principal King at Arms, called *Garter*, whose chief business is to manage and marshal their Solemnities at their yearly Feasts and Installations. Lastly, The Usher of the *Garter*, who is also the Usher of the *Black-Rod*. The scite of this Colledge is the Castle of *Windsor*, with the Chappel of St. *George*, erected by *Edward* the Third, and the Chapter-House in the said Castle, and their Solemnity upon St. *George*'s day. *Camden* saith, This Order receiv'd great Ornament from *Edward* the Fourth. *Fernes Glory of Generosity*, pag. 120. And that most Pious Prince *Charles* the First, as an addition to their Splendor, ordered all the Companions of the Order to wear on the left side of their upper Garment, the Cross of *England* encircled with the *Garter* and Motto, from whence round about are cast beams of Silver like the Rays of the Sun in full lustre. See *Garter*. I hear of a large Tract concerning this Order, written by *Elias Ashmole* Esq; which see for further satisfaction.

Knights Banneret, See *Baneret*.

Knights of the Bath, *Milites balnei vel de balneo*, Are an Order of *Knights* made within the Lists of the *Bath*, and girded with a Sword in the Ceremony of his Creation, *Fernes Glory of Generosity*, 105. These are spoken of 8 E. 4. *cap.* 2. For the Antiquity and Ceremony of their Creation, see Mr. *Dugdales Description of Worcestershire*, *fol.* 531, 532. They are so called from *Bathing* the night before their Creation. They take place of *Knights Batchelors*, but come after Baronets.

Knights of the Order of St. John of Jerusalem, *Milites Sancti* Johannis Hierosolymitani, were an Order of *Knight-hood* that began about the year of our Lord, 1120. *Honorius* being Pope, they had their denomination from *John* the Charitable Patriarch of *Alexandria*, though vowed to St. *John the Baptist* their Patron, *Fernes Glory of Generosity*, pag. 127. They had their Primary abode at first in *Jerusalem*, and then in the *Isle of Rhodes*, until they were expelled thence by the *Turks*, *Anno* 1523. Since which time their chief Seat is in the *Isle of Malta*, where they have done great Exploits against the *Infidels*, but specially in the year 1595. They live after the Order of Fryers, under the Rule of St. *Augustine*. Of whom mention is made in the Stat. 25 *H.* 8. *cap.* 2. and 26 *H.* 8. *cap.* 2. They had in *England* one general Prior that had the Government of the whole Order within *England* and *Scotland*, *Reg. Orig. fol.* 20 and was the first Prior of *England*, and sate in the Lords House of Parliament. But towards the end of *Henry* the Eighths days, they in *England* and *Ireland* being found overmuch to adhere to the Pope against the King, weee suppressed, and their Lands and Goods given to the King, by 32 *H.* 8. 24. The occasion and propagation of this Order more especially described, you may read in the Treatise, entituled, *The Book of Honor and Arms*, lib. 5. cap. 18. written by Mr. *Richard Jones*.

Knights of Malta. See *Knights of the Order of St.* John *of* Jerusalem.

Knights of the Rhodes, 32 *H.* 8. 24. See *Knights of the Order of St.* John *of* Jerusalem.

Knights of the Temple, *Templarii*, Otherwise called *Templers*, was an Order of *Knight-hood* instituted by Pope *Gelasius*, about the year of our Lord, 1117. and so called, because they dwelt in a part of the Building belonging to the *Temple* at *Jerusalem*, not far from the Sepulchre of our Lord. They entertained Christian Strangers and Pilgrims charitably, and in their Armor led them through the Holy Land, to view the Sacred Monuments of Christianity, without fear of Infidels. This Order increasing and continuing by the space of 200 years, was far spred in Christendom, and namely here in *England*; but in process of time, some of them at *Jerusalem* being (as some report) found to fall away to the *Saracens* from Christianity, or rather, because they grew too potent, the whole Order was suppressed by *Clemens Quintus*, 1309. and by the Council of *Vienna*, 1312. and their Substance given partly to the *Knights* of St. *John* of *Jerusalem*, and partly to other Religious, *Cassan. de gloria Mundi*, part. 9. consid. 5. and *Anno* 1. *cap.* 24. These flourished here in *England* from *Henry* the Seconds days, till they were supprest. They had in every Nation a particular Governor, whom *Bracton lib.* 1. *cap.* 10. calls *Magistrum militiæ Templi*. The Master of the Temple here was summoned to Parliament, 49 *H.* 3. *m.* 11. *in Schedula*; and the chief Minister of the *Temple* Church in *London* is still called *Master of the Temple*. Of these *Knights*, read *Dugdales Antiquities of Warwickshire*, fol. 706. In ancient Records, they were also called *Patres Militiæ Templi Solomonis*, Mon. Ang. 2 part. fol. 554.

Knights of the Chamber, *Milites Cameræ*, mentioned in 2 *Inst. fol.* 666. And in *Rot. Pat.* 29 *E.* 3. *part.* 1. *m.* 29. seem to be such *Knights* Batchelors as are made in time of Peace, because *Knighted* commonly in the Kings *Chamber*, and not in the Field, as in time of War.

Knights of the Shire, *Milites Comitatus*, otherwise called *Knights of the Parliament*, are two *Knights*, or other Gentlemen of worth, that are chosen in *Pleno Comitatu*, by the Free-holders of every County that can dispend 40 s. *per annum*, and be resident in the *Shire*, *Anno* 1 *H.* 5. *cap.* 1. & 10 *H.* 6. *cap.* 2. upon the Kings Writ, to be sent to the Parliament, and there to consult and advise concerning the Publick Affairs of the Realm: These, when every Man that had a *Knights* Fee, were constrained to be *Knights*, were of necessity to be *Milites gladio cincti*, and so the Writ still runneth, *Cromp. Jur. fol.* 1. But now Custom allows Esquires to be chosen to this Office, 23 *H.* 6. 6. So that they be resident in the County. For the choice of these *Knights*, See the Statutes, 7 *H.* 4. 15. 11 *H.* 4. 1. 6 *H.* 6. 4. 8 *H.* 6. 7. 23 *H.* 6. 15. with others; and the *New Book of Entries, verbo* Parliament. Their Expences are to be born by the County during the Parliament, 35 *H.* 8. 11. but that is of late disused in some measure.

Knight Marshal, *Marescallus Hospitii Regis*, Is an Officer in the Kings House, having Jurisdiction and Cognisance of any Transgression within the Kings House and Verge, as also of Contracts made there, whereunto one of the House is Party, *Reg. Orig. fol.* 185. & 191. and *Spelmans Gloss. in verbo* Marescallus.

Knight-service, *Servitium militare*, was a

Tenure whereby several Lands in this Nation were held of the King, which drew after it Homage, Escuage, Wardship, Marriage, &c. but taken away by 12 *Car.* 2 *cap.* 24. In *Doomsday Book* some Land holden by *Knights-service* is called *Tainland*, and Land holden by Socage, *Reveland*, fol. 86. a.

Knights Fee, *Feodum militare*, Is so much Inheritance as is sufficient yearly to maintain a *Knight* with convenient Revenue, which in *Henry* the Thirds days was 15 li. *Camd. Brit. pag.* 111. But Sir *Thomas Smith* in his *Repub. Angl. lib.* 1. *cap* 18. rateth it at forty pounds. And I find in the Statute for *Knights, Anno* 1 E. 2. *cap.* 1. that such as had twenty pounds in Fee, or for term of Life, might be compelled to be *Knights*; but this Statute is repealed 17 *Car.* 1. *cap.* 20. *Stow* in his *Annals*, pag. 285. saith, There were found in *England*, at the time of the *Conqueror*, 60211 *Knights Fees*: Others say 60215, whereof the Religious Houses, before their suppression, were possessed of 28015,—*unde octo Carucatæ terræ faciunt feodum unius militis*, Mon. Ang. 2 par. fol. 825. Of this you may read more in *Seldens Titles of Honor*, fol. 691. and *Bract. lib.* 5. *tract.* 1. *cap.* 2. and *Co.* on *Lit. fol.* 69. A *Knights Fee* contained twelve Plow-lands, 2 *par. Inst. fol.* 596. or six hundred Acres of Land. *Knights Fee* is sometime used for the Rent that a *Knight* payeth for his *Fee* to his Lord, of whom he holdeth; and this was uncertain, as appears by *Bracton, lib.* 5. *tract.* 1. *cap.* 2.

Knighten-gyld, Was a Guild in *London*, consisting of nineteen *Knights*, which King *Edgar* founded, giving unto them a Portion of void Ground, lying without the Walls of the City, now called *Port-soken Ward*, *Stows Annals*, *pag.* 151. This in *Mon. Ang.* 2 *par. fol.* 82. is written *Cnittenegild*.

Kyddiers, 13 *Eliz. cap.* 25. See *Kidder*.

Kylyw, —*Et sint quieti de pastu* & Kylyw & *omnibus aliis exactionibus, quas Forestarii* & *alii ballivi solent exigere*, Mon. Ang. 1 *par. fol.* 722, Perhaps it might signifie some Liquid thing, exacted by Foresters. See Scotale. We have to this day in the North the word *Kele*, which the Country people use for liquid Victuals.

L.

Laborariis, Is a Writ that lies against such as having not whereof to live, do refuse to serve, or for him that refuseth to serve in Summer where he served in Winter, *Reg. Orig. fol.* 189.

Laches, Cometh of the French *Lascher*, id est, *Laxare*; or *Lascke*, *ignavus*, and signifies slackness or negligence, as appears in *Littleton*, *sect.* 403 & 726. where *Laches* of Entry is nothing else but a neglect in the Heir to enter; whereupon, I take liberty to guess, that it may be an old English Word, as when we say, There is *Laches* of Entry, it is all one as if we should say, There *lack* is of Entry, or there is *lack* of Entry; and indeed it hath no other signification, for so is it used, *Lit. fol.* 136. and *Old Nat. Brev. fol.* 110. So where a man ought to make or do a thing, and he makes or does it not, I of his *Laches* can not have an Assise, but must take an Action upon the Case. See *Co.* on *Lit. fol.* 246. & 380.

Laford swick, Is derived from the Saxon *Hlaford Dominus* & *swic proditio*, *Infidelitas erga Dominum*, a betraying ones Lord or Master. In the Laws of *Henry* the First, *cap.* 13. *Quædam Placita emendari*, (i. *Quædam crimina expiari*) *non possunt*, Husbrech, Bernet, Opentheofe, Ebermath, and *Lafordswick*, which word is also found in *Canutus* Laws, *cap.* 61. which some Authors have written corruptly *Labordsith*.

Laga, *Lex*, The Law, *Lagam Regis* Edwardi *vobis reddo*, *cum illis emendationibus*, *quibus Pater meus eam emendavit*, says *Magna Charta*. Hence we deduce *Saxon-lage*, *Mercen-lage*, *Dane-lage*, &c.

Lageman, *Homo habens legem*, or as we term it, *Homo legalis*, such as we now call *Good men of the Jury*, which in the Writ are stiled, *Probos* & *legales homines*. The word is frequently used in *Doomsday*, and in the Laws of *Edward the Confessor*, *cap.* 38. Thus *Postea inquisisset Justicia per* Lagamannos, & *per meliores homines de burgo*, &c.

Lagen, *Lagena*, *Fleta*, *lib.* 2. *cap.* 8, 9. In ancient time it was a Measure of six *Sextarii*. *Donatio insuper de sex* Lagenis *olei annuatim*. Carta, 2 E. 3. m. 25. n. 82. See *Minstrel*.

Lagon or Lagan, Is such a parcel of Goods as the Mariners in danger of Shipwrack cast out of the Ship, and because they know they are heavy and sink, they fasten to them a Buoy or Cork, that so they may find and have them again. If the Ship be drowned, or otherwise perish, these Goods are called *Lagan* or *Ligan*, *a ligando*; and so long as they continue upon the Sea, they belong to the Admiral, but if they are cast upon the Land, they are then called a *Wreck*, and belong to him that hath the *Wreck*, as appears in *Co. lib.* 5. *fol.* 106.

Lacerta, Is a Word mentioned in *Doomsday* Book, and there signifies a Fathome.

Lahslite, Lagslite, Laghslite, *Transgressio Legis*, A breach of the Law, and sometimes the punishment for breaking the Law. *Si quis Dei rectitudines per vim teneat*, *solvat* Lahslite *cum Dacis*, *plenam* Wytam *cum Anglis*, Leg. Hen. 1. cap. 13. Lamb. Explic. of Saxon Words, verbo *Mulcta*.

Lairwite, Lecherwite and Legergeldum, *Pœna vel mulcta offendentium in Adulterio* & *fornicatione*, which Priviledge did anciently belong to some Lords of Mannors, in reference to their Villains and Tenants, which *Fleta*, *lib.* 1. *cap.* 47. seems to infer. See *Co.* 4. *Inst. fol.* 206.

Laised-lists, *Anno* 1 R. 3. *cap.* 8.

Lammas-day, Is the first of *August*, so called, *quasi Lamb-mas*, on which day the Tenants that held Lands of the Cathedral Church of *York*, which is dedicate to St. *Peter ad vincula*, were bound by their Tenure to bring a living Lamb into the Church at High Mass. See *Gule of August*.

Landa, An open Field without wood.

Land-boc, A Charter or Deed, whereby Lands or Tenements are given, or held, *sic Anglo Saxone*,

Saxones Chartas & instrumenta, nuncuparant, prædiorum Sessiones, jura & firmitates continentia, says the Learned *Spelman*; And we read in *Concil. Synodal. apud Clouesho*, Anno Dom. 822. *ut præfata Abbatissa prænominatam terram & cum libris quos Angli dicunt* Land-boc,— *in perpetuam hæreditatem traderet.*

Landegandman, Was according to *Spelman* one of the inferior Tenants of a Mannor; the word is used in *Custumar. de Hecham.*

Land-cheap, An ancient customary Fine paid either in Cattel or Money at every alienation of *Land* lying in some peculiar Mannor, or the liberty of some Borough. As at *Maldon* in *Essex*, there is yet a custom, that for certain Houses and Lands sold within that Borough, thirteen pence in every Mark of the Purchase-Money shall be paid to the Town; and this Custom of *Land-cheap* they claim *inter alia*, by a Grant made to that Town by the Bishop of *London*, *Anno* 5 *H*.4. *Sommer* in his *Saxon Dictionary* says, *Landceap est fortasse pretium fundi pacto datum vel debitum.* The word is also read in *Spel. de concil. vol.* 1. *fol.* 502.

Land-gable, Is a Tax or Rent issuing out of *Land*, according to *Doomsday*, *Census prædialis vel tributum quod a prædiis colligitur*; that is, says *Spelman*, a peny for every House; the *Welsh* use *Pridgavel* for *Landgavel*.

Landimers, *Agrimensores*, Measures of *Land* so called of old, *Landimera autem est terra limes vel meta.*

Land-man, *Terricola*, The *Terre-Tenant*.

Land-tenant, Is he that actually possesses the *Land*, or hath it in his manual Occupation, 14 *E*. 3. *Stat*. 5. *cap*. 3. 23 *E*. 3. *cap*. 1. 26 *Ed*. 3. *Stat*. 5. *cap*. 2. See *Terre-Tenant*, & 12 R. 2. *cap*. 4. & 4 *H*. 4. *cap*. 8. it is joyned with this word Possessor, as *Synonymon*, *Anno* 1 H. 6. *cap*. 5. See *Terre-tenant*.

Langemanni, *Item in ipsa civitate erant* 12 Langemanni, i. *habentes Socam & Sacam*, Doomsday, *tit. Lincolnshire.*

Land, *Terra*, in a general and legal signification, includeth not only all kinds of Grounds, as Meadow, Pasture, Arable, Wood, &c. but Houses and all Edifices whatsoever; but in a more restrained sense it is taken only for Arable Ground, *Co.* on *Lit. lib.* 1. *cap*. 2. *sect*. 14. says, *Terra est nomen Generalissimum & comprehendit omnes species terræ*, but properly *terra dicitur a terendo, quia vomere teritur*; and anciently it was written with a single *r*, and in that sense includes whatever may be Plowed. The Earth hath in Law a great extent upwards, for *Cujus est solum ejus usque ad cœlum*, Co. 9. Rep. *Alureds* Case.

Lanis de crescentia Walliæ traducendis absque Custuma, &c. Is a Writ that lyeth to the Custumer of a Port, for the permitting one to pass over Wools without Custom, because he hath paid Custom in *Wales* before. See the *Register*, *fol*. 279.

Lapse, *Lapsus*, Is the omission of a Patron to present to a Church, within six months after voidable; by which neglect, title is given to the Ordinary to collate to the said Church: We say that Benefice is in *lapse*, or *lapsed*; whereunto he that ought to present hath omitted or slipped his opportunity, 13 *Eliz. cap*. 12. This *Lapse* happens, as well the Patron being ignorant of the avoidance, as Privy, except only upon the resignation of the former Incumbent, or the deprivation upon any cause comprehended in the Statute 13 *Eliz*. 12. *Panor. in cap. quia diversitatem*, num. 7. *de concess. Prabend. &c.* In which cases the Bishop ought to give notice to the Patron.

Larceny, *Latrocinium*, Is a wrongful taking away another mans Goods, with a mind to steal them; and it is derived of the French *Larcen*, i. *furtum*; and in respect of the thing stollen is of two sorts, *viz*. Great, which is called *Theft* simply, where the things stollen exceed the value of twelve pence, and that is Felony. And *Petit Larceny*, when the Goods stollen exceed not the value of twelve pence, *West. part*. 2. *Symb. tit. Inditements.* But he differeth from *Bracton*, *lib*.3. *tract*. 2. *cap*. 32. *num*. 1. Of this see more *Stamf. Pl. Cor. lib*. 1. *cap*. 15, 16, 17, 18, 19. See also *Spelman*, who calls *Minuta furta*, *Petty* Larcenies, ex Assisis, Hen. 2. *Clarendoniæ editis*, &c.

Larons, Is the French Word for Thieves. In the Statute for view of *Frank-pledge* made 18 *E*. 2. the fourteenth Article, to be given in charge at a Leet, is of *Petty Larons*, as of Geese, Hens, &c.

Lashlite, It denoted the Danish common Forfeiture, which was twelve Ores, every Ore valuing about sixteen pence sterling, *Seldens History*, *of Tythes*, pag. 203.

Last, Signifies in general a Burden, and particularly a certain Weight or Measure. As a *Last* of Pitch, Tar or Ashes, contains fourteen Barrels, 32 *H*. 8. 14. A *Last* of Hides or Skins, twelve dozen, 1 *Jac*. 33. A *Last* of Codfish, twelve Barrels, 15 *Car*. 2. 7. A *Last* of Herring contains twenty Cades, or ten thousand, every thousand ten hundred, and every hundred sixscore, 51 *H*. 3 *stat*. 2. *cap*. 2. A *Last* of Corn, &c. is ten Quarters. A *Last* of Wool is twelve Sacks. A last of Leather is twenty Dickers, and every Dicker ten Skins; Of unpack'd Herrings, eighteen Barrels make a *Last*: Also *Last* in the Marshes of *East Kent*, signifies a Court held by twenty four Jurats, and summoned by the two Bayliffs thereof, wherein they make Orders, lay and levy Taxes, &c. for the preservation of the Marshes. See the *History of Imbanking and Drayning*, fol. 54.

Last heyre, *Ultimus hæres*, Is he to whom Land comes by Escheat, for want of lawful *Heirs*, that is, the Lord of whom they held in some cases, but in others the King. *Quippe Rex omnium hæredum ultimus est, uti Oceanus omnium fluviorum receptaculum*, Bract. lib. 7. cap. 17.

Lastage or Lestage, *Lastagium*, Is a Custom exacted in some Fairs and Markets, to carry things where one will, according to *Rastal*. But 21 R. 2. *cap*. 18. it is taken for the Ballast of a Ship. In a Charter of *Hen*. 3. to the Monastery of *Semplingham*, we read—*Et sint quieti de Theolonio & Pontagio, & Passagio, & Pedagio*, & Lestagio, &c. where we must take it in the former signification. So also in *Diplom*. H. 1. *de libertatibus* London, we find, *Omnes homines* London *sint quieti & liberi & omnes res eorum per totam Angliam & per portus maris, de Theolonio, & Passagio, &* Lastagio,

gio, & *ab omnibus aliis consuetudinibus*, Lastage, according to others, is properly a Custom paid for Wares sold by the *Last*.

Lathe, *Læstum*, Is a great part of a County, sometimes containing three or more Hundreds, as in *Kent* and *Sussex*. See *Leges Edw. Conf. cap.* 35. & *sint quieti de sectis Comitatuum*, Leth, Hundred & *auxiliis Vice-comitum*, Pat. 1 H. 4. part. 8. m. 8.

Latimer, Seems to be used by Sir *Edward Coke* for an Interpreter, 2. *par. Inst. fol.* 515. I suppose the word is mistaken, and should be *Latiner*, because heretofore he that understood Latine, which, in the time of the *Romans*, was the prevailing Language, might be a good Interpreter.

Latitat, Is the name of a Writ, whereby all men in personal Actions are called originally to the King's Bench, *F. N. B. fol.* 78. And it hath the Name, as supposing that the Defendant doth lurk and lie hid; and therefore being served with this Writ, he must put in security for his appearance at the day, for *Latitare est se malitiose occultare, animo fraudandi creditores suos agere volentes*. But the true original of this Writ was this, In ancient time, while the King's Bench was moveable, and followed the King's Court, the Custom was, upon the commencing of a Suit, to send forth a Writ to the Sheriff of the County where the Court lay, for the calling him in, and if the Sheriff returned, *Non est inventus in Balliva mea*, &c. then was there a second Writ sued forth, that had these words, *Cum testatum est quod* Latitat, &c. and thereby the Sheriff commanded to attach him in any other place where he may be found. Now when the Tribunal of the King's Bench came to be setled at *Westminster*, the former course of Writ was held for a long time, first sending to the Sheriff of *Middlesex* to summon the Party, and if he could not be found there, then to apprehend him wheresoever; but afterwards upon pretence of easing the Subject, and expediting Justice, it was contrived to put both these Writs into one, and so originally to attach the Party complained of, upon a supposal or fiction, that he was not within the County of *Middlesex*, but lurking elsewhere, and that therefore he was to be apprehended in any place else, where he was presumed to lye hid, by a Writ directed to the Sheriff of the County where he is suspected to be. And by this Writ a man being brought in, is committed to the Marshal of the King's Bench, in whose Custody, when he is, he may be sued upon an Action in that Court.

Latine, False *Latine* shall not quash an Indictment, nor abate any Declaration; for although the original Writ shall abate for false *Latine*, yet judicial Writs, or a Fine, shall not be impeached for false *Latine*. See *Co.* 5. *Rep.* Long's Case. But if the word be not *Latine*, nor a word allowed by the Law, as *Vocabulum artis*, (as every Art and Science hath its proper terms) but be insensible; and if it be in a material point, this makes the Indictment insufficient, as *Burglaritèr, murdrum, felonicè*, and the like, be terms of Art well known in the Law; and therefore if these words, or the like, be mistaken in an Indictment, so that in a material place there is an insensible word, which is not *Latine*, nor any word known in the Law, this will make the Indictment vitious and insufficient.

Launcegayes, *Anno* 7 *R.* 2. *cap.* 13. Were a sort of Weapons now disused, being prohibited by the said Statute.

Law, *Lex*, In the general signification is plain, and by *Bracton* thus defined, *Lex est sanctio justa, jubens honesta & prohibens contraria*: And the divine School-man sayes, *Lex humana est quoddam dictamen rationis, quo diriguntur humani Actus*. This in our Land hath been variable. First, *Molmutius* Laws, translated out of the *Brittish* Tongue into Latine by *Gildas*, of which we find no obscure Remanets in our *Laws* now in use. See *Mag. Cart. cap.* 1. & 14. Secondly, *Merchenlage*, mentioned in *Camd. Brit. pag.* 94. and *Polyd. in Hist. Angl. lib.* 5. Thirdly, *West-Saxon lage*. And fourthly, *Danelage*, All reduced into a Body, and made one by *Edward the Confessor*. At present the *Law* of *England* is divided into three parts: 1. The Common *Law*, which is the most ancient and general *Law* of the Realm. 2. Statutes, or Acts of Parliament. And 3. Particular Customs, *Co.* on *Lit. fol.* 15. *Law* hath an especial signification also, wherein it is taken for that which is *lawful* with us, and not else-where: As Tenant by the Curtesie of *England*, 13 *E.* 1. 3. And again, to wage *Law*, *Vadiare legem*, and to make or do *Law*, *Facere legem*, Bracton, lib. 3. tract. 2. cap. 37. whereof the first, *sc. Vadiare legem* is to put in security, that he will make *Law* at a day assigned, *Glanvil. lib.* 1. *cap.* 9 And to make *Law*, is to take an Oath, that he oweth not the Debt challenged at his hand, and also to bring with him so many men as the Court shall assign to avow upon their Oath, that in their Consciences he hath sworn tuly. And this *Law* is used in Actions of Debt, without speciality; as also where a man coming to the Court after such a time, as his Tenements, for default, be seized into the Kings hands, will deny himself to have been summoned, *Glanvile, lib.* 1. *cap.* 9. & 12. *Kitchin, fol.* 164. This is borrowed from *Normandy*, as appeareth by the *Grand Custumary*, *cap.* 85. But *Coke* in his 4. *Rep. fol.* 95. *Slade*'s Case, sayes, It springs originally from the Judicial *Law* of God, alledging for it the twenty second Chapter of *Exodus*, verse 7. The *Feudists* call them that come to purge the Defendants, *Sacramentales, lib. feud. tit.* 4. *sect.* 3. & *tit.* 10. & 26. And the *Civilians* call them *Purgatores*. *Spelman* sayes, *Legem vadiare est cautionem dare de perimplendo legis exigentiam in re litigata; ut de præstando Sacramento ad indictam diem cum indicto consacramentalium seu conjuratorum numero*. Anciently *Laga* was used as Latine for *Law*, as *Lagam Regis* Edwardi *vobis reddo*, &c. Magna Charta, H. 1. 1 R. 3. cap. 2. 31 H. 6. cap. 6. Our Common *Laws* are properly and aptly termed *Leges Angliæ*, because they are appropriate to this Kingdom of *England*, and have no dependance upon any Foreign *Law* whatsoever, *Co.* 2. *par. Inst. cap.* 9. These are the Birth-Right, and the most ancient and best Inheritance the Subjects have. *Co.* on *Lit. lib.* 2. *cap.* 12. *sect.* 213. and in his *Preface to the sixth Report*. All Books written in the *Law* are either Historical, as the *Year-Books*; Explanatory, as *Stamford*'s *Treatise of the Prerogative*: *Miscellaneous*, as the *Abridgments*; Or *Monological*, being of one certain Subject,

ject, as *Stamford's Pleas of the Crown*, Lambert's *Justice of Peace*. See *Fulbeck's Parallels*, cap. 3.

Lawyer, *Regis peritus*, *Juris consultus*, The Saxons called him *Lahman*.

Law of Armes, *Jus militare*, Is a *Law* that giveth Precepts and Rules concerning War, to make and observe Leagues and Truce, to punish Offendors in the Camp, and such like; for farther knowledge whereof, read such as write *De Jure Belli*.

Law of Merchants, *Lex Mercatoria*, Is a Priviledge, or special *Law*, differing from the Common *Law* of *England*, proper to *Merchants*, and summary in Proceedings, 27 *E*. 3. *Stat*. 8. 9, 19. 20. 13 *E*. 1. *Stat*. 3. See *Co*. on *Lit*. fol. 182.

Law Spiritual, *Lex Spiritualis*, Is the *Ecclesiastical Law*, allowed by the *Laws* of this Realm, being not against the Common *Law*, nor against the Statutes and Customs of the Realm, according to which the Ordinary, and other Ecclesiastical Judges do proceed in Causes within their Cognisance, *Co*. on *Lit*. fol. 344.

Law of the Staple, 27 E. 3. *Stat*. 2. *cap*. 22. Is the same with the *Law of Merchants*. See 4. *Inst*. fol. 237, 238. and *Staple*.

Law of Marque. See *Reprisals*. This word is used *Anno* 27 E. 3. *stat*. 2. *cap*. 17. and cometh from the *German* word *March*, i. *limes*, a Bound or Limit, because they that are driven to this *Law* of Reprisal, do take the Ships and Goods of him by whom they have received wrong, and cannot get ordinary Justice, when they meet with them in their own Precincts or Territories. See 9 *H*. 7. *fol*. 21. & *Smith de Rep. Ang. lib*. 2. *cap*. 21.

Lawday, Is otherwise called *View of Frank-Pledge*, or Court-Leet, *Cromp. Jur. fol*. 160. and is used for the County-Court. 1 *E*. 4. *cap*. 2.

Lawing of Dogs, *Expeditatio canum*, Mastiffs must be *lawed* every three year, *Cromp. Jur. fol*. 163. that is, three Clawes of the Fore-foot shall be cut off by the Skin, *Charta Forestæ*, *cap*. 6. or the Ball of the Fore-foot cut out. See *Expeditate* & *Pellota*.

Lawless Court, On *Kingshill* at *Rochford* in *Essex*, on *Wednesday* Morning, next after *Michaelmas* day, at Cock-crowing, is held a *Court*, vulgarly called *The lawless Court*. They whisper, and have no Candle, nor any Pen and Ink, but a Coal, and he that owes Suit or Service, and appears not, forfeits double his Rent every hour he is missing. This *Court* belongs to the Honor of *Ralegh*, and to the Earl of *Warwick*, and is denominated *lawless*, because held at an unlawful or *lawless* hour: The Title of it in the Court-Rolls runs thus,

Kingshill *in* Rochford } ss. *Curia de Domino Rege*
Dicta sine lege,
Tenta est ibidem
Per ejusdem consuetudinem,
Ante ortum solis
Luceat nisi Polus,
Senescallus solus
Nil scribit nisi colis,
Toties voluerit
Gallus ut cantaverit,
Per cujus soli sonitus
Curia est summonita:
Clamat clam pro Rege
In Curia sine lege,
Et nisi cito venerint
Citius pœnituerint,
Et nisi clam accedant
Curia non attendat,
Qui venerit cum lumine
Errat in regimine,
Et dum sunt sine lumine
Capti sunt in crimine,
Curia sine cura
Jurati de injuria.

Tenta ibidem die Mercurii (ante diem) proximi post festum Sancti Michaelis Archangeli *Anno Regni Regis*, &c. This Court is mentioned in *Camden's Britannia*, *fol*. 431. though imperfectly, which see.

Lawless-man, Is he *qui est extra legem*, *Bract. lib*. 3. *tract*. 2. *cap*. 11. *num*. 1. See *Outlaw*.

Lawe, According to *Doomsday*, by the interpretation of Mr. *Agar* of the Receit in the Exchequer, signifies an Ascent, or easie Summit.

Lawnd or **Lound**, In *Doomsday* signifies a Plain between Woods.

Lawne. See *Landa*.

Layland, *Terra inculta*, *Land* that lies fallow.

Leap-year. See *Bissextile*.

Lease, *Dimissio*, From the French *Laisser*, *permittere*, Is a demise or letting, or Lands or Tenements, right of Common, Rent, or any Hereditament unto another for term of Years or Life, for a Rent reserved: And a *Lease* is either written, called *a Lease by Indenture*, or *a Lease Parol*. The Party that letteth this *Lease* is called *The lessor*, and the Party to whom it is let is the *Lessee*: And a *Lease* hath in it six Points, 1. Words sufficient to import a Demise. 2. A Lessee named. 3. A commencement from a day certain. 4. A term of years. 5. A determination. 6. A reservation of Rent, *Co. lib*. 6. *fol*. 55. *Knight's* Case. *Co*. on *Lit. lib*. 1. *cap*. 7. *sect*. 58. *Co*. 5. *Rep*. Case of *Leases*.

Lecherwite alias **Legerwite**. See *Lairwite*.

Leccator, A debauched Person, a Tavern-hunter.

Leet, *Leta*, *visus Franci Plegii*, Is otherwise called *a Lawday*, *Smith de Rep. Ang. lib*. 2. *c*. 18. and seems to have grown from the Saxon *Lec*, which, as appears by the Laws of King *Edward*, set out by *Lambert*, *num*. 34. was a Court of Jurisdiction above the Wapentake or Hundred: Many Lords, together with their Courts Baron, have likewise *Leets* adjoyned, and thereby do enquire of such Transgressions as are subject to the enquiry and correction of this Court; whereof you may read in *Kitchin*, from the beginning of his Book to the Fifth Chapter, and *Britton*, *cap*. 28. But this Court in whose Mannor soever it be kept, is accounted the King's Court, because the Authority thereof originally belongs to the Crown, *Kitchin*, *fol*. 6. *Dyer*, *fol*. 64. saith, That this *Leet* was first derived from the Sheriffs Turn. And it inquireth of all Offences under High-Treason, committed against the Crown and Dignity of the King, though it cannot punish many, but must certifie them

them to the Justices of Assise, by the Statute of 1 *E.* 3. *cap. ult.* But what things be only inquirable, and what punishable, see *Kitchin* in the Charge of a Court *Leet*, from *fol.* 8. to *fol.* 20. See also the Statute 8 *E.* 2. and 4. *Inst. fol.* 261. *Hæc est Curia prisca illa*, (saith *Spelman*) *quæ inter Saxones ad Friburgos, Decanias, Tenementalas pertinebat.* The Jurisdiction of Bayliffs within the Dutchy of *Normandy*, in the compass of their Provinces, seems to be the same, or very like our *Leet*, *cap.* 4. of the *Grand Custumary*.

Legacy, *Legatum*, Is a particular thing given by a last Will and Testament; for if a man transfer his whole Right or Estate upon another, that the *Civilians* call *Hæreditas*, and he to whom it is so transferred, they term *Hæres*; but we call him *Heir* only, to whom all a mans Lands and Hereditaments descend by right of Blood. See *Heir.* See more *Devise*.

Legatee, Is the person to whom any *Legacy* is given by a last Will and Testament.

Legalis homo, Is taken for a person that stands *Rectus in Curia*, and in this sense are those words so often used *Probi & legales homines.* Hence *legality* is taken for the condition of such a man,---*Ipse tamen malefactor tradat fidejussores de pace & legalitate tuend.* Sureties for his good Behaviour, *Leg. Ed. Conf. cap.* 18. See *Yeoman*.

Legatary, *Legatarius*, He or she to whom any thing is bequeathed, a *Legatee*.

Legatory, The same with *Legatary*, *Anno* 27 *Eliz. cap.* 16.

Legergild, *Legergildum*, The same with *Lairwite*. But in the Laws of *Hen.* 1. it seems to have a different signification, *Si quis Dei fugitivum habet, injuste reddat eum ad rectum & persolvat ei cujus erit & Regi emendet secundum* Legergildum.

Legespend. See *Lespegend*.

Legitimation, *Legitimatio*, A making lawful.

Legruita, Or rather *Lethervita*, but more usually *Lierwith*, is the punishment for lying with a Woman unlawfully, according to *Doomsday*.

Lent, *Quadragesima*, A set time of fasting and abstinence for forty dayes next before *Easter*, mentioned in the Statute 2 & 3 *E.* 6. 19. and first commanded to be observed in *England* by *Ercombert*, seventh King of *Kent*, before the year 800. See *Baker's Chron. fol.* 7.

Lep and Lace, *Leppe & Lassee*, Is a Custom in the Mannor of *Writtle* in *Essex*, that every Cart that comes over a part thereof called *Greenbury* (except it be the Cart of a Nobleman) payes 4 *d.* to the Lord of the Mannor. Mr. *Tobias Edmonds* Steward there.

Leporarius, A Greyhound for the Hare, *Mon. Ang.* 2. *part*, *fol.* 283.

Leproso amovendo, Is a Writ that lies for a Parish, to remove a Leper or Lazar that thrusteth himself into the Company of his Neighbors, either in Church, or other publick Meetings, to their annoyance or disturbance, *Reg. Orig. fol.* 267. and *F. N. B. fol.* 234.

Lespegend, *Sint sub quolibet horum quatuor ex mediocribus hominibus* (*quos Angli* Lespegend *Dani vero* yoong-men *vocant*) *locati qui curam & onus tum viridis tum veneris suscipiant*, *Charta de Foresta Canuti Regis*, Art 2.

Lenna, In *Doomsday*, but corruptly for *Leura. Spel. Gloss.* verb. *Leuca.* See *Leuca*.

Lessor and Lessee, The *Lessor* is he that leases Lands or Tenements to another for term of Life, Years, or at Will: And he to whom the Lease is made is the *Lessee*.

Lestage or Lastage, *Lastagium*, Proceeds from the Saxon word *Last*, *onus*, and is a Custom challenged in Fairs or Markets for carrying of things, *Rastal's Exposition of words*, *Saxton* in the *Description of* England, *cap.* 11. Lastage *Anno* 21 *R.* 2. *cap.* 18. seemeth to be the ballance of a Ship. *Fleta* termeth it *lesting*, saying, *Quod significat acquietantiam* Lestagii, *lib.* 1. *cap.* 47. *sect.* Lesting.

Lesues or Leswes, Is a word used in *Doomsday* to signifie Pastures, and is still used in many places of *England*, and often inserted in Deeds and Conveyances.

Leth. See *Lath*.

Lethewite, 2. *Inst. fol.* 488. See *Lairwite*.

Letters of Exchange, *Literæ Cambitoriæ*, *vel literæ Cambii*, *Reg. Orig. fol.* 194.

Letters Patent, *Literæ Patentes*, Are Writings sealed with the Great Seal of *England*, whereby a man is authorised to do or enjoy any thing, that otherwise of himself he could not, 19 *H.* 7. 7. And they be so termed of their form, because they be open with the Seal affixed, ready to be shewed for confirmation of the Authority given by them. Common persons may grant *Letters Patent*, *F. N. B. fol.* 35. but they are rather call'd *Patentes* than *Letters Patent*. *Letters Patents* to make *Denizens*, 32 *H.* 6. 16. yet, for difference sake, those granted by the King are called *Letters Patent Royal*, 2 *H.* 6. 10. *Letters Patent* conclude with *Teste meipso*, &c. Charters with *His testibus*, 2. *par. Inst.* 78. There is likewise a Writ *Patent* mentioned in *F. N. B. fol.* 1, &c.

Letter of Attorney, *Litera Attornati*, Is a writing authorizing an Attorney, that is, a man appointed to do a lawful Act in our steads, *West*, *Symbol. part* 1. *lib.* 2. *sect.* 559. As a *Letter of Attorney* to give seisin of Lands, to receive Debts, to sue a third person, &c. See the Stat. 7 *R.* 2. 13.

Letters of Marque. See *Marq* and *Reprisals*, 14 H. 6. 7.

Levant and Couchant, Is, when Cattel have been so long in another mans Ground, that they have layne down, and are risen again to feed; in Records in Latine, they say, *Levantes & Cubantes*.

Letters Patent of Summons of Debt, *Anno* 9 *H.* 3. *cap.* 18.

Levari facias, Is a Writ directed to the Sheriff, for the levying of a Sum of Money upon Lands and Tenements of him that hath forfeited a Recognisance, *Reg. Orig. fol.* 298. & 300. and also *F. N. B.* 265.

Levari facias damna de disseisitoribus, Is a Writ directed to the Sheriff, for the levying of Damages, wherein the *Disseisor* hath formerly been condemned to the *Disseisee*, *Reg. Orig. fol.* 214.

Levari facias residuum debiti, Is a Writ directed to the Sheriff, for levying the remnant of a Debt upon Lands and Tenements, or Chattels of the Debtor, that hath in part satisfied before, *Reg. Orig. fol.* 299.

Levari facias, quando Vicecomes retornavit quod non habuit emptores, Is a Writ commanding the Sheriff to sell the Goods of the Debtor which he hath already taken, and returned that he could not sell them, and as much more of the Debtors Goods as will satisfie the whole Debt, *Reg. Orig. fol.* 300.

Levy, *Levare*, Signifies to collect or exact, as to *levy* Money; sometimes to set up any thing, as to *levy* a Mill, *Kitchin, fol.* 180. Sometimes to cast up, as to *levy* a Ditch, *Old Nat. Brev. fol.* 110. And to *levy* a Fine, which is now a frequent and most usual term.

Leuca, Leuva, Leuga, *Viæ spatium. Spel. Gloss.* verb. *Leuca*, They are often used in *Doomsday* for a Measure or Mile of Land. And *Leunides* hath the same signification there.

Lex Bretoyse, The Law of the *Britains*, or of the Marches of *Wales*, *Lex Marchiarum*. See *Bretoyse*.

Lex Brehonia, The *Brehon* Law, was a Law peculiar to *Ireland*, overthrown by King *John* in the Twelfth Year of his Reign, and the English Laws setled in stead thereof.

Lex Deraisnia, But more truly *Deraisina*, is the proof of a thing, which one denies to be done by him, and his Adversary affirms it: This was used among the *Normans*, and in their *Grand Custumary* thus defined, *cap.* 126. *Deraisina autem est* Lex *quædam in* Normania *constituta, per quam in simplicibus querelis, insecutus, factum quod à parte adversa ei objicitur, se non fecisse declarat.* Vide *Plura ibidem & Dereyn.*

Lex-gager, *Anno* 1 *Car.* 1. *cap.* 3. Wager of Law. See *Law*.

Ley, *Lex*. See *Law*. We also term Pasture by a frequent Name in several Countries, *Leys*, and so is it used in *Doomsday*.

Libell, *Libellus*, Literally signifieth a little Book, but by use it is the original Declaration of any Action in the Civil Law, 2 *H.* 5. 3. and 2 *E.* 6. 13. It signifies also a criminous Report of any Man cast abroad, or otherwise unlawfully publisht, and then called *Famosus Libellus*: And this is either *in scriptis, aut sine scriptis*: *In scriptis*, is when an *Epigram* or other Writing, is composed or publisht to anothers disgrace, which may be done *Verbis aut Cantilenis*; as where this is maliciously repeated or sung in the presence of others, or else *Traditione*, when the *Libell*, or any Copy of it is delivered over to scandalize the Party. *Famosus* Libellus *sine scriptis* may be two-fold; 1. *Picturis*, as to paint the Party in a shameful and ignominious manner. Or, 2. *Signis*, As to fix a Gallows, or other ignominious signs at the Door of the Party, or else-where, *Co.* 5. *Rep. de famosis* Libellis.

Libello habendo. See *Copia* Libelli *deliberanda*.

Libera Batella, A free Boat,---*Per liberam* Batellam, *hoc est habere unam cimbam ad piscand. sub ter pontem Cestriæ & supra Etonam, & ibidem cum omni genere retium*, Plac. in Itin. apud Cestriam, 14 H. 7.

Libera Chasea habenda, Is a Writ Judicial granted to a Man, for a free Chace belonging to his Mannor, after he hath by a Jury proved it to belong to him, *Reg. Orig. fol.* 36. 37.

Liberate, Is a Writ issuing out of the Chancery, to the Treasurer, Chamberlains, or Barons of the Exchequer, or Clerk of the *Hamper, &c.* for the payment of any annual Pension, or other Sums granted under the Great Seal. See *Broke*, tit. *Tayle d' Exchequer*, num. 4. *Reg. Orig. fol.* 193. Or sometime to the Sheriff, &c. *Nat. Brev. fol.* 132. For the delivery of any Lands or Goods taken upon forfeits of Recognisance. See *Co. lib.* 4. *fol.* 64, 66, 67. *Fullwood*'s Case. It lies also to a Gaoler, for the delivery of a Prisoner, that hath put in Bayl for his Appearance, *Lamb. Eirenarch. lib.* 3. *cap.* 2.

Libertate probanda, Is a Writ that lay for such as were challenged for Slaves, and offer to prove themselves free, directed to the Sheriff, that he take security of them, for the proving of their Freedom before the Justices of Assise, and provide that in the mean time they be quiet from the Vexation of those that challenge them, *F. N. B. fol.* 77. Villenage, and the Appendixes thereof, *viz.* Infranchisement, Writs *de Nativo habendo*, *libertate probanda*, *&c.* Were of old great Titles in the Books, but now antiquated. See *Nativo habendo*.

Libertatibus allocandis, Is a Writ that lies for a Citizen, or Burgess of any City or Borough, that contrary to the *Liberties* of the City or Town whereof he is, is impleaded before the King's Justices, or Justices Errant, or Justice of the Forest, &c. to have his Priviledge allowed, *Reg. Orig. fol.* 262. *F. N. B. fol.* 229.

Libertatibus exigendis in Itinere, Is a Writ, whereby the King willeth the Justices in *Eyre* to admit of an Attorney, for the defence of another mans *liberty* before them, *Reg. Orig. fol.* 19.

Liberty, *Libertas*, Is a Priviledge held by Grant of Prescription, whereby men enjoy some benefit or favour beyond the ordinary Subject. *Liberties* Royal, what they be, see in *Bract. lib.* 2. *cap.* 5. and *Broke hoc titulo*. See *Franchise*.

Librata terræ, Contains four Oxgangs, and every Oxgange fifteen Acres, *Skene de verbor.* Signif. *verbo* Bovata terræ. See *Farding-deal of Land*.

Licence to go to Election, *Licentia eligendi*, Regist. fol. 294. See *Conge d' eslire*.

Licence to arise, *Licentia surgendi*, Is a liberty given by the Court to a Tenant that is essoined *de malo lecti*, in a real Action: For the Law is, that in this Case he may not arise out of his Bed, or at least go out of his Chamber, until he have been viewed by Knights thereto appointed, and have a day assigned him to appear: And the reason of this is, that it may appear whether he caused himself to be essoined deceitfully or not; and therefore if the Demandant can prove that he was seen abroad before the View, or *licence* of the Court, he shall be adjudged to be deceitfully essoined, and to have made default: Of this, see *Bracton, lib.* 5. *tract.* 2. *cap.* 7. 10. & 12. and *Fleta, lib.* 6. *cap.* 10. and *Horne*'s *Mirrour of Justices*, lib. 2. cap. *des Essoynes*.

Licentia

Licentia surgendi, Is the Writ whereby the Tenant essoined *de malo lecti*, obtaineth liberty to rise.

Licentia transfretandi, Is a Writ or Warrant directed to the Keepers of the Port at *Dover*, *&c.* willing them to let some pass quietly beyond Sea, who have formerly obtained the King's *Licence* thereunto, *Reg. Orig. fol.* 193.

Licentia Concordandi, 12 *Car.* 2. 12. See *King's Silver.*

Lidford Law, Is a proverbial Speech, intending as much as to hang men first, and judge them after. The like is said of *Halifax* in *Yorkshire*, I suppose, because their Proceedings are summary.

Liefetenant or Lieutenant, *Locumtenens*, Is compounded of *lieu*, *locus & tenir*, *tenere*, and signifies him that occupyeth the Kings, or any other Persons place, or representeth his person, as the *Lieutenant* of *Ireland*, 4 *H.* 4. 6. So also is it used 2 & 3 E. 6. *cap.* 2. whence that Officer seems to take his beginning.

Lieutenant of the Ordnance, 39 *Eliz. cap.* 7. We use the word *Lieutenant* also for a military Officer, next in Command to the Captain, whose Place and Duty is so well known, that I need not here inlarge upon it.

Life-rent, Is a Rent or Exhibition which a man receives either for term of Life, or for sustentation of Life, *Skenæus ad Quon. Attach. cap.* 18. *vers.* 5.

Liege, *Ligeus*, Is a word borrowed from the *Feudists*, and hath two several significations in the Common Law, sometimes being used for *Liege* Lord, as 34 & 35 *H.* 8. *cap.* 1. and 25 *H.* 8. 3. and sometimes for *liege-man*, as 10 R. 2. 1. and 11 R. 2. *cap.* 1. *Liege* Lord is he that acknowledgeth no Superior, *Duarenus in Commentar. de consuetud. feudorum*, cap. 4. num. 3. *Liege-man* is he that oweth Allegiance to his *Liege*-Lord. *Skene de verbo* Signif. *verb.* Ligeantia, saith, That it is derived from the Italian word *Liga*, a Bond or Obligation: In whom read more of this matter. See 8 *H.* 6. *cap.* 10. 14 *H.* 8. *cap.* 2.

Lierwit est mulcta adulteriorum, *Fleta*, *lib.* 1. *cap.* 7. It is used for a Liberty, whereby a Lord challengeth the penalty of one that lyeth unlawfully with his Bond-woman. See *Legruita* and *Lotherwit.*

Ligeancy, *Ligeantia*, Is such a Duty or Fealty as no Man may owe to more than one Lord, and therefore it is most commonly used for that Duty and Allegiance which every good Subject owes to his *Liege* Lord the King. And it is thus defined in the *Grand Custumary* of *Normandy*, cap. 13. *Ligeantia est, ex qua Domino tenentur Vassalli sui contra omnes homines qui mori possunt & vivere, proprii corporis præbere consilii & auxilii juvamentum & ei se in omnibus innocuos exhibere, nec ei adversantium partem in aliquo confovere, &c.* This is otherwise called *Legietas*, *Cassan. de consuetud. Burgund.* pag. 420, 421. This word is often used in our Statutes, as 14 *H.* 8. *cap.* 2. and several other.

Ligeance, *Ligeantia*, Is a true and faithful Obedience of the Subject to his Soveraign; Sometimes it signifies the Dominions or Territory of the *Liege* Lord, as 25 E. 3. *Stat.* 2. Children born out of the *ligeance* of the King: Also the same with *ligeancy*. See *Co.* on *Lit. fol.* 129. and 7. *Rep. Calvin's* Case.

Limitation of Assise, *Limitatio Assisæ*, Is a certain time set down by Statute, wherein a man must alledge himself, or his Ancestor, to have been seized of Lands, sued for by a Writ of Assise. See the Statute of *Merton*, *cap.* 8. *Anno* 20 *H.* 3. and *Westm.* 1. *cap.* 38. 32 *H.* 8. 2. 1 *M.* 1. *Par. cap.* 5. *Theloals Digest of Writs*, lib. 10. cap. 2. So it is used in *Old Nat. Brev. fol.* 77. in these words, The Writ *De consuetudinibus & servitiis* lyeth, where I, or mine Ancestors, after the *limitation of Assise* were not seized of the Customs, &c. But before the *limitation of Assise*, we were seized, &c.

Linarium, A place where Flax groweth.

Lindwood, Was a Doctor both of the Civil and Canon-Laws, and Dean of the Arches: He was Embassador for *Henry* the Fifth into *Portugal*, *Anno* 1422. as appeareth by the *Preface to his Commentary upon the Provincials.*

Littleton, VVas a famous Lawyer living in the dayes of King *Edward* the Fourth, as appeareth by *Stamf. Prær. cap.* 21. *fol.* 72. He wrote a Book of great Account called *Littleton's Tenures.*

Literæ ad faciendum attornatum pro secta facienda, Reg. Orig. fol. 172. *Literæ de annua pensione*, Ibid. fol. 266. & 307. *Literæ patens ad faciendum generalem attornatum quia infirmus*, Ibid. fol. 21. *Litera per quam Dominus remittit curiam suam Regi*, Ibid. fol. 4. *Literæ de requestu*, Ibid. fol. 129. *Literæ Canonici ad exercendam jurisdictionem loco suo*, Ibid. fol. 305. *Literæ Patentes ad conferendum Beneficia, Domino in remotis agente*, Ibid. *Literæ procuratoriæ*, Ibid. fol. 205. 206. *Literæ Regiæ deprecatoriæ pro annua pensione*, Ibid. fol. 307. See these in their proper places.

Littera, As *Tres Carectatas* Litteræ, Three Cart-loads of Straw or Litter, *Mon. Ang.* 2. *par. fol.* 33. *b.*

Livery, *Liberatura*, Is derived from the French *Livre*, that is, *insigne*, *gestamen*, or else from *livrer*, id est, *tradere*, and accordingly hath three significations. In one it is used for a Suit of Cloth or Stuff that a Gentleman giveth in Coats, Cloaks, Hats or Gowns, with Cognisance, or without, to his Servants or Followers; and is mentioned in 1 R. 2. 7. 20 R. 2. 1, 2. 7 *H.* 4. 14. 8 E. 4. 2. 13 E. 4. 3. 8 *H.* 6. 4. 3 *H.* 7. 1. 12. 11 *H.* 7. 3. 19 *H.* 7. 14. 3 *Car.* 1. *cap.* 4. In the other signification, it betokened a delivery of possession to those Tenants which held of the King *in Capite*, or Knights-service; for the King, by his Prerogative, hath *primer seisin* of all Lands and Tenements so holden of him, *Stamf. Prærog. fol.* 12. & *cap.* 3. *Livery*, in the third signification, is the Writ which lies for the Heir, to obtain the Possession or Seisin of his Land, at the King's Hands, which see in *F. N. B. fol.* 155. But by the Statute, 12 *Car.* 2. *cap.* 24. All Wardships, *Liveries*, *&c.* are utterly taken away, and absolutely discharged.

Livery of Seisin, *Deliberatio seisinæ*, Is a delivery of Possession of Lands or Tenements, or other things corporeal, unto one that hath right, or a probability of right to them: For as *Bracton* saith, *Traditio debet esse vestita & non nuda, sc. quod traditione præcedat vera causa, &c.* lib. 2. cap. 18. num. 3. *West*, Symb. part 1. lib. 2. sect. 169. calls this *a Ceremony* in the Common-Law, used in the Conveyance of Lands or Tenements, &c. where an Estate in Fee-simple, Fee-tail, or a Free hold shall pass: And is a Testimonial of the willing departing of him who makes the *Livery*, from the thing whereof *Livery* is made; and the receiving of the *Livery*, is a willing acceptance of the other Party. And it was invented, that the common people might have knowledge of the passing or alteration of Estates from man to man, that thereby they might be the better able to try in whom the right of Possession of Lands and Tenements were, if they should be impannelled in Juries, or otherwise have to do concerning the same. Of this *Livery* there be two kinds, *viz.* A *Livery in Deed*, and a *Livery in Law*; A *Livery in Deed* is, when the Feoffor taketh the Ring of the Door, or Turf or Twig of the Land, and delivereth the same to the Feoffee in the name of *Seisin* of the Land. A *Livery in Law* is, when the Feoffor saith to the Feoffee, being in view of the House or Land, *I give to you yonder Land, to you and your Heirs, and therefore enter into the same, and take possession thereof accordingly*; And the Feoffor doth accordingly in the life of the Feoffor enter, this is a good Feoffment, *Co.* on *Lit. lib.* 1. *cap.* 7. *sect.* 59. and 5 *Reports*, *Sharpe's* Case. For the form of words, and manner thereof, you may see them in *West, Symbol. part.* 1. *lib.* 2. *sect.* 169. and *Termes de la Ley.*

Lieutenant. See *Liefrenant.*

Lieutenant of the Tower, Seemeth to have been an Officer under the Constable.

Locus partitus, Signifies a Division made between two Towns or Countries, to make out in which the Land or place in question lies, *Fleta, lib.* 4. *cap.* 15. *num.* 1.

Local, *Localis*, signifieth in a legal sense as much as tyed or annexed to a place: For example. The thing is *local*, and annexed to the Freehold, *Kitchin, fol.* 180. And again, in the same place, An Action of Trespass for Battery, &c. is transitory, not *local*, that is, not needful that the place of the Battery should be set down as material in the Declaration, or if it be set down, that the Defendant should traverse it, by saying he did not commit the Battery in the place mentioned in the Declaration, and so avoid the Action. And again, *fol.* 230. the place is not *local*, that is, not material to be set down in certain. The guard of the person, and of the Lord differ in this, because the person being transitory, the Lord may have his ravishment *de gard*, before he be seised of him, but not so of the Land, because it is *local*, *Perkin's Grants*, 30.

Lobbe, A great kind of North Sea-fish, *Anno* 31 *E.* 3. *Stat.* 3. *cap.* 2.

Lodemanage, Is the Hire of a Pilot, for conducting a Ship from one place to another.

Lode ship, A kind of fishing Vessel, mentioned 31 *E.* 3. *Stat.* 3. *cap.* 2.

Lode works, Is one of the *Works* belonging to the *Stanneryes* in *Cornwall*, for which see *Camden's Brit.* tit. *Cornwall.* See *Streme-works.*

Logating, An unlawful Game, mentioned 33 H. 8. *cap.* 9. now disused.

Logwood, Otherwise called *Blockwood*, brought from divers remote parts, and prohibited by the Statute of 23 *Eliz. cap.* 9. and 39 *Eliz. cap.* 11. but since by 14 *Car.* 2. *cap.* 11. The importation and use of it is allowed.

Loich-fish, As Lob, Ling, Cod, mentioned 31 *E.* 3. *Stat.* 3. *cap.* 2.

Lollardy, 1 & 2 *P. & M. cap.* 6. The Doctrine and Opinion of the *Lollards*, *Rogerus Acton miles pro proditione &* Lollardia *distrahatur & suspendatur, & sic suspensus pendeat ad voluntatem Regis.* Middlesex, Plac. Hill. 1 H. 5. Rot. 7. & Trin. 2 H. 5. Rot. 6.

Lollards, *Lollardi*, So called (says *Tritemius*) from one *Walter Lolhard a German*, the first Author of that Sect, about the year of our Lord 1315. were in account of those times Hereticks, that abounded here in *England* in the dayes of *Edward* the Third and *Henry* the Fifth, and mentioned 2 *H.* 5. 7. whereof *Wickliff* was the chief, as *Stow* saith in his *Annals, pag.* 425. Against these *Thomas Arundel* Archbishop of *Canterbury*, in a Councel at *Oxford*, made several Decrees. *Spotswood* in his *History of Scotland*, fol. 61. sets forth their Tenets; Their intent was, to subvert the Christian Faith, the Law of God, the Church and the Realm, so said the fore-mentioned Statute of 2 *H.* 5. 7. which was repealed by 1 *E.* 6. 12. The high Sheriff of every County is bound by his Oath to suppress them. See *Co.* 3. *Inst. fol.* 41. and *Cawdrye's* Case.

Lord, *Dominus*, Is a word of honor with us, and is diversly used: Sometimes attributed to a Man noble by Birth or Creation, and are otherwise called *Lords of Parliament*; sometimes to those that be so called by the curtesie of *England*, as all the Sons of a Duke, or the eldest Son of an Earl. Sometimes to Men honourable by Office, as Lord chief Justice, &c. and sometime to a mean man that hath Fee, and so consequently the Homage of Tenants within his Mannor. In which last signification, it is most frequently used by the Writers of the Law, and divided into *Lord Paramount* and *Lord Mesne*; *Lord Mesne* is he that is Owner of a Mannor, and by vertue thereof hath Tenants holding of him in Fee, and by Copy of Court-Roll, and yet holdeth himself of a Superior *Lord*, called *Lord Paramount*, Old Nat. Brev. fol. 79. We read likewise of *very Lord* and *very Tenant*, Ibid. fol. 42. and *Bro.* tit. *Heriot*, num. 1. Where *very Lord* is he which is immediate *Lord* to his Tenant, and *very Tenant* he that holds immediately of that *Lord*; so that if there be *Lord Paramount*, *Lord Mesne* and *Tenant*; The *Lord Paramount* is not *very Lord* to the *Tenant*, nor the *Tenant very Tenant* to him.

Lord in grosse, *F. N. B. fol.* 3. Is he that is *Lord*, having no Mannor, as the King in respect of his Crown, *Ibid. fol.* 5. and *fol.* 8. where is a Case wherein a private man is *Lord in grosse*, *viz.* A man makes a Gift in tayl of all the Land he hath, to hold of him, and dyeth; his Heir hath but a Seigniory *in gross.*

Lorimers or **Loriners**, May well be deduced from the Latine *Lorum*: They are one of of the Companies of *London* that make Bits for Bridles, Spurs, and such like small Iron Ware, 1 *R*. 2. *cap*. 12.

Lot or Loth, Is the thirteenth Dish of Lead in the *Derbishire* Mines, which belong to the King *pro Dominio suo*. See *Rot. Rageman & de Quo Warranto de* Itin. *de* Derbi. 9 E. 1. See *Cope*.

Lotherwite alias **Leyerwit**, Is a Liberty or Priviledge to take amends of him that defileth your Bond-woman without licence, *Rastall's Exposition of words*; so that it is an amends for lying with a Bond-woman. *Saxtons* in his *Description of England*, cap. 11. See *Lairwit*. Some think it should rather be written *Legerwit*, for *Leger* is the Saxon word for a Bed; or *Lecherwite* a punishment for *Lechery*. See *Bloodwit* and *Lyerwit*.

Lourgulary, *In Statuto pro stratis London*, Printed *Anno* 1573. *Art*. 45. Casting any corrupt thing, or appoysoning the Water, is *Lowrgulary* and Felony. Some think it a corruption of Burglary. See *Gloss. in* X. *Scriptores*, *verbo* Burglaria.

Lowbellers, 23 *Eliz. cap*. 10. Are such as go with light and a *Bell*, by the sight whereof Birds sitting on the Ground, become somewhat stupified, and so are taken with a Net. This name is derived from the word *Low*, which in the Saxon, or old English, signifies a Flame of Fire. See the *Antiquities of Warwickshire*, pag. 4.

Lufernes. See *Furre*.

Lushborow or **Lushburgh**, Was a base sort of Coyn used in the dayes of King *Edward* the third; coyned beyond Sea to the likeness of *English* Money, and brought in to deceive the King and his Subjects. To prevent and avoid which, it was made Treason for any man wittingly to bring any such into the Realm, as knowing it to be false, by the Statute made *Anno* 25 *Edw*. 3. *Statut*. 4. *cap*. secrudo, and *Co. Inst*. 3. *par. fol*. 1.

Lupulicetum, A place where Hops grow, *Co*. 1. *inst*. 4. *b*.

M.

M. Is a numeral letter, and stands for a Thousand; Also every person convicted for Murder (Manslaughter) and admitted to the benefit of his Clergy, must be marked on the brawn of the left Thumb with an M. by 4 *H*. 7. *cap*. 13.

Mace griefe alias **Mace-greffs**, *Machecarii*, Are such as willingly buy and sell stollen Flesh, knowing the same to be stollen, *Britton*, cap. 29. and *Crompton's Justice of Peace*, fol. 193. Vide *Leges Inæ*, cap. 20. *de carnem furtivam tenente*.

Madning money, Old *Roman* Coynes, sometimes found about *Dunstable*, are so called by the Country-people; they seem to retain this Name from *Magintum*, used by the Emperor *Antoninus* in his *Itinerary* for *Dunstable*. *Camd*.

Maeremium, Is derived from the old *Norman* word *Marisme* or Timber.

Magbote or **Mægbote**, A recompence for the slaying or murder of ones Kinsman; for anciently in this Nation, corporal punishments for Murder, and other great Offences, were sometimes transmuted into pecuniary Fines, if the Friends of the Party slain were so content, *Leg. Canuti Regis*, part 1. cap. 2.

Magna Assisa eligenda, Is a Writ directed to the Sheriff, to summon four lawful Knights before the Justices of *Assise*, there upon their Oaths to chuse twelve Knights of the Vicinage, &c. to pass upon the great *Assise* between *A*. Plaintiff, and *B*. Defendant, &c. *Reg. Orig. fol*. 8.

Magna Charta, The *Great Charter* was granted the Ninth Year of *Henry* the Third, and confirmed by *Edward* the First. The reason why it was termed *Magna Charta*, was either for that it contained the sum of all the Liberties of *England*, or else because there was another *Charter* call'd *Charta de Foresta* establisht with it, which was the less of the two; or because it contained more than many other Charters, or more than that of King *Henry* the First, or of the great and remarkable solemnity in the denouncing Excommunication, and direful *Anathema's* against the Infringers of it. We read in *Holinshed*, that King *John*, to appease his Barons, yielded to Laws or Articles of Government, much like to this *Great Charter*: But we have now no ancienter written Law than this, which was thought to be so beneficial to the Subject, and a Law of so great equity, in comparison of those which were formerly in use, that King *Henry*, for the granting it, had the fifteenth peny of all the moveable Goods, both of the *Spirituality* and *Temporalty* throughout the Realm. *Spelman* in his *Gloss*. on this word, calls it *Augustissimum Anglicarum libertatum diploma & sacra Anchora*. It is *Magnum in Parvo*, and hath been above *thirty times confirmed* sayes *Coke* upon *Littleton*, fol. 81.

Mayhim or **Mayhem**, *Mahemium*, Cometh of the French word *Mehaigne*, and signifies a corporal hurt, by which a man loseth the use of any Member, that is or might be any defence unto him in Battel: As if a Bone be taken out of the Head, or broken in any other part of the Body, or Foot, or Hand, or Finger, or Joynt of a Foot, or any Member be cut, or by Wound the Sinews be made to shrink; or if any Eye be put out, fore-teeth broke, or any other thing hurt in a mans body, whereby he is disabled to defend himself, or offend his Enemy, *Glanvile*, *lib*. 14. *cap*. 7. See *Bracton* at large, *lib*. 3. *tract*. 2. *cap*. 24. *num*. 3. *Britton*, *cap*. 25. and *Stamf. Pl. Cor. lib*. 1. *cap*. 41. and *The Mirrour of Justices*, cap. *de Homicide*. But the cutting off an Ear or Nose, the breaking of the hinder Teeth, or such like, was no *Mayhem*, it being rather a deformity of Body, than diminishing of Strength. But now by the *Stat*. of 22. & 23. *Car*. 2. *cap*. 1. the cutting off a Nose, or cutting off or disabling any Limb or Member, is made Felony without benefit of the Clergy: *Mayhem* is commonly tryed by the *Justices* inspecting the Party: And if they doubt whether it be a *Mayhem*, or not, they use to take the Opinion of some able Chirurgion in the point. The *Grand Custumary* of *Normandy*, cap. 6. calls it *Mahaignium*, and the *Canonists Membri mutilationem*; but all agree, that it is the loss of a Member, or the use thereof; and *Membrum*, *Cassan. de Conf. Burg. pag*. 168. defines thus, *Est pars corporis habens destinatam operationem in corpore*. See

Skene de verborum significatione, *verbo* Machanium. See *Co.* on *Lit. lib.* 2. *cap.* 11. *sect.* 194.

Magistrate, *Magistratus*. He is *Custos utriusq; tabulæ*, the Keeper or Preserver of both Tables of the Law; therefore if any *Magistrate*, or Minister of Justice, in execution of their Office, or keeping of the Peace, according to the duty of their Office, be slain; this is *murder*, for their Contempt and Disobedience to the King and the Law, for it is *contra potestatem Regis & Legis*, Co. 9. Rep. *Mackallye*'s Case.

Maiden Rents, Is a noble paid by every Tenant in the Mannor of *Builth* in *Radnorshire*, at the Marriage of a Daughter, and was anciently given to the Lord for his quitting the Custom of *Marcheta*, which I suppose was a Fine paid to the Lord, for a licence to marry a Daughter: Sir *Edw. Sawyer* is now Lord of this Mannor. See *Marcheta*.

Maignagium, Derives it self from the French *Maignen*, i. *Faber ærarius*, and signifies a Brasier's Shop. See *Cotland*. But *Co.* 4. *Inst. fol.* 338. confounds *Managium* with *Mesuagium*.

Maile, Anciently a kind of Money, but more largely signifies not only Money, but any proportion of Grain, or other Rent; This later in the *North* is called *Blackmaile*, *Inquis. capt. post mortem* Will. *de* Conwey, *Anne* 20 E. 3. *num.* 63. Lanc. *Spelman* says, There is in *Ulverstone quoddam proficuum vocat. Geesemales & quoddam proficuum apud Plumpton vocat. Cowmale*. See *Blackmaile*.

Mainour, alias **Manour**, alias **Meinour**, From the French *Manier*, i. *manu tractare*: In a legal sense, denotes the thing that a Thief taketh away, or stealeth. As to be taken with the *Mainour*, *pl. cor. fol.* 179. is to be taken with the thing stollen about him: And again, *fol.* 194. it was presented, That a Thief was delivered to the Sheriff or Viscount, together with the *Mainour*: And again, *fol.* 186. If a man be indited, That he feloniously stole the Goods of another, where, in truth, they be his own Goods, and the Goods be brought into the Court as the *Mainour*; and it be demanded of him, what he saith to the Goods, and he disclaim them; though he be quitted of the Felony, he shall lose the Goods: And again, *fol.* 149. If the Defendant were taken with the *Manour*, and the *Manour* be carried to the Court, they, in ancient times; would arraign him upon the *Manour*, without any Appeal or Indictment. I find this word used in the *Old Nat. Brev. fol.* 110 In this sort, where a man maketh a thing by *Manour*, or levying, or estopping; in such case he shall have an Assise, where it signifies handy-labor, and is but an abbreviation of *Mainovery*.

Mainure. See *Minovery*.

Mainpernable, That may be let to *bayl*. See the Statute of *Westm.* 1. *cap.* 15. made *Anno* 3 *E.* 1. what persons be *mainpernable*, and what not.

Mainpernors, *Manucaptores*, Are those Persons to whom a person is delivered out of Custody or Prison, and they become security for him, either for appearance or satisfaction; they are called *Manucaptores*, because they do it as it were *manu capere & ducere captivum é custodia vel prisona*. And the Prisoner is said to be delivered to *Bail*, from the words of the *Bail-piece*, viz. *A. B. &c. traditur in Ballium* J. D. & R. R. &c. See *Mainprise*.

Mainprise, *Manucaptio*, Is compounded of two French words, *viz. Main*, *manus*, & *Prins*, *captus*: It signifies in our Law, the taking or receiving a man into friendly custody, that otherwise is or might be committed to Prison, upon security given for his forth-coming at a day assigned: And they that thus undertake for any, are called *Main pernors*, because they do receive him into their hands, *Stamf. Pl. Co. fol.* 178. from hence comes the word *Mainpernable*, which denotes him that may thus be bailed; For in many Cases a man is not *mainpernable*, whereof see *Bro.* tit. *Mainprise per totum*, and *F. N. B. fol.* 249. *Manwood* in his *Forest Laws*, pag. 167. makes a great difference between Bail and *Mainprise*; for he that is *mainprised* (saith he) is alwayes said to be at large, and to go at his own liberty out of Ward until the day of his appearance; but otherwise it is, where a man is *let to bail* to four or two men by the *Lord chief Justice in Eyre* of the Forest, until a certain day; for there he is always accounted by the Law to be in their Ward and Custody for the time: And they may, if they will, keep him in Ward or in Prison all that time, or otherwise at their will; so that he that is so bailed, shall not be said by the Law to be at large, or at his own liberty: Thus far *Manwood*. The *Mirror of Justices* distinguishing between *Pledges* and *Mainpernors*, saith, That Pledges are more general, and that *Mainpernors* are Body for Body, *lib.* 2. *cap. de Trespass venial*, and *lib.* 3. cap. *des Pledges &* Mainpernors. When *Mainprises* may be granted, and when not; see *Cromp. Just. of Peace*, fol. 136. *and* 141. and *Lamb. Eiren. lib.* 3. *cap.* 2. *pag.* 336, 337, 338, 339, 340. See also *Britton*, *fol.* 37. cap. *des Pledges & Mainpernors*. Lastly, The *Mirror of Justices* saith, That *Pledges* be those that bail or redeem any thing but the Body of a Man, but *Mainpernors* are those that free the Body of a Man; and therefore that *Pledges* belong properly to real and mixt Actions, and *Mainpernors* to personal.

Mainport, Is a small Duty, which, in some places, the Parishioners pay to the Rector of their Church, in recompence of certain *Tythes*. See *Wax shot*. *Spelman* in his *Glossary* saith, That *Vicaria de Wragly* (*in Com* Lincoln) *consistit in toto Altaragio & in Ceragio*, *vulgariter dict.* Waxshot, *in panibus*, *vulgariter dict.* Mainport, *& in incremento denariorum sancti* Petri, *vulgariter dict.* Fireharth.

Malesworne, In the North signifies as much as *Forsworne*, *Brownloe*'s *Rep.* 4. *Hobart*'s *Rep.* 8.

Maintainor, 19 *H.* 7. 14. Is he that supports or seconds a Cause depending in Suit between others, either by disbursing Money, or making Friends for either Party towards his help.

Maintenance, *Manutentio & manutenentia*, Signifies the upholding of a Cause or Person, metaphorically drawn from succoring a young Child, that learns to go by ones hand: In Law it is taken in the worst sense, as appears by 32 *H.* 8. 9. And when a mans act in this kind is by Law accounted *Maintenance*, and when not. See *Broke*, tit. *Maintenance*, and *Kitchin*, fol. 202. and *F. N. B.* 172.

172. and *Cromp. Jurisd. fol.* 38. The *Writ* that lies against a man for this Offence, is called *Maintenance.* See *Co.* on *Lit. fol.* 368. *Special maintenance*, Kithcin, fol. 204. Seemeth to be *maintenance*, most properly so termed. Of this see *Cromp. Just. of Peace, fol.* 155. and the *New Book of Entries, verbo* Maintenance.

Maison dieu, Is the French Name for an Hospital or Almes-house. See *Meason dieu.*

Make, *Facere*, Signifies to perform or execute; as to *make his Law*, is to perform that Law which he hath formerly bound himself to: that is, to clear himself of an Action commenced against him by his Oath, and the Oaths of his Neighbours, *Old Nat. Brev. fol.* 161. *Kitchin, fol.* 192. Which Law seemeth to be borrowed of the *Feudists*, who call those men that come to swear for another in this case *Sacramentales.* Of whom *Hotoman* saith thus in verbis Feudal. *Sacramentales a Sacramento*, id est, *juramento dicebantur ij, qui quamvis rei de qua ambigebatur, testes non fuissent, tamen ex ejus, cujus res agebatur, animi sententia, in eadem quæ illi verba jurabant; illius videlicet probitate & innocentia confisi, &c.* The formal words used by him that *makes* his Law, are commonly these, *Hear O ye Justices, that I do not own this sum of Money demanded, neither in all nor any part thereof in manner and form declared. So help me God, and the Contents of this Book.* To make Services or Custome, is nothing else but to perform them, *Old Nat. Brev. fol.* 14. To make Oath, is to take Oath.

Malediction, *Maledictio*, A Curse which was of old usually annexed to Donations of Land made to Churches and Religious Houses. See the Charter of King *Athelstane* to the Monastery of *Wiltune, Anno* 933. and the Charter of King *Eadred*, in *Mon. Ang.* 2. *par. fol.* 867.

Male fesance, A doing of evil, *Cro. Rep.* 2. *par. fol.* 266. It is derived from the French *Mal-faire*, to offend or transgress.

Maletent or Maletolte, *Malum vel indebitum Telonium*, In the Statute called *The Confirmation of the Liberties, &c.* 25 *E.* 1. *cap.* 7. Is interpreted to be a Toll of forty shillings for every Sack of Wool. *Stow* in his *Annals* calls it a *Maletot*, pag. 461. See also the *Statute de Tallagio non concedendo, Anno* 35 *E.* 1. Nothing from hence-forth shall be taken of Sacks of Wool, by colour or occasion of *maletent.* In *France* they had an extraordinary Tax called *Maletoste.*

Malin. See *Marle.*

Malveis procurors, *In Artic. super Chart. cap.* 10. Is understood of such as use to pack Juries by nomination, or other Practice, 2. *Inst. fol.* 561.

Manbote, Signifies a Recompence for *Homicide*, or a pecuniary compensation for killing a man. *Spelman* in his First Volume, *concil. fol.* 622. sayes, *Manbote*, i. *compensatio Domino persolvenda pro homine suo occiso, Anglorum lege Regi & Archiepiscopo tres marcas de hominibus eorum propriis sed Episcopo ejusdem comitatus & Consuli & Dapifero Regis, Viginti solidos, Baronibus autem aliis decem solidos, &c.* See *Lambert* in his *Explication of Saxon words*, verbo *Æstimatio*, and *Hovedem* in parte poster. annal. suor. fol. 344. & *Bote.*

Manca, Was a square piece of Gold, commonly valued at thirty pence; and *Mancusa* was as much as a mark of Silver. See the Notes upon *Canutus* Laws, where it was called *Mancusa, quasi manu cusa*, coined with the Hand.

Manciple, *Manceps*, A Caterer, An Officer anciently in the Temple, now called *The Steward.* Of whom our ancient Poet *Jeoffry Chaucer*, sometimes a Student there, thus writes,

> A Manciple *there was in the Temple,*
> *Of which all Catours might take ensemple.*

This Officer still remains in Colledges in the Universities.

Mandamus, Is a Writ that lyeth after the Year and Day, whereas in the mean time the Writ called *Diem clausit extremum* hath not been sent out to the Escheator for the same purpose for which it should have been sent forth, *F.N.B. fol.* 253. See *Diem clausit extremum.*

Mandamus, Is also a Charge to the Sheriff, to take into the Kings hands all the Lands and Tenements of the Kings Widow, that against her Oath formerly given, marryeth without the Kings consent, *Reg. fol.* 295. See *Widow.*

Mandatary, *Mandatarius*, He to whom a Charge or Commandment is given. Also he that obtains a Benefice by *Mandamus.*

Mandate, *Mandatum*, Is a Commandment of the King, or his Justices, to have any thing done for dispatch of Justice, whereof you shall see diversity in the Table of the *Register Judicial, verbo* Mandatum. The Bishops *Mandates* to the Sheriff, 31 *Eliz.* 9.

Manentes, Was of old used for *Tenentes* or *Tenants, Council. Synodal. apud* Cloveshoo, *Anno* 822.

Manning, *Manopera*, A dayes work of a Man; in some ancient Deeds there is a reserve of so much Rent, and so many *mannings.*

Manor, *Manerium*, Seems to be derived of the French *Manour, habitatio*, or rather from *manendo*, of abiding there, because the Lord did usually reside there. *Skene de verb.* Signif. saith, It is call'd *Manerium quasi manurium*, because it is laboured by handy-work: It is a noble sort of Fee granted partly to Tenants for certain Services to be performed, and partly reserved to the use of his Family, with Jurisdiction over his Tenants for their Farms. That which was granted out to Tenants, we call *Tenementales*; those reserved to the Lord, were *Dominicales*: The whole Fee was termed a Lordship, of old a Barony; from whence the Court, that is always an Appendant to the Mannor, is called *The Court Baron.* Touching the original of the *Manors*, it seems that in the beginning there was a circuit of Ground granted by the King to some Baron, or Man of worth, for him and his Heirs to dwell upon, and to exercise some Jurisdiction more or less within that compass, as he thought good to Grant, performing such Services, and paying such yearly Rent for the same, as he by his Grant required, and that afterward this great man parcelled his Land to other meaner men, injoyning them such Services and Rents as he thought good, and so as he became Tenant to the King, the inferiors became Tenants to him.

See *Perkins Reservations*, 670. and *Hornes Mirror of Justices*, lib. 1. cap. *de roy Alfred*, and *Fulbeck*, *fol.* 18. And according to this our Custome, all Lands holden in Fee throughout *France* are divided into *Fieffs* and *arrieri fiefs*, whereof the former are such as are immediately granted by the King; the second, such as the Kings *Feudataries* do again grant to others, *Gregorii Syntagm. lib.* 6. *cap.* 5. *num.* 3. In these days a *Manor* rather signifieth the Jurisdiction and Royalty incorporeal, than the Land or Scite. For a man may have a *Manor in gross*, (as the Law termeth it) that is, the right and interest of a Court Baron, with the perquisites thereto belonging, and another or others have every Foot of the Land, *Kitchin*, *fol.* 4. Broke, *hoc titulo per totum*, Bracton, *lib.* 4. *cap.* 31. *num.* 3. divideth *manerium* into *capitale & non capitale*. See *Fee*. A *Manor* may be compounded of divers things, as of a Horse, arable Land, Pasture, Meadow, Wood, Rent, Advowson, Court Baron, and such like; and this ought to be by long continuance of time, beyond the memory of man. For at this day a *Manor* cannot be made, because a Court Baron cannot now be made, and a *Manor* cannot be without a Court Baron, and Suiters or Free-holders, two at the least; For if all the Free-holds, except one, eschet to the Lord, or if he purchase all, except one, there his *Manor* is gone *causâ qua supra*, although in common speech it may be so called.

Manpygarnon, VVillielmus VValcote *tenet manerium de* Adington *in Com.* Sur. *per servitium inveniendi, ad Coronationem Regis quoddam Potaginum vocat.* Manpygarnon.

Mansion, *Mansio, a manendo*, According to the definition of *Bracton*, *lib.* 5. *cap.* 28. *num.* 1. Is a dwelling consisting of one or more Houses: It is most commonly taken for the Lords chief dwelling-house within his Fee, otherwise called *The Capital messuage*, or chief Mannor-place, *Bracton*, *lib.* 2. *cap.* 26. *Mansion*, amongst the ancient *Romans*, was a place appointed for the lodging of the Prince, or Souldiers in their Journey; and in this sense we read *Primam mansionem, &c.* It is probable, That this word *Mansion* doth in some construction signifie so much Land as *Bede* calleth *Familiam* in his *Ecclesiastical History*. For *Lambert* in his *Explication of Saxon words*, verb. *Hida terræ*, saith, That that which he calleth *Familiam*, others since call *Manentem vel mansam*, *mansus & mansum*, you may read in the *Feudists*, and in *Skene de verbor.* Significat. *verbo* Mansus. The Latine word *mansio* hath the same signification in the Charter granted by King *Kenulphus* to *Ruchin* the Abbot of *Abington*, mentioned by Sir *Edward Coke* in his Book *de jure Regis Ecclesiastico*; And in a Charter of *Edward the Confessor*, it is written *Mansa*. See *History of Pauls*, fol. 189.

Mansura & Masura, Are used in *Doomsday*, and other ancient Records, for *mansiones vel habitacula villicorum*.

Manslaughter, *Homicidium*, Is the unlawfull killing of a man, without prepensed malice. As when Two, that formerly meant no harm one to another, meet together, and upon some sudden occasion falling out, the one killeth the other, *West*, *part* 2. *Symbol.* tit. *Inditements*, *sect.* 44. It differeth from *Murder*, because it is not done with fore-going malice: And from *Chance-Medley*, because it hath a present intent to kill. And this is Felony, but admitted to the benefit of Clergy for the first time, *Stamf. pl. cor. lib.* 1. *cap.* 9. and *Britton*, *cap.* 9. Yet is confounded with Murder in the Statute, *Anno* 28 *E.* 3. *cap.* 11.

Mansus, Anciently a Farm, *Seldens History of Tythes*, pag. 62. *Mansum* or *mansus*, Is sometimes confounded with *messuagium*: *Spelman.*

Mantyle, *Mantile*, May be drawn from the French word *Manteau*, and signifies with us a long Robe, *Anno* 24. *H.* 8. *cap.* 13.

Manubrium, The handle or haft of a Sword or Dagger, *Jur. præsentant, quod* A. de C. *Aurifaber* 2. Junii, 2 Jac. *apud* S. *prædict. quoddam* Manubrium *Pugionis ferreum*, *Anglicè* a Dagger hilt of Iron, &c. *apud* Maidston.

Manucaptio, Is a VVrit that lies for a man, who, taken upon suspition of Felony, and offering sufficient Bail for his Appearance, cannot be admitted thereto by the Sheriff, or other having Power to let to Mainprise, *F. N. B. fol.* 249. See *Mainprise*. How diversly it is used, see the *Reg. Origin.* in the Table, and *Prynns Animadversions*, fol. 268.

Manuel, *Manuelis*, Any thing whereof present profit may be made, or that is employed or used by the hand, *Stamf. Prærog. fol.* 54. As a thing in the *manuel* Occupation of one, *i.* actually used or employed by him.

Manumission, *Manumissio*, Is the freeing of a Villain or Slave out of his Bondage: The form of it, in the *Conquerors* time, *Lambert* in his Ἀρχαιονομία, *fol.* 126. setteth down in these words, *Si quis velit servum suum liberum facere, tradat eum Vicecomiti, per manum dextram in pleno Comitatu & quietum illum clamare debet a jure servitutis suæ per* manumissionem; *& ostendat ei liberas portas & vias & tradat ei libera arma* scilicet, *Lanceam & gladium & deinde liber homo efficitur.* Some also were wont to be *manumitted* by Charter. *Vide Broke*, tit. *Villenage*, *fol.* 305. The *Termes of the Law* make two kinds of *manumission*, one *expressed*, the other *implyed*: *Manumission expressed* is, when the Lord makes a Deed to his Villain, to infranchise him by this word *Manumittere*; The manner of which in old time was thus, The Lord, in the presence of other persons, took the Bond-man by the Head, saying, *I will that this man be free*, and thereupon shoved him forward out of his hand. *Manumission implyed* is, when the Lord makes an Obligation for payment of money to him at a certain day, or sueth him, when he might enter without Suit; or granteth him an Annuity, or leaseth Land to him by Deed, for Years, or for Life, and such like. See *Neif.*

Manupastus, We often find it in the Law *Dialect*, to signifie a Domestick Servant, *Spelm. Erit culpabilis tanquam de* Manupasto *Manwood*, *cap.* 16. *num.* 6. That is, he shall be culpable as of a thing done by one of his Family, *Gloss.* in 10. *Scriptor.*

Manutenentia, Is a Writ used in case of Maintenance, *Reg. Orig. fol.* 182. & 189. See *Maintenance.*

Manworth, The price or value of a mans Life or Head; for of old every man was rated at a certain price, according to his Quality, which price

price was paid to the Lord in satisfaction for killing him.

Marches, *Marchia*, Be the Bounds and Limits between Us and *Wales*, or between Us and *Scotland*. 24 *H*. 8. *cap*. 9. *Camd. pag*. 453. & 606. And the *Marches of Scotland* are divided into West and Middle *marches*, 4 *H*. 5. 7. 22 *E*. 4. *cap*. 8. The word is used in the Statute of 24 *H*. 8. 12. generally for the Borders of the Kings Dominions; And may be derived from the German *March*, i. *limes*, or from the French *Marque*, that is, *Signum*, being the notorious distinction between two Countries or Territories.

Marchers, Were the Noblemen that lived on the Marches of *Wales* or *Scotland*, who, in times past, as *Camden* saith, *pag*. 453. had their private Laws, as if they had been petty Kings, which are now abolish't by 27 *H*. 8. *cap*. 26. Of these *Marchers* you may read 2 *H*. 4. 18. 26 *H*. 8. 6. 1 *E*. 6. 10. where they are called *Lords-marchers*. See also 1 & 2 P. & M. *cap*. 15.

Marchet, Marchetum, *Consuetudo pecuniaria, in mancipiorum filiabus maritandis*, Bract. lib. 2. tit. 1. cap. 8. num. 2. This Custome is in divers parts of *England* and *Wales*, as also in *Scotland* and the *Isle of Guernsey*. See *Spelman* at large of it. *Coke* on *Lit. fol*. 140. says, It is called *Marchet*, as it were a *Chete* or *Fine* for Marriage. In the Mannor of *Denever in Com. Carmarthen*, every Tenant at the marriage of his Daughter, pays by Custome ten shillings to the Lord, which, in the *Brittish* Language, is call'd *Gwabr merched*, that is, a Maids Fee. See *Maiden Rents*, and *Gwabr merched*.

Mareshall, *Marescallus*, Is a French word signifying as much as *Tribunus militum* with the ancient *Romans*, or πολέμαρχος with the Greek, or ἵππαρχος. *Trinquel. de nobilitate*, cap. 8. pag. 42. num. 17. The French word may seem also to proceed from the German *Marschalk*, i. *Equitum magister*, which *Hotoman in verbis feudalibus verbo* Marchalkus, derived from the old word *March*, signifying a Horse. Others make it of the two Saxon words, *Mar*. i *equus*, and *Scalch*. i. *præfectus*; or according to *Verstegan*, from *Mare*, the general appellation of all Horses, (as Horse is now in *English*) and *Scale*, which in the ancient *Teutonick*, he affirms, to signifie a kind of Servant, as *Scalco* doth at this day among the *Italians*. With us there be divers Officers of this Name, but one most noble of all the rest, who is called *Lord* or *Earl Marshal of England*, of whom mention is made in divers Statutes, 1 *H*. 4. 7. & 14. and 13. *Rich*. 2. *cap*. 2. His Office consists especially in matters of War and Arms, as well with us as in other Countries, whereof you may read *Lupanus de Magistratibus Franciæ. lib*. 1. *cap*. Mareshallus, and *Tilius*, lib. 2. cap. *de Conestabili Mariscallo*, &c. The next to this is the *Marshal* of the Kings House, whose special Authority is (according to *Britton* and *Gwin* in the *Preface to his Readings*,) in the Kings Place to hear and determine all Pleas of the Crown, and to punish faults committed within the Verge, and to hear and judge of Suits between those of the Kings Houshold, &c. *Cromp. Jur. fol*. 192. of him you may read *F. N. B. fol*. 241. & 18 *E*. 3. *stat*. 2. *cap*. 7. and 27 *E*. 3. *stat*. 2. *cap*. 6. and 2 *H*. 4. 13. and divers others. Whoever desires to know farther of this Officer, and his Duty, may find it in *Fleta*, *lib*. 2. *cap*. 4. & 5. There be other inferior Officers of this Name, as *Marshal* of the Justices *in Eyre*, 3 *E*. 1. 19. *Marshal* of the Kings Bench, 5 *E*. 3. *cap*. 8. and this hath the Custody of the Kings Bench Prison in *Southwark*, *F. N. B. fol*. 251. And these inferior *Marshals* be either *ad placitum*, or in Fee, *Kitchin, fol*. 143. *Fleta* also, *lib*. 2. *cap*. 15. mentions a *Marshal* of the Kings Hall, whose Office is, when the Tables be prepared, to call out both those of the Houshold and Strangers, according to their worth, and decently to place them, &c. There is also a *Marshal* of the Exchequer, 51. *H*. 3. *stat*. 15. to whom the Court committeth the Custody of the Kings Debtors during the Term time, for securing the Debts. He also assigneth Sheriffs, Escheators, Customers, and Collectors, their Auditors before whom they shall account. He hath all Inquisitions taken before Escheators *virtute Officii*, delivered unto him to be redeliver'd by him to the Treasurers Remembrancer in the Exchequer.

Marshallee, *Marescaltia*, Is the Court or Seat of the *Marshal*, of whom see *Cromp. Jur. fol*. 102. It is allowed for the Prison in *Southwark*; the reason whereof may be, because the *Marshal* of the King House was wont perhaps to sit there in Judgment, or keep his Prison. See the Stat. 9 *R*. 2. *cap*. 5. and 2 *H*. 4. *cap*. 23. King *Charles* the First erected a Court by Letters Patents under the Great Seal, by the Name of *Curia Hospitii Domini Regis*, &c. which takes Cognisance more at large of all Causes than the *Marshalsee* could; of which the Knight *Marshal* or his Deputy are Judges.

Mariage, *Maritagium*, Signifies not only the lawful conjunction of Man and Wife, but also the Interest of bestowing a Ward or a Widow in *Marriage*, *Magna Cart. cap*. 6. and *Bracton*, *lib*. 2. *cap*. 3. And also it signifies Lands given in *Marriage*, *Bracton*, *lib*. 2. *cap*. 34. 39. And in this signification the same Author saith, That *Maritagium est, aut liberum, aut servitio obligatum*, lib. 2. cap. 7. num. 3. 4. *Liberum* maritagium *dicitur, ubi Donator vult quod terra sic data quieta sit & libera ab omni seculari servitio, quod ad Dominum feudi possit pertinere, & ita quod ille, cui sic data fuerit, nullum omnino inde faciat servitium usq; ad tertium Hæredem & usq; ad quartum gradum*, &c. See *Skene de verb*. Signif. *verb*. Maritagium, (which according to *Glanvile*, *lib*. 7. *cap*. 1.) is that portion which the Husband receives with his Wife. See *Dower*.

Maritagio amisso per defaltam, Is a Writ for the Tenant in *Frank-Marriage*, to recover Lands, &c. whereof he is divorced by another, *Reg. fol*. 171.

Maritagio forisfacto, Is a Writ. See *Forisfactura maritagii*.

Marke, *Merca*, From the Saxon *Mearc*, *signum*, was a piece of Silver money worth thirty pence, *Lamb. Explication of Saxon words*, *verbo* Mancusa. In old time a *mark of Gold* was the quantity of eight ounces, *Stowes Annals*, *pag*. 32. and *pag*. 691. Twelve *marke* of Gold Troy-weight was two hundred pounds of *English* Money, after which rate every *marks* weighed sixteen pounds, thirteen shillings, four pence. *Skene de verb*. Sgnif. *verb*. Mark, saith, That in *Tractatu* *de ponderibus & mensuris*; a *mark* signifieth an ounce Weight, or half a pound, whereof the dram is the eighth part, as the ounce is the eighth part of a *mark*, citing *Cassanæus de consuetud. Burg. Rub. prim.* sect. 7. verb. *Solz Turnoys.* A *mark* of Silver every man knows is now thirteen shillings and four pence.

Marketzeld, more truly **Marketgeld**, It signifies Toll of the Market. The word *Zeld* denoting a payment. It is else-where written *Markethgald. Plac. apud Cestriam*, 31 E. 3.

Mark-peny, Every Inhabitant at *Maldon* who had Pipes or Gutters laid out of their Houses into the Street, paid one peny, *Hill.* 15 *E.* 1. Mr. *Phillips* of *Purveyance.*

Market, *Mercatus*, May be derived from the French *Marche*, i. *Emporium*; it signifies with us the same thing, and also the liberty or priviledge whereby a Town is enabled to keep a *Market*, *Old Nat. Brev. fol.* 149. So doth *Bracton* use it, *lib.* 2. *cap.* 24. *num.* 6. & *lib.* 4. *cap.* 46. where he shews, That one *Market* ought to be distant from another, *Sex Leucas & dimidiam & tertiam partem dimidiæ.* The reason thereof both he and *Fleta* give in these words, *Quia omnes rationabiles dietæ constant ex 20. milliaribus. Dividatur ergo Dieta in tres partes, prima autem matutina detur euntibus versus mercatum, secunda detur ad emendum & vendendum; quæ quidam sufficere debet omnibus nisi sint forte mercatores statarii, qui merces deposuerint & exposuerint venales, quibus necessaria erit prolixior mora in* mercatu. *& tertia pars relinquitur redeuntibus de* mercatu *ad propria, &c.* lib. 4. cap. 28. sect. *Item refert.* By the Statute 27 *H.* 6. 5. all *Fairs* and *Markets* are forbidden to be kept upon any *Sunday*, or upon the Feasts of the *Ascension* of our Lord; *Corpus Christi*, or the *Assumption* of our blessed Lady; *All-Saints* or *Good-Friday*, except for necessary Victual, and in the time of Harvest.

Marle, *Marla*, Is a kind of Earth or Mineral, which men in divers Counties of this Kingdom cast upon their Land to make it more fertile: It is also called *Malin*, 17 *E.* 4. *cap.* 4.

Marlerium or **Marletum**, A *Marlepit*, Mr. *Dugdale* hath an old Deed by him, wherein is mentioned this word, *Sciant, &c. quod ego Rog. la Zouch. dedi, &c. & quod habeant omnem libertatem, &c. in boscis, in planis, &c. in* marleriis *& omnibus aliis locis ad prædict. Manerium de Tonge spectant. Et quod capiant* marlam *pro voluntate sua ad terram suam* marlend, *&c. Reddendo, &c.* And else we may read twenty *Acras terræ* Marlatas, that is, *marled* Land.

Marque, From the Saxon *Mearc*, *signum*: We use the word in the same sense to this day, when we say, Give such a thing a *mark* or sign; but in our ancient Statutes it signifies as much as *Reprisals*, as *Anno* 4 *H.* 5. *cap.* 7. where *Marque* and *Reprisal* are used as *Synonyma*; and *Letters of Marque* are found in the same signification in the same Chapter. See *Reprisals*, and see also *Marches.*

Marquis or **Marquesse**, *Marchio*, Is now a Title of Honor next before an Earl, and next after a Duke; by the opinion of *Hotoman*, verb. *Marchio in verbis feudalibus*: The Name is derived from the German *March*, i. *Limes*, signifying originally as much as *Custos limitis*, or *Comes & præfectus limitis.* It was an ancient Custome among the *Britains*, and after them of the *Saxons*, to give the Title of *Reguli* to all Lords that had the Charge and Custody of *Marches* and Limits. See *Seldens Mare Clausf.* lib. 2. *cap.* 19. From hence it was, that in the time of *Richard* the Second, came up first the Title of *Marquesses*, which is a Governor of the *Marches*; for before that time, those that governed the *Marches*, were called commonly *Lords Marchers*, and not *Marquesses*, as *Judge Dodaridge* hath observed in his *Law of Nobility and Peerage*, under the Title of *Marquesses*, pag. 31.

Marsum, A word used in *Doomsday* Book, and interpreted by Mr. *Agar* of the Receit of the Exchequer, to signifie a quantity of Coyn, *sed quære.*

Mariscus, A word frequent in *Doomsday*, and signifies *Palus*, or *locus Paludosus*, a marshy or fenny Ground. See *Doomsday Book.*

Marrow, Was a Lawyer of great Account in *Henry* the Sevenths days, whose learned Readings are extant, but not in Print, *Lamb. Eirenarch. lib.* 1. *cap.* 10.

Marshall. See *Mareshall.*

Marternes. See *Furre.*

Martial Law, Is the Law of War, depending upon the Pleasure of the *King*, or his Lieutenant: for though the King in time of Peace never makes any Laws, but by common consent in *Parliament*; yet in War he useth absolute Power, insomuch that His word is a Law, *Smith de Repub. Anglor. lib.* 2. *cap.* 4. See *Law of Arms.*

Mast, *Glans*, *Glandis nomine continentur glans, castanea, fagino, ficus & alia quæq; quæ edi & pasci poterunt præter herbam*, Bracton, lib. 4. 226. See *Pessona.*

Master of the Rolls, *Magister Rotulorum*, Is an Assistant to the *Lord Chancellor*, or *Lord Keeper*, of the Great Seal of *England*, in the high Court of *Chancery*, and, in his absence, heareth Causes there, and giveth Orders, *Cromp. Jur. fol.* 41. His Title in his Patent is, *Clericus parvæ Bagæ, Custos Rotulorum & domus conversorum.* This *Domus conversorum* is the House where the *Rolls* are kept, so call'd, because the *Jews* that were converted to Christianity inhabited there: But his Office seems to take denomination from the safe keeping of the *Rolls* of all Patents and Grants that pass the Great Seal, and of all Records of the Court of Chancery, *&c.* He is called *Clerk of the Rolls*, 12 R. 2. cap. 2. and in *Fortescue*, *cap.* 24. and no where *Master of the Rolls*, until 11 *H.* 7. 20. and yet 11 *H.* 7. *cap.* 25. he is also called *Clerk*: Sir *Thomas Smith de Rep. Ang. lib.* 2. *cap.* 11. saith, He might not unfitly be called *Custos Archivorum*: The Offices of the six Clerks, Clerks of the Petty-bag, Examiners of the Court, and Clerks of the Chappel, are all in his dispose, *Anno* 14 & 15 *H.* 8. *cap.* 1. See *Rolls.*

Master of the Mint, *Anno* 2 *H.* 6. 14. Is now called the *Warden of the Mint*; and his Office is to receive in the Silver and Bullion to be Coyned, and to take care thereof, *&c.*

Master of the Court of Wards and Liveries, *Magister Curiæ Wardorum & Liberationum*,

rationum, was the chief Officer and Judge of the *Court*, named and assigned by the King, to whose Custody the Seal of the *Court* was committed. See *Anno* 33 *H.* 8. *cap.* 33. But this *Court* with the Officers, Members, Power and Appurtenances thereof is taken away and dissolved by the Statute made in *Anno* 12 *Car.* 2. *cap.* 24.

Master of the Horse, Is he that hath the Rule and Charge of the King's Stable, being an Office of high Account, and alwayes bestowed upon some Noble-man of great Merit. He is mentioned 39 *Eliz.* 7. and 1 *E.* 6. 5. This Officer, under the *Roman* Emperors, was called *Comes sacri stabuli*.

Master of the Posts, Was an Officer of the King's Court, that had the appointing, placing and displacing of all such through *England* as provide *Post-horse*, for the speedy passing of the King's Messages, and other Business, in the thorow-fair Towns where they dwell; as also to see that they keep a certain number of convenient Horses of their own, and when occasion is, that they provide others wherewith to furnish such as have warrant from him to take *Post-horses* either from or to the Seas, or other border or places within the Realm: He likewise hath the care to pay them their Wages, and make them allowance accordingly as he shall think meet: This Officer is mentioned *Anno* 2 *E.* 6. 3. But now by a Statute made 12 *Car.* 2. *cap.* 34. One *General Letter-Office* or *Post-Office* is setled in *London*, the *Master* of which is appointed by the King by *Letters Patent*, with Rates and Rules prescribed in the Act for carriage of *Letters*. The *Master* thereof at present is his Royal Highness *James* Duke of *York*.

Master of the Armory, Is he that hath the Care and Over-sight of His Majestie's *Armor* in any standing *Armoryes*, with Power of placing and displacing all inferior Officers thereto appertaining: Mention is made of him 39 *Eliz.* *cap.* 7.

Master of the Jewel-House, Is an Officer in the King's Houshold, of great Credit, being allowed *Bouge of Court*, that is, Dyet for himself and inferior Officers, *viz.* Clerks of the *Jewel House*, and a special Lodging in Court, having Charge of all Plate of *Gold*, of *Silver* double or parcel gilt, used for the King or Queens Table, or to any Officer of Account that attends in Court, and of all *Plate* remaining in the *Tower* of *London*, of Chains and loose *Jewels*, not fixed to any Garment: He is mentioned 39 *Eliz.* *cap.* 7.

Master of the King's Houshold, *Magister Hospitii Regis*, Is otherwise called *Grand Master of the King's Houshold*, and also *Lord Steward of the King's most honourable Houshold*, 32 H. 8. 39. But in the first of Queen *Mary*, and ever since he is called *Lord Steward of the King's Houshold*, under whom there is a principal Officer called the *Master of the Houshold*, of great Authority as well as Antiquity.

Master of the Ordnance, 39 *Eliz.* 7. Is a great Officer, to whose Care all the King's *Ordnance* and Artillery is committed, being some great man of the Realm, and expert in Martial Affairs.

Masters of the Chancery, *Magistri Cancellariæ*, are Assistants in *Chancery* to the *Lord Chancellor*, or *Lord Keeper*, of the Great Seal, in matters of Judgment. Of these, there are some *Ordinary*, some *Extraordinary*: Of *Ordinary* there are twelve (whereof the *Master of the Rolls* is accounted one) whereof some sit in Court every day in each Term, and have referred to them (at the *Lord Chancellors*, *Lord Keepers*, or *Master of the Rolls* discretion) interlocutory Orders, for stating Accounts, computing Damages, and the like; taking of Oaths, Affidavits, and acknowledgments of Deeds and Recognisances. The *Extraordinary* do Act in all the Country ten miles from *London*, by taking Recognizances and Affidavits, acknowledgment of Deeds, &c. for the ease of the Subject.

Master of the King's Musters, Is a Martial Officer in all Royal Armies most necessary, as well for maintaining the Forces compleat, well armed and trained, as also for prevention of such Frauds as otherwise may exceedingly wast the *Princes* Treasure, and extremely weaken the Forces: He hath the over-sight of all the *Captains*, and their *Companies*, and ought to have at the beginning delivered unto him by the *Lord General* perfect *Lists and Rolls* of all the Forces both Horse and Foot, &c. He is mentioned *Anno* 2 *E.* 6. *cap.* 2. and called *Muster-Master-General*, 35 *Eliz.* 4.

Master of the Wardrobe, *Magister Garderobæ*, Is a great and principal Officer in Court, having his Habitation and Dwelling-house belonging to that Office, called *The Wardrobe near Puddle-wharf in London*: He hath the Charge and Custody of all former Kings and Queens ancient Robes remaining in the Tower of *London*, and of all Arras and Tapistry Hangings, Bedding, &c. He hath also the Charge and delivering out of all Velvet or Scarlet for Liveries, to any of his Majestie's Servants, &c. mention is made of him 39 *Eliz.* 7.

Masura terræ, *Sunt in eisdem masuris* 60. *Domus plus quam antè fuerunt*, Doomsday. It is a quantity of Ground, containing about four Oxgans.

Matter in Deed, and **Matter of Record**, Are said to differ thus, In *Old Nat. Brev. fol.* 19. *Matter in Deed* seems to be nothing else but a Truth to be proved, though not by any Record: And *Matter of Record* is, that which may be proved by some Record: For example, If a man be sued to an *Exigent*, during the time he was in the King's Wars; this is *matter in Deed*, and not *matter of Record*: And therefore he that will alledge this for himself, must come before the *Scire facias* for execution be awarded against him, for after that nothing will serve but *matter of Record*; that is, some Error in the Process appearing upon Record. *Kitchin, fol.* 216. maketh also a difference between *matter of Record*, and *a specialty* and *nude matter*; Where he saith, That *nude matter* is not of so high a nature as either *matter of Record* or a *specialty*, otherwise there called *matter in Deed*; whereby it seems, That *nude matter* is a naked allegation of a thing done, to be proved only by Witnesses, and not either Record or other specialty in writing under Seal.

Maugre, Is a Compound of the two French words *Mal* and *Gre*, i. *iniquo animo*; so

that

that it is as much as to say, with an unwilling mind, or in despight of another, and so it is used in *Lit. sect.* 672. Where it is said, That the Husband and Wife shall be remitted *maugre* the Husband, that is, in despight, or against the Will of the Husband.

Maund, A kind of great Basket or Hamper containing eight Bales, or two Fats. See the *Book of Rates*, fol. 3.

Maxims in Law, Are Positions and *Theses*, being conclusions of Reason, and universal Propositions, so sure and perfect, that they may not be impugned or disputed. For *Co.* upon *Lit.* saith, That *Principia probant non probantur*, and therefore *contra negantem Principia non est disputandum*: It is another *maxim*, That *as no Estate can be vested in the King, without matter of Record, so none can be divested out of him, but by matter of Record*; For things are dissolved as they are contracted, *Co. Rep.* 1. *Cholmeye's* Case. Another, That *an Obligation, or other matter in Writing, cannot be discharged by an Agreement by word.* And *Argumentum ab authoritate fortissimum est in Lege*, Co. *on* Lit. *pag.* 141. and many other. See *Co.* on *Lit. fol.* 11. And see also *Doctor and Student.*

Mayor, Is the chief Magistrate of a City, and anciently among the *Britains* call'd *Meyr*, which is derived from the *Brittish* word *Miret*; which signifies *Custodire*, to keep and preserve; and not from the Latine *Major*, greater, *Anno* 1189. *Richard* the First changed the Bayliff of *London* into a *Mayor*, and by that example 1204. King *John* made the Bayliff of *Kings Lyn* a *Mayor*, while *Norwich* obtained not that Title till the Seventh of *Henry* the Fifth 1419. See more of this word in *Spelm. Gloss.*

Meal-rents, Are certain *Rents* still so called, but now paid in *money*, which heretofore, by some Tenants, in the honour of *Clun*, were paid in *meal*, to make *meat* for the Lord's Hounds.

Meane, *Medius*, Signifies the middle, between two extreams, and that either in time or dignity. For example of the first, His Action was mean betwixt the Disseisin made to him and his recovery, that is in the *interim*, (or as we usually say in the mean time.) Of the second, there is Lord *Mean* or *Mesne*, (mentioned in the Statute of *Amortising Lands*, made *tempore* E. 1.) and *Tenant*. See *Mesne*.

Mease, *Messuagium*, Seemeth to come from the French *Maison*, or rather *Meix*, which word you read in *Cassanæus de Consuet. Burgund.* pag. 1195. and interpreted by him *Mansus*. What *Mansus* is, see *Mansion*: It signifies a Messuage or Dwelling-house, *Kitchin, fol.* 139. and *F. N. B. fol.* 2. *Stat.* Hiberniæ, 14 *H.* 3. and 21 *H.* 8. 13. In some places called corruptly a *Mise* or *Miseplace*. See *Mise*, and *Mese*, and *Mesuage*.

Measne. See *Mesne*.

Meason-due, In French *Maison de dieu*, *Domus Dei*; A House of God, A Monastery, Religious House or Hospital; the word is mention'd 2 & 3 *P. & M. cap.* 23. 39 *Eliz.* 5. and 15 *Car.* 2. 7.

Measure, *Mensura*, According to the 25th Chapter of *Mag. Chart.* and the Stat. 17 *Car.* 1. *cap.* 19. all Weights and Measures in this Kingdom ought to be the same, and according to the King's *Standard*. See 4 *Inst.* 273. & *Mensura*.

Measurer. See *Alneger*.

Medfee, The *Saxon Dictionary* interprets it to be a Bribe or Reward; it also signifies that Compensation given in an Exchange, where the things exchanged are not of equal value; as in 4 E. 3. *Hoc scriptum fact.* 20. *die* Decemb. *inter Dominum Hugonem de Courtenay ex parte una &* Rich. Stanlake, & Johannam *uxorem ejus ex altera parte testatur, quod idem Dominus* Hugo *in excambium----remisit, &c.* and at last it follows, *Quod ipsi non dabunt* Medfee. See *Arrura*.

Medietas Linguæ, Denotes a Jury impanelled upon any Cause, wherein a Stranger is party, whereof the one half consists of Denizens, the other of Strangers, and is used in Pleas, where one party is a Denizen, and the other a Stranger; and this manner of Tryal was first given by the Statute of 27 *E.* 3. *Stat.* 2. *cap.* 8. and 8 *H.* 6. *cap.* 29. And by the Statute of 28 *E.* 3. *cap.* 13. it was granted in Cases where the King himself was party with an Alien: Before the first of these Statutes was made, this was wont to be obtained of the King, by Grant made to any Company of Strangers, *Stamf. Pl. Cor. lib.* 3. *cap.* 7. and is called a *Party-Jury*, *Anno* 14 *Car.* 2. *cap.* 11.

Medio Acquietando, Is a Writ Judicial, to distrain a Lord for the *acquitting* a *mean* Lord from a Rent which he formerly acknowledged in Court not to belong to him, *Reg. Jud. fol.* 29.

Mediterranean, Is that which passeth through the midst of the Earth. And for that reason, the Sea which stretcheth it self from West to East, dividing *Europe*, *Asia* and *Africa*, is called *The Mediterranean Sea*; It is mentioned 12 *Car.* 2. in the Statute of *Tonnage*.

Medium Tempus, Was of old taken to signifie the mean Profits, as *Annum, diem & medium* tempus. See *Flem*.

Medlefe, *Cromp. Just. of Peace, fol.* 193. Is that which *Bracton* calleth *Medletum*, lib. 3. tract. 2. cap. 35. It signifies Quarrels, scuffling or brawling, and to be derived from the French *Mesler*, i. *miscere*, *Culpa dicitur quam quis inopinatè commiserit non rixando solum & pugnando sed immiscendo se pacifice rei cuivis vel negotio*, saith *Spelman*. Hence our usual Phrase *To meddle with other Folks business*.

Meere, *Merus*, Though an Adjective, yet is used as a Substantive, to signifie *meere right*, *Old Nat. Brev. fol.* 2. in these words. This Writ hath but two Issues, *viz.* joyning the *mise* upon the *meere*, and that is to put himself in the *great Assise* of our Soveraign Lord the King, or to joyn Battel. See *Mise*.

Megbote. See *Magbote*.

Meld-feot, The reward and recompence due and given to him that made the discovery of any breach of penal Laws committed by another. The Promoter or Informers Fee, see the *Saxon Dictionary*.

Meliores. See *Tales*.

Meiny, *Menagium*, French *Mesnie*, As the Kings *meiny*, 1 R. 2. *cap.* 4. That is, the King's Family or Houshold-Servants.

Melius inquirendo, Is a Writ that lyeth for

for a second *inquiry* of what Lands and Tenements a man died seized, where partial dealing was suspected upon the Writ of *Diem clausit extremum*, *Fitz. Nat. Brev. fol.* 255.

Memories, Are some kind of Remembrances or Obsequies for the dead, in Injunctions to the *Clergy*, 1 E. 6.

Menials, As *menial Servants*, (a derivative from *Mœnia*, signifying the Walls of a House, or other place,) are Houshold-Servants, that is, such as live within the Walls of their Master's House, mentioned in the Stat. 2 *H.* 4. 21.

Mensura, In a legal sense is taken for a Bushel, as *Mensura Bladi*, a Bushel of Corn. So in the *Register* of the *Priory of Cokesford*, it is used to the same purpose, *viz. Prior habet* mensuras *tam aridorum quam liquidorum signatas signo Domini Regis & quod nullus debet vendere nec emere in foro nisi per eas.*

Mensura Regalis, The King's *Standard-measure* kept in the *Exchequer*, according to which all others are to be made. See 17 *Car.* 1. *cap.* 19. Vide *Measure.*

Merchenlage, Is one of those three Laws out of which the *Conqueror* framed our *Common Laws* with a mixture of the Laws of *Normandy*, and was the Law of the *Mercians*, when they governed the third part of this Realm. For *Camden* in his *Britannia*, pag. 94, &c. saith, That in the year 1016. this Land was divided into three parts, whereof the *West Saxons* had one, governing it by the Law called *West-Saxonlage*, and that contained these nine Shires, *Kent*, *Sussex*, *Surrey*, *Barkeshire*, *Hampshire*, *Wiltshire*, *Somerset*, *Dorset* and *Devonshire*. The second by the *Danes*, which was ruled by the Laws called *Danelage*, and that contained these fifteen Shires, *York*, *Derby*, *Nottingham*, *Leicester*, *Lincoln*, *Northampton*, *Bedford*, *Buckingham*, *Hertford*, *Essex*, *Middlesex*, *Norfolk*, *Suffolk*, *Cambridge* and *Huntington*. The third was possess'd and govern'd by the *Mercians*, whose Law was called *Merchenlage*, and held these eight, *Glocester*, *Worcester*, *Hereford*, *Warwick*, *Oxford*, *Chester*, *Salop* and *Stafford*. Out of these three (which relate not at all to a *different Law*, *Custome or Usage*, but to *several* sorts of *Amerciaments*, *Mulcts and Fines*, for the transgression of one and the same Law,) as we said, with some additions, was framed, that which now we call *The Common Law of England*.

Mercimoniatus Angliæ, Was of old time used for the Impost of *England* upon Merchandise.

Mercy, *Misericordia*, Signifies the Arbitrement or discretion of the King, Lord or Judge, in punishing any Offence, not directly censured by the Law: As to be in the *grievous mercy* of the King, 11 *H.* 6. 6. is to be in hazard of a great Penalty. See *Misericordia.*

Mertlage. See 9 *H.* 7. *fol.* 14. *b.* Seems to be a corruption of, or a Law French word for *Martyrologe.*

Mese. See *Mease.*

Mesn or **Measn**, *Medius*, May be deduced from the French *Maisne*, i. *minor natu*, and signifies him that is Lord of a Mannor, and so hath Tenants holding of him; yet himself holds of a Superior Lord, and therefore not absurdly drawn from the French *Maisne*, because his Tenure is inferior and *minor* to that of which he holds. *Mesne* also signifies a Writ which lyeth, where there is *Lord*, *Mesne* and *Tenant*. The *Tenant* holdeth of the *Mesne* by the same Services, whereby the *Mesne* holdeth of the *Lord*; and the *Tenant* of the *mesne* is distrained by the superior *Lord*, for that his Service or Rent which is due to the *mesne*, *Fitz. Nat. Brev. fol.* 135. 13 E. 1. *cap.* 9.

Mesnalty, *Medietas*, Cometh of *mesn*, and signifies nothing but the right of the *Messne*, as the *Mesnalty* is extinct; *Old Nat. Brev. fol.* 44. if the *mesnalty* descend of the Tenant. *Kitchin*, *fol.* 147. For farther understanding whereof, take these words out of the *Custumary* of *Normandy*, *Medietati tenentur feuda, quando aliqua persona intervenerit Dominum & tenentes; Et hoc modo tenent omnes Postnati, mediante ante-nato.*

Messarius, A Mower or Reaper, one that works Harvest-work, *Fleta*, *lib.* 2. *cap.* 75.

Messenger of the Exchequer, Is an Officer in that Court, of which there are four, who as *Pursuivants* attend the *Lord Treasurer*, to carry his Letters and Precepts. See *Pursuivant.*

Messuage, *Messuagium*, Is properly a dwelling-house, with some adjacent Land assigned to the use thereof, *West*, *part* 2. *Symb. tit.* Fines, *sect.* 26. *Bract. lib.* 5. *cap.* 28. and *Plowden*, *fol.* 169. 170. Where it is said, That by the Name of a *Messuage* may pass also a Curtilage, a Garden, an Orchard, a Dove-house, a Shop, a Mill, a Cottage, a Toft, a Chamber, a Cellar, &c. yet may they be demanded by their single Names. *Messuagium* in *Scotland*, signifies the principal place or Dwelling-house within a Barony, which we call a *Mannor house*. *Skene de verbo.* Signif. *verbo* Messuagium; In some places it is called the *scite of a Mannor*. A *Præcipe* lies not *de domo*, but *de messuagio*, Co. *on* Lit. cap. 8.

Mestilo, **Messine**, Or rather *Mescellane*, That is, Wheat and Rye mingled together,--*Et nonam garbam frumenti*, mestilonis, *siliginis & omnis generis bladi*, Pat. 1 E. 3. par. 1. m. 6.

Metegavel, *Cibi gablum seu vectigal*, A Rent paid in Victuals, a thing usual of old, as well with the King's Tenants as others, till *Henry* the First changed it into money, *Taylor's Hist. of Gavelkind*, pag. 118.

Metheglin, A kind of Drink made of Water, Herbs, Spice and Honey boyled together: 'Twas an old *Brittish* Drink, and still continues from *Wales*, in repute in *England*, and mentioned in the Act for Excise, 15 *Car.* 2. 9.

Michis, A sort of White-loaves paid as a Rent in some Mannors.

Mile, *Miliare*, Is the distance of one thousand paces, otherwise eight Furlongs, every Furlong to contain forty Lugs or Poles, and every Lug or Pole sixteen Foot and a half, 35 *Eliz.* 6.

Milvernir, Are a kind of *Canvas*, whereof Sayl-Clothes, or other Furniture for Ships, are made, *Anno* 1 *Jac. cap.* 24.

Militia, The Furniture and Habiliments for War, 12 *Car.* 2. *cap.* 2.

Milleate, A Trench to convey Water to or from a Mill, more truly a *Mill-eate.*

Mineral Courts, *Curiæ Minerales*, Are peculiar *Courts* for regulating the Concerns of *Lead-Mines*, as *Stannary Courts* are for *Tin*.

Miniments, *Minumenta*, Are the Evidences or Writings, whereby a man is enabled to defend the Title of his Estate, 5 *R*. 2. 8. and 35 *H*. 6. 37. *Wangford* says, This word *Miniment* includes all manner of Evidences. See *Muniment*.

Ministri Regis, Extend to the Judges of the Realm, as well as to those that have *Ministerial* Offices, *Co*. 2. *Inst*. *fol*. 208.

Miniver. See *Furre*.

Minovery, 7 *R*. 2. 4. Seemeth to be compounded of two French words, *Main*, i. *manus*, and *Ouvrer*, i. *operari*, and signifies some Trespass or Offence committed by a man's Handy-work in the Forest, as en Engine to catch Deer: *Britton* uses the word *Main-overer* to occupy and manure Land, *cap*. 40. and *cap*. 62. *Mainoure* for Handy-work. Our English word *Manure* hath a great similitude with it.

Minstrel, *Minstrellus*, From the French *Menstrel*, a Fidler or Piper, mentioned 4 *H*. 4. *cap*. 27. *Lit. Pat*. 24. *April*, 9 E. 4. *Quod marescalli & Ministrelli prædicti per se forent & esse deberent unum corpus & una communitas perpetua*, &c. See *King of the Minstrells*.

Mint, Is the place where the King's Coyn is formed, be it Gold or Silver, which is at present, and long hath been the *Tower of London*, though it appear by divers Statutes, that in ancient times the *Mint* hath been also at *Caleys*, 21 *R*. 2. 16. 9 *H*. 5. *Stat*. 5. *cap*. 5. The Officers belonging to the *Mint* have not always been alike: At present they are these, *The Warden* who is the chief of the rest, and is by his Office to receive the Silver of the Goldsmiths, and to pay them for it, and to Over-see all the rest belonging to this Function: His Fee is a hundred pound *per annum*. *The Master-worker*, who receiveth the Silver from the Warden, causeth it to be melted, and delivereth it to the Moniers, and taketh it from them again when it is made; His allowance is not any set Fee, but according to the pound weight. The third is *the Controller*, who is to see that the Money be made to the just assise, to over-see the Officers, and control them, if the Money be not as it ought to be; his Fee is a hundred Marks *per annum*. Then is *the Master of Assay* who weigheth the Silver, and seeth whether it be according to the Standard; his yearly Fee is likewise a hundred Marks: Then is *the Auditor* to take the Accounts. *The Surveyor of the melting*, who is to see the Silver cast out, and not to be alter'd after it is delivered to the *Melter*, which is after the Assay-Master hath made trial of it. *The Clerk of the Irons*, who seeth that the Irons be clean, and fit to work with. *The Graver*, who graveth the Stamps for the Money. *The melters*, that melt the Bullion before it come to the Coyning. *The Blanchers*, who do anneal, boyl and cleanse the Money. *The Porters*, who keep the Gate of the *Mint*. *The Provost of the Mint*, who is to provide for all the Moniers, and to over-see them. Lastly, *The Moniers*, who are some to shear the Money, some to forge it, others to beat it broad; some to round it, and some to stamp or coyn it. Their Wages is uncertain, according to the weight of Money coyned by them.

Minute Tythes, *Minutæ sive minores Decimæ*, Small *Tythes* such as usually belong to the Vicar, as Herbs, Seeds, Eggs, Honey, Wax, &c. See 2. *par*. *Inst*. *fol*. 649. and *Udal* and *Tindales* Case, *Hill*. 22 *Jac*. Where the *Tyth* of Woad was adjudged *Minuta Decima*, *Cro*. *Rep*. *fol*. 21. See *Tythes*.

Misaventure or **Misadventure**, *Infortunium*, Has in Law a special signification for the killing of a man, partly by negligence and partly by chance. As if one thinking no harm, carelesly throws a stone, or shooteth an Arrow, &c. wherewith he killeth another: In this case he commits not Felony, but only looseth his Goods, and hath pardon of course for his life, *Stamf*. *pl*. *cor*. *lib*. 1. *cap*. 8. *Britton*, *cap*. 7. distinguisheth between *Aventure* and *Misaventure*: *Aventure* he maketh to be meer chance; as if a man being upon or near the Water, be taken with some sudden Sickness, and so fall in and is drowned, and into the Fire and be burned to death. *Misadventure* he maketh, where a man cometh to his death by some untoward violence, as the fall of a Tree, or of a Gate, the running of a Cart-wheel, the stroke of a Horse, or such like: So that *Misaventure* in *Stamford*'s Opinion is construed somewhat more largely than *Britton* understandeth it, *West*, *Symbol*. *part* 2. *tit*. Inditement, *sect*. 48. makes *Homicide casual* to be *meerly casual* or *mixt*. *Homicide* by meer chance he defineth *sect*. 49. to be, when a man is slain by meer fortune, against the mind of the Killer; as if one hewing, the Ax flyeth off the haft, and killeth a man, and this is all one with *Britton*'s *Misaventure*, *Homicide by chance mixed* he defineth *sect*. 50. to be, when the Killers ignorance or negligence is joyned with the chance; as if a man lop Trees by the High-way-side, by which many usually travel, and cast down a Bough, not giving warning, &c. by which a man passing by is slain.

Miscognisant, Ignorant, or not knowing. In the Stat. 32 *H*. 8. *cap*. 9. against *Champerty* and Maintenance. *It is Ordained*, *That the Justices of Assise shall twice every year*, *in every County*, *cause open Proclamation to be made of this present Act*, *to the intent no person should be ignorant or* miscognisant *of the dangers and penalties therein contained*.

Miscontinuance, *Kitchin*, *fol*. 231. Is the same with Discontinuance. See *Discontinuance*.

Mise, *Misa*, Is a French word signifying as much as *Expensum* in Latine, and the Latine word *Misa* is so used in *Kitchin*, *fol*. 144. & *West*, *Symbol*. *part* 2. tit. *Proceedings in Chancery*, *sect*. 21. This word has divers significations, as first it is a Gift or Customary present which the People of *Wales* give to every new King or Prince at their entrance into that Principality. It was formerly given in Cattel, but when that Dominion was annexed to the English Crown, the Gift was changed into Money, and that is now 5000 *li*. or more, which happened to be thrice paid in King *James* his Reign. First, At his own coming to the Crown, and that Principality. Secondly, When Prince *Henry* was created *Prince of Wales*. And thirdly, When King *Charles the First* succeeded him in that Principality. *Misæ etiam dicuntur præstationes illæ quas ob fruendas pristinas immunitates Cestriæ Palatinatus subditi novo cuiq; Comiti impendunt*, that is, 3000 Marks for that County. By 27 *H.* 8. It is Ordain'd, That *Lord Mayors shall have all such* Mises *and Profits of their Lands as they have had in times past*, *&c.* See 2 *&* 3 *E.* 6. 36. 33 *H.* 8. 13. 4 *&* 5 P. *&* M. *cap.* 11. Sometimes *Mises* are taken for Taxes or Tallages, *Anno* 25 *E.* 1. 5. Sometimes for *Costs and Expenses*, as *pro* misis *& custagiis*, for Costs and Charges ordinarily used in the Entries of Judgments in personal Actions. *Mise* is also *vocabulum artis*, appropriated to a *Writ of Right* so called, because both Parties have put themselves upon the meer right to be tryed by the *Grand Assise*, or by *Battel.* So as that which in all other Actions is called an *Issue*, in a *Writ of Right* is called a *Mise*, unless a collateral point be tryed, and there it is called an *Issue*, *Co.* on *Lit. fol.* 294. *Lit. fol.* 102. and *Old Nat. Brev. fol.* 2. 37 *E.* 3. 16. *To joyn the* Mise *upon the meere*, is as much to say as to joyn the *mise* upon the clear Right, and that in more plain termes, is nothing else but to joyn upon this point, whether hath the more Right the Tenant or Demandant, *Lit. lib.* 3. *cap.* 8. *fol.* 101. This word is also sometimes used for a Particle, signifying as much as *cast or put upon*, Co. 6. Rep. fol. 124. *Saffin's* Case. And sometimes corruptly for *Mease*, a Messuage or Tenement, as a *Mise place* in some Mannors is taken to be such a Messuage or Tenement as answers the Lord a Heriot at the death of its owner, 2 *Inst. fol.* 285. which in our Law-French is written *Mees.*

Miserere, Is the Name, and first word of the 51. *Psalm*, being most commonly that which the Ordinary gives to such guilty Malefactors as have the benefit of Clergy allowed them by the Law, and is usually called the *Psalm of Mercy.*

Misericordia, is in Law used for an arbitrary Amerciament imposed on any for an Offence; for where the Plaintiff or Defendant in any Action is amerced, the Entry is *Ideo in* Misericordia. *Bracton*, *lib.* 4. *tract.* 5. *cap.* 6. hath these words, *Item si quis in* misericordiam *inciderit pro disseisina*, *non remanebit* misericordia *exigenda*, *si ille qui amiserit*, *quæsiverit convictionem.* Kitchin, fol. 78. out of *Glanvile* saith thus, *Est autem* misericordia, *quia quis per juramentum legalium hominum amerciatus est ne aliquid de suo honorabili contenemento amittat.* See *Glanvile*, *lib.* 9. *cap.* 11. *Fitzherbert* sayes in his *Nat. Brev. fol.* 75. That it is called *Misericordia*, because it ought to be very moderate, and rather less than the Offence, according to the tenour of *Magna Charta*, *cap.* 14. Therefore if a man be unreasonably amerced in a Court not of Record, as in a *Court Baron*, *&c.* there is a Writ called *Moderata Misericordia*, directed to the Lord, or his Bayliff, commanding them that they take moderate Amerciaments. Sometimes *misericordia* is to be quit, and discharged of all manner of Amerciaments that a man may fall into in the Forest. See *Cromp. Jur. fol.* 196. Vide *Amerciament*, *Mercy*, *and moderata misericordia.*

Misfeasans, Misdeeds or Trespasses, ------ *Jury to enquire of all Purprestures* and Misfeasans, *Cro. Car. fol.* 498. and *Misfeasor* a Trespasser, *Co.* 2. *Inst. fol.* 200.

Missering. See *Abisbersing* and *Miskering.*

Miskening, (*Meskenninga*, Leg. H. 1. cap. 12.) *iniqua vel injusta in jus vocatio*; *inconstanter loqui in Curia*----*Renovamus etiam & confirmamus privilegia antiquorum Regum atq; ob reverentiam Dominæ nostræ perpetuæ Virginis* Mariæ, *sanctique Benedicti*, *sanctarumq; virginum*, *omnibusq; futuris ibidem Abbatibus in tota possessione Monasterii* Sacham *&* Socham, *Theloniumq; suum in terra & in aqua concedo & consuetudines ut ab omnibus apertius & plenius intelliguntur*, *Anglicè scriptas*, *scilicet*, Mundbriche, Feardwite, Fitwite, Blodwite, Miskening, Frithsoke, Hamsockne, Forstal, Forphange, Theifephang, Hangwite, Frithbrich, Utlepe, Infongenthef, Supbriche, Tol et Tem *aliasq; omnes leges & consuetudines quæ ad me pertinent tam plene & tam libere*, *sicut eas in manu mea habebam*, Confirm. fundationis Monast. de Ramesey per S. Edw. Conf. *Mon. Ang.* 1. par. fol. 237.

Miskering, *Hoc est quietus esse pro querelis coram quibuscunq; in transumptione probata*, M.S. L.L. Rob. Cot. pag. 262. See *Mishering.*

Misnomer, Compounded of the French *Mes*, which, in composition, alwayes signifies amiss, and *nomer*, i. *nominare*, it signifies the using of one Name for another, or misterming. See *Broke*, tit. *Misnomer.*

Misprision, *Misprisio*, Cometh of the French *Mespris*, *contemptus*, and signifies in our Law neglect or over-sight. As for example, *Misprision of Treason or Felony*, is a neglect or light account shewed of Treason or Felony committed, by not revealing it, when we know it to be committed, *Stamf. pl. cor. lib.* 1. *cap.* 19. Or by letting any Person committed for Treason or Felony, or suspition of either, to go before he be indited. *Misprision of Clerks*, 8 H. 6. 15. Is a neglect of Clerks in writing, or keeping Records: By the *misprision of Clerks* no Process shall be annulled or discontinued, 14 *E.* 3. *cap.* 6. *Stat.* 1. *Misprision of Treason* is the concealment, or not disclosing of known Treason, for which the Offenders are to suffer imprisonment during the King's Pleasure, lose their Goods, and the profits of their Lands during their lives, *Cromp*, *Justice of Peace*, cap. *Misprision of Felony*, *fol.* 40. *West*, *Symbol. part* 2. tit. *Indictments*, sect. 63. *in fine.* *Misprision of Felony* is only finable by the Justices, before whom the Party is attainted, *Cromp. ibid.* The Justices of the Common-Pleas have Power to assess Fines and Amerciaments upon persons offending by *misprisions*, contempts or neglects for not doing or misdoing any thing in or concerning Fines, *West Symbol.* part 2. tit. *Fines*, *sect.* 133. *Justices of Assise* shall amend the defaults of Clerks *misprising* of a Syllable, or Letter, or Writing, *Cromp. Jur. fol.* 20. But here we are to observe, That other Faults may be accounted *Misprisions of Treason or Felony*, because some later Statutes have inflicted that punishment upon them, that of old were inflicted upon misprisions, whereof you have an example, *Anno* 14 *Eliz. cap.* 3. Of such as Coyn foreign Coyns, not currant in this Realm, and of their Procurers, Ayders and Abetters. *Misprision* also signifies a mistaking, 14 *E.* 3. *Stat.* 1. *cap.* 6. Here note, That *misprision* is included in every Treason or Felony; and where any man hath committed Treason or Felony, the King may cause him to be indited and arraign'd of *misprission* only if he please. See more hereof *Stamf. lib.* 1. *cap.* 39. *Vide etiam* 3. *Inst. fol.* 36. & 139.

Misses. See *Mise*.

Mistryal, A false or erroneous Tryal, *Cro. Car. fol.* 284. *Delves* Case.

Misuser, Is an abuse of Liberty or Benefit; As *he shall make Fine for his* Misuser, *Old Nat. Brev. fol.* 149.

Missall, *Missale*, Is a Book containing all things to be daily said in the *Mass*, Lindw. *Provincial*, lib. 3. tit. *De Ecclesiis ædificandis*, cap. 2. *Parochiani Ecclesiarum tenentur invenire rei divinæ supellectilem*, viz. *Antiphoriarium*, *Gradale*, *Psalterium*, Missale, *Manuale*, &c. See *Spelmans Glossary*.

Mystery, *Mysterium*, *Vitæ modus*, A Trade or Occupation, derived from the French *Mestier*, i. *ars*, *artificium*.

Mitta, From the Saxon *Mitten*, *mensura*, a Measure of ten Bushels, M. S. *In Wich. Salina redd.* 30. *mittas salis.* Doomsday *Book* tit. *Wirec. scire. In Libro Rames*, M. S. sect. 38. &. 143. *Ego Wulfrum* (*uxor Anketelli*) *singulis annis vitæ meæ ad festum sancti Benedicti quod est in æstate decem* mittas *de brasio* & 5. *de gruto*, & 5. mittas *farinæ triticiæ*, & 8. *pernas*, & 16. *caseos*, & 2. *vaccas pingues*, *de terra mea Hichelings pro respectu annuo eidem Ecclesiæ* (*Ramesiensi*) *procurari decerno.* Spelm.

Mittendo manuscriptum pedis finis, Is a Writ Judicial, directed to the Treasurer and Chamberlains of the Exchequer, to search and transmit the foot of a Fine acknowledged before *Justices in Eyre* into the *Common-Pleas*, &c. Reg. Orig. fol. 14.

Mittimus, Is a Writ by which Records are transferred from one Court to another: Sometimes immediately, as appears by the Stat. 5 *R.* 2. *cap.* 15. As out of the Kings Bench into the Exchequer, and sometimes by a *Certiorari* into the Chancery, and from thence by a *Mittimus* into another Court, as you may see in 28 *H.* 8. *Dyer*, *fol.* 29. and 29 *H.* 8. *Dyer*, *fol.* 32. This word is also used for the Precept that is directed by a Justice of Peace to a Gaoler, for the receiving and safe keeping a Felon, or other Offendor, by him committed to the Gaol. Of divers other Uses and Applications of this word, see *Reg. Orig.* in the *Table*.

Mixt Tythes, *Decimæ mixtæ*, Are those of Cheese, Milk, &c. and of the young of Beasts, *Co.* 2. *par. Inst. fol.* 649. See *Tyth*.

Mockadoes, A kind of Stuff made in *England*, and else-where, concerning which see 23 *Eliz. cap.* 9.

Moderata misericordia, Is a Writ for him that is amerced in a *Court-Baron*, or other, being not of Record for any Transgression or Offence beyond the quality of a Fault. It is directed to the Lord of the Court, or his Bayliff, commanding them to take a *moderate amerciament* of the Party, and is founded upon *Magna Charta*, cap. 14. *Quod nullus liber homo amercietur nisi secundum qualitatem delicti*, &c. The rest touching this Writ, see in *F. N. B. fol.* 75. See *Misericordia*.

Modo & Forma, Are words of Art in Process and Pleadings, and namely, in the answer of the Defendant, whereby he denyeth himself to have done the thing laid to his charge, *modo & forma declarata*, Kitchin, fol. 232. It signifies as much as that clause in the Civil Law, *Negat allegata prout allegantur, esse vera.* Where *modo & forma* are of the substance of the Issue, and were but words of course. See *Co.* on *Lit. fol.* 281.

Modius, We take it usually to signifie a Bushel, and it is a Measure, but various according to the Custome of several Countries, in some places containing more, in some places less.

Modius villæ, Donatio A Rthmail Regis Gwentiæ Landavensi Ecclesiæ circa *Annum* 986. *Largitus est*, &c. *Villam Lann-Mihargel Lichrit cum tertia parte prati*--*Et* 4. *Modios Villæ stifilat.* M. S. Cod. Landaven. fol. 102. col. 2.

Moer, It is a *Danish* word, signifying a *Virgin* or *Maiden*; the People of *Norfolk* in some measure retain the word to this day. The occasion of their first using it was this, *Norfolk* (which among other *English* Counties, was given by King *Alfred* to the *Danes*, *Anno* 876.) was totally inhabited by them, and their Customs, Laws and Speech there used. Now they call Virgins and young Maids *Moer*, and accordingly (as *Olaus Wormius* testifies, *Fast. Dan. lib.* 1. *cap.* 6.) they named such as were excellent Singers of the worthy Deeds of their Heroes, *Scaldmoer*, id. est, *Virgines cantratrices*, and those that by Valor won Reputation *Scioldmoer*, that is, *Scutiferas Virgines*, by which name also they signifie the *Amazons*: But this, I confess, by the ignorant Rustick is corrupted, they pronouncing instead of *Moer*, a Virgin, *Mother*, a word well known to be of a different nature.

Modus Decimandi, Is when either Land, a sum of Money, or yearly Pension is given to the Parson, &c. by composition, as satisfaction for his Tythes in kind. See 2. *Inst. fol.* 490.

Molendinum Bladonicum, *A Cornmill*, Ancient Charters have it *Molendinum bladum & molendinum de blado*: So a *Fulling-Mill* hath several *Latine* Appellations, as *Molendinum fullonicum* Molend. *fullanicum*, Molend. *fullere*, Molend. *fullarium*, &c. A Wind-Mill, *Molendinum ad ventum, vel ventriticum.* A Water-Mill, *Molendinum aquaticum.* A Horse-Mill, *Molendinum equitium.* A grinding or Griest-Mill, *Molendinum molare.* We read also for a Mill, *Molinum* and *Molinus*, *Doomsday*, tit. *Sudsex. Terra Comitis Rogeri*, num. 11. *Castrum Harundel*, T. R. E. *reddebat de quodam* Molino 40 s. & *ibidem alibi* T. R. E. *reddebat Oxenford*,-- *Comiti verò Algaro* 10. *libras adjuncto* molino, *quem infra civitatem habebat.*

Moyety, *Medietas*, Cometh of the French *Moitie* i. *coæqua vel media pars*, and signifies the half of any thing, *Lit. fol.* 125.

Molasses, Is the refuse Sirrup in the boyling of Sugar, which the Statute 12 *Car.* 2. *cap.* 25. prohibits to be mingled with Wine.

Molman, According to *Spelman*, signifies the Servants of a Monastery, *Fideles Ecclesiarum Ministeriales. Prior Lewens*, pag. 16. *Item omnis* Molman *inveniet equum si habuerit ad portandum corrodium Prioris*, &c. And again, pag. 21. *Omnis* Lanceta, *omnis* Toftman, & *omnis* Molman, (*qui* *non ſedet ſuper* Ogeland) *debent ſpargere unam* reiam de fiens, *&c.*

Monks Clothes, A certain kind of courſe Cloth, mentioned 20 *H.* 6. 20.

Monetagium, Mintage, The right and propriety of Coyning or Minting Money.

Moniers, *Monetarii*, Are Miniſters of the Mint, which make and Coyn the King's *Money*, *Reg. Orig. fol.* 262. and 1 *E.* 6. 15. It appears in ancient Authors, That the Kings of *England* had Mints in ſeveral Counties of this Realm; and in the *Tractate* in the *Exchequer*, written by *Ockham*, I find, that whereas Sheriffs were uſually obliged to pay into the King's Exchequer the King's ſterling *Money*, for ſuch Debts as they were to anſwer; they of *Cumberland* and *Northumberland* were admitted to pay in any ſort of *money* ſo it were Silver: And the reaſon is there given, becauſe thoſe two Shires *Monetarios de antiqua inſtitutione non habent.* Of later dayes the Title of *Moniers* hath been given to *Bankers*, that is, ſuch as make it their Trade to deal in *Monies* upon returns.

Money, *Moneta*, *Pecunia*, Is that Metal, be it Gold or Silver, that receives an authority by the Princes *Impreſa* to be currant; For as Wax is not a Seal without print, ſo Metal is not *Money* without Impreſſion, *Co.* on *Lit. pag.* 207.

Monopoly, May not improperly be derived from the Greek Μόνος *Solus*, and πωλέω *Vendo*, which ſignifies to ſell alone, and ſo is a Priviledge of the King (as ſome interpret it) by his Grant, Commiſſion, or otherwiſe, to any perſon or perſons of or for the ſole buying, ſelling, making, working, or uſing any thing, whereby any perſon or perſons are reſtrained of any freedom or liberty that they had before, declared againſt Law by 21 *Jac.* 3. except in ſome particular Caſes, concerning which ſee 3. *Inſt. fol.* 181. All *Monopolies* againſt *Magna Charta*, &c. *Co.* 2. *par. Inſt. cap.* 29. So then all incloſing is a *Monopoly*, which is poſitively contradicted in *More's Rep. fol.* 675. *Darcy* and *Allen's* Caſe, becauſe any Grant made by the King *pro bono Publico* is not a *Monopoly*. See *Grotius de jure belli & pacis.* 233.

Monſter, *Monſtrum*, A *Monſter* born within lawful Matrimony, that hath not humane ſhape, cannot purchaſe, much leſs retain any thing; but if he have humane ſhape, he may be Heir, though he have ſome deformity in any part of his Body.

Monſtrans de droit, Is as much as to ſay, The *ſhewing of Right*; In a legal ſenſe it denotes a Suit in *Chancery*, for the Subject to be reſtored to Land and Tenements, which he ſhews to be his Right, though by Office found to be in the poſſeſſion of another lately dead; by which Office the King is intituled to a Chattel, Freehold or Inheritance in the ſaid Lands. And this *Monſtrans de droit* is given by the Statutes 34 *E.* 3. *cap.* 14. and 36 *E.* 3. 13. See *Stamf. prærog. cap.* 21. and *Broke*, tit. *Petition*, and *Co.* 4. *Rep. fol.* 54. *Caſe of the Wardens and Commonalty of* Sadlers.

Monſtrans de faits ou Records, *Shewing of Deeds or Records is thus*, Upon an Action of Debt brought upon an Obligation, after the Plaintiff hath declared, he ought to ſhew his Obligation, and ſo it is of *Records*. And the difference between *Monſtrans de fait*, and *Oyer de faits* is this, He that pleads the Deed or *Records*, or declares upon it, ought to *ſhew* the ſame; and the other, againſt whom ſuch Deed or *Record* is pleaded, may demand *Oyer* of the ſame.

Monſtraverunt, Is a Writ that lies for the Tenants in *ancient Demeſne*, being diſtrained for the payment of any Toll or Impoſition, contrary to their liberty which they do or ſhould enjoy. See more in *F. N. B. fol.* 14.

Month or **Moneth**, *Menſis*, In Saxon *Monath*, is a ſpace of time containing by the week 28 dayes, by the *Calendar* ſometimes 30, ſometimes 31. See *Co. lib.* 6. *fol.* 61. and *Kalendar-moneth*. Some have derived it from μὴν, *menſis*, and that from μήνη, *Luna*, but we ſuppoſe more truly from the German *Mon* or *Man*, one of their antique Deities and Kings, mentioned by *Tacitus*, *Ex hoc*, ſayes the learned *Spelman*, *maſculino* (*ut Hebræi*) *Lunam dicunt genere*, Der mon, *dominamq; ejus & amaſiam è cujus aſpectu alias languet, alias reſipiſcit*, Die ſon *quaſi hunc Lunam, hanc ſolem, Hinc & Idolum Lunæ, viri fingebant ſpecie; non ut* Verſtegan *opinatur, fæminæ, ex quo & veſtem miram ad genua vix dimiſſam.*

Moot, Mota, *Curia*, *placitum*, *conventus*, From the Saxon *Gemote*, *conventus*, which may be deduced from the Saxon *Motian*, *placitare*. It is a Term well underſtood in the Inns of Court, to be that exerciſe, or arguing of Caſes, which young Students perform at appointed times, the better to enable them for practice and defence of Clients Cauſes. The places where *Moot-Caſes* were argued, was anciently called a *Moot-hall*. In the Inns of Courts there is a *Bayliff or Surveyor of the Moots* yearly choſen by the *Bench*, to appoint the *Mootmen* for the Inns of Chancery, and to keep account of performance of exerciſes both there and in the Houſe. See *Orig. Judiciales*, *fol.* 212.

Mootmen, Are thoſe that argue Readers Caſes (call'd alſo *Moot-caſes*) in the Houſes of Chancery, both in Term-time, and alſo in Vacations, *Coke's Rep.* 3. *par. in Proæmio.*

Moratur or **Demoratur in Lege**, Signifies as much as *He demurres*, becauſe the Party goes not forward in Pleading, but reſts upon the Judgment of the Court in the Point, who deliberate and take time to argue and adviſe thereupon, *Co.* on *Lit. fol.* 71. See *Demurrer*.

Moriam, Is all one in ſignification with the French *Morion*, i. *Caſſis*, a Head-piece, and that ſeems to be derived from the Italian *Morione*, *Anno* 4 & 5 P. & M. *cap.* 2. now called a *Pot*.

Morling alias **Mortling**, Is that Wooll taken from the ſkin of a dead Sheep, either dying of the Rot, or killed, 4 *E.* 4. 2. & 3. 27 *H.* 6. 2. This is written *Morkin*, 3 *Jac.* 18. *Morling or Shorling*, 3 *E.* 4. 1. and 14 *Car.* 2. 18. See *Shorling*.

Mort-dancestor. See *Aſſiſe*.

Mortgage, *Mortgagium*, *vel mortuum vadium*, Is compounded of two French words, *viz. Mort*, i. *Mors*, and *Gage*, i. *Pignus*: In Law it ſignifies a Pawn of Land or Tenement, or any thing moveable, laid or bound for Money borrowed, to be the Creditors for ever, if the Money be not paid at the day agreed upon: And the Creditor holding Land or Tenement upon this Bargain, is called *Tenant in Mortgage*. Of this we read in the

Grand Customary of *Normandy*, cap. 113. which see. *Glanvile* likewise, *lib.* 10. *cap.* 6. defineth it thus, *Mortuum vadium dicitur illud, cujus fructus vel reditus interim percepti in nullo se acquietant.* So you see it is called a *Dead Gage*, because whatsoever profit it yieldeth, yet it redeemeth not it self by yielding such profit, except the whole sum borrowed be paid at the day. See *Skene de verbor. Signif. verbo* Mortgage. He that pledgeth this Pawn or Gage, is called *The Mortgager*, and he that taketh it *The Mortgagee*, *West Symb.* part 2. tit. *Fines*, sect. 145. This, if it contain excessive Usury, is forbidden by 37 *H.* 8. *cap.* 9.

Mortmaine, *Manus mortua*, Is compounded of two French words, *Mort*, i. *mors*, & *maine*, i. *manus*: It signifies an alienation of Lands and Tenements to any Guild, Corporation or Fraternity, and their Successors, as Bishops, Parsons, Vicars, &c. which may not be done without the King's Licence, and the Lord of the Mannor, or of the King alone, if it be immediately holden of him. The reason of the name may be deduced from hence, because the Services, and other profits due, for such Lands as Escheats, &c. cometh into a *dead hand*, or into such a hand as holdeth them, and is not of power to deliver them, or any thing for them back again, *Magna Charta*, *cap.* 36. and 7 E. 1. commonly called *The Statute of Mortmaine*, and 18 *E.* 3. *Stat.* 3. *cap.* 3. and 15 *R.* 2. *cap.* 5. *Polydore Virgil* in the Seventeenth Book of his *Chronicles* mentions this Law, and giveth this reason of the Name, *Et Legem hanc manum mortuam vocarunt, quod res semel datas collegiis sacerdotum, non utiq; rursus venderentur, velut mortuæ, hoc est, usui aliorum mortalium in perpetuum adeptæ essent. Lex diligenter servatur, sic ut nihil possessionum ordini sacerdotali à quoquam detur, nisi Regio permissu*; But the forementioned Statutes be in some manner abridged by 39 *Eliz. cap.* 5. by which the Gift of Lands, &c. to Hospitals is permitted, without obtaining *Licenses in Mortmaine. Hotoman* in his Commentaries *De verbis feudalibus*, verbo *Manus mortua*, hath these words, *Manus mortua locatio est, quæ usurpatur de iis, quorum possessio (ut ita dicam) immortalis est, quia nunquam hæredem habere desinunt: Quâ de causâ res nunquam ad priorem dominum revertitur, nam manus pro possessione dicitur, mortua pro immortali, &c. Petrus Belluga in speculo principum*, fol. 76. *Jus amortizationis est licentia capiendi ad manum mortuam*: To the same effect read *Cassan. de consuet. Burgund. pag.* 348. 387, 1183, 1185, 1201, &c. *Skene de verb.* Signif. saith, *Dimittere terras ad* manum mortuam *est idem atq; dimittere ad multitudinem sive universitatem, quæ nunquam moritur, idq; per ἀνἴιφεασιν, seu à contrario sensu*, because Commonalties never die. The President and Governors for the Poor within the Cities of *London* and *Westminster*, may without *licence in Mortmain*, purchase Lands, &c. not exceeding the yearly value of 3000 pound, &c. by the Statute made 14 *Car.* 2. *cap.* 9.

Mortuary, *Mortuarium*, Is a Gift left by a man at his death to his Parish Church, for the recompence of his personal Tythes and Offerings not duly paid in his life-time. A *Mortuary* is not properly and originally due to an Ecclesiastical Incumbent from any, but those only of his own Parish. But by Custom in some places of this Kingdom, they are paid to the Parsons of other Parishes, as the Corps passes through them. *Mortuaries* formerly were payable in Beasts, but by 21 *H.* 8. *cap.* 6. an Order and Rate is set down for the payment of *mortuaries* in money. Their payment was enjoyned by the Statute of *Circumspecte agatis*. made 13 *E.* 1. and also by several Constitutions. *Mortuarium*, sayes *Linwood*, *sic dictum est, quia relinquitur Ecclesiæ pro anima defuncti*; In old time a *Mortuary* was called a *Corps-present*, (because the Beast was presented with the Body at the Funeral,) concerning which see *Dugdale's Antiquities of Warwickshire*, fol. 679. *Selden's History of Tythes*, pag. 287. 2. par. Inst. fol. 491. *Constit. Rob. Dunelm.* Ep. anno 1276. in Rubr. *De rebus liberorum Decimandis &* Mortuariis *inde solvendis. Et in textu---- De bonis propriis si existant* mortuarium *matrici Ecclesiæ solvere teneantur.*

Motbell, *Campana quâ Saxonibus nostris indici solebat conventus publicus qui* Folcmote *dicitur*, derived from *Mot*, *conventus*, and *Bell*, *campana.* Vide Leg. Edw. Conf. cap. 35.

Mosstroopers, A rebellious sort of Malefactors in the furthest North of *England*, that live by Robbery and Spoyl, not unlike the *Toryes in Ireland*, or the *Banditi in Italy*, for whose suppression, were made the Statutes 4 *Jac.* 1. 7 *Jac.* 1. and 14 *Car.* 2. *cap.* 22.

Mote, *Mota*, From the Saxon *Gemote*, *Curia*, *placitum*, *conventus*: As *Mota de Hereford*, i. *Curia vel placita Comitatus de Hereford.* In the Charter of *Maud*, the Empress Daughter of King *Henry* the First, we read thus, *Sciatis me fecisse Milonem de* Glocest. *Comitem de* Hereford *& dedisse ei* moram Herefordiæ *cum toto castello, &c.* Hence *Burgemote*, *curia vel conventus Burgi*; Swaingemot *curia vel conventus ministrorum scil. Forestæ, &c.* From this also we draw our word *Mote* or *Moot*, To plead. The *Scots* say to *Mute*, as the *Mute Hill at Scone*, i. *Mons placiti de Scona*; We commonly apply the word *Moot*, to that arguing of Cases used by young Students in the *Inns of Court* and *Chancery*. In the Charter of Peace between King *Stephen* and Duke *Henry*, afterwards King, it is taken to signifie a Fortress, as *Turris de* London *&* Mota *de* Windsor. The Tower of *London*, and Fortress of *Windsor*. *Mote* also signifies a standing Pool or Water to keep Fish in, or a great Trench of Water encompassing a Castle, or other Dwelling-house.

Muchehunt, *Habeant hi quatuor unam regalem potestatem (salva semper nobis nostra præsentia) quaterq; in anno Generales Forestæ demonstrationes & viridis & veneris forisfactiones quas* Muchehunt *dicunt, &c.* Vide Leg. de Foresta, R. Canuti, cap.

Mulier, As it is used in the Common Law, seems to be a word corrupted, and used for *Melior*, or the French *Melieur*, and signifies the *lawful Issue* preferred before an elder Brother born out of Matrimony, *Anno* 9 H. 6. 11. *Smith de Repub. Anglorum*, lib. 3. cap. 6. But by *Glanvile*, lib. 7. cap. 1. *The lawful Issue* seems rather *mulier* than *melior*, because it is begotten *è muliere*, and not *è concubina*; for he calls such Issue *Filios mulieratos*, opposing them to Bastards, and *Britton*, *cap.* 70. hath *frere mulier*, i. the Brother begotten of the Wife, opposite to *frere Bastard.* This appears to be used in *Scotland* also, For *Skene de verbor. Signific.*

Signific. sayes, That *Mulieratus filius* is a lawful Son begotten of a lawful Wife. A man hath a Son by a Woman before Marriage, that is, a *Bastard*, and unlawful, and after he Marries the Mother of the *Bastard*, and they have another Son; this second Son is called *Mulier*, that is to say *lawful*, and shall be Heir to his Father; but the other cannot be Heir to any man, because in Judgment of Law he is said to be *nullius filius*, or *filius populi*, according to the old Verses.

Cui pater est populus, Pater est sibi nullus & omnis,
Cui pater est populus, non habet ipse patrem.

And you alwayes find them distinguisht with this addition *Bastard eigne* and *Mulier puisne*. See *Co.* on *Lit. fol.* 170. & 243.

Mulierty, The being or condition of a *Mulier* or lawful Issue, *Co.* on *Lit.* fol. 352.

Mulmutius Laws, See *Law*.

Mulcta or **Multura Episcopi**, Is derived from the Latine word *Mulcta*, for that it was a Fine given to the King, that the Bishop might have power to make his last Will and Testament, and to have the Probate of other mens, and the granting Administrations, 2. *Inst. fol.* 491.

Multiplication, *Multiplicatio*, Multiplying or increasing; By a Statute made 5 *H.* 4. cap. 4. *It is Ordained and Established, That none from henceforth shall use to* multiply *Gold or Silver, nor use the craft of* Multiplication, *and if any the same do, he shall incur the pain of Felony*; And it was made upon a presumption that some persons skilful in Chymistry, could *multiply* or augment those Metals. And *Henry* the Sixth granted Letters Patent to some persons (who undertook to perform the same, and to find out the Philosophers Stone,) to free them from the penalty of the said Statute, *Rot. Pat.* 34. *Hen.* 6. *m.* 13. *Co.* 3 *Inst. fol.* 74.

Multitude, *Multitudo*, Must, according to some Authors, consist of ten persons, or more. But *Co.* on *Lit.* fol. 257. says, He never found it limited to any certain number, but left to the Discretion of the Judges.

A multo fortiori, Or *a minori ad majus*, Is an Argument often used by *Littleton*, and is framed thus. If it be so in a Feoffment passing a new Right, much more is it for the restitution of an ancient Right, &c. *Co.* on *Lit. fol.* 253. & 260.

Multure, *Molitura vel multura*, Is the Toll that the Miller takes for grinding of Corn; *Et totam sequelam Custumariorum meorum qui ad dictum molendinum bladum suum molent, ad sextum decimum vas & braseum suum sine multura*, Mon. Ang. 2 par. fol. 825.

Mundbrech, A compound of the Saxon *Mund*, i. *tutela*, *defensio*, and *Brice*, *fractio*, *violatio*; *Si Rex Ecclesiam, monasterium, burgum, hominem aliquem vel societatem, eorumve res aut prædia in suam susceperat protectionem dicebatur hoc omne & ejusmodi quicquid in Regis esse mundio* (in Saxon **On Cynings munde**,) *cujus violatio etiam* Mundbrice *dicta est q. protectionis violatio, aut datæ pacis fractio quæ in Anglorum lege* 5. *libris plectebatur*, Spelman's Gloss. *verbo* Mund. Some would have *Mundbrech* to signifie an infringement of Priviledges; others would that it denotes *Montis fracturam*, because *Mund* also is *mons*. But of later time it is expounded *clausarum fractio*, for *Mund* signifies *Clausarum munitio*, the fencing of Lands, therefore *Mundbrech* must be the breaking of those Fences which in many parts of *England* we call *Mounds*; and we say when Lands are fenced in and hedged, that they are *mounded*.

Mundeburde, *Mundeburdium*, A Saxon Compound of *Munde*, *defensio*, and *Bord* or *Borh*, i. *fidejussor*, so that *Mundeburd sit defensionis vel Patrocinii fidejussio*; from whence *Mundeburdus*, *advocatus*.

Muniments, *Munimenta*, Are authentick Deeds and Writings, by which a man may defend the Title to his Lands, *Episcopus cum munimentorum inspectionem habere non potuit, &c. Mat. Paris*, fol. 311. See *Minimentes*.

Muniment house, *Munimen*, In Cathedrals, Collegiate Churches, Castles, &c. is a little Room purposely made for keeping the Seal, Evidences, Charters, &c. of such Church, Colledge, &c. such Evidences being called *Muniments*, from *munio*, to defend, 3 *par. Inst. fol.* 170. 35 *H.* 6. *fol.* 37. *b.*

Murage, *Muragium*, Is a Toll or Tribute to be levyed, for the building or repairing of publick Walls, *F. N. B. fol.* 227. It is due either by Grant or Prescription, *Co.* 2. *par. Inst. fol.* 222. *Murage* seemeth also to be a liberty granted to a Town by the King, for the collecting money towards the walling of the same, *Anno* 3 *E.* 1. *cap.* 30.

Murder, *Murdrum*, May be derived either from the French *Meurtre*, *internecio*, or the Saxon *Mordren*, signifying the same thing; and according to our Law, is a wilful and felonious killing of another upon prepensed malice, whether secretly or openly, 52 *H.* 3. *cap.* 25. *West Symbol.* part 2. tit. *Indictments*, sect. 47. *Bracton*, *lib.* 3. *tract.* 2. *cap.* 15. *num.* 1. defineth it thus, *Homicidium quod nullo præsente, nullo audiente, nullo vidente clam perpetratur. Britton*, *cap.* 6. is of the same Opinion, so is *Fleta*, *lib.* 1. *cap.* 30. adding besides, that it was not *murder*, except it were proved the party slain was English, and no Forreiner: But *Stamf. pl. cor. lib.* 1. *cap.* 2. says, The Law in this point is altered by the Statute 14 *E.* 3. *cap.* 4. For now it is *murther*, when a man upon fore-thought malice kills another, whether privately or publickly, English-man or Foreigner living under the King's Protection. And this prepensed malice is two-fold; 1. Express, when it may be evidently proved that there was ill will. 2. Implyed, when one killeth another suddenly, having nothing to defend himself, as going over a Stile, or such like, *Cromp. Justice of Peace*, cap. *Of murder*, fol. 19. *Bro.* tit. *Quo warrant.* 2. See *Were*.

Murengers, Are two ancient Officers in the City of *Chester*, being two of the principal Aldermen, yearly elected to see the Walls kept in good repair; for the maintaining whereof, they receive several Tolls and Customs.

Muster, Cometh of the French *Moustre*, i. *specimen*, *exemplum*, as *Faire moustre Generale de tout son armie*, is as much as *lustrare exercitum*. The signification is well known to *muster an Army*. So *mustred of Record*, 18 H. 6. cap. 19. is to be enrolled

rolled in the number of the King's Souldiers, *Master of the King's Musters*, 2 E. 6. 2. See in *Muster*.

Muster-Master General, *Anno* 35 *El. cap.* 4. See *Master of the King's Musters*.

Mute, *Mutus*, Speechless, or that refuses to speak; A Prisoner may stand *mute* two manner of wayes, 1. When he stands *mute*, without speaking of any thing, and then it shall be enquired whether he stood *mute* of Malice, or by the act of God; and if it be found that it was by the act of God, then the Judge of the Court *ex Officio* ought to inquire whether he be the same Person, and of all other Pleas, which he might have pleaded, if he had not stood *mute*. 2. When he pleads, Not Guilty, or doth not answer directly, or will not put himself upon the Enquest, to be tryed by God and the Country, *Co.* 2. *par. Inst. cap.* 12. 32 *H.* 8. 3. See *Paine fort et dure*. *Mute* also signifies a *Kennel, or cry of Hounds*, as *Bailler la meute & rovi à un Cerfe*, to follow after him with a full cry, *Spelman*.

Mysterium, Vide *Misterium*.

N.

Naam, *Namium*, From the Saxon *Name*, *captio*, signifies the taking another mans moveable Goods, and is either lawful or unlawful; *Lawful Naam* is a reasonable Distress, proportionable to the value of the thing distrained for; and this *Naam* was anciently called either *vif*, or *mort*, quick or dead, according as it is made of dead or living Chattels: *Lawful Naam* is so, either by the Common Law, or by a mans particular Fact: By the Common Law, as when one taketh another mans Beasts Damage feasant in his Ground. By a mans particular Fact, as by reason of some Contract made, that for default of payment of an Annuity agreed upon, it shall be lawful to distrain in such and such Lands, &c. *Horne's Mirror of Justices*, lib. 2. cap. *De Naam*. See *Withernam*. From hence comes *Namatio*, the taking or impounding. *Namatus* distrained, see *Skene de Verb.* Signif. *verbo* Namare. In the Laws of *Canutus*, M. S. *cap.* 18. we read *Et nemo* Namium *capiat in Comitatu vel extra Comitatum, priusquam ter in Hundredo suo rectum sibi perquisierit*. And in the *Charter of Henry the First*, of the Liberties of *London*, *Quod si reddere noluerint (debitores) nec ad disrationandum venire, tunc cives quibus debita sua debent, capiant in civitate* Namia *sua vel de Comitatu in quo manet qui debitum debet*. and in *Mon. Angl.* 2. par. fol. 256. *Non licebit* Namium *sumere vel vadimonium nec averia sua imparchiare*, Spelm. Gloss. *verbo* Namium.

Nabulum, *Merces nautica*, Spelman.

Nasse, Seems to be the proper name of *Orford* Haven, 4 *H.* 7. 22.

Nathwayte, ——*Quod nec dictus Philippus de Avery nec hæredes sui de cætero petere possint aliqua tallagia nec etiam Francum plegium nec etiam aliam demandam quæ vocatur* Nathwite: *Charta* 55 H. 3. m. 6.

Nativity, *Nativitas*, Birth, casting the *Nativity*, or by Calculation, seeking to know how long the Queen should live, &c. made Felony, 23 *Eliz.* 2. *Nativitas* was anciently taken for *Bondage* or *Villenage*, *Terram quam* nativi *sui tenueruut de se in* nativitate, Mon. Ang. 2. par. fol. 643.

Nativo habendo, Was a Writ that lay to the Sheriff for a Lord, whose Villain claimed for his Inheritance, run from him, for the apprehending and restoring him to his Lord again, *Reg. Orig. fol.* 87. *F. N. B. fol.* 77. See the Charter of *Richard* the Second, by which he manumitted all in the County of *Hertford*, *Walsingham*, pag. 254.

Nativus, He that is born a Servant, and so differs from him that suffers himself to be sold; of which Servants there are three sorts, *Bondmen*, *Natives* and *Villeins*; *Bondmen* were those who bound themselves by Covenants to serve, and took their name from the word *Bond*. *Natives*, we spoke of just before; And *Villains* were such who belonging to the Land, till the Lords Demesnes, nor may depart thence without the Lords Licence, *Spelman's Gloss.* ——*Quod si aliquis* Nativus *alicujus in præfato Burgo manserit & terram in eo tenuerit & fuerit in prædicta Gilda & Hansa &* Loth *&* Scoth *cum eisdem Burgensibus nostris per unum annum & unum diem sine calumpnia, deinceps non possit repeti à Domino suo, ut in eodem Burgo liber permaneat*, Carta, Hen. 3. *Burgensibus Mungumery*.

Native tenentes, *Sunt (ipsi etiam liberi) qui terram tenent* Nativam, *hoc est*, nativorum *servitiis obnoxiam*, Spelman.

Naturalization, *Naturalizatio*, Is when an Alien born, is made the King's *natural* Subject. See *Denizen*. And this saith *Spelman*, *Regio diplomate & Senatus-consulto expetendum est. Potest autem virtute Regii Diplomatis denizationem, hoc est, Municipium consequi, quo prædia comparet, possideat, disponat, muniaq; omnia subeat uti* naturalis *indigena*; *hæreditariè tamen nil adeat simplici hoc nomine: Sed* naturalizationis *pallio indutus omnem adipiscitur plenitudinem*.

Ne admittas, Is a Writ that lyeth for the Plaintiff in a *Quare Impedit*, or him that hath an Action of Darrein Presentment depending in the Common-Bench, and feareth that the Bishop will admit the Clerk of the Defendant, during the Suit between them; which Writ must be sued within six Months after the avoidance, because after six Months the Bishop may present by Lapse, *Reg. Orig. fol.* 31. *F. N. B. fol.* 37.

Neatland, *Terra Villanorum*, Land let or granted out to the Yeomanry, *Ex vet. Charta*.

Negative pregnant, *Negativa prægnans*, Is a *negative* implying also an affirmative: As if a man being impleaded to have done a thing on such a day, or in such a place, denyeth that he did it *modo & forma declarata*, which implyeth nevertheless, that in some sort he did it; Or if a man be said to have aliened Land in Fee, and he saith he hath not aliened in Fee, this is a *negative, pregnant*; for though it be true that he hath not aliened in fee, yet it may be, he hath made an Estate in tail, *Dyer*, *fol.* 17. *num.* 95. And *Brook hoc titulo*, and *Kitchin*, *fol.* 232. and the *Termes of the Law*. We read also in some Civilians of *Affirmativa prægnans*, and that is, *quæ habet in se inclusivam* negativam *& hoc importare videntur dictiones (solum & tantum) qua implicant* negativam.

Pacianus

Pacianus de probationibus, lib. 1. cap. 31. num. 16. fol. 93.

Neife, *Nativa*, From the French *Naif*, *naturalis*, Is a Bond-woman, *Anno* 1 E. 6. 3. and 9 R. 2. *cap.* 2. But if she marry a Free-man, she is thereby made free; and if she be once free, and clearly discharged of all Bondage, she cannot be *Neif* after, without some special act done by her, as Divorce, or Confession in Court of Record; and that is in favour of liberty, and therefore a free Woman shall not be bound by taking a Villain to her Husband; but their Issue shall be Villains as their Father was, which is contrary to the Civil Law, which sayes, *Partus sequitur ventrem.* See *Manumission.*

Writ of Neifty, Was a Writ whereby the Lord claimed such a Woman for his *Neif*, wherein but two *Neifs* could be put; but it is now quite out of use.

Neophyte, A Learner in any thing, *Tyro*; we call such a one a *Novice.*

Ne injuste vexes, Is a Writ which lies for a Tenant that is distrained by his Lord, for other Services than he ought to make, and is a prohibition to the Lord in it self, commanding him not to distrain: The special use of it is, where the Tenant hath formerly prejudiced himself, by performing more Services, or paying more Rent, without constraint, than he needed; for in this Case, by reason of the Lords Seisin, he cannot avoid him in *Avowry*, and therefore is driven to this Writ as his next remedy, *Reg. Orig. fol.* 4. *F.N.B. fol.* 10.

Nesse. See *Nasse.*

Ne vice-comes colore mandati Regis quenquam amoveat à possessione Ecclesiæ minus justè, Regist. Orig. fol. 61.

Niderling, alias **Nidering**, alias **Nithing**, *Gulie. Malmes*, pag. 121. In the life of *William Rufus*, hath these words, *Anglos suos appellat (Rex) & jubet ut compatriotas advocent ad obsidionem venire, nisi si qui velint sub nomine* nidering *quod* nequam *sonat remanere; Angli qui nihil miserius putarunt quam hujusce vocabuli dedecore aduri, catervatim ad Regem confluunt & invincibilem exercitum faciunt.* And *Mat. Paris* in Anno 1088. pag. 14. *Ut ad obsidionem veniant jubet, nisi velint sub nomine* Nithing *quod Latinè* nequam *sonat recenseri, &c.*

Nient comprise, Is an exception taken to a Petition as unjust, because the thing desired is not contained in that Act or Deed whereon the Petition is grounded. For example, One desireth of the Court to be put into possession of a House, formerly among other Lands, &c. adjudged unto him: The adverse party pleadeth, That this Petition is not to be granted, because though he had a Judgment for certain Lands and Houses, yet the House, into the possession whereof he desireth to be put, is not contained among those for which he had Judgment. See the *New Book of Entries, titulo* Nient comprise.

Nifle, *Anno* 3 *E.* 4. *cap.* 5. The word is mentioned, and seems to signifie a thing of little value; It may be a corruption of *nihil*, but neither *Cowell* nor *Spelman* have given it any interpretation.

Nihil or **Nichil**, Is a word which the Sheriff answers, that is apposed concerning Debts illeviable, and that are nothing worth, by reason of the insufficiency of the Parties from whom they are due; 5 R. 2. *Stat.* 1. *cap.* 3. and 27 *Eliz. cap.* 3. *Accounts of* Nihil *shall be put out of the Exchequer*, 5 R. 2. Stat. 2. cap. 13.

Nihil dicit, Is a fayling to put in Answer to the Plea of the Plaintiff by the day assigned, which if a man omit, Judgment passeth against of course by *nihil dicit*, that is, because he sayes nothing in his own defence, why it should not.

Nihil capiat per Breve, Is the Judgment given against the Plaintiff, either in bar of his Action, or in abatement of his Writ, *Co.* on *Lit.* fol. 363.

Nihil capiat per billam, See *Nihil capiat per breve.*

Nisi prius, Is a Writ judicial, which lyeth in case where the Jury is impannell'd, and returned before the Justices, the one Party or the other requesting to have this Writ for the ease of the Country, whereby the Sheriff is willed to cause the Enquest to come before the Justices in the same County at their coming. See 14 *E.* 3. *cap.* 15. The form of the Writ you have in the *Old Nat. Brev. fol.* 159. and in the *Register Judicial, fol.* 7. & 28. & 75. *New Book of Entries, verbo* Nisi Prius. And it is called a Writ of *Nisi Prius*, of these words, whereby the Sheriff is commanded to bring to *Westminster* the men impannelled at a certain day, or before the Justices of the next Assises, *Nisi die Lunæ apud talem locum* prius *venerint, &c.* And the Justices of *Nisi Prius* must be one of them before whom the Cause is depending in the Bench, *F.N.B. fol.* 240. which he taketh from the *Statute of York*, *Anno* 12 *E.* 2. See *Westm.* 2. *cap.* 30. 13 *E.* 1. and 27 *E.* 1. *cap.* 4. 2 *E.* 3. *cap.* 17. & 4 *E.* 3. *cap.* 11. & 14 *E.* 3. *cap.* 16. 7 R. 2. *cap.* 7. and 18 *Eliz. cap.* 12.

Niger Liber, Is the *Black-Book* in the Exchequer so called.

Nobilis, A Noble, an ancient kind of English-money now not in use; the value thereof, in the thirty fourth year of *Edward* the Third, being 1360. appears in the Letters of *John* King of *France*, upon the Treaty of Peace between the same two Kings, where *Art.* 13. you have these words, ---- *Item accorde est, que le Roy de* France *payera au Roy d' Angleterre trois milions d'escus d'or, dont les deux valent un* noble *de la money d' Angleterre.* We at this day value a *noble* at six shillings eight pence, but have no peculiar Coyn of that name.

Nobilitas, Nobility compriseth all degrees of Dignity above a Knight, so that a Baron is the lowest Order thereof, *Smith* de Repub. Ang. lib. 1. cap. 17. *Bartolus* in his *Tract de Nobilitate*, lib. 12. defines it thus, *Nobilitas est qualitas illata*, &c.

Noctes & noctem de firma, We often meet in *Doomsday* with *Tot* noctes *de firma*, *vel firma tot* noctium, which is to be understood of entertainment for so many nights. See *Doomsday, tit.* Essexa. *Rex Hundred de* Chemeresford *writelam tunc reddit hoc manerium decem* noctes *de firma & 10. lib. &c.* Our Ancestors, the English *Saxons*, were accustomed to reckon their times by the Nights, which Custome we still retain, when we say

say for a single Week, a **Senight**, quasi *seven-night*, that is, *septem noctes*; and so for two weeks, a **Fornight**, quasi *fourteen-nights*, (i.) *quatuordecem* noctes.

Nocumentum. See *Nusance.*

Nodfyrs alias **Nedfri**, Was a word well known among the *Saxons* to signifie necessary Fire, being derived from the Saxon Neb, that is, necessary and *fyr*, *ignis*: But the learned *Spelman* is of opinion from the old Saxon *Neod*, (i.) *obsequium*; so that *Nodfyrs* were Fires made in honour of the Heathenish Deities. Vide *Proemium Eadgari Regis de Cœnobitis Regularibus introducendis, &c.*----

Nomenclator, One that enucleates and opens the Etymologies of Names. *Spelman* verbo *Nomenclator*, interprets it to be *Thesaurarius*.

Nomination, *Nominatio*, Is used as well by the Canonists as Common-Lawyers, and taken for a Power, that a man by vertue of a Mannor, or otherwise, hath to appoint a Clerk to a Patron of a Benefice, by him to be presented to the Ordinary.

Nons, **Nonæ**, According to the *Romans* Account were those dayes which at the beginning of some Months had six, of others had four dayes, according to the Verses,

> *Sex* Nonas *Maius, October, Julius & Mars,*
> *Quatuor at reliqui, &c.*----

Spelman in his *Glossary* interprets it for *Meridies*, Midday, Dinner-time, which we in English call *Noon* and *Noontide*, which is as much as if we should say in Latine *Horam nonam*, id est, *Pomeridianam tertiam, non meridiem*, and as he inferrs, *Ratio à Romanorum cœna ducta est, quæ hora diei* nona *est, nec solenniter antè comedebant.*

Nonability, Is an exception taken against the Plaintiff or Defendant, upon some cause why he cannot commence Suit in Law, as *Præmunire, Outlary, Profest in Religion, Excommunicate, or a Stranger born*, which last holds only in Actions real and mixt, and not in personal, except he be a Stranger and an Enemy. The *Civilians* say, That such a man hath not *Personam standi in judicio*. See *Bro. hoc titulo*, and F. N. B. *fol.* 35. 65. & 77.

Non admittas. See *Ne admittas.*

Nonage, Is all that time of a mans age, under one and twenty years in some Cases, and fourteen in others, as Marriage. See *Broke*, tit. *Age*. Vide *Age*.

Non capiendo Clericum. See *Clericum non capiendo.*

Nonclaime, Is the omission, or neglect, of him that ought to challenge his Right within a time limited, by which neglect he is either barred of his Right, as at this day upon *Nonclaime* within five years after a Fine, and Right to him accrued, by the Statute of 4 *H.* 7. 24. Or of his Entry by his descent, for want of *Claime*, within five years after the *Disseisin*, made by the Stat. 32 *H.* 8. 33. Vide *Co. lib.* 4. *in Proœm.* and *Continual Claim.*

Non compos mentis, That is, not of sound memory or understanding, which are four-fold, 1. An *Ideot à Nativitate*, is *non compos mentis*. 2. He that by accident afterwards wholly loseth his memory and understanding. 3. A Lunatick, that hath *Lucida intervalla*, sometimes his understanding, and sometimes not. 4. He that by his own act for a time depriveth himself of his right mind, as a Drunkard; but this last kind shall give no priviledge to him or his Heirs. See *Co. lib.* 4. *fol.* 124. *Beverlye's* Case.

Non distringendo, Is a Writ comprising under it divers particulars, according to divers Cases, which see in the Table of *Reg. Orig.* verb. *Non distringendo.*

Non est Culpabilis, Is the general Plea to an Action of Trespass, whereby the Defendant doth absolutely deny the Fact imputed to him by the Plaintiff, whereas in other special Cases the Defendant but alledgeth some reason in his own defence: And therefore when the Rhetoricians comprise the substance of their Discourses under three Questions, *An sit, quid sit, quale sit.* This Answer falleth under the first of the three, and as it is the general answer in an Action of Trespass, that is, an Action criminal civilly prosecuted; so is it also in all Actions criminally followed, either at the Suit of the King, or other, wherein the Defendant denyeth the Crime objected unto him. See the *New Book of Entries*, tit. *Non culpabilis*, and *Stamf. Pl. Cor.* lib. 2. cap. 62.

Non est factum, Is an Answer to a Declaration, whereby a man denyeth that to be his Deed, whereupon he is impleaded, *Bro. hoc tit.*

Non implacitando aliquem de libero tenemento sine brevi, Is a Writ to inhibit Bayliffs, &c. from distraining any man without the King's Writ touching his Free-hold, *Register, fol.* 171.

Non intromittendo, quando breve de Præcipe in Capite subdole impetratur, Is a Writ directed to the Justices of the Bench, or in *Eyr*, willing them not to give one that hath under colour of intituling the King to Land, &c. as holding of him *in Capite*, deceitfully obtained the Writ called *Præcipe in Capite*, but to put him to this Writ of Right, if he think good to use it, *Reg. Orig. fol.* 4. *b.*

Non Mercandizando Victualia, Is a Writ directed to the *Justices of Assise*, commanding them to inquire whether the Officers of such a Town do sell Victuals in gross, or by retail, during their Office, contrary to the Statute, and to punish them if they find it true, *Register of Writs, fol.* 184.

Non molestando, Is a Writ that lyeth for him which is *molested* contrary to the King's Protection granted him, *Register of Writs, fol.* 24.

Non obstante, (Which signifies Notwithstanding,) Is a Clause frequent in Statutes and Letters Patent. *All Grants of such Pensions, and every* non obstante *therein contained shall be void*, 14 Car. 2. cap. 11. *Croke's* Rep. 3. par. fol. 196. and *Plowd. Com. fol.* 501, 502. In the Reign of King *Henry* the Third, (sayes Sir *Richard Baker*.) The Clause *non obstante* (first brought in by the *Pope*) was taken up by the King in his Grants and Writings. See *Prynne's Animadversions* on 4. *Inst. fol.* 129.

Non

Non omitt. propt. aliquam libertat. Is a Writ that lies where the Sheriff returns upon a Writ to him directed, that he hath sent to the Bayliff of such a Franchise which hath the return of Writs, and he hath not served the Writ, then the Plaintiff shall have this Writ directed to the Sheriff to enter into the Franchise, and execute the King's Process himself, *Old Nat. Brev. fol.* 44. Of this the *Register Original* hath three sorts, *fol.* 82. & 151. and the *Register Judicial* one, *fol.* 5. & 56. Also the Sheriff shall warn the Bayliff, That he be before the Justices at the Day contained in the Writ, and if he come not, then all the *Judicial* Writs during the same Plea issuing, shall be Writs of *non omittas*, and the Sheriff shall execute the same. See *Termes de la Lay, hoc tit.*

Non Ponendis in Assisis & Juratis, Is a Writ founded upon the *Statute of Westm.* 2. *cap.* 38. and *Articuli super Chartas*, cap. 9. which is granted upon divers Causes to Men, for the freeing them from *Assises* and *Jurors*. See *F. N. B. fol.* 165. and the *Register*, *fol.* 100. 119, 181, 183.

Non Procedendo ad Assisam Rege inconsulto, Is a Writ to stop the Tryal of a Cause appertaining unto one that is in the King's Service, &c. until the King's Pleasure be farther known, *Register*, *fol.* 220.

Non residentia pro Clericis Regis, Is a Writ directed to the Ordinary, charging him not to molest a Clerk imployed in the King's Service, by reason of his *non-residence*, *Reg. Orig. fol.* 58.

Non Residence, 28 *H.* 8. 13. Is applyed to such spiritual Persons as are not resident, but do absent themselves for the space of one or two Months at several times in one Year from their Benefices; for *Personal residence* is required of Ecclesiastical Persons upon their Cures. See 2. *par. Inst. fol.* 625.

Non solvendo pecuniam ad quam Clericus mulctatur pro non residentia, Is a Writ prohibiting an Ordinary to take a pecuniary mulct imposed upon a Clerk of the King for *non Residence*, Reg. Orig. fol. 59.

Non suite, Is a renouncing of the *Suit* by the Plaintiff or Demandant, most commonly upon the discovery of some Error or Defect, when the matter is so far proceeded in, as the Jury is ready at the Bar to deliver their Verdict, 2 *H.* 4. 7. See the *New Book of Entries*, verbo *Nonsuit*. The *Civilians* term it *Litis renunciationem*, See 23 *H.* 8. *cap.* 15. 8 *Eliz. cap.* 2. and 4 *Jac. cap.* 3. whereby he that is *non suit* shall pay Costs to the Defendant.

Non sum informatus. See *Informatus non sum.*

Non sane memory, *Non sanæ memoriæ*, Is an exception taken to an Act declared by the Plaintiff or Demandant, to be done by another, whereupon he grounds his Plaint or Demand: And the effect of it is, that the Party that did that Act was mad, or not well in his Wits when he did it. See the *New Book of Entries*, titulo *Non sanæ memoriæ & dum non fuit compos mentis.* See also before *Non compos mentis.*

Non tenure, Is an exception to a Count, by saying, That he holdeth not the Land specified in the Count, or at least some part of it, 25. *E.* 3. *Stat.* 4. *cap.* 16. *West Symbol.* part 2. tit. *Fines*, sect 138. makes mention of *non tenure general*, and *non tenure special*. See the *New Book of Entries* verbo *Non tenure*, where 'tis said, That *special non tenure* is an exception, alledging that he was not Tenant the day when the Writ was purchased. *Non tenure general*, is when one denies himself ever to have been Tenant to the Land in question.

Non terme, *Non terminus*, Is the time of Vacation between *Term* and *Term*: It was wont to be called the time or Dayes of the King's Peace, *Lamb. Archaionom.* fol. 126. and that these were in the time of King *Edward* the Confessor, see there. This time, by the *Romans*, was called *Justitium* or *Feriæ*, or *dies nefasti*; *Feriæ appellari notum est tempus illud, quod forensibus negotiis & jure dicendo vacabat; Earum autem aliæ solennes erant, aliæ repentinæ, Brisson. de verb.* Signif. *lib.* 6. *Wesenbec. paratit. de feriis*, num. 6.

Nooke of Land, *Noka terræ. universis pateat quod ego* J. *quæ fui uxor* W. B. ---- *tradidi, &c.* H. A. *unum mess. & unam* Nokam *terræ cum pertin. in villa de* M. Dat. *apud Sodynton*, 5 E. 3.

Norroy, As much to say as *Northroy*, that is, the Northern King: The third of the three Kings at Arms, and his Office, lies on the North-side of *Trent*, as *Clarentius* on the South: He is mentioned in the Statute 14 *Car.* 2. *cap.* 33. See *Herald.*

Notary, *Notarius*, Mentioned 27 *E.* 3. 1. Is a Scribe, or Scrivener, that makes short draughts of Writings and other Instruments. At this day we call him a *Notary*, or *Publick Notary*, that attests Deeds or Writings to make them authentick in another Country, but principally in business relating to Merchants.

Note of a Fine, *Nota finis*, Is a brief of a *Fine* made by the *Chirographer*, before it be ingrossed; the form whereof see in *West Symbol.* part 2. tit. *Fines*, sect. 117.

Not Guilty. See *Non est Culpabilis.*

Novale, Seems to be Land newly plowed, that without memory of man had not been tilled. *Item nota quod* Novale *est ager nunc primum præcisus & quod* Novale *semel fuit, semper erit* Novale, *quo ad decimarum retentionem vel solutionem.* Ex cartulario Abbathiæ de Furnesse in Com. Lanc. in Officio Ducat. Lanc. fol. 41. b.

Novel Assignment, *Nova assignatio*, Is an *assignment* of Time, Place, or such like, otherwise than as it was before *assigned*, *Bro.* tit. *Deputy*, num. 12. See *Novel assignment of Trespass* in a new place, after Bar pleaded, *Bro.* tit. *Trespass* 122. and *Novel assignment* in a Writ *de ejectione custodiæ*, tit. *Ejectione custodiæ*, num. 7. See *Assignment.*

Noyles, *No person shall put any* Noyles, *Flocks, Thrums, Hair, or other deceiveable thing into any broad Wollen Cloth, &c.* 22. Jac. 18.

Nude Contract, *Nudum Pactum*, Is a bare promise of a thing, without any consideration; and therefore we say, *Ex* nudo pacto *non oritur actio.*

Nude Matter. See *Matter.*

Nummata terræ, Is the same with *Denariatus terræ*, and thought to contain an Acre, *Sciatis me*

(*sc.* Will. Longespee) *dedisse & concessisse Ecclesiæ S.* Mariæ *de* Walsingham *et Canonicis ibidem Deo Servientibus in perpetuam Eleemosynam* 40. Nummatas terræ *in* Walsingham, *quæ fuit Archetel & Brinig fratris ejus de socca Wihctune, libere, quiete & honorifice absque omni servitio & omni consuetudine.* Spelman.

Nuncupative Will. See *Will.*

Nunne, *Nonna,* Signifies a holy or consecrated Virgin, or a Woman that hath by Vow bound her self to a single and chast Life in some Place and Company of other Women, separated from the World, and devoted to an especial Service of God by Prayer, Fasting, and such like holy Exercises. St. *Hierome* tells us, This is an *Egyptian* Word, as *Hospinian* recordeth of him in the Book *De Origine & Progressu Monachatus,* fol. 2.

Nuncius, We may call him an *Apparitor, Sergeant,* or *Beadle.*

Nuper obiit, Is a Writ that lies for a Coheir, being deforced by her Co-parcener of Lands or Tenements, of which the Grand-Father, Father, Uncle or Brother to them both, or any other their common Ancestor, died seised of an Estate in Fee-simple. See the Form of the Writ, *Reg. Orig. fol.* 226. *&c.* and *Fitzh Nat. Brev. fol.* 197. But if the Ancestor died seised in fee tayl, then the Co-Heir deforced shall have a *Formedon, ibid.* But where the Ancestor was once seised, and died not seised of the Possession, but in Reversion; in such case a Writ of *Rationabli parte* lies for the Party.

Nusance, (*Nocumentum,*) Cometh of the French *Nuire,* i. *Nocere,* and signifies not only a thing done whereby another Man is annoyed in his free Lands or Tenements, but the Assise or Writ lying for the same, *Fitz. Nat. Brev. fol.* 183. And this Writ *de Nocumento,* or of *Nusance,* is either simply *de Nocumento,* or *de parvo nocumento,* and then it is *Vicountiel,* Old Nat. Brev. *fol.* 108. 109. *F. N. B. fol.* 183. 184. *Britton* calls it *Nosance,* whom read *cap.*61,62. *Manwood* in his *Forest Laws,* cap. 17. makes three sorts of *Nusance* in the Forest: The first is, *Nocumentum commune.* The second, *Nocumentum speciale.* The third, *Nocumentum generale,* which you may read there, (for I will not insist upon the distinction.) See *Reg. Orig. fol.* 197. & 199. *Co. Rep. Williams* Case. In stead of this, now generally are brought Actions of Trespass, and upon the Case.

Nutmegs, *Nuces muscatæ,* Is a Spice well known to all, described in *Gerards Herbal,* lib. 3. cap. 145. and mentioned among Spices that are to be garbled, 1 *Jac.* 19.

O.

O *Ni.* In the Exchequer, as soon as a Sheriff enters into his Accounts, for Issues, Amerciaments, and mean Profits, they set upon his Head this mark *O Ni.* which denotes *Oneratur, nisi habet sufficientem exonerationem,* and thereupon he forthwith becomes the King's Debtor, and a *Debet* set upon his Head, and then the Parties *Peravayle,* become Debtors to the Sheriff and discharged against the King, *Co.* 4. *Inst. fol.* 116.

Oale-Gavel. See *Gavel-fester.*

Oate-Gavel. See *Gavel.*

Oath, *Juramentum,* Is an Affirmation, or denyal by any Christian of any thing lawful and honest before one or more that have Authority to give the same, for the advancement of Truth and Right, calling Almighty God to Witness, that his Testimony is true: It is called a *Corporal Oath,* because he toucheth with his Hand some part of the *Holy Scripture,* Co. 3. par. Inst. cap. 74. The Law esteems it the best means to search out the Truth, by the *Oaths of honest, lawful, and indifferent Persons*; and therefore it is fitly termed *Sacramentum,* an holy Band, or sacred Tye, or godly Vow. Some do call it *Firmamentum veritatis,* the foundation and ground of Truth; Others *Vinculum pacis,* and if it be taken and found by a whole Jury, it is called *Veredictum,* a Verdict. *Pulton de Pace Regis & Regni.* See the Book of *Oaths,* lately set out and Printed.

Obedientia, Was a Rent, as appears out of *Roger Hoveden, parte poster. annal. suor.* pag. 430. in these words, *Ut ergo eis (sc. regularibus) adimatur opportunitas evagandi, prohibemus, ne redditus quod* Obedientias *vocant ad firmam teneant, &c.* In the Common-Law it is used for an Office, or administration of an Office; and thereupon the word *Obedientiales* is used in the Provincial Constitutions, for those which have the execution of any Office under their Superiors, *cap. prim. de Statu regulæ.* For thus saith *Linwood* in his gloss upon that Word, *Hi sunt qui sub* Obedientia *suorum Prælatorum sunt et habent certa Officia administranda interius vel exterius.* It may be that some of these Offices call'd *Obedientia,* consisted in the collection of Rents or Pensions, and that therefore those Rents were by a *Metonymie,* call'd *Obedientia quia colligebantur ab Obedientialibus.*

Obit, A latine Word signifying a Funeral Solemnity, or an Office for the Dead, most commonly performed at the Funeral, when the Corps lye in the Church uninterred: Also the Anniversary Office, *Cro.* 2. *par. fol.* 51. *Holloway's* Case. It was held 14 *Eliz. Dyer* 313. That the tenure of *Obit* or *Chantry* Lands held of Subjects, is extinct by the Act of 1 *E.* 6. 14. See 15 *Car.* 2. *cap.* 9.

Oblata, Properly Offerings: But in the Exchequer it signifies old Debts, brought together from precedent Years, and put to the present Sheriffs Charge. See the *Practice of the Exchequer,* pag. 78. Also Gift made to the King by any of his Subjects, which were so carefully taken notice of in the Reigns of King *John* and *Henry* the Third, that they were entred in the fine Rolls under the Title *Oblata*; concerning which see Mr. *Philips* his Book of the Antiquity and Legality of Royal Purveyance, *Spelmans Glossary,* and *Prynnes Aurum Reginæ.*

Oblations, *oblationes,* Are thus defined in the Canon Law, *Oblationes dicuntur, quæcunque a piis fidelibusque Christianis offeruntur Deo & Ecclesiæ sive res soli sive mobiles sint; nec refert an tegentur testamento, an aliter donentur,* cap. *Clerici* 13. quæst. 2. Read more thereof in *Duarenus de sacr. Eccl. Minister. ac. benefi.* cap. *tertio,* 12 Car. 2. cap. 11.

Obligation, *Obligatio,* Is a Bond containing a Penalty, with a Condition annext, either for payment

payment of Money, performance of Covenants, or the like, and so differs from a Bill that hath no Penalty nor Condition; and yet a Bill may be Obligatory. See *Co.* on *Lit. fol.* 172. and *West Symbol.* part 1. lib. 2. sect. 146.

Obligor, Is he that enters into such an *Obligation*, and *Obligee* the Person to whom it is entred into. In the *Saxons* Time, Writings were made firm with Golden Crosses, but the *Normans* put to them a Seal of Wax, and the testimony of three or four Witnesses.

Obolata terræ, In the Opinion of some contains half an Acre of Land, Others but half a Perch. *Thomasius* sayes, *Obolum terræ* is ten foot in length, and five in breadth. See *Fardingdele*, and *Spelman's Glossary* more at large upon this Word.

Obventions, *Obventiones*, Offerings, 2. *Inst. fol.* 661. Also Rents or Revenues properly of Spiritual Livings, 12 *Car.* 2. *cap.* 11.

Occasio, Is, according to *Spelman*, taken for an Impediment in the Charter of Liberties of *Henry* the First, We have these Words, *Quorum Regnum oppressum erat injustis* occasionibus *& exactionibus*, and in Chart. Forest, cap. 12. *unusquisque liber homo de cætero sine* occasione *faciat in bosco suo vel in terra sua —— molendina, vivaria, &c.*

Occationes, (in some Authors corruptly written *Occasiones*) are *Assarts*, whereof *Manwood* speaks at large; The word is derived *ab Occando*, i. e. Harrowing or breaking Clods: See *Spelman's Glossary*, verbo *Essartum.*

Occupant, If Tenant *pur terme de auter vie* dies, living *Cestuy que vie*; he that first enters shall hold the Land, during that other Man's Life, and he is in Law call'd an *Occupant*, because his Title is by his first *occupation*; and so if Tenant for his own Life, grant over his Estate to another, if the Grantee dies, there shall be an *Occupant*, *Co.* on *Lit. cap.* 6. *sect.* 56. and *Bulstrods Rep.* 2. *par. fol.* 11, 12.

Occupation, *Occupatio*, Signifies the putting a Man out of his Free-hold in time of War, and is all one with *Disseisin* in time of Peace, saving that it is not so dangerous. *Co.* on *Lit. fol.* 249. Also use or tenure, so we say such Land is in the Tenure or *Occupation* of such a man, that is, in his possession. See *Terre-Tenant*. Also Trade or *Occupation*, 12 *Car.* 2. *cap.* 18. But *occupationes, in the Stat. de bigamis*, cap. 4. are taken for Usurpations upon the King, and is when one Usurps upon the King, by using Liberties which he ought not. And as an unjust Entry upon the King into Lands or Tenements is an *Intrusion*, so an unlawful using of Franchises is a *Usurpation*. See 2. *Inst. fol.* 270.

Occupavit, Is a Writ that lyeth for him which is ejected out of his Land or Tenement in times of War, as a Writ of *Novel Disseisin* lies for one ejected in time of Peace, *Ingham*, sect, *Brief de Novel Disseisin.*

Octave, *Octava*, The eighth day following some peculiar Feasts. See *Utas.*

Octo tales. See *Tales*. See *Bro.* tit. *Octo tales.*

Odio & atia, Is an old Writ mentioned in the Statute of *Westm.* 1. made 3 *E.* 1. *cap.* 11. And it was directed to the Sheriff, to inquire whether a Man committed to Prison upon Suspition of Murder, be committed upon just Cause of suspition, nor onely upon Malice, *Register, fol.* 133. *Bracton, lib.* 3. *part.* 2. *cap.* 20. And if upon inquisition it were found, That he was not Guilty, then there came another Writ to the Sheriff to bail him. But now that course is taken away by the Statute of 28 *E.* 3. *cap.* 9. as appears in *Stamford, Pl. Cor. fol.* 77. and *Co. lib.* 9. *fol.* 56. and *Spelman* verbo *Atia.*

Office, *Officium*, Doth signifie not only that Function, by vertue whereof a Man hath some Imployment in the Affairs of another, as of the King, or of another common Person; but also an Inquisition made to the King's Use of any thing by vertue of his *Office* who inquireth. And therefore we oftentimes read of an Office found, which is nothing else but such a thing found by Inquisition made *ex Officio*. And in this Sense it is used, 33 *H.* 8. 20. and in *Stamf. Prærog.* fol. 6, 61. where to *traverse an Office*, is to traverse the Inquisition taken of *Office*, and in *Kitchin, fol.* 177. *To return an Office*, is to return that which is found by vertue of the *Office*. See also the *New book of Entries*, tit. *Office pur le Roy*, and this is by a *Metonymie* of the Effect. And there be two sorts of *Offices* in this signification issuing out of the *Exchequer* by Commission, *viz. An* Office *to intitle the King to the thing inquired of, and an* Office *of Instruction*, for which see *Co.* 6. *Rep. fol.* 52. *Pages* Case. *Office in fee* is that which a Man hath to himself and his Heirs, 13 *E.* 1. *cap.* 25. *Kitch. fol.* 152. See *Clerk.*

Ofer-hyrnesse and Over hernessa, In the Councel holden at *Winchester*, in the Time of Archbishop *Lanfranc*, *Anno* 1076. we read, *Si autem post excommunicationem & satisfactionem venerint forisfacturam suam quæ Anglice vocatur* Oferhynesse *seu* Cahslite *pro unaquaque vocatione Episcopo suo reddant.* See *Gloss. in* 10. *Scripter.* verbo *Overhernessa.*

Official, *Officialis*, Is a Word very diversly used; for sundry *Civilians* of other Countries, that write in these Dayes, apply it to such as have the sway of Temporal Justice, *Egidius Bossius in pract. crim.* tit. *De* Officialibus *corruptis, &c.* But by the ancienter Civil Law it signifies him that is the Minister or Apparitor of a Magistrate or Judge, *lib.* 1. sect. *si quis ultro.* In the Canon Law, it is especially taken for him to whom any Bishop doth generally commit the Charge of his Spiritual Jurisdiction, and in this Sense one in every Diocess is *Officialis Principalis*, whom the Statutes and Laws of this Kingdom call *Chancellor*, 32 H. 8. 15. The rest, if they be more, are by the Canon Law called *Officiales Foranei, Gloss. in Clem.* 2. *de Rescriptis*, but with us termed *Commissaries, Commissarii*, or sometimes *Commissarii Foranei.* The difference of these two Powers you may read in *Linwood*, tit. *De sequestra possess.* cap. 1. *verbo* Officialis. But this Word *Official* in our Statutes and Common-Law, signifies him whom the Arch Deacon substituteth in the executing of his Jurisdiction, as appears by the said Statute.

Officiariis non faciendis vel amovendis, Is a Writ directed to the Magistrates of a Corporation, willing them not to make such a Man an Officer, and to put him out of the Office he hath, until Inquiry be made of his Manners, according to an Inquisition

Inquisition formerly Ordained, *Reg. Orig. fol.* 126.

Ofgang-fordell, *Spelman* thinks it should rather be read *Ofgang* for *Ordal*, i. *transitus ad ordalium. Eantq; (rei) ad trpilex judicium quod Angli* Ofgangfordell *Vocant*. Constit. Canuti Reg. de Foresta, *cap.* 11.

Oleron Laws, Are so called, because made when King *Richard* the First was there, and have respect to Maritime Affairs, *Co.* on *Lit. fol.* 260. This *Oleron* is an Island in the Bay of *Acquitayne*, at the mouth of the River *Charent*, now belonging to the French King. See *Seldens Mare clausum*, fol. 222. & 254. and *Prynnes Animadversions* on *Co.* 4. *Inst. fol.* 126.

Olympiad, *Olympias*, The space of five years: *Ethelred*, King of the *English Saxons*, reckon'd his Reign by *Olympiads*, as appears by a certain Charter of his, having these Words, *Consentiens (inquit) signo sanctæ Crucis subscripsi in* Olympiade 4. *Regni mei.* And this, by Contemporary Writers, seems to have been the sixteenth Year of his Reign, and the Year of our Lord, 994. or thereabouts, *Spelman*.

Onerando pro rata portionis, Is a Writ that lies for a Joynt-Tenant, or Tenant in Common, that is distrained for more Rent than his proportion of the Land cometh to, *Reg. Orig. fol.* 182.

Onus importandi, The Charge of *importing* mentioned, 12 *Car.* 2. *Art.* 28.

Onus probandi, The burden of proving spoken of, 14. *Car.* 2 *cap.* 11.

Open Law, *Lex manifesta seu apparens*, Is making *Law*, which by *Magna Charta*, cap. 28. Bayliffs may not put Men unto upon their own bare Assertions, except they have witness to prove the truth thereof. See *Law*.

Open Thef, That is, *open Theft*, *Quædam placita vel crimina emendari non possunt quæ sunt* Husbrech, Bernet, Open Thef, Eberemord *and* Lafordswick, *Leg. Hen.* 1. *cap.* 13. *Hoc in emendationibus* Williel. *pri.* Ran. *dicitur*, saith *Spelman*.

Ora, Was a sort of Saxon Money of the value of Sixteen Pence; 'tis often mentioned in *Doomsday*, 15. *Oræ libram faciunt*, say some. In the Laws of *Edward the Confessor*, cap. 12. *Manbote in Denelaga de Villano & Sokeman* 12. Oras, *de liberis autem hominibus* 3. *marcas*; you may read of it in *Doomsday* in *Landgable*, and in the same Book, *Linc.* In *Stanford*, T. R. E. 12. *Lagemanni qui habent infra domos suas Sacam et Socam, et super homines suos præter Geld & Heriete & forisfacturam corporum suorum de* 40 Oris *argenti*, &c. See more of this in *Spelman*.

Orchel, *Anno* 1 *R.* 3. *cap.* 8. *Orchall*, 24 H. 8. *cap.* 2. and 3 & 4 *E.* 6. *cap.* 2, seems to be all one with *Corke*.

Orbis, *Anglice*, A **Wenney**, A swelling or knot in the Flesh caused by a Blow, *Bract. lib.* 3. tit. *De Corona*, cap. 23. num. 2. —— *Arma moluta plagam faciunt, sicut gladius, bisacuta & hujusmodi; Ligna vero & lapides faciunt Brusuras*, Orbes *& ictus, qui judicari non possunt ad plagam.*

Ordeffe or Ordelfe, *Effossio metalli*, Is a Word derived from the Saxon **Ore** *Metallum*, and **Delfan** *effedere*, and often used in Charters of Priviledges, being taken for a Liberty, whereby a man claims the *Ore* found in his own Ground, but properly is the *Ore* lying under ground: As also a *Delfe* of Coal is Coal lying in Veins under ground, before it is digged up.

Ordel, *Ordalium*, Is a Saxon Word compounded of *Or*, *magnum*, and *deal*, alias *dele*, *Judicium*, or as others from *Or*, which in that Language is *privative*, and *del*, *part*, that is, *expers criminis*, or not Guilty; but is used for a kind of purgation practised in ancient Times, and in the Canon Law called *Purgatio vulgaris*. There were of this two sorts, one by Fire, another by Water. Of these see Mr. *Lambard* in his *Explication of Saxon Words*, *verbo Ordalium*: Of this you may read likewise *Holinshed*, *fol.* 98. and *Hotoman* especially *Disput. de Feud.* pag. 41. where of five Kinds of Proofs, which he calleth *Feudales probationes*, he maketh this the fourth, calling it *Explorationem & hujus furiosæ probationis* 6. *genera fuisse animadvertit*, viz. *per flammam, per aquam, per ferrum candens, per aquam vel gelidam vel ferventem, per sortes & per corpus Domini*, of all which he alledgeth several Examples out of History, very worthy the reading. See *Skener de* verb. *Significat.* verbo *Machanium.* This seems to have been in use in *Henry* the Second's Time, as appeareth by *Glanvile*, *lib.* 14. *cap.* 1, 2. See also *Verstegan*, *cap.* 3. *pag.* 63, &c. See also *Hoveden* 556. This *Ordalian* Law was condemned by Pope *Stephen* the Second, and afterwards here totally abolisht by Parliament, as appears by *Rot. Paten. de Anno* 3 Hen. 3. *Membr.* 5. See *Spelman* at large upon this Subject, *verbo* Ordalium, *Co. lib.* 9. *De strata Marcella*, and the *Saxon Dictionary*.

Ordinance of the Forest, *Ordinatio Forestæ*, Is a Statute made touching *Forest* Causes in the thirty fourth year of *Ed.* 1. See *Assise*.

Ordinary, *Ordinarius*, Is a civil Law Term, and there signifies any Judge that hath Authority to take Cognisance of Causes in his own Right; as he is a Magistrate, and not by Deputation; but in the Common Law, it is taken for him that hath exempt and immediate Jurisdiction in Causes Ecclesiastical, as appears in *Co. lib.* 9. *fol.* 36. *Hensloe's* Case. And the Statute of *Westm.* 2. *cap.* 19. 31. *E.* 3. *cap.* 11. and 21 *H.* 8. *cap.* 5. *Co.* 2. *Inst. cap.* 19. See *Broke*, *hoc tit.* and *Linwood* in cap. *Exterior.* tit. *De constitutionibus*, verbo *Ordinarii*, saith, *Ordinarius habet locum principaliter in Episcopo, & aliis superioribus, qui soli sunt universales in suis jurisdictionibus, sed sub eo sunt alii* ordinarii, *his viz. quibus competit Jrisdictio* ordinaria *de jure, privilegio, vel consuetudine*, &c.

Ordinatione contra servientes, Is a Writ that lyeth against a Servant, for leaving his Master against the Statute, *Reg. Orig. fol.* 189.

Orfgild alias **Cheapgeld**, Is a Saxon Word compounded of *Orf*, *pecus* and *Gild*, *solutio*, and signifies a Payment, or restoring of Cattel. But *Lamb.* in his *Archaion*, pag. 125, 126. sayes, 'Tis a restitution made by the Hundred or County, of any wrong done by one that was *in Plegio*.

Orgild, *Sine solutione*, *sine compensatione*, Spelman.

Orfrayes, *Aurifrisium*, A sort of Cloth of Gold made and used in *England*, both before and since the Conquest, worn by our Kings and Nobility, as appears by a Record in the Tower, where the King Commands the *Templers* to deliver such Jewels, Garments and Ornaments, as they had of his in keeping, among which he names *Delmaticum velatum de Orefreis*, that is, a Garment guarded with *Orfrayes*; And of old, the Coat Armors of the Kings Guard were also termed **Orfrayes**, because adorned with *Goldsmiths* work.

Orgallous, But more truly *Orguillous*, that is, proud and high-minded; derived from the French *Orgueil*, i. *pride*.

Orgeys, 31 *E*. 2. *stat*. 3. *cap*. 3. Is the greatest sort of North-Sea-fish, which we now call *Organ-Ling*, corruptly from *Orkney-Ling*, because the best are near that Island.

Originalia, In the Treasurers Remembrancers Office, in the Exchequer, are Records or Transcripts sent thither out of the Chancery, and are distinguisht from *Recorda*, which contains the Judgments and Pleadings in Suits tryed before the Barons of that Court.

Ortelli, Is a word used in the Book termed *Pupilla oculi*, cap. *De Chart. Forest*, part 5. cap. 22. and signifies the Claws of a Dogs-foot, being taken from the French *Orteils des pieds*, i. *digiti pedum*, the Toes.

Osmonds, 32 *H*. 8. 14. Is that Ore of which Iron is made, and it seems was anciently brought into *England*.

Oath of the King, *Juramentum Regis*, Is that which the King taketh at his Coronation, mentioned by *Bracton*, and divers others.

Oath of the Kings Justices, Is the *Oath* they take at the entrance into their Office, mentioned *Anno* 18 *Ed*. 3. *stat*. 4.

Otho, Was a Deacon-Cardinal of St. *Nichens*, *in carcere Tulliani*, a Legate for the Pope here in *England*, 22 H. 3. whose Constitutions we have at this day, *Stowe's Annals*, pag. 303.

Othobonus, Was a Deacon-Cardinal of St. *Adrian*, and the Pope's Legate here in *England*, 15 *H*. 3. as appeareth by the Award made betwixt the said King and his Commons at *Kenelworth*; his Constitutions we have at this day in use.

Ouch, 24 *H*. 8. 13. A kind of Collar of Gold, worn by Women about their Necks. It is sometimes also used for a Boss or Button of Gold set with some rich stone.

Oversamessa, This seems to have been anciently a Fine (before the Statute of *Hue-and-Cry*) laid upon those, who hearing of a Murder or Robbery, did not pursue the Malefactor, 3. *Inst*. *fol*. 116. and to be the same, which is else-where written **Overlegenesse** and **Oversenesse**. *Si quis furi obviaverit & sine vociferatione eum dimiserit*, *emendet secundum* Weram *ipsius furis vel plena* lada *se adlegiet*, *quod cum eo falsum nescivit*; *siquis audito clamore supersedit*, *reddat* **Oversamessa** *Regis*, *&c*.

Ovealty of Services, Is equality of *Services*, as when the Tenant Paravail owes as much to the Mesne, as the Mesne does to the Lord Paramount, *F. N. B. fol*. 36. See *Owelty of Partition*, Co. *on* Lit. fol. 169.

Overt act, *Factum apertum*, An open act, *Co*. 3. *Inst*. fol. 12. which must be manifestly proved.

Overt word, An open plain Speech, derived from the French *Ouvert*, *open*, Anno 1 *Mar*. *Sess*. 2. *cap*. 3.

Ouster le maine, *Amovere manum*, Signifies to take off the hand, though in true French it should be *Ouster la main*; In a legal sense, it denotes a Judgment given for him that traversed or sued *a Monstrans le droit*, and is indeed a delivery of Lands out of the King's hands; for when it appeareth upon the matter discussed, that the King hath no Right or Title to the thing seised, then Judgment shall be given in the Chancery, That the King's hands be amoved, and thereupon an *Amoveas manum* shall be awarded to the Escheatour, which is as much as if the Judgment were given, that he shall have again his Land, *Stamf*. *Prærog*. *cap*. 24. See 28 *E*. 1. *Stat*. 3. *cap*. 19. It was also taken for the Writ granted upon this Petition, *F. N. B. fol*. 256. It is written *Oter le maine*, 25 H. 8. 22. But now all Wardships, Liveries, Primer-seisins, and *Ouster le mains*, *&c*. are taken away and discharged by 12 *Car*. 2. *cap*. 24.

Ouster le mer, *Ultra mare*, Is a cause of excuse or essoine, if a man appear not in Court upon Summons. See *Essoine*.

Ousted, Derived from the French *Oster*, to remove, as *ousted* of the Possession, that is, removed or put out of possession, *Mich*. 9. *Car*. 1. *Cro*. 3. *Rep*. *fol*. 349. *Pocke's* Case.

Outfangthef, Is thus defined by *Bracton*, *lib*. 3. *tract*. 2. *ca*. 34. *Utfangthefe dicitur latro extraneus veniens aliunde de terra aliena & qui capus fuit in terra ipsius qui tales habet libertates*: But *Britton* hath it otherwise, *fol*. 91. It is a Compound of three Saxon words, *viz*. *Out*, *extra*; *Fang*, *capio vel captus*, and *Thef*, i. *fur*. It is used in the Common-Law for a Liberty or Privilege, whereby a Lord is enabled to call any man dwelling within his own Fee, and taken for Felony in any other place, and to Judge him in his own Court, *Rastall's Exposition of words*, and 1 & 2 *P*. & *M*. *cap*. 15.

Outlaw, *Utlagatus*, One deprived of the benefit of the Law, and out of the King's Protection, *Fleta*, *lib*. 1. *cap*. 47. calls him *Bannitum extra legem*, and *Bracton*, *lib*. 3. *tract*. 21. *cap*. 11. *num*. 1. & 3. says, *Forisfacit utlagatus omnia quæ panis sunt quia à tempore quo utlagatus est caput gerit Lupinum ita quod ab omnibus interfici possit & impune*; *maxime si se defenderit vel fugerit ita quod difficilis sit ejus captio*: But in the Reign of *Edward* the Third, all the Judges agreed, That none but the Sheriff only, having lawful warrant therefore, should put to death any man *outlawed*, *Co*. on *Lit*. *fol*. 128. See *Utlary*, and *Capias utlagatum*.

Outlawry, *Utlagaria*, Is the loss of the benefit of a Subject, that is of the King's Protection. See *Utlawry*.

Outparters, A kind of Theeves in *Riddes-*

 dale

dale, that stole Cattel, or other things without that Liberty: Some are of Opinion, That those which in the fore-named Statute are termed *Outparters*, are now called *Outputers*, being such as set Matches for the robbing any Man or House. See *Intakers*.

Outriders, Are Bayliffs Errant, imployed by the Sheriffs, or their Deputies, to *ride* to the farthest places of their Counties or Hundreds, with the more speed to summon such as they thought good to their County or Hundred Courts, 14 *E.* 3. *Stat.* 1. *cap.* 9.

Owelty, Is, when there is Lord, Mesne and Tenant, and the Tenant holds of the Mesne by the same Service that the Mesne holds over of the Lord above him; this is called *Owelty* of Services. See *Ovelty*.

Owdel. See *Ordeal*.

Oxgange of Land, *Bovata terræ*, Six *Oxganges of Land* is so much as six Oxen can Plough, *Cromp. Jur. fol.* 220. But an *oxgange* seemeth properly to be spoken of such *Land* as lyeth in Gaynour, *Old Nat. Brev. fol.* 117. *Skene* de verb. *Signif.* verbo *Bovata terræ*, saith, That an Oxengate of Land should always contain thirteen Acres, and that 4 Oxengates extend to a pound Land. *Spelman* says, *Bovatus terræ est quantum sufficit ad iter vel actum unius bovis.* Ox *enim est bos & gang vel gate, iter.* See *Co.* on *Lit. fol.* 69.

Oyer and Terminer, *Audiendo & terminando*, In true French *Ovir & Terminer*, Is a Commission especially granted to some eminent persons, for the hearing and determining one or more Causes: This formerly was used only upon some sudden Outrage or Insurrection in any place, *Cromp. Jur. fol.* 131, 132. *Westm.* 2. *cap.* 29. 13 *E.* 1. by which you may see who might grant this Commission, and for the form thereof, and to whom it may be granted, *F. N. B. fol.* 100. and *Broke hoc tit.* A Commission of *Oyer* and *Terminer* is the first and largest of the five Commissions by which our Judges of Assise do sit in their several Circuits.

Oyer de Record, *Audire recordum*, Is a Petition made in Court, that the Judges, for better proofs-sake, will be pleased to hear or look upon any *Record*. So when an Action is brought upon an Obligation, the Defendant may pray *Oyer* of the Bond; or if Executors sue any one, the Party sued may demand *Oyer* of the Testament. See *Monstrans de faits*.

O yes, Corrupted from the French *Oyez*, i. *Audite*, Hear ye, Is known to be used by our Cryers, as well in Courts as else-where, when they make Proclamation of any thing.

P.

Paagium, *Mat. Paris*, fol. 767. *Fecit equos meos & homines restare donec* Paagium *extorsisset. Spelman* thinks it should be read *Passagium sive telonium exactum pro transitu*, &c.

Pack of Wooll, Is a Horse-load which consists of seventeen Stone and two pound, *Fleta, lib.* 2. *cap.* 12. See *Sarplar*.

Packers, Are those that barrel, or *pack up* Herrings, and they are sworn to do it according to the Statute made 15 *Car.* 2. *cap.* 14.

Packing whites, A kind of Cloth so called, mentioned 1 *R.* 3. *cap.* 8.

Pacification, *Pacificatio*, A making of Peace, spoken of 17 *Car.* 1. *cap.* 17. relating to the Wars between *England* and *Scotland*, *Anno* 1638.

Padnage, *Idem quod Pannagium.* Vide *Chartam Regis* Hen. 1. *Ecclesiæ S. Martini de Bello.*

Pagumentis, A Frize Cloth, mentioned in the Journal Book of the House of Lords, in a Statute made 1 *Eliz.* not printed.

Paine fort & dure, *Pæna fortis & dura*, It signifies an especial punishment for those that being arraigned of Felony, refuse to put themselves upon the ordinary Tryal of God and the Country, and thereby are mute by the interpretation of the Law. *Britton* mentions it in his fourth Chapter, *fol.* 11. And *Stamford* in his Pleas of the Crown, founding it upon the Statute of *Westm.* 1. *cap.* 12. describes it thus,

He shall be sent back to the Prison whence he came, and laid in some low dark House, where he shall lye naked on the Earth, without any Litter, Rushes, or other Clothing, and without any Rayment about him, but only something to cover his privy Members: And he shall lye upon his back with his Head covered and his Feet, and one Arm shall be drawn to one quarter of the House with a cord, and the other Arm to another quarter, and in the same manner let it be done with his Legs; and let there be laid upon his Body Iron and Stone as much as he may bear, or more; and the next day following he shall have three morsells of Barley-bread without drink, and the second day he shall have drink three times, and as much at each time as he can drink of the water next unto the Prison, except it be running water, without any bread: And this shall be his Dyet till he dye.

This kind of Punishment called by the Law *Paine fort et dur*, is that which we vulgarly call *Pressing to death.*

Pais, A Country or Region; *Triall per Pais*, which *Spelman* in his *Glossary* saith, *Non intelligendum est de quovis populo, sed de compagensibus, hoc est eorum qui ex eodem sunt comitatu, quem majores nostri pagum dixere & incolas, inde* pais.

Palatine. See *County-Palatine*, and read *Cassan. de consuetud.* Burg. pag. 14.

Palfrey, *Palfredus, Palafredus, Palefredus, Palifrædus*, Is one of the better sort of Horses used by Noble-men and others for State: And sometimes of old taken for a Horse fit for a woman to ride. *Camden* sayes, That *W. Fauconberge* held the Mannor of *Cukeney*, in the County of *Nottingham*, in Sergeanty, by the Service of shooing the King's *Palfry*, when the King shall come to *Mansfeld*. See *Co.* on *Lit.* fol. 149.

Palfrey Silver, *Custumam ibidem* (speaking of *Belvoir* Castle) *vocant* Palfrey silver, *quæ levari debet annuatim de villis de* Batelesford, Nor-

Normanton, Herdeby, &c. *Escaet.* 23 E. 3. *Post mortem* Gul. *de* Roos *de* Hamlake.

Palingman, 11 *H.* 7. 22. This word is mentioned both by *Cowell* and *Spelman*, and by both left without interpretation; but by the ſenſe of the Statute it ſeems to be a Merchant Denizen, one born in *England*.

Palls, *Pallia*, 25 *H.* 8. 20. Are Veſtures made of Lambs-wooll, in breadth not exceeding three Fingers, and having two Labels hanging down before and behind, which the Pope gives or ſends to Archbiſhops and Metropolitans, who wear them about their Neck, at the Altar, above their other Ornaments. The *Pall* was firſt given to the Biſhop of *Oſtia*, by Pope *Marcus* the Second, *Anno* 336. And the *Prefaceto* an ancient Synod here in *England*, wherein *Odo* Archbiſhop of *Canterbury* preſided, begins thus,---*Ego* Odo *humilis & extremus, divina largiente clementia, almi Præſulis &* Pallii *honore ditatus*, &c. Selden's *Hiſtory of Tythes*, pag. 17. See more of this in *Spelman*'s *Gloſſary*, verbo *Pallium*.

Palmers, Are ſuch as uſed to go in Pilgrimage out of devotion; but of late time, he that can deceitfully coſen at Cards or Dice, by keeping ſome of them in his hand unſeen, we call a *Palmer*.

Palmata alias **Palmada**, A blow upon the hand with a *Ferula*, a thing frequently uſed in Schools. *Beda de remedio peccatorum*, cap. 14. *Si quis intinxerit manum in aliquo cibo & non idonea manu centum* Palmadis *emendetur*.

Panagia, Quaſi *panis* ἅγιος, Holy Bread, *Reg. Eccleſ.* Hereford *differentias referens Orientalis Eccleſ. a Romana*, Artic. 10. *Item* (dicunt Græci) *panem noſtrum* Panagium.

Pandoxatrix, In a Manuſcript Book concerning the Laws, Statutes, and Cuſtoms of the free Borough of *Mountgomery*, from the times of *Hen.* 2. *fol.* 12. *b.* We read theſe words, *Item utimur de* Pandoxatricibus, *quod nemo poteſt braſiare ſive* Pandoxare *in villa & Burgo noſtro niſi per redemptionem aliquam factam ad voluntatem Comburgenſium noſtrorum & ſi talis* Pandoxatrix *braſiaverit & aſſiſam Domini noſtri Regis in Burgo & villa poſitam & proclamatam fregerit, debet capi per Ballivos, amerciari ad voluntatem Ballivorum noſtrorum & non per pares ſuos primo & ſecundo & ſi tertia vice Aſſiſam fregerit debet capi per Ballivos capitales & publice duci ad locum ubi ſituatur* **le Gogingstole**, *& ibi debet eligere unum de duobus*, viz. *an Velit* **le Gogingstole** *aſcendere, an illud judicium redimere ad voluntatem Ballivorum.* In the Dictionary *Pandox* is made to ſignifie a Drunkard, and *Pandoxatorium* a Brew-houſe; but in this place it ſeems to ſignifie an Ale-wife that both brews and ſells Ale and Beer.

Panell, *Panella vel Panellum*, ſo written both by *Forteſcue* in his Book *de Laudibus legum, Ang.* cap. 25. and *Co.* on *Lit.* pag. 158. who ſays, It denotes a little Part. But the learned *Spelman* in his *Gloſſary* ſays, *Hoc eſt minus congruè*: It properly ſignifying *Schedula vel pagina*, or rather *Pagella*, a Schedule or Page; and thence deduced *g* in *n tranſeunte, ſic veteres quidan Manificat pro Magnificat.* Hence comes the Law term *Impannellare*, to impanel; and *to impanel a Jury*, that is, to write in a Schedule or Roll the Names of ſuch Jurors as the Sheriff returns to paſs upon any Tryal, *Reg. Orig. fol.* 223. *Kitchin, fol.* 266 So we ſay a *Panel of Parchment*, and the *Counterpane* of an Indenture. See 8 *H.* 6. *cap.* 12. and *Spelman*, verbo *Panella*.

Pannage or **Pawnage**, *Pannagium*, Which is that Food that the Swine feed on in the Woods, as Maſt of Beech, Acorns, &c. which ſome have called **Pawnes**: It is alſo the Money taken by the *Agiſtors*, for the food of Hogs, with the Maſt of the King's Foreſt, *Cromp. Jur. fol.* 155. *Weſtm.* 2. *cap.* 25. *Manwood* in his *Foreſt Laws*, cap. 12. ſayes, It is moſt properly taken for the Maſt of the Woods within the Foreſt, or the Money due to the Owner of the ſame for it. *Linwood* defines it thus, *Pannagium eſt paſtus pecorum in nemoribus & in ſylvis utpote de glandibus & aliis fructibus arborum ſylveſtrium, quarum fructus aliter non ſolent colligi. Tit. de Decimis*, mentioned alſo 20 Car. 2. cap. 3. *Quiſquis villanus habens* 10. *porcos, eat unum porcum in Paſnagio*, Doomſday. This word is variouſly written *Pannagium, Panagium, Pathnagium, Patnagium, Paunagium & Pennagium*; and ſometimes *Paſnagium*, from the French *Paſnag*. Breve Regis *Henrici* 1. lib. Rameſiens, ſect. 313. *Henricus Rex Angliæ Juſticiariis & omnibus Baronibus & fidelibus ſuis de Huntedonſchire, ſalutem, Præcipio quod Abbas de Rameſia teneat omnes boſcos ſuos bene & in pace & quietè & honorificè ſicut unquam melius tenuit; & nullus ſuper hoc eos capiat vel invaſiet ſine licentia Abbatis & ſi quid ei debetur de* panagio, *reddatur ei juſte & ſi aliquis ei inde ſuper hoc injuriam vel contumeliam fecerit, faciatis ei habere plenum rectum.* Teſte Milone Gloc. *apud* Winton, and Chart. 1. fundat. Waldens Cænobii, *Clamo etiam quietum* panagium *de omnibus Dominicis porcis*, &c.

Pape or **Pope**, *Papa*, May with eaſe enough be derived from the old Greek word πάππας, intending a Father, and was anciently applyed to other Clergy-men in the *Greek* Church, but by uſage is particularly appropriated in the *Latine* Church to the *Biſhop of* Rome: A Name very frequent in our Year-Books, eſpecially in the times of thoſe Kings, who too much abandoning their Imperial Authority, and abaſing themſelves beneath their Eſtate, ſuffered an Alien, a foreign Biſhop, that dwelt 1000 miles diſtant, to deprive them of the diſpoſition of many Spiritual Promotions; ſometimes by Lapſe, ſometimes by Proviſion, or otherwiſe: For redreſs whereof, divers Statutes were made, while this Kingdom was of the *Roman* Communion, but his power was not wholly taken away till towards the latter end of King *Henry* the Eight's Reign.

Parage, *Paragium*, From the French *Parag*, that ſignifies an equality of Name of Blood, Dignity, and alſo of the partition of Lands: Hence we have *Diſparagement*, and to *diſparage*. See *Parcenery*.

Parafredus. See *Palfrey*.

Paramount, Cometh of two French words *Par*, that is, *Per*, and *Monter*, *aſcendere*: It ſignifies in our Law the Supreme Lord of the Fee; for there may be a Tenant to a Lord, that holdeth over of another Lord, the former of which is called *Lord Meſne*, and the ſecond *Lord Paramount*, *F. N. B. fol.* 135. And a *Lord Paramount*

mount (saith *Kitch. fol.* 289.) consisteth only in comparison, as one man may be great being compared to a less, and little being compared with a greater; so that none seemeth simply to be *Lord Paramount* but only the King, who is *Patron Paramount* to all the Benefices of *England*, *Doct.* and *Stud.* cap. 36. See *Paravaile*, *Manor*, *Mesn* and *Fee*.

Paraphanalia, Or according to the Civil Law *Paraphernalia*, from παρὰ *præter* and φερνὴ *dos*, are those Goods which a Wife, besides her *Dower* or *Joynture*, is after her Husband's death allowed to have, as Furniture for her Chamber, wearing Apparel, and Jewels if she be of quality, which are not to be put into her Husbands Inventory, especially in the Province of *York*. See *Touchstone of Wills*, fol. 201.

Paragraph, *Paragraphus*, Is the division of one matter from another in several lines; It is said to be *Scripturæ divisio*. Per Isid. not. in princip. Decretorum.

Paranymph, *Paranymphus*, A Bride-man, derived from παρὰ, (i.) *juxta* & νυμφὴ, *sponsa*, as much as to say, *Assidens sponsæ*, Assistant to the Bride and Bridegroom; *Vocabular. utriusq; juris*, verbo *Paranymphi*.

Parathalassia, *Walsingham* in the County of *Norfolk*, so stiled by *Erasmus*.

Paracium, The tenure that is between Parceners, *viz.* that which the youngest oweth to the eldest. *Doomsday*.

Paravaile, Is a Compound of two French words, *Par.* i. *Per*, and *Avayler*, *demittere*: It signifieth in our Common Law the lowest Tenant, or him that is Tenant to one who holdeth his Fee over of another, and is called *Tenant paravayle*, because it is presumed he hath profit and *avayle* by the Land, 2. *Inst. fol.* 296. and *Co.* 9. Rep. *Conye*'s Case; For the use of this word, see *F. N. B. fol.* 135.

Parcella terræ, A small piece of Land, *Sciant*, &c. *quod ego* Stephanus Wington *de* Bromyard *dedi*, &c. Roberto *de* Dunapton *pro triginta solidis argenti unam* parcellam terræ *meæ cum pertin. jacen. in* Bromyard, &c. sine Dat.

Parcel-makers, Are two Officers in the *Exchequer* that make the *parcells* of the *Escheators* Accounts, wherein they charge them with every thing they have levyed for the King's use within the time of their Office, and deliver the same to one of the *Auditors* of the Court, to make an Account with the Escheator thereof. See *The Practice of the Exchequer*, pag. 99.

Parceners, Quasi *Parcellers*, i. *Rem in parcellas dividens*. *Parceners* therefore are according to the course of the Common Law, or according to Custome; *Parceners* according to the Common Law are, where one seised of an Estate of Inheritance, hath Issue only Daughters, and dies, and the Lands descend to the Daughters; then they are called *Parceners*, and are but as one Heir. The same Law is, if he have not any Issue, but that his Sisters be his Heirs. *Parceners* according to Custom are, where a man is seised of Lands in *Gavelkind*, as in *Kent*, and other places Franchised, and hath Issue divers Sons, and dies, then the Sons are *Parceners* by the Custome. See *Co.* on *Lit. lib.* 3. *cap.* 1. *sect.* 241.

Parcinary, *Participatio*, Cometh of the French *Partir*, i. *dividuum facere*, and signifies in a legal sense a holding or occupying of Land *pro indiviso*, by Joynt-tenants, otherwise called *Coparceners*, of the French *Parsonier*, i. *Particeps*; for if they refuse to divide their common Inheritance, and choose rather to hold it joyntly, they are said to hold in *Parcinery*, Lit. *fol.* 56, 57. This, by the *Feudist* and *Lombards*, is termed *Adæquatio vel peragium*; and accordingly in *Doomsday* it is said, *Duo fratres tenuerunt in Paragio, quisq; habuit aulam suam, & potuerint ire quo voluerint*; The ancient *Romans* stiled such *Particulones*, *sic enim authore Nonnio, à veteribus cohæredes inter se dicebantur, quod partes invicem facerent.* Spigelius.

Pardon, *Pardonatio*, Is a French word signifying as much as *Venia*, and used in the Common Law for the remitting or forgiving of a Felony, or other Offence committed against the King; And this is two-fold, one *ex gratia Regis*; the other, *per course de la ley*, by course of the Law, *Stamf. pl. cor. fol.* 47. *Pardon ex gratia Regis*, is that which the King, in some special regard of the person, or other circumstance, affordeth upon his absolute Prerogative. *Pardon by the course of Law*, is that which the Law in equity affordeth for a light Offence; as *Homicide casual*, when one killeth a man, having no such meaning, *West Symbol.* part 2. tit. *Indictments*, sect. 46. See more of this in the *New Book of Entries*, verbo *Pardon*.

Pardoners, *Anno* 22 *H.* 8. Were persons that carried about the Pope's Indulgences, and sold them to any that would buy them: But we have none at present in *England* that are known.

Park, *Parcus*, From the French *Parc*, or *Parque*, *locus conclusus*: It signifies with us a piece of Ground inclosed, and stored with wild Beasts of Chace, which a man may have by Prescription, or the King's Grant, *Cromp. Jur. fol.* 148. *Manwood* in his *Forest Laws* defines it thus, *A Park is a* place for priviledge for wild Beasts of Venery, and also for other wild Beasts that are Beasts of the Forest and of the Chace, *tam sylvestres quam campestres*; and such a *Park* differs from a Chase or Warren, in that it must be inclosed, and may not lye open for if it do, that is a good cause of Seisure into the hands of the King, as a thing forfeited, as a free Chase is if it be enclosed; besides, the Owner cannot have an Action against such as hunt in his *Park*, if it lye open. See *Forest*, see *Chace*, see *Warren*, *Gulielm. Conq. liberam fecit Ecclesiam de Bello, de apere parcorum*, Spelman's Gloss. And *Hen.* 1. had a *Park* at *Woodstock*, wherein were Lyons, Leopards, Camels, &c. brought thither from foreign parts, *Stow*, *An.* 1117. See 13 *Car.* 2. *cap.* 10.

Parco fracto, Is a Writ that lies against him that violently breaketh a Pound, and taketh out Beasts thence, which, for some Trespass done upon another man's Ground, are lawfully impounded, *Reg. Orig. fol.* 166. *F. N. B. fol.* 100.

Parkbote, Is to be quit of enclosing a *Park*, or any part thereof, *Co.* 4. *Inst. fol.* 308.

Parish, *Parochia*, Signifies the Precinct of a Parish-Church, and the particular charge of a Secular Priest; for every Church is either *Cathedral*, *Conventual*, or *Parochial*; *Cathedral*, is where there is a Bishop seated, so called. *Conventual*, consisteth of regular Clerks, professing some Order of Religion, or of Dean and Chapter, or other

other Colledge of Spiritual persons. *Parochial*, is that which is instituted for the saying of Divine Service, and ministring the holy Sacraments, to the people dwelling within a certain compass of ground near it. Our Kingdom was first divided into Parishes by *Honorius Archbishop of Canterbury*, in the year of our Lord, 636. *Camd. Brit.* pag. 104. whose number at present is esteemed to be nine thousand two hundred eighty four; though many Authors differ much herein. See *Hotoman* in his *Disputations*, *De feudis*, cap. 2. concerning this word *Parochia*,---*Ego* Ceolwulfus *Dei gratia Rex Merciorum, rogatus à* Werfritho *Episcopo* Hwicciorum, *istam libertatem donavi, ut tota* Parochia Hwicciorum *à pastu equorum Regis & eorum qui eos ducunt libera sit, &c.* Charta Ceolwulfi Regis, Anno 872.

Parle-Hill, *Spelman* in his *Glossary* gives us this Description of it, It is (sayes he) *Collis vallo plerunq; munitus, in loco campestri, ne insidiis exponatur, ubi convenire olim solebant centuriæ aut viciniæ incolæ ad lites inter se tractandas & terminandas; Scotis reor* **Grith-hail** *q. mons pacificationis, cui Asyli privilegia concedebantur, & in Hibernia frequentes vidimus the* **Parle** *and* **Parling-Hills**.

Parliament, *Parliamentum*, Is deduced from a French Ground, *viz. Parler* to speak, and *Ment*, *Mens* the Mind, *quasi parler la ment*, to speak ones mind; and the Writ which summons it, sayes, *Ad consulendum, &c. de arduis Regni negotiis*; It is indeed a Solemn Conference of all the States of the Kingdom summoned together by the King's only Authority, to Treat of the weighty Affairs of the Realm. The ancient *Brittans* had no such Assemblies, for *Tacitus* avers, That although *Olim Regibus parebant, nunc per Principes factionibus & studiis trahuntur; nec aliud adversus validissimas gentes pro nobis utilius quam quod in commune non consulunt; Rarus, duabus tribusve civitatibus ad propulsandum commune periculum, conventus; ita dum singuli pugnant, universi vincuntur.* That the *Saxons* had something like it, will appear from King *Inas* Laws, who flourisht *Anno* 712. *Consilio* (inquit) *& documento Cenredi patris mei, Heddæ & Erkenwoldi Episcoporum meorum omniumq; Aldermannorum meorum & seniorum sapientum populi mei, magnâ etiam servorum dei frequentiâ.* But to come a little nearer, *William* the *Conqueror* divided this Land among his Followers, in such manner, that every one of them should hold their Lands of him *in Capite*; and they again distributed part thereof among their Friends and Servants, who, for the same, were bound to do them Suit and Service in their Courts: The chief of these were called *Barons*, who thrice every year assembled at the King's Court, *viz.* at *Christmass*, *Easter* and *Whitsontide*; amongst whom the King was wont to come in his Royal Robes, and his Crown on his Head, and to consult about the Publick Affairs of the Kingdom: But this ancient Custom (say some) was changed by *Henry* the First, who, in the Sixteenth year of his Reign, summoned of the *Commons* to the great Council at *Salisbury*. But see Sir *Walter Ralegh* in his Book of the *Prærog. of Parliaments*, and *Cotton*'s *Posthuma*, fol. 15. and *Co.* 2. *Inst. fol.* 268. At this day it is the greatest Assembly of the Kingdom, consisting of the King and the three Estates of the Realm, *viz.* The Lords Spiritual, the Lords Temporal, and the Commons, for the debating of Matters touching the Common-wealth, especially the making and altering of Laws, *Smith de Rep. Anglor.* lib. cap. 1. & 2. and *Camd. Brit.* pag. 112. Concerning which *Co.* on *Lit. lib.* 2. *cap.* 10. *sect.* 164. and in the Fourth Part of his Institutes saith, *Si vetustatem spectes est antiquissima, si dignitatem est honoratissima, si jurisdictionem est capacissima.* This in an ancient Charter of King *John*, was called *Commune concilium Regni*,----*Nullum scutagium vel auxilium ponam in Regno nostro nisi per Commune concilium Regni nostri*, &c. But besides this Supreme Court, there are other inferior *Parliaments*, The Abbot of *Croyland* was wont to call a *Parliament* of his Monks, to consult about the Affairs of his Monastery: These are the words in the Book of *Croyland*, *Concessimus etiam tunc Serjentium nostræ Ecclesiæ* Semanno de Lek, *qui veniens coram conventu in nostro Publico* Parliamento *similiter juramentum præstitit, quod fidus & fidelis nobis existeret*, &c. And at this day the Societies of the two *Temples*, or Inns of Courts, do call that Assembly *a Parliament*, wherein they consult of the Common Affairs of their several Houses. See *Cromp. Jur. fol.* 1. See *King*, and *Royal Assent*.

Parliamentum insanum, So called in History was a *Parliament* held at *Oxford*, *Anno* 41 *H.* 3. M. S. *in Bibl. Cotton. sub. tit.* Vitellius, C. 9.

Parliamentum indoctorum, Was a *Parliament* held at *Coventry*, 6 H. 4. whereunto, by special precept to the Sheriffs in their several Counties, no *Lawyer*, or person skill'd in the *Law*, was to come, and therefore it was so called. *Walsing.* pag. 412. n. 30. *Rot. Parl.* 6 *Hen.* 4.

Parol, (*Loquela*) Is a French word, *Kitch. fol.* 193. uses it for a Plea in Court. It is sometime joyned with *Lease*, as *Lease-parol*, that is, *Lease per parol*; a Lease by word of mouth, to distinguish it from a Lease in writing.

Parson, *Persona*, Signifies the Rector of a Church, because, for his time, he represents his Church, and sustaineth the person thereof, as well in suing, as being sued in any Action touching the same, *Fleta, lib.* 9. *cap.* 18.

Parson imparsonee, *Persona impersonata*, Is he that is in possession of a Church whether appropriated, or not appropriated. For in the *New Book of Entries*, verb. *Ayd in Annuity*, you have these words, *Et prædictus* A. *dicit quod ipse est persona prædicta Ecclesiæ de* S. impersonata *in eadem ad præsentationem* F. *Patronissæ*, &c. So that *persona* seems to be the Patron, or he that hath right to give the Benefice, by reason that before the *Laterane Councel* he had right to the Tythes, in respect of his liberality used in the erecting and endowing the Church, *Quasi sustineret personam Ecclesiæ*; And *persona impersonata*, to be he to whom the Benefice is given in the Patrons right; for we may read in the *Register Judicial Personam impersonatam*, for the Rector of a Benefice presentative, and not appropriated, *fol.* 34. and *Dyer*, *fol.* 40. *num.* 72. saith, That a Dean and Chapter be *persons impersonees* of a Benefice appropriated unto them, and *fol.* 221. expresly shews, That *persona impersonata* is he that is inducted, and in possession of a Benefice. So that *persona* seems to to be termed *imperſonata*, in reſpect of the poſſeſſion that he hath of the Benefice or Rectory, be it appropriate, or otherwiſe, by the act of another, *Co.* on *Lit. fol.* 300.

Parters of Gold and Silver. See *Finors.*

Partes finis nihil habuerunt, &c. Is an exception taken againſt a Fine levyed, *Co.* 3. *Rep. fol.* 88. *The Caſe of Fines.*

Partitione facienda, *Anno* 31 *H.* 8. *c.* 1. Is a Writ that lies for thoſe who hold Lands or Tenements *pro indiviſo*, and would ſever to every one his part, againſt him or them that refuſe to joyn in *partition*, as *Coparceners*, &c. *Old Nat. Brev. fol.* 142. *F. N. B. fol.* 61. And *New Book of Entries*, verbo *Partition.* See *Partition.*

Partition, *Partitio*, Is a dividing of Land deſcended by the Common Law, or by Cuſtom, among *Co-heirs* or *Parceners*, where there are two at leaſt; and this *Partition* is made four wayes, whereof three are by Agreement, the fourth by Compulſion: The firſt *partition* by Agreement is, when they themſelves divide the Land equally into ſo many parts as they are Coparceners, and each to chuſe one ſhare or part according to order. The ſecond is, when they chuſe certain of their Friends to make the diviſion for them: The third is, by drawing Lots thus, having firſt divided the Land into as many parts as there be Parceners; they write every part ſeverally in a diſtinct Scroll, and wrapping it up, throw each of them into a Hat, Baſon, or ſuch thing, out of which each *Parcener* draws one, according to their ſeniority, and ſo the Land is ſeverally allotted. The fourth *partition*, which is by compulſion, when one or more of the Parceners, by reaſon of the refuſal of ſome other, ſues out a Writ of *Partitione facienda*, by force whereof they ſhall be compelled to part. In *Kent*, where the Land is of *Gavelkind* nature, they call their partition *Shifting*, from the Saxon *Shiftan*, to divide: In Latine it is called *Herciſcere*; *Partition* alſo may be made by Joynt-tenants, or Tenants in Common by aſſent, by Deed, or by Writ, 31 *H.* 8. 1. 32 *H.* 8. 32.

Parricide, *Parricida*, Properly ſignifies him that kills his Father, and may be applyed to him that murders his Mother.

Parties, Are thoſe which are named in a Deed, or Fine, as parties to it, as thoſe that levy the Fine, and to whom the Fine is levyed: So they that make any Deed, and they to whom it is made are called *Parties to the Deed.*

Particata terræ. See *Perticata.*

Party-Jury, 14 *Car.* 2. *cap.* 11. See *Medietas Linguæ.*

Partlet, Was ſome part of the Attire, a kind of Band, or Neck-kerchief, which in ſome places ſtill retains the name: This word is read in the Statute of 24 *H.* 8. *cap.* 13.

Parviſe. See *Perviſe.*

Parvo nocumento, Is a Writ of *Nuſance.* See *Nuſance.*

Paſchal Rents, Are Rents or annual Duties paid by the inferior Clergy to the Biſhop, or Arch-deacon, at their *Eaſter* Viſitation; They are alſo termed *Synodals.* See *Synodals.*

Paſſage, *Paſſagium*, Is a French word ſignifying *Tranſitum*: By the Statutes of 4 *E.* 3. *cap.* 7. and *Weſtm.* 2. *cap.* 25. It denotes the hire that a man pays for being tranſported over Sea, or over any River. In the Charter of *Henry* the Firſt, of the Liberties of *London*, we find theſe words, *Et omnes res eorum per totam Angliam & per portus Maris, de Tholonio &* paſſagio, *& Laſtagio, & omnibus aliis conſuetudinibus, per* paſſagium *Clamat eſſe quiet. de omnibus in Com. Ceſtriæ & Flint pro omnibus careƐtis, cariag. ejus ſervientibus & ſummagiis ſuis oneratis.* Pl. in Itin. apud Ceſtriam, 14 *H.* 7.

Paſſagio, Is a Writ directed to the Keepers of the Ports, to permit a man to paſs over Sea that hath the King's Licence, *Reg. Orig. fol* 193, 194.

Paſcua. See *Paſture.*

Paſcuage, *Paſcuagium*, in French *Paſuage*, the feeding or paſturing of Cattel: ---*Et habere viginti porcos quietos de* paſcuagio, *& fualium ad panem ſuum & cibos coquendos, &c.* Chart. Rich. de Muntfichet Priorat. de Tremhale in Mon. Ang. 2. par. fol. 23. Alſo the ſame with *Pannage.*

Paſſe-port, A Compound of two French words, *viz.* of *Paſſer*, *tranſire*, and *Port*, *portus*, a Haven: It ſignifies a Licence made by any that hath Authority for the ſafe paſſage of any man from one place to another, 2 *E.* 6. *cap.* 2.

Paſture, *Paſtura*, Feeding for Cattel; and therefore we call Feeding-Grounds *Common of Paſture. Linwood* in *lib.* 3. Provincial, Ang. tit. *De Decimis*, cap. *Quoniam*, ſays, That *Differunt paſcua &* paſtura, *nam* paſtura *omne genus paſcendi ſignificat, ſive fiat in pratis, ſive in ſtipula, ſive in agris, ſive in campis, ſed paſcua eſt locus principaliter deputatus pecoribus paſcendis, utputa in montibus, moris, mariſcis & planis non cultis nec aratis.*

Patents, *Literæ Patentes*, Differ from Writs, *Cromp. Jur. fol.* 126. The Coroner is made by Writ, and not by *Patent.* See *Letters Patent*, and alſo *Literæ Patentes*; In the Table of the *Regiſter*, where you may find the form of divers.

Patentee, Is he to whom the King grants his *Letters Patent*, 7 *E.* 6. *cap.* 3.

Paſuage or **Paſnage**, Money taken for Maſt, or the feeding of Hogs, *Doomſday. BraƐton* calls it *Peſſona*, and we *Pannage.* See *Pannage.*

Patria, Properly ſignifies the Country, but in the Law it denotes the men of a Neighbourhood; ſo when we ſay *Inquiratur per patriam*, we mean a Jury of Neighbourhood; in like manner *Aſſiſa vel recognitio per Aſſiſam, idem eſt quod Recognitio* patriæ.

Patriarch, *Patriarcha*, Is a Greek word ſignifying a chief Father, *Anno* 385. In the General-Councel holden at *Conſtantinople*, it was decreed, That the Biſhop of *Conſtantinople* ſhould for ever be called a *Patriarch.*

Patrinus, *Fidejuſſor in Baptiſmate*, Anglicè a God-father, *uti Paulus ſe dixit Oneſimum genuiſſe & Corinthios.*

Patron, *Patronus*, Is uſed in the Civil Law for him that hath manumitted a Servant, and thereby is both juſtly accounted his great Benefactor, and challengeth certain Reverence and Duty of him during his life. See the Title *De Jure Patronatus*

natus in the Digest, with the *Feudists pro authore feudi. Hotoman* verbo *Patronus*, in his *Comment de verbis feudal.* Both in the Canon and Common Law it signifies him that hath the Gift of a Benefice, and the reason is, because the Gift of Churches and Benefices belonged unto such good men as either built, or else endowed them with some great part of their Revenue. And *Corasius* in his Paraphrase *Ad sacerdotiorum materiam*, part. prim. cap. 2. & part 4. cap. 6. writes thus of them, *Patroni in jure Pontificio dicuntur qui alicujus Ecclesiæ extruendæ aut alterius cujuscunq; fundationis Ecclesiasticæ authores fuerunt, ideoq; præsentandi & offerendi clericum jus habent quem Ecclesiæ vacanti præesse & in ea collatis redditibus frui velint. Acquirunt autem hoc jus qui vel fundant Ecclesiam vel dotant, &c.*

Paviage, *Rot. Par.* 10 *Ed.* 3. *m.* 32. Money paid towards the paving of the Streets or High-ways.

Pawnage. See *Pannage*.

Pax Dei. See *Peace of God*.

Pax Ecclesiæ, *Dicitur, cum salva sunt Ecclesiæ omnia Privilegia, & Immunitates, servi, famuli, Ministri, &c.* Vide Leg. Edw. Conf. cap. 8.

Pax Regis, The King's Peace, *Nam longè debet esse* Pax Regis *à parte sua, ubi residens fuerit à quatuor partibus loci illius, hoc est quatuor miliaria & tres quarentenæ & novem acræ latitudine, & novem pedes, & novem palmæ, & novem grana hordei, &c.* Leg. Ed. Conf. cap. 12. See *Spelman*.

Pauper, Signifies properly a poor man, according to which we have a term in Law to sue in *Forma pauperis*; that is, if a Man or Woman having Cause of Action, and not having ability to sue, the Cause of Action being certified under Counsels hand, with a Petition of the party, setting forth their Case and Poverty; the Judge of the Court, whether in Common Law or Equity, will admit the party, to sue in *Forma pauperis*, that is, assign them an Atturney or Clerk, and Counsel to defend their Cause, and plead for them without Fees.

Peace, *Pax*, In the general signification is opposite to War or Strife: But particularly with us it intends a quiet and harmless behaviour toward the King and his People, *Lamb. Eirenarch.* lib. 1. cap. 2. pag. 7. And if any man goes in danger of harm, or bodily prejudice from another, and makes Oath of it before a Justice of *Peace*, he shall be secured by good Bond, which is called *Binding to the Peace*, Lamb. Eiren. *lib.* 2. *cap.* 2. *pag.* 77. *Cromp. Just. of Peace*, fol. 118. ad 129. And also *Frank-pledge* and *Conservator of the Peace*. Time of *Peace* is, when the Courts of Justice are open, and the Judges and Ministers of the same may by Law protect Men from wrong and violence, and administer Justice to all, *Co.* on *Lit. fol.* 249.

Peace of God and the Church, *Pax Dei & Ecclesiæ*, Was anciently used for that rest and cessation which the King's Subjects had from trouble and suit of Law between the Terms. See *Vacation*, and *Pax Dei. Tempus dicitur cultui divino adhibitum, eaq; appellatione omnes dies Dominici, festa & vigiliæ censentur.* Spelman.

Peace of the King, *Pax Regis*, 6 R. 2. Stat. 1. cap. 13. Is that *peace* and security both for Life and Goods, which the *King* promiseth to all his Subjects, or others taken to his Protection. See *Suit of the King's Peace.* This point of policy seemeth to have been borrowed by us from the *Feudists*, which in the second Book of the *Feuds*, *cap.* 53. entituled *De pace tenenda*, &c. *Hotoman* proveth. Of this *Hoveden* setteth down divers Branches, *par. poster. suorum annal.* in *H.* 2. *fol.* 144. & 430. There is also *Peace of the Church*, for which see *Sanctuary*. And the *Peace of the King's High way* to be free from all Annoyance or Molestation. See *Watling street. The Peace of the Plough*, whereby the Plough and Plough-Cattel are secured from Distresses; for which see *F. N. B. fol.* 90. So Fairs may be said to have their *Peace*, because no man in them may be troubled for any Debt else-where contracted. See *Fairs*.

Pectorell, 14 *Car.* 2. *cap.* 3. Armor for the Breast, a Breast-plate, derived from *Pectus*, a Breast.

Peculiar, In French *Peculier*, that is, proper; it signifies a particular Parish, or Church, that hath Jurisdiction within its self, for *probat* of Wills, &c. exempt from the Ordinary, and the Bishops Courts. The King's Chappel is a Royal *peculiar*, exempt from all Spiritual Jurisdiction, and reserved to the Visitation and immediate Government of the King himself, who is Supreme Ordinary. It is an ancient Priviledge of the See of *Canterbury*, that wheresoever any Mannors or Advowsons do belong to it, they forthwith become exempt from the Ordinary, and are reputed *Peculiars*, and of that, see *Canterbury*.

Pecunia, Properly Money, but was anciently used for Cattel, and sometimes for other Goods as well as Money; So we find often in *Doomsday*, *Pastura ibidem ad* pecuniam *villæ*, that is, Pasture-Ground for the Cattel of the Village. And in Emendat. Willielmi primi ad Leg. Edw. Conf. *Intenti simus etiam ut nulla viva* pecunia *vendantur, aut emantur nisi infra Civitates & hoc ante* 3. *fideles testes*, Et Leg. Ed. Conf. cap. 10. *Qui habuerit* 30. *denariatus vivæ* pecuniæ.

Pea, *Mons*, A Hill. *Doomsday*.

Pedage, *Pedagium*, Signifies Money given for the passing by Foot or Horse through any Country, *Pupilla oculi*, part. 9. cap. 7. *Pedagia dicuntur quæ dantur à transeuntibus in locum constitutum à principe*, says Spelman, *Et capiens* pedagium *debet dare salvum conductum, & territorium ejus tenere securum.* So Baldus. *Cassan.* de consuetud. Bur. pag. 118. hath these words, *Pedagium à pede dictum est, quod à transeuntibus solvitur*, &c.

Peere, *Pera*, Is a Fortresse made against the Force of the Sea, for better security of Ships that lye at Harbor in any Haven; so is the *Peere* of *Dover* described, *Camd. Brit.* pag. 259. See 14 *Car.* 2. *cap.* 27.

Peerage, The Dignity of the Lords or Peers of the Realm; also an Imposition for the Maintenance of a Sea-Peer.

Peeres, *Pares*, Signifie in our Common Law those that are impannelled in an Enquest upon any man, for the convicting or clearing him of any Offence for which he is called in question; and the reason thereof is, because the course and custom of our Nation is to try every Man in such

such case by his Equals or *Peers*, *Westm.* 1. *cap.* 6. So *Kitchin* useth it, *fol.* 78. in these words, *Mais si le amerciament soit affirre per pares.* And this word in this sense is not in use with us only, but with other Nations also. For *Pares sunt convassalli quorum sententia vasallus propter feloniam est condemnatus*, Bartilayus de Regno, lib. 4. cap. 2. *Et* pares *sunt qui ab eodem Domino feudum tenent*, lib. 1. Feudor. cap. 26. But this word is most principally used for those that be of the Nobility of the Realm, and Lords of the Parliament, *Stamf. pl. cor.* lib. 3. cap. *Tryal per les Peers*, the reason whereof is, that although there be a distinction of degrees in our Nobility, yet in all publick Actions they are equal, as in their Votes in Parliament, and in passing in Tryal upon any Nobleman, &c. This appellation seems to be borrowed from *France*, and from those twelve *Peers* that *Charlemaine* instituted in that Kingdom; of whom you may read *Vincent. Lupanus de Magist. Franciæ*, lib. 1. cap. *Pares Franciæ.* And though we have borrowed the Appellation, and applyed it with some reason to all Lords of Parliament, yet we have no set number, for our Nobles may be more or less, as the King pleaseth.

Pegen. See *Forath.*

Peyne fort & dure. See *Payne fort & dure.*

Pelfe, *Pelfra*, Tho. Venables *Ar. Clamat*, *Quod si aliquis tenent. sive resident. infra Dominium sive Manerium de* Kinderton *feloniam fecerit & corpus ejus per ipsum* Thomam *super factum illud captum & convict. fuerit*, *habere* pelfram, *viz. Omnia bona & catalla hujusmodi seisire*, Plac. in itin. apud Cestr. 14 H. 7.

Pellicia, A Pilch, *Tunica vel indumentum* pelliceum *hinc super-pelliceum*, A Sur-pilch or Surplice, *Spelm.*

Pellota, French *Pelote*, The ball of the Foot, Charta de Foresta, cap. 7. *Talis autem expeditatio* (viz. canum,) *fiat per assisam communiter usitatam*, viz. *quod tres ortelli abscindantur*, *sive* pellota *de pede anteriori.* See *Co. Inst.* part 4. fol. 308.

Pelt-wooll, Is the *wooll* pulled off the Skin of dead sheep, 8 *H.* 6. *cap.* 22.

Penigeldum, *Denarii alicujus ex quavis consuetudine pro facultate aliqua vel privilegio habendo puta in foresta aut alibi*, Spelm. Gloss.

Penistons, A kind of course woollen Cloth mentioned 43 *Eliz. cap.* 10.

Penne. See *Baye.*

Penon, 11 *R.* 2. *cap.* 1. Is a Standard, Banner or Ensign, carried in War: It is borrowed from *France*, for *Pennon* in the French Language signifies the same thing.

Pension, *Pensio.* That which in the two *Temples* is called a *Parliament*, and in *Lincolns Inn* a *Councel*, is in *Grayes-Inn* termed a *Pension*; that is, an Assembly of the Members of the Society to consult of the Affairs of the House. And in the Inns of Court, *Pensions* are certain annual payments of each Member to the House.

Pension-writ, When a *Pension-writ* is once issued, none sued thereby in an Innes of Court, shall be discharged or permitted to come into Commons, till all Duties be paid. *Order in Grayes-Inn*, wherein it seems to be a peremptory Order against such of the Society as are in arrear for *Pensions*, and other Duties.

Pensioners, *Pensionarii*, Are a Band of Gentlemen so called, that attend as a Guard upon the King's Person: They were instituted *Anno* 1539. and have an allowance of fifty pound a year to maintain themselves and two Horses for the King's Service. See *Stowe's Annals*, 973.

Pentecostalls, *Pentecostalia*, Were certain pious Oblations made at the Feast of *Pentecost* by Parishioners to their Parish-Priest, and sometimes by inferior Churches or Parishes to the principal Mother-Church. Which Oblations were also called *Whitson Farthings*, and were divided into four parts, one to the Parish-Priest, a second to the Poor, a third for repair of the Church, and a fourth to the Bishop. *Stephens of Procurations and Pentecostalls.*

Peny, Was our ancient currant Money, 2. *Inst. fol.* 575. In a Charter of *H.* 7. to the Abbot and Covent of the Church of St. *Peter* in *Westminster*, dated the Nineteenth year of his Reign, we read, *Et quod sint quieti de omnibus misericordiis & Warda, & Ward peny, Aver-peny, & Hundred-peny, Tything-peny, & Borthal peny, & de omnibus operibus castellorum, pontium, &c.*

Pepper, *Piper*, Is a Spice well known, of whose diversities and nature you may read *Gerard's Herbal*, lib. 3. cap. 146. This is set among Merchandise to be garbled, *Anno* 1 *Jac. cap.* 19.

Per cui et post. See *Entry.*

Perambulation of the Forest, *Perambulatio Forestæ*, Is the surveying or walking about the *Forest*, or the Limits of it, by Justices, or other Officers thereto appointed, to set down the Metes and Bounds thereof, and what is within the *Forest*, and what without, 17 *Car.* 1. *cap.* 16. 20 *Car.* 2. *cap.* 3. 4. *Inst. fol.* 30. See *Purliew.*

Perambulatione facienda, Is a Writ that is sued out by two or more Lords of Mannors lying near one another, and consenting to have their Bounds severally known. It is directed to the Sheriff, commanding him to make *perambulation*, and to set down their certain Limits, *F. N. B. fol.* 133. See *Rationabilibus divisis.* See *Reg. Orig. fol.* 157. and the *New Book of Entries*, verbo *Perambulatione facienda.*

Peravayle. See *Paravayle.*

Perch, *Pertica*, Is used with us for a Rod or Pole of sixteen foot and a half in length; whereof forty in length and four in breadth make an Acre of Ground, *Cromp. Jur. fol.* 222. Yet by the Custom of the Country it may be longer, as he there saith; and several Counties differ herein, for in *Stafford shire* it is twenty four foot, In the Forest of *Sherwood* twenty five. In *Hereford-shire* a *perch* of Walling is sixteen foot and a half: a *perch* of Ditching twenty one foot: In the Forest of *Canke* twenty five: in the Forest of *Clarendon* twenty, &c. *Skene de verbor. Signif. verbo* Particata terræ, saith, That *Particata terræ* is a Rood of Land; and a little after to this effect, Three Barley-corns without tayls set together in length make one inch; of the which Corns, one should be taken off the middle ridge, another off the side of the ridge, and one off the furrow: Twelve inches make a foot of measure, three foot and

and an Inch make an Elln, six Elnes make one Fall; which is the common lineal Measure, and six Elnes long and six broad make a Square, and superficial Fall of Land measured. And it is to be understood, that one Rod, one Raip, one lineal fall of Measure, are all one, each of them containing six Elns in length; Howbeit a Rod is a Staff or Pole of Wood, a Raip is made of Tow or Hemp, and so much Land as falleth under the Rod or Raip at once, is called a *Fall of measure*, or a *lineal fall*, because it is the measure of the line or length only; like as the superficial fall is the measure of length and breadth. *Item*, ten falls in length and four in breadth make a Rood, four Roods make an Acre, &c. This is the measure of *Scotland*.

Perdonatio utlagariæ, Is a pardon for him, who for contempts in not coming to the King's Court, is Out-lawed, and afterwards, of his own accord, yieldeth himself to prison, *Reg. Judicial*, fol. 28. *Leg. Edw. Confess.* cap. 18. & 19.

Pere & pite, In the Constitutions of *Canutus* concerning the Forest, *cap.* 17. We have these Words, *Si quis autem contra primarium pugnaverit, in placito emendet secundum pretium sui ipsius quod Angli* **Pere & pite** *dicunt & solvat. primario* 40. *sol.* See *Were*.

Peremptory, *Peremptorius*, Cometh of the Verb *perimere*, to cut off, and joyned with a Substantive (as Action or Exception) signifies a final and determinate Act, without hope of renewing or altering. So *Fitzherbert* calleth a *Peremptory Action*, *Nat. Brev. fol.* 35. 38. 104. 108. and *Nonsute peremptory*, Idem. fol. 5. 11. A *peremptory exception*, Bracton, lib. 4. cap. 20. *Smith de Rep. Anglor.* lib. 2. cap. 13. calleth that a *Peremptory exception*, which makes the State and Issue in a Cause.

Perinde valere, Is a term that belongs to the *Ecclesiastical Law*, and signifies a Dispensation granted to a Clerk, that being defective in his capacity to a Benefice, or other Ecclesiastical Function, is *de facto*, admitted to it, and it hath the Appellation from the Words, which make the faculty as effectual to the party dispensed with, as if he had been actually capable of the thing for which he is dispensed with at the time of his Admission, 25 *Hen.* 8. *cap.* 21. It is called *a Writ*.

Perjury, *Perjurium*, Is a Crime committed, when a lawful Oath is ministred by any that hath Authority to any Person in any judicial proceedings, who swearing absolutely and falsly in a matter material to the Issue, or Cause in question, either of their own accord, or by the subornation of others. And if a man call me *perjur'd Man*, I may have my Action upon the Case, but for calling me a *forsworn Man*, no Action lies, *Co. Inst.* 3. par. fol. 163. 23 *H.* 8. 3. It is excepted out of the Act *Of General Pardon*, 12 Car. 2. cap. 8. How it is punished in *Wales*, see 26 *H.* 8. 4. and 5 *Eliz.* cap. 9.

P[illegible]kins Was a learned Lawyer, a Fellow and Bencher of the *Inner Temple*, that lived in the dayes of *Edward the Sixth* and Queen *Mary*. He wrote a very excellent Book upon divers points of the Common-Law.

Per my et per tout, A Joynt-Tenant is said to be seised of the Land that he holds Joyntly *Per my & per tout*; that is, he is seised by every parcel, and by the whole, *Littl. Tenures*, sect. 281.

Permutatione Archidiaconatus & Ecclesiæ eidem annexæ cum Ecclesia et præbenda, Is a Writ to an Ordinary, commanding him to admit a Clerk to a Benefice, upon exchange made with another, *Reg. Orig. fol.* 307.

Pernor of profits, Is derived of the French *Prenuer*, a Taker or Receiver is he that takes or receives the *profits*, as *Pernor of profits*, 1 H. 7. 1. *Pernor of profits*, and *Cestuy que use*, is all one, *Co. Rep.* 1. *fol.* 123. *Chudley*'s Case. See 21 *R.* 2. cap. 15. and *Co.* on *Lit. fol.* 589. *b.*

Pernancy, A taking or receiving Tythes in *Pernancy*; that is, Tythes taken, or that may be taken in kind.

Per quæ servitia, Is a Writ Judicial, issuing from the Note of a Fine, and lyeth for Cognisee of a Mannor, Seigniory, chief Rent, or other Services, to compel him that is Tenant of the Land at the time of the Note of the Fine levyed, to attorn unto him, *West Symbol.* part 2. tit. *Fines*, sect. 126. *Old Nat. Brev. fol.* 155. *New Book of Entries*, verbo *Per quæ servitia*.

Peaquisite, *Perquisitum*, Is any thing gotten by a Man's own Industry, or purchased with his own Money, different from that which descends to him from his Father or Ancestors; and so *Bracton* uses it, when he sayes, *Perquisitum facere*, lib. 2. cap. 30. num. 3. & lib. 4. cap. 22.

Perquisites of Court, Be those profits that grow to a Lord of a Mannor, by vertue of his Court Baron, over and above the certain yearly profits of his Land, as Fines of Copy holds, Hariots, Amerciaments, Waifes, Strayes, &c. *Perkins*, *fol.* 20, 21.

Person. See *Parson*.

Personable, *Personabilis*, Signifies as much as inabled to maintain plea in Court: As for Example, The Defendant was judged personably to maintain this Action, *Old Nat. Brev. fol.* 142. And in *Kitchin*, *fol.* 214. The Tenant pleaded, That the Wife was an Alien born in *Portugal*, without the Legiance of the King, and Judgment was demanded, whether she should be answered: The Plaintiff saith, She was made *personable* by Parliament, that is, as the *Civilians* would speak it, *Habere personam standi in judicio*. *Personable* is also as much as to be of capacity to take any thing granted or given, *Plowden*, *fol.* 27. *Colthirst*'s Case.

Personal, *Personalis*, Being joyned with the Substantives, Things, Goods or Chattels, as Things *personal*, Goods *personal*, Chattels *personal*; signifies any moveable thing belonging to a man, be it quick or dead: So is it used in *West Symbol.* part 2. tit. *Enditements*, sect. 58. in these Words, Theft is an unlawful felonious taking away another Man's moveable *personal* Goods, so also 61. And *Kitchin. fol.* 139. saith, Where *personal* things shall be given to a Corporation, as a Horse, a Cow, Sheep, or other Goods, &c. And *Stamf. pl. cor. fol.* 25. *Contrectatio rei alienæ*, is to be understood of things *personal*; for in things real it is

 not

not Felony, as the cutting of a Tree is not Felony. See *Chattels*.

Personal Tythes, Are *Tythes* paid of such profits as come by the labor of a Man's Person, as by buying and selling, gains of Merchandise and Handicrafts, *&c.* See *Tythes*.

Personalty, *Personalitas*, Is an Abstract of *Personal*. The Action is in the *Personalty*, *Old Nat. Brev. fol.* 92. that is to say, it is brought against the right Person, or the Person against whom in Law it lies. *In vocabulario utriusque juris*, I find the word *impersonalitas*; For sayes that Author *Personalitas significatur per has dictiones, (tu mihi, ego tibi) cum alio significato quod probabiliter concluditur, & si nullo modo concludatur tunc est impersonalitas.*

Persons ne Prebendaries ne seront chargee as quinsimes, &c. Is a Writ that lyes for *Prebendaries*, or other spiritual Persons, being distrained by the Sheriff, or Collectors of Fifteens, for the Fifteenth of their Goods, or to be contributary to Taxes, *F. N. B. fol.* 176.

Perticata terræ, Is the fourth part of an Acre, which in the whole Superficies contains forty *Perticas*. See *Perches*.

Perticulas, The King granted to *Luke Margnin de insula de Man Scholari, quandam eleemosynam vocatam* Perticulas *ad sustentationem cujusdam pauperis Scholaris de insula prædicta ad exercend. Scholas, per progenitores nostros, quondam Reges Angliæ datam & concessam*, Pat. 5. Hen. 4. m. 16.

Pertinens, Was anciently used for a Kinsman or Kinswoman, *Si quis cum* pertinente *sua jaceat, emendet hoc secundum cognationis modum sit Werâ, sit Witâ, sit omni pecuniâ*, Leg. Canuti Regis M. S. cap. 48.

Pervise or **Parvise**, *Pervisus*, *Parvisia*, Is derived from the French *Le parvis*. *Fortescue. de laudibus legum Angliæ*, cap. 51. pag. 124, hath these words, *Sed tunc placitantes (i. post meredIem) se divertunt ad* pervisum *& alibi consulentes cum servientibus ad legem & aliis consiliariis suis.* Of which *Chaucer* thus, *Prolog.* 9.

A Serjeant at Law, ware and wise,
That often had been at the Parvise.

Nam ibi Legis periti convenere ut clientibus occurrerent, non ad tyrocinia juris, quas motas vocant exercenda, sayes *Spelman*. *Selden* in his Notes on *Fortescue*, pag. 56. sayes, It signifies an Afternoons Exercise or Moot, for the Instruction of young Students, bearing the same Name originally with the *Parvisiæ* in *Oxford*. Mr. *Somner* sayes, *Pervise* signifies *Palatii Atrium vel Area illa a fronte Aulæ* Westm. *hodie*, the Palace-yard. See his *Gloss. in* 10. *Scriptores*, verbo *Triforium*.

Pes Forestæ, —— *Notandum est quod* pes forestæ *usitatus tempore* Ric. Oysell *in arrentatione vastorum, factus est, signatus & sculptus in pariete Cancellæ Ecclesiæ de* Edwinstone *& in Ecclesia* B. Mariæ *de* Nottingham, *& dictus* pes *continet in longitudine octodecem pollices, & in arrentatione quorundam vastorum pertica* 20, 21. *&* 24. *pedum usa fuit, &c.* Ex Regist. Abb. de Novo-loco in Com. Not. penes Rob. Comitem Kingstoniæ, Anno 1630. See *Spelman eodem verbo*.

Pesage, *Pesagium*, A Duty paid for the weighing of Merchandise, and other Wares, we may, without any straying, draw **Poisage** or **Popsing** for *Pondus*, and to **Peise** or **Poise** for *ponderare*.

Pessona, *Mast*, Or, according to *Bracton*, the Money taken for *Mast*, or feeding of Hogs; in the first signification, *Tempore pessonæ* denotes *Mast-time*, or the Season when *Mast* is ripe, which in *Norfolk* they call *Shacking time*.

Pesturable Wares, Seem to be such *Wares* or Merchandise as *pester* and take up much room in a Ship, 32 *H.* 8. *cap.* 14.

Peter-Corn, *Rex* Athelstanus *concessit Deo & beato* Petro *Ebor*, *& colideis prædictis de qualibet Caruca arante in Episcopatu Eboraci unam Travam bladi*, Anno Domini 936. *quæ usque in præsentem diem dicitur* **Peter-Corn**. Ex Reg. S. Leonardi Ebor. in Bibl. Cottoniana, fol. 5. a.

Peter-Pence, *Denarii Sancti* Petri, otherwise call'd in the Saxon Tongue *Romefeoh*, the Fee of *Rome*, or due to *Rome*; and also **Romescot** and **Rome-pennyng** was a Tribute given by *Inas* King of the *West-Saxons*, being in Pilgrimage at *Rome* in the Year of our Lord, 720. which was a penny for every House, *Lamb. Explication of Saxon Words*, verbo *Nummus*, and *fol.* 128. in St. *Edward*'s Laws, *num.* 10. where we may read these Words, *Omnes qui habent* 30. *denariatus vivæ pecuniæ in domo sua de suo proprio, Anglorum lege dabit denarium sancti* Petri, *& lege Danorum dimidiam marcam*; *Iste verò debet summoniri in solenitate Apostolorum* Petri *&* Pauli *et Colligi ad festivitatem quæ dicitur* ad vincula, *ita ut ultra illum diem non detineatur, &c.* See also King *Edgars Laws*, *fol.* 78. *cap.* 4 which contain a sharp constitution touching this matter. *Stow* in his *Annals*, pag. 67. saith, That he had twenty peny-worth of Goods of one sort in his House, was to give a Penny at *Lammas* yearly. See *Romescot*.

St. Peter ad vincula, *Anno* 4. Ed. 4. cap. 1. & 17. Ed. 4. cap. 5. See *Gule of August*.

Petit cape. See *Cape*.

Petit Larceny, *Parvum Latrocinium*. See *Larceny*.

Petit Treason, *Parva proditio*, In French *Petit trahizon*, i. *proditio minor*, Treason of a lesser or lower Kind; for whereas *Treason* in the highest Kind, is an Offence done against the security of the Common-wealth, *West Symbol.* part 2. tit. *Indictment*, sect. 63. So is *Petit Treason*, though not so expresly. *Petit Treason* is, If a Servant kill his Master, a Wife her Husband, a secular or religious Man his Prelate, 25 *E.* 3. *ca.* 2 whereof see more in *Stamf. pl. cor.* lib. 1. cap. 1. *Crompton's Justice of Peace*, *fol.* 2. And for the punishment of it, see the Statute 22 *H.* 8. 14. and *Cromp. ubi supra*.

Petit Sergeanty, *Parva Sergeantia*; To hold by *Petit Sergeanty*, is to hold Lands or Tenements of the King, yielding him a Knife, a Buckler, an Arrow, a Bow without a String, or other like Service, at the Will of the first Feoffer; and there belongs not Ward, Marriage or Relief; And here observe, That none can hold by *Grand* or *Petit Sergeanty*, but of the King. But see the Statute *Car.* 2. *ca.* 24.

Petition, *Petitio*, Hath a general signification for all kinds of Supplications made by an Inferior to a Superior, and especially to one having Jurisdiction and Authority. See *Stamf. prær.* cap. 15. 22.

Petra, Is a sort of Weight, we call it a *Stone*, but differing in many Places of *England*; somewhere consisting of 16, other-where of 14, 12, or 8 pound.

Petra Lanæ, A Stone of Wooll. See *Stone*.

Petty-fogger, An irregular Compound, from the French *Petite*, small; and the Saxon *Fogere*, a Suitor or Sollicitor: So that a *Petty fogger* is an Inferior Atturny or Lawyer, or rather a Troble-Town, having neither Law nor Conscience.

Pharos, A Watch-Tower; no Man may build or erect any Light-houses, *Pharos*, Sea-marks or Beacons, without lawful Warrant and Authority, 3. *Inst. fol.* 204.

Philizer. See *Filacer*.

Picards, A sort of Boats of fifteen Tun, or upwards, used on the River of *Severne*, mentioned 34 & 35 *H.* 8. *ca.* 3. Also a Fisher-boat, 13 *Eliz.* 11.

Piccage, *Piccagium*, From the French *Piquer*, *effodere*; Money paid in Fairs, for breaking of the Ground to set up Booths or Stalls, *Aliquis veniens ad forum nostrum de Rudham cum rebus ejus & frangendo vel pictando aliquam placeam in dicto foro, Prior habebit inde redemptionem. Ex Registro Priorat. de* Cokesford.

Pickards, No Person shall use any Iron Cards or *Pickards* in rowing any Wollen Cloth, upon pain to forfeit the same, and 20s. for every Offence, *Anno* 3 & 4 *E.* 6. *ca.* 2.

Picle alias **Pightell**, *Pictellum*, A small parcel of Land inclosed with a Hedge, which the common People of *England* do in some Places call a *Pingle*, and may perhaps be derived from the Italian Word *Picciola*, i *parvus*.

Pie-powder Court, *Curia pedis pulverizati*, From the French *Pied*, i. *pes*, and *Pouldreux*, i. *Pulverulentus:* Is a Court held in Fairs, to yeild Justice to Buyers and Sellers, and for Redress of all Disorders committed in them; and so called, because they most usally are in Summer, and the Suiters commonly are Countrey-People with dusty Feet; or from the expedition intended, in the hearing of Causes proper thereunto before the dust goes off the Plaintiffs or Defendants feet; it is held *De hora in horam. Skene de verber.* Signif. *verbo* Pede-pulverosus, sayes the word, signifies a Vagabond; especially a Pedler, which hath no place of dwelling, and therefore must have Justice summarily administred to him, *viz.* within three ebbing and three flowing of the Sea. *Bracton*, lib. 5. tract. 1. cap. 6. num. 6. calleth it *Justitiam pepoudrous.* Of this *Court*, read the Statute 17 *E.* 4. *ca.* 2. *Co.* 4. *Inst. fol.* 272. and *Cromp. Jur. fol.* 221. See *Justices of the Pavilion.*

Pig of Lead. See *Fother*.

Pike or **Picke.** See *Polein*.

Pille of Foddray or **Foulrey**, In the County-Palatine of *Lancaster*, *Anno* 2 *H.* 6. *ca.* 5. seems to be a Defence built on a Creek of the Sea, and call'd *Pille* by the *Idiome* of the Country for a *Pile*. This Pile was erected there by the Abbot of *Fornesse*, in the first year of *Ed.* 3. Cam. Brit. *Rex* —— *Dedimus* Henrico *Comiti* Northumberland *insulam*, *castrum*, **Pelam** & *Dominium de Man &c.* Rot Pat. 1 Hen. 4. m. 36.

Pillory, *Collistrigium*, As it were *Collumstringens*, and *Pillorium*, from the French *Pelori*, and that may seem to be derived from the Greek πύλη, *Janua*, a Door, because one standing on the Pillory, puts his Head, as it were, through a Door, and Ὁράω *video*: It is an Engine of Wood made to punish Offendors. There is a Statute made of the *Pillory*, 51 *H.* 3. wherein you may see, who were then subject to this punishment: This, among the *Saxons*, was called *Healsfang*, of *Heals*, a Neck, and *fang*, to take. *Lamb Explication of Saxon Words*, verbo *Mulcta*. In the Laws of *Canutus* it is call'd *Halsfang*, cap. 42. The learned *Spelman* in his *Glossary* sayes, that it is *Supplicii machina ad ludibrium magis quam pœnam*. See more there. *Vide etiam Healfang*.

Pileus supportationis, A Cap of Maintenance; Pope *Julius* sent such a Cap with a Sword to *Hen.* 8. *An.* 1514. *Hollinsh.* pag. 827. but there is mention made of such a Cap by *Hoveden* pag. 656. at the Coronation of *Richard* the First, where it is said, —— *Deinde venerunt* Godofridus *de Luci portans pileum Regium &* Johannes Marescallus *juxta eum portans duo calcaria aurea, &c.*

Pinsinochium, A Bake-house, *Locus pinsandi ubi panes conficiunt*, The Book of St. *Albans* in the Life of *Paul* the fourth Abbot there, sayes, *Iste hanc Ecclesiam cæteraque ædificia, præter Pistrinam et* Pinsinochium *reædificavit ex Lapidibus et tegulis veteris civitatis Verolamii*, &c. by which it seems that many of the Ruines of that ancient City remained until that Abbots time, who dyed *Anno* 1093.

Pioneeres, Cometh of the French *Pionier*, i. *fossor*, and signifieth such Laborers, as are taken up for the King's Army, to cast Trenches, and undermine Forts, 2 & 3 *E.* 6. *ca.* 20.

Pipe, *Pipa*, Is a Roll in the Exchequer, otherwise called *The great Roll*, Anno 37 E. 3. cap. 4. See *Clerk of the Pipe*. It is also a Measure of Wine or Oyl, containing half a Tun, that is, six score and six Gallons, 1 *R.* 3. 3.

Pirata, A *Pirate*, Is now taken for one who maintaines himself by Pillage and Robbing at Sea. But in former times the word was used in a better sense, being attributed to such Person to whose Care the Mole or Peer of a Haven was intrusted. And sometimes for a Sea-Soldier, *Asser. Menevens. Epist. in vit.* Ælfredi —— *Rex* Ælfredus *jussit cymbas et galeas*, i. *longas naves fabricari per Regnum, ut Navali prælio hostibus adventantibus obviaret: Impositisque piratis in illis, vias maris custodiendas commisit.*

Piscary, *Piscaria*, Cometh of the French *Peschary*, i. *Piscatio*, and denotes a liberty of fishing in another Man's Waters.

Pitell alias **Pightell.** See *Picle*.

Pitt, It is a Hole wherein the *Scots* use to drown Women-Theeves, *Skene*.

Pittance, *Pitancia*, A small repast of Fish or Flesh, *Rot. Char. de Anno*, 1 *Reg. Joh.* pag. 2. num. 115. *Johannes Dei Gratia*, &c. *Noverit*, &c.

nos

nos assensum nostrum præbuisse, &c. de Manerio de Milde-Hall, *quod Manerium sancto* Edmundo *sicut jus suum concessimus, &c. ita quod, qui pro tempore Sacrista fuerit,* 12. *de redditu altaris annuatim persolvat Hospitali* S. *Salvatoris quod est extra muros Sancti* Edmundi, *&c. in usus pauperum,* &c. *&* 40 s. *ad refectionem Monachorum, qui illis diebus Officia divina pro defunctis celebrabant, quæ refectio* pittania *vocatur.* See *Spelman* verb. *Pittanciarius.*

Pitching pence, Is that Money which is paid for *pitching* or setting down every Sack of Corn, or pack of any other Merchandise in Fairs or Markets.

Placard, *Anno* 2 *&* 3 *P. & M.* cap. 7. Is a Licence, whereby a Man is permitted to shoot in a Gun, or use unlawful Games: In French it signifies a Table, where Orders are written, and hung up; and **Placcaert** in Dutch is an Edict or Proclamation. See 33 *H.* 8. 6.

Placeta, Seems to signifie a piece or parcel, if of Lands; and a place, if a House or Messuage; as *Placeta Messuagii,* Placeta *Patri,* and Placeta *Pasturæ.*

Playnt, *Querela,* Is used for the propounding or exhibiting of any Action personal or real in writing, and so it is used, *Bro.* tit. *Playnt in Assise*; and the party making this *Playnt,* is called *The party Plaintiff,* Kitchin, *fol.* 231.

Plate, A Hoy, or Water-Vessel so called, *Anno* 13 *Eliz.* cap. 15.

Plea, *Placitum,* Signifies that which either party alledgeth for himself in Court, which was wont to be done in French from the Conquest untill *Edward* the Third, who Ordained them to be done in English in the six and thirtieth year of his Reign, *cap.* 15. These are divided into Pleas of the Crown and Common-Pleas. Pleas of the Crown of *Scotland* be four, *viz.* Robbery, Rape, Murder and wilful Fire, *Skene de* verb. *Signif.* verbo *Placitum.* With us they be all Suits in the King's Name, against Offences committed against his Crown and Dignity, *Stamf. pl. cor.* cap. 1. Or against his Crown and Peace, *Smith de Rep. Angl.* lib. 2. cap. 9. And those seem to be Treasons, Felonies, Misprisions of either, and *Mayhem, Co.* 4. *Inst.* cap. 10. *Edward* the First enfeoffed *Walter de Burgo* in the Land of *Ulster* in *Ireland,* excepting the Pleas of the Crown, to wit, Rape, Horstal, wilful Firing and Treasure trove, *Camd.* tit. *Ireland.* Common-Pleas be those that be held between common Persons; yet by the former definitions they must comprise all other, though the King be a party. Plea may farther be divided into as many Branches as Action; which see, for they signifie all one. Then is there a foreign Plea, whereby Matter is alledged in any Court, that must be tryed in another. As if one should lay Bastardy to another in Court-Baron, *Kitchin, fol.* 75. The Word *Placitum* is used by the *Commentators* upon the *Feuds* in the same signification that Pleas be with us, and *placitare* with them is *Litigare & Causas agere,* Hotom. *in verb.* Feudal. *verb.* Placitare.

Pleas of the Sword, *Placita ad gladium*: *Ranulph* the third Earl of *Chester,* in the Second year of *Henry* the Third, granted to his Barons of *Cheshire* an ample Charter of Liberties, *Exceptis placitis ad gladium meum pertinentibus,* &c. Rot. Pat. *in archivis Regis infra castellum Cestriæ,* 3 E. 4. m. 9. The Reason was, because King *William the Conqueror* gave the Earldome of *Chester* to his Kinsman *Hugh,* commonly called *Lupus, Ancestor* to this Earl *Ranulph, Tenere ita liberè per gladium, sicut ipse Rex* Willielmus *tenuit Angliam per Coronam.* And consonant thereunto in all Indictments for Felony, Murder, &c. in that County-Palatine, the form was anciently, *Contra pacem Domini Comitis, Gladium & dignitates suas.*

Pleadings, Are all the sayings of the parties to Suits after the Count or Declaration, to wit, whatever is contained in the Bar, Replication and Rejoynder, and not in the Count it self; and therefore Defaults in the matter of Count are not comprised within *mispleading,* or insufficient *pleading,* nor are remedyed by the Statute of *Jeofayles,* 32 H. 8. but onely the *mispleading* or insufficient *pleading* committed in the Bar, Replication and Rejoynder; but those are now remedied also by 18 *Eliz. ca.* 13.

Pledge, *Plegius,* May be derived from the French *Pleige, fide jussor,* as *Pleiger aucum,* i. *fide jubere pro aliquo,* in the same signification is *Plegius* used by *Glanvile,* lib. 10. cap. 5. and *Plegiatio* for the act of Suretiship in the Interpreter of the *Grand Custumary* of *Normandy,* cap. 60. *legii dicuntur personæ, quæ se obligant ad hoc, ad quod qui eos mittit, tenebatur*; And in the same Book, *cap.* 89, 90. *Plegiatio* is used in the same Sense with *Glanvile, Salvi plegii* be used for *plegii,* Pupil. oculi. part. 5. cap. 22. *Charta de Foresta.* This Word *plegius* is used also for *Frank pledge* sometime, as in the end of *William the Conqueror*'s Laws, set out by *Lambert* in his *Archaionom.* fol. 125. in these Words, *Omnis homo qui voluerit se teneri pro libero, sit in plegio, ut plegius eum habeat ad justitiam, si quid offenderit,* &c. And these be called *Capital pledges, Kitchin,* fol. 10. See *Frank-pledge,* and *Co.* 4. *Inst. fol.* 180.

Plegiis acquietandis, Is a Writ that lies for a Surety, against him for whom he is a Surety, if he pay not the Money at the day, *F. N. B. fol.* 137. *Regist. of Writs,* fol. 158.

Plena forisfactura & plena wita. See *Forfeiture.*

Plenarty, Is an Abstract of the Adjective *Plenus,* and is used in the Common-Law in matters of Benefices, where *Plenarty* and Vacation are direct contraries, *Stamf. prærog.* cap. 8. fol. 32. *Westm.* 2. cap. 5. Institution is a good *plenatry* against a common Person, but not against the King without induction, *Co.* on *Lit. fol.* 344.

Plevin, *Plevina,* from the French *Pleuvine,* A Warrant or Assurance. See *Replevin.*

Plite of Lawne, *Anno* 3 *E.* 4. *ca.* 5. Seems to be a Measure then in use, as a Yard or an Ell now.

Plonkets, 1 *R.* 3. *ca.* 8. A kind of course wollen Cloth, otherwise call'd *Vervise.*

Plow-Almes, *Eleemosynæ aratrales,* Anciently every *Plow-Land* paid a penny to the Church, — *De qualibet caruca juncta inter Pascham & Pentecosten, unum denarium, qui dicitur* Plow-Almes, *Mon. Ang.* 1. par. fol. 256.

Plow-Land, *Carucata terræ,* The same with a Hide of *Land,* which see.

Pluralitp,

Plurality, *Pluralitas*, 21 *Hen.* 8. *cap.* 13. The having more than one, chiefly applyed to some Church-men, who have two, three or more Benefices. *Selden* in his *Titles of Honor*, fol. 687. mentions *Trialities* and *Quadralities*.

Pluries, Is a Writ that goeth out in the third place, after two former Writs have had no effect; for first the original *Capias* issues, and if that speed not, then goeth out the *Alias*, and if that also fail, then the *Pluries*. See *Nat. Brev. fol.* 33. in the Writ *De Excom. capiendo*. See in what diversity of Cases it is used in the Table of the *Original Register*.

Pocket of Wooll, Is half a sack, 3. *Inst. fol.* 96. See *Sack of Wooll*.

Pole, See *Perch*.

Poledavis, A kind of course Canvas used by the Salesmen, in making up their Ware, 1 *Jac. cap.* 24.

Poleine, Was a sort of Shooe, sharp or picked, and turned up at the Toe; They first came in fashion in the Reign of *William Rufus*, and by degrees came to be of that excessive length, that in *Richard* the Second's time they were tyed up to the Knees with Gold or Silver Chains, according to the dignity of the Wearer: They were forbidden by *Edward* the Fourth, in the fifth year of his Reign, under a great penalty, to be worn so long: but were not utterly laid aside till the Reign of *Henry* the eight. *Malmesbury*, in the Life of the fore-mentioned *William Rufus*, speaking of the Excesses of those times hath these Words, *Tunc fluxus crinium, tunc luxus vestium, tunc usus calceorum cum arcuatis aculeis inventus est*.

Policy of Assurance, *Assecuratio*, Is a course taken by those who do adventure Wares or Merchandise to Sea, whereby, they unwilling to lose the whole adventure, do give unto some other a certain rate or proportion, as ten in the hundred, or such like, to secure the safe arrival of the Ship, and so much Wares at the place agreed upon; So that if the Ship and Wares do miscarry, the Assurer maketh good to the Adventurer so much as he promised to secure; if the Ship arrive safely, he gaineth that clearly which the Merchant compoundeth to pay him. And for the more even dealing between the Merchant and the Assurer in this Case, there is a Clerk or Officer Ordained to set down in writing the sum of their Agreement; and this is called *Pollicy*, to prevent any difference that might after happen between them. This is mentioned 43 *Eliz. cap.* 12. and 14 *Car.* 2. *cap.* 23. And is now many times used to insure Mens lives in Offices, who have paid great Sums of Money for the purchase thereof, and are insured from that Adventure by a certain Company of Merchants or Citizens, for three or four *per cent.* subscribing or underwriting the Agreement, Policy or *Insurance*, who do among them share the *Præmium* or Money given, and run the hazard of it.

Pollex, Properly signifies the Thumbe, but metaphorically it signifies an Inch, *Pollex in omni mensura debet mensurari ad radicem unguis & debet stare ex longitudine trium granorum hordei boni sine caudis.* Spelm.

Pollard, A sort of spurious Coyn, which with *Crocards* were long since prohibited, *Mat. Westm. in An.* 1299. *pag.* 413. *Pollards*, *Crocards*, *Staldings*, *Eagles*, *Leonines* and *Steepings*, were heretofore several sorts of Money used in *England*, but long since disused, 2 *Inst. fol.* 577. We also call those Trees *Pollards* or *Pollengers*, which have been usually cropt, and therefore distinguisht from Timber-Trees. See *Plowden*, *fol.* 469.

Pollinctors, The Embalmers of dead Bodies, such as prepare them for their Funeral and Interment, *Ulp. de Inst. Act. l. quicunque Si libitinarius inquit servum* pollinctorem *habuerit, isque mortuum spoliaverit, dandam in eum quasi actionem institoriam*.

Polygamus, Is he that is marryed to two, or more Wives together, 3. *Inst. fol.* 88.

Pondage. See *Poundage*.

Pone, Is a Writ, whereby a Cause depending in the County-Court, or other inferior Court, is removed in the Common-Pleas, *Old Nat. Brev. fol.* 2. See in what diversity of Cases it is used in the Table of the *Original Register*.

Poll-money, *Capitatio*, Was a Tax Ordained by Act of Parliament, 18 *Car.* 2. *cap.* 1. & 19. *Car.* 2. *cap.* 6. By the first of which every Subject in this Kingdom was Assessed by the Head or *Poll*, according to his degree, *viz.* every Duke 100 *li.* every Marquess 80 *li.* &c. Baronets 30 *li.* Knight 20 *li.* Esquire 10 *li.* &c. and every single Person 12 *d.* &c. And that this is no new Tax, appears by former Acts of Parliament, where, *Quilibet tam conjugatus, quam solutus utriusque sexus pro capite suo solvere cogebatur*, Parliam. Anno 1380. Walsingham Ypod. 534. There was anciently (sayes *Camden* in his Notes upon Coynes) a personal Tribute called *Capitatio* (*Poll-silver*) imposed upon the *Poll* or Person of every one, of Women from the twelfth, of Men from the fourteenth year of their age.

Pone per Vadium, Is a Writ commanding the Sheriff to take Surety of one for his appearance at a day assigned. Of this see five sorts in the Table of the *Register Judicial*, verbo *Pone per Vadium*.

Ponendis in Assisis, Is a Writ founded upon the Statute of *Westm.* 2. *cap.* 38. and upon the Statute of *Articuli super Chartas*, cap. 9. which Statutes do shew what persons Sheriffs ought to impannel upon *Assises* and Juries, and what not; as also what number, which see in *Reg. Orig. fol.* 178. *F. N. B. fol.* 165.

Ponendum in Ballium, Commanding a Prisoner to be bailed in causes bailable, *Reg. Orig. fol.* 133.

Ponendum sigillum ad exceptionem, Is a Writ, whereby the King willeth the Justices, according to the Statute of *Westm.* 2. to put their Seals to Exceptions laid in by the Defendant against the Plaintiffs Declaration, or against the Evidence, Verdict, or other Proceedings before the Justices.

Pontage, *Pontagium*, Is a Contribution towards the maintenance or re-edifying of Bridges, *Westm.* 2. *cap.* 25. *Anno* 13 *Ed.* 1. It may also signifie Toll taken to this purpose of those that pass over Bridges, 39 *Eliz. cap.* 24. 1 *H.* 8. *cap.* 9. 22 *H.* 8. *cap.* 5. *Per* pontagium *clamat* *esse quit de operibus* pontium, Plac. in Itin. apud Cestriam, 14 *H.* 7.

Pontibus reparandis, Is a Writ directed to the Sheriff, *&c.* willing him to charge one, or more, to repair a Bridge, to whom it belongeth, *Reg. Orig. fol.* 153.

Porca, A Ridge of Land. See *Ridge of Land.*

Porcary, *Porcaria*, A Swinesty. *Doomsday.*

Porter of the Door in the Parliament House, Is an Officer belonging to that High and Honorable Court, and injoys the Priviledges accordingly, *Cromp. Jurisd. fol.* 11.

Porter in the Circuit of Justices, Is an Officer that carries a white Rod before the Justices *in Eyre*, so called a *Portando virgam*, Anno 13 *Ed.* 1. cap. 41. See *Vergers.* There is also a *Porter* bearing *Verge* before the Justices of either Bench.

Portgreve, *Portgrevius*, In *Saxon* Popꞇgrepeꝼe, that is, *urbis vel portus præfectus*; Signifies with us a Magistrate in certain Sea-Coast Towns; and as *Camden* in his *Brit. pag.* 325. saith, The chief Magistrate of *London* was so called, as appears by a Charter of King *William the Conqueror* to the same City, in these Words.

William King, Greet William Bishop and Godfry Portgreve, and all the Burgeis within London, French and English: And I grant you, That I will that you be all your Law-worth that ye were in Edwardis dayes the King: And I will that each Child be his Faders Eyer, and I nil suffer, that eny man you any wrongys beed. And God you keep.

In whose stead *Richard* the First Ordained two Bayliffs, but presently after him King *John* granted them a Mayor for their yearly Magistrate.

Portioner, *Portionarius*, Where a Parsonage is served sometimes by two, or sometimes by three Ministers alternately: The Ministers are called *Portioners*, because they have but their portion or proportion of the Tythes or Profits of the Living.

Portmen, *Anno* 13 *Eliz. cap.* 24. The twelve Burgesses of *Ipswich* are so called. So also are the Inhabitants of the *Cinque-Ports*, according to *Camden.*

Portmote, Is a compound of Popꞇe, *portus*, and ꝫemoꞇ, *conventus*, and signifies a Court kept in Haven-Towns, as *Swainemote* in the Forest. It is called the *Portmote Court*, 43 Eliz. cap. 15. *Curia* portmotorum *est curia in civitate Cestriæ coram majore in aula Motorum tenenda*, Pl. in Itin. Ibid. 14 *Hen.* 7.

Portsale, *Anno* 35 *H.* 8. *cap.* 7. Is the sale of Fish, as assoon as it is brought into the Haven.

Posse, Is an Infinitive Mood, but used substantively to signifie a Possibility, as we say, such a thing is in *posse*, that is, such a thing may possibly be; but of a thing in being, we say it is *in esse.*

Possession, *Possessio*, Is two-fold, actual and in Law: actual *Possession* is, when a man actually enters into Lands and Tenements to him descended. *Possession* in Law is, when Lands or Tenements are descended to a Man, and he hath not as yet actually entred into them, *Stamf. pl. cor. fol.* 198. As for example, Before or until an Office be found of Lands escheated by an Attainder, the King hath only a *possession* in Law, and not in Deed, *Stam. prærog.* fol. 54. 55. There is also a Unity of *possession*, which the *Civilians* call *Consolidationem.* See an example of this in *Kitchin, fol.* 134. If the Lord purchase the Tenancy held by Heriot-service, then the Heriot is extinct by unity of *Possession*, that is, because the Seigniory and the Tenancy be now in one man's *possession*: Many other divisions of *possessions* you may read in *Bracton*, lib. 2. cap. 17 *per totum.*

Post. See *Per.*

Posta, In French *Poste*, a swift or speedy Messenger, *Sic dictus* (saith *Spelman*) *quasi posita, quod in viâ publicâ ponitur ad stationem debitam decurrendum.*

Post conquestum, Was first inserted into the King's Title by *Edward* the Third, *Anno* 1328. *Claus.* 2 Ed. 3. *in Dorso. m.* 33.

Post diem, Is the return of a Writ after the day assigned, for which the *Custos brevium* hath four Pence, where as he hath nothing if it be returned at the Day; sometimes it is taken for the Fee it self.

Post Disseisin, *Post Disseisina*, Is a Writ given by the Statute of *Westm.* 2. *cap.* 26. and lies for him that having recovered Lands or Tenements by *Præcipe quod reddat*, upon default or reddition is again disseised by the former Disseisor, *F. N. B. fol.* 190. See the Writ that lies for this in the *Register, fol.* 208.

Post fine, Is a Duty belonging to the King, for a Fine formerly acknowledged before him in his Court, which is paid by the Cognisee, after the same is fully passed, and all things performed touching the same; the Rate thereof is so much, and half so much as was paid to the King for the Fine, and is collected by the Sheriff of the County, where the Land, *&c.* lies whereof the Fine was levyed; to be answered by him into the Exchequer.

Post terme, *Post terminum*, Is a return of a Writ, not only after the day assigned for the return thereof, but after the *terme* also, for which the *Custos brevium* takes the Fee of twenty pence. Sometimes also it is taken for the Fee it self.

Postea, Is the return of the proceedings by *Nisi prius* into the Court of Common-Pleas after a Verdict, and there afterwards recorded, see *Plowden, fol.* 211. *Saunder's* Case. See also an example of it in *Cokes Reports*, vol. 6. fol. 41, 42. See *Custos brevium.*

Posteriority, *Posterioritas*, The coming after or being behind, is a word of comparison, and relation in tenure, the correlative whereof is Priority; for a man holding Lands or Tenements of two Lords, holdeth of his ancienter Lord by Priority, and of his later Lord by *Posteriority*, *Stam. prærog.* fol. 10, 11. When one Tenant holdeth

holdeth of two Lords, of the one by Priority, of the other by *Posteriority*, &c, *Old Nat. Brev. fol.* 94. *Co.* 2. *Inst. fol.* 392.

Postnati, In the Seventh year of King *James*, after many Arguments, and long debates, It was by all the Judges Resolved, That such as were born in *Scotland*, after the descent of the Crown of *England* to King *James*, were no Aliens in *England*: But the *Antenati*, that is, such as were born before that descent, were Aliens in regard of the time of their Birth, *Co.* 7. *Reports*, *Calvine*'s Case.

Pot, A Head-piece for War, 13 *Car.* 2. *cap.* 6.

Pot-Ashes, Are made of the best *Ashes*, *Anno* 12 *Car.* 2. *cap.* 4. and are used in making of Soap; some are made in *England*, but the best are brought from beyond Sea.

Potionatus, Poysoned, *Vita* M. S. *Vulsigi* 3. *Abbatis* S. *Albani*.—— *Postea in brevi migravit ab incolatu hujus mundi, ut dicitur* portionatus, *cum odio conventus & maledictione*.

Pound, *Parcus*, Signifies a place of strength to keep Cattel in that are distrained, and put there for any Trespass done, until they be replevyed or redeemed; and this is called a *Pound*, Overt or Open *Pound*; and because it is built upon the Lord's wast, the Lord's *Pound*, see *Kitchin*, *fol.* 144. It is divided into open and close; An open or overt *Pound*, is not only the Lord's *Pound*, but a Backside, Court, Yard, Pasture-Ground, or whatever place else, whither the Owner of the Beasts impounded may come to give Meat and Drink, without offence, for their being there, or his coming thither. A close *Pound* is contrary, whither the Owner cannot come for the purposes aforesaid, without Offence.

Pound-breach. See *Pundbrech*.

Poundage, Is a Subsidy to the value of twelve pence in the *Pound*, granted to the King, of all manner of Merchandise of every Merchant, as well Denizen as Alien, either exported or imported, and of such Subsidies. See the Statutes 1 & 2 *Ed.* 6. *cap.* 13. and 1 *Jac. cap.* 33. 12 *Car.* 2. *cap.* 4. and 14 *Car.* 2. *cap.* 24.

Pourallee. See *Purlieu*.

Pourchase, *Perquisitum*, Cometh of the French *Pourchasser*, *sollicitare*; it signifieth the buying of Lands or Tenements with Money, or by any other Agreement, and not the obtaining of it by descent, *Conjunctum perquisitum*, a Joynt-purchase, *Reg. Orig. fol.* 143.

Pour fair proclamee, que null inject fimes ou ordures en fosses, ou rivers pres Cityes, &c. Is a Writ directed to the Mayor, Sheriff or Bayliff, of a City or Town, commanding them to proclaim, That none cast filth into the Ditches or Places near adjoyning; and if any cast already, to remove it. This is founded upon the Statute, 12 *R.* 2. 13. *F. N. B. fol.* 176.

Pourparty, *Propars*, *Propartis*, *Propartia*, Is contrary to *pro indiviso*; for to make *Pourparty*, is to divide and sever the Lands that fall to Parceners, which before partition they hold joyntly, and *pro indiviso*, *Old Nat. Brev. fol.* 11.

Pourpresture, *Pourprestura*, From the French *Pourpris*, *conseptum*, an inclosure: It is thus defined by *Glanvile*, lib. 9. cap. 11. *Pourprestura est proprie quando aliquid super Dominum Regem injuste occupatur; ut in Dominicis Regis, vel in viis publicis obstructis, vel in aquis publicis transversis a recto cursu, vel quando aliquis in civitate super Regiam plateam aliquid ædificando occupaverit, & generaliter quoties aliquid fit ad nocumentum Regii tenementi vel Regiæ viæ vel civitatis*. *Crompton* in his *Jurisd.* fol. 152. defines it thus, *Pourpresture* is properly when a Man taketh unto himself, or incroacheth any thing that he ought not, whether it be in any Jurisdiction, Land or Franchise; and generally when any thing is done to the Nusance of the King's Tenants. See *Kitchin*, *fol.* 10. and *Manwoods Forest Laws*, cap. 10. *Skene de* verbor. *Signif.* verbo *Purpresture*, makes three sorts of this offence, one against the King, a second against the Lord of the Fee, the third against a Neighbour by a Neighbour. See *Co.* 2. *Inst. fol.* 38. & 272.

Pour seisir terres la feme que tient en Dower, &c. Was a Writ whereby the King seised upon the Land which the Wife of his Tenant that held *in Capite*, deceased, hath for her Dowry, if she marryed without his leave; and is grounded upon the Statute of the King's Prerogative, *Cap.* 3. See *F. N. B. fol.* 174.

Poursuivant, From the French *Poursuivre*, i. *persequi*, Signifies the King's Messenger attending upon him in his Wars, or at the Council-Table, Exchequer, in his Court, or his Chamber, to be sent upon any Occasion or Message; as for the apprehending of a person accused, or suspected of any Offence: Those that be used in Martial Causes are call'd *Pursuivants at Arms*, 24 *H.* 8. 13. whereof there be four of special Names, which see in the word *Herald*. And *Stow* speaking of *Richard* the Third's death, *pag.* 784. hath these Words, *His Body was naked to the Skin, not so much as one Clout about him, and was trussed behind a* Poursuivant *at Arms like a Hog, or a Calf*, &c. The rest are used upon other Messages in time of Peace, and especially in matters touching Jurisdiction. See *Herald*.

Pourveyor, *Provisor*, Derived from the French *Pourvoire*, i. *providere*, Signifies an Officer of the King or Queen, or other great Personage, that provideth Corn and other Victual for their House. See *Mag. Charta*, cap. 22. and 3 *Ed.* 1. *cap.* 7. & 31. & *anno* 28. *ejusdem*, *Articuli super Chartas*, 2. and other Statutes; but this Office is limited by 12 *Car.* 2. *cap.* 24. See *Pourveyance* and *Achate*.

Pourveyance, Is the providing Corn, Fuel, Victual, and other Necessaries for the King's House. By 12 *Car.* 2. *cap.* 24. It is provided, **That no** Person or Persons, by any Warrant, Commission or Authority, under the Great Seal, or otherwise, by colour of buying or making provision or *Purveyance* for his Majesty, or any Queen of *England* for the time being, or that shall be, or for his, their, or any of their Housnold, shall take any Timber, Fuel, Cattel, Corn, Grain, Malt, Hay, Straw; Victual, Cart, Carriage, or other thing whatsoever of any the Subjects of his Majesty, his Heirs or Successors, without the full and free consent of the Owner or Owners thereof, had and obtained without Menace

or

or Enforcement, &c. See the Antiquity of Pre-emption and *Purveyance*, &c. and 3. *Inst. fol.* 82.

Power of the County, *Posse Comitatus*, In the Opinion of *Lambert* in his *Eirenarcha*, lib. 3. cap. 1. fol. 309. containeth the Ayd and Attendance of all Knights, Gentlemen, Yeomen, Laborers, Servants, Apprentices, and all others, above the Age of fifteen Years within the County, because all of that Age are bound to have Hardness by the Statute of *Winchester*: But Women, Ecclesiastical Persons, and such as are decrepit, or labor of an Infirmity, shall not be compelled to attend. And the Statute of 2 *H.* 5. *cap.* 8. sayes, *That Persons able to travel, shall be assistant in this Service*, which is used where a Possession is kept upon a Forcible Entry, or any Force or Rescue used, contrary to the Command of the King's Writ, or in opposition to the Execution of Justice.

Powledavis. See *Poledavis*, 1 Jac. 24.

Poynings Law, Is an Act of Parliament made in *Ireland* by *Hen.* 7. and so called, because Sir *Edward Poynings* was Lieutenant there when it was made, whereby all the Statutes in *England* were made of force in *Ireland*, which before that time were not, neither are any now in force there which were made in *England* since that time. See *Cokes* 12. *Rep. fol.* 190. *Hill.* 10 *Jac.*

Pray age. See *Age prior.*

Pray in ayd. See *Ayd.*

Pratum falcabile, A Meadow or Ground fit for Mowing, *Juratores dicunt quod prædicta placea a tempore quo, &c. fuit* pratum falcabile *usque ad prædictum annum quod* W. *prædictus illud aravit*, Trin. 18 Ed. 1. *in Banco Rot.* 50.

Preamble, *Proœmium*, Takes name from the Preposition *præ*, before, and *ambulo* to walk; as if we would say, To walk before: And hereof the beginning of an Act is called *The preamble*, which is as a Key to open the intent of the Makers of the Act, and the Mischiefs which they would remedy by the same. As for example, the Statute made at *Westminster* the First, *chap.* 37. which gives an Attaint: The *preamble* is thus, forasmuch as certain people doubt very little to give false Verdicts or Oaths, which they ought not to do, whereby many People are disherited, and lose their Right. It is provided, &c.

Prebend, *Præbenda*, Is the portion which every Member, or Canon, of a Cathedral-Church receiveth in the right of his Place for his Maintenance: So *Canonica portio* is properly used for that share, which every *Canon* or *Prebendary* receiveth yearly out of the common Stock of the Church; And *Præbenda* is a several Benefice, rising from some Temporal Land, or Church appropriated, towards the Maintenance of a Clerk, or Member of a Collegiat-Church, and is commonly sirnamed of the place whence the profit groweth. And these *Prebends* be either *simple*, or *with dignity*; *Simple Prebends* be those that have no more but the Revenue towards their Maintenance. *Prebends with dignity* are such as have Jurisdiction annext to them, according to the divers Orders in every several Church. Of this, see more in the *Decretals*, tit. *De* præbendis & *dignitat. Præbenda* was also in old Deeds used for Provender, as the learned *Spelman* saith, *Ex lib.* M. S. *Roffensis Ecclesiæ*, cap. *Quid mensuræ granarii continent*.

Prebendary, *Præbendarius*, Is he that hath a *Prebend*, and is so called, *a Præbendo auxilium aut consilium Episcopo vel Decano.*

Precariæ, Are Dayes-Works, which the Tenants of some Mannors are bound, by reason of their Tenure, to do for the Lord in Harvest; and in divers places are vulgarly call'd **Bind-dayes** for **Biden-dayes**, which in the Saxon *Dies precarias sonat*. For **Biden** is to pray or intreat. This Custome is plainly set forth in the great Book of the Customs of the Monastery of *Battell*, tit. *Apelderhan*, fol. 60. *Johannes Aylmer tenet per irrotulamentum Curiæ, unum Mess. & unam Virgatam terræ*, &c. *& debet invenire unum hominem*, &c. *& etiam debet venire, quolibet anno ad duas precarias carucæ cum caruca sua si habeat integram carucam, vel de parte quam habeat carucæ quum habet, si carucam non habeat integram & tunc arare debet utroque die quantum potest a manè usque ad meridiem, & uterque tentor*, viz. *carucæ & fugatorum habeant unum pastum solempnem utroque die prædictarum* precariarum, *&c. & debet invenire ad* 3. precarias *in Autumpno* 2. *homines, &c.* See more in *Spelmans Glossary*, verbo *Precariæ*. See *Bederepe*.

Prece partium, Is when a Suit is continued by the prayer, assent or agreement of both Parties, *Anno* 13 *E.* 1. *cap.* 27.

Precept, *Præceptum*, Is diversly taken in Law as sometime for a Commandment in Writing, sent out by a Justice of Peace, or other like Officer, for the bringing of a Person or Records before him, of which you have divers examples in the Table of the *Register Judicial*. And in this sense it seems to be borrowed from the Customs of *Lombardy*, where *præceptum* signifieth *Scripturam vel instrumentum*, Hotom. in verb. *Feudal.* & lib. 3. *Commentar in libros feudor in præfatione.* Sometimes it is taken for the provocation, whereby one man incites another to commit a Felony, as Theft, Murder, *&c.* *Stamf. pl. cor.* fol. 105. *Bracton*, lib. 3. tract. 2. cap. 9. calls it *Præceptum* or *Mandatum*. Whence we may observe three diversities of offending in Murder, *Præceptum, Fortia, Consilium. Præceptum* being the instigation used before-hand: *Fortia*, the assistance in the Fact, as to help to bind the party murdered or robbed; *Consilium*, advice either before or in the Fact. The *Civilians* use *Mandatum* in this Case.

Preceptories, *Præceptoriæ*, *Anno* 32 *H.* 8. cap. 24. Were Benefices in a kind, and termed *Præceptories*, because they were possessed by the more eminent sort of the Templers, whom the chief Master by his Authority created and called, *Præceptores templi. Joach. Steph. de Jurisdict.* lib. 4 cap. 10. num. 27. Sixteen of these are recorded, viz. *Cressing-Temple, Balshall, Shengay, Newland, Yeveley, Witham, Temple Bruere, Wallington, Rothely, Ovenington, Temple Combe, Trebigh, Ribstan, Mount St.* John, *Temple-Newsum*, and *Temple-hurst*. Monast. Ang. 2. par. fol. 543.

Præcipe quod reddat, Is a Writ of great diversity both in its form and use, for which see *Ingressus* and *Entry*. This form is extended as well to a *Writ of Right*, as to other Writs of *Entry* or Possession, *Old Nat. Brev. fol.* 13. and

F. N. B. fol. 5. It is called sometime a *Writ of Right close*, as a *Præcipe in Capite*, where it issueth for a Tenant holding of the King in chief, as of his Crown; and not of the King, as of any Honor, Castle or Mannor, *Reg. Orig. fol.* 4. and *F. N. B. fol.* 5. Sometime a *Writ of Right Patent*, as when it issues out of the Chancery *Patent*, that is, open to any Lords Court for any of his Tenants deforced against the Deforceor, and must be determined there. Of which read more at large *F. N. B. cap.* 1.

Præcipe in Capite, *Mag. Chart.* cap. 24. Was a Writ issuing of the Court of Chancery, for a Tenant holding of the King in chief, as of his Crown, and not as of any Honor, Castle or Mannor, *Regist. fol.* 4.

Precontract, 2 & 3 *Ed.* 6. *cap.* 23. Is a *Contract* made before another *Contract*, but hath relation especially to Marriages.

Predial Tythes, *Decimæ Prædiales*, Are those which are paid of things arising and growing from the Ground onely, as Corn, Hay, Fruit of Trees, and such like, 2 *E.* 6. 13. See *Co.* 2. *Inst. fol.* 649.

Pre-amption, *Praemptio*, Was a Priviledge allowed the King's Purveyor, to have the first buying of Corn and other provision, before others, for the King's House, which is taken by a late Statute made 12 *Car.* 2. *cap.* 24.

Prelate, *Prælatus*, We usually interpret to be an Arch-Bishop or Bishop: But *Spelman* in his *Glossary* sayes, *Prælati Ecclesiæ vocantur nedum superiores ut Episcopi, sed etiam inferiores, ut Archidiaconi, Presbyteri, Plebain & Rectores Ecclesiarum, sic enim in Bulla Privileg. apud* Mat. Par. *in* Hen. 3. *sub* anno 1246. *Innocentius, &c. universis tam Cathedralium quam aliorum Prælatis, necnon Patronis Ecclesiarum Clericis & Laicis per Regnum Angliæ constitutis salutem, &c.* pag. 476.

Premisses. See *Habendum*.

Premium, *Præmium*, A Reward; Amongst Merchants it is used for that sum of Money which the ensured gives the Ensurer for ensuring the safe return of any Ship or Merchandise, *Anno* 19 *Car.* 2. *cap.* 1.

Præmunire, Is either taken for a Writ so called, or for the Offence whereupon the Writ is granted. The one may be sufficiently understood by the other; We may therefore take notice, That heretofore the Church of *Rome*, under pretence of her Supremacy, and the Dignity of St. *Peter*'s Chair, took upon her to bestow most of the Bishopricks, Abbathies, and other Ecclesiastical Livings of worth here in *England*, by Mandates, before they were void, pretending therein a great Care to see the Church provided of a Successor before it needed: Whence it sprung, That these Bulls were called *Gratiæ Expectativæ*, or *Provisiones*, whereof you may read a learned Discourse in *Duarenus*, in his Tractate *De Beneficiis*, lib. 3. cap. 1. and in his Treatise *De immunitate Ecclesiæ Gallicanæ*. These Provisions were so frequent with us, that at last King *Edward* the Third, not digesting so intollerable an Encroachment, made a Statute the in twenty fifth year of his Reign, *Stat.* 5. *cap.* 22. and another *Stat.* 6. *cap.* 1. and a third *Anno* 27. Against those that drew the Kings people out of the Realm, to answer touching things belonging to the King's Court: And another *Anno* 28. *stat.* 2. *cap.* 1, 2, 3, 4. whereby he much restrained this Usurpation of the *Pope*; nevertheless he still adventured the Continuation of these *Provisions*, insomuch that King *Richard the Second* likewise made a Statute against them in the Twelfth year of his Reign, *cap.* 15. and likewise in his thirteenth year, *stat.* 2. *cap.* 2. wherein, mentioning the said first Statute of *Edward the Third*, he ratified the same, and appointed the punishment of those that offended against it, to be **Perpetual Banishment, Forfeiture of their Lands, Tenements, Goods and Chattels, &c.** And again, in the sixteenth year of his Reign, to meet more fully with all the Shifts invented to defraud these former Statutes, he set forth the Offence more particularly, with the same punishment for it, as in the former Statute. After him, King *Henry the Fourth* in like manner vexed with these and other Abuses not fully met with in the former Statutes, in the second year of his Reign, *cap.* 3, 4. addeth certain new cases, and lays upon the Offendors in them the same censure, whereto I refer you, as also to 9 *H.* 4. *cap.* 8. and 3 *H.* 5. 4. concerning which, and the danger that hath been threatned thereby, with the necessity thereof since the uniting of the Supremacy, both Ecclesiastical and Temporal in the King, read Sir *Thomas Smith de Repub. Angl.* lib. 3. cap. 9. 'Tis true, some later Statutes do cast this punishment upon other Offendors, as namely, the Statute of 1 *Eliz. cap.* 1. upon him that denies the King's Supremacy the second time, &c. And the Stat. 13 *Eliz. cap.* 2. upon him that affirms the Authority of the Pope, or refuseth to take the Oath of Supremacy. And the Stat. 13 *Eliz. cap.* 1. such as be Seditious Talkers of the Inheritance of the Crown, or affirms the Queen to be an Heretick. And the Statute 13 *Car.* 2. *cap.* 1. upon such as affirm the Parliament begun at *Westm.* 3. *Novemb.* 1640. is not yet dissolved: Or that there is any Obligation by *Oath, Covenant or Engagement* whatsoever, to endeavor a change of Government either in Church or State: Or that both, or either House of Parliament, have or hath a Legislative Power without the King. And the Word is applyed most commonly to the Punishments first Ordained by the Statutes before-mentioned, for such as transgressed them, but in later times (as we have shewn) imposed upon other Offences; For, where it is said, That any Man for an Offence committed, shall incur a *præmunire*, it is meant, that he shall incur the same punishment which is inflicted upon those that transgress the Statute made 16 *R.* 2. *cap.* 5. commonly called the Statute of *Præmunire*, which kind of reference is not unusual in our Statutes: As to the *Etymology* of this word *Præmunire*, some think it proceedeth from the strength given to the Crown by the former Statutes, against the Usurpation of a Foreign Power, which Opinion may receive Ground from the Statute, 25 *E.* 3. *stat.* 6. *cap.* 1. But others think it may be deduced from the Verb *Præmonere*, being barbarously turned into *Præmunire*; which corruption is taken from the rude Interpreters of the Canon Law, who indeed do put the effect *Præmunire* many times for the sufficient cause *Præmonere*, according to the Proverb, *He* *that is well warned, is half armed.* Of which a reason may be gathered from the form of the Writ, *Præmunire facias præfatum Præpositum & J. R. Procuratorem, &c. quod tunc sint coram nobis, &c.* which words can be referred to none, but the parties charged with the Offence. See 3. *Inst. fol.* 119.

Prender, Is the power or right of taking a thing before it is offered; from the French *Prendre*, id est, *accipere* : *It lies in* Render, *but not in* Prender, *Co. Rep.* 1. *par.* Sir *John Peter's* Case.

Prender de Baron, Signifies literally to take a Husband; but it is used as an Exception, to disable a Woman from pursuing an Appeal of Murder against the Killer of her former Husband, *Stamf. pl. cor.* lib. 3. cap. 59.

Prepensed, *Præpensus*, Fore-thought; as Malice *prepensed*, *Malitia præcogitata*, when a Man is slain upon a sudden Quarrel; yet if there were *Malice prepensed* formerly between them, it makes it *Murder*; or, as it is called in the Statute 12 *Hen.* 7. *cap.* 7. *prepensed Murder.* See *Murder*, and 3. *Inst. fol.* 51.

Præpositus Ecclesiæ. See *Church Reve.*

Præpositus Villæ, Is sometimes used for the Constable of a Town, or Petit Constable, *Cromp. Jur. fol.* 205. Howbeit the same Author, *fol.* 194. seemeth to apply it otherwise, for there *Quatuor homines præpositi* be those four men, that for every Town must appear before the Justices of the Forest in their Circuit: It is used sometime for a *Reve*, or for a chief Officer of the King in a Town, Mannor or Village. See *Reeve. Animatia & res inventæ coram* ipso *& sacerdote ducendæ erant*, Leg. Edw. Conf. cap. 28.

Prærogative of the King, *Prærogativa Regis*, Derived from *Præ, ante*, and *Rogare*, to ask or demand: Is that special Power, Pre-eminence or Priviledge, which the King hath over and above other Persons, and above the ordinary course of the Common Law, in the right of his Crown, *Potest Rex ei, lege suæ dignitatis, condonare si velit, etiam mortem promeritam*, Leg. Ed. Conf. cap. 18. And the *Civilians* use this Word *Prerogative* in the same sense: Among the *Feudists* it is termed, *Jus regalium, jus regaliorum, vel à nonnullis jus Regaliarum.* And as the Feudists, *Sub jure Regalium.* So our Lawyers, *Sub prærogativa Regis* do comprise all that absolute heighth of power that the *Civilians* call *Majestatem vel potestatem, vel jus imperii*, subject only to God. Which *Regalia* the *Feudists* divide into two sorts, *Majora & minora regalia*; for to use their own Words, *Quædam regalia dignitatem*, prærogativam *& imperii præeminentiam spectant; quidam verò ad utilitatem & commodum pecuniarium immediate attinent, & hæc propriè fiscalia sunt & ad jus fisci pertinent.* Peregr. de jure fisci, lib. 1. cap. 1. num. 9. See also *Arnoldus Chapmarius, de arcanis imperii*, lib. 1. cap. 11. By which it appears, That the Statute of the King's *Prerogative* made 17 *E.* 2. contains not the King's whole *Prerogative*, but onely so much thereof as concerns the profit of his Coffers, growing by vertue of his Regal Power and Crown; for it is more than manifest, That his *Prærogative* extends much farther, yea even in the matters of his profit, which that Statute especially consisteth of; For the King hath many Rights of Majesty peculiar to himself, which the learned in the Law term *Sacra sacrorum*, that is, sacred; and *individua*, inseparable, because they cannot be sever'd, which are many and various; and if you would satisfie your self therein, read *Stamf. prærog.* the Stat. *Prærogativa Regis*, 17 E. 2 *Plowden in the Case of Mines*, F. N. B. fol. 31. 31 H. 8. cap. 13. Co. lib. 10. tit. 1. The learned *Spelman* calls it *Lex Regiæ dignitatis.*

Prerogative of the Bishop of Canterbury or York, *Prærogativa Archiepiscopi Cantuariensis sive Eboracensis*, Is an especial Pre-eminence that these Sees have in certain Cases above ordinary Bishops within their Province, of which whoever desires to receive more full Information, may read the Book intituled, *De Antiquitate Britannicæ Ecclesiæ, & nominatim de privilegiis Ecclesiæ Cantuariensis historia*, and especially in the Eighth Chapter of that Book, *pag.* 25.

Prerogative Court, *Curia prærogativa Archiepiscopi Cantuariensis*, Is the *Court* wherein all Wills be proved, and all Administrations taken, that belong to the Archbishop by his *Prærogative*; that is, in case where the deceased had Goods of any considerable value out of the Diocess, wherein he died; and that value is ordinarily 5*li.* except it be otherwise by composition between the said Archbishop and some other Bishop, as in the Diocess of *London* it is ten Pound: And if any Contention grow between Two, or more, touching any such Will or Administration, the Cause is properly debated and decided in this Court: the Judge whereof is termed *Judex Curiæ* Prærogativæ *Cantuariensis*, the Judge of the *Prerogative Court* of *Canterbury.* The Archbishop of *York* hath also the like *Court*, which is termed *His Exchequer*, but far inferior to this in power and profit.

Prescription, *Præscriptio*, Is a Title, taking his substance of use, and time allowed by the Law, which is beyond the memory of Man, *Kitchin, fol.* 104. saith thus, *Prescription* is, when for continuance of time, *ultra memoriam hominis*, a particular Person hath particular right against another particular person; With whom agrees *Co. lib.* 4. *fol.* 32. and *Co.* on *Lit. fol.* 140. But as in the *Civil Law*, so likewise in the *Common: Prescription* may be in a shorter time, at least in some special Cases. As for example, Where the Statute 1 *H.* 8. *cap.* 9. saith, That all Actions popular must be sued within three years after the Offence committed: And the Stat. 7 *H.* 8. 3 that four years being past after the Offence committed in one case, and one year in another, no Suit can be commenced. And the Stat. 31 *Eliz. cap.* 5 saith, That all Actions, *&c.* brought upon Statute, the penalty whereof belongs to the King, shall be brought within two years after the Offence committed, or else be void. And the Stat. 39 *Eliz. cap.* 1. 2. saith, That Actions brought after two Years by any common person, or after three years by the King alone for decay of Husbandry, shall be of no force: Whosoever offendeth against any such Statute, and escapes unquestion'd for two years or three, of the two later of the three fore-mentioned Statutes, may justly be said to have *prescribed* against that Action. The like may be said of the Statute made 23 *Eliz. cap.* 1. which saith, That all Offences comprised in that Statute, made in the thirteenth year of *Eliz. cap.* 2, are inquirable before both *Justices of Peace and Assise* within a year and a day after the Offence committed: Also the Title that a man attaineth by the passing of five years, after a Fine acknowledged of any Lands or Tenements, may justly be said to be obtained by *prescription*: And whereas the Statute made 8 R. 2. *cap.* 4. saith, That a Judge, or Clerk, convicted for false entring of Pleas, may be fined within two years; the two years being past, he *prescribeth* against the punishment of the said Statute: And whereas the Statute 11 *H.* 7. sayes, That he which will complain of Maintenance or Embracery, whereby perjury is committed by a Jury, must do it within six dayes, those six dayes ended, the Parties *prescribe*; and divers other Statutes have the like limitation of time, whence may arise a like *prescription.* See *Action perpetual and temporal.* See *Lam. Eiren.* lib. 4. cap. 5. pag. 469. *Cromp. Just. of Peace*, fol. 173. Of this *prescription*, and the learning touching the same, see *Co. Rep.* 4. *Lutterell's* Case, *fol.* 84. *Præscriptio est jus quoddam, ex tempore congruens, authoritate legum vim capiens, pœnam negligentibus inferens & finem litibus imponens* — *Quadragenalis* præscriptio *omnem prorsus actionem excludat. Reformatio Legum Eccles.* pag. 246. See 2 *Inst. fol.* 653. *Stamf. prærog.* cap. 8. and *Co.* 7. *Rep. Baskervile's* Case.

Presentation, *Præsentatio*, Is used properly for the Act of a Patron, offering his Clerk to the Bishop, to be instituted in a Benefice of his Gift; the form whereof, See in *Reg. Orig. fol.* 322.

Presentee, Is the Clerk that is so presented by the Patron: In the Stat. 13 *R.* 2. *ca.* 1. mention is made of the King's *Presentee*, that is, he whom the King *presents* to a Church.

Presentment, Is a meer denunciation of the *Jurors* themselves, or some other Officer, as *Justice, Constable, Searcher, Surveyor*, &c. (without any information) of an Offence inquirable in the Court whereunto it is presented, *Lamb. Eiren.* lib. 4, cap. pag. 467.

President, *Præses*, In a legal sense denotes the King's *Lieutenant* in a Province or Function, as the *President of Wales, York, Berwick, or of the King's Council*, 22 H. 8. cap. 8. and 24 *H.* 8. 3. 14.

Prest, Is used for a Duty in Money to be paid by the Sheriff, upon his account in the *Exchequer*, or for Money left, or remaining in his hands 2, & 3 *Ed.* 6. *ca.* 4.

Prest-Money, Is so called of the French word *Prest*, that is, *promptus expeditus*, for that it binds those that receive it, to be ready at all times appointed, being meant commonly of Soldiers, 18 *H.* 6. 19. 7 *H.* 7. 1. 3 *H.* 8. 5. and 2 *E.* 6. 2.

Prestation-Money, *Præstatio*, A paying or performing, is a Sum of *Money* paid by Archdeacons yearly to their Bishop *pro exteriori Jurisdictione* — *Et sint* quieti *a præstatione* Muragii, Cart. H. 7. Burgens. Mount-Gomer. *Præstatio* was also anciently used for *Purveyance.* See Mr. *Phillip's* Book on that Subject, *pag.* 222. And see *Spiritualties.*

Presumption, *Præsumptio*, Is of three sorts, 1. *Violent*, which is many times a full proof; as if one be kill'd in a House, and a Man is seen to come out of the House with a bloody Sword, and no other Person was at that time in the House; this, though but a *presumption*, is as a proof. 2. *Probable*, which hath but a small effect. 3. *Levis, seu temeraria*, which is of no prevalency at all: So in case of a Charter or Feoffment, if all the Witnesses to the Deed be dead; the *violent presumption*, which stands for a proof, is continual and quiet possession, *Co.* on *Lit.* lib. 1. cap. 1. sect. 1. *Præsumptio stat in dubio*, it is doubted of yet accounted *Veritatis comes, quatenus in contrarium nulla est probatio, ut regula se habet, stabitur* præsumptio *donec probetur in contrarium. Presumption* was anciently taken for intrusion. — *Assultus, Roberia, Sterbrech*, præsumptio *terræ vel pecuniæ Regis, Thesaurus inventus, &c.* Leg. Hen. 1. cap. 11. *De his quæ sunt jure Regis.*

Pretensed Right or Title, *Jus prætensum*, Is, where one is in possession of Lands or Tenements, and another who is out claims it, and sues for it: Here the *pretensed right and title* is said in him who doth so claim and sue.

Prevaricate, *Prævaricare*, Is, when a Man falsly and deceitfully seems to undertake a thing, *eâ intentione*, that he may destroy it, *Dicitur* prævaricator *quasi varicator, a varia certatione, quia adversam partem ad juvat proditâ suâ propriâ causâ, dum huic instat corpore ex una parte & illi mente & corde ex altera parte.* Vocabul. utriusque juris. *verb.* Prævaricatores.

Price. See *Value.*

Pricked-Bread, — *Molendinario septem panes de conventu & septem panes de* **Pricked-Bread**, *Monast. Angl.* 1. par. fol. 498.

Pride-gavel, In the Lordship of *Rodeley*, in the County of *Gloucester*, is used and paid unto this day, as a Rent to the Lord of the Mannor by certain Tenants, in duty and acknowledgement to him for their liberty and priviledge of fishing in the River *Severne* for Lamprayes, *Taylors History of Gavel-kind*, cap. 9. fol. 112, 113.

Primo beneficio. See *Beneficio.*

Pridie, Is sometimes joyned to an Accusative, and sometimes to a Genitive Case, as *Pridie Calendas*, and *Pridie Calendarum*, is the day before the *calends*, that is, the last day of every Month.

Primage, Is a Duty due to the Mariners and Saylers, for the loading of any Ship at the setting forth from any Haven, *Anno* 32 *H.* 8. ca. 14. which, in some places, is a penny in the pound, in others six pence for every Pack or Bayl, or otherwise, according to the Custom of the place.

Primier seisin, *Prima seisina*, The first possession or *seisin* was heretofore used as a branch of the *King's Prerogative*, whereby he had the first possession, that is, the intire profits for a year of all the Lands and Tenements, whereof his Tenant (that held of him *in Capite*) dyed *seised* in his Demesne as of Fee, his Heir then being at full age; until he do his Homage, or if under age, until he were of Age; *Stamf. prærog.* cap. 3. and *Bracton*, lib. 4. tract. 3. cap. 1. But all the charges arising by *Primer seisins* are taken away by the Stat. made 12 *Car.* 2. *ca.* 24.

Primitiæ, *First-Fruits*, Are properly the first of our increase offered to God; but in our Law, are the profits after avoidance of every spiritual Living for one year. See 26 *H.* 8. *ca.* 3. 32 *H.*

32 *H.* 8. 45. 1. *Mar. Seʃʃ.* 2. *ca.* 10. and 1 *Eliz. ca.* 4. See *First Fruits.*

Primogeniture, *Primogenitura*, The Title of an Elder Brother in right of his Birth: The reason of which, *Co.* upon *Lit.* sayes is, *Qui prior est tempore, potior est jure*, affirming moreover, *That in King* Alfred's *time, Knights Fees descended to the* Eldest Son, *for that by the division of such Fees between Males, the defence of the Realm might be weakned.* And Judge *Dodderidge* in his Treatise of *Nobility* saith, *pag.* 119. It was anciently Ordained, That all Knights Fees should come unto the eldest Son by Succession of Heritage, whereby he succeeding his Ancestors in the whole Inheritance, might be the better enabled to maintain the Wars against the King's Enemies, or his Lords. And that the *Soccage* should be partible among the Male-Children, to enable them to increase into many Families, for the better furtherance in and increase of Husbandry.

Prince, *Princeps*, Is sometimes at large taken for the King himself, but more properly for the King's Eldest Son, who is **Prince of Wales**, as the eldest Son to the French King, is called *Dauphine*; both being born Princes, *Fernes Glory of Generosity*, pag. 138. Before *Edward the Second*, who was born at *Caernarvon*, and *the first English* Prince *of Wales*, the King's Eldest Son was stiled *Lord Prince*, Stamf. prærog. *ca.* 22. *fol.* 75. See 27 *H.* 8. *ca.* 26. and 28 *H.* 8. 3. and *Stows Annals*, pag. 303.

Principal, *Principalium*, A Heyrloome, which see. In *Urchenfield*, in the County of *Hereford*, certain *Principals*, as the best Beast, the best Bed, best Table, &c. pass to the Eldest Child, and are not lyable to partition. Also the chief person in some of the Inns of *Chancery*, is called *Principal* of the House. See *Ancient.*

Principality of Chester, *Anno* 21 *Rich.* 1. *ca.* 9. See *County Palatine* and *Cromptons* divers *Jurisdictions*, fol. 137.

Prior perpetual, or Dative and removeable, *Anno* 9 *Rich.* 2. *ca.* 4. and 1 *E.* 4. *cap.* 1. *Lord* Prior *of St.* Johns *of* Jerusalem, 26 *H.* 8. *ca.* 2.

Priors aliens, *Priores alieni*, Were Religious Men born in *France*, and Governors of Religious Houses, erected for Outlandish Men here in *England*, which were by King *Henry* the Fifth, after his Conquests in *France*, thought no good Members for this Land, and therefore suppressed them; whose Livings afterwards were by King *Henry the Sixth* given to other Monasteries and Houses of Learning, *Stows Annals*, pag. 582. and 1 *H.* 5. *ca.* 7. but especially to the erecting of those two famous Colleges called the one *Kings College in Cambridge*, the other *Eaton*, 2. *par. Inst. fol.* 584.

Priority, *Prioritas*, Signifies an Antiquity of Tenure, in comparison of another not so ancient, as *to hold by priority*, is to hold of a Lord more anciently than of another, *Old Nat. Brev. fol.* 94. So *to hold by Posteriority* is used *in Stamf. prærog.* cap. 2. fol. 11. And *Crompton* in his *Jurisd. fol.* 117. useth this Word in the same signification. The Lord of the *Priority* shall have the custody of the Body, &c. and *fol.* 120. If the Tenant hold by *Priority* of one, and by *Posteriority* of another, &c. to which effect, see also *F. N. B. fol.* 142. *Bartolus* in his Tractate *De insigniis & armis*, useth these words, *Prioritas & posterioritas*, concerning Two that bear one Coat-Armor.

Prisage, Is that custome or share that belongs to the King, out of such Merchandise as are taken at Sea by way of lawful *prise*, *Anno* 31 *Eliz. ca.* 5.

Prisage of Wines, *Anno* 1 *H.* 8. *ca.* 5. Is a word almost out of use, being now call'd *Butlerage*, (because the King's chief Butler receives it;) It is a Custome whereby the Prince challengeth out of every Bark laden with Wine, containing less than forty Tun, two Tun of Wine, the one before, the other behind the Mast at his own price, which is twenty shillings a Tun, yet this varies according to the Custom of the Place: For at *Boston*, every Bark laden with ten Tuns of Wine, or above, pays *Prisage.* See *Butlerage* and *Calthrop*'s *Reports*, fol. 20. and 4. *par. Inst. fol.* 30.

Memorandum, *Quod Rex habet ex antiqua consuetudine de qualibet Nave mercatoris vini 6. carcat applican. infra aliquem portum Angliæ de viginti doliis, duo dolia & de decem doliis unum de prisa Regis pro quodam certo ab antiquo constitut. solvend.* P. Rec. 20. R. 2.

Prise, *Prisa*, From the French *Prendre, capere*, signifies in our Statutes the things taken of the King's Subjects by *Purveyors*, *Anno* 13 E. 1. *ca.* 7. and 28 E. 1. *stat.* 3. *ca.* 2. It signifies also a *Custome* due to the King, 25 E. 1. *ca.* 5. *Reg. Orig. fol.* 117. *In foraneis paginis antiquis* (sayes the learned *Spelman*) *Prisæ plerumque intelliguntur de annonæ reique frumentariæ captionibus aliis etiam necessariis, ob alenda, instruendaque castrorum præsidia, necnon et Regiam familiam minori quam justo pretio agricolis arreptis*, &c. In Rescripto quodam, *Anno* 3 E. 1. Norfolk. — Rogerus de Monte alto *qui sororem & hæredem Hugonis de Albeney, &c. desponsaverat, clamat habere libertates has subscriptas*, viz. *Castellum suum de Risinge cum* Prisis 40. *dierum, &c.* Ubi clausulam *cum* prisis 40. *dierum* intelligo *de libertate capiendi victualia quæ vocant ad sustentationem præsidiarii militis castri sui, ita quod pretium reddat infra* 40. *dies.* See 12 *Car.* 2. *ca.* 24.

Prison, *Prisona*, Is a place of restraint for the safe custody of a person to answer any Action personal or criminal; And here we are to note, That this *salva custodia* must onely be *custodia non pæna*, for *carcer ad homines custodiendos non ad puniendos dari debet*, Co. on Lit. *lib.* 3. *ca.* 7. *sect.* 438.

Prisoner, *Prisonarius, captivus*, From the French *Prisonnier*, signifies a man restrained of his Liberty upon any Action civil or criminal, or upon Commandement: And a Man may be a *Prisoner* upon matter of *Record*, or matter of *Fact.* *Prisoner* upon matter of *Record* is he, which being present in Court, is by the Court committed onely upon Arrest, be it by the Sheriff, Constable, or other, *Stamf. pl. cor.* lib. 1. cap. 32. fol. 34. & 35.

Privation, *Privatio*, A bereaving or taking away, most commonly applyed to a Bishop or Rector of a Church, when, by Death, or other

act

act, they are deprived of their Bishoprick or Benefice. See *Co.* on *Lit.* fol. 329.

Privy, Derived of the French *Prive*, i. *Familiaris*, Signifies him that is partaker, or hath an interest in any Action or thing, as *privies of Blood*, *Old Nat. Brev. fol.* 117. be those that are linked in Consanguinity; every Heir in tail is *privy* to recover the Land intailed, *Id. fol.* 137. No *privity* was between me and the Tenant, *Littleton*, *fol.* 106. If I deliver Goods to a man, to be carried to such a place, and he after he hath brought them thither, doth steal them; it is Felony, because the *privity* of delivery is determined as soon as they are brought thither, *Stamf. pl. cor.* lib. 1. cap. 15. fol. 25. *Merchants-privy* be opposite to *Merchants-strangers*, 2 E. 3. 9. & 14. The Author of the *New Termes of the Laws* maketh divers sorts of *privies*, viz. Privies *in Estate*, Privies *in Deed*, Privies *in Law*, Privies *in Right*, *and* Privies *in Blood*; where you may read examples of each of them in the word *Privy*. See *Perkins* 831, 832, 833. and *Co. lib.* 3. *fol.* 23. *Walker's* Case, and *lib.* 4. *fol.* 123, 124. mentions four kinds of *Privies*, viz. *Privies in Blood*, as the Heir to his Father. *Privies in Representation*, as Executors or Administrators to the deceased. *Privies in Estate*, as he in the Reversion, and he in the Remainder, when Land is given to one for life, to another in fee, for that their Estates are created both at one time. The fourth is *privy in Tenure*, as the Lord by escheat, that is, when the Land escheateth to the Lord for want of Heirs. See *Co.* on *Lit. lib. cap.* 8. *sect.* 161.

Privy-Seal, *Privatum sigillum*, Is a *Seal* that the King useth to such Grants, or other things, as pass the *Great Seal*; first they pass the *Privy-Signet*, then the *Privy-Seal*; and lastly, the *Great Seal of England*. The *Privy Seal* is sometimes used in things of less consequence, that never pass the *Great Seal*. No Writs shall pass under *the Privy Seal*, which touch the Common Law, 2. *Inst. fol.* 555.

Priviledge, *Privilegium*, Is defined by *Cicero* in his Oration *pro domo sua*, to be *lex privata homini irrogata*. It is, says another, *Jus singulare*, whereby a private man, or a particular Corporation, is exempted from the rigor of the Common Law. It is sometimes used in the Common Law for a place that hath any special immunity, *Kitchin, fol.* 118. *Priviledge* is either personal or real; a *personal priviledge* is that which is granted to any person either against or beyond the course of the Common Law: As for Example, A Member of Parliament may not be arrested, nor any of his Servants, during the sitting of the Parliament; nor for a certain time before and after. *A priviledge real*, is that which is granted to a place, as to the *Universities*, that none of either may be called to *Westminster-Hall*, upon any Contract made within their own Precincts, or prosecuted in other Courts: And one belonging to the *Court of Chancery* cannot be sued in any other Court, certain Cases excepted, and if he be, he may remove it by *Writ of Priviledge*, grounded upon the Stat. 18 *E.* 3. See the *New Book of Entries*, verbo *Priviledge*.

Privity, *Privitas*, Private Familiarity, inward Relation: If there be Lord and Tenant, and the Tenant holds of the Lord by certain Services, there is *a privity* between them in respect of the Tenure. See *Privy*.

Probate of Testaments, *Probatio Testamentorum*, Is the exhibiting and proving Wills and *Testaments* before the Ecclesiastical Judge, delegated by the Bishop, who is Ordinary of the place, when the party dies. And the Ordinary is known by the guantity of the Goods that the deceased hath out of the Diocess wherein he departed; for if all his Goods be in the same Diocess, then the Bishop of the Diocess, or the Arch-deacon (according as their composition or prescription leads) hath the *probate of the Testament*: But if the Goods be disperst in divers Diocesses, so that there be any sum of note (as five pounds ordinarily) out of the Diocess where the party lived; then is the Archbishop of *Canterbury* the Ordinary by his *Prerogative*. See *Prerogative of the Archbishop*. This *Probate* may be made in two sorts, *in common form*, or *per testes*. *The proof in common form* is only by the Oath of the Executor or party exhibiting the Will, who sweareth upon his belief, That the Will exhibited by him, is the last Will and *Testament* of the deceased. The proof *per testes* is, when over and besides his own Oath, he also produces Witnesses, or makes other proof to confirm the same, and that in the presence of such as may pretend any interest in the Goods of the deceased, or at least in their absence, after they have been lawfully summoned to see such a Will proved, if they think good. And the later course is taken most commonly when there is fear of strife, or dispute about the deceaseds Goods. For some hold that a *Will proved in common form* only, may be called in question any time within thirty years after. And where a Will disposes of Lands and Tenements of Free-hold, it is now frequently *proved by Witnesses* in *Chancery*.

Procedendo, Is a Writ whereby a Plea or Cause, formerly called from a base Court to the *Chancery*, *Kings Bench*, or *Common-Pleas*, by Writ of *Priviledge* or *Certiorari*, is released and sent down again to the same Court, to be proceeded in there, after it appeareth that the Defendant hath no cause of *Priviledge*, or that the matter comprised in the Bill be not well proved, *Bro. hoc titulo*, and *Co. vol.* 6. *fol.* 63. In 21 *Rich.* 2. *cap.* 11. *in fine*; Letters of *Procedendo* granted by the Keeper of the *Privy-Seal*. See in what divers manners it is used in the Table of the *Original* and *Judicial Writs*, Anno 21 *Jac. cap.* 23.

Processe, *Processus*, So also *a procedendo ab initio usq; ad finem*, is the manner of proceeding in every Cause, being the Writs and Precepts that go forth upon the *Original* upon every Action, being either Original or Judicial, *Britton, fol.* 138. wherein there is great diversity, as you may see in the Table of *F. N. B.* verbo *Processe*, and *Broke hoc tit.* Sometimes that only is called *The processe*, by which a man is called into the Court, because it is the beginning or the principal part thereof, by which the rest of the business is directed, according to that saying of *Aristotle*, ἡ ἀρχὴ ἥμισυ τοῦ παντός. Divers kinds of *Processe* upon Inditements, see in *Cromp. Just. of Peace*, fol. 133, 134, 135. and *Lamb.* in his Tractate of *Processes*, adjoyning to his *Eirenarcha*. *Special Processe* is that which is especially appointed for the Offence by Statute, for which he refers his Reader to the Eighth Chapter of his Fourth Book. The difference between *process and precept*, *or warrant* of the Justices, is this, The *precept or warrant* is only to attach and convent the party before any Indictment or Conviction, and may be made either in the Name of the King, or the Justice. But *the process* is alwayes in the King's Name, and usually after an Indictment, *Co.* 8. *Rep. Blackmore's* Case.

Prochein amy, *Proximus amicus vel propinquior*, The next Friend; is used in the Common Law for him that is next of Kin to a Child in his Nonage, and is in that respect allowed by Law to deal for him in the managing his Affairs, as to be his *Guardian*, if he hold any Land in *socage*, and in the redress of any wrong done to him, Stat. *Westm.* 1. *cap.* 48. and *Westm.* 2. *cap.* 15. and is in the prosecution of any Action at Law *per Guardianum*, where the Plaintiff is an Infant; *& per proximum amicum*, where the Infant is Defendant. See *Co.* 2. *Inst. fol.* 261.

Processum continuando, Is a Writ for the continuance of a *process*, after the death of the chief Justice, or other Justices in the Writ of *Oyer and Terminer*, Regist. Orig. *fol.* 128.

Profe alias **Prove**, Is used for an Enquest, *Anno* 28 *E.* 3. *cap.* 13.

Proclamation, *Proclamatio*, Is a notice publickly given of any thing, whereof the King thinks fit to advertise his Subjects, and so it is used, 7 *Rich.* 2. *cap.* 6.

Proclamation of Rebellion, Is a publick Notice given by the Officer, that a man not appearing upon a *Subpœna*, nor *an Attachment* in the *Chancery*, shall be reputed a Rebel, unless he render himself by a day assigned in this Writ, *Cromp. Jur. fol.* 92. See *Commission of Rebellion.*

Proclamation of a Fine, Is a Notice openly and solemnly given at all the *Assises* held in the County, within one year after the engrossing it. And these *Proclamations* are made upon transcripts of the Fine, sent by the Justices of the Common Pleas to the Justices of Assise and the Justices of Peace. *West Symbol.* 2. par. tit. *Fines*, sect. 132. where also you may see the form of the *Proclamation*, *Proclamare est valde & palam clamare*, F. N. B. fol. 85. sayes, That the *King's Proclamation* is sufficient to stay a Subject from going out of the Realm. See the strength of *Proclamations*, *Anno* 31 *H.* 8. *cap.* 8. See also *Proclamations* in divers cases, *New Book of Entries*, verbo *Proclamations.*

Proctor, *Procurator*, Is he who undertakes to manage another mans Cause in any Court of the Civil Law or Ecclesiastical, for his Fee, *Qui aliena negotia gerenda suscipit.*

Pro confesso, Is, when upon a Bill exhibited in *Chancery*, the Defendant appears, and is in contempt for not answering, and is in custody; upon a *Habeas Corpus* (which is granted by Order) to bring him to the Bar, the Court assigns him a day to Answer, which being expired, and no Answer put in, a second *Habeas Corpus* is granted, and a further day assigned; by which day, if he Answer not, the Bill, upon the Plaintiffs motion, shall be taken *pro confesso*, unless cause be shewed by a day, which the Court usually gives; and for want of such cause shewed upon motion, the substance of the Plaintiffs Bill shall be decreed, as if it had *been confessed* by the Defendants Answer. As it was in the Case of *Filmore* and *Denny*, Hill. 1662. Or after a fourth insufficient Answer to the Bill, the matter of the Bill not sufficiently answer'd unto, shall be taken *pro confesso.*

Proctors of the Clergy, *Procuratores Cleri*, Are those who are chosen and appointed to appear for the Cathedral, or other Collegiate Churches; as also for the Common Clergy of every Diocess at the Parliament, to sit in the Lower-House of *Convocation*; and this is the manner of their Election. First, The King directeth his Writ to the Archbishop of each Province, for the summoning of all Bishops, Deans, Arch-deacons, Cathedral and Collegiate-Churches, and generally of all the Clergy of his Province, assigning them the time and place in the said Writ: Then the Archbishops proceed according to custom; One example shall serve for both. The Archbishop of *Canterbury* upon his Writ received, directeth his Letters to the Bishop of *London*, as his Dean Provincial: First, citing himself peremptorily, and then willing him to cite in like manner all the Bishops, Deans, Archdeacons, Cathedral and Collegiate Churches, and generally all the *Clergy* of his Province to the place, and against the day prefixed in the Writ; but directeth withall, that one *Proctor* be sent for every Cathedral or Collegiate, and Two for the Body of the inferior *Clergy* of each Diocess: And by Vertue of these Letters authentically sealed, the said Bishop of *London* directeth his like Letters severally to the Bishop of every Diocess of the Province, citing them in like sort, and commanding them not only to appear, but also to admonish the said Deans and Arch-deacons personally to appear, and the Cathedral or Collegiate Churches, as also the Common *Clergy* of the Diocess to send their *Proctors* to the place at the day appointed; and also willeth them, to certifie the Archbishop the Names of all and every so warned by them in a Schedule annexed to their Letter certificatory. The Bishops proceed accordingly, and the Cathedral and Collegiate Churches, and also the *Clergy* make choice of their *Proctors*; which done, and certified to the Bishop, he returneth all at the day. These *Proctors of the Clergy* had heretofore place and suffrage in the Commons House of Parliament, as appears by the Statute 21 *R.* 2. *cap.* 2. *&* 12. See *Prolocutor and Convocation*, and see 4. *Inst. fol.* 4.

Procurations, *Procurationes*, Are certain sums of Money which Parish Priests pay yearly to the Bishop or Arch-deacon, *ratione visitationis.* They were anciently paid in necessary Victuals, for the Visitor and his Attendants, but afterwards turn'd into Money. *Procuratio* is defined by *Valensis* to be *Necessariorum sumptuum exhibitio, quæ ratione visitationis, debetur ab Ecclesia vel Monasterio ei cui ex officio incumbit jus & onus visitandi, sive is sit Episcopus, sive Archidiaconus, sive Decanus, sive Legatus summi Pontificis*, Anno 1290. Memorandum, *Quod die Mercurii in festo sanctæ Lucæ Evang. Dominus Episcopus cepit* procurationem *suam in cibis & potibus apud* Bordesley *& pernoctavit ibidem*, Giff. fol. 226. See an Historical Discourse of *Procurations and Synodals*, Printed 1661. These are also called *Proxyes*, see *Dyer*, *fol.* 273. and *Claus. Rot.* 31 *E.* 1. *m.* 15. *Dorso.*

Procurator,

Procurator, Is used for him that gathereth the Fruits of a Benefice for another man, *Anno* 3. *R.* 2. *stat.* 1. *cap.* 3. and *Procuracy*, for the Writing or Instrument whereby he is authorised: They are at this day in the West parts called *Proctors*. See *Proctor*.

Procurors. See *Malveye's Procurors.*

Profer, *Profrum vel proferum*, From the French *Proferer*, i. *producere*, Is the time appointed for the Accounts of Sheriffs, and other Officers in the Exchequer, which is twice in the year, *Anno* 51 *Hen.* 3. *stat.* 5. which may be gathered also out of the *Register*, *fol.* 139. in the Writ *De Atturnato Vice-comitis pro* profro *faciendo.* We read also of *proffers*, 32 *H.* 8. 21. in these words, **Trinity Term shall begin the Monday next after Trinity-Sunday, whensoever it shall happen to fall, for the keeping of the Essoines, Profers, Returns, and other Ceremonies heretofore used and kept.** In which place *profer* signifies the offer or indeavor to proceed in an Action by any man concerned so to do. See *Britton*, *cap.* 28. *fol.* 50. & 55. & 80. and *Fleta*, *lib.* 1. *cap.* 38. *sect.* *Utlagati*, &c.

Profer the half-mark. See *Half mark.*

Profession, *Professio*, Is in the Common Law used particularly for the entring into any Religious Order of Fryers, &c. *New Book of Entries*, verbo *Profession.*

Profits apprendre. See *Prender.*

Prohibition, *Prohibitio*, Is a Writ to forbid any Court, either Spiritual or Secular, to proceed in any Cause there depending, upon suggestion, that the Cognisance thereof belongeth not to the same Court, *F. N. B. fol.* 39. But is now most usually taken for that Writ which lyeth for one that is impleaded in the *Court Christian*, for a Cause belonging to the Temporal Jurisdiction, or the Conusance of the *Kings Court*, whereby as well the party and his Council, as the Judge himself and the Register are forbidden to proceed any further in that Cause. In what Cases this lyeth, see *Bro. hoc tit.* & *F. N. B. fol.* 93. Of this *Prohibition*, *Bracton*, lib. 5. tract. 5. cap. 3, 4, 5, 6. 7, 8, 9, 10, 11, 12. saith, That it lies not after Sentence given in any Cause: And the Statute of 50 *E.* 3. Ordains, That there should lie no more than *one prohibition* in one Cause. See the diversity of *Prohibitions* in the Table of the *Register Original*, and the *New Book of Entries*, verbo *Prohibition*, and *F. N. B. fol.* 39.

Prohibitio de vasto directa parti, Is a Writ Judicial directed to the Tenant, prohibiting him from making wast upon the Land in controversie, during the Suit, *Reg. Judic. fol.* 21. It is sometimes made to the Sheriff; the example whereof you have in the same Book following.

Pro indiviso, Is a possession or occupation of Lands or Tenements, belonging to two or more persons, whereof none knows his several portion, as *Coparceners* before partition, *Bracton*, *lib.* 5. *tract.* 2. *cap.* 1. *num.* 7.

Proles, In English *Progeny*, Is properly such as proceed from a lawful Marriage; though, if the word be taken at large, it may well denote the issue of an unlawful Bed.

Prolocutor of the Convocation-House, *Prolocutor Domus Convocationis*, Is an Officer chosen by persons Ecclesiastical, publickly assembled by Vertue of the King's Writ for every Parliament; and as there be two Houses of *Convocation*, so there are two *Prolocutors*, one of the Lower, and one of the Higher House; He of the lower House, presently upon the first Assembly, by the motion of the Bishops, being chosen by the Members of the said lower House, is presented to the Bishops for *Prolocutor*, that is, the person by whom they intend to deliver their Resolutions to the higher House, and to have their own House especially ordered and governed. His Office is to cause the Clerk to call the Names of such as are of that House, when he sees cause, to read all things propounded, gather Suffrages, and the like.

Promise, *Promissio*, Is, when upon a valuable consideration, we bind our selves by our words to do or perform such an Act as is agreed upon and concluded, upon which an Action may be grounded; whereas, if it be without consideration, it is called *Nudum pactum, ex quo non oritur actio.*

Pramooters, or rather **Promoters**, *Promotores*, Are those, who in popular and penal Actions do prosecute Offendors in their own Name and the Kings, having part of the Fines or Penalties for their reward. These, among the *Romans*, were called *Quadruplatores* or *Delatores.* They belong especially to the *Exchequer and Kings Bench*, *Smith de Rep. Angl.* lib. 2. cap. 14. *Coke* calls them *Turbidum hominum genus*, 3. Inst. fol. 191.

Promulge a Law, *Promulgare Legem*, Is first to make a *Law*, and then to declare, publish, and proclaim the same to publick View, and so **Promulged**, *promulgatus* is published, proclaimed, 6 *H.* 8. 4.

Pronotary or **Protonotary**, *Protonotarius vel primus notarius*, Is a chief Officer of the Common-Pleas and King's Bench, derived from two French words *Prime*, *primus*, & *Notayre*, *notarius*. See 5 *H.* 4. 14. He is termed a chief Clerk of the Common-Pleas. He of the King's Bench Records all Actions civil sued in that Court, as the *Clerk of the Crown Office* doth all criminal Causes. Those of the Common-Pleas, since the Order of 14 *Jac.* upon an Agreement made between the *Prothonotaries* and *Filacers* of that Court (who before did enter all Declarations and Pleas, whereto a Sergeants hand was not required,) do enter and enroll all manner of Declarations, Pleadings, Assises, Judgments and Actions: Also they make out all Judicial Writs, as the *Venire facias* after issue joyned, and *Habeas corpus* for the bringing in of the Jury, and *Distringas Jurator.* They also make out Writs of Execution and Seisin; Writs of *Supersedeas* for appearance to *Exigents*, as well as the *Exigents* and *Writs of Priviledge*, for removing Causes from other Inferior Courts of Record, where the party hath cause of priviledge; also Writs of *Procedendo* and *Scire facias* in all Cases, and Writs to *enquire of Damages*, and all process upon *Prohibitions*, and upon Writs of *Audita Querela*, and *false Judgment*, with

with many others. Laſtly, They enroll all Recogniſances acknowledged in that Court, and all common Recoveries, and may make exemplifications of any Record in the ſame Term, before their Rolls are made up and delivered into the Treaſury of Records of that Court.

Proofe, *Probatio: Bracton* ſayes, There is *Probatio duplex*, viz. *viva*, as by Witneſſes, *viva voce*; and *Mortua*, by Deeds, Writings, &c. A Wife cannot be produced either againſt or for her Husband, *quia duæ ſunt animæ in carne una*, and it might be a cauſe of irreconcilable diſcord, and a mean of great inconveniencies, *Co.* on *Lit. lib.* 1. *cap.* 1. *ſect.* 1.

Pro partibus liberandis, Is a Writ for the partition of Lands between Co-heirs, *Reg. Orig. fol.* 316.

Property, *Proprietas*, Is the higheſt Right that a man hath, or can have to any thing, and no wayes depending upon any other mans curteſie. And this none in our Kingdom can be ſaid to have in any Lands or Tenements, but only the King in the right of his Crown; Becauſe all the Lands throughout the Realm are in the nature of Fee, and hold either mediately or immediately of the Crown. This word nevertheleſs is uſed for that right in Lands and Tenements that common perſons have, becauſe it importeth as much as *Utile Dominium*, though not *directum*. See *Fee*. And there are three manners of Rights of *property*, that is, Property *abſolute*, Property *qualified*, and Property *poſſeſſory*. Of which ſee at large *Co. lib.* 7. *fol.* 17. Caſe of *Swans*.

Proporcitas, *Skene de verbor.* Signif. latines it *Proportatio aſſiſæ*, the Declaration or Deliverance of an Aſſiſe; otherwiſe called *Veredictum Aſſiſæ*, the Verdict of an Aſſiſe, becauſe the Aſſiſors are ſworn to declare the Truth, and therefore are called *Juratores*, Jurors.

Prophecies, *Prophetiæ*, Are by our Statutes reputed for wizardly foretelling of things to come in dark and ambiguous Speeches, whereby great Commotions have been often cauſed in this Kingdom, and great Attempts made by thoſe to whom thoſe Speeches promiſed good ſucceſs, *Anno* 3 E. 6. *cap.* 15. and 7 *Ejuſd. cap.* 11. and 5 *Eliz. cap.* 15. But theſe for diſtinction ſake are called *Fond, falſe and fantaſtical Prophecies*, 3. Inſt. fol. 128.

Proprietary, *Proprietarius*, Is he that hath a property in any thing, *quæ nullius arbitrio eſt obnoxia*; but was heretofore chiefly uſed for him that hath the Fruits of a Benefice to himſelf, and his Heirs or Succeſſors, as in time paſt *Abbots and Priors* had to them and their Succeſſors. See *Appropriation*.

Propounders, The 85 Chapter of *Coke's* 3. *Inſtitutes*, is entituled, *Againſt Monopoliſts*, Propounders *and Projectors*; where it ſeems only to be uſed as a *Synonima* to *Monopoliſts*.

Proprietate probanda, Is a Writ that lies for him that would prove a *property* before the Sheriff, *Reg. Orig. fol.* 83. 85. For where a *Property* is alledged, a *Replegiare* lyeth not, *Broke*, *Property* 1.

Pro rata, That is, *pro proportione*, 16 Car. 2. cap. 6.----*Pro rata portionis*. See *Onerando* pro rata *portionis*.

Prorogue, *Prorogare*, To prolong, or put off to another day, *Anno* 6 H. 8. *cap.* 8. The difference between a *Prorogation* and an *Adjournment*, or continuance of the Parliament, is, That by the *prorogation* in open Court there is a Seſſion, and then ſuch Bills as paſſed in either Houſe, or both Houſes, and had not the Royal aſſent to them, muſt at the next Aſſembly begin again; for every Seſſion of Parliament is in Law a ſeveral Parliament, but if it be but adjourned or continued, then is there no Seſſion, and conſequently all things continue in the ſame ſtate they were in before the *Adjournment*, 4. *Inſt. fol.* 27

Proſecutor, Is he that follows a cauſe in anothers Name. See *Promooters*.

Protection, *Protectio*, Hath a general and a ſpecial ſignification: In the general, it is uſed for that benefit and ſafety which every Subject, Denizen or Alien, eſpecially ſecured hath by the King's Laws, and ſo it is uſed 25 *E.* 3. 22. *Protection* in the ſpecial ſignification, is uſed for an Exemption or Immunity given by the King to a perſon againſt Suits in Law, or other Vexations, upon reaſonable Cauſes him thereunto moving, which is a branch of his *Prerogative*. And of this *Fitzherbert* in his *Nat. Brev. fol.* 28. maketh two kinds, the firſt he calls a *Protection, cum clauſula Volumus*, whereof he mentions four particulars; 1. A *protection quia profecturus*, for him that is to paſs over Sea in the King's Service. 2. A *Protection quia moraturus*, for him that is abroad in the King's Service upon the Sea, or in the Marches, 7 *H.* 7. *cap.* 2. 3. A *Protection* for the King's Debtor, that he be not ſued or attached till the King be paid his Debt. This ſome *Civilians* call *Moratoriam*. And 4. A *Protection* in the King's Service beyond the Sea, or on the Marches of *Scotland*, *Anno* 1 *R.* 2. *cap.* 8. *Reg. Orig. fol.* 23. and *Britton*, cap. 123. The ſecond form of *Protection*, is *cum clauſula Nolumus*, which is granted moſt commonly to a Spiritual Company for their Immunity, from taking of their Cattel by the King's Miniſters: But it may be granted alſo to one man Spiritual or Temporal, *Reg. Orig. fol.* 22, 23. None of theſe *Protections* extend to *Pleas of Dower*, *Quare Impedit*, *Aſſiſe of Novel Diſſeiſin*, *Darrein Preſentment, and Attaints and Pleas before Juſtices in Eyre*. See the *Termes of the Law*, verbo *Protection*, and *New Book of Entries* of this word.

Proto-foreſtarius, Was he whom our King heretofore made chief of *Windſor Foreſt*, to hear all Cauſes of *Death* or *Mayhem* there, *Cam. Brit. pag.* 213. A kind of a Lord chief Juſtice *in Eyre*.

Protonotary, *Protonotarius*. See *Pronotary*.

Proteſtation, *Proteſtatio*, Is (as Juſtice *Walſh* defines it) a defence of ſafeguard to the party which maketh it from being concluded by the act he is about to do, that iſſue cannot be joyned by it, *Plowd. fol.* 276. whereof ſee *Reg. Orig. fol.* 306. And ſee *Proteſt*.

Proteſt, *Proteſtari*, Hath two divers Applications; one is by way of Caution, to call Witneſs (as it were) or openly to affirm, That he doth either not at all, or but conditionally yield his conſent to any act, or unto the proceeding of a Judge in a Court, wherein his Juriſdiction is doubtful, or to anſwer upon his Oath further than by Law he is bound. See *Plowden, fol.* 276. *Gresbrooks* Case, and *Reg. Orig. fol.* 306. The other is by way of complaint, *to protest* a mans Bill. for example, If I give Money to a Merchant in *France*, taking his Bill of Exchange to be repaid in *England* by one whom he assigneth; if at my coming, I find not my self satisfied, but either delayed or denyed, then I go to the *Exchange*, or other open Concourse of Merchants, and *protest*, That I am not paid; and thereupon if he hath any Goods remaining in any mans hands within the Realm, the *Law of Merchants* is, that I be paid out of them to my full satisfaction.

Prover, *Probator*, *Anno* 28 E. 1 and 5 *H.* 4. *cap.* 2. See *Approvors*, and 3. *par Inst. fol.* 129. A man became an *Approver*, and appealed five, and every of them joyned battel with him: *Et duellum percussum fuit cum omnibus & probator devicit omnes quinque in duello, quorum quatuor suspendebantur, & quintus clamabat esse clericum & allocatur, &* probator *pardonatur*, Mich. 39 E. 3. *coram Rege.* Rot. 97. Suff.

Province. *Provincia* Was used among the *Romans* for a Country, without the limits of *Italy*, gained to their subjection by the Sword: Whereupon that part of *France* next the *Alpes* was so called of them, and still retains the Name: But with us a *Province* is most usually taken for the Circuit of an Archbishops Jurisdiction. as the *Province of Canterbury, and the* Province of *York*, 32 *H.* 8. 23. and 33 *H.* 8. 31. yet it is also divers times used in our Statutes for several parts of the Realm, and sometimes for a County. *In placito Agnetis quæ fuit uxor* Radulphi de Buttiler *versus priorem de* Repindon, *pro terra in* Pykinton, *Prior. dicit, quod nulla villa est in* Provincia *illa quæ sic vocatur*, Placit. de Juratis & Assistis apud Derby Pasch. 53 H. 3. Rot. 2.

Provincial, *Provincialis*, Is a chief Governor, of a Religious Order of Fryers, &c. 4 *H.* 4. 17.

Provision, *Provisio*, Is used with us as in the Canon Law, for the providing of a Bishop, or any other person, an Ecclesiastical Living, by the Pope, before the Incumbent be dead: It is also called *Gratia expectativa*, or *Mandatum de providendo*: The great abuse whereof you may read not only in *Duarenus de sacris Ecclesiæ Ministeriis & beneficiis*, lib. 3. cap. 2. but also in divers Statutes of this Realm, *viz* 35 *E.* 3. 22 *stat* 4. & 5. commonly called the Statute *De provisionibus*, & 27 *E.* 3. *cap.* 1. & 38 *E.* 3. *stat.* 2. *cap.* 1. 2. 3. 4. & 2 *Rich.* 2. *cap.* 7. 3. *R.* 2. *cap.* 3. 7 *R.* 2. 12. 12 *R.* 2. *stat.* 2. *cap.* 2. 3. 4. & 3. *H.* 5. *cap.* 4. See *Præmunire.*

Provisor, Is he that sues to the Court of *Rome* for a *provision*, which is called *Gratia expectativa* according to *Spelman.* See also *Old Nat. Brev.* fol. 143. they were prohibited by Proclamation 42 *Hen.* 3 *Anno* 1258. *Hill. Pag* 259. It is sometimes also taken for him that hath the care of *providing* things necessary, a Purveyor. See *Provision.*

Proviso, Is a Condition inserted into any Deed, upon the observance whereof the validity of the Deed depends: Sometimes it is only a Covenant, *Co.* 2 *Rep.* Lord *Cromwel*'s Case. It hath also another signification in matters Judicial, as if the Plaintiff or Demandant desist in prosecuting an Action by bringing it to a Tryal: The Defendant or Tenant may take out a *Venire facias* to the Sheriff, which hath in it these words, *Proviso quod*, &c. to this end, that if the Plaintiff take out any Writ to that purpose, the Sheriff shall summon but one Jury upon them both: In which Case we call going to Tryal by *Proviso.* See *Old Nat. Brev. fol.* 159. in the Writ *Nisi prius.*

Purchase. See *Pourchase.*

Provost Marshal, An Officer in the King's Navy, who hath charge of the Prisoners taken at Sea, 13 *Car.* 2. *cap.* 9. and is sometimes used for the like purpose at Land, or to seise or arrest any within the Jurisdiction of his place or Office.

Proregę. See *Senege*, Haply it may be the payment of *Proxyes or Procurations, sed quære.*

Proxyes, Are yearly payments made by Parish-Priests to their Bishop or Arch-deacon, *ratione visitationis.* See *Procurations*, and the Case between the *King* and Sir *Ambrose Forth*, 2 Jac. in the *Exchequer.* See also Sir *Jo. Davis Rep. fol.* 4.

Pryk, Is a kind of Service or Tenure.— *Nicholas filius & hæres* Nich. *de* Longford *Chivalier, tenet* 4. *Messuagia*, 40. *Acras terræ*, 10 *Acras prati &* 60 s. *redditus cum pertinentiis in* Kinwaldmersh *de Rege in Capite, per servitium inveniendi unum* equum, *unum* saccum *& unum* **Pryk** *in Guerra Walliæ quandocunque contigerit Regem ibi guerrare*, Mich. Fines, 1 Rich. 2. Derb. fol. 204.

Publick Faith, *Fides publica*, 17 Car. 1. cap. 18. Was a Rebellious Cheat to get Money from the seduced People, upon (as they call'd it) *The publick Faith* of the Nation to make a most abhorrid and causless Rebellion against a most Religious and Gracious Soveraign, which was about the Year, 1642.

Pucellage, *Pucellagium*, French *Pucelage*, Virginity— *Quod tenuit eam, dum idem* B. *abstulit* pucellagium *suum vel quod concubuit cum ea*, Bract. lib. 3. tract. 2. cap. 28. num. 2, 3, & 5. In an ancient *M. S.* it is written *Puellagium.* *In placito pro raptu sic continetur—quod ipsam de* puellagio *suo felonice & totaliter desloravit.* Inter Placit. Mich. 19. *E.* 3. *London* 159.

Pudhepec. *Si Pudhepec* (i. nemoris læsio) *parco Regis vel Forestæ fiat* 30. *manc. emendetur, nisi propositio propensior amplius exigat.* Leg. Hen. 1. cap. 38. But the learned *Spelman* thinks it is miswritten, for the Saxon pudhepec, i. *Wudhepec*; the *w* in that Character being like the *p* in Ours.

Pudzeld, The same with *Wordgeld*, *Co.* on *Lit. fol.* 233. And haply the like mistake in the first Letters of this as of the former word.

Puisne, Younger, *Puny.* See *Mulier.*

Pundbrech, Derived from the *Pund*, *Parcus*, and *Brech*, *fractura.* *Si* Pundbrech *fiat in Curia Regis plena* wyta *sit, alibi quinque mancæ*, Leg. Hen. 1. cap. 40. It is the illegal taking of Cattle out of the Pound by any means whatsoever.

Purfles of a Womans Gown, From the French word *Pourfiler*, 33 *H.* 8. 5. A sort of Trimming for *Womens Gowns* then in use; it was made of Tinsel or Gold-Threed, and was also called *Baudkin-work.* So *Camden*, tit. *Ireland*, speaks of a Mantle or shag Rug, with a deep fringed *purfle.*

Purgation, *Purgatio*, is the clearing a mans ſelf of a Crime whereof he is generally ſuſpected, and of the ſame accuſed before a Judge. Of this there was great uſe in *England* touching matter of Felony, imputed to Clerks in former time, as appeareth by *Stamf. pl. cor.* lib. 2. cap. 48. See *Clergy* and *Weſtm.* 1. cap. 2. It is ſtill obſerved for matters pertaining to the Eccleſiaſtical Court, as ſuſpition, or common fame of incontinency, or ſuch like. And here note, That *Purgation* is either *Canonical*, *Canonica*, or *Vulgar*, *Vulgaris*. *Canonical*, is that which is preſcribed by the *Canon Law*; the form whereof is uſually thus in the Spiritual Court, The man ſuſpected takes his Oath, That he is clear of the fault objected, and brings ſo many of his honeſt Neighbors, being not above Twelve, as the Court ſhall aſſign him, to ſwear upon their Conſciences and Credulity, That he ſweareth truly. *Vulgar purgation* was by *Fire*, or *Water*, or by *Combat*, uſed both by Infidels and Chriſtians, till by the Canon Law aboliſht. But *Combat* may be ſtill practiſed by the Laws of the Realm in Cauſes doubtful; and where there is a want of Evidence, or other proof, if the Defendant chuſe rather the *Combat* than other Tryal. See *Ordel* and *Combat*.

Purificatio beatæ Mariæ Virginis, *Anno* 32 *H*. 8. *cap*. 21. See *Candlemas*.

Purlue or **Purlieu**, From the French *Pur*, i. *purus*, and *Lieu*, *locus*, is all that ground near any Foreſt, which being made Foreſt by *Henry* the Second, *Richard* the Firſt, or King *John*, were by perambulation granted, but by King *Henry* the Third ſevered again from the ſame, and became *Purlieu*, *Manwood Foreſt Laws*, cap. 20. And he calleth this Ground either *pouralee*, i. *perambulationem*, or *purliu*, *purluy*, which, he ſaith, are miſtaken for *pourallee*, ibid. num. 3. And with our firſt derivation it may conſiſt, becauſe ſuch things as were by thoſe fore-mentioned Kings ſubjected to the Laws and Ordinances of the Foreſt, are now cleared and freed from the ſame. And as the *Civilians* call that *purum locum*, *qui ſepulchrorum Religioni non eſt obſtrictus*. So our Anceſtors called this *purleiu*, i. *purum locum*, becauſe it was exempted from that Servitude that was formerly laid upon it. And whereas *Manwood* and *Crompton* call it *Pourallee*, we may derive it from *pur*, *purus*, and *alee*, *ambulatio*, becauſe he that walketh or courſeth within thet Circuit, is not lyable to the Laws or Penalties incurred by them which hunt within the Precincts of the Foreſt. See the Stat. 33 *Ed*. 1. *ſtat*. 5.

Purlieu man, Is he that hath Ground within the *Purleiu*, and being able to diſpend forty ſhillings by the year of Free-hold, is upon theſe two points licenſed to hunt in his own *Purlieu*, *Manwood's Foreſt Laws*, pag. 151. 157. But what he muſt obſerve in his hunting, ſee the ſame *pag*. 180. 181. 186. and *cap*. 20. *num*. 5. 8, 9, *&c*. See *Purlieu*.

Purpreſture, *Purpreſtura*, From the French *Pourprendre*, i. *integrè arripere*, is properly *ſubtractio clandeſtina terræ alienæ*, *ejuſdemque vicinæ aſcriptio*. See *Skene de verbor*. Signif. *verbo* Purpreſture, and ſee *Pourpreſture*.

Purpriſum, French *Pourpris*, A Cloſe or Encloſure, alſo the whole compaſs of a Mannor. —— *Donavi eis meum* Purpriſum *de Kirkeham & domos meas*, *&c*. Carta Walteri Eſpee Priorat. de Kirkeham in Mon. Ang. 2. par. fol. 1. 06. n. 40.

Purrell, 25 *Eliz*. *cap*. 10. A Liſt ordained to be made at the end of Kerſies, to prevent deceit in diminiſhing their length.

Purſy, A Term among Clothiers, 43 *Eliz*. 10. See *Rewey*.

Purſuivant. See *Pourſuivant*.

Purveyance. See *Pourveyance*.

Purveyors. See *Pourveyors*.

Purview, Is a French word, ſignifying a Gift or Grant, and *Pourveu que*, a condition; that Sir *Edward Coke* often uſes it for that part of an Act of Parliament which begins with *Be it Enacted*. The Stat. of 3 *H*. 7. ſtands upon a Preamble and a *Purview*, 12. *Rep*. *fol*. 20.

Putage, Putagium, *Fornicatio ex parte fœminæ*, *quod vox nulla Latina exprimit*, *quaſi* Puttam agere; from the French *Puttee*, or the Italian *Putta*, i. *meretrix*. This Crime was ſo odious amongſt our Anceſtors, that if any Heir-Female under Gardianſhip were guilty thereof, they forfeited their part to their Co-heirs; or if ſhe were as onely Heireſs, the Lord of the Fee took it by Eſcheat. *Spelman*, *Quod autem generaliter ſolet dici* putagium *hæreditatem non adimit*, *illud intelligendum eſt de* putagio *matris*; *quia filius hæres legitimus eſt*, *quem nuptiæ demonſtrant*, Glanvile, lib. 7. cap. 12.

Puteus, A pit, in former times the *Scots* were wont to hang Men-delinquents, and to caſt the Women Offendors into a pit full of water to drown; and, 'tis a wonder, this puniſhment, or execution, is not found among the *Britains*, or rather *Engliſh Saxons*, ſince 'tis evidently met with among the *Germans*, from whence they came, as appears by *Tacitus*, in his Book *De German. moribus*, where he ſayes, *Proditores transfugas arboribus ſuſpendunt*, *ignavos & imbelles & corpore infames* (i. *fornicantes*) *cœno ac palude*, *injecta inſuper crate mergunt*, pag. 484.

Putura, A Cuſtome claimed by Keepers, in Foreſts, and ſometimes by Bayliffs of Hundreds, to take Mans-meat, Horſe-meat and Dogs-meat, of the Tenants *gratis*, within the perambulation of the Foreſt, or Liberty of the Hundred. *Communia de* Anno 16 E. 1. Ter. Paſch. Rot. 10. in Dorſo *Rex mandat Baronibus quod allocent* Roberto *de* Chadworth *Vic. Linc.* 56 s. 7 d. *quos per præceptum Regis liberavit Jo. de Bellovento pro* Putura *ſeptem leporariorum & trium falconum & Alanerarium*, &c. *viz*. *pro* Putura *cujuſlibet leporarii & falconis per diem* 1 d. ob. *& pro vadiis*, *&c*. Plac. Coron. in Com. Ebor. 21 E. 1. Rot. 21. —— *In libertate de* Knaresburgh *præſentatur*, *quod parcarii Comitis Cornubiæ percipient* Puturam *ſuam*, viz. *bis comedendo in die vel capiendo pro* Putura *ſua* 2 d. *de tenentibus in diverſis villis ibidem nominatis*, *ſed nunc fecit dictus Comes ipſas villatas ſolvere* 3 d. *pro* putura. See 4. *Inſt*. *fol*. 307.

Pyker alias **Pycar**, A kind of Ship ſpoken of 31 *E*. 3. *ſtat*. 2. *cap*. 2.

Pyrate. See *Pirate*.

Q.

Q.

QUadrans, A Farthing, the fourth part of a Peny.

Quadrantata terræ, Is the fourth part of an Acre. See *Denariata terræ & Obolata*. Item Fardel of Land.

Quadragesima Sunday, Is the first *Sunday* in *Lent*, so called, because it is about the fortieth day before *Easter*: The three preceding *Sundays* are, *Quinquagesima*, *Sexagesima* and *Septuagesima*; all which see in their proper Places.

Quadrugata terræ, A Team of Land, which may be till'd with four Horses.

Quæ plura, Was a Writ that lay where an Inquisition had been made by an Escheator in any County, of such Lands or Tenements as any Man died seised of, and all that was in his possession was imagined not to be found by the Office; the form whereof, see in *Reg. Orig. fol.* 293. and in *F. N. B. fol.* 255. It differs from the Writ called *Melius inquirendum*, according to the same *Fitzherbert*, because this is granted, where the Escheator formerly proceeded by vertue of his Office; and the other, where he found the first Office by vertue of the Writ named *Diem clausit extremum*. See the *New Book of Entries*, verbo *Quæ plura*.

Querens non invenit plegium, Is a return made by the Sheriff upon a Writ directed to him, with this condition inserted, *Si A. fecerit B. securum de clamore suo prosequendo*, F. N. B. *fol.* 38.

Quæ servitia, Is a Writ, see per *quæ servitia*.

Quale jus, Is a Writ Judicial, that lies where a man of Religion hath Judgment to recover Land, before execution be made of the Judgment; for this Writ must go forth to the Escheator, between Judgment and Execution, to inquire whether the Religious person hath any Right to recover, or whether the Judgment be obtained by collusion between the Demandant and the Tenant, to the intent, that the true Lord be not defrauded. See *Westm.* 2. *cap.* 32. the form of this Writ you have *Reg. Judic. fol.* 8. 16, 17, & 46. And in the *Old* Nat. *Brev. fol.* 161. See the *New Book of Entries*, verb. *Quale jus*.

Quam diu se bene gesserit, Is a Clause often used in Letters Patent of the Grant of Offices, as in those to the *Barons of the Exchequer*, which must be intended onely as to matters concerning their Office; and is nothing but what the Law would have implyed, if the Office had been granted for life, *Co.* 4. *Inst. fol.* 117.

Quantum meruit, That is, How much he has deserved; Is an Action of the Case so called, grounded upon a promise to pay a Man for doing any thing, so much as he should deserve or *merit*.

Quare ejecit infra terminum, Is a Writ that lyeth for a Lessee, where he is cast out of his Farm before his Terme be expired, against the Feoffee or Lessor that ejecteth him: And it differs from the *Ejectione firmæ*, because this lies where the Lessor, after the Lease made, infeoffeth another, which ejecteth the Lessee; And the *Ejectione firmæ* lyeth against any other Stranger that ejects him. But the effect of both is all one, that is, to recover the residue of the Terme, F. N. B. *fol.* 197. *Reg. Orig. fol.* 227. and the *New Book of Entries*, verbo *Quare ejecit infra terminum*.

Quare Impedit, Is a Writ that lies for him that hath purchased a Mannor, with an Advowson thereto belonging, against him that disturbs him the Right of his Advowson, by presenting a Clerk thereto when the Church is void: And it differs from the Writ call'd a *Darreine presentment*, *Assisa ultimæ præsentationis*, because that lies where a Man, or his Ancestors, formerly presented; and this for him that is the Purchaser himself. See the *Expositor of the Terms of the Law*, *Old Nat. Brev. fol.* 27. *Bract. lib.* 4. *tract.* 2. *cap.* 6. *Britton*, *cap.* 92. and *F. N. B. fol.* 32. and *Reg. Orig. fol.* 30. And here note, That where a man may have an Assise of Darrein Presentment, he may have a *Quare Impedit*, but not contrariwise. See the *New Book of Entries* on this Writ.

Quare incumbravit, Is a Writ that lyeth against the Bishop, who, within six Months, after the Vacation of a Benefice, conferreth it upon his Clerk, while two others are contending in Law for the Right of presenting. And here note, This Writ alwayes lies depending the Plea, *Old Nat. Brev. fol.* 30. *F. N. B. fol.* 48. and *Reg. Orig. fol.* 32.

Quare intrusit matrimonio non satisfacto, Is a Writ that lies for the Lord against his Tenant being his Ward, who after convenable Marriage offer'd him, marries another, and enters nevertheless upon his Land, without agreement first made with his Lord and Guardian. But all Wardships being taken away by the Statute 12 *Car.* 2. *cap.* 24. This Writ is become useless.

Quare non permittit, Is a Writ that lies for one that has Right to present for a turn against the Proprietary, *Fleta*, *lib.* 5. *cap.* 6.

Quare non admisit, Is a Writ that lies against a Bishop, refusing to admit his Clerk that hath recovered in a Plea of *Advowson*. F. N. B. *fol.* 47. and *Reg. Orig. fol.* 32. See the *New Book of Entries*, verbo *Quare non admisit*.

Quarel, *Querela*, *à querendo*, and extends not only to Actions personal, but also to mixt, and the Plaintiff in them is called *Querens*, and in most of the Writs it is said *Queritur*; So that if a man release all *Quarrels* (a Man's Deed being taken most strongly against himself) it is as beneficial as all Actions; for by it all Actions real and personal are released, *Co. lib.* 8. *fol.* 153. and *Co.* on *Lit. lib.* 3. *cap.* 8. *sect.* 511.

Quarentine, *Quarentina*, Is a benefit allowed by the Law of *England* to the Widow of a Man dying seised of Land, whereby she may challenge to continue in his Capital Messuage, or chief Mansion-house, (so it be not a Castle) by the space of forty Dayes after his Decese, *Bracton*, *lib.* 2. *cap.* 40. And if the Heir, or any other attempt to eject her, she may have the Writ *De quarentina habenda*, F. N. B. fol. 161. *Maneat vidua in Capitali Messuagio mariti sui per quadraginta dies post obitum mariti sui, infra quos dies assignetur ei dos, nisi prius* *us assignata fuerit, vel nisi domus illa sit castrum*, Magna Charta, cap. 7. See *Britton*, cap. 103. and *Fleta*, lib. 5. cap. 23. *Skene de* verborum *Signif.* verb. *Quarentena viduarum*, derives this word from the French *Quaresme*, who also have this Custome called *La quaresme des vefues*, granted to Widows after the decease of their Husbands. *Quarentene* also signifies a Furlong, being a quantity of Land containing forty Perches, and so haply derived from the French *Quarente*, forty. In a Charter of *Withlafe* King of the *Mercians*, mentioned by *Ingulphus*, we have these Words, -- *uatuor arucatas terræ arabilis continentes in longitudine.* 8. quarentenas *et* 8. quarentenas *in latitudine. Quarentine* is also the space of forty dayes, wherein any Person, coming from foreign Parts infected with the Plague is not permitted to land, or come on shore, until so many dayes are expired.

Quarentina habenda, Is a Writ that lies for Widow to enjoy her *Quarentine*, *Reg. Orig. fol.* 175.

Quare obstruxit, Is a Writ that lies for him, who having a liberty to pass through his Neighbors Ground, cannot injoy his Right, for that the Owner has so strengthened it, *Fleta*, lib. 4. cap. 26. sect. *Item si minus.*

Quareria, A Quarry of Stone,— *Præterea dedi eis Turbariam & Petrariam &* quateriam *ubicunque invenire potuerint in territorio villæ de Hepp, &c.* Mon. Ang. part. 2 fol. 595.

Quarter, *Quarterium*, Eight Bushels striked make the *Quarter* of Corn, *Anno* 15 *Rich.* 2. cap. 4.

Quarter Sessions, Is a Court held by the Justices of Peace in every County once every quarter of a Year. How far the Jurisdiction thereof exceedeth, see *Lamb. Eiren.* lib. 4. and *Smith de Repub. Anglor.* lib. 2. cap. 19. To which you may add the several Statutes of this Realm, by which its power is greatly increased: Originally it seems to have been erected onely for matters touching the Peace, but now it extends much farther. The holding these *Sessions* Quarterly, was first ordained by the Statute 25 *E.* 3. *stat.* 1. *cap.* 8.

Quash, *Quassare*, Cometh of the French word *Quasser*, id est, *cassum facere*, to overthrow or annul, *Bracton*, lib. 5. tract. 2. cap. 3. num. 4. *As if the Bayliff of a Liberty return any out of his Franchise, the Array shall be* quasht. And *Co.* on *Lit.* fol. 156. *An Array returned by one that hath no Franchise shall be* quasht.

Quechord, *Anno* 17 *E.* 4. *cap.* 2. A kind of Game prohibited by the same Statute, perchance the same with that we now call *Shovelboard*; And it may be **Quechorde** quasi **Quickbord**, because the pieces wherewith they play run upon the Table with great celerity.

Que Estate, Translated *verbatim*, signifies *Quem statum*: In our Common Law it is a Plea, whereby a man intitling another to Land, &c. saith. Tha the same *Estate* he had, he hath from him: For Example, In a *Quare Impedit*, The Plaintiff alledges, That such four Persons were seised of Lands whereunto the Advowsor in question was appendant in Fee, and did present to the Church, and afterward the Church became void *que estate del, &c.* that is, *which estate* of the four Persons he has now during the Vacation, by vertue whereof he presented, &c. *Bro.* tit. *Que estate*, fol. 175, 176. *New Book of Entries*, verb, *Que estate*, and *Co.* on *Lit.* fol. 121.

Que est mesme, *Verbatim*, Is the same thing, but is used in a legal sense a as Word of art in an Action of Trespass, or such like, for a positive justification of the very Act complained of by the Plaintiff as a wrong: For example, in an Action upon the Case, the Plaintiff sayes, That the Lord threatned his Tenants at will in such sort, that he forced them to give up their Tenures. The Lord, for his defence, pleadeth, That he said unto them, That if they would not depart, he would sue them at Law: This being the same threatning that he used, or to speak artificially, *que est le mesne*, the defence is good. Of this, see *Kitchin*, cap. *Que est le mesine*, fol. 236.

Queen, *Regina*, Is either she that holdeth the Crown of this Realm by right of Blood, or else she that is marryed to the King; which last is called *Queen Consort.* In the former sense she is in all construction the same with the King, and hath the like Power in all respects: In the other signification she is inferior, and a person exempt from the King, for she may sue or be sued in her own Name; yet that she hath is the Kings, and whatever she loses, the King loses, *Stamf. prærog.* cap. 2. fol. 10. *in fine*, *Kitchin*, fol. 1, *Co.* lib. 4. *Copyhold Cases*, fol. 23.

Queen Gold, *Aurum Reginæ*, Is a Royal Duty or Revenue belonging to every *Queen of England* during her Marriage to the King, both by Law, Custom and Prescription, payable by sundry Persons in *England* and *Ireland* (upon divers Grants of the King) by way of Fine or Oblation, amounting to ten Marks, or upwards, to wit, one full tenth part above the entire Fine, as ten pounds upon every hundred pound Fine, upon Pardons, Contracts or Agreements; which becomes a real Debt to the *Queen* by the Name of *Aurum Reginæ*, upon the parties bare Agreement with the King for his Fine, and recording it, without any Promise or Contract for this tenth part exceeding it, *Lib. Nig. Scac.* pag. 43, 44. *Co.* 12. *Rep.* fol. 21, 22. and *Prynnes Tractate* on this Subject thorowout.

Quem redditum reddat, Is a Writ Judicial, that lies for him to whom a Rent-seck or Rent-charge is granted, by Fine levied in the King's Court against the Tenant of the Land that refuseth to attorn to him, thereby to cause to attorn, *Old Nat. Brev.* fol. 126. *West Symbol.* part 2. tit. *Fines.* sect. 156. and the *New Book of Entries*, verb. *Quem redditum reddit.*

Querela frescæ fortiæ, Is a Writ of *Fresh force*.. See *Fresh force.*

Querela coram Rege & consilio discutienda & terminanda, Is a Writ whereby one is called to justifie a Complaint of a Trespass made to the King himself, before the King and his Council, *Reg. Orig. fol.* 124.

Questus or rather **Quæstus**, A *quæro*, to seek or get, is taken for that Land which does not descend to us by Hereditary Right, but is gained by our own Labour and Industry; this we call **Purchased Lands.** In Lib. *Ramus* sub

sub *Stephano Rege conscript.* sect. 140. sub tit. *Quæstus Ædnothi qui floruit tempore Reg. Æthelredi,* We thus read, *Erat illis diebus quidam* Ælfstanus *habens duas hidas apud* Stapleford, *quas frater* Ædnothus *numeratis eidem centum solidis argenti, reliquis* questibus *suis in possessionem Ecclesiæ Remensis adjunxit.* And *Glanvile*, lib. 7. cap. 1. speaking of Lands, saith, *Aut habet hæreditatem tantum, aut* questum *tantum, aut hæreditatem & questum.*

Questus est nobis, Is the form of a Writ of *Nusance*, which, by the Statute 13 *E.* 1. *cap.* 24. lies against him to whom the House, or other thing that breeds the *Nusance* is alienated, whereas before the *Statute*, this Action lay only against him that first levyed the thing to the Annoyance of his Neighbour. See the *said Statute.*

Quia improvide, Seems to be a *Supersedeas* granted in the behalf of a Clerk of the Chancery, sued against the Priviledge of that Court in the Common-Pleas, and pursued to the *Exigent*, or in many other cases where a Writ is erroneously sued out. See *Dyer*, *fol.* 33. *n.* 18.

Quid juris clamat, Is a Writ Judicial, issuing out of the Record of the Fine, which remaineth with the *Custos brevium* of the Common-Pleas, before it be engrossed; and it lies for the Grantee of a Reversion or Remainder, when the particular Tenant will not atturn, *West Symbol.* part 2. tit. *Fines*, sect. 118. *Reg. Judic.* 36. 57. and the *New Book of Entries* on this Writ.

Quid pro quo, Signifies *verbatim*, what for what, and is an Artificial Speech, signifying as much as the Greek συνάλλαγμα among the *Civilians*, which is a reciprocal performance of both Parties to a Contract, and thereupon the giving of one thing of a value for another thing of like value, as 10 *li.* for a Horse, &c. *Kitchin*, *fol.* 184.

Quietantia sectæ, Hundredi & Wichmote, -----*Per hæc verba* Johannes Stanley *Arm. clamat quod ipse & tenentes sui non teneantur venire ad curiam istam,* Plac. in Itin. apud *Cestriam*, 14 *H.* 7. See *Acquietantia.*

Quietancia Assisarum super Assisam, -----*Per hæc verba* Johannes Stanley *clamat quod ipse & tenentes & residentes sui non ponantur in* Assisis, *Jurat. nec magnis* Assisis, Plac. ubi surpra.

Quietus, *Quiet*, *fine*, acquitted, Is a word used by the Clerk of the Pipe, and Auditors in the Exchequer, in their Acquittances or Discharges given to Accomptants; usually concluding with an *abinde recessit quietus*, which is called a *Quietus est*, and mentioned in the Act *Of General Pardon*, 12 *Car.* 2. 11. and 14 *Car.* 2. *cap.* 21. A *Quietus est* granted to the Sheriff, shall discharge him of all Accounts due to the King, 21 *Jac. cap.* 5.

Quinquagesima-Sunday, Is that we call *Shrove Sunday*, and was so named, because it is about the fiftieth day before *Easter*. The reason of the Name you may find in *Durandi rationali Divinorum*, *capit. de* quinquagesima; and we mention it here, because they are frequently spoken of in our ancient Law-writers, as *Britton* 33. and divers others.

Quinsieme or **Quinzime**, *Decima quinta*, A fifteenth with us, it is a Tax so called, because it is raised upon the fifteenth part of Mens Lands and Goods. See *Fifteenth* and *Tax*, 7 *H.* 7. *cap.* 5. *Crompton* in his *Jurisd. fol.* 21. saith, That it is more commonly of late raised upon Land, though in some places by Goods also; and it is well known by the Exchequer Roll, what every Town through *England* is to pay for a *Fifteenth.* Sometime this word *Quinzime* is used for the fifteenth day after any Feast, as *Quinsieme* of St. *John Baptist*, 13 *E.* 1. 3. & 18 *E.* 1. *cap.* 1.

Quintane, *Quintana*, French *Quintayne & Bersant*, a kind of Exercise that young men did, and still do use in some places of this Nation, to try the agility of the Country youth. *Spelman* in his *Glossary* describes it thus from his own Observation, -----*Ejus forma (ut semel aliquando puerulus vidi) hæc est, Erectæ trabi pertica incumbit versatilis uno fine peram dimittens arenâ gravidam; altero tabulam affixam, qua dum à currenti equite fortius hastâ impellitur, pera violentius circumacta, impellentis collum (in citacius evaserit) fortiter verberat.* But what it was anciently *Mat. Paris in* Hen. 3. *sub initio*, Anno 1253. thus delivers, *Eo tempore juvenes* Lond. *statuto pavone pro Bravio ad stadium quod* quintana *vulgariter dicitur vires proprias & equorum cursus sunt experti.*

Quint-Exact, *Quinto Exactus*, 31 Eliz. cap. 3. Is the last call of a Defendant, who is sued to the Outlary, where, if he appear not, he is by the Judgment of the Coroners returned *Outlawed*, if a Woman, *waved*. See *Exigent.*

Quinque Portus, *The Cinque-Ports*, Which are *Hastings*, *Romene*, *Hethe*, *Dover* and *Sandwich*; to the first *Winchelsea* and *Rye* belong, which are reckoned as parts or members of the *Cinque-Ports*; other members belonging to the same are, *Seford*, *Pevensel*, *Hedney*, *Hamme*, *Wekesborne*, *Crenethe*, and *Forthelpye*. This Port of *Hastings* is bound to find twenty one Ships, and in each Ship twenty one Men with a Boy. The second Port is *Romene*, and that finds five Ships, in each Ship twenty four Men and a Boy, to this as members belong, *Brombelle*, *Lyde*, *Oswareston*, *Dengemares* and *Romenhalle*. The third, *Hethe*, finds five Ships, in each Ship twenty one Men and a Boy, to this belongs *Westmethe*. *Dover* the fourth, finds twenty one Ships, in each Ship twenty one Men with a Boy, to which are members, *Folkstan*, *Feversham* and *Mergate*. Lastly, *Sandwich* finds five Ships, in each Ship twenty one Men and a Boy, and it hath as Members *Fordwick*, *Reculver*, *Serrè* and *Dale*, the number of all the Ships are 57, the Men in them 1188, the Boys 57. And the Service that the Barons of the *Cinque-Ports* acknowledge to owe, upon the King's Summons every year, if it shall happen, to attend with these Ships fifteen days at their own proper Costs and Charges; so that the first day be reckoned from the time when they put up their Sails, to set out to those parts whither they are to go: And to stay as long as the King pleases at his own charge.

Quite Clayme, *Quieta clamantia*, Is a Release, or acquitting of a Man, for any Action that he hath, or might, or may have against him. Also a *quitting of ones Claime or Title*, Bracton, *lib.* 5. *tract.* 5. *cap.* 9. *num.* 9. *lib.* 4. *tract.* 6. *cap.* 13. *num.* 1.

Quit-Rent, *Quietus redditus*, Is a certain small *Rent*, payable yearly by the Tenants of most Mannors; upon the payment whereof they are quit and free, till it becomes due again: This in some ancient Records, according to *Spelman*, is written *white Rent*, because paid in *Silver*. Hither may be referred what we find in *Lambards Itinerary*, pag. 212. concerning the Tenants of *Christ-Church* in *Canterbury*, dwelling without the Weald.

De redditu	7 s.	6 d.
De viginti ovis	0 s.	1 d.
De Gallinis & Benerth	0 s.	16 d.

The sum of the whole *Quit-rent* is 8 s. 11 d.

Quod ei Deforceat, Is a Writ that lies for the Tenant in Tail, Tenant in Dower, or Tenant for terme of Life, having lost by default against him that Recovered, or against his Heir. See *Broke, hoc tit. Reg. Orig. fol.* 171. and the *New Book of Entries*, verb. *Quod ei Deforceat.*

Quod permittat, Is a Writ that lies for the Heir of him that is disseised of his Common of Pasture against the Heir of the Disseisor being dead, *Termes de la Ley* 526. *Britton, cap.* 8. sayes, That this Writ lies for him, whose Ancestor dyed seised of Common of Pasture, or other like thing annexed to his Inheritance against the *Deforceor*. See *Broke hoc titulo, Reg. Orig. fol.* 155. and the *New Book of Entries*, verb. *Quod permittat.*

Quod Clerici non eligantur in Officio Ballivi, &c. Is a Writ that lies for a *Clerk*, which, by reason of some Land he hath, is made, or in doubt to be made *Bayliff, Bedle, Reeve*, or some such like Officer. See *Clerico infra sacros, &c.* Reg. Orig. fol. 187. and *F. N. B. fol.* 175.

Quod Clerici beneficiati de Cancel. Is a Writ to exempt a Clerk of the *Chancery* from Contribution towards the Proctors of the Clergy in Parliament, *Reg. Orig. fol.* 261.

Quod Persona nec Prebendarii, &c. Is a Writ that lies for spiritual Persons that are distrained in their spiritual Possessions, for the payment of a *Fifteenth* with the rest of the Parish, *F. N. B. fol.* 176.

Quod non permittat. See *Consuetudinibus* and *Servitiis.*

Quo Jure, Is a Writ that lies for him that has Land, wherein another challengeth *Common of Pasture* time out of mind: And it is to compel him to shew *by what Title* he challenges it, *F. N. B. fol.* 128. and *Britton* more largely, *cap.* 59. *Reg. Orig. fol.* 156 and the *New Book of Entries*, verb. *Quo jure.*

Quo minus, Is a Writ that lies for him that hath a Grant of *House-bote-* and *Hay-bote* in another mans Woods against the Grantor, making such wast as the Grantee cannot enjoy his Grant, *Old Nat. Brev. fol.* 148. and *Kitchin, fol.* 178. This Writ also lies for the Kings Farmer in the Exchequer, against him to whom he selleth any thing by way of Bargain touching his Farm, or against whom he hath any Cause of personal Action, *Perkins Grants* 5. For he supposeth by the Vendees detaining any due from him, he is made *less able* to pay the Kings Rent. And under this pretence, any one who pays the King a Fee-Farm Rent, may have this Writ against any other person for any Debt or Damage, and bring the Cause to tryal in the *Exchequer*.

Quorum, Is a word often mentioned in our Statutes, and much used in Commissions both of Justices of the Peace, and others. As for example, Where a Commission is directed to seven Persons, or to any three of them, *Whereof A. B.* and *C. D.* to be Two, there *A. B.* and *C. D.* are said to be of the *Quorum*, because the rest cannot proceed without them: So a *Justice of the Peace and Quorum* is one without whom the rest of the Justices in some Cases cannot proceed, *Anno* 3 *H.* 7. *cap.* 3. and 32 *Hen.* 8. *cap.* 43.

Quo Warranto, Is a Writ that lies against him that usurps any Franchise or Liberty against the King, as to have *Waife, Stray, Fair, Market, Court-Baron, Leet*, or such like, without good Title, *Old Nat. Brev. fol.* 149. Or else against him that intrudeth himself as Heir into Land, *Bracton, lib.* 4. *tract.* 1. *cap.* 2. *num.* 3. Bro. *hoc tit.* 18 *E.* 1. *stat.* 2 & 3. & *Anno* 30. *ejusdem.* And the *New Book of Entries*, verb. *Quo Warranto.*

Quyke, Was anciently used for a living or quick Beast, as appears by the Will of *John Bracebrige* of *Kinnersbury* Esq; dated 7 *H.* 8. wherein it is appointed, *That his best* Quyke *should be taken in the name of his Mortuary.*

The Quyre of a Boar, Is the Hounds Fee, but what part it is we are unsatisfied; but if we may guess, we think it may denote the Heart, and then doubtless a word corrupted from the French *Cœur, Skynners Etymologicon, Ling. Angl.*

R.

R. Is called *Litera canina*, the Dogs Letter, because it has a jarring sound, such as Dogs use when they snarle; and *Pomponius* writes, That it was first invented by *App. Claudius*, in *L.* 2. *de Orig. Jur.* See *Vocab. utriusq; juris.*

Rachet, *Rachetum* or (as *Skene*) *Rachatum*, Derived from the French *Rachater* or *Racheter, redimere*; It is the same with **Theftbote**, which is the compensation or redemption of a Thief. *Rachetum est thieftbute vel redemptio capta pro venditione furum, latronum vel aliorum malefactorum*, Skene de verb. *Sign.* verb. *Rachetum.*

Racke, *Fidicula*, So called, because Persons are there tortured *ut* fides *inveniatur*. An Engine in the Tower with Cords and Strings to extort confession from Delinquents: *John Holland* Earl of *Huntington* was by King *Henry* the Sixth created *Duke of Exeter*, and made Constable of the Tower: He and *William de la Poole* Duke of *Suffolk*, and others, intended to have brought in the Civil Laws; for a beginning whereof, the Duke of *Exeter* first brought into the Tower the *Racke* or *Brake*, allowed in many Cases by the Civil Law, and thereupon it was called *The Duke of* Exeter's *Daughter*, 3 *Inst. fol.* 35.

Rackevintage, *Anno* 32 *H.* 8. 14. Is a second *Vintage*, or Voyage, for Wines by our Merchants into *France, &c.* for *rack't* Wines, cleansed and drawn from the Lees: From this Voyage our Merchants commonly return about

the

the end of *December*, or beginning of *January*.

Rad-knights. Vide *Rodeknights*.

Radechenistres, In *Doomsday* Book, *Interpretatur pro liberis hominibus*, as *fol.* 18. *tit. Glouc.* Berchelay---*Hii* Radechemistr. *arabant & hirciabant ad Curiam Domini*, & ibidem tit. Derhurst, *De terra hujus Manerii tenebant* Radechenistres, i. *liberi homines, forte* (saith *Spelman*) *sit idem quod* Bractono Radeknights. See *Co.* on *Lit. sect.* 117. verb. *Socagium*, pag. 86.

Radman, *Doomsday*, *tit.* Herefscire, 15. *Bordar. Præpositus & unus* Radman, *&c.* It seems to be the same with *Rodeknight*, unless peradventure it be derived from Reade Counsel, and so *Readmans* signifies Counsellors.

Rageman, Is a Statute so called of Justices, assign'd by *Edward* the First and his Council, to go a Circuit through all *England*, and to hear and determine all Complaints of injuries done within five years next before *Michaelmas*, in the fourth year of his Reign.

Ragmans-Roll, Sir *Richard Baker* in his *Chronicle*, *fol.* 127. saith, That *Edward* the Third surrendred, by his Charter, all his Title of Soveraignty to the Kingdom of *Scotland*, restored divers Deeds and Instruments of their former Homages and Fealties, with the famous Evidence called *Ragmans Roll*.

Ragloria, Is a word mentioned in the Charter of *Edward* the Third, whereby he made his eldest Son *Edward Prince of Wales* in Parliament at *Westminster* the Seventeenth year of his Reign, recited by *Selden* in his *Titles of Honour*, pag. 597.——*Cum Forestis, Parcis, Chaseis, Boscis, Warenis, Hundredis, Comotis*, Ragloriis, *Ringeldiis, Wodewardis, Constabulariis, Ballivis, &c. Davies* in his *Dictionary* sayes, That **Rhaglaw** among the Welsh signifies *Seneschallus*, *Surrogatus*, *Præpositus*.

Ramhundt, In the Constitutions of King *Canutus*, touching the Forest, *Art.* 30. 'tis said, *Item de canibus quod* Ramhundt *vocant*.

Ran, Is a Saxon word, and signifies *aperta rapina*, open or publick Theft, *Lamb. Archai.* fol. 125. defines it thus, *Ran dicitur aperta rapina, quæ negari non potest.* In the Saxon Laws of King *Canute*, *cap.*58. ——*Si in profectione militari* Ran *commiserit, pro facti ratione emendato. Hoveden* in the later part of *H.* 2. speaking of some things which *William the Conqueror* mended in the Laws of *England*, saith, *Decretum est etiam ibi, ut si Francigena appellaverit Anglicum, de perjurio aut murdro, furto, homicidio*, Ran *quod dicunt apertam rapinam quæ negari non potest, Anglicus se defendet, per quod melius voluerit, aut judicio ferri aut duello.* So we still say, when a man takes away the Goods of another by open Violence, he hath taken all he could *Rap and Run*.

Range, From the French *Ranger*, to order, dispose of. It is used in the *Forest Laws* both as a Verb, as to *Range*; and a Substantive, as *to make Range, Charta de Foresta*, cap. 6. To *Range* also signifies to wander and stray about.

Ranger, Is a sworn Officer of the Forest, of which there are twelve, *Id. cap.* 7. whose Authority is in part described by his Oath set down by *Manwood*, *part* 1. *pag.* 50. but more particularly *part* 2. *cap.* 20. *num.* 15, 16, 17. His Office chiefly consists in three points, To walk daily through his Charge, to see, hear and inquire, as well of Trespasses as Trespassers in his Bayliwike; To drive the Beasts of the Forest both of Venery and Chace out of the deafforested into the forested Lands: And to present all Trespasses of the Forest at the next Courts holden for the Forest. This *Ranger* is made by the King's Letters Patent, and hath a Fee of twenty or thirty pound paid yearly out of the *Exchequer*, and certain Fee-Deer.

Ransome, *Redemptio*, Is derived of the French *Rancon* or *Rencon*, *redemptio* signifies properly the Sum that is paid for the *redeeming* one that is taken Prisoner in War: But it is used also for a sum of Mony paid for the Pardoning some great Offence, as in the Statute of 1 *H.* 4. *cap.* 7. 11 *H.* 6. 11. and 23 *H.* 8. *cap.* 3. where *Fine and Ransome* are joined together: But here note, That when one is to make a *Fine and Ransome*, the *Ransome* shall be treble to the Fine, *Cromp. Just. of Peace*, fol. 142. and *Lamb. Eiren. lib.* 4. *cap.* 16. *pag.* 556. *Horne* in his *Mirror of Justices* makes this difference between *Amerciament and Ransome*, that *Ransome* is the redemption of a corporal punishment due by Law to any offence, *Lib.* 3. cap. *De Amerciament. taxable.* See *Co.* on *Lit. fol.* 127.

Rape, *Rapa & Rapus*, Is a part of a County, being in a manner the same with a Hundred, and sometimes contains in it more Hundreds than one. As all *Sussex* is divided into six *Rapes* only, *viz.* Of *Chichester, Arundel, Brember, Lewis, Pevensey* and *Hastings*; every of which, besides their Hundreds, hath a Castle, River and Forest belonging to it, *Camd. Brit. pag.* 225, and 229. These, in other Counties, are called *Hundreds, Tythings, Lathes* and *Wapentakes*, Smith *de Rep. Ang.* lib. 2. cap. 16.

Rape, *Raptus*, Is a Felony committed by a Man, in the violent deflouring of a Woman against her will, be she old or young, *Britton. cap.* 1. *West. Symbol.* part 2. tit. *Inditements*, sect 54. hath these words, Copulation violent is termed a *Rape* or Ravishment of the Body of a Woman against her will, which is carnal knowledge had of a Woman, who never consented thereunto before the Fact or after. And this in *Scotland* ought to be complain'd of the same day or night that the Crime is committed, *Skene de verbor.* Signif. *verb.* Raptus, and his reason is, *quia lapsu diei hoc crimen præscribitur. Co.* on *Lit.* lib. 2. cap. 11. sect. 190. says, If the Woman conceive, it is no *Rape*; for she cannot conceive, unless she consent. This Offence is Felony both in the Principal and his Ayders, 13 *R.* 2. *stat.* 2. *cap.* 1. 11 *H.* 4. *cap.* 13. 1 *E.* 4. *cap.* 1. and *Westm.* 2. *cap.* 13. and shall not be allowed the benefit of Clergy, 18 *Eliz. cap.* 7. And *Fleta* sayes, The Complaint must be made within forty days, or else the Woman may not be heard, *lib.* 3. *cap.* 5. sect. *Præterea.* And carnal knowledge of a Woman under ten years old is Felony, 8 *Eliz.* 6. Of the diversity of *Rapes*, see *Cromp. Justice of Peace*, fol. 43. 44. the Offender is called *Raptor*, a Ravisher, and in *Bracton*'s time was punisht with the loss of his Eyes and Stones, *Quia calorem stupri induxerunt*, 3 Inst. fol. 60. see *Ravishment.* The Civil Law useth *Raptus* in the same signification,

And *rapere virginem vel mulierem est ei vim inferre & violare.* See *Dyer*, *Term. Mich.* 13 & 14 *Eliz. pag.* 304.

Rape of the Forest, *Raptus Forestæ*, Is reckoned among those Crimes, whose Cognisance belongs onely to the King. *Violentus concubitus*, Raptus Forestæ, *relevationes baronum suorum, &c.* Leg. Hen. 1. cap. 10. Trespass committed in the *Forest* by violence.

Rapine, *Rapina*, To take a thing in private against the Owners will, is properly Theft; but to take it openly, or by violence, is *Rapine*, 14 *Car.* 2. *cap.* 22. and 18 *Car.* 2. *cap.* 3.

Raptu hæredis, Is a Writ lying for the taking away of an Heir holding in Socage; of which there are two sorts, one when the Heir is married, the other when he is not; of both these, see the *Reg. Orig. fol.* 163.

Rase, *Raseria*, It seems to have been a measure of Corn now disused. **Toll shall be taken by the** Rase, **and not by the Heape or Cantel,** *Ordinance* for *Bakers*, *Brewers*, *&c.* cap. 4. *Debentur ei annuatim decem & octo* Raseriæ *avenæ*, *& sex* Raseriæ *hordei*, *&c.* Spelman.

Rastall, Was an eminent and learned Lawyer that lived in Queen *Maries* days, and was a Justice of the Common-Pleas; he made an Abridgment of the Statutes, which bears his name to this day. He was also the Author of the *New Book of Entries.*

Rate-tythe, Is, when Sheep, or other Cattel, are kept in a Parish for a less time than a year, the Owner must pay *Tith* for them *pro rata*, according to the Custom of the Place, *F. N. B. fol.* 51. *Broke*, *Dis
mes* 26. *Pro rata dicimus, pro proportione vel proportionaliter.* Linwood.

Ratification, *Ratificatio*, A ratifying or confirming; It is used for the confirmation of a Clerk in a Prebend, &c. formerly given him by the Bishop, &c. where the right of Patronage is doubted to be in the King. See *Reg. Orig. fol.* 304.

Ratio, Properly signifies reason; but we take it mostly for an Account, as *reddere rationem*, to give an Account, and so it is frequently used.

Rationabili parte bonorum, Is a Writ that lies for the Wife against the Executors of her Husband, denying her the third part of her Husband's Goods, after Debts and Funeral Charges defrayed, *F. N. B. fol.* 222. who there cites the Eighteenth Chapter of *Magna Charta*, and *Glanvile*, to prove that according to the Common Law of *England*, the Goods of the Deceased, his Debts first paid, should be divided into three parts, whereof his Wife to have one, his Children the second, and the Executors the third; and this Writ lies as well for the Children as Wife, which appears by *Reg. Orig. fol.* 142. Yet it seems to be in use no where, unless the Custom of the Country leads to it. See the *New Book of Entries*, verb. *Rationabili parte bonorum.*

Rationabilibus divisis, Is a Writ that lies where two Lords, in divers Towns, have Seigniories joyning together, for him that findeth his wast by little and little to have been encroached upon, against the other that hath encroached, thereby to rectifie their Bounds; in which respect *Fitzherbert* calls it in its own nature a *Writ of Right.* The *Old Nat. Brev.* says, That this is a kind of *Justicies*, and may be removed by a *Pone* out of the County to the Common-Bench. See the form and use hereof in *F. N. B. fol.* 128. and *Reg. Orig.* fol. 157. and *New Book of Entries*, verb. *Rationabilibus divisis.* The *Civilians* call this *Judicium finium Regundorum.*

Ravishment, *Raptus*, Signifies an unlawful taking away either a Woman, or an Heir in ward: Sometimes also it is used in the same sense with *Rape*, which see.

Ravishment de gard, Was a Writ that lay for the Guardian by Knights service, or in Socage, against him that took from him the Body of his ward. See *F. N. B. fol.* 140. See 12 *Car.* 2. *cap.* 24.

Ravisher, *Raptor*, He that defloures a Woman by Violence. See the Penalty for *ravishing*, or being ravisht, afterwards consenting, in the Statute 6 *R.* 2. *cap.* 6. See *Rape.*

Rawe, Is a word mentioned *Anno* 4 *E.* 4. 1.

Rawnge and **Rawnger.** See *Range* and *Ranger.*

Ray, Is a word appropriated to Cloth never coloured or dyed, 17 *R.* 2. *cap.* 3. 11 *H.* 4. *cap.* 6. and 1 *R.* 3. *cap.* 8.

Reafforested, Is where a Forest hath been *disafforested*, and again made Forest, as the Forest of *Deane*, by the Statute of 20 *Car.* 2. *cap.* 3.

Realty, Is an abstract of *real*, and distinguished from *Personalty.*

Reasonable ayde, *Rationabile auxilium*, Was a Duty that the Lord of the Fee claimed of his Tenants holding by Knights service, or in Socage, to marry his Daughter, or make his Son Knight, *Westm.* 1. *cap.* 39. but taken away now. See the Stat. 12 *Car.* 2. *cap* 24.

Reattachment, *Reattachiamentum*, Is a second *attachment* of him that was formerly attached and dismissed the Court without day, as by the not coming of the Justices, or some such casualty, *Broke*, *hoc titulo*, where he makes *reattachment General and Special*: *General*, is where a man is reattached for his appearance upon all Writs of Assize lying against him, *Bro. ibid. num.* 18. Then *Special* must be for one or more certain, *Reg. Judic.* fol. 35. and *New Book of Entries*, hoc verbo.

Rebellion, *Rebellio*, Is a French word, or rather Latine, signifying the taking up of Arms trayterously against the King, be it by natural Subjects, or by others once subdued: Among the *Romans* it denoted a second resistance of such as formerly being overcome in Battel, yielded to their Subjection. The word *Rebel* is sometimes attributed to him that wilfully breaks a Law, 25 *E.* 3. 6. and 31 *E.* 3. *stat.* 3. *cap.* 2. Sometime to a Villain disobeying his Lord, *R.* 2. cap. 6. *Commission of Rebellion.* See in *Commission.*

Rebellious Assembly, Is a gathering together of Twelve persons, or more, intending or going about, practising or putting in ure unlawfully of their own Authority, to change any Laws or Statutes of this Realm; or to destroy the Enclosure of any Park or Ground inclosed, or Banks of any Fish-Pound, Pool or Conduit, to the intent the same shall remain void; or to the Intent unlawfully to have Common, or way in any of the said Grounds; or to destroy the Deer in any Park, or any Warren of Conies or Dove-houses, or Fish in any Ponds; or any House, Barns, Mills, or Bayes; or to burn Stacks of Corn, or to abate Rents, or prises of Victuals, *Anno* 1 *Mar.* 12. & 1 *Eliz.* 17. See *West Symbol.* part 2. tit. *Indictments*, sect. 65. and *Cromp. Justice of Peace*, fol. 21.

Rebutter, Cometh of the French *Bouter*, *repellere*, and signifies the same in the Common Law. For example, A man grants Land to the use of himself, and the Issue of his Body, to another in Fee with warranty. And the Donee leaseth out his Land to a third for years; The Heir of the Donor impleadeth, the Tenant alledging, that the Land was in tail to him: The Donee comes in, and by vertue of the warranty made by the Donor, repelleth the Heir, because though the Land was intailed to him, yet he is Heir to the Warrantor likewise; and this is call'd a *Rebutter*, *Bro. tit.* Barre, *num.* 23. And again, If I grant to my Tenant, to hold *sine impetitione vasti*, and afterward I implead him for wast made; he may debar me of this Action, by shewing my grant: And this also is a *Rebutter*, Bro. *ib. num.* 25. *New Book of Entries*, verb. *Rebutter*, and *Co.* on *Lit. fol.* 365.

Recaption, *Recaptio*, Signifies a second Distress of one formerly distrained for the same Cause, and also during the Plea grounded on the former Distress: It likewise signifies a Writ, lying for the party thus distrained; the form and farther use thereof, you may see in *F. N. B. fol.* 71. and *Reg. Orig. fol.* 86. *Reg. Judic. fol.* 69. and the *New Book of Entries*, verbo *Recaption*.

Receiver, *Receptor*, Is with us as with the *Civilians*, commonly used in the evil part for such as receive stollen Goods from Thieves, and conceal them. But annexed to other words, as *the Receiver of Rents*, &c. It signifies many times an Officer of great account belonging to the King, or other great person, *Cromp. Jur.* fol. 18. There is also an Officer called *The Receiver of Fines*, who receives the Money of all such as compound with the King upon Original Writ in *Chancery*, *West Symbol.* part 2. tit. *Fines*, sect. 106. *Receiver* of all Offices accountable, 1 *E.* 4. *cap.* 1.

Receiver-General of the Dutchy of Lancaster, Is an Officer belonging to the *Dutchy Court*, that gathers in all the Revenues and Fines of the Lands of the said *Dutchy*, and of all Forfeitures and Assesments, or what else is thence received, *Anno* 39 *Eliz. cap.* 7.

Receiver-General of the Court of Wards and Liveries, Was an Officer belonging to that *Court*; but the *Court* being taken away by the Stat. 12 *Car.* 2. *cap.* 24. that Officer is also out of Doors.

Receiver-General of the Muster Rolls, *Anno* 35 *Eliz. cap.* 4.

Receit. See *Resceit*.

Recluse, *Reclusus*, Is one that by reason of his Order in Religion, is shut up, and may not stir out of the House or Cloyster, of whom *Littleton* speaks, *sect.* 434.

Recognisance, *Recognitio*, Cometh of the French *Recognoissance*, and is as a Bond or Obligation of Record, testifying the *Recognisor* to owe to the *Recognisee* a certain sum of Money, and is acknowledged in some *Court of Record*, or before some Judge, Master of the Chancery, or Justice of Peace, &c. 23 *H.* 8. 6. and those that be meer *Recognisances* are not sealed but enrolled, and execution by force thereof is of all the *Recognisors* Goods or Chattells (except draught Beast and Implements of Husbandry) and the moyety of his Lands, *West Symbol. part.* 1. *lib.* 2. *sect.* 149. and *Reg. Orig.* fol. 146. 151. & 252. See also *Statute-Merchant and Statute Staple*. *Recognisance* hath yet another signification, as appears by these words in the Statute, *Westm.* 1. *cap.* 36. For it is there provided and agreed, That if any man be attainted of *Disseisin* done in the time of the King that now is, with robbery of any manner of Goods or Moveables, by *Recognisance of Assise* of *Novel Disseisin*, the Judgment shall be, &c. where it is used for the *Verdict* of the twelve men impannelled upon an *Assise*, which twelve are also called *Recognitors* of the *Assise*, *Lit. fol.* 72. So also *Bracton* names them, *lib.* 5. *tract.* 2. *cap.* 9. *num.* 2. and *lib.* 3. *tract.* 1. *cap.* 11. *num.* 16. See the Stat. 20 *E.* 1. *Stat.* 4. and *New Book of Entries*, verbo *Recognisance*.

Recognisee, Is he to whom one is bound in a *Recognisance*, 11 *H.* 6. *cap.* 10.

Recognition, *Recognitio*, An acknowledgment; It is the Title of the first Chapter of the Statute made in the first year of King *James*. See *Skene de verb. Signif. verb.* Recognition.

Recognitione adnullanda per vim & duritiem facta, Is a Writ to the Justices of the Common Bench, for the sending of a Record touching a *Recognisance*, which the *Recognisor* suggests to have been acknowledged by force and duresse, that if it be so, it may be annulled, *Reg. Orig. fol.* 183.

Recognitors, *Recognitores*, Is a word frequently used for the Jury impannelled upon an Assise: The reason why they are so called, is, because they acknowledge a Disseisin by their Verdict, *Bracton*, *lib.* 5. *tract.* 2. *cap.* 9. *num.* 2. & *lib.* 3. *tract.* 1. *cap.* 11. *num.* 16.

Record, *Recordum*, Cometh of the Latine *Recordari* to remember, and signifies an authentick and uncontroulable Testimony in writing, contained in Rolls of Parchment, and preserved in Courts of Record, and they are said to be *Vetustatis & veritatis vestigia*, *Co. Preface to his* 8. *Rep.* Britton, *cap.* 27, and *Lamb. Eiren.* lib. 1. cap. 13. An Act committed to writing in any of the Kings Courts, during the Term wherein it is written, is alterable, being no *Record*; but that Term once ended, and the Act duly enrolled, it is a *Record*, and of that credit, that admits no alteration or proof to the contrary, *Bro. tit.* Record, *num.* 20. 22. yet see *Co.* 4. *Rep. Rawlins* Case. *fol.* 52. The King may make a *Court of Record* by his Grant, *Glanvile*, lib. 8. cap. 8. *Britton*, cap. 121. As Queen *Elizabeth* by her Charter, dated the 26. of

April, in the third year of her Reign, made the Consistory Court of the University of *Cambridge*, a Court of *Record*, *Bro. tit.* Record, seems to insinuate that no Court Ecclesiastical is of *Record*, yet we see that Bishops certifying, *Bastardy, Bigamy, Excommunication, a Marriage, Divorce, or the like*, are credited without farther inquiry, *Fleta, lib.* 6. *cap.* 39, 40, 41, 42. *Lamb. Eiren. lib.* 1. *cap.* 13. *Glanvile, lib.* 7. *cap.* 14, 15. *Reg. Orig. fol.* 5. *Bracton, lib.* 5. *tract.* 5. *cap.* 20. *num.* 5. *Britton, cap.* 92. 94, 106, 107, & 109. *Doct. & Stud. lib.* 2. *cap.* 5. And a Testament shewed under Seal of the Ordinary is not traversable, 36 *H.* 6. *cap.* 31. *Perkin's Testament* 491. *Fulbecke's Parallels*, fol. 61. The reason of which Opinion may be, because by the *Civil or Canon Law* no *Record* is held so firm but that it may be checked by Witnesses able to depose it to be untrue; whereas in our *Common Law* against a *Record* of the King's Court, after the Term wherein it is made, no Witness can prevail, *Britton, cap.* 109. *Co. lib.* 4. *fol.* 71. *Hind's* Case, *Lib. Ass. fol.* 227. *nota* 21. We reckon three sorts of *Records*, viz. A *Record Judicial*, as Attainder, &c. A *Record Ministerial* upon Oath, as an Office or Inquisition found. And a *Record* made by conveyance and consent, as a Fine or Deed enrolled, or the like, *Co. lib.* 4. *fol.* 54. *b. Ognell's* Case.

Recordare facias, or Recordari facias, Is a Writ directed to the Sheriff, to remove a Cause depending in an inferior Court, as Court of ancient Demesne, Hundred or County, to the King's Bench or Common Pleas, *F. N. B. fol.* 71. where, and in what Cases this Writ lies, read *Broke*, tit. *Recordare & Pone.* It seems to be called a *Recordare*, because it commands the Sheriff to whom it is directed to make *a record* of the Proceedings by himself and others, and then to send up the Cause. See the Table of the *Reg. Orig.* verbo *Recordare.* See also *Certiorari*, and *Accedas ad Curiam.*

Recorder, *Recordator*, Is he whom the Mayor, or other Magistrate of any City or Town Corporate having Jurisdiction, or a Court of Record within their Precincts, by the King's Grant, doth associate unto him for his better direction in matters of Justice and Proceedings according to Law: And is therefore for the most a man versed and experienced in the Law. What they call a *Recorder* in other Foreign parts, see in the *Grand Custumary* of *Normandy*, cap. 107, & 121.

Recordo & processu mittendis, Is a Writ to call a Record together, with the whole proceeding in the Cause out of an inferior Court into the King's Court: which see in the Table of the *Reg. Orig.* how diversly it is used.

Recordo utlagariæ mittendo, Is a Judicial Writ, which see in *Reg. Judic. fol.* 32.

Recovery, *Recuperatio.* May be extracted from the French *Recouvrer*, i. *recuperare*, and signifies in a legal Acceptation an obtaining any thing by Judgment or Tryal of Law, as *Evictio* doth among the *Civilians.* And here note, That there is a *true recovery*, and a *feigned* one. A *true recovery* is an actual or real *recovery* of any thing, or the value thereof by Judgment; as if a man sued for any Land, or other thing moveable or immoveable, and have a Verdict and Judgment for him. A *feigned recovery* is (as the *Civilians* call it) *Quædam fictio Juris*, a certain form or course set down by Law, to be observed, for the better assuring of Lands or Tenements unto us; and the end and effect thereof, is (according to *West Symbol.* part 2. tit. *Recoveries*, sect. 1.) to discontinue and destroy Estates tail, Remainders and Reversions, and to bar the Intails thereof. And in this formality are required three persons, *viz. The Demandant, Tenant* and *Vouchee.* The *Demandant*, is he that brings the Writ of Entry, and may be termed *the Recoverer. The Tenant*, is he against whom the Writ is brought, and may be termed *the Recoveree. The Vouchee*, is he whom the Tenant voucheth, and calls to warranty for the Land in demand. *A recovery with double Voucher*, is, where the Tenant voucheth one, who voucheth another, or the common Vouchee. And a *recovery with treble Vouchers*, is, where three are vouched. But to explain this point a little more, A man that is desirous to cut off an Estate tail in Lands or Tenements, to the end, to sell, give, or bequeath it, causeth (by the contrivance of his Council or Attorney) a feigned Writ of Entry, *sur disseisin en le Post*, to be brought for the Lands of which he intends to cut off the entail, and in a feigned Count or Declaration thereupon made, pretends he was disseised by him, who by a feigned Fine, or Deed of Bargain and Sale, is named and supposed to be the Tenant of the Land. This feigned Tenant, if it be *a single recovery*, is made to appear and vouch the *Bagbearer of Writs* for the *Custos brevium* in the *Common Pleas* (for there onely can such *recoveries* be suffred) who makes default. Whereupon the Land is *recovered* by him that brought the Writ, and a Judgment is by such fiction of Law entred, that the Demandant shall *recover*, and have a *Writ of Seisin* for the possession of the Lands demanded, and that the Tenant shall recover the value of the Lands against the Lands of the *Vouchee. Bagbearer*, a poor unlanded and illiterate person, which is feigned to be a satisfaction to the Heir in tail, though he is never to have or expect it. This *feigned recovery* is also called *a common recovery*, because it is a beaten and common path to that end for which it is appointed, *viz.* to cut off the Estates above specified. See *New Book of Entries*, verb. *Recovery.* But a true *recovery* is as well of the value, as of the thing: For example, If a man buy Land of another with warranty, which Land a third person afterwards by Suit of Law recovereth against me; I have my remedy against him that sold it me, to recover in value, that is, to recover so much in Money as the Land is worth, or so much other Land by way of exchange, *F. N. B. fol.* 134. To *recover a warranty*, *Old Nat. Brev.* fol. 146. is to prove by Judgment, that such a man was his warrant against all men for such a thing.

Recoupe, From the French *Recouper*, to cut again; also to reply quickly and sharply to a peremptory Demand: we use it to defalke or discount. As if a man hath ten pounds issuing out of certain Lands, and he disseises the Tenant of the Land in an Assise brought by the Disseisee, the Disseisor shall *Recoupe* the Rent in the Damages.

Recreant, French Cowardly, Faint-hearted. See *Cravent*.

Rectatus, *Spelman* interprets it *Suspectus, ad rectum vocatus. Officium Coronatoris edit*, Anno 3 E. 1. -----*De Thesauro invento debet Coronator inquirere qui fuerint Inventores & similiter quis inde* rectatus *est, & hoc potest scire eo quod vixerit delicate & tabernam frequentat & diu sic se habuit, pro tali suspicione attachiari debent, &c.* See *Bracton* 123. *num.* 8.

Recto, Is a Writ of Right, which is of so high a nature, that whereas other Writs in real Actions are only to recover the possession of the Land or Tenements in question, which have been lost by our Ancestor or our selves; this aimeth to recover both the Seisin which some of our Ancestors or we had, and also the property of the thing whereof the Ancestor died not seised, as of Fee; and whereby are pleaded and tryed both their rights together, *viz.* as well of Possession as Property: So that if a man once lose his Cause upon this Writ, either by Judgment, Assise or Battel, he is without all remedy, and shall be excluded *per exceptionem rei judicatæ*, Bracton, *lib.* 5. *tract.* 1. *cap.* 1. *& seq.* It is divided into two kinds, 1. *Rectum Patens*, a Writ of right Patent, and *Rectum Clausum*, a Writ of right Close. This the *Civilians* call *Judicium Petitorum*. The *Writ of right Patent* is so called, because it is sent open, and is in nature the highest Writ of all other, lying always for him that hath Fee-simple in the Land or Tenements sued for, and not for any other. And when it lyeth for him that challengeth Fee-simple, and in what Cases. See *F.N.B. fol.* 1. 6. where he speaks of a *special Writ of Right* in *London*, otherwise called a *Writ of Right*, according to the Custom of *London*. This Writ also is called *Breve Magnum de recto*, Reg. Orig. *fol.* 9. and *Fleta* lib. 5. cap. 32. sect. 1. A *Writ of right Close*, is a Writ directed to a Lord of *Ancient Demesne*, and lyeth for those which hold their Lands and Tenements by Charter in Fee-simple, or in Fee-tail, or for term of Life, or in Dower, if they be ejected out of such Lands, *&c.* or disseised: In this case a Man, or his Heirs, may sue out this *Writ of right Close*, directed to the Lord of the *Ancient Demesne*, commanding him to do him right, *&c.* in his Court. This is called *Breve parvum de recto*, Reg. Orig. *fol.* 9. and *Britton. crp.* 120. *in fine*, also *F. N. B. fol.* 11. *& seq.* Yet note, That the Writ of right Patent seemeth farther to be extended in use than the original intention; For a *Writ of right of Dower* which lies for the Tenant in Dower, and only for term of Life, is *Patent*, as appears by *F. N. B. fol.* 7. The like may be said in divers other cases, of which see the Table of the *Register Original*, verbo *Recto*. This Writ is properly tryed in the Lords Court between Kinsmen that Claim by one Title from their Ancestor. But how it may be thence removed, and brought either to the County, or to the Kings Court, see *Fleta, lib.* 6. *cap.* 3, 4, *&* 5. *Glanvile* seems to make every Writ, whereby a man sues for any thing due unto him, a Writ of right, *lib.* 10. *cap.* 1. *lib.* 11. *cap.* 1. and *lib.* 12. *cap.* 1.

Recto de dote, Is *a Writ of right of Dower*, which lieth for a Woman that hath received part of her *Dower*, and purposes to demand the remainder in the same Town, against the Heir, or his Guardian, if he be a Ward. Of this see more in *Old. Nat. Brev. fol.* 5. and *Fitzherbert, fol.* 7. Reg. Orig. *fol.* 3. and the *New Book of Entries*, verb. *Droyt*.

Recto de dote unde nihil habet, Is a *Writ of right*, which lies in case where the Husband having divers Lands or Tenements, hath assured no *Dower* to his Wife, and she thereby is driven to sue for her Thirds against the Heir, or his Guardian, *Old Nat. Brev. fol.* 6. *Reg. Orig. fol.* 170.

Recto de rationabili parte, Is a Writ that lies alway between privies of Blood, as Brothers in *Gavelkind*, or Sisters, or other Coparceners; as Nephews or Neeces, and for Land in Fee-simple. For example, If a man lease his Land for term of Life, and afterward dies, leaving Issue two Daughters, and after that the Tenant for term of life dieth also, the one Sister entring upon all the Land, and so deforcing the other, the Sister so deforced shall have this writ to recover part, F. N. B. *fol.* 9. *Reg. Orig.* fol. 3.

Recto quando Dominus remisit, Is a *Writ of Right*, which lies in case where Lands or Tenements that be in the Seigniory of any Lord, are in demand by a *Writ of Right*; for if the Lord hold no Court, or otherwise at the prayer of the Demandant, or Tenant, shall send to the Court of the King his writ, to put the Cause thither for that time, (saving to him at other times the right of his Seigniory,) then this writ issues out for the other Party, and hath the name from the words contained, being the true occasion thereof: This writ is *close*, and must be returned before the Justices of the *Common Banke*, Old Nat. Brev. *fol.* 16. Reg. Orig. *fol.* 4.

Recto de Advocatione Ecclesiæ, Is a *Writ of Right*, lying where a man hath right of *Advowson*, and the Parson of the Church dying, a Stranger presents his Clerk to the Church, and he not having brought his Action of *Quare Impedit*, nor *Darrein Presentment* within six Months, but suffered the Stranger to usurp upon him. And this writ he only may have that claimeth the *Advowson* to himself, and to his Heirs in Fee. And as it lies for the whole *Advowson*, so it lies also for the half, third or fourth part, *Old Nat. Brev. fol.* 24. *Reg. Orig. fol.* 29.

Recto de custodia terræ & hæredis, Was a Writ that lay for him whose Tenant holding of him in Chivalry, died in Nonage, against a Stranger that entred upon the Land, and took the Body of the Heir; but by the Statute of 12 *Car.* 2. *cap.* 24. it is become useless as to Lands holden *in Capite*, or by *Knights-service*, but not where there is Guardian in *Socage*, or appointed by the last Will and Testament of the Ancestor. The form of it, see in F. N. B. *fol.* 139. and *Reg. Orig.* fol. 161.

Recto sur Disclaymer, Is a Writ that lies where a Lord in the Kings *Court of Common Pleas* avow upon his Tenant, and the Tenant *disclaimeth* to hold of him; upon which *disclaimer* he shall have this writ, and if the Lord aver and prove, that the Land is holden of him, he shall recover the Land for ever, *Old. Nat. Brev.* fol. 150. which is grounded upon the Statute *Westm.* 2. *cap.* 2.

Rector, Is both Latine and English, signifying a Governor, and *Rector Ecclesiæ parochialis*, Is he that hath the Charge or Cure of a Parish-Church, *Qui tantum jus in Ecclesia Parochiali habet, quantum Prælatus in Ecclesia Collegiata*: It has of late been over-ruled, that *Rector Ecclesiæ Parochialis*, is he that hath a *Parsonage* where there is a *Vicaridge* endowed; and he that has a *Parsonage* without a *Vicaridge*, is called *Persona*, but this distinction seems to be new and subtile. *Bracton* certainly uses it otherwise, *lib.* 4. *tract.* 5. *cap.* 1. in these words, *Et sciendum quod rectoribus Ecclesiarum parochialium competit Assisa qui instituti sunt per Episcopos & Ordinarios ut Personæ*; Where it is plain, that *Rector* and *Persona* be confounded. Observe also these words there following, *Item dici possunt* Rectores *Canonici de Ecclesiis Præbendatis. Item dici possunt* Rectores *vel quasi Abbates, Priores & alii, qui habent Ecclesias ad proprios usus.* See *Vicar*.

Rectory, *Rectoria*, Is taken for an entire Parish-Church, with all its Rights, Glebes, Tythes, and other profits whatsoever. *Spelman.*

Rectus in Curia, Is *verbatim*, right in Court, and signifies one that stands at the Bar, and no man Objects any thing against him, *Smith de Repub. Angl. lib.* 2. *cap.* 3. We take it also, that when a man is Outlawed, he is *extra legem positus*; So when he hath reversed the Outlawry, and can participate of the benefit of the Law, he is *Rectus in Curia.*

Reddendum, Is used substantively for the Clause in a Lease, &c. whereby the Rent is reserved to the Lessor, *Co. lib.* 2. *fol.* 72. *Cromwels* Case.

Redisseisin, *Redissisina*, Is a *disseisin* made by him, that once before was found and adjudged to have *disseised* the same man of his Lands or Tenements; for the which there lies a special Writ, called a Writ of *Redisseisin*, *Old. Nat. Brev. fol.* 106. *F. N. B.* fol. 188. *New Book of Entries*, *eodem verbo*. The Punishment for *redisseisin*, see in the Statute 52 *H.* 3. *cap.* 8. It is also taken for the Writ lying for a *redisseisin*, Reg. Orig. 206, 207.

Redmans or **Radmans**, *Doomsday in fine* Cestre-scire, tit. *Lanc.* **Blackburne Hundret**, *Rex* E. *tenuit* **Peneverdant**, *Ibi* 11 Car. *sunt in Dominio & 6. Burgenses &* 3. Radmans, & 8. *vill. &* 4. *bovar.* These *Redmans* may be the same with *rad Knights*, who, by the Tenure or Custom of their Lands, were to ride with or for the Lord of the Mannor about his business or affairs.

Redubbors, Be those which buy stollen Cloth, knowing it such, and change it into some other form or colour that it may not be known, *Britton*, cap. 29. *Crompton*'s *Vicount*, fol. 193. and 3. *Inst. fol.* 134.

Re-entry, May be deduced from the French *Rentrer*, i. *rursus intrare*, to enter again, and signifies the resuming or retaking that Possession which we had lately foregone. For example, If I make a Lease of Land or Tenement, I do thereby forego the Possession; and if I do condition with the Lessee, That for non-payment of the Rent at the day, it shall be lawful for me to re-enter; this is as much as if I conditioned to take again the Lands, &c. into mine own Hands, and to recover the Possession by my own Fact, without the assistance of Judge, or other Process.

Reere-County. See *Reir-County*.

Re-extent, Is a *second extent* made upon Lands or Tenements, upon Complaint made, that the former *extent* was partially performed, *Bro.* tit. *Extents*, fol. 313.

Refectory, *Refectorium*, That place in Monasteries where the Monks used to eat. So the *Halls* in *Colledges and Inns of Courts* may properly be called *Refectories*, places wherein the Schollars and Students eat and refresh themselves.

Referendary, *Referendarius*, Is the same as the *Masters of Request* are to the King among us; they were so called by the old *Saxons*, as appears by the Charter of the Endowment of the Monastery of St. *Peter* and *Paul* in *Canterbury*, dated *Anno Dom.* 605. where it is thus endorsed, ✠ *Ego Augemandus* Referendarius *approbavi.* ✠ *Ego Graphio Comes benedixi.* ✠ *Ego Tangisilus Regis Optimas confirmavi*, &c. And in another Charter of the same King, *Testibus reverendissimo Patre Augustino Dorobernensis Ecclesiæ Archiepiscopo Primo*, &c. *Ædbaldo filio meo, Hamigisilo (Duce Landavi) Augemundo* Referendario *Hocca comite*, &c. See *Spelman hoc verbo.*

Reforciuncula, *Walsingham in* Ed. 2. *Anno Dom.* 1317. saith, *In* Reforciuncula *sua de* **Horton** latens *vicinis similẽ injuriam inferebat.*

Regal Fishes, Are *Whales and Sturgions*, *Anno* 1 *Eliz. cap.* 5. some add *Porpusses.* The King, by his Prerogative, shall have every Whale cast on shore in all places within this Realm, unless granted to Subjects by special words. The King himself shall have the Head and Body, and the Queen the Tayle, to make Whale-bones for her Royal Vestments, *Pat.* 1 *E.* 1. *m.* 25. *dorso.* See *Tract. de Auro Reginæ*, pag. 127.

Regalia, *Dicuntur jura omnia ad fiscum spectantia*, saith *Spelman.* The Royal Rights of a King, the *Civilians* reckon to be six, 1. Power of Judicature. 2. Power of Life and Death. 3. Power of War and Peace. 4. Masterless Goods, as Wayfes, Estrayes, &c. 5. Assessments. And 6. Minting of Money. See *Royalties.* Also the Crown, Scepter with the Cross, Scepter with the Dove, St. *Edwards* Staff, four several Swords, the Globe, the Orbe with the Cross, and other such like things used at the Coronation of our Kings, are called *Regalia.* See the relation of the Coronation of King *Charles the Second* in *Baker*'s *Chron.*

Regalis Justicia, —— *Item præfati Barones* (scil. quinq; Portuum) *habere debent ut asserunt per chartam suam* **Regalem Justiciam** *in villa* Gernemuth, *tempore feriæ unà cum Ballivo seu Præposito villæ prædictæ, viz. cognitionem Assisæ panis ulnarum, ponderum, & alaorum mensurarum, & similiter* **voyde strand & Denne** *secundum consuetudines suas usitatas*, &c. Rot. Parl. 8 E. 2. num. 262.

Regardant, As *Villain regardant* was called *Regardant* to the Mannor, because he had the Charge to do all base Services within the same, and to see the same freed of all things that might annoy

annoy it, *Co.* on *Lit. fol.* 120. This word is only applied to a *Villain* or *Neif*, yet in old Books it was sometimes attributed to Services, *ibid.*

Regard, *Regardum & Rewardum*, Is borrowed of the French *Regarder*, i. *Aspectus, respectus*; and though it hath a general signification of any care or diligent respect, yet it hath also a special acceptation, wherein 'tis only used in matters of the Forest; and there two wayes, one for the Office of *Regarder*, the other for the compass of the ground belonging to that Office, *Cromp. Jur. fol.* 175. 199. Touching the former, thus saith *Manwood* in his *Forest Laws*, part 1. pag. 194. & 198. *The Eyre, General Sessions of the Forest, or Justice-Seat is to be kept every third year; and of necessity before any such Sessions or Justice-Seat can be holden, the* Regarders *of the Forest must make their* regard, *and this making of the* regard *must be done by the King's Writ, and the* Regarder *is to go through the whole Forest, to see and inquire of the Trespasses therein*, viz. *ad videndum, ad inquirendum, ad imbreviandum & ad certificandum.* Touching the second signification, the compass of the *Ragarders* Charge is the whole Forest, that is, all the ground which is parcel of the Forest; for there may be Woods within the limits of the Forest, that be no parcel thereof, and those be without the *regard, Manwood*, part 2. cap. 7. num. 4. *Anno* 20 *Car.* 2. *cap.* 3.

Regarder, *Regardator*, Cometh of the French *Regardeur*, i. *spectator*, and signifies an Officer of the Forest, *Cromp. Jurisd.* 153. where it is thus defined. A *Regarder* is an Officer of the Forest, appointed to supervise all other Officers, and was ordained in the beginning of King *Henry* the Second's dayes. *Manwood* thus describes him, A *Regarder* is an Officer of the King's Forest, that is, sworn to make the *regard* of the Forest, as the same hath been used to be made heretofore: And also to view and enquire of all Offences or Defaults of the Foresters, and of all other Officers of the King's Forest concerning the execution of their Offices. This Officer may be made either by the King's Letters Patents, or by any one of the King's Justices of the Forest, at his discretion, in the General *Eyre*, or at such time as the *regard* is to be made, by vertue of the King's Writ directed to the Sheriff of the County for that purpose. More particulars of the *Regarders* Office, how he is chosen, and the form of his Oath, see in *Manwood*, pag. 188. 192, 195, 207. In a Charter of *Henry the Third*, To the Masters, Canons, Brethren, &c. of the Order of the House of *Sempling-ham*, made in the Eleventh year of his Reign, 'tis said, *Et sint quieti tam ipsi quam homines eorum de misericordiâ forestæ & de escapis, & de* Rewardo *& vasto ubiq; in Marisco de* **Retstovene, &c.**

Regio Assensu, Is a Writ whereby the King gives his Royal Assent to the Election of a Bishop or Abbot, *Reg. Orig. fol.* 294.

Registry, *Registrum*, Is properly derived from an old French word *Gister*, i. *in lecto reponere, suo loco constituere.* So that *registrum* is properly the same with *repositorium*, a place where any thing is laid up; and from hence Publick Books, in which various things are inserted, are properly termed *Registers*; and accordingly the Office, Books and Rolls, wherein the proceedings of the Chancery, or any spiritual Court are recorded: The Writer and Keeper of which is called *The Register*, in Latine *registarius.*

Register, Is also the name of a Book, wherein are mentioned most of the forms of the Writs used at Common Law, of which *Spelman* writes thus, *Codex dicitur quo brevia Regia tam originalia quam judicialia formularum muneri inscribuntur; In hoc enim si non extiterit brevis alicujus formula, vel si ab eo variatum fuerit breve illud cassum habetur: Nec de novo condi potest breve aliquod hujusmodi non publico Parliamenti decreto, Hujus Codicis meminit*, Westm. 2. cap. 25. And *Co.* on *Lit. fol.* 159. affirms, That this *Register* is one of the most ancient Books of the Common Law.

Register of the Parish Church, *Registrum Ecclesiæ Parochialis*, Is that Book, wherein Baptisms, Marriages, and Burials are in each *Parish* every year *registred*; which was laudably instituted by the Lord *Cromwel*, in the moneth of *September*, 1538. being the Thirtieth year of *Henry* the Eighth, while he was his Vicar-General.

Regius Professor, *Anno* 12 *Car.* 2. *cap.* 17. *Henry* the Eighth founded five Lectures in each University, *viz.* Of *Divinity, Hebrew, Greek, Law* and *Physick*; The Readers of which Lectures are called in the University Statutes, *Regii Professores.*

Regrator, *Regratarius*, May be deduced from the French *Regrateur*, and signifies him that buys Wares or Victuals, on purpose to enhance the prices; formerly such as bought by great, and sold by retail, came under that notion, 27 *E.* 3. *Stat.* 1. *cap.* 3. But now that Name denotes him that buys and sells any Wares or Victuals in the same Market or Fair, or within five Miles thereof, whereof see the Stat. 5 *E.* 6. *cap.* 14. 5 *Eliz.* 12. and 13 *Eliz.* 25. In the Civil Law such is called *Dardanarius, a* Dardano *quodam hujus sceleris authore*, saith *Spelman.* Heretofore both the *Ingrosser* and *Regrator* were comprehended under the word *Forestaller*, 3. *Inst.* 195. and as such shall be punisht. See *Forestallers and Ingrossers.*

Regulars, *Regulares*, Are such as profess to live under some certain rule; such as *Monks*, or *Canon Regulars*, who ought alwayes to be under some rule of Obedience.

Rehabere facias seisinam quando Vicecomes liberavit seisinam de majore parte quam deberet, Is a Writ Judicial; *Reg. Judic. fol.* 13. 51. There is another Writ of this name and nature, *fol.* 54.

Rehabilitation, *Rehabilitatio*, *Anno* 25 *H.* 8. *cap.* 21. Is one of those Exactions mentioned in that Statute, to be claimed by the Pope heretofore in *England*, and seems to signifie a *Bull* or *Breve*, for *reinabling* a spiritual person to exercise his Function, who was formerly disabled, or a *restoring* to a former *ability.*

Reia, French *Raye*, i. *radius, linea, tractus*, In English a **Rew** or raw, *Prior Lewens*, pag. 21. *Omnis Lanceta, omnis Toftman, & omnis Molman (qui non sedet super Ogeland) debent spergere unam* reiam de fiens, &c. that is, saith *Spelman* in his *Glossary, unum strigam, tractum vel versum stercoris*, Anglice **a rew of muck or dunge,** *ad stercorandum terras Domini.*

Rejoynder, *Rejunctio*, Signifies an Answer

 or

or exception to a Replication; For first the Defendant puts in an Answer to the Plaintiffs Bill, which is sometimes called *An Exception*. The Plaintiffs Answer to that is called a *Replication*, and the Defendants to that a *Rejoynder*, especially in Chancery, *West Symbol.* part 2. tit. *Chancery*, sect. 56. The *Civilians* call it *Duplicatio*, of which *Spigelius* hath these words, *Est autem rejunctio seu Duplicatio vel allegatio, quæ datur reo ad infirmandam replicationem actoris & confirmandam exceptionem rei.*

Reippus, *Precium viduæ emptæ Matrimonii causa. A quo fortè* (saith Spelman) *lex nostra antiqua de maritagiis viduarum, sumpserit initium formâ licet diversâ.* And it may seem to be derived from the Saxon ꞃippan *vel* ꞃypan, *i. metere, rapere, colligere, quasi id quod capitur vel colligitur ob maritandas viduas.*

Reif, According to *Skene*, *Leg. Alexandri* R. C. 2. *paragr.* 3. signifies *Robbery*, and may be derived from the Saxon Reaꝼ, *rapina*, Reaꝼian, *spoliare*, as both from the Latine *rapere*.

Riens per discent, is a form of Pleading, when an Heir is sued for a Debt of his Ancestor, and he hath not *Assets* in his Hand, nor any Lands liable to be extended.

Rekpenis, Constit. Rob. Dunelm. Episc. Anno 1276. cap. 3. *Porro huic Sanctioni adjicimus, quod si plures liberi proprium habentes, in parentum pariter familia vivant, ad denarios qui vocantur* **Rekpenis** *minime arceantur, cum si communiter intrinsecis aluntur à parentibus, sic in extrinsecis ab eisdem lætentur pariter se defendi.*

Relation, *Relatio*, *idem quod fictio Juris*, To make a nullity of a thing from the beginning (for a certain intent) which had essence, *Co. lib.* 3. *fol.* 28. *Butler* and *Baker*'s Case: But more plainly thus, *Relation* is, where, in consideration of Law two times, or other things are considered, so as if they were all one, and by this the thing subsequent is said to take his effect by *relation* at the time preceding. As if *A.* deliver a writing to *B.* to be deliver'd to *C.* as the Deed of *A*, when *C.* hath paid a sum of Money. Now when the Money is paid, and the writing delivered, this shall be taken as the Deed of *A.* at the time when it was first delivered. So Bills of Parliament, to which the King assents on the last day of Parliament, shall relate and be of force from the first day of the beginning of the Parliament, and so it is of divers other like things.

Release, *Relaxatio*, Is an Instrument whereby Estates, Rights, Tythes, Entries, Actions, and other things be sometime extinguished, sometime transferred, sometime abridged, and sometime enlarged, *West Symbol. part* 1. *lib.* 2. *sect.* 509. and there is a *release in Fact*, and a *release in Law*, Perkins *Grants* 71. A *release in Fact*, is that which the very words expresly declare. A *release in Law*, is that which doth acquit by way of consequence or Intendment of Law; an example whereof you have in *Perkins ubi supra*. How these are available, and how not, see *Littleton at large*, lib. 3. cap. 8. And of the divers sorts of *Releases*, see the *New Book of Entries*, verb. *Release*.

Relief, *Relevamen*, But in *Doomsday*, *Relevatio*, *relevium*, signifies a certain sum of Money which the Tenant holding by Knights-service, Grand-sergeanty, or other Tenure, for which Homage or regal Service is due; or by Socage, for which no Homage is due, and being at full age at the death of his Ancestor, paid unto his Lord at his Entrance, *Mag. Chart. cap.* 2. and 28 *E.* 1. *stat.* 1. *Bracton*, lib. 2. cap. 36. affirms, That is called *a relief*, *quia hæreditas quæ jacens fuit per antecessoris decessum, relevatur in manus hæredum, & propter factam relevationem, facienda erit ab hærede quædam Præstatio quæ dicitur* relevium, and *Britton*, cap. 69. Of this also speaks the *Grand Custumary* of *Normandy*, cap. 34. *The Lord of the Fee ought to have* relief *of the Lands, which are held of him by Homage, when those die of whom he had Homage. Hotoman* in his *Commentaries, De verbis Feudalibus*, verb. *Relevium*, defines it thus, Relevium, *est honorarium, quod novus vassallus Patrono introitus causa largitur, quasi morte vassalli alterius vel alio quo casu feudum ceciderit, quod jam à novo sublevetur.* What a legal and just *relief* was in the time of *Hen.* 2. appears partly from *Glanvile*, lib. 9. cap. 4. *Dicitur autem rationabile* relevium *alicujus juxta consuetudinem Regni, de feodi unius militis centum solid. de Socagio vero quantum valet census illius socagii per unum annum; De Baroniis vero nihil certum statutum est, quia juxta voluntatem & misericordiam Domini Regis solent Baroniæ capitales de* Releviis *suis Domino Regi satisfacere.* But it was more certainly set out afterwards by *Magna Charta* in these words, *Si quis Comitum vel Baronum nostrorum, sive aliorum tenentium, de nobis in Capite per servitium militare mortuus fuerit & cum decesserit hæres ejus plenæ ætatis fuerit &* Relevium *nobis debeat, Habeat hæreditatem suam per antiquum* relevium, *scil. Hæres vel hæredes Comitis de integro Comitatu per centum libras; hæres vel hæredes Baronis de Baronia integra, per centum marcas, hæres vel hæredes militis de feodo militis integro, per centum solidos ad plus; & qui minus habuerit, minus dei, secundum antiquam consuetudinem feodorum.* See *Old Nat. Brev.* fol. 94. *Kitchin*, fol. 145. cap. *Relief*, and *Glanvile*, lib. 7. cap. 9. See *Heriot*. *Skene de verbor.* Signif. *verb.* Relevium, saith, *Relief* is a French word, from the Latine *relevare*, which is to relieve, or take up that which is fallen; for it is given by the Tenant or Vassal that is of perfect age, after the expiring of the Wardship to his Superior Lord, of whom he held his Lands by Knight-service, that is, by Ward and *Relief*; For by payment thereof he relieves, and, as it were, raiseth up again his Lands after they were fallen down into his Superiors hands, by reason of Wardship, &c. See him at large. See 12 *Car.* 2. *cap.* 24.

Relegation, *Relegatio*, A banishing, or sending away; as *Abjuration* is a forswearing of the Realm for ever, so *Relegation* is taken for a Banishment for a time onely, *Co.* on *Lit. fol.* 133.

Religious men, *Religiosi*, Are such as enter into a Monastery or Convent, there to live devoutly. In ancient Deeds of Sale of Land, we often find the Vendee restrain'd from giving or alienating it *Viris religiosis vel Judæis*, to the end the Land might not fall into *Mortmaine*. See Judaisme. *Rex Vice-com. &c. Præcipimus tibi quod clamari facias sine dilatione per comitatum tuum quod nulli sicut diligunt corpora & catalla sua, malum faciant vel dicant* viris religiosis & clericis *contra pacem nostram: Et si quem inde attingere possimus, ad*

proximum

proximum quercum eum suspendi faciemus T. *meipso apud Marlebergh* xi. *Apr.* Clauf. 9. Joh. m. 3.

Religious Houses, *Religiosa Domus*, Are *Houses* set apart for Pious Uses, such as are *Monasteries, Churches, Hospitals*, and all other places where Charity is extended to the relief of the Poor and Orphans, or for the use or exercise of Religion.

Reliques, *Reliquiæ*, Are some remainders of Saints that are dead, preserved by some living with great veneration, as sacred Memorials of them; forbidden to be used or brought into *England* by several of our later Statutes.

Remainder, *Remanentia*, Is an Estate limitted in Lands, Tenements or Rents, to be enjoyed after the expiration of another particular Estate: For example, A man may let to one for term of his Life, and the remainder to another for term of his Life, *Littl.* cap. *Atturnment, fol.* 133. And this remainder may be either for a certain term, or in Fee-simple, or Fee-tail, as appears by *Broke*, tit. *Donee & remainder*, fol. 245. and *Glanvile*, lib. 7. cap. 1. where, towards the end, he hath these words, *Notandum quod nec ejus corpus nec Abbas, quia eorum Baroniæ sunt de Eleemosyna Domini Regis & Antecessorum ejus, non possunt de Dominicis suis aliquam partem dare ad remanentiam sine assensu & confirmatione Domini Regis*, where it appears, That *Dare ad remanentiam* is to give away for ever, and again, *cap.* 9. In like sort doth *Bracton* use it, *lib.* 2. *cap.* 23. and *lib.* 4. *tract.* 2. *cap.* 4. *num.* 4. and the *New Book of Entries*, verb. *Remainder.* The difference between a Remainder and Reversion, according to *Spelman*, is this, that by a *Reversion*, after the appointed term, the Estate returns to the Donor, or his Heirs, as the proper Fountain; whereas by *Remainder* it goes to some third, or a stranger.

Remembrancer of the Exchequer, *Rememoratores Scaccarii*, Are three Officers or Clerks there, one called *The King's Remembrancer*, 35 Eliz. cap. 5. The second, *The Lord Treasurer's Remembrancer*, upon whose Charge it lies, to put the Lord Treasurer and the rest of the Judges of that Court in remembrance of such things as are to be called on, and dealt in, for the King's behoof. The third is called *The Remembrancer of the First-Fruits*, 5 R. 2. stat. 1. cap. 14, 15. These in 37 *E.* 3. *cap.* 4. be called *Clerks of the Remembrance. The King's Remembrancer* enters in his Office all Recognisances taken before the Barons for any the King's Debts, for Appearances, or for observing of Orders: He takes all Bonds for the King's Debts, or for Appearance, or for observing Orders, and maketh out Process for the breach of them. He writes Process against the Collectors of Customs, Subsidies, and Fifteenths, for their Accounts: All Informations upon penal Statutes are entred in his Office, and there all matters upon English Bills in the Exchequer-Chamber remain: He makes the Bills of Compositions upon penal Laws, takes the stalment of Debts, has delivered into his Office all manner of Indentures, Fines, and other Evidences whatsoever, that concern the assuring of any Lands to the Crown: He every year *in Crastino animarum* reads in open Court the Statute for election of Sheriffs, and gives them their Oath; and he reads in open Court the Oath of all the Officers of the same when they are admitted, besides many other things. *The Lord Treasurer's Remembrancer* makes Process against all Sheriffs, Escheators, Receivers and Bailiffs, for their Account. He makes Process of *Fieri facias and Extent* for any Debts due to the King either in the Pipe, or with the Auditors, makes Process for all such Revenue as is due to the King, by reason of his Tenures: He makes Record, whereby it appears, whether Sheriffs or other Accountants pay their *Profers* due at *Easter* and *Michaelmas.* He makes another Record, whether Sheriffs and other Accountants keep their dayes of Prefixion. All Estreats of Fines, Issues and Amerciaments, set in any Courts at *Westminster*, or at the Assises or Sessions, are certified into his Office, and are by him delivered to the Clerk of the Estreats, to write Process upon them, &c. See the *Repertory of Records*, fol. 121. The *Remembrancer* of the first Fruits takes all Compositions and Bonds for first Fruits and Tenths, and makes Process against such as do not pay the same.

Remitter, *Remittere*, To restore; in a legal sense intends a Restitution of one that hath two Titles to Lands or Tenements, and is seised of them by his later Title, which proving defective, he is restored to the former and more ancient Title, *F.N.B. fol.* 149. *Dyer, fol.* 68. *num.* 22. In what case this may be granted, see *Bro.* tit. *Remitter*, and in *Doctor and Student*, cap. 9. fol. 19. 'tis said, That if Land descend to him that hath right to that Land before, he shall be *remitted* to his better Title if he will. See *Termes de la Ley* on this word, and the *New Book of Entries*, and *Co.* on *Lit. lib.* 3. *cap.* 12.

Renant, *Anno* 32 *H.* 8. *cap.* 2. But it may be supposed a mistake for **Reniant**, i. *Negans*, a Participle of the French Verb *Renier, negare.*

Render, Cometh of the French *Rendre*, i. *reddere, retribuere*, and signifies with us the same thing: For example, This word is used in levying of a *Fine*, which is either *single*, whereby nothing is granted or *rendred* back again by the Cognisee to the Cognisor; or *double*, which containeth a Grant or *Render* back again of some Rent, Common, or other thing, out of the Land it self to the Cognisor, &c. *West Symbol.* part. 2. tit. *Fines*, sect. 21. & 30. Also there be some things in a Mannor that lye in *Prender*, that is, which may be taken by the Lord or his Officer, when they chance, without any offer made by the Tenant, as Escheats, and the like; and some that lye in *Render*, that is, must be delivered or answered by the Tenants, as Rents, Reliefs, Heriots, and other Services, *ibid. sect.* 126. Also some Service consists in Seisance, some in *Render, Perkin's Reservations* 696.

Renegeld, *Per* **Renegeld** Johannes Stanley *Arm. Clamat habere de qualibet bovata terræ infra feodum de* Aldford 1 d. *exceptis Dominicis terris, & terris in feodo prædicto infra Hundred de Macclefeld*, Rot. Plac. in Itin. apud Cestr. 14 *H.* 7.

Renovant, From *Renovo*, To renew: The Parson sued one for Tythes, to be paid of things *renovant*, but this Horse being only for labor and travel would not *renew*, &c. *Cro.* 2. *par. fol.* 430.

Rent, *Reditus*, Signifies with us a sum of

 Money,

Money, or other consideration issuing yearly out of Lands or Tenements, *Plowden*, *fol.* 132. 138, 141. *Browning*'s Case; of which there are three sorts, *viz.* *Rent-service*, *Rent-charge*, *and Rent-seck.* *Rent-service* is, where a man holds his Lands of his Lord by Fealty and certain Rent or by Fealty, Service, and certain Rent, *Lit. lib.* 2. *cap.* 12. or that which a man making a Lease to another for term of years, reserveth yearly to be paid him for them. In the *Terms of the Law*, this reason is given for it, because it is at his pleasure either to Distrain, or bring an Action of Debt. *Rent-charge* is, where a man makes over his Estate to another, by Deed indented, either in Fee, or Fee-tail, or for term of Life, yet reserves to himself, by the same Indenture, a sum of Money yearly to be paid to him, with clause of Distress for non-payment. See *Littleton ubi supra.* *Rent seck*, otherwise a dry Rent, is that, which a man making over his Estate by Deed indented, reserveth yearly to be paid him without Clause of Distress mentioned in the Indenture, *Lit. ibid.* See the difference between a *Rent* and an Annuity in *Doctor and Student*, pag. 30. Dial. primo.

Rents resolute, *Reditus resoluti*, Are accounted among the Fee-farm *rents*, to be sold by the Statutes of 22 *Car.* 2. *cap.* 6. And are such *Rents* or Tenths as were anciently payable to the Crown, from the Lands of Abbyes and Religious Houses; and after their dissolution, notwithstanding the Lands were demised to others, yet the *rents* were still reserved, and made payable again to the Crown.

Reneez, A *Renegado*, Is derived from the French *Renier*, *renegare*, and is a Title given to such who Apostatise from Christianity to *Mahumetanisme*. *Hoveden* in Rich 1. sub Anno 1192. *Cepit* (saith he) *in equitatione illa* 24. *Paganos & unum* Reneez *qui quondam Christianus fuerat & Dominum nostrum Jesum Christum negaverat*; *& Rex posuit eum ad sagittandum & sagittatus est.*

Renusiator, *Et sunt Communes Latrones &* Renusiatores *hominum*, *&c.* Trin. 28 E. 3. Ebor. 37. q.

Reparatione facienda, Is a Writ which lies in divers Cases, whereof one is, where Three be Tenants in Common, or Joynt-tenants, or *pro indiviso* of a Mill or House which is fallen into decay, and the one being willing to repair it, the other Two will not: In this Case the party willing shall have this Writ against the other Two, *F. N. B. fol.* 127. Of the various uses of it, read *Reg. Orig. fol.* 153.

Repeale, Cometh from the French *Rappell*, *revocatio*, and hath the same signification among us; as the *repeal of a Statute* is the revoking it, *Rastall*, tit. *Repeal.* *Broke* useth *repellance* in the same sense.

Repleader, (*Replacitare*) Is to plead again that which was once pleaded before, *Rastall* tit. *Repleader*, and *New Book of Entries*, Eodem tit.

Replegiare, Is properly to redeem a thing detained or taken by another, by putting in legal Sureties. See *Replevin* and *Second Deliverance.*

Replegiare de averiis, Is a Writ brought by one whose Cattel are distrained, or put in the Pound, upon any cause by another, upon Surety given to the Sheriff to Prosecute or Answer the Action in Law, *Anno* 7 *H.* 8. *cap.* 4. *F.N.B. fol.* 68. See the *Register Orig.* divers sorts of this Writ in the Table, and also in the *Register Judicial*, *fol.* 58. 70. The *New Book of Entries*, verb. *Replevin*, and *Dyer*, *fol.* 173. *num.* 14.

Replevin, *Plevina*, Is a derivation of *replegiare*, to deliver to the Owner upon Pledges, and is the bringing of the Writ called *Replegiare facias* by him that has his Cattel, or other Goods distrained, by an other, for any cause, and putting in Surety to the Sheriff, that upon delivery of the thing distreined, he will prosecute the Action against the Distrainor, *Co.* on *Lit. lib.* 2. *cap.* 12. *sect.* 219. Goods may be *replevyed* two manner of wayes, *viz.* by Writ, and that is by the Common Law, or by Plaint, and that is by Statute Law, for the more speedy having again of their Cattel and Goods. *Replevie* is also used for the Bayling of a man, *Stamf. pl. cor. fol.* 72. 74. and *Westm.* 1. *cap.* 11. *&* 15. *Replegiare est reposcere bona mobilia dato apud Præfectum Vade sive fide-jussore*; *sane & Anglis breve per quod bona ea reposcerent, to* **Replevin**, &c. *Vossius de Vitiis sermonis*, lib. 2. cap. 25. See *Skene eod. verbo.*

Replevish, *Replegiare*, Is to let one to Mainprise upon Surety, *Anno* 3. *E.* 1. *cap.* 11.

Replication, *Replicatio*, Is an Exception of the second degree, made by the Plaintiff upon the first Answer of the Defendant, *West Symbol.* part 2. tit. *Chancery*, sect. 55. and *Westm.* 2. *cap.* 36. It is also that which the Plaintiff *replyes* to the Defendants Answer in *Chancery*; and this is either *General or Special.* *Special*, is grounded upon matter arising out of the Defendants Answer, &c. *General*, is so called from the general words therein used.

Report, *Reportus*, Is a publick relation of Cases Judicially argued, debated, resolved, or adjudged in any of the King's Courts of Justice, with the Causes and Reasons of the same delivered by the Judges, *Coke* on *Lit. fol.* 293. Also when the *Chancery*, or other Court, refer the stating of some Case, or comparing an Account, &c. to a *Master of Chancery*, or other Referree, his Certificate therein is called a *Report.*

Reposition of the Forest, *Repositio Forestæ*, Was an Act whereby certain *Forest* Grounds being made *Purlieu* upon view, were by a second view laid to the Forest again, *Manwood*, *part* 1. *pag.* 178.

Reprisells, *Reprisalia*, May be deduced from the French *Reprise*, i. *resumptio*, and are all one both in the Common and Civil Law, *Reprisalia est potestas pignorandi contra quemlibet de terra debitoris data creditori pro injuriis & damnis acceptis*, *Vocabular, utriusq; juris.* This among the ancient *Romans* was called *Clarigatio*, of the Verb *Clarigo*, i. *res clare repetere.* It is named in the Stat. 27 E. 3. *stat.* 2. *cap.* 17. *Law of Marque*, because one for defect of Justice in another Territory, redresseth himself by the Goods belonging to Men of that Territory, taken within his own Bounds.

Reprises, Is commonly taken for Deductions and Duties which are yearly paid out of a Mannor and Lands, as *Rent-charge*, *Rent seck*, *Pensions*, *Corrodies*, *Annuities*, *Fees of Stewards or Bayliffs*, *&c.* Wherefore when we speak of the clear yearly value of a Mannor, we say it is so much

much *per annum ultra reprisas*, besides all *reprises*.

Reprive, May be derived from the French *Repris*, that is, taken back: So that to *reprive*, is properly to take back, or suspend, a Prisoner from the Execution and Proceeding of the Law for that time.

Requests, *Curia requisitionum*, see in Court. It is utterly taken away by Act of Parliament; But you may read of it in *Gwin's Preface to his Readings*, and else-where.

Resceit, *Receptio*, Is an admission, or receiving a third person to plead his right in a Cause formerly commenced between other Two, *New Book of Entries*, verb. *Resceite*, as if Tenant for Life or Years brings an Action, he in the Reversion comes in, and prays to be *received* to defend the Land, and to plead with the Demandant. See *Bro.* tit. *Resceit, fol.* 205. and *Perkin's Dower*, 448. The *Civilians* call this *Admissionem tertii pro suo interesse. Resceit* is also applied to an admittance of Plea, though the Controversie be only between Two. See *Broke*, tit. *Estoppell*, and *Co.* on *Lit. fol.* 192.

Resceit of Homage, *Receptio Homagii*, Is the Lords receiving *Homage* of his Tenant at his admission to the Land, *Kitchin, fol.* 148. See *Homage*.

Rescous, *Rescussus*, Comes from the French *Rescousse*, i. *Liberatio*, is a resistance against lawful Authority; as if a Bailiff, or other Officer, upon a Writ do arrest a Man, and others by Violence take him away, or procure his Escape; this is a *Rescouse in Fact.* So if one distrain Beasts for Damage-feasant in his Ground, and as he drives them in the High-way towards the Pound, they enter into the Owner's House, and he with-holds them there, and will not deliver them upon demand; this detainer is a *Rescous in Law*, *Co.* on *Lit. lib.* 2. *cap.* 12. *Cassanæus* in his Book *De Consuetud.* Burg. fol. 294. hath the same word coupled with *resistentia*: It is also used for a Writ which lies for this Fact called *Breve de Rescussu*, whereof you may see both the form and use in *F. N. B. fol.* 101. *Reg. of Writs, fol.* 125. and *New Book of Entries*, verb. *Rescous.* This in matters relating to Treason, is Treason; and in matters concerning Felony, is Felony, *Cromp. Just. fol.* 54.

Rescussor, Is he that commits such a *Rescous*, *Cro. Rep.* 2. *par. fol.* 419.

Reseiser, *Reseisire*, Is a taking again of Lands into the hands of the King, whereof a general Livery, or *Ouster le maine*, was formerly mis sued, contrary to the form and order of Law, *Stamf. Prærog.* 26. See *Resumption.*

Reservation, *Reservatio*, A keeping or providing, as when a man lets his Land, he *reserves* a Rent to be paid to himself for his Maintenance. Sometimes it signifies as much as an Exception; as when a man lets a House, and *reserves* to himself one Room, that Room is excepted out of the Demise. See *Perkin's* Reservations *per totum*, and *Termes de la Ley* eodem verbo.

Reset, *Skene* hath that in, and **Resetter** in another place; in both which he expounds it to signifie the receiving or receiver of a Proscribed or Outlawed Person, and may be derived from our English word *Receit.*

Resiance, *Resiantia*, Seemeth to come from the French *Resseant* or *Reseant*, Resident, and signifies a mans abode or continuance in a place, *Old Nat. Brev. fol.* 85. Whence also comes the Participle *resiant*, that is, continually dwelling or abiding in a place, *Kitchin, fol.* 33. It is all one in Deed with residence, but that custom tyes this only to persons Ecclesiastical. *Veteri autem jure nostro* (saith *Spelman*) *etiam & Scotico aliud significat, utpote morbum validum seu veteranum, quo quis exire de suis ædibus prohibetur*: Essonium *igitur quod* de malo lecti *nuncupatur, hoc est* excusatio *quod ratione infirmitatis sistere se in foro non valeat*, essonium *nuncupant* de reseantisa, *Glanvile*, lib. 1. cap. 11. *Quandoq; intervenit* (essonium) *ex infirmitate* de reseantisa. *Ubi in margine notatur*, essonium de reseantisa *idem valet quod* essonium de malo lecti. And all these seem to be drawn from the French, who say, *Exoine de mal resseant.* See *Skene de* verb. *Signif.* verb. *Reseantisa.*

Residence, *Residentia*, Is derived from the Latine word *residere*, and is peculiarly used both in the Common and Canon Law, for the continuance or abode of a Parson or Vicar upon his Benefice. The default whereof (except the Party be qualified and dispensed with) is the loss of ten pounds every month, *Anno* 28 *H.* 8. *cap.* 13.

Resignation, *Resignatio*, Is used particularly for the giving up of a Benefice into the hands of the Ordinary, otherwise by the *Canonists* termed *Renunciatio.* And though it signifie all one in nature with the word *Surrender*, yet it is by custome restrained to the yielding up a Spiritual Living, and *Surrender* to the giving up of Temporal Lands into the hands of the Lord. And a *resignation* may now be made into the hands of the King, as well as of the Diocesan, because he hath *Supremam Authoritatem Ecclesiasticam*, as the *Pope* had here in times past, *Plowden*, fol. 498. *Grendon's* Case.

Resort or **Ressort**, Is a word properly used in a Writ of *Tayle* or *Cousenage*, as *descent* is in a *Writ of right.* In French it signifies the Authority or Jurisdiction of a Court; *Salvo tamen tam ressorto quam aliis jure nostro & etiam jure alieno*, Lit. Pat. Phillippi le Hardy Reg. Franciæ, mentioned by *Spelman* in his *Glossary.*

Respectu computi Vice-comitis habendo, Is a Writ for the *respiting* of a Sheriffs Account, upon just occasion directed to the Treasurer and Barons of the Exchequer, *Register, fol.* 139. & 179.

Respite, *Respectus*, Is used for delay, forbearance or continuance of time, *Glanvile, lib.* 12. *cap.* 9. in breve Regis. *Præcipio tibi quod poni facias in* respectum; *usq; ad aliquem terminum competentem.*

Respite of Homage, *Respectus Homagii*, Is the forbearing of *Homage* which ought first of all to be performed by the Tenant that holdeth by *Homage*; and it had the most frequent use in such as held by Knights service *in Capite*, who did pay into the Exchequer every fifth Term some small sum of Money, to be *respited* the doing of their *Homage.* See the Stat. 12 *Car.* 2. *cap.* 24. whereby this is taken away as a charge incident or arising from *Knight-service*, &c.

Respondeat superior, Where the Sheriffs are removeable for insufficiency, (as in *London*) *respondeat Superior*, that is, the Mayor and

Commonalty of *London Pur insufficiency del Bayliff d'un liberty*, respondeat *Dominus libertatis*, 44 E. 3. 13. 4. *Inst. fol.* 114.

Responsalis, *Qui responsum defert*; He who gives an Answer, is he that appears for another in Court at a day assigned, concerning whom hear *Glanvile*, lib. 12. cap. 1. — *Placita in superioribus exposita*—*Prosequi quis potest sicut & alia quælibet placita civilia*, *tam per seipsum quam* responsalem *suo loco positum*, &c. But *Fleta* makes a difference between *attornatum*, *essoniatorem & responsalem*, lib. 6. cap. 11. sect. *Officium*. As if *essoniator* came only to declare the Cause of the Parties absence, whether Demandant or Tenant; And *Responsalis* came for the Tenant, not only to excuse his absence, but also signifie what Tryal he meant to undergo, *viz*. the Combat or the Country. A man in ancient time could not appoint an Attorney for him, without warrant from the Court, *Fleta*, lib. 6. cap. 13. See *Atturney*. This word is used in the Canon Law, *Et significat Procuratorem vel eum qui absentem excusat*.

Responsions, *Responsiones*, Seems to be a word chiefly used by the *Knights of St. John of Jerusalem*, for certain Accounts made to them by such as held their Lands or Stocks, *Anno* 32 *H*. 8. *cap*. 24.

Restitution, *Restitutio*, Is the yielding up again, or restoring of any thing unlawfully taken from another. But it is most frequently used in the Common Law for the setting him in possession of Lands or Tenements that hath been unlawfully disseised of them; which when it is to be done, and when not. See *Crompton's Justice of Peace*, fol. 144. *usq; ad* 149.

Restitutione extracti ab Ecclesia, Is a Writ to restore a Man to the Church, which he had recovered for his Sanctuary, being suspected of Felony, *Reg. Orig. fol.* 69.

Restitutione temporalium, Is a Writ that lies, where a man being elected and confirmed *Bishop* of any Diocess, and hath the King's Royal assent thereto for the *recovery of the Temporalties*, or Barony of the said Bishoprick: And it is directed from the King to the Escheator of the County, the form whereof may be read in *Reg. Orig. fol.* 294. and *F. N. B. fol.* 169.

Resummons, *Resummonitio*, Is a Decompound of *Re*, *sub* and *moneo*, and signifies *a second Summons*, and calling of a man to Answer an Action, where the first Summons is defeated upon any occasion, as the death of the Party, or such like. See *Bro*. tit. *Resummons*, fol. 214. Of these there are four sorts, according to four divers Cases in the Table of the *Register Judicial*, fol. 1. and *New Book of Entries*, verb. *Reattachment and Resummons*.

Resumption, *Resumptio*, Is a word used in the Statute of 31 *H*. 6. *ca*. 7. particularly to signifie the taking again into the King's hands such Lands or Tenements as before, upon false suggestion, or other Error, he had delivered to the Heir, or granted by Letters Patents to any Man, *Bro*. tit. *Repellance & Resumption*, fol. 298. and 19 *H*. 7. *ca*. 10. See *Reseiser*.

Retaile, That is, to buy by great, and sell by parcels, *Anno* 3 & 4 E. 6. cap. 21. *Qui rem integram ementes per minutiores eam partes distrahebunt*.

Reteiner, From the Latine *retinere*, signifies in a legal sense a Servant, but not Mænial or Familiar, that is, not continually dwelling in the House of his Master, but only wearing his Livery, and attending sometimes upon special Occasions. This *Livery* was wont to consist of Hats, (or Hoods) Badges, or other Suits of one Garment by the year; and were many times given by Lords and Great Men, upon design of Maintenance and Quarrels, and therefore justly forbidden by several Statutes, as 1 R. 2. *ca*. 7. upon pain of Imprisonment, and grievous forfeiture to the King; and again, 16 *R*. 2. *ca*. 4. 20 *R*. 2. *ca*. 1. and 1 *H*. 4. *ca*. 7. by which the Offendors should make ransome at the King's will; and any Knight or Esquire thereby duly attainted, should lose his said Livery, and forfeit his Fee for ever, &c. Which Statute is further confirmed and explained by 2 *H*. 4. *ca*. 21. 7 *H*. 4. *ca*. 3. and 8 *H*. 6. *ca*. 4. And yet this Offence was so deeply rooted, that *Edward* the Fourth was necessitated to confirm the former Statutes, and further to extend their meaning, as appears by 8 *E*. 4. *ca*. 2. adding a special Penalty of five pounds upon every man that gives such *Livery*, and as much on every one so *retained* either by Writing, Oath or Promise, for every month. These are by the *Feudists* call'd *Affidati*, *sic enim dicuntur qui in alicujus fidem & tutelam recepti sunt*. And as our *Retainers* are here forbidden, so are those Affidats in other Countries. But most of the above-mentioned Statutes are repealed by 3 *Car*. 1. *ca*. 4.

Retaining Fee, *Merces retinens*, Is the first *Fee* given to any Serjeant or Counsellor at Law, whereby to make him sure that he shall not be on the contrary part, it is *Honorarium seu præmium causidici præcedaneum*, *quo clienti suo obligatur ne adversarii causam agat*.

Retraxit, Is so called, because that word is the effectual word in the Entry, and is where the Plaintiff or Demandant comes in person into the Court, and says, *He will proceed no further*. And this is a bar of all other Actions of like or inferior nature, *Qui semel actionem renunciavit amplius repetere non potest*, Co. *on* Lit. *lib*. 2. *ca*. 11. *sect*. 288. The difference between a *Nonsuit* and a *Retraxit*, is, that a *Retraxit* is ever when the Demandant or Plaintiff is present in Court; but a *Nonsuit* is upon a demand made, when he should appear, and he makes default. *Retraxit* (as we said) is a bar, so is not *Nonsuit*, for he may commence an Action of like nature again.

Return, *Returna vel retorna*, Cometh of the French *Retour*, i. *reversio*, *recursus*, and in our Law hath two particular Applications; the one is, the *return* of Writs by Sheriffs and Bailiffs, which is only a Certificate made to the Court of that which he hath done, touching the execution of their Writ directed to him. And this among the *Civilians* is termed *Certificatorium*; of *returns* in this signification speaks the Statute of *Westm*. 2. *ca*. 39. So is the *return* of a Commission a Certificate or Answer to the Court of that which is done by the Commissioners, Sheriff, Bayliff, or other, to whom such Writs, Commissions, Precepts or Mandats are directed. Also certain days in every Term are called *return dayes*, or days in Bank; and

and so *Hillary* Term hath four *Returns*, viz. *Octabis Hillarii*, *Quindena Hillarii*, *Crastino Purificationis & Octabis Purificationis*. Easter Term five, *viz. Quindena Pasche*, *Tres Pasche*, *Mense Pasche*, *Quinq; Pasche*, and *Crastino ascensionis Domini*. Trinity Term four, i. *Crastino Trinitatis*, *Octabis Trinitatis*, *Quindena Trinitatis*, *Tres Trinitatis*, and Michaelmas Term six, to wit, *Tres Michaelis*, *mense Michaelis*, *Crastino animarum*, *Crastino Martini*, *Octabis Martini*, *Quindena Martini*. See the Statutes of dayes in Bank, 51 *H.* 3. 32 *H.* 8. *cap.* 21. and 17 *Car.* 1. *cap.* 6. The other application of this word is in case of *Replevin*; for if a man distrain Cattel for Rent, &c. and afterwards justifie or avow his Act, so as it is found lawful, the Cattel before delivered unto him that was distrained, upon security given to follow the Action, shall now be *returned* to him that distrained them, *Bro.* tit. *Returns d' avers & hommes*, fol. 218. and *F. N. B.* in his Table *verb.* Return.

Returno habendo, Is a Writ that lies for him that has avowed a Distress made of Cattel, and proved his Distress to be lawfully taken, for *returning* to him the Cattel distrained, which before were *replevyed* by the Party distrained, upon Surety given to prosecute the Action; or when the Plaint or Action is removed by *Recordari*, or *Accedas ad Curiam* into the Court of *Common-Pleas*, and he whose Cattel were distrained makes default, and doth not prosecute his Suit.

Returnum averiorum, Is a Writ Judicial, granted to one impleaded for the taking the Cattel of another, and unjust detaining them *contra vadium & Plegios*, and appearing upon Summons, is dismissed without day, because the Plaintiff makes default; and it lies for the *return* of the Cattel to the Defendant, whereby he was summoned, or which were taken for security of his Appearance upon the Summons, *Register Judicial*, *fol.* 4. *a.*

Returnum irreplegiabile, Is a Writ Judicial, sent out of the *Common-Pleas* to the Sheriff, for the final restitution or *return* of Cattel to the Owner, unjustly taken by another, as *Damage-feisant*, and so found by the Jury before Justices of Assise in the County, or otherwise by default of Prosecution, *Reg. Judic. fol.* 27.

Reve alias **Greve**, From the Saxon word *Grefa*, *præfectus*, Lambs *Explication of Saxon words*, verb. *Præfectus*, signifies with us the Bayliff of a Franchise or Mannor, especially in the Western parts of *England*: Hence *Shire-reve* for Sheriff. See *Kitchin*, *fol.* 43. See *Greve* and *Sheriff*, and *Vestegan*, *cap.* 10. See also *Church reve*.

Revells, Signifie with us Sports of Dancing, Masking, &c. used in Princes Courts, the Inns of Court, or other Noblemens Houses, which are commonly performed by Night; and there is an Officer to order and supervise them, who is intituled *Master of the Revells*.

Revelland. See *Tein-land*.

Revenue, Is a French word, signifying as *Reditus*, and denotes properly the yearly Rent that accrews to every man from his Lands and Possessions.

Reversion, *Reversio*, A returning again; It is *Nomen Verbale*, and derived of the Verb *Revertor*, *& apte dici non potest* reversio *antequam revertatur in facto*; And therefore *Co.* on *Lit. fol.* 142. says, *Reversio terræ est tanquam terra revertens in possessione Donatori sive hæredibus suis post donum finitum.* It hath a double acception in Law, the one is, *Jus revertendi cum status possessionis defecerit*, and this is but an interest in the Land when the Possession shall fall. 2. When the Possession and Estate which was parted with for a time, ceaseth, and is determined in the persons of the Alienees, Assignees, Grantees, or their Heirs, or effectually returns to the Donor, his Heirs or Assigns, whence it was derived. The difference between a *Reversion and a Remainder*, is, that a *Remainder* is general, and may be to any man, but he that granteth or conveyeth the Land, &c. for term of Life only, or otherwise. A *Reversion* is to himself, from whom the Conveyance of the Land, &c. proceeded, and is commonly perpetual, as to his Heirs also, *Lit. lib.* 2. *cap.* 12. See *Co. lib.* 2. *fol.* 51. Sir *Hugh Cholnleye*'s Case; and yet a *Reversion* is sometimes confounded with a *Remainder*, *Co. lib.* 2. *fol.* 67. *Tooker*'s Case, *Plowden*, *fol.* 170. *Hill*'s Case. What this word *Reversion* in a Deed does carry, see *Littleton*, *lib.* 2. *cap.* 12.

Review, *A Bill of* Review *in Chancery* is, where a Cause hath been heard, and the *Decree* signed and enrolled; and some Error in Law appears upon the *Decree*, or new matter discovered in time after the *Decree* made, which Bill cannot be exhibited, but by licence of the Court. See *Collection of the Chancery Orders*, pag. 69.

Reviving, Is a word metaphorically applyed to Rents and Actions, and signifies a renewing of them after they be extinguished. Of which see divers examples in *Broke*, tit. *Revivings of Rents*, *Actions*, *&c.* fol. 223.

Bill of Reviver, Is, where a *Bill* hath been exhibited in *Chancery* against one, who Answers, and before the Cause is heard, or if heard, before the Decree enrolled, either Party dies: In this Case a *Bill of Revivor* must be brought, that the former proceedings may stand revived, and the Cause be finally determined.

Revocation, *Revocatio*, Is the calling back of a thing granted, of which you have divers in *Reg. Orig.* as *Revocationem brevis de audiendo & terminando*, fol. 124. *Revocationem præsentationis*, fol. 304, 305. *Revocationem Protectionis*, fol. 23. *Revocationem specialium Justiciariorum quia*, *&c.* fol. 205.

Reward. See *Regard*.

Rewey, Anno 43 Eliz. cap. 10. *So as some Clothes being put in water are found to shrink*, Rewey *equally cockling*, *light and notable faulty*, *&c.* it is as much as unevenly wrought, and full of *Rewes*.

Rhandir, Is a part in the division of the Country in *Wales* before the Conquest, as first a *Cantref* consisted of a hundred Towns, under which were so many *Commots*, each *Commot* had twelve *Mannors* or *Circuits*, and two *Townships*; there were four *Townships* to every *Mannor*, every *Township* comprehended four *Gavels*, every *Gavel* had four **Rhandirs**, and four *Tenements* were constituted under every **Rhandir**. This word **Rhandir** admits not of any proper signification in English, but is by Doctor *Davis* render'd *Pars aut sors hæreditaria*, from the verb, **Rhannu**, *Partire*, *distribuere*. Taylor's *Hist. of Gavelkind*, pag. 69.

Ribaud, *Ribaldus*, French *Ribauld*, A Vagrant, luxurious Spend-thrift, a Rogue, a Whoremonger, a person given to all kinds of wickedness and looseness. Petition against *Ribauds* and sturdy Beggars, *Rot. Parl.* 50 E. 3. *num.* 61.

Ric, Is a *Saxon* word, signifying as much as *Regnum* in Latine, *Cambd. Brit.* pag. 346.

Rider-Roll. See in *Roll*.

Ridge or Rig of Land, Riga, *Terram quam è pluribus sulcis in aggerem efferunt arantes, ita ut sicca sedes frumenti habeatur, Romani* strigam (*atq; inde* agros strigatos) *nos* a Rigd of Land, *Spelman.* However it is sometime called *Porca terræ*.

Ridings, Be Names of the Divisions of *Yorkshire*, which are three, *viz.* the East-riding, the West-riding, and the North-riding, mentioned in the Statute 22 *H.* 8. *cap.* 5. and 23 *H.* 8. *cap.* 18. In Indictments in that County, 'tis requisite that the Town and the *Riding* be exprest, *West Symbol.* part 2. tit. *Indictments*, sect. 70. Q.

Riens passe per le fait, Is the form of an Exception taken in some Cases to an Action. See *Bro.* tit. *Estraunger al fait ou Record*.

Riens arreare, Is a kind of Plea used to an Action of Debt upon *arrearages* of Account, whereby the Defendant does alledge, There is *nothing arrear*.

Riens deins le gard, Was a Challenge to a Jury or Enquest of *London*, for that four sufficient Men, &c. were not impannelled: But it is abrogated by the Stat. 7 *H.* 7. *cap.* 4.

Rier County, *Retro-comitatus*, Comes from the French *Arrier*, *posterior*, and in the Stat. 2 *E.* 3. *cap.* 5. is opposite to *Open County*; and by comparing that Statute with *Westm.* 2. *cap.* 38. it appears to be some publick place, which the Sheriff appoints for the receit of the King's Money after the end of his County. *Fleta* says, That it is *Dies crastinus post comitatum*, lib. 2. ca. 67.

Right, *Jus*, In general signification includes not only a *right*, for which a *Writ of right* lies, but also any Title or Claim either by vertue of a Condition, Mortgage, or the like, for which no Action is given by Law, but only an Entry, *Co.* on *Lit. lib.* 3. *cap.* 8. *sect.* 445. There is *Jus proprietatis*, a right of Propriety; *Jus Possessionis*, a right of Possession, and *Jus Proprietatis & Possessionis*, a right both of Propriety and Possession, and this is anciently called *Jus duplicatum*: For example, If a man be disseised of an Acre of Land, the Disseisee hath *Jus proprietatis*, the Disseisor hath *Jus possessionis*; and if the Disseisee release to the Disseisor, he hath *Jus proprietatis & possessionis*, Co. *on* Lit. *lib.* 3. sect. 447. *Jus est sextuplex.* 1. *Jus recuperandi.* 2. *Intrandi.* 3. *Habendi.* 4. *Retinendi.* 5. *Percipiendi.* 6. *Et Possidendi*, Co. 8. Rep. *Edward Altham*'s Case.

Right in Court. See *Rectus in Curia*.

Rime, *Rithmus*, Is taken for a mean kind of Verse, commonly made by some unskilful person, of which we need not give you any example, so many paltry Ballads being every day to be seen.

Ring-head, 43 *Eliz. cap.* 10. An Engine used in the stretching of woollen Cloth.

Riot, *Riota & riottum*, Derived from the French *Riotte quod non solum rixam & jurgium significat sed vinculum etiam, quo plura in unum, fasciculorum instar colligantur*, signifies the forcible doing of an unlawful thing by three, or more persons assembled together for that purpose, *West Symbol.* part 2. tit. *Indictments*, sect. 65. The differences between a *Riot*, *Rout*, and an *unlawful Assembly*, see in *Lamb. Eiren.* lib. 2. cap. 5. *Stat.* 1. *Mar.* cap. 12. and *Kitchin* 19. who gives these examples of *Riots*, The Breach of Inclosures, Banks, Conduits, Parks, Pounds, Houses, Barns, the burning of Stacks of Corn, &c. *Lamb. ubi supra* mentions these, To beat a Man, to enter upon a Possession forcibly. See *Rout* and *Unlawful Assembly*. See also in *Cromp. Just. of Peace* divers Cases of *Riots*, *Anno* 17 R. 2. *cap.* 8. and 13 *H.* 4. *cap.* 7. See *Rout*.

Ripariæ, From *Ripa*, a Bank; In the Stat. *Westm.* 2. *cap.* 47. Signifies Water or River running between the Banks, be it salt or fresh, 2. *Inst. fol.* 478. The word occurs also in *Rot. Cart.* 9 *E. num.* 12.

Ripiers, *Riparii*, Had their Name *a fiscellâ qua in deveehndis piscibus utuntur*, in English a **Ripp**, and are such as are to bring Fish from the Sea-coast to the inner parts of the Land, *Cambd. Brit.* pag. 234.

Rise, *Orisa*, Is a kind of Corn growing in *Asia* and the *Indies*, of which you may read in *Gerard*'s *Herbal*, *lib.* 1. *cap.* 52. This is mentioned among Spices to be garbled in the Stat. 1 *Jac. cap.* 19.

Roather Beasts, *Anno* 7 *E.* 6. *cap.* 11. See *Rother Beasts*.

Roba, Ital. signifies *Vestis*, in English *Robe*.

Robbery, *Robaria*, Is a felonious taking away of another Mans Goods from his person or presence against his will, putting him in fear, and of purpose to steal the same, *West Symb.* part 2. tit. *Indictments*, sect. 60. And this Offence was called *Robbery*, either because they bereaved the true man of some of his *Robes* or Garments, or because his Money or Goods were taken out of some part of his Garment or *Robe* about his person, *Co.* 3. *Inst. cap.* 16. This is sometimes called *Violent Theft*, *West Symbol. ibid.* which is felony of two pence, *Kitchin*, *fol.* 16. and 22 *lib. Ass.* 39. See *Skene de verborum* Signif. *verb.* Reif, and *Cromp. Justice of Peace*, fol. 30.

Robbers, 5 *E.* 3. 14. and 7 *R.* 2. *cap.* 5. *Lamb. Eiren. lib.* 2. *cap.* 6. interpreteth them to be mighty Thieves; they are called in Latine *Robatores*, saith *Spelman*, being *Latrones validi qui in personas hominum insilientes bona sua diripiunt*.

Robersmen or Roberdsmen, Were another sort of great Thieves, mentioned 5 *E.* 3. 14. and 7 *R.* 2. *cap.* 5. *Co.* 3. *Inst. fol.* 197. says, *Robinhood* lived in *Richard* the First's time on the Borders of *England* and *Scotland* by Robbery and Spoil, and that these *Roberdsmen* took Name from him.

Rod, *Roda Terræ*, Is otherwise called a *Perch*, and is a Measure of sixteen foot and a half, and in *Staffordshire* twenty foot, to measure Land with. See *Perch*.

Rodknights alias Radknights, (Is derived from the Saxon *Rad*) in English *Road*, i. *equitatus*, and Cnyꞇ, *Minister*, were certain Servitors

vitors, which held their Land by serving their Lords on Horse-back, *Bract. lib.* 2. *cap.* 36. *num.* 6. saith of them, *Debent equitare cum Domino suo de Manerio in Manerium, vel cum Domini uxore*, Fleta, lib. 3. cap. 14. sect. *Continetur.*

Rose-tyle alias **Creast-tile**, Is that *Tile* which is made to lay upon the ridge of the House, 17 *E*. 4. 4.

Rogation week, *Dies Rogationum*, Is a time well known to all, and is so called, because of the special Devotion of Prayer and Fasting then enjoyned by the Church to all Men, for a Preparative to the joyful remembrance of Christs Ascension, from which time to *Trinity-Sunday* Matrimony is forbidden to be celebrated.

Rogue, *Rogus*, May be deduced from the French *Rogue*, i. *Arrogans*, and signifies an idle sturdy Beggar, who wandreth from place to place without licence, after he hath been by Justices bestowed, or offered to be bestowed on some certain place of abode; who, for the first Offence is called *a Rogue of the first degree*, and punisht by whipping and boring through the gristle of the Ear with a hot Iron, an inch in compass. And for the second Offence, is termed *a Rogue of the second degree*, and put to death as a Felon, if he be above Eighteen years old. See the Stat. 14 *Eliz*. 5. 18 *Eliz*. 3. and 36 *Eliz*. 17. and *Lamb. Eiren.* lib. 4. cap. 4.

Rogus, Is the Latine word for a great Fire, and there it is *congeries lignorum ad comburendum, vocab. utriusq; juris.* Sometimes it is taken only for a Pyle or Stalk of Wood, as *Mandatum est Constabulario castri de Divis. Et custodi forestæ de Cippeham quod fieri fac. unum* rogum *in Foresta prædict' ad operationes castri prædicti, &c.* T. 10. Maii. Claus. 5 Hen. 3. m. 8.

Roll, *Rotulas*, Signifies a Schedule of Paper or Parchment, which may be turned or wound up with the hand to the fashion of a Pipe, *Stamf. pl. cor. fol.* 11. of which there are in the Exchequer several kinds. As *the great Wardrobe* Roll, *the Cofferers* Roll, *the Subsidy* Roll, *&c.* Of which see the *Practice of the Exchequer-Court*, fol. 75.

Ridder-roll, *Noy*'s Rep. *fol.* 84. The Court *Ex Officio*, may award a *Certiorari ad informandam conscientiam*; and that which is certified shall be annexed to the Record, and is called a *Ridder-roll*. Or *a Ridder-roll* is a Schedule, or small piece of Parchment, added to some part of a Roll or Record.

Rolls, Or the Office of the *Rolls* in *Chancery-Lane*, anciently called *Domus Conversorum*, Is the House that was built by King *Henry* the Third, for *Jews* converted to the Christian Faith; but *Edward* the Third expulsed them for their wickedness, and deputed the place for the custody of the *Rolls* and Records of the *Chancery*, the Master whereof is the second in *Chancery*, and in the absence of the Lord Chancellor, or Lord Keeper, sits, as Judge, being commonly called, *The Master of the Rolls*, which see.

Romescote, Is a Saxon word signifying *Nummum Romæ datum*, for peoh, in Saxon is *Nummus*, that is, Money in English. See *Romescot.*

Romepeny, In Saxon pompening, i. *Romæ denarius*, for the Saxon Pening, is the same as **Peny** with us, or *denarius* in Latine. See *Romescot.*

Romescot, Is compounded of *Rome* and *Scot*, as if you would say, The Tribute due to *Rome*. *Mat. Westminster* says it was *Consuetudo Apostolica, a qua neq; Rex, neq; Archiepiscopus vel Episcopus, Abbas vel Prior aut quilibet in Regno immunis erat.* It was annual Tribute of one Peny from every Family, paid yearly to *Rome* at the Feast of St. *Peter ad vincula*; being the first of *August*. *Camden* in his *Brit.* sayes, *Offa* the Saxon first granted it; but others, that *Inas*, a King of the *West Saxons*, being in Pilgrimage at *Rome*, *Anno* 725. gave it as an Alms, and was first forbidden by *Edward* the Third. It amounted to three hundred Marks, and a Noble yearly. See *Leg. Hen.* 1. *cap.* 12. *Rog. Hoveden par. poster. suor. annal. fol.* 344. *in vita Hen.* 2. and see *Peter-pence* and *Hearth-peny*. This Payment was abrogated 25 *H*. 8. 25. restored 1 *&* 2 *P. & M.* but utterly abolisht 1 *Eliz*. 1. See *Spelmans Glossary*, verbis *Romascot, Romfeah, Rompeny.*

Rood of Land, *Roda terræ*, The Fourrh part of an Acre, 5 *Eliz. cap.* 5.

Rother-beasts, Under this Name are comprehended Oxen, Cows, Steers, Heifers, and such like horned Beasts, 21 *Jac. cap.* 28. And in *Herefordshire* the Dung of such Beasts is called *Rothersoyle.*

Rotulus Wintoniæ, *Doomsday* Book so called, because it was of old kept at *Winchester*. See *Doomsday*. *Spelman* in his *Glossary* says, There was another Roll called *Rotulus Wintoniæ*, made long before that by King *Alfred*; concerning which, hear *Ingulphus* speaking of *Doomsday*-Book. *Talem* (says he) *Rotulum & multum similem ediderat quondam Rex* Alfredus *in quo totam terram Angliæ per Comitatus, Centurias, & Decurias descripserat*, &c.

Rotulus Cancellariæ, *Bracton*, lib. 3. cap. 24. *Omnia Brevia de pace* (quæ sunt prohibitiones) *irrotulari debent in* Rotulo *de Cancellaria.* See M. P. in an. 1110. p. 61.

Rouge Crosse. See *Herald.*

Roundlet. See *Runlet.*

Rout, *Routa, Turma, Cohors*, A Company or Number, but in a legal sense signifies an Assembly of three persons, or more, going forcibly to commit an unlawful Act, though they do it not, *West. Symb.* part 2. tit. *Indictment*, sect. 65. says, A *Rout* is the same which the *Germans* yet call *Rot*, meaning a Band, or great Company of Men gathered together, and going to execute, or indeed executing any Riot or unlawful Act. But the Statute of 18 *E*. 3. *stat.* 1. *cap. unico.* which gives Process of Outlawry against such as bring *Routs* into the presence of the Justices, or in affray of the People. And the Statute of 2 *R*. 2. *cap.* 6. that speaks of riding in great *Routs* to make entry into Lands, and beat others, *&c.* do seem to understand it more largely, *Bro.* tit. *Riot* 4, 5. So that *a Rout* seems to be an *unlawful Assembly*, and *a Riot* the disorderly Fact committed by such *unlawful Assembly*. Howbeit two things are common both to *Riot*, *Rout*, and *unlawful Assembly*. The one, That three persons at least be gather'd together. The other, That being together, they do disturb the Peace, either by words, shew of Arms, turbulent Gesture, or actual Violence,

lence, &c. *Lamb. Eiren.* lib. 2. cap. 5. See *Riot and unlawful Assembly.*

Rowing of Clothes, 27 *H.* 8. 13. It may perhaps be derived from the French *Rover, versare, Rotare quia rotâ circumductâ pannos complanare solebant.*

Royal Assent, *Regius Assensus,* Is that *assent* which the King gives to a thing formerly done by others, as to the Election of a Bishop by Dean and Chapter, which given, then he sends a special Writ for the taking of *Fealty.* The form of which you may see in *F. N. B. fol.* 170. And to a Bill passed in both Houses of Parliament, *Cromp. Jur. fol.* 8. which *Assent* in Parliament being once given, the Bill is endorsed with these words, *Le Roy le veult,* i. *It pleases the King*; but if he refuse to agree to it, then thus, *Le Roy S'avisera,* i. *The King will advise.*

Royalties, *Regalia vel Regalitates,* Are the Rights of the King, *Jura Regis,* otherwise called *The Kings Prerogative.* Some of these be such as the King may grant unto common persons; some so high, that they may not be separated from his Crown *privativè,* as the *Civilians* call it, though *Cumulativè* they may. See *Bracton,* lib. 2. cap 5. and *Mathæum de afflictis,* upon the Title of the *Feuds, Quæ sint regalia,* where he reckons up twenty five special particulars of *Royalties.* See also *Hotomans Commentaries,* in lib. 2. *Feudor.* cap 56. and see *Prerogative & regalia.*

Rugi, Rusians, *Leg. Ed. Conf.* tit. *De L. Noricorum*—*Aufugit ad regnum* Rugorum *quod nos melius vocamus* Russiam; And afterwards speaking of *Margaret* the Sister of *Edgar,* and Queen of *Scots, Ex parte verò matris, ex genere & sanguine regum* Rugorum.

Rudge washed Kersey, Is that which is made of Fleece-wool, washt only on the Sheeps back, 35 *Eliz. cap.* 10.

Runcilus & Runcinus, Is used in *Doomsday* (says *Spelman*) for a Load-Horse, *Equus operarius colonicus,* or a Sumpter-Horse; and sometimes for a Cart Horse, which *Chaucer* in the Seamans Tale calls a **Rowncy.**

He rod upon a Rowncy as he could.

Rune, From the Saxon *Rununge,* i. a course or running a Water-course, so called in the Marshes of *Somerset shire*: History of imbanking and drayning, *fol.* 106.

Runlet alias **Roundlet,** Is a certain Measure of Wine, Oyl, &c. containing eighteen Gallons and a half, *Anno* 1 *R.* 3. *cap.* 13.

Ruoda, Leg. Saxonum, tit. 2. sect. 1. —*Qui nobilem occiderit* icccxl. *sol. componat.* Roda *quod dicitur apud Saxones* cxx. *sol. & inter premium* cxx. *ad* Ruod *veteri lingua Saxonica crucem significat.* For it is most certain, that our Ancestors the Saxons called the Cross *Rode* or *Roode*; hence came the *Rode loft,* and we still call *Diem Sanctæ Crucis,* **Holy-rod-day.**

Rupta, Is the same with *Routa,* which see *Mat. Paris* in *Anno* 1199. use it for a Troop of Soldiers. — *Qui duces fuerunt catervæ* (*quam* Ruttam *vocamus*) *militantes sub Comite Jo. fratre Regis* Richardi *equitationem facerent, &c.*

Ruptarii, *Milites,* Soldiers, Mat. Par. in Anno 1199. *Sed quoniam idem Episcopus* (*Belluacensis*) *contra ordinis sui dignitatem captus fuerat in armis, ut miles vel* Ruptarius, *non prius est abire permissus donec* 6000. *argenti carucis ad pondus sterlingorum numeratis & fisco commendatis Regiæ concupiscentiæ satisfecisset. Hollinshead,* pag. 243. calls them *Rutters,* and *pag.* 98, 99. *Ruptarii.*

Rural Deanes, *Decani rurales,* Of whom *Spelman* gives this account, *Sunt Decani temporales ad aliquod Ministerium sub Episcopo vel Archiepiscopo exercendum constituti; qui nec habent institutionem Canonicam secundum Doctores.* And this *Rural Dean* he supposes to be the same, which in the Laws of *Edward the Confessor,* cap. 31. is called *Episcopi Decanus.* See *Deane.* Each Diocess hath in it one or more Arch-deaconries, for dispatch of Ecclesiastical business, and every Arch-deaconry subdivided into fewer or more *Rural Deanries,* Heylins *Cosmog. fol.* 304. and he says, they were anciently called *Arch-Presbyteri & Decani Christianitatis.*

Rusca, In *Doomsday* Book, tit. *Cestre,* we find these words in substance, *When the King himself came in person to* Chester, *every* Carucata *yielded him two hundred* Hestae's, *and one Tun of Ale, and one* Rusca *of Butter*; but what quantity that *Rusca* contained appears not: *Rusca apum* signifies a Hive of Bees.

Rusche, *Mellarium, alveare,* For so it seems to signifie in a Charter of *Will. Bray* Knight, made to the Canons of *Osney,*— *Ita tamen, ut tantum de apicibus, quas ipse* Will. *& hæredes qui & homines sui in Curiis habebant, decimas percipiant, scil. de* Ruschis. It may be derived from the French *Ruche,* that signifies in Latine *Alveare.*

Rymmers about, They seem to be Vagabonds, q. d. *Roamers about, Skene,* lib. *De Crimin. Capital.* tit. 2. C. 14. *Paragr.* 2. F. 135. p. 2.

S.

Sabbatum, In *Doomsday,* tit. *Sudsex,* Is used for Peace, *Terra* Will. *Episcopi de* Tetford, *Bisedes* hundred, *num.* 18. *Postquam* Willielmus *Rex advenit & sedebat in* Sabbato, *&* Willielmus Mallet *fecit suum mastellum de Eia,* &c.

Sables. See *Furre.*

Sac, *Saccha vel saucha.* This *Minshew* renders to signifie a Royalty or Priviledge touching Plea, or Correction of Trespasses of men within a Mannor; and that the word **Sac** in the Saxon Tongue properly signifies as much as (*Causa* with the Latines.) *Sake,* whence we in *English* still retain the Expression, For whose sake, &c. that is, for whose Cause: But in the Laws of *Edward the Confessor* thus, *Sacha est quod si quilibet aliquem nominatim, de aliquo calumniatus fuerit & ille negaverit, forisfactura probationis vel negationis* (*si evenerit*) *sua erit.* I will also exhibit an Exposition both of *Socha & Sacha* out of a very ancient Manuscript Book, in which are registred several Donations to a Cathedral Church in *England,* being in the Custody of *Silas Taylor* Gent. where, after the recital of a certain Charter granted by *Edward the Confessor* to them, *Cum* Saka *&*

cum Sokna; There follows an Expofition of them both in red Letters thus,

Sequitur expofitio illorum Terminorum Soka *&* Saka.

Soka, Hoc eft fecta de hominibus in curia veftra fecundum confuetudinem Regni.

Saka, Hoc eft placitum & emenda de tranfgreffionibus hominum in Curia veftra.

The firft is only the Suit of Court due by the Inhabitants of a Lordfhip or Mannor, and *Sac* is the liberty of holding Pleas, and impofing Mulcts and Forfeitures upon Tranfgreffors in that Court. But *Raftal*, and fome others, define *Sac* to be the Forfeiture it felf. *Bracton, lib.* 3. *tract.* 2. *cap.* 8. quoted by *Stamford* in his *Pleas of the Crown*, lib. 1. cap. 23. ufes the word, but both of them leave the fignification undetermined. *Skene de verbor. Signif. verb.* Sack, writes, That in fome old Books it is called *Placitum de tranfgreffione hominum in curia noftra*, fee him at large, and *Hoveden, part fuor. annal. fol.* 345. See *Keilwayes Rep.* fol. 145. *Et Breve* Hen. 2. *Jufticiariis de Norfolc. Præcipio ut fanctus Benedictus de Ramefia ita bene & libere habeat* Socam *&* Sacam *fuam, &c.* See *Saka*.

Sakaburth alias **Sakebere**, Is he that is robbed, or by Theft deprived of his Goods, *Britton, cap.* 15. *&* 29. with whom agrees *Bracton, lib.* 3. *tract.* 2. *cap.* 32. *num.* 2. thus, *Furtum vero manifeftum eft ubi latro deprehenfus fit, feifitus de aliquo Latrocinio, fcil.* **Hondhabend** & **Backberende**, *& infecutus fuerit per aliquem cujus res illa fuerit qui dicitur* **Sacaburth**, *& fine fecta cognoverit fe inde effe Latronem coram Vice-comite, vel Coronatore, vel ferviente Domini Regis cum teftimonio proborum hominum, extunc furtum dedicere non poffit, quia tales in hoc habent recordum.* The *Scots* term it **Sacreborgh** & **Sikerborgh**, that is, *certum vel fecurum plegium vel pignus*; For with them **Siker** fignifies *Securus*, and **Borgh**, *Plegius*; As if one fhould fay, He that is taken flying with the thing ftollen about him, feems thereby, as by a certain Token, to have betrayed his Guilt. But **Sacaburth** may more reafonably be derived from *Sac* or *Saca*, that is, *lis* or *caufa*, and *burh* pignus, *Propterea quod res furtiva fit quafi caufæ pignus*, fo fays *Spelman*. Sir *Edw. Co.* 3 *Inft.* fol. 69. will have it come from *Sak* and *Bere*, that is, He that bears the Bag; from which *Spelman* differs not much, when he fays the word *Sacaber* is *quafi facam ferens vel lator*.

Saccus cum Brochia, Was a Service or Tenure of finding a Sack and a Broach to the King, for the ufe of his Army, *Bracton, lib.* 2. *tract.* 1. *cap.* 6. hath thefe words, *Si quis teneat per fervitium inveniendi Domino Regi certis locis & certis temporibus unum hominem & unum equum &* Saccum cum Brochia *pro aliqua neceffitate vel utilitate exercitum fuum contingentem.*

Sacreborgh alias **Sikerborgh**, *Securus plegius vel pignus*, A good Pledge or fufficient Caution. See *Sacaburth*.

Sack of Wool, *Saccus Lanæ*, Is a quantity of *Wool* containing twenty fix ftone, and every ftone fourteen pounds, 14 *E.* 3. *ftat.* 1. *cap.* 2. See *Sarplar*. In *Scotland* it is twenty four ftone, and each ftone fixteen pound. See *Skene*.

Sacrafield Rents, Are certain fmall *Rents* paid by fome Tenants of the Mannor of *Chuton* in *Somerfetfhire*, to Sir *Charles Waldgrave* Lord thereof; but he cannot tell why they are fo called.

Sacramento recipiendo, quod vidua Regis fe non maritabit fine licentia Regis, Is a Writ or Commiffion to one, for the taking of an Oath of the King's Widow, that fhe fhall not marry without the King's Licence, *Reg. Orig. fol.* 298.

Sacramentum plenum, *Dictum reor* (fays *Spelman*) *de completo numero duodenario, ut in Leg.* Edw. Confeff. *ab Ingulpho datis*, cap. 17.

Sacrobarra, Lib. M. S. de Officio Coronatoris, *Inquirendum eft per* 12 *juratores pro lege fuper Sacramentum fuum quod fideliter præfentabunt fine ullo concelamento omnes fortunas* (i. fortaffe occifos) *abjurationes, appella murdra* Sacrobarra, *felonias factas, per quos & quæ, &c. Quære*, faith *Spelman*, if *Sacrobarra* be not the fame with *Sacrilegia*.

Safe Conduct, *Salvus Conductus*, Is a Security given by the Prince, under the Great Seal of *England*, for his quiet coming in and paffing out of the Realm; touching which, read the Statutes, 15 *H.* 6. 3. 18 *H.* 6. 8. *&* 28 *H.* 8. *cap.* 1. and the form of it, *Reg. Orig. fol.* 25.

Safe guard. See *Salva gardia*.

Safe pledge, *Salvu plegius*, Is a Surety given for a Man's Appearance againft a day affigned, *Bracton, lib.* 4. *cap.* 2. *num.* 2. where it is alfo called *certus plegius*.

Sagibaro alias **Sachbaro**, The fame that at prefent is called *Jufticiarius*; for *Sagibarones* were *caufarum judices qui in publicis conventibus jus dicebant litefq; dirimebant*; from whence alfo the Name may be derived; For *Sac* or *Sag* fignifies *Caufam* or *litem*, and *Baro*, *virum vel hominem*, as one would fay, *Vir caufarum*, a Judge.

Sagitta Barbata, A bearded Arrow, fuch as we ufually call *A broad Arrow*.

Sailing ware, *Anno* 1 R. 3. *cap.* 8. May be Canvas, or fuch other Cloth as Sails for Ships are made of.

Saka. See *Sac*.

Salary, *Salarium*, Is a recompence or confideration made to a Man, for his pains or induftry beftowed on another mans bufinefs. The word is ufed 23 *E.* 3. *cap.* 1.

Salet, Is a Head-piece, 4 *&* 5 *P. & M.* From the French *Salut*, i. *Salus*, mentioned alfo 20 *R.* 2, *cap.* 1. See **Sallet** or **Scul of Iron**, otherwife called a *Morion* or *Pot*.

Sallarium, Is the Latine word for Cuftome paid for Salt, according to *Camden*.

Saio & Saiones, fori vel Magiftratus Minifter, A Tipftaff or Sergeant at Arms, *qui reus protrahunt in judicium.* It may be derived from the Saxon ſagol, *Faftis*, becaufe they ufe to carry a Rod or Staff of Silver.

Salina, A Salt-pit, a Houfe or Place where Salt is made, *In Herbagiis & Pifcariis, in* falinis

& Fabricis, in maneriis ferreis, &c. Carta 17 E. 2. num. 28.

Salique Law, *Lex* salica, *De terra* salica *nulla portio hæreditatis mulieri veniat, sed ad virilem sexum tota terræ hæreditas perveniat, &c.* Was an ancient Law made by *Pharamond* King of the *Franks*, part of which seems to have been borrowed by our *Henry* the First in compiling his Laws, as *cap.* 89. *Qui hoc fecerit secundum Legem* salicam *moriatur, &c.*

Salmon-Pipe, 25 *H.* 8. *cap.* 7. Is an Engine to catch *Salmons*, or such like Fish.

Salmon sewse, Seems to be the young fry of *Salmon*, *Quasi* salmon *issue*, 13 R. 2. *stat.* 1. *cap.* 19.

Saltatorium, A Deer-leap, *Clamat habere liberum parcum suum apud Halton cum duobus* saltatoriis *in eodem*, Pl. apud Cestriam, 31 E. 3.

Saltus, Highwood. See *Boscus*.

Salva gardia, Is a security given by the King to a stranger, fearing the violence of some of his Subjects, for seeking his Right by course of Law; the form whereof, see in *Reg. Orig. fol.* 26.

Salvage Money, Is a recompence allowed by the Civil Law, in lieu of all Damages sustained by that Ship that saves or rescues another which was set upon by Pyrats or Enemies.

Salute, *Salus*, was a Coyn of Gold stamped by King *Henry* the Fifth in *France*, after his Conquests there: Whereon the Arms of *England* and *France* were stamped quarterly, see *Stow's Chr. pag.* 589.

Salvus Plegius. See *Plegius*.

Sanctuary, *Sanctuarium*, Is a place priviledged by the Prince, for the Safeguard of Mens Lives that are Offenders, being founded upon the Law of Mercy, and upon the great Reverence, Honour and Devotion, which the Prince beareth to the place whereto he granted such a Priviledge, *Stamf. Pl. Cor. lib.* 2. *cap.* 38. This seems to have taken beginning from the Cities of Refuge, mention'd *Exod. cap.* 21. In imitation whereof, first the *Athenians*, then *Romulus*, erected such a place of Immunity, which they called *Asylum. Polydor Virgil. de inventione rerum*, lib. 3. cap. 12. The like did the *Roman* Emperors, as appears, *Cod. lib.* 1. *tit.* 15. But among all others, our ancient Kings of *England* attributed most to these *Sanctuaries*, permitting them to shelter such, as had committed both Felonies and Treasons, so that within forty days they acknowledged their Fault, and submitted themselves to Banishment: During which time, if any Lay-man expelled them, he was excommunicated; if any Clerk, he was made irregular: But after forty days, no man might relieve them, *Stamf. Pl. Cor. lib.* 2. *cap.* 38. See of this the *New Book of Entries*, verb. *Sanctuary*, and *Fleta lib.* 1. *cap.* 29. and how by degrees they have been taken away, read 26 *H.* 8. 13. 28 *H.* 8. 7. 32 *H.* 8. 12. 33 *H.* 8. 15. 1 *E.* 6. 12. 2 *E.* 6. 2 & 33. 5 *E.* 6. 10. See *Abjuration*. Of these there were many in *England*, but one more famous than the rest at St. *Johns* of *Beverley*, which the Saxons called *Fridstoll*, which had this Inscription, *Hæc sedes Lapidea* **Freedstoll**, *dicitur* i. *Pacis Cathedra ad quam reus fugiendo perveniens, omnimodo habet securitatem.*

Sandall, 2 *R.* 2. *cap.* 1. Is a Merchandise brought into *England*, and is a kind of Wood brought out of *India*; for *scandal* in French so signifies, and the like does *santalum* in Latine.

Sand gavel, In the Lordship of *Redeley in Com. Glouc.* the Tenants pay to the Lord a certain Duty of *Sand-gavel*, for liberty granted to them to dig up *sand* for their uses, *Taylor's History of Gavelkind*, pag. 113.

Sarclin time, Is the time when the Husbandman weeds his Corn. And it proceeds from the French *Sarcler*, or the Latine *sarclare*, both which signifies to weed; from whence also proceeds *sarclum*, a weeding Hook.

Sarplar, *Sarplera Lanæ*, otherwise called a *Pocket*, is half a Sack; a Sack eighty Tod, a Tod two stone, and a stone fourteen pound, *Fleta, lib.* 2. *cap.* 12. This in *Scotland* is called *Serpliath*, and contains fourscore stone. For the Lords of the Council, *Anno* 1527. decreed four *Serpliaths* of packed Wooll to contain sixteen score stone of Wooll. See *Skene de verbor.* Signif. *verb.* Serpliath, and 3 *par. Instit. fol.* 96.

Sarum, Is intended for the City of *Salisbury*; It was a form of Church-Service called *Secundum usum Sarum*, and was composed by *Osmund* the second Bishop of *Sarum* in the time of *William the Conqueror*, Hollinshead, *pag.* 17. *col. B.*

Sasse, *Anno* 16 & 17 *Car.* 2. *Cap.* 12. Is a kind of Wear with Flood-gates, most commonly in cut Rivers, for the shutting up and letting out the Water, as occasion requires, for the more ready passing of Boats and Barges, to and fro. This in some places, as *Guilford* River is called a *Lock*, in others less properly a *Turnpike*, and in others a *Sluce*.

Saturdayes-stop, Is a space of time in which of old it was not lawful to take Salmons in *Scotland* and the North of *England*, that is, from Even-song on *Saturday* till Sun-rising on *Monday*.

Saver default, Is word for word to excuse a *default*: This is properly, when a man having made a *default* in Court, comes afterwards and alledges a good Cause why he did it, as Imprisonment at the same time, or such like, *New Book of Entries*, verb. *Saver de default*.

Saunkefine, May be derived from the French *Sang*, *sanguis*, and *Fin*, *finis*; and is a Phrase used by *Britton*, *cap.* 119. for the determination or final race of a descent of Kindred.

Saxonlage, *Seaxenlaga*, *Lex Saxonum*. See *Merchenlage*.

Scabini, Wardens, was a word used by the Wardens of *Linne* in *Norfolk* in a Charter in these words. *Sciant præsentes & futuri quod nos* Richardus Bowghere *Aldermannus*, Edw. Baker, Joh. Browne, Rob. Some, & Will. Hall, *Draper*, *Custodes sive* scabini *& fratres fraternitatis sive Gildæ Mercatoriæ sanctæ Trinitatis villæ* Lenne Episcopi *in Com.* Norf. *pro quadam pecuniæ summa inter nos præfatum Aldermanum & Custodes sive* scabinos, *& fratres &* Thomam Miller *de* Lenne *prædictâ mercatorem concordati, tradidimus, Dimissimus & Feoffavimus, &c. totum illud Messuagium nostrum, &c.* Dat. 20 die Apr. Anno Reg. Regis Hen. 8. 18.

Scandalum Magnatum, Is the special name of a wrong done to any high Personage of the Land, as Prelates, Dukes, Earls, Barons, and other Nobles; and also of the Chancellor, Treasurer, Clerk of the Privy-Seal, Steward of the House, Justice of one Bench or other, and other great Officers of the Realm, by false News, or horrible or false Messages, whereby debates and discords betwixt them and the Commons, or any scandal to their persons might arise, *Anno* 2 R. 2. *cap.* 5. and hath given Name to a Writ, granted to recover damage thereupon.

Scavage, *Scavagium*, It is otherwise called **Echevage**, **Shewage** and **Scheauwing**, may be deduced from the Saxon ꞅeaꝑian, *ostendere*, and is a kind of Toll or Custom exacted by Mayors, Sheriffs, &c. of Merchant-strangers, for Wares *shewed* or offered to sale within their Precincts, which is prohibited by the Statute 19 *H.* 7. 8. In a Charter of *Henry* the Second to *Canterbury* it is written **Scewinga**. The City of *London* still retain the Custom, of which *in an old Printed Book of the Customs of London*, We read thus, **Of which Custom halfen del appertaineth to the Sheriffs, and the other halfen del to the Hostys in whose Houses the Merchants been lodged: And it is to wet that** Scavage **is the Shew, by cause that Merchantys shewen unto the Sheriffs Merchandises, of the which Customs ought to be taken ore that ony thing thereof be sold, &c.**

Scavenger, From the *Belgick* **Scavan**, to scrape. Two of every Parish within *London* and the Suburbs, are yearly chosen into this Office, who hire men called *Rakers*, and Carts to cleanse the Streets, and carry away the Dirt and Filth thereof, mentioned 14 *Car.* 2. *cap.* 2.

Schaffa, A sheaf, as *Schaffa sagittarum* a sheaf of Arrows. See *Skene de verbor.* Sign. *eod. verbo.*

Schildpeny, *Tributum singulo scuto impositum* escuagium, scutagium, *vide*.

Scarcalla, It was especially given in charge by the Justices *in Eyre*, that all Juries should inquire *De his qui piscantur cum Kiddellis & Skarcallis*, *Co.* 2. *par. Inst. fol.* 38.

Scire facias, Is a Writ Judicial, most commonly to call a Man to shew cause to the Court whence it issues, why Execution of a Judgment passed, should not be made out: This Writ is not granted until a year and a day be elapsed after a Judgment given, *Old Nat. Brev. fol.* 151. *Scire facias* upon a Fine lies not, but within the same time after the Fine levyed, otherwise it is the same with the writ of *Habere facias seisinam*, *West Symbol.* part 2. tit. *Fines*, sect. 137. and 25 Ed. 3. *stat.* 5. *cap.* 2. & 39 Eliz. *cap.* 7. Other Diversities of this Writ you may find in the Table of the *Register Judicial and Original* See also the *New Book of Entries*, verb. *Scire facias.*

Scite, 32 *H.* 8. *cap.* 20. See *Site.*

Scot, A part or portion, according to *Rastall*, is a certain Custom, or common Tallage, made to the use of the Sheriff, or his Bayliffs: *Scot* (says *Camden* out of *Mat. Westm.*) *Illud dicitur quod ex diversis rebus in unum acervum aggregatur*, Anno 22 H. 8. cap. 3. **Bearing neither Scot, Lot nor other Charges, &c.** *Et Anno* 33 *H.* 8. *cap.* 9. See *Doomsday* & Spelman. *Scot* and *Lot*, 39 *H.* 8, 9. signifies a Customary Contribution laid upon all Subjects, according to their Ability. *Hoveden* (in the beginning *Hen.* 2.) writes it **Anlote** and **Anscote**. See Leg. Gul. Conq. cap. 125. the same words. And *Hoveden* in *Anno* 1088. *Rex omne injustum* scottum *interdixit.----Foret Ballivus ad* scotta *pro reparatione & sustentatione Walliarum, &c. assessa levandum*, Ordinatio Marisci Romeneiensis, *pag.* 56. And again, *pag.* 64. *Ballivus habeat pro labore suo dupla levanda quæ tempore suo de* scottis *assessis & levatis contingant*; And afterwards, *pag.* 69. *Tam generales* scottas *quam seperales aquagangias assessas ut prædictum est onerabit.* And at last, *pag.* 73. *Statuerunt quod quilibet* scottus *assessus proclamaretur.* Nor are these old words grown *obsolete*, for who ever in like manner (though not by equal portions) are assessed to any Contribution, are generally said to pay *Scot and Lot.*

Scotall alias **Scotale**, *Scotalla & scotalium*, Is a word used in the Charter of the Forest, in these words, cap. 7. *Nullus forestarius vel Bedellus faciat* scotallas *vel Garbas colligat vel aliquam collectam faciat*, Manwood's Forest Law, *Part* 1. *pag.* 216. A *Scotale* is, where any Officer of the Forest keeps an Ale-house within the Forest, by colour of his Office, causing men to come to his House, and there to spend their Money for fear of having displeasure. It is a compound of *Scot* and *Ale*, which is otherwise called an *Aleshot*, *Memorandum quod prædicti tenentes* (*de* Southmalling) *debent de consuetudine inter eos facere* scotalium *de* 16. *denar. & ob. Ita quod de singulis sex denariis*, 1. *denar. & ob. ad potandum cum Bedello Domini Archiepiscopi super prædictum feodum*, Ex vet. Consuetudinario de *Southmalling* in Archivis Archiep. Cant.

Scrudland, A Saxon word, and is *Terra cujus proventus vestibus emendis assignati sunt.* Land allotted for buying Apparel. See the *Saxon Dictionary hoc verbo.*

Scutage, *Scutagium*; *Henry* the Third for his Voyage to the Holy Land, had a Tenth granted by the Clergy, and *scutage*, three Marks of every Knights Fee by the Layety, *Baker's Chron. in vita*, Hen. 3. This was also granted to *Henry* the *Second*, Richard *the First*, and King *John*.

Scutagio habendo, Was a Writ that lay for the King, or other Lord, against the Tenant that holdeth by *Knights-service*, to serve by himself, or else to send a sufficient Man in his place, or pay, &c. where the King intends to make a Warlike Expedition against the *Scots* or *French*, *F. N. B. fol.* 83. It is used in the *Register Original*, for him to recover *Escuage* of others, that hath either by Service or Fine performed his own to the King, *fol.* 88. *a*.

Scutum Armorum, A Coat of Arms, *-----Noverint universi per præsentes me* Johannam *nuper uxorem* Will. Lee *de* Knightley *Dominam & rectam hæredem de* Knightley *dedisse, &c.* Richardo Peshale *filio Humfridi Peshale* scutum armorum meorum. *Habend. & tenend. ac portand. & utend. ubicunq; voluerit sibi & hæredibus suis in perpetuum*;

Ita quod nec ego nec aliquis alius nomine meo aliquod jus vel clameum vel calumpniam in prædicto scuto *habere potuerimus, sed per præsentes sumus exclusi in perpetuum, In cujus, &c.* Dat. apud Knightley, *Anno* 14 *H.* 6.

Scyre-gemot, Is a mere Saxon word, and signifies a Court held twice every year (as the Sheriffs Turn is now) by the Bishop of the Diocess and the *Ealdorman* (in Shires that had *Ealdormen*) and by the Bishops and Sheriffs, in such as were committed to the Sheriffs that were immediate to the King, wherein both the Ecclesiastical and Temporal Laws, were given in charge to the Country, *Selden's Titles of Honor*, fol. 520. See *Consistory*.

Scangium, In *Doomsday* is used for Exchange, according to the Interpretation of Mr. *Agar* of the *Exchequer*.

Seale, *Sigillum*, Is a thing now well known, but not so heretofore: For the first *sealed Charter* we find in *England*, was that of King *Edward the Confessor*, when he founded *Westminster Abbey*. And *Taylor* in his History *Of Gavelkind*, fol. 73. asserts other of the same King's *Seals*; *Edward the Confessor* (says he) made a Grant of some Priviledges to the Church of *Hereford*, and firmed it with a *Seal*, which in one of their Register Books is described to be preserved in *Panno serico*, and a *Memorandum* also of the Circumscription of the said *Seal*, to be this, *Hoc est sigillum Regis Edwardi*. And in many places of *Doomsday* Book it is recorded, That Lands did pass to several People under the *Seal* of King *Edward*; as in *Berkshire*, under the Title of *Terra* Henrici *de Ferieres*; *Godricus Vice-comes tenuit de Rege* Edwardo, *Hanc terram dedit Rex* Edwardus *de sua firma Godrico, & inde viderunt* sigillum *ejus homines de Comitatu, præter istas hidas accepit ipse Godricus de firma Regis unam* V s. *terræ, de qua non viderunt* sigillum *Regis*; By which it appears, that the *Saxons* looked upon *sealing* as of great strength and efficacy to their validating of Deeds and Conveyances. See *Wange*. Anno 1536. *Domini etiam atq; generosi, relictis imaginibus equitum in* sigillis *posuerunt Arma sua in parvis scutis*, Chron. Joh. Rossi in Biblioth. Cotton

Sealer, *Sigillator*, Is an Officer in Chancery appointed by the Lord Chancellor, or Lord Keeper, of the Great Seal of *England* to seal the Writs and Instruments there made in his presence.

Seame, Saxon. See *Seme*.

Seane fish, Seems to be a sort of Fish which is taken with a very great and long Net called a *Seane*.

Searcher. See *Alneger*.

Sea-rover, *Anno* 16 *Car.* 2. *cap.* 6. See *Pyrate*.

Second deliverance, *Secunda deliberatione*, Is a Writ that lies for him, who, after a return of Cattel, replevied; Adjudged to him that distrained them, by reason of a default in the Party that replevied, for the replevying of the same Cattel again, upon security put in for the redelivery of them in case the Distress be justified, *New Book of Entries*, verbo *Replevin in second deliverance*, fol. 522. See *Dyer*, *fol.* 41. *num.* 4, 5.

Second Marriage, *Secundæ Nuptiæ*, Is when after the decease of one, he marries a *second* Wife. This our Law terms *Bigamus*, and had so little favour too, that it admitted not such to holy Orders.

Secta ad Curiam, Is a Writ that lies against him who refuses to perform his Suit either to the *County or Court Baron*, *F. N. B. fol.* 158.

Secta facienda per illam quæ habet æniciam partem, Is a Writ to compel the Heir that hath the elders part of the Co-heirs to perform Service for all the Coparceners, *Reg. Orig. fol.* 177.

Secta Molendini, Is a Writ lying against him that was wont to grind at the Mill of *B*, and after goes to another Mill with his Corn, *Reg. Orig.* fol. 153. *F. N. B. fol.* 122. But it seems by him, that this Writ lies especially for the Lord against his Frank-tenement, who held of him by making suit to his Mill. See the *New Book of Entries* on this word *Secta ad molendinum, and Assises of Nusance* are at present much turned into Trespasses and Actions upon the Case. See *Balduinus ad titulum de servitutibus prædiorum in Instit.*

Sectam proferre, *Est testimonium legalium hominum qui contractui inter eos habito interfuerint præsentes producere, Fleta*, lib. 2. cap. 63. sect. *Nullus*, and *secta* is used for a Witness, *Id. lib.* 4. *cap.* 16. *sect.* final. *Habes tamen* sectam *unam vel plures*, &c.

Secta ad justitiam faciendam, Is a Service which a Man is bound to perform by his Service, *Bracton*, lib. 2. cap. 16. num. 6.

Secta unica tantum facienda pro pluribus hæreditatibus, Is a Writ that lies for that Heir that is distrained by the Lord to more Suits than one, in respect of the Land of divers Heirs descended unto him, *Reg. Orig. fol.* 177. *a.*

Secta shirarum, *Per* sectam shirarum *clamat esse quiet. de* secta *in Com. Cestriæ & Flint coram Justic. Domini Principis in communi aula Placitorum*, Plac. in Itin. apud Cestriam, 14 *H.* 7.

Sectis non faciendis, Is a Writ that lies for a Woman, who, for her Dower, ought not to perform suit of Court, *Reg. Orig. fol.* 174. It lay also for one in Wardship, to be freed of all suits of Court during his Wardship, *Reg. Orig. fol.* 173. but see 12 *Car* 2. *cap.* 24.

Secunda superoneratione pasturæ, Is a Writ that lies where admeasurement of *Pasture* hath been made; and he that first surcharged the Common, doth again surcharge it, notwithstanding the Admeasurement, *Reg. Orig. fol.* 157. *Old Nat. Brev. fol.* 73.

Secundary, *Secundarius*, That Officer who is the second, or next to the chief Officer; as the *secundary* of the Fine-Office: The *secundary* of the Compters, who is the next to the Sheriff of *London* in each of the two Compters; *secundary* of the Office of the Privy-Seal, *Anno* 1 *E.* 4. *cap.* 1. *Secundaries* of the Pipe two: *Secundary* to the Remembrancers, which are two Officers in the Exchequer, *Camd. pag.* 113.

Securitatem inveniendi quod se non divertat ad partes exteras sine licentia Regis, Is a Writ that lies for the King against any of his Subjects, to stay them from going out of his Kingdom; The ground of which is, That every man is bound to serve and defend the

the Common-wealth, as the King shall think meet, *F. N. B. fol.* 85.

Securitate pacis, Is a Writ that lies for one who is threatned Death or Danger, against him that so threatneth, and is taken out of the Chancery, and directed to the Sheriff; the form and farther use whereof, you may see in *Reg. Orig. fol.* 88. and *Fitz. Nat. Brev. fol.* 79.

Se defendendo, Is a Plea for him that is charged with the death of another, saying, He was necessitated to do that which he did in his own Defence: The other so assaulting him, That if he had not done as he did, he must have been in hazard of his own life: But this danger ought to be so great, that it seems inevitable, *Stamf. Pl. Cor. lib.* 1. *cap.* 7. And though he justifie it to be done in his own defence, yet he is driven to procure his Pardon of course from the Lord Chancellor, and forfeits his goods to the King, according to the same Author.

Seignior, *Dominus*, Is borrowed of the French *Seigneur*, and denotes in the general signification as much as Lord; but particularly it is used for the Lord of the Fee, or of a Mannor, even as *Dominus* or *Senior* among the *Feudists* is he who grants a Fee, or Benefit, out of the Land to another: And the reason is, as *Hotoman* saith, because having granted the use and profit of the Land to another; yet the Property, that is, *Dominium*, he still retains in himself. See *Hotoman in verbis feudal*, verb. *Dominus & senior.*

Seignior in grosse, Seemeth to be one that is a Lord, but of no Mannor, and therefore can keep no Court, *F. N. B. fol.* 3.

Seignourage, *9 H. 5. Stat. 2. cap.* 1. Seems to be a Royalty or Prerogative of the King, whereby he challengeth allowance of Gold and Silver brought in the masse to his Exchange for Coyn.

Seignory, *Dominium*, Is borrowed from the French *Seigneurie*, i. *dominatus, imperium, principatus*; and signifies with us a Mannor or Lordship, *Seignory de Sokemans*, Kitch. fol. 80. *Seigniory in gross*, which seems to be the Title of him who is not Lord by means of any Mannor, but immediately in his own person, as *Tenure in Capite*, whereby one holds of the King as of his Crown, is *seigniory in gross*, Kitchin, *fol.* 206. See *Seignior.*

Seisin, *Seisina*, From the French *Seisine*, *possessio*: So *primer seisin* is the first Possession, and *to seise*, is to take Possession. See *Primier seisin*, of the French word *Seisir*, is made the Latine *seisire* used both by the *Canonists* and *Civilians*; *Seisin* according to the Common Law is two-fold, *seisin in Fact*, and *seisin in Law*, Perkins Dower, 369, 370. *Seisin in Fact* is, when a corporal Possession is taken; *Seisin in Law* when something is done, which the Law accounteth a *seisin*, as an Inrolment: And this *seisin in Law* is as much as a right to Lands and Tenements, though the Owner be by wrong disseised of them, *Perkin's Tenant per le curtese* 457. 478. And it seems by *Ingham*, That he who hath had an hours possession quietly taken, hath *seisin de droit et de claime*, whereof no man may disseise him by his own force or subtilty, but must be driven to his Action, *sect. Briefe de Novel Disseisin.* Coke, *lib.* 4. *fol.* 9. calls it *seisin in Law*, or *Actual seisin*. The *Civilians* call the one *Civilem possessionem*, the other *Naturalem.*

Seisina habenda, quia Rex habuit annum, diem & Vastum, Is a Writ that lies for delivery of *seisin* to the Lord of his Lands or Tenements, that was formerly convicted of Felony, after the King, in the right of his Prerogative, hath had the year, day and wast, *Regist. Orig. fol.* 165.

Selda, May be deduced from the Saxon Selde, seat or stool. *Assisa mensurarum, Anno* 9 Rich. 1. *apud* Hoveden,----*Prohibemus ne quis mercator prætendat* seldæ *suæ rubros pannos vel nigros vel scuta vel aliqua alia, per quæ visus emptorum sæpe decipiuntur, ad bonum pannum eligendum*, In Majoribus Chronicis ubi locus hic vertitur. *Spelman* says, *Selda* is expounded for a **Window**: It signifies also a shop, shed, or stall, *Sciant, &c. quod ego* Thomas Pencombe *de* Bromyard *dedi, &c.* Thomæ *Forsenet vicario Ecclesiæ de* Bromyard *præd. unam* seldam *meam jacentem in* Bromyard *præd. &c. Dat. &c.* Anno 10 H. 6.----*Et medietatem unius* seldæ *vocat. Le Unicorne in* London. Mon. Ang. 2. par. fol. 322. *Selda* also signifies a Wood of Sallows, Willows and Withyes, *Co.* on *Lit. fol.* 4.

Selion of Land, *Selio terræ*, May be derived from the French *Seillon*; ground rising between two Furrows, in Latine *Porca*, in English a ridge of Land, and contains no certain quantity, but sometimes more, and sometimes less: Therefore *Crompton* in his *Jurisdictions of Courts*, fol. 221. saith, That a *selion of Land* cannot be demanded, because it is a thing uncertain: It may not without some probability be deduced from the Saxon *Sul or syl*, i. *aratrum*; whence also the French *Seillonner*, id est, *arare*, to Plough.

Seme, *Summa*, A Horse-load; A *seme* of Corn is eight Bushels,-----*Fratres Prædicator.* (Heref) *pro* 2. *summagiis vocat.* **Semes**, *de focali percipiend. quotidie de bosco de* Heywood *pro termino* 20. *annorum*, 3 H. 5. part 2. m. 18. See *Sumage*----*Habebunt etiam duas* summas *frumenti, pro pastellis, cum voluerint faciend.* Mon. Ang. 2. par. fol. 935. *Et sint quieti de summagiis & Murdro, & Tenniggs, & Wapentake, & Auxiliis Vicecomitum*, Ibid. fol. 201.

Sendal, *Anno* 2 Rich. 2. *cap.* 1. Seems to be fine Linnen; but *sandal* is a kind of Physical wood brought from the *Indies.*

Senege, *There goes out yearly in* Proxege *and* Senege 33 *s.* 6 *d.* Perhaps *senege* may be Money paid for Synodals, as *Proxege* for Proxyes or Procurations.

Seneshal, *Seneschallus*, Is a French word, but borrowed from *Germany*, being derived from **Sein**, a House or Place, and **Schale**, *servus*; We English it a Steward, and so doth *Co.* on *Lit. fol.* 61.

As the high *Seneshal* or Steward of *England*, *Stamf. Pl. Cor. fol.* 152. High *Seneshal* or Steward, and *South Seneshal* or Under-steward, *Kitchin, fol.* 83. is understood of the Stewards or Under-stewards of Courts; *Seneshal de l'hostell de Roy*, Steward of the King's Houshold, *Cromp. Jurisd. fol.* 102. See 25 Ed. 3. stat. 5. cap. 21. *In Purificatione Beatæ* Mariæ, *fuit filius Regis Anglorum Parisiis & servi-* vit

vit Regi Francorum ad mensam ut Seneschallus *Franciæ*, Rob. de Monte in Anno 1170. pag. 649.

Senescallo et Mareshallo quod non teneant placita de libero tenemento, &c. Is a Writ directed to the Steward or Marshal of *England*, inhibiting them to take Cognisance of any Action in their Court that concerns either Free-hold, Debt or Covenant, *Reg. Orig. fol.* 185. 191.

Senie alias **Sene**, *Sena*, Is a Medicinal Herb, the use and vertues whereof you may read in *Gerard's Herbal*, lib. 3. cap. 8. This is mentioned among other Drugs and Spices to be garbled, *Anno* 1 *Jac. cap.* 19.

Seneucia, **Widowhood**, If a *Widow*, having Dower after the Death of her Husband shall marry *vel filium*, *vel filiam in* Seneucia *peperit*, she shall forfeit and lose her Dower in what place soever, in *Kent Tenen. in Gavelkind*, Plac. Trin. 17 E. 3.

Separation, *Separatio*, Is the living asunder of Man and Wife. See *Mulier*.

Septum, An Inclosure, a Close, and is so called, because it is encompassed *cum sepe & fossa*, with a Hedge and a Ditch, or at least with a Hedge.

Septuagesima, Mentioned *Westm.* 1. *cap.* 51. Is alwayes the third *Sunday* before *Quadragesima* exclusive, from which, until the *Octaves* after *Easter*, the solemnizing of Marriage is forbidden by the Canon Law. It is called *Septuagesima*, as being above seventy dayes before Easter, as *Sexagesima* and *Quinquagesima*, because the first is accounted sixty, the latter fifty dayes before the same Feast, & are dayes appointed by the Church to acts of Penance and Mortification, and are preparative to the devotion of *Lent* then approaching. See *Quinquagesima*.

Sepulchre, *Sepulchrum*, Is the place where any dead Body lies interred; but a Monument is a place where something is set up for the Memorial of the deceased, though the Corps lye not there.

Sequatur sub suo periculo, Is a Writ that lies where a Summons *ad Warrantisandum* is awarded, and the Sheriff returns, That he hath nothing whereby he may be summoned; then goes out an *Alias* and *Pluries*, and if he come not at the *Pluries*, then goes out this Writ, *Old Nat. Brev. fol.* 163. *Co.* on *Lit. fol.* 101.

Sequela Curiæ, Suit of Court, —— *Et quod sint liberi à* Sequela Curiæ, *Mon. Ang.* 2. par. fol. 253.

Sequester, Is a term used in the Civil Law for renouncing, as when a Widow comes into Court, and disclaims to have any thing to do, or to intermeddle with her Husband's Estate who is deceased; she is said to *Sequester*.

Sequestration, *Sequestratio*, Is a separating of a thing in controversie from the possession of both those that contend for it: And it is of two kinds, *Voluntary* or *Necessary*; *Voluntary*, is that which is done by consent of each Party: *Necessary*, is that which the Judge doth of his Authority, whether the Parties will or not. It is used also for the act of the Ordinary, disposing the Goods and Chattels of one deceased, whose Estate no man will meddle with, *Dyer, fol.* 232. *num.* 5. & *fol.* 256. *num.* 8. & *fol.* 260. *num.* 42. & *fol.* 271. *num.* 26. As also for the gathering the Fruits of a Benefice void, to the use of the next Incumbent, 28 *H.* 8. *cap.* 11. *Fortescue*, *cap.* 50. and in divers other Cases.

Sequestro habendo, Is a Writ Judicial, for the dissolving a Sequestration of the Fruits of a Benefice made by a Bishop at the King's Command, thereby to compel the Parson to appear at the Suit of another; for the Parson upon his appearance may have this Writ for the discharge of the Sequestration, *Reg. Judic. fol.* 36.

Sergeant, *Serviens*, Cometh of the French *Sergeant*, i. *satelles*, a Man of the Guard, so called, because he was *sæpe accitus ad res necessarias in exercitu peragendas*, so *Calepine*. But *Skene de verbor.* Signif. *verb.* Sergeant, saith, It is, *vox composita de* ferrer, *quod est includere &* Gent, *quod pro gente, plebe vel populo usurpatur*. This word is diversly used in our Law, and applyed to sundry Offices and Callings. First, a *Sergeant* at Law (or of the Coyf) is the highest degree taken in that Profession, as that of a Doctor is in the Civil Law. And to these, as Men best learned, and most experienced of all others, one Court is set apart for them to plead in by themselves, which is the Court of Common-Pleas, where the Common Law of *England* is most strictly observed; and though they have this Court to themselves, yet are they not restrained from pleading in any other Courts, where the Judges (who cannot have that Honor, till they have taken the degree of *Sergeant* at Law,) call them *Brothers*, and hear them with great respect next to the King's Attorney and Sollicitor-General. These are made by the King's Mandate, or Writ, directed unto them, commanding them, upon a great penalty, to take upon them that degree by a day certain therein assigned, *Dyer, fol.* 72. *num.* 1. See *Count*. And of these one is the King's *Sergeant*, being chosen commonly out of the rest, in respect of his great Learning, to plead for him in all Causes, especially in those of Treason, *Stamf. Pl. Cor. lib.* 3. *cap.* 1. And of these there may be more, if it please the King. This, in other Kingdoms, is called *Advocatus Regius*, *Cassan. de consuet. Burgund*, pag. 850. With what Solemnity these *Sergeants* be created, read *Fortescue*, *cap.* 50. *Cro.* 3. *par. fol.* 1. and 2. *Inst. fol.* 213. These were called anciently *Servientes Narratores*. *Et prædictus* Thomas *le Mareschall dicit quod ipse est communis* Serviens Narrator *coram Justic. & alibi ubi melius ad hoc conduci poterit, &c.* Trin. 25 E. 1. coram Rege Oxon. 22. This word *Sergeant* is used in *Britton* for an Officer belonging to the County, and the same which *Bracton* in his Fifth Book, *cap.* 4. *num.* 2. calls *Servientem Hundredi*, and is in truth no other than the Bayliff of the Hundred; And the Steward of a Mannor is called *Serviens Manerii*, *Coke*, *vol.* 4. *Copyhold Cases*, *fol.* 21. *a.* Then the next is a *Sergeant* at Arms, *Serviens ad Arma*, whose Office is to attend the Person of the King, *Anno* 7 *H.* 7. *cap.* 3. to Arrest Traytors, or Persons of Quality offending, and to attend the Lord High Steward of *England* sitting in Judgment upon any Traytor, and such like, *Pl. Cor. lib.* 3. *cap.* 1. Of these by the Statute 13 *Rich.* 2. *cap.* 6. There may not be above thirty in the Realm: Two of these, by the King's Allowance, attend on the two Houses of *Parliament*; The Office of him in the House of Commons is the keeping of the Doors, and the Execution of such Commands especially touching the Apprehension of any Offendor, as that House shall enjoyn him, *Cromp. Jurisd. fol.* 9. Another of them attends on the Lord Chancellor, or Lord Keeper, in the Chancery; and one on the Lord High Treasurer of *England*: One attendeth upon the Lord President of *Wales*, and another upon the Lord President of the North. Another sort of *Sergeants* are chief Officers, who execute several Functions in the King's Houshold, of which you may read many in the Statute 33 *H.* 8. *cap.* 12. There is also a more inferior kind of *Sergeants of the Mace*, whereof there is a Troop in the City of *London*, and other Corporate Towns, that attend the Mayor, or other chief Officer, both for menial Attendance, and chiefly for Matters of Justice. These are called *Servientes ad Clavam*, *New Book of Entries*, verb. *Scire facias in Mainpernors*, cap. 3. fol. 538.

Sergeants of Peace, —*Et etiam habere ibidem* (i. Dunham) *sex servientes qui vocantur*, **Sergeants of Peace** *qui servient Cur. Manerii & facient Attach. & executiones omnium Placitorum & querelarum in dicta Caria Placitorum, &c.* Pl. de Quo Warranto apud Cestriam, 31 *Ed.* 3.

Serjeanty, *Serjeantia*, Signifies in Law a Service that cannot be due to any Lord from his Tenant, but to the King only; and this is either Grand or Petit: The first is, where one holds Land of the King by Service, which he ought to do in his own person. *Petit sergeanty* is, where a man holds Land of the King, to yield him yearly some small thing towards his Wars, of which read *Bracton*, *lib.* 2. *cap.* 16. & 37. & *Britton*, *cap.* 66. *num.* 1, 2. *Inter feodalia servitia summum est & illustrissimum, quod nec Patronum aliquem agnoscit præter Regum*, sayes the learned *Spelman*. And *Camden*, tit. *Suffolk*, speaks of *Baldwin le Pettour qui tenuit terras in Henningston in Com.* Suffolk *per* serjantiam, *pro qua debuit facere die natali Domini singulis annis coram Domino Rege Angliæ*, Saltum, Sufflum & Pettum, *alias unum* saltum, *unum* sufflatum, & *unum* bombulum. And Sir *Richard Rockesly* held Lands at *Seton* by *Sergeanty*, to be *Vautrarius Regis*, The King's Forefootman when he went into *Gascoigne Donec perusus fuit pari solutarum precii* 4*d.* until he had worn out a pair of Shooes of four pence price. This Service being to be performed when the King went to *Gascoigne* to make War is *Knights-service*, *Co.* on *Lit. fol.* 69. See the Stat. 12 *Car.* 2. *cap.* 24. whereby all Tenures, &c. are turned into free and common *Socage*; but the Honorary Services of *Grand Sergeanty* are therein excepted. See *Skene de verbor.* Signif.

Servage, *Anno* 1 R. 2. *cap.* 26. See *Service.*

Service, *Servitium*, Is that Service which the Tenant, by reason of his Fee, oweth unto his Lord. *Hotoman* thus defines it, *Servitium est munus obsequii clientelaris*, De verbis Feudal. It is sometime called *Servage*, as 1 R. 2. *cap.* 6. Our ancient Law-Books make many Divisions of it, as *Bract. lib.* 2. *cap.* 16. And *Britton*, cap. 66. into Personal and Real, also into Military and Base, and *Bracton*, *ubi supra*, num 7. into intrinsick and extrinsick, *servitium intrinsecum* is due to the Capital Lord of the Mannor: *Forinsecum* is that which is due to the King, and not to the Capital Lord. *Service* is also divided into *Frank* and *Base*, the one termed *liberum servitium*, the other *Villenagium*. It is also divided into continual or annual, and casual or accidental; the former is the seisin of Rent, the other seisin of Relief, *Co.* 4. *Rep. fol.* 9. *Bevill*'s Case. See *Copy-hold.* See *Socage*. *Thomas Leigh* Esq; at the Coronation of King *Charles* the Second, brought up to the King's Table a Messe of Potage called **Dillogrout**, which Service had been adjudged him by the Court of *Claims* in right of the Mannor of *Addington* in *Surrey*, whereupon the Lord High Chamberlain presented him to the King, who accepted the service, and afterwards Knighted him.

Servientibus, Are certain Writs touching Servants and their Masters, violating the Statutes made against their Abuses, which see in *Reg. Orig. fol.* 189, 190, 191.

Service secular, *Anno* 1 E. 4. *cap.* 1. Is Wordly *service*, contrary to Spiritual and Ecclesiastical.

Servitium ferrandi, The service of shooing Horses. See *Palfrey.*

Servitiis acquietandis, Is a Writ Judicial, that lies for one distrained for Services to *F*, who owes and performs to *R.* for the acquital of such services, *Reg. Judic. fol.* 27. & 36.

Servitors of Bills, Are such Servants or Messengers of the Marshal belonging to the King's Bench, as were sent abroad with *Bills* or Writs to summon Men to that Court; they are now more ordinarily called *Tipstaves*, *Anno* 2. *H.* 4. *cap.* 23.

Session of Parliament, The passing any Bills, by giving the *Royal Assent* thereto, doth not make a *Session*; but the *Session of Parliament* continues till it be prorogued or dissolved. See 4. *par. Inst. fol.* 27. *Sessio Parliamenti*, is the sitting of the Parliament.

Sessions, *Sessiones*, Is a sitting of Justices in Court upon Commission, as the *Sessions of Oyer and Terminer*, Pl. Cor. fol. 67. *Quarter-Sessions*, otherwise called the *General-Sessions*, 5 Eliz. 4. or *Open-Sessions*, ibid. Opposite, whereto are *especial*, otherwise called *Privy-Sessions*, which are procured upon some special occasion, for the more speedy dispatch of Justice in some, *Cromp. Just. of Peace*, fol. 110. What things be inquirable in *Sessions*, see *Ibid. fol.* 109. *Petit-Sessions* or *Statute-Sessions* are kept by the High Constable of every Hundred for the placing of Servants, 5 *Eliz.* 4. See *Statute-Sessions.*

Sesseur, 25 *E.* 3. 6. Seems to signifie the assessing or rating of Wages.

Sentuetum, A Land full of Brambles.

Set Clothes, Are mentioned in the Statute made *Anno* 27 *H.* 8. *cap.* 13. which see.

Setwell, *Valeriana*, Is a Medicinal Herb; the nature and divers kinds whereof you have in *Gerard*'s *Herbal*, lib. 2. cap. 424. The root of this is mentioned among Drugs to be garbled, 1 *Jac.* 19.

Severance, Is the singling or severing of Two, or more, that are joyned in one Writ: For example, If two joyn in a Writ *de libertate probanda*, and the one afterward be Non-suit, here *severance* is permitted; so that notwithstanding the Non-suit of the one, the other may severally proceed, *F. N. B. fol.* 78. and *Bro.* tit. *Severance and summons*, fol. 238. There is also *severance* of the Tenants in an Assise, when as one or two, or more Disseisors appear upon the Writ, and not the other, *New Book of Entries*, fol. 81. And *severance* in Attaints, *Ibid. fol.* 95. And *severance* in Debt, where two, or more, Executors are named Plaintiffs, and the one refuses to prosecute, *Ibid. fol.* 220. *Severance* of Corn, is the cutting and carrying it off from the Ground, and sometimes the setting out the Tythe from the rest of the Corn is called *Severance.* See *Cro. Rep.* 2 *par. fol.* 225. There is also *severance* in *Quare Impedit*, Co. Rep. 5. fol. 97.

Several tayle, *Tallium separatum*, Is that whereby Land is given and entayled *severally* to Two: For example, Land is given to two Men and their Wives, and to the Heirs of their Bodies begotten; the Donees have joynt Estate for their two Lives, and yet they have *several* Inheritance, because the Issue of the one shall have his moyety, and the Issue of the other the other moyety.

Several tenancy, *Tenura separalis*, Is a Plea or Exception taken to a Writ that is said against Two as joynt, which are several, *Broke*, tit. *Several tenancy*, fol. 273.

Sevantly woven, That is, well and honestly *woven*, *Anno* 35 *Eliz. cap.* 10.

Sewer, *Severa & sewera, Est fossa in locis Palustribus ducta ad aquas ejiciendas, &c.* A Passage or Gutter to carry water into the Sea or a River, 6 *H.*6. *cap.* 5. and 12 *Car.* 2. *cap.* 6. And *Commissioners of Sewers* are such as, by Authority under the Great Seal, see Drayns and Ditches well kept and maintained in marishy and fenny Countries, for the better conveyance of the Water into the Sea, and preserving Grass upon the Land for the feeding of Cattel. See the Statutes 15 *Car.*2. *cap.* 17. and 17 *Car.* 2. *cap.* 11. touching the drayning the great Level in the Fens called *Bedford Levell*, and the Authority of the Governor, Bayliff, &c. as *Commissioners of Sewers.*

Sexagesima. See *Septuagesima.*

Sextary, *Sextarius*, Was an ancient Measure, containing about our Pint and a half (according to our Latine *Dictionary*). The Town of *Leicester* paid among other things to the King yearly twenty five Measures called *Sextaries of Honey*, as we read in *Doomsday*. And in *Clauf.* 4 *E.* 3. *m.* 26. We find *Tresdecem* sextarios *vini.---Et unum* sextarium *salis apud Wainflete*, Mon. Ang. 2. par. fol. 849. *A sextary of Ale* contained sixteen *Lagenas*. See *Tolcester*.

Shacke, Is a Custom in *Norfolk* to have Common for Hogs from the end of Harvest till Seed-time, in all Mens Grounds without contradiction, *Co.* 7. *Rep. fol.* 5. *Corbet*'s Case: And in that County, *To go at shacke*, is as much as to go at large.

Shanke. See *Furre.*

Shares. See *Flotzon.*

Sharping Corn, Is a customary Gift of *Corn*, which, at every *Christmas*, the Farmers in some parts of *England* give to their Smith, for *sharpning* their Plough-Irons, Harrow-tines, and such like, and exceeds not half a Bushel for a Plough-Land.

Sherbet, Is a compound Drink, late brought into *England* from *Turkie* and *Persia*, and is made of juyce of Lemons, Sugar, and other Ingredients, &c. *Sherbet* in the *Persian*-Tongue signifies Pleasant Liquor, 15 *Car.* 3. *cap.* 11.

Shermans craft, Is an Art used at *Norwich*; the Artificers whereof do *sheere* as well *Worsteads*, *Stamins*, and *Fustians*, as all other woollen-Cloth. It is mentioned *Anno* 19 *H.* 7. *cap.* 17.

Shewing, Is to be quit of Attachments in any Court, and before whomsoever in Plaints shewed, and not avowed. See *Scavage.*

Shilling, (In Saxon ſcilling) among our English *Saxons* consisted but of five pence, *Si in capillis sit vulnus longitudinis unius unciæ* V. *denariis* i. *uno solido componatur*, Leg. H. 1. cap. 39.

Ship-money, Was an ancient Imposition that had lien Dormant many years, and was charged upon the Ports, Towns, Cities, Boroughs and Counties of this Realm; which was revived by King *Charles* the first in 1635. and 1636. and by Stat. 17 *Car.* 1. *cap.* 14. was declared to be contrary to the Laws and Statutes of this Realm, &c.

Shipper, Is a Dutch word signifying the Master of a *Ship*, *Anno* 1 *Jac. Sess.* 1. *cap.* 33. We commonly say *Skipper*, and use it for any common Seaman.

Shire, *Comitatus*, Derived from the Saxon *Scyran*, i. *partiri*, is well known to be a portion of Land called a *County*; Who first divided this Land into *Shires*, see in *Camden*'s *Brit.* pag. 102. Of which there are in *England* forty, and in *Wales* twelve, in all fifty two. *In Privilegiorum chartis* (says *Spelman*) *ubi conceditur* quietum esse à shiris, *intelligendum est de immunitate, qua quis eximitur à secta vel clientela curiis Vice-comitum* (*quas etiam* shiras *vocant*) *præstanda vel perficienda.* The Assises of the *Shire* was by the *Saxons* of old called *Scire-gemot.*

Shireve, Or as vulgarly Sheriff, *Vicecomes*, is the chief Officer of the King in his Shire or County. *Camden* in his *Brit. pag.* 104. describes his Office in this manner,

Singulis verò annis, nobilis aliquis ex incolis præficitur, quem Vicecomitem, quasi vicarium Comitis, & nostra Lingua **Shyreve**, i. *Comitatus præpositum vocamus; qui etiam Comitatus vel Provinciæ Quæstor rectè dici potest: Ejus enim est publicas provinciæ suæ pecunias conquirere, mulctas irrogatas, vel pignoribus ablatis colligere & ærario inferre, Judicibus præsto adesse & eorum mandata exequi, duodecem viros cogere qui in causis de facto cognoscunt & ad Judices referunt (Judices enim apud nos juris solum, non facti sunt Judices) condemnatos ad supplicium ducere, & in minoribus litibus cognoscere, in majoribus autem Jus dicunt Justiciarii, quos itinerantes ad assisas vocant, qui quotannis hos comitatus, bis adeunt, ut de causis cognoscant*

cant & carceratis sententiam ferant: Henricus *Secundus* hos itinerantes *instituit, vel potius* restituit. *Ille (ut inquit Mat. Par.) consilio filii sui & episcoporum constituit Justitiarios, per sex partes Regni, in qualibet parte tres, qui jurarent quod cuilibet jus suum conservarent illæsum.*

Of the Antiquity and Authority of this Officer, read *Co. Rep. lib.* 4. *Mitton's* Case, and *Spelman's Glossary*, verb. *Vicecomes*. The Sheriff was heretofore chosen in the County Court by the Suffrages of the People, as Knights of the *Shire* for Parliament yet are, but now he is nominated by the King. See *Fortescue*, *cap.* 24. *fol.* 53. *Et dicitur* Vicecomes *quod* vicem Comitis *supplet*, &c. *Niger lib. Scaccar.* The form of his Oath, see in *Reg. Orig. fol.* 331. Of this read also *Skene de verb.* Signif. *voce Shyreve*, where he at large describes of the Sheriff in *Scotland*, in a Discourse worth the reading.

Shiriff-tooth,—*Per* shirif-tooth, *Johannes Stanley Ar. clamat habere de quolibet tenente infra feodum de* Aldford *unum denarium & quadrantem per annum, exceptis Dominicis terris propriis & terra in feodo & Manerio prædicto Maner. & Hundred. de Macclesfield*, Rot. Plac. in Itin. apud Cestriam, 14 H. 7.

Shireeve of Winchester and Essex, Is the extent of a Sheriffs Authority, 21 *R.* 2. *cap.* 10, 11. Sheriffwicks, 13 *Eliz. cap.* 22.

Sheriffalty, The time of a mans being *Sheriff*, 14 *Car.* 2. *cap.* 21.

Shire-clerke, Seems to be the Under-sheriff, *Anno* 11 *H.* 7. *cap.* 15. It is sometimes taken for a Clerk in the County Court, that is Deputy to the Under-sheriff. See *Co.* 4. *Rep. Mitton's* Case.

Shire-mote. Se *Shire* and *Turn*.

Shop, *Shopa, Omnibus,&c.* Johannes Horseret *de* Hereford *Bochour salutem*; *Noveritis me præfatum* Johannem *dedisse*, *&c.* Rogero Smith *de* Bromeyard, *unam* shopam *cum pertin. suis in* Bromeyard *prædict. scituat. in le Market place ibidem*, *&c.* Dat. 27. Feb. 9 Ed. 4. See *Selda*.

Shorling and **Morling,** Seem to be words to distinguish Fells of Sheep; *shorling* signifying the Fells after the Fleeces are shorn off, and *Morling* alias *Mortling*, the Fells flead off after they be killed, or die alone, 3 *E.* 4. *cap.* 1. 4 *E.* 4. 3. 12 *E.* 4. 5. and 14 *E.* 4. 3. See *Mortling* and *Morling*.

Shot, From the Saxon *Sceat*, signifying *Pecuniam aut Vectigal*. See *Lambart's Explication of Saxon words*, verb. *Primitia*. It is still used among Alehouse-Keepers and Vinters; as to pay the *shot*, is to pay the Money due for the reckoning.

Sich, *Sichetum & Sikettus*, A little currant of Water that uses to be dry in the Summer, *Inter duos* sikettos, &c. *Mon. Ang.* 2. *par. fol.* 426. Also a Water-furrow or Gutter.

Sicut alias, Is a second Writ sent out, where the first was not executed, *Co. lib.* 4. *fol.* 85. It takes name from those words in it. As for example, *Carolus Secundus Dei Gratia*, *&c. Vicecom. Midd. salutem. Præcipimus tibi* (sicut alias *præcepimus*) *quod non omittas*, *&c.* and so as in the *Capias*. *Lambert* in his *Tract of Processes*, in the end of his *Eirenarcha*.

Sidemen alias **Questmen,** Be those that are yearly chosen, according to the Custom of every Parish, to assist the Church-wardens in the inquiry and presenting such Offendors to the Ordinary, as are punishable in the *Court-Christian*.

Sigillum,—*Notum sit omnibus Christianis quod ego* Johannes *de* Gresley *non habui potestatem* sigilli mei, *per unum annum integrum ultimò præteritum*, *jam notifico*, *&c. quod scripto* sigillo meo *contradico*, *&c. In cujus rei testimonium* sigillum *Deconatus de* Repingdon *apposui*, *&c. Dat. apud Drakelew*, 18 Ric. 2. See *Seal* and *Tabellion*.

Significavit, Is a Writ *de Excommunicato capiendo*, which issueth out of the *Chancery* upon a Certificate given by the Ordinary, of a man that stands obstinately Excommunicate, by the space of forty days, for the laying him up in Prison without Bayl or Mainprise, until he submit himself to the Authority of the Church. And it is so called, because the word *Significavit* is an Emphatical word in the Writ; there is also another Writ in the *Register*, fol. 7. directed to the Justices of the Bench, commanding them to stay any Suit depending between such and such, by reason of any Excommunication alledged against the Plaintiff, because the Sentence of the Ordinary that did Excommunicate him, is appealed from, and the Appeal yet depends undecided. See *F. N. B. De excommunicato capiendo*, fol. 62. 66. where you may find Writs of this Name in other Cases.

Signet, Is one of the King's Seals, wherewith his private Letters are sealed, and is alwayes in the custody of the King's Secretaries: And there are four Clerks of the *Signet-Office* alwayes attending, 2. *Inst. fol.* 556.

Silk thrower and **Throwster,** *Anno* 14 *Car.* 2. *cap.* 15. Is a Trade or Mystery that winds, twists and spins, or *throws* Silk, so fitting it for use, who are incorporated by the said Act; wherein there is mention also of *Silkwinders and Doublers*, which are members of the same Trade. See 20 *Car.* 2. *cap.* 6.

Silva cedua. See *Sylua cædua*.

Simnell, *Siminellus*, From the Latine *simila*, which signifies the finest part of the flower; *Panis similageneus*, Simnel-Bread. It is mentioned *Assisa panis* (and is still in use specially in *Lent*) **Bread made into** a Simnel *shall weigh two shillings less than Wastell-bread*, Stat. 51 H. 3. See *Cocket*.

Simony, *Simonia*, *Venditio rei sacræ*, so called from *Simon Magus*: It was agreed by all the Justices, *Trin.* 8. *Jac.* That if the Patron present any person to a Benefice with Cure, for Money, that such Presentation, &c. is void, though the Presentee were not privy to it, and the Statute gives the Presentation to the King, *Co.* 12. *Rep. fol.* 74. *Simony* may be by compact between Strangers, without the privity of the Incumbent or Patron, *Cro.* 1. *par. fol.* 331. *Bawderoke's* Case, *Hob. Rep. fol.* 165. *Noy's Rep. fol.* 22. *Pascall's* Case, and 3. *Inst. fol.* 153.

Simpler,—*Carta simplex*, A Deed-Poll or single Deed.

Sine assensu capitali, Is a Writ that lies where a Dean, Bishop, Prebendary, Abbot, Prior or Master of an Hospital, alien the Land holden in the right of his House, *without the consent of the Chapter, Covent or Fraternity*; In which Case his Successor shall have this Writ, *F. N. B. fol.* 195.

Sine die, Without day: When Judgment is given against the Plaintiff, he is said to be *in misericordia pro falso clnmore suo*; But when for the Defendant, then 'tis said, *Eat inde sine die.*

Si non omnes, Is a Writ of Association, whereby, if all in Commission cannot meet at the day assigned, it is allowed, That two, or more, of them may finish the business. See *Association*, and *F. N. B. fol.* 185. & 111. and *Reg. Orig. fol.* 202. 206, *&c.*

Si Recognoscant, Is a Writ that lies for a Creditor against his Debtor, for Money numbred, that hath before the Sheriff in the *County Court* acknowledged himself to owe his Creditor such a sum, received of him *in pecuniis numeratis.* The form of which Writ is this,---*Rex Vicecomiti salutem Praec. tibi quod si* A. *recognoscat se debere* R. 40. *solid. sine ulteriori dilatione, tunc ipsum distringas ad praedictum debitum eidem* R. *sine dilatione reddendum. Teste, &c.* Old Nat. Brev. fol. 68.

Site or **Scite**, *Situs*, The standing of any Place, the scituation of a Capital House or Messuage, a Territory, or part of a Country, as *the site* of the late dissolved Monastery of, &c. i. the place where it stood: The word is mentioned in the Statute 32 *Hen.* 8. *cap.* 20. and 22 *Car.* 2. *cap.* 11. and is there written *Scite*,---*Dedi situm loci in quo domus sua sita est*, Mon. Ang. 2. par. fol. 278.

Sithcundman, A Saxon word, *Et custos Paganus interpretatur*, Lamb. Explic. verb. pag. 5. And was such a one as had the Office to lead the Men of a Town or Parish: *E classe nobilium erat*, saith *Somner.*

Skaw, Is a word mentioned in the Statute made 4 *E.* 4. *cap.* 1.

Skybinage, Is a proper Name, signifying the Precincts of *Caleys*, 27 *H.* 6. *cap.* 2.

Sluse, *Exclusa*, Is a frame to keep or let water out of a Ground.

Smalt, Is that which Painters make blue Colour, *Anno* 21 *Jac. cap.* 3. and *Pat.* 16. *Feb.* 16 *Jac.* in Italian *Smalto.*

Smoke-silver, *Tenementum Newstede cum pertin. &c. in villa de* Staplehirst *in Com. Cant. tenetur de Manerio de* Eastgreenwich *per fidelitatem tantum in libro socagio*, Per Pat. Dat. 3. Feb. 4. Ed. 6. *And by the payment of* **Smoke-silver** *to the Sheriff yearly the sum of Six pence.* Notes for Lord *Wooton*'s Office, 1628. There is *Smoke-silver* and Smoke-peny paid to the Ministers of divers Parishes, and though to be paid in lieu of Tythe-wood; or it may, as in many places at this day, be a continued payment of the *Romescot* or *Peterpence.* See *Chimney-money.*

Soc, *Soca*, According to *Minshew*, is a word signifying a power or liberty of Jurisdiction; whence our Law-Latine word *Soca*, for a Seigniory enfranchised by the King, with liberty of holding a Court of his *Sockmen* or *Socagers*, i. his Tenants, whose Tenure is hence called *Socage. Skene de verbor.* Interp. sayes, *Soc* is called *Secta de hominibus suis, in curia, secundum consuetudinem Regni.* See more there: And *Bracton*, *lib.* 3. *tract.* 2. *cap.* 8. mentions divers Liberties, as *Soc and Sac, Toll and Thean, Infangthef & Utfangthef, & isti qui habent talem libertatem, possunt judicare in curia sua eum qui inventus fuerit infra libertatem suam, seisitus de aliquo latrocinio manifesto.* The same interpretation *Lambard* gives it in his translation of the *Saxon Laws*: For among the rest in those of King *Ina* (*Leg.* 24.) Be Cyric socnum, is rendred *De immunitate fani*; And in the Laws of *Henry* the First, It is said, *Nullus socnam habet impune peccandi*, that is, none hath liberty of sinning without punishment. And in the same sense it is used in *Doomsday*, for in *Essex*, under the Title of *Terra Rogeri Bigoti* it is thus recorded, *Westunam tenet* Hugo de Hosdene *quod tenuerunt* iv. *liberi homines* T. R. E. *qui fuerant de* soca *Algari, &c.*

Socage or **Soccage**, *Socagium*, May be derived from the French *Soc*, that is, *Vomer* a Coulter or Plowshare, and is a Tenure of Lands by or for certain inferior Services of Husbandry to be performed to the Lord of the Fee. See *Institutes of the Common-Law*, 31. *Bracton*, *lib.* 2. *cap.* 35. *num.* 1. describes it thus, *Dici poterit* socagium *a* socco *& inde tenentes qui tenent in* soccagio socmanni *dici poterunt, eo quod deputati sunt, ut videtur, tantummodo ad culturam & quorum custodia & maritagia ad propinquiores parentes jure sanguinis pertinebit. Et si aliquando inde facto capiatur homagium, quod plures contingit, non tamen habebit propter hoc Dominus capitalis custodiam & maritag. Quia non semper sequitur homagium, licet aliquando sequatur. Skene de verbor.* Signif. says, *Socage* is a Tenure of Lands, when a Man is infeoffed freely, without any Service, Ward, Relief or Marriage, and pays to his Lord such Duty as is called *Petit Sergeanty, &c.* There is *free socage* and *base socage*, otherwise call'd *Villenage.*----And, according to *Bracton, Socagium liberum est, ubi fit servitium in denariis Dominis capitalibus, & nihil inde omnino datur ad scutum & servitium Regis.* This *free socage* is also called *Common socage*, Anno 37 H. 8. cap. 20. Other Divisions there are in our Books, *viz. Bract. lib.* 2. *cap.* 8. *num.* 3. *Old Nat. Brev. fol.* 94. and others. But by the Statute 12 *Car.* 2. *cap.* 24. All Tenures shall be adjudged and taken to be turned into *free* and *common socage.*

Socmans alias **Sokemans**, *Socmanni*, Are such Tenants as hold their Lands and Tenements by *socage* tenure, of which there are several kinds, *viz. Sokeman*'s of Frank-tenure, *Kitchin*, fol. 81. *Sokeman*'s of Base-tenure, *Ibid.* and *Sokemans* of ancient Demesne, which last seem most properly to be called *Socmans*, *F. N. B. fol.* 14. *Britton*, cap. 66. num. 2. The word *Sokeman* is found in the Statute of Wards and Relief, 28 *E.* 1.

Socna, In Saxon *Socne*, a Priviledge, or Liberty, and Franchise,-----*Volo, ut ipsi sint eorum* sacae & socnae; Theolonii *etiam &* Teami (*privilegiorum, scilicet & jurium sic appellatorum*) *digni infra tempus & extra tempus*, &c. Charta Canuti Regis in Hist. Eccles. Catch. S. Pauli, fol. 189. See *Soc.*

Socome, Signifies a Custom of grinding at the Lord's Mill: And there is *Bond-socome*, where the Tenants are bound to it, and *Love-socome*, where they do it freely out of *love* to their Lord.

Soke, *Anno* 32 H. 8. cap. 15. & cap. 28. *Significat libertatem Curiæ tenentium quam* socam *appellamus*, Fleta, lib. 1. cap. 47. sect. *Soke. Per* **Soke** Will. Stanley *in Manerio suo de* Knottsford *clamat cognitionem placitorum debiti, transgressionis, conventionis & detentionis infra summam* 40. *sol.* Pl. Itin. apud Cestr. 14 H. 7. **Soke**, id est, *over fraunch Court de ses homes* M.S. See *Soc*.

Soken, *Soca*. See *Soc and Hamsoken*.

Soke-reeve, Seems to be the Lord's Rent-gatherer in the *soke* or soken, *Fleta lib.* 2. *cap.* 55.

Solda, It seems to be the same with *selda*, a Shop or Shed.

Sole-Tenant, *Solus tenens*, Is he or she that holds only in his or her own right, without any other joyned: For example, If a Man and Wife hold Land for their Lives, the Remainder to their Son; Here the Man dying, the Lord shall not have Heriot, because he dyeth not *sole Tenant*. See *Kitchin, fol.* 134.

Sollicitor, *Sollicitator*, Is a man imploy'd to take care of, and follow Suits depending in Courts of Law or Equity; formerly allowed only to Nobility, whose menial Servants they were, but now too frequently used by others, to the Damage of the People, and the increase of Champerty and Maintenance.

Solet & debet. See *Debet & solet*.

Solidata terræ. See farding-deal of Land. *Solidata* also signifies the pay or stipend of a Souldier, *Et qui terram non habent & arma habere possunt, illuc veniant ad capiendum* solidatas *nostras*. Breve Regis Johannis Vicecomitibus Angliæ, Anno 1213.

Solinus terræ, In some places of *Doomsday* Book is said to contain two Plow-Lands, and sometimes less than half a one; for there it is said *Septem* solini terræ *sunt* 17. *Carucat.*

Soller or **Solar**, *Solarium*, A Chamber or Upper-Room; *Dedi--unam shoppam cum* solario *super-ædificato*, Ex Vet. Carta.

Solutione feodi militis Parliamenti, and **solutione feodi Burgens Parliamenti**, Are Writs whereby Knights of the Shire and Burgesses may recover their allowance, if it be denied, *Anno* 35 *Hen.* 8. *cap.* 11.

Solvendo esse, Is a term of Art, signifying that a man hath wherewith to pay, or as we say, is a person *solvent*.

Sommons alias **Summons**, *Summonitio*, Signifies in our Common Law as much as *Vocatio in jus*, or *Citatio* among the *Civilians*: And thence is our word *Somner*, which in French is (*Semoneur*, i. *vocator*, *Monitor*. The *Custumary* of *Normandy* for our *Summons* hath *Semonse*, cap. 61. *Summons* of the Exchequer, 3 *E.* 1. 19. 10 *E.* 1. 9. How *Summons* is divided, and what circumstances it hath to be observed. See *Fleta, lib.* 6. *cap.* 6, 7.

Sontage, Was according to *Stow*, *pag.* 284. A Tax of forty shillings laid upon every Knights Fee: In some places the word is used for course Cloth, as bagging or Hops, or the like. See *Systema Agriculturæ*.

Sorcery, *Sortilegium*, Divination by Lots, which is Felony by 1 *Jac. cap.* 12. Sortilegus, *quia utitur sortibus in cantationibus Dæmonis*, 3. Inst. fol. 44. *Sorcery & devinal sont Members de Heresy.* Mirror. cap. 1. sect. 5. *Sortilegi sunt divinatores, vel isti qui sub nomine fictæ Religionis per quasdam, quas Sanctorum vel Apostolorum vocant sortes vel divinationes, sententiam vel scientiam profitentur; sive divinatione, aut quarumcunq; scripturarum inspectione futura promittunt*, Vocab. utriusq; juris.

Sorting Kersies, 3 *Jac. cap.* 16. A sort of Cloth so called.

Sothale, Mistaken without doubt for *Scotale*, yet in *Bracton, lib.* 3. *tract.* 1. *cap.* 1. it is written *Sothaile*, and he says, It is so called *Fictale*, and was a kind of Entertainment made by Bayliffs to those of their Hundred for gain, which the same *Bracton* says was taken away in the Reign of *Henry* the Third. See *Scotale*.

South Viscount, *Sub Vicecomes*, Is the Under Sheriff, *Cromp. Jur. fol.* 5.

Sowne, Is a word corrupted from the French *Souvenu*, i. remembred; for the Stat. 4 *Hen.* 5. *cap.* 7. In the Original French hath *Des estreats nient souvenu*, and such Estreats and Casualties as are not to be remembred, run not in demand, that is, are not leviable: It is a word of Art used in the *Exchequer*, where *Estreats that sowne not*, are such as the Sheriff by his industry cannot get, and *Estreats that sowne* are such as he may gather, 4. *Par. Inst. fol.* 107.

Speaker of the Parliament, Is an Officer in that High Court, who is, as it were, the common mouth of the rest: And as that Honourable Assembly consists of two Houses, so there are two *Speakers*, the one termed the *Lord Speaker of the House of Peers*, and is most commonly the *Lord Chancellor*, or *Lord Keeper of the Great Seal of* England. The other (being a Member of the House of Commons) is called *The Speaker of the House of Commons*; both whose Duties you have particularly described in a Book entituled, *The Order and Usage of keeping the Parliament*. See *Parliament*.

Special matter in evidence. See *General Issue*, and *Bro.* tit. *General Issue and special Evidence*.

Specialitas, A Specialty is taken for a Bond, Bill, or such like Instrument. But it hath heretofore been taken for particular acquaintance, as appears Inter Pl. coram Rege apud Ebor. Mich. 1 E. 3. Rot. 123. *Presentatum fuit per Juratores——quod quidam* Johannes de Pratis *habuit quandam uxorem amicabilem de cujus* specialitate, Willielmus *filius* Henrici Molendinarii *& similiter quidam alii malefactores fuerunt; ita quod prædicti malefactores venerunt ad lectum ipsius* Johannis *ubi jacebat & ipsum traxerunt ab eadem & ipsum abinde duxerunt & tenuerunt dum prædictus* Willielmus *concubuit cum ea.*

Spinster, It is the addition usually given to all unmarried Women, from the Viscounts Daughter downward: Yet Sir *Edward Coke* says,

Generosa is a good addition for a Gentlewoman, and that if they be named *Spinster* in any Original Writ, Appeal or Inditement, they may abate and quash the same, 2. *Inst. fol.* 668.---Pollard *Miles & Judic. habuit* 11. *filios gladiis cinctos in tumulo suo & totidem filias fusis depictas. Spelman* in his *Aspilogia* sayes, ----*Antiquis temporibus ipsæ Reginæ fusis usæ sunt, unde hodie omnes fœminæ* Spinsters *dictæ sunt.*

Spiritualities of a Bishop, *Spiritualia Episcopi*, Are those Profits which he receives as a Bishop, not as a Baron of the Parliament, *Stamf. Pl. Cor. fol.* 132. Such are the Duties of his Visitation, his benefit growing from ordaining and instituting Priests, Prestation Money, that is, *subsidium charitativum*, which upon reasonable cause he may require of his Clergy, *Johannes Gregor. de Benefic.* cap. 6. num. 9. and the benefit of his Jurisdiction, *Joachimus Stephanus de Jurisd. lib.*4. *cap.* 14. *num.* 14.

Spikenard, *Spica Nardi, vel Nardus*, Is a medicinal Herb, whereof read *Gerard's Herbal*, lib. 2. cap. 415. The Fruit or Ear of this (for it brings forth an Ear like *Lavender*) is a Drug garbleable, by 1 *Jac. cap.* 19.

Spittle-house, Mentioned in the Act for Subsidies, 15 *Car.* 2. *cap.* 9. Is a corruption from Hospital, and signifies the same thing; or it may be taken from the *Teutonick* **Spital**, which denotes an Hospital or Almes-house.

Spoliation, *Spoliatio*, Is a Writ that lies for one Incumbent against another, in any case where the right of the Patronage cometh not in debate: As if a Parson be made a Bishop, and hath dispensation to keep his Rectory, and afterward the Patron present another to the Church, which is instituted and inducted. The Bishop shall have against this Incumbent a Writ of *spoliation* in *Court-Christian*, *F. N.B. fol.* 36. See *Benevolence*, and *Termes de la Ley*, hoc verbo.

Spullars of Yarn, Are Tyers of Yarn, to see if it be well spun, and fit for the Loom, *Anno* 1 *Mar. Parl.* 1. *cap.* 7.

Squilley, *Anno* 43 *Eliz. cap.* 10. See *Rewey*. It is a note of faultiness in the making of Cloth.

Squires. See *Esquires*.

Stablestand, Is one of the four Evidences or Presumptions whereby a man is convicted, to intend the stealing the King's Deer in the Forrest, *Manwood*, *part* 2. *cap.* 18. *num.* 9. The other three are **Dog-draw**, **Back-bear**, and **Bloody-hand.** This **Stablestand** is, when a man is found *in stabili statione*, at his *standing* in the Forest with a Cross-bow or Long-bow bent, ready to shoot at any Deer, or else *standing* close by a Tree with Greyhounds in a Leash, ready to slip.

Stagnarium, *Vel potius* Stannarium, a Tin-Mine, *Rex, &c. Concessimus Dominæ Reginæ matri nostræ cuneum &* stagnarium *Devon. ad se sustinendum*, Pat. Anno 1 Hen. 3.

Stagnes, *Stagna*, Ponds, Pools, or standing-waters, mentioned 5 *Eliz. cap.* 21.

Stadium, Is in *Doomsday Book* accounted for a furlong of Land, which is the eighth part of a Mile.

Stall-boat, A kind of Fishers *Boat*, *Anno* 27 *Eliz. cap.* 21.

Stalkers, A kind of fishing Nets, mentioned 13 *Rich.* 2. *stat.* 1. *cap.* 20. & 17 *Rich.* 2. *cap.* 9.

Stallage, *Stallagium*, May be derived from the Saxon *Stal.* i. *statio*; or the French *Estaller*, i. *merces exponere*: It signifies Money paid for pitching of stalls in Fairs or Markets, or the right of doing it. See *Scavage*. This in *Scotland* is call'd *Stallenge*, according to *Skene de verbor*. Interpret. *verb.* Stallangiatores. Among the *Romans* it was termed *Siliquaticum*, *a siliqua primo & minimo omnium pondere apud illam nationem.*

Standard. See *Estandard*.

Standell, Is a young store Oak-Tree, which may in time make Timber, twelve such are to be left standing in every Acre of Wood at the felling thereof, 35 *H.* 8. 17. and 13 *Eliz. cap.* 25.

Stannaries, *Stannaria*, Comes from the Latine *stannum*; Tinne, and signifies the Mines and Works where this Metal is digged and purified; as in *Cornwall*, and other places: Of this read *Cambd. Brit. pag.* 119. The liberties of the *stannary-men* granted by *Edward* the First, before they were abridged by the Statute 50 *E.* 3. See in *Plowden's* Case *Of Mines*, fol. 327. and *Co.* 12. *Rep. fol.* 9. And further, for the Liberties of the *Stannary-Courts*, see 17 *Car.* 1. *cap.* 15.

Staple, *Stapellum*, Signifies this or that Town or City, whither the Merchants of *England* were, by Act of Parliament, to carry their Wooll, Cloth, Lead and Tinne, and such like *staple* Commodities of this Land, for the utterance of them by the great. The word may either be derived from the Saxon *Staple*, which signifies the stay or hold of any thing, according to *Lambart* in his *Duties of Constables*, num. 4. because the place is certain and setled; or else from the French *Estape*, i. *forum vinarium*, a Market or *Staple* for Wines; the chief Commodity of *France*. And accordingly in a French Book we find it written, ---*A Calais y avoit* Estape *de la laine*, &c. which is as much as to say, as the *staple* for Wools. You may read of many places appointed for this *staple* in our Statutes, according as the King thought fit to alter them, from the second year of *Edward* the Third, to the Fifth of *Edward* the Sixth, *cap.* 7. What Officers the *staples* had belonging unto them, you may see in *Anno* 27 *E.* 3. *stat.* 3. *cap.* 21. The *staple* Commodities of this Realm, are Wooll, Leather, Woollfells, Lead, Tin, Butter, Cheese, Cloth, &c. as appears by the Statute 14 *Rich.* 2. *cap.* 1. though some allow only the five first, see 4. *Inst. fol.* 238.

Star-Chamber, *Camera stellata*, otherwise called *Chamber des estoyells*, was a *Chamber* at *Westminster* so called (as Sir *Tho. Smith de Rep. Anglor.* lib. 2. cap. 4. conjectures,) because at first the ceiling thereof was adorned with Images of gilded *stars*. And in the 25 of *Hen.* 8. *cap.* 1. It is written the *starred Chamber*. *Henry* the Seventh and *Henry* the Eighth ordained by two several Statutes, *viz.* 3 *Hen.* 7. *cap.* 1. and 21 *Hen.* 8. *cap.* 2. That the Chancellor assisted by others there named, should have Power to punish *Routs*, *Riots*, *Forgeries*, *Maintenances*, *Embraceries*, *Perjuries*, and such other *Misdemeanors* as were not sufficiently

sufficiently provided for by the Common Law, and for which the inferior Judges are not so proper to give Correction: And because that place was before set apart to the like Service, it was still used accordingly. Touching the Officers belonging to this Court, see *Cambd. pag.* 112, 113. But by the Statute 17 *Car.* 1. *cap.* 10. this Court commonly call'd *The Star-Chamber*, & all Jurisdiction, Power and Authority thereto belonging, are from and after the first of *August*, 1641. clearly and absolutely dissolved and determined, and so continues dissolved and determined to this day.

Starling. See *Sterling*.

Statute, *Statutum*, Has divers significations; as first, it signifies an Act of Parliament made by the King and the three Estates of the Realm, in which sense it is either general or special, *Co. lib.* 4. *Holland*'s Case, *fol.* 76. *Statute* in another signification, is a short writing called a *Statute-Merchant*, or a *Statute Staple*, which are in nature of Bonds, *Anno* 5 *H.* 4. *cap.* 12. and are called *Statutes*, because made according to the forms expresly provided by *Statutes*, which direct both before what persons, and in what manner they ought to be made. *West Symb. part* 1 *lib.* 2. *sect.* 151. where he defines a *Statute Merchant* thus, A *Statute Merchant* is a Bond acknowledged before one of the Clerks of the *Statutes* Merchant and Mayor, or chief Warden of the City of *London*, or two Merchants of the said City for that purpose assigned, or before the Mayor, chief Warden, or Master of other Cities or good Towns, or other sufficient men for that purpose appointed, sealed with the Seal of the Debtor and of the King, which is of two pieces; the greater is kept by the Mayor, chief Warden, &c. and the lesser piece thereof by the said Clerks: The form of which you may see in *Fleta*, lib. 2. *cap.* 64. sect. 2. thus, *Noverint universi me* N. *de tali Comitatu teneri* P. *in quadraginta marcis solvendis eidem ad festum Pasch. Anno Regni Regis*, *&c.* *&* *nisi fecero, concedo quod currant super me & hæredes meos districtio & pœna provisa in* statuto *Domini Regis Edito apud Westm. Dat.* London. *tali die Anno supradicto*. The Fee for the Seal is, for *Statutes* acknowledged in Fairs for every pound a half-peny, and out of Fairs a farthing. The execution upon *Statute-Merchant* is, first to take the Body of the Debtor, if he be Lay, and can be found, if otherwise upon his Lands and Goods, and is founded on the Statute made 13 *E.* 1. *stat.* 4. See the *New Book of Entries*, verb. *Statute-Merchant*.

Statute-Staple is so called either properly or improperly. A *Statute Staple* properly so called is a Bond of Record, acknowledged before the Mayor of the *Staple*, in the presence of one of the two Constables of the same *Staple*, for which Seal the Fee is of every pound, if the sum exceed not 100 *li.* an half-peny, and if it exceed 100 *li.* a farthing; and by vertue of such *Statute-Staple*, the Creditor may forthwith have execution of the Body, Lands and Goods of the Debtor: And this is founded upon the Statute 27 *E.* 3. *cap.* 9. A *Statute Staple* improper is a Bond of Record, founded upon the Statute 23 *H.* 8. *cap.* 6. Of the nature of a proper *Statute-Staple* as to the force and execution of it, and acknowledged before one of the chief Justices, and in their absence, before the Mayor of the *Staple* and Recorder of *London*. The forms of all these Bonds or Statutes, see in *West Symbol. part* 1. *lib.* 2. *sect.* 152, 153, 154, 155.

Statutes are also vulgarly taken for the *Petit-Sessions*, which are yearly kept for the disposing of Servants in Service, by 5 *Eliz. cap.* 4. See *Recognisance* and these *Statute Sessions*, otherwise called *Petit-Sessions*, are a meeting in every Hundred of all the Shires in *England*, where by Custom they have been used, whereto the Constables and others, both Housholders and Servants repair, for the debating of Difference between Masters and Servants, the rating of Servants Wages, and bestowing such people in Service as being fit to serve, either refuse to seek, or get Masters, *Anno* 1 *Eliz. cap.* 4.

Statuto Stapulæ, Is a Writ that lies to take his Body to Prison, and seize upon his Lands and Goods, that hath forfeited a Bond called *Statute Staple*, *Reg. Orig. fol.* 151.

Statutum de Laborariis, Is a Writ Judicial, for the apprehending of such *Laborers* as refuse to work according to the Statute, *Reg. Judic. fol.* 27.

Statuto Mercatorio, Is a Writ for the imprisoning of him that has forfeited a Bond called *Statute-Merchant*, until the Debt be satisfied, *Regist. Orig. fol.* 146. And of these there is one against Lay-persons, and another against Ecclesiastical, *Ibid. &* 148.

Staves-aker, *Staphys agria vel herba Pedicularis*, Is a medicinal Herb; the kinds and vertues whereof you have in *Gerard's Herbal*, lib. 1. cap. 130. The seed of this is mentioned among Drugs to be garbled, *Anno* 1 *Jac. cap.* 19.

Stemnifreoch, ----*Necnon libertate multuræ suæ in molendino ipsius* Roberti, *&c. quod sint* **temnefreoch** and **Tholfreoch**, *Mon. Ang.* 2. *par. fol.* 293.

Stennery, Is used for the same with Stannaries in the Statute 4 *H.* 8. *cap.* 8. See *Stannaries*.

Sterbrech alias **Strebrech**, Is the breaking, obstructing, or making less of a way, *Siquis viam frangat, concludendo, avertendo vel fodiendo*: It may be derived from the old English word **Stre**, i. *Via*, and **Brech**, i. *Fractio*; Hence probably to go *astray*, or as now we write *astray*, that is, to go out of the way.

Stanlaw, A stony Hill, *Doomsday*.

Stealing, Is the fraudulent taking away of another mans Goods, with an intent to *steal* them against, or without, the will of him whose Goods they be. The Civil Law judges open Theft to be satisfied by the recompence of fourfold and privy theft, by the recompence of double; but the Law of *England* adjudges both those Offences to death, if the value of the thing stollen be above twelve pence.

Sterling, *Sterlingum*, Was and is the Epithete for Silver-money currant within this Realm. And took name from this, that there was a pure Coyn stamped first in *England* by the *Easterlings*, or Merchants of *East-Germany*, by the Command of King *John*, and accordingly *Roger Hoveden parte poster. suor. annal, fol.* 377. writes it *Esterling*. See the Statute *Of Purveyors*, cap. 13. By the Statute 31 *Ed.* 1. the peny which is called the

the *ſterling*, round, and without clipping, weighs thirty two grains of Wheat, well dryed, and twenty pence make an ounce, twelve ounces a pound, and eight pound a gallon of Wine, and eight gallons a Buſhel, which is the eighth part of a Quarter, 17 *E.* 2. *cap.* 19. The word is not yet out of uſe; for though we ordinarily ſay Lawful Money of *England*, yet in the Mint, and the like, they ſay *ſterling* Money.

Stewes, Are thoſe places which were permitted in *England* to Women of profeſſed Incontinency, and that for him would proſtitute their Bodies to all Comers. It is derived from the French *Eſtuves*, i. *Thermæ, vel Balneum*, becauſe diſſolute perſons are wont to prepare themſelves for venerious acts by bathing. And that this is not new, *Homer* ſhews in the Eighth Book of his *Odyſſ.* where he reckons hot Baths among the effeminate ſort of Pleaſures, of theſe read 11 *H.*6.1. But King *Henry* the Eighth about the year 1546. prohibited them for ever.

Steward, *Seneſcallus*, Is compounded of *ſtede*, place and ward; as much as to ſay, as a man appointed in my place or ſtead, and hath many ſeveral Applications, but alwayes ſignifies a principal Officer within his Juriſdiction. The greateſt of theſe is the *Lord High Steward of* England, whoſe Power formerly was of great extent, but of later time ſo abridged, that he has not uſually been appointed, but only for the diſpatch of ſome ſpecial buſineſs, as the Arraignment of ſome Nobleman in caſe of Treaſon, or ſuch like, which once ended, his Commiſſion expires. Of the Court of the *High Steward of* England, you may read 4. *Inſt. fol.* 59. Then is the Lord *Steward* of the King's moſt Honorable Houſhold, 24 *H.* 8. *cap.* 13. whoſe name was changed to that of *great Maſter* by 32 *H.* 8. *cap.* 39. But this Statute was repealed by 1 *Mar.* 2. *Parl. cap.*4. and the Office and Name of the *Lord Steward of the King's Houſehold* revived, where you may read much concerning him, as alſo in *F. N. B. fol.* 241. Of his ancient Power, read *Fleta, lib.* 2. *cap.* 3. There is alſo a *Steward* of the *Marſhalſey*, *Pl. Cor. fol.* 52. and 33 *H.* 8. *cap.* 12. In brief, this word is of ſo great diverſity, that there is in moſt Corporations, and in all Houſes of Honour throughout the Realm, an Officer of this Name and Authority. What a Steward of a Mannor or Houſhold is, or ought to be, *Fleta* fully deſcribes, *lib.* 2. *cap.* 71, 72.

Stilyard, *Guildhalda Teutonicorum*, *Anno* 19 *H.* 7. *cap.* 32. 22 *H.* 8. *cap.* 8. and 32 *H.* 8. *cap.* 14. Was a place in *London*, where the Fraternity of the *Eaſterling Merchants*, otherwiſe called *The Merchants of the Hanſe and Almaine*, Anno 1 E. 6. cap. 13. had their abode. See *Geld.* It was at firſt ſo denominated of a broad Place or Court where *ſteel* was ſold, upon which place that Houſe was founded. See *Hanſe.*

Stoc and Stovel, —*Præterea ſi homines de ſtanhall dicti Abbatis inventi fuerint in boſco prædicti* W. *cum foriſfacto ad* **ſtoc**, *&* *ad* **ſtovel** *alias* **ſtovene**, *& aliquis quærens corporaliter in terram per eos ſeiſit. fuerit, malefactor pro delicto, qui taliter inventus fuerit, reddet tres ſolidos,*---*ſimiliter conceſſum eſt quod ſi aliquis inventus fuerit cum brachiis quercuum vel cum aliis minutis boſcis, cum foriſfacto illo ad* **ſtoc** *& ad* **ſtovell**, *Malefactor ille reddet ſex denarios*, E quadam Cart. Conventionum, inter *Will.* de *Bray* & Abbat. & Convent. de Oſney. See *Zuche.*

Stockikind. See *Gavelkind.*

Stotall, — **Alſo moreover we have granted in amendment of the City, that they bin all quit of** Bryztchel, of Childwit, Zereſgen, **and of** Stotall : **So that no Sheriff of** London, **neither none other Bayly make** Stotall **in the Francheis aforeſaid**, &c. This is in an old Printed Book, which delivers it (among other things) as the Charter of *Henry* the Firſt to the City of *London*: But the word is thought to be miſtaken for *Scotale.*

Stola, Was a Garment which Matrons wore, and reached down to their Buttocks. *Ovid* in his Second Book *De Triſtibus* mentions the word

Quæ ſtola *continguit &* ſtola *ſumpta decet.*

And *Ulpian* alſo *de Auro & argento*, Leg. I. Veſtis. Muliebria, inquit, ſunt, veluti *ſtolæ*, pallia, tunicæ, &c.

Stone of Wooll, *Petra Lanæ*, Anno 11 H. 7. *cap.* 4. Ought to weigh fourteen pounds; yet in ſome places it is more, and in others it is but twelve and a half, *Le charre de plumbo conſtat ex* 30. *formellis & qualibet formella continet* 6. *petras exceptis duabus libris*, *& qualibet Petra conſtat ex* 12. *libris.* Compoſitio de Ponderibus. A *ſtone* of Wax is but eight pound, nor is the *ſtone* of Beef at *London* any more. See *Weights and Sarpler*, and alſo *Crompton's Juſtice of Peace*, fol. 83.

Stovene. See *Zuche.*

Stowage, From the Saxon *Stow*, i. *locus, villa*, is the place or part where Goods are laid, or the Money that is paid for ſuch a place.

Stowe, According to *Doomſday* Book ſignifies *Villam*, a Village.

Straits or **Streits**, *Anno* 18 *H.* 6. and 1 *Rich.* 3. *cap.* 8. A ſort of narrow Cloth or Kerſey ſo called.

Stranded, (From the Saxon **Strand**, A ſhore or bank of the Sea, or any great River,) Is, when any Ship is either by Tempeſt, or ill Sterage, run on ground, and ſo periſhes, Stat. 17 *Car.* 1. *cap.* 14. See *Strond.*

Stray, If any Beaſt do by chance go *aſtray*, and come within the Liberty of the *Prior*, and ſhall be taken by his Bayliffs, it ſhall be carried to the *Pinfold*, and there kept a year and a day; if no man claim it within that time, then the *Prior* ſhall have it: But if any one come, and ſhall lawfully prove it to be his, he ſhall give for every foot one peny, and pay the charges of keeping, and then he ſhall have his Beaſt again. *Ex Regiſt. Priorat. de Cokesford.* See *Eſtray.*

Stranger, May be derived from the French *Eſtrangier, aliena.* It ſignifies generally in our Language a Man born out of the Land, or unknown; but in the Law it hath a ſpecial ſignification, for him that is not privy or party to an act. As a *ſtranger* to a Judgment, *Old Nat. Brev.*

fol.

fol. 128. is he to whom a Judgment doth not belong; and in this sense it is directly contrary to *party* or *privy*. See *Privy*.

Stream-works, Is a kind of *Works* in the *Stannaries*, which you may find mentioned 27 *H.* 8. *cap.* 23. Concerning these, *Camden* in his *Britan.* tit. *Cornwall*, hath these words, *Horum stannariorum sive metallicorum operum duo sunt Genera: Alterum* Lode-works, *alterum* Stream-works *vocant hoc in locis inferioribus est cum fossis agendis stanni venas sectantur & fluviorum alveos subinde deflectunt; illud in locis æditioribus, cum in montibus Puteos, quos* shafts *vocant in magnam altitudinem desodiunt & cuniculos agunt.*

Street-gavel or **Stret-gavel**, *Quilibet tenens in Manerio de* Cholington *dabit* 2s. *pro ita & reditu* M.S. de temp. E. 4. Every Tenant of that Mannor (*in Com. Sussex*) paid yearly two shillings for his going out and returning into it, to the Lord of the Mannor by the Name of *Stret-gavel*, *Mich.* 4 E. 1. *Coram Rege*, *Antiquity of Purveyance*, fol. 222.

Strip, *Strepitus*, Destruction, Mutilation, from the French *Estropier*, i. *Mutilare*, *strepitum & vastum facere*, i. To make *strip* and wast, or *strop* and wast. See *Estrepement*.

Streteward, *Per* streteward *Johannes Stanley Armiger*, *Clamat quod servientes pacis & Ministri sui infra feodum de Aldford capere debent de qualibet fuga catallorum* 4 d. Rot. Pla. in Itin. apud Cestriam, 14 *H.* 7. See *Market zelde*.

Strond, Is a Saxon word signifying a shore or bank of a Sea, or any great River. In a Charter of King *Richard*, Dated at *Canterbury* the 4th of *November*, in the first year of his Reign, we find these words, *Richardus Rex*, *&c. Notum facimus vobis nos concessisse*, *&c. Deo & sancto* Albano *Ecclesiæ suæ sancti* Oswini *de* Tynemuth, *cellæ sancti* Albani *& Monachis ibidem Deo servientibus omnes terras suas & omnes homines suos*, *cum sacha*, *soca*, **Over strond et streme, on wode & felde**, *Toll*, *Them & Grithburge*, *Hamsocne*, *Murdrum & Forestall Danegeld*, *Infangenethef & Utfangenethef*, *Fleminefrenieth*, *Blodwit*, *Wrecke*, *&c.* And the *Gloss.* in 10. *Scriptores* interpreting these words, **On strond et streame, on wode & feld**, saith,--*Voces Anglicæ veteres & in antiquioris ævi chartis crebro repertæ; Privilegium sapiunt seu potius Privilegii latitudinem sive amplitudinem & sic Latine legantur*, *in Littore*, *in Fluvio*, *in Sylva & Campo*.

Strumpet, *Meretrix*, Was heretofore used for an addition, *Jur. præsentant*, *&c. quod* Johannes *de* Mainwaring *de* Whatcroft *de Com. Cest. Esq; Laurentiuus de* Warren *de* Davenham *Esq; &c.* Hugo *de* Sondebach *Yoman*, *Hopkin*, *Norman de Com. Cestr.* Husbond-Knave, *Willielmus le Birchwood de* Clyve-Knave *cum plurimis* aliis & Agnes Cawes de medio Wico de Com. Cestr. **Strumpet**, --*Tali die domum* Ranulphi Madocke, *vi & armis*, *&c. fregerunt*, *&c.* Pla. apud Cestr. 6. H. 5. m. 2. in Dorso.

Stud, Freely to buy and sell as well in *Chester* as in the County and Wiches, where there was no Law, all things with *Toll* and *Stud*, besides Salt and Horses, *Mon. Ang.* 2. *par. fol.* 187. haply it may be the same with *stuth*, which see.

Stuth, *Per* Stuth *clamat esse quiet. de exactione pecuniæ à singulis villis*---*per vicecom. comitat. Cestriæ*, Pl. in Itin. ibid. 14 *H.* 7.

Submarshal, *Submarescallus*, Is an Officer in the *Marshalsea*, who is Deputy to the chief *Marshall* of the King's House, commonly called *The Knight-Marshal*, and hath the custody of the Prisoners there, *Cromp. Jur. fol.* 104. He is otherwise called *Under-Marshal*.

Subornation, *Subornatio*, A secret or under-hand preparing, instructing or bringing in a false Witness, or corrupting or alluring to do such a false act. Hence *subornation of Perjury* mentioned in the Act *Of General Pardon*, 12 Car. 2. cap. 8. Is the alluring to Perjury, *subornation of Witnesses*, 32 H. 8. *cap.* 9. and 3. *par. Inst. fol.* 167.

Subpæna, Is a Writ whereby all persons under the degree of Peerage are called into Chancery, in such case only where the Common Law fails, and hath made no provision; so as the Party who in equity hath wrong, can have no ordinary remedy by the Rules and course of the Common Law, *West Symbol.* part 2. tit. *Proceedings in Chancery*, sect. 18. But Peers of the Realm in such cases are called by the Lord Chancellors, or Lord Keepers Letters, giving notice of the Suit intended against them, and requiring them to appear. There is also a *Subpæna ad testificandum*, for the summoning of Witnesses as well in Chancery as other Courts. There is also a *Subpæna* in the Exchequer, as well in the Court of Equity there as in the Office of Pleas. And these Names proceed from the words in the Writ, which charge the Party summoned to appear at the day and place assigned, *Subpæna Centum Librarum*. See *Cromp. Jurisd. fol.* 33. and *Anno* 15 *Hen.* 6. *cap.* 4.

Subsidium Cathedraticum, See *Cathedratick*.

Subsidy, *Subsidium*, Signifies an Ayd, Tax or Tribute, granted by Parliament to the King, for the urgent Occasions of the Kingdom, to be levyed of every Subject, according to the rate of his Land or Goods, after four shillings in the pound for Land, and two shillings eight pence for Goods. No History mentions, that the *Saxon* Kings had any *Subsidies* after the manner of Ours at present; but they had both Levies of Money and personal Services towards the building and repairing of Cities, Castles, Bridges, Military Expeditions, &c. which they called **Burg-bote**, **Brigbote**, **Herefare**, **Heregeld**, **&c.** But when the *Danes* harassed the Land, King *Ethelred* yielded to pay them for redemption of Peace several great sums of Money yearly. This was called **Danegeld**, for the levying of which, every Hide of Land was taxed yearly at twelve pence, Lands of the Church only excepted, and thereupon it was after called *Hydagium*, and that Name remained afterward upon all Taxes and *Subsidies* imposed on Lands; for sometimes it was laid upon Cattel, and then was termed *Hornegeld*. The *Normans* called these sometimes *Taxes*, sometimes *Tallages*, other-whiles *Auxilia & subsidia*. The *Conqueror* had these *Taxes*, and made a Law for the manner of their levying, as appears in *Emendationibus ejus*, pag. 125. sect. *Volumus & hoc firmiter*, *&c.* many years after the Conquest they were levyed otherwise than now, as every ninth

Lamb, every ninth Fleece, and every ninth Sheaf, 14 *E.* 3. *stat.* 1. *cap.* 20. Of which you may may see great variety in *Rastall's Abridgment*, tit. *Taxes, Tenths, Fifteens, Subsidies, &c.* and 4. *Inst. fol.* 26. & 33. Whence we may gather there is no certain Rate, but as the Parliament shall think fit. *Subsidy* is in our Statutes, sometimes confounded with *Customs*, 11 *H.* 4. *cap.* 7. See *Benevolence*, and 15 *Car.* 2. *cap.* 7.

Subgrundæ, The Eaves of a House, *Tegulæ proyendentes extra tectum domus ad parietum defensionem, ne imbribus corrumpantur*, Vocab. utriusq; juris.

Substitute, *Substitutus*, One placed under another to transact, or do some business.

Succinum, *Gemma est ex gummi arboris Glessariæ congelatæ, quam diximus appellari à Græcis electrum.* Of which *Juvenal.*

In cujus manibus ceu pinguia Succina *tritas*
Cernis Ephemeridas.

And Martial, *Inclusit tenuem* succina *gemma feram.*

Sucking, *Per* Sucking, *hoc est fore quiet. de illis amerciamentis quando* **le Burlimen**, *id est, supervisores del* Ringyord, *id est clausur, quæ vocat. le* **Chiminfildes** *vel* **Common Medowes**, *& præmonit. fuerint ad imparcand. & faciend. clausuras illas simul cum vicinis suis, ille qui non venit ad talem præmonitionem, amerciatus erit ad pretium unius vomeris, Anglicè* **a Sucke** *pretii quatuor denari & hoc quotiescunq; præmonit. non venerit.* Plac. in Itin. apud Cestriam, 14 Hen. 7.

Suffragan, *Suffraganus*, Is a titular Bishop appointed to aid and assist the Bishop of the Diocess. *Co.* 2. *Inst. fol.* 79. calls him *a Bishops Vicegerent. Spelman* says, *Dicuntur Episcopi qui Archiepiscopo* suffragari *& assistere tenentur, &* suffraganei *dicuntur quia eorum* suffragiis *causæ Ecclesiasticæ judicantur.* By the 26 *H.* 8. *cap.* 14. The Diocesan may elect two honest and discreet spiritual persons, &c. and that every such person shall be called *Bishop Suffragan.*

Suit or **Sute**, *Secta*, Signifies a following another, but in divers senses. The first is a *Suit in Law*, and is divided into *real and personal*, and is all one with *action real and personal*, Kitch. *fol.* 74. Secondly, *Suit of Court*, or *Suit-service*, is an Attend that Tenants owe to the Court of their Lord, 7 *H.* 7. *cap.* 2. Thirdly, *Suit-Covenant* is, when your Ancestor hath *covenanted* with mine *to sue* to his Court. Fourthly, *Suit-Custome*, when I and my Ancestors have been seised of your own and your Ancestors *suit* time out of mind. Fifthly, *Suit real or regal*, when Men come to the Sheriffs Turn or Leet. See *Leet.* Sixthly, *Sute*, signifies the following one in Chace, as *Fresh-suit*, *Westm.* 1. *cap.* 46. Lastly, it signifies a Petition made to the King, or any great person.

Suit of the Kings Peace, *Secta pacis Regis*, Is the pursuing a Man for breach of the *King's Peace* by Treasons, Insurrections or Trespasses, 6 *Rich.* 2. *stat.* 2. *cap.* 1. and 27 *R.* 2. *cap.* 15. and 5 *H.* 4. *cap.* 15.

Suit-silver. See *Sute-silver.*

Suling. See *Swoling.*

Summage. See *Sumage* and *Seme.*

Sumage, *Sumagium & summagium*, A Horse-load, also Toll for Carriage on Horseback, *Cromp. Jur. fol.* 191. For where the Charter of the Forest, *cap.* 14. hath these words, For a Horse that bears loads every half year a halfpeny: The Book called *Pupilla Oculi*, useth these words, *Pro uno equo portante* summagium, *per dimidium annum obolum*, Chart. E. 1. num. 17. It is otherwise called *a Seame*: And *a Soame* in the Western parts is a Horse-load.

Summoneas, Is a Writ Judicial, of great diversity, according to the divers Cases wherein it is used, which see in the Table of the *Register Judicial.*

Summoner, *Summonitor*, Is a petty Officer, that calls or cites a Man to any Court; these ought to be *boni homines*, that is in *Fleta's* Judgment, *Liberi homines & ideò boni, quia terras tenentes, quod sint coram talibus Justiciariis ad certos diem & locum secundum mandatum Justiciariorum vicecomiti directum, parati inde facere recognitionem*, lib. 4. cap. 5. sect. *Et cum.*

Summons, *Summonitio*, With us as much as *Vocatio in jus*, or *citatio* among the *Civilians*; And thence is our word *Sumner*, which in French is *Somoneur*, i. *vocator, monitor. Summons* of the Exchequer, 3 *E.* 1. *cap.* 19. How *Summons* is divided, and what circumstances it has to be observed. See *Fleta, lib.* 6. *cap.* 6, 7.

Summons in terra petita, *Kitchin, fol.* 286. Is that *Summons* which is made upon the Land, which the Party (at whose Suit the *Summons* is sent forth) seeks to have.

Summons ad Warrantizand, And *sequatur sub suo periculo*, Dyer, *fol.* 69. num. 35. *Summoneas ad Warrantizandum*, Is the Process whereby the Vouchee is called. See *Co.* on *Lit. fol.* 101. *b.*

Sumptuary Laws, Are Laws made to restrain excess in Apparel, and prohibit costly Clothes; of which we have heretofore had many in *England*, but all repealed, *Anno* 1 *Jac.* See 3. *Inst. fol.* 199.

Super-institution, *Super-institutio*, One *Institution* upon another; as where *A.* is admitted and instituted to a Benefice upon one Title, and *B.* is admitted, instituted, &c. by the Presentment of another. See *Hutchins* Case in *Co. Rep.* 2. *par. fol.* 463.

Superoneratione pasturæ, Is a Writ Judicial, that lies against him who is impleaded in the County, for the overburdening of a Common with his Cattel, in case where he was formerly impleaded for it in the County, and the Cause is removed into the King's Court at *Westminster.*

Super Prærogativa Regis, Is a Writ which lay against the King's Widow, for marrying without his Licence, *F. N. B. fol.* 173.

Supersedeas, Is a Writ in divers Cases, and signifies in general a Command to stay, or forbear the doing of that which ought not to be done, or in appearance of Law were to be done, were it not for that whereon the Writ is granted. For example, A Man regularly is to have surety of Peace against him of whom he will swear, He is afraid, and the Justice required hereunto cannot deny him; yet if the Party be formerly bound to the Peace, either in Chancery, or elsewhere; this Writ lies, to stay the Justice from doing that which otherwise he ought not to deny. See the Table of the *Reg. Orig.* and *Judic.* and *F. N. B. fol.* 236. for preventing the superseding of Executions. See the Statute 16, 17 *Car.* 2. *cap.* 8.

Super statutum Edward. 3. **versus Servants & Laborers**, Is a Writ that lies against him who keeps my *Servants*, departed out of my Service, against Law, *F. N. B. fol.* 167.

Super statuto de York, **quo nul serra Viteller, &c.** Is a Writ lying against him that uses Victualling either in gross, or by Retail, in a City or Borough Town, during the time he is Mayor, &c. *F. N. B. fol.* 172.

Super statuto, 1 *E.* 3. *cap.* 12, 13. Is a Writ that lay against the King's Tenant holding in chief, which alienateth the King's Land without his Licence, *F. N. B. fol.* 175.

Super statuto facto pour Seneshal & Marshal de Roy, &c. Is a Writ lying against the Steward, or *Marshal*, for holding Plea in his Court of Free-hold, or for Trespass or Contracts not made within the King's Houshold, *F. N. B. fol.* 241.

Super statuto de Articulis Cleri, *Cap.* 6. Is a Writ against the Sheriff or other Officer, that distrains in the King's High-way, or in the Glebe-Land, anciently given to Rectories, *F.N.B. fol.* 173.

Supervisor, Is a Latine word signifying a Surveyor or Overseer: It was anciently, and still is a Custom among some, especially of the better sort, to make a *Supervisor* of a Will, but it is to little purpose; However the first might be good, that he should *supervise* the Executor, and see the Will truly performed.

Supervisor, *Or as now* Surveyor of the High-ways, *Anno* 5 *Eliz. cap.* 13. See *Surveyor.*

Superficies, Is the surface or top of the Earth, and whatsoever is upon the face thereof, *Vocab. utriusq; juris.*

Supplicavit, Is a Writ issuing out of the *Chancery*, for taking the Surety of Peace against a Man: It is directed to the Justices of Peace of the County and the Sheriff, and is grounded upon the Statute, *Anno* 1 *E.* 3. *cap.* 16. which Ordains, That certain persons in Chancery shall be assigned to take care of the Peace. See *F.N.B. fol.* 80. This Writ was of old called *Breve de minis*, as *Lambert* saith in his *Eirenarcha*, out of the *Regist. Orig. fol.* 88.

Sur cui in vita, Is a Writ that lies for the Heir of that Woman, whose Husband has aliened her Land in Fee, and she brings not the Writ *Cui in vita* for the recovery of her own Land; In this case her Heir may have this Writ against the Tenant after her decease, *F. N. B. fol.* 193.

Surcharge of the Forest, *Superoneratio Forestæ*, Is, when a Commoner puts on more Beasts in the *Forest* than he has right to, *Manwood, part* 2. *cap.* 14. *num.* 7. And is taken from the Writ *De secunda superoneratione Pastura* in the same sense, when the Commoner surchargeth. 3. *Inst. fol.* 293.

Surety of the Peace, *Securitas Pacis* (so called, because the Party that was in fear is thereby secured,) Is an acknowledging of a Bond to the Prince, taken by a competent Judge of Record, for the *keeping of the Peace.* This *Peace* may a *Justice of the Peace* Command, either as a Minister, when he is commanded thereto by a higher Authority; or as a Judge, when he doth it of his own Power, derived from his Commission. Of both these, see *Lamb. Eiren. lib.* 2. *cap.* 2. *pag.* 77. See *Peace.* See *Supplicavit. Securitas de bono gestu*, *Surety* of the good abearing differs from this, that whereas the *Peace* is not broken without an Affray, or such like; the surety *de bono gestu* may be broken by the number of a Man's Company, or by his or their Weapons and Harness.

Surplusage, *Surplusagium*, Cometh of the French *Surplus*, i. *corolarium*; and signifies in the Common Law a superfluity, or addition, more than needeth, which sometimes is a cause that a Writ abateth, *Broke*, tit. *Nugation and Superfluity*, fol. 100. *Plowden*, fol. 63. *Dives* and *Maningham*'s Case. It is sometimes also applyed to matter of Account, and denotes a greater disbursement than the charge of the Accountant amounteth unto; *Satisfaciant in omnibus quod conjunctum fuerit per prædictum computum inter eos de* surplusagio *recepto de averiis venditis, &c.* Ordinatio de marisco Romeneiensi, pag. 38.

Sullings, In *Doomesday* Book, according to Mr. *Agar*'s Interpretation, are taken for *Alders*. But in 1. *Inst. fol.* 4. for *Elders.*

Sullery, Denotes a Plough-land, as the same Mr. *Agar* interprets it out of *Doomesday.*

Surgeon, *Chirurgus*, May be deduced from the French *Chirurgeon*, signifying him that dealeth in the Mechanical part of Physick, and the outward Cures performed with the hand; and therefore is compound of two Greek words, *viz.* χεὶρ *manus*, ἔργον, *opus*: And for this cause are they not allowed to minister inward Medicine. See the Statute 32 *H.* 8. *cap.* 4. and *Polton*'s *Abridgment*, tit. *Surgeons.*

Surrejoynder, Is a second defence of the Plaintiffs Action, opposite to the Defendants Rejoyner, *West Symb.* part 2. tit. *Supplications*, sect. 57. and therefore *Hotoman* calls it *Triplicationem, quæ est secunda actoris defensio contra rei duplicationem opposita.*

Surrebutter, Is a second *Rebutter*, or a *Rebutting* more than once. See *Rebutter.*

Surrender, *Sursum-redditio*, Is an Instrument in writing, testifying with apt words, that the particular Tenant of Lands or Tenements for life, or years, doth sufficiently consent and agree, That he which has the next or immediate remainder or reversion thereof, shall also have the present Estate of the same in possession, and that he yields and gives up the same unto him: for every *Surrender* ought forthwith to give possession of the things *surrendred*, *West, Symbol. part* 1. *lib.* 2. *sect.* 503. where are several Presidents: There may be also a *surrender* without writing; and therefore there is said to be a *surrender in Deed*, and a *surrender in Law*; A *surrender in Deed* is, that

 which

which is really and sensibly performed. A *surrender in Law* is, in intendment of Law by way of consequent, and not actual. See of this *Perkins, cap.* 9. & *fol.* 606. As if a man have a Lease of a Farm, and during the term, he accept of a new Lease; this Act is in Law a *Surrender* of the former, *Co.* 6. *Rep. fol.* 11. There is also a *customary Surrender* of the Copyhold-Land, for which see *Coke sup. Littleton*, sect. 74.

Surrogate, *Surrogatus*, One that is substituted or appointed in the room of another, most commonly of a Bishop, or of a Bishops Chancellor.

Sursise, *Supersisa*, 32 *H.* 8. *cap.* 48. Seems to be an especial name used in the Castle of *Dover*, for such Penalties and Forfeitures as are laid upon those that pay not their Duties or Rent for *Castleward* at their dayes. *Bracton* hath it in a general signification, *lib.* 5. *tract.* 3. *cap.* 1. *num.* 8. and *Fleta*, *lib.* 6. *cap.* 3. *in princ.*

Surveyor, *Supervisor*, Is a French compound of *sur*, i. *super* and *veoir*, *cernere*, *videre*. It signifies with us one that has the over-seeing or care of some great persons Lands or Works. As the *Surveyor-General* of the Kings Mannors, *Cromp. Jur. fol.* 39. And in this sense it is taken, 33 *H.* 8. *cap.* 39. where there is a Court of *Surveyors* erected: And the *Surveyor* of the Wards and Liveries. But he is taken away with the Court of Wards and Liveries, by the Statute made *Anno* 12 *Car.* 2. *cap.* 24.

Surveyor of the Kings Exchange, 9 *H.* 5. *stat.* 2. *cap.* 4. Was an Officer whose name seems in these days to be changed into some other; for there is none such now, or else the Office now disused.

Survivor, From the French *Surviure*, i. *superesse*, Signifies the longer liver of two Joynt-Tenants. See *Bro.* tit. *Joynt-tenants*, or of any two joyned in the Right of any thing.

Suskin. See *Gally-half-pence.*

Suspension or Suspense, *Suspensio*, Is a Temporal stop of a Mans Right; as when a Seigniory, Rent, &c. by reason of the Unity of possession thereof, and of the Land out of which they issue are not *in esse* for a time, & *tunc dormiunt*, but may be revived or awaked, and so differs from extinguishment, which dies for ever, *Bro.* tit. *Extinguishment and Suspension*, fol. 314. and *Co.* on *Lit. lib.* 3. *cap.* 10. *sect.* 559. *Suspension* is also used sometimes by us, as it is in the Canon Law *pro minori Excommunicatione*, Anno 24 *H.* 8. *cap.* 12. See *Vocab. utriusq; juris.*

Suspiral, (From the Latine *suspirare*, i. *ducere suspiria*,) and seems to be a spring of Water passing under the ground toward a Conduit or Cistern, 35 *H.* 8. *cap.* 10. And indeed the word is an absolute French word; for *Suspiral* in that Tongue signifies *spiramentum Cavernæ*, the mouth of a Cave or Den.

Sute. See *Suit.*

Sute-silver, Is a small Rent, or sum of Money, which, if paid, does excuse the Freeholders from the appearance at the *Court-Barons* within the Honor of *Clun* in *Shropshire*.

Swan, *Cygnus*, He that stealeth the Eggs of *Swans* out of their Nests, shall be imprisoned for a year and a day, and fined according to the King's Pleasure; one moyety to the King, and the other to the Owner of the Land where the Eggs were so taken; and it was a Custom in ancient time, That he which stole a *Swan* in an open and common River, lawfully marked, the same *Swan* (if it may be) or another *Swan* shall be hanged in a House by the beak: And he which stole it in recompence thereof, compelled to give the Owner as much Corn as may cover all the *Swan*, by putting and turning the Corn upon the head of the *Swan*, until the Head of the *Swan* be covered with Corn. See *Co.* 7. *Rep.* Case of *Swans.*

Swanherd. See *Kings Swainherd.*

Swanimote alias **Swainmote**, *Swainmotus*, Signifies a Court touching matters of the Forest, and held by the Charter of the Forest thrice in the year, before the Verderors as Judges, *Anno* 3 *H.* 8. *cap.* 18. What things are inquirable in the same, you may read in *Cromp. Jurisd. fol.* 180. And it is as incident to a Forest as a Court of Pye-Powder to a Fair; *Nullum* Swainmotum *de cætero teneatur*, *in Regno nostro nisi ter in Anno*, viz. *in Principio quindecim dierum ante festum sancti* Michael, &c. *circa festum sancti* Martini, & *initio quindecim dierum ante festum sancti* Johannis Baptistæ, &c. Charta de Foresta tam Regis Johan. quam Hen. 3. cap. 9. See 4. *Inst. fol.* 289. This word is compounded of the Saxon ꞅpanꝫ, a Country Swain or Boclandman, and Gemot. *Conventus*, as Mr. *Lambert* thinks in his *Explication of Saxon words*, verb. *Conventus*; with whom agrees *Manwood* in his *Forest Law*, pag. 11.

Swarffmoney, **The** *Swarffmoney* **is one peny half-peny, it must be paid before the rising of the Sun; the party must go thrice about the Cross, and say the Swarff-money, and then take Witnesse, and then lay it in the hole: And when you have so done, look well that your Witnesse do not deceive you: For if it be not paid, you give a great Forfeiture xxx s. and a white Bull.** This Exposition was found in an old M. S. containing the Rents due to the *Catesbyes* in *Lodbrooke*, and other places of *Warwickshire*; but supposed to be mistaken, or to signifie the same with *Warth-money*. See *Ward-peny.*

Swepage, Is the Crop of Hay got in a Meadow, called also *The swepe* in some parts of *England*, *Co.* on *Lit.* fol. 4.

Swoling or suling of Land, *Sulinga*, *solinga* vel *swolinga terræ*, in Saxon *Sulung*, from *sul* or *suth*, *aratrum*; as to this day in the Western parts, a Plough is called a *Sul*, and a Ploughstaff a *Sulpaddle*. It is the same with *Carucata terræ*, that is, as much as one Plough can Till in a year: A Hide of Land, though others say it is an uncertain quantity. ---*Terram trium aratrorum quam Cantiani Anglice dicunt*, **Three swolings.**

Syb and som, *Pax* & *securitas*, And accordingly we read in the Laws of King *Canutus*, *cap.* 17. *Eallum*, Cyrꞇenum, *Mannum* ꞅyб, ꞅom ꝫemene, that is, *Omnibus Christianis Pax* & *securitas communis esto.*

Sylva cædua, Wood under twenty years growth;

growth; Coppice-wood. See the Statute 45 *E.* 3. *cap.* 3. It is otherwise called in Law-French *Sub-bois*, 2 *Inst. fol.* 642.

Synod, *Synodus*, A Meeting or Assembly of Ecclesiastical persons concerning Religion, of which there are four kinds: 1. *General*, where Bishops, &c. meet of all Nations. 2. *National*, where those of one Nation only come together. 3. A *Provincial*, where they of one only Province meet. 4. *Diocesan*, where those of but one Diocess meet. See *Convocation*, which is all one with a *Synod*, only the one is a Greek, and the other a Latine word.

Synodal, *Synodale*, Is a Tribute in Mony, paid to the Bishop, or Arch-deacon, by the Inferior Clergy at *Easter* Visitation; and it is called *Synodale quia in* synodo *frequentius dabatur*. The Impropriation of *Derehuit* in *Com. Glouc.* pays yearly 7 s. 9 d. *Pro* Synodalibus *& Procurationibus.* Pat. 20. July 34 H. 8. *Et quod sint quieti a* Synodalibus *& ab omni Episcopali consuetudine excepto denario beati Petri*, Mon. Ang. 2. par. fol. 276. See the *Historical Discourse of Procurations and* Synodals, *pag.* 66. *&* 98. These are called otherwise *Synodies* in the Statute of 32 *Hen.* 8. *cap.* 16. yet in the Statute of 25 *H.* 8. *cap.* 19. *Synodals Provincial* seem to signifie the Canons or Constitutions of a *Provincial Synod.* And sometimes *Synodale* is used for the *Synod* it self.

T.

T. Every Person convict of any other Felony (save Murder) and admitted to the benefit of his Clergy, shall be marked with a T. upon the brawn of his left Thumb, *Anno* 4 *H.* 7. *cap.* 13.

Tabellion, *Tabellio*, A Notary, Publick or Scrivener, allowed by Authority to ingross and register private Contracts and Obligations, *Mat. Paris fol.* 424. *De anno* 1236. hath these words, *Quoniam* Tabellionum *usus in Regno Angliæ non habetur, propter quod magis ad sigilla authentica credi est necesse, ut eorum copia facilius habeatur, statuimus ut sigillum habeant non solum Archiepiscopi sed eorum officiales.*

Tabling of Fines, Is the making a Table for every County where his Majesties writ runs, containing the Contents of every *Fine* passed in any one Term, as the name of the County, Towns and Places, wherein the Lands or Tenements lye; the name of the Demandant and Deforceant, and of every Mannor named in the *Fine*. This is to be done properly by the Chirographer of *Fines* of the *Common Pleas*, who every day of the next Term, after the ingrossing any such *Fine*, must fix every of the said *Tables* in some open place of the said Court, during its sitting. And the said Chirographer is to deliver to the Sheriff of every County, his Under-Sheriff or Deputy, fair written in Parchment, a perfect content of the Table so made for that Shire, in the Term next before the Assises for that County, or else between the Term and the Assises, to be set up every day of the next Assises in some open place of the Court, where the Justices of Assises shall then sit, and to continue there during their sitting: And if either the Chirographer or Sheriff fail herein, he shall forfeit 5 *li.* And the Chirographers Fee for every such tabling is four pence, 23 *Eliz.* cap. 3. and *West. Symbol.* part 2. tit. *Fines*, sect. 130.

Tayle, *Tallium*, May come from the French word *Taille*, i. *sectura*, and in our Law signifies two several things, both grounded upon one reason, *Plowden*, *fol.* 251. *Willions* Case. First, It is used for the *Fee*, which is opposite to *Fee-simple*, by reason it is so minced or parted as it were, that it is not in the Owners free power to dispose, but is by the first Giver *cut or divided* from all others, and tyed to the issue of the Donee, *Co. lib.* 4. in *Proœmio*: And this limitation of *tail* is either *general* or *special*. *Tail general*, is that whereby Lands or Tenements are limited to a Man, and to the Heirs of his Body begotten; and it is so called, how many Wives soever the Tenant holding by this Title shall have, one after another in Lawful Marriage; his Issue by them all have a possibility to inherit one after another. *Tail special*, is when Lands or Tenements are limited to a Man and his Wife, and the Heirs of their two Bodies begotten; and hath this term of *special*, because if the Man bury his Wife before Issue, and take another, the Issue by his second Wife cannot inherit the Land, &c. Also if Land be given to a Man and his Wife, and to their Son *Thomas* for ever; this is *Tail special*. See more of this in *Fee*, and *Lit. lib.* 1. *cap.* 2. and the *New Book of Entries*, verb. *Tail*. *Tail* in the other signification is that we vulgarly call a *Tally*; For *une taille de bois* is a cloven piece of wood, to set up an account upon by Nicks; for in the Statute 10 *E.* 1. *cap.* 11. and 27 *E.* 1. *stat.* 1. *cap.* 2. It is termed a *Tail*, and 38 *E.* 3. *cap.* 5. and so in *Brokes Abridgment*, tit. *Tail d' Exchequer*, fol. 247. See *Tailes*.

Tayl after possibility of Issue extinct, Is, where Land is given to a Man and his Wife, and to the Heirs of their two Bodies engendred, and one of them over-lives the other without Issue between them begotten; He shall hold the Land for term of his own life, as Tenant in the *tail after possibility of Issue extinct*, and notwithstanding that he do wast, he shall never be impeached of it. And if he alien, he in the Reversion shall not have a Writ of Entry *in consimili casu*, but he may enter, and his Entry is lawful, by *R. Thorpe* chief Justice, 28 *E.* 3. 96. *&* 45 *E.* 3. 25.

Tailes, *Talliæ*, Are Tallies, of which we spoke before: Of these two sorts are mentioned in our Statutes, to have been long used in the Exchequer, the one is termed *tailes* of Debt, *Anno* 1 *Rich.* 2. *cap.* 5. which are a kind of Acquittance for Debt paid to the King. As for example, The University of *Cambridge* payeth yearly ten pounds for such things as are by their Charter granted them in Fee-farm, *viz.* 5 *li.* at the *Annunciation*, and 5 *li.* at *Michaelmas*. He that pays these sums, receiveth for his Discharge a *Taile* or *Tally* at each day, with both which, or notes of them, he repairs to the Clerk of the Pipe-Office, and there, instead of them, receiveth an Acquittance in Parchment for his full Discharge. The other are *Tailes of Reward* spoken of 27 *H.* 8. 11. *&* 33 *&* 34 *H.* 8. 16. and 2 *&* 3 *E.* 6. *cap.* 4. which seem to be *Tailes* or *Tallies* of allowances, or recompence made to Sheriffs for such matters, as to their Charge they have performed in their Office, or for such Monies as they by course have cast upon them in their Accounts, but cannot levy, &c. See 2 & 3 *E. 6. cap.* 4. There are also *Tallies* of Debt used among Subjects, *Et si creditor habet* Talleam, *oportet creditorem probare illam per convicinos suos vel per alios, per quorum fidelitatem Ballivi & alii præsentes illo tempore in Curia notitiam habere possunt, & si Creditor petat debitum per vocem suam simplicem tunc debitor potest esse ad suam legem manifestatam.* M.S. Codex de LL. Statutis, &c. Burgi villæ Montgomer. à temp. H. 2.

Tailage. See *Tallage.*

Taint, *Attinctus*, Cometh of the French *Teinct*, i. *infectus*, and signifies substantively, either a Conviction, or Adjectively a person convicted of Felony or Treason, &c. See *Attaint.*

Tales, Is a Latine word of known signification, and used in our Law for a supply of Men impannelled upon a Jury or Inquest, and not appearing, or at their appearance challenged by either Party as not indifferent; in which case the Judge, upon motion, grants a supply to be made by the Sheriff of one or more such there present; and hereupon the very act of supplying is called a *Tales de circumstantibus.* But he that hath had one *Tales* either upon default or challenge, may not have another to contain so many as the former: For the first *Tales* must be under the principal Panel, except in a Cause of Appeal, and so every *Tales* less than other, until the number be made up of Men present in Court, and such as are without exception; yet this general Rule is not without some exceptions, as appears by *Stamford, Pl. Cor. lib.* 3. *cap.* 5. These commonly called *Tales*, may in some sort, and indeed are called *Meliores, viz.* when the whole Jury is challenged, as appears by *Bro.* tit. *Octo* tales, *& auter* tales, *fol.* 105. See *Co. lib.* 10. *fol.* 99. *Bewfage's* Case.

Tales, Is also the Name of a Book in the King's-Bench Office, of such Jury-men as were of the *Tales, Co. lib.* 4. *fo.* 93.

Tallage, *Tallagium*, May be derived of the French *Taille*, which properly signifies a piece cut out of the whole, but metaphorically is used for a share of a mans Substance paid by way of Tribute, Toll or Tax, *Stat. de* Tallagio *non concedendo temp.* E. 1. And *Stow's Annals*, pag. 445. Thence come *Talaigiers* in *Chaucer* for *Tax or Tollgatherers.* See *Subsidy. Tallage*, says *Coke*, is a general word for all Taxes, 2 *Inst. fo.* 532. But Tenants in *ancient Demesne* are quit of these Taxes and Tallages granted by Parliament, except the King do Tax ancient Demesne, as he may when he thinks good, for some great cause.

Tallyes. See *Tailes.*

Talshide. See *Talwood.*

Talwood, Is Fire-wood cleft, and cut in Billets of a certain length. See the Statutes 34 & 35 H. 8. *cap.* 3. 7 *E.* 6. *cap.* 7. **Every Talshide marked one, being round bodied, shall contain sixteen inches of Assise in compass, &c.** See *Anno* 43 *Eliz. cap.* 14.

Tangier, An ancient City of *Barbary*, lying within the Kingdom of *Fesse*, mentioned in the Statute 15 *Car.* 2. *cap.* 7. and is now part of the Dominion belonging to the Crown of *England.*

Tanistry, Is a Law or Custome in some parts of *Ireland*, of which Sir *John Davies* in his *Reports, fo.* 28. thus, *Quant ascun person seisie de ascuns Castles, Mannors, Terres ou Tenements del nature & tenure de* Tanistry, *que donques mesme les Castles, &c. doent descender, & de temps dont memory ne court ont use de descender,* Seniori & Dignissimo viro Sanguinis & cognominis, *de tiel person issint morant seisie & que le file ou les files de tiel person issint morant seisie de touts temps avant dit, ne fueront inheritables de tiels terres ou tenements, ou de ascun part de eux.* The Name seems to be derived from *Thanus.* See Sir *James Ware's Antiquitates Hiberniæ*, pag. 38.

Tappa. See *Bosiunus.*

Tare and Tret, The first is the weight of Box, Straw, Cloths, &c. wherein Goods are packed. The other is a consideration allowed in the weight for wast, in emptying and reselling the Goods. See *the Book of Rates.*

Tasels, Is a kind of hard Bur used by Clothiers and Clothworkers, in dressing of Cloth, *Anno* 4 *E.* 4. *cap.* 1.

Tassum, A Mow or Heap from the French *Tasser*, to pile up. *Commissio facta fuit* Roberto Hadham *ad vendend. blada & alia bona diversarum Abbatiarum alienigenarum, qui venit & cognovit, quod vendidit blada Prioris de* Tickeford *in garbis in duobus* tassis *existen.* pro 10 li. &c. Hill 25 *E.* 3. *Coram Rege*, Rot. 13.

Tax, *Taxa*, May be fetched from the Greek τάξις, *Ordo*, because it was a thing done orderly and moderately. It was such a Tribute as being certainly rated upon every Town, was wont to be yearly paid, but now not without consent in Parliament, which was first granted by *Edward* the First, in the Twenty Fifth year of his Reign, *cap.* 5. It differs from a Subsidy in this, that is alway certain, as it is set down in the Exchequer-Book, and levyed in general of every Town, and not particularly of every Man. It is also called *a Fifteenth, Anno* 14 *E.* 3. *stat.* 1. *cap.* 20. and 9 *H.* 4. *cap.* 7. See *Gilde, Subsidy and Fifteen*, and also *Camd. Brit.* pag. 304.

Taxatio Bladorum, An Imposition laid upon Corn.

Taxers, Two Officers yearly chosen in *Cambridge*, to see the true Gage of all weights and Measures: The Name took beginning from taxing or rating the Rents of Houses, which was anciently the Duty of their Office.

Tea, Is a kind of potable Liquor, lately used in *England*, and introduced from *China* and the *East-Indies*, being made of the Leaf of a Shrub, growing in those parts. See 12 *Car.* 2. *cap.* 15.

Teame and Theame, Or **Tem and Theme,** Signifies a Royalty granted by the King's Charter to the Lord of a Manner, for the having, restraining and judging Bondmen, Neifes, and Villains, with their Children, Goods and Chattels in his Court. *Theme est quod habeatis totam generationem villanorum vestrorum cum eorum* *fectis & catallis ubicunque inventi fuerint, excepto quod si nativus quietus manserit per unum annum & unum diem in aliqua Civitate vel villa privilegiata, ita quod in eorum communitatem & libertatem transierit —— Qui autem jurisdictionem habent hujusmodi curiam de* **Theme**, i. *de nativis vel servis dicuntur habere, &c. Spelman* in the Laws of *Edward the Confessor*, cap. 21. & 25. says, *Significare videtur jurisdictionem cognoscendi in Curia sua de advocationibus sive interciatis*, i. *de vocatis ad Warrantiam.* See *Glanvil*, lib. 5. cap. 2. and *Gloss. in* 10 *Scriptores.* See also *Bracton*, lib. 3. tract. 2. cap. 8. num. 25. and *Skene de verbor.* Signif. *verb.* Theme.

Teinland, *Teinlanda*, Tainland or Thainland, as if we should say the Land of a *Thane* or Noble Person. Breve Regis Willielmi Junioris, *lib.* Rames, *sect.* 178.——*Willielmus Rex Angliæ* W. *de Cabaniis salutem*; *Præcipio tibi ut facias convenire shiram de* Hamtona *& judicio ejus cognosce si terra de* Isham *reddidit firmam Monachis sancti Benedicti tempore Patris mei*; *& si ita invent. fuerit, sit in Dominio Abbatis. Si vero* **Teinlanda** *tunc fuisse invenietur, qui eam tenet de Abbate, teneat & recognoscat, quod si noluerit, eam Abbas in Dominio habeat & vide ne clamor inde amplius ad nos redeat, Teste* W. *Episc. Dunelm.* Where **Teinlanda** seems to signifie *Terra Hæreditaria & colonorum servituti obnoxia.* According to *Doomsday*, Land holden by *Knights service* was called **Tainland**, and Land holden in *Socage*, **Reveland**, *Co.* on *Lit. sect.* 117.

Teirs. See *Tierce.*

Teller, Is an Officer of the Exchequer, of which there are four; whose Office is to receive all Monies due to the King, and to give the *Clerk of the Pell* a Bill to charge him therewith. They also pay to all persons any Money payable by the King, by Warrant from the *Auditor of the Receit*, and make weekly and yearly Books, both of their Receipts and Payments, which they deliver to the *Lord Treasurer.*

Telonium. See *Thelonium.*

Templers, or **Knights of the Temple**, *Templarii*, Was a Religious Order of Knighthood, instituted about the year 1119. and so called, because they dwelt in a part of the Building belonging to the *Temple of Jerusalem*, and not far from the *Sepulchre of our Lord.* They flourisht here from *Henry the Second's* Days till they were suppressed. See *Knights of the Temple.*

Temporalties of Bishops, *Temporalia Episcoporum*, Be such Revenues, Lands, and Tenements, and Lay-fees, as have been laid to Bishop Sees, by Kings and other great Personages of this Land from time to time, as they are Barons, and Lords of the Parliament. See *Spiritualties of Bishops.*

Tempus pinguedinis & firmationis, *Et sciendum quod* **tempus pinguedinis** *his computatur inter festum beati Petri ad Vincula & Exaltationem Sanctæ Crucis, &* tempus firmationis *inter festum sancti* Martini *& Purificationem Beatæ* Mariæ. The first is the Season of the Buck, the later of the Doe. See *Firmisona.*

Tenancies, Are Houses of Habitation, or places to live in, held of another. See 23 *Eliz. cap.* 4.

Tend, Seems to signifie as much as to offer, shew forth or endeavour; as to *tend* the Estate of the Party of the Demandant, *Old. Nat. Brev. fol.* 123. To *tend* an Averment, *Britton, cap.* 76. To *tend* to traverse, *Stamf. prærog.* fol. 96.

Tender, May seem to come from the French *Tendre*, i. *tener, delicatus*, and used adjectively, signifies the same with us in *English*: But in a legal sense it denotes as much as carefully to offer, or circumspectly endeavour the performance of any thing belonging to us. As to *tender Rent*, is to offer it at the time and place where and when it ought to be paid. To *tender his Law of Summons*, Kitchin, fol. 197. Is to offer himself ready to make his Law, whereby to prove that he was not summoned. See *Law.* See *Make.*

Tenementis Legatis, Is a Writ that lies to *London*, or any other Corporation, (where the Custome is, That Men may demise Tenements as well as Goods and Chattels by their last Will,) for the hearing any controversie touching the same, and for rectifying the wrong, *Reg. Orig.* fol. 244.

Tenant or **Tenent**, *Tenens* From the Latine *Tenere*, to hold; Signifies one that holds or possesses Lands or Tenements by any kind of Right, be in Fee, for Life, Years, or at Will. The word in Law is used with divers additions, as *Tenant in Dower*, which is she that possesses Land by virtue of her *Dower, Kitchin*, fol. 160. *Tenant per Statute-Merchant*, that holds Land by virtue of a Statute forfeited to him, *Ibid. fol.* 172. *Tenant in Frank-marriage*, Ibid. fol. 158. He that holds Lands or Tenements by virtue of a Gift thereof made to him upon Marriage between him and his Wife. *Tenant by the Courtesie*, Id. fol. 159. That holds for his Life, by reason of a Child begotten by him of his Wife, being an Inheritrix, and born alive. *Tenant by Elegit*, that holds by virtue of the Writ called an *Elegit. Tenant in Mortgage*, that holds by means of a *Mortgage. Tenant by the Verge* in ancient Demesne (*Id. fol.* 81.) is he that is admitted by the Rod in a Court of ancient Demesne. *Tenant by Copy of Court Roll*, Is one admitted *Tenant* of any Lands, &c. within a Mannor, which time out of mind have been demisable, according to the Custome of the Mannor, *West. Symbol. part* 1. *lib.* 2. *sect.* 646. *Tenant by Charter*, Is he that holdeth by Feoffment in Writing, or other Deed, *Kitchin, fol.* 57. There was also *Tenant by Knight-service*, Tenant *in Burgage*, *Tenant in Socage*, Tenant *in Franck-fee*, Tenant *in Villenage.* So is there *Tenant in Fee-simple*, Kitchin, fol. 150. *Tenant in Fee-tail*, Id. fol. 153. *Tenant at the will of the Lord, according to the Custome of the Mannor*, Id fol. 132. & 165. *Tenant at Will by the Common Law*, Ibid. *Tenant upon Sufferance*, Ibid. *Tenant of Estate of Inheritance*, Stamf. Prærog. *fol.* 6. *Tenant in Chief*, that holdeth of the King in Right of his Crown, *F. N. B. fol.* 5. *Tenant of the King*, Is he that holds of the Person of the King, *Ibid.* or as some Honor, *Ibid. Very Tenant*, that holds immediately of his Lord, *Kitchin*, fol. 99. For if there be Lord, Mesne and *Tenant*, the *Tenant* is *very Tenant* of the Mesne, but not to the Lord above: *Tenant Peravayle.* See *Peravayle*, Pl. Cor. 197. and *F. N. B. fol.* 136. See *Dyer's Com.* fol. 25. num. 156. So there are also *Joynt-tenants*, that

 have

have equal Right in Lands and Tenements, by virtue of one Title, *Lit. lib.* 3. *cap.* 3. *Tenents in Common*, that have equal Right, but hold by divers Titles, *Ibid.* cap. 4. *Particular tenant*, *Stamf. Prærog. fol.* 13. that holds only for his term. See *Coke* in Sir *Will. Pelham*'s Case, *lib.* 1. *fol.* 15. called *Termor for Life or Years*. See *Plowd. Cothrist*'s Case, *fol.* 23. *Sole tenant*, Kitchin, fol. 134. He that hath no other joyned with him. *Several tenant* is opposite to *Joynt-tenant*, or *Tenants in Common*. *Tenant al Præcipe*, Is he against whom the Writ *Præcipe* is to be brought, *Co. Rep. lib.* 3. Case *of Fines*, fol. 88. *Tenant in Demesne*, 13 *E.* 1. *cap.* 9. 32 *H.* 8. *cap.* 37. Is he that holdeth the Demeans of a Mannor for a Rent without Service. *Tenant on Service*, 20 *Ed.* 1. stat. 1. Is he that holdeth by Service. Vide *Britton*, *cap.* 79. *in principio* & cap. 96. *Car fealty*, &c. *Tenant by Execution*, 32 H. 8. cap. 5. that holds Land by virtue of an Execution upon any Statute, Recognisance, &c. with divers others.

Tenheved, A Saxon word signifying *Decanus, caput vel Princeps, decuriæ* Leg. Edw. Conf. cap. 29. *Statuerunt Justiciarios super quosq; decem friborgos, quos* Decanos *possumus appellare, Anglicè verò* tienheofod, *dicti sunt*. See *Frank-pledge*.

Tenement, *Tenementum*, Signifies most properly a House or Home-stall; but more largely either for a House or Land that a Man holdeth of another, and joyned with the Adjective *Frank*, it contains Lands, Houses, and Offices, wherein we have Estate for term of Life or in Fee: And in this sense, *Kitchin*, fol. 41. makes *Frank-Tenement* and *base Estate* opposite to each other. In the same sort *Britton* uses it, *cap.* 27. as also *Bracton* doth the Latine *liberum tenementum*, lib. 1. cap. 5. & 6.

Tenentibus in assisis non onerandis, &c. Is a Writ that lyeth for him to whom a Disseisor hath alienated the Land, whereof he disseised another, that he be not molested for the Damages awarded, if the Disseisor have wherewith to satisfie them himself, *Reg. Orig.* 214.

Tenmantale, A Saxon word signifying *Decuria Tythinga*, Leg. Edw. Conf. cap. 20. *Et sint quieti de Geldis & Danegeldis &* thenemanatale *& concelationibus & scottis*, &c. Cart. 29 Ed. 1. Abbat. de Thorneton. See *Friburgh*.

The tenor of these presents, *Tenore præsentium*, Is the matter contained therein, or rather the true intent and meaning thereof, as to do such a thing according to the *tenor* of a writing, is to do the same according to the true intent and meaning thereof.

Tenore indictamenti mittendo, Is a Writ whereby the Record of an Indictment and the Process thereupon is called out of another Court into the Chancery, *Reg. Orig.* fol. 169.

Tenths, *Decimæ*, Are that yearly Portion or Tribute which all Ecclesiastical Livings pay to the King; for though the Bishop of *Rome* does originally pretend Right to this Revenue, by the example of the High Priest among the *Jews*, who had *Tenths* from the *Levites*, *Numb. cap.* 8. *Hierom. in Ezech.* Yet we read in our *Chronicles*, That these were often granted to the King by the Pope upon divers occasions. Sometimes for one year, sometimes for more, till by the Stat. 26 *H. cap.* 3. they were annexed perpetually to the Crown. See *Dismes*. It signifies a Tax also levyed of the Temporalty, 4 *Inst. fol.* 34.

Tentor, A stretcher, tryer or prover, which Dyers and Clothiers use, *Anno* 1 *R.* 3. *cap.* 8. But prohibited by 39 *Eliz. cap.* 20.

Tenure, *Tenura*, And is properly derived from the Latine *tenere*, to hold, and accordingly in the *Grand Custumary of Normandy*, cap. 28. It is thus defined, *Tenure* is the manner whereby Tenements are *holden* of their Lords; What may make a *Tenure*, and what not, see *Perkins cap.* 10. *Reservations* 70. And in that Chapter you shall find the most of those *tenures* recited that be now usually in *England*. See *Cromp. Jur. fo.* 200. *New Book of Entries*, verb. *Tenure*. Mr. *Fabian Philips*'s Book entituled, *Tenenda non tollenda*, and the Stat. 12 *Car.* 2. *cap.* 24. In *Scotland* there be four manner of *tenures*, the first is *pura Eleemosina*, proper to spiritual Men, paying nothing for it but *devota Animarum suffragia*. The second, they call *Few* or Few-ferme, which holds of the King, Church, Barons, or others, paying a certain Duty called *Feuda firma*. The third, is a hold in *Blench*, as they term it, by payment of a Peny, a Rose, or such like thing, if demanded in the name of *Blench*, id est, *nomine albæ firmæ*. The fourth is by Service of Ward and Relief, where the Heir being minor, is in the custody of his Lord, &c. *Skene de verborum* Signif. *verb.* Haubert.

Terme, *Terminus*, Commonly signifies the bounds and limitation of time, as a Lease for terme of Life or Years, *Bract. lib.* 2. *cap.* 6. *num.* 4. But more notedly is it used for that time wherein the Tribunals, or Places for Judgment are open to all that think fit to complain of wrong, or seek their own by due course of Law or Action, the rest of the year is called *Vacation*. Of these *Termes* there be four in every year, during which time Matters of Justice are dispatched. One is called *Hillary Term*, *Terminus sancti Hillarii*, which begins the 23 of *January*, or if that be Sunday, then the next day after, and endeth the 12 of *February* following. The second is, *Terminus Paschæ*, *Easter Term*, which begins the *Wednesday* fortnight after *Easter-day*, and ends the *Monday* next after *Ascension-day*. The third is, *Terminus Trinitatis*, *Trinity Term*, beginning the *Friday* next after *Trinity-Sunday*, and ending the *Wednesday* fortnight after. The fourth is, *Michaelmas Term*, *Terminus sancti Michaelis*, which anciently began the Ninth of *October*; but by the Statute made 17 *Car.* 1. *cap.* 6. reduced to the twenty third of *October*, unless it be *Sunday*, and then to the day after, and ends the twenty eighth of *November* following. *Termini apud nos dicuntur certæ anni portiones agendis litibus designatæ*. See Spelman, *De origine & ratione* terminorum *forensium*.

Termonland, Seems to be the Glebe-land, or land belonging to the Church, anciently so called.

Termor, *Tenens ex termino*, Is he that holds for term of years or life, *Kitchin*, fol. 151. *Littleton*, *fol.* 100.

Terra Gilliforata, Land held by the tenure of paying a Gilliflower, M.S.

Terra

Terra extendenda, Is a Writ directed to the Escheator, &c. willing to inquire and find out the true yearly value of any Land, &c. by the Oath of twelve men, and to certifie the extent into the Chancery, &c. *Reg. Orig. fol.* 293.

Terra Frusca, Fresh Land, or such as hath not lately been plowed, ——*Continens* 40. *Acras* terræ frusca, *pasturæ*, *&c.* Mon. Ang. 2. par. fol. 327. This is else-where written *terra Frisca.*

Terra nova, *Sæpe legitur in Chartis feodalibus & in sensualibus schedulis*, *vel pro* terra *noviter concessa*, *vel noviter assarta*, Prior Lew. pag. 1. *Reddat pro* nova terra, 2. *sol.* Spelm.

Terra vestita, Is used in old Charters for Land sown with Corn.

Terra sabulosa, Gravelly or sandy Ground: *Et prædictæ* 24. *acræ terræ valent per Annum* 13 *sol. &* 4. *denar. & non plus*, *quia est* terra sabulosa, *Inqu.* 10 *E.* 3. *n.* 3. *Norf. in Turr. Lond.*

Terra Puturata. See *Putura.*

Terra Lucrabilis, Land that may be gained from the Sea, or enclosed out of a Wast to particular use. ---*Tam in Mora quam in* terra Lucrabili *& Marais cum omnibus Piscariis suis*, Mon. Ang. part 1. fol. 406.

Terra excultabilis, Land that may be tilled or plowed, ---*Totam illam* terram excultabilem, *quam habuit apud Norwicum in campis*, Mon. Ang. part 1. fol. 426.

Terra culta, Land that is tilled or manured, and *terra inculta*, uncultivated Land. See *Wacnoth.*

Terrage, *Terragium*, *Edward the Third* granted to *John of Gaunt*, *and Blanck* his Wife for their Lives, *Quod sint quieti de Theolonio*, *Passagio*, *Saccagio*, *Lastagio*, *Tallagio*, *Caruagio*, *Priscagio*, *Pickagio &* Terragio, which seems to be an exemption, *à Precariis*, *viz.* Boons of Ploughing, reaping, &c. and perhaps from all Land Taxes.

Terrar, *Terrarium vel catalogus terrarum*, Is a Book or Roll, wherein the several Lands either of a single Person, or of a Town, are described, containing the quantity of Acres, Boundaries, Tenants Names, and such like, 18 *Eliz. cap.* 17. In the Exchequer there is a *Terrar* of all the Glebe-lands in *England* made about 11 *E.* 3.

Terris bonis & catallis rehabendis post purgationem, Is a Writ that lies for a Clerk, to recover his Lands, Goods or Chattels, formerly seised, after he hath cleared himself of that Felony, upon suspition whereof he was formerly convicted and delivered to his Ordinary to be purged, *Reg. Orig.* fol. 68.

Terris liberandis, Is a Writ that lies for a man convicted by Attaint, to bring the Record and Process before the King, and to take a Fine for his Imprisonment, to deliver him his Lands and Tenements again, and to release him of the *Strip* and *Wast*, *Reg. Orig.* fol. 232. It is also a Writ for the delivery of Lands to the Heir after Homage and Relief performed, *Ibid.* fol. 293. Or upon security taken that he shall perform them, *Ibid.* fol. 313.

Terris & catallis tentis ultra debitum levatum, Is a Writ Judicial, for the restoring of Lands or Goods to a Debtor that is distrained above the quantity of the Debt, *Reg. Jud. fol.* 38.

Terre tenant, *Terræ tenens*, Is he who has the actual possession of the Land, which we otherwise call the *Occupation*, 39 *Eliz.* 7. For example, A Lord of a Mannor hath a Free-holder, who letteth out his Free-hold to another to be occupyed; this Occupyer (having the actual possession) is called the *Terre-tenant*, *West Symbol.* part 2. tit. *Fines*, sect. 137. *Cromp. Jur. fol.* 194. *Britton*, *cap.* 29. *Perkins Feoffments* 231. *Terse* is a certain Measure of liquid things, as Wine, Oyl, &c. containing the sixth part of a Tun, 32 H. 8. 14. or the third part of a Pipe.

Testament, *Testamentum*, Is thus defined by *Plowden*, Testamentum *est testatio mentis*, A *Testament* is a Witness of the Mind: But *Aulus Gellius*, *lib.* 6. *chap.* 12. denies it to be a Compound word, and saith, It is *Verbum simplex*, as *Calceamentum*, *Paludamentum*, &c. And therefore it may be thus better defined, *Testamentum*, *est ultimæ voluntatis justa sententia*, *eo quod quis post mortem suam fieri vult*, *&c.* Of *Testaments* there are two sorts, viz. a *Testament in writing*, and a *Testament in words*, which is called a *Nuncupative Testament*, which is, when a Man being sick, and for fear lest death, want of Memory or Speech should come so suddenly upon him, that he should be prevented if he stay'd the writing of his *Testament*, desires his Neighbours and Friends to bear witness of his last Will, and then declares the same before them by words, which after his decease is proved by Witnesses, and put in writing by the Ordinary, and then stands in as good force as if it had at the first in the life of the Testator been put in writing, except only for Lands, which are devisable but by a *Testament* put in writing in the life of the Testator. See *Co.* on *Lit. lib.* 2. *cap.* 10. *sect.* 167. *Plowd. fol.* 541. *Paramore* and *Jurdlye*'s Case, *Co.* 6. *Rep. Marquess of Winchester*'s Case. *Testament* was anciently used (according to *Spelman*) *pro Scripto*, *Charta vel Instrumento*, *quo prædiorum rerumve aliarum transactiones perficiuntur*, *sic dictum quod de ea re vel testimonium ferret vel testium nomina contineret*---*Si quis contra hoc meæ authoritatis* testamentum *aliquod machinari impedimentum præsumpsit*, Charta Croylandiæ ab Æthelbaldo Rege, Anno Domini 716.

Testator, Lat. He that makes a Testament. See *Swinburne of Wills and Testaments.* See *Wills.*

Testatum, Is a Writ in personal Actions, as if the Defendant cannot be arrested upon a *Capias* in the County where the Action is laid, but is returned *Non est inventus* by the Sheriff. This Writ shall be sent out into any other County, where such person is thought to have wherewith to satisfie: And this is termed a *testatum*, because the Sheriff hath formerly *testified*, that the Defendant was not to be found in his Bayliwick. See *Kitchin*'s *Return of Writs*; fol. 287.

Teste, Is a word commonly used in the last part of every Writ, wherein the Date is contained, which begins with these words, *Teste meipso*, *&c.* If it be an original Writ; or if Judicial, *Teste Matthæo Hale milite*, or *Johanne Vaughan milite*, according to the Court whence it issues. Yet we read in *Glanvile*, *lib.* 1. *cap.* 6. *&* 13. and

 lib.

ib. 2. cap. 4. the last Clause of an Original Writ to be *Teste Radulpho de Glanvilla apud Clarendon, &c.* and divers times in the *Register of Writs*, Teste *Custode Angliæ*, as namely in the Title *Prohibition*, fol. 42. and *Consultation*, fol. 54.

Testimonial, 39 *Eliz.* 17. Is a Certificate under the Hand of a Justice of Peace, testifying the place and time when and where a Souldier or Mariner landed, and the place of his Dwelling and Birth, unto which he is to pass, or such like, 3. *Inst.* fol. 85.

Teston, 2 & 3 *E.* 6. *cap.* 17. A sort of Money which, among the French, did bear the value of 18. *Denar.* But in *Henry* the Eighth's time, being made of Brass, lightly gilt with Silver, it was reduced to 12 *d.* and in the beginning of *Edward* the Sixth to 9 *d.* and afterwards to 6 *d.*

Thacktile, 17 *E.* 4. 4. Otherwise called *Plaintiles*, which are laid on the side of a House.

Thanage of the King, *Thanagium Regis*, Signified a certain part of the *King's* Land or Property, whereof the Ruler or Governor was called *Thane*, *Domania Regis & Thanagia idem significant*, says *Skene*.

Thane or **Theyne**, *Thanus*, Signifies sometimes a Nobleman, sometime a Free-man, sometime a Magistrate, but more properly an Officer or Minister of the King, *Lamb.* in his *Exposition of Saxon words*, verb. *Thanus*. And *Skene de verb.* Signif. saith, That it is a name of Dignity, equal with the Son of an Earl. This Appellation was in use among us after the *Norman* Conquest, as appears by *Doomsday*, and by a certain Writ of *William the First*, *Willielmus Rex salutat Hermannum Episcopum, & Stewinum, & Britwi, & omnes* thanos *meos in Dorsestrensi pago amicabiliter*, M. S. de Abbatsbury. *Camden* says, They were enabled only by the Office which they administred. See *Mill's de Nobilitate*, fol. 132.

Theft, *Furtum*, Is an unlawful felonious taking away of another mans moveable and personal Goods against the Owners will, with an intent to steal them; and this is divided into *Theft* simply so called, and *Petit theft*, whereof the one is of Goods above the value of twelve pence, and is felony: The other under that value and is no Felony, but called *Petit Larceny*. See *Larceny* and *Felony*. *Theft* from the Person, or in the presence of the Owner, is properly called *Robbery*, *West Symbol.* part 2. tit. *Inditements*, sect. 58, 59, 60.

Theftbote, May be derived from the Saxon *Theof*, i. *furtum*, and *Bote*, i. *compensatio*, and signifies properly the receiving of Goods from a Thief, to favor and maintain him, *Est quant home prist Chatell de Larons de luy favourer & mainteyner & nemy autrement*, 42. Ass. pag. 2. And the punishment thereof is Ransome and Imprisonment, and not loss of Life and Member, *Stamf. Pl. Cor. lib.* 1. *cap.* 43. and the *Mirror of Justices*, lib. cap. *Des Perches criminals al suit le Roy. Antiquè dicebatur pretium quo furti reus se eximeret à dispendio vitæ; hodie vero de iis dicitur qui furtiva bona à latrone susceperint, sceleris sui fovendi gratia, quo sensu* **Bote** *pro præda ut alias solet intelligendum est. In privilegiorum chartis ubi* **Theftbote** *conceditur, intelligitur alias esse emenda furti sine consideratione Curiæ Domini Regis.* **Theftbote** *(inquit statutum Walliæ Anno* 12 E. 1. ---*Hoc est, emenda furti sine consideratione Curiæ Domini Regis*, Spelm. And see 3. *Inst. fol.* 134.

Thegne. See *Thanus* and *Thingus*.

Thelonium, or Breve essendi quieti de thelonio, Is a Writ lying for the Citizens of any City, or Burgesses of any Town, that have a Charter or Prescription to free them from *Toll*, against the Officers of any Town or Market, who would constrain them to pay *Toll* of their Merchandise contrary to their said Grant or Prescription, *F. N. B. fol.* 226.

Thelonia rationabili habendo pro Dominis habentibus Dominica Regis ad firmam, Is a Writ that lies for him that hath of the King's demesne in Fee-farm, to recover reasonable *Toll* of the King's Tenants there, if his Demesne have been accustomed to be *tolled*, *Reg. Orig. fol.* 87.

Them. See *Teame*.

Then, *Significat servum*, Fleta, lib. 1. cap. 47.

Thenecium, *Quod Prædicti Parochiani* ---*Decimas inferius annotatas Ecclesiis suis persolvant, scilicet, Decimam lactis, ovorum* thenecii agrorum, *apum, mellis*, &c. Const. Rob. Winchelsey Archiep. Cant. tit. de Decimis. *Ibi Lindwode* thenecii agrorum, i. *Arborum crescentium circa agros pro clausura eorum*, vulgarly called **Hedgrowes** or **Dike-rowes**.

Thew, *Georgius Grey comes Cantii clamat in Maner. de* Bushton & Ayton *punire delinquentes contra Assisam panis & cervisiæ per tres vices per amerciamenta & quarta vice pistores per* Pilloriam, *Braciatores per tumbrellam, & rixatrices per* **Thewe**, hoc est, *ponere eas super scabellum vocat. a* **Cuckingstool**, Pl. in Itin. apud Cestr. 14 *H.* 7.

Thingus, (*Thanus*) A Nobleman, a Knight, or Free-man; *Sciatis me concessisse omnibus militibus & omnibus* thingis, *& omnibus liberè tenentibus, qui manent in Foresta mea de Honore de Lancaster quod possunt*, &c. Cromp. Jur. fol. 197.

Thirdborow, Is used for a Constable, *Anno* 28 *H.* 8. *cap.* 10. And *Lambert's Duty of Constables*, pag. 6. and seems to be corruptly used for the Saxon ꝼꞃeoboꞃoᵹ, i. *ingenuus fidejussor*.

Thirdings, The *third* part of the Corn or Grain growing on the Ground at the Tenants Death, due to the Lord for a Heriot within a certain Mannor, and Lands belonging to the Mannor of *Turfat* in the County of *Hereford*.

Third night awn-hinde, *Trium noctium Hospes*: By the Laws of St. *Edward* (cap. *De Hospitibus*) If any Guest lay a *third night* in an Inn, he was accounted a Domestick, and his Host was answerable for what Offence he should commit. **Forman night uncuth, Twa night Gueste, Third night awne-hinde**, that is, *the first* night *a Stranger*, *the second* night *a Guest*, *the third* night *a Domestick*, Bract. lib. 3. tract. 2. cap. 10. num. 2. writs *Hogenhyne* for *Agenhine*.

Item utimur quod si extranei morantur in Burgo prædicto

prædicto ultra tres dies invenient fidejussores de bene gerendo se erga Burgenses & communitatem dum moram inter ipsos fecerint, M. S. Codex de L. Statut. & Consuetud. liberi Burgi Villæ Mountgom. fol. 26. See *Uncuth*.

Thirdpeny, *Denarius tertius est ea pars mulctarum forensiumq; molumentum quæ in Comitatu olim cedebat comiti, Rege alias duas percipiente*, Leg. Ed. Conf. cap. 31. *Rex habebit* 100. *solidos & Consul. comitatus* 50. *qui tertium habebit danarium de forisfacturis, &c.* and was anciently so fixt, and appropriate to an Earldom; as the Earldom of *Oxford*, in the Reign of King *Henry the Second*, passed by the Grant of *Tertium denarium comitatus* Oxon. *ut sit inde Comes.* Of which see *Selden's Titles of Honor.*

Thokes, Fish with broken Bellies, 22 *E.* 4. *cap.* 2. which by the said Statute are not to be mixt or packt with *Tale fish*.

Thol, *Thollonium est libertas emendi & vendendi in terra sua*, Lamb. Archaion, fol. 132.

Thol, i. *quod Prior habet in mercato suo die Lunæ quandam mensuram de bladis Venditis & quoddam certum de animalibus & cæteris similibus venditis*, Reg. Priorat. Cokeford. See *Toll*.

Thorough-Toll, At a place called *Borrogh* in *York-shire*; in times past the Earls of *Richmond* had a Castelet, and a certain Custom called *Thorough-toll*, says *Camden*. See *Toll*.

Thrave of Corn, In most parts of *England* consists of twenty four Sheaves, or four Shocks, six Sheaves to every Shock, 2 *H.* 6. *cap.* 2. yet in some Counties they reckon but twelve Sheaves to the *thrave*: As in the matter concerning the Burgesses of *Derby*,---*Hi autem ad festum sancti* Martini *reddebant Regi duodecem* trabes *annone*, Doomsday Book *de Burgensibus Derb.* See *Peter-corne*.

Thrimsa, From the Saxon ðrim, which signifies three, was an old piece of Money of three shillings, according to *Lambert*, or rather (as *Selden* thinks) the third part of a shilling, *Titles of Honor*, fol. 604. See *Weregild*.

Thrithing, *Thrithingum*, In the Statute of *Merton* signifies a Court which consists of three or four hundreds, *Co.* 2. *Inst. fol.* 99.

Thrower. See *Silk-thrower*.

Thwertnik, *Edwardus, &c. Concessimus etiam quod Vicecomes noster aut hæredum nostrorum qui pro tempore fuerit in dicto comitatu, de cætero faciat executiones pro debitis recuperatis & recognitis in Comitatu vel Scaccario Cestriæ aut in itinere Justiciariorum, qui pro tempore fuerit, absq; aliquo capiendo pro executione facienda, licet etiam præteritis temporibus usum sit, prout per chartam habet ipsa communitas, (scilicet Cestresciræ) quod si aliquis in curia nostra culpatus fuerit, per* thwertnik *se defendere possit; quia hæc defensio est contraria legi Communi, nutrix malorum, pacis æmula & damnosa populo pacifico: Volumus etiam de consensu & requisitione dictæ communitatis, Ordinamus & præcipimus quod dicta defensio per* thwertnik *de cætero non allocetur sed annulletur totaliter & damnetur, &c.* Rot. Cart. de Anno 11, 12, 13 Rich. 2. num. 11. per Inspex.

Tidesmen, Are certain Officers that belong to the *Custome-house*, and are appointed to watch or attend upon Ships, till the Custom of the Fraight be paid; and they are so called, because they go aboard the Ships at their arrival in the mouth of the *Thames*, and come up with the *Tide*.

Tierce. See *Ters*.

Tigh or **Teage**, A Close or Enclosure, a Croft; which word *Tigh* is still used in *Kent* in the same sense. And in an old Charter of the Church of *Canterbury*, we find this Clause,---*Mansionem quoq; quæ est in Aquilonali parte* Doroberniæ & *clausulam quam Angli vocant* teage *quæ pertinent ad prædictam mansionem*, &c.

Tilsen of Satten, Is mentioned *Anno* 1 *H.* 8. *cap.* 14. but not expounded.

Timber of Skins, Is forty *Skins*, *De qualibet* Timber *de Fitcheux venal.* Ob. Pat. 10 R. 2. pars 1. m. 10. *Hæc civitas* (sc. Cestriæ) *tunc reddebat de firma* 45. *libras & tres* timbres *pellium Martrinarum*, Leg. Edw. Conf.

Timberlode, *Servitutis genus, quo Vassallus obligatur materiam sive lignum de sylva, ubi prosternitur, ad Domini sui domum deferre*, Gloss. in 10. Script.

Tineman or **Tienman**, Was of old a petty Officer in the Forest, who had the Nocturnal Care of Vert and Venison, and other servile Employments, *Constitution. Forestæ Canuti Regis*, cap. 4.

Tipstaffe, Is one of the Warden of the Fleets Men, that attends the King's Courts with a painted Staff, for the taking such into Custody as are committed by the Court, and to attend such Prisoners as go at large by Licence: These are otherwise called *Bastons*, *Anno* 1 *Rich.* 2. *cap.* 12. and 5 *Eliz. cap.* 23. They also are called *Tipstaves*, that attend the Judges with a kind of Rod tipt with Silver, and take into their charge all Prisoners either committed or turned over at the Judges Chamber.

Tissue, Is a French word signifying as much as Cloth of Silk and Silver, or of Silk and Gold woven together.

Tithes, *Decimæ*, Are the tenth part of all Fruits, *Predial*, *Personal* and *Mixt*, which are due to God, and consequently to his Churches Ministers for their Maintenance, *Levit.* 27. *vers.* 30. *Omnium bonorum licite quæsitorum quota pars deo, Divina constitutione debita.* And it was of later times Resolved, *viz.*

Paschæ 1 Jac. Rot. 1119. in Communi Banco.

Quod decimarum tres sunt species, quædam Personales, *quæ debentur ex opere personali, ut Artificio, scientia, Militia, Negotiatione*, &c. *Quædam* Prædiales *quæ proveniunt ex prædiis, i. ex fructibus prædiorum, ut Blada, vinum, fænum, linum, cannabum*, &c. *seu ex fructibus arborum, ut Poma, Pyra, Pruna, Volema, Cerasa & fructus hortorum*, &c. *Quædam* mixtæ, *ut de Caseo, Lacte*, &c. *aut ex fœtibus animalium quæ sunt in pascuis & gregatim pascuntur, ut in Agnis, Vitulis, Hædis, Capreolis, Pullis*, &c. *Ex prædialibus quædam sunt* Majores, *quædam* Minutæ. Majores, *ut frumentum, siligo, zizania, fænum*, &c. Minores *sive* minutæ, *quidam dicunt, sunt qui proveniunt ex mentha, aneto, oleribus & similibus juxta illud dictum Domini Luc.* 11. 42. Væ qui decimatis

matis Mentham & Rutham, &c. *Alii dicant quod in Anglia consistunt* decimæ minutæ *in lino, quæ sunt prædiales & lana, lacte, caseis & in Decimis animalium, agnis, pullis & ovibus; Decimæ etiam mellis & ceræ numerantur inter* Minutas, *quæ sunt* Mixtæ. *Vide* Linwood, *cap.* De Decimis. But Laymen in these later times, by with-drawing or with-holding their *Tythes*, occasions the Statutes of 27 *H.* 8. 20. 32 *H.* 8. 7. and 2 *E.* 6. 13. which were made to enforce the payment thereof, which former times required not, when more was often given than was either due or demanded. Nay, anciently many men were so scrupulously careful in their payment of *Tythes*, that at their Death they bequeathed **Soulesceat** to their Parish-Priest, in lieu of any *Tythes* forgotten, and at their Funerals caused their best Oxe or Horse to be led with the Corps, and as a Mortuary or Oblation given to the Priest, in recompence of any *Tythes* which might have been forgotten.

Tithing, *Tithingum*, From the Saxon *Teothunge*, which signifies *Decuriam*: It signifies (according to *Lambert* in his *Duty of Constables)* the number or company of ten Men with their Families, knit together in a Society, all being bound to the King for the peaceable Behavior of each other. Of these Companies, there was one chief or principal Person, who, from his Office was called **Teothung-man**, at this day in some places *Tithing-man*, but is indeed a Constable, for the old way of *Tithings* is long since left off. It is also used for a Court, *Magna Chart, cap.* 25. *Merton, cap.* 10. and 23 *E.* 3. *cap.* 4. See *Chief Pledge, Frank-pledge, Decennier and Trithing.*

Tithingpeny alias **Tithpeny**, alias **Thethingpeny**, *Et sint quieti de* Thethingpeny, *Tympenny, & de omnibus forisfactis quacunque occasione emerserunt, &c.* In Mem. Scac. de anno 20 E. 3. Trin. Rot. 3. *Abbati & Monachis Rading.* **Tithingpeny** *hoc est quieti de Tallagio Decennæ sive* Tithing *per consuetudinem*, M. S. in Biblioth. Cotton. sub tit. *Vitellius*, C. 9. fol. 221.

Tillage, *Agricultura*, Is of great account in Law, as very profitable for the Commonwealth; and therefore arable Land hath the precedence before Meadows, Pastures, Woods, Mines, and all other Ground whatsoever. And by laying of Lands used in *tillage* to Pasture, six grand Inconveniences ensue.

1. Idleness, which is the ground and beginning of all mischief.

2. Depopulation and decay of Towns, for where in some Towns two hundred persons were imployed and lived by their lawful Labours, by converting Tillage into Pasture, only two or three Herd-men are maintained.

3. Husbandry is decayed.

4. Churches are destroyed, by diminution of Church-Livings.

5. Injury and wrong done to Patrons and Ministers.

6. The Defence of the Land against foreign Enemies enfeebled and impaired; the Bodies of Husbandmen being more strong and able, and patient of cold, heat, and hunger than any other.

Title, *Titulus*, Properly is when a man hath lawful cause of Entry into Lands whereof another is seised, for which he can have no Action, as *title* of Mortmain, or *title* to enter for breach of Condition: But legally this word *Title* includes a Right also, and *Title* is the more general word, for every Right is a *Title*, but every *Title* is not such a Right for which an Action lyeth, and therefore *Titulus est justa causa possidendi quod nostrum est*, and signifies the means whereby a man cometh to Land, as his *title* is by Fine or Feoffment. And as by a Release of a *Right* a *Title* is released, so by release of a *Title*, a *Right* is released also. See *Co.* 4. *Rep. Edward Althem's* Case.

Title of Entry, Is, when one is seised of Land in Fee, makes a Feoffment thereof on condition, and the condition is broken; after which the Feoffor hath *title* to enter into the Land, and may do so at his pleasure, and by his *Entry* the Free-hold shall be said to be in him presently. And it is called *Title of Entry*, because he cannot have a Writ of Right against his Feoffee upon condition, for his Right was out of him by the Feoffment, which cannot be reduced with *Entry*, and the *Entry* must be for the breach of the condition.

Tod of Wooll, Contains twenty eight pound, or two stone, mentioned in the Statute 12 *Car. cap.* 32. See 3. *Inst. fol.* 96.

Toft, *Toftum*, A Messuage, or rather a place where a Messuage hath stood, *West Symbol.* part 2. tit. *Fines*, sect. 26. And is a word much used in *Fines*, —*Capitale* Toftum & Croftum *quod fuit Walteri Patris sui*, Cart. Petri de Brus in Biblioth. Cotton. Scites & Toftes, *Anno* 22 *Car.* 2. *cap.* 11.

Toftman, *Toftmannus*, The Owner of a Toft, *Toftmanni similiter operabantur à Sancto* Michaele *usq; ad Autumpnum & in autumno per* 6. *hebdomadas unaquaq; hebdomade per* 2. *dies, &c.* Pri.Lew. pag. 18. See *Molman.*

Toile, Cometh of the French *Toile*, i. *tela*, and signifieth with us a Net or Cord to compass or take Deer. *Tol. tolleror*, as it is a Verb signifieth to defeat or take away, *Anno* 8 *H.* 6. *cap.* 9. as to *Toll* the Entry is to take away the Right of Entry.

Toll alias **Tholl**, *Tolnetum* alias *Theolonium*, Is a Saxon word, and hath in our Common Law two significations. First, It is used for a Liberty to buy and sell within the Precincts of a Mannor, *Lamb. Arch. fol.* 132. Secondly, For a Tribute or Custom paid for passage, &c. *Bract. lib.* 2. *cap.* 24. *num.* 3. Interprets it to be a Liberty as well to take as to be free from *toll*; for they who are enfeoffed with *Toll*, are Custom-free, saith *Skene*. *Toll* hoc est *quod vos & homines vestri de toto Homagio vestro sint quieti de omnibus mercatis & de* Tolneto *de omnibus rebus emptis & venditis.* Of this freedom from *Toll* the City of *Coventry* boasts of an ancient Charter, granted by *Leofrich* (or *Lurich*) *Merciorum Comes*, who at the importunity of *Godeva* his vertuous Lady, granted this Freedom to that City; and in *Richard* the Second's time (as *Dugdale* saith in his *Description of Warwickshire*) the Picture of him & his Lady was set up in the South Window of *Trinity* Church there, holding in his right Hand a Charter, with these words written thereon.

I Jurich, for the Love of Thee,
Do make Coventry Toll-free.

Some Authors make mention of *Tolthrough*, which is Money paid for passage in or *through* some High-ways, or over Ferries, Bridges, &c. *Toll-traverse*, for passing over a private Man's Ground, and **Toll-turne**, which is *Toll* paid at the return of Beasts from Fair or Market, though they were not sold, *Plowd.fo.*236. *Willion*'s Case. *Kitchin, fol.* 104. By the Ancient Law of the Land, the Buyers of Cattle or Corn in Fairs or Markets ought to pay *Toll* to the Lord of the Market, *Horn's Mirror of Just.* lib. 1. cap. *De articles.* The made Latine word *Theolonium*, *Cassanæus de consuet.* Burg. pag. 118. deriveth a *Tollendo*, but it is more properly deduced from the Greek τελώνια or τελωνεῖα, id est, *vectigalium redemptio vel exactio.* See *Fleta, lib.* 1. *cap.* 47.

Tollage, *Anno* 17 *Car.* 1. *cap.* 12. See *Tallage.*

Tolsester, ---*Per* Tolsester, *clamat esse quiet. de reddend. unum Sextarium Cervisiæ quod continet* 16. *Lagenas de nova cervisia mensurata, desultus le* Shakcliff *pro licentia brasiandi cervis, Per totum annum.* Ex Rot. Plac. in Itin. apud Cest. 14 H. 7. The same word occurs in a Charter, 55 *H.* 3. *m.* 6. See *Gavelcester.*

Tolt, *Tolta*, Is a Writ whereby a Cause depending in a Court-Baron, is removed to the County Court, *Old Nat. Brev. fol.* 2. and so called, because it does *tollere loquelam* from the one Court to another. *Preface* to *Co. Rep.* 3. *Plac. coram Rege Pasch.* 22 *E.* 1. *Rot.* 18. Tolla placiti *significat processum per quem causa a jurisdictione curiæ temporalis* tollitur.

Tolsray, ---*Venditio salis quæ debet solvi*, 1. *Bushel & dimid. salis per mensuram*, 4 s. M. S. *de temp.* Edw. 1.

Tonne. See *Tunne.*

Tonnage, *Tonnagium*, Is a Custome or Impost paid to the King for Merchandise carried out, or brought in Ships, or such like Vessels, according to a certain Rate upon every Tun; and of this you may read in the Statutes 12 *E.* 4. *cap.* 3. 6 *H.* 8. *cap.* 14. 1 *E.* 6. *cap.* 13. 1 *Jac.* 33. but especially 12 *Car.* 2. *cap.* 4.

Torney. See *Turney.*

Tort, Is a *French* word for injury or wrong, as *de son tort mesne*, in his own wrong, *Cro. Rep. fol.* 20. *White*'s Case. Wrong or injury is properly called *Tort*, because it is wrested or crooked, *Co.* on *Lit. fol.* 158.

Tortfeasor, a Wrong-doer, a Trespasser, *Cro.* 2. *par. fol.* 383. *num.* 11.

Toties-quoties, *Anno* 19. *Car.* 2. *cap.* 4. and signifies As often as.

Totted, A good Debt to the King, is by the *foreign Opposer*, or other Officer in the Exchequer, noted for such, by writing this word *Tot* to it, *Anno* 42 *E.* 3. *cap.* 9. and 1 *E.* 6. 15. See *Practice of the Exchequer*, pag. 71.

Totteray, Was a Customary payment of four pence for every Bushel and a half of Corn, sold at *Maldon* in *Essex*, *Hill.* 15 E. 1.

Tourne, See *Turn.*

Tout temps prist & uncore est, That is always ready, and is so at this present. This is a kind of Plea in way of excuse or defence for him that is sued for any Debt or Duty belonging to the Plantiff. See *Broke's Abridgment, fol.* 258.

Towage, *Towagium*, Is the rowing or drawing a Ship or Barge along the water by Men, or Beasts on Land, or by another Ship or Boat fastned to her. Also that Money, or other recompence, which is given by Bargemen to the Owner of the Ground next a River where they *tow* a Barge, or other Vessel, *Dominus Rex habeat & habere debeat* Throwagium *navium & Battellorum majorum & minorum in aqua de Tyne, &c.* Pla. coram Rege & ejus concil. Parl. 18 E. 1. in Tur London.

Traylbaston, See *Justices of Traylboston.*

Traytor, *Proditor*, See *Treason.*

Trayterous position, Of taking Arms by the King's Authority against his Person, and those that are commissioned by him, condemned by the Stat. 14 *Car.* 2. *cap.* 3.

Transcript, *Anno* 34 & 35 *H.* 8. *cap*, 14. Is the Copy of any Original written again or exemplified, as the *Transcript* of a Fine.

Transcripto Recognitionis factæ coram Justiciariis itinerantibus, &c. Is a Writ for the certifying of a Recognisance taken before *Justices in Eyre* into the *Chancery*, *Reg. Orig. fol.* 152.

Transcripto pedis finis levati mittendo in Cancellarium, Is a Writ for the certifying the foot of a Fine levyed before *Justices in Eyre*, &c. into the *Chancery*, *Reg. Orig.* fol. 169. & *Reg. Judic.* fol. 14.

Transgressione, Is a Writ commonly called a Writ or Action of Trespass, of which *Fitzherbert* reckons two sorts, one *Vicountiel* so called, because it is directed to the Sheriff, and is not returnable, but to be determined in the County; the form whereof differs from the other, because it hath not these words, *Quare vi & armis*, &c. *F. N. B. fol.* 84. The other is termed *a Writ of Trespass* upon the Case, which is to be sued in the King's Bench or Common Pleas, in which are used always these words, *Vi & armis, F. N. B. fol.* 92. See *Trespass.*

Transire, *Anno* 14. *Car.* 2. *cap.* 11. Is used for a Custom-house Warrant or Let-pass from *Transeo*, to go forth or let pass.

Transitory, Is passing away or flitting, the opposite to *Local.* See *Local.*

Trantery, So in some Mannors they call the Money arising by Amerciaments of Ale-sellers and Victuallers, for breaking the Assise of Bread and Ale, as *Luston*, and other Mannors in *Herefordshire*, especially those belonging to the Bishoprick of *Hereford.*

Translation, *Translatio*, In common sense signifies the version out of one Language into another; but in a more confined, denote the setting from one place to another; as to remove a Bishop from one Diocess to another is called *Translating*, and such a Bishop writes not *Anno Consecrationis*, but *Anno* translationis *nostræ.*

Traverse, (A derivative from the French

Traverser, i. *Transfigere*, signifies sometimes to deny, sometimes to overthrow or undo a thing, or to put one to prove some matter; much used in Answers to Bills in *Chancery*, or it is that which the Defendant pleadeth, or saith in Bar to avoid the Plaintiffs Bill, either by confessing and avoiding, or by denying and *traversing* the material parts thereof, *West Symbol.* part 2. tit. *Chancery*, sect. 54, 55. The formal words of which *Traverse* are in our French *Sans ceo*, in Latine *absq; hoc*, and in English *without that*. See *Kitchin*, fol. 227. and 240. *Stamf. Prærog.* cap. 20. To *traverse an Office*, is nothing else but to prove, That an Inquisition made of Lands or Goods by the Escheator is defective, and untruly made. So to *traverse an Indictment*, is to take Issue upon the chief Matter, and to contradict or deny some point of it. As in a Presentment against *A.* for a High-way overflown with Water, for default of scouring a Ditch, &c. *A.* may *traverse* either the Matter, that there is no High-way there, or that the Ditch is sufficiently scoured; or otherwise he may *traverse* the Cause, *viz.* That he hath not the Land, or that he and they whose Estate, &c. have not used to scour the Ditch, *Lamb. Eiren. lib.* 4. *cap.* 13. *pag.* 521, 522. See the *New Book of Entries*, verb. *Traverse*.

Treason, *Proditio*, Of the French *Trahison*, and it is divided into *High Treason* and *Petty Treason*; *High Treason* is defined to be an Offence committed against the Security of the King or Kingdom, whether it be by Imagination, Word or Deed; as to compass or imagine the death of the King, Queen or Prince; or to deflower the Kings Wife, or his eldest Daughter unmarried, or his eldest Sons Wife: or levy War against the King in his Realm, adhere to his Enemies, counterfeit his Great Seal, Privy Seal, or Money: Or wittingly to bring false Money into this Realm counterfeited, like the Money of *England*, and utter the same. To kill the Kings Chancellor, Treasurer, Justices of either Bench, Justices in Eyre, of Assise, or of Oyer and Terminer, being in their place doing their Office, *Anno* 25. *E.* 2. *cap.* 2. Forging the Kings Seal Manual or Privy Signet, Privy Seal, or foreign Coyn currant here, *Anno* 2 *Mar. Cap.* 6. Or diminishing or impairing currant Money, 5 *Eliz.* 11. 14 *Eliz. cap.* 3. 18 *Eliz.* 1. Or to say the King is an *Heretick* or *Papist*, or that he intends to introduce *Popery*, &c. *Anno* 13 *Car.* 2. *cap.* 1. And many others, which you may read there, and in other places particularly expressed. In case of this *Treason*, a Man shall be drawn, hanged and quartered, and forfeit his Lands and Goods to the King. It is called also *Treason Paramount*, *Anno* 25 *E.* 3. *cap.* 2. *Petit Treason* is, when a Servant kills his Master, a Wife her Husband: or when a Secular or Religious Man kills his Prelate or Superior, to whom he owes Faith and Obedience: and in how many other Cases *Petit Treason* may be committed, see *Cromp. Just. of Peace*. This kind of *Treason* gives forfeiture of Escheats to every Lord within his own Fee. See *Bract. lib.* 3. *tract.* 2. *cap.* 3. *num.* 1, 2. There is also mention of *Accumulative Treason* and *Constructive Treason* in the Statute 14 *Car.* 2. *cap.* 29. And here observe, that in *Majori proditione omnes sunt Principales*, there are no Accessaries in *Treason*, all are Principals. And *Voluntas non reputabitur pro facto nisi in causa Proditionis*, for Petty *Treason*. See *Co.* 1. *Rep. Shellyes* Case.

Treasure, *Thesaurus*, The Kings *treasure* is the Sinews of War, and the Honor and Safety of the King in time of Peace, *Firmamentum Belli & ornamentum Pacis*. If any Mine of base Metal be found in any Ground, it belongs to the Lord of the Soyl, but if it be of Gold or Silver, it appertains to the King, in whose Ground soever they be found.

Treasure trove, *Thesaurus inventus*, Signifies in our Common Law as it does in the Civil, *Veterem depositionem pecuniæ, cujus non extat memoria, ut jam Dominum non habeat*, with which definition *Bracton* agrees: And though the Civil Law give it to the finder, according to the Law of Nature, yet the Law of *England* gives it to the King by his Prerogative, or to some other who Claim by the Kings Grant, or by Prescription, as appears *Bract. lib.* 3. *tract.* 2. *cap.* 3. *num.* 4. The Punishment for concealing *Treasure found*, is Imprisonment and Fine, *Stamf. Pl. Car. lib.* 1. *cap.* 42. *Fitzherb. Abridgment*, *pag.* 187. But if the owner may any ways be known, then it does not belong to the Kings Prerogative. *Britton*, *cap.* 17. says, 'Tis every Subjects part as soon as he has found any *Treasure* in the Earth, to make it known to the Coroners of the County, &c. See *Kitchin*, *fol.* 40. *Anno* 1 & 2 *P.* & *M. cap.* 15. This was anciently called **Findaringa**, of finding the *Treasure*, *Leg. Hen.* 1. *cap.* 11. See 3. *Inst. fol.* 132.

Treasurer, *Thesaurarius*, Is an Officer to whom the treasure of another is committed to be kept, and truly disposed of: The chiefest of these with us is the *Treasurer* of *England*, who is a Lord by his Office, and one of the greatest Men of the Land, under whose Charge and Government is all the Princes Wealth contained in the Exchequer, as also the Clerk of all Officers any way imployed in the collecting of the Imposts, Tributes, or other Revenues belonging to the Crown, *Smith de Rep. Anglor. lib.* 2. *cap.* 14. See more belonging to this Office, 20 *E.* 3. 6. 31. *H.* 6. 5. 4 *E.* 4. 1. 17 *E.* 4, 5. 21 *H.* 8. 20. and 1 *E.* 6. 13. This high Officer hath by vertue of his Office, the nomination of all Escheators yearly throughout *England*, and giveth the Places of all Customers and Searchers in all the Ports of the Realm, with divers other matters, &c. There is also the *Treasurer of the Kings Houshold*, who is of the Privy-Council, and in the absence of the *Steward of the Kings Houshold* hath Power with the *Controller and Steward of the Marshalsea*, without Commission, to hear and determine Treasons, Misprisions of Treason, Murder, Homicide and Bloodshed committed within the Kings Palace, *Stamf. Pl. Cor. lib.* 3. *cap.* 5. *In Westm.* 2. *cap.* 8. There is mention of the *Treasurer of the Exchequer*, *Treasurer of the Navy or War*, 27 *E.* 3. *stat.* 2. *cap.* 18. 35 *Eliz. cap.* 4. *Treasurer* of the Kings Chamber, 26 *H.* 8. 3. 33 *H.* 8. 39. *Treasurer* of the Wars, 7 *H.* 3. 1. 3 *H.* 8. 5. *Treasurer* of the Kings Wardrobe. 15 *E.* 3. *stat.* 1. *cap.* 3. 25 *E.* 3. *stat.* 5. *cap.* 21. Whose Office you have well set out in *Fleta*, *lib.* 2. *cap.* 14. *Treasurer* of the County for Poor Souldiers, 25 *Eliz. cap.* 4. And most Corporations through the Kingdom have an Officer of of this Name that receiveth their Rents, and disburseth their common Expences, and is of great Credit among them.

Treat, Cometh of the French *Traire*, i. *emulgere*; or rather from *tractus* drawn, and signifies as much as taken out or withdrawn: As a Juror was challenged, because he could not dispend forty pound, and for that cause he was *treate*, (that is with-drawn) by the Statute *Old Nat. Brev. fol.* 159.

Trebuchet, *Terbichetum*, A Tumbrel or Cuckingstool, 3. *par. Inst. fol.* 219. See *Tribuch*.

Treete, *Triticum*, Wheat; In the Statute 5. *H.* 3. Bread of *treete* seems to be that Bread which was made of fine Wheat. See *Cocket*.

Trental, *Trentale*, An Office for the dead that continued thirty days, or consisting of thirty Masses, from the Italian *Trenta*, that is, *triginta*, mentioned 1 *E.* 6. 14.

Trespass, *Transgressio*, Signifies any transgression of the Law under Treason, Felony, or Misprision of either, *Stamf. Pl. Cor. fol.* 38. where he says, That for a Lord of the Parliament to depart from the Parliament without the Kings Licence, is neither Treason nor Felony, but *trespass*. But it is most commonly used for that wrong or damage which is done either to the King in his Forest, or by one private Man to another; and in this signification it is of two sorts, *Trespass general*, otherwise termed *trespass vi & armis*; and *Trespass special*, otherwise called *Trespass upon the Case*; and this seemeth to be without force, howbeit sometimes they are confounded. How to distinguish the forms of these Writs or Actions, see *F. N. B. fol.* 86, 87. In an Action of *Trespass*, the Plaintiff always sues for Damages, or the value of the hurt done him by the Defendant. There is also *Trespass local*, and *Trespass transitory*. *Trespass local* is that which is so annexed to a place certain, that if the Defendant joyn issue upon the place, and traverse the place only by saying *absq; hoc*, that he did the *trespass* in the place mentioned in the Declaration, and aver it, it is enough to defeat the Action: *Trespass transitory*, is that which cannot be defeated by the Defendants traverse of the peace, because the place is not material; but Actions of *trespass quare clausum fregit* ought to be local, *Bracton, lib.* 4. *cap.* 34. *num.* 6. divides *Transgressionem in Majorem & Minorem*. See also *New Book of Entries*, verb. *Trespass*.

Trespassants, Is used by *Britton, cap.* 29. for Passengers.

Trial, *Triatio*, Is used for the Examination of all Causes civil or criminal, according to the Laws of the Realm, before a proper Judge; of which there are divers kinds, as matters of Fact shall be tryed by the Jurors, matters of Law by the Justices, matters of Record by the Record it self. A Lord of Parliament upon an Indictment of Treason or Felony, shall be tryed without any Oath by his Peers upon their Honors and Allegiance; but in appeal at the Suit of any Subject they shall be tryed *per bonos & legales homines*. If ancient Demesne be pleaded of a Mannor, and denyed, this shall be tryed by the Record of *Doomsday*. Bastardy, Excommengement, lawfulness of Marriage, and other Ecclesiastical Matters shall be tryed by the Bishops Certificate. Of the ancient Manner of *tryal by Combate* and *great Assise*, see *Combat and Assise*. See also *Stamf. Pl. Cor. cap.* 1, 2, 3. And *twelve men*. *Triatio est exactissima, litis contestatæ, coram Judice per duodecemvirale Sacramentum exagitatio*, Pat. 3 R. Joh. m. 3. in fidelitate Leulini. *Statuitur de triatione differentiarum, dicti Leulini*, &c.

Tribuch and **Trebuchet**, *Terbichetum*, A Tumbrel or Cuckingstool; *Hæc omnia concedimus deo & Ecclesiæ Sancti* Albani *cum Soca & Saca* **on Strond & Streme, on Wude & Feld.** *Toll & Teym*, Tribuch, *Hamsoken, Murdre, Forestal, &c.* Carta Joh. Regis, Dat. 11. Jun. Anno Regni 1.

Trihing & Trithing, *Trithinga* contains three or four Hundreds, or the third part of a Shire or Province: Also a Court held within that Circuit, which was the same we call *a Court Leet*, which is above a Court Baron, and inferior to the County Court. See *Camden*, pag. 102. *Breve de Attornato de loquelis, &c.* Regist. 266. *Provisum est quod quilibet liber homo liberè possit facere Atturnatum suum ad loquelas prosequendas & defendendas motas in* trithingis, *Comitatibus, Warpentachiis & aliis Curiis sine breve nostro*, Sur le Statute de Merton, *cap.* 10. *Fiat autem visus Francii Plegii sic*, viz. *quod pax nostra teneatur & quod* trithinga *sit integra, sicut esse consuevit*, Mag. Charta, cap. 36. See *Fleta*, lib. 2. cap. 61. Sect. *Final. & Origin. Jurisdict.* fol. 26. See *Lath*. See *Pupilla oculi, part* 5. *cap.* 22. and *Roger Hoveden, parte poster. suor. annal. fol.* 346.

Treswel of double soled shooes, 2 & 3 *E.* 6. *cap.* 9. It should rather be written *Creswel*, signifying the broad edge of the shooe-sole round about.

Trinity-house, Is a *House* at *Debtford*, which belongs to a Company or Corporation of Seamen, that have Power, by the Kings Charter, to take knowledge of those that destroy Seamarks, and to redress their doings; as also to correct the Faults of Saylors, &c. and to take care of divers other things belonging to Navigation, and the Seas, *Anno* 8 *Eliz.* 13. and 35. *Eliz.* 6.

Trinke, Is a kind of Net to catch Fish withal, *Anno* 2. *H.* 6. *cap.* 15.

Triours, Are such as be chosen by the Court to examine whether a Challenge made to the Panel, or any of the Panel, be just or no, *Bro.* tit. *Challenge*, fol. 122. and *Old Nat. Brev. fol.* 158.

Tristis, *Tristris & Trista*. From **Traist**, i. *Trust*, Is an immunity, whereby a man is freed from his attendance on the Lord of a Forest, when he is disposed to chase within the Forest, and shall not be compelled to hold a Dog, follow the Chace, nor stand at a place appointed, which otherwise he might be under pains of Amerciament, *Manwood*, part 1. pag. 86. *Et sint quieti*, &c. *de Chevagio, Hondpeny, Buckstall, &* Tristris, *& de omnibus misericordiis*, &c. Priviled. de Sempligham, 4. *Inst. fol.* 306.

Thrithing. See *Trihing*, 2 Inst. fol. 99.

Tronage, *Tronagium*, Is a Custome or Toll taken for weighing of Wooll. *Fleta*. lib. 2. cap. 12. sect. *Item Ulnas*, says, That *Trona* is a Beam to weigh with, mentioned in *Westm.* 2. *cap.* 25.

Tronator, From *Trona*, i. *statera*, An Officer in the City of *London*, who weighs the Wool that it brought thither. See his Oath in the Book *Of Oaths*, fol. 231.

Trover, Cometh of the French *Trover*, i. *invenire*, I. an Action which a man hath against one, that having found any of his Goods, refuseth to deliver them upon demand. See the *New Book of Entries*, verb. *Trever*. Actions of Detinue are of late much turned into Actions upon the Case, *Sur* Trover *& Conversion*, Preface to *Roll's Abridgment*.

Troy weight, *Pondus Trojæ*. See *Weight*.

Trug, --*Tres* Truggæ *frumenti vel avenæ faciunt* 2. *Bushels infra Prebendam de* Hunderton *in Eccles. Heref.* M. S. de temp. E. 3. And at *Lempster* at this day the Vicar has *Trug-Corn* allowed him for officiating at some Chappels of Ease (as *Stoke* and *Dorkelay*) within that Parish.

Tumbrell, *Tumbrellum*, *Turbichetum*, Is an Engine of Punishment, which ought to be in every Liberty that hath view of Frank-pledge, for the Correction of Scolds and unquiet Women, *Kitchin, fol.* 13. See *Cuckingstool*, *New Book of Entries, Franchise* 2. *Et quo warranto* 1. *Item si aliquis qui in lib rtatem nostram, per assensum & consensum Combargensium nostrorum admissus fuerit, fecerit aliquod delictum, per quod ad pœnam publicam seu vile Judicium, ut ad Collistrigium vel* tumbrellum, *vel aliquod alud hujusmodi adjudicatus fuerit, pro perjuro reputabitur, & ipso facto amittet libertatem suam*, M. S. Codex de Leg. Stat. & consuetud. Burgi villæ Montgom. fol. 11.

Tun, Is a Measure of Wine or Oyl containing twelve score and twelve Gallons, 1 *Rich.* 3. *cap.* 12. 2 *H.* 6. 11. and 12 *Car.* 2. *cap.* 4. A *Tun* of Timber is forty solid Feet, a Load fifty.

Tunnage. See *Tonnage*. It began in the five and fortieth year of *Edw.* 3. *Cottoni Posthuma*, fol. 172. See 4 *Inst. fol.* 32.

Tungreve, A Reeve or Bayliff, *Qui in villis (quæ dicimus Maneriis,) Domini personam sustinet ejusque vice omnia dispcnat & moderatur*. See *Spelman*.

Turbary, *Turbaria*, From *turba*, an obsolete Latine word for a Turf: Is a right to dig turves on another Man's ground, *Kitchin, fol.* 94. And *Common of Turbary* is a liberty which some Tenants have by prescription to dig on the Lords Wast. *Turbaria* is also taken sometimes for the Ground where Turves are digged. And you shall find an Assise brought of *Common of Turbary* in 5. *Ass. Pl.* 9. & 7 *E.* 3. *fol.* 43.

Turmerick, *Turmerica*, Is the Root of an Herb growing in *Arabia*, Medicinal against divers Diseases in Horses, and sometimes used for a Man also in case of the yellow Jaundice. It is reckoned among the garbleable Drugs, *Anno* 1 *Jac. cap.* 19.

Turne, *Turne*, Is the Sheriffs Court kept twice every year, *viz.* within a Moneth after *Easter*, and within a Moneth after *Michaelmas*, *Magna Charta, cap.* 35. and 3 *E.* 3. *cap.* 15. From this Court are exempted onely Archbishops, Bishops, Abbots, Priors, Earls, Barons, all religious Men and Women, and all such as have Hundreds of their own to be kept, *Anno* 25 *H.* 3. *cap.* 10. *Britton, cap.* 29. calls it *Tour*, id est, *ambitus circuitus*: It is a Court of Record in all things that pertains to it. It is the King's Leet through all the County, and the Sheriff is Judge, and this Court is incident to his Office. See *Cromp. Jur. fol.* 230. and 4 *Inst fol.* 260. See *Fleta, lib.* 2. *cap.* 52. and *Mirror of Just.* lib. 1. cap. *De turnes.*

Turney or **Tournment**, *Turneamentum*, Comes from the French *Tourney*, i. *Decursorium*, and signifies a Martial Exercise of Knights or Gentlemen fighting on Horse-back one with another in disport, and is thus defined, *Torneamenta dicuntur Nundinæ vel feriæ in quibus milites ex condicto convenire & ad ostentationem virium suarum & audaciæ, temerè congredi solent.* This word is used in the Statute *Anno* 24 *H.* 8. 13. But the thing it self is now totally disused.

Turno Vicecomitum, Is a Writ that lies for those that are called to the *Sheriffs turn* out of their own Hundred, *Reg. Orig. fol.* 174.

Twaite, Signifies a Wood grubbed up, and turned to Arable, *Co.* on *Lit. fol.* 4.

Twa nights Geste, *Hospes duarum noctium*, If he did any harm to any, his Host was not answerable for it, but himself, *Hoveden part. poster. suor. annal.* fol. 345. See *Third Nights-awne-hinde.*

Twelve Men, *Duodecim homines legales*, Otherwise called the *Jury* or *Enquest*, is a number of twelve persons, or upwards, to the number of twenty four, by whose Oath as to matter of Fact all Trials pass, both in civil and criminal Causes through all Courts of the Common Law in this Realm. First, In civil Causes, when proof is made of the matter in question, then the point of the Fact (that they are to give their Verdict upon) is delivered likewise unto them, which we call *the Issue*; then they are put in mind of their Oath to do right, and are by the Judges, who sum up the Evidence, sent out of the Court by themselves, to consider upon the Evidence on both sides, until they be agreed, which done, they return to the Court, and deliver their Verdict by the mouth of their Fore-man; according to which (if the matter be not arrested or stay'd by the Court) the Judgment passeth. See *Glanvile, lib.* 2. *cap.* 14, 15. In *Causes criminal* there are two sorts of *Enquests*, one called the Grand *Enquest*, the other the *Enquest of Life and Death.* The *Grand Enquest* is so called, either because it consists of sixteen at the least, or else because all Causes criminal or penal pas first through them; whereas the other Enquest is especially appointed for one or few matters touching Life and Death committed to their consideration. Those of the *Grand Enquest* are called by *Bracton Duodecim milites*, lib. 3. tract. 2. cap. 1. num. 2. Because they were wont to be Knights, if so many could be had: And their business is to receive all Presentments of any Offence, and accordingly to give their Opinion generally, either by writing these words, *Billa vera* upon the Bill of Presentment, which is an Inditement of the Party presented; or else this word *Ignoramus*, which is a doubting of the Fact presented. Now as criminal Causes be of two sorts, either capital or finable, so is there a double course of these Inditements; for in Causes only finable, the Party indited must either traverse the Inditement by denying it, and so it is referred to a *Petit Jury*, whereby he is either convicted or discharged of the Crime, or else if he confess it, the Court setteth a Fine upon him without more ado. But in matters of Life and Death, the Party indited is commanded to hold up his hand, and answer, *Guilty* or *Not Guilty*; If *Guilty*, he standeth convicted by his own Confession; If *Not Guilty*, he is farther referred to the Jury of Life and Death, who consider upon the Proof brought against the Prisoner, and accordingly bring in their Verdict; according to which he is either condemned or acquitted. Of this read more in *Inditement*, *Assise*, *Jury*. See the Stat. 35 *H*. 8. *cap*. 6. & 37 *H*. 8. 22. 2 E. 6. 32. and 5 *Eliz*. *cap*. 25.

Tylwith, Is a Brittish word signifying *Familia*, *famulitium*; *Tribus*, and is derived either from **Tyle**, i. e. *locus ubi stetit domus vel locus ædificandæ domui aptus*, or else from **Tylath**, which signifies *Trabs*, *tignus*; In the first derivation it signifies a place whereon to build a House, and in the second a Beam in the building. And **Tylwith** is a Tribe or Family branching or issuing forth of another, which we in our English Heraldry call *Second or third Houses*: So that in case the great Paternal Stock branched it self into several **Tylwiths** or *Houses*, they carry no second or younger House further his **Tylwith**, and the use of these **Tylwiths** was to shew not only the Originals of Families, as if their work had been meerly to run over a Pedegree, but the several distinctions and distances of Birth, that in case any Line should make a Fayler, the next in degree may make an unconfounded use of their interest, according to the Rules of Partition in *Gavelkind*.

Tymber of Skins, Is forty Skins, *Book of Rates*, fol. 18.

Tympeny, *Abbas & Monachi Rading---sint quieti de tributis & lastagiis & stallagiis de Thethingpeny &* Tympeny, *de summonitionibus de assisis & super assisis*, *&c*. In Memorand. Scac. de Anno 20 E. 3. int. Record. de Trin. Rot. 3. It is elsewhere written *Tynpeny*, Mon. Ang. 1. par. fol. 419.

V.

V. Is a numeral Letter, and stands in reckoning for five; And among the ancient *Romans* was usually written alone as a *Prænomen*, as *M. V.* for *Marcus Valerius*, and the like; whereof, among Latine Writers, you may find plentiful Examples.

Vacation, *Vacatio*, Is all the respective time betwixt the end of one Term and the beginning of another. When such times began and ended in our Ancestors days, see *Roger Hoveden*'s *Annalls*, *part*. *poster*. fol. 343. where you shall find that this intermission was called *Pax Dei & Ecclesiæ*. Also the time from the death of a Bishop, or other Spiritual Person, till the Bishoprick, or other Dignity, be supplyed with another, is called *Vacation*, *Westm*. 1. *cap*. 21. & 14 *E*. 3. *cap*. 4, 5. See *Plenarty*.

Vaccary or **Vacchary**, *Vaccharia* alias *Vacheria*, Is a House or Place to keep Cows in, *Fleta*, *lib*. 2. *cap*. 41. *sect*. Item inquiratur 12. *Domus sive locus quo* vaccæ *aluntur vel quo negotium quod ad eas pertinet*, *perficitur*, saith *Spelman*. A Dairy-house without warrant no Subject may have a *vacary* within the Forest, *Cromp*. *Jur*. *fol*. 194. But in the Stat. 37 *H*. 8. *cap*. 16. *Vacchary* seems to be a special Name of a certain compass of Ground within the Forest of *Ashdown*.

Vaga. See *Waga*.

Vagabond, *Vagabundus*, Is one that wandreth about, having no certain dwelling, *Rogues*, Vagabonds, *and sturdy Beggars* are all one, and mentioned in divers Statutes, *De* Vagabundis *& aliis hominibus mendicantibus qui se nominant* **Travelling men**, &c. Carta 22 *H*. 6. m. 3. n. 36. *Item utimur quod nullus* Vagabundus *vagetur seu deambulet de nocte in villa seu suburbio ejusdem post pulsationem campanæ nostræ communis*, *vocata* **Coverfew**, &c. M. S. Codex de Leg. & Statut. Burgi Villæ Montgomer à tempore Hen. 2.

Valect, **Valet** or **Vadelect**, *Valettus vel valecta*, *Qui juxta Dominum* Vadit *seu ministrat*. It is a French word: A Servitor or Gentleman of the Privy Chamber, according to *Camden*: In the Accounts of the *Inner-Temple*, it is used for a Benchers Clerk or Servant: The Butler of the House corruptly call them *Varlets*; In the *Register of Writs* 25. *Valettus*. *If the Sheriff be a* Vadelect *of the Crown*, *&c*. *Co*. on *Lit*. fol. 156. *Valet* was anciently a Name specially denoting young Gentlemen, though of great Descent or Quality, but now given to those of the rank of Yeomen, *Selden*'s *Titles of Honor*, fol. 831.

Value, *Valentia*, *Valor*; Is a known word, yet *West* in his *Symbol*. part 2. tit. *Inditements*, sect. 70. Nicely distinguishes between *Value* and Price, His words are these, The *value* of those things in which Offences are committed is usually comprised in Inditements, which seems necessary in *Theft* to make a difference from *Petit Larceny*, and in *Trespass* to aggravate the Fault, and increase the Fine: But no price of things *feræ naturæ* may be expressed, as of Deer, Hares, &c. if they be not in Parks and Warrens, which is a liberty, *Anno* 8 *E*. 4. *fol*. 5. nor of Charters of Land. And where the number of the things taken are to be expressed in the Inditement, as of young Doves in a Dove-house, young Hawkes in a Wood, there must be said (*pretii*) or (*ad valentiam*) but of divers dead things *ad valentiam*, and not *pretii*, of Coyn not currant, it shall be *pretii*; but of Coyn currant it shall neither be said *pretii* nor *ad valentiam*, for the *value* and price thereof is certain.

Value of Marriage, *Valore maritagii*, Is a Writ that lies for the Lord, having proffered covenable *Marriage* to the Infant, without disparagement, if he refuse to take the Lords offer, to recover the *value of the Marriage*, *Reg. Orig. fol*. 164. *Old Nat. Brev. fol*. 90. See *Palmer*'s Case, *Co*. *lib*. 5. *fol*. 126. and the Statute 12 *Car*. 2. *cap*. 24.

Vantarius, *Præcursor*, As *Vantarius Regis*, the King's Fore-foot-man: *Richardus Rockesle miles tenebat terras Seatoniæ per Serjantiam esse* Vantarium

tarium *Regis in Gascoigne, donec perusus fuit pari soluta-rum pretii* 4 d. i. *dum trivisset par calceorum pretii* 4 d. Rot. de finibus, Term. Mich. 2 Ed. 2.

Variance, *Variatio*, Signifies an alteration or change of condition after a thing done: As the Commonalty of a Town make a Composition with an Abbot, and after obtain Bayliffs by Grant from the King. In this case, if the Abbot commence any Suit for breach of the Composition, he must *vary* from the word (*Commonalty*) set down in the Composition, and use *Bayliffs and Commonalty*, *Bro.* tit. *Variance*, *fol.* 292. It is also used for an alteration of something formerly laid in a Plea. See *Variance* in the *New Book of Entries*.

Varlets, By a repealed Statute of 20 *Rich.* 2. *cap.*2. were used for Yeomen or Yeomen-Servants. See *Valects*, and the Stat. 3 *Car.* 1. *cap.*4. *Will. Hunt* Varlet del Chambre *nostre Seigneur le Roy*, Clauf. 12 *Rich.* 2. *M.* 43. *in Dorso*. I suppose it miswritten for *Valet*.

Vaslet, *Vaslettus*, Seems to signifie ward, as appears by a Par. 1 H. 3. *in Dorso* M. 13. *Concordia inter Regem & Radulphum de* Normanvil, *viz. quod* Rad. *tenebit in servitio Regis* Geroldum & Radulphum *milites filios suos, quamdiu guerra sua duraverit, per sic, quod Rex ei remittat* 200. *Marcas quas debebant Regi* Johanni *de fine pro redemptione dicti Geroldi & per sic deberetur*; Thomas *filius dicti Radulphi* Vaslettus *in custodia Regis, qui similiter morabatur in servitio Regis cum prædictis Geroldo Radulpho fratribus suis.*

Vassall, *Vassallus*, Signifies him that holds Land in Fee of his Lord, we call him more usually *a Tenant in Fee*, whereof some owe Fidelity and Service, and are called *Vassalli Jurati. Skene de verbor.* Signif. *verb.* Ligeantia, saith, That *Vassallus* is divided into *Homologum & non Homologum. Homologus* is he that sweareth Service with exception of a higher Lord, and *non Homologus*, is he that sweareth without exception, all one with *Ligeus*. And the same Author, verb. *Vassallus*, saith, That it is *Vassallus quasi Basallus*, i. *inferior socius*, because the *Vassall* is inferior to his Master, and must serve and reverence him; and yet he is in a manner his Companion, because each of them is obliged to the other.

Vasto, Is a Writ that lies for the Heir against the Tenant for term of Life or of Years, for making Wast, or for him in the Reversion or Remainder, *F. N. B. fol.* 55. *Reg. Orig. fol.* 72. & 76. and *Reg. Judic. fol.* 17 21, 23. & 69. Vide 6 *E.* 1. *cap.* 5.

Vavasor alias **Valvasor**, Is one that in Dignities is next to a Baron, *Camb. Brit.* pag. 109. *Bracton*, *lib.* 1. *cap.* 8. says thus of them, —— *Sunt & alii potentes Rege, qui dicuntur Barones, hoc est, robur Belli: Sunt & alii qui dicuntur* Vavasores, *viri magnæ dignitatis.* Vavasor *enim, nihil melius dici poterit quam vas sortitum ad valetudinem.* And *Cambd.* pag. 188. says, *Primis etiam Normannorum temporibus & Thani proximi à Comitibus in dignitate censebantur &* Valvasores *majores (si illis qui de feudis scribunt, credimus) iidem fuerunt Barones.* See more largely of these in *Spelman's Glossary.*

Vavasory, *Vavasoria*, The Lands that a *Vavasor* held,----*Quod dicitur de Baronia non est observandum in* Vavasoria *vel aliis minoribus feodis quam Baronia, quia caput non habent sicut Baronia*, *Bract.* lib. 2. cap. 39.

Veale money or **Veale noble money**, The Tenants of one of the Tythings within the Mannor of *Bradford* in *Wiltshire*, pay a yearly Rent by this Name to their Lord, the Marquess of *Winchester*, which is in lieu of *veale* paid formerly in kind.

Vejours, *Visores*, May be derived from the French *Veoir*, *videre*, *intueri*, are such as are sent by the Court to take view of any place in question, for the better decision of the Right, *Old Nat. Brev. fol.* 112. So likewise *Bracton* uses it, *lib.* 5. *tract.* 3. *cap.* 8. It signifies also such as are sent to view those that Essoine themselves *de malo lecti*, whether they be in truth so sick as they cannot appear, or whether they counterfeit, *Bract. lib.* 5. *tract.* 2. *cap.* 10. & 14. Lastly, It is used for those that are appointed to view an Offence, as a Man murdered, or a Virgin ravished. See *View*.

Venditioni exponas, Is a Writ Judicial, directed to the Under-Sheriff, commanding him to sell Goods which he hath formerly by Commandment taken into his Hands, for the satisfying a Judgment given in the King's Court, *Reg. Judic. fol.* 33. and *Anno* 14 *Car.* 2. *cap.* 21.

Venire facias, Is a Writ Judicial directed to the Under-Sheriff, and goeth out of the Record, and lies where two Parties plead, and come to Issue; for then the Party Plaintiff or Defendant shall have this Writ directed to the Sheriff, to cause twelve Men of the same County to say the truth upon the *Issue* taken. And if this Enquest come not at the day of the Writ returned, then shall go a *Habeas Corpora*, and after a Distress, until they come, *Old Nat. Brev. fol.* 157. See how diversly this Writ is used in the Table of the *Register Judicial*. There is also a Writ of this Name, that is *Original*, as appears in *Reg. Orig. fol.* 200. Which *Lamb.* in his *Processes* annex'd to his *Eirenarcha*, says, Is the common Process upon any Presentment, not being Felony, nor specially appointed for the Fault presented by Statute, whereof he sets down an example in the same place. See also the *New Book of Entries*, verb. *Enquest*, fol. 253. and 35 *H.* 8. *cap.* 5.

Venire facias tot matronas. See *Ventre inspiciendo*, and *Lamb. Eiren. lib.* 4. *cap.* 14. *pag.* 532.

Ventre inspiciendo, Is a Writ for the search of a Woman that saith she is with Child, and thereby with-holdeth Land from him that is next Heir at Law, *Reg. Orig. fol.* 227.

Venue or **Venew**, *Vicinetam* alias *Visnetam*, Is taken for a Neighbouring place, *Locus quem vicini habitant.* For example, Twelve of the Assise ought to be of the same *venew* where the Demand is made, *Old Nat. Brev. fol.* 115. and *Anno* 4 *Hen.* 4. *cap.* 26. and 25 *Hen.* 8. *cap.* 6. **And also shall return in every such Panel upon the** Venire Facias **six sufficient Hundreders at the least, if there be so many within the Hundred where the** Venue **lies.** See *Visne*.

Verd. See *Vert.*

Verderor, *Viridarius*, From the French *Verdeur*, i. *Custos nemoris*, Is a judicial Officer of the King's Forest, chosen by the King's Writ in the full County of the same Shire, within the Forest where he dwells, and is sworn to maintain and keep the Assises of the Forest, and to view, receive and enrol the Attachments and Presentments of all manner of Trespasses of Vert and Venison in the Forest, *Manwood, part* 1. *pag.* 332. His Office is properly to look to the Vert, and see it well maintained, *Cromp. Jur. fol.* 165. His Oath, Fee and Authority you may see in *Manwood, part* 1. *pag.* 51. He is to sit in the *Court of Attachment*, to see the Attachments of the Forest, to receive the same of the Foresters and Woodwards that present them, and then to enter them into their Rolls.

Verdict, *Veredictum quasi dictum veritatis*, Is the Answer of a Jury made upon any Cause civil or criminal committed by the Court to their Examination: And this is two-fold, *General* or *Special*; A *General Verdict* is that (*Stamf. Pl. Cor. lib.* 3. *cap.* 9.) which is given or brought into the Court in like *general* terms to the *general Issue*, as in an Action of Disseisin, the Defendant pleadeth, *No wrong, no Disseisin*; then the Issue is general, whether the Fact be a wrong or not, which being committed to the Jury, they upon consideration of their Evidence come in and say either for the Plaintiff, that it is a Wrong and Disseisin; or for the Defendant, that it is no wrong, no disseisin. A *special Verdict* is, when they say at large, that such a thing and such a thing they find to be done by the Defendant or Tenant so declaring the course of the Fact, as in their Opinion it is proved; and as to the Law upon the Fact, they pray the Judgment of the Court: And this *special Verdict*, if it contain any ample Declaration of the Cause from the beginning to the end, is also called a *Verdict* at large, whereof read Examples in *Stamf. ubi supra*, *New Book of Entries*, verb. *Verdict*, and *Co.* on *Lit. fol.* 228.

Verectum, According to *Doomsday* Book signifies Fallow-ground.

Verge, *Virgata*, May seem to come from the French *Verger*, *viridarium*, and is used here in *England* for the compass of the King's Court, which bounds the Jurisdiction of the Lord Steward of the King's Houshold, and of the Coroner of the King's House, and that seems to have been twelve Miles compass, *Anno* 13 *Rich.* 2. *stat.* 1. *cap.* 3. *F. N. B. fol.* 24. *Britton, fol.* 68, 69. *Co. Rep. lib.* 4. *fol* 47. See also 33 *H.* 8. 12. *Fleta, lib.* 2. *cap.* 4. *sect.* 1. says, This compass about the Court is called *Virgata*, *à virga quam Marishallus portat ut signum suæ potestatis. Verge* hath also another signification, and is for a Stick or Rod, whereby one is admitted Tenant, and holding it in his Hand, swears Fealty to the Lord of a Mannor, who for that cause is called *Tenant by the Verge*, *Old Nat. Brev. fol.* 17. and *Lit. lib.* 1. *cap.* 10.

Verge of Land, *Virgata terræ*, 28 E. 1. *Statute of Wards.* See *Yard land.*

Vergers, *Virgatores*, Are such as carry white Wands before the Justices of either Bench, *Fleta, lib.* 2. *cap.* 38. Otherwise called *Portatores Virgæ.*

Very Lord and **very Tenant**, *Verus Dominus & verus Tenens*, Are they that be immediate *Lord* and *Tenant* one to the other, *Bro. tit. Hariot, fol.* 23. In the *Old Nat. Brev.* and in the Writ *Replegiari de averiis*, you may read these words. And know ye, That in taking of Leases six things are necessary, that is to say, *very Lord and very Tenant*, Service behind, the day of the taking, Seisin of the Services, and within his Fee. And that a Man is not *very Tenant*, until he have atturned to the Lord by some Service. See 19 *H.* 7. *cap.* 15. And see *Tenant.*

Vert, *Viride.* Is made of the French *Verd viridis*, Otherwise called *Green-hue*, signifies in the Forest Laws every thing that grows and bears *green* leaf within the Forest that may cover a Deer, *Manwood*, 2. *par. fol.* 6. & 33. And it is divided into *Over-vert* and *Nether-vert*. *Over-vert* is that which our Law Books call *Hault Bois* and *Nether-vert* is that which they call *South Bois.* And of this you may read *Manwood*'s 2. *par. cap.* 6. *per totum.* There is also a *Vert* called *Special vert*, and that is all Trees that grow in the King's Woods within the Forest, and all the Trees that grow there in other mens Woods, if they be such Trees as bear Fruit to feed Deer; which are called *Special vert*, because the destroying of such *vert* is more grievously punished than the destruction of other *vert* is. See *Manwood, cap.* 6. *num.* 2. *fol.* 35.

Vervise, Otherwise called *Plonkets*, *Anno* 1 *R.* 3. *cap.* 8. a kind of Cloth.

Vesses, *Anno* 1 *R.* 3. *cap.* 8. and 14 & 15 *H.* 8. *cap.* 11. Otherwise called *Set-Clothes*, most commonly made in *Suffolk.*

Vest, Vestire, *Plenam possessionem terræ vel prædii tradere, seisinam dare, infeodare*, saith Spelman.

Vestry-men, *Anno* 15 *Car.* 2. *cap.* 5. Are a select number of the chief Parishioners in every Parish within the City of *London* and Suburbs, and else-where, who yearly choose Officers for the Parish, and take care of its Concernments; so called, because they usually meet in the *Vestry* of the Church.

Vesture, *Vestura*, Signifies a Garment, but in the Law, metaphorically turned to betoken a Possession, or an admittance to a Possession or Seisin; so it is taken in *Westm.* 2. *cap.* 25. And in this signification 'tis borrowed of the *Feudists*, with whom *Investitura* signifies a delivery of Possession by a Spear or Staff, and *Vestura* Possession it self, *Hotoman in verb.* Feudal. *verb.* Investitura.

Vesture of an Acre of Land, *Anno* 14 *E.* 3. *stat.* 1. Is the profit of it. So in *extenta Manerii*, 4 Ed. 1. It is inquirable, **How much the** Vesture **of an Acre is worth, and how much the Land is worth when the Wood is felled.**

Vetitum Namium, *Namium*, Signifies a taking or distress, and *Vetitum* forbidden; as when the Bayliff of a Lord distrains Beasts or Goods, and the Lord forbids his Bayliff to deliver them when the Sheriff comes to Replevy them, and to that end drives them to places unknown; or when without any words they are so eloined, as they cannot be replevyed, divers Lords of Hundreds and Courts Baron have power to hold Plea *De vetito namio*, in old Books called *De vet.* 2. *Inst. fol.* 140. *Spelman* says it is, *Antiqua juris nostri locutio & brevis Regis nomen.* See *Naam.*

Vicario deliberando occasione cujusdam Recognitionis, &c. Is a Writ that lies for a Spiritual Person imprisoned, upon forfeiture of a Recognisance, without the King's Writ, *Register of Writs*, fol. 147.

Vicis & venellis mundandis, Is a Writ that lies against a Mayor or Bayliffs of a Town, &c. for the clear keeping their Streets, *Reg. of Writs*, fol. 267.

Vicar, *Vicarius*, The Priest of every Parish is called *Rector*, unless the Prædial Tythes be impropriated, and then he is called *Vicar*, *quasi vice fungens rectoris. Sciant---quod ego Johannes Webbe* perpetuus Vicarius *Ecclesiæ Parochialis de* Bromyard, *dedi----Domino David Hay* perpetuo Vicario *Ecclesiæ Parochialis de* Anenebury *duas acras terræ, &c.* Dat. 8 H. 5. They stiled themselves *Perpetui vicarii*, because every *Vicaridge* hath a constant succession, as a Corporation, and never dies. *Quidam sunt* Perpetui *ad Parochiales Ecclesias constituti*; *Quidam non* perpetui, *sed ad aliquos actus constituti, ut temporales*; *& isti dicuntur* mercenarii : *Quidam sunt* speciales, *non ad curam sed ad certum locum, articulum vel actum constituti* : *Quidam nec* perpetui, *nec ad curam, nec ad certum actum, sed generaliter dantur ad omnia.* See *Vocab. utriusq; juris*, verb. *Vicarius.*

Vice-Chamberlain; Called *Under-Chamberlain*, 13 R. 2. *stat.* 2. *cap.* 1. Is a great Officer in Court next under the Lord Chamberlain, and in his absence hath the control and command of all Officers whatsoever appertaining to that part of his Majestie's Houshold, which is called *The Chamber*, or above stairs.

Vice-gerent, *Locum-tenens*, A Deputy or Lieutenant, *Anno* 31 *H.* 8. *cap.* 10.

Vice-Treasurer of the Exchequer, 1 *Jac.* 26. See *Under-Treasurer of England*, and see also *Treasurer of the Exchequer.*

Vicinetum. See *Venew.*

Vicinage, *Vicinetum*, French *Voisinage*, Neighborhood, near Dwelling, *Mag. Charta, cap.* 14. See *Venew.*

Vicount alias **Viscount**, *Vicecomes*, Signifies as much as *Sheriff*: Between which two words there is no other difference, but the one comes from our Conquerors the *Normans*, the other from our Ancestors the *Saxons*, of which see more in *Sheriff. Viscount* also signifies a degree of Nobility next unto an Earl, which *Camden Brit. pag.* 170. says, Is an old Name of Office, but a new one of Dignity, never heard of among us till the Reign of *Henry* the Sixth, who in his Eighteenth year, in Parliament, created *John Lord Beaumont, Viscount Beaumont*; But it is far more ancient in other Countries, *Cassan. in gloria mundi, part.* 5. *consid.* 55. See *Selden's Titles of Honor*, fol. 761.

Vicontiel, Is an Adjective made of Vicount, and signifies as much as belonging to the Sheriff; as *Writs vicontiel*, are such Writs as are tryable in the County, or Sheriffs Court, *Old Nat. Brev. fol.* 109. Of this kind you may see divers *Writs of Nusance* set down by *Fitzherbert* in his *Nat. Brev. fol.* 184. *Vicontiels, Vice-comitilia*, are certain Fermes which the Sheriff pays a Rent to the King, and makes what profit he can of them. See the Stat. 33 & 34 *H.* 8. *cap.* 16. 2 & 3 *E.* 6. *cap.* 4. 4 *H.* 5. *cap.* 2. 6 R. 2. *cap.* 3.

Vicontiel Rents, Mentioned 22 *Car.* 2. *cap.* 6. See *Vicontiel.*

Vidimus. See *Innotescimus*, *Anno* 15 *H.* 6. *cap.* 3.

View, *Visus*, Signifies the Act of Viewers; for when an Action real or personal is brought, and the Tenant knows not well what Land it is that the Demandant asks, then may he pray *the view*; which is, that he may *see* the Land which is claimed; of this *Britton* writes, *cap.* 45. This course of proceeding we have received from the *Normans*, as appears by the *Grand Custumary, cap.* 96. 80. & 96. This *view* is used as in other cases, so in an Assise of Rent-service, Rent-charge, or Rent-seck, *F. N. B. fol.* 178. and in a Writ *De Curia claudenda.* Ibid. fol. 128. In a Writ of *Nusance*, Ib. fol. 183. In a Writ *Quo jure*, Ib. fol. 128. In the Writ *De rationabilibus divisis*, Ib. fol. 129. and in the Writ *De secta ad Molendinum*, Ib. 123. See the *New Book of Entries*, verb. *View*, and how this *view* is made in *Fleta*, lib. 4. cap. 6. See *Vejours*, and *Westm.* 2. *cap.* 48.

View of Frank-pledge, *Visus Franci plegii*, Is the Office which the Sheriff in his County Court, or the Bayliff in his Hundred performs in looking to the King's Peace, and seeing that every man be in some *Pledge.* This is called by *Bracton*, lib. 2. cap. 5. num. 7. *in fine, Res quasi sacra, quia solam personam Regis respicit & quod introductus sit pro pace & communi utilitate*, Ibid. cap. 16. num. 8. See *Frank-pledge, Leet and Decennier.* Also see the *New Book of Entries* on this word.

Vi laica removenda, Is a Writ that lies where debate is between two Parsons or Provisors for a Church, and one of them enters into it with a great number and Lay-men, and holds the other out *vi & armis* : He that is holden out shall have this Writ directed to the Sheriff, that he remove the force. And this Writ is returnable, and shall not be granted, until the Bishop of the Diocess, where such Church is, hath certified into the *Chancery* such resisting and force. For the several forms of this Writ, see *F. N. B. fol.* 54. and *Reg. Orig. fol.* 59.

Vigill, *Vigilia*, Is used for the Eve or day next before any Solemn Feast, because then Christians of old were wont to *watch*, fast and pray in their Churches. See *Anno* 2 & 3 *E.* 6. *cap.* 19.

Vill, *Villa*, Is sometimes taken for a Mannor, and sometimes for a Parish, or part of it. Villa *apud Saxones nostros antiquos* Romano *sensu accipi videtur, pro prædio unius alicujus in rure, cum idoneis ædibus ad reponendos ejusdem fructus honestato. Non autem primitus pro multarum mansionum connexione, quod in oppidis potius expectandum esset & successivis temporibus* villis *postea introductum est*, Spelman. *Vill* and *Parish* shall be intended all one, *Cro. Rep.* 2. *par. fol.* 263. *Wraye's* Case, yet there may be two *Vills* in one *Parish*, Id. fol. 120. *Storke's* Case.

Villaine, *Villanus*, Signifies as much as *Servus* among the *Civilians.* A man of servile or base degree, from the French *Vilain*, *vilis*, or from the Latine *villa*, a Country Farm, whereto they were

were deputed to do Service: Of these Bondmen or *Villains* there were two sorts in *England*, one termed a *Villain in gross*, who was immediately bound to the person of his Lord and his Heirs. The other a *Villain* regardant to a Mannor, whom the Civilians term, *Glebæ ascriptitium*, being bound to his Lord as a Member belonging and annexed to a Mannor, whereof the Lord was Owner, *Smith de Rep. Anglor. lib.* 3. *cap.*8. *Old Nat. Brev. fol.* 8. and *Bracton, lib.* 1. *cap.*6.*num.*4. He was properly a pure *Villain*, of whom the Lord took Redemption to marry his Daughter, and to make him free; and whom the Lord might put out of his Lands and Tenements, Goods and Chattels, at his will, and Beat and Chastise, but not Maim him. There are not truly any *Villains* now, though the Law concerning them stands unrepealed. We have hardly heard of any Case in Villenage since *Crouche's* Case in *Dyer*. And *Spelman* says, *Servorum & Nativorum apud nos sublata est conditio, & quas ideò possidebant terras vel prædia, hodie liberè tenent sub antiquæ servitutis consuetudinibus.*

Villanis Regis subtractis reducendis, Is a Writ that lay for the bringing back of the King's Bondmen, that had been carried away by others out of his Mannors, whereto they belonged, *Reg. Orig. fol.* 87.

Villein Fleeces, Are *fleeces* of Wool that are shorn from scabbed Sheep, 31 *E.* 3. *cap.* 8.

Villeinous Judgment, *Villanum judicium*, Is that which casts the Reproach of Villany and Shame upon him against whom it is given as a Conspirator, &c. *Stamf. Pl. Cor. lib.* 3. *cap.* 3. *cap.* 12. *fol.* 175. This *Lamb.* in his *Eirenarch. lib.* 1. *cap.* 13. *pag.* 63. calls *Villainous Punishment*, and says, It may be well call'd *Villainous*, because the *Judgment* in such case shall be like the ancient *Judgment* in *Attaint*, as is said, *Anno* 4 *H.* 5. *Fitzh. Judgment* 220. And in 27. *Lib. Ass. Pl.* 59. set down to be, That they shall not be of any Credit afterward, nor lawful for them in Person to approach the King's Court, and that their Lands and Goods be seised into the King's Hands, their Trees rooted up, and their Bodies imprisoned, &c. And at this Day the Punishment appointed for Perjury (having somewhat more in it than Corporal or Pecuniary pain, stretching to the discrediting the Testimony of the Offendor for ever) may be partaker of this Name. This, and such like is else-where termed *Vile & odibile judicium.* Vide *Pillory.*

Villenage, *Villenagium*, Cometh of Villain, and signifies a Servile kind of Tenure belonging to Lands or Tenements, whereby the Tenant was bound to do all such Services as the Lord commanded, or were fit for a Villain to do; For every one that held in *Villenage*, was not a Villain or Bondman: *Villenagium vel servitium nihil detrabit libertatis, habita tamen distinctione, utrum tales sunt* Villani *& tenuerint in* Villano *soccagio de Dominico Domini Regis*, Bract. lib. 1. cap. 6. num. 1. The division of *Villenage* was into *villenage by Blood*, and *villenage by Tenure.* Tenure in *villenage* could make no Freeman *Villain*, unless it were continued time out of Mind, nor free Land make a *Villain* free. *Bracton, lib.* 2. *cap.* 8. *num.* 3. divides it into *Purum* villenagium, *à quo præstatur servitium incertum & indeterminatum ubi scire non poterit vespere, quale servitium fieri debet manè*, viz. *Ubi quis facere tenetur quicquid ei præceptum fuerit*; The other he calls *Villanum soccagium*, and was tyed to the performance of certain Services agreed upon between the Lord and Tenant, and was to carry the Lord's Dung into his Fields, to plough his Grounds at certain days, to reap his Corn, plash his Hedges, &c. As the Inhabitants of *Bickton* were bound to do for those of *Clun Castle* in *Shropshire*, which was afterwards turned into a Rent, now called *Brickton-Silver*, and the Service excused. *Will. Maynard qui tenuit terras in Hevist cognoscit se esse* Villanum *Abbatis de* Abbendon *& tenere de eo in* Villenagio, *& per* Villanas *consuetudines*, viz. *per servitium* 18 d. *per annum & dandi Maritagium & Marchetum pro filia & sorore sua, ad voluntatem ipsius Abbatis & faciendo omnes* Villenas *consuetudines.* Copy-holders is but a new Name, for anciently they were called *Tenants in villenage*, or, *of base Tenure*, *F. N. B. fol.* 28. But the slavery of this Custom hath received its Deaths Wound, *in favorem libertatis*: For Sir *Edward Coke* out of *Fortescue* hath this Note, *Impius & crudelis judicandus qui libertati non favet*; And gives this as the reason of it, *Angliæ jura in omni casu dant favorem libertati*; The sense of Liberty was of so great force and power, and the favor due unto it according to *Law* and *Right* of so great respect, that those and the like Pressures have received change and alteration.

Vinnet, A kind of Flower or Border, which Printers use, to beautifie printed Leaves in the beginning of Books. See *Anno* 14 *Car.*2.*cap.*33.

Virgata terræ, Otherwise *Virga terræ*, A Yard-land, *Reg. Orig. fol.* 167. *Decem acræ* terræ *faciunt secundùm antiquam consuetudinem, unam ferdellam, & quatuor ferdellæ faciunt* virgatam, M. S. *Codex.* See *Yard-land.*

Viridario eligendo, Is a Writ that lies for the Choice of a *Verderor* in the Forest, *Reg. Orig. fol.* 177.

Virilia, The privy parts of a Man, the cutting off, which was Felony by the Common-Law, whether the Party consented or not, *Bract. lib.* 3. *fol.* 44. Henricus Hall *& A. uxor ejus capti & detenti in Prisona de* Evilchester, *eo quod rectati fuerint, quod ipsi absciderunt* virilia *Johannis Monachi, quem idem* Henricus *deprehendit cum prædicta* A. *uxore ejus*, Rot. Claus. 13 H. 3. m. 9.

Virga ferrea,---*Sciant*, &c. *Quod ego* Hamundus *vi i dedi. &c.* Nich. *filio Edde pro* 8 s. *sterlingis quos mihi dedit præ manibus, unam placetam terræ meæ in vico versus Dustelee, quæ jacet inter terram meam & terram* Philippi *filii* Heylin, *cujus latitudo in fronte continet in se* 16. Virgas ferreas *præter unum quarterium & totidem à retro, &c.* Ex libr. Cart. Prior. Leominstr. This was so many *yards* according to the King's Standard in the Exchequer, which anciently it seems was of *Iron*, but now of Brass.

Vis, Force; So we say, *Vi & armis*, By force of Arms, and this force is five-fold, *vis impulsiva, ablativa, expulsiva, turbativa & inquietativa*: vis *ablativa* is the taking away of moveable things: And hence accrues an Action, *quare vi & armis, &c.* Vis *compulsiva*, by which a man is compelled to do that which otherwise he would not do of his own free will. And from this also accrues an Action; *Vis expulsiva* is, when any one is cast out of his Possession by Force and Arms. *Vis turbativa* is, when any one is disturbed in his Possession, as when two strive to possess the same thing. *Vis inquietativa* is, when one Man will not suffer another quietly to enjoy his Right, or to do a thing in his own Bounds or Limits. And from all these, some sort of Action will arise.

Visitation, *Visitatio*, Is that Office or Action that is performed by a Bishop in every Diocess once every three years, or by the Archdeacon once a year, by *visiting* the Churches and their Rectors, &c.

Visitation of Manners, *Visitatio morum*, Was wont to be the Name of the *Regarders* Office in ancient time, *Manwood, part* 1. *pag.* 195. See *Regarder.*

Visne, *Vicinetum*, Signifies a Neighbour-place, or a place near at hand, *Anno* 16 R. 2. cap. 6. *Dicitur* Vicinetum, *in jure nostro locus quem vicini habitant, qui olim intelligebantur de eadem villa sive ad jacentibus atq; alias de eodem Hundredo vel proximis; modo vero de eodem pago, sive Comitatu, hoc est compagenses.* Spelman, see *Venew.*

Visu Franci plegii, Is a Writ to exempt him from coming to the *view of Frank-pledge*, who is not resident within the Hundred; for Men are bound to this *view*, by reason of their Habitation, and not of Lands held where they dwell not, *Reg. Orig. fol.* 175.

Vitteler or **Victualer**, *Victualarius* or *Vitellarius*, Is he that sells Victuals; for whom there is a Writ in *F. N. B. fol.* 172. If they exercise their Trade, bearing a Magistracy in any Town Corporate. We call now all Common Alehouse-Keepers generally by the name of *Victuallers.*

Viva pecunia, Anciently used for live Cattel. See *Pecunia.*

Viva voce. See *Deposition.*

Vivary, *Vivarium*, Signifies a place of Land or Water, where living Creatures are kept. In Law it signifies most commonly a Park, Warren, Fish-pond or Piscary, *Co.* 2. *Inst. fol.* 100.

Ulnage. See *Alnage.*

Uncore prist, Is a Plea for the Defendant, being sued for a Debt due at a day past, to save the forfeiture of his Bond, saying, That he tendred the Debt at the time and place, and that there was none to receive, and that he is still ready to pay the same, 7 *E.* 6. 6. 83. *Dyer.* See *Unques Prist.* See also *Perkins*, sect. 783, 784. and *Co. lib.* 9. *fol.* 79. *Peytor's* Case.

Uncuth, Is a Saxon word signifying as much as *Incognitus*, unknown, and is used in the old *Saxon* Laws for him that cometh to an Inn Guestwise, and lies but one Night. In such case his Host was not bound to answer for any Offence that he committed, whereof he was guiltless himself; but if he lay there a second Night, then he was called *Guest*, *Hospes*, and then must the Host answer for him, as for one of his own Family. And if he tarried any longer, then he was called **Agenhine**, that is, *Familiaris*, whom if he offend against the King's Peace, his Host was to see him forth-coming; or if he could not bring him out within a Month and a day, he must satisfie for his Offences, *Lamb. Archaion, fol.* 133. *num.* 7. And *Bracton, lib.* 3. *cap.* 10. *num.* 2. writes thus of the same, *Item secundum antiquam consuetudinem dici poterit de familia alicujus qui Hospes fuerit cum alio per tres noctes; quia prima nocte poterit dici* **Uncuth**; *secunda vero*, **Gust**, *tertia nocte* **Hogenehine**. See *Third-night-awne-hine.*

Unde nihil habet, Is a Writ, concerning which, see *Date unde nihil habet.*

Under-Chamberlain of the Exchequer, Is an Officer there that cleaves the Tallies, written by the Clerk of the Tallies, and reads the same, that the Clerk of the Pell, and the Controllers thereof may see their Entries be true. He also makes Searches for all Records in the Treasury, and hath the Custody of *Doomsday* Book. There be two Officers there of this Name.

Under-Escheater, *Subescheator*, *Anno* 5 *Ed.* 3. *cap.* 4. See *Escheator.*

Under-Sheriff, *Sub-vicecomes.* See *Sheriff.*

Undersitter, Is an Inmate. See *Inmate.*

Undertakers, Were such as the King's Purveyors employed as their Deputies, *Anno* 2 & 3 *Ph. & Mar. cap.* 6. And such as *undertake* any great Work, as drayning of Fens, &c. *Anno* 43 *Eliz. cap.* 11. See 12 *Car.* 2. *cap.* 24. 13 *Car.* 2. *cap.* 8. 14 *Car.* 2. *cap.* 20.

Under-Treasurer of England, *Vicethesaurarius Angliæ*, Anno 39 Eliz. 7. This Officer, as some think, was first created in the time of *Henry* the Seventh, to Chest up the King's Treasure at the end of every Term, and to note the content of Money in each Chest, and to see it carried into the King's Treasury in the Tower, for the ease of the Lord *Treasurer*, as being a thing too mean for him to be troubled with, and yet fit to be performed by a Man of great Secrecy and Trust. He, in the vacancy of the Lord *Treasurers* Office, doth all things in the Receit, &c. But this Officer, in the Opinion of others, is far more ancient. Yet named *Treasurer of the Exchequer* in the Statute till Queen *Elizabeth's* time, where he is termed *Under-Treasurer of* England. Yet *Anno* 35 *Eliz.* he is also written *Treasurer of the Exchequer*; Read the Statutes 8 *E.* 3. *stat.* 2. *cap.* 17. 27 *E.* 3. *stat.* 2. *cap.* 18. 1 *Rich.* 2. *cap.* 5. 4 *H.* 4. *cap.* 18. 8 *H.* 6. *cap.* 17. 27 *H.* 8. *cap.* 11.

Uniformity, *Uniformitas*, One form of Publick Prayers and Administration of Sacraments, and other Rites and Ceremonies of the Church of *England*, to which all must submit; prescribed by the Statutes, 1 *Eliz. cap.* 2. and 14 *Car.* 2. *cap.* 4.

Union, *Unio*, Is a combining or consolidating of two Churches into one, which is done by the consent of the Bishop, the Patron, and the Incumbent: But there are two other sorts of it, as when one Church is made subject to the other, and when one Man is made Rector of both, and when a Conventual is made Cathedral, as you may read in the Chapter *Licet de Locato & conducto*, in *Linwood's Provincials*, sect. & *quia.* In the first signification by the Statute 37 *H.* 8. *cap.* 21. It was made lawful to make an *union*, or conso-

consolidation of two Churches in one, whereof the one is not above six pounds in the King's Book of the First-Fruits, and not above one mile distant from the other. And by another Statute made 17 *Car.* 2. *cap.* 3. It shall be lawful for the Bishop of the Diocess, Mayor, Bayliff, &c. of any City or Corporate-Town, and the Patron or Patrons to *unite* two Churches or Chappels in any such City, Town, or the Liberties thereof: Provided such *union* shall not be good, if the Churches so *united* exceed the sum of one hundred pounds *per annum*, unless the Parishioners desire otherwise, &c.

Unity of Possession, *Unitas possessionis*, Is called *Consolidatio fructus & proprietatis* in the Civil Law, and signifies Joynt *Possession* of two Rights by several Titles: As for example, If I take a Lease of Land from One upon a certain Rent, and afterwards I buy the Fee-simple; this is an *unity of Possession*, by which the Lease is extinguished, by reason that I, which before had the Occupation only for my Rent, am become Lord of the same, and am to pay my Rent to none but my self.

University, *Universitas*, Is most usually taken for those two Bodies which are the Nurses of Learning and liberal Sciences in this Kingdom, viz. *Oxford* and *Cambridge*, endowed with great Priviledges, as appears not only by *Anno* 2 *&* 3 *P. & M. cap.* 15. 13 *Eliz. cap.* 21. 18 *Eliz.* 6. but much more by their several Charters granted by divers Pious and Munificent Kings of this Land. See 14 *Car.* 2. *cap.* 4.

Unlage, A Saxon word denoting a wicked or unjust Law, in which sense the word is read in *Leg. Hen.* 1. *cap.* 34. 84.

Unlawful Assembly, *Illicita Congregatio*, Is the meeting of three or more Persons together, by force, to commit some *unlawful* Act, and abiding together, though not endeavouring the Execution of it, as to assault or beat any Person, to enter into his House or Land, &c. *West Symbol.* part 2. tit. *Inditement*, sect. 65. *Lamb. Eiren.* cap. 19. And by the Statute of 16 *Car.* 2. *cap.* 4. and 22 *Car.* 2. *cap.* 1. If five Persons, or more, shall be assembled together, above those of the Family, at any Conventicle or Meeting, under colour of any exercise of Religion, it is *unlawful*, and punishable by Fines, and otherwise, as in the said Statute is expressed.

Unques prist, *Alwayes ready*, Is a Plea whereby a Man professeth himself *alwayes ready* to do or perform that which the Demandant requires. For example, A Woman sues the Tenant for her Dower, and he coming in at the day, offers to aver, That he was alwayes ready, and still is to perform it. In this case, except the Demandant will aver the contrary, he shall recover no Damages: When this Plea will serve to avoid Charges, and when not, see *Kitchin, fol.* 243. See *Uncore prist.*

Voydance, *Vacatio*, Is a want of an Incumbent upon a Benefice, and this is double, either *in Law*, as when a Man hath more Benefices incompatible; or *in Deed*, as when the Incumbent is dead, or actually deprived, *Bro.* tit. *Quare Impedit*, num. 51.

Volumus, Is the first word of a Clause in the King's Writs of Protection and Letters Patent, *Anno* 1 *Rich.* 2. *cap.* 8. and 13 *Rich.* 2. *cap.* 16. Of Protections, some are *Cum clausula volumus*, and of these there are four kinds, *viz.* 1. *Quia Profecturus.* 2. *Quia Moraturus.* 3. *Quia indebitatus nobis existit.* 4. When any one sent into the King's Service beyond Sea in War, is imprisoned, *Co.* on *Lit.* sect. 199.

Volunt, *Voluntas*, Is, when the Tenant holds at the will of the Lessor, or Lord, and that is in two manners; one is, when I make a Lease to a Man of Lands, to hold at my *will*, then I may put him out at my pleasure, but if he sow the Ground, and I put him out, then he shall have his Corn with egress and regress till it be ripe to cut, and carry it out of the Ground. And such Tenant at will is not bound to sustain and repair the House as Tenant for years is. But if he make wilful wast, the Lessor shall have against him an Action of Trespass. The other *Tenant at will of the Lord* is, by Copy of Court-Roll, according to the Custom of the Mannor; and such a Tenant may surrender the Land into the hands of the Lord, according to the Custome, to the use of another for life, in fee, or in tail; and then he shall take the Land of the Lord, or his Steward, by Copy, and shall make Fine to the Lord.

Voucher, *Vocans*, Is *vocabulum artis*, and signifies when the Tenant calls another into the Court, that is bound to him to warranty, *New Book of Entries*, verb. *Voucher*; *Voucher de Garranty*, Brit. cap. 75. And that is either to defend the Right against the Demandant, or to yield him other Lands, &c. in value and extend to Lands or Tenements of Free-hold or Inheritance: He that *voucheth* is called *Voucher*, (*vocans*) and he that is called *Vouchee*, (*Warrantus*). *Bracton* writes of this at large, *lib.* 5. *tract.* 4. *per totum.* And *Littleton* in his Tenures, *cap. ult.* also *F. N. B. fol.* 134. And this seems in some measure to agree to the contract in the Civil Law, whereby the Vendee bindeth the Vendor, sometimes in the simple value of the things bought, sometime in the double, to *warrant* the secure enjoying the thing bought; yet there is this difference between *the Civil* and the *Common Law*, that *the Civil Law* binds every Man to warrant the security of that which he selleth, which the *Common Law* doth not, except it be specially covenanted. The Process whereby *the Vouchee* is called, is a *Summoneas ad warrantisandum.* And if the Sheriff return upon that Writ, that the Party hath nothing whereby he may be summoned, then goes out another Writ called *Sequatur sub suo periculo.* See *Lamb. Explic. of Saxon words*, verb. *Advocare.* A Recovery with a *single Voucher*, is, when there is but *one Voucher*: And with a *double Voucher*, is, when the *Vouchee* voucheth over, and so *a treble voucher.* There is also a *Foreign voucher*, when the Tenant being impleaded in a particular Jurisdiction, as in *London*, or the like; *voucheth* one to warranty, and prays, that he may be summoned in some other County, out of the Jurisdiction of that Court, which might more aptly be called a *Voucher* of a Foreigner. *De forinsecis vocatis ad warrantizandum*, Co. on Lit. fol. 101. also *Co. Rep.* 2. fol. 50. Sir *Hugh Cholmelye's* Case. *Voucher* is also used in the Statute 19 *Car.* 2. *cap.* 1. for a Leiger Book, or Book of Account, wherein are entred the Acquittances or Warrants for the Accountants Discharge.

Upland, *Uplanda*, High ground, or as some call it *Terra firma*, contrary to Moorish, Marsh or Low Ground,---*Duramq; terram novem Miliariis per aquam, de* uplanda, *id est de superiori terra, scaphis deferri & paludibus commisceri jussit*, Ingulph. Hist. Croyland.

Usage. See *Prescription*.

Use, *Usus*, In the Original signification is evident enough, but it hath also a Proper Application in Law, and that is the profit or benefit of Lands or Tenements, *West Symbol. lib.* 1. *sect.* 48, 49, 50, 51, 52. Every Deed consists of two principal parts, namely, *the Premisses* and *the Consequents*; *the Premisses* is the former part thereof, being all that which precedeth *the Habendum* or Limitation of the Estate, which are the persons contracting, and the things contracted. *The Consequent* is that which follows the Premisses, and that is the *Habendum*, in which are two Limitations: The one of the Estate or Property, which the Party passive shall receive by the Deed: The other of *the use*, which is to express in the said *Habendum* to or for what use and benefit he shall have the same Estate, and of the limitation of such *uses*, many Presidents are set down: In the same *West Symbol. part* 1. *lib.* 2. *sect.* 308. & 327. These *uses* were invented upon the Statute of *Westm.* 3. *Quia emptores terrarum*, before which Statute no such *uses* were known, *Perkin's Devises* 528. And because in time many Deceits were invented, by setling the Possession in one Man, and the *use* in another; to avoid which, and divers other Mischiefs and Inconveniences, was the Statute 27 *H.* 8. *cap.* 10. provided, which unites the *use* and Possession together. See *Co. lib.* 3. *Chudleye's Case*, *fol.* 121.

User de Action, Is the pursuing or bringing an *Action*, which in what Place and County it ought to be, See *Bro.* tit. *Lieu & County*, fol. 64.

Usher, *Ostiarius*, From the French *Huissier*, A Door-keeper of a Court; Is an Officer in the Exchequer, of which sort there are four that attend the chief Officers and Barons at the Court at *Westminster*, and Juries, Sheriffs, and all other Accountants, at the pleasure of the Court. There are also *Ushers* in the King's House, as of the Privy-Chamber, &c. See *Black-Rod*.

Usact, *In Privilegio de Semplingham---sint quieti tam ipsi quam homines eorum, &c. de omnibus misericordiis & amerciamentis & forisfacturis, &c. & de murdro, & Latrocinio, & conceiles, &* **Usact**, *& Hamsoka, Grithbrech, &c.* In *Kelwaye's Reports* it is written **Outlatch**.

Usucaption, *Usucaptio*, The enjoying a thing by continuance of time, or receiving the Profits, long Possession or Prescription.

Usufructuary, *Usufructuarius*, One that hath the use, and reaps the profit of any thing.

Usury, *Usura*, Is the gain of any thing above the Principal, or that which was lent, exacted only in consideration of the Loan, be it as well Corn, Apparel, Wares, or such like, as Money. And it is derived *ab usu & ære, quasi usu æra, id est usus æris, &* Usura *est commodum certum quod propter usum rei mutuatæ accipitur*, Co. 5. Rep. *Payton's* Case. The Statute 13 *Eliz. cap.* 8. alloweth not *usury*, but punisheth the excess of it. And that of 21 *Jac. cap.* 17. expresly Ordains, That no word in that Law shall be construed and expounded to allow the practice of *usury* in point of Religion or Conscience. And by the Statute 12 *Car.* 2. *cap.* 13. No man must take above six pound for the forbearance of one hundred pounds for a year, under the penalties therein contained. See *Co.* 3. *Inst. fol.* 151. By the Stat. 3 & 11 *H.* 7. It is called *Dry Exchange*.

Utas, *Octava*, Is the eighth day following any Term or Feast, as the *Utas of St. Michael*, *the* Utas *of St. Hillary*, *the* Utas *of St. John Baptist, &c.* As you may read 51 *Hen.* 3. concerning general days in the Bench; and any day between the Feast and *the Octave*, is said to be within *the Utas*. The use of this is in the return of Writs, as appears by that Statute. **At the** Utas **of the Holy Trinity**, Preamble to the Statute 43 *E.* 3.

Utensil, *Utensile*, Any thing necessary for our Use and Occupation; Housholdstuff.

Utfangthef, That is, *Fur extra captus*, scilicet, *extra Dominium vel jurisdictionem*, Is an ancient Priviledge or Royalty granted to a Lord of a Mannor, by the King, which gives him power to punish a *Thief* dwelling out of his Liberty, and committing *Theft* without the same, if he be taken within his Fee, *Bracton, lib.* 2. *tract.* 2. *cap.* 35. says thus, **Utfangthef** *dicitur extraneus latro, veniens aliunde, de terra aliena & qui captus fuit in terra ipsius qui tales habet libertates.* See *Outfangtheif*.

Utlagh, *Uthlagus*, An Outlaw, signifies *Bannitum extra legem, Fleta, lib.* 1. *cap.* 47. And in *Mon. Ang.* 2. *par. fol.* 618. we read *Fuit quidam* Uthlagus *famosissimus partes istas frequentans propter iter commeantium inter* Nottingham & Derby *per forestam*. See *Outlaw*.

Utlagato capiendo quando utlagatur in uno comitatu & postea fugit in alium, Is a Writ, the nature whereof is sufficiently exprest by the name. See *Reg. Orig. fol.* 133.

Utland, *Terra extra* dicebatur *terra servilis seu tenementalis, quod de procinctu terrarum Dominicalium quæ* **Inland** *nuncupata sunt, in exteriorem agrum rejiciebantur.* Vide *Inland*.

Utlary or **Utlawry**, *Utlagaria vel utlagatio*, Is a punishment for such as being called into Law, and lawfully sought, do contemptuously refuse to appear, after an *Original Writ* with a *Nihil habet*, three Writs of *Capias, Alias & Pluries*. returned by the Sheriff *Non est inventus*, and an *Exigent* with a *Proclamation* thereupon awarded. And *Bracton* says, He must be called at five Counties, a Month being between every County, *lib.* 3. *tract.* 2. *cap.* 11. And if he appear not within that time *pro exlege tenebitur, cum Principi non obediat nec legi & extunc utlagabitur*; that is, he shall be pronounced out of the King's Protection, and deprived of the benefit of the Law. The effect of this is divers; for if he be *Outlawed* at the Suit of another in a Civil Cause, he shall forfeit all his Goods and Chattels to the King; If upon Felony, then he shall forfeit all his Lands and Tenements which he hath in Fee, or for Life, and his Goods and Chattels; *Et tunc gerit caput lupinum, ita quod sine judiciali inquisitione ritè pereat & secum suum judicium portet, & meritò sine lege pereat, qui secundum legem vivere recusaverit, &c.* Bract. lib. 3. tract. 2. cap. 11. And the same *lib.* 3. *tract.* 2. cap. 14. And *Fleta, lib.* 1. *cap.* 27, 28. say, A Minor or Woman cannot be Outlawed: For where a Man is said to be *Outlawed*, a Woman is termed *waived*, F. N. B. *fol.* 161. How an *Outlaw* is *inlawed* again, and restored to the King's Peace and Protection. See *Bracton*, and *Fleta, ubi supra.*

Utlepe, *Significat escapium, hoc est, evasionem latronum*, Fleta, lib. 1. cap. 47. and 18 Hen.6. Pat. 2. m. 22.

Utrum. See *Assise.*

Utter-Barristers, *Juris consulti*, Are such, who for their long study, and great industry bestowed upon the Knowledge of the Common Law, be called from their Contemplation to Practice, and in the face of the World, to take upon them the Protection and Defence of Clyents; These in other Countries are called *Licentiati in jure.* The time before any one ought to be called to the Bar by the ancient Orders, was heretofore eight years, now reduced to seven, and the Exercises done by him (if he were not called *Ex gratia*) was twelve *Grand Moats* performed in the Inns of Chancery in the time of the Grand Readings, and twenty four *petty Moats* at the Inns of Chancery in the Term-times, before the Readers of the respective Inns of Chancery. A *Barrister* newly called is to attend the six next long Vacations the Exercise of the House, *viz.* in *Lent* and *Summer*, and is therefore for those three years called a *Vacation Barrister.* And they are called *Utter Barristers*, i. Pleaders without the Bar, to distinguish them from Benchers, or those who have been Readers, who are sometimes admitted to plead within the Bar, as the King, Queen, or Princes Council are.

W.

WAftors, *Waftores*, *Edward* the Fourth Constituted a Triumvirate of Officers with Naval Power, whom the Patent, 22 *E.* 4. *membr.* 2. stiles *Custodes, Conductores* and *Waftores*; and these were chiefly to guard our Fishermen on the Coast of *Norfolk* and *Suffolk*. We still retain the word to *waft over*, that is, to conduct or convey over Sea.

Waga alias **Waga**, A *weigh*, which is a measure of Cheese, Wooll, &c. containing two hundred fifty six pound of *Averdupois*: For by the Statute 9 *H.* 6. *cap.* 8. a *weigh of Cheese* ought to contain thirty two Cloves, and each Clove eight pound, though some say but seven; *Unam* wagam *salis de salinis suis de Terineton.* Mon. Ang. 1. par. fol. 515. See *Weigh.*

Wage, *Vadiare*, From the French *Gager*, *dare pignus*; Signifies the giving Security for the performance of any thing; as to *wage Deliverance*, which see in *Gage*, to *wage Law.* See in *Law.* None *wages Law* against the King, *Bro.* tit. *Chose in Action*, num. 9. See *Co.* on *Lit.* fol. 294. tit. *Ley-gager.*

Wager of Law. See *Law.*

Waife or **Weyfe**, *Waivium*, Goods *waived* are such as a Thief having feloniously stollen, and being newly followed with Hue-and-Cry, or else over-charged with the burden or trouble of the Goods, for his own Ease, and more speedy Flight, flies away, and leaves the Goods behind him; then the King's Officer, or the Bayliff of the Lord of the Mannor (within whose Jurisdiction they be left) who by Prescription, or Grant from the King, hath the Franchise of *waife*, may seize the Goods so *waived* to his Lord's use, except the Owner come with fresh Suit after the Felon, and sue an Appeal within a year and a day, or give Evidence against him at his Arraignment, and he be attainted, &c. In which cases the first Owner shall have restitution of his Goods so stollen and *waived.* And though *waife* is properly spoken of Goods stollen, yet it may be also of Goods not stollen: As if a man be pursued with *Hue-and-Cry* as a Felon, and he flies, and leaves his own Goods; these shall be forfeit as Goods stollen, and are properly called *Fugitives Goods*, which are not forfeited, till it be found before the Coroner, or otherwise of Record, that he fled for Felony. A thing *pro derelicto habita*, *waived* and forsaken is *nullius in bonis.* See 29 *E.* 3. *Waifes*, things lost and Estrayes, must by the Lord of the Franchise where they are found, be caused to be cryed and published in Markets and Churches near about, else the year and day does not run to the prejudice of the Loser, *Britton, cap.* 17. And further, Inter Plac. coram Joh. de Berewell & sociis suis Justic. Itin. apud Salop. in Octab. Sancti Michaelis, 20 E. 1. Rot. 29. in Dorso. *Richardus filius Alani comes Arundell summonitus fuit ad respondend. Domino Regi de placito quo warranto clamat habere placita Coronæ & habere* **Waife** *de Manerio suo de* Upton *subtus* Hawman, *&c. in Com.* Salop *& comes dicit quod ipse clamat habere* **Infangenethef** & **Wayfe**, *& eadem placita & libertates habuerunt ipse & omnes antecessores sui & eisdem usi sunt à tempore, quo non extat memoria & eo warranto clamat, &c. Et* Hugo *de* Lowther *qui sequitur pro Domino Rege dicit, quod* **Wayfe** *est quoddam grossum de Corona, ita Coronæ Domini Regis annexum quod nullus eo gaudere possit, nisi inde habeat speciale warrantum à Domino Rege vel antecessoribus suis concessum.*

Wainable, That may be ploughed or manured, tillable, ---*Dedimus, &c. in loco qui vocatur* Shiplade *la Moreis & la terre* wainable *& la Bruere, &c.* Carta Rogeri de scales sine dat.

Wainage, *Wainagium*, May be derived from the Saxon *Wæn*, id est, *Plaustrum.* **And any others Villain than ours shall be amerced saving his Wainge, if he fall into our Mercy.** Mag. Cart. cap. 14. Sir *Edward Coke*. 2. *par. Inst. fol.* 28. says, It signifies the countenance of a Villain; but why not rather the furniture of his Cart or Waine. See *Gainage* and *Wannage.*

Waitefee, Tho. Spelman *filius* Johannis, *&c. dicitur tenuisse Manerium de* Narborough, *cum tertia parte advocationis Ecclesiæ, &c. de Domina*

Regina ut de Manerio suo de Wingrave *per servitium militare & per redditum* 14 s. *pro* **waitefee** *& Castlegarde & valet clarè per annum* 34 li. 17 s. 10 d. *quadrant.* Patet in Schedula liberationis *Joh. Spelman* fratris sui, 7. *Aug.* 5. *Eliz.* This might probably be a *Fee* to excuse his *waiting* at the Castle.

Waive, *Waiviare*, Is to forsake, *Reg. Orig.* 277. The *Civilians* term it *Habere pro derelicto*, and so *Waiviare feudum suum* signifies. To *waive* the Company of Theeves, *Stamf. Pl. Cor. fol.* 26. But this word properly belongs to a Woman, who is said to be *waived*, as a Man to be *Outlawed*, *Reg. Orig. fol.* 132. **Many of the Kings Liege People** Outlawed, **and many** Waived **by erroneous Processe**, *Anno* 7 *H.* 4. *cap.* 13. See *Utlary*.

Wakeman, The chief Magistrate of the Town of *Rippon* in *Yorkshire* so called, *quasi* Watchman, *Camd. Brit.*

Wald, *Walda.* See *Weald.*

Wales, *Wallia*, Is a part of *England* on the West side, inhabited by the Offspring of the ancient *Britans*, chased thither by the *Saxons*, called in to assist them against the *Picts* and *Scots*: But now they are incorporated to *England*, see *Lamb. Explication of Saxon words*, verb. *Wallus.*

Walkers, Are such as are otherwise called *Foresters*, *Cromp. Jur. fol.* 145. There are Foresters assigned by the King, who are *Walkers* within a certain space of Ground assigned to their Care.

Waiviaria mulieris, Is as much as *Utlagatio viri*, *Reg. Orig. fol.* 132.

Wall or Sea-wall. See *Water-gage.*

Wallesheria or Walecheria, ——*Quod quatuor villatæ propinquiores loco ubi casus Homicidii vel infortunium contigerit, veniant ad proximum Comitatum una cum inventore &* Wallesheria, i. *Parentela hominis interfecti & ibidem præsentent factum feloniæ & casum infortunii, &c.* I find, (saith *Spelman*) in a certain Note, A Wallesheria, i. *Parentela interfecti, scil. unus ex parte patris & alius ex parte matris*, and concludes that *significat* wallica *pars ut videtur.*

Wang, Properly signifies in the Saxon Tongue a Field, but we use it also for the Cheek or Jaw-teeth, which *Chaucer* calls *Wangs* and *wangteeth*, according to these Verses,

And in witness that this is sooth,
I bite the wax with my wang **tooth.**

Wangenetheof,---*Sit quietum de* **Gelth** & **Scoth**, *de wrecchο*, *& de* **Wangenethof** & **Danegelde**, Pat. 22 H. 4. par. 1. m. 33.

Wannage, Wannagium, *Eodem anno* (viz. 1198.) *Rex Angliæ accepit de unaquaq; carucata terræ sine Hyda totius Angliæ*, 5. *sol. de auxilio, ad quos colligendos misit idem Rex per singulos Comitatus Angliæ, unum Clericum & etiam unum Militem, &c. Qui fecerunt venire coram se Senescallos Baronum illius Comitatus, qui juraverunt quot carucarum* wannagia *fuerint in singulis Villis, &c. Ipsi vero qui electi fuerant, & constituti ad hoc negotium Regis faciendum, statuerunt per æstimationem legalium hominum ad uniuscujusq; Carucæ* wannagium *centum acras terræ, Hoveden's* Annal. part. poster. fol. 443. num. 30. See *Wainage. Wannagium* sometimes seems to signifie *Wain houses*, or necessary Out-houses for Husbandry.

Wapentake, *Wapentachium*, Is all one with that we call a *Hundred*, as appears by *Bracton, lib.* 3. *tract.* 2. *cap.* 1. *num.* 1. *Convocentur* (saith he) *servientes & Ballivi Hundredorum, & per ordinem irrotulentur Hundredarii sive* wapentachia *& nomina servientium*, &c. And *Lambert* in his *Explication of Saxon words*, verb. *Centuria*; Is of the same mind, adding that this word is specially used in the North Countries beyond the River *Trent*. And in the Laws of King *Edward the Confessor*, are these words, *Et quod Angli vocant* Hundredum, *supradicti comitatus vocant* wapentachium. The original of the Name *Hoveden* derives *à tactu armorum*, because *cum quis accipiebat præfecturam* wapentachii, *die Statuto in loco ubi consueverant Congregari, omnes majores contra eum conveniebant & descendente de equo suo, omnes assurgebant ei. Ipse vero, erecta lancea sua, ab omnibus secundum morem fœdus accipiebat: Omnes enim quotquot venissent cum lanceis suis ipsius hastam tangebant, & ita confirmabant per contactum armorum pace palam concessa, &c.* But we take it from hence, *Quod quoties novus esset Hundredi Dominus ei in subjectionis signum arma redderent Vassalli*, Ranulph. Cestr. lib. 1. cap. 5. See *Fleta*, lib. 2. cap. 61. sect. *universimode.* Sir *Thomas Smith de Rep. Anglor. lib.* 2. *cap.* 16. says, That anciently Musters were taken of the Armor and *Weapons* of the several Inhabitants of every several *wapentake*, and from those that could not find sufficient Pledges for their good abearing, their Weapons were taken away, and given to others. The Statutes 3 *H.* 5. *ca.* 2. 9 *H.* 6. *ca.* 10. and 15 *H.* 6. *cap.* 7. make mention of *Stainctiffe wapentake* and *Frendless wapentake* in *Craven*, in the County of *York.* See *Camd. Brit. fol.* 159. and *Co.* 2 *par. Inst. fol.* 99. Wapentake *hoc est quietancia de sectis & Hundredis quod dicitur* wapentake. *M. S. in Biblioth. Cotton. sub tit.* Vitellius.

Ward, *Custodia*, Hath divers significations, as a *ward* in *London*, in Latine *warda*, which is a portion of the City, committed to the special charge of one of the Aldermen of the City. See *Stowe's Survey of London*: Also a Forest is divided into *wards*, *Manwood, part* 1. *pag.* 97. Thirdly, A Prison is also called a *ward*. Lastly, The Heir of the King's Tenant, that held by *Knights service* or *in Capite*, was called a *ward* during his Nonage, 32 *H.* 8. 46. But this last is taken away by the Stat. 12 *Car.* 2. *cap.* 24.

Wards and Liveries, *Wardi & Liberaturæ*, Was a Court first erected by King *Henry the Eighth*, and afterwards augmented by him with the Office of *Liveries*, and therefore stiled *The Court of Wards and Liveries*; But it is absolutely taken away and abolished by the Statute made *Anno* 12 *Car.* 2. *cap.* 24.

Warden, *Gardianus*, Is the same with the French *Gardein*, and signifies him that hath the keeping or charge of any Person, or thing by Office; as *Wardens* of the Societies in *London*, 14 *H.* 8. *cap.* 2. *Warden-Courts*, 31 *H.* 6. *cap.* 3. *Warden* of the Marches, 4 *H.* 7. *cap.* 8. *Warden's and Commonalty* of the Lands contributary to *Rochester* Bridge,

Bridge, 18 *Eliz.* 7. *Warden of Peace*, 2 E. 3. 3. *Stat. Northampton.* *Warden* of the West Marches, *Camd. Brit.* pag. 606. *Warden* of the Forest, *Manwood*, *part.* 1. *pag.* 42. & 111. *Warden* of the *Alnage.* 18 H. 6. 16. *Warden* of the King's Wardrobe, 51 *H.* 3. *stat.* 5. *Wardens* of the Tables of the King's Exchange, 9 *E.* 3. *stat.* 2. *cap.* 7. & 9 *H.* 5. *stat.* 2. *cap.* 4. *Wardens* of the Rolls in the Chancery, 1 *E.* 4. *cap.* 1. 5. *Warden* or Clerk of the Hanaper in Chancery, *Ibid.* *Warden* of the King's Writs and Records of his Common Bench, *Ibid.* *Warden* of the King's Armor in the Tower, 1 *E.* 4. 1. *Warden* of the House of the Converts, 12 *Car.* 2. *cap.* 30. And *Warden* of the Stannaries, 14 *Car.* 2. *cap.* 3. See *Gardian.*

Wardmote, *Wardmotus*, Is a Court kept in every *ward* in *London*, 32 *H.* 8. 17. ordinarily called among them *The Wardmote-Court* or *Inquest.* See 4 *Inst. fol.* 249.

Wardpeny alias **Warpen**, and **Warthpeny**, Is Money contributed to watch and *ward*; *Denarii vicecomiti vel aliis castellanis persoluti ob castrorum præsidium vel excubias agendas.* And in a Charter of *William the Conqueror* to the Church of St. *Martine* in *Battell*, we find these words, *Concedo etiam eidem Ecclesiæ leugam circumquaq; adjacentem liberam & quietam ab omni Geldo, & Secto, & Hydagio, & Danegeldo, & opere Pontium, & Castellorum, & Parcorum, & omnibus auxiliis, placitis & querelis, &c. cum Saca & Soca & Thol & Theam, & Infangtheof &* **Warpeny, &c.**

Wardage, *VVargium*, It seems to be the same with the *wardpeny*, which see.

Wardstaff, *Lamborne* Mannor in *Essex* is held by Service of the **Wardstaff**, viz. to carry a Load of *Straw* in a Cart with six Horses, two Ropes, two Men in Harness to watch the said **Wardstaff**, when it is brought to the Town of *Aibridge*, &c. *Camd.* tit. *Essex.*

Wardfeoh or **Wardfegh**, Signified the value of a *ward*, or the Money paid to the Lord for his Redemption from *wardship.*

Wardwite, *Significat quietantiam misericordiæ in casu quo non invenerit, quis hominem ad* wardam *faciendam in castro vel alibi*, Fleta, lib. 1. cap. 7. And Spelman says it is, *Immunitas à præsidiis faciendis vel ab eorum contributione.*

Warranty, Warrantia *est securitas à venditore præstita emptori, quo tranquillè aliquid possideat. Eaq; à significatione* warrantizare *dicitur* warrantus, *sive venditor quando se empto obligat per acta Curiæ, aut chartam, aut contractus instrumentum*, Vossius de vitiis Sermonis, *lib.* 2. *ca.* 20. It is a Promise or Covenant by Deed made by the Bargainor, for himself and his Heirs, to *warrant* or secure the Bargainee and his Heirs against all Men, for the enjoying any thing agreed on between them. And he that makes this *warranty* is called *warrantus*, by *Bracton*, *lib.* 2. *cap.* 19. *and* 37. And this *warranty* passeth from the Seller to the Buyer, from the Feoffor to the Feoffee, from him that releaseth, to him that is released from an Action real, and such like: And the form of it is in this manner, *Et ego præfatus* J. *& hæredes mei prædictas decem acras terræ cum pertinentiis suis, præfato* H. *hæredibus & assignatis suis contra omnes gentes* warrantizabimus *in perpetuum per præsentes*, West Symbol. part 1. lib. 3. tit. *Feoffments*, sect. 287, 288. See *Glanvile*, *lib.* 3. *per totum. Bracton*, *lib.* 5. *tract.* 4. *Brition*, *cap.* 105. and *Co.* 4. *Rep. fol.* 81. *Nokes* Case. *Warranty* is either *real* or *personal*; *Real*, when it is annexed to Lands or Tenements granted for life, &c. And this is either *in Deed*, as by the word *warrantizo* expresly; or *in Law*, as by the word *Dedi*, or some other amplification: *Personal*, which either respects the property of the thing sold, or the quality of it. *Real warranty* in respect of the Estate, is either *Lineal*, *Collateral*, or *commencing by Disseisin*, for which see *Littleton* in the last Chapter of his Tenures, and *Co. lib.* 3. *Fermor's* Case, *fol.* 78. So then under the word *Hæredes* are comprehended all such as the first *warranters* Lands afterwards come unto either by descent, or otherwise, *Bracton*, *lib.* 5. *tract.* 4. *cap.* 1. *num.* 2. saith, *Imprimis videndum est quid sit* warrantizatio; *Et sciendum quod* warrantizare, *nihil aliud est quam defendere & acquietare tenentem, qui* warrantum *vocabit in seisina sua.* With whom agrees *Fleta*, lib. 5. cap. 15. sect. 1. & lib. 6. cap. 23. *per totum.* By what words in a Feoffment a Feoffor shall be bound to *warranty.* See the *Statute of Bigamy*, 4 *E.* 1. cap. 6. and see *Co.* on *Lit. fol.* 365. and 383. There is also a *warrant of Attorney*, whereby a Man appoints another to do some thing in his Name, and *warranteth* his *Action*; which seems to differ from a *Letter of Atturney*, which passeth usually under the Hand and Seal of him that makes it, before any credible Witnesses; whereas a *warrant of Atturney* in personal, mixt, and some real Actions, is put in of course by the Attorneys for the Plaintiffs or Demandants, Tenants or Defendants. But a *warrant of Atturney* to suffer a common Recovery by the Tenant or Vouchee, is acknowledged before such Persons as a Commission for the doing thereof directs, *West Symb.* 2. par. tit. *Recoveries*, sect. 1. See *Attorney.*

Warrantia Chartæ, Is a Writ that lies properly for him, who being infeoffed in Lands or Tenements, with a Clause of warranty, and is impleaded in an *Assise* or *writ of Entry*, wherein he cannot vouch or call to *warranty*: For in this Case his remedy is to take out this Writ against the Feoffor, or his Heirs, *Reg. Orig. fol.* 157. *F. N. B. fol.* 134. *Fleta*, lib. 6. cap. 35. and *West Symbol.* part 2. tit. *Fines*, sect. 156.

Warrantia diei, Is a Writ lying in case where a Man having a day assigned personally to appear in Court to any Action wherein he is sued, is in the mean time, by Commandment, employ'd in the King's Service, so that he cannot come at the day assigned: The Writ is directed to the Justices to this end, that they neither take nor Record him in default for that day, *Reg. Orig. fol.* 18. Of this read more *F. N. B. fol.* 17. and *Glanvile*, *lib.* 1. *cap.* 8.

Warrantia custodiæ, Is a Writ Judicial, and lay for him who was challenged to be a Ward to another, in respect of Land said to be holden in Knights service, which when it was bought by the Ancestors of the Ward, was warranted to be free from such thraldome, and it lay against the Warrantor and his Heirs, *Reg. Jud. fol.* 36. But now by the Statute made 12 *Car.* 2. *cap.* 24. It is become altogether out of use.

Warrant of Attorney. See *Letter of Attorney* and *warranty.*

Warectum & terra wareta, Land that has been neglected, and long untilled, fallow Ground: *Tem us warecti* in ancient Records signifies the time wherein Land lies fallow. --- *In* warectis, *in Brueriis, in Boscis, in Mariscis, in Defensis, & in omnibus terris, &c.* Mon. Ang. 2. par. fol. 253. And in the same, *part* 1. *fol.* 525. we read 25. *Acras uno-quoq; anno ad seminandum & totidem ad* warectandum. See also *Yvernagium.*

Warren, *Warrenna* alias *Varrenna*, Cometh of the French *Garenne*, i. *Vivarium, vel locus in quo vel aves, vel pisces, vel feræ continentur, quæ ad victum duntaxat pertinent, Calepine* out of *Aulus Gellius*, lib. 2. *Noct. Attic.* cap. 20. But a *Warren* as we use it, is a Franchise or place priviledged, either by Prescription or Grant from the King, to keep Beasts and Fowl of *warren*, which are Hares and Conyes, Partridges and Phesants: And if any Person be found an Offendor in any such *Fee-warren*, he is punishable for the same at the Common Law, and by the Statute 21 *Ed.* 3. called the Statute *De malefactoribus in parcis & chaceis*, &c. A *Fee warren* may lie open, for there is no necessity of inclosing the same as there is of a Park; which ought to be seised into the King's Hands, if it be not inclosed.

Warnoth, Is an ancient Custom, whereby if any Tenant holding of the Castle of *Dover*, fail'd in paying his Rent at the day, he should forfeit double, and for the second fayler treble, &c. [illegible] *Recept, Scac. Trin.* 33 *E.* 1. *Linc.* 46. *coram* [illegible] And in Mon. Ang. 2. par. fol. 589. *Terris cul-* [illegible] *terris de* **Warnoth**.

Warscot, Was the Contribution wont to be made towards Armor in the *Saxons* time. *Sint omnes tam primarii quam mediocres & minuti, immunes, liberi & quieti ab omnibus Provincialibus, summonitionibus & popularibus placitis quæ* **Hundred-laghe** *Angli dicunt, & ab omnibus armorum oneribus quod* **Warscot** *Angli dicunt & forinsecis querelis*, Leg. Forest. Canuti Reg. num. 9.

Warwite. See *Wardwite.*

Wast, *Vastum*, Hath divers significations: First, It is a spoyl made either in Houses, Woods, Lands, &c. by the Tenant for Life or Years, to the prejudice of the Heir, or of him in the Reversion or Remainder, *Kitchin, fol.* 168. Whereupon the Writ of *wast* is brought, for the recovery of the thing wasted and treble Damages. See *Vasto*. *Wast* of the Forest is most properly where a man cuts down his own Woods within the Forest, without Licence of the King, or Lord chief *Justice in Eyre*. See *Manwood, part* 2. *cap.* 8. *num.* 4. & 5. Secondly, *Wast* is taken for those Lands which are not in any Mans Occupation, but lie Common; which seem to be so called, because the Lord cannot make such profit of them as of his other Lands, by reason of that use which others have of it in passing to and fro; upon this none may Build, cut down Trees, Dig, &c. without the Lord's Licence. Thirdly, *Year, day and wast*, (*Annus, dies & vastum*,) Is a Punishment or Forfeiture belonging to Petit Treason or Felony, whereof you may read *Stamf. Pl. Cor. lib.* 3. *cap.* 30. And see *Year, day and wast.*

Wast ground, *Vastus fundus*, Is so called, because it lies as *wast*; with little or no profit to the Lord of the Mannor, and to distinguish it from the Demesnes in the Lord's Hands, 2. *par. Inst. fol.* 656. See *Wast.*

Wastors, Were a kind of Theeves so called, *Anno* 5 *E.* 3. *cap.* 14. **There have been divers Manslaughters, Felonies and Robberies done by People called Roberdsmen**, Wastors, **and Draw-latches**, 4 *H.* 4. *cap.* 27.

Wastel Bread, *Anno* 51 *H.* 3. *Statute of Bread* seems to be the finest *Bread*: But whence the word *wastel* is derived, *Non liquet*, says the *Glosse in* 10. *Scriptores*. See *Cocket.*

Water-Bayliffs, Seem to be Officers in Port-Towns, for the searching of Ships, 28 *H.* 6. *cap.* 5. Also an Officer belonging to the City of *London*, who hath the supervising and search of Fish brought thither, and the gathering of the Toll rising from the *Thames*. He also attends on the Lord Mayor for the time being, and hath the principal care of marshalling the Guests at the Table; and doth Arrest Men for Debt, or other personal or criminal Matters, upon the River of *Thames*, by Warrant of his Superiors, and the like.

Watergage, *Watergagium & Aquægagium*, A Sea-wall or Bank to distrain the Current or Overflow of the Water: Also an Instrument to *gage* or measure the quantity or Deepness of any Waters.

Water-gang, *Watergangium*, A Trench or Course to carry a Stream of Water, such as are usually made in Sea-walls to loose and drain Water out of the Marishes. Some confound this with *watergage*, but they seem to differ in signification; *Carta* H. 3. *De ordinatione Marisci de* Romeney, *&c. Ad reparandum wallias & Watergangias ejusdem Marisci contra Maris periculum. Omnibus Ballivis de* Besinstone, Robertus *de Curci, salutem, Mando vobis atq; præcipio, quatenus justicietis meos homines de Margate, ut faciant wallas &* watergangas, *& clausuras wallarum sicut debent facere*, Mon. Ang. 2 par. fol. 920.

Water gavel, Was a Rent paid for fishing in, or other benefit received from some River or Water, Henricus---Rex salutem; *Sciatis nos dedisse*, &c. *dilecto & fideli nostro* Huberto de Burgo *comiti Cantiæ & Margeriæ uxori suæ redditum* 32 s. & 4 d. *quem homines eorundem* Huberti & Margeriæ *de Manerio suo de* Elmour *nobis reddere solebant singulis annis per manum Ballivi nostri de* Menstreworth *nomine* **Water-gavel** *Habend.* Dat. 15 H. 3.

Watling-street, Is one of those four wayes which the *Romans* are said to have made here, and called them *Consulares, Prætorias, Militares & Publicas*. This *Street* is otherwise called *Werlam-street*. See *Hoveden. part. prior. Annal. fol.* 248. This *Street* leads from *Dover* to *London*, Saint *Albans*, *Dunstable*, *Towcester*, *Atherston*, and the *Severne*, near the *Wrekin* in *Shropshire*, extending it self to *Anglesey* in *Wales*, *Anno* 39 *Eliz. cap.* 2. The second is called *Ikemild-street*, so called *ab Icenis* stretching from *Southamton* over the River *Isis*, at *Newbridge*; thence by *Camden* and *Litchfield*, then it passeth the River *Derwent* by *Derby*, so to *Bolseover* Castle, and ends at *Tinmouth*. The third was called *The Fosse*, because in some places it was never perfected, but lies as a large Ditch, leading from *Cornwall* through *Devonshire*, by *Tetbury*, near *Stow in the wolds*, and besides

Coventry to *Leicester*, *Newark*, and so to *Lincoln*. The fourth was called *Ermine* or *Erminage-street*, beginning at St. *David's* in *West-Wales*, and going to *Southampton*. See the Laws of *Edward the Confessor* whereby these four Publick wayes had the Privilege of *Pax Regis*. See *Holinshed's Chron. vol.* 1. *cap.* 19. and *Henry* of *Huntington*, *lib.* 1. *in principio*.

Warshot or **Warscot**, *Ceragium*, This was anciently paid thrice a year towards the charge of Candles in Churches. *Tributum quod in Ecclesiis pendebatur ad subministrationem ceræ & Luminarium. Hac autem solutione multi se contendunt immunes esse à minoribus quibusdam decimis persolvendis ejusdemq; generis sunt quæ alias* **Cock & War**, *alias* **Mainepozt** *appellantur*. Spelman.

Way. See *Chimin*.

Weald or **Weld**, A Saxon word signifying *Sylva*, is the woody part of a Country, as the *weald of Kent*, Camd. Brit. *pag.* 247. *Anno* 26 *H.* 8. *cap.* 7. In the *Collection of Statutes*, 14 Car. 2. *cap.* 6. It is misprinted *wildes of Sussex*, *Surrey or Kent*, for *Wealds*.

Weare or **Were**, *Wera & wara*, A Stank, or great Dam in a River, well known, accommodated for the taking of Fish, or to convey the Stream to a Mill. *Unam* warram *& duas Cotlandas cum Dominio & Prato*, Mon. Angl. 2. par. fol. 128. See *Kiddell*.

Weif. See *Waife*.

Weigh, *Waga*, Is a weight of Cheese or Wooll containing two hundred fifty six pounds of *Aver-du-pois*. See *Waga*. *Co.* 12. *Rep. fol.* 17. mentions eighty *weigh* of *Bay-Salt*.

Weights, *Pondera*, There are two sorts of them in use with us; The one called *Troy-weight*, having twelve ounces in the pound, by which Pearl, Pretious Stones, Electuaries, and medicinal things, Gold, Silver and Brede be weighed. The other is termed *Averdupois*, and contains sixteen ounces in the pound, by which all other things be weighed that pass by weight. *Geo. Agricola* in his learned Tractate *De Ponderibus & mensuris*, pag. 339. terms the pound of twelve ounces *Libram medicam*, and the other of sixteen ounces *Libram civilem*, saying thus of them both, *Medica & civilis libra numero non gravitate unciarum differunt*. The second seems so to be termed, by reason of the more full *weight*. But by these words *Aver du pois* are sometimes signified such Merchandise as are bought and sold by this kind of *weights*. The first Statute of *York*, made 9 *E.* 3. *in Proœm.* 27 *E.* 3. *stat.* 2. *cap.* 10. and 24 *H.* 8. *cap.* 13. See *Skene de Verbor.* Signif. *verb.* Serplathe. All our *Weights* and Measures have their first Composition from the Penny-Sterling, which ought to weigh thirty two wheat Corns of a middle sort; twenty of which Pence make an Ounce, and twelve such Ounces a Pound; but fifteen Ounces make the Merchants Pound, *Fleta*, *lib.* 2. *cap.* 12. which though an ounce less should probably be all one in signification with *Aver dupois*, and the other Pound called by *Fleta*. *Trone weight* plainly appears to be the same with that we now call *Troy weight*. See *Tronage*. **From henceforth there shall be one weight, one Measure, and one Yard, according to the Standard of the Exchequer through all the Realm, &c.** *Anno* 17 *Car.* 1. *cap.* 19.

Weights of Auncel, *Anno* 14 *E.* 3. *stat.* 1. *cap.* 12. See *Auncell weight*.

Weythe,----*Et omnia animalia advenientia fugitiva, Gallicè* **Weyth** *in toto Hundredo de Halton*, Mon. Ang. 2. par. fol. 187. See *Waif*.

Wend, *Wendus*, i. *perambulatio*, From the Saxon *Wendam*, *ire*, to go. *Procinctus terræ amplior plurima juga in se continens*, Rentale Regalis Manerii de Wye, *pag.* 31. -- *Tres sunt* wendi, *viz.* **Doun-wend**, **Chiltones wend**, **et Brons-fordwend**, *& in quolibet* wendo *sunt decem juga & sic in tribus* wendis *sunt* 30. *juga*, *quorum* 26. *juga & dimid. sunt in wye* & infra. *Quilibet* wendus *faciet* 10. *avoragia semper de tribus septimanis in tres*, &c.

Were alias **Werræ**, According to *Lambert* in his *Explication of Saxon words* signifies *æstimatio capitis aut pretium hominis*. That is so much as one paid in ancient time for killing a Man, when such Crimes were punisht with pecuniary Mulcts, not Death. In *Leg. Ed. Conf. cap.* 11. we read *Were suum*,---id est, *pretium suæ redemptionis*, his ransome. ---*Siquis ante Comitem in placito pugnaverit*, *emendat secundum pretium sui-ipsius*, *& forisfacturum quod Angli dicunt* were *&* wite, Leg. Canut. M. S. pag. 150. In which words the Saxon *W.* is often mistaken for *P.* and written *Pere and Pite*. See *Pere and Pite*. See also *Gavelet*.

Weregelt-thef, Signifies a *Theif* that may be redeemed, *Fleta*, *lib.* 1. *cap.* 47.

Weregild, **Wergeld**, Wergildus, *Pretium seu valor hominis occisi, homicidii pretium*, which was paid partly to the King, for the loss of his Subject, partly to the Lord whose Vassal he was, and partly to the next of Kin. *De unoquoq; fure per totam Scotiam est* **wergelt** 30. *Vaccæ & una juvenca*, *sive fuerit liber homo*, *sive servus*, Reg. Majest. lib. 4. cap. 19. The **weregild** of an Archbishop and of an Earl was 15000 *Thrimsa's*, Selden's *Titles of Honor*, fol. 604.

Weretoffe, ---*Et sint quieti de communi misericordia Comitatus*, *de Ward-peny*, *& Aver peny*, *de Hundred-peny & Thirding-peny*, *de* Weretoffe, *& de Forefeng*, Carta Hen 1. See *Were*.

Wervagium, --*Cum omnibus aliis consuetudinibus*, *legibus & libertatibus suis &* wervagio *suo* **bi land & bi strand**, Carta Hen. 3. Leveshamensi cænob. *concess.*

West-Saxonlage, Was the Law of the West-Saxons. See *Merchenlage*.

Westminster, *Westmonasterium*, Was the ancient Seat of our Kings, and is now the well-known place, where the High Court of Parliament and Courts of Judicature sit. It had great Privileges granted by Pope *Nicholas* among others. *Ut amplius in perpetuum Regiæ constitutionis locus sit atq; Repositorium Regalium Insignium*. Ep. ejus ad div. Edovard. Tom. 3. B. fol. 1228. See *City*, and 4. *Inst. fol.* 255.

Wetecroft, *Habebit mensuram unam*, *sc.* **wetecroft** *cum orto ubi possit manere*, *&c.* Mon. Ang. 2. par. fol. 40.

Wharfe, *Wharfa*, Is a broad plain place near a *Creek* or *Hith* of the Water, to lay Wares on, that are brought to or from the Water, *New Book of Entries*, fol. 3. *Anno* 12 *Car*. 2. *cap*. 4.

Wharfage, *Wharfagium*, Is money paid for landing Wares at a *Wharf*, or for shipping or taking Goods into a Boat or Barge from thence. It is mentioned 27 *H*. 8. *cap*. 26. And 22 *Car*. 2. *cap*. 11, &c.

Wharfinger, Is he that owns or keeps a Wharfe, or hath the over-sight or management of it, *Anno* 7 *E*. 6, 7. 12 *Car*. 2. *cap*. 4. and 22 *Car*. 2. *cap*. 11.

Wheelage, *Rotagium*; *Tributum est quod Rotarum nomine penditur, hoc est pro plaustris & carris transeuntibus*. Spelm.

Whitehart Silver, *Candidi cervi argentum*, Is a mulct paid into the *Exchequer* out of certain Lands in or near the Forest of *Whitehart*, which hath continued from *Henry* the Third's time, who imposed it upon *Thomas de la Linde*, for killing a most beautiful *White Hart*, which that King before had purposely spared in hunting, *Camd. Brit. pag*. 150.

White Rent, *Redditus albus*. See *Quit-Rent*.

White-Spurs, A sort of Esquires so called. See *Esquires*.

White-Straits, A kind of course Cloth made in *Devonshire*, about a yard and half a quarter broad, raw, mentioned 5 *H*. 8. *cap*. 2.

Whitson-farthings. See *Pentecostalls*, mentioned in Letters Patent of *Henry the Eighth* to the Dean of *Worcester*.

Widow of the King, *Vidua Regis*, Was she, that after her Husband's death, being the *Kings* Tenant *in Capite*, was forced to recover her Dower by the Writ *De Dote assignanda*, and could not marry again without the King's consent, *Stamf. Prærog. cap*. 4. See the Statute of the *Prærog. Anno* 17 *E*. 2. *Mag. Chart. cap*. 7. and 32 *Hen*. 8. *cap*. 46. See *F. N. B. fol*. 263.

Widow-hood, *Viduitas*, The state or condition of a *Widow*.

Wife, *Uxor*, After Marriage, all the will of the *Wife*, in Judgment of the Law, is subject to the will of the Husband, and it is commonly said *A feme covert hath no will, sed fulget radiis mariti*, Co. 4. Rep. *Forse* and *Hembling*'s Case. See *Perkins*, *fol*. 2, 3, 4. *Plowd. Comment*. 344. *Bret* and *Rigdon*'s Case, *Doctor and Student*, fol. 13. and 4 *H*. 6. 31.

Will, or **last Will**, *Testamentum*, *ultima voluntas*, Is of two sorts, A *Will in writing*, called also a *Testament*; and a *Will* by word of Mouth, only called a *Nuncupative will*, which being proved *per Testes*, may be of as good force as that in writing, except only for Lands, which are not devisable, but by a *Testament* in writing made in the life of the Testator. See *Touchstone of Wills*, pag. 2. See *Testament*.

Wigreve, A Saxon word, derived from **Wig** or **Wic**, which signifies *Sylvam*, and *Greve præpositus*, and denotes the Overseer of a Wood, according to *Spelman*: But *Wia* in Saxon more truly signifies *Vir*, and so it may more properly intend an Overseer of the High-wayes.

Winches, A kind of Engine to draw Barges up the Water against the Stream, *Anno* 21 *Jac. cap*. 32.

Winter-heyning, Is that Season comprehended between the Eleventh day of *November* and the Three and twentieth of *April*, which time, by the Act made 20 *Car*. 2. *cap*. 3. is excepted from the liberty of commoning in the *Forest of Dean*.

Wisgilthef, *Vale Royal*, pag. 113. Perhaps mistaken for *Weregelthef*, which see.

Windsore, A *Herald*. See *Herald*.

Wite, A *Saxon* word signifying Punishment, Pain, Penalty, Fine or Mulct: Hence **Wite** or **Witfree**, one of the terms of Priviledge granted to our *Portsmen*, denoting a Freedom or Immunity from Fines or Amerciaments, and not (as they vulgarly accept) from being liable to be beg'd for Fools, for lack of *wit* or understanding, *Saxon Dict*. See *Wyte* & *Gloss. in* 10. *Script*.

Witerden alias **Witereden**, & **Winterden**, Was a kind of Taxation among the *West-Saxons*, imposed by the Publick Council of the Kingdom: For *Wite* and *Witan* signifie *Majores Regni* and *Rædan Concilium*. See Charta Ethelvulphi Regis Catholica apud Malm. de Gest. R. lib. 1. pag. 41. *Mansio* (sc. quævis Ecclesiæ assignata) *sit tuta & libera ab omnibus secularibus servitiis, Necnon regalibus tributis majoribus & minoribus sive taxationibus, quæ nos dicimus* **Witereden**.

Withernam, *Vetitum Namium*, May be compounded of the Saxon *Wyther*, *altera*, & *Nam*, *captio*, and is a forbidden taking, as the taking or driving a Distress to a Hold, or out of the County, so that the Sheriff cannot upon the Replevin make deliverance thereof to the Party distrained. In which case the Writ of *Withernam*, or *de Vetito Namio* is directed to the Sheriff, for the taking as many of his Beasts that did thus unlawfully distrain, or as much Goods of his into his keeping, till he hath made deliverance of the first Distress: Also if the Beasts be in a Fortlet or Castle, the Sheriff may take with him the *posse Comitatus*, and beat down the Castle, as appears by the *Statute of Westm*. 1. *cap*. 20. and *Britton*, *cap*. 27. *Withernam* according to *Bracton*, *lib*. 3. *tract*. 2. *cap*. 37. And in *Westm*. 2. *cap*. 2. seems to signifie an unlawful Distress made by him that has no right to distrain, *Anno* 13 *E*. 1. *cap*. 2. See the *New Book of Entries*, *hoc verb*. and see *F. N. B. fol*. 73. *Reg. Orig. fol*. 82, 83. *Reg. Judic. fol*. 29. and *Smith de Repub. Anglor. cap*. 10. This *withernam* (saith he) is in Dutch and likewise in Saxon *Withernempt*, that is *alternum accipere*, and signifies all one with *Reprisalia*, *Reprisals*. See *Skene de verbor*. Signif. *verb*. Averia.

Woad, *Glastum*, Is an Herb like Plantane, growing in many places of *England*, formerly brought from *Tholouse* in *France*, and from *Spain* much used, and very necessary for the dying of a blue colour, *Anno* 7 *H*. 8. *cap*. 2. We call it *Woad*, from the Italian *Guedo*.

Wold, *Walda*, A Doun, or Champaigne-ground, hilly, and void of wood; as *Stow in the wolds*, and *Cotswold* in *Gloucestershire*.

Wong,

Wong, A Saxon word, written otherwise *Wange*, and signifying a Field; *Tres acras terræ jacentes in lez* **wongs**, i. *in campis opinor seminalibus, magis quam pascuis*, saith *Spelman*. So in an ancient Charter of *Garradon Abbey* in *Leicestershire*, Dat. 14 *E*. 3. There is mention of the **wicketwong**, which is a large piece of inclosed Ground lying before the Abby Gate. See *Wang*.

Woodgeld, *Woodgeldum*, Seems to be the gathering or cutting of wood within the Forest, or Money paid for the same to the Foresters; and the immunity from this by the King's Grant is by *Crompton* called *Woodgeld*, *fol*. 157. *Co*. on *Lit*. *fol*. 233. says, It signifies to be free from payment of Money for taking wood in any Forest.

Woodmen, Are those in the Forest that have charge especially to look to the King's Wood, *Cromp*. *Jurisd*. *fol*. 146.

Woodmote, Is the old Name of that Court of the Forest, which is now since the Statute of *Charta de Foresta* called the *Court of Attachments*, and by that Statute is held every forty days, but was wont to be held at the will of the chief Officers of the Forest, without any certain time. See *Manwood*'s *Forest Law*, cap. 22. fol. 207.

Woodplea-Court, Is a *Court* held twice in the year in the Forest of *Clun* in *Con*. *Salop*, for determining all matters of *wood* and agistment there, and perhaps was anciently the same with *Woodmote Court*.

Woodward, *Woodwardus*, Is an Officer of the Forest, whose Function you may understand by his Oath set down in *Cromp*. *Jur*. fol. 201.

You shall truly execute the Office of a Woodward *of* B. *woods within the Forest of* W, *so long as you shall me* Woodward *there; you shall not conceal any Offence either in Vert or Venison, that shall be committed or done within your Charge, but you shall truly present the same, without any Favour, Affection or Reward. And if you see or know any Malefactors, or find any Deer killed or hurt, you shall forthwith do the Verderor to understand thereof, and you shall present the same at the next Court of the Forest, be it* Swainmote, *or Court of* Attachments. *So help you God*.

Woodwards May not walk with Bow and Shafts, but with Forest Bills, *Manwood*, part 1. pag. 189. *Arcum & calamos gestare in Foresta non licet, sed* (*ut rescripti utar verbo*) Hachettum *tantummodo*. Sic. Term. Hill. Anno 13 *E*. 3. Ebor. Rot. 106.

Wooll drivers, *Anno* 2 & 3 *P*. & *M*. *cap*. 13. Are such as buy *wooll* abroad in the Country of the Sheep-Masters, and carry it on Horseback to the Clothiers, or to Market-Towns to sell again.

Woolferhefod, *Caput Lupinum*, Is the condition of such as were Outlawed in the Saxons time, for not submitting themselves to Justice: For if they could be taken alive, they should have been brought to the King, and if, upon fear of Apprehension, they defended themselves, they might be killed, and their Heads brought to the King; for they carried a *Wolves head*, that is to say, their Head was no more to be accounted of than a *Wolves head*, being a Beast so hurtful to Man. So the Laws of King *Edward*, by *Lambert*, *fol*. 127. *num*. 7. and *Bract*. *lib*. 3. *tract*. 2. *cap*. 11. This is miswritten *Wulveshevod* by *Roger Hoveden*, part. poster. suor. *Annal*. *fol*. 343.

Woolstaple, *Anno* 51 *H*. 3. *stat*. 5. That City or Town where *wooll* was sold. See *Staple*.

Woollwinders, Are such as wind up every Fleece of *wooll*, that is to be packed and sold by weight, into a kind of bundle, after it is cleansed in such manner as it ought to be by Statute, and to avoid such deceit as the Owners were wont to use by thrusting in locks of refuse *wooll*, and other dross, to gain weight. They are sworn to perform that Office truly between the Owner and the Merchant. See the Stat. 8 *H*. 6. *cap*. 22. 23 *Hen*. 8. *cap*. 17. and 18 *Eliz*. 25.

Wormseed, *Semen Sanctonicum*, Is a medicinal *seed*, produced by that Plant which we call *Holy-wormwood*, whereof you may read in *Gerard*'s *Herbal*, *lib*. 2. *cap*. 435. This is a Drug to be garbled, *Anno* 1 *Jac*. *cap*. 19.

Wranglands, Seem to be misgrown Trees, that will never prove Timber, *Kitchin*, *fol*. 169.

Wrecke, *Wreccum maris*, Is, where a Ship is perished on the Sea, and no Man escapes alive out of it: The *Civilians* call it *Naufragium*. This *wrecke* being made, the Goods that were in the Ship being brought to Land by the Waves, belong to the King by his Prerogative, or such other persons to whom the King hath granted *wrecke*. But if a Man, or a Dog, or a Cat escape alive, so that the Party to whom the Goods belong come within a year and a day, and prove the Goods to be his, he shall have them again by the Provision of the Statute of *Westm*. 1. *cap*. 4. and 17 *E*. 2. *cap*. 11. *Co*. *vol*. 6. *fol*. 106. *Bracton*, *lib*. 2. *cap*. 5. *num*. 7. This in the *Grand Custumary of Normandy*, *cap*. 17. is called *Varech*, and latined *veriscum*, and in some ancient Charters it is written **Seupwerpe**, *quasi* **Sea up-werpe**, that is, *ejectus maris*, from **Up-werpen**, *ejicere*. By which, and other Antiquities, it appears, that *wreck* did not only comprehend Goods that came from a perishing Ship, but whatever else the Sea did cast up upon the Land, were it pretious Stones, Fishes, or the like, as by the Statute made 17 *E*. 2. *cap*. 11. called *Statutum Prærogativæ Regis*, appears in these words, *Item Rex habebit* wreccum maris, *per totum Regn*. *Balenas*, & *Sturgiones captas in mari vel alibi infra regnum*, *exceptis quibusdam locis privilegiatis per Regem*. In the Stat. 27 *H*. 8. *cap*. 26. it is called *wreck de mer*. See 2. *Inst*. *fol*. 167.

Writ, *Breve*, Is the King's Precept, whereby any thing is commanded to be done touching a Suit or Action, as the Defendant or Tenant to be summoned, a Distress to be taken, a Disseisin to be redressed, &c. And these Writs are diversly divided in divers respects, some in respect of their Order, or manner of granting are termed *Original*, and some *Judicial*. *Original* Writs are these, that are sent out for the summoning of the Defendant in a personal, or the Tenant in a real Action, before the Suit begins, or rather to begin the Suit: Those are *Judicial*, which are sent out by

Order of the Court where the Cause depends, upon occasion after the Suit begun, *Old Nat. Brev. fol.* 51. & 147. And the *Judicial* are known from the *Original* thus, because the *Teste* of that bears the Name of the chief Justice of that Court whence it Issues, whereas the *Original* in the *Teste* has the Name of the Prince; and according to the nature of the Action, they are either *personal* or *real*: *Real* are either touching the *possession* called *writs of Entry*, or the *property* called *writs of Right*. Some *writs* are at the Suit of the Party, some of Office, some Ordinary, some of Privilege: A *writ of Privilege*, is that which a privileged brings to the Court for his exemption, by reason of some Privilege. See *Procedendo*, and the *New Book of Entries*, verb. *Privilege*. See *Breise*.

Writ of Rebellion. See *Commission of Rebellion*.

Writ of Assistance, Issues out of the Exchequer, to authorize any person to take a Constable, or other publick Officer, to seize Goods or Merchandize prohibited and un-customed, Stat. 14 *Car.* 2. *cap.* 11. There is also a *writ of Assistance* out of the Chancery to give a Possession.

Writer of the Tallyes, *Scriptor Talliarum*, Is an Officer in the Exchequer, being Clerk to the Auditor of the Receit, who *writes* upon the *Tallyes* the whole Letters of *Tellers* Bills.

Wudhepec. See *Pudhepec*.

Wyke, *Wyka*, A Farm, or little Village, *Et totam* wykam *cum hominibus*, &c. Mar. Ang. 2. par. fol. 154.

Wyte or Wite, *VVyta vel wita*, In Latine *Mulcta Saxones duo mulctarum genera statuere* **weram & wytam**, Wera *mortis reos & gravissime peccantes liberabat.* Wyta *mediis & levioribus delictis statuta fuit, non certa sed pro qualitate commissi, aliàs gravior, aliàs levior; salvo tamen semper contenemento delinquentis (ut lex loquitur in* Mag. Chart. cap. 14.*) hoc est, æstimatione ejus Anglicè* **his Countenance**. ---*Ex his placitis quædam emendantur centum solidis, quædam* wera *quædam* wyta, *quædam emendari non possunt*, Leg. H. 1. cap. 13. *Emendet juxta ordinis dignitatem, sive per redemptionem*, i. **were**; *per forisfacturam*, i. **wyte**: *per legis transgressionem*, i. **Lashlite**. M. S. de Leg. Canuti in Biblioth. Cotton. sub tit. *Vitellius*, C. 9.

Wrong, *Injuria*, Is in French aptly called *Tort*, because *wrong* is wrested or crooked, being contrary to that which is right and strait, *Co.* on *Lit. lib.* 2. *cap.* 1.

X.

XEnia, *Dicuntur Munuscula quæ à Provincialibus rectoribus Provinciarum offerebantur. Vox est in Privilegiorum Chartis non insueta, ubi* quietus esse à Xeniis *immunes notat ab hujusmodi muneribus aliisq; donis Regi vel Reginæ præstandis quando ipsi per prædia Privilegiatorum transierint*, ut in Chart. domus Semplingham. *Principibus enim olim fuit in more, à subditis vel invitis munera extorquere. Itaq; ab hoc jugo liberos fecit Ecclesiasticos*, Æthelbaldus *Rex Merciorum*, Anno 747. ut ab exemplari Chartæ suæ tum apud *Ingulphum Sax.* tum *Will. Malmesb. lib. de Gest. Reg. Angl.* p. 29. l. 4. his verbis habetur. *Concedo ut omnia Monasteria & Ecclesiæ Regni mei à Publicis vectigalibus, operibus & oneribus absolvantur. ---Nec munuscula præbeant Regi vel principibus nisi voluntaria*, Spelm. So in Memorand. Scacc. de anno 20 E. 3. Trin. Rot. 3. *Nulla autem persona parva vel magna ab hominibus & terræ Radingensis Monasterii exigat non equitationem sive expeditionem, non summagia, non vectigalia, non navigia, non opera, non tributa, non* Xenia, &c.

Xenodochium, *Interpretatur hospitium*, An Inn by Publick Licence allowed, for the entertainment of Strangers, and other Guests. It may also be interpreted an Hospital, *In quæ valetudinarii & senes, id est, infirmi recipiuntur & aluntur*. See *Vocab. utriusq; juris*, verb. *Eodem*.

Y.

YA et Nay, ---*Quod homines sui* (Ripponienses) *sint credendi per suum* Ya *& per suum* Nay *in omnibus Querelis & Curiis, licet tangen.* **Freedmortell**, &c. Charta Athelstani Regis.

Yard, *Virga*, Is a well known Measure, three Foot in length, which (Sir *Rich. Baker* in his *Chronicle* says) *Henry the First* Ordained by the length of his own Arm. See *Virga ferrea*.

Yardland, *Virgata Terræ*, Is a quantity of Land various, according to the place; as at *Wimbleton* in *Surrey* it is but fifteen Acres, in other Counties twenty; in some twenty four, in some thirty, and in others forty Acres: Virgata terræ *continet* 24. *Acras &* 4. Virgatæ *constituunt unam Hydam, & quinq; Hydæ constituunt feodum militare*, M. S. Abbatiæ Malmesb. This *Yardland Bracton*, lib. 2. cap. 10. & 27. calls *Virgatam terræ*, but expresses no certainty what it contains. It is called a *Verge of Land*, Anno 28 E. 1. *Statute of Wards*. See *Selden's Titles of Honor*, fol. 622.

Year and Day, *Annus & Dies*, Is a time that determines a right in many Cases; and in some Works an usucaption, in others a Prescription; as in case of an Estray, if the Owner (Proclamations being made) challenge it not within that time, it is forfeit: So is the *year and day* given in case of Appeal, in case of Descent after Entry or Claim; of no Claim upon a Fine or Writ of right at the Common Law, so of a Villain remaining in ancient Demeasn: Of a Man so bruised or wounded: Of Protections, Essoins in respect of the King's Service; of a Wreck, and divers other cases, *Co. vol.* 6. *fol.* 107. And that touching the death of a Man, seemeth an imitation of the Civil Law. *Nam si mortifere fuerit vulneratus & postea post longum intervallum mortuus fit inde annum numerabimus*; Secundum Julianum l. ait lex. π ad legem Aquil.

Year, Day and Wast, *Annus, Dies & Vastum*, Is a part of the King's Prerogative, whereby he challengeth the Profits of their Lands and Tenements for a *year and a day* that are attainted of Petty Treason or Felony, whoever is Lord of the Mannor whereto the Lands or Tenements

nements belong; and not only so, but in the end may wast the Tenements, destroy the Houses, root up the Woods, Gardens, Pasture, and Plough up the Meadows, except the Lord of the Fee agree with him for redemption of such Wast, afterwards restoring it to the Lord of the Fee, whereof you may read at large in *Stamf. Prærog. cap.* 16. *fol.* 44.

Yeelding and Paying, *Reddendo & solvendo*, Is a corruption from the Saxon gelдan and gylдan, *solvere, præstare*. And in *Doomsday* Book, *Gildare* is used for *solvere*.

Yeme, Is an old Corruption from *Hieme*, and that from *Hiems* winter; So some old Deeds have it, *Reddendo--ad festum S.* Martini *in* **yeme**, &c. And in another of 4 *E.* 3. thus,--*Reddend. quando dict.* 4. *acræ terræ seminantur semine* **yemali** *duodecim* Bushell. *boni & legalis frumenti ad festum Purificationis*, &c.

Yeven or yoven, So some old Indentures say, *Yeoven the day and year first above written*: It is the same with *Given*, and perhaps corrupted from the Saxon Geopian, i. *Dare*. So *Dictum de Kenelworth* concludes----*Yeoven, and proclaimed in the Castle of* Kenelworth *the day before the Calends of* Novemb. *Anno* 1256.

Yeman, or yeoman, or yoman, A derivative of the Saxon geman, i. *Communis*. These *Camden* in his *Brit. pag.* 105. placeth next in order to Gentlemen, calling them *Ingenuos*, whose Opinion the Statute affirms, *Anno* 6 *Rich.* 2. *cap.* 4. and 20 *R.* 2. *cap.* 2. Sir *Thomas Smith* in his *Republ. Anglorum, lib.* 1. *cap.* 23. calls him a *Yeoman*, who our Law calls *Legalem hominem*, which (says he) is in the English a Free-born man, that may dispend of his own free Land in yearly Revenue to the sum of forty shillings sterling. *Verstegan* in his *Restitution of decayed Intelligence*, cap. 10. writes, That *Gemen* among the ancient *Teutonickes*, and *Gemein* among the modern signifies as much as *Common*, and the letter *G*. being turned into *Y*. is written *Yemen*, which therefore signifies a *Commoner*. *Yeoman* also signifies an Officer in the King's House, in the middle-place between the Sergeant and the Groom, as *Yeoman* of the *Chandry*, *Yeoman* of the *Scullery*, 33 *H.* 8. cap. 12. *Yeoman* of the *Crown*, 3 *E.* 4, 5. The word *Yongmen* is used for *yeomen* in the Statute 33 *H.* 8. *cap.* 10. See *Jemen*.

Yingman, Leg. H. 1. cap. 16. *Danagildum quod aliquando* **yingeman** *dalatur*, i. 12 d. *de unaquaq; hida per annum; si ad terminum non reddatur*, wita *emendetur*. *Spelman* thinks this may be mistaken for *Inglishman*, or as we say now *Englishman*, though he finds it written **yingeman** both in Sir *Robert Cotton's Codex* and his own.

Yvernagium, (From the French *Hyvernee*, that is, the Winter-Season,) was anciently used for the Winter-seednes, or season for sowing of Corn; *Dictus verò* Willielmus *& hæredes sui arabunt unum seilonem ad* yvernagium, *& unum seilonem ad semen Quadragesimale, & unum seilonem ad warectum, &c.* Charta *Richardi* de *Harecourt* penes *Tho. Wallascot* Arm. sine Dat.

Yule, Deep in the North parts of *England*, the Country People call the *Feast of the Nativity of our Lord*, usually termed *Christmas*, **yule**, and the Sports used at *Christmas*, here called *Christmas Gamboles*, they stile **Yule-Games**.

Z.

Zealot, *Zelotes*, Is for the most part taken in *pejorem sensum*, and so we term one that is a *Separatist or Schismatick* from the Church of *England*, a *Zealot*, or a Fanatick; which are well known terms of Separation.

Zuche, Zucheus, *Stips siccus & aridus*, A withered or dry stock of Wood, *Rex, &c. Quia accepimus per Inquisitionem quod non est ad dampnum seu præjudicium nostrum aut aliorum, si concedimus dilecto valecto nostro* Ric. de Stelley *omnes* Zuches *aridos qui Anglice vocantur* **stovenes** *infra Haiam nostram de* Beskewood, *quæ infra forestam nostram de* Shirewood, *&c.* Pla. Forest. in Com. Nott. de Anno 8 H. 3.----*Auxilium faciend. Burgensibus Salop. de veteribus* Zuchis, *& de mortuo bosco, &c.* Clauf. 4 Hen. 3. m. 10.

FINIS.

AN APPENDIX

CONTAINING

The ancient Names of Places here in *England*, very Necessary for the Use of all young STUDENTS, who intend to Converse with Old *Records*, *Deeds*, or *Charters*.

A.

Ancient Name	Modern Name
ABlato-Bulgio,	*Bulnesse* or *Bolnesse* in *Cumberland.*
Aballaba, Applebeia,	*Appleby* in *Westmerland.*
Abbandunum, Abbendoma, Abendonia,	*Abington* in *Berk-shire*, *formerly called Sewsham.*
Abone, Abonis,	*Avington* or *Aventon* in *Glocestershire.*
Abrevicum,	*Barwick* on *Tweed.*
Abbus æstuarium,	*Humber* in *York-shire.*
Achelanda,	*Bishops Aukland* in the Bishoprick of *Durham.*
Adelingia,	*Athelney* in *Somersetshire.*
Ad-Lapidem,	*Stoneham* in *Hampshire*, near *Redbridge.*
Ad-murum,	*Waltown.*
Ad-Pontem,	*Pawnton* in *Lincolnshire.*
Adros, vel Andros, vel Andium,	*Bardsey Island* betwixt *Wales* and *Ireland.*
Adurni portus,	*Ederington* in *Suffolk.*
Æbudæ,	*The Isles* of *Hebrides* to the West of *Scotland.*
Ætona,	*Eaton* in *Berk-shire.*
Afena, Agelocum,	See *Segelocum.*
Ager Maridunensis,	*Carmarthenshire.*
Alannius,	The River *Avon* in *Wilshire.*
Alaunicus portus,	*Milford Haven.*
Alaunicus Pons, Alaunodunum,	*Maidenhead* in *Berk-shire.*
Alaunus, flu.	The River *Alne* in *Northumberland.*
Album Monasterium,	*Whitchurch* in *Shropshire.*
Alenus, flu.	The River *Alen* in *Dorsetshire*, another in *Denbishire*, also the River *Alne* in *Warwick shire.*
Alion, Alione, Alone	*Lancaster*, also *Whitby Castle* in *Cumberland.*
Alone flu.	The River *Alon* in *Northumberland.*
Amboglanna,	*Amblesside* in *Westmerland.*
Ambrosii burgus,	*Amesbury* in *Wilts.*
Amænissima montana de de Balsham,	*Gogmagog* Hills near *Cambridge.*
Ancalites,	The Hundred of *Denby* in *Oxfordshire.*
Anderida,	*Newenden* in *Kent.*
Andevera,	*Andover* in *Hantshire.*
Anglesega, Mona,	*Anglesey.*
Anguillaria insula,	*The Isle* of *Ely.*
Anguillarianum Monasterium,	*The City* of *Ely.*
Antivestæum,	*The Lands end.*
Autona vel Aufona,	*Aufon* or *nen* in *Northamptonshire.*
Apiacum,	*Pap Castle* in *Cumberland.*
Aquæ calidæ, Aquæ solis, Akeman-cester,	*Bath City* in *Somersetshire.*
Aquædon,	*Eidure vulgo Eatoun.*
Aquædunensis saltus,	*Waterdon.*
Aquævadensis pons,	*Eiford.*
Aquædunum,	*Aieton.*
Aquilædunum,	*Hoxton* in stead of *Eagles-Town.*
Arbeia,	*Ireby* in *Cumberland.*
Ariconium,	*Kenchester* near *Hereford.*
Arundelia, Arundellum, Aruntina vallis,	*Arundel* in *Sussex.*
Arundinis vadum,	*Redbridge* in *Hantshire.*
Arunus, fl.	The River *Arun* in *Sussex.*
Arvonica.	*Carnarvonshire.*
Arus, flu.	The River *Are* in *Yorkshire.*
Asaphensis episcopatus,	*The Bishoprick* of St. *Asaph.*
Athanaton,	*The Isle* of *Thanet* in *Kent.*
Athesis flu.	*The River Tees* in the *Bishoprick* of *Durham.*
Attrebatii,	*Berkshire Men.*
Avalonia,	*Glastonbury* in *Somersetshire.*
Augusta Trinobantum,	*London.*

Avena flu.	*Aven* in *Wiltshire.*
Avona, flu.	*The River Avon, that runs by Malmesbury, Bradford, Bathe, Bristoll.* *The River Nen, that runs through Northamptonshire* by *Oundle, Peterborough, and into the Sea near Lin.* *The Avon that flows by Amesbury, Salisbury, and so into Dorsetshire.* *The wavency that divides Norfolk* and *Suffolk runs by Bongay, corruptly so called for Avoney.* *The Avon rising not far from Naseby in Northamptonshire, runs by Warwick, Stratford, Evesham, and into the Severn at Tewkesbury.*
Avona,	*Bungey* in *Norfolk.*
Avona,	*Hampton Court* according to *Leland.*
Avondunum,	
Avonæ vallis,	*Avondale* or *Oundle* in *Northamptonshire.*
Axelodunum,	*Hexam* in the *Bishoprick* of *Durham.*

B.

Bachelaganæ sylvæ,	*Bagley.*
Badiza,	*Bath* in *Somersetshire.*
Badonicus mons,	*Bannes-down, a hill over a little Village near Bath called Bathstone.*
Bainardi castellum,	*Baynards Castle* in *London.*
Bainus pons	*Bainbridge* in *Yorkshire.*
Balnea,	
Batha,	*Bath City.*
Bathonia,	
Bannavenna,	*Northampton,* or rather *Weedon on the street.*
Bannaventa,	
Banus, flu.	*The River Ban* in *Lincolnshire.*
Basenga,	*Basing* in *Hantshire.*
Basingum,	
Batersega,	*Battersey.*
Bearrocscira,	*Berkshire.*
Bedeforda,	*Bedford.*
Bedfordia,	
Belgæ,	*The Inhabitants of Somerset, Wilts* and *Hantshire.*
Belerium prom.	See *Antivestæum.*
Bellinus sinus,	*Bellings Gate.*
Belisama,	*Rhiqelmouth* in *Lancashire.*
Bellelanda,	*Biland* in *Yorkshire.*
Belloclivum,	
Bello desertum,	*Beldesert* in *Warwickshire.*
Bellus locus,	
Berceia,	*Berkshire.*
Bercheria,	
Berechingum,	*Barking* in *Essex.*
Berclea,	*Berkley* in *Gloucestershire.*
Bermundi insula,	*Bermondsey* in *Surrey.*

Bernardi Castellum,	*Bernard Castle* in the *Bishoprick of Durham.*
Bernicia,	*Was a Province reaching from the River Tees* to *Edenborough Frith* in *Scotland.*
Berwicus,	*Berwick upon Tweed.*
Beverlea,	*Beverley* in *Yorkshire.*
Beverlacensis,	*Of or belonging to* Beverley
Bibrocassi,	*The Hundred of* Bray *in* Yorkshire.
Bibroci,	
Bimonium vinocium,	
Brinonium vinovia,	*Binchester* in the *Bishoprick* of *Durham.*
Binovia,	
Binovium,	
Bishamum,	*Bisham* in *Berkshire.*
Blacamora,	*Part of the Northbriding of* Yorkshire.
Blancoforda,	*Blandford* in *Dorsetshire.*
Blancum castrum,	*Blanc-Castle* in *Monmouthshire.*
Blatum Bulgium,	*Bulnesse* or *Balnesse* in *Cumberland.*
Blestium,	*Old-town* in *Herefordshire.*
Boccinum,	*Buckingham* and *Buckenham.*
Bodiamum,	*Bodiam* in *Sussex.*
Bodotria,	*Edenborough Frith.*
Bolerium Prom.	*See Antivestæum.*
Bonium seu Bovium,	*Boverton* or *Cowbridge* in *Glamorganshire,* also *Bangor* or *Banchor* in *Flintshire.*
Boræum Prom.	St. *Ellens Cape.*
Borcovicum,	*Berwick upon Tweed.*
Borcovicus,	
Botelega,	*Botley* near *Oxford.*
Braboniacum,	*Brougham* in *Westmerland.*
Bracchium,	*Burgh* in *Yorkshire.*
Brachilega,	*Brackly* in *Northamptonshire.*
Bramptonia,	*Brampton* near *Huntington.*
Brannodunum,	*Branchester* in *Norfolk.*
Branovium,	
Branoricum,	
Bravinum,	*The City of* Worcester.
Branconium,	
Brannovium,	
Brechinia,	*Brecknock.*
Bremenium,	*Rochester* in *Northumberland.*
Brementonacum,	*Overborow* in *Lancashire.*
Brementuracum,	*Brampton* in *Cumberland.*
Brentæ Vadus,	*Brentford* in *Middlesex.*
Brigantes,	*Inhabitants of Yorkshire, Lancashire, Bishoprick* of *Durham, Westmerland* and *Cumberland.*
Brigantium,	*York City.*
Bridge vel Brage,	*Broughton* in *Hantshire.*
Bristolia,	*The City of* Bristol.
Bristowa,	
Brocavum,	
Brocave,	
Broconiacum,	*Brougham* in *Westmerland.*
Brovonacis,	
Brovonacum,	
Bromfelda,	*Bromfield* in *Denbighshire.*
Bucostenum,	*Buxton* in *Derbishire.*

Budeforda,

Budeforda,	*Bedforda.*
Bullæum ſilurum,	*Buelth in Brecknockshire.*
Burrium,	*Vske* in *Monmouthſhire.*
Buſtelli domus.	*Buſtleham* or *Biſham* in *Berks.*

C.

CAcaria, Calcaria,	*Tadcaſter* or *Helcaſter* in *Yorkshire.*
Calatum,	
Caermardinia,	*Carmardin.*
Caerperis,	*Portcheſter.*
Caer-ſeverus,	*Sarisbury.*
Caer Lincoit,	*Lincoln.*
Cæſaria,	*Jarſey Iſle.*
Cæſaro-magus,	*Burgſted,* alſo *Burnt-wood* in *Eſſex.*
Calacum, Calagum,	*Overborow* in *Lancaſhire,* alſo *Whealpe-Caſtle* in *Cumberland.*
Calaterium nemus,	*The Foreſt of* Galtres *in* Yorkſhire.
Calderus flu.	*The River* Calder *in* Yorkſhire.
Caledonia,	*Scotland.*
Caledonius Oceanus,	*The Scottiſh-Sea.*
Caleva vel Calena,	*Wallingford* in *Berkshire.*
Calna,	*Calne* in *Wiltſhire.*
Calonia,	*Coldingham.*
Camaletum,	*Camalet-Caſtle.*
Cambodunum,	*Ruines* near *Almondbury* in *Yorkshire.*
Camboricum, Camboritum,	*Grandceſter.* *Cambridge.*
Cambretonium, Cambretovium,	*A place by* Breton Spring *in* Suffolk.
Cambria,	*Wales.*
Camoladunum, Camolodunum, Camudolanum, Camulodunum,	*Maldon* in *Eſſex.*
Campordunum,	See *Cambodunum.*
Candalia,	*Kendal* in *Weſtmerland.*
Candida caſa,	*Whiteherne* in *Scotland.*
Canonium,	*Canonden* in *Eſſex,* alſo *Clemesford in the ſame County.*
Cantabrigia,	*Cambridge Univerſity.*
Cantium,	*Kent.*
Cantium prom.	*The Northforeland.*
Cantuaria,	*Canterbury City.*
Capræ-caput,	See *Gabroſentum.*
Carboriarius callis,	*Coleſhill* in *Flintſhire.*
Carleolum,	*The ancient City of* Carliſle *in* Cumberland.
Cardigania, Carmarthinia, Carnarvonia,	*Cardigan*, *Carmarthin*, *Carnarvon* in *Wales.*
Caſſi, Caſſii,	*The Hundred* of *Cayſhow* in *Hertfordshire.*
Caſſiterides,	*The Iſlands of* Sylly.
Caſeivelauni oppidum,	*The Old City of* Verulam.
Caſtra alata vel Caſtrum alatum, Caſtrum puellarum,	*Edenborough City* in *Scotland.*

Caſtra exploratorum,	*Burgh* on the Sands in *Cumberland.*
Caſtrum de vies, Caſtrodunum,	*The Deviſes* in *Wiltſhire.*
Cataracta flu.	*The River* Swale *in* Richmondſhire.
Cataracta, Cataractonium,	*Catarick Bridge,*
Catuellani, Cattidudani, Cathricludani, Cattieuchlani,	*The People of Buckingham, Bedford* and *Hertford ſhires.*
Caveda,	*Cawood* in *Yorkshire.*
Cauna,	See *Convennos.*
Cauſennæ, Cauſennis,	See *Gauſennæ.*
Cavum Deiram,	*Holderneſſe* in *Yorkshire.*
Ceangi & Cangi,	*People about* Cheſhire, *as* Camden *ſuppoſes.*
Cenion, Cemo flu.	*The River by Tergeny* in *Cornwall.*
Centum fontes,	*Hundreds kelde.*
Cerdici vadum,	*Chardford* in *Hantſhire.*
Ceretica,	*Cardiganſhire.*
Cerneliensa Cænobium,	*Cerne* in *Dorſetshire.*
Ceroti inſula, Certeſia,	*Chertſey* in *Surrey.*
Cervi inſula,	*Hartlepoole.*
Ceſtria, Cheſtrum,	*Cheſter City.*
Chineglishi caſtrum,	*Kenelworth-Caſtle.*
Cheva,	*Kew* in *Surry.*
Chirca,	*Chirke* in *Denbighshire.*
Ciceaſtria, Ciceſtria,	*Chicheſter* in *Suſſex.*
Cilurinum, Cilurnum,	*Collerton* or *Cellerford* in *Northumberland.*
Cirenceſtria,	*Ciceſter* or *Cirenceſter* in *Glouceſterſhire.*
Clara-fontanus, Clarus fons,	*Shirburne.*
Claudia, Claudioceſtria, Clevum, Glevum,	*Glouceſter City.*
Clauſentum,	*Southampton.*
Coccium,	*Ribblecheſter* in *Lancashire.*
Cokarus, Cocarus,	*The River Cocar* in *Lancashire* and *Coke* in *Yorkshire.*
Colonia, Coludi, Coldania,	*Coldingham* in *Scotland.*
Colceſtria, Colonia,	*Colcheſter* in *Eſſex.*
Colonia victricenſis,	*Maldon* in *Eſſex.*
Colunum,	*Colebrooke* in *Middleſex.*
Combeſetonium, Combretovium,	*Brettenham* in *Suffolk.*
Concangium,	*The Barony* of *Kendale.*
Condate,	*Congleton* in *Cheſhire.*
Condercum,	*Cheſter upon the Street* in the *Biſhoprick* of *Durham.*
Cononium,	*Chelmesford* in *Eſſex.*
Conovium,	*Caerhean* upon *Conway* in *Carnarvonshire.*

Convennon, Convennos insula,	Convey Island at the Thames mouth in Essex.
Conventria, Coventria,	Coventry City in Warwickshire.
Coqueda insula,	The Isle of Coquet.
Coria & Curia,	Corebridge in Northumb.
Corinia,	Cornwall.
Corinium,	Cirencester in Gloucestershire, as Camden thinks.
Corinus flu.	The River Churne that runs by Cirencester.
Coritani vel Coritavi,	People of Northampton, Leicester, Rutland, Derby, and Nottinghamshire.
Cornavii vel Cornabii,	Inhabitants of Warwick, Worcester, Stafford, Shropshire and Cheshire.
Cornubia,	Cornwall.
Cornutum Monasterium,	Horn-Church in Essex.
Corstopilum, Corstopitum, Curia,	Corbridge upon Tyne, says Talbot, Morpit in Northumberland, as Camden, Curebridge by H. Huntington, and Corebridge by Hoveden.
Cotteswoldia,	Cotswold in Gloucestershire.
Covi Berchelega,	Coverley in Gloucestershire.
Cranburna, Craneburgum, Burginatium,	Cranborn in Dorsetshire, or Cronenburgh in Cleveland.
Craven,	The County of Craven in Yorkshire.
Crecolada vel Græcolada,	Creeklade in Wiltshire.
Cridea,	Crediton or Kirton in Devonshire.
Crococalana, Crocolana,	Ancaster in Lincolnshire.
Croylandia,	Crowland in Lincolnshire.
Cumbria, Cumberlandia,	Cumberland.
Cunetio,	Marleborow in Wiltshire.

D.

DAnmonii vel Damnonii,	PEople of Devonshire and Cornwall.
Danica Sylva,	Andredswald Forest in Sussex: Also the Forest of Dean in Gloucestershire.
Danmoniorum Promontorium,	The Lizard in Cornwall.
Danubiæ,	The Forest of Dean in Gloucestershire.
Danum,	Dancaster in Yorkshire.
Danus flu.	The Dane in Lincolnshire. The Dan or Daven in Cheshire. The Don or Dun in Yorkshire.
Darbia vel Derbia,	The Town of Darby.
Darbiensis comitatus,	Darbishire.
Darvernum,	Rochester in Kent.
De alto Pecco,	The Castle in the Peake in Derbishire.
Deilocum,	Godsto in Oxfordshire.

Deira,	That part of the Kingdom of the Northumbers that lay on this side Tyne.
Deira sylva,	Deirharst in Gloucestershire.
Dela,	Dele in Kent.
Delgovitia,	Godmanham in Yorkshire.
Demetæ,	People of West-wales.
Demetia,	West wales.
Denbighia,	Denbigh in Denbighshire.
Derentivadum,	Dertford in Kent.
Derwentio,	Auldby upon Derwent in Yorkshire.
Deva flu.	The River Dee in Cheshire.
Deva seu Devana urbs,	Chester or West-Chester.
Devonia,	Devonshire.
Dictum,	Diganwey in Carnarvonshire.
Divisæ, Divisio, Castrum de Vies,	The Vies or Devises in Wiltshire.
Dotuni,	People of Gloucester and Oxford shires.
Dorfris vel Dubris, Doris,	Dover in Kent.
Dorcestria, Dorkestra, Dorcinni civitas,	Dorchester, either in Oxford or Dorsetshire.
Dorpendunum,	Orpington in Kent.
Durobrevum,	Rochester in Kent.
Dorobernia, Dorovernum,	Canterbury.
Dorventania,	Darbishire.
Dorus flu.	The Dor in Hartfordshire.
Dovus flu.	The Dove in Derbishire.
Dunelmensis comitatus,	The County of the Bishoprick of Durham.
Dunelmia, Dunelmum, Dunelmus, Dunholmum,	Durham City.
Dunum vel Dunus sinus,	The Creek at Dunsbey near Whitby in Yorkshire.
Dunvicus aliàs felicis oppidum,	Dunmock aliàs Flixton in Suffolk.
Duria provincia,	Dorsetshire.
Durvonovaria,	Dorchester in Dorsetshire.
Dorcinia civitas, Duracastrum, Hydropolis,	Dorchester in Oxfordshire.
Durobrevis, Durobrevum,	Rochester in Kent.
Durobrivæ,	Dornford near Walmeford in Huntingtonshire.
Durocobrivæ,	Redburne in Hertfordshire.
Durolenum,	Leneham in Kent.
Durolipons,	Gormanchester in Huntingtonshire.
Durolitum,	Layton in Essex.
Durotriges,	People of Dorsetshire.

E.

EAst-fexena, Effexia,	*ESſex.*
Ebodia,	*The Iſle* of *Alderney.*
Eboracum, Eburacum,	*York City.*
Edmundi Burgus,	St. *Edmondsbury in Suffolk.*
Eilecuriana vallis,	*The Vale of Alisbury* in *Buckinghamshire.*
Eimotus flu.	*The River Eimot* in *Cumberland.*
Elienſis inſula,	*The Iſle of Ely.*
Elteſhamum,	*Eltham* in *Kent.*
Ellandunum,	*The old name of Wilton* in *Wiltshire.*
Eminentior,	*Eaton-neſſe* in *Suffolk.*
Eoveſum, Eveſtamum,	*Evesham* or *Evesholme* in *Worceſtershire.*
Epeiacum vel Epiacum,	*Pap-Caſtle* in *Cumberland.*
Etocetum,	*Uttoxeter* in *Staffordshire*, according to *Camden.*
Eilimenon Gabrantonicorum,	*Everby* in *Yorkshire.*
Eubonia,	*The Iſle of Man.*
Evenlodus flu.	*The River Evenlode* in *Oxfordshire.*
Excambium Regium, Periſtilium ſive Burſa,	*The Royal Exchange* in *London.*
Exa. flu.	*The River Exe* in *Devonshire.*
Exonia,	*Exceſter City* in *Devonshire.*
Exploratorum Caſtra,	*Burgh upon Sands* in *Cumberland.*

F.

FAla flu.	*THe River Vale* in *Cornwall.*
Falenſis portus,	*Falemouth* in *Cornwall.*
Fanum Albani,	St. *Albans* in *Hertfordshire.*
Fanum Iltuti,	St. *Lantwit* in *Glamorganshire.*
Fanum Ivonis Perſa,	St. *Ives* in *Huntingtonshire.*
Fanum Leonis,	*Leominſter.*
Fanum Neoti,	St. *Neots* in *Huntingtonshire.*
Fanum Reguli,	St. *Andrews* in *Scotland.*
Fanum Stephani,	*Kirkby Stephen* in *Weſtmerland.*
Fauſtini villa,	St. *Edmonsbury* in *Suffolk.*
Fawenſes,	*Inhabitants of Foy* in *Cornwall.*
Fibrilega, Fibrolega,	*Beverley* in *Yorkshire.*
Flintia,	*Flint town.*
Fons Brigidæ,	*Bridewell* in *London.*
Fons clarus,	*Shireburne* in *Dorſetshire.*
Fontanenſis Eccleſia,	*Wells* in *Somerſetſhire.*
Fretum Britannicum, Fretum Gallicum, Fretum Morinorum,	*The ſtraight of* Callis.
Fromus flu.	*The River Frome* in *Glouceſterſhire* that runs to *Briſtol*; alſo another in *Dorſetſhire.*

G.

GAbrantonicorum, Salutaris portus, Gabrantovicorum, Portuoſus ſinus,	*Suerby* in *Yorkshire.*
Gabrocentum vel Gabroſentum,	*Gateſhead in the Biſhoprick* of *Durham*, hard by *New-Caſtle.*
Galva vel Gallava,	*Wallwick* in *Northumberland.*
Gallatum vel Gallagum,	*Whealp* or *Whealop Caſtle* in *Cumberland.*
Ganganorum Prom.	*Lheyne* in *Carnarvonshire.*
Garionomum,	*Yarmouth* in *Norfolk.*
Garrienis vel Gargenus flu.	*Yare River* in *Norfolk.*
Gauſennæ,	*Brig-caſterton* in *Lincolnshire.*
Geldeforda,	*Guilford* in *Surrey.*
Genumia,	*North-wales.*
Geſſoriacum,	*The ſtraight between Britain and the Iſle of Wight.*
Geviſſi,	*People over againſt the Iſle of Wight.*
Girvii,	*Inhabitants of the Fens.*
Glamorgania vel Glamorgantia,	*Glamorganshire.*
Glaſconia, Glaſtonia,	*Glaſtonbury* in *Somerſetshire.*
Glavorna, Glevum, Glocestria,	*Glouceſter.*
Glenus flu.	*The Glen* in *Northumberland.*
Gloveceaſtria, Glovernia,	*Glouceſter City.*
Gobanium,	*Abergavenny* in *Monmouthſhire.*
Goderici caſtrum,	*Goodrich Caſtle* in *Herefordshire.*
Granta,	*Cambridge as ſome think.*
Graveſenda, Greva,	*Graveſend* in *Kent.*
Grenovicus, Grenovicum, Greenwicum,	*Greenwich* in *Kent.*
Gualæ,	*Wales.*
Guerfa fl.	*The River wharf* in *Yorkshire.*
Guldonicus clivus,	*Guy-cliffe* near *Warwick.*
Guinethia,	*Wales.*
Guldforda,	*Gildford* in *Surrey.*
Gumicaſtrum, Gumicaſter.	*Godmancheſter* near *Huntington.*

H.

Habitancum,	*Risingham* in *Northumberland.*
Hadriani murus,	*The Picts wall.*
Hagulstadia,	*Auston upon Tyne* in *Northumberland.*
Hagulstadunum,	*Hexham* in the *Bishoprick* of *Durham.*
Hamptunia,	*Southampton* in *Hantshire.*
Hansus flu.	*The River Hans* in *Staffordshire.*
Hantonia,	*Hantshire.*
Harefordia,	*Hereford City.*
Hastingæ,	*Hastings* in *Sussex.*
Helenum prom.	*The Lands end.*
Heliense cænobium,	*Ely City* in *Cambridgeshire.*
Henlega,	*Henley upon Thames.*
Herculis prom.	*Hertey point* in *Devonshire.*
Herefordia,	*Hereford City* in *Herefordshire.*
Hertfordia,	*Hertford.*
Hertfordiæ comitatus,	*Hertfordshire.*
Hesperides,	*The Sorlings* or *Scilly Isles.*
Hibernia,	*Ireland.*
Hinchesega,	*Hinkesey* near *Oxford.*
Hithinus portus,	*Hith* in *Kent.*
Hodneius flu.	*The Hodney* in *Brecknockshire.*
Hollandia vel Hoilandia,	*Holland*, a part of *Lincolnshire.*
Homelea flu.	*The River Humble* over against *the Isle of Wight* in *Hantshire.*
Hrofi civitas,	*Rochester* in *Kent.*
Humbra flu.	*The River Humber* in *Yorkshire.*
Hundesdena, Hunsdona,	*Hunsdon* in *Herefordshire.*
Hungreforda,	*Hungerford* in *Berkshire.*
Huntingdonia,	*Huntington Town.*
Huntingdonensis ager,	*Huntingtonshire.*
Hurstelega,	*Hurstley.*
Hwiccii,	*People of Worcestershire*, and about *Severne.*
Hydropolis,	*Dorchester* in *Oxfordshire.*
Hymbronenses,	*People of Northumberland.*

I.

Jamesa, Iamissa,	*The Thames* according to *Ptolomy.*
Iccius portus,	*Callis Withsand.*
Inceni,	*People of Suffolk, Norfolk, Cambridge* and *Huntington shires.*
Iciani vel Isianos,	*Ichborow* in *Norfolk.*
Icta,	The *Isle of Wight.*
Idumania,	The *River Stone.*
Idumanum æstuarium, Idumanus flu.	The *River Blackwater* in *Essex.*
Ingiruum,	*Iarrow* in *Bishoprick* of *Durham*, where *Beda* flourished.
Insula,	*Egnesham* or *Enisham* in *Oxfordshire.*
Insula siturum,	The *little Isle of Silley* in *Severn.*
Insula vecta, Vectis vectesis,	The *Isle of Wight.*
Interamna,	*Twinamburne* in *Dorsetshire.*
	Christ-Church in *Hantshire.*
Isaca vel Isca,	The *River Exe* in *Devonshire.*
Isannavantia, Isannavaria, Isannavatia,	*Northampton*, or rather *Wedon on the street* in *Northamptonshire.*
Isca Danmoniorum,	*Excester City.*
Isca, legio Augusta, Isce legua Augusti,	*Caerleon City* in *Glamorganshire.*
Ischalis,	*Inelchester*, commonly called *Ilchester* in *Somersetshire.*
Isidis insula,	*Ousney* by *Oxford.*
Isidis vadum,	*Ouseford* or *Oxford.*
Isis flu.	The *River Isis* by *Oxford.*
	The Ouse that runs by Buckingham.
	Another Ouse that runs by York.
Isuria.	*Yorkshire.*
Isurium,	*Aldburgh* or *Oldburrow* in *Yorkshire.*
Itium Galliæ,	*Vitsan* or *Whitsan* near *Callis* in *France.*
Ituma flu.	The River *Eden* in *Westmerland* and *Cumberland.*
Julia strata,	*A high way not far from* Carleon *in* Wales.

K.

Kanus flu.	The *Kin* in *Westmerland.*
Keneta flu.	The *River Kened* in *Wiltshire.*
Keresburga,	*Carisbrooke-Castle* in the *Isle of Wight.*
Kestevena,	*Kesteven*, a part of *Lincolnshire.*
Kinebantum castrum,	*Kimbolton-Castle* in *Huntingtonshire.*

L.

Lactodorum, Lactodurum,	*Lutterworth* or *Loughborough.*
Lactorodum, Lactorudum,	*Bedford. Stony-Stratford.*
Lagecium,	*Castleford* near *Pomfret* in *Yorkshire.*
Lamitha,	*Lambeth* in *Surrey* near *London.*
Lancastria,	*Lancaster-Town*,
Lancastrensis Comitatus.	*Lancashire.*
Landava,	*Landaffe* in *Wales.*
Langanum prom.	*Lheyne Promontory* in *Carnarvonshire.*

Lavatres,

Levatres, Levatres, Levatris, Levatris,	*Browes* upon *Stanemore* in *Richmondshire.*
Lea flu.	*The River Lea* in *Hertfordshire.*
Legeceſtria, Legaceſtria,	*The Town of* Leiceſter *in* Leiceſterſhire.
Legio 2. Auguſta,	*Carleon* in *Wales.*
Legio 6. Nicephorica, Legio 6. Victrix,	*York City.*
Legio 20. Victrix,	*Cheſter City.*
Legra,	*The River at* Leiceſter.
Lemaus portus,	*Lime* in *Kent.*
Lemanii,	*Lime hill* or *Lime* in *Kent.*
Leogoria,	*Leiceſter* in *Leiceſterſhire.*
Leonenſe cænobium, Leovenſe, Leofenſe, Leonis Monaſtrium,	*Lemſter* in *Herefordshire.*
Leonis caſtrum,	*Lyons,* alias *Holt-Caſtle* in *Denbighshire.*
Levarum,	*Loghor* in *South-Wales.*
Lhoegria,	*England.*
Lichfeldia,	*Lichfield.*
Lideforda,	*Lidford* in *Devonſhire.*
Limenus flu.	*The River* Rother.
Limnos,	*The Iſle of* Ramſey.
Limodomus,	*Lime-houſe* near *London.*
Limpida ſylva,	*Shirwood Foreſt* in *Nottinghamshire.*
Lincolnia, Lindecollinum,	*Lincoln City.*
Lindesfarna, Lindisfarnum,	*Holy-Iſland* or *Farn-Iſle on the Coaſt of* Northum.
Lindeſeia, Lindiſia,	*Lindſey,* a third part of *Lincolnſhire.*
Lindocolina, Lindon,	*Lincoln City.*
Linnum Regis, vel Linum,	*Linne* in *Norfolk.*
Liſia,	*An Iſle called* Gulfe *near the utmoſt part of* Cornwall.
Lomithis vel Lonuthis,	*Lambeth* in *Surrey.*
Londinum, Londinium, Londinia, Londonia, Lundonia,	*The famous City of* London.
Loncaſtria, Longovcium,	*Lancaſter* or *Loncaſter.*
Lucopibia,	
Luguballia, Luguballum, Luguvallum,	*Carliſle City* in *Cumberland.*
Lychefeldia,	*Lichfield City* in *Staffordſhire.*

M.

MAdus,	*Maydſton* in *Kent.*
Magæ, Magi,	*Old Rudnor.*
Mageſetæ,	*People of* Radnorſhire.
Magnitum, Magioninium, Magiovinium, Magiovintum,	*Dunſtable* in *Bedfordſhire.*
Maglova, Maglona,	*Maclenith* in *Montgomeryshire.*
Magna,	*Cheſter in the Wall* near to *Haltweſſell* in *Northumberland.*
Magnus portus,	*Portſmouth* or *Porcheſter.*
Maidulphi curia, Maidulphi urbs, Maldunenſes Monaſterium, Malmesburium,	*Malmesbury* in *Wiltshire.*
Mala Platea,	*Ilſtreet* in *Cheſhire.*
Mailoria wallica,	*Bromfield* in *Denbighshire.*
Malvernia, Malvernum,	*Malverne* in *Worceſtershire.*
Malus paſſus,	*Malpas* in *Cheshire.*
Mammucium, Mancunium,	*Mancheſter* in *Lancashire.*
Mandueſſedum,	*Mancheſter* in *Warwickshire.*
Mannia,	*The Iſle of Man.*
Mannenſes,	*People of that Iſland.*
Manucium,	*Man-Caſtle* in *Lancaſter.*
Mare Britannicum,	*The Brittish Sea.*
Mare ſabrinianum,	*The Severne Sea.*
Margidunum, Margitudum,	*A place near* Belvoyr *Caſtle in* Lincolnſhire.
Maridunenſis ager,	*Carmarthenshire.*
Maridunenſes,	*The people of that Shire.*
Maridunum,	*Carmarthen Town.*
Maſſamenſis pons,	*Masham-Bridge* in *Yorkshire.*
Mauditi caſtrum,	St. *Mawes-Caſtle* in *Cornwall.*
Mealdunum & Camalodunum,	*Maldon* in *Eſſex.*
Meandari,	*People of part of* Hantſhire.
Meatæ,	*People of* Northumberland *about the Wall.*
Meanuari,	*Meanborow,* alſo *Eaſtmean* and *Weſtmean Hundreds* in *Hantshire.*
Medeguaia flu.	*The River Medway* in *Kent.*
Medena,	*New-Port* in the *Iſle of Wight.*
Mediolanium,	*Middleham* in *Yorkshire.*
Mediterranei, Angli,	*Staffordshire-men.*
Melanclani,	*People of* Silley.
Meldunum,	*Malmesbury* in *Wiltshire.*
Menavia,	*The Iſle of Man.*
Menevia,	St. *Davids* in *Wales.*
Mercia,	*Middle England.*
Mercii,	*Middle Engliſhmen.*
Merionithia, Mervinia,	*Merionethshire.*
Merlebrigia,	*Marleborough.*
Metaris æſtuarium,	*The Waſhes* in *Norfolk.*
Mevania,	*The Iſle of Man.*
Michelnia,	*Michelney* in *Somerſetshire.*
Middleſexia,	*Middleſex.*
Mitfordia,	*Mitford* in *Northumberland.*
Molis flu.	*The Mole* in *Surrey.*

Mona,	*The Isle of Anglesey.*
Monabia,	*The Isle of Man*, according to *Pliny.*
Monasterium de Bello,	*Battell Abbey.*
Monasterium de Melsa,	*Meaux Abbey* in *Yorkshire.*
Monmuthia,	*Monmouth.*
Monochapolis,	*New-Castle* in *Northumberland.*
Monoeda,	*The Isle of Man*, according to *Ptolomy.*
Mons acutus,	*Montacute* in *Somersetshire.*
Mons dives,	*Richmond* in *Surrey.*
Mons Gomericus, Montgomeria,	*Montgomery* in *Wales.*
Mons Michaelis,	St. *Michaels Mount* in *Cornwall.*
Mons rosarum,	*Montrose* in *Scotland.*
Monumetha, Monumethia,	*Monmouth.*
Morbium,	*Morsby* in *Cumberland.*
Moricamba, Moricambe æstuarium,	*The Bay of Cardronack* in *Cumberland.*
Moridunum, vel Ridunum,	*Seaton* in *Devonshire.*
Mortuus Lacus,	*Mortlake* in *Surrey.*
Muridunum, *see* Maridunum,	*Carmarthen.*
Murimintum pro Murivindum,	*Silcester* in *Hantshire.*

N.

Nauesbia,	*Naseby* in *Northamptonshire.*
Nauticus sinus,	*Reather* or *Rother hith*, vulgarly called *Redriff.*
Neomagus vel Noviomagus,	*According to* LLhuiid *is* Guilford, *according to* Talbat Croydon, *by* Camden *and* Somner, Woodcot *about* Croyford. — in *Surrey.*
Neoportus,	*Newport.*
Neoportus Paganellicus,	*Newport Paganel* in *Buckinghamshire.*
Nidum, Nidus,	*Neath* in *Glamorganshire.*
Nigera,	*Blackney* in *Norfolk.*
Nivicollini,	*Snowdon Hills* in *Carnarvonshire.*
Nordhumbra,	*Northumberland.*
Nordovolca, Norfolcia,	*Norfolk.*
Northanimbria,	*Northumberland.*
Northantonia,	*Northampton.*
Northantoniensis ager,	*Northamptonshire.*
Northimbria, Northumbria,	*Northumberland.*
Nortobricum, Nordoricum,	*Norton-Hall* in *Yorkshire.*
Nottinghamia,	*Nottingham.*
Nottinghamiensis ager,	*Nottinghamshire.*
Novantum prom.	*Cockermouth.*
Noviodunum,	*Newenden* in *Kent* upon the *Rother.*
Novius,	*Conwey.*
Novus Burgus,	*Newport* in the *Isle of Wight.*
Novum castellum,	*New-Castle* in *Northumberland.*
Novum forum, Novum mercatum,	*New Market* in *Suffolk.*
Novus portus,	*New-Port.*
Nubiria,	*Newberry* in *Berkshire.*
Nulla ejusmodi, Nulli par, Nulli secunda,	*Nonsuch* in *Surrey.*

O.

Oceanus virgivius,	*The Virgivian* or *Westerne Ocean.*
Occidentales Britones,	*Western Britains*, or *Inhabitants* of *Cornwall.*
Occidua wallia,	*Cornwall.*
Occellum prom.	*Holdernesse*, also *Kelnesy* in *Yorkshire.*
Ockhamptonia,	*Ockhampton* in *Devonshire.*
Ocrinum prom.	*The Lizard point* in *Cornwall.*
Octopitarum prom.	St. *David's head* in *Pembrokeshire* in *Wales.*
Olenacum,	*Edenborow* in *Cumberland.*
Olicana,	*Ilkely*, also *Halifax*, both in *Yorkshire.*
Ordevices, Ordovices,	*People of Northwales.*
Orus flu.	*The River* Ore *in* Suffolk.
Osca flu.	*The River* Uske *in* Wales.
Othona,	*Ithancester* in *Essex.*
Ottadeni, Ottadini, Ottalini, Ottatini,	*People of Northumberland.*
Ottaforda,	*Otford* in *Kent.*
Ovinia insula,	*The Isle of* Shepey *in* Kent.
Oxenforda, Oxonia, Oxonium,	*Oxford City.*
Oxinaga,	*Oxney Isle* in *Kent.*

P.

Palus salsa,	*Pulchely* in *Carnarvonshire.*
Parathalassia,	*Walsingham* in *Norfolk.*
Parisi,	*People of Holdernesse.*
Pegelandia,	*Peckirke* not far from *Crowland.*
Penbrochia,	*Pembroke* in *Wales.*
Pendinas,	*Pendennys-Castle* in *Cornwall.*
Penguernum,	*Shrewesbury-Town.*
Penlinnia,	*A place in* Merionethshire, *where is the Lake* Tagit, *whence rises the River* Dee.
Pennocrucium,	*Penkridge* in *Staffordshire.*
Pennorinum,	*Penrin* in *Cornwall.*
Pente flu.	*The River* Pant *in* Essex.
Perscora, Persora.	*Pershore* in *Worcestershire.*

Peterillus, Peterus flu.	*The Peterill* in *Cumberland.*
Petriburgus, Petropolis,	*Peterborow City* in *Northamptonshire.*
Petuaria vel Petuaria Parisiorum,	*Bevely* in *Yorkshire.*
Pevensea,	*Pevensey* in *Sussex.*
Pictavia,	*The Countrey of the* Picts.
Picti,	*The* Picts, *a people of* Britain.
Placentia,	*The Royal Palace at* Greenwich.
Pontes,	*Reading* in *Berkshire,* also *Colebrooke* in *Buckinghamshire.*
Pons Burgensis,	*Burrowbridge* in *Yorkshire.*
Ad Pontem,	*Paunton* in *Lincolnshire.*
Pons Ælii,	*Pont-Eland* in *Northumberland.*
Pontus flu.	*The Pont* in *Northumberland.*
Portesmutha,	*Portesmouth* in *Hantshire.*
Portlandia, Portunia insula,	*Portland Isle.*
Portus magnus, Portus Ostium,	*Portsmouth* or *Portchester.*
Portus salutis,	*Cromarty.*
Powisia,	*Powys,* a part of *Wales.*
Præsidium,	*Warwick Town.*
Prætorium,	*Patrington* in *Yorkshire.*
Procolitia, Protolitia,	*Prudhow* or *Prodhow-Castle* in *Northumberland.*
Profundum vadum,	*Depeford.*
Putenega,	*Putney* in *Surrey.*

R.

Radnoria,	*Radnor* in *Radnorshire.*
Raga, Ragæ,	*Ratiford* or *Ratford.*
Raganeia,	*Ralegh* in *Essex.*
Ramesburia,	*Ramesbury* in *Wiltshire.*
Ratæ,	*Leicester Town.*
Rato stabius flu.	*The* Taffe *in* Glamorganshire.
Readingum,	*Reading* in *Berkshire.*
Regiodunum, Hullinum,	*Kingston upon Hull* in *Yorkshire.*
Regiodunum Thamesinum,	*Kingston upon Thames.*
Regis Burgus,	*Queenborow* in *Kent.*
Regni.	*People of* Surrey, Sussex, *and the Sea-Coasts of* Hantshire.
Regulbium,	*Reculner* in *Kent.*
Repandunum,	*Repton* in *Derbishire.*
Rhedus flu.	*The Read in* Northumberland.
Rhibellus flu.	*The Rhibell* in *Lancaster.*
Ritubi portus, Rhutubi portus, Rhutupiæ statio, Rhitupis portus, Rutupius portus,	*Reptacester, Ruptimuth, Richberge,* now *Richborow* near *Sandwich* in *Kent.*
Rhobogdium prom.	*Faire foreland.*
Rebodunum,	*Riblechester* in *Lancashire.*
Richmundia, Richmondia,	*Richmund* in *Yorkshire,* also the same in *Surrey.*
Ripadium,	*Repton* in *Derbishire.*
Ripodum,	*Rippon* in *Yorkshire.*
Robertinus pons,	*Rother Bridge* in *Sussex.*
Rodecotanus pons,	*Radcot-Bridge* on the *River Isis* in *Oxfordshire.*
Roibis, Roffa,	*Rochester City* in *Kent.*
Roisiæ oppidum,	*Royston* in *Cambridgeshire.*
Rossia,	*Rosse-land* in *Cornwall,* also *Rose* in *Pembrokeshire.*
Rugnitunia, Ruitonia, Rutunia,	*Riton upon Dunsmore* in *Warwickshire.*
Ruber clivus,	*Redcliffe* near *London,* vulgarly *Ratcliffe.*
Rupis aurea,	*Gold cliffe* in *Monmouthshire.*
Ruthunia,	*Ruthin* in *Denbighshire.*
Rutlandia,	*Rutlandshire.*
Rutunium,	*Rowton* in *Shropshire.*

S.

Sabaudia,	*The Savoy* in *London.*
Sabriana vel Sabrina,	*The River Severne.*
Sabulovicum,	*Sandwich* in *Kent.*
Sacra insula,	*Holy Isle* by *Northumberland.*
Sacra sylva,	*Halifax* in *Yorkshire.*
Salenæ, Salinæ,	*Saludy* in *Bedfordshire.*
Salisburria, Sarisburia,	*Salisbury City* in *Wiltshire.*
Salopesbiria, Salopia,	*Shrewsbury.*
Salopiæ comitatus,	*Shropshire.*
Saltria,	*Sawtry* in *Huntingtonshire.*
Sandicum, Sandovicus, Sanwicum,	*Sandwich* in *Kent.*
Sarnia,	*Garnesey Island.*
Saverna,	*The Severne.*
Sceptonia,	*Shaftsbury* in *Dorsetshire.*
Schelsega,	*Chelsey* by *London.*
Schirburnia,	*Shirburne* in *Dorsetshire.*
Scona,	*Scone* in *Scotland.*
Scoti,	*Scots.*
Scotia,	*Scotland.*
Scorberia, Scorbesberia,	*Shrewsbury Town.*
Sebasta, altera, Legio,	*Liskard* in *Cornwall.*
Secandunum,	*Seckington in* Warwickshire.
Segedunum,	*Seghill* in *Northumberland.*
Segelocum, Segelogum,	*Aulert* in *Shirwood* in *Nottinghamshire.*
	Agle in *Lincolnshire.*
	Littleborow in *Nottinghamshire.*
Segontium,	*Caer-sejont* near *Carnarvon Town.*
Seguntium,	*Silchester* in *Hantshire.*
Selburgi tumulus,	*Selbury Hill* in *Wiltshire.*
Seolesia,	*Seolsey* or *Selsey* in *Sussex,* whence the best *Cockles.*

Setantiorum Palus,	*Winander Meere* in *Lancashire.*
Seteia æstuar,	*Dee-mouth.*
Severia,	*Salisbury City.*
Sharpernoria,	*Sharpnore* in the *Isle of Wight.*
Shenum,	*Shene* or *Richmond* in *Surrey.*
Sigdeles, Sillinæ insulæ,	*The Isles* of *Scilly.*
Silesia,	*Seolsey* or *Selsey* in *Sussex,* sometimes a *Bishops See.*
Silura,	*The little* Isle *of* Silley *in* Severne, *as* Camden *thinks.*
Silures,	*People of* Southwales.
Sinnodununum,	*Sinnodum Hill* near *Wallingford* in *Berkshire.*
Sitomagus, Simomagus, Sinomagus,	*Thetford* in *Norfolk.*
Slepa,	*The old Name of* St. Ives *in* Huntingtonshire.
Snawdonia,	*Snowdown Forest* in *Carnarvonshire.*
Somaridunum,	*Somerton* in *Lincolnshire.*
Somersetensis comitatus, Somertunensis comitatus,	*Somersetshire.*
Sorbiodunum, Sorviodunum, Sorurodunum,	*Old Salisbury.*
Southamptonia,	*Southampton.*
Southeria, Surria,	*The County of* Surrey.
Southerlandia,	*Southerland* in *Scotland.*
Southria, Southriana,	*Surrey.*
Southregienses,	*People of* Surrey.
Southsexena, Southsexia,	*The County of* Sussex.
Southwella,	*Southwell* in *Nottinghamshire.*
Spinarum insula,	*Thorney Isle* the old name of *Westminster.*
Spinæ,	*Newberry* in *Berkshire,* and *Spene* near *Newbury.*
Staffordia,	*Stafford Town.*
Stanfordia,	*Stanford* in *Lincolnshire.*
Stenum,	*Stene* in *Northamptonshire.*
Stringulia,	*Cherpstow* in *Monmouthshire.*
Strivillina,	*Sterling* in *Scotland.*
Stuccia vel Stucia flu.	*Ystwith* in *Cardiganshire.*
Sturodunum,	*Stourton* and *Sturminster* in *Dorsetshire.*
Sturus flu.	*The Stoure* in *Derbishire.*
Sulcalva flu.	*The Swale* in *Yorkshire.*
Sudoverca,	*Southwark.*
Suffolcia, Suffolicia,	*Suffolk.*
Sullomacæ. Sullonicæ,	*Brockley-Hill* near *Ellestre* in *Hertfordshire*, also *Barnet* or *Edgworth Shelney.*
Sunningum,	*Sanning* by *Reading.*
Salimnos insula,	*Salmey Isle* not far from *Mildford Haven.*

T.

Taffus flu.	*The Taffe* in *Glamorganshire.*
Taizalos & Vernicones,	*People of* Northumberland.
Tama flu.	*The River Tame* in *Oxfordshire,* another in *Staffordshire.*
Tama oppid.	*Tame,* a Town in *Oxfordshire.*
Tamara flu.	*The River Tamar* in *Cornwall.*
Tamawordina,	*Tamworth* in *Staffordshire.*
Tamara oppid.	*Tamarton* in *Cornwall.*
Tamisis,	*The Thames.*
Tanfelda,	*Tanfield* in *Yorkshire.*
Tavistokia,	*Tavestocke* in *Devonshire.*
Tedfordia,	*Thetford* in *Norfolk.*
Teesis & Teesa,	*The River Tees* in the *Bishoprick* of *Durham.*
Tegæus Lacus.	*The Lake Tagit* or *Pemble Meere* in *Merionithshire* in *Wales.*
Terentus flu.	*The River* Trent.
Tetocuria,	*Tedbury* in *Gloucestershire.*
Thanaton Thanatos insula,	*The Isle of* Tanet *in Kent.*
Theobaldenses ædes,	*Theobalds House* in *Hertfordshire.*
Theodorunum,	*Wells* in *Somersetshire.*
Theoci curia, Theokesberia,	*Tewksbury* in *Gloucestershire.*
Thermæ,	The *Bath City.*
Thongum,	*Thong-Castle* in *Lincolnshire.*
Thonodunum,	*Taunton* in *Somersetshire.*
Thornega,	*Thornege,* the old name of *Westminster.*
Thorneia,	*Thorney* in *Cambridgeshire.*
Tichfelda,	*Tichfield* in *Hantshire.*
Tina & Tinna,	*The River* Tine *in* Northumberland.
Tindolana,	*Winchester* in the *Wall.*
Tinemutha,	*Tinmouth* in *Northumberland.*
Tintagium,	*Tintagell* in *Cornwall.*
Toliapis, Toliatis,	*The Isle of Shepey* in *Kent.*
Torcestria,	*Towcester* in *Northamptonshire.*
Totonesium,	*Totnesse* in *Devonshire.*
Trehenta,	*The River* Trent.
Trenovantum,	*London.*
Trimontium,	*Atterith,* a Town in *Scotland.*
Trinoantes, Trinobantes, Trinovantes,	*People of Middlesex and Essex.*
Tripontium,	*Towcester* in *Northamptonshire.*
Trisanton, Trinsantonis portus,	*Southampton.*
Tuesis,	*Berwick upon Tweed.*
Tunnocellum, Tunocellum,	*Tinmouth* in *Northumberland.*

V.

VAdum pulchrum,	*Fairford* in *Glouceſter-ſhire.*
Vaga flu.	The River *Wye* in *Herefordshire.*
Vagniacæ,	*Wrotham* in *Kent.*
Vagniacum,	*Maidſton* in *Kent.*
Vallis aurea,	*Golden Vale* in *Herefordshire.*
Vallis crucis,	*The Vale of the Croſs in* Denbighſhire.
Vallum,	The *Picts wall.*
Vandalis flu.	*The River Wandle* in *Surrey.*
Vandelbiria,	*Wandlesbury*, a Fort on the Hills near *Cambridge.*
Vanatinga,	*Wantage* in *Berkshire.*
Varia flu.	The *Frome* at *Dorcheſter* in *Dorſetshire.*
Varis,	*Boduary* in *Flintshire.*
Vecta,	
Vecteſis,	The *Iſle of Wight.*
Victeſis,	
Venantodunia,	*Huntingtonshire.*
Venantodunum,	
Venatorum mons,	*Huntington Town.*
Venedotia,	*North wales.*
Venta Belgarum,	*Wincheſter* in *Hantshire.*
Venta Icenorum,	*Caſter* near *Norwich.*
Venta ſilurum,	*Caer went* in *Monmouthshire.*
Verlucio,	*Warmiſter* in *Wiltshire.*
Vernemetum,	
Vernometum,	*Burrow-hill* in *Leiceſtershire.*
Verometum,	
Verolamium,	
Virolamium,	*Verulam City* near St. *Albans* in *Hertfordshire.*
Verulamium,	
Verovicum,	*Warwick Town.*
Veteleganus pons,	*Wheatly-Bridge* near *Oxford.*
Verteræ,	*Burgh* upon *Stanemore* in *Weſtmerland.*
Vertilingiana via,	*Watling-ſtreet way.*
Vexala,	*Juellmouth* in *Somerſetshire.*
Vicus Malbanus,	*Namptwich* in *Cheſhire.*
Vicus ſaxeus,	*Standrop* in the *Biſhoprick* of *Durham.*
Vigornia,	*Worceſter City.*
Villa Fauſtini,	St. *Edmundsbury* in *Suffolk.*
Vilugiana provincia,	*Wiltshire.*
Vinchelſega,	
Vindagora,	*Winchelſey* in *Suſſex.*
Vindelis,	*Old Winchelſey.*
Vindeliſora,	*Windſor* in *Berkshire.*
Vindobala,	
Vindomora,	*Walls end* in *Northumberland.*
Vindogladia,	
Vindugladia,	*Wimburne* in *Dorſetſhire.*
Vindolana,	*Old Wincheſter* in *Northumberland.*
Vindonum,	
Vindonus,	*Silcaſtre* in *Hantshire.*
Vindugleſſus,	*Vandeles* in the *Biſhoprick* of *Durham.*
Virecinum,	
Virecium,	*Wroxceſter* in *Shropshire.*
Viridis ſinus,	*Greenwich.*
Viroſidum,	*Werewic* upon *Eden* near *Carliſle* in *Cumberland.*
Vitrea inſula,	*Glaſtonbury* in *Somerſetshire.*
Vituli inſula,	*Selſey.*
Ulmetum,	*Elmeſly* in *Yorkshire.*
Umber flu.	The *River Humber* in *Yorkshire.*
Valdia,	*Cotſwold* in *Glouceſtershire.*
Voliba,	*Bodman.*
Voluba,	*Falmouth* in *Cornwall.*
Volucrum domus,	*Fulham* in *Middleſex.*
Voreda,	*Old Perith* in *Cumberland.*
Univallis,	*Jorval* in *Yorkshire.*
Uſoconna,	*Oken yate* in *Shropshire.*
Uxela,	*Crekeborne well.*
Uzella,	*Leſtythiell* in *Cornwall.*
Uzela æſtuarium,	*Juel mouth* in *Somerſetſhire.*

W.

WAkefeldia,	*Wakefield* in *Yorkshire.*
Waldena,	*Saffron-Walden* in *Eſſex.*
Wallia,	*Wales.*
Wara,	*The Town of* Ware *in* Hertfordſhire.
Warwicana provincia,	*Warwickshire.*
Warwici Comitat,	
Wiableia,	*Webly Town* in *Hertfordshire.*
Wellæ,	*Wells City* in *Somerſetſhire.*
Wentana civitas,	*Wincheſter City.*
Weſtberia,	*Weſtbury* near *Briſtoll.*
Weſtmaria,	
Weſtmoria,	*Weſtmerland.*
Weſtmorlandia,	
Weſtmonaſterium,	*Weſtminſter City.*
Wetha,	*The Iſle of Wight*, according to W. *Malmesbury.*
Wichcombia,	*Wickham* in *Buckinghamshire.*
Wichum,	*Wich* in *Worceſterſhire.*
Wiccia,	*Worceſterſhire.*
Wigornia,	*Worceſter City.*
Wiltonia,	*Wiltshire.*
Wimundhamia,	*Wimundham* in *Norfolk.*
Winburna,	*Winburne* in *Dorſetſhire.*
Wincelcumba,	*Winchcombe* in *Glouceſtershire.*
Winchelcumba,	
Windeſora,	
Windleſora,	*Windſor* in *Berkshire.*
Windeſoria,	
Witleſia,	*Wittleſey* in *Huntingtonſhire.*

Y.

Yarum, Garienis, Garienus, } *Yare* in *Yorkshire*. *Yare River* in *Norfolk*.

Yarmuthia, Jernmuthia, Garanonum, Garienis ostium, } *Yarmouth* in *Norfolk*.

FINIS.